STEVEN WASSERSTROM

P9-DVY-921

THE OTHER BIBLE

THE OTHER BIBLE

Edited by Willis Barnstone

1817

Harper & Row, Publishers, San Francisco
Cambridge, Hagerstown, New York, Philadelphia
London, Mexico City, São Paulo, Sydney

Grateful acknowledgment is made to the following for permission to reprint selections:

E. J. Brill

Excerpts from *Gnosis* by Robert Haardt, trans. J. F. Hendry, 1971. Reprinted by permission.

Fortress Press

Excerpts from Cartlidge/Dungan, *Documents for the Study of the Bible*. Copyright © 1980 by Fortress Press. Used by permission.

Harper & Row, Publishers

Excerpts from *The Nag Hammadi Library in English*, ed. James M. Robinson. Copyright © 1977 by E. J. Brill. Reprinted by permission. Excerpts from *Gnosticism* by Robert M. Grant. Copyright © 1961 by R. M. Grant. Reprinted by permission. Excerpts from Moses Hadas, ed. and trans., *The Third and Fourth Book of Maccabees*. Copyright © 1953 by Dropsie College. Reprinted by permission. Excerpts from Moses Hadas, ed. and trans., *Aristeas to Philocrates*. Copyright © 1951 by Dropsie College. Reprinted by permission.

Oxford University Press

Excerpts from Gnosis: *A Selection of Gnostic Texts*, ed. Werner Foerster; trans. and ed. R. McL. Wilson, 1972. Reprinted by permission of Artemis Publishers Ltd., Zurich.

Schocken Books

Reprinted by permission of Schocken Books, Inc., from *Zohar: The Book of Splendor*, by Gershom Scholem. Copyright © 1949, 1977 by Schocken Books, Inc.

SPCK

Reprinted by permission of The Society for Promoting Christian Knowledge, from *Some Authentic Acts of the Early Martyrs*, by E. L. E. Owen. Copyright © 1933 by SPCK.

Viking Penguin, Inc.

Selections from *The Dead Sea Scrolls* by Millar Burrows. Copyright © 1955 by Millar Burrows. Copyright renewed © 1983 by E. G. Burrows. Reprinted by permission of Viking Penguin, Inc.

Continued on page vi

The Other Bible. Copyright © 1984 by Willis Barnstone. All rights reserved. Printed in the United States of America. No part of this book may be used or reproduced in any manner whatsoever without written permission except in the case of brief quotations embodied in critical articles and reviews. For information address Harper & Row, Publishers, Inc., 10 East 53rd Street, New York, NY 10022. Published simultaneously in Canada by Fitzhenry & Whiteside, Limited, Toronto.

FIRST EDITION

Designed by Design Office Bruce Kortebein

Library of Congress Cataloging in Publication Data
Main entry under title:

THE OTHER BIBLE.

A collection of ancient, esoteric texts from Judeo-Christian traditions, excluded from the official canon of the Old and New Testaments.
  Bibliography: p.
  1. Apocryphal books. 2. Gnostic literature.
3. Cabala. I. Barnstone, Willis, 1927–
BS1695.087   1984   229'.052   83-48416
ISBN 0-06-250031-7
ISBN 0-06-250030-9 (pbk.)

84 85 86 87 88 10 9 8 7 6 5 4 3 2 1

For Marija Dionisia Maddock

Credits—Continued

Westminster Press

Reprinted from *The Other Gospels: Non-Canonical Gospel Texts*, ed. Ron Cameron. Copyright © 1982 by Ron Cameron. Reprinted and used by permission of The Westminster Press, Philadelphia, PA. Reprinted from *New Testament Apocrypha: Volume One: Gospels and Related Writings*, ed. Edgar Hennecke and Wilhelm Schneemelcher, copyright © 1959 by J. C. B. Mohr (Paul Siebeck), Tübingen; English Translation copyright © 1963 by Lutterworth Press. Published in the United States by The West-minster Press, Philadelphia, PA. Reprinted and used by permission. Reprinted from *New Testament Apocrypha: Volume Two: Writings Relating to the Apostles, Apocalypses and Related Subjects*, ed. by R. McL. Wilson. Copyright © 1964 by J. C. B. Mohr (Paul Siebeck), Tübingen. English Translation © 1965 by Lutterworth Press. Published in the United States by The Westminster Press, Philadelphia, PA. Reprinted and used by permission.

Contents

2/Histories and Narratives

3/Wisdom Literature and Poetry

4/Gospels

5/Infancy Gospels

6/Acts

7/Apocalypses

8/Diverse Gnostic Texts

9/Manichaean and Mandaean Gnostic Texts

10/Mystical Documents

Introduction

William Blake's wife, Catherine Boucher, once complained that she had very little of Mr. Blake's company for he was always in Paradise. When the English poet was not in the Paradise of an imagined Jerusalem or in the Hell of his native London, he was recording those revelations in a personal bible that he wrote throughout his life. His was a rebellious scripture, influenced by the canonical Bible as well as such texts as *The Book of Enoch*, a pseudepigraphical text from the intertestamental period. Other poets—Walt Whitman, Charles Baudelaire, Jorge Guillén—gave themselves to one book, to recording their personal religion, sacred or profane, in a bible for their times.

The word bible, from *biblía*, Greek for "small books," signifies broadly a collection of books by which a person or people can live. The ancient Bible was sacred, for its composition was held to be inspired by God. Similarly, if we believe the text, William Blake's prophetic books were divinely inspired. So the act of inspired composition, whether of a Blake or a Whitman or a biblical patriarch, whether of the West or East, appears to be a universal human endeavor, not restricted to one people or religion. After the closing of the Old Testament and during the first centuries of the Common Era, inspired authors continued to write sacred scriptures. They were written by Jews, Christians, Gnostics, and Pagans. Many of these texts were of amazing beauty and religious importance and competed with books within the canon. The Jewish texts are in large part called pseudepigrapha, which includes the Dead Sea Scrolls; the Christian texts are called Christian Apocrypha; the Gnostic scriptures, today so fascinating and even modish, were called by their orthodox rivals heretical. These Jewish, Christian, and Gnostic books are presented here under the title of *The Other Bible*. Had events been otherwise and certain of these inspired texts incorporated in our Bible, our understanding of the tradition of religious thought would have been radically altered. Today, free of doctrinal strictures, we can read the "greater bible" of the Judeo-Christian world.

The Other Bible, then, is a book of holy texts that were not included in the Old or New Testaments. It contains creation and Eden myths, psalms and romances, gospels and epistles, prophecies and apocalypses, histories and mystical documents. Every genre of the Bible is represented. It also has works from early Kabbalah, Haggadah, Hermes Trismegistus, and Plotinus.

Why did the specifically Jewish and Christian texts fail to find a place in the Bible? Was it a question of divine authority, period, doctrine? These errant scriptures are often aesthetically and religiously the equal of books in the canon and offer vital information, such as infancy gospels on Jesus' childhood, as well as alternate versions of major biblical stories. In a Manichaean version of Genesis it is Eve who gives life to Adam, while the serpent, the Luminous Jesus, is a liberating figure urging the first couple to take the first step toward salvation by eating from the Tree of Gnosis. The exclusion of many texts was often as arbitrary and dubious as was the inclusion of such magnificent and dangerous books as Ecclesiastes and the Song of Songs.

At times the cause of exclusion was fierce political and religious rivalry between sects, between factions, between Jew, Christian, and Gnostic. The antiquity of a book was a primary factor influencing inclusion, and for this reason many competing texts were attributed to great figures of the Bible—to Enoch, Isaiah, Thomas, Paul—to give them both age and authority. For similar reasons pseudonymous books of the Bible—the Song of Songs, the Psalms, and certain Epistles—assumed the names of Solomon, David, and John in their titles. As for the abundant Gnostic scriptures, these were excluded precisely because of their Gnosticizing tendencies. Indeed, it is said that the early Gnostic Marcion of Sinope so angered the followers of the new religion of Jesus Christ that he provoked the Christian Fathers into establishing a New Testament canon.

The Gnostics were serious rivals of orthodox Christians. The most systematized and organized Gnostic cult was Manichaeism, which spread from Mesopotamia through Asia Minor to North Africa and the European territories of the Roman Empire. It extended to eastern Iran and into Chinese Turkestan, where it became the state religion of the Uigur Empire. Western China remained Manichaean until the thirteenth century. In the West it rose here and there as various medieval sects, such as the Bogomils and Cathari, and the Albigensians in southern France. Today in Iran and southwest Iraq the Mandaeans, a Gnostic offshoot of heterodox Jewish sects originally from eastern Syria and Palestine, continue in the Gnostic faith.

The most serious conflict between Christians and Gnostics was in the first four centuries of the Common Era. In the second century Valentinus, a major Gnostic thinker, sought election as Pope of Rome. Surely the fixation of the New Testament in Carthage in 397 would have been drastically different had Valentinus succeeded; and what would have been the views of that former Gnostic, Saint Augustine, whose words so affected the conciliar decisions at Carthage? Leaving aside speculations, we can say categorically that the Bible, with the absence of sacred texts from the entire intertestamental period, with its acceptance of a small and repetitious canon for the New Testament, with the exclusion of all later Christian Apocrypha, and the total rejection of Gnostic scriptures, has given us a highly censored and distorted version of ancient religious literature.

Deprived of all scriptures between the Testaments, the common reader is left with the impression that somehow Christianity sprang self-generated like a divine entity, with no past, into its historical setting. Yet a reading of the texts between the Testaments shows how major eschatological themes of the New Testament—the appearance of the Son of Man, the imminence of the End, the apocalyptic vision in the Book of Revelation, the notion of salvation through the messiah— are all the preoccupation of intertestamental literature. In the *Genesis Apocrypon* from the Dead Sea Scrolls, Abram heals the Pharaoh by laying hands on his head, thus proving that this New Testament "innovation" existed earlier and was recorded in earlier scriptures. Edmund Wilson observes:

> This laying-on hands is often mentioned in the New Testament as a feature of the healing of Jesus, but it does not occur in the Old Testament or, so far as is known, in rabbinical literature. Yet its occurrence in the Genesis apocryphon, this copy of which is supposed to have been made either during the lifetime of Jesus or a little earlier, would seem to indicate that the practice was not peculiar to Jesus but was a recognized method of effecting cures.[1]

In regard to the New Testament, the Acts, Epistles, and Book of Revelation could be increased, if not replaced, by other works in these genres. Noncanonical Christian Apocrypha conveys a lucid picture of the life and ideals of early Christendom. We see the wanderings of the apostles in Asia Minor and India, and note their legendary adventures, the sermons of chastity, the bloody accounts of much-desired martyrdom. The Apocrypha is particularly rich in apocalypses, which immediately informs the reader that the canonical Apocalypse is not really an odd and obscure text, but rather one that is perfectly consistent with noncanonical Jewish and Christian scriptures. In these wondrous texts we witness visionary journeys to Heaven and Hell, which feed stock images into the tradition that Dante followed in the *Commedia* when he himself was translated to Hell, Purgatory, and Heaven.

As for the Gnostics, their scriptures were anathema to orthodox Christians, for they reversed fundamental notions of Christian theology—although they thought themselves the true and uncorrupted Christians. As a result of conflict between these two major sects of primitive Christianity and the victory of the orthodox, the Gnostic texts disappeared; they were destroyed or left uncopied, achieving the same end. Until a few years ago the loss appeared so complete that we relied for information largely on the works of early Christian Fathers, such as Irenaeus, Hippolytus, Clement of Alexandria, and Augustine, who wrote refutations of the Gnostics. Then, in 1945, extensive Gnostic treatises were discovered in earthenware jars buried in a field at Nag Hammadi in Egypt. The fifty-two scriptures were in Coptic, translated from Greek. Just as the discovery of the Dead Sea Scrolls at Qumran in 1947 gave us for the first time Essene scriptures, so the startling appearance of these Egyptian documents gave us at last the actual words of the Gnostics. The books are rich in cosmogonies and anthropogonies. They contain apocalyptic visions and secret scrolls of Jesus' life and sayings. The magnificent *Gospel of Truth* and *Gospel of Thomas* add greatly to the information provided by the New Testament.

Most of the texts in *The Other Bible* are from the third century B.C. to the fourth and fifth centuries A.D. In addition to Old Testament pseudepigrapha, New Testament Apocrypha, and early Gnostic scriptures, the book contains a few examples of early Kabbalah and excerpts from Hermes Trismegistus, a Gnostic Pagan, and Plotinus, a Neoplatonist. Gershom Scholem, the editor of the kabbalistic texts, traces these medieval Spanish versions of Kabbalah back to pre-Christian times. Hermes Trismegistus (more likely a tradition than a person) is included because the Hermetic theology and lexicon reveal Jewish, Christian, and Gnostic parallels and exemplify in extraordinary texts the syncretic nature of religious traditions in the first centuries of the Common Era. Plotinus, a thoroughly Hellenized Egyptian Neoplatonist, gives us the vocabulary and system of mystical introspection and ascension to God that anticipates the last Christian scripture in our volume, *The Mystical Theology* of Pseudo-Dionysius. Pseudo-Dionysius, also referred to incorrectly but less pejoratively as Dionysius the Areopagite, elaborated the three-stage spiritual journey of the negative way—the *viae* of purgation, illumination, and union—which is further elaborated in medieval theology and provides the mystical structure for Saint John of the Cross, the greatest of renaissance mystical poets.

The literary quality of these diverse texts is often astonishing. *The Book of the Secrets of Enoch* retells the creation of the world. We hear God speaking to Enoch. Enoch is overwhelmed by what he has heard from the Lord's lips, and he recounts what he has seen from beginning to end. With the cosmic grandeur of Genesis and poetic drama of Job, the book tells us of the origin of things. Enoch experiences the ecstasy of rapture into Heaven. He has seen "the Lord's limitless and perfect compass":

> I know all things and have written them into books concerning the heavens and their end, their plenitude, their armies, and their marching. I have measured and described the stars, their great and countless multitude. What man has seen their revolutions and entrances? Not even the angels see their number, yet I have recorded all their names.

Enoch measures the sun's circle, records the sweet smells of every grass and flower and the wings of the rain, and knows all their names. Further, he knows about cold and the winds of Hell:

> I wrote of the treasure houses of the snow, the storage houses of the cold and of freezing winds, and I observed how the key-holder of the seasons fills the clouds with its snows and winds but never exhausts their treasure houses.
>
> And I wrote of the resting places of the winds and observed how the key-holders hold scales and measures. They weight the

seasons in the pans and release them cunningly over the whole earth, its mountains, hills, fields, trees, stones, rivers. I recorded the height from earth to the seventh heaven and down to the very lowest Hell, the judgment place, the great, open, and weeping Hell.

In another apocalypse we read of Enoch's visionary ascent to Heaven. Dramatically and fearfully Enoch climbs to the unseeable. The apocalyptic flights in Revelation and vision in Isaiah find an analogue in Enoch's declarations. In full, luminous speech, he says:

> This vision was shown to me. The vision clouds invited me and a mist summoned me, the course of the stars and lightning sped me, and the winds in the vision caused me to fly, lifting me upward and bearing me into heaven. I went in till I came near a wall built of crystals and surrounded by tongues of fire. It began to frighten me. I went into the tongues of fire and came near a large house built of hailstone crystals. The walls of the house were like a tesselated floor of crystals, its floor also was crystal. Its ceiling was the path of stars and lightning. Between them were fiery cherubim. Their Heaven was clear as water. A fire surrounded the walls and its portals blazed. I entered that house and it was hot as fire, cold as ice. There were no delights of life therein. Fear covered me, and trembling seized me. I quaked, fell on my face, and beheld a vision!

Elsewhere the Sibylline oracle speaks her fearful prophecies, and in the Dead Sea Scrolls we have a detailed report on the laws and behavior of an ultraconservative community that had retreated from the Hellenizing corruption of the city to live an austere life of obedience, duties, and rhapsodic prayer in the desert.

As we move into the first centuries of the Common Era we encounter a mixture of several traditions, often in the same scripture. The *Gospel of John*, an excellent example of such syncretic tendencies, begins with the haunting logic of, "In the beginning was the Word, and the Word was with God, and the Word was God." The Word or logos in the Fourth Gospel comes from Philo of Alexandria (ca. 20 B.C.–A.D. 40) who linked the Stoic logos with the Platonic world of ideas, making logos the means of knowing the transcendent God. So in one famous Christian passage we see clear currents of Greek Platonism through the intermediary of a Hellenized Alexandrian Jew who, among other contributions, invented allegorical exegesis of the Bible, which Christian apologists soon adopted.

Many of the Christian Apocrypha are Jewish scriptures with a Christian overlay. So the Son of Man, a common messianic term in Jewish pseudepigrapha, obviously becomes in Christian recension Jesus the Messiah. Often the Apocrypha have a Gnostic dimension, as do passages of the Gospels. *The Odes of Solomon*, a Syriac text discovered in 1909, is a Jewish hymnbook, in Christian redaction, subjected to Gnostic interpolations. The original text was almost certainly composed in Greek. The odes are profound and of immense poetic beauty. In Ode 35 we read:

> The dew of the Lord rinsed me with silence
> and a cloud of peace rose over my head,

Salvation and ascension to God is a typical preoccupation of texts of the period. The same ode ends with a correlation of physical and spiritual gestures as the narrator rises upward into perfection:

> I spread my hands out as my soul pointed
> to the firmament
> and I slipped upward to him
> who redeemed me.

In these strange, eclectic poems we find examples of the Gnostic tendency to view God as an androgynous figure:

> The Holy Ghost opened the Father's raiment
> and mingled the milk from the Father's two breasts. (Ode 19)

The Other Bible reveals the great diversity of ancient thought. Each view, it seems, is contradicted by a second and a third. The reader has several perspectives to aid in interpretations and judgments. In contrast to Old Testament concern with the historical destiny of a people, the scriptures between the Testaments emphasize salvation, eternity, and otherworldly *topoi*. We may find three conflicting views of a single event. Thus after Jesus Christ is crucified the Jews think him another man and go on seeking the messiah, the Christians proclaim the crucified Jesus both man and God, and the Gnostics take the Docetic view that Jesus was only a simulacrum on the cross, for God is always God. In fact, in the Gnostic works *The Second Treatise of the Great Seth* and *The Apocalypse of Peter*, Jesus the Savior stands above the cross, laughing at the ignorance of his would-be executioners who think that men can kill God.

While the New Testament speaks of a Jesus who rewards the faithful with salvation and condemns "the men of little faith" to eternal damnation, the Apocrypha depict a much more compelling picture of these rewards: we find Jesus on his throne of glory in seventh heaven or descending into Hell to torture sinners with his breath of fire. One of the literary masterpieces is the martyrdom narration of *Felicity and Perpetua*, in which we witness the death of a beautiful young woman whose execution, an erotic and spiritual event, is described in exquisite detail; then we have the Gnostic counterview, which derides martyrdom as cowardice. While the Christian Pseudo-Dionysius sought the "divine ray of darkness" in order to ascend to God, the Gnostic looked for light. While the Christian mystic searched through the dark night of ignorance, the Gnostic replaced faith and ignorance with *gnosis*, that is, knowledge and inner illumination. While the Judeo-Christian view held that our Fall occurred when Eve and Adam ate from the Tree of Knowledge, the Gnostics held that the Fall occurred earlier and Adam and Eve were innocent of wrongdoing. The great error took place when the Creator God himself (as opposed to the alien God) fell into sin by creating the world, by trapping divine sparks of spirit in the darkness, in the material prison of the human body.

I have listed a few random notions from this volume to suggest that original diversity of scriptures which ultimately disappeared when Jewish pseudepigrapha, Christian Apocrypha, and Gnostic scriptures were rejected and the present canon established as the Holy Bible.

In *The Other Bible* we see the full richness of religious speculation as we move from creation myths and tribal prophecy to acosmic visionary journeys; as we follow the apostles in their legendary and miraculous adventures, or learn of Jesus' childhood or Mani's martyrdom; as we study the method of Jewish, Christian, and Gnostic meditation, which, in discrete ways, sought the same end: ecstatic union with the godhead. The volume also moves in emphasis from the great Jewish dualism of earthly beings and God to other dualisms of body and soul, and ultimately of human spirit and divine spirit. In these later texts the speculations of Jews, Christians, and Gnostics, as exemplified in Kabbalah, Christian mystical theology, and Gnostic meditations, articulate the common end of most universal religions: peace, detachment, and entry into the realm of light.

All text introductions are by the editor unless otherwise indicated. Those that are taken from other sources are reproduced here by permission.

WILLIS BARNSTONE

Note

1. Edmund Wilson, *The Dead Sea Scrolls* (London: W. H. Allen, 1969), p. 145.

Had Alexandria triumphed and not Rome,
the extravagant and muddled stories that I have summarized here
would be coherent, majestic,
and perfectly ordinary.

—Jorge Luis Borges (on the Gnostics)

1
CREATION MYTHS

The Book of the Secrets of Enoch

(2 Enoch) (Jewish Pseudepigrapha)

The Book of the Secrets of Enoch (2 Enoch) is an apocalypse describing Enoch's ascent through the seven heavens,[1] his personal vision of God in the throne room, and his return to earth, where he fulfills his commission to write 366 books in order to instruct his sons in his personally acquired ethical and eschatological knowledge. It was probably written by a Hellenistic Jew from Alexandria in the first century A.D. There may have been a Hebrew original for parts of the book, but the present versions, two texts surviving in Old Church Slavonic, are translations from the Greek.

The text, *2 Enoch,* is a Jewish pseudepigraph, that is, a scripture, usually from the intertestamental period, attributed to an assumed great name of the Old Testament. The pseudepigrapha are noncanonical and were composed largely in Palestine or in Egypt, where the Diaspora gave rise to a flourishing Graeco-Jewish literature. The tale told in *2 Enoch*—not to be confused with *1 Enoch,* a related but earlier apocalypse—is a poetic and visionary tract of a journey through Heaven and Hell; it also retells fantastically the Genesis myths of creation and Paradise; and finally it serves as a wisdom book of the good life. Its admonitions to love God and humanity—to hate people would be to hate God's creations in his own image—to help the poor and the weak, to feed the hungry and clothe the poor, to disdain worldly goods in favor of heavenly redemption of the soul, are all themes of intertestamental scriptures. Such themes link Old and New Testaments. The messianic obsession of the Jews of this period of Roman Palestine and the Diaspora is found in *1 Enoch,* and also serves to fill in the gap between Old Testament Judaism and first century Jewish Christianity. So in the books of Enoch as well as in the Dead Sea Scrolls, the *Wisdom of Solomon,* and the *Odes of Solomon,*[2] we encounter again and again the phrases the "Son of Man," the "shepherd of peace," the "resurrection of the righteous" through the coming of the messiah. At the same time Enoch's apocalyptic journey into Sheol (Hell) evokes both Old and New Testament descriptions of that place of torment.

Throughout 2 Enoch, Enoch himself serves as a surrogate messiah, frequently asserting the divine origin and universality of his knowledge. He quotes words he has heard from God's own lips. After his audience with God in Heaven, God orders his initiate to return to earth and to put in his "handwriting" books revealing the divine creation of the cosmos and the ethics of salvation.

The Enoch creation myth is placed together with other Jewish and Gnostic versions at the beginning of this volume, while Enoch's ascent to Heaven is included in the later section of apocalypses.

For more information on Enoch the patriarch who "vanished" or was "translated" into Heaven by God, Genesis 5:21–24, and the revelational elements of the Enoch books, see introductions to sections of 1 Enoch and 2 Enoch in Part 7, Apocalypses.

Notes

1. There are seven heavens in recension B, ten in recension A.
2. In the Odes of Solomon, as well as other pseudepigrapha, there is, in addition to these phrases that anticipate New Testament terms, a direct Christian interpolation. The pseudepigrapha were well known in the first centuries A.D. and were often altered and emended to make them into Christian scriptures.

THE CREATION OF THE WORLD*

Of the Great Secrets of God, Which God Revealed and Told Enoch, Face to Face
And the Lord summoned me, and put me on his left near Gabriel. And I bowed down to the Lord. And he spoke to me: "All those things you have seen, Enoch, completed by me, I shall tell you now what they were before they were formed. First, I created all things from nonexistence into existence, and from invisible into visible. And I have not informed my angels of my secrets, nor of their origins, nor of my endless, unfathomable thinking of creation. Yet I opened up the light and rode through it

*Chapters 24B–68. R. H. Charles, The Apocrypha and Pseudepigrapha of the Old Testament (Oxford: Clarendon Press, 1906), pp. 444–51, 455–56, 461, 469.

as one of the invisible, as the sun rides from east to west. And I conceived the notion of laying foundations and creating the visible creation.

"Deep down I commanded the great Idoil[1] to come forth, having a great stone in his belly. And I spoke to him: 'Burst asunder, Idoil, and let the visible be born from you.'

"And he burst asunder. A great stone came out of him, bearing all creation which I had wished to create. I saw that it was good. And I set a throne[2] up for myself and sat down on it. I said to the light, 'Go higher, become firm, and be a foundation for the highest.' But there is nothing higher than the light. All this I saw, having raised myself up from my throne.

"From deep down I summoned a second time one thing more to come out from the invisible into the one firm visible thing. Then the formation came out

4

firm and heavy and very black. And I saw that it was good."

How God Founded the Water, and Surrounded It with Light, and Established on It Seven Islands

"Having surrounded some things with light, I made those things thick and stretched forth a road of water over the darkness, below the light, and then I made the waters firm. I made them bottomless, with a foundation of light. And I created seven circles from inside, and made the water like wet and dry crystal, like glass, and made a circle of waters and other elements. And I showed each one its road, and I ordered the movement of each of the seven stars in its heaven, and I saw that it was good. I separated the light from the darkness. I told the light to be day, and the darkness to be night, and there was evening and there was morning, and it was day one.

"And then I made firm the heavenly circle and commanded the lower water, under Heaven, to collect itself together into one whole, and the chaos to become dry, and it became so. Out of the waves I created rocks hard and big, and from the rock I piled up the dry, and the dry I called earth. The middle of the earth I called abyss, the bottomless. I collected the sea in one place and bound it together with a yoke. And I said to the sea, 'Behold. I give you eternal limits, and you shall not break loose from your component parts.' Thus I made fast the firmament. On this day I called myself the first created. Then it became evening, and then again morning, and it was the second day."

The Fiery Essence

"For all the heavenly troops I made the image and essence of fire. My eye looked at hard rock and, from the gleam of my eye, the lightning received its wonderful nature, which is both fire in water and water in fire. The water does not put out the fire nor the fire dry the water. The lightning is brighter than the sun, softer than water, and firmer than rock. And from the rock I cut off a great fire, from which I created the orders of ten troops of incorporeal angels. Their weapons are fiery and their raiment a burning flame. I commanded that each one stand in order."

How Satanail[3] with His Angels Was Thrown Down from the Height

"And one of the angels, having turned away with the order that was under him, conceived an impossible thought: to place his throne higher than the clouds above the earth that he might become equal in rank to my power. And I threw him out from the height, and he was flying in the air continuously above the abyss.

"And then I created all the heavens, and it was the third day.

"On the third day I commanded the earth to grow great and fruitful trees, and hills, and I made seed for sowing, and I planted Paradise. I enclosed it, placing flaming angels there as armed guardians. Thus I created renewal.

"Then came evening and came morning, and it was the fourth day.

"On this day I commanded there to be great lights placed on the heavenly circles. On the uppermost circle I placed the star Kruno,[4] on the second circle I placed Aphrodit, on the third Aris, on the fifth Zeus, on the sixth Ermis, on the seventh the diminished moon adorned with the lesser stars. And on the lower circle I placed the sun to illuminate the day and the moon and stars to illuminate the night. That the sun should go according to each animal of the zodiac, I appointed the succession of twelve months and their names and lives, their thunderings, their hour markings, and how they follow each other. Then evening came and morning came, and it was the fifth day.

5

"On the fifth day I commanded the sea to bring forth fishes, and I created feathered birds of many varieties, all animals creeping over the earth, four-legged animals running on the earth, and I made those beasts which soar in the air, both male and female, and every soul breathing the spirit of life.

"Then evening came and morning came, and it was the sixth day.

"On the sixth day I commanded my wisdom to create man from seven consistencies: one, his flesh from the earth; two, his blood from the dew; three, his eyes from the sun; four, his bones from stone; five, his intelligence from the swiftness of the angels and from cloud; six, his veins and his hair from the grass of the earth; seven, his soul from my breath and from the wind. And I gave him seven natures: flesh for hearing, eyes for sight, the soul for smell, blood for touch, bones for endurance, and intelligence for sweetness and joy.

"I conceived a cunning saying: I created man from invisible and visible nature. From both come his death, his life, and image. He knows speech like some created thing, small in greatness and great in smallness. And I placed on the earth a second angel, honorable, great, and glorious, and appointed him as ruler on earth to have my wisdom. And there was none like him on earth of all my existing creatures. And I gave him a name from the four component parts, from east, west, south, and north, and I assigned him four special stars. I called his name Adam. I showed him the two ways, the light and the darkness, and told him, 'This is good and that bad,' to learn whether he has love or hatred for me, to know who among his people love me.

"Although I have seen his nature, he has not seen his own nature. Therefore, because of not seeing he will sin worse, and I said, 'After sin what is there but death?'

"And I put sleep into him and he fell asleep. And I took a rib from him, and created a wife for him that death should come to him by his wife, and I took his last word and called her name mother, that is, Eva.

"Adam has life on earth, and I created a garden in Eden, in the east, so he might observe the testament and keep the command. I made the heavens open before him so he might see the angels singing the song of victory and of the gloomless light. He remained in Paradise, and the Devil understood that I wanted to create another world, because Adam was lord on earth, which he ruled and controlled.

"The Devil is the evil spirit of the lower places, a fugitive. He made Sotona from the heavens, so his name was Satomail. Thus he became different from the angels, but his nature did not change his intelligence in regard to understanding right and wrong. And he understood his condemnation and the sin which he had sinned. Therefore he nurtured thoughts against Adam. He entered his world and seduced Eva but did not touch Adam. I cursed ignorance. But what I had blessed previously, that I did not curse—not man, nor the earth, nor other creatures, but man's evil fruit and works.

"I said to him 'You are earth, and into the earth from which I took you, you shall go, and I shall not destroy you but send you away from where I placed you. Then I can take you to me again at my second coming.'

"And I blessed all my creatures, visible and invisible. And Adam was five-and-a-half hours in Paradise. I blessed the seventh day, the Sabbath on which I rested from all my works.

God Shows Enoch the Age of the World
"And I assigned the eighth day to be the first day created after my work, and the first seven to revolve in the form of seven thousand. At the beginning of the eighth thousand I appointed an uncounted time, an infinity, unmeasured by years, months, weeks, days, or hours.

"And now, Enoch, I invented all things I have told you about, all you have seen on earth, all things you have written in these books. I created everything from the highest to the lowest. There is no counselor here. I am eternal and not made with hands. My thought is counselor, my word is deed, my eyes see all. What I look on stands. What I turn away from will be destroyed. So apply your mind, Enoch, and know him who speaks to you, and care for the books you have written.

"I give you the angels Semil and Rasuil[5] and him who brought you up to me. Go down to earth and tell my sons all things I have spoken to you and all you have seen from the lowest heaven up to my throne. Of all the troops I have created, none opposes me or does not submit to me. All submit to my monarchy and serve my power.

"Pass on the books of your handwriting, from child to child, from kinsman to kinsman, from race to race, you Enoch, mediator of my general Michael, for your writing and the writing of your fathers Adam and Seth will not be destroyed till the end of time. I have told my angels Orioch[6] and Marioch how I have put a chart on earth and ordered the ages to be preserved, and the writing of your fathers to be preserved that it will not perish in the flood I shall unleash on your people."

Enoch's Pitiful Warning to His Sons

My children, my loved ones, hear your father's warning in keeping with the Lord's will. Not from my lips but from the Lord's lips I announce all that is and was and will be till judgment day. For the Lord has let my lips come to you. You hear the words of my lips, of a man made larger for you. I have seen the Lord's face. Like iron made to glow from fire, it sends forth sparks and burns.

You look into my eyes, the eyes of a man great with meaning for you. I have seen the Lord's eyes shining like the sun's rays and filling the eyes of man with wonder. My children, you see the right hand of a man who helps you, but I have seen the Lord's right hand filling Heaven as he helped me. You see the compass of my work like your own, but I have seen the Lord's limitless and perfect compass. You hear the words of my lips, as I heard the words of the Lord, like incessant great thunder and hurling clouds.

Now hear the discourses of the father of the earth. And know how fearful it is to come before the face of the ruler of the earth. Think how much more terrible and awful it is to come before the face of the ruler of Heaven, the controller of living and dead, and of the heavenly troops. Who can endure that unending pain? Now hear those things I know from the Lord's lips, what my eyes have seen from beginning to end.

I know all things and have written them into books concerning the heavens and their end, their plenitude, their armies and their marchings. I have measured and described the stars, their great and countless multitude. What man has seen their revolutions and entrances? Not even the angels see their number, yet I have recorded all their names.

And I measured the sun's circle, measured its rays, counted the hours. I wrote down all that exists on earth—how things are nourished, how all seeds that the earth produces are sown and unsown, and about all plants, and every grass and flower, and their sweet smells, and their names, and the dwelling places of clouds, their composition and their wings, and how they bear raindrops.

I wrote of the road taken by the thunder and lightning, and they showed me their keys and guardians, their rise, their movement. Thunder and lightning are released by a chain in strict measure lest a reckless heavy chain of violence hurl down angry clouds and destroy all things on earth.

I wrote of the treasure houses of the

snow, the storage houses of the cold and of freezing winds, and I observed how the key-holder of the seasons fills the clouds with its snows and winds but never exhausts their treasure houses.

And I wrote of the resting places of the winds and observed how the key-holders hold scales and measures. They weigh the seasons in the pans and release them cunningly over the whole earth, lest heavy breathing rock the earth. And I measured out the whole earth, its mountains, hills, fields, trees, stones, rivers. I recorded the height from earth to the seventh heaven and down to the very lowest Hell, the judgment place, the great, open, and weeping Hell. And I saw how its prisoners are in pain, expecting never-ending judgment. And I recorded all who have been judged by the judge, all their punishments, and all their deeds.

Enoch Instructs His Sons from God's Lips and Hands Them This Book

Children, hear your father whose words come from God's lips. Take these books your father has written and read them. In these many books you will learn all the Lord's works, from the beginning of creation till the end of time. And if you read well, you will not sin against the Lord. There is no other like the Lord in Heaven, on earth, in the very lowest places, and in the one foundation.

The Lord placed foundations in the unknown, and spread forth both visible and invisible heavens. He fixed the earth on the waters, and created countless creatures. Who has counted the water and the foundation of the unfixed or the dust of the earth or the sand of the sea or the drops of the rain or the morning dew or the wind's breathings? Who has filled earth and sea and in the indissoluble winter?

He cut the stars out of fire, decorated the firmament, and placed it in our midst.

How God Bids Us to Be Meek, to Endure Attack and Insult, and Not to Offend Widows and Orphans

I have put every man's work in writing and none born on earth can remain hidden nor his works remain concealed. I see all things. Therefore, my children, in patience and meekness spend the number of your days that you may inherit endless life. For the sake of the Lord, endure every wound and injury, every evil word and attack. If ill-requitals befall you, do not return them to neighbor or enemy, because the Lord will return them for you and be your avenger on the day of great judgment that there be no avenging here among men.

Whoever spends gold or silver for his brother's sake, he will receive ample treasure in the world to come. Do not injure widows or orphans or strangers, lest God's wrath come upon you.

Enoch Instructs His Sons Not to Hide Treasures in the Earth, but Bids Them Give Alms to the Poor

Stretch out your hands to the poor according to your strength. Do not hide your silver in the earth. Help the faithful man in affliction and affliction will not find you in the time of your trouble. And every grievous and cruel yoke that come upon you bear all for the sake of the Lord, and thus you will find your reward in the day of judgment.

It is good to go morning, midday, and evening into the Lord's dwelling, for the glory of your creator. Every breathing thing glorifies him, and every creature visible and invisible returns him praise.

Enoch Taken Up on High

When Enoch had talked to the people, the Lord sent darkness onto the earth, and there was darkness, and it covered those men standing and talking with Enoch, and they took Enoch up onto the highest heaven, where the Lord was, and he received him and placed him before his face, and darkness left the earth, and light came again.

But the people did not see and understand how Enoch had been taken to glorify God. They found a roll in which was traced: "the invisible God," and all went to their homes.

Enoch was born on the sixth day of the month Tsivan, and lived three hundred and sixty-five years.

He was taken up to Heaven on the first day of the month Tsivan and remained in heaven sixty days. He wrote all these signs of all creation, which the Lord created, and wrote three hundred and sixty-six books, and handed them over to his sons and remained on earth thirty days, and was again taken up to Heaven on the sixth day of the month Tsivan, on the very day and hour when he was born. As every man's nature in this life is dark, so also are his conception, birth, and departure from this life. At the hour he was conceived, at that hour he was born, and at that hour too he died.

Methosalam[7] and his brethren, all the sons of Enoch, made haste, and erected an altar at the place called Achuzan, whence and where Enoch had been taken up to Heaven.

All people were summoned and they took sacrificial oxen and sacrificed them before the Lord's face.

All people, the elders of the people, and the whole assembly, came to the feast and brought gifts to the sons of Enoch.

And they made a great feast, rejoicing, and they were merry for three days, praising God, who had given them a sign through Enoch, who had found favor with God. All people rejoiced that this sign could be passed on to their sons and from generation to generation and from age to age.

Notes

1. Idoil. In Slavonic A it occurs as Adoil. R. H. Charles suggests "the hand of God." The word occurs nowhere else.

2. Throne. The throne was created before the world, according to *Bereshith rabba c.*

3. Satanail. Satan.

4. Kruno, Aphrodit, Aris, Ermis are Chronos, Aphrodite, Ares, Hermes.

5. Semil and Rasuil. In Slavonic A they occur as Samuil and Raguil. In *1 Enoch* 20:4, Raguil is a holy angel who takes vengeance on the world of luminaries. In *2 Enoch* Samuil and Rasuil escort Enoch on his journey through the heavens.

6. Orioch. A name found as Arioch in Genesis 14:1, 9; Daniel 2:14.

7. Methosalam. Methuselah.

The Book of Jubilees

(Jewish Pseudepigrapha)

The *Book of Jubilees* is an extensive retelling of Genesis and Exodus in which the author's emphasis on *Halakhah* (the teachings and ordinances of biblical law) suggests both opposition to the Hellenizing spirit in Israel and an affinity with the Qumran community, the so-called Essenes of the Dead Sea Scrolls. The emphasis on halakhic commentary is seen in references to "commandments written down on heavenly tablets."

In this "Little Genesis"—an alternate title to a book longer than Genesis as well as any book of the pseudepigrapha—God secretly reveals to Moses on Mount Sinai the history of the Jews from the creation of the world to the passage through the Red Sea. God's agent is the "angel of the presence," who orders Moses to write down God's exact words. Events in the book follow a solar calendar, and dates and numbers are specific and emphatic. For example, the regulations governing the uncleanness of a woman after the birth of a son or daughter specify the number of days of the mother's separation from the sanctuary, and God gives this information to Adam directly on his arrival in Eden from the land of his creation. The emphasis on the prohibition of nakedness, on Adam and Eve's shame and God's gift of clothing to them, all reflect an attempt to protect Israel from the Greek *gymnasion* and *ephebeion*, which were popular in Jerusalem and even among its Maccabean rulers. A notable richness in the book is its angelology—angels of the winds and of the waters—which is referred to in Matthew, Acts, and Revelation. In the final section (not given here), the righteous live a mythical existence and enjoy a prediluvian longevity of a thousand years or more. Their souls will enjoy immortality.

The date of composition is uncertain, but most scholars indicate the middle of the second century B.C. *Jubilees* was written in Hebrew, then translated into Greek, and from Greek into Ethiopic. The complete text exists in Ethiopic today, edited by R. H. Charles. Fragments of a Latin translation are also extant.[1]

Notes

1. George W. E. Nickelsburg announces in *Jewish Literature between the Bible and the Mishnah* (Philadelphia: Fortress Press, 1981) a new translation of *Jubilees* by Orval S. Wintermute in Nickelsburg's forthcoming *The Pseudepigrapha of the Old Testament* (Garden City, New York: Doubleday).

THE CREATION OF THE WORLD*

On the first day[1] he created the tall heavens and the earth and waters and all the spirits who served him: the angels of the presence, the angels of sanctification, the angels of the spirit of fire, the angels of the spirit of the winds, of the clouds, of darkness, of snow, hail, and hoarfrost, the angels of the voices of thunder and lightning, the angels of the spirits of cold and heat, of winter, spring, autumn, and summer, and of all spirits of his creatures in Heaven and on the earth. He created the abysses and darkness, twilight and night, and light, dawn, and day, and he prepared them in the knowledge of his heart. Thereupon we saw his works, and praised him.

He created seven great works on the first day. On the second day he created the firmament in the midst of the waters, and on that day the waters were divided, half of them going above, half below, the firmament hanging over the face of the entire earth. This was God's only work on the second day. On the third day he commanded the waters to roll off the face of the earth, to gather in one place, and for dry land to appear. The waters did as he commanded and rolled off the face of the earth, and in a single place the dry land appeared. On that day he created all the seas according to their separate gathering places, all rivers, waters in the mountains and along the earth, the lakes and dew, seed which is sown, and all sprouting things, fruit trees, trees of the forest, and the Garden of Eden. In Eden he formed every manner of plant. These were his great works on the third day.

And on the fourth day he created the sun and moon and stars, and placed them in the firmament of heaven to give light on earth, to rule over day and night, to separate light from darkness. And God appointed the sun to be a great sign on the earth for days and for sabbaths and for months, for feasts, years, sabbaths of years, for jubilees, and every season of the years. The sun divided light from darkness so that all things may prosper which shoot and grow in the earth. These three things he made on the fourth day.

And on the fifth day he created great sea monsters in the depths of the waters —these were the first things of flesh created by his hands—the fish and everything that moves in the waters, and everything that flies—all the birds. The sun rose above them to enrich all his creations—plants shooting on the earth, trees, and flesh. These three things he created on the fifth day.

And on the sixth day he created all the animals of the earth, cattle, and all moving things. And after all this he created man, a man and woman, and he gave him dominion over all on the earth, in the seas, in the air, over beasts and cattle he gave him dominion. And these four species he created on the sixth day. There were altogether twenty-two kinds.

*Chapter 2. All selections in this chapter are modern revisions of R. H. Charles, *The Book of Jubilees* (Oxford: Clarendon Press, 1902), pp. 40–43, 46–51.

He finished his work on the sixth day—in Heaven and earth, in the waters and abysses, in light and darkness. And he gave us a great sign, the Sabbath: that we should work six days but on the Sabbath, the seventh day, we should keep from all work.

ADAM, EVE, AND PARADISE*

During six days of the second week, according to God's word, he brought Adam all beasts, cattle, all birds and things creeping on the earth and moving in the water. Beasts were on day one, cattle on day two, birds on day three, all that creeps on the earth on day four, all that moves in the water on day five. And Adam named them. As he called them so was their name. And during these five days Adam saw that each species had male and female, but he was alone. He had no helpmate. The Lord said to us: "It is not good for the man to be alone. I will make him a helpmate." Our God caused a deep sleep to fall on him, and while he slept God took one of his ribs as a woman. This was the origin of woman. And he built up the flesh on it. He constructed woman. And he woke Adam from his sleep, and on this sixth day he brought her to the rising Adam, and Adam knew her and said, "She is now bone of my bones and flesh of my flesh. She will be called my wife because she was taken from her husband." So man and wife will be one, so a man will leave his father and mother and cleave to his wife, and they will be one flesh.

Adam was created in the first week, and his wife, his rib, in the second week. God showed her to him, and so the commandment was given for a male to keep in his defilement for seven days and for a female twice seven days.

_____
*Chapter 3.

After Adam had completed forty days in the land where he was created, he was brought into the Garden of Eden to till and to keep it. His wife was brought in on the eightieth day. For that reason the commandment is written on the heavenly tablets in regard to the mother: "She who bears a male shall remain in her uncleanness seven days, and thirty-three days in the blood of purification. She shall not touch any hallowed things, nor enter in the sanctuary until the days for the male or female child are accomplished." This is law and testimony written down for Israel.

In the first week of the first jubilee, Adam and his wife were in the Garden of Eden for seven years tilling and reaping. He was given work and instructed how to farm correctly. He tilled the Garden and was naked, but he did not know it, and was not ashamed. He protected the Garden from birds and beasts and cattle, and gathered fruit and food, which he stored for himself and his wife. After exactly seven years, in the seventeenth day of the second month, the serpent came and said to the woman, "Did God command you not to eat of any tree in the Garden?" She said, "God told us to eat fruit from all trees in the Garden, except for the fruit of the tree in the middle of the Garden. God said to us: 'You must not eat from it, nor touch it, or you will die.'"

And the serpent said to the woman, "You will surely not die. For God knows that on the day you eat of that tree your eyes will be opened. You will be like gods and know good from evil." And the woman looked at the tree, which was pleasant to her eye, and its fruit good for food, and she picked a fruit and ate. She covered her shame with a fig leaf and gave Adam what she had taken from the tree. He ate, and his eyes were opened and he saw that he was naked. He took fig leaves, sewed them together, made an apron for himself, and covered his shame.

Then God cursed the serpent and was

forever angry with it. He was angry with the woman, for she had listened to the serpent and had eaten. He said to her: "I will greatly multiply your sorrows and your pains. In sorrow you will bring forth children. You will return to your husband, who will rule over you." To Adam he said: "Because you listened to your wife's voice and ate from the tree I commanded you not to touch, let the ground be cursed under you. Thorns and thistles will grow in it, and you will eat your bread in the sweat of your face until you return to the earth from which you were taken. You are earth and to earth you will return." He made them coats out of skins, clothed them, and sent them out of the Garden of Eden.

On the day Adam left the Garden, he made an offering of sweet-smelling frankincense, galbanum, and stacte, and spices of the morning. And on that day was closed the mouth of all beasts, of cattle, birds, whatever walks and crawls, so that they could not speak. They had all spoken to each other with one lip and one tongue. He sent out of the Garden all flesh that was there, and all flesh was scattered according to its kinds in the places created for them. He gave only Adam the means of covering his shame, not any of the beasts and cattle. And so those who know the judgment of law prescribed on the heavenly tablets know to cover their shame. They should not uncover themselves as the Gentiles do.[2]

On the new moon of the fourth month Adam and his wife left the Garden of Eden and dwelled in the land of Elda, in the land of their creation. Adam called his wife Eve. They had no son till the first jubilee, and after this he knew her. Now he farmed the land as he had been instructed to in the Garden of Eden.

Notes

1. *The Book of Jubilees* is presented as a secret revelation given to Moses by God's angels on Mount Sinai. The first line of chapter 2, omitted in the above text, introduces the retelling of the Genesis creation: "And the angel of the presence spoke to Moses according to the word of the Lord, saying: 'Write the complete history of the creation, how in six days the Lord God finished all his works and all that he created, and kept Sabbath on the seventh day and hallowed it for all ages, and appointed it as a sign for all his works.' "

2. This passage suggests opposition to stripping by Greeks (as well as Jews) for athletic games. In a larger sense it suggests opposition to Hellenizing Jews and Hellenization in Palestine.

Haggadah

(Jewish Legend from Midrash, Pseudepigrapha, and Early Kabbalah)

The Haggadah, often translated as "legend," derives from an oral tradition of stories, biblical commentary, and biblical exegesis (the Midrash), and is usually contrasted with the Halakhah, which derives from oral law. Both Haggadah and Halakhah are originally associated with the Talmud, a vast collection of Jewish writing compiled from the post-biblical period of the fourth century A.D. for the Palestinian Talmud, and the fifth and perhaps sixth century for the Babylonian Talmud. The text of the Talmud is the Mishnah (in Hebrew) and the Gemara (in Aramaic), the former the text itself, the latter usually a commentary. But the Haggadah has come to include not only the Midrashic elaborations of the Talmud but the entire didactic, ethical, and narrative traditions of the pseudepigrapha and the early Kabbalah. The popular, spontaneous character of the Haggadah is its prominent feature and, even preserved in its written form, it retains that Socratic freshness of oral debate, narration, and speculation.

The Haggadah treats many aspects of Jewish life—friendship, animals, dreams, love, education, health, justice, and the nature of a caring, personal God. Above all it is an elegant and mythical homage to the *book:* the Torah. Before God creates the earth and Heaven, he creates the book. In fantastic vision, the Haggadah informs us that the Torah is "written with black fire on white fire, and [is] lying on the lap of God." As in the later *Zohar*, the *Book of Radiance* of the Spanish Kabbalah, before God creates the world by his word he must devise the twenty-two letters of the alphabet. When man is made from the dust, the dust is of various colors: "red for the blood, black for the bowels, white for the bones and veins, and green for the pale skin." The Haggadah has stunning literary passages, graced with clarity and an often humorous fantasy. For the Jews it is, to use the title of George Seferis's famous Homeric retelling, *Mythistorema*, "the myth of our history."

THE CREATION OF THE WORLD*

The First Things Created

In the beginning, two thousand years before the Heaven and the earth, seven things were created: the Torah written with black fire on white fire, and lying in the lap of God; the Divine Throne, erected in the Heaven which later was over the heads of the Hayyot; Paradise on the right side of God, Hell on the left side; the Celestial Sanctuary directly in front of God, having a jewel on its altar graven with the Name of the messiah, and a Voice that cries aloud, "Return, you children of men."

When God resolved upon the creation of the world, he took counsel with the Torah. Her advice was this: "O Lord, a king without an army and without courtiers and attendants hardly deserves the name of king, for none is nigh to express the homage due to him." The answer pleased God exceedingly. Thus did he teach all earthly kings, by his divine example, to undertake naught without first consulting advisers.

The advice of the Torah was given with some reservations. She was skeptical about the value of an earthly world, on account of the sinfulness of men, who would be sure to disregard her precepts. But God dispelled her doubts. He told her that repentance had been created long before, and sinners would have the opportunity of mending their ways. Besides, the Temple service would be invested with atoning power, and Paradise and Hell were intended to do duty as reward and punishment. Finally, the messiah was appointed to bring salvation, which would put an end to all sinfulness.

*Chapters 1–2. The text used here is translated by Henrietta Szold from Louis Ginzberg's classic rendering into German of specific Talmudic, pseudepigraphic, and kabbalistic texts. All selections in this chapter are from Louis Ginzberg, *The Legend of the Jews* (Philadelphia: Jewish Publication Society of America, 1909).

Nor is this world inhabited by man the first of things earthly created by God. He made several worlds before ours, but he destroyed them all, because he was pleased with none until he created ours. But even this last world would have had no permanence, if God had executed his original plan of ruling it according to the principle of strict justice. It was only when he saw that justice by itself would undermine the world that he associated mercy with justice, and made them to rule jointly. Thus from the beginning of all things prevailed divine goodness, without which nothing could have continued to exist. If not for it, the myriads of evil spirits had soon put an end to the generations of men. But the goodness of God has ordained that in every Nisan, at the time of the spring equinox, the seraphim shall approach the world of spirits, and intimidate them so that they fear to do harm to men. Again, if God in his goodness had not given protection to the weak, the tame animals would have been extirpated long ago by the wild animals. In Tammuz, at the time of the summer solstice, when the strength of behemoth is at its height, he roars so loud that all the animals hear it, and for a whole year they are affrighted and timid, and their acts become less ferocious than their nature is. Again, in Tishri, at the time of the autumnal equinox, the great bird ziz flaps his wings and utters his cry, so that the birds of prey, the eagles and the vultures, blench, and they fear to swoop down upon the others and annihilate them in their greed. And again, were it not for the goodness of God, the vast number of big fish had quickly put an end to the little ones. But at the time of the winter solstice, in the month of Tebet, the sea grows restless, for then leviathan spouts up water, and the big fish become uneasy. They restrain their appetite, and the little ones escape their rapacity.

Finally, the goodness of God manifests itself in the preservation of his people Israel. It could not have survived the enmity of the Gentiles if God had not appointed protectors for it, the archangels Michael and Gabriel. Whenever Israel disobeys God, and is accused of misdemeanors by the angels of the other nations, he is defended by his designated guardians, with such good result that the other angels conceive fear of them. Once the angels of the other nations are terrified, the nations themselves venture not to carry out their wicked designs against Israel.

That the goodness of God may rule on earth as in Heaven, the angels of destruction are assigned a place at the far end of the heavens, from which they may never stir, while the angels of mercy encircle the throne of God, at his behest.

The Alphabet

When God was about to create the world by his word, the twenty-two letters of the alphabet descended from the terrible and august crown of God whereon they were engraved with a pen of flaming fire. They stood round about God, and one after the other spake and entreated, "Create the world through me!"

After the claims of all these letters had been disposed of, Bet stepped before the Holy One, blessed be he, and pleaded before him: "O Lord of the world! May it be your will to create your world through me, seeing that all the dwellers in the world give praise daily unto you through me, as it is said, 'Blessed be the Lord forever. Amen, and Amen.'" The Holy One, blessed be he, at once granted the petition of Bet. He said, "Blessed be he that comes in the name of the Lord." And he created his world through Bet, as it is said, "Bereshit God created the Heaven and the earth."

The only letter that had refrained from urging its claims was the modest Alef, and God rewarded it later for its humility by giving it the first place in the Decalogue.

The First Day

On the first day of creation God produced ten things: the heavens and the earth, Tohu and Bohu, light and darkness, wind and water, the duration of the day and the duration of the night.

Though the heavens and the earth consist of entirely different elements, they were yet created as a unit, "like the pot and its cover." The heavens were fashioned from the light of God's garment, and the earth from the snow under the divine throne. Tohu is a green band which encompasses the whole world, and dispenses darkness, and Bohu consists of stones in the abyss, the producers of the waters. The light created at the very beginning is not the same as the light emitted by the sun, the moon, and the stars, which appeared only on the fourth day. The light of the first day was of a sort that would have enabled man to see the world at a glance from one end to the other. Anticipating the wickedness of the sinful generations of the deluge and the Tower of Babel, who were unworthy to enjoy the blessing of such light, God concealed it, but in the world to come it will appear to the pious in all its pristine glory.

Several heavens were created, seven in fact, each to serve a purpose of its own. The first, the one visible to man, has no function except that of covering up the light during the nighttime; therefore it disappears every morning. The planets are fastened to the second of the heavens; in the third the manna is made for the pious in the hereafter; the fourth contains the celestial Jerusalem together with the Temple, in which Michael ministers as high priest, and offers the souls of the pious as sacrifices. In the fifth heaven, the angel hosts reside, and sing the praise of God, though only during the night, for by day it is the task of Israel on earth to give glory to God on high. The sixth heaven is an uncanny spot; there originate most of the trials and visitations ordained for the earth and its inhabitants. Snow lies heaped up there and hail; there are lofts full of noxious dew, magazines stocked with storms, and cellars holding reserves of smoke. Doors of fire separate these celestial chambers, which are under the supervision of the archangel Metatron. Their pernicious contents defiled the heavens until David's time. The pious king prayed God to purge his exalted dwelling of whatever was pregnant with evil; it was not becoming that such things should exist near the Merciful One. Only then they were removed to the earth.

The seventh heaven, on the other hand, contains naught but what is good and beautiful: right, justice, and mercy, the storehouses of life, peace, and blessing, the souls of the pious, the souls and spirits of unborn generations, the dew with which God will revive the dead on the resurrection day, and, above all, the divine throne, surrounded by the seraphim, the ofanim, the holy Hayyot, and the ministering angels.

Corresponding to the seven heavens, God created seven earths, each separated from the next by five layers. Over the lowest earth, the seventh, called Erez, lie in succession the abyss, the Tohu, the Bohu, a sea, and waters. Then the sixth earth is reached, the Adamah, the scene of the magnificence of God. In the same way the Adamah is separated from the fifth earth, the Arka, which contains Gehenna, and Sha 'are Mawet, and Sha 'are Zalmawet, and Beer Shahat, and Tit ha-Yawen, and Abaddon, and Sheol, and there the souls of the wicked are guarded by the angels of destruction. In the same way Arka is followed by Harabah, the dry, the place of brooks and streams in spite of its name, as the next, called Yabbashah, the mainland, contains the rivers and the springs. Tebel, the second earth, is the first mainland inhabited by living creatures, three hundred and sixty-five species, all essentially different from those of our own earth. Some have human heads set on the body of a lion, or a serpent, or an ox; others have human bodies topped by the head of one of these animals. Besides, Tebel is inhabited by human beings with two heads and four hands and feet, in fact with all their organs doubled excepting only the trunk. It happens sometimes that the parts of these double persons quarrel with each other, especially while eating and drinking, when each claims the best and largest portions for himself. This species of mankind is distinguished for great piety, another difference between it and the inhabitants of our earth.

Our own earth is called Heled, and, like the others, it is separated from the Tebel by an abyss, the Tohu, the Bohu, a sea, and waters.

Thus one earth rises above the other, from the first to the seventh, and over the seventh earth the heavens are vaulted, from the first to the seventh, the last of them attached to the arm of God. The seven heavens form a unity, the seven kinds of earth form a unity, and the heavens and the earth together also form a unity.

When God made our present heavens and our present earth, "the new heavens and the new earth" were also brought forth, yea, and the hundred and ninety-six thousand worlds which God created unto his own glory.

It takes five hundred years to walk from the earth to the heavens, and from one end of a heaven to the other, and also from one heaven to the next, and it takes the same length of time to travel from the east to the west, or from the south to the north. Of all this vast world only one-third is inhabited, the other two-thirds being equally divided between water and waste desert land.

Beyond the inhabited parts to the east is Paradise with its seven divisions, each assigned to the pious of a certain degree. The ocean is situated to the west, and it is dotted with islands upon islands, inhabited by many different peoples.

Beyond it, in turn, are the boundless steppes full of serpents and scorpions, and destitute of every sort of vegetation, whether herbs or trees. To the north are the supplies of hell-fire, of snow, hail, smoke, ice, darkness, and windstorms, and in that vicinity sojourn all sorts of devils, demons, and malign spirits. Their dwelling place is a great stretch of land, it would take five hundred years to traverse it. Beyond lies Hell. To the south is the chamber containing reserves of fire, the cave of smoke, and the forge of blasts and hurricanes. Thus it comes that the wind blowing from the south brings heat and sultriness to the earth. Were it not for the angel Ben Nez the Winged, who keeps the south wind back with his pinions, the world would be consumed. Besides, the fury of its blast is tempered by the north wind, which always appears as moderator, whatever other wind may be blowing.

In the east, the west, and the south, Heaven and earth touch each other, but the north God left unfinished, that any man who announced himself as a god might be set the task of supplying the deficiency, and stand convicted as a pretender.

The construction of the earth was begun at the center, with the foundation stone of the Temple, the Eben Shetiyah, for the Holy Land is at the central point of the surface of the earth, Jerusalem is at the central point of Palestine, and the Temple is situated at the center of the Holy City. In the sanctuary itself the Hekal is the center, and the holy Ark occupies the center of the Hekal, built on the foundation stone, which thus is at the center of the earth. Thence issued the first ray of light, piercing to the Holy Land, and from there illuminating the whole earth. The creation of the world, however, could not take place until God had banished the ruler of the dark. "Retire," God said to him, "for I desire to create the world by means of light." Only after the light had been fashioned, darkness arose, the light ruling in the sky, the darkness on the earth.

The power of God displayed itself not only in the creation of the world of things, but equally in the limitations which he imposed upon each. The heavens and the earth stretched themselves out in length and breadth as though they aspired to infinitude, and it required the word of God to call a halt to their encroachments.

The Second Day
On the second day God brought forth four creations, the firmament, Hell, fire, and the angels.

The firmament is not the same as the heavens of the first day. It is the crystal stretched forth over the heads of the Hayyot, from which the heavens derive their light, as the earth derives its light from the sun. This firmament saves the earth from being engulfed by the waters of the heavens; it forms the partition between the waters above and the waters below. It was made to crystallize into the solid it is by the heavenly fire, which broke its bounds, and condensed the surface of the firmament. Thus fire made a division between the celestial and the terrestrial at the time of creation, as it did at the revelation on Mount Sinai. The firmament is not more than three fingers thick, nevertheless it divides two such heavy bodies as the waters below, which are the foundations for the nether world, and the waters above, which are the foundations for the seven heavens, the divine throne, and the abode of the angels.

The separation of the waters into upper and lower waters was the only act of the sort done by God in connection with the work of creation. All other acts were unifying. It therefore caused some difficulties. When God commanded, "Let the waters be gathered together, unto one place, and let the dry land appear," certain parts refused to obey. They embraced each other all the more closely. In his wrath at the waters, God determined to let the whole of creation resolve itself into chaos again. He summoned the Angel of the Face, and ordered him to destroy the world. The angel opened his eyes wide, and scorching fires and thick clouds rolled forth from them, while he cried out, "He who divides the Red Sea in sunder!"—and the rebellious waters stood. The all, however, was still in danger of destruction. Then began the singer of God's praises: "O Lord of the world, in days to come your creatures will sing praises without end to you, they will bless you boundlessly, and they will glorify you without measure. You will set Abraham apart from all mankind as your own; one of his sons you will call 'My firstborn'; and his descendants will take the yoke of your kingdom upon themselves. In holiness and purity you will bestow your Torah upon them, with the words, 'I am the Lord your God,' whereunto they will make answer, 'All that God has spoken we will do.' And now I beseech you, have pity upon your world, destroy it not, for if you destroy it, who will fulfill your will?" God was pacified; he withdrew the command ordaining the destruction of the world, but the waters he put under the mountains, to remain there forever.

Hell has seven divisions, one beneath the other. They are called Sheol, Abaddon, Beer Shahat, Tit ha-Yawen, Sha 'are Mawet, Sha 'are Zalmawet, and Gehenna. It requires three hundred years to traverse the height, or the width, or the depth of each division, and it would take six thousand three hundred years to go over a tract of land equal in extent to the seven divisions.

Each of the seven divisions in turn has seven subdivisions, and in each compartment there are seven rivers of fire and seven of hail. The width of each is one thousand ells, its depth one thousand, and its length three hundred, and they flow one from the other, and are supervised by ninety thousand angels of destruction. There are, besides, in every compartment seven thousand caves, in every cave there are seven thousand crevices, and in every crevice seven thousand scorpions. Every scorpion has three hundred rings, and in every ring seven thousand pouches of venom, from which flow seven rivers of deadly poison. If a man handles it, he immediately bursts, every limb is torn from his body, his bowels are cleft asunder, and he falls upon his face. There are also five different kinds of fire in Hell. One devours and absorbs, another devours and does not absorb, while the third absorbs and does not devour, and there is still another fire, which neither devours nor absorbs, and furthermore a fire which devours fire. There are coals big as mountains, and coals big as hills, and coals as large as the Dead Sea, and coals like huge stones, and there are rivers of pitch and sulphur flowing and seething like live coals.

The Third Day

Up to this time the earth was a plain, and wholly covered with water. Scarcely had the words of God, "Let the waters be gathered together," made themselves heard, when mountains appeared all over and hills, and the water collected in the deep-lying basins. But the water was recalcitrant, it resisted the order to occupy the lowly spots, and threatened to overflow the earth, until God forced it back into the sea, and encircled the sea with sand. Now, whenever the water is tempted to transgress its bounds, it beholds the sand, and recoils.

The waters did but imitate their chief Rahab, the Angel of the Sea, who rebelled at the creation of the world. God had commanded Rahab to take in the water. But he refused, saying, "I have enough." The punishment for his disobedience was death. His body rests in the depths of the sea, the water dispeling the foul odor that emanates from it.

19

The main creation of the third day was the realm of plants, the terrestrial plants as well as the plants of Paradise. First of all the cedars of Lebanon and the other great trees were made. In their pride at having been put first, they shot up high in the air. They considered themselves the favored among plants. Then God spake, "I hate arrogance and pride, for I alone am exalted, and none beside," and he created the iron on the same day, the substance with which trees are felled down. The trees began to weep, and when God asked the reason of their tears, they said: "We cry because you have created the iron to uproot us therewith. All the while we had thought ourselves the highest of the earth, and now the iron, our destoyer, has been called into existence." God replied: "You yourselves will furnish the axe with a handle. Without your assistance the iron will not be able to do aught against you."

The most important work done on the third day was the creation of Paradise. Two gates of carbuncle form the entrance to Paradise, and sixty myriads of ministering angels keep watch over them. Each of these angels shines with the luster of the heavens. When the just man appears before the gates, the clothes in which he was buried are taken off him, and the angels array him in seven garments of clouds of glory, and place upon his head two crowns, one of precious stones and pearls, the other of gold of Parvaim, and they put eight myrtles in his hand, and they utter praises before him and say to him, "Go your way, and eat your bread with joy." And they lead him to a place full of rivers, surrounded by eight kinds of roses and myrtles. Each one has a canopy according to his merits, and under it flow four rivers, one of milk, the other of balsam, the third of wine, and the fourth of honey. Every canopy is overgrown by a vine of gold, and thirty pearls hang from it, each of them shining like Venus. Under each canopy there is a table of precious stones and pearls, and sixty angels stand at the head of every just man, saying unto him: "Go and eat with joy of the honey, for you have busied yourself with the Torah, and she is sweeter than honey, and drink of the wine preserved in the grape since the six days of creation, for you have busied yourself with the Torah, and she is compared to wine." The least fair of the just is beautiful as Joseph and Rabbi Johanan, and as the grains of a silver pomegranate upon which fall the rays of the sun. There is no light, "for the light of the righteous is the shining light."

And they undergo four transformations every day, passing through four states. In the first the righteous is changed into a child. He enters the division for children, and tastes the joys of childhood. Then he is changed into a youth, and enters the division for the youths, with whom he enjoys the delights of youth. Next he becomes an adult, in the prime of life, and he enters the division of men, and enjoys the pleasures of manhood. Finally, he is changed into an old man. He enters the division for the old, and enjoys the pleasures of age.

There are eighty myriads of trees in every corner of Paradise, the meanest among them choicer than all the spice trees. In every corner there are sixty myriads of angels singing with sweet voices, and the tree of life stands in the middle and shades the whole of Paradise. It has fifteen thousand tastes, each different from the other, and the perfumes thereof vary likewise. Over it hang seven clouds of glory, and winds blow upon it from all four sides, so that its odor is wafted from one end of the world to the other. Underneath sit the scholars and explain the Torah. Over each of them two canopies are spread, one of stars, the other of sun and moon, and a curtain of clouds of glory separates the one canopy from the other. Beyond Paradise begins Eden, containing three hundred and ten worlds and seven compartments for seven different classes of the pious. In the first are "the martyr victims of the government," like Rabbi Akiba and his colleagues; in the second those who were drowned; in the third Rabbi Johanan ben Zakkai and his disciples; in the fourth those who were carried off in the cloud of glory; in the fifth the penitents, who occupy a place which even a perfectly pious man cannot obtain; in the sixth are the youths who have not tasted of sin in their lives; in the seventh are those poor who studied Bible and Mishnah, and led a life of self-respecting decency. And God sits in the midst of them and expounds the Torah to them.

The Fourth Day

The fourth day of creation produced the sun, the moon, and the stars. These heavenly spheres were not actually fashioned on this day; they were created on the first day, and merely were assigned their places in the heavens on the fourth. At first the sun and the moon enjoyed equal powers and prerogatives. The moon spoke to God, and said: "O Lord, why did you create the world with the letter Bet?" God replied: "That it might be made known unto my creatures that there are two worlds." The moon: "O Lord, which of the two worlds is the larger, this world or the world to come?" God: "The world to come is the larger." The moon: "O Lord, you created two worlds, a greater and a lesser world; you created the Heaven and the earth, the Heaven exceeding the earth; you created fire and water, the water stronger than the fire, because it can quench the fire; and now you have created the sun and the moon, and it is becoming that one of them should be greater than the other." Then spoke God to the moon: "I know well, you would have me make you greater than the sun. As a punishment I decree that you may keep but one-sixtieth of your light." The moon made supplication: "Shall I be punished so severely for having spoken a single word?" God relented: "In the future world I will restore your light, so that your light may again be as the light of the sun." The moon was not yet satisfied. "O Lord," she said, "and the light of the sun, how great will it be in that day?" Then the wrath of God was once more enkindled: "What, you still plot against the sun? As you live, in the world to come his light shall be sevenfold the light he now sheds."

The suns runs his course like a bridegroom. He sits upon a throne with a garland on his head. Ninety-six angels accompany him on his daily journey, in relays of eight every hour, two to the left of him, and two to the right, two before him, and two behind. Strong as he is, he could complete his course from south to north in a single instant, but three hundred and sixty-five angels restrain him by means of as many grappling-irons. Every day one looses his hold, and the sun must thus spend three hundred and sixty-five days on his course. The progress of the sun in his circuit is an uninterrupted song of praise to God. And this song alone makes his motion possible. Therefore, when Joshua wanted to bid the sun stand still, he had to command him to be silent. His song of praise hushed, the sun stood still.

The sun is double-faced; one face, of fire, is directed toward the earth, and one, of hail, toward Heaven, to cool off the prodigious heat that streams from the other face, else the earth would catch afire. In winter the sun turns his fiery face upward, and thus the cold is produced. When the sun descends in the west in the evening, he dips down into the ocean and takes a bath, his fire is extinguished, and therefore he dispenses neither light nor warmth during the night. But as soon as he reaches the east in the morning, he laves himself in a stream of flame, which imparts warmth and light to him, and these he sheds over the earth. In the same way the moon and the stars take a bath in a stream of hail before they enter upon their service for the night.

As the sun sets forth on his course in

the morning, his wings touch the leaves on the trees of Paradise, and their vibration is communicated to the angels and the holy Hayyot, to the other plants, and also to the trees and plants on earth, and to all the beings on earth and in heaven. It is the signal for them all to cast their eyes upward. As soon as they see the Ineffable Name, which is engraved in the sun, they raise their voices in songs of praise to God. At the same moment a heavenly voice is heard to say, "Woe to the sons of men that consider not the honor of God like unto these creatures whose voices now rise aloft in adoration." These words, naturally, are not heard by men, as little as they perceive the grating of the sun against the wheel to which all the celestial bodies are attached, although the noise it makes is extraordinarily loud. This friction of the sun and the wheel produces the motes dancing about in the sunbeams. They are the carriers of healing to the sick, the only health-giving creations of the fourth day, on the whole an unfortunate day, especially for children, afflicting them with disease.

When God punished the envious moon by diminishing her light and splendor, so that she ceased to be the equal of the sun as she had been originally, she fell, and tiny threads were loosed from her body. These are the stars.

The Fifth Day

On the fifth day of creation God took fire and water, and out of these two elements he made the fishes of the sea. The animals in the water are much more numerous than those on land. For every species on land, excepting only the weasel, there is a corresponding species in the water, and, besides, there are many found only in the water.

The ruler over the sea animals is leviathan. With all the other fishes he was made on the fifth day. Originally he was created male and female like all the other animals. But when it appeared that a pair of these monsters might annihilate the whole earth with their united strength, God killed the female. So enormous is leviathan that to quench his thirst he needs all the water that flows from the Jordan into the sea. His food consists of the fish which go between his jaws of their own accord. When he is hungry, a hot breath blows from his nostrils, and it makes the waters of the great sea seething hot. Formidable though behemoth, the other monster, is, he feels insecure until he is certain that leviathan has satisfied his thirst. The only thing that can keep him in check is the stickleback, a little fish which was created for the purpose, and of which he stands in great awe. But leviathan is more than merely large and strong; he is wonderfully made besides. His fins radiate brilliant light, the very sun is obscured by it, and also his eyes shed such splendor that frequently the sea is illuminated suddenly by it. No wonder that this marvelous beast is the plaything of God, in whom he takes his pastime.

There is but one thing that makes leviathan repulsive, his foul smell, which is so strong that if it penetrated thither, it would render Paradise itself an impossible abode.

The real purpose of leviathan is to be served up as a dainty to the pious in the world to come. The female was put into brine as soon as she was killed, to be preserved against the time when her flesh will be needed. The male is destined to offer a delectable sight to all beholders before he is consumed. When his last hour arrives, God will summon the angels to enter into combat with the monster. But no sooner will leviathan cast his glance at them than they will flee in fear and dismay from the field of battle. They will return to the charge with swords, but in vain, for his scales can turn back steel like straw. They will be equally unsuccessful when they attempt to kill him by throwing darts and slinging stones; such missiles will rebound without leaving the least impression on his body. Disheartened, the angels will give up the combat, and God will command leviathan and behemoth to enter into a duel with each other. The issue will be that both will drop dead, behemoth slaughtered by a blow of leviathan's fins, and leviathan killed by a lash of behemoth's tail. From the skin of leviathan God will construct tents to shelter companies of the pious while they enjoy the dishes made of his flesh. The amount assigned to each of the pious will be in proportion to his deserts, and none will envy or begrudge the other his better share. What is left of leviathan's skin will be stretched out over Jerusalem as a canopy, and the light streaming from it will illumine the whole world, and what is left of his flesh after the pious have appeased their appetite will be distributed among the rest of men, to carry on traffic therewith.

On the same day with the fishes, the birds were created, for these two kinds of animals are closely related to each other. Fish are fashioned out of water, and birds out of marshy ground saturated with water.

As leviathan is the king of fishes, so the ziz is appointed to rule over the birds. His name comes from the variety of tastes his flesh has; it tastes like this, *zeh*, and like that, *zeh*. The ziz is as monstrous of size as leviathan himself. His ankles rest on the earth, and his head reaches to the very sky.

It once happened that travelers on a vessel noticed a bird. As he stood in the water, it merely covered his feet, and his head knocked against the sky. The onlookers thought the water could not have any depth at that point, and they prepared to take a bath there. A heavenly voice warned them: "Alight not here! Once a carpenter's axe slipped from his hand at this spot, and it took it seven years to touch bottom." The bird the travelers saw was none other than the ziz. His wings are so huge that unfurled they darken the sun. They protect the earth against the storms of the south;

without their aid the earth would not be able to resist the winds blowing thence. Once an egg of the ziz fell to the ground and broke. The fluid from it flooded sixty cities, and the shock crushed three hundred cedars. Fortunately, such accidents do not occur frequently. As a rule the bird lets her eggs slide gently into her nest. This one mishap was due to the fact that the egg was rotten, and the bird cast it away carelessly. The ziz has another name, Renanim, because he is the celestial singer. On account of his relation to the heavenly regions he is also called Sekwi, the seer, and, besides, he is called "son of the nest," because his fledgling birds break away from the shell without being hatched by the mother bird; they spring directly from the nest, as it were. Like leviathan, so ziz is a delicacy to be served to the pious at the end of time, to compensate them for the privations which abstaining from the unclean fowls imposed upon them.

The Sixth Day

As the fish were formed out of water, and the birds out of boggy earth well mixed with water, so the mammals were formed out of solid earth, and as leviathan is the most notable representative of the fish kind, and ziz of the bird kind, so behemoth is the most notable representative of the mammal kind. Behemoth matches leviathan in strength, and he had to be prevented, like leviathan, from multiplying and increasing, else the world could not have continued to exist; after God had created him male and female, he at once deprived him of the desire to propagate his kind. He is so monstrous that he requires the produce of a thousand mountains for his daily food. All the water that flows through the bed of the Jordan in a year suffices him exactly for one gulp. It therefore was necessary to give him one stream entirely for his own use, a stream flowing forth from Paradise, called Yubal. Behemoth too, is destined to be served to the pious

23

as an appetizing dainty, but before they enjoy his flesh, they will be permitted to view the mortal combat between leviathan and behemoth, as a reward for having denied themselves the pleasures of the circus and its gladiatorial contests.

Leviathan, ziz, and behemoth are not the only monsters; there are many others, and marvelous ones, like the reem, a giant animal, of which only one couple, male and female, is in existence. Had there been more, the world could hardly have maintained itself against them. The act of copulation occurs but once in seventy years between them, for God has so ordered it that the male and female reem are at opposite ends of the earth, the one in the east, the other in the west.

The act of copulation results in the death of the male. He is bitten by the female and dies of the bite. The female becomes pregnant and remains in this state for no less than twelve years. At the end of this long period she gives birth to twins, a male and a female. The year preceding her delivery she is not able to move. She would die of hunger, were it not that her own spittle flowing copiously from her mouth waters and fructifies the earth near her, and causes it to bring forth enough for her maintenance. For a whole year the animal can but roll from side to side, until finally her belly bursts, and the twins issue forth. Their appearance is thus the signal for the death of the mother reem. She makes room for the new generation, which in turn is destined to suffer the same fate as the generation that went before. Immediately after birth, the one goes eastward and the other westward, to meet only after the lapse of seventy years, propagate themselves, and perish. A traveler who once saw a reem one day old described its height to be four parasangs, and the length of its head one parasang and a half. Its horns measure one hundred ells, and their height is a great deal more.

One of the most remarkable creatures is the "man of the mountain," Adne Sadeh, or, briefly, Adam. His form is exactly that of a human being, but he is fastened to the ground by means of a navel-string, upon which his life depends. Once the cord is snapped, he dies. This animal keeps himself alive with what is produced by the soil around about him as far as his tether permits him to crawl. No creature may venture to approach within the radius of his cord, for he seizes and demolishes whatever comes in his reach. To kill him, one may not go near to him, the navel-string must be severed from a distance by means of a dart, and then he dies amid groans and moans.

Once upon a time a traveler happened in the region where this animal is found. He overheard his host consult his wife as to what to do to honor their guest, and resolve to serve "our man," as he said. Thinking he had fallen among cannibals, the stranger ran as fast as his feet could carry him from his entertainer, who sought vainly to restrain him. Afterward, he found out that there had been no intention of regaling him with human flesh, but only with the flesh of the strange animal called "man."

As the "man of the mountain" is fixed to the ground by his navel-string, so the barnacle-goose is grown to a tree by its bill. It is hard to say whether it is an animal and must be slaughtered to be fit for food, or whether it is a plant and no ritual ceremony is necessary before eating it.

Among the birds the phoenix is the most wonderful. When Eve gave all the animals some of the fruit of the tree of knowledge, the phoenix was the only bird that refused to eat thereof, and he was rewarded with eternal life. When he has lived a thousand years, his body shrinks, and the feathers drop from it, until he is as small as an egg. This is the nucleus of the new bird.

The phoenix is also called "the guardian of the terrestrial sphere." He runs with the sun on his circuit, and he spreads out his wings and catches up the fiery rays of the sun. If he were not there to intercept them, neither man nor any other animate being would keep alive. On his right wing the following words are inscribed in huge letters, about four thousand stadia high: "Neither the earth produces me, nor the heavens, but only the wings of fire." His food consists of the manna of Heaven and the dew of the earth. His excrement is a worm, whose excrement in turn is the cinnamon used by kings and princes. Enoch, who saw the phoenix birds when he was translated, describes them as flying creatures, wonderful and strange in appearance, with the feet and tails of lions, and the heads of crocodiles; their appearance is of a purple color like the rainbow; their size nine hundred measures. Their wings are like those of angels, each having twelve, and they attend the chariot of the sun and go with him, bringing heat and dew as they are ordered by God. In the morning when the sun starts on his daily course, the phoenixes and the chalkidri sing, and every bird flaps its wings, rejoicing the Giver of light, and they sing a song at the command of the Lord.

Man and the World

With ten Sayings God created the world, although a single Saying would have sufficed. God desired to make known how severe is the punishment to be meted out to the wicked, who destroy a world created with as many as ten Sayings, and how goodly the reward destined for the righteous, who preserve a world created with as many as ten Sayings.

The world was made for man, though he was the lastcomer among its creatures. This was design. He was to find all things ready for him. God was the host who prepared dainty dishes, set the table, and then led his guest to his seat. At the same time man's late appearance on earth is to convey an admonition to humility. Let him beware of being proud, lest he invite the retort that the gnat is older than he.

The superiority of man to the other creatures is apparent in the very manner of his creation, altogether different from theirs. He is the only one who was created by the hand of God. The rest sprang from the Word of God. The body of man is a microcosm, the whole world in miniature, and the world in turn is a reflex of man. The hair upon his head corresponds to the woods of the earth, his tears to a river, his mouth to the ocean. Also, the world resembles the ball of his eye: the ocean that encircles the earth is like unto the white of the eye, the dry land is the iris, Jerusalem the pupil, and the Temple the image mirrored in the pupil of the eye.

But man is more than a mere image of this world. He unites both heavenly and earthly qualities within himself. In four he resembles the angels, in four the beasts. His power of speech, his discriminating intellect, his upright walk, the glance of his eye—they all make an angel of him. But, on the other hand, he eats and drinks, secretes the waste matter in his body, propagates his kind, and dies, like the beast of the field. Therefore God said before the creation of man: "The celestials are not propagated, but they are immortal; the beings on earth are propagated, but they die. I will create man to be the union of the two, so that when he sins, when he behaves like a beast, death shall overtake him; but if he refrains from sin, he shall live forever." God now bade all beings in Heaven and on earth contribute to the creation of man, and he himself took part in it. Thus they all will love man and, if he should sin, they will be interested in his preservation.

The Angels and the Creation of Man

God in his wisdom having resolved to create man, he asked counsel of all around him before he proceeded to execute his purpose—an example to man, be he never so great and distinguished, not to scorn the advice of the humble and lowly. First God called upon Heaven and earth, then upon all other things he had created, and last upon the angels.

The angels were not all of one opinion. The Angel of Love favored the creation of man, because he would be affectionate and loving; but the Angel of Truth opposed it, because he would be full of lies. And while the Angel of Justice favored it, because he would practice justice, the Angel of Peace opposed it, because he would be quarrelsome.

To invalidate his protest, God cast the Angel of Truth down from Heaven to earth, and when the others cried out against such contemptuous treatment of their companion, he said, "Truth will spring back out of the earth."

The objections of the angels would have been much stronger had they known the whole truth about man. God had told them only about the pious, and had concealed from them that there would be reprobates among mankind, too. And yet, though they knew but half the truth, the angels were nevertheless prompted to cry out: "What is man, that you are mindful of him? And the son of man, that you visit him?" God replied: "The fowl of the air and the fish of the sea, what were they created for? Of what avail a larder full of appetizing dainties, and no guest to enjoy them?" And the angels could not but exclaim: "O Lord, our Lord, how excellent is your name in all the earth! Do as is pleasing in your sight."

The Creation of Adam
When at last the assent of the angels to the creation of man was given, God said to Gabriel: "Go and fetch me dust from the four corners of the earth, and I will create man therewith." Gabriel went forth to do the bidding of the Lord, but the earth drove him away, and refused to let him gather up dust from it. Gabriel remonstrated: "Why, O earth, do you not hearken unto the voice of the Lord, who founded you upon the waters without props or pillars?" The earth replied,

and said: "I am destined to become a curse, and to be cursed through man, and if God himself does not take the dust from me, no one else shall ever do it." When God heard this, he stretched out his hand, took of the dust of the ground, and created the first man therewith.

Of set purpose the dust was taken from all four corners of the earth, so that if a man from the east should happen to die in the west, or a man from the west in the east, the earth should not dare refuse to receive the dead, and tell him to go whence he was taken. Wherever a man chances to die, and wheresoever he is buried, there will he return to the earth from which he sprang. Also, the dust was of various colors—red, black, white, and green—red for the blood, black for the bowels, white for the bones and veins, and green for the pale skin.

At this early moment the Torah interfered. She addressed herself to God: "O Lord of the world! The world is yours, you can do with it as seems good in your eyes. But the man you are now creating will be few of days and full of trouble and sin. If it be not your purpose to have forbearance and patience with him, it were better not to call him into being." God replied, "Is it for naught I am called long-suffering and merciful?"

The grace and lovingkindness of God revealed themselves particularly in his taking one spoonful of dust from the spot where in time to come the altar would stand, saying, "I shall take man from the place of atonement, that he may endure."

The Soul of Man
The care which God exercised in fashioning every detail of the body of man is as naught in comparison with his solicitude for the human soul. The soul of man was created on the first day, for it is the spirit of God moving upon the face of the waters. Thus, instead of being the last, man is really the first work of creation.

This spirit, or, to call it by its usual

name, the soul of man, possesses five different powers. By means of one of them she escapes from the body every night, rises up to Heaven, and fetches new life thence for man.

With the soul of Adam the souls of all the generations of men were created. They are stored up in a promptuary, in the seventh of the heavens, whence they are drawn as they are needed for human body after human body.

The soul and body of man are united in this way: When a woman has conceived, the Angel of the Night, Lailah, carries the sperm before God, and God decrees what manner of human being shall become of it—whether it shall be male or female, strong or weak, rich or poor, beautiful or ugly, long or short, fat or thin, and what all its other qualities shall be. Piety and wickedness alone are left to the determination of man himself. Then God makes a sign to the angel appointed over the souls, saying, "Bring me the soul so-and-so, which is hidden in Paradise, whose name is so-and-so, and whose form is so-and-so." The angel brings the designated soul, and she bows down when she appears in the presence of God, and prostrates herself before him. At that moment, God issues the command, "Enter this sperm." The soul opens her mouth, and pleads: "O Lord of the world! I am well pleased with the world in which I have been living since the day on which you called me into being. Why do you now desire to have me enter this impure sperm, I who am holy and pure, and a part of your glory?" God consoles her: "The world which I shall cause you to enter is better than the world in which you have lived hitherto, and when I created you, it was only for this purpose." The soul is then forced to enter the sperm against her will, and the angel carries her back to the womb of the mother. Two angels are detailed to watch that she shall not leave it, nor drop out of it, and a light is set above her, whereby the soul can see from one end of the world to the other. In the morning an an-

gel carries her to Paradise, and shows her the righteous, who sit there in their glory, with crowns upon their heads. The angel then says to the soul, "Do you know who these are?" She replies in the negative, and the angel goes on: "These whom you behold here were formed, like you, in the womb of their mother. When they came into the world, they observed God's Torah and his commandments. Therefore they became the partakers of this bliss which you see them enjoy. Know, also, you will one day depart from the world below, and if you will observe God's Torah, then will you be found worthy of sitting with these pious ones. But if not, you will be doomed to the other place."

In the evening, the angel takes the soul to Hell, and there points out the sinners whom the angels of destruction are smiting with fiery scourges, the sinners all the while crying out "Woe! Woe!" but no mercy is shown unto them. The angel then questions the soul as before, "Do you know who these are?" and as before the reply is negative. The angel continues: "These who are consumed with fire were created like you. When they were put into the world, they did not observe God's Torah and his commandments. Therefore have they come to this disgrace which you see them suffer. Know, your destiny is also to depart from the world. Be just, therefore, and not wicked, that you may gain the future world."

Between morning and evening the angel carries the soul around, and shows her where she will live and where she will die, and the place where she will be buried, and he takes her through the whole world, and points out the just and the sinners and all things. In the evening, he replaces her in the womb of the mother, and there she remains for nine months.

When the time arrives for her to emerge from the womb into the open world, the same angel addresses the soul, "The time has come for you to go

27

abroad into the open world." The soul demurs, "Why do you want to make me go forth into the open world?" The angel replies: "Know that as you were formed against your will, so now you will be born against your will, and against your will you shall die, and against your will you shall give account of yourself before the King of kings, the Holy One, blessed be he." But the soul is reluctant to leave her place. Then the angel fillips the babe on the nose, extinguishes the light at his head, and brings him forth into the world against his will. Immediately the child forgets all his soul has seen and learnt, and he comes into the world crying, for he loses a place of shelter and security and rest.

When the time arrives for man to quit this world, the same angel appears and asks him, "Do you recognize me?" And man replies, "Yes; but why do you come to me today, and you came on no other day?" The angel says, "To take you away from the world, for the time of your departure has arrived." Then man falls to weeping, and his voice penetrates to all ends of the world, yet no creature hears his voice, except the cock alone. Man remonstrates with the angel, "From two worlds you took me, and into this world you brought me." But the angel reminds him: "Did I not tell you that you were formed against your will, and you would be born against your will, and against your will you would die? And against your will you will have to give account and reckoning of yourself before the Holy One, blessed be he."

The Ideal Man

Like all creatures formed on the six days of creation, Adam came from the hands of the Creator fully and completely developed. He was not like a child, but like a man of twenty years of age. The dimensions of his body were gigantic, reaching from Heaven to earth, or, what amounts to the same, from east to west.

Among later generations of men, there were but few who in a measure resembled Adam in his extraordinary size and physical perfections. Samson possessed his strength, Saul his neck, Absalom his hair, Asahel his fleetness of foot, Uzziah his forehead, Josiah his nostrils, Zedekiah his eyes, and Zerubbabel his voice. History shows that these physical excellencies were no blessings to many of their possessors; they invited the ruin of almost all. Samson's extraordinary strength caused his death; Saul killed himself by cutting his neck with his own sword; while speeding swiftly, Asahel was pierced by Abner's spear; Absalom was caught up by his hair in an oak, and thus suspended met his death; Uzziah was smitten with leprosy upon his forehead; the darts that killed Josiah entered through his nostrils, and Zedekiah's eyes were blinded.

The generality of men inherited as little of the beauty as of the portentous size of their first father. The fairest women compared with Sarah are as apes compared with a human being. Sarah's relation to Eve is the same, and, again, Eve was but as an ape compared with Adam. His person was so handsome that the very sole of his foot obscured the splendor of the sun.

His spiritual qualities kept pace with his personal charm, for God had fashioned his soul with particular care. She is the image of God, and as God fills the world, so the soul fills the human body; as God sees all things, and is seen by none, so the soul sees, but cannot be seen; as God guides the world, so the soul guides the body; as God in His holiness is pure, so is the soul; and as God dwells in secret, so does the soul.

When God was about to put a soul into Adam's clod-like body, he said: "At which point shall I breathe the soul into him? Into the mouth? Nay, for he will use it to speak ill of his fellow man. Into the eyes? With them he will wink lustfully. Into the ears? They will hearken to slander and blasphemy. I will breathe her into his nostrils; as they discern the unclean and reject it, and take in the fragrant, so the pious will shun sin, and will cleave to the words of the Torah."

The perfections of Adam's soul showed themselves as soon as he received her, indeed, while he was still without life. In the hour that intervened between breathing a soul into the first man and his becoming alive, God revealed the whole history of mankind to him. He showed him each generation and its leaders; each generation and its prophets; each generation and its teachers; each generation and its scholars; each generation and its statesmen; each generation and its judges; each generation and its pious members; each generation and its average, commonplace members; and each generation and its impious members. The tale of their years, the number of their days, the reckoning of their hours, and the measure of their steps, all were made known unto him.

Of his own free will Adam relinquished seventy of his allotted years. His appointed span was to be a thousand years, one of the Lord's days. But he saw that only a single minute of life was apportioned to the great soul of David, and he made a gift of seventy years to her, reducing his own years to nine hundred and thirty.

The wisdom of Adam displayed itself to greatest advantage when he gave names to the animals. Then it appeared that God, in combating the arguments of the angels that opposed the creation of man, had spoken well, when he insisted that man would possess more wisdom than they themselves. When Adam was barely an hour old, God assembled the whole world of animals before him and the angels. The latter were called upon to name the different kinds, but they were not equal to the task. Adam, however, spoke without hesitation: "O Lord of the world! The proper name for this animal

is ox, for this one horse, for this one lion, for this one camel." And so he called all in turn by name, suiting the name to the peculiarity of the animal. Then God asked him what his name was to be, and he said Adam, because he had been created out of Adamah, dust of the earth. Again, God asked him his own name, and he said: "Adonai, Lord, because you are Lord over all creatures"— the very name God had given unto himself, the name by which the angels call him, the name that will remain immutable evermore. But without the gift of the holy spirit, Adam could not have found names for all; he was in very truth a prophet, and his wisdom a prophetic quality.

The names of the animals were not the only inheritance handed down by Adam to the generations after him, for mankind owes all crafts to him, especially the art of writing, and he was the inventor of all the seventy languages. And still another task he accomplished for his descendants. God showed Adam the whole earth, and Adam designated what places were to be settled later by men, and what places were to remain waste.

The Fall of Satan

The extraordinary qualities with which Adam was blessed, physical and spiritual as well, aroused the envy of the angels. They attempted to consume him with fire, and he would have perished, had not the protecting hand of God rested upon him, and established peace between him and the heavenly host. In particular, Satan was jealous of the first man, and his evil thoughts finally led to his fall. After Adam had been endowed with a soul, God invited all the angels to come and pay him reverence and homage. Satan, the greatest of the angels in Heaven, with twelve wings, instead of six like all the others, refused to pay heed to the behest of God, saying, "You created us angels from the splendor of the Shekinah, and now you command us to cast ourselves down before the creature which you fashioned out of the dust of the ground!" God answered, "Yet this dust of the ground has more wisdom and understanding than you." Satan demanded a trial of wit with Adam, and God assented thereto, saying: "I have created beasts, birds, and reptiles. I shall have them all come before you and before Adam. If you are able to give them names, I shall command Adam to show honor unto you, and you shall rest next to the Shekinah of my glory. But if not, and Adam calls them by the names I have assigned to them, then you will be subject to Adam, and he shall have a place in my garden, and cultivate it." Thus spoke God, and he betook himself to Paradise, Satan following him. When Adam beheld God, he said to his wife, "O come, let us worship and bow down; let us kneel before the Lord our Maker." Now Satan attempted to assign names to the animals. He failed with the first two that presented themselves, the ox and the cow. God led two others before him, the camel and the donkey, with the same result. Then God turned to Adam, and questioned him regarding the names of the same animals, framing his questions in such wise that the first letter of the first word was the same as the first letter of the name of the animal standing before him. Thus Adam divined the proper name, and Satan was forced to acknowledge the superiority of the first man. Nevertheless he broke out in wild outcries that reached the heavens, and he refused to do homage unto Adam as he had been bidden. The host of angels led by him did likewise, in spite of the urgent representations of Michael, who was the first to prostrate himself before Adam in order to show a good example to the other angels. Michael addressed Satan: "Give adoration to the image of God! But if you do not, then the Lord God will break out in wrath against you." Satan replied: "If he breaks out in wrath against me, I will exalt my throne above the stars of God, I will be like the Most High!" At once God flung Satan and his host out of Heaven, down to the earth, and from that moment dates the enmity between Satan and man.

Woman

When Adam opened his eyes the first time, and beheld the world about him, he broke into praise of God, "How great are your works, O Lord!" But his admiration for the world surrounding him did not exceed the admiration all creatures conceived for Adam. They took him to be their creator, and they all came to offer him adoration. But he spoke: "Why do you come to worship me? Nay, you and I together will acknowledge the majesty and the might of him who has created us all. 'The Lord reigns,'" he continued, "'he is apparelled with majesty.'"

And not alone the creatures on earth, even the angels thought Adam the lord of all, and they were about to salute him with "Holy, holy, holy, is the Lord of hosts," when God caused sleep to fall upon him, and then the angels knew that he was but a human being.

The purpose of the sleep that enfolded Adam was to give him a wife, so that the human race might develop, and all creatures recognize the difference between God and man. When the earth heard what God had resolved to do, it began to tremble and quake. "I have not the strength," it said, "to provide food for the herd of Adam's descendants." But God pacified it with the words, "I and you together, we will find food for the herd." Accordingly, time was divided between God and the earth; God took the night, and the earth took the day. Refreshing sleep nourishes and strengthens man, it affords him life and rest, while the earth brings forth produce with the help of God, who waters it. Yet man must work the earth to earn his food.

The divine resolution to bestow a companion on Adam met the wishes of man, who had been overcome by a feeling of isolation when the animals came to him in pairs to be named. To banish his loneliness, Lilith was first given to Adam as wife. Like him she had been created out of the dust of the ground. But she remained with him only a short time, because she insisted upon enjoying full equality with her husband. She derived her rights from their identical origin. With the help of the Ineffable Name, which she pronounced, Lilith flew away from Adam, and vanished in the air. Adam complained before God that the wife he had given him had deserted him, and God sent forth three angels to capture her. They found her in the Red Sea, and they sought to make her go back with the threat that, unless she went, she would lose a hundred of her demon children daily by death. But Lilith preferred this punishment to living with Adam. She takes her revenge by injuring babes—baby boys during the first night of their life, while baby girls are exposed to her wicked designs until they are twenty days old. The only way to ward off the evil is to attach an amulet bearing the names of her three angel captors to the children, for such had been the agreement between them.

The woman destined to become the true companion of man was taken from Adam's body, for "only when like is joined unto like the union is indissoluble." The creation of woman from man was possible because Adam originally had two faces, which were separated at the birth of Eve.

When God was on the point of making Eve, he said: "I will not make her from the head of man, lest she carry her head high in arrogant pride; not from the eye, lest she be wanton-eyed; not from the ear, lest she be an eavesdropper; not from the neck, lest she be insolent; not from the mouth, lest she be a tattler; not from the heart, lest she be inclined to envy; not from the hand, lest she be a meddler; not from the foot, lest she be a gadabout. I will form her from a chaste portion of the body," and to every limb and organ as he formed it, God said, "Be chaste! Be chaste!" Nevertheless, in spite of the great caution used, woman has all the faults God tried to obviate. The daughters of Zion were haughty and walked with stretched-forth necks and wanton eyes; Sarah was an eavesdropper in her own tent, when the angel spoke with Abraham; Miriam was a talebearer, accusing Moses; Rachel was envious of her sister Leah; Eve put out her hand to take the forbidden fruit, and Dinah was a gadabout.

The physical formation of woman is far more complicated than that of man, as it must be for the function of childbearing, and likewise the intelligence of woman matures more quickly than the intelligence of man. Many of the physical and psychical differences between the two sexes must be attributed to the fact that man was formed from the ground and woman from bone. Women need perfumes, while men do not; dust of the ground remains the same no matter how long it is kept; flesh, however, requires salt to keep it in good condition. The voice of women is shrill, not so the voice of men; when soft viands are cooked, no sound is heard, but let a bone be put in a pot, and at once it crackles. A man is easily placated, not so a woman; a few drops of water suffice to soften a clod of earth; a bone stays hard, and if it were to soak in water for days. The man must ask the woman to be his wife, and not the woman the man to be her husband, because it is man who has sustained the loss of his rib, and he sallies forth to make good his loss again. The very differences between the sexes in garb and social forms go back to the origin of man and woman for their reasons. Woman covers her hair in token of Eve's having brought sin into the world; she tries to hide her shame; and women precede men in a funeral cortege, because it was woman who brought death into the world. And the religious commands addressed to women alone are connected with the history of Eve. Adam was the heave offering of the world, and Eve defiled it. As expiation, all women are commanded to separate a heave offering from the dough. And because woman extinguished the light of man's soul, she is bidden to kindle the Sabbath light.

Adam was first made to fall into a deep sleep before the rib for Eve was taken from his side. For, had he watched her creation, she would not have awakened love in him. To this day it is true that men do not appreciate the charms of women whom they have known and observed from childhood up. Indeed, God had created a wife for Adam before Eve, but he would not have her, because she had been made in his presence. Knowing well all the details of her formation, he was repelled by her. But when he roused himself from his profound sleep, and saw Eve before him in all her surprising beauty and grace, he exclaimed, "This is she who caused my heart to throb many a night!" Yet he discerned at once what the nature of woman was. She would, he knew, seek to carry her point with man either by entreaties and tears, or flattery and caresses. He said, therefore, "This is my never-silent bell!"

The wedding of the first couple was celebrated with pomp never repeated in the whole course of history since. God himself, before presenting her to Adam, attired and adorned Eve as a bride. Yea, he appealed to the angels, saying: "Come, let us perform services of friendship for Adam and his helpmate, for the world rests upon friendly services, and they are more pleasing in my sight than the sacrifices Israel will offer upon the altar." The angels accordingly surrounded the marriage canopy, and God pronounced the blessings upon the bridal couple, as the Hazan does under the Huppah. The angels then danced and played upon musical instruments before Adam and Eve in their ten bridal chambers of gold, pearls, and precious stones, which God had prepared for them.

Adam called his wife Ishah, and himself he called Ish, abandoning the name Adam, which he had borne before the creation of Eve, for the reason that God added his own name Yah to the names of the man and the woman—Yod to Ish and He to Ishah—to indicate that as long as they walked in the ways of God and observed his commandments, his name would shield them against all harm. But if they went astray, his name would be withdrawn, and instead of Ish there would remain Esh, fire, a fire issuing from each and consuming the other.

Adam and Eve in Paradise

The Garden of Eden was the abode of the first man and woman, and the souls of all men must pass through it after death, before they reach their final destination.

In Paradise stands the Tree of Life and the Tree of Knowledge, the latter forming a hedge about the former. Only he who has cleared a path for himself through the Tree of Knowledge can come close to the Tree of Life, which is so huge that it would take a man five hundred years to traverse a distance equal to the diameter of the trunk, and no less vast is the space shaded by its crown of branches. From beneath it flows forth the water that irrigates the whole earth, parting thence into four streams, the Ganges, the Nile, the Tigris, and the Euphrates. But it was only during the days of creation that the realm of plants looked to the waters of the earth for nourishment. Later on God made the plants dependent upon the rain, the upper waters. The clouds rise from earth to Heaven, where water is poured into them as from a conduit. The plants began to feel the effect of the water only after Adam was created. Although they had been brought forth on the third day, God did not permit them to sprout and appear above the surface of the earth, until Adam prayed to him to give food unto them, for God longs for the prayers of the pious.

Paradise being such as it was, it was, naturally, not necessary for Adam to work the land. True, the Lord God put the man into the Garden of Eden to dress it and to keep it, but that only means he is to study the Torah there and fulfill the commandments of God. There were especially six commandments which every human being is expected to heed: man should not worship idols; nor blaspheme God; nor commit murder, nor incest, nor theft and robbery; and all generations have the duty of instituting measures of law and order. One more such command there was, but it was a temporary injunction. Adam was to eat only the green things of the field. But the prohibition against the use of animals for food was revoked in Noah's time, after the deluge. Nevertheless, Adam was not cut off from the enjoyment of meat dishes. Though he was not permitted to slaughter animals for the appeasing of his appetite, the angels brought him meat and wine, serving him like attendants. And as the angels ministered to his wants, so also the animals. They were wholly under his dominion, and their food they took out of his hand and out of Eve's. In all respects, the animal world had a different relation to Adam from their relation to his descendants. Not only did they know the language of man, but they respected the image of God, and they feared the first human couple, all of which changed into the opposite after the fall of man.

The Fall of Man

Among the animals the serpent was notable. Of all of them he had the most excellent qualities, in some of which he resembled man. Like man he stood upright upon two feet, and in height he was equal to the camel. Had it not been for the fall of man, which brought mis-

fortune to them, too, one pair of serpents would have sufficed to perform all the work man has to do, and, besides, they would have supplied him with silver, gold, gems, and pearls. As a matter of fact, it was the very ability of the serpent that led to the ruin of man and his own ruin. His superior mental gifts caused him to become an infidel. It likewise explains his envy of man, especially of his conjugal relations. Envy made him meditate ways and means of bringing about the death of Adam. He was too well acquainted with the character of the man to attempt to exercise tricks of persuasion upon him, and he approached the woman, knowing that women are beguiled easily. The conversation with Eve was cunningly planned, she could not but be caught in a trap. The serpent began, "Is it true that God hath said, 'You shall not eat of every tree in the Garden?'" "We may," rejoined Eve, "eat of the fruit of all the trees in the Garden, except that which is in the midst of the Garden, and that we may not even touch, lest we be stricken with death." She spoke thus, because in his zeal to guard her against the transgressing of the divine command, Adam had forbidden Eve to touch the tree, though God had mentioned only the eating of the fruit. It remains a truth, what the proverb says, "Better a wall ten hands high that stands, than a wall a hundred ells high that cannot stand." It was Adam's exaggeration that afforded the serpent the possibility of persuading Eve to taste of the forbidden fruit. The serpent pushed Eve against the tree, and said: "You see that touching the tree has not caused your death. As little will it hurt you to eat the fruit of the tree. Naught but malevolence has prompted the prohibition, for as soon as you eat thereof, you shall be as God. As he creates and destroys worlds, so will you have the power to create and destroy. As he slays and revives, so will you have the power to slay and revive. He himself ate first of the fruit of the tree, and then he created the world. Therefore he forbids you to eat thereof, lest you create other worlds. Everyone knows that 'artisans of the same guild hate one another.' Furthermore, have you not observed that every creature has dominion over the creature fashioned before itself? The heavens were made on the first day, and they are kept in place by the firmament made on the second day. The firmament, in turn, is ruled by the plants, the creation of the third day, for they take up all the water of the firmament. The sun and the other celestial bodies, which were created on the fourth day, have power over the world of plants. They can ripen their fruits and flourish only through their influence. The creation of the fifth day, the animal world, rules over the celestial spheres. Witness the ziz, which can darken the sun with its pinions. But you are masters of the whole of creation, because you were the last to be created. Hasten now and eat of the fruit of the tree in the midst of the Garden, and become independent of God, lest he bring forth still other creatures to bear rule over you."

To give due weight to these words, the serpent began to shake the tree violently and bring down its fruit. He ate thereof, saying: "As I do not die of eating the fruit, so will you not die." Now Eve could not but say to herself, "All that my master"—so she called Adam—"commanded me is but lies," and she determined to follow the advice of the serpent. Yet she could not bring herself to disobey the command of God utterly. She made a compromise with her conscience. First she ate only the outside skin of the fruit, and then, seeing that death did not fell her, she ate the fruit itself. Scarce had she finished, when she saw the Angel of Death before her. Expecting her end to come immediately, she resolved to make Adam eat of the forbidden fruit, too, lest he espouse another wife after her death. It required tears and lamentations on her part to prevail upon Adam to take the baleful step. Not yet satisfied, she gave of the fruit to all other living beings, that they, too, might be subject to death. All ate, and they all are mortal, with the exception of the bird malham, who refused the fruit, with the words: "Is it not enough that you have sinned against God, and have brought death to others? Must you still come to me and seek to persuade me into disobeying God's command, that I may eat and die thereof? I will not do your bidding." A heavenly voice was heard then to say to Adam and Eve: "To you was the command given. You did not heed it; you did transgress it, and you did seek to persuade the bird malham. He was steadfast, and he feared me, although I gave him no command. Therefore he shall never taste of death, neither he nor his descendants—they all shall live forever in Paradise."

Adam spoke to Eve: "Did you give me of the tree of which I forbade you to eat? You gave me thereof, for my eyes are opened, and the teeth in my mouth are set on edge." Eve made answer, "As my teeth were set on edge, so may the teeth of all living beings be set on edge."

The first result was that Adam and Eve became naked. Before, their bodies had been overlaid with a horny skin, and enveloped with the cloud of glory. No sooner had they violated the command given them than the cloud of glory and the horny skin dropped from them, and they stood there in their nakedness, and ashamed. Adam tried to gather leaves from the trees to cover part of their bodies, but he heard one tree after the other say: "There is the thief that deceived his Creator. Nay, the foot of pride shall not come against me, nor the hand of the wicked touch me. Hence, and take no leaves from me!" Only the fig tree granted him permission to take of its leaves. That was because the fig was the forbidden fruit itself. Adam had the same experience as that prince who seduced one of the maid-servants in the palace. When the king, his father, chased him out, he vainly sought a refuge with the other maid-servants, but only she who had caused his disgrace would grant him assistance.

The Punishment

As long as Adam stood naked, casting about for means of escape from his embarrassment, God did not appear unto him, for one should not "strive to see a man in the hour of his disgrace." He waited until Adam and Eve had covered themselves with fig leaves. But even before God spoke to him, Adam knew what was impending. He heard the angels announce, "God betakes himself unto those that dwell in Paradise." He heard more, too. He heard what the angels were saying to one another about his Fall, and what they were saying to God. In astonishment the angels exclaimed: "What! He still walks about in Paradise? He is not yet dead?" Whereupon God: "I said to him, 'In the day that you eat thereof, you shall surely die!' Now, you know not what manner of day I meant—one of my days of a thousand years, or one of your days. I will give him one of my days. He shall have nine hundred and thirty years to live, and seventy to leave to his descendants."

When Adam and Eve heard God approaching, they hid among the trees—which would not have been possible before the Fall. Before he committed his trespass, Adam's height was from the heavens to the earth, but afterward it was reduced to one hundred ells. Another consequence of his sin was the fear Adam felt when he heard the voice of God: before his fall it had not disquieted him in the least. Hence it was that when Adam said, "I heard your voice in the Garden, and I was afraid," God replied, "Before you were not afraid, and now you are afraid?"

God refrained from reproaches at first. Standing at the gate of Paradise, he but asked, "Where are you, Adam?" Thus did God desire to teach man a rule of polite behavior, never to enter the house of another without announcing himself. It cannot be denied, the words "Where are you?" were pregnant with meaning. They were intended to bring home to Adam the vast difference between his latter and his former state—between his supernatural size then and his shrunken size now; between the lordship of God over him then and the lordship of the serpent over him now. At the same time, God wanted to give Adam the opportunity of repenting of his sin, and he would have received divine forgiveness for it. But so far from repenting of it, Adam slandered God, and uttered blasphemies against him. When God asked him, "Have you eaten of the tree whereof I commanded you should not eat?" he did not confess his sin, but excused himself with the words: "O Lord of the world! As long as I was alone, I did not fall into sin, but as soon as this woman came to me, she tempted me." God replied: "I gave her unto you as a help, and you are ungrateful when you accuse her, saying, 'She gave me of the tree.' You should not have obeyed her, for you are the head, and not she." God, who knows all things, had foreseen exactly this, and he had not created Eve until Adam had asked him for a helpmate, so that he might not have apparently good reason for reproaching God with having created woman.

As Adam tried to shift the blame for his misdeed from himself, so also Eve. She, like her husband, did not confess her transgression and pray for pardon, which would have been granted to her. Gracious as God is, he did not pronounce the doom upon Adam and Eve until they showed themselves stiff-necked. Not so with the serpent. God inflicted the curse upon the serpent without hearing his defense; for the serpent is a villain, and the wicked are good debaters. If God had questioned him, the serpent would have answered: "You gave them a command, and I contradicted it. Why did they obey me, and not you?'' Therefore God did not enter into an argument with the serpent, but straightaway decreed the following ten punishments: The mouth of the serpent was closed, and his power of speech taken away; his hands and feet were hacked off; the earth was given him as food; he must suffer great pain in sloughing his skin; enmity is to exist between him and man; if he eats the choicest viands, or drinks the sweetest beverages, they all change into dust in his mouth; the pregnancy of the female serpent lasts seven years; men shall seek to kill him as soon as they catch sight of him; even in the future world, where all beings will be blessed, he will not escape the punishment decreed for him; he will vanish from out of the Holy Land if Israel walks in the ways of God.

Furthermore, God spoke to the serpent: "I created you to be king over all animals, cattle and the beasts of the field alike; but you were not satisfied. Therefore you shall be cursed above all cattle and above every beast of the field. I created you of upright posture; but you were not satisfied. Therefore you shall go upon your belly. I created you to eat the same food as man; but you were not satisfied. Therefore you shall eat dust all the days of your life. You sought to cause the death of Adam in order to espouse his wife. Therefore I will put enmity between you and the woman." How true it is—he who lusts after what is not his due, not only does he not attain his desire, but he also loses what he has!

As angels had been present when the doom was pronounced upon the serpent —for God had convoked a Sanhedrin of seventy-one angels when he sat in judgment upon him—so the execution of the decree against him was entrusted to angels. They descended from heaven, and chopped off his hands and feet. His suffering was so great that his agonized cries could be heard from one end of the world to the other.

The verdict against Eve also consisted of ten curses, the effect of which is noticeable to this day in the physical, spiritual, and social state of woman. It was not God himself who announced her fate to Eve. The only woman with whom God ever spoke was Sarah. In the case of Eve, he made use of the services of an interpreter.

Finally, also the punishment of Adam was tenfold: he lost his celestial clothing —God stripped it off him; in sorrow he was to earn his daily bread; the food he ate was to be turned from good into bad; his children were to wander from land to land; his body was to exude sweat; he was to have an evil inclination; in death his body was to be a prey of the worms; animals were to have power over him, in that they could slay him; his days were to be few and full of trouble; in the end he was to render account of all his doings on earth.

These three sinners were not the only ones to have punishment dealt out to them. The earth fared no better, for it had been guilty of various misdemeanors. In the first place, it had not entirely heeded the command of God given on the third day, to bring forth "tree of fruit." What God had desired was a tree the wood of which was to be as pleasant to the taste as the fruit thereof. The earth, however, produced a tree bearing fruit, the tree itself not being edible. Again, the earth did not do its whole duty in connection with the sin of Adam. God had appointed the sun and the earth witnesses to testify against Adam in case he committed a trespass. The sun, accordingly, had grown dark the instant Adam became guilty of disobedience, but the earth, not knowing how to take notice of Adam's fall, disregarded it altogether. The earth also had to suffer a tenfold punishment: independent before, she was hereafter to wait to be watered by the rain from above; sometimes the fruits of the earth fail; the grain she brings forth is stricken with blasting and mildew; she must produce all sorts of noxious vermin; thenceforth she was to be divided into valleys and mountains; she must grow barren trees, bearing no fruit; thorns and thistles sprout from her; much is sown in the earth, but little is harvested; in time to come the earth will have to disclose her blood, and shall no more cover her slain; and, finally, she shall, one day, "wax old like a garment."

When Adam heard the words, "Thorns and thistles shall it bring forth," concerning the ground, a sweat broke out on his face, and he said: "What! Shall I and my cattle eat from the same manger?" The Lord had mercy upon him, and spoke, "In view of the sweat of your face, you shall eat bread."

The earth is not the only thing created that was made to suffer through the sin of Adam. The same fate overtook the moon. When the serpent seduced Adam and Eve, and exposed their nakedness, they wept bitterly, and with them wept the heavens, and the sun and the stars, and all created beings and things up to the throne of God. The very angels and the celestial beings were grieved by the transgression of Adam. The moon alone laughed, wherefore God grew angry, and obscured her light. Instead of shining steadily like the sun, all the length of the day, she grows old quickly, and must be born and reborn, again and again. The callous conduct of the moon offended God, not only by way of contrast with the compassion of all other creatures, but because he himself was full of pity for Adam and his wife. He made clothes for them out of the skin stripped from the serpent. He would have done even more. He would have permitted them to remain in Paradise, if only they had been penitent. But they refused to repent, and they had to leave, lest their godlike understanding urge them to ravage the Tree of Life, and they learn to live forever. As it was, when God dismissed them from Paradise, He did not allow the divine quality of justice to prevail entirely. He associated mercy with it. As

they left, he said: "O what a pity that Adam was not able to observe the command laid upon him for even a brief span of time!"

To guard the entrance to Paradise, God appointed the cherubim, called also the ever-turning sword of flames, because angels can turn themselves from one shape into another at need. Instead of the Tree of Life, God gave Adam the Torah, which likewise is a tree of life to them that lay hold upon her, and he was permitted to take up his abode in the vicinity of Paradise in the east.

Sentence pronounced upon Adam and Eve and the serpent, the Lord commanded the angels to turn the man and the woman out of Paradise. They began to weep and supplicate bitterly, and the angels took pity upon them and left the divine command unfulfilled, until they could petition God to mitigate his severe verdict. But the Lord was inexorable, saying, "Was it I that committed a trespass, or did I pronounce a false judgment?" Also Adam's prayer, to be given of the fruit of the Tree of Life, was turned aside, with the promise, however, that if he would lead a pious life, he would be given of the fruit on the day of resurrection, and he would then live forever.

Seeing that God had resolved unalterably, Adam began to weep again and implore the angels to grant him at least permission to take sweet-scented spices with him out of Paradise, that outside, too, he might be able to bring offerings unto God, and his prayers be accepted before the Lord. Thereupon the angels came before God, and spoke: "King unto everlasting, command you us to give Adam sweet-scented spices of Paradise," and God heard their prayer. Thus Adam gathered saffron, nard, calamus, and cinnamon, and all sorts of seeds besides for his sustenance. Laden with these, Adam and Eve left Paradise, and came upon earth.

They had enjoyed the splendors of

Paradise but a brief span of time—but a few hours. It was in the first hour of the sixth day of creation that God conceived the idea of creating man; in the second hour, he took counsel with the angels; in the third, he gathered the dust for the body of man; in the fourth, he formed Adam; in the fifth, he clothed him with skin; in the sixth, the soulless shape was complete, so that it could stand upright; in the seventh, a soul was breathed into it; in the eighth, man was led into Paradise; in the ninth, the divine command prohibiting the fruit of the tree in the midst of the garden was issued to him; in the tenth, he transgressed the command; in the eleventh, he was judged; and in the twelfth hour of the day, he was cast out of Paradise, in atonement for his sin.

This eventful day was the first of the month of Tishri. Therefore God spoke to Adam: "You shall be the prototype of thy children. As you have been judged by me on this day and absolved, so thy children Israel shall be judged by me on this New Year's Day, and they shall be absolved."

Each day of creation brought forth three things: the first, Heaven, earth, and light; the second, the firmament, Gehenna, and the angels; the third, trees, herbs, and Paradise; the fourth, sun, moon, and stars; and the fifth, fishes, birds, and leviathan. As God intended to rest on the seventh day, the Sabbath, the sixth day had to do double duty. It brought forth six creations: Adam, Eve, cattle, reptiles, the beasts of the field, and demons. The demons were made shortly before the Sabbath came in, and they are, therefore, incorporeal spirits—the Lord had no time to create bodies for them.

In the twilight, between the sixth day and the Sabbath, ten creations were brought forth: the rainbow, invisible until Noah's time; the manna; water-springs, whence Israel drew water for his thirst in the desert; the writing upon the two tables of stone given at Sinai; the pen with which the writing was written; the two tables themselves; the mouth of Balaam's she-ass; the grave of Moses; the cave in which Moses and Elijah dwelt; and the rod of Aaron, with its blossoms and its ripe almonds.

Manichaean Creation Myths (Gnostic)

(Manichaeism and Other Gnostic Sects)

Among all the Gnostic cults—those systems of self-knowledge, cosmic alienation, and salvation into light—only Manichaeism survived beyond the first three centuries A.D. to continue as a strong historic force. Manichaeism follows the teaching of Mani, a Persian born about A.D. 216 in Babylonia, then part of the Parthian kingdom. From Zoroastrianism Mani took the dualism of Light and Darkness, Knowledge and Ignorance, Good and Error. In his Iranian type of Gnosticism he emphasized the conflict between these polar forces and preached the freeing of Light caught in Darkness, and of the divine spirit caught in the human body.

By contrast, the so-called Syrian-Egyptian type of Gnostic speculation, based on the writings of Valentinus, was more concerned with illumination through knowledge. Through each private act of knowledge the individual self moves toward the divine realm. In his *Against the Gnostics* Irenaeus sums up the Valentinian speculation in a few words: "knowledge is the salvation of the inner man" and "perfect salvation is the cognition itself of the ineffable greatness."[1] So the process itself "of knowing the universal being" is the end. Such is the tenet of most subsequent western mystical doctrine.

But however attractive the most elitist and individual Valentinian system was, it was not an organized religious group like the Manichaeans and did not survive. Manichaeism, however, was elaborately structured, with apostles, bishops, and priests. One of its early officers was Saint Augustine, a Manichaean for nine years until his conversion. In fact, with its missionary zeal and wide following, it was a serious rival to the Catholic Church and largely prevailed in western Asia and eastern Europe during the fourth and fifth centuries. In the sixth it was violently suppressed in the territories of the old Roman

Empire, but in the East it spread to the eastern provinces of Persia and into Chinese Turkestan where, in 762, it became the state religion of the Uigar Empire. It remained the dominant religion in western China until it was wiped out by the invasion of Genghis Khan. In the west its last important outbreak was the "Albigensian heresy," from the eleventh to thirteenth centuries, which occurred simultaneously with the flowering of Provençal culture. Pope Innocent III (1198–1216) ordered a crusade to clean the Manichaean "scourge of God" from the earth, and effectively turned southern France into a gothic desert.

The Manichaeans were Gnostics, and many of them claimed to be the only true Christians. But there were also Jewish Gnostics—Gershom Scholem has an excellent book on the Jewish Gnostics[2]—and Pagan Gnostics, notably Hermes Trismegistus, from whom the "hermetic" tradition is derived. The Greek word *gnosis* (from which we have "Gnosticism") and the Sanskrit *bodhi* (from which we have "Buddhism") have exactly the same meaning, "knowledge."[3] In making this observation, Joseph Campbell tells us further that *gnosis* and *bodhi* refers to a knowledge that transcends "that derived either empirically from the senses or rationally by way of the categories of thought. Such ineffable knowledge transcends, as well, the terms and images by which it is metaphorically suggested." Moreover, the Gnostic esteem of *gnosis*, knowledge, was often accompanied by a certain disdain for its opposite, *pistis*, faith, which they associated with ignorance and an external imposition of belief by the clergy. But knowledge is necessary for salvation. The Gnostic sects were essentially eschatological, that is, concerned with salvation, with transcendence from this world of error (as opposed to sin) to a knowledge of the Living God, who is knowable only through a revelationary experience. The object of *gnosis* is God—into whom the soul is transformed monistically. This notion of assimilation into a divine essence—as opposed to theistic adherence to a God figure—is the aim and claim of much mysticism, including that of Plotinus, who wrote *against* the Gnostics.

But beyond soteriological yearnings of the Gnostic sects, there is an elaborate cosmogony and anthropogony, defiantly opposed to traditional Jewish and Christian beliefs. For the Jew and the Christian a good God created Adam and Eve, who, through their own sin, fell into corruption. But for the Gnostics God was not good at all, at least the traditional God worshiped in church and synagogue. He was associated with the Zoroastian devil, Angra Mainyu, a secondary god below Mother Sophia and the Father of All. The Old and New Testament God was called variously the Demiurge (after Plato's Demiurge), Ialdabaoth, Sabaoth, and Saclas, and it was his evil act of creation, an attempt to catch spiritual light in ignorance and darkness, rather than Adam and Eve's disobedience, which brought on misery and corruption. Indeed, Adam and Eve were heroic in their disobedience, aided by the Promethean figure of the serpent, who gave them knowledge, and who will later return in some sects as Jesus, the serpent Jesus, to redeem humanity by teaching disobedience to the curse of the laws of Yahweh the Creator. "Christ redeemed us from the curse of the law," Saint Paul himself had written (Gal. 3:13). The Gnostics sought to free us not only from the laws, but their Maker, and the world he created, usually through a method of extreme asceticism and meditation. Augustine, the former Manichaean, describes Gnostic beliefs with clarity and indignation:

> They assert, however, that Christ was the one called by our Scriptures the Serpent, and they assure us that they have been given insight into this in order to open the eyes of knowledge and to distinguish between Good and Evil. Christ came in the latter days to save souls, not bodies. He did not really exist in the flesh, but in mockery of the human senses proffered the simulated appearance of fleshly form, and thereby also produced the illusion not only of death, but also of resurrection. God, who issued the Law through Moses, and who spoke through Hebrew prophets, was not the true God but one of the Archons of Darkness.[4]

Upon his conversion Augustine also adopted a principal distinction in his new Christian faith: he opposed the notion of *emanation*, that is, the Manichaean doctrine of the immanence of divine light as the light within all beings, in favor of the separate act of *creation*. For the Gnostic that divine spark imprisoned in the human body is the hope of salvation. As in Plotinus or any system based on divine emanation, the ray of God is in all of us, and to free ourselves of delusion, of matter, and to return to that ray's source is the purpose of life.

The divine hierarchy of the Gnostics, like their theology, represents a reversal of traditional Christian notions. Foremost in these contradictions is the role of Yahweh the Creator. The Creator God is low in the hierarchy of transcendent forces. Above him is Mother Sophia, the Mother of Life, and the thirty Aeons or good angels of the Pleroma. Mother Sophia emanates from the highest God, the Father of Light—called variously Father of Truth, Father of All, Father of Greatness, or the Unknown Father. Opposed to all these forces of spirit and light is the traditional God of Jews and Christians, the Creator, a Prince of Darkness, surrounded by Archons or Rulers. This God is engaged in a precosmic struggle with the God of Light to trap Light in his Darkness, to trap spirit in matter. The Father sends his emissary, the Primal Man and his sons, to fight against the Darkness and to liberate the Light. But the Primal Man (the Manichaeans call him Ormuzd, a version of Ahura Mazda, the Zoroastrian God of Light) is defeated by the Creator God, and his spirit is held by impure matter; is swallowed up by Darkness. Yet in the conquest of spirit or soul by matter, matter itself was lured into a trap, for when the soul (which precedes the existence of matter) is ultimately freed and redeemed from matter, matter will die. As for the actual creation of Heaven and earth, there are several versions—as there are several versions of all the Gnostic myths—but a common notion is that the world was created by the Archons, including its master Yahweh, the Prince of Darkness. The flesh and skin of the Archons were stretched out to form the firmaments and the mountains were formed from their flesh and bones. Into this impure matter the soul was mingled: thus Manichaean pessimism, which finds human life a prison of the soul in the powers of Darkness.

The most pessimistic version of creation concerns the creation of Adam and Eve. They are pawns of the King of Darkness in his strategy to defeat the Unknown Father. Their birth is described by the Manichaeans as an abomination, an abortion, a ruse, in which the Creator reveals cannibalism for his own offspring. Hans Jonas writes:

> The King of Darkness produces Adam and Eve in the image of the glorious forms and pours into them all the Light left at his disposal. This procreation is described with much repulsive circumstance, involving copulation between the male and female demons, devouring of the progeny by their King, etc.[5]

With the creation of man and woman, the struggle between Light and Darkness concentrate on human beings. In one version the Archons create Adam, with the Creator God breathing life into his face. In Origen's version (recounted in this volume in "The Origin of the World") Mother Sophia sends her daughter Zoë (Life) who is called Eve (Life) to raise up Adam. She sees Adam on the earth, an inert lump of mud, and, pitying him, breathes spirit into his face. Adam rises immediately, and on opening his eyes declares Eve the "mother of the living" for having given him life. In the Gnostic versions of the anthropogony, not only is Eve usually a figure of goodness,[6] but the serpent-instructor is the Luminous Jesus, who induces Eve to obtain knowledge and rebel against the King of Darkness. Jesus the serpent will appear once again as the Christ on the cross, a phantom figure who does not suffer and offers promise of the realm of Light.

Who were the Gnostics? What were the sources of their ideas? Mani (A.D. 216–276), a later Gnostic, preached a syncretic doctrine combining, as many scholars have observed, Zoroastrian, Buddhist, and Judeo-Christian ideas. As stated earlier, the Old Testament Creator God was identified with the Zoroastrian figure of darkness and error, Angra Mainyu. Error and delusion are in turn related to the Buddhist principle of delusion (māyā). Through meditation and knowledge (bodhi), delusion fades and one achieves total illumination. From Christianity came, with radical changes, the notion of a divine godhead and his son Jesus, who descended to Adam and Eve to teach them disobedience to the Creator God; he promised them freedom into light.

Manichaean Gnosticism is permeated with Zoroaster's dualistic doctrine of the struggle of light and darkness, soul and matter, which in turn represent the conflict of good and evil. Mani was, after all, a Persian, and the mingling of eastern and western religions was natural; as A. V. Williams Jackson writes, in the east, Buddhistic elements came more to the front, in the west, the Christian elements were emphasized.[7]

As for the earlier Gnostics in the Hellenized Syrian-Egyptian world, they were largely ex-Jews (as were the early followers of Orthodox Christianity), renegades from their religion. R. M. Grant writes, "The Gnostic teachers may have regarded themselves as the only true Jews, but certainly authoritative rabbinic teachers did not regard them so."[8] Grant speculates that after the destruction of Jerusalem by the Romans in A.D. 70 and the failure of Jewish apocalyptic hopes—that is, the messianic hope of God's intervention—the Jews looked inside for revelation and illumination. Whatever the cause, there is no question that all the Gnostic sects are more self- than God-oriented. The light was to be found inside. Today one custom of ordinary life still recalls the Gnostics: shaking hands. The Manichaeans had the peculiarity of grasping right hands when meeting each other "in sign that they themselves are of those saved from the Darkness."[9]

Until relatively recently our main sources for studying the Gnostics were in works of Church Fathers who wrote against the Gnostics. These were Justin at Rome (150?–165?), Irenaeus at Lyons around 180, Hippolytus at Rome about 230, Epiphanius in Cyprus around 375. The main sources of our knowledge of the Manichaeans came from Saint Augustine (354?–430) and Theodore bar Konai. Towards the end of the eighth century, Theodore bar Konai of Kashkar in Babylonia produced a *Commentary* in Syriac. "Concerning the Impure Doctrine" is from the eleventh book of this *Commentary*. It presents extracts from an original manuscript by Mani, which are introduced on each occasion in the text by the words: "He (i.e., Mani) says. . . ." Theodore's source may be considered to be the "Circular Letter concerning the Two Principles," which is placed first among Mani's documented works by Ibn an-Nadim in the Fihrist. This manuscript may prove to be identical with the "Epistula fundamenti" known to Augustine. In the last century many original texts have turned up, mainly in Coptic. The *Pistis Sophia*, the *Gospel of Mary*, and the *Apocryphon of John* finally gave us works by, as opposed to works against, the Gnostics. Important Manichaean documents were found in Central Asia, written in Turfan Pahlavi (Middle Persian), in the first decade of the twentieth century. But the most important find, by far, occurred in Nag Hammadi in upper Egypt, where a Coptic Gnostic library was discovered, containing forty-eight Gnostic treatises of more than seven hundred pages. These texts were published in English translation in 1977 in James M. Robinson, ed., *The Nag Hammadi Library* (San Francisco: Harper & Row, 1977). There have been numerous studies and books on the Nag Hammadi documents. Among the most readable are John Dart, *The Laughing Savior: The Discovery and Significance of the Nag Hammadi Gnostic Library* (New York: Harper & Row, 1976), and Elaine Pagels, *The Gnostic Gospels* (New York: Random House, 1979).

Notes

1. Irenaeus I.21.4
2. Gershom Scholem, *Jewish Gnosticism, Merkabah Mysticism, and Talmudic Tradition* (New York: Schocken Books, 1960).
3. Joseph Campbell, *The Masks of God: Creative Mythology* (1968; reprint, New York: Penguin Books, 1980), p. 158.
4. Augustine, *de haeresibus ad quodvultdeum* 46.4.
5. Hans Jonas, *The Gnostic Religion*, 2d ed., rev. (1958; reprint, Boston: Beacon Press, 1970), p. 224.
6. Eve fares much better among the Syrian-Egyptian Gnostics. As Hans Jonas writes (*The Gnostic Religion*, p. 93), since the serpent persuades Eve to disobey the Creator, she is helping counteract the designs of the Demiurge. Thus she represents redemption as the biblical God represents degradation and cosmic oppression. For the Manichaeans, however, Eve is a symbol of the body

and sexuality to which the Manichaeans are completely hostile. In A. V. Williams Jackson's *Researches in Manichaeism* (New York: Columbia University Press, 1965), p. 11, Jackson comments: "Our first parents were demon-born, offspring of the execrated union of the Arch-Fiend and his mate. In Adam, however, the luminous particles predominated, while Eve was composed wholly of dark elements."

7. Jackson, *Researches in Manichaeism*, p. 7.

8. R. M. Grant, *Gnosticism and Early Christianity*, 2d ed. (1959; reprint, New York: Columbia University Press, 1966), p. 26.

9. Hans Jonas explains (see *The Gnostic Religion*, p. 223), that clasping hands had been used in antiquity as a symbolic act for concluding legal documents, similar to today's "Let's shake on it." The early Christians had the kiss of brotherhood, but the custom soon disappeared.

THE PRIMAL MAN*

The good God, the highest of the gods,
a diadem and eternal glory,
blissful among the lights,
was proud and happy when you were born in his realm.
The twelve sons and the Aeons of the Aeons
of the vast air were also happy.
All gods and inhabitants of his realm—
the mountains, trees, springs,
the broad strong palaces and halls,
were happy through you, Friend.
When the lovely women and girls
born of the Sense saw you,
they praised you, blessed you,
perfect youth.
Songs filled the air. Tambourine, harp, and flute
exploded.
All gods stood before you, Prince, son of a king.
Voices ring from the vast air,
songs from the Light-Earth
tell the Father of Light:
Born is the battler who makes peace.
The all-good highest of the gods
gives you three tasks:
Destroy death, strike the enemies,
and cover the whole Paradise of Light!
You paid homage and went out for battle
and covered the whole Paradise of Light.
The tyrant prince was bound forever
and the dwelling place of the Dark Ones was destroyed.
The Light Friend, Primal Man,
remained
until he carried out the Father's will.

---

*Version by W.B.

ADAM, CHILD OF DEMONS, AND HIS SALVATION*

Az,
the evil mother of all demons,
grew angry and raged
for her own purposes.
From the dirt of male and female demons
she made this body
and entered it.
Then from the five elements of Light,
Lord Ohrmuzd's armor,
she formed the good soul
and chained it into the body.
She made the first man like someone blind and deaf,
unconscious and deluded
that from the beginning he might not know
his true origin and family.
She created the body as a prison
and chained the grieved soul into it.
"My jailers are robbers,
male and female demons, witches!"
Firmly she chained the soul
into the fraudulent body
and made it hateful and evil,
angry and vengeful.
But Lord Ohrmuzd
had mercy on the souls,
and came down to earth
in human form.
He maimed the evil Az.
Then he revealed to man and woman
all that was and will be.
He quickly showed
that this body of flesh
was not made by Lord Ohrmuzd,
nor was the soul chained by him.
The wise soul of the fortunate
was resurrected;
he believed in the knowledge
of Ohrmuzd, the good Lord.
All injunctions and orders
and seals of peace
he fully accepted
like a hero.
He put off the body of death
and was saved for eternity.
He ascended into Paradise,
into the land of the blessed.

*Version by W.B.

CONCERNING HIS IMPURE DOCTRINE (FROM THEODORE BAR KONAI)*

In this volume we must present some of the senseless doctrine and blasphemous views of the godless Mani, to the shame of the Manichaeans.

He says: Before Heaven and Earth and all that lies therein existed, there were two principles: one good and one evil. The principle of good dwelt in the region of Light, and he calls it the Father of Greatness. And he says: Apart from him there were his five dwelling-places: Reason, Knowledge, Thought, Imagination, Reflection. And he calls the Evil Principle the King of Darkness. He says: He lives in his land, the Darkness in his five Aeons which are there: the Aeon of Smoke, the Aeon of Fire, the Aeon of Wind, the Aeon of Water, the Aeon of Darkness. And he says: When the King of Darkness thought of ascending to the Place of Light, the five Dwelling Places were afraid. And he says the Father of Greatness reflected and said: I shall not send any of these five dwelling places, which are my Aeons, into battle, for I created them for quiet and for peace, rather shall I myself go and fight." And he says: "The Father of Greatness called forth the Mother of Life; the Mother of Life called forth Primary Man; and the Primary Man called forth his five sons, like a man girding himself for the fight.

And he says: Then an angel called Nachashbat came to meet him with a wreath of victory in his hand. And he says: He shone the light in front of the Primal Man and when the King of Darkness saw it, he reflected and said: "What I sought far off, I have found close by." Thereupon the Primal Man with his

*Liber Scholiorum XI (Scher 313–318). Translation by Kurt Schubert, based on the Syriac text edited by A. Scher, Corpus Scriptorum Christianorum Orientalium, Scriptores Syri, Series II, Tomus 66, Paris-Leipzig 1912, 313–318. From Robert Haardt, Gnosis (Leiden: Brill, 1971), pp. 289–296.

five sons gave himself to the five sons of darkness, as food, just as a man who has an enemy, mixes a deadly poison in a kitchen and gives it to him. And he says: When the sons of darkness had consumed the sons of Primal Man, the five light-gods lost their reason. Through the poison of the sons of darkness they became like a man who has been bitten by a mad dog or a snake. And he says: Primal Man regained his reason and said a prayer to the Father of Greatness seven times. The latter, in a second summons, called forth the Friend of the Lights; the Friend of the Lights called forth the Great Architect; the Great Architect called forth the Living Spirit; the Living Spirit called forth his five sons: the Adornment of the Light from his Reason; the great King of Honor from his Knowledge; the Light Adamas, from his Thought; the King of Glory, from his Imagination; and the "Bearer" from his Reflection. These came to the Land of Darkness and found Primal Man swallowed up by Darkness, him and his five sons. Then the Living Spirit called with his voice, and the voice of the Living Spirit took on the aspect of a sharp sword, and he allowed his shape to become visible to Primal Man, and said to him:

"Greeting, O Good Man in the midst of Evil,

O Creature of Light in the midst of Darkness!

God dwells in the midst of the animals of anger

Who do not know his Honor."

And the Primal Man answered him and said:

"Come with Salvation, since you bring the burden of Salvation and Peace."

And he said to him:

"How goes it with our Fathers the Sons of Light, in their City?"

And the Call answered him: "They are doing well." And the Call and the Answer accompanied one another and ascended to the Mother of Life and the Living Spirit. And the Living Spirit clothed itself with the Answer, its beloved Son. And they descended together to the Land of Darkness, to the Place where dwelt Primary Man and his sons. Then the Living Spirit commanded his three sons[1] that one of them should kill the Archons, the Sons of Darkness, and another flay them and that they should bring them to the Mother of Life. The Mother of Life spread out the heavens from their skins; she made ten[2] heavens, and she cast their bodies into the Land of Darkness. And they made eight earths and each of the five sons of the Living Spirit completed his work: It was the Adornment of the Light who seized the five Light Gods by their haunches, and the heavens were spread out beneath their haunches. It was the "Bearer" who down on one knee held up the earths. When the heavens and the earths had been created, the great King of Honor sat down in the center of the sky and watched over them all. Thereupon the Living Spirit disclosed to the Sons of Darkness his shapes, and from the light which had been swallowed up by the Demons, he purified the light, and made out of it the sun and moon and over a thousand stars. And he formed the Spheres which are there: wind, water, and fire. He descended and set them on their paths below, by the "Bearer." The King of Glory called out and erected on them strata so that they stepped on these Archons which were imprisoned on the earths, to serve the five Light Gods, and not to burn them through the poison of the Archons.

And he says: Thereupon the Mother of Life, Primal Man, and the Living Spirit raised their prayers and pleaded with the Father of Greatness. And the Father of Greatness heard them and in a third summons called forth the messenger. The messenger called forth the twelve Virgins in their garments, crowns, and attributes. The first was Authority, the second Wisdom, the third Victory, the fourth Power of Conviction, the fifth Venerableness, the sixth Truth, the sev-

enth Faith, the eighth Forbearance, the ninth Integrity, the tenth Goodness, the eleventh Righteousness, the twelfth Light.

When the emissary came to these vessels, the sun and moon, he ordered the three servants to set the vessels in motion. He commanded the Great Architect to construct the New Earth and the three Spheres to raise themselves up. And when the vessels moved and had reached the center of the sky, the emissary caused his shapes to appear, male and female, and he was seen by all the Archons, the sons of darkness, male and female.

And at the sight of the emissary, who was lovely in his forms, all the Archons were seized with desire for him: the male ones desired his feminine form, and the women his masculine form. And in their desire, they began to eject the Light which they had swallowed from the five Light Divinities. Thereupon the Sin, which was locked up in them like spoiled food,[3] mingled with the Light which was streaming from the Archons. They wished to enter the emissary's ship. The emissary therefore concealed his shapes and separated the Light of the five Light Divinities from the Sin which was with them. And it, which had come out of the Archons, fell back upon them, but they did not take it up, like a man who feels disgust at his own vomit. They fell upon the ground, half on the wet part and half on the dry. And it[4] turned itself into a fearful animal, which resembled the King of Darkness. The Light-Adamas was sent out against this animal. He fought with it, conquered it, and turned it on its back, struck home at the aorta of its heart, threw his shield on its jaws, placed one foot on its thigh and the other on its breast. And the Sin, which had fallen on the dry ground, began to sprout in the form of five trees.

And he says: Those Daughters of Darkness became pregnant here before, by virtue of their own nature. As a result of the beauty of the forms of the emissary, whom they had seen, they had abortions, and the fruits of their body fell upon earth and consumed the blossoms of the trees.

And the abortions held council together and remembered the figure of the emissary whom they had seen. They said: "Where is the figure we caught sight of?" And Ashaklun, Son of the King of Darkness, said to the abortions: "Give me your sons and your daughters and I shall make you a figure like the one you have seen." They brought them and gave them to him. He ate the male ones and handed the female ones over to Nekbael, his companion. Nekbael[5] and Ashaklun came together; Nekbael became pregnant and bore Ashaklun a son to whom she gave the name Adam. And she became pregnant again and bore a daughter to whom she gave the name Havva [Eve]. And he says: The Light-Jesus approached unsuspecting Adam and awakened him out of mortal sleep so that he should be delivered from many spirits. And like a just man who finds a human being possessed of a terrible demon, and calms him down by his art, so it was with Adam, since the friend discovered him sunk in deep sleep, wakened him, set him in motion, aroused him, drove away the enticing demons from him, and chained up[6] the many Archons far away from him. Then Adam examined himself and recognized who he was. And the Light-Jesus showed him the Fathers in the heights and his own self, his soul, cast into the midst of all, exposed to the teeth of panthers, the teeth of elephants, devoured by the devourers, consumed by the consumers, eaten by the dogs, mingled with and imprisoned in everything that exists, shackled in the stench of darkness. And he says: The Light-Jesus raised Adam up and made him eat of the Tree of Life. Then Adam glanced upward and wept, raising his voice powerfully like a lion roaring. He tore his hair, beat his breast, and said: "Woe, woe unto him, the Sculptor of my Body, woe unto him who

has shackled my soul, and woe to the rebellious ones who have enslaved me!"

MANICHAEAN MYTH (FROM THE SPEECH ON GEHMURD AND MURDIYANAG)*

And also in the beginning, when the gods had distributed zones, places, and frontiers according to the revolution and the protecting control and the waxing and the waning of the sun and the moon and made day and night and month and year visible, and when they had purified Light out of the universe, then this Az of defeated offspring, Az, who had fallen down from the sky and put on trees and plants as a garment and by the help of the trees and the plants put on as a garment the abortions of the Mazans and Asreshtars that had fallen down from the sky—and by them that splendor and nobleness of God Narisah, the Third Messenger, was seen; yes, thereupon Az observed the sun and the moon giving protection; and likewise she also saw the gods and the sun and the moon continuously releasing and purifying that Goodness and Light of God that she had captured from the bondage of Greed and up from the universe leading it, protected, to the chariots and transporting it to Paradise.

Then that tricked Az was filled with heavy anger. She began to desire to make a step forward, and she thought: "After those two forms—the female and the male—of God Narisah that I have seen, I will form those two creatures, the male and the female, so that they become my garment and veil; by me these two creatures shall not be taken away, and I will let no misery and wretchedness come over them." There-

*From Jes P. Asmussen, *Manichaean Literature* (Delmar, New York: Scholars' Facsimiles & Reprints, 1975), pp. 127–131.

upon the Az from all that progeny of the demons that had fallen down unto the earth from the sky put on as a garment these two, the male Asreshtar and the female Asreshtar, lion-shaped, lustful and wrathful, sinful and terrible. She made them her own veil and garment and raged within them. And just as the Az herself from the primeval beginning in that Hell of Darkness, her abode, had taught the demons and witches, the demons of wrath, the Mazans and Asreshtars, male and female, lewdness and copulation, so again thereafter Az began to teach also these, the other male and female, Mazans and Asreshtars, that had fallen upon the earth from the sky, lewdness and copulation so that they might become lewd and copulate and, with joined bodies, be mixed together so that dragon progeny might be born from them, and so that Az then might take and devour that progeny in order to make herefrom two creatures, a man and a woman.

Then this Mazan and Asreshtar, the male and the female, taught all the others lewdness and copulation. And they were mixed together, with joined bodies. And their progeny was born and fostered. And they gave their own progeny to these two Asreshtars, the male and the female, lion-shaped, with the garment of Az, and full of lust. And Az devoured that progeny and made these two Mazans, the male and the female, lewd and made them copulate, and they were mixed together, with joined bodies. And that mixture which they, from that progeny of Mazans and Asreshtars which she devoured, had put on as a garment, that mixture she formed by her own lasciviousness and made one body of male form, with bones, sinews, flesh, veins, and skin.

And part of that Light and Goodness of God that, through fruits and buds was mixed with that progeny of Mazans, was bound into this body as a soul. And in the body of the first man was inserted their greed and lust, salaciousness and copulation and enmity and calumny, envy and sinfulness, wrath and impurity, senselessness and wickedness of soul and doubt, stealing and lying, robbery and ill-doing, obstinacy, revenge, sorrow and grief, pain and toothache, poverty and begging, illness and old age, stench, and brigandage.

And those various words and voices of these Mazan abortions from which that body was built, Az gave to this creature, the first man, that he might speak and understand the varied words.

And that male descendant of the gods that came from the chariot and was seen by her, exactly after him, with him as a model, she formed and built the first man. And also from above, from the sky, she joined for him a binding connection with the Mazans and the Asreshtars and the zodiac and the planets so that upon him might rain wrath, lust, and sinfulness from the Mazans and the zodiac, and so that the will might penetrate him to become more cruel and more Mazan-like, greedy and lustful. And when that male creature had been born, then she gave it the name of the "first man," namely Gehmurd. And then those two Asreshtars, the male and the female, lion-shaped, again ate from the very same progeny of their friends and they were penetrated by lewdness and copulation, and they were mixed together, with joined bodies. And Az, who had filled them from that progeny of the Mazans that they ate, she again in the same way formed and built another body, a female one, with bones, sinews, flesh, veins and skin.

And after that female-formed descendant of the Gods (i.e., the Maiden of Light) that came from the chariot and was seen by the Az, so she had formed and built the first woman. And also for her, from the sky she joined binding and connection with the zodiac and the planets so that also upon her might rain wrath, lewdness, and sinfulness from the Mazans and the zodiac, and so that the will might penetrate her to become more cruel and more sinful, filled with lewdness and lust, and so that she might deceive this man through lust, and so that from these two creatures mankind might be born in the world, and so that they might become greedy and lustful and behave wrathfully and maliciously and mercilessly, and so that they might strike water and fire, trees and plants and worship greed and lust, do what the demons want, and go to Hell.

Thereafter, when that female creature had been born, then they gave her the name of the "Female of Glories," namely Murdiyanag. And when those two creatures, the male and the female, had been born in the world and fostered and had become older, then great joy came to Az and to the Asreshtars of the demons. And this leader of the Asreshtars made a gathering of the Mazans and the Asreshtars. He said to these two human beings: "For your sake I have created the earth and the sky, the sun and the moon, water and fire, trees and plants, and wild and tame animals so that you thereby might become joyful and happy and glad and do my will." And a terrible dragon, Mazan, he set over these two children as a guard, thinking: "He shall protect them and not allow anybody to lead them away from us. For these Mazans and Asreshtars fear the gods and are afraid that they should come over us and strike us or bind us. For these two children have been formed and built after the appearance and form of the gods."

Thereafter, that "first man" and that "Female of Glories," the first woman, began ruling over the earth. Then greed was awakened in them. And wrath penetrated them, and they began filling up springs, striking trees and plants, and ruling, in very great wrath, over the earth, and becoming greedy. And the gods they did not fear. And these five Elements of Light through which the world has been arranged they did not recognize, but hurt incessantly.

Notes

1. The textual detail is wrong, since the Living Spirit—as is shown above and below—has five sons; probably this should read "three of the sons."

2. The text has "eleven," which should no doubt be altered to "ten" (cf. Augustine c. Faustum, 32, 19); Schaeder in Reitzenstein-Schaeder, Studien, 344, Fr. Cumont, Recherches sur le Manichéisme, Bruxelles, 1912.

3. This is an extremely difficult passage. Schaeder (Reitzenstein-Schaeder, Studien, 345 f.) translates: "Then the 'sin' (which) (was) in them was snared and mixed, in accordance with the captured part, with the Light which was emitted from the Archons." Adam, Texte zum Manichäismus, 20, gives it as follows: "Then however the sin which was in them was added and mixed like a hair into the (bread)-dough into the moon which came out of the Archons (-Spheres)."

4. I.e., the "sin" that has fallen on the damp part of the earth.

5. The text here has Nebroel, essentially identical with the Supreme She-Devil Nekbael.

6. Another version: "And captured the mighty female Archon turned away from him" (Schaeder in Reitzenstein-Schaeder, Studien, 347).

The Secret Book of John

(Gnostic)

The Secret Book of John is a key Gnostic theogony as well as a retelling of early Genesis as the Gnostics saw God, Adam, Eve, the serpent, and Noah. The book was well known during the first centuries A.D.—Irenaeus knew its teaching when he composed *Against Heresies* (A.D. 185)— and the book was still known in the eighth century by the Audians of Mesopotamia.

Of course the confusing word for most of us is "God." For the Gnostics the highest deity is the Father of Light. God the Creator, the Yahweh of the Bible, is below him in the divine hierarchy, and he is a "jealous God" because he knows that he is not the sole divine power. The Gnostics called Yahweh Ialdabaoth, and they characterized him as "a monstrous abortion of darkness" who has trapped the Light-spirit of man in darkness and matter. Moreover, they believed that sin and evil came about not through Adam and Eve's original disobedience but through God's very act of creation of the world and Adam, which he did with arrogance, vanity, and in ignorance. God took light particles from his mother, Sophia, and trapped them in his human creation, but Adam and Eve struggle to return to the Father of Light. They began the process of redemption through their first act of disobedience to the Creator God, by eating from the Tree of Gnosis (knowledge), also called the Tree of the Thought of Light.

Clearly, the most elementary assumptions of Judeo-Christian theologies are reversed in the Gnostics. How did the God of the Bible become the monstrous Ialdabaoth? In *The Secret Book of John* Mother Sophia, the first female principle emanating from the Father of Light, desired to bring forth a likeness out of herself, but did so without the consent of her Consort. The result was the First Archon, the Ruler of

Darkness, the Creator of the world. The myth of the birth of God, our God, is a key Gnostic tale:

> Sophia's thought could not remain unproductive, and her work came forth, imperfect and ugly in appearance, because she had made it without her Consort. . . . When she considered it she saw that it was a copy of another appearance, since it had the appearance of a snake and a lion. Its eyes were shining with fire. She pushed it away from herself, outside those places, so that none of the Immortals might see it, because she had brought it to birth in ignorance; she joined a cloud of light with it, and set a throne in the middle of the cloud, so that no one might see it except the Holy Spirit, which is called Life, the Mother of All.

Thereupon Ialdabaoth created the world. Man was created in the image of the perfect Father, whose reflection was mirrored on the water, and the Creator God was tricked into breathing Light-power into him. But man was imprisoned in a material body. God attempted to divert him from a knowledge of the true God by preventing him from looking upward to the true God's perfection. When Adam and Eve rebelled by eating the fruit of *gnosis*, they were expelled from Paradise. Then God seduced Eve twice, and she brought forth Cain and Abel. Finally, Christ was sent down to save humanity by directing them to a knowledge of the light. The ascetic life provides the way to the realm of light. Those who fall, as in the Buddhist cycles, are fated to reincarnation until they come to saving knowledge.

The Secret Book of John exists in several Coptic versions found in the Nag Hammadi collection. These recensions are translations from an unknown Greek text. As James M. Robinson, editor of *The Nag Hammadi Library*, comments, the Gnostic documents reflect the ecumenical and syncretistic nature of the early Gnostics. The *Apocryphon of John* (here called *The Secret Book of John*) was "originally composed as a non-Christian text"[1] whose Christian thrust was added by a later Christian editor. As it now stands, the tract uses the device of a revelation delivered by the resurrected Christ to John the son of Zebedee, though they themselves offer nothing other than the Socratic frame of questions and answers.

Note

1. James M. Robinson, ed., *The Nag Hammadi Library* (San Francisco: Harper & Row, 1977), p. 9.

OF SOPHIA, MOTHER OF THE MONSTROUS CREATOR IALDABAOTH, YAHWEH*

It happened one day when John, the brother of James (these are sons of Zebedee), went up to the temple there a Pharisee named Arimanius approached him and said to him, "Where is your master whom you followed?" He said to him, "He has returned to the place from which he came." The Pharisee said to him, "This Nazarene deceived you with deception and hardened your hearts and estranged you from the tradition of your fathers."

When I, John, heard this, I went away from the temple to the mountain,[1] to a desert place, and with great grief in my heart I said, "How then was the Savior appointed? And why was he sent into the world by his Father who sent him? And who is his Father? And what is the nature of that Aeon to which we shall go? He told us, 'This Aeon received the type of that imperishable Aeon,' but he did not reveal to us what its nature is."

As I had these thoughts the heavens were opened and the whole creation shone with a light not of earth, and the universe was shaken. I was afraid and fell down, and behold, a child appeared to me; but I saw the form of an old man in whom was light. When I looked upon him I did not comprehend this wonder. If it is a unity with many forms because of the light? Then its forms appear. If it is a unity, how would it have three aspects?

He said to me, "John, why do you doubt [cf. Matt. 28:17]? For it is not foreign to you. Do not be of little faith; I am the one who is with you always. [Matt. 28:20]. I am the Father, I am the Mother, I am the Son. I am the eternally Existent

[Exod. 3:14], the unmixable, for there is no one who mixed himself with him. Now I have come to reveal to you that which is, that which has been, and that which will be [cf. Rev. 1:19], so that you may know the things which are seen and the things not seen and to reveal to you about the perfect Man [cf. Eph. 4:13]. Now lift up your face and come and hear and learn what I shall tell you today, so that you yourself may reveal it to spirits of the same sort, who are of the unwavering race of the Perfect Man and are able to understand."

He said to me, "The Spirit is a Unity, over which no one rules. It is the God of Truth, the Father of the All, the Holy Spirit, the invisible one, the one who is over the All, the one who exists in his imperishability, the one who exists in pure light into which no sight can look.

"One must not consider the Spirit as God or as of a specific quality, for it is more excellent than the gods. It is a Beginning that none precedes, for no one existed before it and it has no need of them. It does not need life, for it is eternal; it needs nothing, for it is not perfectible, since it has no deficiency which might be perfected, but is beyond all perfection. It is light. It is illimitable because no one is before it to give it limits; undifferentiated, because no one is before it to differentiate it; immeasurable, because no one has measured it as though existing before; invisible, because no one has seen it [John 1:18]. It is the eternal which always exists, the indescribable because no one has apprehended it so as to describe it, the one whose name no one can tell because no one existed before it to name it.

"It is the immeasurable Light, the holy and pure purity, the indescribable, perfect and imperishable. It is not perfection or beatitude or deity, but something far more excellent. It is not boundless nor are limits set to it; it is something more excellent. It is neither corporeal nor incorporeal, not great, not small, not a quantity, not a creature; no one can think

---

*Pages 19–77 of the Berlin Coptic Papyrus. All selections in this chapter are from Robert M. Grant, *Gnosticism* (New York: Harper & Brothers, 1961), pp. 69–85.

it. It is not anything existent, but something prior—not as if in itself it were prior, but because it is its own. It has no part in an Aeon. Time does not belong to it, for one which participates in an Aeon has been formed by others. Time is not allotted to it, since it receives nothing from any other which allots. It makes use of nothing. In short, there is nothing before it. It seeks only itself in the perfection of Light, and comprehends the pure Light. The immeasurable greatness, the eternal, the giver of eternity, the Light, the giver of light, the life, the giver of life, the blessed one, the giver of blessedness, the knowledge, the giver of knowledge, the eternal good, the giver of good, the benefactor; that which is not of such a kind because it is such, but it gives qualities; the merciful mercy, the grace-giving grace, the immeasurable Light.

"What shall I say to you of It, the incomprehensible—the vision of the light —corresponding to what I shall be able to comprehend? For who will ever comprehend It as I can discuss It with you?

"Its Aeon is imperishable, existing in rest and reposing in silence. It existed before the All. It is the head of all Aeons. If another were with It—for no one among us has recognized that which belongs to the immeasurable one except the one who dwelt in it. He told this to us [cf. John 1:18], he who alone understands himself in his own light which surrounds him, he who is the fount of the water of life, the light full of purity.

"The fount of the Spirit flowed out of the living water of light [cf. John 7:38]. And it supplied all Aeons and all worlds in every way. It understood Its own image, when It saw it in the pure water of light which surrounds It. And Its Thought became operative and revealed herself. She stood before It out of the splendor of the light, which is the Power which is before the All, the Power which has revealed itself and is the perfect Forethought of the universe, the Light, the copy of Light, the image of the invisible. She is the perfect Power, the Barbelo, the perfect Aeon of glory. She praises It because she appeared through It and understands It. She is the First Thought, Its Image; she became a First Man, i.e., the Virginal Spirit, the thrice-male one, which has three powers, three names, three acts of generation; the Aeon which does not age, the male-female which came out of Its Forethought.

"And Barbelo asked It to give her First Knowledge. It consented, and when It had consented, First Knowledge revealed herself and placed herself with Thought, i.e., Forethought, while they praised the Invisible One and the Perfect Power, Barbelo, because they originated through her. And again, First Knowledge asked this Power to give her Imperishability. And when It had consented, Imperishability revealed herself and placed herself with Thought and First Knowledge, while they praised the Invisible One and Barbelo, because it was through her that they had originated. She asked that Eternal Life might be given her. It consented, and when It had consented, Eternal Life revealed herself, and they stood there while they praised It and Barbelo, because it was through her that they had originated in the revelation permitted by the Invisible Spirit. This is the Five of the Aeons of the Father—First Man [the image of the Invisible One, i.e., Barbelo] and Thought and First Knowledge and Imperishability and Eternal Life. This is the male-female Five, the tenth of the Aeons, the Father of the ungenerated Father.

"Barbelo looked intensely into the pure Light and she turned to It and gave birth to a blessed Spark of Light; but he was not equal to her in greatness. This is the Monogenes, who revealed himself to the Father, the divine Self-born, the first-born Son of the All, from the Spirit of the pure Light. And the Invisible Spirit rejoiced at the Light which came into existence, which appeared through the First Power [Forethought, Barbelo]. It anointed him with Its goodness so that he became perfect, faultless, and Christ anointed because It has anointed him with the goodness of the Invisible Spirit. He appeared before it and received anointing through the Virginal Spirit; and he stood before It while he praised the Invisible Spirit and the perfect Forethought, this Spirit in which he had dwelt. And he asked It to give him one thing only, Mind. The Invisible Spirit consented; Mind revealed itself and stood with Christ while they praised It and Barbelo. All these, however, came into existence in silence and a Thought. The Invisible Spirit willed to make something; its Will became corporeal; Will revealed itself and stood with Mind and the Light while it praised It. Logos followed Will for through the logos, Christ created all things. The divine Self-born, Eternal Life, a Will, and Mind and First Knowledge placed themselves while they praised the Invisible Spirit and Barbelo. For it was through her that they came into existence, and through the Spirit of the eternal Self-born—son of Barbelo because he came to the eternal Virginal and Invisible Spirit—the Self-born God, Christ, whom the Spirit honored with great honor because he came into existence from Its First Thought. The Invisible Spirit appointed him as God over the All [cf. Rom. 9:5]. The true God gave him all power and subjected to him the Truth which was in it, so that he might comprehend the All. His name will be told to those who are worthy of him.

"But out of the Light, which is Christ, and out of Imperishability, through the working of the Invisible Spirit, the four great Lights revealed themselves from the divine Self-born, in order to place themselves by him and by the three. Will and Thought and Life. Now these four are Grace, Comprehension, Perception, and Prudence. Grace is at the first Light, Harmozel, which is the angel of light in the first Aeon; and there are three Aeons with it—Grace, Truth, and Form. At the

second Light, Oroiael, which he has appointed over the second Aeon, there are three Aeons—Forethought, Perception, and Memory. At the third Light, Daueithe, which he has appointed over the third Aeon, there are three Aeons—Comprehension, Love, and Idea. At the fourth Light, Eleleth, which he has appointed over the fourth Aeon, there are three Aeons—Perfection, Peace, and Sophia. These are the four Lights which stand by the Self-generator of the gods, the twelve Aeons, which stand by the child, by the great Self-generator-Christ, through the good pleasure of God, the Invisible Spirit. The twelve Aeons belong to the Son, the Self-generated. All things are made fast according to the will of the Holy Spirit through the Self-born.

"Out of First Knowledge and perfect Mind, through God, through the good pleasure of the great Invisible Spirit, and through the good pleasure of the Self-born, came forth the perfect true Man, the first appearance. He called him Adam, and appointed him over the first Aeon with the great God, the Self-generator Christ, in the first Aeon of Harmozel; and his powers are with him. And the Invisible Spirit gave him an invincible, intelligible Power. The Man said, 'I glorify and praise the Invisible Spirit, for because of thee all things came into existence, and all things aspire to thee. But I praise thee and the Self-born with the Aeons, the Three—the Father and the Mother and the Son, the perfect Power.'

"And he appointed his son Seth over the second Light, Oroiael. In the third Aeon was placed the seed of Seth, the souls of the saints who are eternally in the third Light, Daueithe. In the fourth Aeon were placed the souls who recognized their perfection and did not immediately repent but persisted; finally they repented. They will remain at the fourth Light, Eleleth, which joined them with itself while they praise the Invisible Spirit.

"Our sister Sophia, being an Aeon, conceived a thought from herself. Thinking of the Spirit and of First Knowledge, she willed to let a copy appear out of herself. The Spirit did not agree with her or consent with her, nor did her Consort, the male Virginal Spirit, approve. She found no more her supporter, when she consented without the good pleasure of the spirit and the knowledge of her own supporter. Because of the Desire [Prunicos] that was in her, she emanated outward. Her thought could not remain unproductive, and her work came forth, imperfect and ugly in appearance, because she had made it without her Consort. It did not resemble its mother's appearance but was of another form. When she considered it she saw that it was a copy of another appearance, since it had the appearance of a snake and a lion. Its eyes were shining with fire. She pushed it away from herself, outside those places, so that none of the Immortals might see it, because she had brought it to birth in ignorance; she joined a cloud of light with it, and set a throne in the middle of the cloud, so that no one might see it except the Holy Spirit, which is called Life, the Mother of All. And she named it Ialdabaoth. This is the First Archon. From his mother he drew great power, and he withdrew from her and turned away from the place where he was born. He took possession of another place; he created for himself an Aeon, flaming with shining fire [cf. Gen. 3:24], where he still is.

"And he joined himself with the Unreason which was with him, and called the Powers into existence, twelve angels under him, each in his Aeon according to the model of the Imperishable Aeons. And for each of them he created seven angels; and the angels with three powers, so that all those under him are three hundred and sixty angelic powers, including their three powers, which correspond to the appearance of the first model which was before him. When the Powers had revealed themselves from the arch-generator, the First Archon of the Darkness, from the Ignorance of the

one who begot them, they had the following names: the first is Iaoth, the second Hermas [the eye of fire], the third Galila, the fourth Iobel, the fifth Adonaios, the sixth Sabaoth, the seventh Kainan and Kae [who is called Cain, which is the sun], the eighth Abiressine, the ninth Iobel, the tenth Harmupiael, the eleventh Adonin, the twelfth Belias. They all have still other names because of lust and wrath; they have still other double names which are given them; these were given them because of the glory of the Heaven. But these names correspond to the truth which reveals their nature. And Saclas called them by these names in a vision and in relation to their power. Through periods of time they withdraw and grow weak; through periods of time they obtain strength and grow powerful.

"And he ordained that seven kings rule over the heavens and five over the chaos of Hades. The names of glory of those who rule over the seven heavens are these: the first is Iaoth, with the face of a lion; the second Eloaios, with the face of an ass; the third Astaphaios, with the face of a hyena; the fourth Iao, with the face of a seven-headed snake; the fifth Adonaios, with the face of a dragon; the sixth Adoni, with the face of an ape; the seventh Sabbataios, with a face of shining flames of fire. This is the Seven of the week; these are the ones who govern the world.

"But Ialdabaoth, Saclas, who possesses many forms in order to reveal himself with diverse forms as he pleases, apportioned to them some of his own fire and power. He did not give them any of the pure light which he had drawn from his Mother. Hence he governed them because of the glory which was in him from the power of the light of the Mother; hence he let himself be called God because he rebelled against the substance out of which he came into existence.

"And he joined seven powers with the Authorities. Because he spoke, they came into existence [Ps. 33:9]; he gave them names, and appointed authorities. He began from above. The first is the Forethought with the first, Iaoth; the second is the Deity with the second, Eloaios; the third is the Goodness with the third, Astaphaios; the fourth is the Fire with the fourth, Iao; the fifth is the Kingdom with the fifth, Sabaoth; the sixth is the Comprehension with the sixth, Adonaios; the seventh is the Sophia with the seventh, Sabbataios. These have a firmament like Heaven and an Aeon according to the Aeon-appearance which from the beginning existed after the model of the Imperishable Ones.

"He saw the creation beneath him, and the multitude of angels beneath him, who came into existence out of him, and he said to them, 'I am a jealous God; there is no other god beside me' [Deut. 5:9, Exod. 20:3]—already indicating to the angels beneath him that another god does exist. For if there were no other, of whom would he be jealous? The Mother then began to be 'borne about' [Gen. 1:2] because she recognised her deficiency. Because her consort had not agreed with her, she had diminished in her perfection."

I said, "Christ, what does 'borne about' mean?" He smiled and said, "Do you think it is, as Moses said, 'above the waters'? Not at all. She saw the wickedness and the apostasy which clung to her son. She repented, and while she went to and fro in the darkness of ignorance, she began to be ashamed and did not venture to return above but went to and fro. This going to and fro is 'to be borne about.' After the self-satisfied one had received a power from the Mother, he did not know many things which were set over his Mother. He thought that his Mother alone existed. He saw the countless army of angels which he had made, and he felt himself exalted above them. But when the Mother knew that the abortion of darkness was imperfect, since her consort had not agreed with

her, she repented and grieved exceedingly. He heard the prayer of her repentance and the brothers petitioned on her behalf. The Holy Invisible Spirit gave permission, and after the Holy Invisible Spirit had given permission, It poured over her a spirit from the Perfection. Her consort came down to her in order to correct her deficiency. He decided in his forethought to correct her deficiency. She was not led back to her own Aeon, but because of the abundant ignorance which had appeared in her, she is in the Nine until she corrects her deficiency.

THE BIRTH OF ADAM AND EVE

"A voice came to her: 'Man exists, and the Son of Man.' The first Archon Ialdabaoth heard it, and he thought that the voice had not come down. To him the holy, perfect Father, the First Man in the form of a man. The Blessed One revealed his appearance to them, and the whole archontic group of the seven Authorities gave permission. They saw in the water the appearance of the image, and they said to one another, 'Let us make a man, after the image and after the appearance of God' [cf. Gen. 1:26]. From one another they created, and from all their powers they formed a formation from themselves. And each one of every power in his power created the soul. They created it after the image which they had seen, by way of an imitation of him who was from the beginning the Perfect Man. They said, 'Let us call him Adam, so that the name of this being and his power may become a light for us.' And the powers began from below. The first is Deity, i.e., a soul of bone; the second is Goodness, i.e., the desire of the soul; the third is Fire, i.e., a flesh-soul; the fourth is Providence, i.e., a marrow-soul, and the whole framing of the body; the fifth is Kingdom, i.e., a blood-soul; the sixth is Understanding,

57

i.e., a head-soul; the seventh is Sophia, i.e., a hair-soul. And they set the whole body in order, and their angels came to them from the number of those who were first prepared by the Authorities, the Soul-substances, for the arrangement of the joined members. And they made the whole body, fitted together from the army of angels, whom I have already mentioned. And it remained inert for a long time, since the seven Authorities could not raise it up, nor could the three hundred and sixty angels who assembled the members.

"And the Mother wanted to recover the power which she had given to the Archon of Prunicos. She came in innocence and prayed to the Father of All, the one rich in mercy, the God of Light. By a holy decree he sent the Self-born and the Four Lights in the form of the angels of the First Archon. They advised him so that they might bring forth the power of the Mother from him. They said to him, "Breathe in his face something of the spirit which is in you, and the object will raise itself up." So he breathed into him some of his spirit— i.e., the power of the Mother—into the body, and he moved. And the other powers were jealous because he originated from them all, and they had given the man the powers which were derived from them, and he had taken to himself the souls of the seven Authorities and their powers. His wisdom was stronger than all of them, stronger than the First Archon. And they knew that he was free from wickedness, since he was more intelligent than they were, and had come in the Light. They took him and brought him down to the region at the bottom of all matter.

"But the blessed Father is a compassionate benefactor. He took pity on the power of the Mother which had been taken from the First Archon so that it might obtain power over the body. He sent out the good Spirit, he and his great compassion, as a helper for the first one who had come down, who was called

Adam—namely the Thought of Light, which by him was called 'Life.' This is she who works at the whole creature, Adam, since she labors with the creature [cf. Rom. 8:22], sets him in his own perfect temple, explains the coming down of his flaw, and shows him his way upwards. And the Thought of Light was hidden in him so that the Archons would not perceive it but our sister Sophia might correct her error through the Thought of Light. And the man shone forth because of the shadow of the Light which is in him, and his thinking rose higher than those who had created him. And they agreed and saw that the man had raised himself above them. They made a resolution with the whole angelic array of the Archons and with the rest of their powers. Then fire and earth united with water and flame. They were confounded with the four winds, so that they blew fierily, united one with another, and caused a great commotion. They brought him into the shadow of death.

"Then they made another formation out of earth, water, fire, and wind; i.e., out of matter, darkness, desire, and the Opposed Spirit. This is the fetter, this is the tomb of the formation, of the body, which was put on man as the fetter of matter. This is the first one who came down, and his first separation. But the Thought of Light is in him and awakens his thought.

The First Archon brought him and placed him in Paradise, of which he said that it would be a 'delight' for him; that means that he tricked him. For their delight is bitter and their beauty is lawless. Their delight is deceit and their tree was hostility. Their fruit is poison, against which there is no healing, and their promise is death for him. Their tree was planted as the 'Tree of Life.' But I will proclaim to you the mystery of their life; that is their Imitation Spirit, which comes from them, so that it will lead him astray, so that he will not know his perfection. That tree is made as follows: its root is bitter; its branches are shadows of death; its leaves are hate and deceit; its sap is an ointment of wickedness and its fruit is the desire of death; its seed drinks up those who taste it; the Hades is their abode.

"But the tree which they call 'of the knowledge of good and evil,' this is the Thought of Light, on whose account the commandment was given not to taste of it, that is, 'do not hear them,' since the commandment was directed against him, so that he might not look up towards his perfection nor know his nakedness in relation to his perfection. But I have brought you to eat of it."

I said to him, "Christ, was it not the serpent who taught her?"

He smiled and said, "The serpent taught her the begetting of desire for pollution and corruption, since these serve him. And he knew that she would not obey him, since she is shrewder than he. He wanted to bring out the power which had been given him by him, and he let lack of perception settle upon Adam."

I said to him, "Christ, what is lack of perception?"

He said, "It is not as Moses said, 'He let him sleep,' [Gen. 2:21], but he enveloped his senses with a veil and burdened him with anesthesia. For he said through the prophet [Isa. 6:10], 'I will harden the ears of your hearts so that you may not understand and may not see.' Then the Thought of Light hid herself in him and in his will he decided to bring her forth out of the rib. But the Thought of Light, since she is unattainable, even though Darkness pursued her, it could not grasp her [cf. John 1:5]. He decided to bring the power out of him and again make a formation with a female form. And he let it arise before him; not as Moses said, 'He took a rib and created the woman for him' [Gen. 2:21–22]. Immediately he became sober from the intoxication of the Darkness. The Thought of Light removed the veil from his mind; and as he recognized in her his essence, he said, 'This is now

bone of my bones and flesh of my flesh' [Gen. 2:23]. For this reason the man will leave his father and his mother and will cleave to his wife and the two will become one flesh [Gen. 2:24]. Because they will send the consort of the Mother, and will raise her up, because of this Adam called her 'Mother of all living' [Gen. 3:20].

"From the Absolute Sovereignty of the Height and of revelation, Thought taught them knowledge through the tree, in the form of an eagle. She taught them to eat knowledge so that he might take care of his perfection, since both had the flaw of ignorance. Ialdabaoth knew that they withdrew from him. He cursed them, and furthermore ordained that the man should be lord over the woman, though he, Ialdabaoth, was ignorant of the mystery [Eph. 5:32] which originated from the decree of the holy Height.

"But Adam and Eve were afraid to curse him and to uncover his ignorance. All his angels drove them out of Paradise and he surrounded it with thick darkness. Then Ialdabaoth saw the virgin who stood beside Adam. Senselessness filled Ialdabaoth and he wanted to let a seed sprout from her. He seduced Eve and begot the first son, and similarly the second: Yahweh, with a face like a bear, and Elohim, with a face like a cat. But one is righteous, while the other is unrighteous. Elohim is the righteous, Yahweh the unrighteous. He set the righteous one over fire and wind; the unrighteous one he set over water and earth. These are the ones who up to the present day are called Cain and Abel among all generations of men. Marital intercourse arose through the First Archon. He planted in Adam a desire for sowing, so that it is of this essence that women produce a copy from their Imitation Spirit. And he set the two Archons over the principalities, so that they might rule over the grave [i.e., body].

"Adam knew his nature and begot Seth [Gen. 4:25]. And as in the generation which is in heaven under the Aeons, so the Mother sent the Spirit which belongs to her. The Spirit descended to her in order to awaken the nature which is like it, after the model of perfection, in order to awaken them from lack of perception and from the wickedness of the grave. So it remained for a time and worked for the seed, so that when the Spirit comes from the holy Aeons it may place them outside deficiency in the arrangement of the Aeon; so that it may become holy perfection, so that deficiency may no longer be with it."

And I said, "Christ, will the souls all live longer than the purity of light?"

He said to me, "You have come to a perception of great things, which are hard to reveal to others than those who are of the generation which does not waver. Those upon whom the Spirit of Life descends, when they are bound together with the power, will be saved and will become perfect and they will become worthy to rise upward to that great light; for they will become worthy to purify themselves with them from every evil and from the temptations of wickedness, so that they no longer direct their glance at anything but the imperishable assembly, and strive for it without anger, envy, fear, desire, and satiety. They will be affected by none of these except only the flesh, which they use while they wait to be led forth and received by the Receiver into the honor of eternal, imperishable life and their vocation, in which they endure all things and suffer all things [1 Cor. 13:7] so that they may pass through the struggle and inherit eternal life."

I said, "Christ, if they have not done this, what will the souls into which the power and the Spirit of Life have entered do so that they too may be saved?"

He said to me "The souls to which that Spirit comes will under all circumstances live, and they come out of evil. For the power enters all men; without it they cannot stand upright. But after the soul is born, then the Spirit of Life will be brought to it. And when it comes this strong, divine Spirit to the life, it strengthens the power—i.e., the soul— and it does not turn aside to wickedness. But in the case of those whom the Imitation Spirit enters, it leads the soul astray and the soul errs."

I said, "Christ, the souls of these, when they come out of the flesh, whither will they go?"

He smiled and said, "To a place for the soul, i.e., the power which is far superior to the Imitation Spirit. This is strong; it escapes from the works of wickedness and through the imperishable guidance it will be saved and raised up to the Rest of the Aeons."

I said, "Christ, those who have not known the All, what are their souls or whither will they go?"

He said to me, "An Imitation Spirit has overgrown them in their stumbling, and so the Imitation Spirit burdens their souls, draws the soul to the works of wickedness, and brings it in this way to lack of perception. After the soul is unclothed, the Imitation Spirit delivers it to the powers which are under the Archon. The souls will once more be cast into fetters and led about until they are saved from lack of perception, attain knowledge, and so will be perfected and saved."

I said, "Christ, how then does the soul gradually shrivel up and return into the nature of the Mother or of the Man?"

He rejoiced when I asked him, and he said, "Blessed are you for a clear understanding. Therefore they will be given together with the other in whom the Spirit of Life is a consequence for him. And because the soul hears through him, it will be saved. It no longer goes into another flesh."

I said to him, "Christ, those who have known but have turned away, what are their souls?"

He said to me, "They will go to the place where the angels of impoverishment [cf. Gal. 4:9] will withdraw, for whom there is no portion of repentance [cf. Heb. 12:17]. They will all be preserved for the day on which they will be punished. All who have blasphemed against the Holy Spirit [Matt. 12:31] will be tormented in eternal punishment" [cf. Heb. 6:4–8].

I said, "Christ, whence came the Imitation Spirit?"

He said to me, "When the merciful Mother and the Holy Spirit, the merciful, which troubled itself with us—that is, the Thought of Light—and the seed which it awakened in the thought of the men of the generation of this perfect and eternal man of light—then the First Archon recognized that she surpassed him in the height of their wisdom. He wanted to get possession of their counsel. Since he is ignorant, he did not know that they are wiser than he is. He took counsel with his powers. They brought Fate into being and through measure, periods, and seasons they imprisoned the gods of the heavens, the angels, the demons, and men, so that all would come into its fetters and Fate would be lord over all: an evil and tortuous plan. And he repented for everything which had come into being through him [cf. Gen. 6:6]. He decided to let a flood come over the whole presumption of men. And the greatness of Providence, i.e., the Thought of Light, informed Noah. He made a proclamation to men, yet they did not believe him. Not as Moses said, 'He hid himself in an ark,' [cf. Gen. 7:16], but he covered himself in a Place. Not only Noah, but other people from the generation which does not waver, went to a Place and covered themselves with a cloud of light. And he recognized the authority from above, together with those who were with him in the light which shone on them; for the darkness was poured out over everything on the earth.

"He took counsel with his angels; they sent their angels to the daughters of men, so that they might let seed generate from them for their pleasure. At first they had no success. They all came to a decision to create the Imitation Spirit, so that they might remember the Spirit which came down. And the angels changed their forms into the appearance of their husbands and they sowed with the spirit which tormented them in the darkness. Out of wickedness they brought them gold, silver, gifts, and metals, copper and iron and all sorts, and they led them into temptation so that they would not remember their Providence, which does not waver.[2] And they took them and begot children [cf. Gen. 6:1] out of the darkness through their Imitation Spirit. Their hearts were hardened, they became hard through the hardening of the Imitation Spirit, even until now.

"The One to be praised, the Father-Mother, the One rich in mercy, takes form in its seed.

"I first came up or down to the perfect Aeon.

"I say this to you, so that you may write it down and give it in secret to your fellow spirits. For this mystery belongs to the generation which does not waver.

"The Mother once descended before me. But these are the things which she effected in the world; she raised up her seed.

"I will proclaim to you what will take place; and indeed I have given you this, so that you may write it down, and it will certainly be deposited."

Then he said to me, "Cursed is anyone who exchanges this for a gift or for food or drink or clothing or anything else of the sort."

He gave John this mystery and forthwith disappeared from him. And John came to his fellow disciples and began to tell them what had been said to him by the Savior.

Notes

1. Mountain. Mount of Olives.
2. Cf. 1 Enoch 7–8.

On the Origin of the World

*(Gnostic)**

The modern title *On the Origin of the World* is used to name a tractate that has been transmitted without a title, but which discusses what this hypothetical title suggests. *On the Origin of the World* is a compendium of essential Gnostic ideas, a work written in the form of an apologetic essay offering to the public an explanation of the Gnostic worldview. Although the treatise does not represent any known Gnostic system, there are reminiscences of Sethian, Valentinian, and Manichaean themes; the author obviously draws upon a variety of traditions and sources. For example, some sort of connection with the *Hypostasis of the Archons* (Codex II, 4) is clear, though the precise nature of this relationship is uncertain. *On the Origin of the World* was probably composed in Alexandria at the end of the third century A.D. or the beginning of the fourth. The place and date of composition are suggested by the juxtaposition of various sorts of materials: the varieties of Jewish thought, Manichaean motifs, Christian ideas, Greek or Hellenistic philosophical and mythological concepts, magical and astrological themes, and elements of Egyptian lore together suggest that Alexandria may have been the place where the original Greek text was composed.

After opening with a reference to the philosophical controversy regarding the origin of Chaos, *On the Origin of the World* proceeds to a detailed portrayal of primeval history. The Genesis story of the creation of the world, the place of the arrogant demiurge Ialdabaoth, and the climactic creation and enlightened transgression of Adam and Eve are described from a Gnostic viewpoint. In addition, important salvific roles are played by Wisdom (Pistis Sophia and Sophia Zoë), the little blessed spirits, and Jesus the logos and Savior. Finally, in a victorious blaze of destruction, light triumphs over darkness, and life over death.

---

*Introduction by Hans-Gebhard Bethge.

The treatise *On the Origin of the World* is an important Gnostic work in several respects. This text provides insight into the thought, methodology, and argumentation of a Gnostic author presenting to the public at large certain information on the origin and end of the world and of man. Furthermore, the tractate also shows the freedom and skill with which such a writer could utilize various materials of a diverse character, all in the service of Gnostic proclamation. *On the Origin of the World* illustrates how the Gnostic worldview can assert itself in dialogue with other spiritual movements and in part even replace them.

THE CREATION OF THE WORLD AND THE DEMIURGE IALDABAOTH*

Since everyone—the gods of the world and men—says that nothing existed prior to Chaos, I shall demonstrate that they all erred, since they do not know the structure of Chaos and its root. Here is the demonstration:

If it is agreed by all men concerning Chaos that it is a darkness, then it is something derived from a shadow. It was called darkness.

But the shadow is something derived from a work existing from the beginning.

So it is obvious that the first work existed before Chaos came into being.

Now let us enter into the truth, but also into the first work, from whence Chaos came; and in this way the demonstration of truth will appear.

After the nature of the immortals was completed out of the boundless one, then a likeness called "Sophia" flowed out of Pistis. She wished that a work should come into being which is like the light which first existed, and immediately her wish appeared as a heavenly

likeness, which possessed an incomprehensible greatness, which is in the middle between the immortals and those who came into being after them, like what is above, which is a veil which separates men and those belonging to the sphere above.

Now the Aeon of truth has no shadow within it because the immeasurable light is everywhere within it. Its outside, however, is a shadow. It was called "darkness." From within it, a power appeared over the darkness. And as for the shadow, the powers which came into being after them called it "the limitless Chaos." And out of it every race of gods was brought forth, both one and the other and the whole place. Consequently, the shadow too is posterior to the first work which appeared. The abyss is derived from the aforementioned Pistis.

Then the shadow perceived that there was one stronger than it. It was jealous, and when it became self-impregnated, it immediately bore envy. Since that day the origin of envy has appeared in all of the aeons and their worlds. But that envy was found to be a miscarriage without any spirit in it. It became like the shadows in a great watery substance.

Then the bitter wrath which came into being from the shadow was cast into a region of Chaos. Since that day a watery substance has appeared, i.e., what was enclosed in the shadow flowed forth, appearing in Chaos. Just as all the useless afterbirth of one who bears a little child falls, likewise the matter which came into

*Codex II, 5 and XIII, 2. Translated by Hans-Gebhard Bethge and Orval S. Wintermute. All selections in this chapter are from James M. Robinson, ed., *The Nag Hammadi Library* (San Francisco: Harper & Row, 1977), pp. 160–179.

being from the shadow was cast aside. And it did not come out of Chaos, but matter was in Chaos, existing in a part of it.

Now after these things happened, then Pistis came and appeared over the matter of Chaos, which was cast off like a miscarriage since there was no spirit in her. For all of that is a boundless darkness and water of unfathomable depth. And when Pistis saw what came into being from her deficiency, she was disturbed. And the disturbance appeared as a fearful work. And it fled in order to dwell in the Chaos. Then she turned to it and breathed into its face in the abyss, which is beneath all of the heavens.

Now when Pistis Sophia desired to cause the one who had no spirit to receive the pattern of a likeness and rule over the matter and over all its powers, a Ruler first appeared out of the waters, lion-like in appearance, androgynous, and having a great authority within himself, but not knowing whence he came into being.

Then when Pistis Sophia saw him moving in the depth of the waters, she said to him, "O youth, pass over here," which is interpreted "Ialdabaoth." Since that day, the first principle of the word which referred to the gods and angels and men has appeared. And the gods and angels and men constitute that which came into being by means of the word. Moreover, the ruler Ialdabaoth is ignorant of the power of Pistis. He did not see her face, but the likeness which spoke with him he saw in the water. And from that voice he called himself "Ialdabaoth." But the perfect ones call him "Ariael" because he was a lion-likeness. And after this one came to possess the authority of matter, Pistis Sophia withdrew up to her light.

When the ruler saw his greatness, he saw only himself; he did not see another one except water and darkness. Then he thought that he alone existed. His thought was made complete by means of the word, and it appeared as a spirit moving to and fro over the waters. And when that spirit appeared, the ruler separated the watery substance to one region, and the dry substance to another region. And from the one matter he created a dwelling place for himself. He called it "Heaven." From the other matter the ruler created a footstool. He called it "earth."

Afterward the Ruler thought within his nature, and he created an androgynous being by means of the word. He opened his mouth and boasted to himself. When his eyes were opened, he saw his father and he said to him "y." His father called him "Yao." Again he created the second son and boasted to himself. He opened his eyes and he said to his father "e." His father called him "Eloai." Again he created the third son and boasted to himself. He opened his eyes, and he said to his father "as." His father called him "Astaphaios." These are the three sons of their father.

Seven appeared in Chaos as androgynous beings. They have their masculine name and their feminine name. The feminine name of Ialdabaoth is Pronoia Sambathas, i.e. the Hebdomad. As for his son, called "Yao," his feminine name is "lordship." Sabaoth's feminine name is "divinity." Adonaios' feminine name is "kingship." Eloaios' feminine name is "envy." Oraios' feminine name is "riches." Astaphaios' feminine name is "Sophia." These are the seven powers of the seven heavens of Chaos. And they came into being as androgynous beings according to the deathless pattern which existed before them and in accord with the will of Pistis, so that the likeness of the one who existed from the first might rule until the end.

You will find the function of these names and the masculine power in "the Archangelike of Moses the Prophet." But the feminine names are in "the First Book of Noraia."

Now since the First Father, Ialdabaoth, had great authority, he created for each of his sons, by means of the word, beautiful heavens as dwelling places, and for each heaven great glories, seven times more exquisite than any earthly glory, thrones and dwelling places and temples and chariots and spiritual virgins and their glories, looking up to an invisible realm, each one having these within his heaven; and also armies of divine, lordly, angelic, and archangelic powers, myriads without number, in order to serve.

The report concerning these you will find accurately in "the First Logos of Noraia."

Now they were completed in this way up to the sixth heaven, the one belonging to Sophia. And the Heaven and his earth were overturned by the troubler who was beneath all of them. And the six heavens trembled. For the powers of Chaos knew not who it was who destroyed the heaven beneath them. And when Pistis knew the scorn of the troubler, she sent her breath, and she bound him and cast him down to Tartaros.

Since that day, the Heaven has been consolidated along with its earth by means of the Sophia of Ialdabaoth, the one which is beneath them all. But after the heavens and their powers and all of their government set themselves aright, the First Father exalted himself and was glorified by the whole army of angels. And all the gods and their angels gave him praise and glory. And he rejoiced in his heart, and he boasted continually, saying to them, "I do not need anything. I am God and no other one exists except me." But when he said these things, he sinned against all of the immortal imperishable ones, and they protected him. Moreover, when Pistis saw the impiety of the chief Ruler, she was angry. Without being seen, she said, "You err, Samael," i.e., "the blind god." "An enlightened, immortal man exists before you. He will appear within your molded bodies. He will trample upon you as potter's clay is trampled. And you will go with those who are yours down to your mother, the abyss. For in the consumma-

tion of your works, all of the deficiency which appeared in the truth will be dissolved. And it will cease, and it will be like that which did not come into being." After Pistis said these things, she revealed the likeness of her greatness in the waters. And thus she withdrew up to her light.

But when Sabaoth the son of Ialdabaoth, heard the voice of Pistis, he worshiped her. He condemned the father on account of the word of Pistis. He glorified her because she informed them of the deathless man and his light. Then Pistis Sophia stretched forth her finger, and she poured upon him a light from her light for a condemnation of his father. Moreover, when Sabaoth received light, he received a great authority against all of the powers of Chaos. Since that day, he has been called "the lord of the powers." He hated his father, the darkness, and his mother, the abyss. He loathed his sister, the thought of the First Father, the one who moves to and fro over the water.

And on account of his light, all of the Authorities of Chaos were jealous of him. And when they were disturbed, they made a great war in the seven heavens. Then when Pistis Sophia saw the war, she sent seven archangels from her light to Sabaoth. They snatched him away up to the seventh heaven. They took their stand before him as servants. Furthermore, she sent him three other archangels and established the kingdom for him above every one so that he might come to be above the twelve gods of Chaos.

But when Sabaoth received the place of repose because of his repentance, Pistis moreover gave him her daughter Zoë with a great Authority so that she might inform him about everything that exists in the eighth heaven. And since he had an Authority, he first created a dwelling place for himself. It is a large place which is very excellent, sevenfold greater than all those which exist in the seven heavens. Then in front of his dwelling place he created a great throne on a four-faced chariot called "cherubin." And the cherubin has eight forms for each of the four corners—lion forms, and bull forms, and human forms, and eagle forms—so that all of the forms total sixty-four forms. And seven archangels stand before him. He is the eighth, having authority. All of the forms total seventy-two. For from this chariot the seventy-two gods receive a pattern; and they receive a pattern so that they might rule over the seventy-two languages of the nations. And on that throne he created some other dragon-shaped angels called "seraphin," who glorify him continually.

Afterward he created an angelic church—myriads belong to her—being like the church which is in the eighth. And a first-born called "Israel," i.e., "the man who sees God," and also having another name, "Jesus the Christ," who is like the Savior who is above the eighth, sits at his right upon an excellent throne. But on his left the virgin of the holy spirit sits upon a throne praising him. And the seven virgins stand before her, while thirty other virgins with lyres and harps and trumpets in their hands glorify him. And all of the armies of angels glorify him and praise him. But he sits on a throne concealed by a great light-cloud. And there was no one with him in the cloud except Sophia Pistis, teaching him about all those which exist in the eighth so that the likeness of those might be created, in order that the kingdom might continue for him until the consummation of the heavens of Chaos and their powers.

Now Pistis Sophia separated him from the darkness. She summoned him to her right. But she left the First Father on her left. Since that day right has been called "justice," but left has been called "injustice." Moreover, because of this they all received an order of the assembly of justice; and injustice stands above all their creations.

Moreover, when the First Father of Chaos saw his son, Sabaoth, and that the glory in which he dwells is more exquisite than all the authorities of Chaos, he was jealous of him. And when he was angry, he begot Death from his own death. It was set up over the sixth heaven. Sabaoth was snatched away from that place. And thus the number of the six authorities of Chaos was completed.

Then since Death was androgynous, he mixed with his nature and begot seven androgynous sons. These are the names of the males: Jealousy, Wrath, Weeping, Sighing, Mourning, Lamenting, Tearful Groaning. And these are the names of the females: Wrath, Grief, Lust, Sighing, Cursing, Bitterness, Quarrelsomeness. They had intercourse with one another, and each one begot seven so that they total forty-nine androgynous demons.

Their names and their functions you will find in "the Book of Solomon."

And vis-à-vis these, Zoë, who exists with Sabaoth, created seven androgynous good powers. These are the names of the males: One-who-is-not-jealous, the Blessed, Joy, the True One, One-who-is-not-envious, the Beloved, the Trustworthy One. As for the females, however, these are their names: Peace, Gladness, Rejoicing, Blessedness, Truth, Love, Faith. And many good and guileless spirits are derived from these.

Their accomplishments and their functions you will find in "the Schemata of the Heimarmene of the Heaven which is beneath the twelve."

But when the First Father saw the likeness of Pistis in the waters, he grieved. Especially when he heard her voice, it was like the first voice which called to him out of the water, and when he knew that this was the one who named him, he groaned and was ashamed on account of his transgression. And when he actually knew that an enlightened, immortal man existed before him, he was very much disturbed, because he had first said to all the gods and their angels, "I am God. No other one exists except me."

For he had been afraid lest perhaps they know that another one existed before him and condemn him. But he, like a fool, despised the condemnation and acted recklessly, and said, "If someone exists before me, let him appear so that we might see his light." And immediately, behold, a light came out of the eighth, which is above, and passed through all the heavens of the earth.

When the First Father saw that the light was beautiful as it shone forth, he was amazed and was very much ashamed. When the light appeared, a human likeness, which was very wonderful, was revealed within it; and no one saw it except the First Father alone and Pronoia who was with him. But its light appeared to all the powers of the heavens. Therefore, they were all disturbed by it.

Then when Pronoia saw the angel, she became enamored of him. But he hated her because she was in the darkness. Moreover she desired to embrace him, but she was not able. When she was unable to cease her love, she poured out her light upon the earth. From that day, that angel was called "Light-Adam," which is interpreted "the enlightened bloody one." And the earth spread over him, Holy Adamas, which is interpreted "the holy steel-like earth." At that time, all the authorities began to honor the blood of the virgin. And the earth was purified because of the blood of the virgin. But especially the water was purified by the likeness of Pistis Sophia, which appeared to be the First Father in the waters. Moreover, with reason they have said "through the waters." Since the holy water gives life to everything, it purifies it too. Out of the first blood Eros appeared, being androgynous. His masculine nature is Himeros, because he is fire from the light. His feminine nature is that of a blood-soul, and is derived from the substance of Pronoia. He is very handsome in his beauty, having more loveliness than all the creatures of chaos. Then when all the gods and their angels saw Eros, they became enamored of him. But when he appeared among all of them, he burned them. Just as many lamps are kindled from a single lamp and the single light remains but the lamp is not diminished, so also Eros was scattered in all the creatures of chaos yet he was not diminished. Just as Eros appeared out of the midpoint between light and darkness, and in the midst of the angels and men the intercourse of Eros was consummated, so too the first sensual pleasure sprouted upon the earth.

The man followed the earth,
The woman followed the man,
And marriage followed the woman,
And reproduction followed marriage,
And death followed reproduction.

After Eros, the grapevine sprouted up from the blood which was poured upon the earth. Therefore those who drink the vine acquire the desire for intercourse. After the grapevine, a fig tree and a pomegranate tree sprouted up in the earth, together with the rest of the trees, according to their kind, having their seed derived from the seed of the authorities and their angels.

Then Justice created the beautiful Paradise. It is outside the circuit of the moon and the circuit of the sun in the luxuriant earth, which is in the east in the midst of the stones. And desire is in the midst of the trees since they are beautiful and tall. And the tree of immortal life, as it was revealed by the will of God, is in the north of Paradise in order to give life to the immortal saints, who will come out of the molded bodies of poverty in the consummation of the Aeon. Now the color of the tree of life is like the sun, and its branches are beautiful. Its leaves are like those of the cypress. Its fruit is like clusters of white grapes. Its height rises up to Heaven. And at its side is the Tree of Knowledge, possessing the power of God. Its glory is like the moon shining forth brilliantly. And its branches are beautiful. Its leaves are like fig leaves. Its fruit is like the good, magnificent dates. And this is in the north side of Paradise in order to raise up the souls from the stupor of the demons, so that they might come to the Tree of Life and eat its fruit and condemn the authorities and their angels.

The accomplishment of this tree is written in "the Holy Book" as follows:

"You are the Tree of Knowledge,
which is in Paradise,
from which the first man ate
and which opened his mind,
so that he became enamored of his
   co-likeness,
and condemned other alien likenesses,
and loathed them."

Now after this there sprouted up the olive tree which was to purify kings and chief priests of justice, who will appear in the last days. Now the olive tree appeared in the light of the first Adam for the sake of the anointing which they will receive.

But the first Psyche (Soul) loved Eros who was with her, and poured her blood upon him and upon the earth. Then from that blood the first rose sprouted upon the earth out of the thorn bush, for a joy in the light which was to appear in the bramble. After this the beautiful, fragrant flowers sprouted up in the earth according to their kind from the blood of each of the virgins of the daughters of Pronoia. When they had become enamored of Eros, they poured out their blood upon him and upon the earth. After these things, every herb sprouted up in the earth according to its kind, and having the seed of the Authorities and their angels. After these things, the Authorities created from the waters all species of beasts and reptiles and birds according to their kind, having the seed of the Authorities and their angels.

But before all these things, when the Light-Adam appeared on the first day, he remained thus upon the earth two days. He left the lower Pronoia in Heaven, and began to ascend to his light. And immediately darkness came upon the whole world. Now when Sophia, who is in the lower heaven, wished to receive an Authority from Pistis, she created great luminaries and all the stars, and put them in the heaven in order to shine upon the earth and to perfect chronological signs and special times and years and months and days and nights and seconds, etc. And thus everything above the heaven was ordered.

Now when Light-Adam desired to enter his light, i.e., the eighth, he was not able because of the poverty which had mixed with his light. Then he created a great Aeon for himself; and in that Aeon he created six Aeons and their worlds, totaling six in number, which are sevenfold more exquisite than the heavens of Chaos and their worlds. But all these Aeons and their worlds exist within the boundless region, which is between the eighth and Chaos, which is beneath it, and they are reckoned with the world which belongs to the poverty.

If you wish to know the arrangement of these, you will find it written in "the Seventh Cosmos of Hieralaias the Prophet."

But before Light-Adam withdrew, the authorities saw him in Chaos. They laughed at the First Father because he lied, saying, "I am God. No one else exists before me." When they came to him they said, "Is this not the god who destroyed our work?" He answered and said: "Yes, but if you desire that he not be able to destroy our work, come, let us create a man from the earth according to the image of our body and according to the likeness of that one, in order that he may serve us so that whenever that one sees his likeness, he may become enamored of it. Then he will no longer ruin our work, but we shall make those who will be begotten from the light servants to ourselves—" through all the time of this Aeon. Now all this which came to pass was according to the foresight of Pistis in order that the man might appear face to face with his likeness and condemn them from within their molded body. And their molded body became a hedge for the light.

THE RAISING OF ADAM FROM THE MUD BY EVE (ZOË-LIFE)

Then the authorities received knowledge necessary to create man. Sophia Zoë, who is beside Sabaoth, anticipated them, and laughed at their decision because they were blind—in ignorance they created him against themselves—and they do not know what they will do. Because of this she anticipated them. She created her man first in order to inform their molded body of how he would condemn them. And in this way he will save them.

Now the birth of the instructor occurred in this way. When Sophia cast a drop of light, it floated on the water. Immediately the man appeared, being androgynous. That drop first patterned the water as a female body. Afterward it patterned itself within the body of the likeness of the mother who appeared, and it fulfilled itself in twelve months. An androgynous man was begotten, one whom the Greeks call "Hermaphrodites." But the Hebrews call his mother "Eve of Life," i.e., "the instructor of life." Her son is the begotten one who is lord. Afterward, the Authorities called him "the beast" in order to lead their molded bodies astray. The interpretation of the "beast" is "the instructor"; he was found to be wiser than all of them. Moreover, Eve is the first virgin, not having a husband. When she gave birth, she is the one who healed herself. On account of this it is said concerning her that she said,

"I am the portion of my mother,
    and I am the mother.
I am the woman,
    and I am the virgin.

I am the pregnant one.
I am the physician.
I am the midwife.
My husband is the one who begot me,
    and I am his mother,
and he is my father and my lord.
He is my potency.
That which he desires he speaks
    with reason.
I am still in a nascent state,
    but I have borne a lordly man."

Now these things were revealed by the will of Sabaoth and his Christ to the souls who will come to the molded bodies of the Authorities; and concerning these, the holy voice said, "Multiply and flourish to rule over all the creatures." And these are the ones who are taken captive by the First Father according to lot and thus they were shut up in the prisons of the molded bodies until the consummation of the Aeon. And then at that time, the First Father gave those who were with him a false intention concerning the man. Then each one of them cast his seed on the midst of the navel of the earth. Since that day, the seven Rulers have formed the man: his body is like their body, his likeness is like the man who appeared to them. His molded body came into being according to a portion of each one of them. Their chief created his head and the marrow. Afterward he appeared like the one who was before him. He became a living man, and he who is the father was called "Adam," according to the name of the one who was before him.

Now after Adam was completed, he left him in a vessel since he had taken form like the miscarriages, having no spirit in him. Because of this deed, when the chief ruler remembered the word of Pistis, he was afraid lest perhaps the man come into his molded body and rule over it. Because of this, he left his molded body forty days without soul. And he withdrew and left him.

But on the fortieth day Sophia Zoë

sent her breath into Adam, who was without soul. He began to move upon the earth. And he was not able to rise. Now when the seven Rulers came and saw him, they were very much disturbed. They walked up to him and seized him, and Ialdabaoth said to the breath which was in him, "Who are you? And from whence have you come hither?" He answered and said, "I came through the power of the Light-man because of the destruction of your work." When they heard, they glorified him because he gave them rest from their fear and concern. Then they called that day "the rest," because they rested themselves from their troubles. And when they saw that Adam was not able to rise, they rejoiced. They took him and left him in Paradise, and withdrew up to their heavens.

After the day of rest, Sophia sent Zoë, her daughter, who is called "Eve [of Life]," as an instructor to raise up Adam, in whom there was no soul, so that those whom he would beget might become vessels of the light. When Eve saw her co-likeness cast down, she pitied him, and she said, "Adam, live! Rise up on the earth!" Immediately her word became a deed. For when Adam rose up, immediately he opened his eyes. When he saw her, he said, "You will be called 'the mother of the living' because you are the one who gave me life."

THE RAPE OF EVE BY THE PRIME RULER (GOD) AND BY HIS ANGELS

Then the Authorities were informed that their molded body was alive, and had arisen. They were very much disturbed. They sent seven archangels to see what had happened. They came to Adam. When they saw Eve speaking with him, they said to one another, "What is this female light-being? For truly she is like the likeness which appeared to us in the light. Now come, let us seize her and let us cast our seed on her, so that when she is polluted she will not be able to ascend to her light, but those whom she will beget will serve us. But let us not tell Adam that she is not derived from us, but let us bring a stupor upon him, and let us teach him in his sleep as though she came into being from his rib so that the woman will serve and he will rule over her."

Then Eve, since she existed as a power, laughed at their false intention. She darkened their eyes and left her likeness there stealthily beside Adam. She entered the Tree of Knowledge, and remained there. But they tried to follow her. She revealed to them that she had entered the tree and become tree. And when the blind ones fell into a great fear, they ran away.

Afterward, when they sobered up from the stupor, they came to Adam. And when they saw the likeness of that woman with him, they were troubled, thinking that this was the true Eve. And they acted recklessly, and came to her and seized her and cast their seed upon her. They did it with a lot of tricks, not only defiling her naturally but abominably, defiling the seal of her first voice, which before spoke with them, saying, "What is it that exists before you?" But it is impossible that they might defile those who say that they are begotten in the consummation by the true man by means of the word. And they were deceived, not knowing that they had defiled their own body. It was the likeness which the Authorities and their angels defiled in every form.

She conceived Abel first from the Prime Ruler; and she bore the rest of the sons from the seven Authorities and their angels. Now all this came to pass according to the foresight of the First Father, so that the first mother might beget within herself every mixed seed which is joined together with the fate of the world and its schemata and fate's justice. A dispensation came into being because of

Eve so that the molded body of the Authorities might become a hedge for the light. Then it will condemn them through their molded bodies.

Moreover, the first Adam of the light is spiritual. He appeared on the first day. The second Adam is soul-endowed. He appeared on the sixth day, and is called "Hermaphrodite." The third Adam is earthy, i.e., "man of law," who appeared on the eighth day after "the rest of poverty," which is called "Sunday." Now the progeny of the earthy Adam multiplied and completed the earth. They produced by themselves every knowledge of the soul-endowed Adam. But as for the All, he was in ignorance of it. Afterwards, let me continue, when the Rulers saw him and the woman who was with him, erring in ignorance like the beasts, they rejoiced greatly. When they knew that the deathless man would not only pass by them, but that they would also fear the woman who became a tree, they were troubled and said, "Is perhaps this one, who blinded us and taught us about this defiled woman who is like him, the true man, in order that we might be conquered by her?"

Then the seven took counsel. They came to Adam and Eve timidly. They said to him, "Every tree which is in Paradise, whose fruit may be eaten, was created for you. But beware! Don't eat from the Tree of Knowledge. If you do eat, you will die." After they gave them a great fright, they withdrew up to their Authorities.

Then the one who is wiser than all of them, this one who was called "the beast," came. And when he saw the likeness of their mother, Eve, he said to her, "What is it that God said to you? 'Don't eat from the Tree of Knowledge'?" She said, "He not only said 'Don't eat from it,' but 'Don't touch it lest you die.' " He said to her, "Don't be afraid! You certainly shall not die. For he knows that when you eat from it your mind will be sobered and you will become like God, knowing the distinctions which exist between evil and good men. For he said this to you, lest you eat from it, since he is jealous."

Now Eve believed the words of the instructor. She looked at the tree. And she saw that it was beautiful and magnificent, and she desired it. She took some of its fruit and ate, and she gave to her husband also, and he ate too. Then their mind opened. For when they ate, the light of knowledge shone for them. When they put on shame, they knew that they were naked with regard to knowledge. When they sobered up, they saw that they were naked, and they became enamored of one another. When they saw their makers, they loathed them since they were beastly forms. They understood very much.

Then when the Rulers knew that they had transgressed their commandment, they came in an earthquake with a great threat into Paradise to Adam and Eve in order to see the result of the help. Then Adam and Eve were very much disturbed. They hid under the trees in Paradise. Then, because the Rulers did not know where they were, they said, "Adam, where are you?" He said, "I am here. But because of fear of you I hid after I became ashamed." But they said to him, in ignorance, "Who is the one who spoke to you of the shame which you put on, unless you ate from the tree?" He said, "The woman whom you gave me, she is the one who gave to me, and I ate." Then they said to that woman, "What is this you have done?" She answered and said, "The instructor is the one who incited me, and I ate." Then the rulers came to the instructor. Their eyes were blinded by him so that they were not able to do anything to him. They merely cursed him since they were impotent. Afterward they came to the woman, and they cursed her and her sons. After the woman they cursed Adam and the earth and the fruit because of him. And everything which they created they cursed. There is no blessing from them. It is impossible that good be produced from evil. Since that day the Authorities knew that truly one who is strong is before them. They would not have known except that their command was not kept. They brought a great envy into the world only because of the deathless man.

Now when the Rulers saw that their Adam had acquired a different knowledge they desired to test him. They gathered all the domestic animals and wild beasts of the earth and the birds of the heaven. They brought them to Adam to see what he would call them. When he saw them, he named these creatures. They were troubled because Adam had sobered from every ignorance. They gathered together and took counsel, and they said, "Behold, Adam has become like one of us, so that he understands the distinction of light and darkness. Now lest perhaps he is deceived in the manner of the Tree of Knowledge, and he also comes to the Tree of Life and eats from it and becomes immortal and rules and condemns us and regards us and all our glory as folly—afterward he will pass judgment on us and the world—come, let us cast him out of Paradise down upon the earth, the place from whence he was taken, so that he will no longer be able to know anything more about us." And thus they cast Adam and his wife out of Paradise. And this which they had done did not satisfy them; rather, they were still afraid. They came to the Tree of Life and they set great terrors around it, fiery living beings called "cherubin"; and they left a flaming sword in the midst, turning continually with a great terror, so that no one from among earthly men might ever enter that place.

After these things, when the Rulers had become jealous of Adam, they desired to diminish their lifetimes, but they were unable because of fate, which was established since the beginning. For their lifetimes were determined: for each one of the men one thousand years according to the circuit of the luminaries. But be-

cause the Rulers were not able to do this, each one of those who engaged in evil diminished his lifespan by ten years, and all of this time amounts to nine hundred and thirty years, and these are spent in grief and weakness and in evil distractions. And from that day, the course of life thus proceeded downward until the consummation of the Aeon.

Then when Sophia Zoë saw that the Rulers of Darkness cursed her co-likeness, she was angry. And when she came out of the first heaven with every power, she chased the Rulers from their heavens, and she cast them down to the sinful world so that they might become there like the evil demons upon the earth. She sent the bird which was in Paradise so that, until the consummation of the Aeon, it might spend the thousand years in the rulers' world, a vital living being called phoenix, which kills itself and reanimates itself for a witness to their judgment because they dealt unjustly with Adam and his race.

There are three men and his descendants in the world until the consummation of the Aeon: the spiritual and the vital and the material. This is like the three shapes of phoenixes of Paradise: the first is immortal, the second attains one thousand years; as for the third, it is written in "the Holy Book" that "he is consumed." Likewise three baptisms exist: the first is spiritual, the second is fire, the third is water.

Just as the phoenix appears as a witness for the angels, so too the crocodiles in Egypt have become a witness to those who come down for the baptism of a true man. The two bulls in Egypt, insofar as they possess the sun and the moon as a mystery, exist for a witness to Sabaoth because he exists above them. Sophia (of Astaphaios) received the universe, since the day when she created the sun and the moon and sealed her heaven until the consummation of the Aeon. Now the worm which is brought forth from the phoenix is also a man. It is written of it, "The just will sprout up like the phoenix." And the phoenix appears first alive, and dies, and again rises up, being a sign of the one who appeared in the consummation of the Aeon. These great signs appeared only in Egypt, not in other lands, signifying that it is like the Paradise of God.

Again let us come to the Rulers of whom we spoke, so that we might present their proof. For when the seven Rulers were cast out of their heavens down upon the earth, they created for themselves angels, i.e., many demons, in order to serve them. But these demons taught men many errors with magic and potions and idolatry, and shedding of blood, and altars, and temples, and sacrifices, and libations to all the demons of the earth, having as their co-worker fate, who came into being according to the agreement by the gods of injustice and justice. And thus when the world came to be in distraction, it wandered astray throughout all time. For all the men who are on the earth served the demons from the foundation until the consummation of the Aeon—the angels served justice and the men served injustice. Thus the world came to be in a distraction and an ignorance and a stupor. They all erred until the appearance of the true man.

Enough for you up to here. And next we will come to our world so that we might complete the discussion of its structure and its government precisely. Then he will appear just as the belief was found in the hidden things, which appear from the foundation to the consummation of the Aeon.

Now I will come to the praiseworthy chapters about the immortal man. I will say why the forms are here. After a multitude of men came into being through this one who was molded from matter, and as soon as the world was filled, the rulers ruled over it, that is to say, they possessed it in ignorance. What is the cause? It is this. Since the immortal Father knows that a deficiency came into being in the Aeons and their worlds out of the truth, therefore when he desired to bring to naught the rulers of destruction by means of their molded bodies, he sent your likenesses, i.e., the blessed little guileless spirits, down to the world of destruction. They are not strangers to knowledge. For all knowledge is in an angel who appears before them. He stands in front of the Father and is not powerless to give them knowledge. Immediately, whenever they appear in the world of destruction, they will first reveal the pattern of indestructibility for a condemnation of the Rulers and their powers. Moreover, when the blessed ones appeared in the molded bodies of the authorities, they were jealous of them. And, because of the jealousy, the Authorities mixed their seed with them in order to defile them, and they were not able. Moreover, when the blessed ones appeared in their light, they appeared distinctively. And each one of them from their land revealed their knowledge of the church which appeared in the molded bodies of destruction. They found it to have every seed because of the seed of the Authorities which was mixed with it. Then the Savior created a deliverance from among all of them. And the spirits of these appeared, being elect and blessed but varying in election, and many others are kingless and more exquisite than anyone who was before them. Consequently, four races exist. There are three which belong to the kings of the eighth heaven. But the fourth race is kingless and perfect, one that is above all of them. For these will enter into the holy place of their father and they will rest themselves in a repose, and eternal, ineffable glory, and a ceaseless joy. Now they are already kings—immortal within the mortal realm. They will pass judgment on the gods of Chaos and their powers.

Moreover, the logos who is more exalted than anyone who was sent for this work only, so that he might announce concerning what is unknown. He said, "There is nothing hidden which will not appear, and what was unknown will be known." [Matt. 10:26]. Now these were sent so that they might reveal that which is hidden and expose the seven Authorities of Chaos and their impiety. And thus they were condemned to be killed. Moreover, when all the perfect ones appeared in the molded bodies of the Rulers, and when they revealed the incomparable truth, they put to shame every wisdom of the gods, and their fate was discovered to be condemnable, their power dried up, their dominion was destroyed, and their foresight and their glories became empty.

Before the consummation of the Aeon, the whole place will be shaken by a great thunder. Then the Rulers will lament, crying out on account of their death. The angels will mourn for their men, and the demons will weep for their times, and their men will mourn and cry out on account of their death. Its kings will be drunk from the flaming sword and they will make war against one another, so that the earth will be drunk from the blood which is poured out. And the seas will be troubled by that war. Then the sun will darken and the moon will lose its light. The stars of the heaven will disregard their course and a great thunder will come out of a great power that is above all the powers of Chaos, the place where the firmament of woman is situated. When she has created the first work, she will take off her wise flame of insight. She will put on a senseless wrath. Then she will drive out the gods of Chaos whom she had created together with the First Father. She will cast them

down to the abyss. They will be wiped out by their own injustice. For they will become like the mountains which blaze out fire, and they will gnaw at one another until they are destroyed by their First Father. When he destroys them, he will turn against himself and destroy himself until he ceases to be. And their heavens will fall upon one another and their powers will burn. Their Aeons will also be overthrown. And the First Father's heaven will fall and it will split in two. Likewise, the place of his joy will fall down to the earth, and the earth will not be able to support them. They will fall down to the abyss and the abyss will be overthrown.

The light will cover the darkness. It will wipe it out. It will become like one which had not come into being. And the work which the darkness followed will be dissolved. And the deficiency will be plucked out at its root and thrown down to the darkness. And the light will withdraw up to its root. And the glory of the unbegotten will appear, and it will fill all of the Aeons, when the prophetic utterance and the report of those who are kings are revealed and are fulfilled by those who are called perfect. Those who were not perfected in the unbegotten Father will receive their glories in their Aeons and in the kingdoms of immortals. But they will not ever enter the kingless realm.

For it is necessary that every one enter the place from whence he came. For each one by his deed and his knowledge will reveal his nature.

The Hypostasis of the Archons

*(Gnostic)**

The *Hypostasis of the Archons* ("Reality of the Rulers") is an anonymous tractate presenting an esoteric interpretation of Genesis 1–6, partially in the form of a revelation discourse between an angel and a questioner. While the treatise illustrates a wide-ranging Hellenistic syncretism, the most evident components are Jewish, although in its present form the *Hypostasis of the Archons* shows clearly Christian features and thus can be considered a Christian work. Its theological perspective is a vigorous Gnosticism of undetermined sectarian affiliation. The tractate was originally composed in Greek, probably in Egypt; and although the date of composition is unknown, some evidence points to the third century A.D. Interestingly, the many parallels between this tractate and the tractate *On the Origin of the World* (Codex II, 5) demonstrate some sort of close connection between the two documents.

After a brief introduction quoting "the great apostle" Paul, the *Hypostasis of the Archons* offers its mythological narrative. The main characters in the mythological drama that unfolds include the blind Ruler Samael, also called Sacla ("Fool") and Ialdabaoth, who blasphemes against the divine; the spiritual Woman, who rouses Adam and outwits the rapacious Rulers; the snake, "the instructor," who counsels the man and woman to eat of the fruit forbidden by the Rulers; and Norea, the daughter of Eve, a virgin pure in character and exalted in knowledge. On page 93 of the tractate the focus changes somewhat: on center stage now is the Great Angel Eleleth, who reveals to Norea the origin and destiny of the archontic powers.

The *Hypostasis of the Archons* proclaims, as its title indicates, the reality of the archontic Rulers: far from being merely fictitious, imaginary

---

*Introduction by Roger A. Bullard.

powers, the Archons are all too real. These Rulers indeed exist. This is a grim reality for the Christian Gnostics, who define their own spiritual nature in opposition to that of the ruling and enslaving Authorities. Yet, as this document promises, the Christian Gnostics can have hope, for their spiritual nature will be more lasting than the Archons and their heavenly destiny will be more glorious. In the end the Rulers will perish, and the Gnostics, the Children of the Light, will know the Father and praise him.

THE HYPOSTASIS OF THE ARCHONS*

On account of the reality [hypostasis] of the Authorities, inspired by the Spirit of the Father of Truth, the great apostle—referring to the "Authorities of the Darkness"—told us that "our contest is not against flesh and blood, rather, the Authorities of the universe and the spirits of wickedness" [Eph. 6:12]. I have sent you this because you inquire about the reality of the Authorities.

Their chief is blind; because of his Power and his ignorance and his arrogance he said, with his Power, "It is I who am God; there is none apart from me."

When he said this, he sinned against the Entirety. And this speech got up to Incorruptibility; then there was a voice that came forth from Incorruptibility, saying, "You are mistaken, Samael"—that is, "god of the blind."

His thoughts became blind. And, having expelled his Power—that is, the blasphemy he had spoken—he pursued it down to Chaos and the Abyss, his mother, at the instigation of Pistis Sophia [Faith-Wisdom]. And she established each of his offspring in conformity with its power—after the pattern of the realms that are above, for by starting from the

invisible world the visible world was invented.

As Incorruptibility looked down into the region of the Waters, her Image appeared in the Waters; and the Authorities of the Darkness became enamored of her. But they could not lay hold of that Image which had appeared to them in the Waters, because of their weakness—since beings that merely possess a soul cannot lay hold of those that possess a spirit; for they were from below, while it was from Above.

This is the reason why "Incorruptibility looked down into the region": so that, by the Father's will, she might bring the Entirety into union with the Light. The Rulers [Archons] laid plans and said, "Come, let us create a man that will be soil from the earth." They modeled their creature as one wholly of the earth.

Now the Rulers took some soil from the earth and modeled their Man, after their body and after the Image of God that had appeared to them in the waters. They said, "Come, let us lay hold of it by means of the form that we have modeled, so that it may see its male counterpart and we may seize it with the form that we have modeled"—not understanding the force of God, because of their powerlessness. And he breathed into his face; and the Man came to have a soul and remained upon the ground many days. But they could not make him arise because of their powerlessness. Like storm winds they persisted in blowing, that they might try to capture that image, which had appeared to them in

*Codex II, 4. Translated by Bentley Layton. From James M. Robinson, ed., *The Nag Hammadi Library* (San Francisco: Harper & Row, 1977), pp. 131–151.

the Waters. And they did not know the identity of its power.

Now all these events came to pass by the will of the Father of the Entirety. Afterwards, the Spirit saw the soul-endowed Man upon the ground. And the Spirit came forth from the Adamantine Land; it descended and came to dwell within him, and that Man became a living soul.

It called his name Adam since he was found moving upon the ground. A voice came forth from Incorruptibility for the assistance of Adam; and the Rulers gathered together all the animals of the earth and all the birds of heaven and brought them in to Adam to see what Adam would call them, that he might give a name to each of the birds and all the beasts.

They took Adam and put him in the Garden, that he might cultivate it and keep watch over it. And the Rulers issued a command to him, saying, "From every tree in the Garden shall you eat; yet from the Tree of Knowledge of Good and Evil do not eat, nor touch it; for the day you eat from it, with death you are going to die."

They do not understand what they have said to him; rather, by the Father's will, they said this in such a way that he might in fact eat, and that Adam might not regard them as would a man of an exclusively material nature.

The Rulers took counsel with one another and said, "Come, let us cause a deep sleep to fall upon Adam." And he slept. Now the deep sleep that they "caused to fall upon him, and he slept" is Ignorance. They opened his side like a living Woman. And they built up his side with some flesh in place of her, and Adam came to be endowed only with soul.

And the spirit-endowed Woman came to him and spoke with him, saying, "Arise, Adam." And when he saw her, he said, "It is you who have given me life; you will be called 'Mother of the Living.' For it is she who is my mother. It is she who is the Physician, and the Woman, and She-Who-Has-Given-Birth."

Then the Authorities came up to their Adam. And when they saw his female counterpart speaking with him, they became agitated and they became enamored of her. They said to one another, "Come, let us sow our seed in her," and they pursued her. And she laughed at them for their witlessness and their blindness; and in their clutches, she became a tree, and left before them her shadowy reflection resembling herself; and they defiled it foully. And they defiled the form that she had stamped in her likeness, so that by the form they had modeled, together with their own image, they made themselves liable to condemnation.

Then the Female Spiritual Principle came in the form of the Snake, the Instructor; and it taught them, saying, "What did he say to you? Was it, 'From every tree in the Garden shall you eat; yet, from the tree of evil and good do not eat'?"

The carnal Woman said, "Not only did he say 'Do not eat,' but even 'Do not touch it; for the day you eat from it, with death you are going to die.' "

And the Snake, the Instructor, said, "With death you shall not die; for it was out of jealousy that he said this to you. Rather, your eyes shall open and you shall come to be like gods, recognizing evil and good." And the Female Instructing Principle was taken away from the Snake, and she left it behind, merely a thing of the earth.

And the carnal Woman took from the tree and ate; and she gave to her husband as well as herself; and these beings that possessed only a soul ate. And their imperfection became apparent in their lack of acquaintance; and they recognized that they were naked of the Spiritual Element, and took fig leaves and bound them upon their loins.

Then the chief Ruler came; and he said, "Adam! Where are you?"—for he did not understand what had happened.

And Adam said, "I heard your voice and was afraid because I was naked; and I hid."

The Ruler said, "Why did you hide, unless it is because you have eaten from the tree from which alone I commanded you not to eat? And you have eaten!"

Adam said, "The Woman that you gave me, she gave to me and I ate." And the arrogant Ruler cursed the Woman.

The Woman said, "It was the Snake that led me astray and I ate." They turned to the Snake and cursed its shadowy reflection, powerless, not comprehending that it was a form they themselves had modeled. From that day, the Snake came to be under the curse of the Authorities; until the All-powerful Man was to come, that curse fell upon the Snake.

They turned to their Adam and took him and expelled him from the Garden along with his wife; for they have no blessing, since they too are beneath the curse.

Moreover they threw Mankind into great distraction and into a life of toil, so that their Mankind might be occupied by wordly affairs, and might not have the opportunity of being devoted to the Holy Spirit.

Now afterwards, she bore Cain, their son; and Cain cultivated the land. Thereupon he knew his wife; again becoming pregnant, she bore Abel; and Abel was a herdsman of sheep. Now Cain brought in from the crops of his field, but Abel brought in an offering from among his lambs. God looked upon the votive offerings of Abel; but he did not accept the votive offerings of Cain. And carnal Cain pursued Abel his brother.

And God said to Cain, "Where is Abel your brother?"

He answered, saying, "Am I, then, my brother's keeper?"

God said to Cain, "Listen! The voice of your brother's blood is crying up to me!

You have sinned with your mouth. It will return to you: anyone who kills Cain will let loose seven vengeances, and you will exist groaning and trembling upon the earth."

And Adam knew his female counterpart Eve, and she became pregnant and bore Seth to Adam. And she said, "I have borne another man through God, in place of Abel."

Again Eve became pregnant, and she bore Norea. And she said, "He has begotten on me a virgin as an assistance for many generations of mankind." She is the virgin whom the Forces did not defile.

Then Mankind began to multipy and improve.

The Rulers took counsel with one another and said, "Come, let us cause a deluge with our hands and obliterate all flesh, from man to beast."

But when the Ruler of the Forces came to know of their decision, he said to Noah, "Make yourself an ark from some wood that does not rot and hide in it— you and your children and the beasts and the birds of heaven from small to large—and set it upon Mount Sir."

Then Norea came to him, wanting to board the ark. And when he would not let her, she blew upon the ark and caused it to be consumed by fire. Again he made the ark, for a second time.

The Rulers went to meet her, intending to lead her astray. Their supreme chief said to her, "Your mother, Eve, came to us."

But Norea turned to them and said: "It is you who are the Rulers of the Darkness; you are accursed. And you did not know my mother; instead it was your female counterpart that you knew. For I am not your descendant; rather it is from the World Above that I am come."

The arrogant Ruler turned with all his might. He said to her presumptuously, "You must render service to us, as did also your mother Eve."

But Norea turned and, in a loud voice, cried out up to the Holy One, the God of the Entirety, "Rescue me from the Rulers of Unrighteousness and save me from their clutches—forthwith!"

The Great Angel came down from the heavens and said to her, "Why are you crying up to God? Why do you act so boldly towards the Holy Spirit?"

Norea said, "Who are you?"

The Rulers of Unrighteousness had withdrawn from her. He said, "It is I who am Eleleth, Sagacity, the Great Angel, who stands in the presence of the Holy Spirit. I have been sent to speak with you and save you from the grasp of the Lawless. And I shall teach you about your Root."

Now, as for that angel, I cannot speak of his power. His appearance is like fine gold and his raiment is like snow. No, truly, my mouth cannot bear to speak of his power and the appearance of his face!

Eleleth, the Great Angel, spoke to me. "It is I," he said, "who am Understanding. I am one of the Four Light-givers, who stand in the presence of the Great Invisible Spirit. Do you think these Rulers have any power over you? None of them can prevail against the Root of Truth; for on its account he appeared in the final ages; and these Authorities will be restrained. And these Authorities cannot defile you and that generation; for your abode is in Incorruptibility, where the Virgin Spirit dwells, who is superior to the Authorities of Chaos and to their universe."

But I said, "Sir, teach me about these Authorities—how did they come into being, and by what kind of genesis, and what material, and who created them and their force?"

And the Great Angel Eleleth, Understanding, spoke to me: "Within limitless realms dwells Incorruptibility, Sophia, who is called Pistis, wanted to create something, alone, without her consort and her product was a celestial thing.

"A veil exists between the World Above and the realms that are below; and Shadow came into being beneath the veil; and that Shadow became Matter; and that Shadow was projected apart. And what she had created became a product in the Matter, like an aborted fetus. And it assumed a plastic form molded out of shadow, and became an arrogant beast resembling a lion." It was androgynous, as I have already said, because it was from Matter that it derived.

Opening his eyes he saw a vast quantity of Matter without limit; and he became arrogant, saying, "It is I who am God, and there is none other apart from me."

When he said this, he sinned against the Entirety. And a voice came forth from above the realm of absolute power saying, "You are mistaken, Samael."

And he said, "If any other thing exists before me, let it become visible to me!" And immediately Sophia stretched forth her finger and introduced Light into Matter; and she pursued it down to the region of Chaos. And she returned up to her light; once again Darkness returned to Matter.

This Ruler, by being androgynous, made himself a vast realm, an extent without limit. And he contemplated creating offspring for himself, and created for himself seven offspring, androgynous just like their parent.

And he said to his offspring, "It is I who am the god of the entirety."

And Zoë [Life], the daughter of Pistis Sophia, cried out and said to him, "You are mistaken, Sacla!"—for which the alternate name is Ialdabaoth. She breathed into his face, and her breath became a fiery angel for her; and that angel bound Ialdabaoth and cast him down into Tartaros below the abyss.

Now when his offspring Sabaoth saw the force of that angel, he repented and condemned his father and his mother Matter.

He loathed her, but he sang songs of praise up to Sophia and her daughter, Zoë. And Sophia and Zoë caught him up and gave him charge of the seventh heaven, below the veil between Above and Below. And he is called 'God of the

Forces, Sabaoth,' since he is up above the Forces of Chaos, for Sophia established him.

Now when these events had come to pass, he made himself a huge four-faced chariot of cherubim and harps and lyres and an infinity of angels to act as ministers.

And Sophia took her daughter, Zoë, and had her sit upon his right to teach him about the things that exist in the Eighth heaven; and the Angel of Wrath she placed upon his left. Since that day, his right had been called life; and the left has come to represent the unrighteousness of the realm of absolute power above. It was before your time that they came into being.

Now when Ialdabaoth saw him in this great splendor and at this height, he envied him; and the envy became an androgynous product; and this was the origin of Envy. And Envy engendered Death; and Death engendered his offspring and gave each of them charge of its heaven; and all the heavens of Chaos became full of their multitudes.

But it was by the will of the Father of the Entirety that they all came into being —after the pattern of all the Things Above—so that the sum of Chaos might be attained.

There, I have taught you about the pattern of the Rulers and the Matter in which it was expressed and their parent and their universe.

But I said, "Sir, am I also from their Matter?"

You, together with your offspring, are from the Primeval Father; from Above, out of the imperishable Light, their souls are come. Thus the Authorities cannot approach them because of the Spirit of Truth present within them; and all who have become acquainted with this Way exist deathless in the midst of dying Mankind. Still, that Sown Element will not become known now.

Instead, after three generations it will come to be known and free them from the bondage of the Authorities' error.

Then I said, "Sir, how much longer?"

He said to me, "Until the moment when the True Man, within a modeled form, reveals the existence of the Spirit of Truth, which the Father has sent.

"Then he will teach them about everything: And he will anoint them with the unction of Life eternal, given him from the undominated generation.

Then they will be freed of blind thought. And they will trample underfoot Death, which is of the Authorities. And they will ascend into the limitless Light where this Sown Element belongs.

Then the Authorities will relinquish their ages. And their angels will weep over their destruction. And their demons will lament their death.

Then all the Children of the Light will be truly acquainted with the Truth and their Root, and the Father of the Entirety and the Holy Spirit. They will all say with a single voice, 'The Father's truth is just, and the Son presides over the Entirety.' And from everyone, unto the ages of ages, 'Holy—Holy—Holy! Amen!' "

The Apocalypse of Adam

(Gnostic)*

The *Apocalypse of Adam* may be termed a Sethian tractate in the sense that Seth and his descendants figure prominently as the recipients and bearers of the Gnostic tradition. Whether there is any connection with the Sethians as depicted by the heresiologists, however, remains uncertain. It is obvious that the *Apocalypse of Adam* depends heavily on Jewish apocalyptic traditions; in fact, the document may represent a transitional stage in the development from Jewish to Gnostic apocalyptic. If this be the case, its date may be very early, perhaps as early as the first or second century A.D. Most interestingly, the *Apocalypse of Adam* does not disclose any explicitly Christian themes. Hence some have concluded that this tractate demonstrates the existence of a sort of Gnosticism which, though non-Christian, yet contains a well-developed myth proclaiming a heavenly redeemer.

In content this work consists of a revelation received by Adam and taught to his son Seth. Father Adam explains how in the Fall he and Eve lost their glory and knowledge, and came under the enslaving power of the lowly Creator and of death itself. Through the revelation imparted to Adam by three heavenly visitors, however, this knowledge is passed on to Seth and his seed; and in spite of the attacks of the Creator, who tries to destroy mankind with a flood and with fire, the knowledge is preserved. Finally, when the mighty "illuminator" comes, "the man upon whom the Holy Spirit has come," he will be persecuted by the worldly powers. But in the end he will triumph, and those who have truly known the living God will live forever.

---

*Introduction by George W. MacRae.

THE REVELATIONS OF ADAM'S ORIGIN AS TOLD TO HIS SON SETH*

The revelation which Adam taught his son Seth in the seven hundredth year, saying, "Listen to my words, my son Seth. When God had created me out of the earth along with Eve, your mother, I went about with her in a glory which she had seen in the Aeon from which we had come forth. She taught me a word of knowledge of the eternal God. And we resembled the great eternal angels, for we were higher than the God who had created us and the powers with him, whom we did not know.

"Then God, the ruler of the Aeons and the powers, divided us in wrath. Then we became two Aeons. And the glory in our hearts left us, me and your mother Eve, along with the first knowledge that breathed within us. And glory fled from us; not from this Aeon from which we had come forth, I and Eve your mother. But knowledge entered into the seed of great Aeons. For this reason I myself have called you by the name of that man who is the seed of the great generation or from whom it comes. After those days the eternal knowledge of the God of truth withdrew from me and your mother Eve. Since that time we learned about dead things, like men. Then we recognized the God who had created us. For we were not strangers to his powers. And we served him in fear and slavery. And after these events we became darkened in our hearts. Now I slept in the thought of my heart.

"And I saw three men before me whose likeness I was unable to recognize, since they were not from the powers of the God who had created us. They surpassed glory, and men, saying to me,

'Arise, Adam, from the sleep of death, and hear about the Aeon and the seed of that man to whom life has come, who came from you and from Eve, your wife.'

"When I had heard these words from the great men who were standing before me, then we sighed, I and Eve, in our hearts. And the Lord, the God who had created us, stood before us. He said to us, 'Adam, why were you both sighing in your heart? Do you not know that I am the God who created you? And I breathed into you a spirit of life as a living soul.' Then darkness came upon our eyes.

"Then the God, who created us, created a son from himself and Eve, your mother. I knew a sweet desire for your mother. Then the vigor of our eternal knowledge was destroyed in us, and weakness pursued us. Therefore the days of our life became few. For I knew that I had come under the authority of death.

"Now then, my son Seth, I will reveal to you the things which those men whom I saw before me at first revealed to me after I have completed the times of this generation and the years of the generation have been accomplished.

"For rain-showers of God the almighty will be poured forth so that he might destroy all flesh of God the almighty, so that he might destroy all flesh from the earth by means of that which is around them, along with those from the seed of the men to whom passed the life of the knowledge, that came from me and Eve, your mother. For they were strangers to him. Afterwards great angels will come on high clouds, who will bring those men into the place where the spirit of life dwells in glory there. Then the whole multitude of flesh will be left behind in the waters.

"Then God will rest from his wrath. And he will cast his power upon the waters, and give power to his sons and their wives by means of the ark along with the animals, whichever he pleased, and the birds of heaven, which he called

---

*Codex V 64, 1–85, 32. Translated by George W. MacRae; edited by Douglas M. Parrott. From James M. Robinson, ed., *The Nag Hammadi Library* (San Francisco: Harper & Row, 1977), pp. 152–160.

and released upon the earth. And God will say to Noah—whom the generations will call Deucalion—'Behold, I have protected you in the ark along with your wife and your sons and their wives and their animals and the birds of heaven, which you called and released upon the earth. Therefore I will give the earth to you—you and your sons. In kingly fashion you will rule over it—you and your sons. And no seed will come from you of the men who will not stand in my presence in another glory.'

"Then they will become as the cloud of the great Light. Those men will come who have been cast forth from the knowledge of the great Aeons and the angels. They will stand before Noah and the Aeons. And God will say to Noah, 'Why have you departed from what I told you? You have created another generation so that you might scorn my power.' Then Noah will say, 'I shall testify before your might that the generation of these men did not come from me nor from my sons.'

"And he will bring those men into their proper land and build them a holy dwelling place. And they will be called by that name and dwell there six hundred years in a knowledge of imperishability. And angels of the great Light will dwell with them. No foul deed will dwell in their hearts, but only the knowledge of God.

"Then Noah will divide the whole earth among his sons, Ham and Japheth and Shem. He will say to them, 'My sons, listen to my words. Behold, I have divided the earth among you. But serve him in fear and slavery all the days of your life. Let not your seed depart from the face of God the almighty.

My seed will be pleasing before you and before your power. Seal it by your strong hand with fear and commandment, so that the whole seed which came forth from me may not be inclined away from you and God the almighty, but it will serve in humility and fear of its knowledge.'

"Then others from the seed of Ham and Japheth will come, four hundred thousand men, and enter into another land and sojourn with those men who came forth from the great eternal knowledge. For the shadow of their power will protect those who have sojourned with them from every evil thing and every unclean desire. Then the seed of Ham and Japheth will form twelve kingdoms, and their seed also will enter into the kingdom of another people, and will take counsel from the great aeons of imperishability. And they will go to Sacla, their God. They will go in to the powers, accusing the great men who are in their glory.

"They will say to Sacla, 'What is the power of these men who stood in your presence, who were taken from the seed of Ham and Japheth, who will number four hundred thousand men? They have been received into another aeon from which they had come forth, and they have overturned all the glory of your power and the dominion of your hand. For the seed of Noah through his son has done all your will, and so have all the powers in the Aeons over which your might rules, while both those men and the ones who are sojourners in their glory have not done your will. But they have turned aside your whole throng.'

"Then the God the Aeons will give them some of those who serve him. They will come upon that land where the great men will be who have not been defiled, nor will be defiled by any desire. For their soul did not come from a defiled hand, but it came from a great commandment of an eternal angel. Then fire and sulphur and asphalt will be cast upon those men, and fire and blinding mist will come over those Aeons, and the eyes of the powers of the illuminators will be darkened, and the Aeons will not see by them in those days. And great clouds of light will descend, and other clouds of light will come down upon them from the great Aeons.

"Abrasax and Sablo and Gamaliel will

descend and bring those men out of the fire and the wrath, and take them above the Aeons and the Rulers of the powers, and take them away there, with the holy angels and the Aeons. The men will be like those angels, for they are not strangers to them. But they work in the imperishable seed.

"Once again, for the third time, the illuminator of knowledge will pass by in great glory, in order to leave something of the seed of Noah and the sons of Ham and Japheth—to leave for himself fruit-bearing trees. And he will redeem their souls from the day of death. For the whole creation that came from the dead earth will be under the authority of death. But those who reflect upon the knowledge of the eternal God in their hearts will not perish. For they have not received spirit from this kingdom alone, but they have received it from one of the eternal angels. The illuminator will come. And he will perform signs and wonders in order to scorn the powers and their ruler.

"Then the God of the powers will be disturbed, saying, 'What is the power of this man who is higher than we?' Then he will arouse a great wrath against that man. And the glory will withdraw and dwell in holy houses which it has chosen for itself. And the powers will not see it with their eyes, nor will they see the illuminator either. Then they will punish the flesh of the man upon whom the holy spirit has come.

"Then the angels and all the generations of the powers will use the name in error, asking, 'Where did the error come from?' or 'Where did the words of deception, which all the powers have failed to discover, come from?'

"Now the first kingdom says of him. . . .
He was nourished in the heavens.
He received the glory of that one and the power. He came to the bosom of his mother.
And thus he came to the water.

"And the second kingdom says about him that he came from a great prophet. And a bird came, took the child who was born and brought him onto a high mountain.

And he was nourished by the bird of Heaven. An angel came forth there. He said to him, 'Arise! God has given glory to you.'

He received glory and strength.
And thus he came to the water.

"The third kingdom says of him that he came from a virgin womb. He was cast out of his city, he and his mother; he was brought to a desert place.
He was nourished there.
He came and received glory and power.
And thus he came to the water.

"The fourth kingdom says of him that he came from a virgin. . . . Solomon sought her, he and Phersalo and Sauel and his armies, which had been sent out. Solomon himself sent his army of demons to seek out the virgin. And they did not find the one whom they sought, but the virgin who was given to them. It was she whom they fetched. Solomon took her. The virgin became pregnant and gave birth to the child there.
She nourished him on a border of the desert. When he had been nourished,
he received glory and power from the seed from which he had been begotten.
And thus he came to the water.

"And the fifth kingdom says of him that he came from a drop from Heaven. He was thrown into the sea. The abyss received him, gave birth to him, and brought him to Heaven.
He received glory and power.
And thus he came to the water.

"And the sixth kingdom says that a [. . .] down to the Aeon which is below, in order to gather flowers. She became pregnant from the desire of the flowers. She gave birth to him in that place.

The angels of the flower garden nourished him.

He received glory there and power.

And thus he came to the water.

"And the seventh kingdom says of him that he is a drop. It came from Heaven to earth. Dragons brought him down to caves. He became a child. A spirit came upon him and brought him on high to the place where the drop had come forth.

He received glory and power there.

And thus he came to the water.

"And the eighth kingdom says of him that a cloud came upon the earth and enveloped a rock. He came from it.

The angels who were above the cloud nourished him.

He received glory and power there.

And thus he came to the water.

"And the ninth kingdom says of him that from the nine Muses one separated away. She came to a high mountain and spent some time seated there, so that she desired herself alone in order to become androgynous. She fulfilled her desire and became pregnant from her desire. He was born.

The angels who were over the desire nourished him.

And he received glory there and power.

And thus he came to the water.

"The tenth kingdom says of him that his god loved a cloud of desire. He begot him in his hand and cast upon the cloud above him some of the drop, and he was born.

He received glory and power there.

And thus he came to the water.

"And the eleventh kingdom says of him that the father desired his own daughter. She herself became pregnant from her father. She cast [. . .] tomb out in the desert.

The angel nourished him there.

And thus he came to the water.

"The twelfth kingdom says of him that he came from two illuminators. He was nourished there.

He received glory and power.

And thus he came to the water.

"And the thirteenth kingdom says of him that every birth of their ruler is a word. And this word received a mandate there.

He received glory and power.

And thus he came to the water, in order that the desire of those powers might be satisfied.

"But the generation without a king over it says that God chose him from all the Aeons. He caused a knowledge of the undefiled one of truth to come to be in him. He said, 'Out of a foreign air, from a great Aeon, the great illuminator came forth. And he made the generation of those men whom he had chosen for himself shine, so that they should shine upon the whole Aeon.'

"Then the seed, those who will receive his name upon the water and that of them all, will fight against the power. And a cloud of darkness will come upon them.

"Then the peoples will cry out with a great voice, saying, 'Blessed is the soul of those men because they have known God with a knowledge of the truth! They shall live forever, because they have not been corrupted by their desire, along with the angels, nor have they accomplished the works of the powers, but they have stood in his presence in a knowledge of God like light that has come forth from fire and blood.

" 'But we have done every deed of the powers senselessly. We have boasted in the transgression of all our works. We have cried against the God of truth because all his work is eternal. These are against our spirits. For now we have known that our souls will die the death.'

"Then a voice came to them, saying 'Micheu and Michar and Mnesinous, who are over the holy baptism and the living water, why were you crying out against the living God with lawless voices and tongues without law over them, and souls full of blood and foul deeds? You are full of works that are not of the truth, but your ways are full of joy and rejoicing. Having defiled the water of life, you have drawn it within the will of the powers to whom you have been given to serve them.

" 'And your thought is not like that of those men whom you persecute. Their fruit does not wither. But they will be known up to the great Aeons, because the words they had kept, of the God of the Aeons, were not committed to the book, nor were they written. But angelic beings will bring them, whom all the generations of men will not know. For they will be on a high mountain, upon a rock of truth. Therefore they will be named "The Words of Imperishability and Truth," for those who know the eternal God in wisdom of knowledge and teaching of angels forever, for he knows all things.' "

These are the revelations which Adam made known to Seth his son. And his son taught his seed about them. This is the hidden knowledge of Adam, which he gave to Seth, which is the holy baptism of those who know the eternal knowledge through those born of the word and the imperishable illuminators, who came from the holy seed: Yesseus, Mazareus, Yessedekeus, the Living Water.

The Gospel of Philip

(Gnostic)*

The Gospel of Philip is a collection of theological statements or excerpts concerning sacraments and ethics. Generally Valentinian in character, this collection was named for Philip the apostle, and was probably written in Syria in the second half of the third century A.D. The various sorts of statements comprising the collection are not organized in a way that can be conveniently outlined by the use of headings and subheadings. Though the line of thought is often rambling and disjointed, some continuity of thought is maintained by means of an association of ideas or through catchwords. This collection of excerpts seems to derive largely from a Christian Gnostic sacramental catechesis. In fact, the voice of the original author may still be heard as he speaks to catechumens preparing for the initiation rite.

While emphasizing the place of the sacraments, the *Gospel of Philip* concerns itself in particular with the bridal chamber: "The Lord did everything in a mystery, a baptism and a chrism and a eucharist and a redemption and a bridal chamber." According to this tractate, the existential malady of humanity results from the differentiation of the sexes. When Eve separated from Adam, the original androgynous unity was broken. The purpose of Christ's coming is to reunite "Adam" and "Eve." Just as a husband and wife unite in the bridal chamber, so also the reunion effected by Christ takes place in a bridal chamber, the sacramental, spiritual one, where a person receives a foretaste and assurance of ultimate union with an angelic, heavenly counterpart. "Christ came to repair the separation which was from the beginning and again unite the two," so that restoration may be accomplished and rest achieved.

The *Gospel of Philip* makes an important contribution to our rather limited knowledge of Gnostic sacramental theology and practice. The sacraments exhibited in the *Gospel of Philip* are similar to those used by

---

*Introduction by Wesley M. Isenberg.

Christians in the Great Church for the initiation of candidates. Thus the Gnostics who wrote and used the present text had not departed radically from orthodox sacramental practice; yet the interpretation provided for the sacraments clearly remains Gnostic.

THE GOSPEL OF PHILIP*

A Hebrew makes another Hebrew, and such a person is called "proselyte." But a proselyte does not make another proselyte. Some both exist just as they are and make others like themselves, while others simply exist.

The slave seeks only to be free, but he does not hope to acquire the estate of his master. But the son is not only a son but lays claim to the inheritance of the father. Those who are heirs to the dead are themselves dead, and they inherit the dead. Those who are heirs to what is living are alive, and they are heirs to both what is living and the dead. The dead are heirs to nothing. For how can he who is dead inherit? If he who is dead inherits what is living he will not die, but he who is dead will live even more.

A Gentile does not die, for he has never lived in order that he may die. He who has believed in the truth has found life, and this one is in danger of dying, for he is alive. Ever since Christ came the world is created, the cities adorned, the dead carried out. When we were Hebrews we were orphans and had only our mother, but when we became Christians we had both father and mother.

Those who sow in winter reap in summer. The winter is the world, the summer the other Aeon. Let us sow in the world that we may reap in the summer. Because of this it is fitting for us not to pray in the winter. Summer follows winter. But if any man reap in winter he will not actually reap but only pluck out,

since this sort of thing will not provide him a harvest. It is not only now that the fruit will not come forth, but also on the Sabbath his field will be barren.

Christ came to ransom some, to save others, to redeem others. He ransomed those who were strangers and made them his own. And he set his own apart, those whom he gave as a pledge in his will. It was not only when he appeared that he voluntarily laid down his life, but he voluntarily laid down his life from the very day the world came into being. Then he came forth in order to take it, since it had been given as a pledge. It fell into the hands of robbers and was taken captive, but he saved it. He redeemed the good people in the world as well as the evil.

Light and darkness, life and death, right and left, are brothers of one another. They are inseparable. Because of this neither are the good good, nor the evil evil, nor is life life, nor death death. For this reason each one will dissolve into its original nature. But those who are exalted above the world are indissoluble, eternal.

Names given to worldly things are very deceptive for they divert our thoughts from what is correct to what is incorrect. Thus one who hears the word "God" does not perceive what is correct, but perceives what is incorrect. So also with "the Father" and "the Son" and "the Holy Spirit" and "life" and "light" and "resurrection"and "the Church" and all the rest—people do not perceive what is correct, but they perceive what is incorrect, unless they have come to know what is correct. The names which are heard are in the world to deceive. If they were in the Aeon, they would at no time be used as names in the world. Nor

---

*Codex II 51, 29–86, 19. Translated by Wesley W. Isenberg. From James M. Robinson, ed., *The Nag Hammadi Library* (San Francisco: Harper & Row, 1977), pp. 131–151.

were they set among worldly things. They have an end in the Aeon.

One single name is not uttered in the world, the name which the Father gave to the Son, the name above all things: the name of the Father. For the Son would not become Father unless he wears the name of the Father. Those who have this name know it, but they do not speak it. But those who do not have it do not know it.

But truth brought names into existence in the world because it is not possible to teach it without names. Truth is one single thing and it is also many things for our sakes who learn this one thing in love through many things. The powers wanted to deceive man, since they saw that he had a kinship with those that are truly good. They took the name of those that are good and gave it to those that are not good, so that through the names they might deceive him and bind them to those that are not good. And afterward, if they do them a favor, they will be made to remove them from those that are not good and place them among those that are good. These things they knew, for they wanted to take the free man and make him a slave to them forever.

There are powers which contend against man, not wishing him to be saved. For if man is saved, there will not be any sacrifices and animals will not be offered to the powers. They were indeed offering them up alive, but when they offered them up they died. As for man, they offered him up to God dead, and he lived.

Before Christ came there was no bread in the world, just as Paradise, the place where Adam was, had many trees to nourish the animals but no wheat to sustain man. Man used to feed like the animals, but when Christ came, the perfect man, he brought bread from heaven in order that man might be nourished with the food of man. The powers thought that it was by their own power and will that they were doing what they did, but

the Holy Spirit in secret was accomplishing everything through them as it wished. Truth, which existed since the beginning, is sown everywhere. And many see it as it is sown, but few are they who see it as it is reaped.

Some said, "Mary conceived by the Holy Spirit." They are in error. They do not know what they are saying. When did a woman ever conceive by a woman? Mary is the virgin whom no power defiled. She is a great anathema to the Hebrews, who are the apostles and the apostolic men. This virgin whom no power defiled; the powers defile themselves. And the Lord would not have said "My Father who is in Heaven" [Matt. 16:17] unless he had had another father, but he would have said simply "My father."

The Lord said to the disciples, "Bring out from every other house. Bring into the house of the Father. But do not take anything in the house of the Father nor carry it off."

"Jesus" is a hidden name; "Christ" is a revealed name for this reason: "Jesus" does not exist in any other language, but his name is always "Jesus," as he is called. "Christ" is also his name: in Syriac it is "Messiah," in Greek it is "Christ." Certainly all the others have it according to their own language. "The Nazarene" is he who reveals what is hidden. Christ has everything in himself— man, angel, mystery, and the Father.

Those who say that the Lord died first and then rose up are in error, for he rose up first and then died. If one does not first attain the resurrection will he not die? As God lives, he would already be dead.

No one will hide a large valuable object in something large, but many a time one has tossed countless thousands into a thing worth a penny. Compare the soul. It is a precious thing and it came to be in a contemptible body.

Some are afraid lest they rise naked. Because of this they wish to rise in the flesh, and they do not know that it is those who wear the flesh who are naked. It is those who [. . .] to unclothe themselves who are not naked. "Flesh and blood shall not be able to inherit the kingdom of God" [1 Cor. 15:50]. What is this which will not inherit? This which is on us. But what is this very thing which will inherit? It is that which belongs to Jesus and his blood. Because of this he said, "He who shall not eat my flesh and drink my blood has not life in him" [John 6:53]. What is it? His flesh is the word, and his blood is the Holy Spirit. He who has received these has food and he has drink and clothing. I find fault with the others who say that it will not rise. Then both of them are at fault. You say that the flesh will not rise. But tell me what will rise, that we may honor you. You say the spirit in the flesh, and it is also this light in the flesh. But this too is a matter which is in the flesh, for whatever you shall say, you say nothing outside the flesh. It is necessary to rise in this flesh, since everything exists in it. In this world those who put on garments are better than the garments. In the Kingdom of Heaven the garments are better than those who have put them on.

It is through water and fire that the whole place is purified—the visible by the visible, the hidden by the hidden. There are some things hidden through those visible. There is water in water, there is fire in a chrism.

Jesus took them all by stealth, for he did not reveal himself in the manner in which he was, but it was in the manner in which they would be able to see him that he revealed himself. He revealed himself to them all. He revealed himself to the great as great. He revealed himself to the small as small. He revealed himself to the angels as an angel, and to men as a man. Because of this his word hid itself from everyone. Some indeed saw him, thinking that they were seeing themselves, but when he appeared to his disciples in glory on the mount he was not small. He became great, but he made the disciples great, that they might be able to see him in his greatness.

He said on that day in the Thanksgiving, "You who have joined the perfect, the light, with the Holy Spirit, unite the angels with us also, the images." Do not despise the lamb, for without it, it is not possible to see the king. No one will be able to go in to the king if he is naked.

The heavenly man has many more sons than the earthly man. If the sons of Adam are many, although they die, how much more the sons of the perfect man, they who do not die but are always begotten. The father makes a son, and the son has not the power to make a son. For he who has been begotten has not the power to beget, but the son gets brothers for himself, not sons. All who are begotten in the world are begotten in a natural way, and the others in a spiritual way. Those who are begotten by him cry out from that place to the perfect man, because they are nourished on the promise concerning the heavenly place. If the word has gone out from that place it would be nourished from the mouth and it would become perfect. For it is by a kiss that the perfect conceive and give birth. For this reason we also kiss one another. We receive conception from the grace which is in each other.

There were three who always walked with the Lord: Mary, his mother, and his sister and Magdalene, the one who was called his companion. His sister and his mother and his companion were each a Mary.

"The Father" and "the Son" are single names, "the Holy Spirit" is a double name. For they are everywhere: they are above, they are below; they are in the concealed, they are in the revealed. The Holy Spirit is in the revealed: it is below. It is in the concealed: it is above.

The saints are served by evil powers, for they are blinded by the Holy Spirit into thinking that they are serving an ordinary man whenever they do something for the saints. Because of this a disciple asked the Lord one day for something of this world. He said to him, "Ask your mother and she will give you of the things which are another's."

The apostles said to the disciples, "May our whole offering obtain salt." They called Sophia "salt." Without it no offering is acceptable. But Sophia is without child. For this reason she is called "a trace of salt." But where they will be in their own way, the Holy Spirit will also be, and her children are many.

What the father possesses belongs to the son, and the son himself, so long as he is small, is not entrusted with what is his. But when he becomes a man his father gives him all that he possesses.

Those who have gone astray, whom the Spirit itself begets, usually go astray also because of the Spirit. Thus, by this one and the same breath, the fire blazes and is put out.

Echamoth is one thing and Echmoth another. Echamoth is Wisdom simply, but Echmoth is the Wisdom of death which is the one who knows death [called "the little Wisdom"].

There are domestic animals like the bull and the ass and others of this kind. Others are wild and live apart in the deserts. Man ploughs the field by means of the domestic animals, and from this he feeds both himself and the animals, whether tame or wild. Compare the perfect man. It is through powers which are submissive that he ploughs, preparing for everything to come into being. For it is because of this that the whole place stands, whether the good or the evil, the right and the left. The Holy Spirit shepherds everyone and rules all the powers, the "tame" ones and the "wild" ones, as well as those which are unique. For indeed he gathers them and shuts them in, in order that these, even if they wish, will not be able to escape.

He who has been created is beautiful, and you would find his sons noble creations. If he was not created but begotten, you would find that his seed was noble.

But now he was created and he begot. What nobility is this? First, adultery came into being, afterward murder. And he was begotten in adultery, for he was the child of the serpent. So he became a murderer, just like his father, and he killed his brother. Indeed, every act of sexual intercourse which has occurred between those unlike one another is adultery.

God is a dyer. As the good dyes, which are called "true," dissolve with the things dyed in them, so it is with those whom God has dyed. Since his dyes are immortal, they are immortal by means of his colors. Now God dips what he dips in water.

It is not possible for anyone to see anything of the things that actually exist unless he becomes like them. This is not the way with man in the world: he sees the sun without being a sun; and he sees the heaven and the earth and all other things, but he is not these things. This is quite in keeping with the truth. But you saw something of that place and you became those things. You saw the Spirit and you became spirit. You saw Christ and you became Christ. You saw the Father and you shall become Father. So in this place you see everything and do not see yourself; but in that place you do see yourself—and what you see you shall become.

Faith receives, love gives. No one will be able to receive without faith. No one will be able to give without love. Because of this, in order that we may indeed receive, we believe; but it is so that we may love and give, since if one does not give in love, he has no profit from what he has given. He who has not received the Lord is still a Hebrew.

The apostles who were before us had these names for him: "Jesus, the Nazorean, Messiah," that is, "Jesus, the Nazorean, the Christ." The last name is "Christ," the first is "Jesus," that in the middle is "the Nazarene." "Messiah" has two meanings, both "the Christ" and "the measured." "Jesus" in Hebrew is "the redemption." "Nazara" is "the truth." "The Nazarene," then, is "the truth." "Christ" has been measured. "The Nazarene" and "Jesus" are they who have been measured.

When the pearl is cast down into the mud it does not become greatly despised, nor if it is anointed with balsam oil will it become more precious. But it always has value in the eyes of its owner. Compare the sons of God, wherever they may be. They still have value in the eyes of their Father.

If you say, "I am a Jew," no one will be moved. If you say, "I am a Roman," no one will be disturbed. If you say, "I am a Greek, a barbarian, a slave, a free man," no one will be troubled. If you say, "I am a Christian," the world will tremble. Would that I may receive a name like that! This is the person whom the powers will not be able to endure when they hear his name.

God is a man-eater. For this reason men are sacrificed to him. Before men were sacrificed animals were being sacrificed, since those to whom they were sacrificed were not gods.

Glass decanters and earthenware jugs are both made by means of fire. But if glass decanters break they are done over, for they came into being through a breath. If earthenware jugs break, however, they are destroyed, for they came into being without breath.

An ass which turns a millstone did a hundred miles walking. When it was loosed, it found that it was still at the same place. There are men who make many journeys, but make no progress towards a destination. When evening came upon them, they saw neither city nor village, neither creation nor nature, power nor angel. In vain have the wretches labored.

The eucharist is Jesus. For he is called in Syriac "Pharisatha," which is "the one who is spread out," for Jesus came crucifying the world.

The Lord went into the dye works of Levi. He took seventy-two different colors and threw them into the vat. He took them out all white. And he said, "Even so has the Son of Man come as a dyer."

As for the Wisdom who is called "the barren," she is the mother of the angels. And the companion of the Savior is Mary Magdalene. But Christ loved her more than all the disciples and used to kiss her often on her mouth. The rest of the disciples were offended by it and expressed disapproval. They said to him, "Why do you love her more than all of us?" The Savior answered and said to them, "Why do I not love you like her?" When a blind man and one who sees are both together in darkness, they are no different from one another. When the light comes, then he who sees will see the light, and he who is blind will remain in darkness.

The Lord said, "Blessed is he who is before he came into being. For he who is, has been and shall be."

The superiority of man is not obvious to the eye but lies in what is hidden from view. Consequently, he has mastery over the animals which are stronger than he is and great in terms of the obvious and the hidden. This enables them to survive. But if man is separated from them, they slay one another and bite one another. They ate one another because they did not find any food. But now they have found food because man tilled the soil.

If one goes down into the water and comes up without having received anything and says, "I am a Christian," he has borrowed the name at interest. But if he receives the Holy Spirit, he has the name as a gift. He who has received a gift does not have to give it back, but of him who has borrowed it at interest, payment is demanded. This is the way it happens to one when one experiences a mystery.

Great is the mystery of marriage! For without it the world would not have existed. Now the existence of the world depends on man, and the existence of man on marriage. Think of the undefiled relationship, for it possesses a great power. Its image consists of a defilement of the form.

As for the unclean spirits, there are males among them and there are females. The males are they which unite with the souls which inhabit a female form, but the females are they which are mingled with those in a male form, through one who was disobedient. And none shall be able to escape them, since they detain him if he does not receive a male power or a female power—the bridegroom and the bride. One receives them from the mirrored bridal chamber. When the wanton women see a male sitting alone, they leap down on him and play with him and defile him. So also the lecherous men, when they see a beautiful woman sitting alone, they persuade her and compel her, wishing to defile her. But if they see the man and his wife sitting beside one another, the female cannot come into the man, nor can the male come into the woman. So if the image and the angel are united with one another, neither can any venture to go in to the man or the woman.

He who comes out of the world can no longer be detained, because he was in the world. It is evident that he is above desire and fear. He is master over nature. He is superior to envy. If anyone else comes, they seize him and throttle him. And how will this one be able to escape the great grasping powers? How will he be able to hide from them? Often some come and say, "We are faithful," in order that they may be able to escape the unclean spirits and the demons. For if they had the Holy Spirit, no unclean spirit would cleave to them. Fear not the flesh nor love it. If you fear it, it will gain mastery over you. If you love it, it will swallow and paralyze you.

Either he will be in this world or in the resurrection or in the places in the middle. God forbid that I be found in them! In this world there is good and evil. Its good is not good, and its evil not evil. But there is evil after this world which is truly evil—what is called "the Middle." It is death. While we are in this world it is fitting for us to acquire the resurrection for ourselves, so that when we strip off the flesh we may be found in rest and not walk in the Middle. For many go astray on the way. For it is good to come forth from the world before one has sinned.

Some neither desire to sin nor are able to sin. Others, even if they desire to sin, are not better off for not having done it, for this desire makes them sinners. But even if some do not desire to sin, righteousness will be concealed from them both—those who desire not and do not.

An apostolic man in a vision saw some people shut up in a house of fire and bound with fiery chains, lying in flaming ointment. And he said to them, "Why are they not able to be saved? They answered, "They did not desire it. They received this place as punishment, what is called 'the outer darkness,' because he is thrown out into it."

It is from water and fire that the soul and the spirit came into being. It is from water and fire and light that the son of the bridal chamber came into being. The fire is the chrism, the light is the fire. I am not referring to that fire which has no form, but to the other fire whose form is white, which is bright and beautiful, and which gives beauty.

Truth did not come into the world naked, but it came in types and images. One will not receive truth in any other way. There is a rebirth and an image of rebirth. It is certainly necessary that they should be born again through the image. What is the resurrection? The image must rise again through the image. The bridegroom and the image must enter through the image into the truth: this is the restoration. It is appropriate that those who do not have it not only acquire the name of the Father and the Son and the Holy Spirit, but that they have acquired it on their own. If one does not acquire the name for himself, the name "Christian" will also be taken from him.

But one receives them in the aromatic unction of the power of the cross. This power the apostles called "the right and the left." For this person is no longer a Christian but a Christ.

The Lord did everything in a mystery, a baptism and a chrism and a eucharist and a redemption and a bridal chamber.

The Lord said, "I came to make the things below like the things above, and the things outside like those inside. I came to unite them in that place." He revealed himself in this place through types and images. Those who say, "There is a heavenly man and there is one above him," are wrong. For he who is revealed in Heaven is that heavenly man, the one who is called "the one who is below"; and he to whom the hidden belongs is that one who is above him. For it is good that they should say, "The inner and the outer, with what is outside the outer." Because of this, the Lord called destruction "the outer darkness"; there is not another outside of it. He said, "My Father who is in secret." He said, "Go into your chamber and shut the door behind you, and pray to your Father who is in secret" [Matt. 6:6], the one who is within them all. But that which is within them all is the fullness. Beyond it there is nothing else within it. This is that of which they say, "That which is above them."

Before Christ some came from a place they were no longer able to enter, and they went where they were no longer able to come out. Then Christ came. Those who went in he brought out, and those who went out he brought in.

When Eve was still in Adam, death did not exist. When she was separated from him, death came into being. If he again becomes complete and attains his former self, death will be no more.

"My God, my God, why, O Lord, have you forsaken me?" [Mark 15:34 and parallels]. It was on the cross that he said these words, for it was there that he was divided.

Everyone who has been begotten through him who destroys did not emanate from God.

The Lord rose from the dead. He became as he used to be, but now his body was perfect. He did indeed possess flesh, but this flesh is true flesh. Our flesh is not true, but we possess only an image of the true.

A bridal chamber is not for the animals, nor is it for the slaves, nor for the defiled women; but it is for the free men and virgins.

Through the Holy Spirit we are indeed begotten again, but we are begotten through Christ in the two. We are anointed through the Spirit. When we were begotten we were united. None shall be able to see himself either in water or in a mirror without light. Nor again will you be able to see in light without water or mirror. For this reason it is fitting to baptize in the two, in the light and the water. Now the light is the chrism.

There were three buildings specifically for sacrifice in Jerusalem. The one facing west was called "the Holy." Another facing south was called "the Holy of the Holy." The third facing east was called "the Holy of the Holies," the place where only the high priest enters. Baptism is "the Holy" building. Redemption is "the Holy of the Holy." "The Holy of the Holies" is the bridal chamber. Baptism includes the resurrection and the redemption; the redemption takes place in the bridal chamber. But the bridal chamber is in that which is superior to it and the others, because you will not find anything like it. Those who are familiar with it are those who pray in "the Holy" in Jerusalem. There are some in Jerusalem who pray only in Jerusalem, awaiting the Kingdom of Heaven. These are called "the Holy of the Holies," because before the veil was rent we had no other bridal chamber except the image of the bridal chamber which is above. Because of this, its veil was rent from top to bottom. For it was fitting for some from below to go upward.

The powers do not see those who are clothed in the perfect light, and consequently are not able to detain them. One will clothe himself in this light sacramentally in the union.

If the woman had not separated from the man, she would not die with the man. His separation became the beginning of death. Because of this Christ came to repair the separation which was from the beginning and to again unite the two, to give life to those who died as a result of the separation and unite them. But the woman is united to her husband in the bridal chamber. Indeed, those who have united in the bridal chamber will no longer be separated. Thus Eve separated from Adam because she was never united with him in the bridal chamber.

The soul of Adam came into being by means of a breath, which is a synonym for spirit. The spirit given him is his mother. His soul was replaced by a spirit. When he was united to the spirit, he spoke words incomprehensible to the powers. They envied him because they were separated from the spiritual union. This separation afforded them the opportunity to fashion for themselves the symbolic bridal chamber so that men would be defiled.

Jesus revealed himself at the Jordan: it was the fullness of the Kingdom of Heaven. He who was begotten before everything was begotten anew. He who was once anointed was anointed anew. He who was redeemed in turn redeemed others.

Is it permitted to utter a mystery? The Father of everything united with the virgin who came down, and a fire shone for him on that day. He appeared in the great bridal chamber. Therefore his body came into being on that very day. It left the bridal chamber as one who came into being from the bridegroom and the bride. So Jesus established everything in it through these. It is fitting for each of the disciples to enter into his rest.

Adam came into being from two virgins, from the Spirit and from the virgin earth. Christ, therefore, was born from a virgin to rectify the Fall which occurred in the beginning.

There are two trees growing in Paradise. One bears animals, the other bears men. Adam ate from the tree which bore animals. He became an animal and he brought forth animals. For this reason the children of Adam worship animals. The tree whose fruit Adam ate is the Tree of Knowledge. That is why sins increased. If he ate the fruit of the other tree, that is to say, the fruit of the Tree of Life, the one which bears men, then the gods would worship man. For in the beginning God created man. But now men create God. That is the way it is in the world—men make gods and worship their creation. It would be fitting for the gods to worship men!

Surely what a man accomplishes depends on his abilities. We even refer to one's accomplishments as "abilities." Among his accomplishments are his children. They originate in a moment of ease. Thus his abilities determine what he may accomplish, but this ease is clearly evident in the children. You will find that this applies directly to the image. Here is the man made after the image, accomplishing things with his physical strength but producing his children with ease.

In this world the slaves serve the free. In the Kingdom of Heaven the free will minister to the slaves: the children of the bridal chamber will minister to the children of the marriage. The children of the bridal chamber have just one name. Together they share rest. They need take no other form because they have contemplation, comprehending by insight. They are numerous because they do not put their treasure in the things below, which are despised, but in the glories which are above, though they did not yet know them.

Those who will be baptized go down into the water. But Christ, by coming out of the water, will consecrate it, so that they who have received baptism in his name may be perfect. For he said, "Thus we should fulfill all righteousness" [Matt. 3:15].

Those who say they will die first and then rise are in error. If they do not first receive the resurrection while they live, when they die they will receive nothing. So also when speaking about baptism they say, "Baptism is a great thing," because if people receive it they will live.

Philip the apostle said, "Joseph the carpenter planted a garden because he needed wood for his trade. It was he who made the cross from the trees which he planted. His own offspring hung on that which he planted. His offspring was Jesus and the planting was the cross." But the Tree of Life is in the middle of the Garden. However, it is from the olive tree that we got the chrism, and from the chrism, the resurrection.

This world is a corpse-eater. All the things eaten in it themselves die also. Truth is a life-eater. Therefore no one nourished by truth will die. It was from that place that Jesus came and brought food. To those who so desired he gave life, that they might not die.

God planted a Garden. Man was put into the Garden. There were many trees there for him, and man lived in this place with the blessing and in the image of God. The things which are in it I will eat as I wish. This garden is the place where they will say to me, "O man, eat this or do not eat that, just as you wish." This is the place where I will eat all things, since the Tree of Knowledge is there. That one killed Adam, but here the Tree of Knowledge made men alive. The law was the tree. It has power to give the knowledge of good and evil. It neither removed him from evil, nor did it set him in the good, but it created death for those who ate of it. For when he said, "Eat this, do not eat that," it became the beginning of death.

The chrism is superior to baptism, for it is from the word "chrism" that we have been called "Christians," certainly not because of the word "baptism." And it is because of the chrism that "the Christ" has his name. For the Father anointed the Son, and the Son anointed the apostles, and the apostles anointed us. He who has been anointed possesses everything; he possesses the resurrection, the light, the cross, the Holy Spirit. The Father gave him this in the bridal chamber; he merely accepted the gift. The Father was in the Son and the Son in the Father. This is the Kingdom of Heaven.

The Lord said it well: "Some have entered the Kingdom of Heaven laughing and they have come out." They do not remain there—the one because he is not a Christian, the other because he regrets his action afterward. And as soon as Christ went down into the water, he came out laughing at everything of this world, not because he considers it a trifle, but because he is full of contempt for it. He who wants to enter the Kingdom of Heaven will attain it. If he despises everything of this world and scorns it as a trifle, he will come out laughing. So it is also with the bread and the cup and the oil, even though there is another one superior to these.

The world came about through a mistake. For he who created it wanted to create it imperishable and immortal. He fell short of attaining his desire. For the world never was imperishable, nor, for that matter, was he who made the world. For things are not imperishable, but sons are. Nothing will be able to receive imperishability if it does not first become a son. But he who has not the ability to receive, how much more will he be unable to give?

The cup of prayer contains wine and water, since it is appointed as the type of the blood for which thanks is given. And it is full of the Holy Spirit, and it belongs to the wholly perfect man. When we drink this, we shall receive for ourselves the perfect man. The living water is a body. It is necessary that we put on the living man. Therefore, when he is about to go down into the water, he unclothes himself, in order that he may put on the living man.

A horse sires a horse, a man begets man, a god brings forth a god. Compare the bridegroom and the bride. Their children were conceived in the bridal chamber. No Jew was ever born to Greek parents as long as the world has existed. And, as a Christian people, we ourselves do not descend from the Jews. There was another people and these blessed ones are referred to as "the chosen people of the living God" and "the true man" and "the Son of man" and "the seed of the Son of man." In the world it is called "this true people." Where they are, there are the sons of the bridal chamber.

Whereas in this world the union is one of husband with wife—a case of strength complemented by weakness—in the Aeon the form of the union is different, although we refer to them by the same names. There are other names, however; they are superior to every name that is named and are stronger than the strong. For where there is a show of strength, there those who excel in strength appear. These are not separate things, but both of them are this one single thing. This is the one which will not be able to rise above the heart of flesh.

Is it not necessary for all those who possess everything to know themselves? Some indeed, if they do not know themselves, will not enjoy what they possess. But those who have come to know themselves will enjoy their possessions.

Not only will they be unable to detain the perfect man, but they will not be able to see him, for if they see him they will detain him. There is no other way for a person to acquire this quality except by putting on the perfect light and becoming perfect oneself. Everyone who has put this on will enter the kingdom. This is the perfect light, and it is necessary that we, by all means, become perfect men before we leave the world. He who has received everything and has not rid

himself of these places will not be able to share in that place, but will go to the Middle as imperfect. Only Jesus knows the end of this person.

The priest is completely holy, down to his very body. For if he has taken the bread, will he consecrate it? Or the cup or anything else that he gets, does he consecrate them? Then how will he not consecrate the body also?

By perfecting the water of baptism, Jesus emptied it of death. Thus we do go down into the water, but we do not go down into death in order that we may not be poured out into the spirit of the world. When that spirit blows, it brings the winter. When the Holy Spirit breathes, the summer comes.

He who has knowledge of the truth is a free man, but the free man does not sin, for "he who sins is the slave of sin." [John 8:34]. Truth is the mother, knowledge the father. Those who think that sinning does not apply to them are called "free" by the world. Knowledge of the truth merely makes such people arrogant, which is what the words "it makes them free" mean. It even gives them a sense of superiority over the whole world. But "love builds up" [1 Cor. 8:1]. In fact, he who is really free through knowledge is a slave because of love for those who have not yet been able to attain to the freedom of knowledge. Knowledge makes them capable of becoming free. Love never calls something its own, and yet it may actually possess that very thing. It never says "This is mine" or "That is mine," but "All these are yours." Spiritual love is wine and fragrance. All those who anoint themselves with it take pleasure in it. While those who are anointed are present, those nearby also profit from the fragrance. If those anointed with ointment withdraw from them and leave, then those not anointed, who merely stand nearby, still remain in their bad odor. The Samaritan gave nothing but wine and oil to the wounded man. It is nothing other than the ointment. It healed the wounds, for "love covers a multitude of sins" [1 Pet. 4:8].

The children a woman bears resemble the man who loves her. If her husband loves her, then they resemble her husband. If it is an adulterer, then they resemble the adulterer. Frequently, if a woman sleeps with her husband out of necessity, while her heart is with the adulterer with whom she usually has intercourse, the child she will bear is born resembling the adulterer. Now you who live together with the Son of God, love not the world, but love the Lord, in order that those you will bring forth may not resemble the world, but may resemble the Lord.

The human being has intercourse with the human being. The horse has intercourse with the horse, the ass with the ass. Members of a race usually have associated with those of like race. So spirit mingles with spirit, and thought consorts with thought, and light shares with light. If you are born a human being, it is the human being who will love you. If you become a spirit, it is the spirit which will be joined to you. If you become thought, it is thought which will mingle with you. If you become light, it is the light which will share with you. If you become one of those who belong above, it is those who belong above who will rest in you. If you become horse or ass or bull or dog or sheep or another of the animals which are outside or below, then neither human being nor spirit nor thought nor light will be able to love you. Neither those who belong above nor those who belong within will be able to rest in you, and you have no part in them.

He who is a slave against his will, will be able to become free. He who has become free by the favor of his master and has sold himself into slavery will no longer be able to be free.

Farming in the world requires the cooperation of four essential elements. A harvest is gathered into the barn only as a result of the natural action of water, earth, wind, and light. God's farming likewise has four elements—faith, hope, love, and knowledge. Faith is our earth, that in which we take root. And hope is the water through which we are nourished. Love is the wind through which we grow. Knowledge then is the light through which we ripen. Grace exists in four ways: it is earthborn; it is heavenly; it comes from the highest heaven; and it resides in truth.

Blessed is the one who on no occasion caused a soul distress. That person is Jesus Christ. He came to the whole place and did not burden anyone. Therefore, blessed is the one who is like this, because he is a perfect man. This indeed is the Word. Tell us about it, since it is difficult to define. How shall we be able to accomplish such a great thing? How will he give everyone comfort? Above all, it is not proper to cause anyone distress—whether the person is great or small, unbeliever or believer—and then give comfort only to those who take satisfaction in good deeds. Some find it advantageous to give comfort to the one who has fared well. He who does good deeds cannot give comfort to such people, for it goes against his will. He is unable to cause distress, however, since he does not afflict them. To be sure, the one who fares well sometimes causes people distress—not that he intends to do so; rather, it is their own wickedness which is responsible for their distress. He who possesses the qualities of the perfect man rejoices in the good. Some, however, are terribly distressed by all this.

There was a householder who had every conceivable thing, be it son or slave or cattle or dog or pig or corn or barley or chaff or grass or castor oil or meat and acorn. Now he was a sensible fellow and he knew what the food of each one was. He himself served the children bread and meat. He served the slaves castor oil and meal. And he threw barley and chaff and grass to the cattle. He threw bones to the dogs, and to the pigs he threw acorns and scraps of bread. Compare the disciple of God: if he is a sensible fellow he understands what discipleship is all about. The bodily forms will not deceive him, but he will look at the condition of the soul of each one and speak with him. There are many animals in the world which are in human form. When he identifies them, to the swine he will throw acorns, to the cattle he will throw barley and chaff and grass, to the dogs he will throw bones. To the slaves he will give only the elementary lessons, but to the children he will give the complete instruction.

There is the Son of man and there is the son of the Son of man. The Lord is the Son of man, and the son of the Son of man is he who is created through the Son of man. The Son of man received from God the capacity to create. He also has the ability to beget. He who has received the ability to create is a creature. He who has received the ability to beget is an offspring. He who creates cannot beget. He who begets also has power to create. Now they say, "He who creates begets." But his so-called "offspring" is merely a creature. Therefore his children are not offspring but creatures. He who creates works openly; he himself is visible. He who begets, begets in private; he himself is hidden, since he is superior to every image. He who creates, creates openly. But one who begets, begets children in private. No one will be able to know when the husband and the wife have intercourse with one another, except the two of them. Indeed, marriage in the world is a mystery for those who have taken a wife. If there is a hidden quality to the marriage of defilement, how much more is the undefiled marriage a true mystery! It is not fleshly but pure. It belongs not to desire but to the will. It belongs not to the darkness or the night but to the day and the light. If a marriage is open to the public, it has become prostitution, and the bride plays the harlot not only when she is impregnated by another man but even if she slips out of her bedroom and is seen. Let her show herself only to her father and her mother and to the friend of the bridegroom and the sons of the bridegroom. These are permitted to enter every day into the bridal chamber. But let the others yearn just to listen to her voice and to enjoy her ointment, and let them feed from the crumbs that fall from the table, like dogs. Bridegrooms and brides belong to the bridal chamber. No one shall be able to see the bridegroom with the bride unless one becomes one.

When Abraham rejoiced that he was to see what he was to see, he circumcised the flesh of the foreskin, teaching us that it is proper to destroy the flesh.

Most things in the world, as long as their inner parts are hidden, stand upright and live. If they are revealed they die, as is illustrated by the visible man: as long as the intestines of the man are hidden, the man is alive; when his intestines are exposed and come out of him, the man will die. So also with the tree: while its root is hidden it sprouts and grows. If its root is exposed, the tree dries up. So it is with every birth that is in the world, not only with the revealed but with the hidden. For so long as the root of wickedness is hidden, it is strong. But when it is recognized, it is dissolved. When it is revealed, it perishes. That is why the word says, "Already the ax is laid at the root of the trees" [Matt. 3:10]. It will not merely cut—what is cut sprouts again—but the ax penetrates deeply until it brings up the root. Jesus pulled out the root of the whole place, while others did it only partially. As for ourselves, let each one of us dig down after the root of evil which is within one, and let one pluck it out of one's heart from the root. It will be plucked out if we recognize it. But if we are ignorant of it, it takes root in us and produces its fruit in our heart. It masters us. We are its slaves. It takes us captive, to make us do what we do not want; and what we do want we do not do. It is powerful because we have not recognized it. While it exists it is active. Ignorance is the mother of all evil. Ignorance will eventuate in death, because those who come from ignorance neither were nor are nor shall be. But those who are in the truth will be perfect when all the truth is revealed. For truth is like ignorance: while it is hidden it rests in itself, but when it is revealed and is recognized, it is praised inasmuch as it is stronger than ignorance and error. It gives freedom. The word said, "If you know the truth, the truth will make you free" [John 8:32]. Ignorance is a slave. Knowledge is freedom. If we know the truth, we shall find the fruits of the truth within us. If we are joined to it, it will bring fulfillment.

At the present time we have the manifest things of creation. We say, "The strong are they who are held in high regard. And the obscure are the weak who are despised." Contrast the manifest things of truth: they are weak and despised, while the hidden things are strong and held in high regard. The mysteries of truth are revealed, though in type and image. The bridal chamber, however, remains hidden. It is the holy in the holy. The veil at first concealed how God controlled the creation, but when the veil is rent and the things inside are revealed, this house will be left desolate, or rather will be destroyed. But the whole inferior godhead will not flee from these places into the holies of the holies, for it will not be able to mix with the unmixed light and the flawless fullness, but will be under the wings of the cross and under its arms. This ark will be its salvation when the flood of water surges over them. If some belong to the order of the priesthood, they will be able to go within the veil with the high priest. For this reason the veil was not rent at the top only since it would have been open only to those above; nor was it rent at the bottom only since it would have been revealed only to those below. But it was rent from top to bottom. Those above opened to us who are below, in order that we may go in to the secret of the truth. This truly is what is held in high regard, since it is strong! But we shall go in there by means of lowly types and forms of weakness. They are lowly indeed when compared with the perfect glory. There is glory which surpasses glory. There is power which surpasses power. Therefore, the perfect things have opened to us, together with the hidden things of truth. The holies of the holies were revealed, and the bridal chamber invited us in.

As long as it is hidden, wickedness is indeed ineffectual, but it has not been removed from the midst of the seed of the Holy Spirit. They are slaves of evil. But when it is revealed, then the perfect light will flow out on everyone. And all those who are in it will receive the chrism. Then the slaves will be free and the captives ransomed. "Every plant which my father who is in heaven has not planted will be plucked out" [Matt. 15:13]. Those who are separated will be united and will be filled. Every one who will enter the bridal chamber will kindle the light, for it burns just as in the marriages which are observed, though they happen at night. That fire burns only at night and is put out. But the mysteries of this marriage are perfected rather in the day and the light. Neither that day nor its light ever sets. If anyone becomes a son of the bridal chamber, he will receive the light. If anyone does not receive it while he is in these places, he will not be able to receive it in the other place. He who will receive that light will not be seen, nor can he be detained. And none shall be able to torment a person like this even while he dwells in the world. And again, when he leaves the world he has already received the truth in the images. The world has become the Aeon, for the Aeon is fullness for him. This is the way it is: it is revealed to him alone, not hidden in the darkness and the night, but hidden in a perfect day and a holy light.

The Paraphrase of Shem

(Gnostic)*

The *Paraphrase of Shem* is the first of the five tractates contained in
Codex VII, the best preserved of all the codices in the Nag Hammadi
library. This tractate takes the form of a revelation given by Derdekeas,
the son and likeness of the perfect Light, to Shem, who is "from an
unmixed power," and is "the first being upon the earth." Interestingly, the tractate has the same sorts of phrases and general outlook as
the report of the heresiologist Hippolytus concerning the Sethian
Gnostics. Hippolytus refers to his source as the *Paraphrase of Seth*, apparently a Christianized version of a tractate similar to the *Paraphrase of
Shem*.

The revelation from Derdekeas to Shem is introduced by Shem's
rapture to Heaven. Shem tells about an ecstatic experience during
which his mind was separated from his body as if in sleep. He was
caught up to the top of creation close to the supreme being, the Light.
This framework is apparently terminated when he "awakens," though
additional revelation to him occurs later in the tractate. The revelation
includes discussion of cosmogony, soteriology, and eschatology. According to the *Paraphrase of Shem*, there are three basic "roots," three
primeval powers: Light, Darkness, and Spirit between them. The mixing of these three powers triggers the cosmic drama: Darkness, realizing his inferiority and yearning for equality, directs his attack at the
Spirit, since the Darkness is ignorant of the Light. The mind of Darkness is the prime tool of Darkness to accomplish his evil schemes in
the world; yet at the same time the mind of Darkness, together with
the light of the Spirit, is the object of the salvific efforts of the redeemer Derdekeas.

*Introduction by Frederick Wisse.

The description of this Gnostic redeemer Derdekeas is particularly significant. Moved by pity, Derdekeas descends to the realm of evil to rescue the fallen and entrapped light of the Spirit and of the mind of Darkness. During his stay in Hades, Derdekeas experiences the hostility of the powers of Darkness, and goes unrecognized. He puts on "the beast," apparently the body, and in that disguise he advances the cosmic work of salvation. After his stay on earth he receives honor from his amazing garments, which provide both protection and glory. Finally, he reveals his saving work as life-giving knowledge to his elect.

The *Paraphrase of Shem* is a non-Christian Gnostic work which uses and radically transforms Old Testament materials, especially from Genesis. The tractate proclaims a redeemer whose features agree with those features of New Testament Christology which may very well be pre-Christian in origin. As such, the *Paraphrase of Shem* is important for the study of Christian origins, and may contribute significantly to the understanding of the development of Christology in the New Testament.

THE CONFLICT OF LIGHT AND DARKNESS*

The paraphrase is about the unbegotten Spirit.

What Derdekeas revealed to me, Shem, according to the will of the Majesty. My mind which was in my body snatched me away from my race. It took me up to the top of the world, which is close to the light that shone upon the whole area there. I saw no earthly likeness, but there was light. And my mind separated from the body of darkness as though in sleep.

I heard a voice saying to me, Shem, since you are from an unmixed power and you are the first being upon the earth, hear and understand what I shall say to you first concerning the great Powers who were in existence in the beginning before I appeared. There was Light and Darkness and there was Spirit between them. Since your root fell into forgetfulness—he who was the unbegot-

*Codex VII 1, 1–49, 9. Translated by Frederick Wisse. From James M. Robinson, ed., *The Nag Hammadi Library* (San Francisco: Harper & Row, 1977), pp. 309–329.

ten Spirit—I reveal to you the truth about the Powers. The Light was mind full of attentiveness and reason. They were united into one form. And the Darkness was wind in waters. He possessed the mind wrapped in a chaotic fire. And the Spirit between them was a gentle, humble light. These are the three roots. They reigned each in themselves, alone. And they covered each other, each one with its power.

But the Light, since he possessed a great power, knew the abasement of the Darkness and his disorder, namely, that the root was not straight. But the crookedness of the Darkness was lack of perception, namely the illusion that there is no one above him. And when he was able to bear up under his evil, he was covered with the water. And he stirred. And the Spirit was frightened by the sound. He lifted himself up to his station. And he saw a great, dark water. And he was nauseated. And the mind of the Spirit stared down; he saw the infinite Light. But he was overlooked by the putrid root. And by the will of the great Light the dark water separated. And the Darkness came up wrapped in vile ignorance, and this was in order that the mind might separate from him because he prided himself in it.

And when he stirred, the light of the Spirit appeared to him. When he saw it he was astonished. He did not know that another Power was above him. And when he saw that his likeness was dark compared with the Spirit, he felt hurt. And in his pain he lifted up to the height of the members of Darkness his mind which was outside the bitterness of evil. He caused his mind to take shape in a member of the regions of the Spirit, thinking that, by staring down at his evil, he would be able to equal the Spirit. But he was not able. For he wanted to do an impossible thing. And it did not take place, so that the mind of Darkness, which is outside the bitterness of evil, might not be destroyed. Since he was made partially similar, he arose and shone with a fiery light upon all of Hades, in order that the equality to the faultless Light might become apparent. For the Spirit benefited from every form of Darkness because he appeared in his majesty.

And the exalted, infinite Light appeared, for he was very joyful. He wished to reveal himself to the Spirit. And the likeness of the exalted Light appeared to the unbegotten Spirit. I appeared, I am the son of the incorruptible, infinite Light. I appeared in the likeness of the Spirit, for I am the ray of the universal Light. And his appearance to me was in order that the mind of Darkness might not remain in Hades. For the Darkness made himself like his mind in a part of the members. When I, O Shem, appeared in the likeness, in order that the Darkness might become dark to himself, according to the will of the Majesty —in order that the Darkness might become free from every aspect of the power which he possessed—the mind drew the chaotic fire, with which it was covered, from the midst of the Darkness and the water. And from the Darkness the water became a cloud. And from the cloud the womb took shape. The chaotic fire which was a deviation went there.

And when the Darkness saw the womb, he became unchaste. And when he had aroused the water, he rubbed the womb. His mind dissolved down to the depths of Nature. It mingled with the power of the bitterness of Darkness. And the womb's eye ruptured at the wickedness in order that she might not again bring forth the mind. For it was a seed of Nature from the dark root. And when Nature had taken to herself the mind by means of the dark power, every likeness took shape in her. And when the Darkness had acquired the likeness of the mind, it resembled the Spirit. For Nature rose up to expel it; she was powerless against it, since she did not have a form from the Darkness. For she brought it forth in the cloud. And the cloud shone. A mind appeared in it like a frightful, harmful fire. The mind collided against the unbegotten Spirit since it possessed a likeness from him, in order that Nature might become emptier than the chaotic fire.

And immediately Nature was divided into four parts. They became clouds which varied in their appearance. They were called Hymen, Afterbirth, Power, and Water. And the Hymen and the Afterbirth and the Power were chaotic fires. And the mind was drawn from the midst of the Darkness and the water—since the mind was in the midst of Nature and the dark power—in order that the harmful waters might not cling to it. Because of this, Nature was divided, according to my will, in order that the mind may return to its power which the dark root, which was mixed with the mind, had taken from it. And the dark root appeared in the womb. And at the division of Nature he separated from the dark power which he possessed from the mind. The mind went into the midst of the power—this was the middle region of Nature.

And the Spirit of light, when the mind burdened him, was astonished. And the force of his astonishment cast off the burden. And the burden returned to its heat. It put on the light of the Spirit. And when Nature moved away from the power of the light of the Spirit, the burden returned. And the astonishment of the light cast off the burden. It stuck to the cloud of the Hymen. And all the clouds of Darkness cried out, they who had separated from Hades, because of the alien Power. He is the Spirit of light who has come from them. And by the will of the Majesty the Spirit gazed up at the infinite Light, in order that his light may be pitied. And the likeness was brought up from Hades.

And when the Spirit had looked, I flowed out—I, the son of the Majesty—like a wave of light and like a whirlwind of the immortal Spirit. And I blew from the cloud of the Hymen upon the astonishment of the unbegotten Spirit. The cloud separated and cast light upon the clouds. These separated in order that the Spirit might return. Because of this the mind took shape. Its repose was shattered. For the Hymen of Nature was a cloud which cannot be grasped; it is a great fire. Similarly, the Afterbirth of Nature is the cloud of silence; it is an august fire. And the Power which was mixed with the mind, it, too, was a cloud of Nature which was joined with the Darkness that had aroused Nature to unchastity. And the dark water was a frightful cloud. And the root of Nature, which was below, was crooked, since it is burdensome and harmful. The root was blind with respect to the light-bondage, which was unfathomable since it had many appearances.

And I had pity on the light of the Spirit which the mind had received. I returned to my position in order to pray to the exalted, infinite Light that the power of the Spirit might be suspended over the place and might be filled without dark defilement. And reverently I said, "You are the root of the Light. Your hidden form has appeared, O exalted, infinite one. May the whole power of the Spirit spread and may it be filled with its light, O infinite Light. Then he will not be able to join with the unbegotten Spirit, and the power of the astonishment will not be able to mix with Nature according to the will of the Majesty." My prayer was accepted.

And the voice of the Word was heard saying through the Majesty of the unbegotten Spirit, "Behold, the power has been completed. What was revealed by me originated from the Spirit. Again I shall appear. I am Derdekeas, the son of the incorruptible, infinite Light."

The light of the infinite Spirit came down to a feeble nature for a short time until all the impurity of nature became void, and in order that the darkness of Nature might be exposed. I put on my garment which is the garment of the light of the Majesty—which I am. I came in the appearance of the Spirit to consider the whole light which was in the depths of the Darkness, according to the will of the Majesty, in order that the Spirit by means of the Word might be filled with his light independently of the power of the infinite Light. And at my wish the Spirit arose by his own power. His greatness was granted to him that he might be filled with his whole light and depart from the whole burden of the Darkness. For what was mentioned before was a dark fire which blew and pressed on the Spirit. And the Spirit rejoiced because he was protected from the frightful water. But his light was not equal to the Majesty—but he who was favored by the infinite Light—in order that in all his members he might appear as a single image of light. And when the Spirit arose above the water, his black likeness became apparent. And the Spirit honored the exalted Light: "Surely you alone are the infinite one, because you are above every unbegotten thing, for you have protected me from the Darkness. And at your wish I arose above the power of darkness."

And that nothing might be hidden from you, Shem, the mind, which the Spirit from the greatness had contemplated, came into being, since the Darkness was not able to restrain his evil. But when the mind appeared, the three roots became known as they were from the beginning. If the Darkness had been able to bear up under his evil, the mind would not have separated from him, and another power would not have appeared.

But from the time it appeared I was seen, the son of the Majesty, in order that the light of the Spirit might not become faint, and that Nature might not reign over it, because it gazed at me. And by the will of the greatness my equality was revealed, that what is of the Power might become apparent. You are the great Power which came into being, and I am the perfect Light which is above the Spirit and the Darkness, the one who puts to shame the Darkness for the intercourse of the impure practice. For through the division of Nature the Majesty wished to be covered with honor up to the height of the mind of the Spirit. And the Spirit received rest in his power. For the image of the Light is inseparable from the unbegotten Spirit. And the lawgivers did not name him after all the clouds of Nature, nor is it possible to name him. For every likeness into which Nature had divided is a power of the chaotic fire which is the hylic seed. The one who took to himself the power of the Darkness imprisoned it in the midst of its members.

And by the will of the Majesty, in order that the mind and the whole light of the Spirit might be protected from every burden and from the toil of Nature, a voice came forth from the Spirit to the cloud of the Hymen. And the light of the astonishment began to rejoice with the voice which was granted to him. And the great Spirit of light was in the cloud of the Hymen. He honored the infinite Light and the universal likeness who I am, the son of the Majesty, saying, "Anasses Duses, you are the infinite Light who was given by the will of the Majesty to establish every light of the Spirit upon the place, and to separate the mind from the Darkness. For it was not right for the light of the Spirit to remain in Hades. For at your wish the Spirit arose to behold your greatness."

For I said these things to you, Shem, that you might know that my likeness, the son of the Majesty, is from my infinite mind, since I am for him a universal likeness which does not lie, and I am above every truth and origin of the word. His appearance is in my beautiful garment of light which is the voice of the immeasurable mind. We are that single, sole light which came into being. He appeared in another root in order that the power of the Spirit might be raised from the feeble Nature. For by the will of the great Light I came forth from the exalted Spirit down to the cloud of the Hymen without my universal garment.

And the Word took me to himself, from the Spirit, in the first cloud—of the Hymen—of Nature. And I put on this of which the Majesty and the unbegotten Spirit made me worthy. And one-third of my garment appeared in the cloud, by the will of the Majesty, in a single form. And my likeness was covered with the light of my garment. And the cloud was disturbed, and it was not able to tolerate my likeness. It shed the first power which it had taken from the Spirit, that which shone on him from the beginning, before I appeared in the word to the Spirit. The cloud would not be able to tolerate both of them. And the light which came forth from the cloud passed through the silence, until it came into the middle region. And, by the will of the Majesty, the light mixed with him, i.e., the Spirit which exists in the silence, he who had been separated from the Spirit of light. It was separated from the light by the cloud of the silence. The cloud was disturbed. It was he who gave rest to the flame of fire. He humbled the dark womb in order that she might not reveal other seed from the darkness. He kept them back in the middle region of Nature in their position, which was in the cloud. They were troubled since they did not know where they were. For still they did not possess the universal understanding of the Spirit.

And when I prayed to the Majesty, toward the infinite Light, that the chaotic power of the Spirit might go to and fro, and the dark womb might be idle, and that my likeness might appear in the cloud of the Hymen, as if I were wrapped in the light of the Spirit which went before me. And by the will of the Majesty and through the prayer I came in the cloud in order that through my garment—which was from the power of the Spirit of the Pleroma of the word, from the members who possessed it in the Darkness. For because of them I appeared in this insignificant place. For I am a helper of everyone who has been given a name. For when I appeared in the cloud, the light of the Spirit began to save itself from the frightful water, and from the clouds of fire which had been separated from dark Nature. And I gave them eternal honor that they might not again engage in the impure practice.

And the light which was in the Hymen was disturbed by my power, and it passed through my middle region. It was filled with the universal mind. And through the word of the light of the Spirit it returned to its repose. It received form in its root and shone without deficiency. And the light which had come forth with it from the silence went in the middle region and returned to the place. And the cloud shone. And from it came an unquenchable fire. And the part which separated from the astonishment put on forgetfulness. It was deceived by the fire of darkness. And the shock of its astonishment cast off the burden of the cloud. It was evil since it was unclean. And the fire mixed with the water in order that the waters might become harmful.

And Nature which had been disturbed immediately arose from the idle waters. For her ascent was shameful. And Nature took to herself the power of fire. She became strong because of the light of the Spirit which was in Nature. Her likeness appeared in the water in the form of a frightful beast with many faces, which is crooked below. A light went down to chaos filled with mist and dust, in order to harm Nature. And the light of the astonishment which is in the middle region came to it after he cast off the burden of the Darkness. He rejoiced when the Spirit arose. For he looked from the clouds down at the dark waters upon the light which was in the depths of Nature.

Therefore I appeared that I might get an opportunity to go down to the nether world, to the light of the Spirit which was burdened, that I might protect him from the evil of the burden. And through his looking down at the dark region the light once more came up in order that the womb might again come up from the water. The womb came up by my will. Guilefully, the eye opened. And the light which had appeared in the middle region and which had separated from the astonishment rested and shone upon her. And the womb saw things she had not seen, and she rejoiced joyfully in the light, although this one which appeared in the middle region, in her wickedness, is not hers. When the light shone upon her, and the womb saw things she had not seen, and she was brought down to the water, she was thinking that she had reached to the power of light. And she did not know that her root was made idle by the likeness of the Light, and that it was to the root that he had run.

The light was astonished, the one which was in the middle region and which was beginning and end. Therefore his mind gazed directly up at the exalted Light. And he called out and said, "Lord, have mercy on me, for my light and my effort went astray. For if your goodness does not establish me, I do not know where I am." And when the Majesty had heard him, he had mercy on him.

And I appeared in the cloud of the Hymen, in the silence, without my holy garment. With my will I honored my garment which has three forms in the cloud of the Hymen. And the light which was in the silence, the one from the rejoicing Power, contained me. I wore it. And its two parts appeared in a single form. Its other parts did not appear on account of the fire. I became unable to speak in the cloud of the Hymen, for its fire was frightful, lifting itself up without humility. And in order that my greatness and the word might appear, I placed likewise my other garment in the cloud of the silence. I went into the middle region and put on the light that was in it, that was sunk in forgetfulness and that was separated from the Spirit of astonishment, for he had cast off the burden. At my wish, nothing mortal appeared to him, but they were all immortal things which the Spirit granted to him. And he said in the mind of the Light, "I have come in a great rest in order that he may give rest to my light in his root, and may bring it out of harmful Nature."

Then, by the will of the Majesty, I took off my garment of light. I put on another garment of fire which has no form, which is from the mind of the power, which was separated, and which was prepared for me, according to my will, in the middle region. For the middle region covered it with a dark power in order that I might come and put it on. I went down to chaos to save the whole light from it. For without the power of darkness I could not oppose Nature. When I came into Nature she was not able to tolerate my power. But I rested myself upon her staring eye which was a light from the Spirit. For it had been prepared for me as a garment and a rest by the Spirit. Through me, he opened his eyes down to Hades. He granted Nature his voice for a time.

And my garment of fire, according to the will of the Majesty, went down to what is strong, and to the unclean part of Nature which the power of darkness was covering. And my garment rubbed Nature in her covering. And her unclean femininity was strong. And the wrathful womb came up and made the mind dry, resembling a fish which has a drop of fire and a power of fire. And when Nature had cast off the mind, she was troubled and wept. When she was hurt and in her tears, she cast off the power of the Spirit and remained as I. I put on the light of the Spirit and rested with my garment on account of the sight of the fish.

And in order that the deeds of Nature might be condemned, since she is blind, manifold animals came out of her, in accordance with the number of the fleeting winds. All of them came into being in Hades, searching for the light of the mind which took shape. They were not able to stand up against it. I rejoiced over their ignorance. They found me, the son of the Majesty, in front of the womb which has many forms. I put on the beast, and laid before her a great request that Heaven and earth might come into being, in order that the whole light might rise up. For in no other way could the power of the Spirit be saved from bondage except that I appear to her in animal form. Therefore she was gracious to me as if I were her son.

And on account of my request, Nature arose, since she possesses the power of the Spirit and the Darkness and the fire. For she had taken off her forms. When she had cast it off, she blew upon the water. The Heaven was created. And from the foam of the Heaven the earth came into being. And at my wish it brought forth all kinds of food in accordance with the number of the beasts. And it brought forth dew from the winds on account of you and those who will be begotten the second time upon the earth. For the earth possessed a power of chaotic fire. Therefore it brought forth every seed.

And when the Heaven and the earth were created, my garment of fire arose in the midst of the cloud of Nature and shone upon the whole world until Nature became dry. The Darkness which was the earth's garment was cast into the harmful waters. The middle region was cleansed from the Darkness. But the womb grieved because of what had happened. She perceived in her parts what was water like a mirror. When she perceived it, she wondered how it had come into being. Therefore she remained a widow. It also was astonished that it was not in her. For still the forms possessed a power of fire and light. The power remained in order that it might be in Nature until all the powers are taken away from her. For just as the light of the Spirit was completed in three clouds, it is necessary that also the power which is in Hades will be completed at the appointed time. For, because of the grace of the Majesty, I came forth to her from the water for the second time. For my face pleased her. Her face also was glad.

And I said to her, "May seed and power come forth from you upon the earth." And she obeyed the will of the Spirit that she might be brought to naught. And when her forms returned, they rubbed their tongues with each other; they copulated; they begot winds and demons and the power which is from the fire and the Darkness and the Spirit. But the form which remained alone cast the beast from herself. She did not have intercourse, but she was the one who rubbed herself alone. And she brought forth a wind which possessed a power from the fire and the Darkness and the Spirit.

And in order that the demons also might become free from the power which they possessed through the impure intercourse, a womb was with the winds resembling water. And an unclean penis was with the demons in accordance with the example of the Darkness, and in the way he rubbed with the womb from the beginning. And after the forms of Nature had been together, they separated from each other. They cast off the power, being astonished about the deceit which had happened to them. They grieved with an eternal grief. They covered themselves with their power.

And when I had put them to shame, I arose with my garment in the power and —which is above the beast which is a light, in order that I might make Nature desolate. The mind which had appeared in the Nature of Darkness and which was outside the heart of Darkness, at my wish reigned over the winds and the demons. And I gave him a likeness of fire: light, and attentiveness, and a share of guileless reason. Therefore he was given of the greatness in order to be strong in his power, independent of the power, independent of the light of the Spirit, and intercourse of Darkness, in order that, at the end of time, when Nature will be destroyed, he may rest in the honored place. For he will be found faithful, since he has loathed the unchastity of Nature with the Darkness. The strong power of the mind came into being from the mind and the unbegotten Spirit.

But the winds, which are demons from water and fire and darkness and light, had intercourse unto perdition. And through this intercourse the winds received in their womb foam from the penis of the demons. They conceived a power in their vagina. From the breathing, the wombs of the winds girded each other until the times of the birth came. They went down to the water. And the power was delivered, through the breathing which moves the birth, in the midst of the practice. And every form of the birth received shape in it. When the times of the birth were near, all the winds were gathered from the water which is near the earth. They gave birth to all kinds of unchastity. And the place where the wind alone went was permeated with the unchastity. Barren wives came from it and sterile husbands. For just as they are born, so they bear.

Because of you, the image of the Spirit appeared in the earth and the water. For you are like the Light. For you possess a share of the winds and the demons, and a mind from the Light of the power of the astonishment. For everything which he brought forth from the womb upon the earth was not a good thing for her, but her groan and her pain, because of the image which appeared in you from the Spirit. For you are exalted in your heart. And it is blessedness, Shem, if a part taken from the soul is given to the mind of the Light. For the soul is a burden of the Darkness, and those who know where the root of the soul came from will be able to grope after Nature also. For the soul is a work of unchastity and an object of scorn to the mind of Light. For I am the one who revealed concerning all that is unbegotten.

And in order that the sin of Nature might be filled, I made the womb, which was disturbed, pleasant—the blind wisdom—that I might be able to bring it to naught. And at my wish, he plotted with the water of Darkness and also the Darkness, that they might wound every form of your heart. For by the will of the light of the Spirit they surrounded you; they bound you securely. And in order that his mind might become idle, he sent a demon that the content of her wickedness might be proclaimed. And he caused a flood, and he destroyed your race, in order to take the light and to take from Faith. But I proclaimed quickly by the mouth of the demon that a tower come to be up to the [. . .] of the light, which was left in the demons and their race—which was water—that the demon might be protected from the turbulent chaos. And the womb planned these things according to my will in order that she might pour forth completely. A tower came to be through the demons. The Darkness was disturbed by his loss. He loosened the muscles of the womb. And the demon who was going to enter the tower was protected in order that the races might continue and might acquire coherence through him. For he possesses power from every form.

Return henceforth, O Shem, and rejoice greatly over your race and Faith, for without body and necessity it is protected from every body of Darkness, bearing witness to the holy things of the greatness which were revealed to them in their mind by my will. And they shall rest in the unbegotten Spirit without grief. But you, Shem, because of this, you remained in the body outside the cloud of light that you might remain with Faith. And Faith will come to you. Her mind will be taken and given to you with a consciousness of light. And I told you these things for the benefit of your race from the cloud of light. And likewise, what I shall say to you concerning everything, I shall reveal to you completely that you may reveal them to those who will be upon the earth the second time.

O Shem, the disturbance which occurred at my wish happened in order that Nature might become empty. For the wrath of the Darkness subsided. O Shem, the Darkness' mouth was shut. No longer does the light which shone for the world appear in it, according to my will. And when Nature had said that its wish was fulfilled, then every form was engulfed by the waters in prideful ignorance. Nature turned her dark vagina and cast from her the power of fire which was in her from the beginning through the practice of the Darkness. It lifted itself up and shone upon the whole world instead of the righteous one. And all her forms sent forth a power like a flame of fire up to Heaven as a help to the corrupted light, which had lifted itself up. For they were members of the chaotic fire. And she did not know that she had harmed herself. When she cast forth the power, the power which she possessed, she cast it forth. And the demon, who is a deceiver, stirred up the womb to every form.

And in her ignorance, as if she were doing a great thing, she granted the demons and the winds a star each. For without wind and star nothing happens upon the earth. For every power is filled by them after they were released from the Darkness and the fire and the power and the light. For in the place where their darkness and their fire were mixed with each other, beasts were brought forth. And in the place of the Darkness

109

and the fire, and the power of the mind and the light, where human beings came from, the Spirit, the mind of the Light, my eye, exists not in every man. For before the flood came from the winds and the demons, came to men that as yet the power which is in the tower might be brought forth, and might rest upon the earth.

Then Nature, which had been disturbed, wanted to harm the seed which will be upon the earth after the flood. Demons were sent to them, and a deviation of the winds, and a burden of the angels, and a fear of the prophet, a condemnation of speech, that I may teach you, O Shem, from what blindness your race is protected. When I have revealed to you all that has been spoken, then the righteous one will shine upon the world with my garment. And the night and the day will be separated. For I shall hasten down to the world to take the light of that place, the one which Faith possesses. And I shall appear to those who will acquire the mind of the light of the Spirit. For because of them my majesty appeared.

When he will have appeared, O Shem, upon the earth, in the place which will be called Sodom, then safeguard the insight which I shall give you. For those whose heart was pure will congregate to you, because of the word which you will reveal. For when you appear in the world, dark Nature will shake against you, together with the winds and a demon, that they may destroy the insight. But you, proclaim quickly to the Sodomites your universal teaching, for they are your members. For the demon of human form will part from that place by my will, since he is ignorant. He will guard this utterance. But the Sodomites, according to the will of the Majesty, will bear witness to the universal testimony. They will rest with a pure conscience in the place of their repose, which is the unbegotten Spirit. And as these things will happen, Sodom will be burned unjustly by a base nature. For the evil will not cease in order that your majesty may reveal that place.

Then the demon will depart with Faith. And then he will appear in the four regions of the world. And when Faith appears in the last likeness, then will her appearance become manifest. For the firstborn is the demon who appeared in the union of Nature with many faces, in order that Faith might appear in him. For when he appears in the world, evil passions will arise, and earthquakes, and wars, and famines, and blasphemies. For because of him the whole world will be disturbed. For he will seek the power of Faith and Light; he will not find it. For at that time the demon will also appear upon the river to baptize with an imperfect baptism, and to trouble the world with a bondage of water. But it is necessary for me to appear in the members of the mind of Faith to reveal the great things of my power. I shall separate it from the demon who is Soldas. And the light which he possesses from the Spirit I shall mix with my invincible garment, as well as him whom I shall reveal in the darkness for your sake and for the sake of your race, which will be protected from the evil Darkness.

Know, O Shem, that without Elorchaios and Amoias and Strophaias and Chelkeak and Chelkea and Aileou, no one will be able to pass by this wicked region. For this is my testimony, that in it I have been victorious over the wicked region. And I have taken the light of the Spirit from the frightful water. For when the appointed days of the demon—he who will baptize erringly—draw near, then I shall appear in the baptism of the demon to reveal with the mouth of Faith a testimony to those who belong to her. I testify of you, Spark the unquenchable, Osei, the elect of the Light, the eye of Heaven, and Faith, the first and the last, and Sophia, and Saphaia, and Saphaina, and the righteous Spark, and the impure light. And you, east, and west, and north, and south, upper air and lower air, and all the powers and authorities, you are in Nature. And you, Moluchtha and Soch, are from every work and every impure effort of Nature. Then I shall come from the demon down to the water. And whirlpools of water and flames of fire will rise up against me. Then I shall come up from the water, having put on the light of Faith and the unquenchable fire, in order that through my help the power of the Spirit may cross, she who has been cast in the world by the winds and the demons and the stars. And in them every unchastity will be filled.

Finally, O Shem, consider yourself pleasing in the mind of the Light. Do not let your mind have dealings with the fire and the body of Darkness which was an unclean work. These things which I teach you are right.

This is the paraphrase: For you did not remember that it is from the firmament that your race has been protected. Elorchaios is the name of the great Light, the place from which I have come, the Word which has no equal. And the likeness is my honored garment. And Derdekeas speaks with the voice of the Spirit. And Strophaia is the blessed glance which is the Spirit. And Chelkeach, who is my garment, who has come from the astonishment, who was in the cloud of the Hymen which appeared, he is a trimorphic cloud. And Chelkea is my garment which has two forms, he who was in the cloud of silence. And Chelke is my garment which was given him from every region; it was given him in a single form from the greatness, he who was in the cloud of the middle region. And the star of the Light which was mentioned is my invincible garment which I wore in Hades; this, the star of the Light, is the mercy which surpasses the mind and the testimony of those who bear witness, and the testimony which has been mentioned, the first and the last, Faith, the mind of the wind of darkness. And Sophaia and Saphaina are in the cloud of those who have been separated from the chaotic fire. And the righteous Spark is

the cloud of light which has shone in your midst. For in the cloud of light my garment will go down to chaos.

But the impure light, which appeared in the Darkness and which belongs to dark Nature, is a power. And the upper air and the lower air, and the powers and the authorities, the demons and the stars, these possessed a [. . .] of fire and a light from the Spirit. And Moluchthas is a wind, for without it nothing is brought forth upon the earth. He has a likeness of a serpent and a unicorn. His protrusions are manifold wings. And the remainder is the womb which has been disturbed. You are blessed, Shem, for your race has been protected from the dark wind which is many-faced. And they will bear witness to the universal testimony and to the impure practice of Faith. And they will become high-minded through the reminder of the Light.

O Shem, no one who wears the body will be able to complete these things. But through remembrance he will be able to grasp them, in order that, when his mind separates from the body, then these things may be revealed to him. They have been revealed to your race. O Shem, it is difficult for someone wearing a body to complete these things, as I said to you. And it is a small number that will complete them, those who possess the mind of the light of the Spirit. They will keep their mind from the impure practice. For many in the race of Nature will seek the security of the Power. They will not find it, nor will they be able to do the will of Faith. For they are seed of the universal Darkness. And those who find them are in much suffering. The winds and the demons will hate them. And the bondage of the body is severe. For where the winds, and the stars, and the demons cast forth from the power of the Spirit, there repentance and testimony will appear upon them, and mercy will lead them to the unbegotten Spirit. And those who are repentant will find rest in the consummation and Faith, in the place of the Hymen. This is the Faith which will fill the place which has been dug out. But those who do not share in the Spirit of light and in Faith will dissolve in the Darkness, the place where repentance did not come.

It is I who opened the eternal gates which were shut from the beginning. To those who long for the best of life, and those who are worthy of the repose, he revealed them. I granted perception to those who perceive. I disclosed to them all the thoughts and the teaching of the righteous ones. And I did not become their enemy at all. But when I had endured the wrath of the world, I was victorious. There was not one of them who knew me. The gates of fire and endless smoke opened against me. All the winds rose up against me. The thunderings and the lightning-flashes for a time will rise up against me. And they will bring their wrath upon me. And on account of me, according to the flesh, they will rule over them according to kind.

And many who wear erring flesh will go down to the harmful waters through the winds and the demons. And they are bound by the water. And he will heal with a futile remedy. He will lead astray, and he will bind the world. And it will not be granted them, when Faith disturbs them in order to take to herself the righteous one.

O Shem, it is necessary that the mind be called by the word in order that the bondage of the power of the Spirit may be saved from the frightful water. And it is blessedness if it is granted someone to contemplate the exalted one, and to know the exalted time and the bondage. For the water is an insignificant body. And men are not released since they are bound in the water, just as from the beginning the light of the Spirit was bound.

O Shem, they are deceived by manifold demons, thinking that through baptism with the uncleanness of water, that which is dark, feeble, idle, and disturbing, he will take away the sins. And they do not know that from the water to the water there is bondage, error, unchastity, envy, murder, adultery, false witness, heresies, robberies, lusts, babblings, wrath, and bitterness. Therefore, there are many deaths which burden their minds. For I foretell it to those who have a heart. They will refrain from the impure baptism. And those who take heart from the light of the Spirit will not have dealings with the impure practice. And their heart will not expire, nor will they curse nor will they be given honor. Where the curse is, there is the deficiency. And the blindness is where the honor is. For if they mix with the evil ones, they become empty in the dark water. For where the water has been mentioned, there is Nature, and the oath, and the lie, and the loss. For only in the unbegotten Spirit, where the exalted Light rested, has the water not been mentioned, nor can it be mentioned.

For this is my appearance: for when I have completed the times which are assigned to me upon the earth, then I will cast from me my garment of fire. And my unequalled garment will come forth upon me, and also all my garments which I put on in all the clouds which were from the astonishment of the Spirit. For the air will tear my garment. For my garment will shine, and it will divide all the clouds up to the root of the Light. The repose is the mind and my garment. And my remaining garments, those on the left and those on the right, will shine on the back in order that the image of the Light may appear. For my garments which I put on in the three clouds, in the last day they will rest in their root, i.e., in the unbegotten Spirit, since they are without fault, through the division of the clouds.

Therefore I have appeared, being faultless, on account of the clouds, because they are unequal, in order that the wickedness of Nature might be ended. For she wished at that time to snare me. She was about to establish Soldas who is the dark flame, who attended on the

[. . .] of error, that he might snare me. She took care of her faith, being vainglorious.

And at that time the light was about to separate from the Darkness, and a voice was heard in the world, saying, "Blessed is the eye which has seen you, and the mind which has supported your majesty at my desire." It will be said by the exalted one, "Blessed is Rebouel among every race of men, for it is you alone who have seen." And she will listen. And they will behead the woman who has the perception, whom you will reveal upon the earth. And according to my will, she will bear witness, and she will cease from every vain effort of Nature and Chaos. For the woman whom they will behead at that time is the coherence of the power of the demon who will baptize the seed of darkness in severity, that the seed may mix with unchastity. He begot a woman. She was called Rebouel.

See, O Shem, how all the things I have said to you have been fulfilled. And the things which you lack, according to my will, will appear to you at that place upon the earth, that you may reveal them as they are. Do not let your mind have dealings with the body. For I have said these things to you, through the voice of the fire, for I entered through the midst of the clouds. And I spoke according to the language of each one. This is my language which I spoke to you. And it will be taken from you. And you will speak with the voice of the world upon the earth. And it will appear to you with that appearance and voice, and all that I have said to you. Henceforth proceed with Faith to shine in the depths of the world.

And I, Shem, awoke as if from a long sleep. I marveled when I received the power of the Light and his whole mind. And I proceeded with Faith to shine with me. And the righteous one followed us with my invincible garment. And all that he had told me would happen upon the earth happened. Nature was handed over to Faith, that Faith might overturn her and that Nature might stand in the Darkness. These things completed her deeds.

Then I rejoiced in the mind of the Light. I came forth from the Darkness and I walked in Faith where the forms of Nature are, up to the top of the earth, to the things which are prepared. Your Faith is upon the earth the whole day. For all night and day she surrounds Nature to take to herself the righteous one. For Nature is burdened, and she is troubled. For none will be able to open the forms of the door except the mind alone who was entrusted with their likeness. For frightful is their likeness of the two forms of Nature, the one which is blind.

But they who have a free conscience remove themselves from the babbling of Nature. For they will bear witness to the universal testimony; they will strip off the burden of Darkness; they will put on the Word of the Light; and they will not be kept back in the insignificant place. And what they possess from the power of the mind they will give to Faith. They will be accepted without grief. And the chaotic fire which they possess they will place in the middle region of Nature. And they will take to themselves, through my garments, these things which are in the clouds. It is they who guide their members. They will rest in the Spirit without suffering. And because of this, the appointed term of Faith appeared upon the earth for a short time, until the Darkness is taken away from her, and her testimony is revealed which was revealed by me. They, who will prove to be from her root, will strip off the Darkness and the chaotic fire. They will put on the light of the mind and they will bear witness. For all that I have said must happen.

After I cease to be upon the earth and withdraw up to my rest, a great, evil error will come upon the world, and many evils in accordance with the number of the forms of Nature. Evil times will come. And when the era of Nature is approaching destruction, darkness will come upon the earth. The number will be small. And a demon will come up from the power who has a likeness of fire. He will divide the heaven, and he will rest in the depth of the east. For the whole world will quake. And the deceived world will be thrown into confusion. Many places will be flooded because of envy of the winds and the demons who have a name which is senseless: Phorbea, Chloerga. They are the ones who govern the world with their teaching. And they lead astray many hearts because of their disorder and their unchastity. Many places will be sprinkled with blood. And five races by themselves will eat their sons. But the regions of the south will receive the Word of the Light. But they who are from the error of the world and from the east will not. A demon will come forth from the belly of the serpent. He was in hiding in a desolate place. He will perform many wonders. Many will loathe him. A wind will come forth from his mouth with a female likeness. Her name will be called Abalphe. He will reign over the world from the east to the west.

Then Nature will have a final opportunity. And the stars will cease from the sky. The mouth of error will be opened in order that the evil Darkness may become idle and silent. And in the last days the forms of Nature will be destroyed with the winds and all their demons; they will become a dark lump, just as they were from the beginning. And the sweet waters which were burdened by the demons will perish. For where the power of the Spirit has gonè there are my sweet waters. The other works of Nature will not be manifest. They will mix with the infinite waters of darkness. And all her forms will cease from the middle region.

I, Shem, have completed these things. And my mind began to separate from the body of darkness. My time was complet-

ed. And my mind put on the immortal memorial. And I said, I agree with your memorial which you have revealed to me, Elorchaios. And you, Amoiaiai, and you, Sederkeas, and your guilelessness, Strophaias, and you, Chelkeak, and you, Chelkea, and Chelke and Elaie, you are the immortal memorial. I testify to you, Spark, the unquenchable one, who is an eye of Heaven and a voice of Light, and Sophaia, and Saphaia, and Saphaina, and the righteous Spark, and Faith, the first and the last, and the upper air and lower air, and you, Chelkeak, Chelke, and Elaie. You are the immortal memorial. I testify to you, Spark, the unquenchable one, who is an eye of Heaven and a voice of Light, and Sophaia, and Saphaia, and Saphaina, and the righteous Spark, and Faith, the first and the last, and the upper air and the lower air, and all the powers and the authorities that are in the world. And you, impure light, and you also, east, and west, and south, and north; you are the zones of the inhabited world. And you also, Moluchtha and Essoch, you are the root of evil and every work and impure effort of Nature.

These are the things which I completed while bearing witness. I am Shem. On the day that I was to come forth from the body, when my mind remained in the body, I awoke as if from a long sleep. And when I arose as it were from the burden of my body, I said, "Just as Nature became old, so is it also in the day of mankind. Blessed are they who knew, when they slept, in what power their mind rested."

And when the Pleiades separated, I saw clouds, which I shall pass by. For the cloud of the Spirit is like a pure beryl. And the cloud of the hymen is like a shining emerald. And the cloud of silence is like a flourishing amaranth. And the cloud of the middle region is like a pure jacinth. And when the righteous one appeared in Nature, then—when Nature was angry—she felt hurt, and she granted to Morphaia to visit Heaven. The righteous one visits during twelve periods that he may visit them during one period, in order that his time may be completed quickly, and Nature may become idle.

Blessed are they who guard themselves against the heritage of death, which is the burdensome water of darkness. For it will not be possible to conquer them in a few moments, since they hasten to come forth from the error of the world. And if they are conquered, they will be kept back from them and be tormented in the darkness until the time of the consummation. When the consummation has come and Nature has been destroyed, then their minds will separate from the Darkness. Nature has burdened them for a short time. And they will be in the ineffable light of the unbegotten Spirit without a form. And thus is the mind as I have said from the first.

Henceforth, O Shem, go in grace and continue in faith upon the earth. For every power of light and fire will be completed by me because of you. For without you they will not be revealed until you speak to them openly. When you cease to be upon the earth, they will be given to the worthy ones. And apart from this proclamation, let them speak about you upon the earth, since they will take the carefree and agreeable land.

The Second Treatise of the Great Seth

*(Gnostic)**

The *Second Treatise of the Great Seth* is a revelation dialogue allegedly delivered by Jesus Christ to an audience of "perfect and incorruptible ones," that is, Gnostic believers. Apart from the title, the name "Seth" never occurs in the text, though perhaps Jesus Christ is meant to be identified with Seth. The treatise presents, in a brief and simple way, the true story of the Savior's commission by the heavenly Assembly, his descent to earth, his encounter with the worldly powers and apparent crucifixion, and his return to the Pleroma. To this story of the Savior are added an exhortation to the Savior's followers and a promise of future blessedness. As the Savior says to the Gnostic believers at the close of his discourse, "Rest then with me, my fellow spirits and my brothers, for ever."

There is no doubt that the *Second Treatise of the Great Seth* is a work that is both Christian and Gnostic. On the one hand, Christian elements are tightly woven into the fabric of the treatise. The tractate accepts the New Testament or parts of it, and claims to be the revelation of Jesus Christ. Furthermore, the crucifixion figures prominently in the tractate; in fact, it is described in three separate scenes within the tractate. On the other hand, the *Second Treatise of the Great Seth* is also clearly Gnostic: knowledge is the means of salvation. The God of this world is evil and ignorant, and can be identified with the God of the Old Testament; in addition, all his minions are mere counterfeits and laughingstocks. The interpretation of the crucifixion is that of the Gnostic Basilides as presented by the heresiologist Irenaeus: Simon of Cyrene is crucified in the place of the laughing Jesus.

The purpose for which the *Second Treatise of the Great Seth* was writ-

*Introduction by Joseph A. Gibbons.

ten is plainly polemical. The entire first part (49, 10–59, 18) describes the true history of Jesus Christ and emphasizes, over against orthodox Christianity, his docetic passion. The second part of the tractate (59, 19–70, 10) is a refutation of orthodoxy's claim to be the true church. Despite the trials and persecutions apparently instigated by the orthodox church, by those ignorant and imitative persons "who think that they are advancing the name of Christ," the Gnostic believers will enjoy true brotherhood on earth, and bliss in the joy and union of eternal life.

THE SECOND TREATISE OF THE GREAT SETH*

And the perfect Majesty is at rest in the ineffable light, in the truth of the mother of all these, and all of you that attain to me, to me alone who am perfect, because of the Word. For I exist with all the greatness of the Spirit, which is a friend to us and our kindred alike, since I brought forth a word to the glory of our Father, through his goodness, as well as an imperishable thought; that is, the Word within him—it is slavery that we shall die with Christ—and an imperishable and undefiled thought, an incomprehensible marvel, the writing of the ineffable water which is the word from us. It is I who am in you, and you are in me, just as the Father is in you in innocence.

Let us gather an assembly together. Let us visit that creation of his. Let us send someone forth in it, just as he visited the Ennoias, the regions below. And I said these things to the whole multitude of the multitudinous assembly of the rejoicing Majesty. The whole house of the Father of Truth rejoiced that I am the one who is from them. I produced thought about the Ennoias which came out of the undefiled Spirit, about the descent upon the water, that is, the regions below. And they all had a single mind, since it is

*Codex VII 49, 10–70, 12. Translated by Roger A. Bullard; edited by Frederik Wisse. From James M. Robinson, ed., *The Nag Hammadi Library* (San Francisco: Harper & Row, 1977), pp. 329–338.

out of one. They charged me since I was willing. I came forth to reveal the glory to my kindred and my fellow spirits.

For those who were in the world had been prepared by the will of our sister Sophia—she who is a whore—because of the innocence which has not been uttered. And she did not ask anything from the All, nor from the greatness of the Assembly, nor from the Pleroma. Since she was first she came forth to prepare Monads and places of the Son of Light, and the fellow workers which she took from the elements below to build bodily dwellings from them. But having come into being in an empty glory, they ended in destruction in the dwellings in which they were, since they were prepared by Sophia. They stand ready to receive the life-giving word of the ineffable Monad and of the greatness of the assembly of all those who persevere and those who are in me.

I visited a bodily dwelling. I cast out the one who was in it first, and I went in. And the whole multitude of the Archons became troubled. And all the matter of the Archons as well as all the begotten powers of the earth were shaken when it saw the likeness of the Image, since it was mixed. And I am the one who was in it, not resembling him who was in it first. For he was an earthly man, but I, I am from above the heavens. I did not refuse them even to become a Christ, but I did not reveal myself to them in the love which was coming forth from me. I revealed that I am a stranger to the regions below.

There was a great disturbance in the whole earthly area with confusion and flight, as well as in the plan of the Archons. And some were persuaded, when they saw the wonders which were being accomplished by me. And all these, with the race that came down, flee from him who had fled from the throne to the Sophia of hope since she had earlier given the sign concerning us and all the ones with me—those of the race of Adonaios. Others also fled, as if from the Cosmocrator and those with him, since they have brought every kind of punishment upon me. And there was a flight of their mind about what they would counsel concerning me, thinking that Sophia is the whole greatness, and speaking false witness, moreover, against the Man and the whole greatness of the assembly. It was not possible for them to know who the Father of Truth, the Man of the Greatness, is. But they who received the name because of contact with ignorance —which is a burning and a vessel—having created it to destroy Adam whom they had made, in order to cover up those who are theirs in the same way. But they, the Archons, those of the place of Ialdabaoth, reveal the realm of the angels, which humanity was seeking in order that they may not know the Man of Truth. For Adam, whom they had formed, appeared to them. And a fearful motion came about throughout their entire dwelling lest the angels surrounding them rebel. For without those who were offering praise, I did not really die lest their archangel become empty.

And then a voice—of the Cosmocrator —came to the angels. "I am God and there is no other beside me." But I laughed joyfully when I examined his empty glory. But he went on to say, "Who is man?" And the entire host of his angels who had seen Adam and his dwelling were laughing at his smallness. And thus did their Ennoia come to be removed outside the Majesty of the heavens, i.e., the Man of Truth, whose name they saw since he is in a small dwelling place, since they are small (and) senseless in their empty Ennoia, namely their laughter. It was contagion for them.

The whole greatness of the Fatherhood of the Spirit was at rest in his places. And I am he who was with him, since I have an Ennoia of a single emanation from the eternal ones and the undefiled and immeasurable incomprehensibilities. I placed the small Ennoia in the world, having disturbed them and frightened the whole multitude of the angels and their ruler. And I was visiting them all with fire and flame because of my Ennoia. And everything pertaining to them was brought about because of me. And there came about a disturbance and a fight around the seraphim and cherubim, since their glory will fade, and the confusion around Adonaios on both sides and their dwelling—to the Cosmocrator and him who said, "Let us seize him"; others again, "The plan will certainly not materialize." For Adonaios knows me because of hope. And I was in the mouths of lions. And the plan which they devised about me to release their error and their senselessness—I did not succumb to them as they had planned. But I was not afflicted at all. Those who were there punished me. And I did not die in reality but in appearance, lest I be put to shame by them because these are my kinsfolk. I removed the shame from me and I did not become fainthearted in the face of what happened to me at their hands. I was about to succumb to fear, and I suffered according to their sight and thought in order that they may never find any word to speak about them. For my death which they think happened, happened to them in their error and blindness, since they nailed their man unto their death. For their Ennoias did not see me, for they were deaf and blind. But in doing these things, they condemn themselves. Yes, they saw me; they punished me. It was another, their father, who drank the gall and the vinegar; it was not I. They struck me with the reed; it was another, Simon, who bore the cross on his shoulder. It was another upon whom they placed the crown of thorns. But I was rejoicing in the height over all the wealth of the Archons and the offspring of their error, of their empty glory. And I was laughing at their ignorance.

And I subjected all their powers. For, as I came downward, no one saw me. For I was altering my shapes, changing from form to form. And therefore, when I was at their gates I assumed their likeness. For I passed them by quietly, and I was viewing the places, and I was not afraid nor ashamed, for I was undefiled. And I was speaking with them, mingling with them through those who are mine, and trampling on those who are harsh to them with zeal, and quenching the flame. And I was doing all these things because of my desire to accomplish what I desired by the will of the Father above.

And the Son of the Majesty, who was hidden in the region below, we brought to the height where I was in all these aeons with them, which height no one has seen nor known, where the wedding of the wedding robe is, the new one and not the old, nor does it perish. For it is a new and perfect bridal chamber of the heavens, as I have revealed that there are three ways: an undefiled mystery in a spirit of this aeon, which does not perish, nor is it fragmentary, nor able to be spoken of; rather, it is undivided, universal, and permanent. For the soul, the one from the height, will not speak about the error which is here, nor transfer from these aeons since it will be transferred when it becomes free and when it is endowed with nobility in the world, standing before the Father without weariness and fear, always mixed with the *nous* of power and of form. They will see me from every side without hatred. For since they see me, they are being seen and are mixed with them. Since they did not put me to shame, they were not put to

shame. Since they were not afraid before me, they will pass by every gate without fear and will be perfected in the third glory.

It was my going to the revealed height which the world did not accept, my third baptism in a revealed image. When they had fled from the fire of the seven Authorities, and the sun of the powers of the Archons set, darkness took them. And the world became poor when he was restrained with a multitude of fetters. They nailed him to the tree, and they fixed him with four nails of brass. The veil of his temple he tore with his hands. It was a trembling which seized the chaos of the earth, for the souls which were in the sleep below were released. And they arose. They went about boldly, having shed zealous service of ignorance and unlearnedness beside the dead tombs, having put on the new man, since they have come to know that perfect Blessed One of the eternal and incomprehensible Father and the infinite light, which is I, since I came to my own and united them with myself. There is no need for many words, for our Ennoia was with their Ennoia. Therefore they knew what I speak of, for we took counsel about the destruction of the Archons. And therefore I did the will of the Father, who is I.

After we went forth from our home, and came down to this world, and came into being in the world in bodies, we were hated and persecuted, not only by those who are ignorant, but also by those who think that they are advancing the name of Christ, since they were unknowingly empty, not knowing who they are, like dumb animals. They persecuted those who have been liberated by me, since they hate them—those who, should they shut their mouth, would weep with a profitless groaning because they did not fully know me. Instead, they served two masters, even a multitude. But you will become victorious in everything, in war and battles, jealous

division and wrath. But in the uprightness of our love we are innocent, pure,
and good, since we have a mind of the
Father in an ineffable mystery.

For it was ludicrous. It is I who bear
witness that it was ludicrous, since the
Archons do not know that it is an ineffable union of undefiled truth, as exists
among the sons of light, of which they
made an imitation, having proclaimed a
doctrine of a dead man and lies so as to
resemble the freedom and purity of the
perfect assembly and joining themselves
with their doctrine to fear and slavery,
worldly cares, and abandoned worship,
being small and ignorant since they do
not contain the nobility of the truth, for
they hate the one in whom they are, and
love the one in whom they are not. For
they did not know the knowledge of the
greatness, that it is from above and from
a fountain of truth, and that it is not from
slavery and jealousy, fear and love of
worldly matter. For that which is not
theirs and that which is theirs they use
fearlessly and freely. They do not desire
because they have authority, and they
have a law from themselves over whatever they will wish.

But those who have not are poor, that
is, those who do not possess him. And
they desire him and lead astray those
who, through them, have become like
those who possess the truth of their freedom, just as they bought us for servitude
and constraint of care and fear. This person is in slavery. And he who is brought
by constraint of force and threat has been
guarded by God. But the entire nobility
of the Fatherhood is not guarded, since
he guards only him who is from him,
without word and constraint, since he is
united with his will he who belongs only
to the Ennoia of the Fatherhood, to make
it perfect and ineffable through the living
water, to be with you mutually in wisdom, not only in word of hearing but in
deed and fulfilled word. For the perfect
ones are worthy to be established in this
way and to be united with me, in order

that they may not share in any enmity,
in a good friendship. I accomplish everything through the Good One, for this is
the union of the truth, that they should
have no adversary. But everyone who
brings division—and he will learn no
wisdom at all because he brings division
and is not a friend—is hostile to them all.
But he who lives in harmony and friendship of brotherly love, naturally and not
artificially, completely and not partially,
this person is truly the desire of the Father. He is the universal one and perfect
love.

For Adam was a laughingstock, since
he was made a counterfeit type of man
by the Hebdomad, as if he had become
stronger than I and my brothers. We are
innocent with respect to him, since we
have not sinned. And Abraham and
Isaac and Jacob were a laughingstock,
since they, the counterfeit fathers, were
given a name by the Hebdomad, as if he
had become stronger than I and my
brothers. We are innocent with respect to
him, since we have not sinned. David
was a laughingstock in that his son was
named the Son of Man, having been influenced by the Hebdomad, as if he had
become stronger than I and the fellow
members of my race. But we are innocent with respect to him; we have not
sinned. Solomon was a laughingstock,
since he thought that he was Christ, having become vain through the Hebdomad,
as if he had become stronger than I and
my brothers. But we are innocent with
respect to him. I have not sinned. The
twelve prophets were laughingstocks,
since they have come forth as imitations
of the true prophets. They came into being as counterfeits through the Hebdomad, as if he had become stronger
than I and my brothers. But we are innocent with respect to him, since we have
not sinned. Moses, a faithful servant,
was a laughingstock, having been named
"the Friend," since they perversely bore
witness concerning him who never knew
me. Neither he nor those before him,

from Adam to Moses and John the Baptist, none of them knew me nor my brothers.

For they had a doctrine of angels to observe dietary laws and bitter slavery, since they never knew truth, nor will they know it. For there is a great deception upon their soul making it impossible for them ever to find a *nous* of freedom in order to know him, until they come to know the Son of Man. Now concerning my Father, I am he whom the world did not know, and because of this, the world rose up against me and my brothers. But we are innocent with respect to him; we have not sinned.

For the Archon was a laughingstock because he said, "I am God, and there is none greater than I. I alone am the Father, the Lord, and there is no other beside me. I am a jealous God, who brings the sins of the fathers upon the children for three and four generations." As if he had become stronger than I and my brothers! But we are innocent with respect to him, in that we have not sinned, since we mastered his teaching. Thus he was in an empty glory. And he does not agree with our Father. And thus through our fellowship we grasped his teaching, since he was vain in an empty glory. And he does not agree with our Father, for he was a laughingstock and judgment and false prophecy.

O those who do not see, you do not see your blindness, i.e., this which was not known, nor has it ever been known, nor has it been known about him. They did not listen to firm obedience. Therefore they proceeded in a judgment of error, and they raised their defiled and murderous hands against him as if they were beating the air. And the senseless and blind ones are always senseless, always being slaves of law and earthly fear.

I am Christ, the Son of Man, the one from you who is among you. I am despised for your sake, in order that you yourselves may forget the difference.

And do not become female, lest you give birth to evil and its brothers: jealousy and division, anger and wrath, fear and a divided heart, and empty, nonexistent desire. But I am an ineffable mystery to you.

Then before the foundation of the world, when the whole multitude of the assembly came together upon the places of the Ogdoad, when they had taken counsel about a spiritual wedding which is in union, and thus he was perfected in the ineffable places by a living word, the undefiled wedding was consummated through the Mesotes of Jesus, who inhabits them all and possesses them, who abides in an undivided love of power. And surrounding him, he appears to him as a monad of all these, a thought and a father, since he is one. And he stands by them all, since he as a whole came forth alone. And he is life, since he came from the Father of ineffable and perfect truth, the father of those who are there, the union of peace and a friend of good things, and life eternal and undefiled joy, in a great harmony of life and faith, through eternal life of fatherhood and motherhood and sisterhood and rational wisdom. They had agreed with *nous*, who stretches out and will stretch out in joyful union and is trustworthy and faithfully listens to someone. And he is in fatherhood and motherhood and rational brotherhood and wisdom. And this is a wedding of truth, and a repose of incorruption, in a spirit of truth, in every mind, and a perfect light in an unnameable mystery. But this is not, nor will it happen among us in any region or place in division and breach of peace, but in union and a mixture of love, all of which are pefected in the one who is.

It also happened in the places under heaven for their reconciliation. Those who knew me in salvation and undividedness, and those who existed for the glory of the father and the truth, having been separated, blended into the One through the living word. And I am in the spirit and the truth of the motherhood, just as he has been there; I was among those who are united in the friendship of friends forever, who neither know hostility at all, nor evil, but who are united by my knowledge in word and peace, which exists in perfection with everyone and in them all. And those who assumed the form of my type will assume the form of my word. Indeed, these will come forth in light forever, and in friendship with each other in the spirit, since they have known in every respect and indivisibly that what is is One. And all of these are one. And thus they will learn about the One, as did the assembly and those dwelling in it. For the father of all these exists, being immeasurable and immutable: *nous* and word and division and envy and fire. And he is entirely one, being the All with them all in a single doctrine because all these are from a single spirit. O unseeing ones, why did you not know the mystery rightly?

But the Archons around Ialdabaoth were disobedient because of the Ennoia who went down to him from her sister Sophia. They made for themselves a union with those who were with them in a mixture of a fiery cloud, which was their envy, and the rest who were brought forth by their creatures, as if they had bruised the noble pleasure of the assembly. And therefore they revealed a mixture of ignorance in a counterfeit of fire and earth and a murderer, since they are small and untaught, without knowledge having dared these things, and not having understood that light has fellowship with light, and darkness, with darkness, and the corruptible with the perishable, and the imperishable with the incorruptible.

Now these things I have presented to you—I am Jesus Christ, the Son of Man, who is exalted above the heavens, O perfect and incorruptible ones, because of the incorruptible and perfect mystery and the ineffable one. But they think that we decreed them before the foundation of the world in order that when we emerge from the places of the world, we may present there the symbols of incorruption from the spiritual union unto knowledge. You do not know it because the fleshly cloud overshadows you. But I alone am the friend of Sophia. I have been in the bosom of the Father from the beginning, in the place of the sons of the truth, and the Greatness. Rest then with me, my fellow spirits and my brothers, forever.

Creation of the World and the Alien Man

(Mandaean Gnosticism)

The Mandaeans are the sole Gnostic sect to survive into our times. Living in southern Iran and southern Iraq, about fourteen thousand to fifteen thousand Mandaeans still inhabit villages near the Tigris and the Euphrates. They have remained relatively untouched by other cultures, although today, as E. S. Drower has written,[1] modernity threatens to remove them from their religious traditions. Yet as recently as shortly after World War I, Lady Drower was able to obtain a handwritten Mandaean prayerbook of 238 pages from an old silversmith. This prayerbook contained canonical prayers used for many centuries, repeating magical texts and secret doctrines from their beginnings in the first centuries A.D. Drower writes:

> That an ancient gnostic sect should have survived into our time is remarkable: that so many of their writings, their magical texts, their secret doctrine in the ritual scrolls and their liturgical literature has been preserved, is little short of a miracle.[2]

These writings, largely concerned with the fundamental human experience of man and woman being in an alien world, estranged from the true World, in life exiled from Life, in light exiled from Light, are poetic documents, with no particular order or consistent system. Their chief holy book is the *Ginza Rabba* (Great Treasure). As Hans Jonas has noted:

> [O]wing to their geographical and social remoteness from Hellenistic influence the Mandaeans were less exposed than most to the temptation to assimilate the expression of their ideas to Western intellectual conventions. In their writings mythological fantasy

abounds, the compactness of its imagery unattenuated by any ambition toward conceptualization, its variety unchecked by care for consistency and system.[3]

Originally, the Mandaeans were an eastern offshoot of Gnostics who came from a background of heterodox Jewish sects in eastern Syria and Palestine. They called themselves "Nazorenes," meanings "Observers." In the Mandaean language, an eastern Aramaic dialect akin to the Aramaic used in the Babylonian Talmud, "Mandaean" means "Gnostic." The group passed into southern Mesopotamia probably as early as the third century A.D. They were a syncretizing religion, reconciling elements of Jewish, Christian, and Gnostic traditions. Werner Foerster observes, "One may indeed say that here gnosis has been grafted on to an old branch of the cultic community of unorthodox Jewry."[4] Baptism was essential and, as Foerster states, "by immersion in the Jordan, [the neophite] enters into close communion (laufa) with the World of Light, thus receiving a share of salvation, and secondly receives an (outer and inner) purification from transgressions and sin."[5]

Like other Gnostic groups they regarded the world as a dualistic scheme, with an acosmic godhead and his Aeons pitted against the Creator God, the Demiurge, the cosmic God of matter, time, and our alien world. While the biblical God in most of the sects is completely evil, ignorant of his errors, and fiendish—in the *Apocryphon of John* the Demiurge is "the abortion of darkness"—for the Mandaeans he is simply a depraved creature of light who will be forgiven and will return to the Realm of Light.

But the emphasis in the Mandaean poems is less on the rival gods and more on human exile. To live in this world is to endure the anguish and terror of separation from the King of Light. The very creation of the world and of human life dispersed particles of light into the darkness of matter. Salvation lies in gathering in the dispersed light and restoring it to the original unity. So life is a falling into darkness and the inhabitants of earthly bodies are forlorn and homesick for the other Life. "How shall I sink within all the worlds";[6] "Who has carried me into captivity away from my place and my abode, from the household of my parents who brought me up?";[7] "Why did you carry me away from my abode into captivity and cast me into the stinking body?"[8]

Life therefore is, as Jonas points out, a numbness, a sleep, a drunkenness, an oblivion.[9] In Gnostic thought the world takes the place of the traditional underworld. And our ignorance is a form of unconsciousness, an infection of the darkness from which we are "awakened" or "called." Knowledge will save us. Knowledge protects the spirit against sexual love and sensual pleasures and other seductions of this world. Jonas writes:

> The ignorance of drunkenness is the soul's ignorance of itself, its origin, and its situation in the alien world: it is precisely the awareness of alienness which the intoxication is meant to suppress; man drawn into the whirlpool and made oblivious of his true being is to be made one of the children of this world. This is the avowed pur-

pose of the powers of the world in proffering their wine and holding their "feast." The drunkenness of ignorance is opposed by the "sobriety" of knowledge, a religious formula sometimes intensified to the paradox of "sober drunkenness."[10]

The sleep of Adam in the Garden becomes a symbol of the human condition on earth. The alien man or woman waits for the call, amid the noise of this world, to wake and to return. Jorge Luis Borges has always been obsessed with the Gnostics and with *el otro*, "the other." Although the Argentine looks for no ultimate redemption, no "call," he shares with the Mandaeans and all Gnostic sects the total challenge to all conventional theological values. Whether he or the Gnostics are right about that other World, they each travel a similar way of personal self-knowledge outrageous to the noisy world. Borges dualistically divides himself into "Borges and I" and sides with the "I." Likewise the Mandaean Gnostics, forlorn in their "stinking bodies," seek illumination for their alien selves. Despite the low value given to the human body, which is debased matter, the Mandaeans were not, however, in contrast to other sects, strongly ascetic. Indeed, they emphasized fertility, which, along with isolation, may have been a factor in their extraordinary survival.

Notes

1. E. S. Drower, *The Canonical Prayerbook of the Mandaeans* (Leiden: E. J. Brill, 1959), p. viii.
2. Drower, *The Canonical Prayerbook*, p. viii.
3. Hans Jonas, *The Gnostic Religion*, 2d ed., rev. (1958; reprint, Boston: Beacon Press, 1970), p. 48.
4. Werner Foerster, ed., R. McL. Wilson, trans., *Gnosis: A Selection of Gnostic Texts*, vol. 2 (Oxford: Oxford Univ. Press, 1974), p. 139.
5. Foerster, *Gnosis*, p. 132.
6. Hans Jonas, *The Gnostic Religion*, p. 63.
7. Hans Jonas, *The Gnostic Religion*, p. 63.
8. Hans Jonas, *The Gnostic Religion*, p. 63.
9. Hans Jonas, *The Gnostic Religion*, p. 68.
10. Hans Jonas, *The Gnostic Religion*, p. 71.

THE WORLD BEYOND*

Before all the worlds came into being,
there was [or: came into being] this great fruit.
When the great fruit was (or: came into being) in the great fruit, the great King of
    Light came into existence.
From the great and glorious King of Light
the great ether of radiance came into being.

*All selections in this chapter are from Werner Foerster, ed., R. McL. Wilson, trans., *Gnosis: A Selection of Gnostic Texts*, vol. 2 (Oxford: Oxford University Press, 1974), pp. 156, 163–164, 165, 170–179, 187–192.

From the great ether of radiance
the living fire was brought into being.
From the living fire
the light came into being.
By the power of the King of Light
life was brought into being and the great fruit.

The great fruit was brought into being,
and in it the Jordan was brought into being.
The great Jordan was brought into being,
there came into being the living water.
The radiant and resplendent water was brought into being and from the living
    water, I, the Life,
was brought into being.
I, the Life, was brought into being,
and then all the uthras were brought into being.

THE WORLD OF DARKNESS

When I stood in the House of Life,
I beheld the rebellious.
I beheld the gates of darkness,
I beheld the depths full of darkness.
I beheld the destructive
and the lords of the gloomy abode.
I beheld the warriors,
who are buried in darkness.
I beheld the gates of fire,
how they burn and glow.
The wicked burn and glow
and deliberate on imperfection and deficiency.
I beheld Hewath the female,
how she speaks in the darkness and malice.
She speaks in malice,
in witchcraft, and sorcery, which she practices.
She speaks with illusory wisdom
and sits enthroned in falsehood.
I beheld the gate of darkness
and the arteries[1] of the earth Siniawis, just as they are there.
I beheld the black water in it,
which rose up, boiled, and bubbled.
Whoever enters there dies,
and whoever beholds it is scorched.
I beheld the dragons,
who were hurled there and writhe about.
I beheld dragons
of every type and every kind.
I beheld the chariots of the sons of darkness,

which do not resemble one another.
I beheld the wicked rebels,
as they are seated in their chariots.
I beheld the wicked rebels,
how they are arrayed with weapons of evil.
They are arrayed in weapons of evil
and plot evil against the Place of Light.

There is no boundary for the light
and it was not known when it came into being.
Nothing was when light was not,
nothing was when radiance was not.
Nothing was when the Mighty Life was not;
there never was a boundary for the light.
Nothing was when the water was not;
the water is prior to the darkness.
Prior to the darkness is the water:
there is nothing without an end.[2]
There is no number of which we could say,
how great it was before the uthras came into being.
The uthras are prior to the darkness,
prior to the darkness are the uthras and more ancient than its inhabitants.
Goodness is prior
to the malice of the Place of Darkness.
Gentleness is prior
to the bitterness of the Place of Darkness.
The living fire is prior
to the consuming fire of the Place of Darkness.
Praise is prior
to sorcery and witchcraft, which the wicked practice.
The third jordan is prior
to the flowing water of the Place of Darkness.
Perception (or: instruction in the faith) is prior
to this or that, which the wicked of the Place of Darkness practice.
The call of the uthras is prior
to that of the powerful wicked ones of the Place of Darkness.
The throne of rest is prior
to the throne of rebellion.
Hymns and recitations (or: books) are prior
to the sorcery of Hewath, the terrible woman.

COSMOGONY

Then the Second[3] was established,
and his uthras rose up and gave him advice.
His uthras rose up and gave him advice
and spoke to him:
"Grant us to call forth a world and establish skinas

127

for you, which shall be named as yours."
And the Second gave them some of his radiance and his light
and some of that which the Life gave him.
He gave them some of his radiance
and ordered them to call forth a world.
The sons of the Second arose,
they went and descended to the Place of Darkness.
They called forth Ptahil-Uthra,
they called him forth and set him in his place.
They called forth the "sons of perfection"
and set them on their thrones.
They called forth and created the skinas
and created uthras in them.
They arrived at the streams,
they saw and beheld the Place of Darkness.
B'haq-Ziwa shone by himself,
and he held himself to be a mighty one.
He held himself to be a mighty one
and abandoned the name that his father had called him by.
And he spoke:
"I am the father of the uthras."[4]
The father of the uthras am I,
I made skinas for the uthras.'
He pondered over the turbid water
and said: 'I shall call forth a world.'
He took no advice
and did not perceive the turbid water.

He called Ptahil-Uthra,
embraced him, and kissed him like a mighty one.
He bestowed names on him,
which are hidden and protected in their place.
He gave him the name "Gabriel, the Messenger,"[5]
he called him, gave command, and spoke to him:
"Arise, go, descend
to the place where there are no skinas or worlds.
Call forth and create a world for yourself,
just like the sons of perfection, whom you saw.
Set up and establish a world,
establish a world for yourself and make uthras in it."
The father of the uthras in his greatness told him
nothing about the adversaries,
he neither armed him nor instructed him.
Ptahil-Uthra rose up,
he went out and descended below the skinas,
to the place where there is no world.
He trod in the filthy mud,
he entered the turbid water.
He spoke with his voice,
as the living fire in him changed.[6]

When the living fire in him changed, he was troubled in his heart and said:
"Since I am a son of the Great One,[7]
why has the living fire in me changed?"
When Ptahil said this,
Ruha took heart.
Ruha took heart,
she herself became arrogant.
She spoke: "His radiance has changed,
his radiance has become deficient and imperfect."
She arose, destroyed her property,
and clothed herself in a capacious robe.
She changed her spirit into arrogance,[8]
she conducted herself, as she was not.
She spoke to the warrior,[9]
the foolish one who has no sense or understanding.
She spoke to him:
"Arise, see how the radiance of the alien Man has diminished,
how his radiance has become deficient and imperfect.
Arise, sleep with your mother,
and you will be released from the chain which binds you,
which is stronger than all the world."
When the evil one[10] heard this
he trembled in his bones.
He slept with Ruha,
and she conceived seven forms by the *one* act.
After seven days she was in labor
and brought forth the despicable ones.
She gave birth to the Seven Planets
from which seven forms emanated.
When she caught sight of them,
her heart fell down from its support.
Ptahil washed his hands in the turbid water
and spoke:
"May an earth come into being
as it did in the house of the mighty ones."
When he immersed his hands
a solidification took place.
A solidification took place,
which was thrown down and ran here and there,
as though there were no solidification.
When no earth came into being and solidified,
his heart was torn with discord.
When his heart was torn with discord,
Ruha again took heart,
and she spoke:
"I will get up and destroy my property,
I will go to the king of the world."
She spoke to him:
"Rise, great monster, rise,
behold, the whole world is yours!"

"I am your sister!
If you sleep with me,
your strength shall be doubled."
When he slept with her,
she conceived twelve monsters by the *one* act.
She conceived twelve monsters by him,
none of which was good for anything.
After twelve days
Ruha was in travail.
She was in labor and gave birth to twelve forms,
none of which resembled any other.
They did not resemble one another,
and each one rose on the other's lap.

Ptahil stood engrossed in thought,
engrossed in thought Ptahil stood and cried;
"I shall leave the world."
When Ruha heard,
her heart righted itself again on its support,
and she spoke:
"The alien is no match for me,
the alien has no more power in the world."

She prepared to go, destroyed her property,
and went to the source[11] of the Place of Darkness.
She spoke to the base warrior,
who is without hands and feet:
"Rise, my father, behold:
I am your daughter!
Embrace me, kiss me,
and sleep with me."

He kissed her and slept with her,
and she became pregnant by him.
She conceived five scoundrels by him,
who disavowed one another.
They disavowed one another
and practiced anything that was unworthy and ugly.
She was in labor and gave birth to five forms,[12]
none of which resembled any other.
None resembled the other,
and they stumbled over one another.
Through them imperfection came into being
with which the worlds are unable to cope.

Ptahil pondered in his mind
he conferred in his wisdom and said:
"I shall get ready, fall at the feet of the Life,
and cast myself before the Great Life.
I long to put on a clothing of living fire,
and walk in the turbid water.
in the turbid water I shall walk
and indicate all that shall take place."

130

When Ptahil in the wisdom which he devised,
had fallen down and praised the Life,
he received a garment of living fire
and walked in the turbid water.
When the living fire intermingled
with the turbid water,
at the aroma of the clothing of living fire
dust ascended from the earth Siniawis.
Dust flew up from the earth Siniawis
and dispersed in all directions.
All the seas were stopped up,
and all the mines were filled.
Dryness came into being,
and solidification took place and fell into the water.
A curtain was raised,
ascended, and was installed in the heart of the sky.
When the firmament was spanned out
Ptahil fell down and praised the man, his planter.
When he saw the lofty throne,[13]
he rejoiced, and his heart was glad.
He seized the navel of the earth
and tried to bind it to the heart of the sky.
When he attempted to seize the navel of the earth
the "perishable ones"[14] surrounded him.
The basket of the cunning ones surrounded him.
which is full of false "wisdom."
It is full of delusions,
and redolent of false "wisdom."
How full it is of delusions,
a woman's market-basket of witchcraft!
The seven Planets encircled him
and the twelve good-for-nothing monsters.
Atarpan and Lufan encircled him,
the two princes of the world,
Urpel and Marpel,
who have dominion over anger in the Tibil.
They encircled the great dragon,
ascended, and were installed in the vault.
When he seized the navel of the earth,
took it up, and pinned it to the vault,
when he seized the lofty circle of the firmament,
took it up, and fixed it to his throne,
then the seven Planets were bound,
they ascended, and took their place in the vault.
The twelve monsters took up position;
they were bound in their thongs.
As for their five leaders,
they wailed: "Alas, alas."
Ptahil sits there in his wisdom
and asks them severally:
"Where do you come from, you wicked,

you whose form is not from the father's house?"
When he said this to them,
Ruha[15] answered him from below:
"We come wishing to be your servants,
we would approach and be your helpers.
We would be your helpers in everything you do,
and leave you on your throne in peace.
On your throne we would leave you in peace,
we would approach and maintain order in the world.
We would be good
and be completely devoted to you."
When the seven planets had thus spoken
he said to them: "You are my sons!
If you perform good deeds
then I will reckon you on my side!"
When Ptahil said this,
his house[16] was taken (away) from him.
His house was taken from him,
and the "perishable ones" gained dominion over it,
as before the firmament was spanned out
and the earth had become compact by solidification.

When Ptahil spoke thus,
Ruha searched into her "wisdom" and said:
"I shall call forth hmurthas and astartes,
who shall be my children in the world.
The planets and their demons
shall rise up in opposition.
The monsters and devs shall rise up[17]
and we shall disorganize the whole world.
The five masters of the house
shall rise up and wage war."
When Ptahil beheld them,
he shone in his wisdom.
He clenched his fist
and beat upon the forecourts of his breast
and said:
"Before I enter the father's house,
I shall appoint a master over this world.
The masters of the house do not know
that this world has a master."[18]

When I, Ptahil, was formed and came into being,
I came into being from the source of the great radiance.
When my father considered and called me forth,
he called me forth from the source of radiance.
He clothed me in a robe of radiance
and wrapped me in a covering of light.
he gave me a great crown
by whose radiance the worlds shine.
He spoke:
"O son, arise, go and betake yourself to the Tibil earth

and make a solidification in the black waters.
Solidify the Tibil earth
and disperse jordans and canals in it."

I set off and came
as far as the boundary of the Tibil earth.
My eyes were filled with black waters.[19]
Up to my knees I stood in the waters,
but the waters did not solidify.
Up to my thighs I stood in the waters,
but the waters did not solidify.
Up to my first mouth[20] I stood in the waters,
but the waters did not solidify.
Up to my last mouth I stood in the waters,
but the waters did not solidify.
I pronounced the name of the Life and of Manda d'Haiye[21] over the waters,
but the waters did not solidify.
Some of the seven garments of radiance, light, and glory,
which my father gave to me, I cast upon the waters,
but the waters did not solidify.

I rose up out of the black waters
and presented myself before Abathur.
I went to my father Abathur,
to speak to him about the mysteries of this world.
When Abathur saw me,
he questioned me.
He said:
"The world which you called forth, what is it like,
and your works, how have you set them up in it?"
Then I answered my father and said:
"You sent me to the world, a foul stench,
which has no ray of light,
to the waters, which consume each other,
and will not accept the name of the Life."

When I had thus spoken to my father Abathur,
he rose up to pray and to praise.
To pray and to praise he rose up,
he prostrated himself and rendered full praise to the Life.
He ascended to the Life, his father,
to speak to him concerning the works of this world.
He called[22] Hibil-Ziwa
and sent him to the flank of the stallion,[23]
and from him he took the solidification.
The solidification he took from him,
he came and gave it to Abathur.
Abathur wrapped it up in his pure wrapping,[24]
he brought it to his son Ptahil and gave it to him.
He spoke to him:
"Go, solidify the Tibil earth
and span out the firmament in perfection."

I rose up from my father Abathur,
and arrived at the boundaries of the Tibil earth.
I cast the solidification, which my father gave to me,
upon the waters, and the waters solidified.

By my [Ptahil's] first cry I solidified the earth
and spanned out the firmament in perfection.
By my second cry I dispersed jordans and canals in it.
By my third cry I called forth the fish of the sea
and feathered birds of every type and variety.
By my fourth cry I made all the plants and seeds,
every single one different from each other.
By my fifth cry evil reptiles came into being.
By my sixth cry the whole structure of darkness came into being.
By my seventh cry came into being
Ruha and her seven sons.
Ruha and her seven sons came into being,
they came and presented themselves before me.
When I beheld them
my heart fell down from its support.

THE CREATION OF MAN

When Ptahil came and said to the[25] planets: "Let us create Adam that he may be king of the world," when he had thus spoken to them, they all conferred together: "We shall tell him that we want to create Adam and Eve,[26] because he belongs to us." They said to him: "Come now, we will create Adam and Eve, the head of the whole family." When the planets spoke thus to him Ptahil was grieved in his heart and said: "If I by myself create Adam and Eve, the head of the whole family, what will Adam then do in the world?" Ptahil-Uthra spoke to the planets and said: "What do we confide in and rely on, and what is our authority in the world?" Ptahil answered and said to them: "You shall be his guardians and render him full service."

They created Adam and laid him down
but there was no soul in him.[27]
When they created Adam
they were unable to cast a soul into him.
They appealed to the ether wind,
that it might hollow out his bones.
That it might hollow out his bones,
and marrow be formed in them.
That marrow be formed in them,
that he might become strong and stand on his feet.
They summoned the splendor of the living fire,
that it might illuminate his raiment.
That it might illuminate his raiment,
and he become strong and stand on his feet.

They summoned the vapors of the streams
and the fumes of the consuming fire,
that they might enter into his trunk.
That he might clench his fists
and beat with his wings [arms].
That he might make a noise in anger and shake himself,
and that he might become strong and stand on his feet.
The Planets gave utterance
and spoke to Ptahil:
"Grant us, that we may cast into him some of the spirit [ruha]
which you brought with you from the father's house."
All the planets exerted themselves,
and the lord of the world[28] exerted himself.
Despite their exertions,
they could not set him on his feet.
Ptahil went in his illumination
and ascended to the Place of Light.
He entered the presence of the "father of the uthras,"
and his father said to him: "What have you accomplished?"
He answered him:
"Everything that I formerly made has been successful,
but my counterpart and yours has not been successful."
The "father of the uthras" raised himself up,
went forth, and hastened to the secret place.
He fetched the great Mana,[29]
that he might illuminate all corruptible things;
that he might illuminate the coat of the body[30]
of every type and variety.
He wrapped him in his pure turban
under invocation of the name which the Life gave to him.
He grasped him by the ends of his turban,
brought him hither, and gave him to Ptahil, his son.
When he had given him to Ptahil-Uthra,
the Life summoned the helpers.
He summoned Hibil, Sitil, and Anos,
the uthras, who are outstanding and without defect.
He summoned them and gave them their orders,
and issued warnings[31] to them concerning the souls.
He said to them:
"You, be a guardian over them,
so that all the worlds may know nothing about them.
Let not the wicked Ptahil know
how the soul falls into the body,
How the soul falls into the body
and how the blood speaks in it.[32]
How the blood in it speaks
and how the channels [veins] permeate it.
The supporter of Adakas-Mana,
let him be its[33] protector.
When Adam is clothed in the radiance of life,

shows stability and stands on his feet,
When he speaks with a pure mouth
you[34] restore him to his place once more.
Restore him to his place once more
and protect him against all and sundry."
Ptahil enveloped him in his pure turban,
he wrapped[35] him in his garment.
The uthra hastens and goes down
and his helpers go down with him.
His helpers, who go down with him,
are men who have been set in charge of souls.
When they reached the Tibil
and the bodily trunk,
When Ptahil wanted to cast it into the trunk,
I, Manda d'Haiye, took it out of his pocket.
While Ptahil lifted Adam up
it was I who raised up his bones.
While he laid his hands on him,
it was I who made him breathe the breath of life.
His body filled with marrow,
and the radiance of the Life spoke in him.
When the radiance of the Life spoke in him,
he opened his eyes in the bodily trunk.
When the radiance of the Life spoke in him,
Adakas-Ziwa ascended to his place.
I made him ascend to his place, to the house of the Mighty Life
to the place where the Great Life is enthroned.
I committed him to the charge of the treasurers,
the uthras who take care of the jordans.[36]
The Life thanked the uthra,[37]
who had brought the soul.
The Great Life summoned me and commanded me,
he said to me: "Go down, bestow a sublime call.
Bestow a sublime call
so that the wicked may learn nothing of the soul."
I came and found the wicked,
all of them, as they sit there.
As they sit there,
and discharge witchcraft over the soul.
Over it they discharge witchcraft,
and the wicked desire to chop the soul into single pieces.
As for me, when I beheld it
I shone forth in my pure raiment.
I appeared to the worlds in my abundant radiance,
which my father had given me.
I appeared to Ptahil-Uthra,
who then howled and lamented.
He howled and lamented,
because of what he had done.
I appeared to Ruha, the seductress,
who seduces all the worlds.

136

I showed her the great mystery,
by which rebels are subdued.
I showed her the great mystery
yet she remained blind and did not see it.
I showed her a second mystery,
then I put a camel's bridle on her.
I showed her a third mystery
and split her head open with a blow.
When they saw me, they were all afraid and declared themselves guilty,
the Seven declared themselves guilty.
They declared themselves guilty,
fell down headlong, and tumbled on their faces.
They fell down headlong and tumbled on their faces,
they put their hands before their faces.
And they said:
"Our master! We have erred and sinned,
forgive us all our sins."
However, when the wicked said this,
I made a breach in their phalanx.
I adjured them by the Great Mystery,
that they should do no wrong against the soul.
I concealed myself before the souls, I restrained myself:
I took on a bodily form.
I took on a bodily form
and told myself I would not frighten the soul.[38]
I would not frighten the soul
and it would not be alarmed in its garment.
I assumed bodily form for its sake
and sat down beside it in splendor.
I spread the radiance of the great Mana over it
out of which Adam had been planted.[39]
I sat beside him and instructed him in that
with which the Life charged me.
I sang hymns to him in a sublime voice,
more sublime and luminous than all the worlds.
I sang hymns to him in a soft voice
and roused his heart from sleep.
I spoke to him in the speech of the uthras
and taught him my wisdom.
I taught him from my wisdom and said to him
that he should arise and prostrate himself and praise the Mighty Life.
That he should praise the lofty place
the abode in which the good sit.
That he should praise Adakas-Ziwa,
the Father from whom he came into being.
As I sat there and gave him instruction,
he rose up, bowed down, and praised the Mighty Life.
He praised his father Adakas-Ziwa,
the Mana, by whom he had been planted.
When he bowed down and praised his father, the uthra,
he appeared to him out of the secret place.

When he beheld his father, the uthra,
he was filled with the most sublime praises.
He sang hymns in a loud voice
and overturned the planets.
He overturned the planets
and overturned the lord of the world.
He disowned the sons of the house [this world]
and all the deeds that they had done.
He bore witness to the name of the Life
and the uthra who had let him hear his voice.
He disowned the works[40] of the Tibil
and raised his eyes to the Place of Light.
When he did this,
the "uthra of life" was full of kindness towards him.
He was full of kindness towards him
and commanded a building to be erected for him.
He commanded a building to be erected for him
and commanded a planting to be planted for him.
He commanded a jordan to be prepared for him
so that, when his measure was full,
he might make him ascend and be set in his building.
That he might set him up in the Place of Light with his father Adakas-Ziwa
and make him an uthra in the Place of Light.

THE HEAD IS ONE WORLD*

(From "The Thousand and Twelve Questions")

The head is one world; one world the neck, one world the breast, and each leg is one world even so, unto the liver, and spleen, bowels, stomach, liver [sic], the male organs and the womb and skin and hair and nails and back and viscera: each one of them is a separate world. And when they converse together it is like talk between persons in whom there is no hatred, envy, or dissension. And if, amongst all these worlds, there be one superfluous or another lacking from the structure, that is in the Body, the whole Body is harmed, for they counterpoise one another, and the Soul dwells in their midst as they dwell with one another.

*Verses 217–226, Book 1, Part 2. From E. S. Drower, ed., *The Thousand and Twelve Questions* (Berlin: Akademie-Verlag, 1960), pp. 164–167.

And if they are not counterpoised, one corrupts the other and they, together with Body and Soul, are not mutually established.

For when the Body was formed, a Soul [nisimla] was formed, and when the Soul took shape in the Body, the Body formed the Vital Spirit [ruha]. And when both had taken shape, the Womb was formed. For the Womb is a great world, there is no world greater or more powerful than It.

And the Blood that is within it is lovely Radiance [or Light], and the Blood that is in its Heart is precious and sublime Radiance, and the blood in its Liver is lovely and plenteous Radiance, that moves in all the Body. And the blood that is in the Veins is flowing Radiance. These are the four Emanations of Light which control the Body, if they had been but three, the Body would not be established. If the juices of the liver imbibe from them, four fluids intermingle, they are become one: fluids which plasma deposits, and they are wholesome, some are gathered from the eyes; other fluids gathered from the ears; further, mingled fluids are gathered from the nostrils.

Moreover, these four humors resemble blood and water; each of which has its own inherent quality. From these, four qualities and four colors arise, and of these four humors one of them is red, one of them yellow, one of them white, and one of them black. And from the black one evil impurities originate which injure spirit and soul, and they fear it and quake before it.

Then there are four other qualities which proceed from the watery humors by which the whole body is interpenetrated. The quality of one is wholesome and pleasing so that the soul gladly sits in its company. And one of them is pungent and its odor hateful, another is salty and of the nature of salt which dries up the mysteries of the body, and one of them is troublesome, bile is its name.

For the blend of mysteries are held together by stability, each one with all its brethren. Four winds are kept within it. And of these four qualities, each one of them has four attributes: thus there are sixteen attributes, and each of these sixteen have thirty-two characteristics, and of those thirty-two characteristics sixty-four qualities tendencies characterize the Body: heating, drying, and consuming; hence they are called sixty-four sins. Every man whose soul is delivered from these cities, sixty-four sins, namely these, shall be loosed from him.

In the name of the Great Life! So, when the soul reaches the seven mysteries, a servant of the seven went forth towards her and came and embraced her and said to her, "Where do you come from and where are you going?"

I will say to him "I come from the Body the name of which is 'earth' and I journey towards the Good *Kimsa*."

And the servant will say to the soul, "Who are you and of whom are you called a messenger?"

I will say to him, "I am the servant of the beloved *Kimsa* and the messenger of Ayar-Sagia."

Then they bless and praise her and say to her: "Every man who knows this saying will rise towards the good *Kimsa* because he seeks to control the mysteries of the body." And they question her and then she rises up towards the good *Kimsa. Finis.*

This is a secret mystery and explanation of the Body, that is esoteric and not revealed, which I have copied who am poor, lowly, striving and childlike, a slave who is all sin. I am Zakia-Zihrun.

The earth is a Body and air [*ayar*] is the soul therein. And its burgeonings-forth are its bones and the rivers are its veins; its blood is the ocean and its womb. . . . The copper earth is the legs upon which the body is supported, and its supporting columns are in the earth . . . the Body and its size, its convexity and its extent . . . and the hair of the head, the eyebrows and eyelashes, hair beneath the buttocks and breasts, and the hair of the whole body.

Moreover, each extremity is the end of one world. The right is a world and the left a world; the breasts are two worlds and the two feet two worlds, and the two shanks two worlds and the knees two worlds. The two thighs are two worlds and the whole trunk is two worlds.

And the male organ is vigorous in its strength and imperial majesty: the body, the earth and heavens and the worlds of light and darkness, are equipped therewith. It is a strong implement, and kingliness resembles it, for the whole Body and the kings are safeguarded thereby and no trees, birds, animals, cattle, or running waters can escape its compulsion.

For seven kings are incorporated therein standing in seven garments and written with seven letters namely, GABA-RUT(A) [virility]—their name. For the male organ is the channel of mysteries, it is a wellspring and hair comes out from it;

139

thereby the senses are held. For it is a great mystery to those who perform its function; who erect it in purity and not to excess. As for those who deprave it, they are cast from the height down to the uttermost limit of the worlds. The eye is not opened which beholds all worlds; their eyes are dazzled and they behold them not!

So, when you release seed and have been orderly in the act and its fount fell upon the mystery of the womb within her, which is responsive to it, seed and blood love one another and seek their vehicle; a soul, a body, and a vital spirit. And by them kings and regents, yea and the whole world, are created. And so, when they approach one another, soul and spirit rejoice at that mystery. As the male seed neared the mystery of the womb, the soul rejoiced and addressed a hymn to it and said:

In the Name of the Great Life!

On the day the Radiance became manifest
And emerged from the Inner Radiance,
The counterpart of the Jordan formed itself in its mirror.
Its counterpart was formed in a jordan that was its mirror,
And in the Ether water was produced.
A jordan issued in radiancy
And water in the Ether was shed abroad;
Shed abroad were the waters in the Ether-air,
And the power of Light divulged itself;
It expressed itself, increased and multiplied.
And the Crown was established, and the Wreath twined;
Twined was the Wreath and the leaves of myrtle flourished,
They flourished, the leaves of the myrtle,
And trees bore their burden of fruit.
Nasirutha spoke in them and twined their purities on kings
From the beginning unto the end.

Notes

1. I.e., river, stream.
2. A Mandean proverb that, according to Lady Drower, means something like "there is always an exception.
3. I.e., the Second Life, also called Yosamin.
4. Mandean etymology of the name Abathur, who is equated with B'haq.
5. A secondary identification.
6. Or "disappeared."
7. An attribute of the heavenly beings of light.
8. Or "Ruha changed her arrogance."
9. The King of Darkness.
10. Ibid.
11. Perhaps with Lidzbarski: "home."
12. The five planets (not counting the sun and the moon).
13. The firmament.
14. The evil demons (planets, signs of the zodiac).
15. One would expect the planets.
16. The world.

17. Another reading: "shall be called forth."
18. The primeval man Adam is referred to.
19. I.e., they saw, as far as they could see, only the black waters.
20. The anus.
21. The formula of baptism.
22. Or, "I called."
23. A circumlocution for the King of Darkness. (cf. Lidzbarski, *Ginza*, 227 n. 3; Jb. ch. 62; Rudolph, *Theogonie*, 147 n. 1, 241, 244). In its original context the solidification which Hibil brings clearly derives from the Life.
24. The meaning of "turban" (Lidzbarski) is uncertain (cf. Drower-Macuch, *Dict.*, s.v. tartbuna).
25. "All" is omitted following Lidzbarski.
26. Eve is clearly a secondary addition to the context.
27. The inability of the demiurge and his powers to make Adam stand up is found frequently in Mandeism; in western Gnosis the motiff is found in Saturnilus, the Ophites, the

Apocryphon of John, and, somewhat differently, also among the Naassenes. Cf. Rudolph, "Ein Grundtyp gnostischer Urmensch-Adam-Spekulation," *Zeitschrift für Religions- und Geistesgeschichte* 9 (1957), 1–20.

28. Ptahil; Lidzbarski: "lords of the world."

29. It is the "hidden" or "great" Adam.

30. The reference is probably to the "bodily Adam." For the metaphor cf. Corp. Herm. VII 2 (vol. I, p. 335).

31. Or "He granted assurances (magical formulae) for the souls.

32. Probably the passage ran originally: "as the radiance filled him."

33. Of the soul or of Adakas-Mana.

34. Adakas or Manda dHaiye?

35. Thus with Lidzbarski instead of "fondled."

36. I.e., are baptized in the heavenly Jordans.

37. Originally Adakas, the "inner Adam," in the present context referring to Manda dHaiye.

38. Cf. the Docetics, Hippolytus *Ref.* VIII 10, 3 (vol. I, p. 310).

39. Note the abrupt change of subject from the soul to Adam.

40. These may refer to rites and magical practices in the cultic sense.

Kabbalah

One legend states that the Kabbalah was brought down from Heaven by angels to teach Adam, after his fall, how to recover his primal nobility and bliss.[1] Others say Moses received it directly from God during his forty days on Mount Sinai, and that then it was transmitted by word of mouth. In reality Kabbalah means tradition, specifically oral tradition, and during much of its history it was, like the midrashic Haggadah, passed down by word of mouth. Its actual origin has its sources, according to Gershom Scholem, the foremost scholar of Jewish mysticism, in the esoteric and theosophical currents existing among the Jews of Palestine and Egypt in the era that saw the birth of Christianity.

We have already seen the apocalyptic and mystical tendencies in the pseudepigraphic literature of the intertestamental period. Such works as the *Book of Enoch*, the Dead Sea Scrolls of the Qumran sect, and the writings of the Jewish Gnostics contained the elements of Kabbalah, which were to characterize its first document, the *Sefer Yezirah (Book of Creation)*. These elements were the mystical Chariot *(Merkabah)* of God,[2] the *Sefirot* (virtues) and their relation to the letters of the Hebrew alphabet, and the cosmogonies and anthropogonies. The throne on its chariot goes back to the first chapter of Ezekiel, and this throne of glory is the source of a long mystical and visionary tradition. As for the *Sefer Yezirah (Book of Creation)*, it was written, Scholem contends, by a Jew in Palestine between the third and sixth centuries. In that first Kabbalah we already find the linguistical-mystical cosmogony, that is, the magical power of letters which precedes the word. So we read about "the letters in which Heaven and earth were created."

The word "kabbalah" was used to designate any secret mysteries or "whispered" statements of sages. But by the time of Isaac the Blind (1200), Kabbalah (also written as "Cabala" in Spanish) superseded other designations for Jewish mystical literature, and the many other names, usually of specific books, were no longer used. For our purposes we are citing the rather late *Sefer Ha-Zohar (Book of Radiance);* the *Zohar,* as it is usually called, has been the best translated work in English, and it is also representative of all the tendencies in Kabbalah tradition.

The *Zohar* is attributed to the Spanish kabbalist Moses de León, who died in 1305. Its source, of course, is in the ancient midrashic works of the first centuries A.D. Much of it is a kabbalistic commentary on the Torah. The language is Aramaic. Its mystical content is related to the *Sefirot,* which Moses de León elaborates, but which Moses de Cordovero, in a later kabbalistic work, the *Tomer Devorah,* develops much further. For each single *Sefirah,* there is a corresponding ethical attribute. To achieve the mystic way on this earth and to adhere to God, to achieve ecstasy and illumination—*devekut*—one must accumulate *Sefirot* and so climb the ladder of *devekut* to God. But kabbalistic union is never complete—that would be blasphemous and monistic; for God is not, as in Plotinus, an emanating force to whom one returns in one's entirety, thus becoming one with or in God. Rather, one cleaves to God, one enters the celestial light of the Creator, and two wills—human and divine—coincide. But there are always two wills: human and divine.

Notes

1. Adolphe Franck, *Kabbalah: The Religious Philosophy of the Hebrews* (1967; reprint, Secaucus, New Jersey: Citadel Press, 1979), p. 13.
2. For more information, see "The Historical Development of Kabbalah" in Gershom Scholem, *Kabbalah* (1974; reprint, New York: New American Library, 1978).

THE BEGINNING*

"In the beginning" [Gen. 1:1]—when the will of the King began to take effect, he engraved signs into the heavenly sphere that surrounded him. Within the most hidden recess a dark flame issued from the mystery of *eyn sof,* the Infinite, like a fog forming in the unformed—enclosed in the ring of that sphere, neither white nor black, neither red nor green, of no color whatever. Only after this flame began to assume size and dimension did it produce radiant colors. From the innermost center of the flame sprang forth a well out of which colors issued and spread upon everything beneath, hidden in the mysterious hiddenness of *eyn sof.*

The well broke through and yet did not break through the ether of the sphere. It could not be recognized at all until a hidden, supernal point shone forth under the impact of the final breaking through.[1]

Beyond this point nothing can be known. Therefore it is called *reshit,* beginning—the first word out of the ten by means of which the universe has been created.

THE UNIVERSE: SHELL AND KERNEL

When King Solomon "penetrated into the depths of the nut garden," as it is written, "I descended into the garden of

---

*The remainder of this chapter is from Gershom Scholem, ed., *Zohar* (New York: Schocken, 1963), pp. 27, 28, 29, 31.

nuts" [Cant. 6:11], he took up a nut shell and studying it, he saw an analogy in its layers with the spirits which motivate the sensual desires of humans, as it is written, "and the delights of the sons of men are from male and female demons" [Eccles. 2:8].

The Holy One, be blessed, saw that it was necessary to put into the world all of these things so as to make sure of permanence, and of having, so to speak, a brain surrounded by numerous membranes. The whole world, upper and lower, is organized on this principle, from the primary mystic center to the very outermost of all the layers. All are coverings, the one to the other, brain within brain, spirit inside of spirit, shell within shell.

The primal center is the innermost light, of a translucence, subtlety, and purity beyond comprehension. That inner point extended becomes a "palace" which acts as an enclosure for the center, and is also of a radiance translucent beyond the power to know it.

The "palace" vestment for the incognizable inner point, while it is an unknowable radiance in itself, is nevertheless of a lesser subtlety and translucency than the primal point. The "palace" extends into a vestment for itself, the primal light. From then outward, there is extension upon extension, each constituting a vesture to the one before, as a membrane to the brain. Though membrane first, each extension becomes brain to the next extension.

Likewise does the process go on below; and after this design, man in the world combines brain and membrane, spirit and body, all to the more perfect ordering of the world. When the moon was conjoined with the sun, she was luminous, but when she went apart from the sun and was given governance of her own hosts, her status and her light were reduced, and shell after shell was fashioned for investing the brain, and all was for its good.

THE FIRST LIGHT

"And God said, Let there be light, and there was light" [Gen. 1:3].

This is the primal light which God made. It is the light of the eye. This light God showed to Adam, and by means of it he was enabled to see from end to end of the world. This light God showed to David, and he, beholding it, sang forth his praise, saying, "Oh how abundant is your goodness, which you have laid up for them that fear you" [Ps. 31:20]. This is the light through which God revealed to Moses the land of Israel from Gilead to Dan.

Foreseeing the rise of three sinful generations, the generation of Enoch, the generation of the Flood, and the generation of the Tower of Babel, God put away the light from their enjoyment. Then he gave it to Moses in the time that his mother was hiding him, for the first three months after his birth. When Moses was taken before Pharaoh, God took it from him, and did not give it again until he stood upon the mount of Sinai to receive the Torah. Thenceforth Moses had it for his until the end of his life, and therefore he could not be approached by the Israelites until he had put a veil upon his face [Exod. 34:33].

"Let there be light, and there was light" [Gen. 1:3]. To whatsoever the word *vayehi* and there was is applied, that thing is in this world and in the world to come.

Rabbi Isaac said: "At the Creation, God irradiated the world from end to end with the light, but then it was withdrawn, so as to deprive the sinners of the world of its enjoyment, and it is stored away for the righteous, as it stands written, 'Light is sown for the righteous' [Ps. 97:11]; then will the worlds be in harmony and all will be united into one, but until the future world is set up, this light is put away and hidden. This light emerged from the darkness which was hewed out by the strokes of the Most Secret; and likewise, from the light which was hidden away, through some secret path, there was hewed out the darkness of the lower world in which inheres light. This lower darkness is called 'night' in the verse, 'and the darkness he called night' [Gen. 1:5].

CREATION OF MAN

Rabbi Simeon then rose and spoke: "In meditating, I have perceived that when God was about to create man, then above and below all creatures commenced to tremble. The course of the sixth day was unfolding when at last the divine decision was made. Then there blazed forth the source of all lights and opened up the gate of the east, from where light flows. The light which had been bestowed on it at the beginning, the south gave forth in full glory, and the south took hold upon the east. The east took hold on the north, and the north awakened and, opening forth, called loud to the west that he should come to him. Then the west traveled up into the north and came together with it, and after that the south took hold on the west, and the north and the south surrounded the Garden, being its fences. Then the east drew near to the west, and the west was gladdened and it said, 'Let us make man in our image, after our likeness' [Gen. 1:26], to embrace like us the four quarters and the higher and the lower.' Thereupon were east and west united, and produced man. Therefore have our sages said that man arose out from the site of the Temple.

"Moreover, we may regard the words 'Let us make man' as conveying this: to the lower beings who derived from the side of the upper world God disclosed the secret of how to form the divine name Adam, in which is encompassed the upper and the lower, in the force of its three letters *alef, dalet,* and *mem* final. When the three letters had come down below, there was perceived in their form, complete, the name Adam, to comprehend male and female. The female was fastened to the side of the male, and God cast the male into a deep slumber, and he lay on the site of the Temple. God then cut the female from him and decked her as a bride and led her to him, as it is written, 'And he took one of his sides, and closed up the place with flesh' [Gen. 2:21]. In the ancient books, I have seen it said that here the word 'one' means 'one woman,' that is, the original Lilith, who lay with him and from him conceived. But up to that time, she was no help to him, as it is said, 'but for Adam there was not found a help meet for him' [Gen. 2:20]. Adam, then, was the very last, for it was right that he should find the world complete when he made his appearance."

"No shrub of the field was yet in the earth" [Gen. 2:5].

Rabbi Simeon went on to say: "The allusion is to the magnificent trees which grew later, but as yet were minute. Adam and Eve, as we have said, were created side by side. Why not face to face? For the reason that Heaven and earth were not yet in complete harmony, 'the Lord God had not caused it to rain upon the earth' [Gen. 2:5]. When the lower union was rendered perfect, and Adam and Eve turned face to face, then was the upper union perfected.

"This we may know from the matter of the Tabernacle: for we have learned that together with it there was put up another tabernacle, nor was the upper one raised until the lower one was erected; and so it was in this case. Moreover, inasmuch as all above was not yet perfectly ordered, Adam and Eve were not created face to face. This is borne out by the order of the verses in the Scripture; first it is written,

'For the Lord God had not caused it to rain upon the earth,' and following, "there was not a man to till the ground" [Gen. 2:5], and it signifies that man was yet imperfect, for only when Eve was made perfect, was he then made perfect too. Further proof is that in the word *va-yisgor* [and he closed], there occurs for the first time in this passage the letter *samekh*, which signifies "support," as much as to say that male and female they now supported the one the other. In like wise do the lower world and the upper sustain each other. Not until the lower world was made perfect, was the other world also made perfect. When the lower world was made to support the upper, by being turned face to face with it, the world was then finished, for previously 'the Lord God had not caused it to rain upon the earth.'

"Then, 'There went up a mist from the earth' [Gen. 2:6], to make up for the lack, by 'watering the whole face of the ground' [Gen. 2:5]; and the mist rising is the yearning of the female for the male. Yet another interpretation says that we take the word "not" from the first verse to use in the second with "mist," and this means that God failed to send rain because a mist had not gone up, for from below must come the impulse to move the power above. Thus, to form the cloud, vapor ascends first from the earth. And likewise, the smoke of the sacrifice ascends, creating harmony above, and the uniting of all, and so the celestial sphere has completion in it. It is from below that the movement starts, and thereafter is all perfected. If the Community of Israel failed to initiate the impulse, the One above would also not move to go to her, and it is thus the yearning from below which brings about the completion above.

Notes

1. This primordial point is identified by the *Zohar* with the wisdom of God [*bokmah*] the ideal thought of Creation.

2
HISTORIES AND NARRATIVES

The Martyrdom of Isaiah

(Jewish Pseudepigrapha)

The legend of Isaiah's martyrdom has a biblical basis in 2 Kings 20:16–21:18 and 2 Chronicles 32:32–33:20, but nowhere in the Bible is there mention of Isaiah's death or martyrdom. The case of martyrdom, however, does appear in writings before the Christian era, in *2 Maccabees*, *4 Maccabees*, and in Daniel in the lion pit; then in the story of Jesus, in the martyrdom Acts of the apostles, and in the exquisite, sensual martyrdom of the beautiful Perpetua in the *Passion of Perpetua and Felicity*. The main ingredients are there for all the narrations: a good prophetic figure foretells his death. He is maligned by a false prophet, urged on by the Satan. The king is himself diabolic or urged on by wickedness. So too are his attendants, his city, and the people, all of whom deride the martyred figure. The martyr has his eyes, in vision, on God, and is indifferent to pain. When he dies, as in Isaiah's story, he delivers his soul to the Holy Spirit.

This version of Isaiah's death is part of a larger document that includes the *Vision of Isaiah* and *The Ascension of Isaiah*, the latter two being much later Christian versions of the tale. *The Martyrdom of Isaiah* also contains some minor Christian interpolations indicated by brackets in the text. The author of the work was a Jew, probably from the second century B.C. Leonhard Rost suggests a connection with the Essenes of the Qumran community,[1] and George W. E. Nickelsburg argues convincingly that such a connection is the most likely explanation for many aspects of the story: "the retreat into wilderness to escape the wickedness of the Jerusalem establishment," the angelic dualism, that is, the struggle of the good angels on earth against Beliar, the wicked angel; and, above all, as Nickelsburg points out, the correspondence between Isaiah and his friends with the Teacher of Righteousness and his Community, between Manasseh and the Wicked Priest, and between Bechira and The False Oracle.[2] For more on the Teacher of Righteousness, see the sections on the Qumran Dead Sea Scrolls.

The original text was probably Hebrew. The translation by R. H. Charles in the following selection is from the Ethiopic, which was based on a Greek translation. Fragments also survive in Latin and Old Slavonic.

Notes

1. Leonhard Rost, ed., David E. Green, trans., *Judaism Outside the Hebrew Canon: An Introduction to the Documents* (1971; reprint, Nashville: Parthenon Press, no date), p.151.

2. George W. E. Nickelsburg, *Jewish Literature between the Bible and the Mishnah* (Philadelphia: Fortress Press, 1981), pp. 143–144.

THE MARTYRDOM OF ISAIAH*

And it came to pass in the twenty-sixth year of the reign of Hezekiah, king of Judah, that he called Manasseh, his son. He was his only son. He called him into the presence of Isaiah, son of Amoz, the prophet and into the presence of Josab, son of Isaiah.

And while Hezekiah gave commands, Isaiah, in the presence of his own son Josab, said to King Hezekiah (but not in the presence of Manasseh): "As the Lord lives, whose name has been sent into this world [and as the Beloved of my Lord lives],[1] and as the Spirit which speaks in me lives, all these commands and these words will be undone by Manasseh, and through the agency of his hands I shall depart amid the torture of my body. And Sammael Malchira[2] will serve Manasseh and execute all his desire, and will become a follower of Beliar[3] rather than of me. And he will cause many in Jerusalem and Judaea to abandon the true faith, and Beliar will dwell in Manasseh, and by his hands I shall be sawed asunder."

When Hezekiah heard these words he wept bitterly, and rent his garments, and

placed earth on his head, and fell on his face. Isaiah said to him, "The counsel of Sammael against Manasseh is consummated, and nothing will avail you." And on that day Hezekiah resolved in his heart to slay his own son Manasseh. But Isaiah said to Hezekiah, "[The Beloved has dissolved your design and] the purpose of your heart will not be accomplished, for with this calling I have been called [and will inherit the heritage of the Beloved]."

And it came to pass that after Hezekiah died and Manasseh became king, he did remember the commands of his father Hezekiah. He forgot them. And Sammael lived in Manasseh and clung fast to him. Manasseh forsook the service of his father's God and served Satan, his angels, and his powers. He turned from his father's house and his wise words. He turned his heart to serve Beliar. The angel of lawlessness who rules this world is Beliar, whose name is also Matanbuchus.[4] And he delighted in Jerusalem because of Manasseh and made him strong in apostatizing Israel and spreading lawlessness. Witchcraft and magic increased, divination and auguration, fornication and adultery, and the persecution of the good by Manasseh and Belchira, and Tobia the Canaanite, by John of Anathoth, and by Zadok, the chief of the works. The rest of the acts are recorded in the Book of the Kings of Judah and Israel.[5]

---

*Verses 1–5. The text is a revision from R. H. Charles, ed., *The Apocrypha and Pseudepigrapha of the Old Testament in English* (Oxford: Clarendon Press, 1913), pp. 159–162.

When Isaiah, son of Amoz, saw the lawlessness in Jerusalem and the worship of Satan and his wantonness, he withdrew from Jerusalem and settled in Bethlehem in Judah. There was also much lawlessness there, and so he withdrew from Bethlehem and settled on a mountain in a deserted place. [And Micaiah the prophet, and the aged Ananias, and Joel and Habakkuk, and his son Josab, and many of the faithful who believed in the ascension into heaven, withdrew and settled on the mountain.] They were all clothed in garments of hair, and were all prophets. They had nothing with them, were naked, and all lamented greatly because of Israel's going astray. They ate nothing but wild herbs gathered on the mountains, and having cooked them they survived on them together with the prophet Isaiah. They spent the days of two years on the mountains and hills.

While they were in the desert, there was a certain man in Samaria named Belchira,[6] of the family of Zedekiah, son of Chenaan, a false prophet who was living in Bethlehem. Now in the days of Ahab, king of Israel, Zedekiah had been the teacher of the four hundred prophets of Baal and had reproved and beaten Micaiah, the son of Amada the prophet.[7] Ahab reproved Micaiah and cast him into prison. During this time Zedekiah was together with Ahab's son, Ahaziah, king of Samaria. But Elijah, the prophet of Tebon of Gilead, was reproving Ahaziah and Samaria, and he prophesied that Ahaziah would die of sickness on his bed, and that Samaria would be delivered into the hands of Salmanassar, because he, Ahaziah, had slain the prophets of God. When the false prophets who were with Ahab's son Ahaziah and their teacher Gemarias of Mount Joel[8] heard this (and Gemarias was Zedekiah's brother), they persuaded King Ahaziah of Samaria to slay Micaiah.

Now Belchira recognized the place where Isaiah was and also the prophets who were with him. He lived in the region of Bethlehem and was an adherent of Manasseh. He prophesied falsely in Jerusalem, and had many confederates in Jerusalem. He himself was a Samaritan. It so happened that when Salmanassar, king of Assyria, came and captured Samaria and took the nine tribes captive and led them away to the mountains of the Medes and the rivers of Gozan, Belchira, who was still a youth, had escaped to Jerusalem. These were the days of Hezekiah, King of Judah, but he did not walk in the ways of his father of Samaria, for he feared Hezekiah. Then he was found speaking words of lawlessness in Jerusalem. Hezekiah's servants accused him and he escaped to the region of Bethlehem.

But in Bethlehem Belchira accused Isaiah and the prophets who were with him: "Isaiah and his cohorts prophesy against Jerusalem and against the cities of Judah, urging that they be laid waste. He speaks against the children of Judah and Benjamin, urging that they be taken into captivity, and against you, O lord our king, that you be bound in hooks and iron chains. But they prophesy falsely against Israel and Judah. Isaiah himself said: 'I see more than the prophet Moses.' Moses had said 'No man can see God and live.' But Isaiah said, 'I have seen God and behold, I live.' Know, therefore, O king, that Isaiah is lying. He called Jerusalem Sodom, and declared that the the princes of Judah and Jerusalem are people of Gomorrah.'' Before Manasseh Belchira brought many accusations and also against the other prophets. Now Beliar dwelled in the heart of Manasseh and in the heart of the princes of Judah and Benjamin, in the heart of the eunuchs and councillors of the king. Belchira's words pleased him, and he sent for and seized Isaiah.

And he sawed him asunder with a woodsaw. When Isaiah was being sawed asunder, Belchira stood up, accusing him, and all the false prophets stood up, laughing and rejoicing because of Isaiah. Belchira, aided by Mechembechus,[9] stood up before Isaiah, deriding him. Belchira said to Isaiah: "Confess that you have lied in everything you said and that the ways of Manasseh are good and right. Say that my ways and my associates are good." He said this to Isaiah while he was being cut in two. But Isaiah was absorbed in a vision of the Lord, and though his eyes were open, he did not see them. Belchira again spoke to Isaiah: "Say what I have told you and I will turn their heart and compel Manasseh and the princes of Judah, all Jerusalem, and the people to reverence you." Isaiah answered, "Insofar as I can utter a word, be damned and cursed, along with all the powers and all your house. For you can take nothing from me but the skin of my body."

They seized and sawed Isaiah in two. Manasseh and Belchira and the false prophets and the princes and the people stood looking on. To the prophets who were with him, he said, as he was being sawed in two: "Go to the region of Tyre and Sidon. God mingled the cup for me alone." While Isaiah was being sawed asunder, he neither shouted aloud nor wept, but his lips spoke with the Holy Spirit until he was sawed in two.

Notes

1. The words in brackets are an addition by a Christian editor, who converts a reference to the transcendence of God into a doctrinal statement about the Trinity. All words in brackets are Christian overlays.

2. Sammael. Satan.

3. Beliar. Satan.

4. Matanbuchus. Also Metanbakas. The name suggests apostatizing.

5. 2 Kings 21:17.

6. Belchira. Perhaps an impersonation of Satan or simply a false prophet.

7. Amada. Imlah.

8. Joel. There are many guesses about the meaning of Joel. R. H. Charles suggests it means Israel.

9. Mechembechus. Matanbuchus (see note 4).

The Fourth Book of Maccabees: Concerning the Sovereignty of Reason

(Jewish Psuedepigrapha)

The *Fourth Book of Maccabees* is an elegant discourse in flawless Hellenistic Greek in which the Stoic cardinal virtues (prudence, temperance, courage, justice) are enlisted in the cause of Jewish orthodoxy. Reason triumphs over the body. Indeed, all the most ingenious and horrible engines of torture can have no effect other than to strengthen resolve when reason in the service of the law is being tested. The reward for such resolve is the immortality of the soul in Heaven. Unlike *2 Maccabees*, from which the story of the martyrs is derived, the souls, rather than the body, are saved after bodily death. In fact, even the souls of the wicked persist—in eternal fire and torment, however, rather than in the eternal happiness promised for the virtuous.

The text of *4 Maccabees* is divided into two main parts: the edifying philosophical discourse on the rule of reason over passions, and the panegyric for the martyred family. The cause of this discourse—Professor C. C. Torrey calls it a Greek diatribe—may be the abuses of Antiochus Epiphanes (the Brilliant), also called Antiochus Epimanes (the Madman). He is the torturer of the book. But a more immediate brilliant madman may have been the intended target: Caligula, who had ordered the erection of his divine statue in the Temple of Jerusalem. Moses Hadas speculates on the mass protests that this order to desecrate the Temple must have provoked and speculates a date of composition around A.D. 40, that is, a date contemporary with the event; he suggests Alexandria, possibly Antioch, as the place of composition.

This text is a wonder of contradictions, or should we say, resolution of contradictions. It is ostensibly directed against a Greek tyrant, Antiochus IV, by a devout orthodox Jew, yet it is written in exquisite Greek by a philosopher trained in Greek thought, and its methods of argument are Socratic or, more specifically, of the Stoics. The opening passage clearly demonstrates the philosophical vein:

> Thoroughly philosophical is the subject I propose to discuss, namely, whether religious reason is sovereign over the emotions; and I may properly advise you to attend earnestly to my philosophical exposition. The theme is essential to everyone as a branch of knowledge, but in addition it embraces a eulogy of the highest virtue—I mean, of course, prudence. If it is demonstrated that reason is sovereign over the emotions which hamper temperance, to wit, gluttony and concupiscence, it is also demonstrated that it rules over the emotions which impede justice, such as malice, and over those which impede courage, to wit, anger and pain and fear.

The narration of 4 *Maccabees* concerns the attempt to force Eleazar and his seven sons to eat unclean food, thus violating Jewish law. Antiochus offers to let Eleazar not eat the unclean meat, not to defile himself personally, if he will confirm to others that he has eaten unclean food. Eleazar will not fall into the trap of betraying his people. Indeed, his own pain and death will serve to expiate the sins of others and to purify the land. His martyrdom will also be a model for others to emulate. So one by one Eleazar and his sons, urged on by their mother, are subjected to excruciating torture—their tongues are ripped out, they are blinded, torn, thrown in the fire—but till the last breath they maintain the calm of philosophic reason and detachment. The mother commits suicide rather than let herself be defiled by the soldiers. Here, in this unusual passage, suicide in the service of virtue is praised.

The tale told in 4 *Maccabees* was widely read by Greeks and early Christians and served as a model for Christian martyrdom stories. The notion of martyrdom, a most desired goal of early Christians, was mocked, however, by the Christian Gnostics, who considered it perverse self-indulgence.

154

THE MARTYRDOM OF ELEAZAR, HIS WIFE, AND SEVEN SONS*

Thoroughly philosophical is the subject I propose to discuss, namely, whether religious reason is sovereign over the emotions; and I may properly advise you to attend earnestly to my philosophical exposition. The theme is essential to everyone as a branch of knowledge, but in addition it embraces a eulogy of the highest virtue—I mean, of course, prudence. If it is demonstrated that reason is sovereign over the emotions which hamper temperance, to wit, gluttony and concupiscence, it is also demonstrated that it rules over the emotions which impede justice, such as malice, and over those which impede courage, to wit, anger and pain and fear. How, some might ask, if reason is sovereign over the emotions, does it not rule over forgetfulness and ignorance? Their attempt at argument is laughable. It is not over its own emotions that reason is sovereign, but over those that are opposed to justice and courage and temperance; and over these it rules not with the design of destroying them, but of not yielding to them. Many and diverse sources would enable me to demonstrate to you that reason is sovereign over emotions, but I could far best prove it from the heroism of those who died for virtue's sake— Eleazar, and the seven brothers, and their mother. All these despised suffering even unto death, and so proved that reason is sovereign over emotions. For their virtues I might indeed eulogize those stalwarts who at this season died with their mother in the cause of what is noble; but I would rather felicitate them for their eminent distinction. By their courage and perseverance they won the admiration not only of all mankind but even of their very torturers, and they became responsible for the dissolution of the tyranny which oppressed our nation; the tyrant they overcame by their perseverance, so that through them the fatherland was purged. But of these things there will be occasion to speak presently; I shall commence, as is my custom, by presenting my general thesis, and then I may address myself to their history, rendering glory to God the All-wise.

Our inquiry, then, is whether reason is sovereign over the emotions. We must determine what reason is, and what emotion is, how many types of emotion there are, and whether reason holds the mastery over all of them. Reason, then, is the intellect choosing with correct judgment the life of wisdom; and wisdom is knowledge of things human and divine and of their cause. Such wisdom is education in the Law, through which we learn things divine reverently and things human advantageously. The types comprised in wisdom are prudence, justice, courage, and temperance. Of these, prudence has the greatest authority of all, for it is through it that reason rules over the emotions. Of the emotions, the two most comprehensive classes are pleasure and pain, and of these each involves both the body and the soul. A numerous suite of emotions attends upon both pleasure and pain: desire precedes pleasure, and joy follows after pleasure; fear precedes pain, and sorrow follows after pain. Anger is an emotion common to both pleasure and pain, if one considers how it affects him. Under pleasure, too, is included malicious temper, which presents the most varied aspects of all the emotions; those of the soul are braggadocio and avarice and publicity seeking and quarrelsomeness and backbiting; those of the body are indiscriminate voracity and gluttony and secret gourmandizing. Pleasure and pain thus being as it were two branches burgeoning from body and soul, there are many offshoots of these emotions.

*Verses 1–18. From Moses Hadas, ed. and trans., *The Third and Fourth Book of Maccabees* (New York: Harper & Brothers, for the Dropsie College for Hebrew and Cognate Learning, 1953), pp. 1–18.

Each of these reason, the universal gardener, purges and prunes and binds up and waters and irrigates by diverse devices; and so tames the wild growth of inclinations and emotions. For reason is the guide of virtues, and of emotions the sovereign.

Observe in the first place how, in the case of deeds which hamper temperance, reason is sovereign over the emotions. Temperance is in fact mastery over desires, of which some pertain to the soul and others to the body; over both of these reason manifestly exercises mastery. How is it that when we are drawn to forbidden foods we turn away from the pleasures they afford? Is it not because reason possesses the power to master the appetites? I think it is. When we crave seafood or fowl or quadrupeds or any sort of food which is forbidden to us according to the Law, it is due to the mastery of reason that we abstain. For the emotions of the appetites are reduced and checked by the temperate intellect, and all the motions of the body are muzzled by reason.

What wonder, then, if the desires of the soul for union with beauty lose their force? It is for this reason that the praise of the temperate Joseph is merited: rationality gave him the upper hand over voluptuousness; though a young man and at the prime of sexual appetite, he frustrated the goad of passion by the force of reason. And not only over the goadings of voluptuousness is reason seen to possess mastery, but over all desire; for the Law says, "You shall not covet your neighbor's wife nor anything that is his." Well, then, if the Law has bidden us not to covet, it becomes easier for me to persuade you that reason is able to exercise rule over the desires.

And so it does over the emotions which hamper justice; for how could a man whose character is that of a secret gourmandizer or a glutton, or even a drunkard, be reformed by education, unless it were evident that reason is lord over the emotions? As soon as a man subjects his conduct to the Law, then even if he be covetous he constrains his own inclination and lends to the needy without interest, canceling the debt at the approach of the seven-year period. And if a man be niggardly, he rules himself through reason to obey the Law, and neither to glean over his harvested fields nor to garner the last grapes on his vines.

And so in other instances also we are enabled to perceive that reason holds mastery over the emotions. For the Law prevails even over benevolence to parents, and will not for their sake betray virture; it maintains the upper hand over love for a wife, and chides her for transgression; it takes precedence over love for children, and punishes their wickedness; and it bears sway over the attachment of friends, and rebukes them for evil. Nor must you regard it as a paradox that reason is able to bear rule even over enmity: the fruit trees of the enemy must not be cut down; one must save cattle of a personal enemy, and help raise up his beast if it has fallen.

Reason manifestly holds mastery also over the more violent emotions—love of authority, vain self-esteem, braggadocio, arrogance, backbiting; all these malicious emotions the temperate intellect thrusts out, as it does anger—for over anger too it holds sway. Moses was indeed angry at Dathan and Abiram, yet he took no measure against them in anger, but regulated his anger by reason. For the temperate intellect, as I have said, is able to triumph over the emotions, and to transform some of them and render others impotent. Why else did our eminently wise father Jacob inculpate Simeon and Levi and their friends for massacring, without employing reason, the whole tribe of Shechemites, and exclaim "Cursed be their anger"? Unless reason were able to master anger, he would not have so spoken. When God fashioned man he implanted in him emotions and inclinations; but at the same time he enthroned intellect, through the agency of the senses, as the sacred guide over all. To the intellect he gave the Law; and he who lives subject to it shall reign over a realm of temperance, and justice, and goodness, and courage.

How is it, then, someone may object, if reason is lord of the emotions, that it has no mastery over forgetfulness and ignorance?

Such logic is altogether laughable, for reason is manifestly master not of its own emotions but of those contrary to justice, courage, temperance, and prudence; and of these it is master not in order to destroy them, but in order not to yield to them. None of you, for example, can extirpate desire; but reason can secure that you be not enslaved to desire. Anger none of you can extirpate from his soul; but reason is able to assuage anger. Malice none of you can extirpate; but reason may be your ally in not submitting to malice. For reason is not the uprooter of emotions, but their antagonist.

This can be explained quite clearly by the story of King David's thirst. David had been fighting against the Philistines for a whole day, and with the soldiers of his own people had slain many of them; and then when evening fell he went to the royal pavilion, around which the entire army of our forebears was bivouacked. All the others addressed themselves to their supper; but the king, intensely parched as he was, though he had abundant springs of water, was not able to allay his thirst from them. An irrational desire for the water which was in the enemy's sector tensed the king and inflamed him, loosed and consumed him. When his guards chafed at the king's desire, two stout young warriors who reverenced it attired themselves in full panoply, and carrying a pitcher, scaled the enemy's ramparts. They eluded the sentries at the gates, and in their search traversed the entire encampment of the enemy; and when they discovered

the spring, they boldly drew from it and conveyed the drink to the king. But he, though feverish with thirst, reasoned that a drink reckoned of like value with blood was a very terrible danger to his soul; and so, setting reason against desire, he made libation of the drink to God. For the temperate intellect is able to vanquish the compulsion of the emotions and quench their flaming goads; to surmount the sufferings of the body, however extreme; and through the nobility of reason to scorn and reject the tyranny of the emotions.

But the season now summons us to the demonstration of the theme of temperate reason. When our fathers were enjoying profound peace because of their observance of the Law, and were prospering to the degree that even the King of Asia, Seleucus Nicanor, furnished them moneys for the Temple service and recognized their polity, at that very time certain persons acting subversively against the communal harmony occasioned manifold disasters.

A certain Simon was at feud with Onias, who currently held the high priesthood with life tenure and was a man of the highest merit; and when despite every sort of calumny he was unable to injure Onias in the eyes of the people, he exiled himself for the purpose of betraying his country. He made his way to Apollonius, governor of Syria, Phoenicia, and Cilicia, and said: "Because I am zealous for the interests of the king, I have come to give information that many thousands in private funds are deposited in the treasury at Jerusalem; the Temple possesses no share in these funds, and they therefore belong to King Seleucus." Apollonius informed himself of the details of this matter, thanked Simon for his care of the king's interests, and went up to Seleucus and informed him concerning those large sums. He obtained full authority to deal with the matter, and proceeded quickly to our country with the accursed Simon and a powerful army; upon his arrival he declared that he had come by the king's command in order to receive the private funds deposited in the treasury. At this speech our people voiced indignant complaints, and protested, maintaining that it would be a scandalous thing if those who had entrusted their deposits to the sacred treasury should be deprived of their property; and they did what they could to prevent him. Apollonius, however, made his way toward the Temple with menaces. The priest and the women and children in the Temple supplicated God to defend the sacred place which was being desecrated; and when Apollonius with his army under arms advanced to seize the money, there appeared from Heaven angels, with flashing armor, mounted on horses, who filled them with dread and terror. Then did Apollonius fall half dead in the Court of the Gentiles; and he stretched his hands to Heaven, and with tears besought the Hebrews to pray for him and propitiate the heavenly host. He had so sinned, he said, as to deserve death; but promised, if he were saved, to hymn the blessedness of the Holy Place before all men. Swayed by these words, and by a special anxiety lest King Seleucus think that Apollonius had been overthrown by a human plot and not by divine justice, the High Priest Onias interceded for him. And when he was thus miraculously saved, he departed to inform the king what had befallen him.

When King Seleucus died his son Antiochus Epiphanes succeeded to the rule. He was an arrogant and terrible man; he deposed Onias from the high priesthood, and appointed as High Priest his brother Jason, who had agreed to pay him three thousand, six hundred and sixty talents annually if he would bestow the office upon him. And so Antiochus appointed Jason to serve as High Priest and to rule over the nation. Jason changed the nation's manner of life and altered its polity, in complete defiance of the Law; not only did he construct a gymnasium upon the very citadel of our country, but he even suppressed the service of the Temple. At these things divine justice was angered, and brought Antiochus himself to war against them. For while he was waging war against Ptolemy in Egypt he heard that upon a rumor of his death being spread abroad the people of Jerusalem had exhibited the very greatest delight, and so he speedily marched against them; and when he had ravaged them he issued a decree to the effect that any who were found living according to the Law of their fathers must die. And when he could in no wise avail to suppress the nation's fidelity to its Law through his decrees, but perceived that all his threats and penalties were utterly disregarded, to the degree that even women who knew this would be their fate were flung headlong from the walls with their babes for having circumcised them—when, as I say, his decrees were utterly despised by the people, he himself endeavored to compel each individual of the nation to taste of unclean food through tortures, and to abjure Judaism.

And so the tyrant Antiochus, sitting with his counselors upon a lofty place and surrounded by his soldiers under arms, ordered his guards to hale the Hebrews one by one, and force them to eat of swine's flesh and of meat consecrated to idols; and those who refused to eat of the contamination he ordered to be broken on the wheel and killed. Many were seized and corralled; and the first of the herd to be haled before the tyrant was a man called Eleazar, a priest by family and an expert in the Law, advanced in age, and known to many of the king's court because of his philosophy. When Antiochus saw him, he said: "Before I commence inflicting torture upon you, graybeard, I would give you this counsel: eat of the swine's flesh and save yourself. I respect your age and your hoary head; but I cannot think you a philosopher when you have so long been an old man and still cling to the religion of the

Jews. Why do you abominate eating the excellent meat of this animal which nature has freely bestowed upon us? It is folly not to enjoy pleasures which are free of reproach, and unrighteous to reject the bounties of nature. To me your conduct will seem even greater folly, if by reason of your empty opinions in regard to truth you despise even me, at the cost of your own punishment. Will you not awaken from your crazy philosophy? Will you not disperse the vaporings of that reasoning of yours, adopt a frame of mind suitable to your years, and adhere to the true philosophy of the advantageous? Will you not yield to my humane benevolence, and show mercy to your own gray hairs? Bethink you, that even if there is some power that watches over that religion of yours, it would pardon you for a transgression arising out of extreme compulsion."

When the tyrant had in this fashion sought to urge him on to the eating of forbidden flesh, Eleazar begged leave to speak; and when he had received permission to do so, he began his discourse as follows: "We, Antiochus, who out of conviction lead our lives in accordance with the divine Law, believe no constraint more compelling than our own willing obedience to the Law; and therefore under no circumstance do we deem it right to transgress the Law. Nay, even if our Law were in good truth, as you suppose, not divine, and we merely believed it to be divine, even so it would not be possible for us to invalidate our reputation for piety. And do not regard the eating of unclean flesh a small offense; transgression is of equal weight in small matters as in large, for in either case the Law is equally despised. You mock at our philosophy, and say our living according to it is contrary to reason. Yet it teaches us temperance, so that we rule over all pleasures and desires; and it inures us to courage, so that we willingly endure any difficulty; and it educates us in justice, so that we keep an even balance whatever our tempers; and it instructs us in piety, so that we reverence the sole living God with due magnificence. Therefore do we not eat unclean foods. We believe that God has established the Law, and we know that the Creator of the world, in giving us the Law, has conformed it to our nature. That which will be appropriate to our souls he has bidden us eat, and that food which is contrary he has prevented us from eating. A tyrant's way it is, to force us not only to transgress the Law but also to eat, so that you may then laugh at us for eating the unclean food we abominate. But in my case you shall have no such joke to laugh at. I shall not violate the sacred oaths of my ancestors in regard to keeping the Law, not even if you cut my eyes out and burn my entrails. I am neither so decrepit, nor so ignoble, that my reason should lose the vigor of youth in the cause of religion. So make ready your torturer's wheel, fan your fires to a fiercer heat. I am not so tender of my old age as to annul by my own act the Law of my fathers. Never, O Law, my teacher, will I be false to you, never will I abjure you, beloved self-control; never will I shame you, philosophic reason; never will I deny you, honored priesthood and knowledge of the Law. You shall not defile the sacred lips of my old age, nor the hoariness of a life spent in the service of the Law. Unsullied shall my fathers welcome me; unafraid of your compulsion even unto death. Tyrannize if you will over the ungodly; neither by word nor by deed shall you lord it over my reason, where religion is at stake."

Such was Eleazar's eloquent response to the exhortations of the tyrant; and then the guards who stood by brutally dragged him to the instruments of torture. First, they stripped the garb of the old man, who was yet attired in the comeliness of his piety; and then they bound his arms on either side, and scourged him with whips, while a herald who faced him cried out, "Obey the bidding of the king!" But the great-spirited and noble man, an Eleazar in very truth, was in no way moved, as though it were in a dream he was tortured. With his eyes raised high to heaven the old man suffered his flesh to be torn by the scourges; he was flowing with blood, and his sides were lacerated. He fell to the ground, when his body was no longer able to endure the torment; but his reason he kept erect and unbent. With his foot one of the savage guards struck his flanks to make him rise up when he fell; but he endured the pain, despised the compulsion, prevailed over the torments, and like a noble athlete under blows outstripped his torturers, old man as he was. With his face bathed in sweat and his panting breath coming hard, his stoutness of heart won the admiration even of his torturers.

Thereupon, partly out of pity for his old age, partly in sympathy because of their earlier intimacy, partly in admiration for his perseverance, some of the king's courtiers approached him and said: "Why, Eleazar, will you so unreasonably destroy yourself with these evils? We will put before you some of the cooked food; do you pretend to taste of the swine's flesh and be saved."

But Eleazar cried out, as if his torments had been rendered only the more cruel by this counsel: "Never may we children of Abraham be so misguided in our thoughts, that out of weakness of spirit we should enact a comedy which becomes us so ill. Contrary to reason indeed would it be, if having lived our lives in accordance with truth, and having, in keeping with the Law, guarded our reputation for so doing, we should now change and ourselves prove to be a model of impiety to the young by setting an example for the eating of forbidden food. Shameful indeed would it be, if, having but a short shrift of life remaining, we should become ludicrous in the eyes of all for our cowardice, and earn the tyrant's contempt as ignoble by failing to protect our divine Law unto death. Therefore do you, children of Abraham,

die nobly for piety's sake; and you, guards of the tyrant, why do you delay?"

When they saw him so lofty of spirit in the face of hard constraint, and wholly unmoved by their own pity, they brought him to the fire, and there they burned him with evilly devised instruments, and flung him under the fire; and into his nostrils they poured a noisome brew. And when he was now consumed to his very skeleton, and on the point of perishing, he raised his eyes to God, and said: "You know, God, that though I might have saved myself, I die in fiery torment for the sake of the Law. Be merciful to your people, and let my punishment be sufficient for their sake. Make my blood an expiation for them, and take my life as a ransom for theirs." Uttering these words, the holy man nobly succumbed to his torments; even in the tortures of death he resisted, by virtue of reason, for the Law's sake.

Confessedly, then, religious reason is master over the emotions. For if the emotions dominated over reason, to them should I have rendered the testimony of their domination. But now that reason has conquered the emotions, fittingly may we attribute to it the authority of leadership. We must needs, then, confess that the sovereignty is reason's, for it rules over external torments. A ridiculous thing it is. And it is not only over torments that I prove the reason sovereign; it rules also over pleasures, and yields to them no whit.

Like an excellent pilot, indeed, the reason of our father Eleazar, steering the bark of religion in the sea of emotion, though he was buffeted by the threats of the tyrant and submerged by the triple wave of torture, in no way swerved the rudder of religion until he had entered the harborage of deathless victory. No city besieged with numerous and ingenious works has offered such resistance as did that perfect saint. When his holy soul was set aflame with rack and torture, he overcame his besiegers through the bulwark of his religion—reason. Making his mind taut like a jutting crag, our father Eleazar shattered the frenzied surge of the emotions. Ah, priest worthy of the priesthood, never did you sully your sacred teeth, never, by eating of abomination, did you defile those entrails which harbored piety and purity. Ah, harmonious music of the Law, philosopher of the divine life! Such is it fitting for functionaries to be—so to defend the Law with their own blood, and with their noble sweat in the face of sufferings unto death. You, father, by your perserverance in the public gaze, have made strong our adherence to the Law; your lofty speech on holiness you did not render vain; by your deeds you gave credit to your words concerning divine philosophy—aged hero, mightier than torture; stalwart Elder, fiercer than flame; king, supreme over suffering; Eleazar! Even as our father Aaron, armed with the censer, ran through the multitude of his people and overcame the angel of fire, so did Aaron's scion Eleazar not swerve in his reason, though consumed in the flame. But most marvelous of all, though he was an old man, and the tautness of his body was already unstrung and his muscles relaxed and his sinews enfeebled, he renewed youth in his spirit by means of reason, and by reason like Isaac's he prevailed over many-headed torture. Ah, blessed old age, hoary head revered, life loyal to the Law, and consummated by the faithful seal of death!

If, then, an aged man despised tortures under death, we must acknowledge that religious reason is leader over the emotions. But some may say that not all men are in control of their emotions, because not all men possess prudent reason. Those who take thought for religion with their whole heart, they alone are able to dominate the passions of the flesh, believing that to God they die not, as neither did our patriarchs Abraham, Isaac, and Jacob, but live to God. No contradiction is then involved in the fact that certain persons seem to be dominated by their emotions because of the weakness of their reason. Could anyone who lives as a philosopher according to the full rule of philosophy, and believes in God, and knows that it is blessed to endure any pain for virtue's sake, fail to control his emotions for the cause of religion? Only the wise man and the courageous is master of his emotions.

Yes, and even young lads have achieved philosophy by religious reason, and so have prevailed over torments yet more cruel. When the tyrant had been so manifestly worsted in his first trial, having proved powerless to compel the old man to eat forbidden food, then with vehement passion he bade others of the Hebrew captives to be brought, to try whether they would eat of the forbidden food: if they would eat, he would release them; but if they refused he would punish them yet more severely. When the tyrant had so bidden, there were brought into his presence seven brothers, along with their aged mother—handsome and modest and well-born and in every way charming. Upon seeing them, posed about their mother in the center like a chorus, the tyrant took pleasure, being smitten by their comeliness and nobility; he smiled upon them, and called them near, and said: "Young men, with right good will do I admire you, each and every one; and because I pay high honor to such beauty and such a numerous band of brothers, I not only counsel you against raging with the same madness as that old man has just been tortured, but I urge you further to yield to me and enjoy my friendship. Just as I am able to punish those who disobey my orders, so am I also able to benefit those who show me obedience. Repose your trust in me; you shall receive executive positions over my domains, if you renounce the ancestral Law of your citizenship. Share in the Greek way; change your mode of life;

161

take pleasure in your youth. If by your intransigence you rouse my anger, you will force me to have recourse to terrible punishments, and to destroy you with torture. Take pity upon yourselves: even I your foe have compassion for your youth and your beauty. Will you not reflect that if you disobey nothing except death upon the rack awaits you?"

When he had said this, he ordered that the instruments of torture be brought forward, so that terror might sway them to eat of the forbidden food. The guards brought forward wheels and instruments for dislocating joints, racks and wooden horses, and catapults, and caldrons and braziers and thumbscrews and iron grips and wedges and bellows; and the tyrant then resumed, and said: "Lads, be afraid; the justice which you revere will be indulgent to transgression under duress."

But they, though they heard his cajoling words and looked upon the frightful implements, not only were not affrighted, but confronted the tyrant with their own philosophy, and by their right reasoning nullified his tyranny. Yet let us now reflect: if some among them had been faint-spirited and cowardly, what arguments might they have used? Surely something like this: "Wretched and exceedingly senseless that we are, when the king invites us and urges our well-being, should we not hearken to him? Why do we entertain ourselves with these vain resolutions, and make foolhardly venture of fatal disobedience? Shall we not, dear brothers, be afraid of these instruments of torture? Shall we not ponder the threats of torment? Shall we not eschew this vainglory and this death-bringing braggadocio? Let us take pity upon our own youth; let us show compassion to our mother's hoary head. Let us lay it upon our hearts that if we disobey we die. We shall be pardoned, even by divine justice, for showing fear of the king under duress. Why do we banish ourselves out of life, that is so sweet; why do we deprive ourselves of the charms of the world? Let us not violate necessity; let us not indulge vainglory at the price of our own torture. Not even the Law itself would willingly condemn us to death for being affrighted by torture. Why does such love of contention inflame us, why does such fatal obduracy attract us, when it is possible for us to lead an untroubled life if we obey the king?"

But none of these arguments did the young men use, though they were on the point of being tortured; none did they lay to heart. For the emotions they despised, and they were sovereign over pain; and so, when the tyrant had ceased counseling them to eat forbidden food, all together with one voice, as from a single spirit, said:

"Why, tyrant, do you delay? Ready are we to die, rather than transgress our forefathers' commandments. Our forebears we should verily shame if we did not show obedience to the Law, and take Moses as our counselor. Tyrant counselor of transgression, do not in your hatred of us pity us more than we pity ourselves. Worse than death itself do we regard that pity of yours, which leads to safety through transgression of the Law. You seek to terrify us by threatening us with death through torture, as if you had learned nothing from Eleazar a short while ago. But if old men of the Hebrews have died for religion's sake, and persevering through torture have abided in their religion, it is even more fitting that we who are young should die, despising the torments of your compulsion, over which our aged teacher triumphed. Proceed, then, with your trial, tyrant; and if you take our lives and inflict upon us a death for religion's sake, do not think that you are injuring us by your torments. We, by our suffering and endurance, shall obtain the prize of virtue; and we shall be with God, on whose account we suffer; but you, for our foul murder, will endure at the hand of divine justice the condign punishment of eternal torment by fire."

When they had said these things, the tyrant was not only indignant, as at men disobedient, but also infuriated, as at men who proved ingrate. At his orders, then, the guards brought up the eldest of the brothers, and ripped off his tunic, and bound his hands and arms on this side and that with thongs. And when they had flogged him with scourges until they were weary and had gained nothing, they cast him upon the wheel. Here the noble youth was racked until his limbs were out of joint. But, though he was maimed in every limb, he broke into denunciations, and said: "Foul tyrant, enemy of heaven's justice, savage of heart, it is not as a murderer that you so torture me, nor as an impious wretch, but as a defender of the divine Law." The guards said to him, "Consent to eat, and save yourself from the torments." But he said to them: "Your wheel is not so strong, you base minions, as to strangle my reason. Slice my members, burn my flesh, twist my joints: through all these torments I will convince you that the children of the Hebrews alone are invincible in virtue's cause." When he said this they strewed fire under him and heaped it with coals, and they made the wheel yet more taut. Besmeared with blood on all sides was the wheel, and the heap of live coals was quenched by the droppings of the fluid, and gouts of flesh whirled around on the axles of the machine. Even when the frame of his body was already dissevered, that great-spirited youth, a true son of Abraham, uttered no groan. As though he were being transformed into incorruption by the fire, he nobly endured the torments, and he said: "Imitate me, my brothers; do not desert your post in my trial, do not abjure our brotherhood in nobility. Fight the sacred and noble fight for religion's sake. Through it may the just Providence which watched over our fathers also become merciful to our people, and exact

punishment from the accursed tyrant." Uttering these words, the saintly young man broke off his life.

All marveled at his firm constancy; and the guards brought up the one next to the eldest in age, and when they had adjusted their iron "hands" with sharp claws, they bound him to the instrument of torture and the catapult. Before torturing him they inquired whether he were willing to eat; and when they heard his noble resolve, they tore out his sinews with their iron hands, and they flayed all his flesh up to his chin and also the skin of his head, like savage leopards. The agony he endured with fortitude, and he said: "How sweet is every form of death for the sake of our ancestral religion." And to the tyrant he said: "Do you not perceive, tyrant most cruel of all, that you are being tormented more than I, when you see that your arrogant reasoning of tyranny is vanquished by our endurance in the cause of religion? In my case, I lighten my pain by the joys which virtue brings; but you are tortured by the threats implicit in wickedness. You cannot, vile tyrant, escape the judgments of divine wrath."

When he too had gloriously endured death, the third was brought forward—amid many exhortations urged by many people that he taste of the food and save himself. But he cried out, and said, "Do you not know that the same father who begot my brothers who have died begot me, and the same mother bore me, and that I was nurtured in the same doctrines? I do not abjure the noble kinship of our brotherhood. Therefore, if you have any means of torture, apply it to my body; my soul you cannot touch, even if you would." The man's free speaking irked them sharply, and with their dislocating instruments they dislocated his hands and his feet, and they pried his members asunder from their joints with levers; his fingers and arms and legs and elbows they shattered. And when they could in no way prevail to strangle his spirit, they abandoned their instruments, and with the tips of their fingers scalped him as the Scythians do. Straightway then they brought him to the wheel, and when his vertebrae were being disjointed upon it he saw his own flesh hanging in shreds, and gouts of blood dropping from his entrails. When he was on the point of death, he said, "We, tyrant most abominable, undergo these sufferings for our teaching and divine virtue; but you will endure torments interminable for your impiety and your cruelty."

And when he had died in a manner worthy of his brothers, they dragged forward the fourth brother, and said: "Do not you too act the madman with that same madness your brothers have shown, but obey the king and save yourself." But he said to them, "No fire you can bring against me is so burning hot as to make a coward of me. By the blessed death of my brothers, by the everlasting destruction of the tyrant, by the glorious life of the pious, I will not deny our noble brotherhood. Contrive novel tortures, tyrant, so that they may teach you further proof that I am brother to those who have already been tortured." Upon hearing this, the bloodthirsty and murderous and utterly abominable Antiochus ordered his tongue to be cut out. But he said, "Even if you take away my organ of speech, yet doth God hear them that are silent. Look, my tongue hangs out, cut it off, for by doing so you will not mutilate my reason to speechlessness. Gladly, for the sake of God, do we suffer our body's members to be amputated. But you God will speedily overtake, for you are cutting out the tongue which hymned the praises divine."

Cruelly racked by the torments, he too died; and then the fifth son leapt forward saying, "I shall not, tyrant, beg off torment for the cause of virtue, but of my own accord have I come forward, so that by killing me also you may be liable to heavenly justice for punishment on ac-

count of misdeeds even more numerous. Ah, enemy of virtue and enemy of mankind, for what action on our part do you destroy us in this manner? Is it because we revere the Creator of all, and live in accordance with his virtuous Law? But such conduct is worthy of honors, not of torments." As he was uttering such words, the guards bound him and dragged him to the catapult. Upon it they fastened him by the knees, and fixed them with iron cramps; and they twisted his loins back upon the circular wedge; thus he was wholly broken upon the wheel like a scorpion, and all his members were disjointed. In this position, struggling for breath and racked in body, "A kindly favor," said he, "have you granted us, you tyrant, though all unwilling, for by these noble sufferings you enable us to show forth our constancy toward the Law."

And when he too was dead, the sixth was led forward a mere lad. When the tyrant asked him whether he were willing to eat and so be released, he declared: "In years, indeed, I am younger than my brethren, but in reason I am their age-fellow. For the same design were we born and brought up, and we are similarly obliged to die also for the same cause. Hence if you are minded to torture one who does not eat of pollution, torture away." When he said this, they brought him to the wheel. They stretched him upon it with care, and disjointed his vertebrae, and roasted him with a slow fire. They heated sharp spits in the flame and applied them to his back; they pierced his sides, and burned away his entrails. But in the midst of his tortures he said, "Holy and seemly is the passion to which we brethren so many have been summoned, a contest of suffering for religion's sake; and we have not been vanquished. For, tyrant, religious knowledge is invincible. Armed with nobility cap-a-pie, I too shall die along with my brethren; and I too shall inflict upon you an additional retribution, you deviser of novel tortures, you enemy of the truly pious. Only six lads, and we have dissolved your tyranny! For when you are not able to sway our reason, nor compel us to eat unclean food, is that not your dissolution? Your fire is to us cold, your catapults painless, your violence impotent. Not a tyrant's guards, but those of the divine Law have been our protectors, and therefore do we retain our reason unvanquished."

And when he too had died a blessed death, having been cast into a caldron, the seventh came up, the youngest of all. Him the tyrant pitied, though he had been vehemently abused by his brothers. When he saw the fetters already laid upon him, he summoned him to approach nearer, and tried to persuade him, saying: "You see how your brothers' folly has ended; for their disobedience they have been tortured, and are dead. Now you too, if you do not obey, you will be tortured miserably, and you will die before your time; but if you do obey, you will be my Friend, and have charge over the affairs of my realm." When he had thus advised him, he summoned the boy's mother, so that in pity of her who had been bereft of so many sons he might urge obedience as salvation for him that was left. But when his mother had encouraged him in the Hebrew tongue, as we shall presently recount, "Loose me," he said, "let me speak to the king and to all his friends that are with him." They were greatly rejoiced at the lad's promise, and speedily loosed him. Then he ran to the nearest of the braziers, and said: "Sacrilegious man, tyrant most impious of all that are wicked, are you not ashamed, when you have received all good things, including your kingdom, from God, to slay his servants, and to torture those who cultivate religion? In recompense for this, justice will keep you in store for intense and eternal fire and torment, and these shall never release you throughout time. Are you not ashamed, being but a man, you

most savage of beasts, to cut out the tongues of men who have like feelings with you, and are begotten of the same elements, and to torment and torture them in this vile manner? They, indeed, have died nobly, and so fulfilled their piety to God; but you will groan lamentably for having slain the blameless champions of virtue." Thereupon, when he too was on the point of death, he declared, "I shall not prove renegade to the heroism of my brothers. I call upon the God of my fathers to prove merciful to our nation. You he will punish, both in the present life and when you are dead." When he had uttered these imprecations he flung himself into the braziers, and so gave up his life.

Now, therefore, if the seven brothers despised sufferings even unto death, it must be universally agreed that devout reason is sovereign over the emotions. For if they had been enslaved to the emotions, and had eaten unclean food, we should have said that they had been vanquished by them. But this was not the case; by the reason which is commended by God they got the better of emotions, over which the superiority of reason is thus made evident; for they overcame both emotion and suffering. How is it then possible not to admit, considering these men, right reason's sovereignty over emotion, when they did not shrink from the agonies of fire? Even as towers constructed at the mouths of harbors break the threatening waves, and render the anchorage calm for those that sail into it, so the seven-turreted right reason of these young men fortified the harbor of religion, and overcame the unruliness of the emotions. A holy choice of religion did they establish; and they gave one another courage, saying, "In a brotherly fashion, brothers, let us die on behalf of the Law. Let us emulate the Three Youths of Assyria who despised a similar ordeal of the furnace. Let us not show cowardice in the demonstration of religion." "Courage, brother!" said one;

and another, "Bear up nobly!" Another, recalling the past, said "Remember where you came from, and at the hand of what father Isaac endured immolation for religion's sake." Each severally and all together, looking upon one another with faces shining and filled with courage, said, "With all our hearts let us consecrate ourselves to God, who gave us our souls; and let us use our bodies for the guardianship of the Law. Let us not fear him who thinks that he kills. Great is the trial of soul, and the danger laid up in eternal tribulation, for those who transgress the commandment of God. Let us then arm ourselves with that mastery over suffering which comes from divine reason. When we have died in such fashion, Abraham and Isaac and Jacob will receive us, and all the patriarchs will praise us." And to each one of the brothers, as they were dragged away, those that remained said, "Do not shame us, brother; do not deceive those of our brothers who have died before."

You cannot be ignorant of the charm of brotherhood, which divine and all-wise Providence has imparted through fathers upon those begotten of them—implanting it, indeed, even in their mother's womb. There do brothers abide for a similar period; and are molded through the same span, and nurtured by the same blood, and brought to maturity through the same vitality. After equal gestation are they brought to birth, and from the same fountains do they imbibe milk; from these embracings are fraternal spirits nourished; and they grow more robust by reason of their shared nurture and daily companionship and their training, both in other respects and in our discipline in the Law of God. The bond of internal affection and sympathy is, we see, firmly fixed; but these seven brothers possessed an ever closer bond of sympathy with one another; for having been trained in the same Law, and having cultivated the same virtues, and having been brought up together in a life of righteousness, they had even greater

love for one another. Their rivalry in all excellence strengthened their affection for one another, and their concord; and the bond of religion made their brotherly love more fervent. Nevertheless, though in their case nature and companionship and the practices of virtue augmented the charms of brotherhood, yet for religion's sake those that survived had the fortitude to look on while their brothers were being outrageously misused and tortured to death.

Nay, they even urged them on to the torments; and so not only despised physical anguish, but also prevailed over the emotion of brotherly love.

O Reason, more kingly than kings, more free than freemen! O sacred and harmonious concord of the seven brothers for religion's sake! Not one of the seven lads turned coward, none shrank in the face of death; but all, as if running the course to deathlessness, sped onward to death by torture. Just as hands and feet move in harmony with the promptings of the soul, so did those holy youths, as if prompted by the deathless spirit of religion, harmoniously accept death on its behalf. O all-sacred hebdomad of brothers in harmony! For just as the seven days of creation move in chorus about religion, so do these youths in chorus circle about the hebdomad, voiding the fear of torment. Even now, we, when we hear of the agonies of those young men, must shudder; but they, not only in looking on, not only in hearing the utterance of the instant threat, but even in suffering, they endured with fortitude, and this in the burning agonies of fire than which what could be more painful? Sharp and incisive is the power of fire, and quickly did it destroy their bodies.

Nay, count it not a marvelous thing that reason prevailed over tortures in the case of those men, when the mind of even a woman despised torments even more manifold. For the mother of the seven youths endured the agonies of every one of her children. Consider how many-skeined is maternal affection, which draws all things to a feeling shared with her own inward parts. Even unreasoning animals have a sympathy and affection for those born of them, as have human beings. Of winged creatures, those that are tame protect their young by nesting in the roofs of houses; and those that build their nests on the peaks of mountains and in clefts of precipices and in the holes or tops of trees— these hatch their young, and repel any intruder; and even when they cannot repel them, they flutter about their nestlings in the anguish of love, and call to them in their own speech, and help their young in whatever way possible. But what need to demonstrate the sympathy of unreasoning animals for their offspring, when even the bees ward off intruders at the season of making honey, and pierce with their sting as with steel those that approach their young, and defend them to the death. But sympathy for her offspring did not move the mother of the youths, whose soul was like Abraham's.

O Reason of the children, master over the emotions! O religion, dearer to the mother than her sons! When two alternatives lay before her, religion, or the immediate salvation of her sons according to the tyrant's promise, she loved religion better, which preserves to eternal life according to God's promise. In what terms can I describe the passionate love of parents for their children? Upon the tender mold of the child we impress a marvelous likeness of soul and of form; and especially mothers, for by reason of their travail they are more sympathetic to offspring than fathers. For mothers are not stalwart in spirit; and in the degree that their offspring is abundant their love of children is more abounding. But of all mothers the mother of the seven sons proved most abounding in love; for by seven travails she implanted in herself a deep affection for them, and because of

the manifold pains in the birth of each she was constrained to cherish a deep bond with them; yet because of her fear of God she disregarded the temporal safety of her children. Nay, more; because of her very nobility, and their ready obedience to the Law, she cherished an even deeper affection for them. For they were just, and temperate, and courageous, and great-spirited, and united by fraternal love; and so loved their mother that in obedience to her they observed the Law even unto death. Nevertheless, though so many considerations affecting maternal love drew the mothers to sympathize with them, yet in the case of none of them did their manifold tortures avail to sway her reason; but each child severally and all together the mother urged on to death for religion's sake. Ah, sacred nature, charm of parental love, filial yearning, nurture, the indomitable emotions of motherhood! One by one the mother saw her sons tortured and burned and swerved not, for religion's sake. The flesh of her children she saw disintegrating in the fire; the fingers of their hands and the toes of their feet quivering on the ground; the flesh of their heads flayed down to the cheeks, exposed like masks. O mother, who did now experience anguish more bitter than in their birth pangs! O woman, who alone did bring perfect religion to birth! Your firstborn, breathing out his life, did not turn your resolution; nor did the second, gazing pitifully upon you in his torment; nor the third, as he breathed his last; nor, when you looked at the eyes of each one, as in his torments he gazed immovable upon the same savage cruelty; nor when you perceived their nostrils revealing the forebodings of approaching death, did you wail. When you saw the flesh of your children burned over the embers of your children's flesh, and severed hands heaped on hands, and flayed skulls upon skulls, and corpses fallen upon corpses; and when you saw the place crowded with spectators of your children's torments, you did not weep. Not the sirens' melodies, nor the notes of the swan, so draw their hearers to the delight of hearing, as the voices of children in torment draw a mother's heart. How numerous, then, and how great, were the torments of the mother, as she suffered with her children as they were racked by the wheel and by fire! But devout reason gave manly courage to her heart in the midst of these emotions, and nerved her to ignore the immediate claims of maternal affection. And although she saw the destruction of seven children, and the manifold variety of their torments, that noble mother counted all these things as naught, because of her faith in God. In the tribunal of her own heart, as it were, she saw clever advocates nature, parentage, maternal love, the torment of children; and she held in her discretion (a mother over her children!) two ballots: a doom of death, and salvation; yet she did not choose that favorable course which would bring safety to her seven sons for a brief space, but rather as a daughter of God-fearing Abraham bethought herself of Abraham's fortitude.

O mother of the nation, champion of the Law, defender of religion, and victor in the contest of the heart! Or noble than men in endurance, O more heroic than heroes in perseverance! Like the ark of Noah, which, bearing the universe in the midst of universal cataclysm, bravely endured the buffetings of the waves, so did you, guardian of the Laws, assailed on all sides in the midst of emotions' cataclysm by the powerful blasts of your sons' torments, with bold persistence withstand the tempests against religion.

If, then, a woman—elderly at that, and the mother of seven sons—endured seeing her children tortured to death, it must be acknowledged that religious reason is sovereign over the emotions. Thus I have demonstrated that not only men have shown mastery over the emotions, but that even a woman could despise the fiercest tortures. Not so savage were lions about Daniel; not so fiercely did Mishael's brazier burn with its greedy flame; as did innate maternal affection burn that woman, as she saw those seven sons of hers subjected to such manifold torments. But by reason which belongs to religion did the mother quench emotions so numerous and so intense.

This, too, you must consider: If the woman had been weak in spirit being, as she was, a mother—she would have lamented over them, and perhaps have spoken as follows: "Ah, miserable woman that I am, repeatedly wretched time and again! Seven children have I borne, and I am the mother of none. In vain were my seven pregnancies; futile the ten-months burden borne seven times; fruitless the nursing, and wretched the suckling. In vain, my children, did I endure those many travails for you; and the harder anxieties of your upbringing. Alas for my sons—some unwedded, others married, but to no purpose; I shall never see your children, nor shall I ever be blessed with the title of grandmother. I had children, both numerous and handsome; and now am a woman forsaken and solitary, with many sorrows. Nor when I die, shall I have any of my sons to bury me."

Yet that holy and God-fearing mother lamented none of them with such a dirge; nor did she urge any of them to avoid death. Nor did she grieve, as they were on the point of dying. On the contrary as though her mind were of adamant, and as though she were again giving birth to her brood of seven sons unto immortality—by her supplications she rather encouraged them to death for religion's sake. Mother, soldier of God through religion, Elder, woman! By your constancy you have vanquished even the tyrant; and by your deeds and your words discovered yourself more stalwart than a man. For when you were seized, along with your children, you stood firm, as you watched Eleazar undergoing torture; and you said to your children—

speaking in Hebrew: "My sons, noble is the contest; and since you are summoned to it in order to bear testimony for your nation, strive zealously on behalf of the Law of our fathers. 'Twere shame indeed that this old man should endure agonies for the sake of religion, and you who are young should be terrified of torments. Remember that it is because of God that you have a share in the world, and have enjoyed life: for this reason you are bound to endure any hardship, for the sake of God. For his sake also was our father Abraham zealous to immolate his son Isaac, the father of a nation; nor did Isaac flinch when he saw his father's hand, armed with a sword, descending upon him. Moreover, Daniel the righteous was thrown to the lions; and Hananiah, Mishael, and Azariah were flung into the fiery furnace, and they endured for the sake of God. Do you, too, therefore, hold the same faith in God, and be not dismayed; for it would be unreasonable for you, who know religion, not to withstand suffering."

With these words the mother of the seven encouraged each of her sons, and bade them die rather than transgress the commandment of God; and they too knew well that those who die for the sake of God live with God, as do Abraham and Isaac and Jacob and all the patriarchs.

Certain of the guards declared that when she too was about to be seized and put to death, she flung herself into the fire, so that no one might touch her body. O mother with your seven sons, who broke the violence of the tyrant, and rendered his evil devices futile, and demonstrated the nobility of faith! Nobly set as a beam upon the pillars of your children, unswervingly did you support the earthquake of the tortures. Be of good courage, then, mother of holy soul, who keep the hope of your endurance firm with God; not so majestic stands the moon in heaven, with its stars, as you stand; lighting the way to piety for your seven starlike sons; honored by God, and with them fixed in heaven. For your childbearing was of our Father Abraham.

If it were possible for us to paint, as on a picture, the story of your religion, would not the spectators shudder when they saw the mother of seven children enduring manifold torments unto death for the sake of religion? Indeed, it would be proper to inscribe upon their very tomb the words following as a memorial to those heroes of our people: HERE LIE BURIED AN AGED PRIEST, AN OLD WOMAN, AND HER SEVEN SONS, VICTIMS OF THE VIOLENCE OF A TYRANT RESOLVED TO DESTROY THE POLITY OF THE HEBREWS. THEY VINDICATED THEIR RACE, LOOKING TO GOD, AND ENDURING TORMENTS EVEN TO DEATH.

Divine indeed was the contest of which they were the issue. Of that contest virtue was the umpire; and its score was for constancy. Victory was incorruptibility in a life of long duration. Eleazar was the prime contestant; but the mother of the seven sons entered the competition, and the brothers too vied for the prize. The tyrant was the adversary, and the world and humanity were the spectators. Reverence for God was the winner, and crowned her own champions. Who did not marvel at the athletes of the divine legislation, who were not astonished by them?

The tyrant himself, and his whole council, were amazed at the constancy whereby they now have their stand before the throne of God, and live the life of eternal blessedness. For Moses says, "All the holy ones are underneath your hands." These, then, having been sanctified by God, are honored not only with this distinction, but also by the fact that because of them our enemies did not prevail over our nation; and the tyrant was chastised, and our land purified— they having become as it were a ransom for the sin of the nation. It was through the blood of these righteous ones, and through the expiation of their death, that divine Providence preserved Israel, which had been ill used. For the tyrant Antiochus, taking as a model the courage of their virtue, and their constancy under torture, advertised their endurance as a pattern to his own soldiers; he thus got them noble and courageous for infantry battle, and for siege; and he ravaged and vanquished all his enemies.

O descendants of the seed of Abraham, children of Israel, obey this Law, and in every respect pursue religion; knowing that religious reason is master over the emotions, and over pains not only from within but also from without. Those men who yielded up their bodies to suffering for the sake of religion were in recompense not only admired by mankind, but were also deemed worthy of a divine portion. And it was because of them that our nation obtained peace; they renewed the observance of the Law in their country, and lifted their enemies' siege. But the tyrant Antiochus was punished upon earth, and is yet chastised after his death. For when he was by no means able to force the people of Jerusalem to change their race, and to depart from the usages of their fathers, he departed from Jerusalem and marched against the Persians.

The mother of the seven children also uttered these righteous sayings to her children: "I was a chaste maiden, and did not depart from my father's house; but I kept guard over the rib fashioned into woman's body. No seducer of the desert or spoiler in the field corrupted me; nor did the seducing and deceitful serpent defile the sanctity of my chastity. All the period of my maturity I abode with my husband. When these sons were grown up, their father died. Happy was he; for he was alive to enjoy the fair season of their birth, but was not grieved at the pangs of childlessness. He, when he was still with you, taught you the Law and the Prophets. He read to you of Abel, done to death by Cain; of Isaac, offered as a holocaust; and of Joseph, in prison. He spoke to you of the zeal of Phineas; and taught you concerning Hananiah, Mishael, and Azariah in the fire. He also glorified Daniel, in the pit of lions, and called him blessed. He admonished you of the Scripture of Isaiah, which declares, 'When you walk through fire the flame shall not burn you.' He chanted to you the psalm of David which says, 'Many are the ills of the righteous.' He recited the proverb of Solomon which says, 'He is a tree of life to them that do his will.' He affirmed the word of Ezekiel, 'Shall these dry bones live?' Nor indeed did he forget, in his instruction, the song that Moses taught, which says, 'I kill and I make alive; for that is your life and the length of your days.' "

Ah, that day—at once bitter and not bitter, when that bitter tyrant of the Greeks quenched fire with fire in his cruel caldrons, and in seething fury brought to the catapults and again to his tortures those seven sons of the daughter of Abraham; the pupils of their eyes he pierced, their tongues he cut off, and he slew them with manifold torments. For these deeds divine justice has pursued that accursed tyrant and shall pursue him. But the children of Abraham, with their mother, who bore off the prize, are ranged in the choir of their fathers; having received souls pure and deathless from God, to whom be glory for ever and ever. Amen.

The Passion of
Perpetua and Felicity

(Christian Acts of Martyrdom)*

The Passion of Perpetua and Felicity stands near the historical beginnings
of an immense body of hagiographical literature that recounts the lives
and deaths of Christian heroes. Our texts fall roughly into the generic
category of *acta* or purportedly historically accurate accounts of the
persecution of Christians based on first-person narratives or legal
records. While the narrative before us is a fiction, it is a fiction that is
at every turn infused with the reality of historical events and everyday
life. It reflects accurately the life situation of the African Christian community at the beginning of the third century. The traditional dating for
the events described here is, in fact, February or March 203. That Perpetua and Felicity were what they purport to be here—mistress and
servant, both recent mothers but more significantly recent converts to
a still fervent Christian community—can hardly be denied. Erich Auer-
bach, the great historian of the presentation of reality in western literature, has singled our text as a document almost unique in its rendering
of life situations. *Perpetua*, he tells us "speaks of things that do not
occur elsewhere in ancient literature. . . . Ancient literature has its An-
tigone, but there was nothing like this, nor could there be; there was
no literary genre capable of presenting such a reality with so much
dignity and elevation."

The inclusion of the *Passion of Perpetua* in the present collection,
however, stems not so much from its historical significance, nor even
from the power with which it cannot fail to move us, but because it
also holds great interest for the reader of apocalyptic literature. Indeed, *Perpetua* is as much apocalypse as it is hagiography. Its writers
have drawn freely from such sources as the *Similitudes of Enoch*, the

*Introduction by C. Clifford Flanigan.

Shepherd of Hermas, the *Apocalypse of Peter*, and the canonical Revelation of St. John. It is perhaps significant that these texts are more in evidence in this work, which calls itself a passion, than the account of Jesus' suffering and death in the Gospels. In any case, the bridge that links the work's hagiographical interests with its apocalyptic elements is the notion, common in the early history of Christianity, that the martyr and saint on his way to martyrdom possesses special powers, including visionary ones. The most striking example of the power of the martyr in our text is found in the seventh and eighth chapters. Here Perpetua realizes that she has special intercessory powers with God ("I saw at once that I was entitled," she says) and has a vision of her dead younger brother Dinocrates, who is suffering in some sort of limbo or hell. Apparently, Dinocrates died unbaptized, a condition symbolized by his gangrenous face. In the vision he tries unsuccessfully to drink of the living water that would transfer him into the realm of the blessed. Some of the details of this vision seem to be inspired by Jesus' story about the rich man and poor Lazarus in Luke 16. In any case, Perpetua's prayer brings about Dinocrates' release.

More striking than this demonstration of Perpetua's powers are the phantasmagoric and erotic visions that symbolize and interpret her situation as martyr. A great deal could—and should—be made of these accounts from a number of different historical, psychological, and literary approaches. But the main point is that Perpetua's experience and the expression of it, in stylistically very colloquial language, acquires a sublimity by its use of extensive, though not necessarily conscious, literary allusion. In her first vision, for example, Perpetua sees a ladder leading to Heaven. Its dangers (sharp weapons on all sides threaten those who attempt to climb it) and its narrowness stress, of course, the difficulty of rising to God thrugh the act of martyrdom. This image is inspired by Jacob's dream of a ladder reaching into Heaven, recounted in Genesis 28. At the top of the ladder is a "vast expanse of garden," which suggests that the road to martyrdom leads back to the Garden of Eden. Presiding over the garden is a tall, old shepherd—perhaps the Good Shepherd of Christian tradition—and he is surrounded by many thousands "clad in white," the martyrs described in the canonical apocalypse. The shepherd provides Perpetua with milk and "something sweet," hinting that the garden is situated in the new Promised Land, the earthly counterpart of which the Hebraic tradition repeatedly describes as "flowing with milk and honey." But the most significant detail in Perpetua's vision is the fact that at the bottom of the ladder there is lurking an enormous dragon upon whose head Perpetua must step if she is ever to climb up to the new Eden. This image of treading on the head of the enemy links this vision with others in the collection. Perpetua steps on the face of her Egyptian opponent, to cite but a single example. The dragon at the bottom of the ladder is, of course, Satan, who appeared to a woman in the first Garden of Eden in the guise of a snake. He is also Leviathan and the great dragon of the Book of Revelation. Perpetua's stepping on his head must be related to the Christian interpretation of Yahweh's words in Genesis 3:15: "I will put enmity between you and the woman, and between your seed and her seed; he shall bruise your head and you shall bruise his heel." Thus Perpetua becomes a new Eve, crushing the Devil by her martyrdom and reversing the effects of the Fall. Her martyrdom creates a new kind of motherhood, as the persistent concern with details about nursing scattered through the text suggests. Perpetua's action is further illuminated by other biblical passages as well, among them Luke 10:19, where Jesus says to his followers, "Behold I have given you authority to tread upon serpents and scorpions and over all the power of the enemy; and nothing shall hurt you." Also relevant are images and themes in the Hebrew Bible, such as those found in Joshua 10:24, Psalm 90:3, and Psalm 109:1. These allusions do not exhaust the richness of the images in Perpetua's vision, but they must suffice here to illustrate the way that the apocalyptic elements in the book are the product of a fusion of Perpetua's life situation and a very rich religious and literary heritage.

The striking visions do not, however, exhaust the significance of this text for our understanding of early Christian apocalyptic. Prefacing them at the beginning is an apology for apocalyptic religion written in a different and more learned Latin style. These prefatory remarks have often been attributed to Tertullian (c.160–c.220), the first Latin theologian. Tertullian's Montanist tendencies toward a morally stern but otherwise ecstatic form of Christianity always put him on the edge of heresy, at least by later orthodox standards. Whether written by him or not, the opening section claims that the seeing of visions and the dreaming of dreams in the author's own time is of equal value to the prophecies and visions that are included in the canonical Scriptures. "Why should not more examples be set out," he asks, "by the one power of the one spirit?" For him experiences like those of Perpetua and her companions demonstrate that the end time is near; logically, he feels that "the more recent things should be deemed the greater, as being later than the last," that is, as occurring after the formative work of the Spirit in establishing the church. Rarely within the history of Jewish and Christian apocalyptic has such a claim for the superiority of noncanonical over canonical versions been so openly and forcefully asserted. This fact alone would justify the inclusion of Perpetua's *Passion* in the present collection. Yet for most readers it is not this doctrinaire claim, but the extraordinary combination of the realistic first-person accounts with phantasmagoric imagery that makes this text one of the most effective and genuinely moving in all of apocalyptic literature.

THE PASSION OF PERPETUA AND FELICITY*

I

If the ancient examples of faith, such as both testified to the grace of God, and wrought the edification of man, have for this cause been set out in writing that the reading of them may revive the past, and so both God be glorified and man strengthened, why should not new examples be set out equally suitable to both those ends? For these in like manner will some day be old and needful for posterity, though in their own time because of the veneration secured to antiquity they are held in less esteem. But let them see to this who determine the one power of the one Spirit by times and seasons; since the more recent things should rather be deemed the greater, as being "later than the last." This follows from the preeminance of grace promised at the last lap of the world's race. For "In the last days, saith the Lord, I will pour forth of my Spirit upon all flesh, and their sons and their daughters shall prophesy: and on my servants and on my hand-maidens will I pour forth of my Spirit: and their young men shall see visions, and their old men shall dream dreams." And so we who recognize and hold in honor not new prophecies only but new visions as alike promised, and count all the rest of the powers of the Holy Spirit as intended for the equipment of the Church, to which the same Spirit was sent bestowing all gifts upon all as the Lord dealt to each man, we cannot but set these out and make them famous by recital to the glory of God. So shall no weak or despairing faith suppose that supernatural grace, in excellency of martyrdoms or revelations, was found among the ancients only; for God ever works what he has promised, to un-

*From Edward Charles Owen, *Some Authentic Acts of the Early Martyrs* (London: SPCK, 1933), pp. 41–51.

believers a witness, to believers a blessing. And so "what we have heard and handled declare we unto you also," brothers and little children, "that you also" who were their eyewitnesses may be reminded of the glory of the Lord, and you who now learn by the ear "may have fellowship with" the holy martyrs, and through them with the Lord Jesus Christ, to whom belong splendor and honor for ever and ever. Amen.

II

Certain young catechumens were arrested, Revocatus and his fellow slave Felicitas, Saturninus, and Secundulus. Among these also Vibia Perpetua, well-born, liberally educated, honorably married, having father and mother, and two brothers, one like herself a catechumen, and an infant son at the breast. She was about twenty-two years of age. The whole story of her martyrdom is from this point onwards told by herself, as she left it written, hand and conception being alike her own.

III

"When I was still," she says, "with my companions, and my father in his affection for me was endeavoring to upset me by arguments and overthrow my resolution, 'Father,' I said, 'Do you see this vessel for instance lying here, waterpot or whatever it may be?' 'I see it,' he said. And I said to him, 'Can it be called by any other name than what it is?' And he answered, 'No.' 'So also I cannot call myself anything else than what I am, a Christian.'

"Then my father, furious at the word 'Christian,' threw himself upon me as though to pluck out my eyes; but he was satisfied with annoying me; he was in fact vanquished, he and his Devil's arguments. Then I thanked the Lord for being parted for a few days from my father, and was refreshed by his absence. During those few days we were baptized, and the Holy Spirit bade me make no other petition after the holy water save for bodily endurance. A few days after we were lodged in prison; and I was in great fear, because I had never known such darkness. What a day of horror! Terrible heat, thanks to the crowds! Rough handling by the soldiers! To crown all I was tormented there by anxiety for my baby. Then Tertius and Pomponius, those blessed deacons who were ministering to us, paid for us to be removed for a few hours to a better part of the prison and refresh ourselves. Then all went out of the prison and were left to themselves. My baby was brought to me, and I suckled him, for he was already faint for want of food. I spoke anxiously to my mother on his behalf, and strengthened my brother, and commended my son to their charge. I was pining because I saw them pine on my account. Such anxieties I suffered for many days; and I obtained leave for my baby to remain in the prison with me; and I at once recovered my health, and was relieved of my trouble and anxiety for my baby; and my prison suddenly became a palace to me, and I would rather have been there than anywhere else."

IV

"Then my brother said to me: 'Lady sister, you are now in great honor, so great indeed that you may well pray for a vision and may well be shown whether suffering or release be in store for you.' And I who knew myself to have speech of the Lord, for whose sake I had gone through so much, gave confident promise in return, saying: 'Tomorrow I will bring you word.' And I made request, and this was shown me. I saw a brazen ladder of wondrous length reaching up to heaven, but so narrow that only one could ascend at once; and on the sides of the ladder were fastened all kinds of iron weapons. There were swords, lances, hooks, daggers, so that if anyone went up carelessly or without looking upwards he was mangled and his flesh caught on the weapons. And just beneath the ladder was a dragon couching of wondrous size who lay in wait for those going up and sought to frighten them from going up. Now Saturus went up first, who had given himself up for our sakes of his own accord, because our faith had been of his own building, and he had not been present when we were seized. And he reached the top of the ladder, and turned, and said to me: 'Perpetua, I await you; but see that the dragon bite you not.' And I said: 'In the name of Jesus Christ he will not hurt me.' And he put out his head gently, as if afraid of me, just at the foot of the ladder; and as though I were treading on the first step, I trod on his head. And I went up, and saw a vast expanse of garden, and in the midst a man sitting with white hair, in the dress of a shepherd, a tall man, milking sheep; and round about were many thousands clad in white. And he raised his head, and looked upon me, and said: 'You have well come, my child.' And he called me, and gave me a morsel of the milk which he was milking and I received it in my joined hands, and ate, and all they that stood around said: 'Amen.' And at the sound of the word I woke, still eating something sweet. And at once I told my brother, and we understood that we must suffer, and henceforward began to have no hope in this world."

V

"After a few days a rumor ran that we were to be examined. Moreover, my father arrived from the city, worn with trouble, and came up the hill to see me, that he might overthrow my resolution, saying: 'Daughter, pity my white hairs! Pity your father, if I am worthy to be called father by you; if with these hands I have brought you up to this your prime of life, if I have preferred you to all your brothers! Give me not over to the reproach of men! Look upon your brothers, look upon your mother and your mother's sister, look upon your son who cannot live after you are gone! Lay aside your pride, do not ruin all of us, for none of us will ever speak freely again, if anything happen to you!' So spoke my father in his love for me, kissing my hands, and casting himself at my feet; and with tears called me by the name not of daughter but of lady. And I grieved for my father's sake, because he alone of all my kindred would not have joy in my suffering. And I comforted him, saying: 'It shall happen on that platform as God shall choose; for know well that we lie not in our own power but in the power of God.' And full of sorrow he left me."

VI

"On another day when we were having our midday meal, we were suddenly hurried off to be examined; and we came to the marketplace. Forthwith a rumor ran through the neighboring parts of the marketplace, and a vast crowd gathered. We went up on to the platform. The others on being questioned confessed their faith. So it came to my turn. And there was my father with my child, and he drew me down from the step, beseeching me: 'Have pity on your baby.' And the procurator Hilarian, who had then received the power of life and death in the room of the late proconsul Minucius Timinianus, said to me: 'Spare your father's white hairs; spare the tender years of your child. Offer a sacrifice for the safety of the Emperors.' And I answered: 'No.' 'Are you a Christian?' said Hilarian. And I answered: 'I am.' And when my father persisted in trying to overthrow my resolution, he was ordered by Hilarian to be thrown down, and the judge struck him with his rod. And I was grieved for my father's plight, as if I had been struck myself, so did I grieve for the sorrow that had come on his old age. Then he passed sentence on the whole of us, and condemned us to the beasts; and

in great joy we went down into the prison. Then because my baby was accustomed to take the breast from me, and stay with me in prison, I sent at once the deacon Pomponius to my father to ask for my baby. But my father refused to give him. And as God willed, neither had he any further wish for my breasts, nor did they become inflamed; that I might not be tortured by anxiety for the baby and pain in my breasts."

VII

"After a few days, while we were all praying, suddenly in the middle of the prayer I spoke, and uttered the name of Dinocrates; and I was astonished that he had never come into mind till then; and I grieved thinking of what had befallen him. And I saw at once that I was entitled, and ought, to make request for him. And I began to pray much for him, and make lamentation to the Lord. At once on this very night this was shown me. I saw Dinocrates coming forth from a dark place, where there were many other dark places, very hot and thirsty, his countenance pale and squalid; and the wound which he had when he died was in his face still. This Dinocrates had been my brother according to the flesh, seven years old, who had died miserably of a gangrene in the face, so that his death moved all to loathing. For him then I had prayed; and there was a great gulf between me and him, so that neither of us could approach the other. There was besides in the very place where Dinocrates was a font full of water, the rim of which was above the head of the child; and Dinocrates stood on tiptoe to drink. I grieved that the font should have water in it and that nevertheless he could not drink because of the height of the rim. And I woke and recognized that my brother was in trouble. But I trusted that I could relieve his trouble, and I prayed for him every day until we were transferred to the garrison prison, for we were to fight with the beasts at the garrison games on the Caesar Geta's birthday. And I prayed for him day and night with lamentations and tears that he might be given me."

VIII

"During the daytime, while we stayed in the stocks, this was shown me. I saw that same place which I had seen before, and Dinocrates clean in body, well-clothed and refreshed; and where there had been a wound, I saw a scar; and the font which I had seen before had its rim lowered to the child's waist; and there poured water from it unceasingly; and on the rim a golden bowl full of water. And Dinocrates came forward and began to drink from it, and the bowl failed not. And when he had drunk enough of the water, he came forward being glad to play as children will. And I awoke. Then I knew that he had been released from punishment."

IX

"Then after a few days Pudens the adjutant, who was in charge of the prison, who began to show us honor perceiving that there was some great power within us, began to admit many to see us, that both we and they might be refreshed by one another's company. Now when the day of the games approached, my father came in to me worn with trouble, and began to pluck out his beard and cast it on the ground, and to throw himself on his face, and to curse his years, and to say such words as might have turned the world upside down. I sorrowed for the unhappiness of his old age."

X

"On the day before we were to fight, I saw in a vision Pomponius the deacon come hither to the door of the prison and knock loudly. And I went out to him, and opened to him. Now he was clad in a white robe without a girdle, wearing shoes curiously wrought. And he said to me: 'Perpetua, we are waiting for you; come.' And he took hold of my hand, and we began to pass through rough and broken country. Painfully and panting did we arrive at last at an amphitheatre, and he led me into the middle of the arena. And he said to me: 'Fear not; I am here with you, and I suffer with you.' And he departed.

"And I saw a huge crowd watching eagerly. And because I knew that I was condemned to the beasts, I marveled that there were no beasts let loose on me. And there came out an Egyptian, foul of look, with his attendants to fight against me. And to me also there came goodly young men to be my attendants and supporters. And I was stripped and was changed into a man. And my supporters began to rub me down with oil, as they are wont to do before a combat; and I saw the Egyptian opposite rolling in the sand. And there came forth a man wondrously tall so that he rose above the top of the amphitheatre, clad in a purple robe without a girdle with two stripes, one on either side, running down the middle of the breast, and wearing shoes curiously wrought made of gold and silver; carrying a wand, like a trainer, and a green bough on which were golden apples. And he asked for silence, and said: 'This Egyptian, if he prevail over her, shall kill her with a sword; and, if she prevail over him, she shall receive this bough.' And he retired. And we came near to one another and began to use our fists. My adversary wished to catch hold of my feet, but I kept on striking his face with my heels. And I was lifted up into the air, and began to strike him in such fashion as would one that no longer trod on earth. But when I saw that the fight lagged, I joined my two hands, linking the fingers of the one with the fingers of the other. And I caught hold of his head, and he fell on his face; and I trod upon his head. And the people began to shout, and my supporters to sing psalms. And I came forward to the trainer, and received the bough. And he kissed me, and said to me: 'Peace be with you, my daughter.'

"And I began to go in triumph to the Gate of Life. And I awoke. And I perceived that I should not fight with beasts but with the Devil; but I knew the victory to be mine. Such were my doings up to the day before the games. Of what was done in the games themselves let him write who will."

XI

But the blessed Saturus also has made known this vision of his own, which he has written out with his own hand. "Methought we had suffered, and put off the flesh, and began to be borne toward the east by four angels whose hands touched us not. Now we moved not on our backs looking upward, but as though we were climbing a gentle slope. And when we were clear of the world below we saw a great light, and I said to Perpetua, for she was by my side: 'This is what the Lord promised us, we have received his promise.' And while we were carried by those four angels, we came upon a great open space, which was like as it might be a garden, having rose-trees and all kinds of flowers. The height of the trees was like the height of a cypress, whose leaves sang without ceasing. Now there in the garden were certain four angels, more glorious than the others, who when they saw us, gave us honor, and said to the other angels: 'Lo! they are come; lo! they are come,' being full of wonder. And those four angels which bare us trembled and set us down, and we crossed on foot a place strewn with violets, where we found Jucundus and Saturninus and Artaxius, who were burned alive in the same persecution, and Quintus who, being also a martyr, had died in the prison, and we asked of them where they were. The other angels said unto us: 'Come first and enter and greet the Lord.'"

XII

"And we came near to a place whose walls were built like as it might be of light, and before the gate of that place were four angels standing, who as we entered clothed us in white robes. And we entered, and heard a sound as of one voice saying: 'Holy, holy, holy,' without ceasing. And we saw sitting in the same place one like unto a man white-haired, having hair as white as snow, and with the face of a youth; whose feet we saw not. And on the right and on the left four elders; and behind them were many other elders standing. And entering we stood in wonder before the throne; and the four angels lifted us up, and we kissed him, and he stroked our faces with his hand. And the other elders said to us: 'Let us stand.' And we stood and gave the kiss of peace. And the elders said to us: 'Go and play.' And I said to Perpetua: 'You have your wish.' And she said to me: 'Thanks be to God, that as I was merry in the flesh, so am I now still merrier here.'"

XIII

"And we went forth, and saw before the doors Optatus the bishop on the right, and Aspasius the priest-teacher on the left, severed and sad. And they cast themselves at our feet, and said: 'Make peace between us, for you have gone forth, and left us thus.' And we said to them: 'Are not you our father, and you our priest? Why should ye fall before our feet?' And we were moved, and embraced them. And Perpetua began to talk Greek with them, and we drew them aside into the garden under a rose-tree. And while we talked with them, the angels said to them: 'Let them refresh themselves; and if you have any quarrels among yourselves, forgive one another.' And they put these to shame, and said to Optatus: 'Reform your people, for they come to you like men returning from the circus and contending about its factions.'

And it seemed to us as though they wished to shut the gates. And we began to recognize many brethren there, martyrs too amongst them. We were all fed on a fragrance beyond telling, which contented us. Then in my joy I awoke."

XIV

Such are the famous visions of the blessed martyrs themselves, Saturus and Perpetua, which they wrote with their own hands. As for Secundulus, God called him to an earlier departure from this world while still in prison, not without grace, that he might escape the beasts. Nevertheless, his body, if not his soul, made acquaintance with the sword.

XV

As for Felicitas indeed, she also was visited by the grace of God in this wise. Being eight months gone with child (for she was pregnant at the time of her arrest), as the day for the spectacle drew near she was in great sorrow for fear lest because of her pregnancy her martyrdom should be delayed, since it is against the law for women with child to be exposed for punishment, and lest she should shed her sacred and innocent blood among others afterwards who were malefactors. Her fellow martyrs too were deeply grieved at the thought of leaving so good a comrade and fellow traveler behind alone on the way to the same hope. So in one flood of common lamentation they poured forth a prayer to the Lord two days before the games. Immediately after the prayer her pains came upon her. And since from the natural difficulty of an eight-months' labor she suffered much in childbirth, one of the warders said to her: 'You who so suffer now, what will you do when you are flung to the beasts which, when you refused to sacrifice, you despised?' And she answered: 'Now I suffer what I suffer: but then another will be in me, be-

cause I too am to suffer for him.' So she gave birth to a girl, whom one of the sisters brought up as her own daughter.

XVI

Since, therefore, the Holy Spirit has permitted, and by permitting willed, the story of the games themselves to be written, we cannot choose but carry out, however unworthy to supplement so glorious a history, the injunction, or rather sacred bequest, of the most holy Perpetua, adding at the same time one example of her steadfastness and loftiness of soul. When they were treated with unusual rigor by the commanding officer because his fears were aroused through the warnings of certain foolish people that they might be carried off from prison by some magic spells, she challenged him to his face: 'Why do you not at least suffer us to refresh ourselves, "the most noble" among the condemned, belonging as we do to Caesar and chosen to fight on his birthday? Or is it not to your credit that we should appear thereon in better trim?' The commanding officer trembled and blushed; and so ordered them to be used more kindly, giving her brothers and other persons leave to visit, that they might refresh themselves in their company. By this time the governor of the prison was himself a believer.

XVII

Moreover, on the day before the games when they celebrated that last supper, called "the free festivity," not as a "festivity," but, so far as they could make it so, a "love-feast," with same steadfastness they flung words here and there among the people, threatening them with the judgment of God, calling to witness the happiness of their own passion, laughing at the inquisitiveness of the crowd. Said Saturus: "Tomorrow does not satisfy you, for what you hate you love to see. Friends today, foes tomorrow. Yet mark our faces well, that when the day comes you may know us again." So all left the place amazed, and many of them became believers.

XVIII

The day of their victory dawned, and they proceeded from the prison to the amphitheatre, as if they were on their way to heaven, with gay and gracious looks; trembling, if at all, not with fear but joy. Perpetua followed with shining steps, as the true wife of Christ, as the darling of God, abashing with the high spirit in her eyes the gaze of all; Felicitas also, rejoicing that she had brought forth in safety that so she might fight the beasts, from blood to blood, from midwife to gladiator, to find in her Second Baptism her childbirth washing. And when they were led within the gate, and were on the point of being forced to put on the dress, the men of the priests of Saturn, the women of those dedicated to Ceres, the noble Perpetua resisted steadfastly to the last. For she said: "Therefore we came to this issue of our own free will, that our liberty might not be violated; therefore we pledged our lives, that we might do no such thing: this was our pact with you." Injustice acknowledged justice; the commanding officer gave permission that they should enter the arena in their ordinary dress as they were. Perpetua was singing a psalm of triumph, as already treading on the head of the Egyptian. Revocatus, Saturninus, and Saturus were threatening the onlookers with retribution; when they came within sight of Hilarian, they began to signify to him by nods and gestures: "You are judging us, but God shall judge you." The people infuriated thereat demanded that they should be punished with scourging before a line of beast-fighters. And they for this at least gave one another joy, that they had moreover won some share in the sufferings of their Lord.

XIX

But he who had said: "Ask and you shall receive" had granted to those who asked him that death which each had craved. For, whenever they talked amongst themselves about their hopes of martyrdom, Saturninus declared that he wished to be cast to all the beasts; so indeed would he wear a more glorious crown. Accordingly at the outset of the show he was matched with the leopard and recalled from him; he was also later mauled on the platform by the bear. Saturus on the other hand had a peculiar dread of the bear, but counted beforehand on being dispatched by one bite of the leopard. And so when he was offered to the wild boar, the fighter with beasts, who had bound him to the boar, was gored from beneath by the same beast, and died after the days of the games were over, whereas Saturus was only dragged. And when he was tied up on the bridge before the bear, the bear refused to come out of his den. So Saturus for the second time was recalled unhurt.

XX

For the young women the Devil made ready a mad heifer, an unusual animal selected for this reason, that he wished to match their sex with that of the beast. And so after being stripped and enclosed in ncts they were brought into the arena. The people were horrified, beholding in the one a tender girl, in the other a woman fresh from childbirth, with milk dripping from her breasts. So they were recalled and dressed in tunics without girdles. Perpetua was tossed first, and fell on her loins. Sitting down she drew back her torn tunic from her side to cover her thighs, more mindful of her modesty than of her suffering. Then having asked for a pin she further fastened her disordered hair. For it was not seemly that a martyr should suffer with her hair disheveled, lest she should seem to mourn in the hour of her glory. Then she rose, and seeing that Felicitas was bruised, approached, gave a hand to her, and lifted her up. And the two stood side by side, and the cruelty of the people being now appeased, they were recalled to the Gate of Life. There Perpetua was supported by a certain Rusticus, then a catechumen, who kept close to her; and being roused from what seemed like sleep, so completely had she been in the Spirit and in ecstasy, began to look about her, and said to the amazement of all: "When we are to be thrown to that heifer, I cannot tell." When she heard what had already taken place, she refused to believe it till she had observed certain marks of ill-usage on her body and dress. Then she summoned her brother and spoke to him and the catechumen, saying: 'Stand fast in the faith, and love one another; and be not offended by our sufferings.'

XXI

Saturus also at another gate was encouraging the soldier Pudens: "In a word," said he, "what I counted on and foretold has come to pass, not a beast so far has touched me. And now, that you may trust me wholeheartedly, see, I go forth yonder, and with one bite of the leopard all is over." And forthwith, as the show was ending, the leopard was let loose, and with one bite Saturus was so drenched in blood that the people as he came back shouted in attestation of his Second Baptism, "Bless you, well bathed! Bless you, well bathed!" Blessed indeed was he who had bathed after this fashion. Then he said to the soldier Pudens: "Farewell! Keep my faith and me in mind! And let these things not con-found, but confirm you." And with that he asked for the ring from Pudens's finger, plunged it in his own wound, and gave it back as a legacy, bequeathing it for a pledge and memorial of his blood. Then by this time lifeless he was flung with the rest on to the place allotted to the throat-cutting. And when the people asked for them to be brought into the open, that, when the sword pierced their bodies, these might lend their eyes for partners in murder, they rose unbidden and made their way whither the people willed, after first kissing one another, that they might perfect their martyrdom with the rite of the Pax. The rest without a movement in silence received the sword, Saturus in deeper silence, who, as he had been the first to climb the ladder, was the first to give up the ghost; for now as then he awaited Perpetua. Perpetua, however, that she might taste something of the pain, was struck on the bone and cried out, and herself guided to her throat the wavering hand of the young untried gladiator. Perhaps so great a woman, who was feared by the unclean spirit, could not otherwise be slain except she willed.

O valiant and blessed martyrs! O truly called and chosen to the glory of Jesus Christ our Lord! He who magnifies, honors, and adores that glory should recite to the edification of the Church these examples also, not less precious at least than those of old; that so new instances of virtue may testify that one and the self-same Spirit is working to this day with the Father, God Almighty, and with his son Jesus Christ our Lord, to whom belong splendor and power immeasurable forever and ever. Amen.

The Story of Ahikar

(Jewish Pseudepigrapha)

The Story of Ahikar is an example of secular wisdom literature. The story is ancient. Our earliest version is contained in fragments of an Aramaic papyrus from the fifth century B.C., discovered at Elephantine, an Aramaic-speaking Jewish colony in Egypt. The tale probably had an Akkadian version from the Assyrian period, for it uses the Akkadian forms of the monarchs Sennacherib and Esarhaddon. In Tobit, a colorful narrative of the standard Apocrypha, the scene is also Assyria and we have a reference to Ahikar, who is Tobit's nephew. Ahikar is also the model for one of the lives of Aesop, and much later appears in the supplementary pages of the *Arabian Nights.*

In this adventuresome romance, the wise Ahikar is the hero. He is Grand Vizier to Sennacherib, King of Assyria (c. 681 B.C.). Despite the sixty wives he has married, Ahikar remains childless and so chooses to make Nadan, his sister's son, heir to his palace and fortune. He brings up Nadan with love, honor, and proverbial wisdom, yet the nephew, anxious to obtain his uncle's position, falsifies documents and succeeds in getting Ahikar condemned to death. But the swordsman in charge of the execution recognizes Ahikar as one who had earlier saved his life and so spares the good vizier by substituting a condemned slave in his place. After an interval of hiding, Ahikar is sorely missed by the Assyrian king. Only he can solve the nation's problems. His astonishing reappearance brings him back to favor. Now Nadan is placed in prison where, as the vizier's recriminating wisdom reaches his ears, he is beaten, starved, and justly left to perish. "He who digs a pit for his brother shall fall in it."

The brilliant descriptions, the intrigues, the moral condemnation of the traitor and reward of the virtuous wise man provide, amid a profusion of moral proverbs, the traditional elements of this father-and-son parable. Here the father's insistent intelligence saves himself and his nation. The text exists in the aforementioned Aramaic fragments. It also occurs in later Syriac, Arabic, Ethiopic, Armenian, and Slavonic versions, as well as in the Greek version in the lives of Aesop. The translation below is a revision of the Arabic version edited by J. Rendel Harris, Agnes Smith Lewis, and F. C. Conybeare in R. H. Charles, *The Apocrypha and Pseudepigrapha of the Old Testament*, Vol. 2 (Oxford: Clarendon Press, 1913).

THE STORY OF AHIKAR*

I

Ahikar (Haiqar), Grand Vizier of Assyria, has sixty wives but is fated to have no son. Therefore he adopts his nephew. He crams him full of wisdom and knowledge more than of bread and water.

The story of Haiqar the Wise, Vizier of Sennacherib the King, and of Nadan, sister's son to Haiqar the Sage.

There was a Vizier in the days of King Sennacherib, son of Sarhadum, King of Assyria and Nineveh, a wise man named Haiqar, and he was Vizier of the king Sennacherib.

He had a fine fortune and much goods, and he was skillful, wise, a philosopher, in knowledge, in opinion, and in government, and he had married sixty women, and had built a castle for each of them.

But with it all he had no child by any of these women, who might be his heir.

And he was very sad on account of this, and one day he assembled the astrologers and the learned men and the wizards and explained to them his condition and the matter of his barrenness.

And they said to him, "Go, sacrifice to the gods and beseech them that perchance they may provide you with a boy."

And he did as they told him and offered sacrifices to the idols, and besought them and implored them with request and entreaty.

*From Frank Crane, *The Lost Books of the Bible and the Forgotten Books of Eden* (New Foundland: Alpha House, 1927), pp. 198–219.

And they answered him not one word. And he went away sorrowful and dejected, departing with a pain at his heart.

And he returned, and implored the Most High God, and believed, beseeching him with a burning in his heart, saying, "O Most High God, O Creator of the Heavens and of the earth, O Creator of all created things!

"I beseech you to give me a boy, that I may be consoled by him, that he may be present at my death, that he may close my eyes, and that he may bury me."

Then there came to him a voice saying, "Inasmuch as you have relied first of all on graven images, and have offered sacrifices to them, for this reason you shall remain childless your life long.

"But take Nadan your sister's son, and make him your child and teach him your learning and your good breeding, and at your death he shall bury you."

Thereupon he took Nadan his sister's son, who was a little suckling. And he handed him over to eight wetnurses, that they might suckle him and bring him up.

And they brought him up with good food and gentle training and silken clothing, and purple and crimson. And he was seated upon couches of silk.

And when Nadan grew big and walked, shooting up like a tall cedar, he taught him good manners and writing and science and philosophy.

And after many days King Sennacherib looked at Haiqar and saw that he had grown very old, and moreover he said to him,

"O my honored friend, the skillful, the trusty, the wise, the governor, my secretary, my vizier, my chancellor and director; truly you are grown very old and weighted with years; and your departure from this world must be near.

"Tell me who shall have a place in my service after you." And Haiqar said to him, "O my lord, may your head live forever! There is Nadan my sister's son, I have made him my child. And I have brought him up and taught him my wisdom and my knowledge."

And the king said to him, "O Haiqar! bring him to my presence, that I may see him, and if I find him suitable, put him in your place; and you shall go your way, to take a rest and to live the remainder of your life in sweet repose."

Then Haiqar went and presented Nadan his sister's son. And he did homage and wished him power and honor.

And he looked at him and admired him and rejoiced in him and said to Haiqar: "Is this your son, O Haiqar? I pray that God may preserve him. And as you have served me and my father Sarhadum, so may this boy of yours serve me and fulfill my undertakings, my needs, and my business, so that I may honor him and make him powerful for your sake."

And Haiqar did obeisance to the king and said to him, "May your head live, O my lord the king, forever! I seek from you that you may be patient with my boy Nadan and forgive his mistakes that he may serve you as it is fitting."

Then the king swore to him that he would make him the greatest of his favorites, and the most powerful of his friends, and that he should be with him in all honor and respect. And he kissed his hands and bade him farewell.

And he took Nadan his sister's son with him and seated him in a parlor and set about teaching him night and day till he had crammed him with wisdom and knowledge more than with bread and water.

II

A "Poor Richard's Almanac" of ancient days. Immortal precepts of human conduct concerning money, women, dress, business, friends.

Thus he taught him, saying: "O my son! Hear my speech and follow my advice and remember what I say.

"O my son! If you hear a word, let it die in your heart, and reveal it not to another, lest it become a live coal and burn your tongue and cause a pain in your body, and you gain a reproach, and are shamed before God and man.

"O my son! If you have heard a report, spread it not; and if you have seen something, tell it not.

"O my son! Make your eloquence easy to the listener, and be not hasty to return an answer.

"O my son! When you have heard anything, hide it not.

"O my son! Loose not a sealed knot, nor untie it, and seal not a loosened knot.

"O my son! Covet not outward beauty, for it wanes and passes away, but an honorable remembrance lasts forever.

"O my son! Let not a silly woman deceive you with her speech, lest you die the most miserable of deaths, and she entangle you in the net till you are ensnared.

"O my son! Desire not a woman bedizened with dress and with ointments, who is despicable and silly in her soul. Woe to you if you bestow on her anything that is yours or commit to her what is in your hand and she entice you into sin, and God be angry with you.

"O my son! Be not like the almond tree, for it brings forth leaves before all the trees, and edible fruit after them all, but be like the mulberry tree, which brings forth edible fruit before all the trees, and leaves after them all.

"O my son! Bend your head low down, and soften your voice, and be courteous, and walk in the straight path, and be not foolish. And raise not your voice when you laugh, for if it were by a loud voice that a house was built, the ass would build many houses every day; and if it were by dint of strength that the plough were driven, the plough would never be removed from under the shoulders of the camels.

"O my son! The removing of stones with a wise man is better than the drinking of wine with a sorry man.

"O my son! Pour out your wine on the tombs of the just, and drink not with ignorant, contemptible people.

"O my son! Cleave to wise men who fear God and be like them, and go not near the ignorant, lest you become like him and learn his ways.

"O my son! When you have a comrade or a friend, try him, and afterwards make him a comrade and a friend; and do not praise him without a trial; and do not spoil your speech with a man who lacks wisdom.

"O my son! While a shoe stays on your foot, walk with it on the thorns, and make a road for your son, and for your household and your children, and make your ship taut before she goes on the sea and its waves and sinks and cannot be saved.

"O my son! If the rich man eat a snake, they say, 'It is by his wisdom,' and if a poor man eat it, the people say, 'From his hunger.'

"O my son! Be content with your daily bread and your goods, and covet not what is another's.

"O my son! Be not neighbor to the fool, and eat not bread with him, and rejoice not in the calamities of your neighbors. If your enemy wrong you, show him kindness.

"O my son! A man who fears God, do you fear him and honor him.

"O my son! The ignorant man falls and stumbles, and the wise man, even if he stumbles, he is not shaken, and even if he falls he gets up quickly, and if he is sick, he can take care of his life. But as for the ignorant, stupid man, for his disease there is no drug.

"O my son! If a man approaches you who is inferior to yourself, go forward to meet him, and remain standing, and if he cannot recompense you, his Lord will recompense you for him.

"O my son! Spare not to beat your son, for the drubbing of your son is like manure to the garden, and like tying the mouth of a purse, and like the tethering of beasts, and like the bolting of the door.

"O my son! Restrain your son from wickedness, and teach him manners before he rebels against you and brings you into contempt among the people and you hang your head in the streets and the assemblies and you be punished for the evil of his wicked deeds.

"O my son! Get yourself a fat ox with a foreskin, and an ass great with its hoofs, and get not an ox with large horns, nor make friends with a tricky man, nor get a quarrelsome slave, nor a thievish handmaid, for everything which you commit to them they will ruin.

"O my son! Let not your parents curse you, and the Lord be pleased with them; for it has been said, 'He who despises his father or his mother let him die the death (I mean the death of sin); and he who honors his parents shall prolong his days and his life and shall see all that is good.'

"O my son! Walk not on the road without weapons, for you know not when the foe may meet you, so that you may be ready for him.

"O my son! Be not like a bare, leafless tree that does not grow, but be like a tree covered with its leaves and its boughs; for the man who has neither wife nor children is disgraced in the world and is hated by them, like a leafless and fruitless tree.

"O my son! Be like a fruitful tree on the roadside, whose fruit is eaten by all who pass by, and the beasts of the desert rest under its shade and eat of its leaves.

"O my son! Every sheep that wanders from its path and its companions becomes food for the wolf.

"O my son! Say not, 'My lord is a fool and I am wise,' and relate not the speech of ignorance and folly, lest you be despised by him.

"O my son! Be not one of those servants, to whom their lords say, 'Get away from us,' but be one of those to whom they say, 'Approach and come near to us.'

"O my son! Caress not your slave in the presence of his companion, for you know not which of them shall be of most value to you in the end.

"O my son! Be not afraid of your Lord who created you, lest he be silent to you.

"O my son! Make your speech fair and sweeten your tongue; and permit not your companion to tread on your foot, lest he tread at another time on your breast.

"O my son! If you beat a wise man with a word of wisdom, it will lurk in his breast like a subtle sense of shame; but if you drub the ignorant with a stick he will neither understand nor hear.

"O my son! If you send a wise man for your needs, do not give him many orders, for he will do your business as you desire: and if you send a fool, do not order him, but go yourself and do your business, for if you order him, he will not do what you desire. If they send you on business, hasten to fulfill it quickly.

"O my son! Make not an enemy of a man stronger than yourself, for he will take your measure, and his revenge on you.

"O my son! Make trial of your son, and of your servant, before you commit your belongings to them, lest they make away with them; for he who has a full hand is called wise, even if he be stupid and ignorant, and he who has an empty hand is called poor, ignorant, even if he be the prince of sages.

"O my son! I have eaten a colocynth, and swallowed aloes, and I have found nothing more bitter than poverty and scarcity.

"O my son! Teach your son frugality and hunger, that he may do well in the management of his household.

"O my son! Teach not to the ignorant the language of wise men, for it will be burdensome to him.

"O my son! Display not your condition to your friend, lest you be despised by him.

"O my son! The blindness of the heart is more grievous than the blindness of the eyes, for the blindness of the eyes may be guided little by little, but the blindness of the heart is not guided, and it leaves the straight path, and goes in a crooked way.

"O my son! The stumbling of a man with his foot is better than the stumbling of a man with his tongue.

"O my son! A friend who is near is better than a more excellent brother who is far away.

"O my son! Beauty fades but learning lasts, and the world wanes and becomes vain, but a good name neither becomes vain nor wanes.

"O my son! The man who has no rest, his death were better than his life; and the sound of weeping is better than the sound of singing; for sorrow and weeping, if the fear of God be in them, are better than the sound of singing and rejoicing.

"O my child! The thigh of a frog in your hand is better than a goose in the pot of your neighbor; and a sheep near you is better than an ox far away; and a sparrow in your hand is better than a thousand sparrows flying; and poverty which gathers is better than the scattering of much provision; and a living fox is better than a dead lion; and a pound of wool is better than a pound of wealth, I mean of gold and silver; for the gold and the silver are hidden and covered up in the earth, and are not seen; but the wool stays in the markets and it is seen, and it is a beauty to him who wears it.

"O my son! A small fortune is better than a scattered fortune.

"O my son! A living dog is better than a dead poor man.

"O my son! A poor man who does right is better than a rich man who is dead in sins.

"O my son! Keep a word in your heart, and it shall be much to you, and beware lest you reveal the secret of your friend.

"O my son! Let not a word issue from your mouth till you have taken counsel with your heart. And stand not betwixt persons quarreling, because from a bad word there comes a quarrel, and from a quarrel there comes war, and from war there comes fighting, and you will be forced to bear witness; but run from there and rest yourself.

"O my son! Withstand not a man stronger than yourself, but get a patient spirit, and endurance and an upright conduct, for there is nothing more excellent than that.

"O my son! Hate not your first friend, for the second one may not last.

"O my son! Visit the poor in his affliction, and speak of him in the Sultan's presence, and do your diligence to save him from the mouth of the lion.

"O my son! Rejoice not in the death of your enemy, for after a little while you shall be his neighbor, and him who mocks you do you respect and honor and be beforehand with him in greeting.

"O my son! If water would stand still in Heaven, and a black crow become white, and myrrh grow sweet as honey, then ignorant men and fools might understand and become wise.

"O my son! If you desire to be wise, restrain your tongue from lying, and your hand from stealing, and your eyes from beholding evil; then you will be called wise.

"O my son! Let the wise man beat you with a rod, but let not the fool anoint you with sweet salve. Be humble in your youth and you shall be honored in your old age.

"O my son! Withstand not a man in the days of his power, nor a river in the days of its flood.

"O my son! Be not hasty in the wedding of a wife, for if it turns out well, she will say, 'My lord, make provision for me'; and if it turns out ill, she will rate at him who was the cause of it.

"O my son! Whosoever is elegant in his dress, he is the same in his speech; and he who has a mean appearance in his dress, he also is the same in his speech.

"O my son! If you have committed a theft, make it known to the Sultan, and give him a share of it, that you may be delivered from him, for otherwise you will endure bitterness.

"O my son! Make a friend of the man whose hand is satisfied and filled, and make no friend of the man whose hand is closed and hungry.

"There are four things in which neither the king nor his army can be secure: oppression by the vizier, and bad government, and perversion of the will, and tyranny over the subject; and four things which cannot be hidden: the prudent, and the foolish, and the rich, and the poor."

III
Ahikar retires from active participation in affairs of state. He turns over his possessions to his treacherous nephew. Here is the amazing story of how a thankless profligate turns forgerer. A clever plot to entangle Ahikar results in his being condemned to death. Apparently the end of Ahikar.

Thus spake Haiqar, and when he had finished these injunctions and proverbs to Nadan, his sister's son, he imagined that he would keep them all, and he knew not that instead of that he was displaying to him weariness and contempt and mockery.

Thereafter Haiqar sat still in his house and delivered over to Nadan all his goods, and the slaves, and the handmaidens, and the horses, and the cattle, and everything else that he had possessed and gained; and the power of bidding and of forbidding remained in the hand of Nadan.

And Haiqar sat at rest in his house, and every now and then Haiqar went and paid his respects to the king, and returned home.

Now when Nadan perceived that the power of bidding and of forbidding was in his own hand, he despised the position of Haiqar and scoffed at him, and set about blaming him whenever he appeared, saying, "My uncle Haiqar is in his dotage, and he knows nothing now."

And he began to beat the slaves and the handmaidens, and to sell the horses and the camels and be spendthrift with all that his uncle Haiqar had owned.

And when Haiqar saw that he had no compassion on his servants nor on his household, he arose and chased him from his house, and sent to inform the king that he had scattered his possessions and his provision.

And the king arose and called Nadan and said to him: "While Haiqar remains in health, no one shall rule over his goods, nor over his household, nor over his possessions."

And the hand of Nadan was lifted off from his uncle Haiqar and from all his goods, and in the meantime he went neither in nor out, nor did he greet him.

Thereupon Haiqar repented him of his toil with Nadan his sister's son, and he continued to be very sorrowful.

And Nadan had a younger brother named Benuzardan, so Haiqar took him to himself in place of Nadan, and brought him up and honored him with the utmost honor. And he delivered over to him all that he possessed, and made him governor of his house.

Now when Nadan perceived what had happened he was seized with envy and jealousy, and he began to complain to every one who questioned him, and to mock his uncle Haiqar, saying: "My uncle has chased me from his house, and has preferred my brother to me, but if the Most High God give me the power, I shall bring upon him the misfortune of being killed."

And Nadan continued to meditate as to the stumbling block he might contrive

for him. And after a while Nadan turned it over in his mind, and wrote a letter to Achish, son of Shah the Wise, king of Persia, saying thus:

"Peace and health and might and honor from Sennacherib king of Assyria and Nineveh, and from his vizier and his secretary Haiqar unto you, O great king! Let there be peace between you and me.

"And when this letter reaches you, if you will arise and go quickly to the plain of Nisrin, and to Assyria and Nineveh, I will deliver up the kingdom to you without war and without battle array."

And he wrote also another letter in the name of Haiqar to Pharaoh king of Egypt. "Let there be peace between you and me, O mighty king!

"If at the time of this letter reaching you, you will arise and go to Assyria and Nineveh to the plain of Nisrin, I will deliver up to you the kingdom without war and without fighting."

And the writing of Nadan was like to the writing of his uncle Haiqar.

Then he folded the two letters, and sealed them with the seal of his uncle Haiqar; they were nevertheless in the king's palace.

Then he went and wrote a letter likewise from the king to his uncle Haiqar: "Peace and health to my vizier, my secretary, my chancellor, Haiqar.

"O Haiqar, when this letter reaches you, assemble all the soldiers who are with you, and let them be perfect in clothing and in numbers, and bring them to me on the fifth day in the plain of Nisrin.

"And when you see me there coming towards you, hasten and make the army move against me as an enemy who would fight with me, for I have with me the ambassadors of Pharaoh king of Egypt, that they may see the strength of our army and may fear us, for they are our enemies and they hate us."

Then he sealed the letter and sent it to Haiqar by one of the king's servants. And he took the other letter which he had written and spread it before the king and read it to him and showed him the seal.

And when the king heard what was in the letter he was perplexed with a great perplexity and was wroth with a great and fierce wrath, and said, "Ah, I have shown my wisdom! what have I done to Haiqar that he has written these letters to my enemies? Is this my recompense from him for my benefits to him?"

And Nadan said to him, "Be not grieved, O king! Nor be wroth, but let us go to the plain of Nisrin and see if the tale be true or not."

Then Nadan arose on the fifth day and took the king and the soldiers and the vizier, and they went to the desert to the plain of Nisrin. And the king looked, and lo! Haiqar and the army were set in array.

And when Haiqar saw that the king was there, he approached and signaled to the army to move as in war and to fight in array against the king as it had been found in the letter, he not knowing what a pit Nadan had dug for him.

And when the king saw the act of Haiqar he was seized with anxiety and terror and perplexity, and was wroth with a great wrath.

And Nadan said to him, "Have you seen, O my lord the king! what this wretch has done? but be not wroth and be not grieved nor pained, but go to your house and sit on your throne, and I will bring Haiqar to you bound and chained with chains, and I will chase away your enemy from you without toil."

And the king returned to his throne, being provoked about Haiqar, and did nothing concerning him. And Nadan went to Haiqar and said to him, "W'allah, O my uncle! The king truly rejoices in you with great joy and thanks you for having done what he commanded you.

"And now he has sent me to you that you may dismiss the soldiers to their duties and come yourself to him with your hands bound behind you, and your feet chained, that the ambassadors of Pharaoh may see this, and that the king may be feared by them and by their king."

Then answered Haiqar and said, "To hear is to obey." And he arose straightway and bound his hands behind him, and chained his feet.

And Nadan took him and went with him to the king. And when Haiqar entered the king's presence he did obeisance before him on the ground, and wished for power and perpetual life to the king.

Then said the king, "O Haiqar, my secretary, the governor of my affairs, my chancellor, the ruler of my state, tell me what evil have I done to you that you have rewarded me by this ugly deed."

Then they showed him the letters in his writing and with his seal. And when Haiqar saw this, his limbs trembled and his tongue was tied at once, and he was unable to speak a word from fear; but he hung his head towards the earth and was dumb.

And when the king saw this, he felt certain that the thing was from him, and he straightway arose and commanded them to kill Haiqar, and to strike his neck with the sword outside of the city.

Then Nadan screamed and said, "O Haiqar, O blackface! what avails you your meditation or your power in the doing of this deed to the king?"

Thus says the story-teller. And the name of the swordsman was Abu Samik. And the king said to him, "O swordsman! Arise, go, cleave the neck of Haiqar at the door of his house, and cast away his head from his body a hundred cubits."

Then Haiqar knelt before the king, and said, "Let my lord the king live for ever! and if you desire to slay me, let your wish be fulfilled; and I know that I am not guilty, but the wicked man has to give an account of his wickedness; nevertheless, O my lord the king! I beg of you and of your friendship, permit the swordsman to give my body to my slaves, that they may bury me, and let your slave be your sacrifice."

The king arose and commanded the swordsman to do with him according to his desire.

And he straightway commanded his servants to take Haiqar and the swordsman and go with him naked that they might slay him.

And when Haiqar knew for certain that he was to be slain he sent to his wife, and said to her, "Come out and meet me, and let there be with you a thousand young virgins, and dress them in gowns of purple and silk that they may weep for me before my death.

"And prepare a table for the swordsman and for his servants. And mingle plenty of wine, that they may drink."

And she did all that he commanded her. And she was very wise, clever, and prudent. And she united all possible courtesy and learning.

And when the army of the king and the swordsman arrived they found the table set in order, and the wine and the luxurious viands, and they began eating and drinking till they were gorged and drunken.

Then Haiqar took the swordsman aside apart from the company and said, "O Abu Samik, do you not know that when Sarhadum the king, the father of Sennacherib, wanted to kill you, I took you and hid you in a certain place till the king's anger subsided and he asked for you?

"And when I brought you into his presence he rejoiced in you: and now remember the kindness I did you.

"And I know that the king will repent him about me and will be wroth with a great wrath about my execution.

"For I am not guilty, and it shall be when you shall present me before him in his palace, you shall meet with great good fortune, and know that Nadan my sister's son has deceived me and has done this bad deed to me, and the king will repent of having slain me; and now I have a cellar in the garden of my house, and no one knows of it.

"Hide me in it with the knowledge of my wife. And I have a slave in prison who deserves to be killed.

"Bring him out and dress him in my clothes, and command the servants when they are drunk to slay him. They will not know who it is they are killing.

"And cast away his head a hundred cubits from his body, and give his body to my slaves that they may bury it. And you shall have laid up a great treasure with me."

And then the swordsman did as Haiqar had commanded him, and he went to the king and said to him, "May your head live for ever!"

Then Haiqar's wife let down to him in the hiding place every week what sufficed for him, and no one knew of it but herself.

And the story was reported and repeated and spread abroad in every place of how Haiqar the Sage had been slain and was dead, and all the people of that city mourned for him.

And they wept and said: "Alas for you, O Haiqar! And for your learning and your courtesy! How sad about you and about your knowledge! Where can another like you be found? And where can there be a man so intelligent, so learned, so skilled in ruling as to resemble you that he may fill your place?"

But the king was repenting about Haiqar, and his repentance availed him naught.

Then he called for Nadan and said to him, "Go and take your friends with you and make a mourning and a weeping for your uncle Haiqar, and lament for him as the custom is, doing honor to his memory."

But when Nadan, the foolish, the ignorant, the hardhearted, went to the house of his uncle, he neither wept nor sorrowed nor wailed, but assembled heartless and dissolute people and set about eating and drinking.

And Nadan began to seize the maid-servants and the slaves belonging to Haiqar, and bound them and tortured them and drubbed them with a sore drubbing.

And he did not respect the wife of his uncle, she who had brought him up like her own boy, but wanted her to fall into sin with him.

But Haiqar had been cast into the hiding place, and he heard the weeping of his slaves and his neighbors, and he praised the Most High God, the Merciful One, and gave thanks, and he always prayed and besought the Most High God.

And the swordsman came from time to time to Haiqar while he was in the midst of the hiding place: and Haiqar came and entreated him. And he comforted him and wished him deliverance.

And when the story was reported in other countries that Haiqar the Sage had been slain, all the kings were grieved and despised king Sennacherib, and they lamented over Haiqar the solver of riddles.

IV
"The Riddles of the Sphinx." What really happened to Ahikar. His return.

And when the king of Egypt had made sure that Haiqar was slain, he arose straightway and wrote a letter to king Sennacherib, reminding him in it "of the peace and the health and the might and the honor which we wish specially for you, my beloved brother, king Sennacherib.

"I have been desiring to build a castle between the Heaven and the earth, and I want you to send me a wise, clever man to build it for me, and to answer me all my questions, and that I may have the taxes and the custom duties of Assyria for three years."

Then he sealed the letter and sent it to Sennacherib.

He took it and read it and gave it to his viziers and to the nobles of his kingdom, and they were perplexed and ashamed, and he was wroth with a great wrath, and was puzzled about how he should act.

Then he assembled the old men and the learned men and the wise men and the philosophers, and the diviners and the astrologers, and everyone who was in his country, and read them the letter and said to them, "Who among you will go to Pharaoh king of Egypt and answer him his questions?"

And they said to him, "O our lord the king! There is none in thy kingdom who is acquainted with these questions except Haiqar, thy vizier and secretary.

But as for us, we have no skill in this, unless it be Nadan, his sister's son, for he taught him all his wisdom and learning and knowledge. Call him to thee, perchance he may untie this hard knot."

Then the king called Nadan and said to him, "Look at this letter and understand what is in it." And when Nadan read it, he said, "O my lord! Who is able to build a castle between the Heaven and the earth?"

And when the king heard the speech of Nadan he sorrowed with a great and sore sorrow, and stepped down from his throne and sat in the ashes, and began to weep and wail over Haiqar.

Saying, "O my grief! O Haiqar, who knew the secrets and the riddles! Woe is me for you, O Haiqar! O teacher of my country and ruler of my kingdom, where shall I find your like? O Haiqar, O teacher of my country, where shall I turn for you? Woe is me for you! how did I destroy you! And I listened to the talk of a stupid, ignorant boy without knowledge, without religion, without manliness.

Ah! and again Ah for myself! Who can give you to me just for once, or bring me word that Haiqar is alive? and I would give him the half of my kingdom.

"Whence is this to me? Ah, Haiqar! that I might see you just for once, that I might take my fill of gazing at you, and delighting in you.

"Ah! O my grief for you to all time! O Haiqar, how have I killed you! And I tarried not in your case till I had seen the end of the matter."

And the king went on weeping night and day. Now when the swordsman saw the wrath of the king and his sorrow for Haiqar, his heart was softened towards him, and he approached into his presence and said to him:

"O my lord! Command your servants to cut off my head." Then said the king to him: "Woe to you, Abu Samik, what is your fault?

And the swordsman said, "O my master! Every slave who acts contrary to the word of his master is killed, and I have acted contrary to your command."

Then the king said, "Woe unto you, O Abu Samik, in what have you acted contrary to my command?"

And the swordsman said, "O my lord! You commanded me to kill Haiqar, and I knew that you would repent concerning him, and that he had been wronged, and I hid him in a certain place, and I killed one of his slaves, and he is now safe in the cistern, and if you command me I will bring him to you."

And the king said unto him. "Woe to you, O Abu Samik! You have mocked me and I am your lord."

And the swordsman said unto him, "Nay, but by the life of your head, O my lord! Haiqar is safe and alive."

And when the king heard that saying, he felt sure of the matter, and his head swam, and he fainted from joy, and he commanded them to bring Haiqar.

And he said to the swordsman, "O trusty servant! if your speech be true, I would fain enrich you, and exalt your dignity above that of all your friends."

And the swordsman went along rejoicing till he came to Haiqar's house. And he opened the door of the hiding place, and went down and found Haiqar sitting, praising God, and thanking him.

And he shouted to him, saying, "O Haiqar, I bring the greatest of joy, and happiness, and delight!"

And Haiqar said to him, "What is the news, O Abu Samik?" And he told him all about Pharaoh from the beginning to the end. Then he took him and went to the king.

And when the king looked at him, he saw him in a state of want, and that his hair had grown long like the wild beasts' and his nails like the claws of an eagle, and that his body was dirty with dust, and the color of his face had changed and faded and was now like ashes.

And when the king saw him he sorrowed over him and rose at once and embraced him and kissed him, and wept over him and said: "Praise be to God! who has brought you back to me."

Then he consoled him and comforted him. And he stripped off his robe, and put it on the swordsman, and was very gracious to him, and gave him great wealth, and made Haiqar rest.

Then said Haiqar to the king, "Let my lord the king live forever! These be the deeds of the children of the world. I have reared me a palm tree that I might lean on it, and it bent sideways, and threw me down.

"But, O my lord! Since I have appeared before you, let not care oppress you." And the king said to him: "Blessed be God, who showed you mercy, and knew that you were wronged, and saved you and delivered you from being slain.

"But go to the warm bath, and shave your head, and cut your nails, and change your clothes, and amuse yourself for the space of forty days, that you may do good to yourself and improve your condition and the color of your face may come back to you."

Then the king stripped off his costly robe, and put it on Haiqar, and Haiqar thanked God and did obeisance to the king, and departed to his dwelling glad and happy, praising the Most High God.

And the people of his household rejoiced with him, and his friends and everyone who heard that he was alive rejoiced also.

V

The letter of the "riddles" is shown to Ahikar. The boys on the eagles. The first "airplane" ride. Off to Egypt. Ahikar, being a man of wisdom also has a sense of humor.

And he did as the king commanded him, and took a rest for forty days.

Then he dressed himself in his gayest dress, and went riding to the king, with his slaves behind him and before him, rejoicing and delighted.

But when Nadan his sister's son perceived what was happening, fear took hold of him and terror, and he was perplexed, not knowing what to do.

And when Haiqar saw it he entered into the king's presence and greeted him, and he returned the greeting, and made him sit down at his side, saying to him, "O my darling Haiqar! Look at these letters which the king of Egypt sent to us, after he had heard that you were slain.

"They have provoked us and overcome us, and many of the people of our country have fled to Egypt for fear of the taxes that the king of Egypt has sent to demand from us."

Then Haiqar took the letter and read it and understood all its contents.

Then he said to the king, "Be not wroth, O my lord! I will go to Egypt, and I will return the answers to Pharaoh, and I will display this letter to him, and I will reply to him about the taxes, and I will send back all those who have run away; and I will put your enemies to shame with the help of the Most High God, and for the Happiness of your kingdom."

And when the king heard this speech from Haiqar he rejoiced with a great joy, and his heart was expanded and he showed him favor.

And Haiqar said to the king: "Grant me a delay of forty days that I may consider this question and manage it." And the king permitted this.

And Haiqar went to his dwelling, and he commanded the huntsmen to capture two young eaglets for him, and they captured them and brought them to him:

and he commanded the weavers of ropes to weave two cables of cotton for him, each of them two thousand cubits long, and he had the carpenters brought and ordered them to make two great boxes, and they did this.

Then he took two little lads, and spent every day sacrificing lambs and feeding the eagles and the boys, and making the boys ride on the backs of the eagles, and he bound them with a firm knot, and tied the cable to the feet of the eagles, and let them soar upwards little by little every day, to a distance of ten cubits, till they grew accustomed and were educated to it; and they rose all the length of the rope till they reached the sky; the boys being on their backs. Then he drew them to himself.

And when Haiqar saw that his desire was fulfilled he charged the boys that when they were borne aloft to the sky they were to shout, saying:

"Bring us clay and stone, that we may build a castle for king Pharaoh, for we are idle."

And Haiqar was never done training them and exercising them till they had reached the utmost possible point of skill.

Then leaving them he went to the king and said to him, "O my lord! The work is finished according to your desire. Arise with me that I may show you the wonder."

So the king sprang up and sat with Haiqar and went to a wide place and sent to bring the eagles and the boys, and Haiqar tied them and let them off into the air all the length of the ropes, and they began to shout as he had taught them. Then he drew them to himself and put them in their places.

And the king and those who were with him wondered with a great wonder: and the king kissed Haiqar between his eyes and said to him, "Go in peace, O my beloved! O pride of my kingdom! To Egypt and answer the questions of Pharaoh and overcome him by the strength of the Most High God."

Then he bade him farewell, and took his troops and his army and the young men and the eagles, and went towards the dwellings of Egypt; and when he had arrived, he turned towards the country of the king.

And when the people of Egypt knew that Sennacherib had sent a man of his privy council to talk with Pharaoh and to answer his questions, they carried the news to king Pharaoh, and he sent a party of his privy councillors to bring him before him.

And he came and entered into the presence of Pharaoh, and did obeisance to him as it is fitting to do to kings.

And he said to him: "O my lord the king! Sennacherib the king hails you with abundance of peace and might, and honor.

"And he has sent me, one of his slaves, that I may answer your questions, and may fulfill all your desire: for you have sent to seek from my lord the king a man who will build you a castle between the Heaven and the earth.

"And I by the help of the Most High God and your noble favor and the power of my lord the king will build it for you as you desire.

"But, O my lord the king! What you have said in it about the taxes of Egypt for three years—now the stability of a kingdom is strict justice, and if you win and my hand has no skill in replying to you, then my lord the king will send you the taxes which you have mentioned.

"And if I shall have answered your questions, it shall remain for you to send whatever you have mentioned to my lord the king."

And when Pharaoh heard that speech, he wondered and was perplexed by the freedom of his tongue and the pleasantness of his speech.

And king Pharaoh said to him, "O man! What is your name?" And he said, "Thy servant is Abiqam, and I a little ant of the ants of king Sennacherib."

And Pharaoh said to him, "Had your lord no one of higher dignity than you, that he has sent me a little ant to reply to me, and to converse with me?"

And Haiqar said to him, "O my lord the king! I would to God Most High that I may fulfill what is on your mind, for God is with the weak that he may confound the strong."

Then Pharaoh commanded that they should prepare a dwelling for Abiqam and supply him with provender, meat, and drink, and all that he needed.

And when it was finished, three days afterwards Pharaoh clothed himself in purple and red and sat on his throne, and all his viziers and the magnates of his kingdom were standing with their hands crossed, their feet close together, and their heads bowed.

And Pharaoh sent to fetch Abiqam, and when he was presented to him, he did obeisance before him, and kissed the ground in front of him.

And king Pharaoh said to him, "O Abiqam, whom am I like? And the nobles of my kingdom, to whom are they like?"

And Haiqar said to him, "O my lord the king! You are like the idol Bel, and the nobles of your kingdom are like his servants."

He said to him, "Go, and come back hither tomorrow." So Haiqar went as king Pharaoh had commanded him.

And on the morrow Haiqar went into the presence of Pharaoh, and did obeisance, and stood before the king. And Pharaoh was dressed in a red color, and the nobles were dressed in white.

And Pharaoh said to him "O Abiqam, whom am I like? And the nobles of my kingdom, to whom are they like?"

And Abiqam said to him, "O my lord! You are like the sun, and your servants are like its beams." And Pharaoh said to him, "Go to your dwelling, and come hither tomorrow."

Then Pharaoh commanded his court to wear pure white, and Pharaoh was dressed like them and sat upon his throne, and he commanded them to fetch Haiqar. And he entered and sat down before him.

And Pharaoh said to him, "O Abiqam, whom am I like? And my nobles, to whom are they like?"

And Abiqam said to him, "O my lord! You are like the moon, and your nobles are like the planets and the stars." And Pharaoh said to him, "Go, and tomorrow be here."

Then Pharaoh commanded his servants to wear robes of various colors, and Pharaoh wore a red velvet dress, and sat on his throne, and commanded them to fetch Abiqam. And he entered and did obeisance before him.

And he said, "O Abiqam, whom am I like? And my armies, to whom are they like?" And he said, "O my lord! You are like the month of April, and your armies are like its flowers."

And when the king heard it he rejoiced with a great joy, and said, "O Abiqam! The first time you compared me to the idol Bel, and my nobles to his servants.

"And the second time you compared me to the sun, and my nobles to the sunbeams.

"And the third time you compared me to the moon, and my nobles to the planets and the stars.

"And the fourth time you compared me to the month of April, and my nobles to its flowers. But now, O Abiqam! Tell me, your lord, king Sennacherib, whom is he like? And his nobles, to whom are they like?"

And Haiqar shouted with a loud voice and said: "Be it far from me to make mention of my lord the king and you seated on your throne. But get up on your feet that I may tell you whom my lord the king is like and to whom his nobles are like."

And Pharaoh was perplexed by the freedom of his tongue and his boldness in answering. Then Pharaoh arose from his throne, and stood before Haiqar, and said to him, "Tell me now, that I may perceive whom thy lord the king is like, and his nobles, to whom they are like."

And Haiqar said to him: "My lord is the God of Heaven, and his nobles are the lightnings and the thunder, and when he wills the winds blow and the rain falls.

"And he commands the thunder, and it lightens and rains, and he holds the sun, and it gives not its light, and the moon and the stars, and they circle not.

"And he commands the tempest, and it blows and the rain falls and it tramples on April and destroys its flowers and its houses."

And when Pharaoh heard this speech, he was greatly perplexed and was wroth with a great wrath, and said to him: "O man! tell me the truth, and let me know who you really are."

And he told him the truth. "I am Haiqar the scribe, greatest of the privy councillors of king Sennacherib, and I am his vizier and the governor of his kingdom, and his chancellor."

And he said to him, "You have told the truth in this saying. But we have heard of Haiqar, that king Sennacherib has slain him, yet you seem to be alive and well."

And Haiqar said to him, "Yes, so it was, but praise be to God, who knows what is hidden, for my lord the king commanded me to be killed, and he believed the word of profligate men, but the Lord delivered me, and blessed is he who trusts in him."

And Pharaoh said to Haiqar, "Go, and tomorrow be here, and tell me a word that I have never heard from my nobles nor from the people of my kingdom and my country."

VI

The ruse succeeds. Ahikar answers every question of Pharaoh. The boys on the eagles are the climax of the day.

And Haiqar went to his dwelling, and

wrote a letter, saying in it on this wise:

"From Sennacherib king of Assyria and Nineveh to Pharaoh king of Egypt.

"Peace be to you, O my brother! And what we make known to you by this is that a brother has need of his brother, and kings of each other, and my hope is that you would lend me nine hundred talents of gold, for I need it for the victualling of some of the soldiers, that I may spend it upon them. And after a little while I will send it to you."

Then he folded the letter, and presented it on the morrow to Pharaoh.

And when he saw it, he was perplexed and said to him, "Truly I have never heard anything like this language from any one.'

Then Haiqar said to him, "Truly this is a debt which you owe to my lord the king."

And Pharaoh accepted this, saying, "O Haiqar, it is the like of you who are honest in the service of kings.

"Blessed be God who has made you perfect in wisdom and has adorned you with philosophy and knowledge.

"And now, O Haiqar, there remains what we desire from you, that you should build us a castle between Heaven and earth."

Then said Haiqar, "To hear is to obey. I will build you a castle according to your wish and choice; but, O my lord! Prepare us lime and stone and clay and workmen, and I have skilled builders who will build for you as you desire."

And the king prepared all that for him, and they went to a wide place; and Haiqar and his boys came to it, and he took the eagles and the young men with him; and the king and all his nobles went and the whole city assembled, that they might see what Haiqar would do.

Then Haiqar let the eagles out of the boxes, and tied the young men on their backs, and tied the ropes to the eagles' feet, and let them go in the air. And they soared upwards, till they remained between Heaven and earth.

And the boys began to shout, saying, "Bring bricks, bring clay, that we may build the king's castle, for we are standing idle!"

And the crowd were astonished and perplexed, and they wondered. And the king and his nobles wondered.

And Haiqar and his servants began to beat the workmen, and they shouted for the king's troops, saying to them, "Bring to the skilled workmen what they want and do not hinder them from their work."

And the king said to him, "You are mad; who can bring anything up to that distance?"

And Haiqar said to him, "O my lord! How shall we build a castle in the air? And if my lord the king were here, he would have built several castles in a single day."

And Pharaoh said to him, "Go, O Haiqar, to your dwelling, and rest, for we have given up building the castle, and tomorrow come to me."

Then Haiqar went to his dwelling and on the morrow he appeared before Pharaoh. And Pharaoh said, "O Haiqar, what news is there of the horse of your lord? For when he neighs in the country of Assyria and Nineveh, and our mares hear his voice, they cast their young."

And when Haiqar heard this speech he went and took a cat, and bound her and began to flog her with a violent flogging till the Egyptians heard it, and they went and told the king about it.

And Pharaoh sent to fetch Haiqar, and said to him, "O Haiqar, why do you flog thus and beat that dumb beast?"

And Haiqar said to him, "O my lord the king! Truly she has done an ugly deed to me, and has deserved this drubbing and flogging, for my lord king Sennacherib has given me a fine cock, and he had a strong true voice and knew the hours of the day and the night.

"And the cat got up this very night and cut off its head and went away, and because of this deed I have treated her to this drubbing."

And Pharaoh said to him, "O Haiqar, I see from all this that you are growing old and are in your dotage, for between Egypt and Nineveh there are sixty-eight parasangs, and how did she go this very night and cut off the head of your cock and come back?"

And Haiqar said to him, "O my lord! If there were such a distance between Egypt and Nineveh, how could your mares hear when my lord the king's horse neighs and cast their young? And how could the voice of the horse reach to Egypt?"

And when Pharaoh heard that, he knew that Haiqar had answered his questions.

And Pharaoh said, "O Haiqar, I want you to make me ropes of the sea-sand."

And Haiqar said to him, "O my lord the king! Order them to bring me a rope out of the treasury that I may make one like it."

Then Haiqar went to the back of the house, and bored holes in the rough shore of the sea, and took a handful of sand in his hand, sea-sand, and when the sun rose, and penetrated into the holes, he spread the sand in the sun till it became as if woven like ropes.

And Haiqar said, "Command your servants to take these ropes, and whenever you desire it, I will weave some like them."

And Pharaoh said, "O Haiqar, we have a millstone here and it has been broken and I want you to sew it up."

Then Haiqar looked at it, and found another stone.

And he said to Pharaoh, "O my lord! I am a foreigner, and I have no tool for sewing.

"But I want you to command your faithful shoemakers to cut awls from this stone, that I may sew that millstone."

Then Pharaoh and all his nobles laughed. And he said, "Blessed be the Most High God, who gave you this wit and knowledge."

And when Pharaoh saw that Haiqar had overcome him, and returned him his answers, he at once became excited, and commanded them to collect for him three

years' taxes, and to bring them to Haiqar.

And he stripped off his robes and put them upon Haiqar, and his soldiers, and his servants, and gave him the expenses of his journey.

And he said to him, "Go in peace, O strength of his lord and pride of his doctors! Have any of the sultans your like? Give my greetings to your lord king Sennacherib, and say to him how we have sent him gifts, for kings are content with little."

Then Haiqar arose, and kissed king Pharaoh's hands and kissed the ground in front of him, and wished him strength and continuance, and abundance in his treasury, and said to him, 'O my lord! I desire that not one of our countrymen may remain in Egypt."

And Pharaoh arose and sent heralds to proclaim in the streets of Egypt that not one of the people of Assyria or Nineveh should remain in the land of Egypt, but that they should go with Haiqar.

Then Haiqar went and took leave of king Pharaoh, and journeyed, seeking the land of Assyria and Nineveh; and he had some treasures and a great deal of wealth.

And when the news reached king Sennacherib that Haiqar was coming, he went out to meet him and rejoiced over him exceedingly with great joy and embraced him and kissed him, and said to him, "Welcome home, O kinsman! My brother Haiqar, the strength of my kingdom, and pride of my realm.

"Ask what you would have from me, even if you desire the half of my kingdom and of my possessions."

Then said Haiqar unto him, "O my lord the king, live forever! Show favor, O my lord the king! To Abu Samik in my stead, for my life was in the hands of God and in his."

Then said Sennacherib the king, "Honor be to you, O my beloved Haiqar! I will make the station of Abu Samik the swordsman higher than all my privy councillors and my favorites."

Then the king began to ask him how he had got on with Pharaoh from his first arrival until he had come away from his presence, and how he had answered all his questions, and how he had received the taxes from him, and the changes of raiment and the presents.

And Sennacherib the king rejoiced with a great joy, and said to Haiqar, "Take what you would have of this tribute, for it is all within the grasp of your hand."

And Haiqar said: "Let the king live forever! I desire naught but the safety of my lord the king and the continuance of his greatness.

"O my lord! What can I do with wealth and its like? But if you will show me favor, give me Nadan, my sister's son, that I may recompense him for what he has done to me, and grant me his blood and hold me guiltless of it."

And Sennacherib the king said, "Take him, I have given him to you. And Haiqar took Nadan, his sister's son, and bound his hands with chains of iron, and took him to his dwelling, and put a heavy fetter on his feet, and tied it with a tight knot, and after binding him thus he cast him into a dark room, beside the retiring-place, and appointed Nebu-hal as sentinel over him and commanded him to give him a loaf of bread and a little water every day.

VII

The parables of Ahikar in which he completes his nephew's education. Striking similes. Ahikar calls the boy picturesque names. Here ends the story of Ahikar.

And whenever Haiqar went in or out he scolded Nadan, his sister's son, saying to him wisely:

"O Nadan, my boy! I have done to you all that is good and kind. And you have rewarded me for it with what is ugly and bad and with killing.

"O my son! it is said in the proverbs: He who listens not with his ear, they will make him listen with the scruff of his neck."

And Nadan said, "Why are you angry with me?"

And Haiqar said to him, "Because I brought you up, and taught you, and gave you honor and respect and made you great, and reared you with the best of breeding, and seated you in my place that you might be my heir in the world, and you treated me with killing and repaid me with my ruin.

"But the Lord knew that I was wronged, and he saved me from the snare which you had set for me, for the Lord heals the broken hearts and hinders the envious and the haughty.

"O my boy! You have been to me like the scorpion which, when it strikes on brass, pierces it.

"O my boy! You are like the gazelle who was eating the roots of the madder, and it said to her, 'Eat of me today and take your fill, and tomorrow they will tan your hide in my roots.'

"O my boy! You have been to me like a man who saw his comrade naked in the chilly time of winter; and he took cold water and poured it upon him.

"O my boy! You have been to me like a man who took a stone, and threw it up to Heaven to stone his Lord with it. And the stone did not hit, and did not reach high enough, but it became the cause of guilt and sin.

"O my boy! If you had honored me and respected me and had listened to my words, you would have been my heir, and would have reigned over my dominions.

"O my son! Know that if the tail of the dog or the pig were ten cubits long it would not approach to the worth of the horse's even if it were like silk.

"O my boy! I thought that you would have been my heir at my death; and you through your envy and your insolence did desire to kill me. But the Lord delivered me from your cunning.

"O my son! You have been to me like a trap which was set up on the dunghill, and there came a sparrow and found the trap set up. And the sparrow said to the trap, 'What are you doing here?' Said the trap, 'I am praying here to God.'

"And the lark asked it also, 'What is the piece of wood that you hold?' Said the trap, 'That is a young oak tree on which I lean at the time of prayer.'

"Said the lark: 'And what is that thing in your mouth?' Said the trap: 'That is bread and victuals which I carry for all the hungry and the poor who come near to me.'

"Said the lark: 'Now, then, may I come forward and eat, for I am hungry?' And the trap said to him, 'Come forward.' And the lark approached that it might eat.

"But the trap sprang up and seized the lark by its neck.

"And the lark answered and said to the trap, 'If that is your bread for the hungry God accepts not your alms and your kind deeds.

" 'And if that is your fasting and your prayers, God accepts from you neither your fast nor your prayer, and God will not perfect what is good concerning you.'

"O my boy! You have been to me as a lion who made friends with an ass, and the ass kept walking before the lion for a time; and one day the lion sprang upon the ass and ate it up.

"O my boy! You have been to me like a weevil in the wheat, for it does no good to anything, but spoils the wheat and gnaws it.

"O my boy! You have been like a man who sowed ten measures of wheat, and when it was harvest time, he arose and reaped it, and garnered it, and threshed it, and toiled over it to the very utmost, and it turned out to be ten measures, and its master said to it: 'O you lazy thing! You have not grown and you have not shrunk.'

"O my boy! You have been to me like the partridge that had been thrown into the net, and she could not save herself, but she called out to the partridges, that she might cast them with herself into the net.

"O my son! You have been to me like the dog that was cold and it went into the potter's house to get warm.

"And when it had got warm, it began to bark at them, and they chased it out and beat it, that it might not bite them.

"O my son! You have been to me like the pig who went into the hot bath with people of quality, and when it came out of the hot bath, it saw a filthy hole and it went down and wallowed in it.

"O my son! You have been to me like the goat which joined its comrades on their way to the sacrifice, and it was unable to save itself.

"O my boy! The dog which is not fed from its hunting becomes food for flies.

"O my son! The hand which does not labor and plough and which is greedy and cunning shall be cut away from its shoulder.

"O my son! The eye in which light is not seen, the ravens shall pick at it and pluck it out.

"O my boy! You have been to me like a tree whose branches they were cutting, and it said to them, 'If something of me were not in your hands, truly you would be unable to cut me.'

"O my boy! You are like the cat to whom they said: 'Leave off thieving till we make for you a chain of gold and feed you with sugar and almonds.'

"And she said, 'I am not forgetful of the craft of my father and my mother.'

"O my son! You have been like the serpent riding on a thorn bush when he was in the midst of a river, and a wolf saw them and said, 'Mischief upon mischief, and let him who is more mischievous than they direct both of them.'

"And the serpent said to the wolf, 'The lambs and the goats and the sheep which you have eaten all your life, will you return them to their fathers and to their parents or no?'

"Said the wolf, 'No.' And the serpent said to him, 'I think that after myself you are the worst of us.'

"O my boy! I fed you with good food and you did not feed me with dry bread.

"O my boy! I gave you sugared water to drink and good syrup, and you did not give me water from the well to drink.

"O my boy! I taught you and brought you up, and you dug a hiding place for me and did conceal me.

"O my boy! I brought you up with the best upbringing and trained you like a tall cedar; and you have twisted and bent me.

"O my boy! It was my hope concerning you that you would build me a fortified castle, that I might be concealed from my enemies in it, and you became to me like one burying in the depth of the earth; but the Lord took pity on me and delivered me from your cunning.

"O my boy! I wished you well, and you rewarded me with evil and hatefulness, and now I would tear out your eyes, and make you food for dogs, and cut out your tongue, and take off your head with the edge of the sword, and recompense you for your abominable deeds."

And when Nadan heard this speech from his uncle Haiqar, he said: "O my uncle! Deal with me according to your knowledge, and forgive me my sins, for who is there who has sinned like me, or who is there who forgives like you?

"Accept me, O my uncle! Now I will serve in your house, and groom your horses and sweep up the dung of your cattle, and feed your sheep, for I am the wicked and you are the righteous: I the guilty and you the forgiving."

And Haiqar said to him, "O my boy! You are like the tree which was fruitless beside the water, and its master was fain to cut it down, and it said to him, 'Remove me to another place, and if I do not bear fruit, cut me down.'

"And its master said to it, 'You being beside the water have not borne fruit, how shall you bear fruit when you are in another place?'

"O my boy! The old age of the eagle is better than the youth of the crow.

"O my boy! They said to the wolf, 'Keep away from the sheep lest their dust should harm you.' And the wolf said, 'The dregs of the sheep's milk are good for my eyes.'

"O my boy! They made the wolf go to school that he might learn to read, and they said to him, 'Say A, B.' He said, 'Lamb and goat in my belly.'

"O my boy! They set the ass down at the table and he fell, and began to roll himself in the dust, and one said, 'Let him roll himself, for it is his nature, he will not change.'

"O my boy! The saying has been confirmed which runs: 'If you beget a boy, call him your son, and if you rear a boy, call him your slave.'

"O my boy! He who does good shall meet with good; and he who does evil shall meet with evil, for the Lord requites a man according to the measure of his work.

"O my boy! What shall I say more to you than these sayings? For the Lord knows what is hidden, and is acquainted with the mysteries and the secrets.

"And he will requite you and will judge betwixt me and you, and will recompense you according to your desert."

And when Nadan heard that speech from his uncle Haiqar, he swelled up immediately and became like a blown-out bladder.

And his limbs swelled and his legs and his feet and his side, and he was torn and his belly burst asunder and his entrails were scattered, and he perished, and died.

And his latter end was destruction, and he went to Hell. For he who digs a pit for his brother shall fall into it; and he who sets up traps shall be caught in them.

This is what happened and what we found about the tale of Haiqar, and praise be to God forever. Amen, and peace.

This chronicle is finished with the help of God, may he be exalted! Amen, Amen, Amen.

The Genesis Apocryphon

(Dead Sea Scrolls)

In December 1945 in Upper Egypt, and in the spring of 1947 on the western shore of the Dead Sea, two astonishing discoveries were made that added a great deal to our information about the ancient world. In a cave of a mountain near the town of Nag Hammadi in Egypt, fifty-two texts were discovered, giving us for the first time substantial writings of the Syrian-Egyptian Gnostic sects. Prior to this discovery, our knowledge of the Gnostics depended largely on writings of the early Church Fathers who wrote against the Gnostics—such as Irenaeus and Saint Augustine.

The second discovery, at Khirbet Qumran near the Dead Sea, is that of the celebrated Dead Sea Scrolls. There in the cave two shepherd boys—in fact, Bedouin smugglers—discovered several tall clay jars inside of which were lumps containing manuscripts wrapped in linen and covered with pitch or wax. Their booty soon found its way to the Syrian Metropolitan at the Monastery of St. Mark in Old Jerusalem. There were more discoveries between 1952 and 1956. Altogether ten almost complete scrolls and thousands of fragments have been found. The documents contain fragments from the whole Hebrew Bible, except for the book of Esther, and the entire book of Isaiah—there are actually fifteen manuscripts of Isaiah—many fragments of Pseudepigrapha, such as *Enoch* and *Jubilees*, and, perhaps most important, the sectarian writings of the particular group at Qumran. The community at Qumran has been called the Essenes, and most scholars, including Geza Vermes, the editor and translator of the texts below, agree with this identification. The Essenes have also been associated with the Zealots, but the connection is vague. We do know that there by the Dead Sea, in one of the lowest spots on the planet, a group of Essenes had retreated to the desert to practice their ultraconservative and rigid religious practice. By contrast, orthodox Judaism appears progressive. The group took refuge in the desert to be free of the "corruption" of Jerusalem, then under Hasmonean rule, that is, the patriotic yet worldly Maccabees. The Wicked Priest referred to in the scrolls is probably Jonathan or Simon (Maccabeus). The good priest mentioned in the scrolls is the Teacher of Righteousness. There have been loud polemical debates about the Teacher of Righteousness (or One who Teaches Righteousness). A. Dupont-Sommer reported sensationally that the Qumran documents, particularly, the Teacher of Righteousness, revealed an anticipation of Christianity in the sect of the Essenes, while the late Theodor H. Gaster claimed such ideas were nonsense.

In a broader sense, since much of the intertestamental writings were apocalyptic and messianic, the appearance of a figure such as Jesus Christ ("Christ" means "messiah") was not unexpected. Indeed, because of the messianic nature of Jewish Pseudepigrapha, they were favorite readings of the early Christians and many of them were altered and "Christianized," falsified if you will, to make them reveal Christian truths. That the Essenes or any other Jewish sect anticipated Christianity should not lead to controversy. The rift between Old and New Testaments is bridged by the intertestamental scriptures in which the messiah is eagerly awaited. The main teachings and notions of early Christianity derive from biblical and intertestamental sources. The earliest Christians were, moreover, Jews. Controversy came about and a discontinuity of traditions was posited and thereafter confirmed when the people representing the religious tendencies in Jerusalem took on different names: Jews and Christians.[1]

The *Genesis Apocryphon* retells, sensitively and with abundant geographical detail, a narrative about the Genesis patriarchs. Of particular interest is the picture of Sarai (Sarah) as a full-blown beauty. Here, for the first time we have a picture of Sarah, in language that recalls the Song of Songs. Edmund Wilson points out that Abram heals the Pharaoh by laying hands on his head. In concordance with the notion of New Testament ideas in earlier writing, Wilson observes:

> This laying-on of hands is often mentioned in the New Testament as a feature of the healing of Jesus, but it does not occur in the Old Testament or, so far as is known, in rabbinical literature. Yet its occurrence in the Genesis apocryphon, this copy of which is supposed to have been made either during the lifetime of Jesus or a little earlier, would seem to indicate that the practice was not peculiar to Jesus but was a recognized method of effecting cures.[2]

Geza Vermes introduces The *Genesis Apocryphon* as follows:[3]

> The first section refers to the miraculous birth of Noah. His father, Lamech, suspects that his wife has consorted with one of the angels who descended from Heaven and married the "daughters of men" (Gen. 6:1–4). Her emphatic denial does not convince him and he asks his father, Methuselah, to find his own father, the omniscient Enoch who lives at Parwain, the site of Paradise, in order to discover the truth from him. A story parallel to this appears in the Book of Enoch.

The second section develops Genesis (7–15) with its account of Abraham's journey to Egypt, his return to Canaan, the war against the Mesopotamian kings, and the renewal of the divine promise. This lively and delightful narrative, devoid of sectarian bias, throws valuable light on the Bible interpretation current in Palestine during the intertestamental period.

Although this Aramaic work was discovered in cave I fifteen years ago, so far only five of its twenty-two columns have been published, mainly because of its poor state of preservation.

Notes

1. There were in the early years of Christianity several Jewish-Christian sects, such as the Ebionites, reported in Epiphanius *Against Heresies*. 30, in which Epiphanius states that the Ebionites took Matthew as a teacher of his Gospel in Hebrew, and he shows how this vegetarian sect accepted Jesus as "begotten of the seed of a man" but was the choice of God and called the Son of God. Christ came into Jesus from above in the likeness of a dove. For more information see under "Gospels" *The Gospel of the Hebrews* and *The Gospel of the Ebionites*.

2. Edmund Wilson, *The Dead Sea Scrolls* (London: W. H. Allen, 1965), p.145.

3. Geza Vermes, *The Dead Sea Scrolls*, 2nd ed. (1962; reprint, New York: Penguin Books, 1975), p. 215.

THE GENESIS APOCRYPHON*

Behold, I thought then within my heart that conception was due to the Watchers and the Holy Ones and to the Giants and my heart was troubled within me because of this child. Then I, Lamech, approached Bathenosh, my wife, in haste and said to her, "By the Most High, the Great Lord, the King of all the worlds and Ruler of the sons of Heaven, tell me this truthfully and not falsely. Is the seed within you mine?"

Then Bathenosh my wife spoke to me with much heat and said, "O my brother, O my lord, remember my pleasure, the lying together and my soul within its body. And I tell you all things truthfully."

My heart was then greatly troubled within me, and when Bathenosh, my wife, saw that my countenance had changed, then she mastered her anger and spoke to me saying, "O my lord, O my brother, remember my pleasure! I swear to you by the Holy Great One, the King of the heavens, that this seed is yours and that this conception is from you. This fruit was planted by you and by no stranger or Watcher or son of Heaven. Why is your countenance thus changed and dismayed, and why is your spirit thus distressed? I speak to you truthfully."

Then I, Lamech, ran to Methuselah my father, and I told him all these things. And I asked him to go to Enoch, his father, for he would surely learn all things from him. For he was beloved, and he shared the lot of the angels, who taught him all things. And when Methuselah heard my words, he went to Enoch, his father, to learn all things truthfully from him.

He went at once to Parwain and he found him there and he said to Enoch, his father, "O my father, O my lord, I say to you, lest you be angry with me because I come here [. . .].

*Columns II and XIX–XXII. From Geza Vermes, *The Dead Sea Scrolls*, 2d ed. (1962; reprint, New York: Penguin Books, 1975), pp. 215–224.

And I said, "Until now, you have not come to the Holy Mountain."

And I departed and traveled towards the south until I came to Hebron at the time when Hebron was being built; and I dwelt there two years.

Now there was famine in all this land, and hearing that there was prosperity in Egypt I went to the land of Egypt. I came to the river Karmon and crossed the seven branches of the River. We passed through our land and entered the land of the sons of Ham, into the land of Egypt.

And on the night of our entry into Egypt, I, Abram, dreamt a dream; and behold, I saw in my dream a cedar tree and a palm tree. Men came and they sought to cut down the cedar tree and to pull up its roots, leaving the palm tree standing alone. But the palm tree cried out, saying, "Do not cut down this cedar tree, for cursed be he who shall fell it." And the cedar tree was spared because of the palm tree and was not felled.

And during the night I woke from my dream, and I said to Sarai, my wife, "I have dreamt a dream and I am fearful because of this dream." She said to me, "Tell me your dream that I may know it." So I began to tell her this dream and told her the interpretation of the dream: that they will seek to kill me, but will spare you. Say to them of me, 'He is my brother, and because of you I shall live, and because of you my life shall be saved.'"

And Sarai wept that night on account of my words.

Then we journeyed towards Zoan, I and Sarai.

And when those five years had passed, three men from among the princes of Egypt came at the command of Pharaoh of Zoan to inquire after my business and after my wife and they gave goodness, wisdom, and truth. And I exclaimed before them because of the famine. And they came to ascertain with much food and drink the wine.

During the party, the Egyptians must have seen Sarai, and on their return they praised her to the king, saying "How beautiful is her face! How fine are the hairs of her head! How lovely are her eyes! How desirable her nose and all the radiance of her countenance. How fair are her breasts and how beautiful all her whiteness! How pleasing are her arms and how perfect her hands, and how desirable all the appearance of her hands! How fair are her palms and how long and slender are her fingers! How comely are her feet, how perfect her thighs! No virgin or bride led into the marriage chamber is more beautiful than she; she is fairer than all other women. Truly, her beauty is greater than theirs. Yet together with all this grace she possesses abundant wisdom, so that whatever she does is perfect."

When the king heard the words of Harkenosh and his two companions, for all three spoke as with one voice, he desired her greatly and sent out at once to take her. And seeing her, he was amazed by all her beauty and took her to be his wife, but me he sought to kill. Sarai said to the king, "He is my brother," and so I, Abram, was spared because of her and was not slain.

And I, Abram, wept aloud that night, I and my nephew Lot, because Sarai had been taken from me by force. I prayed that night and I begged and implored, and I said in my sorrow while my tears ran down: "Blessed are you, O Most High God, Lord of all the worlds, You who are Lord and King of all things and who rules over all the kings of the earth and judges them all! I cry now before you, my Lord, against Pharaoh of Zoan the king of Egypt, because of my wife who has been taken from me by force. Judge him for me that I may see your mighty hand raised against him and against all his household, and that he may not be able to defile my wife this night and that they may know you, my Lord, that you are Lord of all the kings of the earth." And I wept and was sorrowful.

And during that night the Most High

God sent a spirit to scourge him, an evil spirit to all his household; and it scourged him and all his household. And he was unable to approach her, and although he was with her for two years he knew her not.

At the end of those two years, the scourges of afflictions grew greater and more grievous upon him and all his household, so he sent for all the sages of Egypt, for all the magicians, together with all the healers of Egypt, that they might heal him and all his household of this scourge. But not one healer or magician or sage could stay to cure him, for the spirit scourged them all and they fled.

Then Harkenosh came to me, beseeching me to go to the king and to pray for him and to lay my hands upon him that he might live, for the king had dreamt a dream. But Lot said to him, "Abram, my uncle, cannot pray for the king while Sarai his wife is with him. Go, therefore, and tell the king to restore his wife to her husband; then he will pray for him and he shall live."

When Harkenosh had heard the words of Lot, he went to the king and said, "All these scourges and afflictions with which my lord the king is scourged and afflicted are because of Sarai, the wife of Abram. Let Sarai be restored to Abram, her husband, and this scourge and the spirit of festering shall vanish from you."

And he called me and said, "What have you done to me with regard to Sarai? You said to me, 'She is my sister,' whereas she is your wife; and I took her to be my wife. Behold your wife who is with me; depart and go hence from all the land of Egypt! And now pray for me and my house that this evil spirit may be expelled from it."

So I prayed for him and I laid my hands on his head; and the scourge departed from him and the evil spirit was expelled from him, and he lived. And the king rose to tell me he had given her much silver and gold and much raiment of fine linen and purple and he ap-

pointed men to lead me out of all the land of Egypt. And I, Abram, departed with very great flocks and with silver and gold, and I went up from Egypt together with my nephew, Lot. Lot had great flocks also, and he took a wife for himself from among the daughters of Egypt.

I pitched my camp in every place in which I had formerly camped until I came to Bethel, the place where I had built an altar. And I built a second altar and laid on it a sacrifice and an offering to the Most High God. And there I called on the name of the Lord of worlds and praised the name of God and blessed God, and I gave thanks before God for all the riches and favors which he had bestowed on me. For he had dealt kindly towards me and had led me back in peace into this land.

After that day, Lot departed from me on account of the deeds of our shepherds. He went away and settled in the valley of the Jordan, together with all his flocks; and I myself added more to them. He kept his sheep and journeyed as far as Sodom, and he bought a house for himself in Sodom and dwelt in it. But I dwelt on the mountain of Bethel and it grieved me that my nephew Lot had departed from me.

And God appeared to me in a vision at night and said to me, "Go to Ramath Hazor which is north of Bethel, the place where you dwell, and lift up your eyes and look to the east and to the west and to the south and to the north; and behold all this land which I give to you and your seed forever."

The next morning, I went up to Ramath Hazor and from that high place I beheld the land from the River of Egypt to Lebanon and Senir, and from the Great Sea to Hauran, and all the land of Gebal as far as Kadesh, and all the Great Desert to the east of Hauran and Senir as far as Euphrates. And he said to me, "I will give all this land to your seed and they shall possess it forever. And I will multiply your seed like the dust of the earth which no man can number; neither shall any man number your seed. Rise and go! Behold the length and breadth of the land for it is yours; and after you, I will give it to your seed forever."

And I, Abram, departed to travel about and see the land. I began my journey at the river Gihon and traveled along the coast of the sea until I came to the Mountain of the Bull [Taurus]. Then I traveled from the coast of the Great Salt Sea and journeyed towards the east by the Mountain of the Bull, across the breadth of the land, until I came to the river Euphrates. I journeyed along the Euphrates until I came to the Red Sea [Persian Gulf] in the east, and I traveled along the coast of the Red Sea until I came to the tongue of the Sea of Reeds [the modern Red Sea] which flows out from the Red Sea. Then I pursued my way in the south until I came to the river Gihon, and returning, I came to my house in peace and found all things prosperous there. I went to dwell at the Oaks of Mamre, which is at Hebron, northeast of Hebron; and I built an altar there, and laid on it a sacrifice and an oblation to the Most High God. I ate and drank there, I and all the men of my household, and I sent for Mamre, Ornam, and Eshkol, the three Amorite brothers, my friends, and they ate and drank with me.

Before these days, Kedorlaomer, king of Elam, had set out with Amrafel, king of Babylon, Ariok, king of Kaptok, and Tidal, king of the nations which lie between the rivers; and they had waged war against Bera, king of Sodom, Birsha, king of Gomorrah, Shinab, king of Admah, Shemiabad, king of Zeboim, and against the king of Bela. All these had made ready for battle in the valley of Siddim, and the king of Elam and the other kings with him had prevailed over the king of Sodom and his companions and had imposed a tribute upon them.

For twelve years they had paid their tribute to the king of Elam, but in the thirteenth year they rebelled against him. And in the fourteenth year, the king of Elam placed himself at the head of all his allies and went up by the Way of the Wilderness; and they smote and pillaged from the river Euphrates onward. They smote the Refaim who were at Ashteroth Karnaim, the Zumzamim who were at Ammon, the Emim who were at Shaveh ha-Keriyyoth, and the Horites who were in the mountains of Gebal, until they came to El Paran which is in the Wilderness. And they returned at Hazazon Tamar.

The king of Sodom went out to meet them, together with the king of Gomorrah, the king of Admah, the king of Zeboim, and the king of Bela; and they fought a battle in the valley of Siddim against Kedorlaomer, the king of Elam, and the kings who were with him. But the king of Sodom was vanquished and fled, and the king of Gomorrah fell into the pits. And the king of Elam carried off all the riches of Sodom and Gomorrah and they took Lot, the nephew of Abram, who dwelt with them in Sodom, together with all his possessions.

Now one of the shepherds of the flocks which Abram had given to Lot escaped from captivity and came to Abram: at that time Abram dwelt in Hebron. He told him that Lot, his nephew, had been taken, together with all his possessions, and that he had not been slain, and that the kings had gone by the Way of the Great Valley of the Jordan in the direction of their land, taking captives and plundering and smiting and slaying, and that they were journeying towards the land of Damascus.

Abram wept because of Lot, his nephew. Then he braced himself; he rose up and chose from among his servants three hundred and eighteen fighting men trained for war, and Ornam and Eshkol and Mamre went with him also. He pursued them until he came to Dan, and came on them while they were camped in the valley of Dan. He fell on them at night from four sides and during the night he slew them; he crushed them and put them to flight, and all of them fled before him until they came to Hel-bon, which is north of Damascus. He rescued from them all their captives, and all their booty and possessions. He also delivered Lot, his nephew, together with all his possessions, and he brought back all the captives which they had taken.

When the king of Sodom learned that Abram had brought back all the captives and all the booty, he came out to meet him; and he went to Salem, which is Jerusalem.

Abram camped in the valley of Sha-veh, which is the valley of the king, the valley of Beth-ha-Kerem; and Mel-chizedek, king of Salem, brought out food and drink to Abram and to all the men who were with him. He was the Priest of the Most High God. And he blessed Abram and said, "Blessed be Abram by the Most High God, Lord of Heaven and earth! And blessed be the Most High God who has delivered your enemies into your hand!" And Abram gave him the tithe of all the possessions of the king of Elam and his companions.

Then the king of Sodom approached and said to Abram, "My lord Abram, give me the souls which are mine, which you have delivered from the king of Elam and taken captive, and you may have all the possessions."

Then said Abram to the king of Sodom, "I raise my hand this day to the Most High God, Lord of Heaven and earth! I will take nothing of yours, not even a shoelace or shoestrap, lest you say, Abram's riches come from my possessions! I will take nothing but that which the young men with me have eaten already, and the portion of the three men who have come with me. They shall decide whether they will give you their portion." And Abram returned all the possessions and all the captives and gave them to the king of Sodom; he freed all the captives from this land who were with him, and sent them all back.

After these things, God appeared to Abram in a vision and said to him, "Be-hold, ten years have passed since you departed from Haran. For two years you dwelt here and you spent seven years in Egypt, and one year has passed since you returned from Egypt. And now ex-amine and count all you have, and see how it has grown to be double that which came out with you from Haran. And now do not fear, I am with you; I am your help and your strength. I am a shield above you and a mighty safeguard round about you. Your wealth and possessions shall multiply greatly." But Abram said, "My Lord God, I have great wealth and possessions but what good shall they do for me? I shall die naked and childless. A child from my house-hold shall inherit from me. Eliezer shall inherit from me." And he said to him, "He shall not be your heir, but one who shall spring from your body shall inherit from you."

The Manual of Discipline

(Dead Sea Scrolls)

As its title implies, *The Manual of Discipline* is a rulebook of behavior. The title given the work by Geza Vermes—*The Community Rule*—conveys a similar idea, although Vermes's title suggests not only personal awareness of discipline, but the notion of the community's rule and discipline over the individual. This handbook of law for the Qumran Community follows the halakhah tradition of documents of law for correct behavior within a strict society. The society at Qumran by the Dead Sea, identified by many scholars as the Essenes, withdrew to the wilderness and established a thoroughly totalitarian sect in which a hierarchy of authority was prescribed and severely enforced. The document details rules of admission for new members, initiation rites for novitiates, a ranking of members, their duties, and punishments for failure to carry out such duties. The tenor is of love and loyalty to members of the brotherhood and hatred for those outside. Consequently, the most infamous of deeds is apostasy.

The members of the community are "the sons of light"; those outside are "the sons of darkness." Within the communal order, in which meals are taken communally and property owned communally, the harshest punishment contained in the penal statutes is banishment. Gossip, lack of respect for the masters, is a grave offense: "A man who gossips about his neighbor shall be separated for a year from the sacred food of the masters; and he shall be punished; and a man who gossips about the masters is to be dismissed from among them and shall not come back again." Even if it is discerned that his spirit wavers, he is considered a traitor: "If a man's spirit wavers from the institution of the community, so that he becomes a traitor to the truth and walks in the stubbornness of his heart; if he repents he shall be punished two years." Acts of personal misbehavior are punished less drastically. Such things as streaking, spitting, flashing, laughing foolishly, and using the left hand to gesticulate (the left hand in the Near East and India, today and anciently, is dirty, since it is used to regulate elimination) are punished merely by days. These injunctions cast significant light on the society:

> One who walks before his neighbor naked when he does not have to do so shall be punished six months. A man who spits into the midst of the session of the masters shall be punished thirty days. One who brings his hand out from beneath his robe when it is torn, so that his nakedness is seen, shall be punished thirty days. One who laughs foolishly, making his voice heard, shall be punished thirty days. One who brings out his left hand to gesticulate with it shall be punished ten days.

The Manual of Discipline is similar in content to *The Zadokite Document* (*The Damascus Document*), a manuscript found in 1896–1897 in the Ezra synagogue in Cairo. *The Zadokite Document*, a twelfth-century copy of a Qumran text, is also a rulebook ordering the brotherhood to keep the law and maintain its covenant with God. Vermes points out that these writings of community rule have no parallel in ancient Jewish sources, "but a similar type of literature flourished among Christians between the second and fourth centuries, the so-called 'Church Orders' represented by the *Didache*, the *Didascalia*, the *Apostolic Constitution*. . . ."[1] Theodor H. Gaster goes further in making comparisons between the Essenes (who he assumes the Brothers to be) and the primitive Christian Church:

> The community calls itself by the same name (*'edah*) as was used by the early Christians of Palestine to denote the Church. There are twelve "men of holiness" who act as general guides of the community—a remarkable correspondence with the Twelve Apostles. These men have three superiors, answering to the designation of John, Peter and James as the three pillars of the Church (Galatians 2:9f). There is a regular system of *mebaqqerim* or "overseers"—an exact equivalent of the Greek *episkopi*, or "bishops" (before they had acquired *sacerdotal* functions). And the Brotherhood describes itself as "preparing the way in the desert"—words which John the Baptist likewise quoted from the Old Testament in defining his mission (John 1:23).[2]

The text dates from between 100 and 75 B.C., and is one of the oldest documents of the sect. It was intended for the Community Teachers, perhaps its "Teacher of Righteousness." The translation by G. Vermes in *The Dead Sea Scrolls* in English is excellent and contains the most recent finds to fill in the text. For our purposes, however, we have reproduced the translation by Millar Burrows (which contains all but the last paragraph of the Vermes's translation), because it is especially beautiful and has a scriptural magnificence.

Notes

1. Geza Vermes, *The Dead Sea Scrolls*, 2d ed. (1962; reprint, London: Penguin Books, 1975), p. 71.

2. Theodor H. Gaster, *The Dead Sea Scrolls in English Translation* (New York: Doubleday Anchor, 1956), p. 35.

THE MANUAL OF DISCIPLINE*

I. Entering the Covenant

... the order of the community; to seek God . . . ; to do what is good and upright before him as he commanded through Moses and through all his servants the prophets; to love all that he has chosen and hate all that he has rejected; to be far from all evil and cleave to all good works; to do truth and righteousness and justice in the land; to walk no longer in the stubbornness of a guilty heart and eyes of fornication, doing all evil; to bring all those who have offered themselves to do God's statutes into a covenant of steadfast love; to be united in the counsel of God and to walk before him perfectly with regard to all the things that have been revealed for the appointed times of their testimonies; to love all the sons of light, each according to his lot in the counsel of God, and to hate all the sons of darkness, each according to his guilt in vengeance of God.

And all who have offered themselves for his truth shall bring all their knowledge and strength and wealth into the community of God, to purify their knowledge in the truth of God's statutes, and to distribute their strength according to the perfection of his ways and all their property according to his righteous counsel; not to transgress in any one of all the words of God in their periods; not to advance their times or postpone any of their appointed festivals; not to turn aside from his true statutes, going to the right or to the left.

And all who come into the order of the community shall pass over into the covenant before God, to do according to all that he has commanded, and not to turn away from following him because of any dread or terror or trial or fright in the dominion of Belial. And when they pass into the covenant, the priests and the Levites shall bless the God of salvation and all his works of truth; and all those who are passing into the covenant shall say after them, "Amen! Amen!"

The priests shall recount the righteous acts of God in his mighty works and tell all the acts of steadfast love and mercy upon Israel; and the Levites shall recount the iniquities of the sons of Israel and all their guilty transgressions and sin in the dominion of Belial. Then all those who are passing into the covenant shall confess after them, saying, "We have committed iniquity, we have transgressed, we have sinned, we have done evil, we and our fathers before us, in walking contrary to the statutes of truth; but righteous is God, and true is his judgment on us and on our fathers; and the mercy of his steadfast love he has bestowed upon us from everlasting to everlasting."

Then the priests shall bless all the men of God's lot, who walk perfectly in all his ways, and shall say: "May he bless you with all good and keep you from all evil; may he enlighten your heart with life-giving prudence and be gracious to you with eternal knowledge; may he lift up his loving countenance to you for eternal peace." And the Levites shall curse all the men of Belial's lot and shall answer and say: "Accursed may you be in all your wicked, guilty works; may God make you a horror through all those that wreak vengeance and send after you destruction through all those that pay recompense; accursed may you be without mercy according to the darkness of your works, and may you suffer wrath in the deep darkness of eternal fire. May God not be gracious to you when you call, and may he not pardon, forgiving your iniquities; may he lift up his angry countenance for vengeance upon you, and may there be no peace for you at the mouth of all those that hold enmity!" And all who are passing over into the covenant shall say after those who bless and those who curse, "Amen! Amen!"

---

*From Millar Burrows, *The Dead Sea Scrolls* (New York: Viking Press, 1951), pp. 390–415.

And the priests and Levites shall continue to say: "Accursed for passing over with the idols of his heart may he be who comes into this covenant and sets the stumbling block of his iniquity before him, turning back with it, and when he hears the words of this covenant blesses himself in his heart, saying, 'May I have peace, because I walk in the stubbornness of my heart!' But his spirit will be swept away, the thirsty together with the sated, without pardon. The wrath of God and the jealousy of his judgments will burn in him to eternal destruction; and all the curses of this covenant will cleave to him; and God will set him apart for evil; and he will be cut off from the midst of all the sons of light, when he turns away from following God with his idols and the stumbling block of his iniquity. He will put his lot in the midst of those accursed for ever." And all who are coming into the covenant shall answer and say after them, "Amen! Amen!"

So shall they do year by year all the days of the dominion of Belial. The priests shall pass over first in order, according to their spirits, one after another; and the Levites shall pass over after them, and all the people shall pass over third in order, one after another, by thousands and hundreds and fifties and tens, so that every man of Israel may know his appointed position in the community of God for the eternal council. And none shall be abased below his appointed position or exalted above his allotted place; for they shall all be in true community and good humility and loyal love and righteous thought, each for his fellow in the holy council, and they shall be sons of the eternal assembly.

Everyone who refuses to enter God's covenant, walking in the stubbornness of his heart, shall not attain to his true community. For his soul has abhorred the discipline of knowledge, the judgments of righteousness he has not confirmed because of his apostasies; and with the upright he will not be reckoned. His knowledge and his strength and his wealth shall not come into the council of community, because in the traffic of wickedness is his devising, and there is pollution in his plans. He will not be justified while giving free rein to the stubbornness of his heart. In darkness he looks at the ways of light, and with the perfect he will not be reckoned. He will not be purified by atonement offerings, and he will not be made clean with the water for impurity; he will not sanctify himself with seas and rivers or be made clean with any water for washing. Unclean, unclean he will be all the days that he rejects the ordinances of God, not being instructed in the community of his counsel.

But in a spirit of true counsel for the ways of a man all his iniquities will be atoned, so that he will look at the light of life, and in a holy spirit he will be united in his truth; and he will be cleansed from all his iniquities; and in an upright and humble spirit his sin will be atoned, and in the submission of his soul to all the statutes of God his flesh will be cleansed, that he may be sprinkled with water for impurity and sanctify himself with water of cleanness. And he will establish his steps, to walk perfectly in all the ways of God, as he commanded for the appointed times of his testimonies, and not to turn aside to right or left, and not to transgress against one of all his words. Then he will be accepted by pleasing atonements before God; and this will be for him a covenant of eternal community.

II. The Two Spirits in Man

The instructor's duty is to make all the sons of light understand and to teach them in the history of all the sons of man as to all their kinds of spirits with their signs, as to their works in their generations, and as to the visitation of their afflictions together with the periods of their recompense. From the God of knowledge is all that is and that is to be; and before they came into being he established all their designing. And when they come into being for their testimony according to his glorious design, they fulfill their work; and nothing is to be changed. In his hand are the ordinances of all; and he provides for them in all their affairs.

He created man to have dominion over the world and made for him two spirits, that he might walk by them until the appointed time of his visitation; they are the spirits of truth and of error. In the abode of light are the origins of truth, and from the source of darkness are the origins of error. In the hand of the prince of lights is dominion over all sons of righteousness; in the ways of light they walk. And in the hand of the angel of darkness is all dominion over the sons of error; and in the ways of darkness they walk. And by the angel of darkness is the straying of all the sons of righteousness, and all their sin and their inquities and their guilt, and the transgressions of their works in his dominion, according to the mysteries of God, until his time, and all their afflictions and the appointed times of their distress in the dominion of his enmity. And all the spirits of his lot try to make the sons of light stumble; but the God of Israel and his angel of truth have helped all the sons of light. For he created the spirits of light and of darkness, and upon them he founded every work and upon their ways every service. One of the spirits God loves for all the ages of eternity, and with all its deeds he is pleased forever; as for the other, he abhors its company, and all its ways he hates forever.

And these are their ways in the world: to shine in the heart of man, and to make straight before him all the ways of true righteousness, and to make his heart be in dread of the judgments of God, and to induce a spirit of humility, and slowness to anger, and great compassion, and eternal goodness, and understanding and insight, and mighty wisdom, which is supported by all the works of God and leans upon the abundance of his steadfast love, and a spirit of knowledge in every thought of action, and zeal for righteous judgments, and holy thought with sustained purpose, and abundance of steadfast love for all the sons of truth, and glorious purity, abhorring all unclean idols, and walking humbly with prudence in all things, and concealing the truth of the mysteries of knowledge.

These are the counsels of the Spirit for the sons of the truth of the world and the visitation of all who walk by it, for healing and abundance of peace in length of days, and bringing forth seed, with all eternal blessings and everlasting joy in the life of eternity, and a crown of glory with raiment of majesty in everlasting light.

But to the spirit of error belong greediness, slackness of hands in the service of righteousness, wickedness and falsehood, pride and haughtiness, lying and deceit, cruelty and great impiety, quickness to anger and abundance of folly and proud jealousy, abominable works in a spirit of fornication and ways of defilement in the service of uncleanness, and a blasphemous tongue, blindness of eyes and dullness of ears, stiffness of neck and hardness of heart, walking in all the ways of darkness and evil cunning. And the visitation of all who walk by it is for abundance of afflictions by all destroying angels, to eternal perdition in the fury of the God of vengeance, to eternal trembling and everlasting dishonor, with destroying disgrace in the fire of dark places. And all their periods to their generations will be in sorrowful mourning and bitter calamity, in dark disasters until they are destroyed, having no remnant or any that escape.

In these two spirits are the origins of all the sons of man, and in their divisions all the hosts of men have their inheritance in their generations. In the ways of the two spirits men walk. And all the performance of their works is in their two divisions, according to each man's inheritance, whether much or little, for all the periods of eternity. For God has established the two spirits in equal measure until the last period, and has put eternal enmity between their divisions. An abomination to truth are deeds of error, and an abomination to error are all ways of truth. And contentious jealousy is on all their judgments, for they do not walk together.

But God in the mysteries of his understanding and in his glorious wisdom has ordained a period for the ruin of error, and in the appointed time of punishment he will destroy it forever. And then shall come out forever the truth of the world, for it has wallowed in the ways of wickedness in the dominion of error until the appointed time of judgment which has been decreed. And then God will refine in his truth all the deeds of a man, and will purify for himself the frame of man, consuming every spirit of error hidden in his flesh, and cleansing him with a holy spirit from all wicked deeds. And he will sprinkle upon him a spirit of truth, like water for impurity, from all abominations of falsehood and wallowing in a spirit of impurity, to make the upright perceive the knowledge of the Most High and the wisdom of the sons of heaven, to instruct those whose conduct is blameless. For God has chosen them for an eternal covenant, and theirs is all the glory of man; and there shall be no error, to the shame of all works of deceit.

Thus far the spirits of truth and of error struggle in the heart of a man; they walk in wisdom and folly; and according to each man's inheritance in truth he does right, and so he hates error; but according to his possession in the lot of error he does wickedly in it, and so he abhors truth. For in equal measure God has established the two spirits until the period which has been decreed and the making new; and he knows the performance of their works for all the periods of eternity. And he causes the sons of

men to inherit them, that they may know good and evil, making the lots fall for every living man according to his spirit in the world until the time of visitation.

III. Rules of the Order

And this is the order for the men of the community who have offered themselves to turn from all evil and to lay hold of all that he commanded according to his will, to be separated from the congregation of the men of error, to become a community in law and in wealth, answering when asked by the sons of Zadok, the priests who keep the covenant, and when asked by the majority of the men of the community, who lay hold of the covenant. At their direction the regulation of the lot shall be decided for every case regarding law, wealth, or justice, to practice truth, unity, and humility, righteousness and justice and loyal love, and to walk humbly in all their ways, that each may not walk in the rebelliousness of his heart or go astray after his heart and his eyes and the thought of his guilty impulse; to circumcise in unity the uncircumcision of impulse and the stiff neck, to lay a foundation of truth for Israel for the community of an eternal covenant, to atone for all who offer themselves for holiness in Aaron and for a house of truth in Israel, and those who joined with them for community and for controversy and for judgment, to condemn all who transgress the statute.

And as for these, this is the regulation of their ways concerning all these ordinances. When they are gathered together, every one who comes into the council of the community shall enter into the covenant of God in the sight of all who have offered themselves; and he shall take it upon himself by a binding oath to turn to the law of Moses, according to all that he commanded, with all his heart and with all his soul, to all that is revealed of it to the sons of Zadok, the priests who keep the covenant and who seek his will, and to the majority of the men of their covenant, who have offered themselves together to his truth and to walking in his good will; and that he will take it upon himself in the covenant to be separated from all the men of error who walk in the way of wickedness. For these are not reckoned in his covenant, for they have not sought or searched for him in his statutes, to know the hidden things in which they have gone astray, incurring guilt, and the things revealed which they have done with a high hand, arousing anger leading to judgment and the wreaking of vengeance by the curses of the covenant, bringing upon themselves great judgments to eternal destruction without remnant.

They shall not enter the water, in order to touch the sacred food of the holy men, for they will not be cleansed unless they have turned from their evil. For there is something unclean in all who transgress his word. And he shall not be united with him in his work and in his wealth, lest he bring upon him guilty transgression, but shall keep far from him in everything, for thus it is written: "From everything false you shall keep far." And no man of the men of the community shall answer when asked by them regarding any law or ordinance. And he shall not eat or drink anything from their wealth, and shall not take from their hand anything at all except for a price, as it is written: "Cease from man, whose breath is in his nostrils, for of what worth is he reckoned?" For all who are not reckoned in his covenant are to be separated with all that is theirs; and a holy man shall not lean upon any works of vanity; for vain are all those who do not know his covenant, and all those who despise his word he will destroy from the world, and all their works are but impurity before him; and there is something unclean in all their wealth.

When he enters the covenant to do according to all these statutes, to be united for a holy congregation, they shall investigate his spirit in the community, between a man and his neighbor, according to his understanding and his works in the law, as directed by the sons of Aaron, who have offered themselves in unity to establish his covenant and to have charge of all his statutes which he commanded men to do, and as directed by the majority of Israel, who have offered themselves to turn in unity to his covenant. They shall be registered in order, each before his neighbor, according to his understanding and his works, so that every one of them shall obey his neighbor, the lesser obeying the greater; and so that they shall have an investigation of their spirits and their works year by year, so as to elevate each one according to his understanding and the perfection of his way or put him back according to his perversions, so that each one may reprove his neighbor in truth and humility and loyal love for each one.

One shall not speak to his brother in anger or in resentment, or with a stiff neck or a hard heart or a wicked spirit; one shall not hate him in the folly of his heart. In his days he shall reprove him and shall not bring upon him iniquity; and also a man shall not bring against his neighbor a word before the masters without having rebuked him before witnesses.

In these ways they shall walk in all their dwellings, every living man, each with his neighbor. The lesser shall obey the greater with regard to wages and property. Together they shall eat, and together they shall worship, and together they shall counsel.

In every place where there are ten men of the council of the community there shall not be absent from them a priest. Each according to his position, they shall sit before him; and thus they shall be asked for their counsel regarding everything. And when they set the table to eat, or the wine to drink, the priest shall stretch out his hand first to pronounce a blessing with the first portion of the bread and the wine. And from the place where the ten are there shall never be absent a man who searches the law day and night, by turns, one after another. And the masters shall keep watch together a third of all the nights of the year, reading the book and searching for justice, and worshiping together.

This is the order for the session of the masters, each in his position. The priests be seated first and the elders second; then all the rest of the people shall be seated, each in his position. And thus they shall be asked concerning justice and every council and matter which comes to the masters, so that each may render his opinion to the council of the community. A man shall not speak in the midst of his neighbor's words, before his brother finishes speaking. And further he shall not speak before his position which is written before him. The man who is asked shall speak in his turn; and in the session of the masters a man shall not speak a word which is not to the liking of the masters. And when the man who is the superintendent over the masters—or any man who has a word to speak to the masters but who is not in the position of the one asking the community's counsel—the man shall stand on his feet and say, "I have a word to speak to the masters." If they tell him, he shall speak.

Everyone who has offered himself from Israel to be added to the council of the community shall be examined by the man appointed at the head of the masters as to his understanding and his works. If he comprehends instruction, he shall bring him into the covenant, to turn to the truth and to turn away from all error; and he shall explain to him all the ordinances of the community. Then later, when he comes in to stand before the masters, they shall all be questioned about his affairs; and as the lot determines, according to the counsel of the masters, he shall be admitted or depart. On being admitted to the council of the community, he shall not touch the sacred food of the masters until they examine him as to his spirit and his deeds when

he has completed a whole year; moreover he shall not participate in the wealth of the masters.

When he has completed a year within the community, the masters shall be questioned about his affairs, as to his understanding and his deeds in the law; and if the lot determines that he shall be admitted to the assembly of the community, as directed by the priests and the majority of the men of their covenant, his wealth and his wages shall be put at the disposal of the man who has supervision over the wages of the masters, and he shall enter it in the account at his disposal, but shall not spend it for the masters.

The new member shall not touch the sacred drink of the masters until he has completed a second year among the men of the community; but when he has completed a second year, he shall be examined with questioning by the masters. If the lot determines that he is to be admitted to the community, he shall be registered in the order of his position among his brethren, for law and for judgment and for the sacred food and for the sharing of his property; and the community shall have his counsel and his judgment.

These are the ordinances by which they shall judge when investigating together concerning cases. If there is found among them a man who lies about his wealth, and knows it, he shall be excluded from the sacred food of the masters for a year, and shall be deprived of a fourth of his food ration. One who answers his neighbor with a stiff neck, or speaks with impatience, breaking the foundation of his fellowship by disobeying his neighbor who is registered before him, his own hand has delivered him; therefore he shall be punished for a year. Any man who mentions anything by the Name which is honored above all shall be set apart. If one has cursed, either when frightened by trouble or for any reason he may have, while he is reading the book or pronouncing a blessing, he shall be set apart and shall not return

215

again to the council of the community. If he spoke in wrath against one of the priests registered in the book, he shall be punished for a year and set apart by himself from the sacred food of the masters. But if he spoke unintentionally, he shall be punished for six months.

One who lies about what he knows shall be punished six months. A man who without justification knowingly denounces his neighbor shall be punished for a year and set apart. One who speaks craftily with his neighbors, or knowingly perpetrates a fraud, shall be punished six months. If he commits a fraud against his neighbor, he shall be punished three months; if he commits a fraud against the wealth of the community, causing its loss, he shall repay it in full. If he is not able to pay it, he shall be punished sixty days.

One who bears a grudge against his neighbor without justification shall be punished six months [inserted above this line: a year]; so also he who takes vengeance for himself for anything. One who speaks with his mouth the word of a fool shall be punished three months. For one who speaks while his neighbor is speaking the punishment shall be ten days. One who lies down and goes to sleep during a session of the masters, thirty days. So also a man who leaves during a session of the masters unadvisedly and without cause as many as three times at one session shall be punished ten days; but if they object and he leaves, he shall be punished thirty days.

One who walks before his neighbor naked when he does not have to do so shall be punished six months. A man who spits into the midst of the session of the masters shall be punished thirty days. One who brings his hand out from beneath his robe when it is torn, so that his nakedness is seen, shall be punished thirty days. One who laughs foolishly, making his voice heard, shall be punished thirty days. One who brings out his left hand to gesticulate with it shall be punished ten days.

A man who gossips about his neighbor shall be separated for a year from the sacred food of the masters, and he shall be punished; and a man who gossips about the masters is to be dismissed from among them and shall not come back again. A man who murmurs against the institution of the community shall be dismissed and shall not come back; but if he murmurs against his neighbor without justification he shall be punished six months.

If a man's spirit wavers from the institution of the community, so that he becomes a traitor to the truth and walks in the stubbornness of his heart; if he repents he shall be punished two years. During the first he shall not touch the sacred food of the masters, and during the second he shall not touch the drink of the masters; and he shall be seated after all the men of the community. When his two years are completed, the masters shall be asked about his case. If they admit him, he shall be registered in his position; and after that he shall be asked for judgment. If any man is in the council of the community for ten full years, and his spirit turns back so that he becomes a traitor to the community and goes out from before the masters to walk in the stubbornness of his heart, he shall not come back again to the council of the community. If any man of the men of the community partakes with him of his sacred food, or of his wealth which he has delivered to the masters, his sentence shall be like his; he shall be dismissed.

There shall be in the council of the community twelve men, and there shall be three priests who are perfect in all that has been revealed of the whole law, to practice truth and righteousness and justice and loyal love and walking humbly each with his neighbor, to preserve faithfulness in the land with sustained purpose and a broken spirit, and to make amends for iniquity by the practice of justice and the distress of tribulation, and to walk with all by the standard of truth and by the regulation of the time.

When these things come to pass in Israel, the council of the community will be established in the truth for an eternal planting, a holy house for Israel, a foundation of the holy of holies for Aaron, true witnesses for justice and the elect by God's will, to make atonement for the land and to render to the wicked their recompense—this is the tested wall, a precious cornerstone; its foundations will not tremble or flee from their place—a most holy dwelling for Aaron with eternal knowledge for a covenant of justice and to offer a pleasing fragrance, and a house of perfection and truth in Israel to establish a covenant for eternal statutes. And they shall be accepted to make atonement for the land and to decide the judgment of wickedness, and there shall be no error. When these men have been prepared in the foundation of the community for two years with blameless conduct, they shall be separated in holiness in the midst of the council of the men of the community; and when anything which has been hidden from Israel is found by the man who is searching, it shall not be hidden from these men out of fear of an apostate spirit.

When these things come to pass for the community in Israel, by these regulations they shall be separated from the midst of the session of the men of error to go to the wilderness to prepare there the way of the LORD; as it is written, "In the wilderness prepare the way of the LORD; make straight in the desert a highway for our God." This is the study of the law, as he commanded through Moses, to do according to all that has been revealed from time to time, and as the prophets revealed by his Holy Spirit.

Any man of the men of the community, of the covenant of the community, who willfully takes away a word from the whole commandment shall not touch the sacred food of the holy men; he shall not know any of their counsel until his works are cleansed from all error, so that he conducts himself blamelessly. Then he shall be admitted to the council as directed by the masters, and afterward he shall be registered in his position. According to this law shall it be done for every one who is added to the community.

These are the ordinances by which the men of perfect holiness shall walk, each with his neighbor, every one who enters the holy council, those who conduct themselves blamelessly as he commanded. Any man of them who transgresses a word of the law of Moses overtly or with deceit shall be dismissed from the council of the community and shall not come back again; and none of the holy men shall participate in his wealth or in his counsel concerning anything. But if he acts unintentionally, he shall be separated from the sacred food and the council; and they shall interpret the ordinance that he shall not judge a man or be asked concerning any counsel for two years. If his conduct is perfect in the meeting, in interpretation, and in counsel as directed by the masters; if he has not again sinned unintentionally by the completion of his two years—because for one unintentional sin he shall be punished for two years—as for him who acts deliberately, he shall not come back again; only he who sins unintentionally shall be tested for two years, that his conduct and his counsel may be perfected under the direction of the masters —after that he shall be registered in his position for the holy community.

When these things come to pass in Israel according to all these regulations, for a foundation of a holy spirit, for eternal truth, for a ransom for the guilt of transgression and sinful faithlessness, and for acceptance for the land more than the flesh of whole burnt offerings and the fats of sacrifice, and an offering of the lips for justice like the pleasing quality of righteousness, and perfect conduct like a willing gift of an acceptable offering; at that time the men of the community shall be set apart, a house of holiness for Aaron, to be united as a holy of holies and a house of community for Israel, those who conduct themselves blamelessly.

Only the sons of Aaron shall administer judgment and wealth, and as they direct the lot shall determine for every regulation of the men of the community. As for the wealth of the holy men, who conduct themselves blamelessly, their wealth shall not be combined with the wealth of the men of deceit, who have not purified their conduct by separating themselves from error and conducting themselves blamelessly. They shall not depart from any counsel of the law, walking in all the stubbornness of their hearts; but they shall be judged by the first judgments by which the men of the community began to be disciplined, until there shall come a prophet and the Messiahs of Aaron and Israel.

These are the statutes for the wise man, that he may walk in them with every living being, according to the regulation of one time and another and the weight of one man and another; to do the will of God according to all that has been revealed for each time at that time; and to learn all the wisdom that has been found, according to the times, and the statute of the time; and to set apart and weigh the sons of Zadok according to their spirit; and to hold firmly to the elect of the time according to his will, as he commanded. According to each man's spirit he is to be given his due; according to the cleanness of each man's hands he is to be admitted; and according to his understanding he is to be accepted; so too his love together with his hate.

There must be no admonitions or contention with the men of the pit, for the counsel of the law must be concealed among the men of error; but there must be admonition of true knowledge and righteous judgment for those who choose the way; each according to his spirit, according to the regulation of the time, to guide them in knowledge and so to give them understanding in the marvelous mysteries and truth among the men of the community, that they may conduct themselves blamelessly, each with his neighbor, in all that has been revealed to them—that is the time of clearing the way to the wilderness—to give them understanding of all that has been found to be done at this time; and to be separated from every man, and not to pervert his way because of any error.

These are the regulations of the way for the wise man in these times, for his love together with his hate, eternal hate for the men of the pit in a spirit of concealment, leaving to them wealth and manual labor like a slave for the man who rules over him, and humility before the man who has the mastery over him. Each one must be zealous for the statute and its time, for the day of vengeance, to do what is acceptable in everything he puts his hands to, and in all his dominion as he commanded; and everything done in it will be accepted freely.

IV. The Closing Psalm

With nothing but the will of God shall a man be concerned,
but with all the words of his mouth shall he be pleased;
he shall not desire anything which he did not command,
but to the ordinance of God he shall look always.
In every period that is to be he shall bless his Maker,
and in whatever state he is he shall tell of his righteousness.
With an offering of the lips he shall bless him
throughout the periods which A has decreed:
at the beginning of the dominion of light, through its circuit,

and at its ingathering to its decreed dwelling;
at the beginning of the watches of darkness,
when he opens his treasury and appoints it for a time;
and at its circuit, together with its ingathering before the light,
when lights appear from the holy habitation,
together with their ingathering to the glorious dwelling;
at the coming in of seasons in days of the new moon,
both their circuit and their connection one with another.
When they renew themselves, the M is large for the holy of holies;
and the letter N is for the key of his eternal, steadfast love.
At the heads of seasons in every period to be,
at the beginning of months for their seasons
and holy days in their fixed order,
for a memorial in their seasons,
with an offering of the lips I will bless him
as a decree engraved forever.
At the heads of years and in the circuit of their seasons,
when the circle of their fixed order completes the day ordained for it,
one leading to another: the season of reaping to summer,
the season of sowing to the season of vegetation,
seasons of years to weeks of them,
and at the head of their weeks for a season of emancipation;
as long as I exist a decree engraved shall be on my tongue
for fruit of praise and for a gift of my lips.
I will sing with knowledge,
and all my music shall be for the glory of God;
my lyre and harp shall be for his holy fixed order,
and the flute of my lips I will raise
in his just circle.

With the coming of day and night
I will enter the covenant of God;
and with the outgoing of evening and morning
I will speak his decrees;
and while they exist I will set my limit
so that I may not turn back.

His judgment I will pronounce, according to my perversity—
for my transgression is before my eyes—like a statute engraved.
And to God I will say, "My righteousness";
to the Most High, "Foundation of my goodness,
Source of knowledge and Fountain of holiness,
Height of glory and Strength of all,
to eternal majesty!"
I will choose as he teaches me,
And I will be pleased as he judges me.

When I begin to put forth my hands and my feet,
I will bless his name;
when I begin to go out or come in,
when I sit down or stand up,
and as I lie on my couch, I will sing aloud to him;

I will bless him with an offering of the utterance of my lips
more than the oblation spread out by men.
Before I raise my hand to satisfy myself
with the delights of what the world produces,
in the dominion of fear and terror,
the place of distress with desolation,
I will bless him, giving special thanks.
On his might I will meditate,
and on his steadfast love I will lean all the day;
for I know that in his hand is the judgment of every living man,
and all his works are truth.
When distress is let loose I will praise him,
and when I am delivered I will sing praise also.

I will not render to a man the recompense of evil;
with good I will pursue a man;
for with God is the judgment of every living man;
and he will repay to a man his recompense.
I will not be jealous of an evil spirit;
wealth got by violence my soul shall not desire;
and the abundance of a man of the pit I will not seize
until the day of vengeance;
but my anger I will not turn back from men of error,
and I will not be pleased until he has established judgment.
I will not remain angry with those who turn from transgression,
but I will not have mercy on any who turn aside from the way,
and I will not show favor to those who are smitten until their conduct is blameless.

I will not keep baseness in my heart,
and folly shall not be heard in my mouth;
iniquitous falsehood, deceits, and lies
shall not be found on my lips;
but the fruit of holiness shall be on my tongue,
and abominable things shall not be found on it.

With thanksgivings I will open my mouth,
the righteous acts of God shall my tongue recount always
and the faithlessness of man until their transgression is complete.
Empty words I will banish from my lips,
unclean things and perversions from the knowledge of my mind.
With wise counsel I will conceal knowledge,
and with knowing prudence I will hedge about wisdom
with a firm limit, to preserve fidelity
and strong justice according to the righteousness of God.
I will exalt the decree with the measuring-line of times,
and will teach the practice of righteousness,
loyal love for the humble,
and strengthening of hands for the fearful of heart;
for the erring in spirit understanding;
to instruct the fainting with doctrine,
to answer humbly before the haughty of spirit,
and with a broken spirit to men of injustice,

who point the finger and speak wickedly
and are envious of wealth.

But as for me, my judgment belongs to God,
and in his hand is the blamelessness of my conduct
together with the uprightness of my heart;
and in his righteousness my transgression will be wiped out.
For from the source of his knowledge he has opened up my light;
my eye has gazed into his wonders
and the light of my heart penetrates the mystery that is to be.
That which is eternal is the staff of my right hand;
on a strong rock is the way I tread;
before nothing will it be shaken.
For the faithfulness of God is the rock I tread,
and his strength is the staff of my right hand.
From the source of his righteousness is my judgment.
A light is in my heart from his marvelous mysteries;
my eye has gazed on that which is eternal,
sound wisdom which is hidden from the man of knowledge,
and prudent discretion from the sons of man,
a source of righteousness and reservoir of strength
together with a spring of glory hidden from the company of flesh.
To those whom God has chosen he has given them for an eternal possession;
he has given them an inheritance in the lot of the holy ones
and with the sons of heaven has associated their company
for a council of unity and a company of a holy building,
for an eternal planting
through every period that is to be.

But I belong to wicked mankind,
to the company of erring flesh;
my iniquities, my transgression, my sin,
with the iniquity of my heart
belong to the company of worms and those who walk in darkness.
For the way of a man is not his own,
a man does not direct his own steps;
for judgment is God's,
and from his hand is blamelessness of conduct.
By his knowledge everything comes to pass;
and everything that is he establishes by his purpose;
and without him it is not done.
As for me, if I slip,
the steadfast love of God is my salvation forever;
and if I stumble in the iniquity of flesh,
my vindication in the righteousness of God will stand to eternity.
If he lets loose my distress,
from the pit he will deliver my soul;
he will direct my steps to the way.
In his mercy he has brought me near,
And in his steadfast love he will bring my vindication.
In his faithful righteousness he has judged me,
and in the abundance of his goodness he will forgive all my iniquities.

And in his righteousness he will cleanse me from the impurity of man,
from the sin of the sons of man.
Thanks be to God for his righteousness,
to the Most High for his majesty!

Blessed are you, O my God,
who opens to knowledge the heart of your servant.
Direct in righteousness all his works
and establish the son of your handmaid,
as you accepted the elect of mankind
to stand before you forever.
For without you conduct will not be blameless,
and apart from your will nothing will be done.
It is you that has taught all knowledge;
and everything that has come to pass has been by your will.
And there is no other beside you
to oppose your counsel,
to understand all your holy purpose,
to gaze into the depth of your mysteries,
or to comprehend all your marvels,
together with the strength of your power.
Who is able to bear your glory,
and what then is he,
the son of man, among your marvelous works;
what shall one born of woman be accounted before you?
As for him, he was kneaded from dust,
and the food of worms is his portion.
He is an emission of spittle, a cut-off bit of clay,
and his desire is for the dust.
What will clay reply, a thing formed by hand?
What counsel will it understand?

The Damascus Document

(Dead Sea Scrolls)

The *Damascus Document* is an austere work of exhortations and commandments regulating the life of the Qumran Community. It is similar in tone and content to the *Manual of Discipline*. The Essene "righteous few" had withdrawn from the temptations of the city to live in the wilderness in strict obedience to the laws of their Covenant with God. The area of Qumran by the Dead Sea where the select faithful lived was a harsh wasteland, below sea level, with soil so acidic and hostile to normal vegetation that in most places no animals, insects, or grasses could survive. There this strict community preserved its religious beliefs and practices, unpolluted by Jerusalem and its Hasmonean high priests; it followed the message of its Teacher of Righteousness, which was preserved in scrolls later found stored in caves; and there while Belial (Satan) was loose in the land, the faithful of the community waited for the coming of God, and glory, and the great joy they would experience. God would replace the Teacher of Righteousness as a Messiah figure, to judge them and bring salvation here on earth.

Internal loyalty was a cardinal virtue for this very closed society, and, by extension, apostasy was the ultimate sin. Temptation came in the form of imitation of the ways of Gentiles and their Pagan, particularly Greek, practices, or any connection with those worldly priests who committed fornication, who profaned the Temple, and transgressed the codes. While the Teacher of Righteousness revealed the proper interpretation of the Scriptures and the calendar, the Scoffer or Wicked Priest (who was probably the Hasmonean Jonathan or Simon) was leading Israel to punishment by God. The faithful of the community were supervised by the Guardians and instructed by Zadokite priests. The exhortations of the first part of the document represent a literary genre that was used by Jewish and Christian religious teachers. An example of the exhortation text is Paul's Letter to the Hebrews. The commandments or statutes of the second part of the document also prefigure a literary genre, that of the Mishnah, the second century codification of Jewish law.

The *Damascus Document* was already known at the end of the last century when two incomplete medieval copies of the text were discovered by Solomon Schechter in 1896–1897 in the storeroom of a Cairo synagogue. Schechter published them in 1910 under the title *Fragments of a Zadokite Work* (Cambridge). They were re-edited by Chaim Rabin in 1954 under the title *The Zadokite Documents* (Oxford). The term Zadokite is derived from "sons of Zadok," the name the members of the community called themselves. The present title given by Millar Burrows, the *Damascus Document*, is rendered as the *Damascus Rule* in Geza Vermes's translation of the scrolls. Both titles are derived from a passage that reads: "according to the decision of those who entered the covenant in the land of Damascus" (VIII). Scholars do not agree whether Damascus stands for exile in Damascus, is a symbol for someplace else, or refers to Qumran. The date of composition of the Qumran texts is thought to be between 100 and 75 B.C.

Many passages of the commandments in the *Damascus Document* indicate a connection with the *Book of Jubilees*. Chaim Rabin cites fifty-eight parallels between the earlier intertestamental book, composed around 168 B.C., and the halakhic interpretation of the laws found in the Torah. Despite all the juridical language, we find a coloring of the supernatural when we read that angels are among the assembly, regarding the faithful. And hope of redemption is always present with the mention of the messiah of Aaron and Israel who will save those who have been saved from the snares of the pit. The main theological sermon comes, however, at the end of the first section of exhortations. Those who hear the Teacher of Righteousness will find joy and salvation:

> [W]ho give ear to the voice of a teacher of righteousness and do not reject the statutes of righteousness when they hear them—they shall rejoice and be glad, and their hearts shall be strong, and they shall prevail over all the sons of the world, and God will forgive them, and they shall see his salvation, because they have taken refuge in his holy name.

THE DAMASCUS DOCUMENT*

History and Exhortation

And now listen, all you who know righteousness and understand the works of God. For he has a controversy with all flesh, and will execute judgment upon all who despise him. For when those who forsook him trespassed, he hid his face from Israel and from his sanctuary, and gave them up to the sword; but when he remembered the covenant of the ancients, he left a remnant to Israel and did not give them up to destruction. And in the period of the wrath—three hundred and ninety years, when he gave them into the hand of Nebuchadnezzar, king of Babylon—he visited them and caused to sprout from Israel and Aaron a root of planting to inherit his land and to grow fat in the goodness of his soil. Then they perceived their iniquity and knew that they were guilty men; yet they were like men blind and groping for the way for twenty years. And God observed their works, that they sought him with a perfect heart; and he raised up for them a teacher of righteousness to lead them in the way of his heart. And he made known to later generations what he did to a later generation, to a congregation of treacherous men, those who turned aside out of the way.

This was the time concerning which it was written, "Like a stubborn heifer, Israel was stubborn," when arose the man of scorn, who preached to Israel lying words and led them astray in a trackless wilderness, so that he brought low their iniquitous pride, so that they turned aside from the paths of righteousness, and removed the landmark which the forefathers had fixed in their inheritance,

so making the curses of his covenant cleave to them, delivering them to the sword that wreaks the vengeance of the covenant. For they sought smooth things, and chose illusions, and looked for breaches, and chose the fair neck; and they justified the wicked and condemned the righteous, transgressed the covenant and violated the statute. And they banded together against the life of the righteous, and all who walked uprightly their soul abhorred, and they pursued them with the sword and exulted in the strife of the people. Then was kindled the wrath of God against their congregation, laying waste all their multitude; and their deeds were uncleanness before him.

And now listen to me, all you who have entered the covenant, and I will uncover your ears as to the ways of the wicked. God loves the knowledge of wisdom; and sound wisdom he has set before him; prudence and knowledge minister to him. Longsuffering is with him, and abundance of pardon to forgive those who turn from transgression, but power and might and great wrath with flames of fire by all the angels of destruction upon those who turn aside from the way and abhor the statute, so that they shall have no remnant or survival.

For God did not choose them from the beginning of the world, but before they were established he knew their works and abhorred their generations from of old, and he hid his face from the land and from his people until they were consumed; for he knew the years of abiding and the number and explanation of their periods for all who exist in the ages, and the things that come to pass even to what will come in their periods for all the years of eternity.

But in all of them he raised up for himself men called by name, in order to leave a remnant to the land, and to fill the face of the world with their seed. And he caused them to know by his anointed his Holy Spirit and a revelation

*From Millar Burrows, *The Dead Sea Scrolls* (New York: Viking Press, 1951), pp. 349–364. The translation is based on two manuscripts, *A* and *B*, of which *A* is prime source; where *B* is used to supplement *A*, *B* is enclosed in brackets.

of truth; and in the explanation of his name are their names. But those he hated he caused to go astray.

And now, my sons, listen to me, and I will uncover your eyes to see and understand the works of God, and to choose what he likes and reject what he hates; to walk perfectly in all his ways, and not to go about with thoughts of a guilty impulse and eyes of fornication; for many went astray in them, and mighty men of valor stumbled in them, formerly and until now. In their walking in the rebelliousness of their hearts the watchers of heaven fell; in it they were caught who did not keep the commandment of God, and their children, whose height was like the loftiness of the cedars, and whose bodies were like the mountains, fell thereby. Yea, all flesh that was on the dry land fell; yea, it perished; and they were as though they had not been, because they did their own will and did not keep the commandment of their Maker, until his anger was kindled against them.

In it the sons of Noah and their families went astray; in it they were cut off. Abraham did not walk in it, and he was accounted as God's friend, because he kept the commandments of God and did not choose the will of his own spirit. And he passed on the commandment to Isaac and Jacob, and they kept it and were recorded as friends of God and possessors of the covenant forever.

The sons of Jacob went astray in them and were punished according to their error, and their sons in Egypt walked in the stubbornness of their hearts, taking counsel against the commandments of God and doing each what was right in his own eyes. They ate blood, and he cut off their males in the desert. And he said to them in Kadesh, "Go up and take possession of the land," but they hardened their spirit and did not listen to the voice of their Maker, the commandments of their Teacher, but murmured in their tents.

Then the anger of God was kindled against their congregation; their children perished by it, their kings were cut off by it, and their mighty men perished by it; and their land was made desolate by it. By it the first that entered the covenant became guilty, and they were delivered to the sword, because they forsook the covenant of God and chose their own will, and went about after the stubbornness of their heart, each doing his own will.

But with those who held fast to the commandments of God, those who were left of them, God established his covenant for Israel to eternity, revealing to them hidden things in which all Israel had gone astray. His holy Sabbaths and his glorious festivals, his righteous testimonies and his true ways, and the desires of his will, by which, if a man does them, he shall live, he opened up before them. And they dug a well for many waters, and he who despises them shall not live. But they defiled themselves with the transgression of man, and in the ways of the unclean woman, and they said, "That is for us." But God in his wondrous mysteries forgave their iniquity and pardoned their transgression, and he built for them a sure house in Israel, the like of which has not existed from of old or until now. Those who hold fast to it are for eternal life, and all the glory of man is theirs; as God established it for them by the prophet Ezekiel, saying, "The priests and the Levites and the sons of Zadok, who kept the charge of my sanctuary when the sons of Israel went astray from me, they shall offer to me fat and blood."

The priests are the captivity of Israel who went forth from the land of Judah, and the Levites are those who joined them; and the sons of Zadok are the elect of Israel, those called by name, who will abide at the end of days. Behold the explanation of their names according to their generations, and the period of their abiding, and the number of their distresses, and the years of their sojourning, and the explanation of their works, the first saints whom God forgave, and who justified the righteous and condemned the wicked.

All who come after them must do according to the explanation of the law in which the forefathers were instructed until the completion of the period of these years. According to the covenant which God established with the forefathers to forgive their sins, so God will forgive them. And at the completion of the period to the number of these years they shall no more join themselves to the house of Judah, but every one must stand up on his watchtower. The wall has been built; the decree is far away.

And during all these years Belial will be let loose in Israel, as God spoke by the prophet Isaiah the son of Amoz, saying, "Terror and the pit and the snare are upon you, O inhabitant of the land." This means the three nets of Belial of which Levi the son of Jacob spoke, in which he caught Israel and set them before them as three kinds of righteousness. The first is fornication; the second is wealth; the third is the pollution of the sanctuary. He who gets out of one will be caught in another, and he who is rescued from one will be caught in another.

The builders of the wall who follow a precept—the precept is a preacher, because it says, "They will surely preach" —they will be caught in two nets: in fornication by taking two wives during their lifetime, whereas the foundation of the creation is, "male and female he created them"; and those who went into the ark, "Two by two they went into the ark." And concerning the prince it is written, "He shall not multiply wives for himself."

But David did not read the sealed book of the law which was in the ark; for it was not opened in Israel from the day of the death of Eleazar and Joshua and the elders who served the Ashtaroth, but was hidden and not disclosed until Zadok arose. The deeds of David were overlooked, except the blood of Uriah, and God left them to him.

Moreover they defile the sanctuary, because they do not separate according to the law, but lie with her who sees the blood of her issue. And they take each his brother's daughter or his sister's daughter; but Moses said "You shall not approach your mother's sister; she is your mother's near kinswoman." And the ordinance of intercourse for males is written, and like them for the women. And if the brother's daughter uncovers the nakedness of the brother of her father; she is a near kinswoman.

Moreover they defiled their holy spirit, and with a tongue of blasphemies they opened the mouth against the statutes of God's covenant, saying, "They are not established." And abominations they speak concerning them. They "all kindle fire and set brands alight!" "The webs of spiders" are their webs, and "adders' eggs" are their eggs. He who is near them shall not be counted innocent; the more he does it, the more shall he be held guilty, unless he was forced.

But of old God punished their works, and his anger was kindled because of their doings. For "it is not a people of understanding"; "they are a nation void of counsel," because there is no understanding in them. For of old arose Moses and Aaron through the prince of lights, and Belial raised Jannes and his brother with his evil device, when Israel was delivered the first time.

In the period of the destruction of the land arose the removers of the landmark and led Israel astray. And the land became desolate, because they spoke rebellion against the commandments of God by Moses, and also by the holy anointed ones; and they prophesied falsehood to turn away Israel from following God.

But God remembered the covenant of the forefathers, and raised up from

Aaron men of understanding, and from Israel wise men. And he made them listen, and they dug the well. "A well which princes dug, which the nobles of the people delved with the staff." The well is the law, and those who dug it are the captivity of Israel, who went out from the land of Judah and sojourned in the land of Damascus, all of whom God called princes, because they sought him, and their glory was not rejected in the mouth of anyone. And the staff (or legislator) is he who studies the law, as Isaiah said, "He produces an instrument for his work." And the nobles of the people are those who come to dig the well with the staves (or rules) which the staff (or legislator) prescribed to walk in during the whole period of wickedness; and without them they shall not attain to the arising of him who will teach righteousness at the end of days.

And all who have been brought into the covenant not to come into the sanctuary to kindle fire on his altar in vain shall become those who shut the door, as God said, "Who among you will shut his door, so that you will not kindle fire on my altar in vain?"—unless they observe to do according to the explanation of the law for the period of wickedness; and to separate from the sons of the pit; and to keep away from the unclean wealth of wickedness acquired by vowing and devoting and by appropriating the wealth of the sanctuary; and not to rob the poor of his people, so that widows become their spoil, and they murder the fatherless; and to make a separation between the unclean and the clean, and to make men know the difference between the holy and the common; and to keep the Sabbath day according to its explanation, and the festivals and the day of the fast, according to the decision of those who entered the new covenant in the land of Damascus; to contribute their holy things according to their explanation; to love each his brother as himself; and to hold fast the hand of the poor and the needy

and the proselyte; and to seek every one the peace of his brother; for a man shall not trespass against his next of kin; and to keep away from harlots according to the ordinance; to rebuke each his brother according to the commandment, and not to bear a grudge from day to day; and to separate from all uncleannesses according to their ordinances; for a man shall not make abominable his holy spirit, as God separated for them.

For all who walk in these things in perfection of holiness, according to all his teaching, God's covenant stands fast, to make them live to a thousand generations. [Ms. B: As it is written, "Who keeps covenant and steadfast love for him who loves him and for those who keep his commandments to a thousand generations.]

And if they dwell in camps according to the order of the earth [Ms. B: which was from of old] and take wives [Ms. B: according to the guidance of the law] and beget sons, they shall walk according to the law and according to the ordinances of the teachings, according to the order of the law, as it says, "between a man and his wife and between a father and his son."

But all who reject it when God visits the land, the recompense of the wicked is to be rendered to them, when the word comes to pass which is written in the words of the prophet Isaiah the son of Amoz, who said, "He will bring upon you and upon your people and upon your father's house such days as have not come since the day that Ephraim departed from Judah." [Ms. B: But all who reject the commandments and the statutes, the recompense of the wicked is to be rendered to them when God visits the land, when the word comes to pass which was written by the prophet Zechariah, "O sword, awake against my shepherd and against the man who stands next to me, says God; smite the shepherd, and the sheep shall be scattered, and I will turn my hand against the little ones." Now "those who give heed to him" are the poor of the flock.]

When the two houses of Israel separated, Ephraim departed from Judah; and all who turned back were given over to the sword, but those who stood firm escaped to the land of the north, as it says, "And I will exile the *sikkuth* of your king and the *kiyyun* of your images from the tents of Damascus." The books of the law are the booth of the king, as it says, "And I will raise up the booth of David that is fallen"; the king is the assembly; and the *kiyyun* of the images are the books of the prophets, whose words Israel despised; and the star is the interpreter of the law who came to Damascus, as it is written, "A star shall come forth out of Jacob, and a scepter shall rise out of Israel." The scepter is the prince of the whole congregation. And when he arises, he "shall break down all the sons of Seth."

These escaped in the period of the first visitation, but those who turned back they delivered to the sword [*Ms. B:* when comes the Messiah of Aaron and Israel; as it was during the period of the first visitation, of which he spake by Ezekiel, "to set a mark upon the foreheads of those who sign and groan," but the rest were delivered to "the sword that executes vengeance for the covenant"]. And such shall be the judgment of all of those who enter his covenant that do not hold fast to the oath, being visited for destruction through Belial. That is the day on which God will visit [*Ms. B:* as he has spoken].

The princes of Judah have become those [*Ms. B:* who remove the landmark; upon whom I will pour wrath like water] upon whom you will pour wrath. For they will hope for healing, but all the rebellious will crush them, [*Ms. B:* for they entered the covenant of repentance]; because they did not turn away from the way of the treacherous, but defiled themselves in the ways of harlots and in the wealth of wickedness and revenge and bearing a grudge, each against his brother, and hating each his neighbor; and they hid themselves each against his near kin, and drew near to unchastity, and behaved arrogantly for wealth and unjust gain; and they did each what was right in his own eyes, and chose each the stubbornness of his heart; and they did not separate from the people [*Ms. B:* and their sin]; and they cast off restraint with a high hand, walking in the way of the wicked, concerning whom God said, "Their wine is the poison of serpents and the cruel venom of asps." The serpents are the kings of the peoples, and their wine is their ways, and the venom of asps is the head of the kings of Greece, who comes to take vengeance upon them.

But all these things those who built the wall and daubed it with whitewash did not understand, for a raiser of wind and preacher of lies [*Ms. B:* one walking in wind and weighing storms and preaching to man for a lie] preached to them, because the anger of God was kindled against all his congregations, and as Moses said, "Not because of your righteousness or the uprightness of your heart are you going in to possess these nations, but because of his love for your fathers, and because of his keeping the oath." And such is the judgment of the captivity of Israel; they turned aside from the way of the people.

In God's love for the forefathers, who stirred up after him [*Ms. B:* who testified against the people after God], he loved those who came after them, for theirs is the covenant of the fathers. But in his hatred of the builders of the wall [*Ms. B:* But God hates and abhors the builders of the wall] his anger was kindled [*Ms. B:* against them and against all who follow them].

And such is the judgment of every man who rejects the commandments of God and forsakes them; and they turn away in the stubbornness of their hearts.

This is the word that Jeremiah spoke to Baruch the son of Neriah, and Elisha to his servant Gehazi. All the men who entered the new covenant in the land of Damascus, [*Ms. B:* but turned back and acted treacherously and departed from the well of living water, shall not be reckoned in the company of the people, and in its book they shall not be written, from the day of the gathering in of the unique teacher until arises a Messiah from Aaron and from Israel. And such is the judgment for all who enter the congregation of the men of perfect holiness, and he abhors doing the precepts of upright men. He is the man who is melted in the furnace. When his deeds become known, he shall be expelled from the congregation as one whose lot has not fallen among those who are taught of God. According to his trespass the men of knowledge shall rebuke him until the day when he comes back to stand in the meeting of the men of perfect holiness. And when his deeds become known, according to the interpretation of the law in which the men of perfect holiness walk, no man shall agree with him in wealth and service; for all the holy ones of the Most High have cursed him.

And such shall be the judgment of every one who rejects the former ones and the latter ones; those who have taken idols into their hearts and walked in the stubbornness of their hearts. They have no share in the house of the law. According to the judgment of their fellows who turned back with the men of scorn shall they be judged, for they spoke error against the statutes of righteousness and rejected the firm covenant which they had established in the land of Damascus, that is, the new covenant. And neither they nor their families shall have a share in the house of the law.

From the day of the gathering in of the unique teacher until the annihilation of all the men of war who returned with the man of the lie will be about forty years; and in that period will be kindled the anger of God against Israel, as it says,

"There is no king and no prince and no judge, and none who rebuke in righteousness." Those who repented of the transgressions of Jacob have kept the covenant of God.

Then each will speak to his neighbor, to strengthen one another, that their steps may hold fast to the way of God; and God will listen to their words and hear, and a book of remembrance will be written before him for those who fear God and think of his name, until salvation and righteousness are revealed for those who fear God. Then you shall again discern between the righteous and the wicked, between him who serves God and him who does not serve him. And he will show kindness to thousands, to those who love him and keep his commandments, to a thousand generations, after the manner of the house of Peleg, who went out from the holy city and leaned upon God during the period when Israel transgressed and polluted the sanctuary; but they turned to God. And he smote the people with few words. All of them, each according to his spirit, shall be judged in the holy council. And all who have broken through the boundary of the law, of those who entered the covenant, at the appearing of the glory of God to Israel shall be cut off from the midst of the camp, and with them all who condemn Judah in the days of its trials.

But all who hold fast to these ordinances, going out and coming in according to the law, and who listen to the voice of a teacher and confess before God, "We have sinned, we have done wickedly, both we and our fathers, in walking contrary to the statutes of the covenant; right and true are your judgments against us"; all who do not lift a hand against his holy statutes and his righteous judgments and his true testimonies; who are instructed in the former judgments with which the men of the community were judged; who give ear to the voice of a teacher of righteousness and do not reject the statutes of righteousness when they hear them—they shall rejoice and be glad, and their hearts shall be strong, and they shall prevail over all the sons of the world, and God will forgive them, and they shall see his salvation, because they have taken refuge in his holy name.]

Community Regulations

Any man who dedicates anything which is the property of the camp, according to the statutes of the Gentiles he must be put to death: And as for what it says, "You shall not take vengeance or bear a grudge against the sons of your own people," any man of those who enter the covenant who brings a charge against his neighbor without having rebuked him before witnesses, and brings it in the heat of his anger, and tells his elders, in order to bring him into contempt, he is an avenger and grudge-bearer; but nothing is written except, "He takes vengeance on his adversaries and bears a grudge against his enemies." If he kept silence about him from day to day, but in the heat of his anger against him spoke against him concerning a capital offense, he has wronged him, because he did not confirm the commandment of God, who said to him, "You shall reprove your neighbor, lest you bear sin because of him."

Concerning the oath: as it says, "Let not your own hand deliver you," if a man makes one take an oath in the open field, not in the presence of the judges or at their command, his own hand has delivered him.

When anything is lost, and it is not known who stole it from the property of the camp in which it was stolen, one shall make its owners take the oath of the curse, and he who hears, if he knows and does not tell, shall be guilty.

When any restitution for guilt is made of something which has no owners, he who makes restitution shall confess to the priest, and it shall all go to him in addition to the ram of the guilt-offering.

And so everything lost which is found and has no owner shall go to the priests, because he who found it does not know the right of it. If no owners are found for it, they shall keep it.

When a man trespasses in any matter against the law and his neighbor sees it and he is alone; if it is a capital offense, he shall tell it in his presence with an accusation to the superintendent, and the superintendent shall write it down with his own hand, until he does it again before one witness; then he shall return and make it known to the superintendent. If he is caught again before one witness, the case against him is complete. But if there are two and they testify concerning one offense (or, but they testify concerning a different offense), the man shall be separated from the sacred food by himself, if they are trustworthy, and on the day that they see the man they shall tell it to the superintendent.

And concerning the statute: They shall accept two trustworthy witnesses, and concerning one offense, to separate the sacred food. And there shall not be accepted a witness by the judges, to have a man put to death on his testimony, whose days have not been fulfilled so as to pass over to those who are numbered, one who fears God. No man shall be believed against his neighbor as a witness who transgresses a word of the commandment with a high hand, until he is cleansed so that he can return.

And this is the order for the judges of the congregation: There shall be as many as ten men chosen by the congregation according to the time, four of the tribe of Levi and Aaron and six from Israel, instructed in the book of *hgw* and in the teachings of the covenant, from five and twenty years to sixty years old. But no one shall take the position from the age of sixty years and upward to judge the congregation; for when man transgressed, his days were diminished, and in the heat of God's anger against the inhabitants of the earth he commanded that their knowledge should depart from them before they completed their days.

Concerning purification with water: Let not a man wash in water that is filthy or not enough for covering a man. Let him not purify in it any vessel. And any pool in a rock in which there is not enough covering, which an unclean person has touched, its water is unclean like the water of a vessel.

Concerning the Sabbath, to observe it according to its ordinance: Let not a man do work on the sixth day from the time when the sun's disk is its full width away from the gate, for that is what it says: "Observe the Sabbath day to keep it holy." And on the Sabbath day let not a man utter anything foolish or trifling. Let him not lend anything to his neighbor. Let them not shed blood over wealth and gain. Let him not speak of matters of work and labor to be done on the morrow. Let not a man walk in the field to do the work of his business on the Sabbath. Let him not walk out of his city more than a thousand cubits. Let not a man eat on the Sabbath day anything but what is prepared. And of what is perishing in the field let him not eat. And let him not drink anything except what is in the camp. If he is on the way and is going down to battle let him drink where he stands, but let him not draw water into any vessel. Let him not send the son of a foreigner to do his business on the Sabbath day. Let not a man put on garments that are filthy or that were put in storage unless they have been washed in water or rubbed with frankincense. Let not a man go hungry of his own accord on the Sabbath. Let not a man walk after an animal to pasture it outside of his city more than two thousand cubits. Let him not lift his hand to strike it with his fist. If it is stubborn, let him not take it out of his house. Let not a man take anything from the house out-of-doors, or from out-of-doors into the house, and if he is in a booth, let him not take anything out of it or bring anything into it. Let him not open a sealed vessel on the Sabbath. Let not a man take on him ointments to go out and come in on the Sabbath. Let him not lift up in his dwelling house rock or earth. Let not the nurse take up the sucking child to go out and come in on the Sabbath. Let not a man provoke his male or female slave or his hired servant on the Sabbath. Let not a man help an animal to give birth on the Sabbath day; and if she lets her young fall into a cistern or a ditch, let him not raise it on the Sabbath. Let not a man rest in a place near to Gentiles on the Sabbath. Let not a man profane the Sabbath for the sake of wealth or gain on the Sabbath. And if any person falls into a place of water, or into a place, let not a man come up by a ladder or rope or instrument. Let not a man bring up anything to the altar on the Sabbath except the burnt offering of the Sabbath, for thus it is written, "beside your Sabbaths."

Let not a man send to the altar burnt offering or meal offering or frankincense or wood by the hand of a man who is unclean with any of the uncleannesses, allowing him to make the altar unclean; for it is written, "The sacrifice of the wicked is an abomination, but the prayer of the righteous is like an acceptable offering." And when anyone enters the house of worship, let him not enter while unclean, requiring washing. And when the trumpets of assembly sound, let him act before or afterward, or so that they shall not stop the whole service on the Sabbath; it is holy. Let not a man lie with a woman in the city of the sanctuary making unclean the city of the sanctuary with their impurity.

Any man in whom the spirits of Belial rule, and who speaks rebellion, shall be judged according to the judgment of the medium and wizard. And every one who goes astray so that he profanes the Sabbath and the feasts shall not be put to death, but the sons of man shall be responsible for taking charge of him; and if he is healed of it, they shall have charge of him seven years, and after that he shall come into the assembly.

Let no one stretch out his hand to shed the blood of a man of the Gentiles on account of wealth and gain; moreover let him not take any of their wealth, lest they blaspheme, unless it is by the counsel of the society of Israel. Let not a man sell animals or birds that are clean to the Gentiles, lest they sacrifice them. And from his threshing-floor or his winepress let him not sell them anything among all his possessions. And let him not sell them his male or female slave who entered with him into the covenant of Abraham.

Let not a man make himself abominable with any living creature or creeping thing by eating of them, from the larvae of bees to any living creature that creeps in the water. And let not fish be eaten unless they have been split alive and their blood has been poured out. And all the locusts according to their kinds shall be put into fire or into water while they are still alive, for this is the law of their creation. And all wood and stones and dust which are polluted by the uncleanness of men shall be considered like them as polluting: according to their uncleanness he who touches them shall be unclean. And every instrument, nail, or peg in the wall which is with the dead in the house shall be unclean with the uncleanness of an implement for work.

The order of the session of the cities of Israel: According to these ordinances separation is to be made between the unclean and the clean, and the difference between the holy and the common is to be made known. And these are the statutes for the wise man, that he may walk in them with every living being according to the law of one time and another. And according to this ordinance the seed of Israel shall walk, and they shall not be cursed.

And this is the order of the session of the camps: Those who walk in these ways during the period of wickedness, until arises the Messiah of Aaron and Israel, must be as many as ten men at least, by thousands and hundreds and fifties and tens. And in a place having ten there shall not be absent a priest learned in the book of *hgw*. According to his word shall they all be ruled. And if he is not qualified in all these ways, but a man of the Levites is qualified in these ways, the decision to go out or come in for all who enter the camp shall be made according to his direction. And if there is a judgment against a man concerning the law of disease, then the priest shall come and stand in the camp, and the superintendent shall instruct him in the explanation of the law. And if he is simple, he shall lock him up; for theirs is the judgment.

And this is the order for the superintendent of the camp: He shall instruct the many in the works of God and make them understand his wondrous mighty acts; and he shall recount before them the things that have been done of old in their divisions. And he shall have mercy on them as a father on his sons, and shall bring back all their erring ones as a shepherd does with his flock. He shall loose all the ties that bind them, so that there shall be none oppressed and crushed in his congregation. And everyone who is added to his congregation he shall examine him as to his works, his understanding, his strength, his might, and his wealth. And they shall register him in his place according to his being in the lot of the truth. No man of the sons of the camp shall have authority to bring a man into the congregation without the word of the superintendent of the camp. And no man of all those who enter the covenant of God shall do business with the sons of the pit except hand to hand. And no man shall make an agreement for buying and selling unless he has told the superintendent who is in the camp.

For all who walk in these ways the

covenant of God stands fast, to rescue them from all snares of the pit; for the simple go on and are punished.

And this is the order of the session of all the camps: They shall all be enrolled by their names; the priests first, the Levites second, the sons of Israel third, and the proselyte fourth. And so they shall sit, and so they shall ask concerning everything. And the priest who is appointed at the head of the many shall be from thirty to sixty years old, instructed in the book of *hgw* and in all the ordinances of the law, so as to speak them rightly. And the superintendent who is over all the camps shall be from thirty years old to fifty years old, proficient in every secret counsel of men and in every tongue according to their number. According to his direction those who enter the congregation shall enter, each in his turn. And any word which any man has to speak he shall speak to the superintendent concerning any controversy and decision.

And this is the order of the many, for settling all their affairs: The wages of the two days for every month at least—and they shall put it into the hand of the superintendent, and the judges shall give from it for orphans, and from it they shall support the poor and the needy, and for the aged man who dies, and for the wanderer, and for him who goes into captivity to a foreign people, and for the virgin who has no redeemer, and for the slave for whom nobody seeks any work of the association.

He shall not swear either by *aleph* and *lamed* or by *aleph* and *daleth*.

If he swears and transgresses, he profanes the Name. And if by the curses of the covenant he has sworn before the judges, and has transgressed, he is guilty; and he shall confess and make restitution, that he may not bear sin and die. The sons of those who enter the covenant for all Israel for an eternal decree,

when they attain to passing into the number of those enrolled, shall be obligated by the oath of the covenant.

And such is the ordinance during the whole period of wickedness for everyone who turns from his corrupt way. On the day that he speaks with the superintendent of the many they shall enroll him with the oath of the covenant which Moses made with Israel, the covenant to return to the law of Moses with the whole heart and with the whole soul, to what one finds to do during the whole period of wickedness. But no man shall tell him the ordinances until he stands before the superintendent, lest he prove simple when he examines him.

Therefore the man shall obligate himself to return to the law of Moses, for in it everything is specified.

The explanation of their periods, for the blindness of Israel to all these, is specified in the *Book of the Divisions of the Times according to their Jubilees and in their Weeks*. And on the day that the man obligates himself to return to the law of Moses the angel of enmity will depart from behind him if he makes good his words. Therefore Abraham was circumcised on the day that he received knowledge. And as for what it says, "What has passed your lips you shall keep," to perform it; no binding oath which a man takes upon himself, to do anything according to the law, shall he redeem even at the cost of death. If a man takes anything upon himself contrary to the law, let him not, even at the cost of death, perform it. As for any oath of a woman, of which it says, "Her husband must annul her oath," let not a man annul an oath of which he does not know whether it should be confirmed or annulled. If it is to transgress the covenant, he shall annul it and not confirm it. And such is the ordinance for her father. Concerning the law of the free will offerings, a man shall not vow for the altar anything taken by force.

The War of the Sons of Light with the Sons of Darkness

(Dead Sea Scrolls)

As the title of these selections suggests, this war is more than an ordinary earthly military combat. The forces of light, of God, are pitted against the Prince of Darkness, against Belial and his hosts. The people of Israel will triumph in battle as a result of God's intervention, and his intervention is guaranteed if the people of Israel hold to the Law and Covenant with God. Yet while the struggle is clearly spiritual, it is expressed in the military language of its time—which helps us place the work in the last decades of the first century B.C. or the beginning of the first century A.D. As Yigael Yadin points out in his definitive edition of the scroll,[1] the art of war is practiced according to the tactics of the Roman legion as well as ancient practices recounted in the Old Testament. The troops are arrayed in three lines, in the Roman *triplex acies*. Of course, missing from the Roman legion is the Jewish priest between the lines, blowing on his ram's horn and urging the troops forward. But the screams and howls of the soldiers to strike terror in the enemy's hearts appear to be a tactic taken from Roman practice.

The main subject of the scroll is the forty-year war that will take place "when the exiles of the sons of light return from the wilderness of the nations to encamp in the wilderness of Jerusalem." The tribes of Israel will fight this war. Kittim is the enemy. This enemy nation may be identified with contemporary foes of Israel, the Romans, the Selucids of Syria, the Egyptians, the descendants of Alexander's empire; or to the more traditional enemies recounted in the Bible, the Ammonites, the Moabites, the Philistines, and so on. But it would be a mistake

235

to treat the battle as an external conflict between Israel and the entire Gentile world. Clearly the holy war is a metaphor for an ethical and theological conflict between the forces of light and the forces of darkness, between those who keep the Law of Moses as well as the laws of the sect at Qumran and those who transgress these laws. In the larger mythical sense, which Theodor H. Gaster elaborates, the combat is another version of the enactment of the new defeating the old, the reformed Noahs defeating the age of corruption, or, in their seasonal enactment, a combat in which "Fertility discomfits Drought, Summer ousts Winter, or Life subdues Death."[2]

The blending of myth and history in the scrolls raises interesting questions. Myth is myth—that is, fantasy as opposed to history—only to skeptical outsiders. To the faithful, the intended audience, myth is revealed truth. A typical device of writers of the fantastic—be it in holy scriptures or in Franz Kafka—is to state the impossible or transcendental and then relentlessly prove its veracity by means of scrupulously realistic detail. Such is the literary device used to recount this mythical war. Extraordinary cosmic events are laced with ordinary realistic details reflecting contemporary times. So while angels fight alongside men, the Sons of Light must follow the biblical camp laws of soldierly purity.

"Any man who is not pure with regard to his sexual organs on the day of battle shall not join them in battle, for holy angels are in communion with their hosts" (vii,6).

One of the most colorful sections of the scrolls concerns the banners carried by each fighting unit. The Romans used banners for organizational purposes and for signaling. The banners carried by the sons of light were used for organizational purposes: they served to distinguish each tribe and the families within the tribe. But, as Yigael Yadin remarks, these banners were also associated with religious and magical concepts.[3] The very proliferation of holy words, of apocalyptic slogans, held high in the midst of battle, suggests that continuous preoccupation with words, with letters and numbers, elaborated endlessly by the Kabbalists, putting the written language, the scroll, at the heart of traditional Judaism.

Notes

1. Yigael Yadin, ed., *The Scroll of the War of the Sons of Light against the Sons of Darkness* (Oxford: Oxford University Press, 1962), 387 pp.

2. Theodor H. Gaster, *The Dead Sea Scrolls in English Translation* (New York: Doubleday Anchor, 1956), p. 275.

3. Yadin, *The Scroll*, p. 64.

THE WAR OF THE SONS OF LIGHT WITH THE SONS OF DARKNESS*

I

At the beginning of the undertaking of the sons of light, they shall start against the lot of the sons of darkness, the army of Belial, against the troop of Edom and Moab and the sons of Ammon, against the people of Philistia, and against the troops of the Kittim of Assyria, and with them as helpers the violators of the covenant. The sons of Levi, the sons of Judah, and the sons of Benjamin, the exiles of the desert, shall fight against them and their forces with all their troops, when the exiles of the sons of light return from the desert of the peoples to encamp in the desert of Jerusalem. And after the battle they shall go up from there against the king of the Kittim in Egypt; and in his time he shall go forth with great wrath to fight against the kings of the north; and his wrath shall destroy and cut off the horn of their strength. That will be a time of salvation for the people of God, and a period of dominion for all the men of his lot, but eternal destruction for all the lot of Belial. And there shall be a great tumult against the sons of Japheth; and Assyria shall fall with none to help him. And the dominion of the Kittim shall come to an end, so that wickedness shall be laid low without any remnant; and there shall be no survivor of the sons of darkness.

II

The chiefs of the priests they shall arrange in rank behind the chief priest and second to him, twelve chiefs to minister continually before God. Twenty-six

---

chiefs of the assignments shall minister in their assignments; and after them the chiefs of the Levites to minister continually, twelve, one to a tribe; and the chiefs of their assignments shall minister, each in his position. The chiefs of the tribes and the fathers of the congregation shall be always in their places in the gates of the sanctuary; and the chiefs of their assignments with their officers shall be in their places at their appointed times, for new moons and for sabbaths and for all the days of the year. From fifty years old and upward, they shall be in their places over the burnt offerings and over the sacrifices, to set out the fragrant incense for God's acceptance, to make atonement for all his congregation, and to make acceptable offerings before him always with an honored table. All these they shall set in order in the appointed time of the year of release. During the thirty-three years of war that are left the men of renown, those acclaimed in the assembly, and all the chiefs of the fathers of the congregation shall choose for themselves men of war for all the lands of the Gentiles from all the tribes of Israel; men of valor shall be equipped for them, to go out for warfare, according to the testimonies of war, year by year. But in the years of release they shall not be equipped to go out for warfare, for that is a sabbath of rest for Israel. During thirty-five years of service the battle shall be set in array six years, and those who set it in array shall be the whole congregation together. And as for the war of the divisions during the twenty-nine years that are left, in the first year they shall fight against Mesopotamia, and in the second against the sons of Lud; in the third they shall fight with the remnant of the sons of Syria, with Uz and Hul, Togar and Mashsha who are across the Euphrates; in the fourth and fifth they shall fight with the sons of Arpachshad; in the sixth and seventh they shall fight with all the sons of Assyria and Persia and the people of the east as far as the great desert; in the eighth year they shall fight against the sons of Elam;

---

*Columns i. 1–7; ii. 1–13; iii. 1–11; iv. 1–14; vi. 1–14; vii. 1–15; viii. 1–14; ix. 1–9; x. 1–10; xi. 1–12; xii. 10–15; xiii. 1–6; xiv. 2–5; and xvii. 5–9. From Millar Burrows, *The Dead Sea Scrolls* (New York: Viking Press, 1951), pp. 390–399.

in the ninth they shall fight against the sons of Ishmael and Keturah; and in the ten years after these the war shall be distributed against all the sons of Ham.

III

... the ranks of battle, and the trumpets of their assembling when the war gates are opened for the champions to go forth, the trumpets of the war-blast over the slain, the trumpets of ambush, the trumpets of pursuit when the enemy is smitten, and the trumpets of reassembly when the battle turns back. On the trumpets of the assembly of the congregation they shall write "The Called of God"; on the trumpets of the assembly of the commanders they shall write "The Princes of God"; on the trumpets of the connections they shall write "The Order of God"; on the trumpets of the men of renown they shall write "The Chiefs of the Fathers of the Congregation." When they are gathered together to the house of meeting they shall write "The Testimonies of God for the Holy Council." On the trumpets of the camps they shall write "The Peace of God in His Holy Camps"; on their trumpets of breaking camp they shall write "The Powers of God for Scattering the Enemy and Putting to Flight Those Who Hate Righteousness and Turning Back Kindness against Those Who Hate God." On the trumpets of the ranks of battle they shall write "The Ranks of the Banners of God for the Vengeance of His Anger against All the Sons of Darkness." On the trumpets of assembly of the champions, when the war gates are opened to go forth to the array of the enemy, they shall write "Memorial of Vengeance in the Assembly of God"; on the trumpets of the slain they shall write "The Mighty Hand of God in Battle to Cast Down all the Faithless Slain"; on the trumpets of ambush they shall write "The Mysteries of God for the Destruction of Wickedness"; on the trumpets of pursuit they shall write "God's Smiting of All the Sons of Dark-ness—His Anger Will Not Turn Back until They Are Destroyed." When they return from the battle to come to the array, they shall write on the trumpets of return "The Gathering of God"; on the trumpets of the way of return from the battle of the enemy to come to the congregation of Jerusalem they shall write "The Rejoicings of God at the Return of Peace."

IV

On the standard of Merari they shall write "The Offering of God," and the name of the prince of Merari and the names of the commanders of its thousands; on the standard of the thousand they shall write "The Anger of God with Fury against Belial and All the Men of His Lot without Remnant," and the name of the commander of the thousand and the names of the commanders of its hundreds; on the standard of the hundred they shall write "The Hundred of God, a Hand of War against All Erring Flesh," and the name of the commander of the hundred and the names of the commanders of its tens; on the standard of the fifty they shall write "The Position of the Wicked Has Ceased by the Power of God," and the name of the commander of the fifty and the names of the commanders of its tens; on the standard of the ten they shall write "Songs of God with a Harp of Ten Strings," and the name of the commander of the ten and the names of the nine men of his command.

When they go to the battle they shall write on their standards "The Truth of God," "The Righteousness of God," "The Glory of God," "The Justice of God," and after these the whole order of the explanation of their names. When they draw near to the battle they shall write on their standards "The Right Hand of God," "The Assembly of God," "The Panic of God," "The Slain of God," and after these the whole explanation of their names. When they return from the battle they shall write on their standards "The Extolling of God," "The Greatness of God," "The Praises of God," "The Glory of God," with the whole explanation of their names.

The order of the standards of the congregation: when they go out to the battle they shall write on the first standard "The Congregation of God," on the second standard "The Camps of God," on the third "The Tribes of God," on the fourth "The Families of God," on the fifth "The Banners of God," on the sixth "The Assembly of God," on the seventh "The Called of God," on the eighth "The Armies of God," and they shall write the explanation of their names with their whole order. When they draw near to the battle they shall write on their standards "The War of God," "The Vengeance of God," "The Strife of God," "The Reward of God," "The Strength of God," "The Peace-Offerings of God," "The Power of God," "The Destruction of God on Every Nation of Vanity," and the whole explanation of their names they shall write on them. When they return from the battle they shall write on their standards "The Deliverances of God," "The Victory of God," "The Help of God," "The Staff of God," "The Comfort of God," "The Praises of God," "The Lauding of God," "The Peace of God."

V

... seven times, and they shall return to their position. And after them three troops of champions shall go out and stand between the ranks. The first troop shall hurl at the rank of the enemy seven war-darts. On the blade of the dart they shall write "The Lightning of a Lance for the Power of God"; and on the second weapon they shall write "Shootings of Blood to make the Slain Fall in the Anger of God"; and on the third dart they shall write "Flashing of a Sword Consuming the Iniquitous Slain in the Judgment of God." All these shall cast seven times and return to their position. After them

two troops of champions shall go out and stand between the two ranks, the first troop, holding lance and shield, and the second troop, holding shield and javelin to make the slain fall in the judgment of God and to lay low the rank of the enemy in the power of God, to pay the recompense of their evil to every nation of vanity. And the God of Israel shall have the kingdom; and among the saints of his people he will display might.

And seven lines of horsemen also shall stand on the right and left of the rank; on this side and that shall their lines stand: seven hundred horsemen on one side and seven hundred on the other side. Two hundred horsemen shall go out with a thousand of the rank of the champions, and so they shall stand on all sides of the camp. The whole shall be four thousand six hundred and a thousand and four hundred chariots for the men of the line of the ranks, fifty to a rank. And the horsemen shall be beside the chariots, men of the line, six thousand five hundred to a tribe. All the chariots that go out to the battle with the champions shall have stallions, swift-footed and tender-mouthed, gentle, and mature, in middle life, trained for battle and able to hear sounds and to see all imaginable sights. The men who ride on them shall be men of valor for war, trained in chariotry, and in middle life, from thirty to forty-five years old. And the horsemen of the line shall be from forty to fifty years old.

VI

The men of the line shall be from forty to fifty years old; and those who set up the camp shall be from fifty to sixty years old; the officers also shall be from forty to fifty years old. And all those who strip the slain and those who take the spoil and those who cleanse the earth and those who keep the weapons and he who sets out the food—all of them shall be from twenty-five to thirty years old.

And no youth or woman shall enter their camps when they go forth from Jerusalem to go to battle until they return. No lame or blind man or halt man, or one with a permanent blemish in his flesh, or a man afflicted with the uncleanness of his flesh—none of these shall go with them to battle; they shall all be volunteers for war, blameless in spirit and flesh, and ready for the day of vengeance. And no man who is not clean from his issue on the day of battle shall go down with them; for holy angels are together with their armies. And there shall be a space between all their camps for the place of the hand, about two thousand cubits. And no indecent, evil thing shall be seen in the vicinity of any of their camps.

When the ranks of battle are drawn up over against the enemy, rank over against rank, there shall go forth from the middle gate to the space between the ranks seven priests of the sons of Aaron wearing garments of white linen, tunics and trousers of linen, and girt with girdles of fine twined linen, blue and purple and scarlet stuff, a varied pattern, the work of a designer, and caps on their heads—garments of war, not to be brought to the sanctuary. One priest shall go before the men of the rank to strengthen their hands in the battle; and in the hands of the other six shall be the trumpets of assembly, the memorial trumpets, the trumpets of the war-blast, the trumpets of pursuit, and the trumpets of reassembly. And when the priests go forth to the space between the ranks there shall go with them seven Levites holding in their hands the seven rams' horns of jubilee, and three officers of the Levites before the priests and the Levites. Then the priests shall sound the two trumpets of assembly.

VII

The trumpets shall continue to sound to direct the slingers until they have finished throwing seven times. After that the priests shall sound for them the trumpets of return, and they shall come beside the first battle line to take their positions. The priests shall sound the trumpets of assembly, and three troups of champions shall come out from the gates and stand between the ranks, and beside them the charioteers to right and left. Then the priests shall sound on the trumpets a prolonged note, the signal for putting the battle in array, and the leaders shall spread out to their lines, each to his position. When they are standing in three lines, the priests shall sound for them a second call, a quiet and sustained note, the signal for advancing until they are near the rank of the enemy. Then they shall take hold of their weapons, and the priests shall sound on the six trumpets of the slain a sharp and agitated note to direct the battle; and the Levites and all those who have the rams' horns shall sound in unison a great war-blast, so that the enemy's heart shall melt. At the sound of the blast, the war-darts shall be let fly to make the slain fall. The sound of the rams' horns shall be accelerated, while with the trumpets the priests are sounding a sharp and agitated note to direct the hands of battle until they have thrown at the rank of the enemy seven times. After that the priests shall sound for them on the trumpets of return a quiet, prolonged, and sustained note. According to this order the priests shall sound for the three troops.

VIII

They shall begin with their hands to make some fall among the slain; and all the people shall make haste with the sound of the war-shout, and the priests shall continue sounding on the trumpets of the slain to direct the battle until the enemy is smitten and they turn their backs. The priests shall sound to direct the battle, and when they are smitten before them the priests shall sound on the trumpets of assembly, and all the champions shall go out to them from the midst of the ranks of persons. Then six troops shall stand, and the troop which is brought near, all of them seven ranks, twenty-eight thousand men of war, and the charioteers six thousand. All these shall pursue to destroy the enemy in the war of God, to eternal destruction. Then the priests shall sound for them on the trumpets of pursuit, and they shall gird themselves against all the enemy, for a pursuit to destruction. And the chariots shall turn them back into the battle until they are utterly destroyed. And while the slain are falling the priests shall keep sounding from afar, but they shall not come in among the slain lest they be defiled by their unclean blood, for they are holy; they shall not profane the anointing oil of their priesthood with the blood of a nation of vanity.

IX

. . . our camps, and to be on guard against every indecent, evil thing; and what he made known to us, that you are in the midst of us, a great and terrible God, to despoil all our enemies before us. And he taught us of old for our generations, saying, "When you draw near to the battle, the priest shall stand and speak to the people, saying, 'Hear, O Israel, you draw near this day to battle against your enemies: do not fear, and let not your heart faint; do not tremble or be in dread of them; for your God goes with you to fight for you against your enemies to save you.'" And our officers shall speak to all those ready for the battle, willing volunteers, to make them strong in the power of God and to turn back all the fainthearted; to make them strong together with all mighty men of valor. And what he spoke through Moses, saying, "When you go to war in your land against the adversary who oppresses you, you shall sound a war-blast on the trumpets, and you shall be remembered before your God and shall be saved from your enemies." Who is like you, O God of Israel, in Heaven or on earth, who has wrought such great works as yours and such mighty power as yours; and who is like your people Israel, whom you chose for yourself from all the peoples of the lands, the people of the saints of the covenant?

X

For yours is the battle, and by the strength of your hand their corpses were scattered without burial. Goliath the Gittite, a mighty man of valor, you delivered into the hand of your servant David, because he trusted in your great name and not in sword and spear, for yours is the battle; and he subdued the Philistines many times in your holy name. Moreover by our kings you saved us many times, because of your mercy and not according to our works, in which we acted wickedly, and the evil deeds of our transgressions. Yours is the battle, and from you is power, and it is not ours; nor has our strength or the might of our hands done valiantly, but it is by your strength and by the power of your great might; as you made known to us of old, saying, "A star shall come forth out of Jacob, and a scepter shall arise out of Israel, and it shall crush the forehead of Moab and break down all the sons of Sheth; and he shall go down from Jacob and destroy the remnant of Seir, and the enemy shall be dispossessed, and Israel shall do valiantly." By your anointed ones, seers of testimonies, you have made known to us the ordering of the battles of your hands, to fight [interlinear correction: to get glory] against our enemies, to make the troops of Belial fall, seven nations of vanity, by the poor whom you have redeemed with strength and with peace, for marvelous power, and a melted heart, for a door of hope. And you did to them as to Pharaoh and the officers of his chariots at the Red Sea. The stricken in spirit you will consume like a flaming torch among sheaves, consuming wickedness; you will not turn back until guilt is destroyed. Of old you

241

caused us to hear the appointed time of the power of your hand against the Kittim, saying, "And Assyria shall fall by a sword, not of a man; and a sword, not of man, shall devour him."

XI

Rise, mighty one; bring back your captives, man of glory!
Seize your plunder, you who does valiantly!
Lay your hand on the necks of your enemies
and your foot on the heaps of the slain;
smite the nations, your adversaries,
and let your sword consume guilty flesh!
Fill your land with glory,
your inheritance with blessing!
Let there be an abundance of cattle in your territories,
silver and gold and precious stones in your palaces.
Rejoice greatly, O Zion;
appear with glad shouts, O Jerusalem;
and exult, cities of Judah!
Open the gate continually,
that the wealth of nations may be brought in to you;
that their kings may minister to you,
and all that have afflicted you may bow down to you
and lick the dust of your feet.
O daughters of my people, cry aloud with the sound of a glad shout;
Adorn yourselves with glorious ornaments!

XII

. . . and his brethren the priests and the Levites, and all the elders of the order with him; and they shall bless in their places the God of Israel and all his faithful works, and his indignation which he has directed against Belial and all the spirits of his lot. And they shall answer and say, "Blessed be the God of Israel with all his holy purpose and all his faithful works. And blessed be all his hosts in righteousness, who know him by faith.

"But cursed be Belial with his hostile purpose, and may he be an object of indignation in his guilty dominion; and cursed be all the spirits of his lot in their wicked purpose, and may they be objects of indignation in all their unclean service of defilement; for they are the lot of darkness, but the lot of God belongs to eternal light."

XIII

After they have gone up from the slain to come to the camp, they shall all sing the psalm of returning. And in the morning they shall wash their garments and be cleansed of the blood of the corpses of guilt; and they shall return to their positions where they set the rank in array before the slain of the enemy fell. There they shall all bless the God of Israel and exalt his name together with joy. And they shall answer and say, "Blessed be the God of Israel, who maintains loyalty to his covenant and testimonies of salvation for the people he has redeemed."

XIV

Today is his appointed time to lay low and to make fall the prince of the dominion of wickedness; and he will send eternal help to the lot he has redeemed by the power of the angel he has made glorious for rule, Michael, in eternal light, to give light in joy to all Israel, peace and blessing to the lot of God, to exalt among the gods the rule of Michael and the dominion of Israel over all flesh. Righteousness shall rejoice in the high places, and all the sons of his truth shall be joyful in eternal knowledge. And you, sons of his covenant, be strong in the crucible of God until he waves his hand and fills his crucibles with his mysteries that you may stand.

The Letter of Aristeas

(Jewish Pseudepigrapha)

The letter of Aristeas to his brother Philocrates is the outstanding apologia of Jewish culture and theology to the Greeks of Egypt. Written in Greek around 130 B.C., as Moses Hadas suggests in the introduction to his masterful translation, it deals with the translation of the Pentateuch into Greek.

The legendary origin of the Septuagint bible, which remains the bible of Eastern orthodoxy today, is as follows: Ptolomy II Philadelphus (283–247 B.C.), a bibliophile, wanted this most important book for the great library of Alexandria. Thus he requested seventy-two scholars from Jerusalem to go to the island of Pharos in the harbor of Alexandria and to translate faithfully the Hebrew scriptures in seventy-two days. In reality, the Septuagint (meaning "seventy") was done over a period of centuries, at first for the Greek-reading Jews of Egypt and later, as more scriptures were added, for the Eastern Christian Church. Aristeas's letter describes not only the great value of the book for Ptolemy's royal collection, but the process itself of translation. In its praise to the translators, its admonitions against mistakes or changes, it is perhaps the first significant treatise on the theory and practice of literary translation.

The author has taken the name Aristeas, allegedly that of an Egyptian courtier. From internal evidence, however, the author is clearly an Alexandrian Jew who is arguing for harmony between Jews and Greeks, who even equates God and Zeus—his disapproval of Greek things is limited to idolatry and sexual immorality—and who not only shows the Greek love for Jewish literature, law, and ethics, but, in a political gesture, persuades the king to free 100,000 Jewish captives and slaves in exchange for the precious volume. The king, in turn, is so enthusiastic about the project that he appeals to Eleazar, high priest in Jerusalem, to appoint a committee of six members from each of the twelve tribes to carry out his request. Ptolemy overwhelms the group with royal presents. Then the letter strays to Jerusalem where the temple, its ceremonies, the city, and surrounding countryside are described in striking detail. Finally, the seventy-two come to Alexandria where they are feted in a great banquet and where the criteria of the translation are irrevocably fixed. Unlike 4 *Maccabees*, which shows the brutal suppression of Jewish customs by Antiochus IV, written ironically as a Platonic debate between reason and passion, in this enlightened work of rapprochement the Jews and Greeks of Alexandria, like Ianthis in Constantine Cavafy's famous poem "Of the Jews, 50 A.D.," share one culture, one vision of the good life. *The Letter of Aristeas* is frequently called an outstanding piece of propaganda about Jewish law, wisdom, and scholarship. It is that. In its digressions it is also a document about Greek justice and tyranny and about the Hellenistic theory of kingship.

ON THE TRANSLATION OF THE SEPTUAGINT*

Inasmuch as the account of our deputation to Eleazar, the High Priest of the Jews, is worth narrating, Philocrates, and because you set a high value, as you constantly remind me, on hearing the motives and purposes of our mission, I have endeavored to set the matter forth clearly. I appreciate your characteristic love of learning, for it is indeed man's highest function "ever to add knowledge, ever to acquire it," either through researches or by actual experience of affairs. It is thus that a pure state of soul is fashioned, by seizing upon what is fairest; and in its pursuit of piety, the greatest good of all, it enjoys an unerring gauge for its guidance. It was because of my predilection for the careful study of religious matters that I offered myself for the embassy to the man mentioned above, who is highly esteemed both by his countrymen and by others for his worth and renown, and who possesses the greatest usefulness for his countrymen, those with him and those in other

places, for the translation of the divine Law, for it exists among them written on parchments in Hebrew characters.

This embassy, then, I undertook with alacrity, when I had seized the opportunity of speaking to the king concerning those who had been transported to Egypt from Judaea by the king's father when he first acquired possession of the city and took over the government of Egypt. It is worthwhile to inform you of these things also. I am confident that you in particular, because of your tendency towards holiness and the outlook of those men who live according to the holy Law, will gladly listen to what I purpose to reveal, for you have only lately come over to us from the island and are eager to hear whatever contributes to the soul's edification. On a previous occasion also I transmitted to you an exposition of matters I deemed worthy of record concerning the race of the Jews which I received from the most erudite high priests in the most erudite land of Egypt. To you who are a lover of learning in matters capable of benefiting the mind it is right to communicate these things. Gladly would I communicate them to all who are likeminded, but in particular to you, whose convictions are genuine and who are not only proven my brother-german in character but also at one with me in striving for the good. For neither the charm of gold nor any other of the embellishments

*From Moses Hadas, ed. and trans., *Aristeas to Philocrates* (New York: Harper & Brothers for the Dropsie College for Hebrew and Cognate Learning, 1951), lines 1–4 and lines 301–321.

prized by the vainglorious confers as great benefit as education and attention devoted to culture. But not to weary you with a long extended introduction, I shall resume the thread of my narrative.

When Demetrius of Phalerum was put in charge of the king's library he was assigned large sums of money with a view to collecting, if possible, all the books in the world; and by arranging purchases and transcriptions he carried the king's design to completion as far as he was able. When he was asked, in my presence, about how many thousands of books were already collected, he replied, "Above two hundred thousand, Your Majesty; and in a short while I shall exert every effort for the remainder, to round out the number of half a million. I am informed that the laws of the Jews also are worthy of transcription and of being included in your library." "What is to prevent you from doing so?" the king replied. "All the necessary means are at your disposal." But Demetrius said, "Translation is required; in the country of the Jews they use a peculiar script, just as the Egyptians employ their arrangement of letters, and they have their own language. They are supposed to use Syrian, but that is not the case, for theirs is another dialect." When the king learned these particulars he gave word that a letter should be addressed to the High Priest of the Jews, in order that the design above mentioned might be carried to completion.

Now, I thought, was the opportune moment for proferring the matter concerning which I had often petitioned Sosibius of Tarentum and Andreas, chiefs of the bodyguard, namely, the emancipation of those who had been carried away from Judaea by the king's father. He had overrun the whole of Coele-Syria and Phoenicia, exploiting his good fortune and prowess, and had transplanted some and made others captive, reducing all to subjection by terror; it was on this occasion that he transported more than a hundred thousand persons from the country of the Jews to Egypt. Of these he armed some thirty thousand chosen men and settled them in garrisons in the country. Previously many had come into the country along with the Persian, and even before this others had been sent out as auxiliaries to fight in the army of Psammetichus against the king of the Ethiopians; but these were not so numerous a body as Ptolemy son of Lagus transported. As has been said, then, he selected and armed those that were fittest in age and outstanding in ruggedness; but the remaining bulk, those too old and too young and also the women, he reduced to bondage, not out of his own individual choice indeed, but because he was overborne by his soldiers, in return for the services which they had rendered in military action.

Now when I had procured a pretext for their release, as signified above, I addressed arguments to the king somewhat as follows: "Surely it would be illogical, Your Majesty, to be proven inconsistent by our deeds. For inasmuch as the legislation which we propose not only to transcribe but also to translate is laid down for all Jews, what justification shall we have for our mission when a large multitude subsists in slavery in your realm? Rather with a perfect and bountiful spirit release those who are afflicted in wretchedness, for the same God who has given them their law guides your kingdom also, as I have learned in my researches. God, the overseer and creator of all things, whom they worship, is he whom all men worship, and we too, Your Majesty, though we address him differently, as Zeus and Dis; by these names men of old not unsuitably signified that he through whom all creatures receive life and come into being is the guide and lord of all. Surpass all men, then, in magnanimity of spirit, and grant liberty to those oppressed in bondage."

The king refrained himself for a little while, and I prayed inwardly to God to dispose his mind for a general release. Human beings, since they are creatures

245

of God, are by him turned and swayed; and therefore repeatedly and in various terms I called upon him who rules the heart that the king might be constrained to fulfill my petition. For I had high hope, in presenting an argument concerning the deliverance of men, that God would effect the fulfillment of my petition; when men piously believe that what they do is for the sake of justice and the promotion of good deeds, then God, who is Lord of all, guides their actions and their designs. The king then raised his head, showing a friendly countenance, and said, "How many thousands do you suppose there will be?" Andreas, who was standing in attendance, declared, "A little more than a hundred thousand." "It is but a small matter indeed," the king said, "that Aristeas asks of us." Sosibius and others of those present said, "Surely it is worthy of your magnanimity that you dedicate the release of these people as a thank-offering to God the Greatest. Greatly as you have been honored by him who rules all things, and greatly as you have been distinguished above your forefathers, it is fitting if you make your thank-offering very great." The king was delighted, and ordered that an addition be made to the soldiers' stipends, that twenty drachmas be paid for each slave, that a decree should be issued concerning these matters, and the registers be constituted forthwith. Generous was the zeal he displayed; God fulfilled our whole desire and constrained him to liberate not only those who had accompanied his father's army, but also any that were there previously or had been brought into the kingdom subsequently. It was pointed out that the donation was in excess of four hundred talents.

I think it not unprofitable to put the text of the decree on record. Thus the munificence of the king, whom God enabled to become a means of deliverance to a numerous multitude, will be far more manifest and explicit. It ran as follows: "All persons who took the field with our father against the regions of Syria and Phoenicia and in the invasion of the country of the Jews came into possession of Jewish slaves and have brought them over to our city and country or have sold them to others—and likewise if any such were in the country previously or introduced subsequently—those holding them shall release them straightway, receiving forthwith compensation of twenty drachmas for each slave, the soldiers with the payment of their stipend, and others from the royal bank. For it is our belief that these persons were made prisoner contrary to the will of our father and to propriety, and that it was to military recklessness that the despoliation of their country and the removal of the Jews themselves to Egypt was due. The booty which accrued to the soldiers on the field of battle was sufficient; hence the further oppression of the people was wholly inequitable. Therefore, since it is our professed purpose to award justice to all men, and more particularly to those who are unreasonably tyrannized, and since we strive in every respect to deal fairly with all men in accordance with justice and piety, we have decreed that so many Jewish persons as are held in bondage in whatever manner anywhere in the kingdom their owners shall release upon receipt of the stipulated sum. No one shall be in any way negligent in the discharge of this obligation. Lists shall be submitted to the officials placed in charge of this matter within three days from the posting up of this decree, and the persons involved shall be produced at once. For we have determined that it is advantageous both for ourselves and for the realm for this business to be accomplished. Any who wish may give information concerning recalcitrants, on condition that the informer acquire ownership of the culprit; the property of the defaulters shall be confiscated to the royal purse."

The decree as submitted to be read over to the king contained all the rest with the exception of the clause, "If any such were in the country previously or introduced subsequently," and the king himself, indulging his munificence and magnanimity, made the addition. He also ordered that the several amounts be assigned in a lump sum to the paymasters of the forces and to the royal bankers. Thus the matter was decreed and went into force in seven days. The grant amounted to more than six hundred and sixty talents, for many children at the breast were emancipated along with their mothers. When the question was raised whether the sum of twenty drachmas should be paid out for these also, the king ordered that this should be done, so completely did he give effect to his decision in every detail.

Now when this business was finished he bade Demetrius to submit a statement concerning the transcription of the Jewish books. These kings used to administer all their business through decrees and with great precaution; nothing was done negligently or casually. I have therefore put on record copies of the memorial and the letters and also an inventory of the lavish gifts and a description of each, for each was outstanding in magnificence and artistic execution. Here is the copy of the memorial:

"To the great king, from Demetrius: At Your Majesty's bidding with respect to the completion of the collection of books in the library, that those which are wanting should be added to the collection and that those in disrepair should receive the proper attention, my efforts in the charge have not been cursory, and I now submit the following statement to you. The books of the Law of the Jews together with some few others are wanting. It happens that they are written in Hebrew characters and in the Hebrew tongue, and they have been committed to writing somewhat carelessly and not adequately, according to the testimony of experts, for they have never benefited by a king's forethought. It is necessary that these books too, in an emended form, should be given a place in your library, for their

legislation is most philosophical and flawless, inasmuch as it is divine. It is for this reason that authors and poets and the mass of historians have abstained from mentioning these aforesaid books and the men who have lived and are living in accordance with them, because the views set forth in them have a certain holiness and sanctity, as Hecataeus of Abdera says. If it seems good to Your Majesty, therefore, a letter shall be written to the High Priest at Jerusalem requesting him to dispatch elders who have led exemplary lives and are expert in their own law, six from each tribe, so that when we have examined wherein the majority agree and have obtained an accurate translation we may lay it up in a distinguished manner worthy of the subject matter and of your benevolence. Fare well forever."

When this memorial has been submitted, the king bade that a letter be written to Eleazar concerning these matters, informing him also of the liberation of the captives. For the construction of bowls and flagons and a table and libation cups he presented gold fifty talents in weight and seventy talents of silver and a great quantity of stones—he bade the treasurers allow the craftsmen to select the materials they preferred—and for sacrifices and other purposes he presented as much as a hundred talents of coined money.

Of the construction of the gifts I shall give you an account when I have done with the copies of the letters. The purport of the king's letter was as follows:

King Ptolemy to Eleazar the High Priest, greeting and good health. Whereas it is come about that many Jews have been settled in our country, some forcibly removed from Jerusalem by the Persians during their period of power and others who came into Egypt as captives in the train of our father—of these he enrolled many in the armed forces at higher than ordinary pay, and likewise when he judged their chief men to be loyal he gave them fortresses which he built, so that the native Egyptians might be in awe of them; and we too, since we have assumed the realm, meet all men in a very humane manner but your countrymen to a special degree—we, then, have given liberty to above a hundred thousand captives, paying their owners proper market prices and making good whatever injury may have been inflicted through the impulses of the mob. Our resolve in this matter was to do a pious deed and to dedicate a thank-offering to God the Most High, who has preserved our kingdom in tranquility and in the mightiest esteem throughout the inhabited world. Those in the flower of their age, moreover, we have enrolled in our forces, and to those capable of being about our person and worthy of the trust of the royal court we have assigned offices of state. Now since we desire to show favor to these and to all the Jews in the world and to their posterity we have resolved that your Law should be translated into Greek writing from the Hebrew tongue in use among you, so that these writings should find place in our library along with other royal books. It will be a courteous act, therefore, and one worthy of our own zeal if you will choose elders of exemplary life who possess skill in the law and ability to translate, six from each tribe, so that it may be discovered wherein the majority agree, for the investigation concerns a matter of great weight. We think that we shall bear off great renown by the accomplishment of this task. We have sent upon this business Andreas, of the keepers of the bodyguard, and Aristeas, men whom we hold in honor, to converse with you. They bring with them dedicatory offerings for the temple, and for sacrifices and other purposes a hundred talents of silver. And if you should write us concerning any desires of yours, you would gratify us and act as friendship requires; be assured that your wishes shall be fulfilled most speedily. Farewell."

To this letter Eleazar replied as well as might be in the terms following: "Eleazar the High Priest to his true friend King Ptolemy, greeting. Yourself fare well, and Queen Arsinoe your sister, and the children: so will it be well and as we wish; we too are in good health. When we received your letter we rejoiced greatly because of your resolution and your goodly plan, and we assembled our entire people and read it out to them, in order that they might know the piety you cherish for our God. We displayed also the flagons which you sent, twenty of gold and thirty of silver, the five bowls, the table for dedication, and for the offering of sacrifices and whatever repairs the temple might require a hundred talents of silver. These gifts were brought by Andreas, who holds a place of honor with you, and by Aristeas, true gentlemen both, outstanding in culture, and in every respect worthy of your own conduct and righteousness. They have also communicated your message to us, and from our lips have heard a reply in accordance with your letter. Whatever is to your advantage, even if it be contrary to nature, we shall hearken; for to do so is a mark of friendship and affection. You too have vouchsafed our countrymen great and unforgettable benefits in many ways. We have therefore straightway offered sacrifices on your behalf and on behalf of your sister and children and friends, and the entire multitude prayed that your affairs might always turn out as you desire, and that God Lord of all might preserve your kingdom in peace with honor, and that the transcription of the holy Law might come about to your advantage and with security. And in the presence of all we selected elders good and true, six from each tribe, with whom we have sent the book of the Law. We shall be obliged to you, righteous king, if you enjoin that when the transcription of the books is completed the men may be restored to us again in safety. Farewell."

After three days Demetrius took the men with him and crossed the breakwater, seven stades long, to the island; then he crossed over the bridge and proceeded to the northerly parts. There he called a meeting in a mansion built by the seashore, magnificently appointed and in a secluded situation, and called upon the men to carry out the business of translation, all necessary appliances having been well provided. And so they proceeded to carry it out, making all details harmonize by mutual comparisons. The appropriate result of the harmonization was reduced to writing under the direction of Demetrius. The sessions would last until the ninth hour, and afterwards they would break up to take care of their bodily needs, all their requirements being lavishly supplied. In addition, everything that was prepared for the king Dorotheus arranged for them also, for he had been so instructed by the king. Every day they would come to the court early in the morning, and when they had made their salutation to the king they departed to their own place. When they had washed their hands in the sea, as is the custom of all Jews, and had offered prayer to God, they addressed themselves to the interpretation and clarification of each passage. I questioned them on this point too, why it was that they washed their hands before praying. And they explained that it was in witness that they had done no wrong, since the hands are the organs of all activity; in such beautiful and holy spirit do they make all things symbols of righteousness and truth. Thus, as we have said before, they foregathered every day to this spot, so delightful for its seclusion and its clear light, and carried out their appointed task. And so it came about that the work of transcription was completed in seventy-two days, as if this coincidence had been the result of some design.

When the work was concluded Demetrius assembled the community of the Jews at the place where the translation was executed, and read it out to the entire gathering, the translators too being present; these received a great ovation from the community also, in recognition of the great service for which they were responsible. And they accorded Demetrius a similar reception, and requested him to have a transcription of the entire Law made and to present it to their rulers. When the rolls had been read the priests and the elders of the translators and some of the corporate body and the leaders of the people rose up and said, "Inasmuch as the translation has been well and piously made and is in every respect accurate, it is right that it should remain in its present form and that no revision of any sort take place." When all had assented to what had been said, they bade that an imprecation be pronounced, according to their custom, upon any who should revise the text by adding or transposing anything whatever in what had been written down, or by making any excision; and in this they did well, so that the work might be preserved imperishable and unchanged always.

When these proceedings were reported to the king he rejoiced greatly, for he thought that the purpose he cherished had been securely carried out. The whole work was read out to him also, and he marveled exceedingly at the intellect of the lawgiver.

To Demetrius he said, "How has it not occurred to any of the historians or poets to make mention of such enormous achievements?" And he said, "Because the Law is holy and has come into being through God; some of those to whom the thought did occur were smitten by God and desisted from the attempt." Indeed, he said, he had heard Theopompus say that when he was on the point of introducing into his history certain matter which had previously been translated from the Law, too rashly, he suffered a derangement of the mind for more than thirty days; upon the abatement of the disorder he implored God that the cause of what had befallen be made plain to him, and when it was signified to him in a dream that it was his meddlesome desire to disclose divine matters to common men, he desisted, and was thereupon restored to health. "And of Theodectes also, the tragic poet, I have heard," he added, "that when he was on the point of introducing into one of his plays something recorded in the Book, his vision was afflicted with a cataract. Conceiving the suspicion that this was the reason for his calamity, he implored God and after many days recovered."

When the king heard the account of these things from Demetrius, as I have said before, he bowed deeply and gave orders that great care be taken of the books and that they be watched over reverently. He also urged the translators to make visits to him, after they had been restored to Judaea. It was but just he said, for them to be sent home; but if they visited him he would treat them as friends, as it was his solemn obligation to do, and they would receive rich marks of his consideration. He ordered that preparations for their sending off be seen to, treating the men munificently. To each he gave three costumes of the highest quality, and two talents of gold, and a sideboard of a talent's weight, and complete furnishings for the dining room. To Eleazar he sent, with their escort, ten couches with legs of silver, and all their appurtenances, and a sideboard of thirty talents, and ten costumes, and a purple robe, and a magnificent crown, and a hundred webs of fine woven linen, and shallow bowls, and plates, and two mixing bowls of gold as a dedicatory offering. He also wrote a letter urging that if any of the men chose to return to him Eleazar might not prevent, for he accounted it a privilege to associate with cultured men, and would rather lavish his wealth upon such men than on vanities.

3
WISDOM LITERATURE AND POETRY

The Psalms of Solomon

(Jewish Pseudepigrapha)

The *Psalms of Solomon* were written around the middle of the first century B.C. Although they are preserved in Syriac and Greek, it is now assumed that the original language was Hebrew. Unlike the *Odes of Solomon*, some of which were strongly Christianized, these psalms are composed in the style of the Davidic Psalter and deal with traditional Jewish themes—human responsibility for one's action, a belief in the resurrection of the body, a deep concern for the life of goodness and piety. Attempts to relate them to any specific group— the Pharisees, the Essenes—are rejected by James H. Charlesworth, who sees them as fitting into no one sectarian category.[1] The eighteen psalms may have been composed in Jerusalem. The attribution to Solomon, as with the Song of Songs, is, of course, false.

Notes

1. Edgar Hennecke and Wilhelm Schneemelcher, eds., R. McL. Wilson, trans., *New Testament Apocrypha*, vol. 2 (Philadelphia: Westminster Press, 1966), p. 440.

When my soul sank from the Lord, I almost fell into the pit,
When I was far from my Lord, my soul was almost poured into death.
I was near the gates of Hell, with sinners.
My soul almost separated from the God of Israel,
but the Lord, in his mercy, helped me.
He pricked me, as a horse is pricked. He was watchful.
He was my helper at all times, and he saved me.
God, I thank you for my redemption. You did not count me among the sinners for
  destruction.
Do not withdraw your mercy.
Do not forget my heart, or I will die.
Save me from wickedness, from lusting women who set traps for the simple,
do not let the beauty of an outrageous woman seduce me.
Establish your works and let me walk before you.
Let words of truth rule my lips and tongue
and may I be free of anger, extreme passion, and rancor.
If I sin, chasten me so I may return to you.
Help my soul with your goodness and joy.
With your strength, I survive.
Without it, who can endure the punishment of poverty?
Poverty tests a man. Yet enduring all, with virtue,
will bring mercy from you, O Lord.

---

*Version by W. B., based on a translation in Rendel Harris and Alphonse
Mingana, *The Odes and Psalms of Solomon*, vol. 2 (London: Longmans, 1920).

The Thanksgiving Psalms

(Dead Sea Scrolls)

The book of psalms contained in one of the scrolls found by the Dead Sea consists of at least twenty-five separate poems.[1] These psalms (or hymns) offer thanksgiving to the Lord who has given the community the secrets of salvation. They were probably learned and sung by initiates when they entered the brotherhood. The majority of scholars believe that many of the psalms are in the voice of the Teacher of Righteousness, and perhaps written by him. Theodor H. Gaster belittles this notion as restrictive and unsubstantiated. He compares their passion and conceits to the work of the great English metaphysical poets Donne, Herbert, and Vaughan, and stresses their mystical component.[2]

The French scholar A. Dupont-Sommer, who views the scrolls as a harbinger of primitive Christianity, sees in the psalms not only their biblical source but ideas connected with the adjacent worlds of the Zoroastrians and the Gnostics. He writes:

> But however close their bond with ancient Jewish piety, the *Hymns* of Qumran constantly betray new ideas which are obviously connected with the religious world of Zoroastrianism and Hellenistic Gnosis. The psalmist is a "man who knows," a Gnostic; knowledge that is the principle of his salvation and the source of his joy.[3]

Whatever the source, whoever the speaker in the psalms, commentators agree that the poems are the literary jewel of the Dead Sea Scrolls. Indeed, they are equal to the very best psalms of the Old Testament. Their magnificent language, their flow and universal passion, their sweeping images of Heaven, Hell, lions, humanity, clay, frequently render them overwhelming. Foremost in the psalms is the certainty of heavenly redemption. But, as in the later traditional mystics, the ascent to God, to another Eden, requires the faith of oblivion and pain, the shuddering in the purgative dark night. The speaker suffers a "negative ecstasy" of virtual extinction before deliverance. So we hear in Psalm 10:

> I am stricken dumb like a ewe lamb,
> my arm is wrenched from its socket,
> my eyes blur from seeing evil,
> my ears are closed from hearing the cry of bloodshed.

As the senses fail and the speaker becomes detached from earthly things, from his or her own body, the body itself manifests this passage through a violent shuddering, which is also typical of the physical signs of passage found in the tales told by other mystics:

> Then my foundations shudder
> and my bones are out of joint.

Finally, the speaker is obliterated by the divine force:

> My heart is utterly sore,
> and in the havoc of transgression
> a whirlwind swallows me up.

But the psalmist is not merely to be obliterated. That oblivion is simply the first step to salvation and its knowledge. While the world casts slime on him, God freshens and redeems him. In Psalm 14:

> I am despised by rioting rivers
> which cast slime upon me.

> But you, God, placed morning rain in my mouth,
> for all seasons,
> and living waters which will not fail.

Finally, the psalmist enters the truth and light of God and that truth and light enter him or her. So there is a commingling, a union with the spirit. In a radiant poem, Psalm 23, we read:

> Your holy spirit
> illuminates the dark places of the heart
> of your servant
> with light like the sun.
> I look to the covenants made by men.
> Worthless.
> Only your truth shines
> and those who live it are wise
> and walk in the glow
> of your light.
> From darkness you raise hearts.
> Let light shine on your servant.
> Your light is everlasting.

The word of God is given and the speaker, mere clay, mere stone, hears: "My heart is amazed/for the word is given me./My heart of stone hears" (Psalm 25). The language in the last of the preserved psalms is utterly simple and direct. The divine promise of joy, of peace, of light, is fulfilled. Psalm 25 ends with a revelational vision of harmony:

You end
my wandering
to bring me into concordance with you
that I may stand, unshaken
before you
in the glow of perfect light
forever,
where no darkness is
forever,
where unsearchable peace is
forever.

For me, a creature of dust.

Paradoxically, in this most sectarian, exclusive brotherhood, the highest expression of their faith in knowledge and salvation raises their words into grand and universal poetry.

Notes

1. See also Thanksgiving Psalm at end of *The Manual of Discipline*.
2. Theodor H. Gaster, *The Dead Sea Scrolls* (New York: Doubleday Anchor, 1956), p. 112.
3. A. Dupont-Sommer, ed., G. Vermes, trans., *The Essene Writings from Qumran* (Oxford: Basil Blackwell, 1961), p. 200.

PSALM 1*

These things I know from your wisdom,
and you have freed my ears to hear wondrous mysteries.
I am a thing
formed of clay and kneaded with water,
the earth of nakedness and well of pollution,
a furnace of iniquity and fabric of sin,
My perverted spirit strays into error,
fearing good judgment.
What can I say that you do not know beforehand?
All things are graven before you with a pen of remembrance,
for all times, for the years of eternity.
From you nothing is absent or obscure.

*Version by W. B. of Psalms 1 through 25
is based on earlier translations by Theodor H.
Gaster, Millar Burrows, and G. Vermes.

257

PSALM 4

I thank you, O Lord,
for your eye is awake and watches over my soul.
You rescue me from the jealousy of liars,
from the congregation of those who seek the smooth way.
But you save the soul of the poor
whom they planned to destroy
by spilling the blood of your servant.

I walked because of you—they didn't know this.
They laughed at me. They shamed me
with lies in their mouth.
But you helped the soul of the poor and the weak,
you saved me from their harsh arms,
you redeemed me
amid their taunts. From the wicked
I do not fear destruction.

PSALM 5

They made my life a ship on the deep sea,
like a fortified city
circled by aggressors.
I hurt like a woman in labor
bearing her first child,
whose belly pangs torture her in the crucible.
Pains of Hell
for a son come on the waves of death.
She labors to bear a man,
and among the waves of death she gives birth to a manchild,
with pains of Hell.
He springs from the crucible,
O wondrous counselor with power.
Yes, a man emerges from the waves . . .

But she who carries dead seed in her womb
suffers waves from a pit of horror.
The foundations of the wall will rock
like a ship on the face of the waters.
Clouds will bellow.
Those who dwell in the dust, like those on the sea,
are terrified by the roar of the waters.

All those wise men are like mariners on the deep:
their wisdom confounded by the roaring seas.
The abyss boils over the fountains of water.
The seas rage.
Hell opens, and arrows fly toward Heaven.
The doors of Hell will close forever on iniquity.
Their eternal bars are bolted.

PSALM 6

I thank you, O Lord,
for you have released my soul from the pit, from Hell,
from the Sheol of Abaddon,
and taken me to the eternal highland of the world.

I walk that limitless plain
and know there is hope for one you formed
out of dust
to share a timeless companionship.
You cleaned a spirit distorted by sin
so it might stand with the host of holy beings,
in communion with the children of Heaven.
You gave man an eternal lot with the souls
of understanding.
Let him praise your name, commonly rejoice,
recount your wonders and your works.

But I am a creature of clay. What am I?
Like bread kneaded with water, what is my worth,
what is my strength?
I stood within the borders of ungodliness
and cast my lot with the damned.
The poor man's soul lived in savage confusion.
Calamity dodged my steps.
When all the snares of the pit were opened,
when the lures of wickedness were set
and nets of the damned were spread on the face
of the waters,
when arrows flew out of the pit, unalterably,
and struck, extinguishing hope,
when the measuring rope of judgment fell
and wrath fell on the forsaken,
when fury devoured the cunning
the cords of death tightened around me. There
was no escape.
The torrents of Belial overflowed their high banks.

Like a devouring fire
it destroyed every green or withered tree in its channel.

It wanders about with burning flames
until all who drink are no more.
It pours over horizons of dry land,
captures the foundations of mountains with fire.
The roots of flint become streams of pitch,
and it even plunges into the great abyss.
The torrents of Belial burst into Hell itself
and roar with eruptions of mud.
The earth groans in anguish
for the havoc in the universe.
The deeps howl. The living scream,
go mad, and perish.
God thunders his raucous voice of power.
His holy residence echoes the truth of his glory.
The armies of Heaven utter their voice
and the world's foundations quake and melt.
The war initiated by the soldiers of Heaven
scourges the cosmos. It sweeps on
until its incomparable extermination, wholly determined,
is complete.

PSALM 8

I thank you, O Lord.
You illuminated my face by your covenant.
I seek you,
As sure as the dawn you appear as perfect light.

Teachers of lies have comforted your people
and now they stumble, foolishly.
They abhor themselves
and do not esteem me through whom your wonders and power
are manifest.
They have banished me from my land like a bird
from its nest, and my friends
and neighbors are driven from me.
They think me a broken pot.
They preach lies. They are dissembling prophets.
They devise baseness against me,
exchanging your teaching, written in my heart,
for smooth words.
They deny knowledge to the thirsty
and force them to drink vinegar

to cover up error. They stumble through mad feasts,
but you, God, spurn the schemes of Belial.
Your wisdom prevails.
Your heart's meditation endures, established forever.

PSALM 9

I thank you, O Lord,
for you have not left my side,
here, while I live among an alien people.
You have not looked on me as guilty,
nor cast me away because of my lust.
You took my life from the pit
but you set me among lions ready to spring on the guilty,
terrible lions who crush the bones of the mighty
and drink their blood.
You have had me live with many fishermen,
spreaders of nets on the face of the water,
and hunters of the children of error.
There you established me for justice,
and in my heart you fortified a counsel of truth
and waters of the covenant for its seekers.
You locked the mouths of the young lions
whose teeth are swords,
whose fangs are sharp spears with the venom of dragons.

Their design is robbery
but their mouths have not opened against me.
O God, you have hidden me
before the sons of man.
Your teaching is hidden in my heart
until that time when you reveal my salvation.

When my soul was low you were with me.
You heard my clamor in the bitterness of my soul.
When I sighed
you discerned the song of my pain.
When I was in the den of lions,
sharpening their tongues like swords,
you delivered me.
You locked their teeth in their jaws
lest they tear out the life of a poor man.
You made their tongues go back
like a sword into its scabbard
lest your servant be killed.

In the presence of the sons of men
you manifest your power
and work miracles in me:
Placed like gold in a furnace,
like silver in a smith's crucible,
refined seven times, purified, I am unhurt.
The wicked rush wildly against me
to trap me,
to pound my soul all through the day.
You, my God,
transform the storm into sweet calm.
In its danger you rescue my soul
like a bird from the net,
like prey from the mouth of young lions.

PSALM 10

I am stricken dumb like a ewe lamb,
my arm is wrenched from its socket,
my foot sinks in filth,
my eyes blur from seeing evil,
my ears are closed from hearing the cry of bloodshed,
my heart is appalled at the thought of evil
when human baseness is revealed.
Then my foundations shudder
and my bones are out of joint.
My entrails heave like a ship in a slamming storm from the East.
My heart is utterly sore,
and in the havoc of transgression
a whirlwind swallows me up.

PSALM 11

You have chosen me father to the sons of kindness,
nurse to men of wonder,
and they have opened their mouths like babies sucking at the breast,
like a tender child playing in its nurse's bosom.
You raised my horn above those who revile me,
who attack
but shake like windy trees.
My enemies are chaff in the wind,
and my domination is over the children of error.

You healed my soul
and raised my horn,
and I will glow in seven folds of light
with beams from your glory.
You are everlasting light
and help me to walk to you.

PSALM 14

I thank you, O Lord. In the wilderness you placed me
beside a flowing brook,
by springs of water in the wasteland,
in a blossoming garden.
You placed me among cypresses and pine, among cedars
like your glory,
There concealed among the trees drinking the water
are other trees of life near springs of mystery,
which issue shoots of an eternal Plant,
and before they flower they expose their roots
to the waters of life
and become the eternal fountain.

All beasts of the forest feed on the leafy branches
of the Plant,
wanderers trample its trunk,
winged fowl perch on its limbs.
Trees by the water exult above the holy tree.

But that tree planted in truth,
destined to flower in branches of holiness,
is sealed and secret, unesteemed and unknown.
O God, you hedged its fruit with enormous angels
and walls of fire
so no stranger might come near the fountain,
nor drink its water
like the eternal tree,
nor bear fruit from the rain of heaven.
The stranger saw but did not believe in the fountain of life.

I am despised by rioting rivers
which cast slime upon me.

But you, God, placed morning rain in my mouth,
for all seasons,
and living waters which will not fail.
When they burst open, they never go dry
but rise like a torrent over its banks.

Bottomless seas, long in secret, gush out in flood,
freshening green and dry forests
and every bird and wild beast in the abyss.
Trees sink like lead in enormous waves,
fire plays on them and shrivels them,
but the rich Plant near the eternal fountain
is a park of glory, is Eden.

Yet when I lift my hands to dig,
the earth is flint, hard and hot.
When I remove my hand,
thistles throng the desert
and great trunks turn into nettles in the saltmarsh,
into thorns and wormwood. Trees on the banks
are stinking weeds.
My soul is diseased
like those who descend into Sheol.
My spirit is jailed with the dead.
My life has entered the pit.

My wound breaks out like fire in my bones,
day after day, turning me feeble,
chewing my flesh.
Gone is my body strength,
my flesh melts like wax,
the power of my loins is terror,
my arm is torn from its socket, worthless,
my knees slide like water,
my feet are shackled, unable to walk,
my tongue—which you made marvelous—is tied!
I cannot talk.
I cannot lift my voice to my disciples.
to encourage with words those who are stumbling.
My circumcised lips are still.

PSALM 15

What is a man? He is earth,
cut from a bit of clay, and he returns to dust.
You startle him with your marvels and the secret of your truth. You inform him,
but I, who am already dust and ashes,
what can I know that you have not determined?
What can I think that you have not willed?
If I am strong, you sustain me.
If I stumble, you stay me.
What can I say, if you do not open my mouth?
How can I reply, if you do not make me wise?

You are the prince of gods, king of glorious beings
and master of every creature.
Without you, nothing is done;
without your will, nothing is known.
No one can be compared to your power and priceless glory.
Who among all your wondrous creatures
can stand in the presence of that glory?
How much less am I who return to dust?
For your glory alone, you made all things,
O blessed God of mercy!

PSALM 23

Your holy spirit
illuminates the dark places of the heart
of your servant
with light like the sun.
I look to the covenants made by men.
Worthless.
Only your truth shines.
and those who love it are wise
and walk in the glow
of your light.
From darkness you raise hearts.
Let light shine on your servant.
Your light is everlasting.

PSALM 25

My heart is amazed
for the word is given me.
My heart of stone hears.
I have come to know
that you did these things for yourself, O God.
You have done miracles for mere flesh.
It is your glory.
You have called into being
a host endowed with knowledge,
and instructed us who are born of women.
In our covenant with you
you open the heart of dust,
and in compassion
you save us from the traps of judgment.

As for me, a creature of clay
and water
with a heart of stone,
how am I worthy of all this?
You set your word
in this ear of dust
and write truths on my heart.
You end
my wandering
to bring me into concordance with you
that I may stand, unshaken,
before you
in the glow of perfect light
forever,
where no darkness is
forever,
where unsearchable peace is
forever.

For me, a creature of dust.

The Odes of Solomon

(Jewish Pseudepigrapha, Jewish Christian)

The *Pistis Sophia*, a Gnostic text preserved in Coptic, contains five odes from *The Odes of Solomon*, and these were all we had of that very important hymnbook until J. Rendel Harris's discovery in 1909 of a 400-year-old Syriac text of the collection. The original language of the Odes was probably Greek, although some scholars argue for a Syriac original. Harris conjectured a Jewish-Christian origin from the first century A.D. Others suggest a Jewish original with a Christian redaction. W. Bauer offers a third possibility: "But more and more the view became established that we have to do with a Gnostic hymn-book from the 2nd century."[1] Whatever the origin, in their present form it is clear that they are based on Jewish hymnal tradition, that many of them have been subjected to a Christian overlay, and that there are also Gnostic references, which are more significant than their mere inclusion in the *Pistis Sophia*. Harris also points out many quotations of the odes in the works of the Early Fathers of the Church. The odes were of particular interest because of their Christology, that is, the use of Christ as a speaker in the Odes. Frequently, the structure of an ode consists of a prologue on the part of the Odist, then an oracular statement *ex ore Christi*, and finally a doxology for the congregation to participate in.

Many of the Odes are hauntingly beautiful. The images soar. The diction is rich with surprising references, such as "milk from the Lord," which apologists explain away as odd symbolism. Actually, the odes are as poetic, profound, and astonishing as the most compelling psalms of the Old Testament. So we read "The dew of the Lord rinsed me with silence/ and a cloud of peace rose over my head" (Ode 35); or, with typical chariot imagery of Jewish mysticism: "I went up to the light of truth as into a chariot/ and truth took me/ across canyons and ravines" (Ode 38). The words are graceful in "My heart was cloven and there appeared a flower,/ and grace spang up" (Ode 11), and the thought of three prevailing traditions, Jewish, Christian, Gnostic, is suggested in Ode 7:

> The father of knowledge
> is the word of knowledge.

> He who created wisdom
> is wiser than his works,

The Odes of Solomon are one of the great poetic and wisdom documents of antiquity.

Note

1. Edgar Hennecke and Wilhelm Schneemelcher, eds., *New Testament Apocrypha*, vol. 2 (Philadelphia: Westminster Press, 1964), p. 809.

ODE 1*

The Lord is on my head like a crown
and I shall not be without him.

The crown of truth was woven for me
and caused your branches to blossom in me.

The crown is not dry and sterile.

You live
and blossom on my head.

Your fruits are full and perfect
and filled with salvation.

ODE 3

I clothe his limbs, his own limbs,
and hang from them.
He loves me.

How would I know how to love the Lord
if he did not love me?
And who can tell us about love?
Only one who is loved.

I love the beloved and my soul loves him
and am where he reposes

---

*Odes 1 through 42 are revisions of earlier translations, particularly: Rendel Harris and Alphonse Mingana, *The Odes and Psalms of Solomon*, vol. 2 (London: Longman, 1920).

and will be no stranger
for he is not petty, my high merciful Lord.

I have gone to join him, for the lover has found
his beloved,
and to love the son
I become a son.

Whoever joins the immortal becomes immortal.
Whoever delights in the living one is living.

This is the spirit of the Lord.
It does not lie. It teaches us his ways.

Be wise. Be understanding, and your eyes
be open.

ODE 4

No man, O my God, may take your holy place, nor alter it,
for no man has such power.

You designed your sanctuary before you drew the world.

What is older will not be undone by the younger.

You gave your heart, O Lord, to your believers
and will not fail
or be fruitless.

One hour of your faith
is more precious than all days and years.

Who will be so hurt
as to put on your grace?

Your seal is known.
Creatures know it. Hosts possess it. Archangels are robed in it.

You gave your fellowship. Not you but we
were in need.

Distill your dews upon us
and open your rich fountains that pour forth milk and honey.

You repent of nothing, of nothing you promised.

And you knew the end
and gave freely
so you might withdraw and give again.

You knew all, God,
and from the beginning set it in order.
And you, O Lord, made all things.

ODE 5

I thank you, O Lord,
because I love you.

O highest one, do not abandon me
for you are my hope.

Your grace I have received freely
and live on it.

My persecutors will come, but let them not see me.
Let a cloud of darkness fall on their eyes
and thick gloom darken them.

Let light be gone and I be invisible
so they will not seize me.

Let their counsel be thick darkness
and their cunning turn on their own heads,
for their counsel
is nothing.

The Lord is my hope,
I will not fear.

He is a garland on my head
and I will not be moved.

Should everything shake,
I stand firm.

If all visible things perish,
I will not die,
for the Lord is with me
and I am with him.

ODE 6

As the hand moves over the harp and the strings speak
so the spirit of the Lord speaks in my members
and I speak by his love,

for he destroys what is foreign
and bitter.

So he was from the beginning
and will be to the end:
nothing will be his adversary
nor resist him.

The Lord multiplied his knowledge
and was zealous to make us know what he gives us
through his grace.

He gave us praise for his name
and our spirits praise his holy spirit.

A stream went forth
and became a long and broad river.
It flooded and broke and carried away the Temple.

Ordinary men could not stop it,
nor could those whose art is to halt the waters.

And it spread over the face of the whole earth,
filling everything,
and the thirsty of the earth drank
and their thirst was quenched.

The drink came from the highest one.

Blessed are the ministers of that drink,
who guard his water.

They assuage dry lips.
They raise up those who have fainted.

Souls that were about to depart
they have drawn back from death,

and limbs that had become crooked
they have made straight.

They gave strength to our feebleness
and light to our eyes.

Everyone knew them in the Lord
and by the water they lived forever.

ODE 7

As anger moves over evil
so joy moves over the beloved
and floods us with fruit.

My joy is the Lord and I move toward him.
The way is excellent.

My helper is the Lord
who in his candor lets me know him thoroughly.
His kindness has humbled his magnitude.

He became like me so I could receive him.
He thought like me so I could become him

and I did not tremble when I saw him,
for he was gracious to me.

He took on my nature so I could learn from him,
took on my form so I would not turn away.

The father of knowledge
is the word of knowledge.

He who created wisdom
is wiser than his works,

and he who created me when I was not
knew what to do when I came into being.

So in his abundant grace he pitied me
and granted me to ask for and receive his sacrifice.

He is incorrupt,
the perfection of the worlds and their father.

He lets himself be seen in his works
that he be recognized as their creator,
that all may not suppose they are self-made.

His way is knowledge.
He has broadened it and made it perfect.

And over it are the traces of his light,
from the beginning to the end.

He was resting in his son, was pleased with his son,
and because of his salvation the Lord took possession of all things.

The highest one will be known in his saints,
sung in songs of the coming of the Lord
and those who sing may go forth to meet him
with joy and a harp of many tunes.

Seers will go before him
and be seen
and praise the Lord for his love.
He is near and sees.

Hatred will leave the earth,
jealousy drown,
ignorance be destroyed,
for the knowledge of the Lord has come.

Let singers sing the grace of the Lord most high,
let them sing,

let their hearts be like day,
their harmonies like the Lord's excellent beauty.

Let there be nothing without life, knowledge
or speech,

for the Lord has given a mouth to his creation.
He opens the voice of our mouth
to praise him.

Confess his power
and reveal his grace.

ODE 11

My heart was cloven and there appeared a flower,
and grace sprang up
and fruit from the Lord,

for the highest one split me with his holy spirit,
exposed my love for him
and filled me with his love.

His splitting of my heart was my salvation
and I followed the way of his peace,
the way of truth.

From the beginning to the end
I received his knowledge.

and sat on the rock of truth
where he placed me.

Speaking waters came near my lip
from the vast fountain of the Lord,

and I drank and was drunk
with the living water that never dies,
and my drunkenness gave me knowledge.

I threw off vanity,
turned to my God
and his bounty made me rich.

I threw off the madness of the earth,
I stripped it from me and cast it away,

and the Lord renewed me in his raiment
and held me in his light.

From above he gave me uncorrupt ease
and I was like land deep and happy in its orchards,
and the Lord was sun on the face of the land.

My eyes were clear,
dew was on my face.

and my nostrils enjoyed
the aroma of the Lord.

He took me to Paradise
where I knew joy
and worshiped his glory.

Blessed are they
planted in your land,
in Paradise,
who grow in the growth of your trees
and change from gloom into light.

Your servants are lovely.
They do good,
they abjure evil and turn to your pleasantness.

They are free of the bitterness of trees
ancient in their land.

You are everywhere,
always before your servants.

There is much space in Paradise
but no wasteland.
All is fruit.

Glory, Lord, and eternal delight of Paradise.

ODE 12

He filled me with words of truth
that I may speak the same.

Like the flow of waters truth flows from my mouth,
and my lips reveal its harvest,

and it gives me the gold of knowledge
for the mouth of the Lord is the true word
and the door of his light.

And the highest one gave the word to his worlds,
which interpret his own beauty,
recite his praise,
confess his thought,
are heralds of his mind,
are instructors of his works.

For the swiftness of the word is ineffable
and like his statement are its swiftness and sharpness.

Its course knows no end,
it never fails, it stands.
Its descent and its way are incomprehensible.

Like his work is its end
for it is the light and the dawn of thought,

and through it worlds converse
and the silent acquire speech,

and from it came love and concord
and candor,
and they were penetrated by the word
and knew him that made it,
for they came into concord.

The mouth of the Highest One spoke to them
and he was made clear by his word.

The dwelling place of the word is man
and its truth is love.

Blessed are they who by it have understood everything
and have known the Lord in his truth.

ODE 14

As the eyes of a son to his father
so my eyes turn to you, O Lord, at all times,
for with you are my consolation and joy.

Do not turn your mercy from me, O Lord,
nor your kindness,
but stretch out your right hand,
and be my guide to the end.

Care for me,
save me from evil,

and let your gentleness
and love be with me.

Teach me to sing of truth
that I may engender fruit in you.

Open the harp of your holy spirit
so I may praise you, Lord, with all its notes.

From your sea of mercy
help me,
help me in my hour of need.

ODE 15

As the sun is joy to those who seek daybreak,
so my joy is the Lord.

He is my sun and his rays have lifted me up
and chased all darkness from my face.

In him I have acquired eyes
and seen his sacred day.

I have acquired eyes
and heard his truth.

I have acquired knowledge
and been made happy by him.

I left the way of error and went to him
and was saved.

According to his bounty he gave me,
according to his beauty he made me.

I found purity through his name,
I shed corruption through his grace.

Death has died before my countenance,
hell is abolished by my word.

A deathless life appears in the land of the Lord,
is known to those with faith,
and is given to those with faith, unceasingly.

ODE 16

As the work of the farmer is the plough
and the helmsman the guidance of the ship
so my work is a song to the Lord.

My art and occupation are in his praise.
His love feeds my heart,
his sweet foods reach my lips.

My love is the Lord
and so I will sing to him.

I grow strong in his celebration.
I have faith.

In my mouth
his spirit talks of
his glory and beauty,

the labor of his hands,
the craft of his fingers,

his horizonless mercy,
the power of his word.

The Lord's word finds the invisible
and reveals his thought.

Our eye sees his labor,
our ear hears his mind.

He spread out the earth
and placed the waters in the sea.

He measured the firmament
and fixed the stars.

He created
and rested.

Created things follow a pattern.
They do not know
rest.

Throngs follow his word.
The gold coin of light is the sun,
the gold coin of darkness is the night.

He made the sun to clarify the day
but evening blurs the face of the earth.

Their alternation
speaks the beauty of God.

And nothing exists without the Lord.
He was before anything was,

and our worlds were made by his word,
his thought and his heart.

Glory and honor to his name.

ODE 17

I was crowned by God,
by a crown alive,

and my Lord justified me.
He became my certain salvation.

I was freed from myself
and uncondemned.
The chain fell from my wrists.

I took on the face and ways of a new person,
walked in him and was redeemed.

The thought of truth drove me.
I walked to it and did not wander off.

Those who saw me were amazed,
supposing me to be a strange person.

He who knew me and brought me up
is the summit of perfection.

He glorified me by kindness
and lifted my thought to truth

and showed me his way.
I opened closed doors,

shattered bars of iron.
My own shackles melted.

Nothing appeared closed
because I was the door to everything.

I freed slaves,
left no man in bonds,

I spread my knowledge
and love

and sowed my fruits in hearts
and transformed them.

I blessed them. They lived.
I gathered them and saved them.

They became the limbs of my body
and I was their head.

Glory to you, our head, our Lord Messiah.

ODE 18

My heart was raised and magnified in the love of the highest one
that I might celebrate his name.

My arms and legs were made powerful
that they might not fall from his power.

He healed my bodily sickness.
His will was firm
as his kingdom.

O Lord, that I may help the weak,
let me keep your word.

For them
do not deny me your perfection.

Let the luminary not be conquered by darkness,
nor truth flee falsehood.

Appoint me to victory. Your right hand
is salvation. Receive
and preserve us who greet temptation.

Falsehood and death are not in your mouth,
my God.
Your will is perfection.

Vanity you do not know,
nor does it know you.

Error you do not know,
nor does it know you.

Ignorance appeared like dust
and like the scum of the sea.

And the vain supposed it was great
and were its child,

but the wise understood and meditated
and were unpolluted in their meditations
for they shared the mind of the Lord.

They laughed at those in error
and spoke truth
breathed into them from the Highest One.

His name is greatly beautiful.

ODE 19

A cup of milk I was offered
and I drank its sweetness as the delight of the Lord.

The Son is the cup
and he who was milked is the Father
and he who milked him is the Holy Ghost.

His breasts were full
and his milk should not drip out wastefully.

The Holy Ghost opened the Father's raiment
and mingled the milk from the Father's two breasts

and gave that mingling to the world, which was unknowing.
Those who drink it are near his right hand.

The Spirit opened the Virgin's womb
and she received the milk.

The Virgin became a mother of great mercy;
she labored, but not in pain, and bore a Son.
No midwife came.

She bore him as if she were a man,
openly, with dignity, with kindness.
She loved him, and swaddled him, and revealed his majesty.

ODE 21

I raised my arms high
to the grace of the Lord,

for he had cast off my bonds.
My helper had lifted me to his grace and salvation.

I discarded darkness
and clothed myself in light.

My soul acquired a body
free from sorrow,
affliction or pain.

The thought of the Lord restored me.
I fed on his incorruptible fellowship.

And I was raised in the light
and went to him,
near him,
praising and proclaiming him.

He made my heart flood into my mouth,
made it shine on my lips.

On my face the exultation of the Lord increased,
and his praise.

ODE 24

The dove flew over the head of the Messiah
who was her head,
and she sang over him
and her voice was heard.

The inhabitants were afraid
and travelers shuddered.

Birds took flight
and all creeping things died in their holes.

Abysses opened and closed.
They were seeking God like women in labor.

They had no food.
None belonged to them.

The abysses sank and were sealed by the Lord
and people perished in their own thought,
ancient and new.

Everyone was imperfect and died.
They could say nothing.

The Lord destroyed the imagination
of all who did not have his truth.

They were weak in wisdom
and were rejected. They lacked his truth.

The Lord disclosed his way,
and spread his grace in alien lands.

Those who understood
know holiness.

ODE 29

The Lord is my hope. With him I shall not be lost,
and through his praise he made me
and through his goodness he gave me common things
and through his mercy he raised me up
and through his beauty he set me on high.
He led me out of the depths of Sheol
and led me out of the mouth of death.

I laid my enemies low
and he justified me through his grace.
I believed in him, I believed in the Messiah,
and he came to me
and he showed me his sign
and led me by way of his light.

And he gave me the rod of his power
to subdue the dreams of others,
to bring down the mighty,
to make war through his word
and come to victory through his power.

And through his word the Lord overthrew my enemy
who was like stubble blown away in the wind.

I praise him. He is most high, and has exalted me
his servant.
He has exalted the son of his handmaid.

ODE 30

Drink deeply from the living fountain of the Lord.
It is yours.

Come, all who are thirsty, and drink,
and rest by the fountain of the Lord.

How beautiful and pure.
It rests the soul.

That water is sweeter than honey.
The combs of bees are nothing beside it.

It flows from the lips of the Lord.
Its name is from the Lord's heart.

It is invisible but has no borders
and was unknown until it was set in our midst.

They who drink are blessed
and they rest.

ODE 34

The simple heart finds no hard way,
good thought finds no wounds.
Deep in the illuminated mind is no storm.

Surrounded on every side by the beauty of the open country,
one is free of doubt.

Below
is like above.

Everything is above.
Below is nothing, but the ignorant think they see.

Now you know grace. It is for your salvation.
Believe and live and be saved.

ODE 35

The dew of the Lord rinsed me with silence
and a cloud of peace rose over my head,

guarding me.
It became my salvation.

Everybody quivered in horror.
They issued smoke and a judgment,

but I was silent, near my Lord,
who was more than shadow, more than foundation.

He carried me like a child by its mother.
He gave me milk, his dew,

and I grew in his bounty,
rested in his perfection.

I spread my hands out as my soul pointed to the firmament
and I slipped upward to him
who redeemed me.

ODE 38

I went up to the light of truth as into a chariot
and truth took me

across canyons and ravines,
and preserved me against waves smashing the cliffs.

It was my haven and salvation
and put me in the arms of immortal life.

It went with me, soothed me, kept me from error,
since it was and is truth . . .

ODE 41

. . .
All who see me will be astonished
for I am an alien among you.

The Father of Truth remembered me.
He possessed me from the beginning.

Through his riches and the thought in his heart
he engendered me.

His word is our way.
The Savior makes us alive and does not forget our souls.

The humbled
are exalted in him.

The son of the highest one
appeared in the Father's perfection.

Light found daybreak in the word
that was earlier his.

The Messiah is one,
known before the foundation of the world.
He saves souls in his truth, in his name.

Let us sing to the Lord. We love him.

ODE 42

I stretched out my hands and came near my Lord.
It is my sign,

stretching my hands as spread on a tree.
That was my way up to the Good One.

I became useless to those who did not take hold of me.
I hide from those who do not love me,

but am with them
who love me.
My persecutors died.
They sought me because I am alive.

I rose up and am with them
and speak through their mouths.

They despised their persecutors.
I locked them in the yoke of love,

like the groom over the bride
so is my love over those who believe in me.

They thought me rejected, perished.
I was not.

Hell saw me and was miserable.
Death cast me up and many others.

I have been gall and bitterness to death.
I went down with it to the utmost depth
and it released my feet and head
for it could not endure my face.

I made a congregation of living men among its dead
and spoke to them with living lips
so my word would not be empty.

The dead ran toward me,
crying: "Son of God, pity us,
be kind,
bring us out of the bonds of darkness.

Open the door
to yourself.
We perceive that our death has not touched you.

Save us,
you are our redeemer."

I heard their voice
and stored their faith in my heart.

I set my name upon their heads,
for they are free men and are mine.

The Gospel of Truth
and the Valentinian
Speculation

(Gnostic)

The *Gospel of Truth* is attributed by some scholars to Valentinus himself, founder of one of the main schools of Gnostic speculation. Valentinus was born in Egypt around A.D. 100–110, educated in Alexandria, and taught in Rome between A.D. 135 and 160. He and his disciples Ptolemaeus and Marcus were heads of schools of the Valentinian doctrine, "a heresy" which infuriated orthodox Christians—particularly Irenaeus, who complained that each day one of those Valentinians invented something new. Much of the first book of Irenaeus' treatise against heresies concerns the writing of Ptolemaeus, who was the great systematizer and exegete of the Valentinian school. Eventually, Valentinus and his followers had to be expelled from the Church, for in reality they reversed all the main tenets of Jewish and Christian teaching. Above all, their hostility to both the Creator and his creation was intolerable. How could God not be considered good, and his act of creating the world be viewed as an act of corruption?

In the Valentinian speculation, the sins of the world, our error, our spirit trapped in ignorance, darkness, and matter are directly caused by God, the God of Jews and Christians. But salvation remains possible in each person. Through illumination and knowledge (*gnosis*), salvation may come to an individual soul. And each "cosmic event" of self-knowledge affects the whole universe, helping to bring grace to the world and to reduce the damage done by God. Hans Jonas writes:

> . . . every individual illumination by "knowledge" helps to cancel out again the total system sustained by that principle [the substantialization of ignorance]; and, as such knowing finally transposes the

individual self to the divine realm, it also plays its part in integrating the impaired godhead itself.[1]

Irenaeus points out the core of Valentinian thought in his words: "Knowledge is salvation of the inner man" (Iren. I.21.4).

The Valentinian system incorporated figures also found in other Gnostic systems. Foremost, above all lower deities is the unbegotten Father of All, the mysterious alien god who is above Yahweh in the Gnostic hierarchy. The invisible Father is sometimes presented as an androgynous combination of Mind (*nous*, which in Greek is masculine) and Thought (*ennoia* or *epinoia*, which are feminine). Mind, particularly in the Simonian system, is the upper principle of great power, the instrument, while Thought is the lower feminine principle of thought and process, who as creator-mother brings forth both Primal Man and God the creator of Heaven and earth. This female principle is also identified with Mother Sophia or Sophia-Prunikos (Wisdom-Whore) and also the Mother of Life. The Mother of Life brings forth the Primal Man, also referred to as Perfect Man or True Man. When Primal Man and his five sons are defeated by the King of Darkness, his spiritual light is caught in their darkness. The lower Sophia's child, God the Creator, the Demiurge, was compelled to make the world to free those particles of light from darkness. By freeing or "unmixing" light from darkness, man or woman is prepared to return to the former state of pure spirit.

In creating the world God first thought himself to be alone, and he arrogantly considered himself the highest god. But his mother Sophia informed him of his place below the Father of All and the thirty Aeons of the Pleroma. God kept the mystery of that high world to himself, however, and passed himself off jealously as the sole God—"Hear, O Israel, the Lord our God, the Lord is one"—a notion which non-Gnostic Jews and Christians shared. We see in Irenaeus' refutation of Valentinianism (as practiced by its head Ptolemaeus) the uneasy relations between Achamoth and the Demiurge,[2] that is, between Mother Sophia and her son God:

> The Demiurge supposed that he made these things of himself, but he made them after Achamoth projected them. He made Heaven without knowing Heaven; he formed man in ignorance of man; he brought earth to light without understanding earth. In every case he was ignorant of the ideas of the things he made, as well as of the Mother; and he thought he was entirely alone. But the Mother was the cause of his creating; she wanted to bring him forth as the head and beginning of her own nature and as lord of the whole operation. (Iren. 5.3)

The Demiurge as Creator acts as Sophia's agent. He is an ignorant Creator, deprived of *gnosis* for his own salvation. But man and woman, through knowledge of their own spiritual light, may ultimately heal and redeem their Creator.

As for Sophia, her role is diverse. Elaine Pagels has written extensively about her major role in the Gnostic systems. A prominent aspect of her condition is her suffering. Sophia split into two persons, an upper and a lower Sophia. The lower Sophia, Mother Achamoth, left the Pleroma in search of the Invisible Father. Finding herself outside the protection of the Pleroma, she wanders in shadow and void, and she suffers and feels desire and passion. Central to the Valentinian system is the suffering of the Mother, rather than of Jesus. Although again systems differ, Jesus' suffering is usually described as that of a phantom, of a simulacrum. Eventually, Sophia will find salvation from her suffering when the spiritual (pneumatic) elements in the world are saved through knowledge. Then she reenters the Pleroma and there takes place the marriage of Sophia and Jesus: "Then our Mother Achamoth will depart from the place of the Middle and will enter into the Pleroma and will receive the Savior as her bridegroom" (Iren. 7.1).

To understand the roles of Mother Sophia and her offspring the Demiurge, we should understand the materials of which they were made. Three kinds of material existed, in descending order of importance: spirit of *pneuma*, soul/mind or *psyche*, and matter or *hyle*. Sophia was pure spirit, which we associate with light, truth, and knowledge. Her creation, the Father of the Earth, was, however, without spirit. Demiurge had a psychic and material nature. Demiurge proceeded to create seven heavens, and heavenly and earthly beings whom he fashioned after himself, that is, with psyche and matter. But Sophia secretly inserted spirit into earthly beings, which is the source of their salvation; because Sophia had this essential role in the creation, God is called "Mother-Father."

There are several versions of how Sophia brought a spiritual nature to earthly beings (as there are several, often contradictory, versions of most Gnostic myths). One Valentinian version is ingenious. Irenaeus writes:

> The embryo of our Mother Achamoth, which she conceived in accordance with the vision of the angels about the Savior was unknown to the Demiurge and was secretly inserted into him while he remained ignorant, so that through him it might be sown into the soul created by him and into the material body, might grow and increase in them, and might become ready for the reception of the perfect Logos. The Demiurge was unaware of the spiritual man who was sown, in his "inbreathing" [Gen. 2:7], by Sophia with ineffable power and foreknowledge. As he did not know the Mother, so he does not know her seed. This seed is the Church, which corresponds to the [Aeon] Church above. Man thus has his soul from the Demiurge, his body from liquid and his flesh from matter, but his "spiritual man" from the Mother Achamoth. (Iren. 7.1)

Robert M. Grant compares the androgynous nature of the Gnostic Creator God to mystical Judaism of the *Zohar*, the classical work of the Kabbalah: "Yahweh is called the Father and Elohim the Mother."[3] But despite all speculation on the nature of the Creator in the Gnostic texts—in the *Gospel of Truth* the Creator is simply alluded to as Error—the very denigration of the traditional God suggests an essential characteristic of all Gnostic systems: a shift from a God-oriented to a self-oriented religion. Self-knowledge, not reverence for a deity, leads to salvation. In short, Gnosticism is a personal religion or philosophy whose eschatological goal is the discovery of divinity within the self. Grant suggests that Gnosticism arose among ex-Jews because of "the failure of Jewish apocalyptic hopes."[4] The people were waiting for the messiah, for divine intervention, during years when the Romans burned the Temple and drove the populace into exile. The failure of their expectations provoked a turn away from apocalyptic Judaism, a turn toward an inward speculation. Hence the Jewish Gnostic speculation.

The fulfillment of Jewish apocalyptic hope was, however, realized in Christianity, which proclaimed the Messiah, thereby redeeming the dream which had obsessed Essenes and Zealots and other groups who despaired of contemporary religious and political realities. But then some Christians sensed a failure in Christian *apokalypsis* (revelation), and rejected Yahweh, Church, and traditional faith, and turned inward to self-knowledge. Hence the Christian Gnostic speculation. Because the Christian Gnostics violently altered orthodox doctrine, they sought justification of their systems through biblical exegesis. As Philo had earlier allegorized the Old Testament, the Gnostics, and particularly the Valentinians, became exegetes of both New and Old Testaments.

The *Gospel of Truth* is a mediating tractate between the synoptic gospels and the fully Gnostic scriptures. Like the Valentinian *Letter to Flora*, the *Gospel of Truth* offers alternatives to orthodox Christian beliefs, but it is not, as other Gnostic works, a violent rejection of Judaism and Christianity. Moreover, it is a gospel only in the sense of "good news," for it does not pretend to deal with the historical Jesus. Yet, as George W. MacRae points out, the *Gospel of Truth* does concern "news" about Jesus, the Word, and all that reveals the Father "and passes on knowledge, particularly self-knowledge."[5] It emphasizes redemption of a mystical nature. When the fog of error vanishes, the Father may be known within. R. M. Grant puts the mystical aspect of the work in its historical background:

> The Gospel of Truth, first published in 1957, is full of Jewish mystical speculation and lacks any explicit criticism of the Jews or of Jewish Christianity. It suggests that Valentinus was trying to reinterpret Jewish apocalyptic Christianity as Jewish Gnostic Christianity, and that the occasion for his work, as for that of Marcion, was the apocalyptic catastrophe in the reign of Hadrian.[6]

The work begins with a proclamation of the joy of receiving the Word from the Pleroma, which derives from the Father, and which ultimately offers joyful union with the Father. Like the Kabbalists, the Gnostics were wonderfully and irredeemably bookish. So the metaphor for that meditation which leads to salvific knowledge is to turn into oneself and to discover the book of the mind of the perfect Father. Speaking of children who possess a knowledge of the Father, the work states: "In their heart, the living book of the living was manifest, the book which was written in the thought and in the mind of the Father." This quiet book, profound and beautiful, was itself obscured from our eyes for nearly two thousand years until its discovery in 1945 at Nag Hammadi, near the ancient Egyptian town of Chenoskeia.

Notes

1. Hans Jonas, *The Gnostic Religion,* 2d ed., revised (1958; reprint, Boston: Beacon Press, 1963), p. 175.

2. Achamoth means "wisdom" in Hebrew; Demiurge means "creator" in Greek. It is appropriate that two major figures in the Gnostic myth have Hebrew and Greek names, since Judaism and Greek Platonic philosophy (the Demiurge appears in Plato's *Timaeus*) are the source of Gnosticism.

3. R. M. Grant, *Gnosticism and Early Christianity,* 2d ed. (1959; reprint, New York: Columbia Univ. Press, 1966), p. 23.

4. Grant, *Gnosticism and Early Christianity,* p. 36.

5. James M. Robinson, ed., *The Nag Hammadi Library* (San Francisco: Harper & Row, 1977), p. 37.

6. Grant, *Gnosticism and Early Christianity,* pp. 128–129.

THE GOSPEL OF TRUTH*

The gospel of truth is joy to those who have received from the Father of truth the gift of knowing him by the power of the Logos, who has come from the Pleroma and who is in the thought and the mind of the Father; he it is who is called "the Savior," since that is the name of the work which he must do for the redemption of those who have not known the Father. For the name of the gospel is the manifestation of hope, since that is the discovery of those who seek him, because the all sought for him from whom it had come forth. You see, the all had been inside of him, that illimitable, inconceivable one, who is better than every thought.

This ignorance of the Father brought about terror and fear. And terror became dense like a fog, that no one was able to see. Because of this, error became strong. But it worked on its hylic substance vainly, because it did not know the truth. It was in a fashioned form while it was preparing, in power and in beauty, the equivalent of truth. This, then, was not a humiliation for him, that illimitable, inconceivable one. For they were as nothing, this terror and this forgetfulness and this figure of falsehood, whereas this

_____
*From Robert M. Grant, *Gnosticism* (New York: Harper & Brothers, 1961), pp. 146–161.

established truth is unchanging, unperturbed and completely beautiful.

For this reason, do not take error too seriously. Thus, since it had no root, it was in a fog as regards the Father, engaged in preparing works and forgetfulnesses and fears in order, by these means, to beguile those of the middle and to make them captive. The forgetfulness of error was not revealed. It did not become light beside the Father. Forgetfulness did not exist with the Father, although it existed because of him.[1] What exists in him is knowledge, which was revealed so that forgetfulness might be destroyed and that they might know the Father. Since forgetfulness existed because they did not know the Father, if they then come to know the Father, from that moment on forgetfulness will cease to exist.

That is the gospel of him whom they seek, which he has revealed to the perfect through the mercies of the Father as the hidden mystery, Jesus the Christ. Through him he enlightened those who were in darkness because of forgetfulness. He enlightened them and gave them a path. And that path is the truth which he taught them. For this reason error was angry with him, so it persecuted him. It was distressed by him, so it made him powerless.[2] He was nailed to a cross. He became a fruit of the knowledge of the Father. He did not, however, destroy them because they ate of it. He rather caused those who ate of it to be joyful because of this discovery.

And as for him, them he found in himself, and him they found in themselves, that illimitable, inconceivable one, that perfect Father who made the all, in whom the all is, and whom the all lacks, since he retained in himself their perfection, which he had not given to the all. The Father was not jealous. What jealousy, indeed, is there between him and his members? For, even if the Aeon had received their perfection, they would not have been able to approach the perfection of the Father, because he retained their perfection in himself, giving it to them as a way to return to him and as a knowledge unique in perfection. He is the one who set the all in order and in whom the all existed and whom the all lacked. As one of whom some have no knowledge, he desires that they know him and that they love him. For what is it that the all lacked, if not the knowledge of the Father?

He became a guide, quiet and at leisure. In the middle of a school he came and spoke the word, as a teacher. Those who were wise in their own estimation came to put him to the test. But he discredited them as empty-headed people. They hated him because they really were not wise men. After all these came also the little children, those who possess the knowledge of the Father. When they became strong they were taught the aspects of the Father's face. They came to know and they were known. They were glorified and they gave glory. In their heart, the living book of the living was manifest, the book which was written in the thought and in the mind of the Father and, from before the foundation of the all, is in that incomprehensible part of him.

This is the book which no one found possible to take, since it was reserved for him who will take it and be slain. No one was able to be manifest from those who believed in salvation as long as that book had not appeared. For this reason, the compassionate, faithful Jesus was patient in his sufferings until he took that book, since he knew that his death meant life for many. Just as in the case of a will which has not yet been opened, the fortune of the deceased master of the house is hidden, so also in the case of the all which had been hidden as long as the Father of the all was invisible and unique in himself, in whom every space has its source. For this reason Jesus appeared. He took that book as his own. He was nailed to a cross. He affixed the edict of the Father to the cross.

Oh, such great teaching! He abases himself even unto death, though he is clothed in eternal life. Having divested himself of these perishable rags, he clothed himself in incorruptibility, which no one could possibly take from him. Having entered into the empty territory of fears, he passed before those who were stripped by forgetfulness, being both knowledge and perfection, proclaiming the things that are in the heart of the Father, so that he became the wisdom of those who have received instruction.[3] But those who are to be taught, the living who are inscribed in the book of the living, learn for themselves, receiving instructions from the Father, turning to him again.

Since the perfection of the all is in the Father, it is necessary for the all to ascend to him. Therefore, if one has knowledge, he gets what belongs to him and draws it to himself. For he who is ignorant, is deficient, and it is a great deficiency, since he lacks that which will make him perfect. Since the perfection of the all is in the Father, it is necessary for the all to ascend to him and for each one to get the things which are his. He registered them first, having prepared them[4] to be given to those who came from him.

Those whose name he knew first were called last, so that the one who has knowledge is he whose name the Father has pronounced. For he whose name has not been spoken is ignorant. Indeed, how shall one hear if his name has not been uttered. For he who remains ignorant until the end is a creature of forgetfulness and will perish with it. If this is not so, why have these wretches no name, why do they have no sound? Hence, if one has knowledge, he is from above. If he is called, he hears, he replies, and he turns towards him who called him and he ascends to him and knows what he is called. Since he has knowledge, he does the will of him who called him. He desires to please him and he finds rest. He receives a certain name.[5] He who thus is going to have knowledge knows whence he came and whither he is going. He knows it as a person who, having become intoxicated, has turned from his drunkenness and having come to himself, has restored what is his own.

He has turned many from error. He went before them to their own places, from which they departed when they erred because of the depth of him who surrounds every place, whereas there is nothing which surrounds him. It was a great wonder that they were in the Father without knowing him and that they were able to leave on their own, since they were not able to contain him and know him in whom they were, for indeed his will had not come forth from him. For he revealed it as a knowledge with which all its emanations[6] agree, namely, the knowledge of the living book which he revealed to the Aeons at last as his letters, displaying to them that these are not merely vowels nor consonants,[7] so that one may read them and think of something void of meaning; on the contrary, they are letters which convey the truth. They are pronounced only when they are known. Each letter is a perfect truth like a perfect book, for they are letters written by the hand of the unity, since the Father wrote them for the Aeons, so that they by means of his letters might come to know the Father.

While his wisdom meditates on the logos, and since his teaching expresses it, his knowledge has been revealed. His honor is a crown upon it. Since his joy agrees with it, his glory exalted it. It has revealed his image. It has obtained his rest. His love took bodily form around it. His trust embraced it. Thus the logos of the Father goes forth into the all, being the fruit of his heart and expression of his will. It supports the all. It chooses and also takes the form of the all, purifying it[8] and causing it to return to the Father and to the Mother, Jesus of the utmost[9] sweetness. The Father opens his bosom, but his bosom is the Holy Spirit. He reveals his hidden self which is his son, so that through the compassion of the Father the Aeons may know him, end their wearying search for the Father[10] and rest themselves in him, knowing that this is rest. After he had filled what was incomplete, he did away with form. The form of it [i.e., what was incomplete] is the world, that which it served. For where there is envy and strife, there is an incompleteness; but where there is unity, there is completeness. Since this incompleteness came about because they did not know the Father, so when they know the Father, incompleteness, from that moment on, will cease to exist. As one's ignorance disappears when he gains knowledge, and as darkness disappears when light appears, so also incompleteness is eliminated by completeness. Certainly, from that moment on, form is no longer manifest, but will be dissolved in fusion with unity for now their works lie scattered. In time unity will make the spaces complete. By means of unity each one will understand itself. By means of knowledge it will purify itself of diversity with a view towards unity, devouring matter within itself like fire and darkness by light, death by life.

Certainly, if these things have happened to each one of us, it is fitting for us, surely, to think about the all so that the house may be holy and silent for unity. Like people who have moved from a neighborhood,[11] if they have some dishes around which are not good, they usually break them. Nevertheless the householder does not suffer a loss, but rejoices, for in the place of these defective dishes there are those which are completely perfect. For this is the judgment which has come from above and which has judged every person, a drawn two-edged sword cutting on this side and that. When it appeared, I mean, the logos, who is in the heart of those who pronounce it—it was not merely a sound but it has become a body—a great disturbance occurred among the dishes, for some were emptied, other filled; some were provided for, others were removed; some were purified, still others were broken. All the spaces were shaken and disturbed for they had no composure nor stability. Error was disturbed not knowing what it should do. It was troubled; it lamented, it was beside itself because it did not know anything. When knowledge, which is its abolishment, approached it with all its emanations, error is empty, since there is nothing in it. Truth appeared; all its emanations recognized it. They actually greeted the Father with a power which is complete and which joins them with the Father. For each one loves truth because truth is the mouth of the Father. His tongue is the Holy Spirit, who joins him to truth attaching him to the mouth of the Father by his tongue at the time he shall receive the Holy Spirit.

This is the manifestation of the Father and his revelation to his Aeons. He revealed his hidden self[12] and explained it. For who is it who exists if it is not the Father himself. All the spaces are his emanations. They knew that they stem from him as children from a perfect man. They knew that they had not yet received form nor had they yet received a name, every one of which the Father produces. If they at that time receive form of his knowledge, though they are truly in him, they do not know him. But the Father is perfect. He knows every space which is within him. If he pleases, he reveals anyone whom he desires by giving him a form and by giving him a name; and he does give him a name and cause him to come into being. Those who do not yet exist are ignorant of him who created them. I do not say, then, that those who do not yet exist are nothing. But they are in him who will desire that they exist when he pleases, like the event which is going to happen. On the one hand, he knows, before anything is revealed, what he will produce. On the other hand, the fruit which has not yet been revealed does not know anything, nor is anything either. Thus each space which, on its part, is in the Father comes from the existent one, who, on his part, has established it from the nonexistent. . . . he who does not exist at all, will never exist.

What, then, is that which he wants him to think? "I am like the shadows and phantoms of the night." When morning comes, this one knows that the fear which he had experienced was nothing. Thus they were ignorant of the Father; he is the one whom they did not see. Since there had been fear and confusion and a lack of confidence and doublemindedness and division, there were many illusions which were conceived[13] by him, the foregoing, as well as empty ignorance—as if they were fast asleep and found themselves a prey to troubled dreams. Either there is a place to which they flee, or they lack strength as they come, having pursued unspecified things. Either they are involved in inflicting blows, or they themselves receive bruises. Either they are falling from high places, or they fly off through the air, though they have no wings at all.[14] Other times, it is as if certain people were trying to kill them, even though there is no one pursuing them; or, they themselves are killing those beside them, for they are stained by their blood. Until the moment when they who are passing through all these things—I mean they who have experienced all these confusions—awake, they see nothing because the dreams were nothing. It is thus that they who cast ignorance from them as sheep do not consider it to be anything, nor regard its properties to be something real, but they renounce them like a dream in the night and they consider the knowledge of the Father to be the dawn. It is thus that each one has acted, as if he were asleep, during the time when he was ignorant and thus he comes to understand, as if he were awakening. And happy is the man who comes to himself and awakens. Indeed, blessed is he who has opened the eyes of the blind.

And the Spirit came to him in haste when it raised him. Having given its hand to the one lying prone on the ground, it placed him firmly on his feet, for he had not yet stood up. He gave them the means of knowing the knowledge of the Father and the revelation of his son. For when they saw it and listened to it, he permitted them to take a taste of and to smell and to grasp the beloved son.

He appeared, informing them of the Father, the illimitable one. He inspired them with that which is in the mind, while doing his will. Many received the light and turned towards him. But material men were alien to him and did not discern his appearance nor recognize him. For he came in the likeness of flesh and nothing blocked his way because it was incorruptible and unrestrainable. Moreover, while saying new things, speaking about what is in the heart of the Father, he proclaimed the faultless word. Light spoke through his mouth, and his voice brought forth life. He gave them thought and understanding and mercy and salvation and the Spirit of strength derived from the limitlessness of the Father and sweetness. He caused punishments and scourgings to cease, for it was they which caused many in need of mercy to astray from him in error and in chains—and he mightily destroyed them and derided them with knowledge. He became a path for those who went astray and knowledge for those who were ignorant, a discovery for those who sought, and a support for those who tremble, a purity for those who were defiled.

He is the shepherd who left behind the ninety-nine sheep which had not strayed and went in search of that one which was lost. He rejoiced when he had found it. For ninety-nine is a number of the left hand, which holds it. The moment he finds the one, however, the whole number is transferred to the right hand. Thus it is with him who lacks the one, that is, the entire right hand which attracts that in which it is deficient, seizes it from the left side and transfers it to the right. In this way, then, the number becomes one hundred. This number signifies the Father.[15]

He labored even on the Sabbath for the sheep which he found fallen into the pit. He saved the life of that sheep, bringing it up from the pit in order that you may understand fully what that Sabbath is, you who possess full understanding.[16] It is a day in which it is not fitting that salvation be idle, so that you may speak of that heavenly day which has no night and of the sun which does not set because it is perfect. Say then in your heart that you are this perfect day and that in you the light which does not fail dwells.

Speak concerning the truth to those who seek it and of knowledge to those who, in their error, have committed sins. Make sure-footed those who stumble and stretch forth your hands to the sick. Nourish the hungry and set at ease those who are troubled. Foster men who love. Raise up and awaken those who sleep. For you are this understanding which encourages.[17] If the strong follow this course, they are even stronger. Turn your attention to yourselves. Do not be concerned with other things, namely, that which you have cast forth from yourselves, that which you have dismissed. Do not return to them to eat them. Do not be moth-eaten. Do not be worm-eaten, for you have already shaken it off. Do not be a place of the devil, for you have already destroyed him. Do not strengthen your last obstacles, because that is reprehensible. For the lawless one is nothing. He harms himself more than the law. For that one does his works because he is a lawless person. But this one, because he is a righteous person, does his works among others. Do the will of the Father, then, for you are from him.

For the Father is sweet and his will is good. He knows the things that are yours, so that you may rest yourselves in them. For by the fruits one knows the things that are yours, that they are the children of the Father, and one knows his aroma, that you originate from the grace of his countenance. For this reason, the Father loved his aroma; and it manifests itself in every place; and when it is mixed with matter, he gives his aroma to the light; and into his rest he causes it to ascend in every form and in every sound. For there are no nostrils[18] which smell the aroma, but it is the Spirit which possesses the sense of smell and it draws it for itself to itself and sinks into the aroma of the Father. He is, indeed, the place for it, and he takes it to the place from which it has come, in the first aroma which is cold. It is something in a psychic form, resembling cold water which is . . .[19] since it is in soil which is not hard, of which those who see it think, "It is earth." Afterwards, it becomes soft again. If a breath is taken, it is usually hot. The cold aromas, then, are from the division. For this reason, God came and destroyed the division and he brought the hot Pleroma of love, so that the cold may not return, but the unity of the perfect thought prevail.

This is the word of the Gospel of the finding of the Pleroma for those who wait for the salvation which comes from above. When their hope, for which they are waiting, is waiting—they whose likeness is the light in which there is no shadow, then at that time the Pleroma is about to come. The deficiency of matter, however, is not because of the limitlessness of the Father who comes at the time of the deficiency. And yet no one is able to say that the incorruptible One will come in this manner. But the depth of the Father is increasing, and the thought of error is not with him. It is a matter of falling down and a matter of being readily set upright at the finding of that one who has come to him who will turn back.

For this turning back is called "repentance." For this reason, incorruption has breathed. It followed him who has sinned in order that he may find rest. For forgiveness is that which remains for the light in the deficiency, the word of the pleroma. For the physician hurries to the place in which there is sickness, because that is the desire which he has. The sick man is in a deficient condition, but he does not hide himself because the physician possesses that which he lacks. In this manner the deficiency is filled by the Pleroma, which has no deficiency, which has given itself out in order to fill the one who is deficient, so that grace may take him, then, from the area which is deficient and has no grace. Because of this a diminishing occurred in the place where there is no grace, the area where the one who is small, who is deficient, is taken hold of.

He revealed himself as a Pleroma, i.e., the finding of the light of truth which has shined towards him, because he is unchangeable. For this reason, they who have been troubled speak about Christ in their midst so that they may receive a return and he may anoint them with the ointment. The ointment is the pity of the Father, who will have mercy on them. But those whom he has anointed are those who are perfect. For the filled vessels are those which are customarily used for anointing. But when an anointing is finished, the vessel is usually empty, and the cause for its deficiency is the consumption of its ointment. For then a breath is drawn only through the power which he has. But the one who is without deficiency—one does not trust anyone beside him nor does one pour anything out. But that which is deficient is filled again by the perfect Father. He is good. He knows his plantings because he is the one who has planted them in his Paradise. And his Paradise is his place of rest.

This is the perfection in the thought of the Father and these are the words of his reflection. Each one of his words is the work of his will alone, in the revelation of his logos. Since they were in the depth of his mind, the logos, who was the first to come forth, caused them to appear, along with an intellect which speaks the unique word by means of a silent grace. It was called "thought," since they were in it before becoming manifest. It happened, then, that it was the first to come forth—at the moment pleasing to the will of him who desired it; and it is in the will that the Father is at rest and with which he is pleased. Nothing happens without him, nor does anything occur without the will of the Father. But his will is incomprehensible. His will is his mark,[20] but no one can know it, nor is it possible for them to concentrate on it in order to possess it. But that which he wishes takes place[21] at the moment he wishes it —even if the view does not please anyone: it is God's will.[22] For the Father knows the beginning of them all as well as their end. For when their end arrives, he will question them to their faces. The end, you see, is the recognition of him who is hidden, that is, the Father, from whom the beginning came forth and to whom will return all who have come from him. For they were made manifest for the glory and the joy of his name.

And the name of the Father is the son. It is he who, in the beginning, gave a name to him who came forth from him— he is the same one—and he begat him for a son. He gave him his name which belonged to him—he, the Father, who possesses everything which exists around him. He possesses the name; he has the son. It is possible for them to see him. The name, however, is invisible, for it alone is the mystery of the invisible about to come to ears completely filled with it through the Father's agency. Moreover, as for the Father, his name is not pronounced, but it is revealed through a son. Thus, then, the name is great.

Who, then, has been able to pronounce a name for him, this great name, except him alone to whom the name belongs and the sons of the name in whom the name of the Father is at rest, and who themselves in turn are at rest in his name, since the Father has no beginning?[23] It is he alone who engendered it for himself as a name in the beginning before he had created the Aeons, that the name of the Father should be over their heads as a lord—that is, the real name, which is secure by his authority and by his perfect power. For the name is not drawn from lexicons nor is his name derived from common name-giving. But it is invisible. He gave a name to himself alone, because he alone saw it and because he alone was capable of giving himself a name. For he who does not exist has no name. For what name would one give him who did not exist? Nevertheless, he who exists also with his name and he alone knows it, and to him alone the Father gave a name. The son is his name. He did not, therefore, keep it secretly hidden, but the son came into existence. He himself gave a name to him. The name, then, is that of the Father, just as the name of the Father is the son. For otherwise, where would compassion find a name—outside of the Father? But someone will probably say to his companion, "Who would give a name to someone who existed before himself, as if, indeed, children did not receive their name from one of those who gave them birth?"

Above all, then, it is fitting for us to think this point over: What is the name? It is the real name. It is, indeed, the name which came from the Father, for it is he who owns the name. He did not, you see, get the name on loan, as in the case of others because of the form in which each one of them is going to be created. This, then, is the authoritative name. There is no one else to whom he has given it. But it remained unnamed, unuttered, till the moment when he, who is perfect, pronounced it himself; and it was he alone who was able to pronounce his name and to see it. When it pleased him, then, that his son should be his pronounced name and when he gave this name to him, he who has come from the depth spoke of his secrets, because he knew that the Father was absolute goodness.[24] For this reason, indeed, he sent this particular one in order that he might speak concerning the place and his place[25] of rest from which he had come forth, and that he might glorify the Pleroma, the greatness of his name and the sweetness of the Father.

Each one will speak concerning the place from which he has come forth, and to the region from which he received his essential being, he will hasten to return once again. And he went from that place —the place where he was—because he tasted of that place, as he was nourished and grew. And his own place of rest is his Pleroma. All the emanations from the Father, therefore, are Pleromas, and all his emanations have their roots in the one who caused them all to grow from himself. He appointed a limit. They, then, became manifest individually in order that they might be in their own thought, for that place to which they extend their thought is their root, which lifts them upwards through all heights to the Father. They reach[26] his head, which is rest for them, and they remain there near to it so that they say that they have participated in his face by means of embraces. But these of this kind were not manifest, because they have not risen above themselves. Neither have they been deprived of the glory of the Father nor have they thought of him as small, nor bitter, nor angry, but as absolutely good, unperturbed, sweet, knowing all the spaces before they came into existence and having no need of instruction.

Such are they who possess from above something of this immeasurable greatness, as they strain towards that unique and perfect one who exists there for them. And they do not go down to Hades. They have neither envy nor moaning, nor is death in them. But they rest in him who rests, without wearying themselves or becoming involved in the search for truth. But they, indeed, are the truth, and the Father is in them, and they are in the Father, since they are perfect, inseparable from him who is truly good. They lack nothing in any way, but they are given rest and are refreshed by the Spirit. And they listen to their root; they have leisure for themselves, they in whom he will find his root, and he will suffer no loss to his soul.

Such is the place of the blessed; this is their place. As for the rest, then, may they know, in their place, that it does not suit me, after having been in the place of rest to say anything more. But he is the one in whom I shall be in order to devote myself, at all times, to the Father of the all and the true brothers, those upon whom the love of the Father is lavished, and in whose midst nothing of him is lacking. It is they who manifest themselves truly since they are in that true and eternal life and speak of the perfect light filled with the seed of the Father, and which is in his heart and in the Pleroma, while his Spirit rejoices in it and glorifies him in whom it was, because the Father is good. And his children are perfect and worthy of his name, because he is the Father. Children of this kind are those whom he loves.

Notes

---

1. Or, "if it existed, then (it existed) because of him."

2. Or, "(so) it crushed him," or "wore him down."

3. Literally, "the name of an individual comes to be his."

4. The meaning of the Coptic word is unknown.

5. Literally, "these are not images of voices nor are they letters which do not lack a voice."

6. Plural, "them," in text.

7. "Last, final, utmost." No need to negativize the adjective to read "limitless, boundless."

8. Literally, "and cease being weary (and) seeking after the Father."

9. Literally, "some places."

10. Literally, "that of him which is hidden."

11. Literally, "done."

12. Literally, "there are no wings there at all."

13. Or, "who are without instruction." The lacuna is of such a nature that it affords both possibilities, opposites though they may be.

14. I.e., "the things which are his."

15. Literally, "the sign of that which is their sound is: this is the Father."

16. Literally, "You are the children of the understanding of the heart."

17. The Coptic word means basically "pluck, draw," but the context seems to require the verb to mean "inspire, encourage, strengthen," as one might do in stretching forth one's hand to the sick, etc.

18. We expect here not *ear* but *nose*. The transposition of several Coptic letters of the word meaning *ear*—a type of mistake common among copyists—gives us the word meaning *nostrils*.

19. The meaning of the Coptic verb is unknown.

20. Literally, "footstep."

21. Literally, "is (there)"

22. Literally, "in the presence of God, the will."

23. That is, he is the one who did not come into existence, because he has always been in existence.

24. Literally, "free of sin."

25. Perhaps *hendiadys:* "concerning his place of rest."

26. Literally, "they have."

The Gospel of Thomas

*(Gnostic)**

The *Gospel of Thomas* is a collection of traditional sayings, prophecies, proverbs, and parables of Jesus. The Coptic *Gospel of Thomas* was translated from the Greek; in fact, several fragments of this Greek version have been preserved, and can be dated to about A.D. 200. Thus the Greek (or even Syriac or Aramaic) collection was composed in the period before about A.D. 200 possibly as early as the second half of the first century, in Syria, Palestine, or Mesopotamia. The authorship of the *Gospel of Thomas* is attributed to Didymos Judas Thomas, that is, Judas "the Twin," who was identified particularly within the Syrian Church as the apostle and twin brother of Jesus.

The relationship of the *Gospel of Thomas* to the New Testament gospels has been a matter of special interest: many of the sayings of the *Gospel of Thomas* have parallels in the synoptic gospels (Matthew, Mark, and Luke). A comparison of the sayings in the *Gospel of Thomas* with their parallels in the synoptic gospels suggests that the sayings in the *Gospel of Thomas* either are present in a more primitive form or are developments of a more primitive form of such sayings. Indeed, the *Gospel of Thomas* resembles the synoptic sayings source, often called "Q" (from the German word Quelle, "source"), which was the common source of sayings used by Matthew and Luke. Hence the *Gospel of Thomas* and its sources are collections of sayings and parables which are closely related to the sources of the New Testament gospels.

The influence of Gnostic theology is clearly present in the *Gospel of Thomas*, though it is not possible to ascribe the work to any particular school or sect. The collected sayings are designated as "the secret sayings which the living Jesus spoke." Thus the collection intends to be esoteric: the key to understanding is the interpretation or secret meaning of the sayings, for "whoever finds the interpretation of these sayings will not experience death." According to the *Gospel of Thomas*, the basic religious experience is not only the recognition of one's divine

---

*Introduction by Helmut Koester.

identity, but more specifically the recognition of one's origin (the light) and destiny (the repose). In order to return to one's origin, the disciple is to become separate from the world by "stripping off" the fleshly garment and "passing by" the present corruptible existence; then the disciple can experience the new world, the kingdom of light, peace, and life.

The numeration of 114 sayings is not in the manuscript but is followed by most scholars today.

THE GOSPEL OF THOMAS*

These are the secret sayings which the living Jesus spoke and which Didymos Judas Thomas wrote down.

(1) And he said, "Whoever finds the interpretation of these sayings will not experience death."

(2) Jesus said, "Let him who seeks continue seeking until he finds. When he finds, he will become troubled. When he becomes troubled, he will be astonished, and he will rule over the All."

(3) Jesus said, "If those who lead you say to you, 'See, the Kingdom is in the sky,' then the birds of the sky will precede you. If they say to you, 'It is in the sea,' then the fish will precede you. Rather, the Kingdom is inside of you, and it is outside of you. When you come to know yourselves, then you will become known, and you will realize that it is you who are the sons of the living Father. But if you will not know yourselves, you dwell in poverty and it is you who are that poverty."

(4) Jesus said, "The man old in days will not hesitate to ask a small child seven days old about the place of life, and he will live. For many who are first will become last, and they will become one and the same."

(5) Jesus said, "Recognize what is in your sight, and that which is hidden from you will become plain to you. For

*II 32, 10–51, 28. From James M. Robinson, ed., *The Nag Hammadi Library* (San Francisco: Harper & Row, 1977), pp. 118–130.

there is nothing hidden which will not become manifest."

(6) His disciples questioned him and said to him, "Do you want us to fast? How shall we pray? Shall we give alms? What diet shall we observe?"

Jesus said, "Do not tell lies, and do not do what you hate, for all things are plain in the sight of Heaven. For nothing hidden will not become manifest, and nothing covered will remain without being uncovered."

(7) Jesus said, "Blessed is the lion which becomes man when consumed by man; and cursed is the man whom the lion consumes, and the lion becomes man."

(8) And he said, "The man is like a wise fisherman who cast his net into the sea and drew it up from the sea full of small fish. Among them the wise fisherman found a fine large fish. He threw all the small fish back into the sea and chose the large fish without difficulty. Whoever has ears to hear, let him hear."

(9) Jesus said, "Now the sower went out, took a handful of seeds, and scattered them. Some fell on the road; the birds came and gathered them up. Others fell on rock, did not take root in the soil, and did not produce ears. And others fell on thorns; they choked the seeds and worms ate them. And others fell on the good soil and produced good fruit: it bore sixty per measure and a hundred and twenty per measure."

(10) Jesus said, "I have cast fire upon the world, and see, I am guarding it until it blazes."

(11) Jesus said, "This heaven will pass

away, and the one above it will pass away. The dead are not alive, and the living will not die. In the days when you consumed what is dead, you made it what is alive. When you come to dwell in the light, what will you do? On the day when you were one you became two. But when you become two, what will you do?"

(12) The disciples said to Jesus, "We know that you will depart from us. Who is to be our leader?"

Jesus said to them, "Wherever you are, you are to go to James the righteous, for whose sake heaven and earth came into being."

(13) Jesus said to his disciples, "Compare me to someone and tell me whom I am like."

Simon Peter said to him, "You are like a righteous angel."

Matthew said to him, "You are like a wise philosopher."

Thomas said to him, "Master, my mouth is wholly incapable of saying whom you are like."

Jesus said, "I am not your master. Because you have drunk, you have become intoxicated from the bubbling spring which I have measured out."

And he took him and withdrew and told him three things. When Thomas returned to his companions, they asked him, "What did Jesus say to you?"

Thomas said to them, "If I tell you one of the things which he told me, you will pick up stones and throw them at me; a fire will come out of the stones and burn you up."

(14) Jesus said to them, "If you fast, you will give rise to sin for yourselves; and if you pray, you will be condemned; and if you give alms, you will do harm to your spirits. When you go into any land and walk about in the districts, if they receive you, eat what they will set before you, and heal the sick among them. For what goes into your mouth will not defile you, but that which issues from your mouth—it is that which will defile you."

(15) Jesus said, "When you see one who was not born of woman, prostrate yourselves on your faces and worship him. That one is your Father."

(16) Jesus said, "Men think, perhaps, that it is peace which I have come to cast upon the world. They do not know that it is dissension which I have come to cast upon the earth: fire, sword, and war. For there will be five in a house: three will be against two, and two against three, the father against the son, and the son against the father. And they will stand solitary."

(17) Jesus said, "I shall give you what no eye has seen and what no ear has heard and what no hand has touched and what has never occurred to the human mind."

(18) The disciples said to Jesus, "Tell us how our end will be."

Jesus said, "Have you discovered, then, the beginning, that you look for the end? For where the beginning is, there will the end be. Blessed is he who will take his place in the beginning; he will know the end and will not experience death."

(19) Jesus said, "Blessed is he who came into being before he came into being. If you become my disciples and listen to my words, these stones will minister to you. For there are five trees for you in Paradise which remain undisturbed summer and winter and whose leaves do not fall. Whoever becomes acquainted with them will not experience death."

(20) The disciples said to Jesus, "Tell us what the Kingdom of Heaven is like."

He said to them, "It is like a mustard seed, the smallest of all seeds. But when it falls on tilled soil, it produces a great plant and becomes a shelter for birds of the sky."

(21) Mary said to Jesus, "Whom are your disciples like?"

He said, "They are like children who have settled in a field which is not theirs. When the owners of the field come, they will say, 'Let us have back our field.'

They will undress in their presence in order to let them have back their field and to give it back to them. Therefore I say to you, if the owner of a house knows that the thief is coming, he will begin his vigil before he comes and will not let him dig through into his house of his domain to carry away his goods. You, then, be on your guard against the world. Arm yourselves with great strength lest the robbers find a way to come to you, for the difficulty which you expect will surely materialize. Let there be among you a man of understanding. When the grain ripened, he came quickly with his sickle in his hand and reaped it. Whoever has ears to hear, let him hear."

(22) Jesus saw infants being suckled. He said to his disciples, "These infants being suckled are like those who enter the Kingdom."

They said to him, "Shall we then, as children, enter the Kingdom?"

Jesus said to them, "When you make the two one, and when you make the inside like the outside and the outside like the inside, and the above like the below, and when you make the male and the female one and the same, so that the male not be male nor the female female; and when you fashion eyes in place of an eye, and a hand in place of a hand, and a foot in place of a foot, and a likeness in place of a likeness; then will you enter the Kingdom."

(23) Jesus said, "I shall choose you, one out of a thousand, and two out of ten thousand, and they shall stand as a single one."

(24) His disciples said to him, "Show us the place where you are, since it is necessary for us to seek it."

He said to them, "Whoever has ears, let him hear. There is light within a man of light, and he lights up the whole world. If he (or: it) does not shine, he is darkness."

(25) Jesus said, "Love your brother like your soul, guard him like the pupil of your eye."

(26) Jesus said, "You see the mote in your brother's eye, but you do not see the beam in your own eye. When you cast the beam out of your own eye, then you will see clearly to cast the mote from your brother's eye."

(27) Jesus said, "If you do not fast as regards the world, you will not find the Kingdom. If you do not observe the Sabbath as a Sabbath you will not see the Father."

(28) Jesus said, "I took my place in the midst of the world, and I appeared to them in flesh. I found all of them intoxicated; I found none of them thirsty. And my soul became afflicted for the sons of men, because they are blind in their hearts and do not have sight; for empty they came into the world, and empty too they seek to leave the world. But for the moment they are intoxicated. When they shake off their wine, then they will repent."

(29) Jesus said, "If the flesh came into being because of spirit, it is a wonder. But if spirit came into being because of the body, it is a wonder of wonders. Indeed, I am amazed at how this great wealth has made its home in this poverty."

(30) Jesus said, "Where there are three gods, they are gods. Where there are two or one, I am with him."

(31) Jesus said, "No prophet is accepted in his own village; no physician heals those who know him."

(32) Jesus said, "A city being built on a high mountain and fortified cannot fall, nor can it be hidden."

(33) Jesus said, "Preach from your housetops that which you will hear in your ear and in the other ear. For no one lights a lamp and puts it under a bushel, nor does he put it in a hidden place, but rather he sets it on a lampstand so that everyone who enters and leaves will see its light."

(34) Jesus said, "If a blind man leads a blind man, they will both fall into a pit."

(35) Jesus said, "It is not possible for anyone to enter the house of a strong man and take it by force unless he binds

his hands; then he will be able to ransack his house."

(36) Jesus said, "Do not be concerned from morning until evening and from evening until morning about what you will wear."

(37) His disciples said, "When will you become revealed to us and when shall we see you?"

Jesus said, "When you disrobe without being ashamed and take up your garments and place them under your feet like little children and tread on them, then will you see the Son of the Living One, and you will not be afraid."

(38) Jesus said, "Many times have you desired to hear these words which I am saying to you, and you have no one else to hear them from. There will be days when you will look for me and will not find me."

(39) Jesus said, "The Pharisees and the scribes have taken the keys of Knowledge and hidden them. They themselves have not entered, nor have they allowed to enter those who wish to. You, however, be as wise as serpents and as innocent as doves."

(40) Jesus said, "A grapevine has been planted outside of the Father, but being unsound, it will be pulled up by its roots and destroyed."

(41) Jesus said, "Whoever has something in his hand will receive more, and whoever has nothing will be deprived of even the little he has."

(42) Jesus, "Become passers-by."

(43) His disciples said to him, "Who are you, that you should say these things to us?"

Jesus said to them, "You do not realize who I am from what I say to you, but you have become like the Jews, for they either love the tree and hate its fruit (or) love the fruit and hate the tree."

(44) Jesus said, "Whoever blasphemes against the Father will be forgiven, and whoever blasphemes against the Son will be forgiven, but whoever blasphemes against the Holy Spirit will not be forgiven either on earth or in heaven."

(45) Jesus said, "Grapes are not harvested from thorns, nor are figs gathered from thistles, for they do not produce fruit. A good man brings forth good from his storehouse; an evil man brings forth evil things from his evil storehouse, which is in his heart, and says evil things. For out of the abundance of the heart he brings forth evil things."

(46) Jesus said, "Among those born of women, from Adam until John the Baptist, there is no one so superior to John the Baptist that his eyes should not be lowered before him. Yet I have said, whichever one of you comes to be a child will be acquainted with the Kingdom and will become superior to John."

(47) Jesus said, "It is impossible for a man to mount two horses or to stretch two bows. And it is impossible for a servant to serve two masters; otherwise, he will honor the one and treat the other contemptuously. No man drinks old wine and immediately desires to drink new wine. And new wine is not put into old wineskins, lest they burst; nor is old wine put into a new wineskin, lest it spoil it. An old patch is not sewn onto a new garment, because a tear would result."

(48) Jesus said, "If two make peace with each other in this one house, they will say to the mountain, 'Move away,' and it will move away."

(49) Jesus said, "Blessed are the solitary and elect, for you will find the Kingdom. For you are from it, and to it you will return."

(50) Jesus said, "If they say to you, 'Where did you come from?', say to them, 'We came from the light, the place where the light came into being on its own accord and established itself and became manifest through their image.' If they say to you, 'Is it you?', say, 'We are its children, and we are the elect of the Living Father.' If they ask you, 'What is the sign of your Father in you?', say to them, 'It is movement and repose.' "

(51) His disciples said to him, "When will the repose of the dead come about,

and when will the new world come?"

He said to them, "What you look forward to has already come, but you do not recognize it."

(52) His disciples said to him, "Twenty-four prophets spoke in Israel, and all of them spoke in you."

He said to them, "You have omitted the one living in your presence and have spoken only of the dead."

(53) His disciples said to him, "Is circumcision beneficial or not?"

He said to them, "If it were beneficial, their father would beget them already circumcised from their mother. Rather, the true circumcision in spirit has become completely profitable."

(54) Jesus said, "Blessed are the poor, for yours is the Kingdom of Heaven."

(55) Jesus said, "Whoever does not hate his father and his mother cannot become a disciple to me. And whoever does not hate his brothers and sisters and take up his cross in my way will not be worthy of me."

(56) Jesus said, "Whoever has come to understand the world has found only a corpse, and whoever has found a corpse is superior to the world."

(57) Jesus said, "The Kingdom of the Father is like a man who had good seed. His enemy came by night and sowed weeds among the good seed. The man did not allow them to pull up the weeds; he said to them, 'I am afraid that you will go intending to pull up the weeds and pull up the wheat along with them.' For on the day of the harvest the weeds will be plainly visible, and they will be pulled up and burned."

(58) Jesus said, "Blessed is the man who has suffered and found life."

(59) Jesus said, "Take heed of the Living One while you are alive, lest you die and seek to see him and be unable to do so."

(60) They saw a Samaritan carrying a lamb on his way to Judea. He said to his disciples, "Why does that man carry the lamb around?"

They said to him, "So that he may kill it and eat it."

He said to them, "While it is alive, he will not eat it, but only when he has killed it and it has become a corpse."

They said to him, "He cannot do so otherwise."

He said to them, "You too, look for a place for yourselves within Repose, lest you become a corpse and be eaten."

(61) Jesus said, "Two will rest on a bed: the one will die, and other will live."

Salome said, "Who are you, man, that you, as though from the One, (or: as whose son), that you have come up on my couch and eaten from my table?"

Jesus said to her, "I am he who exists from the Undivided. I was given some of the things of my father."

Salome said, "I am your disciple."

Jesus said to her, "Therefore I say, if he is undivided, he will be filled with light, but if he is divided, he will be filled with darkness."

(62) Jesus said, "It is to those who are worthy of my mysteries that I tell my mysteries. Do not let your left hand know what your right hand is doing."

(63) Jesus said, "There was a rich man who had much money. He said, 'I shall put my money to use so that I may sow, reap, plant, and fill my storehouse with produce, with the result that I shall lack nothing.' Such were his intentions, but that same night he died. Let him who has ears hear."

(64) Jesus said, "A man had received visitors. And when he had prepared the dinner, he sent his servant to invite the guests. He went to the first one and said to him, 'My master invites you.' He said, 'I have claims against some merchants. They are coming to me this evening. I must go and give them my orders. I ask to be excused from the dinner.' He went to another and said to him, 'My master has invited you.' He said to him, 'I have just bought a house and am required for the day. I shall not have any spare time.'

He went to another and said to him, 'My master invites you.' He said to him, 'My friend is going to get married, and I am to prepare the banquet. I shall not be able to come. I ask to be excused from the dinner.' He went to another and said to him, 'My master invites you.' He said to him, 'I have just bought a farm, and I am on my way to collect the rent. I shall not be able to come. I ask to be excused.' The servant returned and said to his master, 'Those whom you invited to the dinner have asked to be excused.' The master said to his servant, 'Go outside to the streets and bring back those whom you happen to meet, so that they may dine.' Businessmen and merchants will not enter the Places of my Father."

(65) He said, "There was a good man who owned a vineyard. He leased it to tenant farmers so that they might work it and he might collect the produce from them. He sent his servant so that the tenants might give him the produce of the vineyard. They seized his servant and beat him, all but killing him. The servant went back and told his master. The master said, 'Perhaps they did not recognize him.' He sent another servant. The tenants beat this one as well. Then the owner sent his son and said, 'Perhaps they will show respect to my son.' Because the tenants knew that it was he who was the heir to the vineyard, they seized him and killed him. Let him who has ears hear."

(66) Jesus said, "Show me the stone which the builders have rejected. That one is the cornerstone."

(67) Jesus said, "Whoever believes that the All itself is deficient is himself completely deficient."

(68) Jesus said, "Blessed are you when you are hated and persecuted. Wherever you have been persecuted they will find no Place."

(69) Jesus said, "Blessed are they who have been persecuted within themselves. It is they who have truly come to know the Father. Blessed are the hungry, for the belly of him who desires will be filled."

(70) Jesus said, "That which you have will save you if you bring it forth from yourselves. That which you do not have within you will kill you if you do not have it within you."

(71) Jesus said, "I shall destroy this house, and no one will be able to rebuild it."

(72) A man said to him, "Tell my brothers to divide my father's possessions with me."

He said to him, "O man, who has made me a divider?"

He turned to his disciples and said to them, "I am not a divider, am I?"

(73) Jesus said, "The harvest is great but the laborers are few. Beseech the Lord, therefore, to send out laborers to the harvest."

(74) He said, "O Lord, there are many around the drinking trough, but there is nothing in the cistern."

(75) Jesus said, "Many are standing at the door, but it is the solitary who will enter the bridal chamber."

(76) Jesus said, "The Kingdom of the Father is like a merchant who had a consignment of merchandise and who discovered a pearl. That merchant was shrewd. He sold the merchandise and bought the pearl alone for himself. You too, seek his unfailing and enduring treasure where no moth comes near to devour and no worm destroys."

(77) Jesus said, "It is I who am the light which is above them all. It is I who am the All. From me did the All come forth, and unto me did the All extend. Split a piece of wood, and I am there. Lift up the stone, and you will find me there."

(78) Jesus said, "Why have you come out into the desert? To see a reed shaken by the wind? And to see a man clothed in fine garments like your kings and your great men? Upon them are the fine garments, and they are unable to discern the truth."

(79) A woman from the crowd said to

him, "Blessed are the womb which bore you and the breasts which nourished you."

He said to her, "Blessed are those who have heard the word of the Father and have truly kept it. For there will be days when you will say, 'Blessed are the womb which has not conceived and the breasts which have not given milk.' "

(80) Jesus said, "He who has recognized the world has found the body, but he who has found the body is superior to the world."

(81) Jesus said, "Let him who has grown rich be king, and let him who possesses power renounce it."

(82) Jesus said, "He who is near me is near the fire, and he who is far from me is far from the Kingdom."

(83) Jesus said, "The images are manifest to man, but the light in them remains concealed in the image of the light of the Father. He will become manifest, but his image will remain concealed by his light."

(84) Jesus said, "When you see your likeness, you rejoice. But when you see your images which came into being before you, and which neither die nor become manifest, how much you will have to bear!"

(85) Jesus said, "Adam came into being from a great power and a great wealth, but he did not become worthy of you. For had he been worthy he would not have experienced death."

(86) Jesus said, "The foxes have their holes and the birds have their nests, but the Son of Man has no place to lay his head and rest."

(87) Jesus said, "Wretched is the body that is dependent upon a body, and wretched is the soul that is dependent on these two."

(88) Jesus said, "The angels and the prophets will come to you and give to you those things you already have. And you too, give them those things which you have, and say to yourselves, 'When will they come and take what is theirs?' "

(89) Jesus said, "Why do you wash the outside of the cup? Do you not realize that he who made the inside is the same one who made the outside?"

(90) Jesus said, "Come unto me, for my yoke is easy and my lordship is mild, and you will find repose for yourselves."

(91) They said to Him, "Tell us who You are so that we may believe in You."

He said to them, "You read the face of the sky and of the earth, but you have not recognized the one who is before you, and you do not know how to read this moment."

(92) Jesus said, "Seek and you will find. Yet, what you asked Me about in former times and which I did not tell you then, now I do desire to tell, but you do not inquire after it."

(93) Jesus said, "Do not give what is holy to dogs, lest they throw them on the dung-heap. Do not throw the pearls to swine, lest they grind it to bits."

(94) Jesus said, "He who seeks will find, and he who knocks will be let in."

(95) Jesus said, "If you have money, do not lend it at interest, but give it to one from whom you will not get it back."

(96) Jesus said, "The Kingdom of the Father is like a certain woman. She took a little leaven, concealed it in some dough, and made it into large loaves. Let him who has ears hear."

(97) Jesus said, "The Kingdom of the Father is like a certain woman who was carrying a jar full of meal. While she was walking on a road, still some distance from home, the handle of the jar broke and the meal emptied out behind her on the road. She did not realize it; she had noticed no accident. When she reached her house, she set the jar down and found it empty."

(98) Jesus said, "The Kingdom of the Father is like a certain man who wanted to kill a powerful man. In his own house he drew his sword and stuck it into the wall in order to find out whether his hand could carry through. Then he slew the powerful man."

(99) The disciples said to Him, "Your brothers and Your mother are standing outside."

He said to them. "Those here who do the will of My Father are My brothers and My mother. It is they who will enter the Kingdom of My Father."

(100) They showed Jesus a gold coin and said to Him, "Caesar's men demand taxes from us."

He said to them, "Give Caesar what belongs to Caesar, give God what belongs to God, and give Me what is Mine."

(101) Jesus said, "Whoever does not hate his father and his mother as I do cannot become a disciple to Me. And whoever does not love his father and his mother as I do cannot become a disciple to me. For my mother gave me falsehood, but my true mother gave me life."

(102) Jesus said, "Woe to the Pharisees, for they are like a dog sleeping in the manger of oxen, for neither does he eat nor does he let the oxen eat."

(103) Jesus said, "Fortunate is the man who knows where the brigands will enter, so that he may get up, muster his domain, and arm himself before they invade."

(104) They said to Jesus, "Come, let us pray today and let us fast." Jesus said, "What is the sin that I have committed, or wherein have I been defeated? But when the bridegroom leaves the bridal chamber, then let them fast and pray."

(105) Jesus said, "He who knows the father and the mother will be called the son of a harlot."

(106) Jesus said, "When you make the two one, you will become the sons of man, and when you say, 'Mountain, move away,' it will move away."

(107) Jesus said, "The Kingdom is like a shepherd who had a hundred sheep. One of them, the largest, went astray. He left the ninety-nine and looked for that one until he found it. When he had gone to such trouble, he said to the sheep, 'I care for you more than the ninety-nine.' "

(108) Jesus said, "He who will drink from my mouth will become like me. I myself shall become he, and the things that are hidden will be revealed to him."

(109) Jesus said, "The Kingdom is like a man who had a hidden treasure in his field without knowing it. And after he died, he left it to his son. The son did not know about the treasure. He inherited the field and sold it. And the one who bought it went plowing and found the treasure. He began to lend money at interest to whomever he wished."

(110) Jesus said, "Whoever finds the world and becomes rich, let him renounce the world."

(111) Jesus said, "The heavens and the earth will be rolled up in your presence. And the one who lives from the Living One will not see death." Does not Jesus say, "Whoever finds himself is superior to the world?"

(112) Jesus said, "Woe to the flesh that depends on the soul; woe to the soul that depends on the flesh."

(113) His disciples said to him, "When will the Kingdom come?"

Jesus said, "It will not come by waiting for it. It will not be a matter of saying 'Here it is' or 'There it is.' Rather, the Kingdom of the Father is spread out upon the earth, and men do not see it."

(114) Simon Peter said to them, "Let Mary leave us, for women are not worthy of Life."

Jesus said, "I myself shall lead her in order to make her male, so that she too may become a living spirit resembling you males. For every woman who will make herself male will enter the Kingdom of Heaven."

The Hymn of the Pearl

(Gnostic)

"The Hymn of the Pearl" is a fabulous narrative poem concerning the adventurous quest for a pearl. Although the tale was probably pre-Gnostic and pre-Christian, in its present form it has been furnished with details that clearly make it Manichaean and, as Günther Bornkamm argues, the young prince and savior is depicted as Mani himself, the founder of Manichaeism.[1] It is a beautiful poem, one of the most attractive documents in Gnostic literature.

On the surface the poem is simply an adventure. But everywhere in it are clues of other meanings. After all, serpents who sleep with pearls in their possession cannot but have an allegorical dimension. "The Hymn of the Pearl" would be impoverished were one not to decode its symbols, which seem to be determined by their usage in earlier Mandaean traditional tales as well as in such Gnostic works as the *Pistis Sophia*. By consensus of most scholars, the main figures—the Father, Mother, and Prince—form a Gnostic trinity, equivalent to the Christian trinitarian formula. They represent the Father of Truth, the Mother of Wisdom, and the Son. The Son, who is redeemer and savior, is not Christ, however, or at least not primarily Christ. Hans Jonas identifies him with the Manichaean pre-cosmic Primal Man. Curiously, he has a double or twin role, for he appears to be both savior and the soul which he saves; he saves and must himself be saved. So too the Pearl, which at first appears to be a symbol of the soul, is also the deity who saves the soul. So, as Jonas points out "the interchangeability of the subject and object of the mission, of savior and soul, of Prince and Pearl, is the key to the true meaning of the poem, and to the gnostic eschatology in general."[2] Other symbols in the poem are more obvious, although the notion of the double, so typically Gnostic, continues. The Prince's garment of glory, which he has taken off in order to assume the unclean robe of the world—obviously the unclean human body—represents his heavenly glory, which he has left behind, yet this garment of glory also operates as an independent being. So too the letter, on which is written the call of redemption, flies down as an eagle from heaven and becomes a messenger of light. As for Egypt, it stands traditionally for the body, for material things, for darkness and error. It is the kingdom of death. Likewise, the serpent is the realm of darkness and ignorance. For the Gnostics, who tend to reverse Judeo-Christian values, ignorance is equivalent to Judeo-Christian sin and evil; *gnosis* (brought about through eating the apple from the Tree of Gnosis, and which Christians speak of as original sin) is good and brings redemption. Thus the food that the Prince carries with him is his *gnosis*, which the soul needs to find itself and return to its heavenly journey. The Father and Mother's home in the east is, of course, Heaven.

As in many Gnostic tales, the woman has an equal or important role in the divine strategy. In key roles such as the creator of Adam's soul, she is not reduced to the non-deity role of mother and housewife as in the family of Jesus or troublemaker during Adam's sojourn in Eden. In "The Hymn of the Pearl" reference is not simply to the "Father," but to the "parents." The Mother is called " The Mistress of the East," that is, the "Mistress of Heaven."

"The Hymn of the Pearl," sometimes called "The Hymn of the Soul," is a fable of redemption. Unlike the traditional Christian myth, here the savior himself must be saved. For a while he forgets who he is and falls into the sleep of earthly things. But the Father of Truth and the Mother of Wisdom (Mother Sophia) do not forget him, and send messages. He wakes from the prison of earthly things, steals the pearl, and returns to his true parents.

The hymn exists in an early Syriac text and a somewhat later Greek version. It is attached to the Apocryphal *Acts of Thomas*, which deal with the deeds of the Apostle Judas Thomas.

Notes

1. Günther Bornkamm, ed., R. McL. Wilson, trans., *The Acts of Thomas*, in Edgar Hennecke and Wilhelm Schneemelcher, eds., *New Testament Apocrypha*, vol. 2 (Philadelphia: Westminster Press, 1965), pp. 434–435.

2. Hans Jonas, *The Gnostic Religion*, 2d ed., rev. (1958; reprint, Boston: Beacon Press, 1963), p. 127.

THE HYMN OF THE PEARL*

When I was a little child
living in my kingdom, in my father's house
happy in the glories and riches
of my family that nurtured me,
my parents gave me provisions

---

*Version by Willis Barnstone, derived from earlier translations. Reliable translations appear in Edgar Hennecke and Wilhelm Schneemelcher, eds., *New Testament Apocrypha*, vol. 2 (Philadelphia: Westminster Press, 1965), pp. 498–504; and in Robert M. Grant, *Gnosticism* (New York: Harper & Brothers, 1961), pp. 116–122.

and sent me forth from our home in the east.
From their treasure house
they made up a bundle for me.
It was big though light
so I might carry it alone,
and it held gold from the House of the Highest Ones
and silver of Gazzak the Great
and rubies of India
and opals from the land of Kushan,
and they girded me with adamant
which can crush iron.
And they took off my bright robe of glory,
which they had made for me out of love,
and took away my purple toga,
which was woven to fit my stature.
They made a covenant with me
and wrote it in my heart so I would not forget:
"When you go down into Egypt
and bring back the One Pearl
which lies in the middle of the sea
and is guarded by the snorting serpent,
you will again put on your robe of glory
and your toga over it,
and with your brother, our next in rank,
you will be heir in our kingdom."
I left the east and went down
with my two royal envoys,
since the way was dangerous and harsh
and I was very young to walk alone.
I crossed the borders of Maishan,
the gathering place of merchants of the east,
and came into the land of Babel
and entered the walls of Sarbug.
I went down into Egypt
and my companions left me.
I went straight to the serpent
and settled in close by his inn,
waiting for him to sleep
so I could take my pearl from him.
Since I was all alone
I was a stranger to others in the inn,
Yet I saw one of my own people there,
a nobleman from the east,
young, handsome, lovable,
a son of kings—an anointed one,
and he came and was close to me.
And I made him my confidante
with whom I shared my mission.
I warned him against the Egyptians
and of contact with the unclean ones.
Then I put on a robe like theirs

lest they suspect me as an outsider
who had come to steal the pearl;
lest they arouse the serpent against me.
But somehow they learned
I was not their countryman,
and they dealt with me cunningly
and gave me their food to eat.
I forgot that I was a son of kings,
and served their king.
I forgot the pearl
for which my parents had sent me.
Through the heaviness of their food
I fell into a deep sleep.
But when all these things happened
my parents knew and grieved for me.
It was proclaimed in our kingdom
that all should come to our gate.
And the kings and princes of Parthia
and all the nobles of the east
wove a plan on my behalf
so I would not be left in Egypt.
And they wrote me a letter
and every noble signed it with his name.
"From your father, the King of Kings,
and your mother, the Mistress of the East,
and from your brother, our next in rank,
to you, our son in Egypt, greetings:
Awake and rise from your sleep
and hear the words of our letter!
Remember that you are a son of Kings
and see the slavery of your life.
Remember the pearl
for which you went into Egypt!
Remember your robe of glory
and your splendid mantle
which you may wear
when your name is named in the book of life,
is read in the book of heroes,
when you and your brother inherit
our kingdom."
And serving as messenger
the letter was a letter
sealed by the king with his right hand
against the evil ones, the children of Babel
and the savage demons of Sarbug.
It rose up in the form of an eagle,
the king of all winged fowl;
it flew and alighted beside me,
and became speech.
At its voice and the sound of its rustling
I awoke and rose from my sleep.

I took it, kissed it,
broke its seal and read.
And the words written on my heart
were in the letter for me to read.
I remembered that I was a son of Kings
and my free soul longed for its own kind.
I remembered the pearl
for which I was sent down into Egypt,
and I began to enchant
the terrible and snorting serpent.
I charmed him into sleep
by naming the name of my Father over him,
and the name of the next in rank,
and of my Mother, the queen of the east.
I seized the pearl
and turned to carry it to my Father.
Their filthy and impure garment
I stripped off, leaving it in the fields,
and directed my way
into the light of our homeland, the east.
On my way the letter that awakened me
was lying on the road.
And as it had awakened me with its voice
so it guided me with its light;
it was written on Chinese silk,
and shone before me in its own form.
Its voice soothed my fear
and its love urged me on.
I hurried past Sarbug,
and Babel on the left,
and came to Maishan,
the haven of merchants,
perched next to the sea.
My robe of glory which I had taken off
and the toga over it
were sent by my parents
from the heights of Hyrcania.
They were in the hands of treasurers
to whom they were committed
because of their faith,
and I had forgotten the robe's splendor
for as a child I had left it
in my Father's house.
As I gazed on it
suddenly the garment seemed to be a mirror
of myself. I saw it in my whole self,
and in it I saw myself apart,
for we were two entities
yet one form.
The treasurers brought me one robe:
they were two of the same shape

with one kingly seal.
They gave me wealth,
and the bright embroidered robe
was colored with gold and beryls,
with rubies and opals,
and sardonyxes of many colors
were fastened to it in its high home.
All its seams were fastened
with stones of adamant;
and the image of the King of Kings
was embroidered on it,
and it glowed with sapphires
of many colors.
I saw it quiver all over
with the movements of *gnosis,*
and as it prepared to speak
it moved toward me,
murmuring the sound of its songs
as it descended:
"I am the one who acted for him
for whom I was brought up in my Father's house.
I saw myself growing in stature
according to his labors."
With regal movements
it was spreading toward me,
urging me to take it,
and love urged me
to receive it,
and I stretched forth and received it
and put on the beauty of its colors.
I cast my toga of brilliant colors
all around me.
Therein I clothed myself and ascended
to the Gate of Salutation and Adoration.
I bowed my head and adored
the majesty of my Father who had sent it to me.
I had fulfilled his commandments
and he had fulfilled what he promised,
and at the gate of his princes
I mingled with his nobles.
He rejoiced in me and received me
and I was with him in his kingdom,
and all his servants praised him
with resounding voices.
He promised me that I would journey quickly
with him to the Gate of the King of Kings,
and with my gifts and my pearl
I would appear with him before our King.

Manichaean Hymn-Cycles

(Gnostic)*

In the community life of the Manichaeans,** hymns played an outstanding part. Through the beauty in art and poetry, skillfully depicted by their painters and poets, the mind was turned to the wonderful
destination of the redeemed. It is quite understandable, therefore, that
the bulk of Middle Persian and Parthian texts are hymns, many of
which are "cantillated," made usable for chanting. Formally they can
be divided into three categories: the long hymn-cycles; the long but
undivided chants of praise (Middle Persian *afurishn*, Parthian *afrivan*);
and the short hymns (Middle Persian *mahr*, Parthian *bashah*). The
manuscript M 1 II from the eighth century is an index with the opening lines of hymns, of which a considerable number has been preserved elsewhere:

> "We will bless and praise" (340)
> "May we find mercy from you" (347)
> "Show mercy to me, Great God" (352)
> May there be well-being, peace and happiness" (378)
> "The blessed day of joy has come" (382)
> "We will bless you, Light Self" (415)
> "Come, brothers, let us sing" (425)

In the extant Manichaean literature the long hymn-cycle is represented by two Middle Persian texts, *The Speech of the Living Self (Govishn
ig griv zindag)* and *The Speech of the Light Self (Govishn ig griv roshn)*, and
by two Parthian texts, *Fortunate for Us (Huvidagman)* and *Rich (Friend) of
the Beings of Light (Angad Roshnan (Friyanag)*, attributed to Ammo, the

---

*Introduction by Jes P. Asmussen.
*For further information see Section 1,
Manichaean Creation Myths (Gnostic).

314

great missionary of the east. Fragments of a Sogdian translation of the Middle Persian as well as the Parthian texts are known, and a fragment of an Uighur Turkish translation of the *Huvidagman* has been published by W. B. Henning.

The Middle Persian cycles are devoted to the Living Self, the divine Light in the prison of matter, Augustine's Jesus *patibilis*, as holy as the sacred fire and water of the Zoroastrians. It suffers, being treated in many different ways, like a slave, like a lord, like a friend, like an enemy, etc. In this situation sin loiters everywhere, but by the help of the world of Light it is washed away, when the redeeming knowledge comes.

The Parthian texts tell about a soul in distress, surrounded by dangers from all sides, its fervent longing for salvation, the coming of the Savior and hence the promise of being able to begin the journey to the new Paradise, the dwelling of the rescued souls until their return to the Eternal Paradise (the Real Paradise in a Sogdian text) at the final victory of Light. The *Huvidagman* in addition has an opening canto describing paradise and a canto entitled "The Punishment of Sinners." It is difficult, from the material at hand, to determine the liturgical use of these texts, but [they] probably have to do with a death-mass of some kind.

FROM THE GOVISHN IG GRIV ZINDAG*

1

a

You buy me like slaves from thieves,
and you fear and implore me as you do lords.
Like disciples from the world you elect me to be among the righteous,
and you show me reverence as you do masters.
You smite and hurt me like enemies,
and you save and vivify me like friends.
However, my Fathers, the Light Gods, have power and might
to offer you thanks in many ways
And as a reward for one day of fasting,
to give you the eternal happiness.
And in order to send you the share that through me is yours
they will send the Gods before you.
And also the share in toil and worry
that you bear and suffer for my sake.

---

*Both selections in this chapter are from Jes P. Asmussen, *Manichaean Literature* (Delmar, New York: Scholars Facsimiles & Reprints, 1975), pp.81–86, 88–97.

b

I am the Fire which Zarathustra built up,
and he bade the righteous build me up.
Build me up . . . do not make!
From the seven consecrated, sweet-smelling fires
bring me, the Fire, purified fuel.
Bring forth clean firewood,
and delicate and fragrant incense.
Kindle me with knowledge,
and give me clean offering!
I am the Water which is fit
that you should give me "the offering to the water" that I may become strong.

2

And my body he, Jesus, the savior shall cure from pain,
and from being despised he shall make me adorable.
And he shall wash me clean from the dirt and the heavy sinfulness,
and he shall bath me and lighten me.
And he is my great intermediator
and my protection and my true refuge.
He is the one who guides me away from all sins
and who frees me.
He is the one who saves me from trouble.

3

And he shall wash my soul with a laving from the land,
And he shall raise me on wings
upwards to dwellings.
And shall set me in the treasure-house of the Father,
where no thieves shall loiter.

FROM THE PARTHIAN
HYMN-CYCLES

Huvidagman

Canto I

It was fortunate for us that through you we knew and accepted your teaching.
Beneficent Sovereign, show mercy to us.
The Envoy of the Father heals souls,
gives joy to all, and removes sorrows.

Lofty and limitless, where darkness never comes,
all the monasteries and the dwelling places are magnificent,
for they are happy in the light and know no pain.
All who enter there stay for eternity.
Neither blows nor torture ever overcome them.
The clothes which they wear none has made by hand.
They are ever clean and bright, and no ants are in them.
Their verdant garlands never fade,
and they are wreathed brightly, in numberless colors.
Heaviness and drooping do not exist in their bodies,
and paralysis does not affect any of their limbs.
Heavy sleep never overtakes their souls,
and deceptive dreams and delusions are unknown among them.
Hunger and anguish are not known in that land.
There is no thirst.
The waters of all its lakes give out a wondrous
fragrance. Floods and drowning are never known among them.
Their walk is quicker by far than lightning.
In the bodies they possess, there is no sickness.
The activities of all dark powers are not in them, nor attacks and conflicts.
Fear and terror do not exist in those places,
and in those lands there is no destruction.
The trees do not shake down
all the fruits.
Decay does not exist in their fruit.
Within and without, it is all full of brightness.
All the gardens give out fragrance.
Bricks and thorns are never found among them.
Each who ascends up to their land, and who has the knowledge,
will praise his manifestation, lauded and beneficent.
None who is among them (?) has a dark shadow.
All the bodies and appearances upon that land are radiant.
Precious are they, with forms that are free from injury.
And feebleness and age do not affect their limbs.
They are joyous, uttering wonderful praises.
They continually do reverence to the Exalted and Beneficent one.
All is filled with happiness and sweet delightful song—
all the monasteries.
The monasteries are all splendid, and fear is unknown there.
Barking of dogs, calls of birds, confusing and troublesome
evil howling—they are not heard in that land.
From any darkness and fog . . . there is nothing within
the pure abodes.
Full of Light is their living self; ever in gladness
and purity loving each other, they are very beautiful.
No Living Self dies among them.

Canto VI a

Who will release me from all the pits and prisons,
in which are gathered lusts that are not pleasing?
Who will take me over the flood of the tossing sea—
the zone of conflict in which there is no rest?
Who will save me from the jaws of all the beasts
who destroy and terrify one another without pity?
Who will lead me beyond the walls and take me over the moats,
which are full of fear and trembling from ravaging demons?
Who will lead me beyond rebirths, and free me from them all—
and from all the waves, in which there is no rest?
I weep for my soul, saying: May I be saved from this,
and from the terror of the beasts who devour one another!
The bodies of men, and of birds of the air,
of fish of the sea, and four-footed creatures and of all insects—
who will take me beyond these and save me from them all,
so that I shall not turn and fall into the perdition of those hells
so that I shall not pass through defilement in them, nor return in rebirth,
wherein all the kinds of plants are taken out.
Who will save me from the swallowing height and
the devouring deeps, which are all hell and distress?

Canto IV b

These will collapse upon the whole structure,
and all the dark powers will perish in agony and perdition.
And wretchedness will overtake all its inhabitants
and perdition of Hell in which there is no mercy.
Who will save me from these and take me beyond them all,
so that I shall not be devoured in the distress of those Hell-deeps?

Canto V

Or who will save me from the pit of destruction,
and from the dark valley where all is harshness?
—where all is anguish and the stab of death.
And helper and friend is there none therein.
Never to eternity is there safety there.
It is all full of darkness and fume-filled fog.
It is all full of wrath and there is no pity there.
All who enter are pierced by wounds.
It is waterless through drought, and hardened by hot winds.
No golden drop of water is ever found there.
Who will save me from this, and from all stabs,
and take me afar from all distress of Hell?
They are struck by merciless blows in the deep.
There is no health for all their sickness.
Not all the lusts and the comfort of wealth

will help them in that hellish place.
Not all their idols, altars, and images
can save them from that Hell.
They shall not find there a pious messenger,
who shall come for them and open the gate of Hell.
Who will take me far from it, that I may not plunge into them;
that I may not tumble and fall into every bitter Hell.

Canto V c

Their fragrant garlands are sacred and immortal;
their bodies are full of living pure drops.
All with one mind praise one another; they bless one another
with living blessings, and become blessed for evermore.
In my mind I remembered; and I wept aloud in misery, saying:
Who will save me from every terror and fear?
Who will take me up to that happy realm,
so that joy shall be mine in union with all its inhabitants?

Canto VI

And while I thus wept and shed tears upon the ground,
I heard the voice of the beneficent King.

Canto VI a

I shall save you from . . .
the rebellious powers who have frightened you with fear.
I shall release you from all deceit and turbulence and the torment of death.
I will make an end of the activity of all forces of destruction,
and all sickness which has dismayed you with death.

Canto VI b

I shall free you from the hands of the guardians of Hell,
who show no mercy to spirit and soul.

Canto VI c

I shall take you eagerly and soar up upon wings,
high over all the dark powers and rebellious princes.
I shall lead you into the primeval calm of that land, the new Paradise
and I shall show you the Fathers, my own divine entity.
You shall rejoice in gladness, in blissful praises,
and you shall be without grief, forgetful of wretchedness.
You shall put on a radiant garment, and gird on light;
and I shall set on your head the diadem of sovereignty.

By a spiritual invocation there was built on that structure the fortress,
high and vast, of the noble Emperor.
A palace is the dominion of the primeval first-born
for in it, the first man, he clothes himself in gladness and binds on the diadem of
    sovereignty.
Upon all his friends he binds the diadem
and clothes their bodies in the garment of gladness.
And all the believers and the pious elect
he clothes in praise, and binds on them the diadem.
They reign now in gladness, even as once they had been fettered for their mere
    name,
and had undergone anguish at the hands of their foes.
The return from the depth was obtained out of the victory;
for the enemies are subdued, and the height lies in front!
That is the day when he will reveal his form,
the beneficent Father, the Lord of the Aeons of Light.
He will show his radiant shape and brilliant, glorious form
to all the Gods who shall dwell there.

Angad Roshnan

I The Ship of God

Rich friend of the beings of light! In mercy
grant me strength and succor me with every gift!
Array my soul, O Lord! respond to me!
Succor me in the midst of the foe!
Make pass from me all the ravages
of their deceitful body that tortures me with pain.
You are the friend, praised and beneficent!
Free me.
My soul weeps within,
and cries out at each distress and stab.
And the hour of life, and this carrion-form
is ended for me, with its turbulent days.
It was tossed and troubled as a sea with waves.
Pain was heaped on pain, whereby they ravage my soul.
On all sides the anguish reached me;
fire was kindled, and the fog was full of smoke.
The wellsprings of darkness had all been opened.
The giant fishes transfixed me with fear.
My soul was dismayed at the sight of their forms,
for they became apparent in their dreadfulness;
for all were hideous and dreadful to behold.
And the human form is not found among their bodies.
All the demons, the banished princes,
transfixed me with fear, and dismayed me with anguish.
Their fury gathered like a sea of fire.
The seething waves rose up that they might engulf me.
For in every region gathered stormy winds
and rain and the fume of all fogs,

lightning and thunder and banked clouds of hail,
the crash and roar of all the waves of the sea.
The skiff rises up, lifted on the crest of the wave,
and glides down into the trough, to be hidden within.
All the clamps become loosened, . . .
the iron rivets are plucked out. . . .
Each yard is dipped by these drownings.
And the masts are flung together in the turmoil.
The rudders had dropped off into the sea.
Fear grips those on board.
The helmsmen and all the pilots
weep bitterly and lament aloud.

I a

Through continual redemptions
every hand, link, and shutter of the prison becomes weakened.
All the comets quivered, and the stars were whirled about,
and each of the planets turned awry its course.
The earth shook, my foundation beneath,
and the height of the heavens sank down above.
All the rivers, the veins of my body, dried up at their source.
All my limbs have connection no longer.
When again they were broken, they reflected on existence.
The reckoning of my days and months is ended.
Harm befell the course of the zodiac's wheel.
The seal of my feet and the joints of my toes—
each link of the life of my soul was loosed.
Each joint of my hands and of my fingers—
each was loosed and its seal taken off.
All the gristly parts—their life grew feeble.
And cold became each one of my limbs.
My knees were fettered through fear,
and strength was drawn out of each leg.

I b

And when I saw the dark, the strength of my limbs collapsed;
and my soul moaned at all its forms.

III a

Who shall save me
and make for me a path?
Who shall make straight for me
by that path?

III b

Who shall free me from . . .
from every blazing fire and the distress of destruction?

III c

Who shall shed this body from me
and clothe me in a new body . . .?

VI

When I had said these words, with soul a-tremble,
I beheld the Savior as he shone before me.
I beheld the sight of all the helmsmen,
who had descended with him to array my soul.
I lifted up my eyes toward that direction,
and saw all deaths were hidden by the envoy.
All ravages had become remote from me,
and grievous sickness, and the anguish of their distress.
The sight of them was hidden, their darkness had fled away.
And all was divine nature, without peer.
There shone forth light, elating and lovely
and full of gladness, pervading all my mind.
In joy unbounded he spoke with me,
raising up my soul from deep affliction.
To me he says, Come, spirit! fear not.
I am your mind, your glad tidings of hope.
And you are the garment of my body,
which brought dismay to the powers of darkness.
I am your light, radiant, primeval,
your great mind and complete hope.
You are my word, and my panoply of war,
which saved me fully from the fight, and from all sinners.
From each dungeon shall I release you,
bearing you afar from all wounds and afflictions.
I shall lead you forth from this torture where
You shall no more fear each encounter.
Beloved! beauty of my bright nature!
From these shall I lead you forth, and from all prisons.
I shall save you from all perdition,
and free you forever from all wounds.
And all the filth and corrosion that you have passed through,
I shall cleanse from you through perfect light.
And the deep of the sea wherein you have gone through these drownings,
I shall deliver you from that and from all the waves.
I shall set you free from every sickness,
and from every distress at which you have wept.
I shall not wish to leave you longer in the hands of the Sinner;
for you are my own, in truth, forever.

You are the buried treasure, the chief of my wealth,
and the pearl which is the beauty of all the gods.
And I am the righteousness sown in your limbs,
and in the stature of your soul—the gladness of your mind.
And you are my beloved, the love in my limbs;
and the heroic mind, the essence of my limbs.
And I am the light of your whole structure,
your soul above and base of life.
And from the holiness of my limbs did you descend in the beginning
into the dark places, and did become their light.
And from you a diadem was bound on all our foes.
And it became apparent and held sway during the hours of tyranny.
And for your sake was there battle and tremor
in all the heavens and the bridges of the earths.
And for your sake all the dark powers ran and sped.
And for your sake the Princes and all the dark powers were bound.
For your sake the apostles shone forth
to reveal the Light above, and uncover the root of darkness.
And for your sake the gods went forth and became apparent,
and they struck down death, and darkness they slew.
And you are the exalted trophy
and the sign of light that puts darkness to flight.
And I am come forth to save you from the Sinner,
to make you whole from pain, and to bring gladness to your heart.
And all you have desired of me I shall bestow upon you,
and I shall make new your place within the lofty Kingdom.
And I shall open before you the gates in all the heavens,
and shall make smooth your path, free from terror and vexation.
And I shall take you with might, and enfold you with love,
and lead you to your home, the blessed abode.
And forever shall I show you the noble Father (the First Man);
and I shall lead you in, into his presence, in pure raiment.
And I shall show to you the mother of the beings of light.
And forever shall you rejoice in lauded happiness.
And I shall reveal to you the holy brethren,
who are filled with happiness.
And forever shall you dwell joyful among them all,
beside all the jewels and the venerable gods.
And fear and death shall never overtake you more,
nor ravage, distress and wretchedness.
And rest shall be yours in the place of salvation,
in the company of all the gods and those who dwell in quietness.

VII

Come, spirit, fear no more!
Death has fallen, and sickness fled away.
And the term of troubled days is ended,
and its terror departed amid clouds of fire.
Come, spirit, step forth!

Let there be no desire for the house of affliction,
which is wholly destruction and the anguish of death.
Truly you were cast out from your native abode.
And all the pangs you have suffered in Hell
you have undergone for this, in the outset and beginning.
Come yet nearer, in gladness without regret;
and lie not content in the dwelling of death.
Turn not back, nor regard the shapes of the bodies,
which lie there in wretchedness, they and their fellows.
And see, they return through every rebirth,
and through every agony and every choking prison.
And see, they are reborn among all kinds of creatures,
and their voice is heard in burning sighs.
Come yet nearer, and be not fond of
this beauty that perishes in all its varieties.
And it falls and melts as snow in sunshine.
And there is no abiding for any fair form.
It withers and fades as a broken rose
that wilts in the sun, its grace destroyed.
Yet come, you spirit, and be not fond
of the sum of hours and the fleeting days.
Do not turn back for every outward show, for
desire is death, and leads to destruction.
Hence, spirit, come! . . .
I shall lead you to the height, to your native abode.
Remember, O spirit! look on the anguish
that you have borne through the fury of all your ravagers.
And regard the world and the prison of creation;
for all desires will be swiftly destroyed.
Terror, fire and ruin will overtake
all those who dwell therein.
The height will be shattered with all its dwellings;
all the heavens will fall down into the deep.
And the trap of destruction will swiftly close
upon those deceivers who brag therein.
And the whole dominion, with the brilliance of all the
stars—ruin will come upon them, and the pang of their indignity.
All the princes and the border rebels will suffer
forever in wretchedness within the blazing fire.
The whole of life, from every seed and stem,
will swiftly be wrecked and brought to perdition.
The parts of the dead souls will be fettered
in the tomb of death where all is blackness.

VIII

My soul is saved from all the sins
which day by day oppressed me, inflicting anguish.
And the dark, hot distress is taken from me
which at the outset, in the beginning, made me captive.

I am clothed with a garment of light . . .
and I am passed beyond the pain and anguish of bodies.
And I am arrayed and succored by the savior of my spirit,
through the power, which was never constricted.
Those who are homomorphic with the demons will pass
again through all the prisons and the cycle of death.
And I saw that the abandoned body became dark, shedding no light;
hideous in appearance and overpowering in form.
The savior said to me: Spirit! behold the husk
you have abandoned in the deep in terror and destruction.
Truly for you it was a deceptive partner,
a distressful prison in every hell.
And truly for you it was an unruly death,
which severed your soul from life forever.
And truly for you it was a path of stumbling
which was wholly deeds of dread, and much sickness.

The Coptic Psalm-Book

(Manichaean Gnostic)[*]

The *Manichean Psalm-Book* in Coptic, from which we take the following fragments, belongs to the Manichean Papyrus Codices discovered in 1930 by the theologian and archaeologist Carl Schmidt, in a second-hand booksellers in Egypt.

The manuscripts, found by natives in Medinet Madì in southwest Fayum, are composed in the Subachmimic dialect of Coptic, and comprise translations of unknown Greek originals, which probably derive from Syriac models.

In general it may be said that the composition of the Coptic texts can probably be dated to the second half of the fourth century, while those of the *Psalm-Book* are probably somewhat earlier. The very badly preserved find, which consisted of seven Codices and the remnants of two Codices (some 3500 pages in all), was apportioned—apart from a few fragments—between the collector Sir A. Chester Beatty, London, and the State Museums in Berlin.

The *Manichean Psalm-Book*, of which only the second part is available in published form, is from the Chester Beatty Collection. The edition was prepared for publication by Charles R. C. Allberry (*A Manichaean Psalm-Book*, Part II, Stuttgart 1938). As regards the versification of the Psalms, comparison should be made with T. Säve-Söderbergh, *Studies in the Coptic Manichaean Psalm-Book, Prosody and Mandaean Parallels*, Uppsala 1949.

The Psalter contains a fairly large number of different meters. In only a few of the psalms has it not been possible so far to indicate a meter (cf. T. Säve-Söderbergh, op. cit. 41), for example Psalm 223, a translation of which is given below. Most psalms (apart from the twenty Thomas Psalms) end with a doxology, in which Egyptian Manichaean martyrs are mentioned, and which is therefore clearly an appendage of local origin. The refrain, which in the original is frequently not written

---

[*]Introduction by Robert Haardt.

out in full, for reasons of space, is completed in the translation where appropriate, no indications being given.

In contrast to Manichaeism, which represents that form of the Gnostic religion which—even by the intent of its founder—attained the highest degree of systematization in its thought, the extensive Mandaean literature contains a considerable number of traditions which have not been reconciled, often overlap, and even at times contradict each other. For this reason and for the purpose of this anthology, it has been sufficient in the matter of selection to consider but a few of the most representative threads of tradition.

The translations used have been taken from the two publications of M. Lidzbarski, *Ginza, The Treasure or the Great Book of the Mandaeans*, Göttingen-Leipzig 1925, and the *Book of John of the Mandaeans*, Part II, Giessen 1915.

For further information on the Mandaeans, see Section 1, "Creation of the World and the Alien Man" (Mandaean).

LET US WORSHIP THE SPIRIT OF THE PARACLETE*

Psalm 223 (Allberry 9–11)[1]

Let us worship the Spirit of the Paraclete:[2]
Let us bless our Lord Jesus
who has sent to us the Spirit of Truth.
He came and separated us from the Error of the World.
He brought us a mirror.
We looked into it, and saw in it the Universe.

When the Holy Spirit came, he revealed to us
the way of truth and taught us that there are two Natures,
that of the Light and that of the Darkness,
separated from each other since the beginning.

The Kingdom of Light consisted of five Greatnesses,
these are the Father and his twelve Aeons
and the Aeons of the Aeons, the Living Air,
the Land of Light; the Great Spirit blows in them
and feeds them with its Light.

The Kingdom of Darkness, however, consists of five Chambers,
these are Smoke, Fire,
Wind and Water and Darkness.
Their resolution crawls in them, moves them
and spurs them on to make war with one another.

---

*Both selections in this chapter are from Robert Haardt, *Gnosis* (Leiden: Brill, 1971), pp. 81–86, 88–97.

Now as they were warring with each other, they made bold
to attack the Land of Light, considering themselves capable
of conquering it. Yet they know not that what
they thought will recoil upon their own heads.

But there was a host of angels in the Land of Light
which possessed the power to issue forth and overcome
the enemy of the Father, whom it pleased that through the Word
that he would send, he should subdue the rebels
who desired to raise themselves above what was more exalted than they.

Like a shepherd who sees a lion approaching
to destroy his sheepfold, he uses guile,
takes a lamb and sets it as a snare that he may catch it with it,
for with a single lamb he saves his sheepfold.
Afterward he heals the lamb that has been wounded by the lion.

In this way too the Father acted, who sent out his stout Son.
He produced out of himself his Maiden,
furnished with the five Powers that she might fight
against the five Abysses of the Dark.

When the Watchman[3] stood fast within the frontiers of Light
he showed the Powers of Darkness his Maiden,
who is his Soul.
They became agitated in their abyss
and wanted to possess her,
they opened their mouths and tried to swallow her.

He seized the Maiden's power
and spread it over the Powers of Darkness,
like nets over fish, he rained her down on them
like purified clouds of water, she penetrated into them
like a piercing lightning stroke.
She crept into their insides and bound them all
without their ever knowing.

When the First Man had ended his struggle
the Father sent his second Son.
He came and helped his brother out of the Abyss.
He built this whole World up out of the mixture
that had come into existence out of Light and Darkness.

All the Powers of the Abyss he spread out to ten Heavens
and to eight Earths, he shut them up into this World
and made it a dungeon for all the Powers of Darkness.
The World is also, however, a place of purification for the soul
which had been swallowed up[4] in the Powers of Darkness.

The Sun and the Moon were set up
and fixed in the heights, to purify the Soul.
They take the refined part daily upward to the heights
but they destroy the deposit.
They convey it up and down.

This whole World stands firm for a Season, since
there is a great Building being erected outside of the World.
At the Hour when that Architect shall complete it,
the entire World shall be dissolved.
It shall be set afire, that fire may melt it away.

All Life, the Remnants of Light in every Place
he shall gather to himself and form[5] of it a Statue.
Even the Resolution of Death also, the whole of the Darkness,
he shall gather in and make an image of itself
along with the Archon.[6]

In a moment the Living Spirit shall come.
[Lacuna] It will succour the Light,
but the Resolution of Death and the Darkness
it shall lock away in the chamber
that was built for it
that it may lie in chains in it forever.

There is no other means save this means to bind the Enemy,
for he shall not be received into the Light
because he is a stranger to it, but he shall also not
be left in his Land of Darkness,
lest he may wage a greater war than the first.

A new Aeon shall be built in place of this World,
which shall be dissolved,
so that in it the Powers of Light may reign
since they have performed and fulfilled the whole of the Father's will.
They have overthrown the hateful one, they have defeated[7] him forever.

This is the Knowledge of Mani,
let us worship him and bless him.
Blessed is every man that shall trust in him
for he shall live with all of the Righteous.

Honor and Victory to our Lord Mani, the Spirit of Truth,
that cometh from the Father and has revealed to us
the Beginning, the Middle, and the End.
Victory to the Soul of the Blessed Mary. Theona, Pshai, Jemnoute.

JOY CAME OVER ME

Joy came over me
and no one will ever be able to tell of it.
  My brethren, I have received my garland.
Take unto you the word of Truth
  O men who love God!
The world is nothing.
There is nothing to be gained in it.
  My brethren, I have received my garland.

Men go on thinking
that they are at rest
and they know not
that trouble is being prepared for them.
    My brethren, I have received my garland.
They run and break forth
till the hour catches up with them.
They have been called and have not understood.
They came empty and go empty.
    My brethren, I have received my garland.
I have despised the world
in order to give life to my soul.
The things of the flesh I have forsaken.
With the things of the Spirit I have made my peace.
    My brethren, I have received my garland.
Since I have found my Savior
I have walked in his steps.
Nothing could keep me
from receiving this garland.
    My brethren, I have received my garland.
How great is the joy
prepared for the perfect!
. . . all of you, my brethren,
we inherit it.
    My brethren, I have received my garland.

Notes

1. This psalm belongs to a collection of songs that were sung at the Bema-Feast, the chief feast of the Manichaean community. During this function the suffering and death of Mani was meditated upon, as well as the upcoming Judgment. The Greek word *Bema* here means, roughly, "seat" or "judge's bench."

2. This verse is a refrain that is repeated after every stanza. Mani considers himself to be the Paraclete foretold by Jesus ("Helper"; see Jos. 16:7).

3. The meaning of this word is uncertain.

4. "Swallowed up": a conjecture of the editor (Haardt).

5. "Zographein": literally, "to paint."

6. "Along with": A conjecture of the editor (Haardt).

4
GOSPELS

The Gospel of the Hebrews

*(Jewish-Christian)**

The *Gospel of the Hebrews* is a syncretistic, Jewish-Christian document, composed in Greek, which presents traditions of Jesus' preexistence and coming into the world, his baptism and temptation, some of his sayings, and the report of a resurrection appearance to his brother, James the Just. This is the Jewish-Christian gospel most frequently mentioned by name in the early church; it is also the only one whose original title has been transmitted from antiquity. The title seems to indicate the identity of the group who used this gospel, and may suggest that this was the gospel of predominately Greek-speaking Jewish Christians. The *Gospel of the Hebrews* has no connection with other Jewish-Christian gospels, displaying no kinship with the Gospel of Matthew. It is instructive to note that most of the extant fragments come from quotations in the writings of persons who lived in Alexandria, Egypt.

The *Gospel of the Hebrews* may have been known to Papias (a church writer who died ca. A.D. 130, whose five-volume "Exegesis of the Sayings of the Lord" is now lost, preserved only in a few quotations in the writings of Eusebius). Hegesippus (late in the second century) and Eusebius (early in the fourth century) attest to the existence of this gospel, but do not quote from it. Fragments are preserved in the writings of Clement of Alexandria (late in the second century), Origen (early in the third century), and Cyril (Bishop of Jerusalem, ca. 350 C.E.). Jerome (ca. 400 C.E.) also preserves several fragments, all of which he probably reproduced from the writings of Origen. The extent of this gospel is no longer known. According to the list of "canonical" and "apocryphal" books drawn up by Nicephorus (Patriarch of Con-

---

*Introduction by Ron Cameron.

stantinople, 806–818 c.e.), the *Gospel of the Hebrews* contained 2200 lines, only 300 fewer than Matthew!

The report of a resurrection appearance of Jesus to his brother, James, indicates the position of authority assigned to James in the *Gospel of the Hebrews*. It is well known that James was the leading figure of the conservative Jewish church in Jerusalem. Reports of his "conversion" by a vision of the risen Lord are well documented in the church (compare 1 Cor. 15:7), and are based on an early, probably sound tradition. According to the report in the *Gospel of the Hebrews*, James was the very first witness of the resurrection, and thus its principal guarantor. He is so distinguished that he is even said to have taken part in the Last Supper of Jesus. The esteem in which James is held in this gospel may be used to locate the authority and secure the identity of the tradition of those communities which appealed to him as their leader.

The accounts of Jesus' preexistence, coming, baptism, and temptation are abbreviated mythological narratives. They presuppose a myth of the descent of divine Wisdom, embodying herself definitively in a representative of the human race for the revelation and redemption of humankind. Such a myth was widespread in the Greco-Roman world and underlies many of the earliest christological formulations of believers in Jesus, as evidenced, for example, in Pauline (Phil. 2:6–11), synoptic (Matt. 11:25–30; Luke 7:18–35; 11:49–51), and Johannine traditions (John 1:1–18), as well as in those of the *Gospel of Thomas*. Moreover, the second saying of the *Gospel of Thomas* is also cited as part of the *Gospel of the Hebrews*, suggesting that this was a free-floating saying at home in Egypt as well as in Syria. The wisdom saying numbered below as fragment 5 may permit the suggestion that the majority of the sayings in the *Gospel of the Hebrews* had the same character as those of the synoptic gospels.

The extant fragments of the *Gospel of the Hebrews* display no dependence upon the writings of the New Testament. Unfortunately, it cannot be determined whether other portions of the text that are no longer preserved are in any way contingent upon these or any other writings which we now possess. The earliest possible date of the composition of the *Gospel of the Hebrews* would be in the middle of the first century, when Jesus traditions were first being produced and collected as part of the wisdom tradition. The latest possible date would be in the middle of the second century, shortly before the first reference to this gospel by Hegesippus and the quotations of it by Clement and Origen. Based on the parallels in the morphology of the tradition, an earlier date of composition is more likely than a later one. Internal evidence and external attestations indicate that Egypt was its place of origin.

In the gospel citations that follow, care should be taken to distinguish between the actual quotations of the text of the *Gospel of the Hebrews* and the interpretive comments of the church writers who recorded the citations.

THE GOSPEL OF THE HEBREWS*

It is written in the Gospel of the Hebrews:

When Christ wished to come upon the earth to men, the good Father summoned a mighty power in Heaven, which was called Michael, and entrusted Christ to the care thereof. And the power came into the world and it was called Mary, and Christ was in her womb seven months.

(Cyril of Jerusalem, *Discourse on Mary Theotokos* 12a)

According to the Gospel written in the Hebrew speech, which the Nazaraeans read, the whole fount of the Holy Spirit shall descend upon him. . . . Further in the Gospel which we have just mentioned we find the following written:

And it came to pass when the Lord was come up out of the water, the whole fount of the Holy Spirit descended upon him and rested on him and said to him: My son, in all the prophets was I waiting for you that you should come and I might rest in you. For you are my rest; you are my firstbegotten Son that reigns forever.

(Jerome, *Commentary on Isaiah* 4 [on Isaiah 11:2])

And if any accept the Gospel of the Hebrews—here the Savior says:

Even so did my mother, the Holy Spirit, take me by one of my hairs and carry me away on to the great mountain Tabor.

(Origen, *Commentary on John* 2.12.87 [on John 1:3])

As also it stands written in the Gospel of the Hebrews:

He that marvels shall reign, and he that has reigned shall rest.

(Clement, *Stromateis* 2.9.45.5)

To those words (from Plato, *Timaeus* 90) this is equivalent:

He that seeks will not rest until he finds; and he that has found shall marvel; and he that has marveled shall reign; and he that has reigned shall rest.

(Clement, *Stromateis* 5.14.96.3)

As we have read in the Hebrew Gospel, the Lord says to his disciples:

And never be you joyful, save when you behold your brother with love.

(Jerome, *Commentary on Ephesians* 3 [on Ephesians 5:4])

In the Gospel according to the Hebrews, which the Nazaraeans are wont to read, there is counted among the most grievous offences:

He that has grieved the spirit of his brother.

(Jerome, *Commentary on Ezekiel* 6 [on Ezekiel 18:7])

The Gospel called according to the Hebrews which was recently translated by me into Greek and Latin, which Origen frequently uses, records after the resurrection of the Savior:

And when the Lord had given the linen cloth to the servant of the priest, he went to James and appeared to him. For James had sworn that he would not eat bread from that hour in which he had drunk the cup of the Lord until he should see him risen from among them that sleep. And shortly thereafter the Lord said: Bring a table and bread! And immediately it is added: he took the bread, blessed it and brake it and gave it to James the Just and said to him: My brother, eat your bread, for the Son of man is risen from among them that sleep.

(Jerome, *De viris inlustribus* 2)

---

*From Ron Cameron, *The Other Gospels* (Philadelphia: Westminster Press, 1982), pp. 83–86.

The Gospel of the Ebionites

(Jewish-Christian)*

The *Gospel of the Ebionites* is a gospel harmony preserved in a few quotations in the writings of Epiphanius (a church writer who lived at the end of the fourth century A.D.). The original title of this gospel is unknown. The designation customary today is based on the fact that this was the gospel probably used by the Ebionites, a group of Greek-speaking Jewish Christians who were prominent throughout the second and third centuries. Epiphanius incorrectly entitles this the "Hebrew" gospel, and alleges that it is an abridged, truncated version of the Gospel of Matthew. Whereas the *Gospel of the Ebionites* is indeed closely related to Matthew, examination of the extant fragments reveals that much of the text is a harmony, composed in Greek, of the Gospels of Matthew and Luke (and, probably, the Gospel of Mark as well). Although Irenaeus (late in the second century) attests to the existence of this gospel, we are dependent solely upon the quotations given by Epiphanius for our knowledge of the contents of the text.

Like Mark and the Synoptic Sayings Source, Q, the *Gospel of the Ebionites* begins with the preaching of John the Baptist and the baptism of Jesus. But though Mark and Q did not know of any birth or infancy stories, the *Gospel of the Ebionites* did, for they were present in its written sources, Matthew and Luke. Evidently the Ebionite community chose to omit these stories from their gospel because the Ebionites rejected the virgin birth.

The theology of the Ebionites can be detected in the other gospel fragments as well. Their gospel makes both John the Baptist and Jesus vegetarians: John's diet is said to consist exclusively of wild honey; and Jesus is made to say that, at the passover meal with his disciples, he does not desire to eat meat. In another context, Jesus makes a legal pronouncement in which he states that he has come to abolish sacrifices. Together with the saying about the passover, this intimates a polemic against the Jewish Temple. Since the *Gospel of the Ebionites* was written after the destruction of the Temple in Jerusalem in A.D. 70, such a polemic may have been intended to address the problem of the continuation of Judaism as a religion. In this respect, this gospel is to be compared especially with Matthew, which also appears to reinterpret Jewish and Jesus traditions to provide, in part, a possible option for Jewish identity after the destruction of the Temple. In opposition to the views of emerging Pharisaic Judaism, both Matthew and the *Gospel of the Ebionites* seem to suggest that faithful Jews are those who have come to believe in Jesus, the true interpreter of the Law. In the *Gospel of the Ebionites*, accordingly, the twelve apostles have been commissioned by Jesus himself to be witnesses for Israel, representatives of the twelve tribes.

The *Gospel of the Ebionites* was composed sometime after the Gospels of Matthew and Luke and before the first reference to it in the writings of Irenaeus (toward the end of the second century). A date of composition in the middle of the second century, when several other gospel harmonies were also being written, is most likely. Its provenance is probably Syria-Palestine, where the Ebionites were at home.

The quotations below are given in the order of their citation by Epiphanius, not necessarily in the order of their occurrence in the gospel itself. Care should be taken to distinguish between the actual quotations of the text of the *Gospel of the Ebionites* and Epiphanius' own interpretive comments.

THE GOSPEL OF THE EBIONITES*

In the Gospel that is in general use among them which is called according to Matthew, which however is not whole and complete but forged and mutilated—they call it the Hebrew Gospel—it is reported:

There appeared a certain man named Jesus of about thirty years of age, who chose us. And when he came to Capernaum, he entered into the house of Simon whose surname was Peter, and opened his mouth and said: As I passed the Lake of Tiberias, I chose John and James the sons of Zebedee, and Simon and Andrew and Thaddaeus and Simon the Zealot and Judas the Iscariot, and

you, Matthew, I called as you sat at the receipt of custom, and you followed me. You, therefore, I will to be twelve apostles for a testimony unto Israel.

(Epiphanius, *Panarion* 30.13.2–3)

And:

It came to pass that John was baptizing; and there went out to him Pharisees and were baptized, and all Jerusalem. And John had a garment of camel's hair and a leathern girdle about his loins, and his food, as it is said, was wild honey, the taste of which was that of manna, as a cake dipped in oil.

Thus they were resolved to pervert the word of truth into a lie and to put a cake in the place of locusts.

(Epiphanius, *Panarion* 30.13.4–5)

And the beginning of their Gospel runs:

It came to pass in the days of Herod the king of Judaea, when Caiaphas was high priest, that there came one, John by

*Introduction by Ron Cameron.
*From Ron Cameron, *The Other Gospels* (Philadelphia: Westminster Press, 1982), pp. 103–106.

name, and baptized with the baptism of repentance in the river Jordan. It was said of him that he was of the lineage of Aaron the priest, a son of Zacharias and Elisabeth; and all went out to him.

(Epiphanius, *Panarion* 30.13.6)

And after much has been recorded it proceeds:

When the people were baptized, Jesus also came and was baptized by John. And as he came up from the water, the heavens were opened and he saw the Holy Spirit in the form of a dove that descended and entered into him. And a voice sounded from Heaven that said: You are my beloved Son, in you I am well pleased. And again: I have this day begotten you. And immediately a great light shone round about the place. When John saw this, it is said, he said unto him: Who are you, Lord? And again a voice from Heaven rang out to him: This is my beloved Son in whom I am well pleased. And then, it is said, John fell down before him and said: I beseech you, Lord, baptize me. But he prevented him and said: Suffer it; for thus it is fitting that everything should be fulfilled.

(Epiphanius, *Panarion* 30.13.7–8)

Moreover, they deny that he was a man, evidently on the ground of the word which the Savior spoke when it was reported to him: "Behold, your mother and your brethren stand without," namely:

Who is my mother and who are my brethren? And he stretched forth his hand towards his disciples and said: These are my brethren and mother and sisters, who do the will of my Father.

(Epiphanius, *Panarion* 30.14.5)

They say that Christ was not begotten of God the Father, but created as one of the archangels . . . that he rules over the angels and all the creatures of the Almighty, and that he came and declared, as their Gospel, which is called Gospel according to Matthew or Gospel according to the Hebrews?, reports:

I am come to do away with sacrifices, and if you cease not from sacrificing, the wrath of God will not cease from you.

(Epiphanius, *Panarion* 30.16.4–5)

But they abandon the proper sequence of the words and pervert the saying, as is plain to all from the readings attached, and have let the disciples say:

Where will you have us prepare the passover? And him to answer to that:

Do I desire with desire at this Passover to eat flesh with you?

(Epiphanius, *Panarion* 30.22.4)

The Secret Gospel of Mark

(Christian Apocrypha)*

The *Secret Gospel of Mark* is a fragment of an early edition of the Gospel of Mark which contains an account of the raising of a young man from the dead, a rite of initiation, and a brief excerpt of an encounter between Jesus and three women. The *Secret Gospel of Mark* is preserved in Greek in a fragment of a letter of Clement of Alexandria (a church writer who lived at the end of the second century), in which he denounces the Carpocratians (a libertine group of Christian gnostics who were prominent throughout the second century). This fragment was discovered by Morton Smith in 1958 at the Monastery of Mar Saba, located roughly twelve miles southeast of Jerusalem in the Judean desert. On paleographical grounds the copy of the letter has been assigned a date in the second half of the eighteenth century, at which time it was copied into the back of a 1646 edition of letters of Ignatius of Antioch (a church writer who lived at the beginning of the second century).

In his letter, Clement responds to certain questions he had received about the text of the *Secret Gospel of Mark*. He presents the following schema of the various alleged editions of the Gospel of Mark: first, Mark wrote "an account of the Lord's doings" for catechumens, in which he selected what he thought was most suitable for beginners in the faith; second, Mark also wrote another, "more spiritual Gospel," to be used by those who were being perfected in the faith; and third, Mark knew of additional, arcane traditions—which he did not write down—which would lead initiates into the "innermost sanctuary" of the truth.

The fragments of the *Secret Gospel of Mark* are located between Mark

---

*Introduction by Ron Cameron.

10:34 and 35 and after Mark 10:46a. In the first fragment, the account of the raising of the young man from the dead is a variant of the story of the raising of Lazarus in the Gospel of John (John 11). On form-critical and redaction-critical grounds, the version of the story in the *Secret Gospel of Mark* is to be judged more primitive than the one preserved in John 11. Immediately following this story is the report of the initiation of this young man. The technical term used to describe this rite, the "mystery of the kingdom of God," suggests that this nocturnal initiation most likely refers to baptism. The second fragment, which comes after Mark 10:46a, seems to be a remnant of an encounter between Jesus and his young initiate's family in Jericho.

The *Secret Gospel of Mark* is an important witness to the history and development of gospel traditions. The close similarity between the stories of the raisings from the dead in the *Secret Gospel of Mark* and in the Gospel of John suggests that Mark and John have drawn upon a shared tradition, and raises the question whether this story came from a common collection, perhaps written in Aramaic, from which Mark and John have also taken their other miracle stories. Moreover, since this story occurs in the same sequence in the structural outline of both the *Secret Gospel of Mark* and the Gospel of John, it is possible that this story is part of a more comprehensive source used independently by both evangelists.

Most of all, the discovery of the *Secret Gospel of Mark* has made us privy to new and unparalleled information about the various editions of the Gospel of Mark, and has brought to our attention the widespread esoteric tradition among the earliest believers in Jesus. It is known that the Gospel of Mark has gone through several stages in its compositional history, including its use of more primitive collections of sayings, stories, parables, an apocalypse, and a passion narrative, as well as the subsequent addition of two separate, longer endings to the last chapter. Furthermore, Matthew and Luke have made full-scale revisions of the Gospel of Mark by independently incorporating it into their own gospels. *The Secret Gospel of Mark* is additional evidence of the instability of gospel texts and gospel manuscripts in the first two centuries A.D. Clement of Alexandria states that the Carpocratians used an edition of the *Secret Gospel of Mark* which differed in a number of respects from the edition which Clement's own church used. Some of this divergent material he termed "falsifications." Clement also states that the *Secret Gospel of Mark* is an expansion of the (now canonical) Gospel of Mark. In fact, the precise opposite may well be the case: the canonical (or "public") Gospel of Mark appears to be an abridgment of the *Secret Gospel of Mark*. The first edition of Mark, which was written ca. A.D. 70, is no longer extant. The *Secret Gospel of Mark* was probably composed around the beginning of the second century, most likely in Syria. Sometime thereafter our present edition of Mark, with only vestiges of the secret tradition still visible (Mark 4:11; 9:25–27; 10:21, 32, 38–39; 12:32–34; 14:51–52), took shape.

THE SECRET GOSPEL OF MARK*

From the letters of the most holy Clement, the author of the Stromateis. To Theodore.

You did well in silencing the unspeakable teachings of the Carpocratians. For these are the "wandering stars" referred to in the prophecy, who wander from the narrow road of the commandments into a boundless abyss of the carnal and bodily sins. For, priding themselves in knowledge, as they say, "of the deep things of Satan," they do not know that they are casting themselves away into "the nether world of the darkness" of falsity, and, boasting that they are free, they have become slaves of servile desires. Such men are to be opposed in all ways and altogether. For, even if they should say something true, one who loves the truth should not, even so, agree with them. For not all true things are the truth, nor should that truth which merely seems true according to human opinions be preferred to the true truth, that according to the faith.

Now of the things they keep saying about the divinely inspired Gospel according to Mark, some are altogether falsifications, and others, even if they do contain some true elements, nevertheless are not reported truly. For the true things being mixed with inventions, are falsified, so that, as the saying goes, even the salt loses its savor.

As for Mark, then, during Peter's stay in Rome he wrote an account of the Lord's doings, not, however, declaring all of them, nor yet hinting at the secret ones, but selecting what he thought most useful for increasing the faith of those who were being instructed. But when Peter died a martyr, Mark came over to Alexandria, bringing both his own notes and those of Peter, from which he transferred to his former book the things suitable to whatever makes for progress toward knowledge. Thus he composed a more spiritual Gospel for the use of those who were being perfected. Nevertheless, he yet did not divulge the things not to be uttered, nor did he write down the hierophantic teaching of the Lord, but to the stories already written he added yet others and, moreover, brought in certain sayings of which he knew the interpretation would, as a mystagogue, lead the hearers into the innermost sanctuary of that truth hidden by seven veils. Thus, in sum, he prepared matters, neither grudgingly nor incautiously, in my opinion, and, dying, he left his composition to the church in 1, verso Alexandria, where it even yet is most carefully guarded, being read only to those who are being initiated into the great mysteries.

But since the foul demons are always devising destruction for the race of men, Carpocrates, instructed by them and using deceitful arts, so enslaved a certain presbyter of the church in Alexandria that he got from him a copy of the secret Gospel, which he both interpreted according to his blasphemous and carnal doctrine and, moreover, polluted, mixing with the spotless and holy words utterly shameless lies. From this mixture is drawn off the teaching of the Carpocratians.

To them, therefore, as I said above, one must never give way; nor, when they put forward their falsifications, should one concede that the secret Gospel is by Mark, but should even deny it on oath. For, "Not all true things are to be said to all men." For this reason the Wisdom of God, through Solomon, advises, "Answer the fool from his folly," teaching that the light of the truth should be hidden from those who are mentally blind. Again it says, "From him who has not shall be taken away," and, "Let the fool walk in darkness." But we are "children of light," having been illuminated by "the dayspring" of the spirit of the Lord "from on high," and "Where the

---

*Folio 1, recto and 2, recto. From Ron Cameron, *The Other Gospels* (Philadelphia: Westminster Press, 1982), pp. 67–70.

Spirit of the Lord is," it says, "there is liberty," for "All things are pure to the pure."

To you, therefore, I shall not hesitate to answer the questions you have asked, refuting the falsifications by the very words of the Gospel. For example, after "And they were in the road going up to Jerusalem," and what follows, until "After three days he shall arise," the secret Gospel brings the following material word for word: "And they come into Bethany. And a certain woman whose brother had died was there. And, coming, she prostrated herself before Jesus and says to him, 'Son of David, have mercy on me.' But the disciples rebuked her. And Jesus, being angered, went off with her into the garden where the tomb was, and straightway a great cry was heard from the tomb. And going near Jesus rolled away the stone from the door of the tomb. And straightway, going in where the youth was, he stretched forth his hand and raised him, seizing his hand. But the youth, looking upon him, loved him and began to beseech

him that he might be with him. And going out of the tomb they came into the house of the youth, for he was rich. And after six days Jesus told him what to do and in the evening the youth comes to him, wearing a linen cloth over his naked body. And he remained with him that night, for Jesus taught him the mystery of the Kingdom of God. And thence, arising, he returned to the other side of the Jordan."

After these words follows the text, "And James and John come to him," and all that section. But "naked man with naked man," and the other things about which you wrote, are not found.

And after the words, "And he comes into Jericho," the secret Gospel adds only, "And the sister of the youth whom Jesus loved and his mother and Salome were there, and Jesus did not receive them." But the many other things about which you wrote both seem to be and are falsifications.

Now the true explanation and that which accords with the true philosophy.

The Apocryphon of James

(Gnostic)*

The Apocryphon of James is a Coptic translation of an originally Greek document that gives an account of the teachings of Jesus in the form of a dialogue between Jesus and two of his disciples, Peter and James. Since the document was untitled in the original, scholars have assigned its title on the basis of the document's own reference to itself as a "secret book" (Greek: *apocryphon*) which allegedly was revealed by Jesus to his brother, James the Just. The *Apocryphon of James* is the second of five tractates of Codex I of the Coptic Gnostic Library, which was buried in the fourth century and discovered in Egypt in 1945. This Codex is commonly known as the Jung Codex, after the name of the Jung Institute in Zurich, which acquired the text in 1952. When first published in 1968, the document was referred to as the *Epistula Iacobi Apocrypha*. Today it is housed in the Coptic Museum of Old Cairo.

Unlike the four gospels that came to be included in the New Testament, the body of the *Apocryphon of James* has no narrative structure. Instead, it preserves sayings, prophecies, parables, and rules for the community which are attributed to Jesus, secondarily inserted into an account of a post-resurrection appearance, and, in turn, embedded into the frame of a letter, allegedly written in Hebrew by James, for the instruction and edification of an unidentified group of Christians. In the first half of the *Apocryphon of James*, sayings are used as the basis of a dialogue between Jesus and his disciples, Peter and James. The use of dialogue is almost completely absent from the discourse of the second half, and, indeed, seems to be a secondary literary technique used throughout the entire document.

The identification of the sources of the traditions used in the *Apocry-*

---

*Introduction by Ron Cameron.

phon of James is a matter of considerable debate. The epistolary frame that serves to introduce the document, however, provides a clue to the use of sources and to the date and nature of composition. The opening paragraphs of the *Apocryphon of James* describe a situation in which scribal activity was taking place. The disciples of Jesus were gathered together after Jesus' resurrection and, remembering what Jesus had said to each one of them, were setting it down in books. This scene suggests that this took place at a time when the literary production of sayings of Jesus was still being vigorously pursued, a time in which written texts with "scriptural" authority were not yet normative. Moreover, only some of the sayings that are in the *Apocryphon of James* are also found in the New Testament. Analysis of each of these sayings provides no evidence that the *Apocryphon of James* either knew of or is literarily dependent upon any of the writings of the New Testament. Most of all, appeals to particular disciples or apostles of Jesus as authorities for local communities were well known in the second, third, and fourth generations of Christianity. The appeal to James suggests that the *Apocryphon of James* dates from a time when written traditions about Jesus were connected with the competitive claims of authority under the names of individual disciples of Jesus.

All of this implies that the *Apocryphon of James* is an early Christian writing based on an independent sayings collection that was contemporary with other early Christian writings that presented sayings of Jesus. The earliest possible date of composition would be sometime in the first century; the latest possible date would be at the end of the second or the beginning of the third century, when the gospels of the New Testament began to be known, read, and used as authoritative texts in the struggle against the "heretics." The freedom in the use of sayings and the role of Peter and James as authority figures in the transmission of the tradition suggest that the *Apocryphon of James* was probably composed in the first half of the second century. Internal evidence intimates that Egypt was its place of origin. The use of individually discrete sayings of Jesus in the composition of discourses and dialogues makes it an important witness to the use and development of sayings traditions. In some instances, sayings that are transmitted as words of Jesus in the synoptic gospels are, in the *Apocryphon of James*, preserved as questions or comments of the disciples. The *Apocryphon of James* can thus be profitably compared with the Gospel of John, which also uses individual sayings to compose Jesus' dialogues in the first half of the gospel as well as his "farewell discourse" in the second half.

THE APOCRYPHON OF JAMES*

James writes to you. Peace be with you from Peace, love from Love, grace from Grace, faith from Faith, life from Holy Life!

Since you asked me to send you a secret book which was revealed to me and Peter by the Lord, I could neither refuse you nor speak directly to you, but I have written it in Hebrew letters and have sent it to you—and to you alone. But inasmuch as you are a minister of the salvation of the saints, endeavor earnestly and take care not to recount this book to many—this which the Savior did not desire to recount to all of us, his twelve disciples. But blessed are those who will be saved through faith in this discourse.

Now I sent you ten months ago another secret book which the Savior revealed to me. But that one you are to regard in this manner, as revealed to me, James.

Now the twelve disciples were sitting all together at the same time, and, remembering what the Savior had said to each one of them, whether secretly or openly, they were setting it down in books. And I was writing what was in my book—lo, the Savior appeared, after he had departed from us while we gazed at him. And five hundred and fifty days after he arose from the dead, we said to him: "Have you gone and departed from us?"

And Jesus said: "No, but I shall go to the place from which I have come. If you desire to come with me, come."

They all answered and said: "If you bid us, we'll come."

He said: "Truly I say to you, no one ever will enter the Kingdom of Heaven if I bid him, but rather because you yourselves are full. Let me have James and

_____
*From Ron Cameron, *The Other Gospels* (Philadelphia: Westminster Press, 1982), pp. 55–64.

Peter, in order that I may fill them." And when he called these two, he took them aside, and commanded the rest to busy themselves with that with which they had been busy.

The Savior said: "You have received mercy. Do you not desire, then, to be filled? And is your heart drunk? Do you not desire, then, to be sober? Therefore, be ashamed! And now, waking or sleeping, remember that you have seen the Son of Man, and with him you have spoken, and to him you have listened. Woe to those who have seen the Son of Man! Blessed are those who have not seen the Man, and who have not consorted with him, and who have not spoken with him, and who have not listened to anything from him. Yours is life! Know, therefore, that he healed you when you were ill, in order that you might reign. Woe to those who have rested from their illness, because they will relapse again into illness! Blessed are those who have not been ill, and have known rest before they became ill. Yours is the Kingdom of God! Therefore I say to you, become full and leave no place within you empty, since the Coming One is able to mock you."

Then Peter answered: "Lord, three times you have said to us, 'Become full,' but we are full."

The Lord answered and said: "Therefore I say to you, become full, in order that you may not be diminished. Those who are diminished, however, will not be saved. For fullness is good and diminution is bad. Therefore, just as it is good for you to be diminished and, on the other hand, bad for you to be filled, so also the one who is full is diminished; and the one who is diminished is not filled as the one who is diminished is filled, and the one who is full, for his part, brings his sufficiency to completion. Therefore, it is fitting to be diminished while you can still be filled, and to be filled while it is still possible to be diminished, in order that you can fill yourselves the more. Therefore become full of the spirit but be diminished of reason. For reason is of the soul; and it is soul."

And I answered and said to him: "Lord, we can obey you if you wish. For we have forsaken our forefathers and our mothers and our villages and have followed you. Grant us, therefore, not to be tempted by the wicked Devil."

The Lord answered and said: "What is your merit when you do the will of the Father if it is not given to you by him as a gift, while you are tempted by Satan? But if you are oppressed by Satan and are persecuted and you do the Father's will, I say that he will love you and will make you equal with me and will consider that you have become beloved through his providence according to your free choice. Will you not cease, then, being lovers of the flesh and being afraid of sufferings? Or do you not know that you have not yet been mistreated and have not yet been accused unjustly, nor have you yet been shut up in prison, nor have you yet been condemned lawlessly, nor have you yet been crucified without reason, nor have you yet been buried shamefully, as was I myself, by the evil one? Do you dare to spare the flesh, you for whom the spirit is an encircling wall? If you contemplate the world, how long it is before you and also how long it is after you, you will find that your life is one single day and your sufferings, one single hour. For the good will not enter the world. Scorn death, therefore, and take concern for life. Remember my cross and my death and you will live."

And I answered and said to him: "Lord, do not mention to us the cross and the death, for they are far from you."

The Lord answered and said: "Truly I say to you, none will be saved unless they believe in my cross. But those who have believed in my cross, theirs is the Kingdom of God. Therefore, become seekers for death, just as the dead who seek for life, for that for which they seek is revealed to them. And what is there to concern them? When you turn yourselves towards death, it will make known to you election. In truth I say to you, none of those who are afraid of death will be saved. For the Kingdom of God belongs to those who have put themselves to death. Become better than I; make yourselves like the son of the Holy Spirit."

Then I questioned him: "Lord, how may we prophesy to those who ask us to prophesy to them? For there are many who ask us and who look to us to hear an oracle from us."

The Lord answered and said: "Do you not know that the head of prophecy was cut off with John?"

And I said: "Lord, it is not possible to remove the head of prophecy, is it?"

The Lord said to me: "When you come to know what 'head' is, and that prophecy issues from the head, then understand what is the meaning of 'Its head was removed.' I first spoke with you in parables, and you did not understand. Now, in turn, I speak with you openly, and you do not perceive. But it is you who were to me a parable in parables and what is apparent in what are open.

"Be zealous to be saved without being urged. Rather, be ready on your own and, if possible, go before me. For thus the Father will love you.

"Become haters of hypocrisy and evil thought. For it is thought which gives birth to hypocrisy, but hypocrisy is far from the truth.

"Let not the Kingdom of Heaven wither away. For it is like a date palm shoot whose fruits poured down around it. It put forth leaves and, when they budded, they caused the productivity of the date palm to dry up. Thus it is also with the fruit which came from this single root: when the fruit was picked, fruits were collected by many harvesters. It would indeed be good if it were possible to produce these new plants now; for then you would find the Kingdom.

"Since I have been glorified in this manner before this time, why do you all restrain me when I am eager to go? You have constrained me to remain with you eighteen more days for the sake of the parables. It sufficed for some persons to pay attention to the teaching and to understand 'The Shepherds' and 'The Seed' and 'The Building' and 'The Lamps of the Virgins' and 'The Wage of the Workers' and 'The Double Drachma' and 'The Woman.'

"Become zealous about the Word. For the Word's first condition is faith; the second is love; the third is works. Now from these comes life. For the Word is like a grain of wheat. When someone sowed it, he believed in it; and when it sprouted, he loved it, because he looked forward to many grains in the place of one; and when he worked it, he was saved, because he prepared it for food. Again he left some grains to sow. Thus it is also possible for you all to receive the Kingdom of Heaven: unless you receive it through knowledge, you will not be able to find it.

"Therefore I say to you, be sober. Do not go astray. And many times I have said to you all together—and also to you alone, James, I have said—be saved. And I have commanded you to follow me, and I have taught you the response in the presence of the rulers. Observe that I have descended, and I have spoken, and I have troubled myself, and I have received my crown, when I saved you. For I have descended to dwell with you in order that you also may dwell with me. And when I found that your houses had no ceilings over them, I dwelt in houses which would be able to receive me when I descended.

"Therefore, obey me, my brothers. Understand what the great light is. The Father does not need me. For a father does not need a son, but it is the son who needs the father. To him I am going, for the Father of the Son is not in need of you.

"Pay attention to the Word. Under-stand knowledge. Love life. And no one will persecute you, nor will any one oppress you, other than you yourselves.

"O you wretched! O you unfortunates! O you dissemblers of the truth! O you falsifiers of knowledge! O you sinners against the spirit! Do you even now dare to listen, when it behooved you to speak from the beginning? Do you even now dare to sleep, when it behooved you to be awake from the beginning, in order that the Kingdom of Heaven might receive you? In truth I say to you, it is easier for a holy one to sink into defilement, and for a man of light to sink into darkness, than for you to reign—or even not to reign!

"I have remembered your tears and your grief and your sorrow. They are far from us. Now, then, you who are outside the inheritance of the Father, weep where it behooves you and grieve and proclaim that which is good, since the Son is ascending appropriately. In truth I say to you, had it been to those who would listen to me that I was sent, and had it been with them that I was to speak, I would have never descended upon the earth. And now, then, be ashamed on account of them.

"Behold, I shall depart from you. I am going and I do not desire to remain with you any longer—just as you yourselves have not desired. Now, then, follow me quickly. Therefore I say to you, for your sake I have descended. You are the beloved; you are those who will become a cause of life for many. Beseech the Father. Implore God often, and he will give to you. Blessed is the one who has seen you with him when he is proclaimed among the angels and glorified among the saints. Yours is life! Rejoice and be glad as children of God. Keep his will in order that you may be saved. Take reproof from me and save yourselves. I intercede on your behalf with the Father, and he will forgive you much."

And when we heard these things, we became elated, for we had been depressed on account of what we had said

347

earlier. Now when he saw our rejoicing, he said: "Woe to you who are in want of an advocate! Woe to you who are in need of grace! Blessed are those who have spoken freely and have produced grace for themselves. Make yourselves like strangers; of what sort are they in the estimation of your city? Why are you troubled when you oust yourselves of your own accord and depart from your city? Why do you abandon your dwelling place of your own accord, readying it for those who desire to dwell in it? O you exiles and fugitives! Woe to you, because you will be caught! Or perhaps you imagine that the Father is a lover of humanity? Or that he is persuaded by prayers? Or that he is gracious to one on behalf of another? Or that he bears with one who seeks? For he knows the desire and also that which the flesh needs. Because it is not the flesh which yearns for the soul. For without the soul the body does not sin, just as the soul is not saved without the spirit. But if the soul is saved when it is without evil, and if the spirit also is saved, then the body becomes sinless. For it is the spirit which animates the soul, but it is the body which kills it—that is, it is the soul which kills itself. Truly I say to you, the Father will not forgive the sin of the soul at all, nor the guilt of the flesh. For none of those who have worn the flesh will be saved. For do you imagine that many have found the Kingdom of Heaven? Blessed is the one who has seen himself as a fourth one in Heaven."

When we heard these things, we became distressed. Now when he saw that we were distressed, he said: "This is why I say this to you, that you may know yourselves. For the Kingdom of Heaven is like an ear of grain which sprouted in a field. And when it ripened, it scattered its fruit and, in turn, filled the field with ears of grain for another year. You also: be zealous to reap for yourselves an ear of life, in order that you may be filled with the Kingdom.

"As long as I am with you, give heed to me and obey me. But when I am to depart from you, remember me. And remember me because I was with you without your knowing me. Blessed are those who have known me. Woe to those who have heard and have not believed! Blessed are those who have not seen but have had faith.

"And once again I persuade you. For I am revealed to you building a house which is very valuable to you, since you take shelter under it; in the same way it will be able to support the house of your neighbors when theirs is in danger of falling. In truth I say to you, woe to those on behalf of whom I was sent down to this place! Blessed are those who are to ascend to the Father. Again I reprove you. You who are, make yourselves like those who are not, in order that you may come to be with those who are not.

"Let not the Kingdom of Heaven become desolate among you. Do not become arrogant on account of the light which illumines. Rather, become to yourselves in this manner, as I am to you. For you I have placed myself under the curse, in order that you may be saved."

And Peter answered to this and said: "Sometimes you urge us on to the Kingdom of Heaven, and other times you turn us away, Lord. Sometimes you persuade us and impel us to faith and promise us life, and other times you expel us from the Kingdom of Heaven."

And the Lord answered and said to us: "I have given you faith many times. Moreover, I have revealed myself to you, James, and you have not known me. Again, now I see you rejoicing many times. And when you are elated over the promise of life, are you nevertheless glum? And are you distressed when you are taught about the Kingdom? But you through faith and knowledge have received life. Therefore, scorn rejection when you hear it, but, when you hear the promise, be the more glad. In truth I say to you, the one who will receive life and believe in the Kingdom will never leave it—not even if the Father desires to banish him!

"These things I shall say to you for the present. But now I shall ascend to the place from which I have come. But you, when I was eager to go, have driven me out, and, instead of your accompanying me, you have pursued me. But give heed to the glory which awaits me, and, having opened your hearts, listen to the hymns which await me up in heaven. For today I am obliged to take (my place) at the right hand of my Father. Now I have said my last word to you. I shall part from you. For a chariot of wind has taken me up, and from now on I shall strip myself in order that I may clothe myself. But give heed: blessed are those who have preached the Son before he descended, in order that, when I have come, I may ascend. Thrice blessed are those who were proclaimed by the Son before they came into being, in order that you may have a portion with them."

When he said these things, he went away. And we knelt down, I and Peter, and gave thanks, and sent our hearts up to heaven. We heard with our ears and saw with our eyes the sound of wars and a trumpet call and a great commotion.

And when we passed beyond that place, we sent our minds up further. And we saw with our eyes and heard with our ears hymns and angelic praises and angelic jubilation. And heavenly majesties were hymning, and we ourselves were jubilant.

After this, we also desired to send our spirits above to the Majesty. And when we ascended, we were permitted neither to see nor to hear anything. For the rest of the disciples called to us and questioned us: "What is it that you have heard from the Master?" And, "What has he said to you?" And, "Where has he gone?"

And we answered them: "He has ascended." And, "He has given us a pledge and has promised us all life and has disclosed to us children who are to come after us, since he has bid us to love them, inasmuch as we will be saved for their sake."

And when they heard, they believed the revelation, but were angry about those who would be born. Then I, not desiring to entice them to scandal, sent each one to another place. But I myself went up to Jerusalem, praying that I may obtain a portion with the beloved who are to be revealed.

And I pray that the beginning may come from you, for thus I can be saved. Because they will be enlightened through me, through my faith and through another's which is better than mine, for I desire that mine become the lesser. Endeavor earnestly, therefore, to make yourself like them, and pray that you may obtain a portion with them. For apart from what I have recounted, the Savior did not disclose revelation to us. For their sake we proclaim, indeed, a portion with those for whom it was proclaimed, those whom the Lord has made his children.

The Gospel of Bartholomew

(Christian Apocrypha)

The *Gospel of Bartholomew* is a passion gospel. It begins with a dramatic description of Christ's descent into Hell and his freeing of Adam and the other great souls imprisoned there. The vivid description of Christ's breaking into Hell parallels the version found in the *Gospel of Nicodemus*. Then Jesus tells Bartholomew how he had the archangel Michael use his flaming sword to rend the temple in Jerusalem in vengeance for his passion. Jesus also informs Bartholomew that of the 30,000 souls which leave the world each day, only three are admitted to Paradise.

A remarkable episode in the Gospel is Mary's divulgence of how she was informed by the angel of her mission to be the vessel for God's son. She tells the story to Bartholomew and, at the point when she is to reveal the final secrets, "fire came from her mouth, and the world was on the point of being burned up" (II, 22). Jesus intervenes to silence her, for the ultimate enigmas—the name of God, the face of God, the indescribable and ineffable—must never be fully revealed. Following Mary's confessions, Jesus takes the apostles to the abyss, the place of truth. Yet he warns them not to look. The "earth was rolled up like a papyrus roll" and the abyss exposed. The apostles fell on their faces. Once more, the sight of truth was too overwhelming. But again and again the apostles ask Mary to reveal the workings of God. They ask about Eve's transgression and finally they ask Jesus about Beliar (Satan). Jesus obliges by bringing Beliar up from Hell, bound with fiery chains and held by 660 angels. He allows Bartholomew to step on Beliar's neck and to question him. Satan offers a meticulously detailed account of organized angelry. He goes on to describe his own world and evil strategems, and the creation of Adam and Eve from his point of view. Finally, Jesus informs Bartholomew of his salvific role. He, Jesus, came to this world to bring immortality to the faithful and eternal punishment to those who, by his judgment, are wicked. This is his mystery, which Bartholomew must not reveal, for Satan's agents are all about. Of course the *Gospel* itself, having survived, remains a vehicle for the revelation of the mysteries of God.

The *Gospel of Bartholomew* in its original form may be assigned to the third century. The texts are preserved in varying degrees of completeness in Greek, Latin, and Old Church Slavonic. There are also Coptic fragments related to the *Gospel of Bartholomew*.

THE GOSPEL OF BARTHOLOMEW*

I

In the time before the passion of our Lord Christ all the apostles were gathered together. And they asked and besought him: "Lord, show us the secrets of the Heaven." But Jesus answered: "I can reveal nothing to you before I have put off this body of flesh."

But when he had suffered and risen again, all the apostles at the sight of him did not dare to ask him, because his appearance was not as it was before, but revealed the fullness of his godhead. But Bartholomew went up to him and said: "Lord, I wish to speak to you." Jesus answered him: "Beloved Bartholomew, I know what you wish to say. Ask then, and I will tell you all you wish to know. And I myself will make known to you what you do not say." Bartholomew said to him: "Lord, when you went to be hanged on the cross, I followed you at a distance and saw how you were hanged on the cross and how the angels descended from heaven and worshiped you. And when darkness came, I looked and saw that you had vanished from the cross; only I heard your voice in the underworld, and suddenly a great wailing and gnashing of teeth arose. Tell me,

Lord, where you went from the cross." And Jesus answered: "Blessed are you, Bartholomew, my beloved, because you saw this mystery. And now I will tell you everything you ask me.

"When I vanished from the cross, I went to the underworld to bring up Adam and all the patriarchs, Abraham, Isaac and Jacob. The archangel—Michael —had asked me to do this. When I descended with my angels to the underworld, in order to dash in pieces the iron bars and shatter the portals of the underworld, Hades said to the devil: 'I perceive that God has come down upon the earth.' And the angels cried to the mighty ones: 'Open your gates, you princes, for the King of glory has come down to the underworld.' Hades asked: 'Who is the King of glory who has come down to us?' And when I had descended five hundred steps, Hades began to tremble violently and said: 'I believe that God has come down. His strong breath goes before him. I cannot bear it.' But the Devil said to him: 'Do not submit, but make yourself strong. God has not come down.'

"But when I had descended five hundred steps more, the strong angels cried out: 'Open, doors of your prince! Swing open, you gates! For see: the King of glory has come down.' And again Hades said: 'Woe is me! I feel the breath of God. And yet you say: God has not come down upon the earth.'

"Beelzebub replied: 'Why are you afraid? It is a prophet, and you think it is God. The prophet has made himself like

*From Edgar Hennecke and Wilhelm Schneemelcher, eds., *New Testament Apocrypha*, vol. 1, trans. R. McL. Wilson (Philadelphia: Westminster Press, 1963), pp. 484–502.

God. We will take him and bring him to those who think to ascend into Heaven.' And Hades said: 'Which of the prophets is it? Tell me. Is it Enoch, the scribe of righteousness? But God has not allowed him to come down upon the earth before the end of the six thousand years. Do you say that it is Elias, the avenger? But he does not come down before the end. What am I to do, for the destruction is from God? For already our end is at hand. For I have the number of the years in my hands.'

"But when the Devil perceived that the Word of the Father had come down upon the earth, he said: 'Do not fear, Hades; we will make fast the gates and make strong our bars. For God himself does not come down upon the earth.' And Hades said: 'Where shall we hide ourselves from the face of God, the great king? Permit me, do not resist; for I was created before you.' And thereupon they dashed in pieces the gates of brass and I shattered the iron bars. And I went in and smote him with a hundred blows and bound him with fetters that cannot be loosed. And I brought out all the patriarchs and came again to the cross." And Bartholomew said to him: "Lord, I saw you again hanging on the cross and all the dead arising and worshiping you. Tell me, Lord, who was he whom the angels carried in their arms, that exceedingly large man? And what did you say to him that he groaned so deeply?"

"It was Adam, the first created, for whose sake I came down from heaven upon the earth. And I said to him: 'I was hanged upon the cross for your sake and for the sake of your children.' And when he heard that, he groaned and said: 'So you were pleased to do, O Lord.'"

Again Bartholomew said: "Lord, I also saw the angels ascending before Adam and singing praises. But one of the angels, greater than the others, would not go up. He had in his hand a fiery sword and looked at you.[1] And all the angels besought him to go up with them; but he would not. But when you commanded

him, I saw a flame issuing out of his hands, which reached as far as the city of Jerusalem." And Jesus said to him: "Blessed are you, Bartholomew my beloved, because you saw these mysteries. This was one of the avenging angels who stand before my Father's throne. He sent this angel to me. And for this reason he would not go up, because he wished to destroy the power of the world. But when I commanded him to go up, a flame issued from his hand, and after he had rent the veil of the temple, he divided it into two parts as a testimony to the children of Israel for my passion, because they crucified me."

And when he had said this, he said to the apostles: "Wait for me in this place; for today a sacrifice is offered in Paradise, that I may receive it after my arrival." And Bartholomew said to him: "Lord, what sacrifice is offered in Paradise?" Jesus answered: "The souls of the righteous, when they leave the body, go to Paradise, and unless I am present there they cannot enter." Bartholomew asked: "Lord, how many souls leave the world every day?" Jesus answered: "Thirty thousand." And again Bartholomew asked: "Lord, when you lived among us, did you receive the sacrifices in Paradise?" Jesus answered: "Truly, I say to you, my beloved, even when I taught among you, I sat at the right hand of the Father and received the sacrifices in Paradise." And Bartholomew said: "Lord, if thirty thousand souls leave this world daily, how many are admitted into Paradise?" Jesus answered: "Only three." Bartholomew again asked: "Lord, how many souls are born into the world every day?" Jesus answered: "Only one over and above those who leave the world." And when he had said this, he gave them the peace and vanished from their sight.

II

Now the apostles were in the place called Chritir with Mary. And Bartholomew came to Peter and Andrew and John, and said to them: "Let us ask Mary, her who is highly favored, how she conceived the incomprehensible or how she carried him who cannot be carried or how she bore so much greatness." But they hesitated to ask her. Therefore Bartholomew said to Peter: "Father Peter, you, as the chief one, go to her and ask her." But Peter said to John: "You are a chaste youth and blameless; you must ask her." And as they all were doubtful and pondered the matter to and fro, Bartholomew came to her with a cheerful countenance and said: "You who are highly favored, tabernacle of the Most High, unblemished, we, all the apostles ask you, but they have sent me to you. Tell us how you conceived the incomprehensible, or how you carried him who cannot be carried or how you bore so much greatness." But Mary answered: "Do not ask me concerning this mystery. If I begin to tell you, fire will come out of my mouth and consume the whole earth." But they asked her still more urgently. And since she did not wish to deny the apostles a hearing, she said: "Let us stand up in prayer." And the apostles stood behind Mary. And she said to Peter: "Peter, chief of the apostles, the greatest pillar, do you stand behind me? Did not our Lord say: 'The head of the man is Christ, but the head of the woman is the man?' Therefore stand in front of me to pray." But they said to her: "In you the Lord set his tabernacle and was pleased to be contained by you. Therefore you now have more right than we to lead in the prayer." But she answered them: "You are shining stars, as the prophet said: 'I lifted up my eyes to the hills, from which comes my help' [Ps. 120:1 LXX]. You, then, are the hills and you must pray." The apostles said to her: "You ought to pray as the mother of the heavenly king." Mary said to them: "In your likeness God formed the sparrows and sent them to the four corners of the world." But they answered her: "He whom the seven heavens scarcely contain was pleased to be contained in you."

Then Mary stood up before them, and spread out her hands to Heaven and began to pray thus. "O God, exceeding great and all-wise, king of the ages, indescribable, ineffable, who created the breadths of the heavens by your word and arranged the vault of heaven in harmony, who gave form to disorderly matter and brought together that which was separated, who parted the gloom of the darkness from the light, who made the waters to flow from the same source, before whom the beings of the air tremble and the creatures of the earth fear, who gave the earth its place and did not wish it to perish, in bestowing upon it abundant rain and caring for the nourishment of all things, the eternal Word of the Father. The seven heavens could scarcely contain you, but you were pleased to be contained in me, without causing me pain, you who are the perfect Word of the Father, through whom everything was created. Glorify your exceedingly great name, and allow me to speak before your holy apostles."

And when she had ended the prayer, she began to say to them: "Let us sit down on the ground. Come, Peter, chief of the apostles, sit on my right hand and put your left hand under my shoulder. And you, Andrew, do the same on my left hand. And you, chaste John, hold my breast. And you, Bartholomew, place your knees on my shoulders and press close my back so that, when I begin to speak, my limbs are not loosed."

And when they had done that, she began: "When I lived in the temple of God and received my food from the hand of an angel, one day there appeared to me one in the form of an angel; but his face was indescribable and in his hand he had neither bread nor cup, as had the angel who came to me before. And immediately the veil of the temple was rent and there was a violent earthquake, and I fell to the earth, for I could not bear the sight of him. But he took me with his hand

and raised me up. And I looked toward Heaven; and there came a cloud of dew on my face and sprinkled me from head to foot, and he wiped me with his robe. Then he said to me: 'Hail, you who are highly favored, the chosen vessel.' And then he struck the right side of his garment and there came forth an exceedingly large loaf, and he placed it upon the altar of the temple, and first ate of it himself and then gave to me also. And again he struck his garment, on the left side, and I looked and saw a cup full of wine. And he placed it upon the altar of the temple, and drank from it first himself and gave it also to me. And I looked and saw that the bread did not diminish and the cup was full as before. Then he said: 'Three years more, and I will send my word and you shall conceive my son, and through him the whole world shall be saved. But you will bring salvation to the world. Peace be with you, favored one, and my peace shall be with you forever.' And when he had said this, he vanished from my eyes and the temple was as before."

As she was saying this, fire came from her mouth, and the world was on the point of being burned up. Then came Jesus quickly and said to Mary: "Say no more, or today my whole creation will come to an end." And the apostles were seized with fear lest God should be angry with them.

III

And he went with them to the mountain Mauria and sat down in their midst. But they hesitated to question him, because they were afraid. And Jesus answered and said: "Ask me what you wish, so that I can teach you and show you. For there are still seven days, and then I ascend to my Father and shall no more appear to you in this form." But they, hesitating, said to him: "Lord, show us the abyss, as you promised us." He answered: "It is not good for you to see the abyss. But if you wish it, I will keep my promise. Come, follow me and see." And he led them to a place called Cherubim, that is, place of truth. And he beckoned to the angels of the West. And the earth was rolled up like a papyrus roll, and the abyss was exposed to their eyes. When the apostles saw it, they fell on their faces. But Jesus said to them: "Did I not say to you that it was not good for you to see the abyss?" And he again beckoned to the angels, and the abyss was covered up.

IV

And he took them and brought them to the mount of Olives. And Peter said to Mary: "You who are favored, ask the Lord to reveal to us all that is in the heavens." And Mary answered Peter: "O rock hewn above, did not the Lord build his church upon you? You therefore should be the first to go and ask him." Peter said again: "You were made the tabernacle of the most high God. You ask him." Mary said: "You are the image of Adam. Was not he formed first and then Eve? Look at the sun. It shines like Adam. Look at the moon. It is full of clay, because Eve transgressed the commandment. For God placed Adam in the East and Eve in the West, and he commanded the two lights to shine, so that the sun with its fiery chariot should shine on Adam in the East, and the moon in the West should shed on Eve its milk-white light. But she defiled the commandment of the Lord, and therefore the moon became soiled, and its light does not gleam. Since, therefore, you are the likeness of Adam, you ought to ask him. But in me the Lord took up his abode, that I might restore the dignity of women."

Now when they came to the top of the mountain, the Lord parted from them for a little while. Then Peter said to Mary: "You made good the transgression of Eve, changing her shame into joy. So you ought to ask." But when Jesus appeared again, Bartholomew said to him:

"Lord, show us the adversary of men, that we may see his form, or what his work is, or where he comes from, or what power he has that he did not even spare you, but caused you to be hanged on the cross." And Jesus looked at him and said: "O bold heart! You ask for that which you cannot look upon." But Bartholomew was frightened, and he fell at Jesus' feet and began to say: "O lamp never extinguished, Lord Jesus Christ, everlasting one, who gave grace for the whole world to those who love you, and gave everlasting light through your appearing on earth, who at the command of the Father gave up your life above and completed your work, who changed the dejection of Adam into joy and overcame the sorrow of Eve with gracious countenance by your birth from a virgin mother, do not be angry with me, and grant me the right to ask." When he said this, Jesus raised him up and asked him: "Bartholomew, do you wish to see the adversary of men? I tell you that, when you see him, not only you, but the apostles with you, and Mary will fall on your faces and will be like the dead." But they all said to him: "Lord, we wish to see him." And he led them down from the mount of Olives, and threatened the angels of the underworld, and beckoned to Michael to sound his mighty trumpet in the height of Heaven. Then the earth was shaken and Beliar came up, held by six hundred and sixty angels and bound with fiery chains.

He was sixteen hundred yards long and forty yards broad. His face was like a lightning of fire, and his eyes like sparks, and from his nostrils came a stinking smoke. His mouth was like a cleft of rock and a single one of his wings was eighty yards long. As soon as the apostles saw him, they fell to the ground on their faces and became like dead men. But Jesus came near and raised up the apostles, and gave them the spirit of power. Then he said to Bartholomew: "Come near to him, Bartholomew, and place your feet on his neck; then he will tell you what his work is, and how he deceives men." And Jesus stood at a distance with the apostles. And Bartholomew raised his voice and said: "O womb more spacious than a city! O womb wider than the span of Heaven! O womb that contained him whom the seven heavens do not contain. You contained him without pain and held in your bosom him who changed his being into the smallest of things. O womb that bore, concealed in your body, the Christ who has been made visible to many. O womb that became more spacious than the whole creation." And Bartholomew was afraid, and said: "Lord Jesus, give me a hem of your garment, that I may venture to approach him." Jesus answered him: "You cannot have a hem of my garment, for it is not the garment which I wore before I was crucified." And Bartholomew said: "Lord, I fear lest, as he did not spare your angels, he will swallow me up also." Jesus answered: "Were not all things made by my word and according to the plan of my Father? The spirits were made subject to Solomon himself. Go therefore, since you have been commanded to do so in my name, and ask him what you wish."

And Bartholomew went and trod upon his neck, and pressed down his face to the earth as far as his ears. And Bartholomew asked him: "Tell me who you are and what is your name." He replied: "Ease me a little, and I will tell you who I am and how I came into this condition and what my work is and how great my power is." Bartholomew eased him and asked him: "Tell me all you have done and all you do." Beliar answered and said: "If you wish to know my name, I was first called Satanael, which means 'angel of God.' But when I rejected the image of God, I was called Satan, which means 'angel of Hell.'" And again Bartholomew asked him: "Reveal everything to me, and conceal nothing from me." And he replied: "I swear to you by the mighty glory of God that even if I wished, I can conceal nothing from you; for he who can convict me stands near me. For if I had the power, I would destroy you as I hurled one of you to destruction.[2] I was the first angel to be created. For when God made the heavens, he took a handful of fire and formed me first, Michael second, the captain of the hosts above, Gabriel third, Uriel fourth, Raphael fifth, Nathanael sixth and six thousand other angels, whose names I cannot tell. There are rod-bearers, lictors of God, and these scourge me seven times a day and seven times a night and never leave me alone and break in pieces all my power. These are the avenging angels, who stand by God's throne. All these belong to the first-created angels.

"And after them was the whole number of the angels created: one hundred myriads for the first heaven, and the same number for the second, third, fourth, fifth, sixth and seventh heavens. Outside the seven heavens there is the first sphere, the firmament; and there dwell the angels of power who influence men. There are also four angels who are set over the winds. The first rules over Boreas. He is called Chairum, and he has in his hand a fiery rod, and restrains the great moisture which this wind has, so that the earth should not dry up. And the angel who rules over Aparktias[3] is called Oertha. He has a torch of fire in his hand, and holds it to him and to his sides and warms his coldness so that he does not freeze the earth. And the angel of the south wind is called Kerkutha, and he breaks his violence' so as not to shake the earth. And the angel who is set over the southwest wind is called Naoutha. He has a rod of ice in his hand and puts it at his mouth, and quenches the fire which comes from his mouth. And if the angel did not quench it at his mouth, it would set the whole world on fire. And another angel rules over the sea, and makes it rough with the waves. I will not tell you more, for he who stands near me does not permit it."

Then Bartholomew asked him: "How do you chastise the souls of men?" Beliar answered: "Am I to describe to you the punishment of the hypocrites, the slanderers, the jesters, the covetous, the adulterers, the sorcerers, the soothsayers, and of those who believe in us, and of all behind whom I stand?" Bartholomew said to him: "I wish you to be brief." And he gnashed his teeth together, and there came up from the abyss a wheel with a sword flashing fire, which had pipes. And I asked him: "What is the sword?" He answered: "It is the sword for the gluttonous. They are put into this pipe because in their gluttony they turn to every kind of sin. Into the second pipe come the slanderers because they secretly slander their neighbors. Into the third pipe come the hypocrites and the rest whom I trip up with my machinations." And Bartholomew said: "Do you do this by yourself?" Satan replied: "If I were able to go out by myself, I would destroy the whole world in three days, but neither I nor any of the six hundred goes out. We have other swift servants whom we command. We equip them with a many-barbed hook, and send them out to hunt, and they catch men's souls for us, enticing them with the sweetness of various allurements, that is, drunkenness, laughter, slandering, hypocrisy, pleasures, fornications, and the other devices in their treasury which weaken men. I will tell you also the rest of the names of the angels. The angel of the hail is called Mermeoth. He holds the hail on his head, and my sevants adjure him and send him wherever they wish. And other angels rule over the snow, and others over the thunder, and others over the lightning, and when a spirit wishes to go forth from among us, either over land or over water, these angels send out fiery stones and set our limbs on fire." Bartholomew said: "Be silent, dragon of the abyss." And Beliar said: "I will tell you much about the angels. Those who run together through the heavenly and earthly regions are Mermeoth, Onoma-tath, Duth, Melioth, Charuth, Grapha-thas, Hoethra, Nephonos, and Chalk-atura. Together they fly through the regions of heaven, of earth, and the underworld."

Bartholomew interrupted him and said: "Be silent and powerless, so that I can entreat my Lord." And Bartholomew fell on his face, and scattered earth on his head, and began: "O Lord Jesus Christ, the great and glorious name. All the choirs of the angels praise you, Lord; and I also, who am unworthy in my lips, praise you, Lord. Hear me, your servant, and as you called me from the custom-house and did not allow me to remain to the end in my former manner of life, hear me, Lord Jesus Christ, and have mercy on the sinners." When he had so prayed, the Lord said to him: "Stand up, turn to him that groans. I will declare the rest to you." And Bartholomew raised up Satan, and said to him: Go to your place with your angels. The Lord has mercy on all his world." But the devil said: "Allow me to tell you how I was cast down here, and how God made man.

"I wandered to and fro in the world, and God said to Michael: Bring me earth from the four ends of the world and water out of the four rivers of Paradise. And when Michael had brought them to him, he formed Adam in the east, and gave form to the shapeless earth, and stretched sinews and veins, and united everything into a harmonious whole. And he showed him reverence for his own sake because he was his image. And Michael also worshiped him. And when I came from the ends of the world, Michael said to me: 'Worship the image of God which he has made in his own likeness.' But I said: 'I am fire of fire. I was the first angel to be formed, and shall I worship clay and matter?' And Michael said to me: 'Worship, lest God be angry with you.' I answered: 'God will not be angry with me, but I will set up my throne over against his throne, and shall

be as he is [Isa. 14:14f.].' Then God was angry with me and cast me down, after he had commanded the windows of heaven to be opened.

"When I was thrown down, he asked the six hundred angels that stood under me whether they would worship Adam. They replied: 'As we saw our leader do, we also will not worship him who is less than ourselves.' After our fall upon the earth we lay for forty years in deep sleep, and when the sun shone seven times more brightly than fire, I awoke. And when I looked around, I saw the six hundred under me overcome by deep sleep. And I awoke my son Salpsan, and took counsel with him how I could deceive the man on whose account I had been cast out of heaven. And I devised the following plan. I took a bowl in my hand, and scraped the sweat from my breast and my armpits, and washed myself in the spring of water from which the four rivers flow.[4] And Eve drank of it, and desire came upon her. For if she had not drunk of that water, I should not have been able to deceive her."

Then Bartholomew commanded him to go into Hades. And he came to Jesus, and fell at his feet, and began with tears to speak thus: "Abba, Father, who cannot be discovered by us, Word of the Father, whom the seven heavens hardly contained, but who were pleased to be contained easily and without pain in the body of the Virgin, without the Virgin knowing that she carried you, while you by your thought ordained everything as it should be, you who give us our daily bread without our asking for it. You who wore a crown of thorns in order to prepare for us repentant sinners the precious heavenly crown, who hung upon the cross and were given gall and vinegar to drink, in order to give us to drink the wine of contrition, and were pierced in the side with the spear, in order to satisfy us with your body and blood. You who gave names to the four rivers, to the first, Phison because of the faith, which you preached after your appearance on earth; to the second, Geon, because man was formed of earth; to the third, Tigris, that by you we might be shown the consubstantial Trinity in Heaven; and to the fourth, Euphrates, because by your coming on earth you made every soul rejoice through the message of immortality. My God, great Father and King; save, Lord, the sinners."

When Bartholomew had uttered this prayer, Jesus said to him: "Bartholomew, the Father named me Christ, that I might come down on earth and anoint with the oil of life everyone who came to me. And he called me Jesus, that I might heal every sin of the ignorant and give to men the truth of God." And again Bartholomew said to him: "Lord, may I reveal these mysteries to every man?" Jesus answered him: "Bartholomew, my beloved, entrust them to all who are faithful and can keep them for themselves. For there are some who are worthy of them; but there are also others to whom they ought not to be entrusted, for they are boasters, drunkards, proud, merciless, idolaters, seducers to fornication, slanderers, teachers of falsehood, and doers of all the works of the devil, and therefore they are not worthy that they should be entrusted to them. These things are also to be kept secret because of those who cannot contain them. For all who can contain them shall have a share in them. As regards this, therefore, my beloved, I have spoken to you, for you are blessed and all who are akin to you in having this message entrusted to them, for all who contain it shall receive all they wish in all times of my judgment."

Notes

1. The archangel Michael.
2. Judas.
3. Aparktis is also a north wind.
4. Here he will have thrown the bowl with his sweat into the water and let it flow into Paradise.

The Gospel of Nicodemus

(Christian Apocrypha)

The *Gospel of Nicodemus* is a passion gospel, purporting to be an official report of the trial, crucifixion, and resurrection of Jesus. It is also called *The Acts of Pilate*, which is actually the first of two main parts of the Gospel. The second part is *Christ's Descent into Hell*, in which Joseph of Arimathaea describes Christ's formidable entry into Hades, the freeing of the dead, and the arrest of Satan. Among other documents and letters appended to the Gospel is the Paradosis, the report of Pilate's surrender of Jesus to the Jews.

The *Gospel of Nicodemus* is one of the most dramatic and moving documents of early Christianity. Argumentative rather than spiritual, it reads like an exciting eyewitness report of murder, miracle, and resurrection. The prologue is in the voice of Ananias, a Roman guard, who claims to have found the official records in Hebrew concerning Jesus' trial and death, which he has translated into Greek and offers as "a memorial of our Lord Jesus Christ done in the time of Pontius Pilate." The Christian apologist Justin spoke of trial records—Pagan, anti-Christian records—but the prevailing opinion today is that if indeed such records were ever current, the Christian counterpart, the *Gospel of Nicodemus*, was not a contemporary work of the first century as it suggests, but a fabricated record of the third or fourth century written specifically as a pious counterblast to Pagan statements concerning Jesus. Among the heroes of the *Gospel of Nicodemus* is Pontius Pilate. His transformation into an innocent and virtuous figure appears to be an act of policy of the Roman Church. Pilate is not only vindicated, but is so Christianized that he passes into Byzantine legend as a saint and is still celebrated today as a martyr in the Coptic Church.

In the *Acts of Pilate* miracles occur in the presence of Pontius Pilate. This introduction of the supernatural is not recorded in the synoptic gospels. Then follows debate about the veracity of the miracles—a frequent controversy in noncanonical apocrypha. Was Jesus born of fornication? Was Joseph betrothed? Was Mary a virgin? Faith or disbelief makes one person's miracles another's sorcery, and so the fierce slander as each side arms itself with proof. Jesus is referred to as *rabboni*, my rabbi, as he is in the New Testament; but the word "Jew" is generally applied not to those who make up Jesus' immediate family, nor to his disciples and apostles, but to those who do not follow him and to the priestly caste. In keeping with other works of the period, the Gospel is virulently anti-Jewish. It attempts editorially to dissociate Jesus as well as early biblical figures from Jewish identity. And it goes so far as to make Moses and the prophets foretell Jesus' death and resurrection. In IV,3, we read "Jesus said: 'Moses and the prophets foretold my death and resurrection.' The Jews had been eavesdropping and heard. . . ." We have Moses and the prophets on the one hand and the Jews on the other, as if somehow the former were not Jews. There are also "good Jews" in the text—the exceptions who turn against the vile Jews in order to follow Jesus. While Old Testament prophets raged against the sins of their people, they spoke self-critically to their own tribe. Here, where the abuse comes from the outside, the term "Jews" becomes a stereotyping device to condemn a rival alien people.

The politico-religious message of the *Acts of Pilate* is foremost. In the rivalry between Christianity and its source religion, Judaism—which, from the Christian point of view, lacked the good grace to disappear or to accept Jesus as its Messiah—the *Acts of Pilate* was, as Ron Cameron states, "a document of Christian apologetics that endeavors to introduce its reader to some of the beliefs of a Christian community and to defend the claim of its members to be the true citizens of the people of God."[1] In keeping with the exoneration of Pilate and "the anti-Jewish polemic," Cameron shows how Jewish scriptures are "cited to prove that Jesus was the true fulfillment of Jewish expectations. In accordance with this view, therefore, Jesus' followers are understood to be the legitimate heirs of the Jewish tradition, the embodiment of the allegedly 'chosen people' of God."[2]

The good Jews of this *Gospel* are Nicodemus and, above all, Joseph of Arimathaea. Joseph, a rich and pious merchant, provided fine linen for Jesus' body and laid him in his own rock tomb. For doing so he was locked in a windowless house. The house was raised into the sky and there follows one of the most passionate revelations in gospel scriptures. With the rapture of the room into the air, and the lightning, smells, fainting, and trembling, Joseph has moved, in a quasi-mystical way, elsewhere. He experiences the *ekstasis*, the ecstasy, of literally "being elsewhere" as he encounters his lord:

> And at midnight as I stood and prayed, the house where you shut me in was raised up by the four corners, and I saw as it were a lightning flash in my eyes. Full of fear I fell to the ground. And someone took me by the hand and raised me up from the place where I had fallen, and something moist like water flowed from my head to my feet, and the smell of fragrant oil reached my nostrils. And he wiped my face and kissed me and said to me: Do not fear,

Joseph. Open your eyes and see who it is who speaks with you. I looked up and saw Jesus. (XV,6)

In *Christ's Descent into Hell* Jesus raises the dead from Hell. The scene shifts to Hell (Hades, in this translation) and Jesus enters like a conqueror. "And immediately at this answer the gates of brass were broken in pieces and the bars of iron were crushed and all the dead who were bound were loosed from their chains, and we with them. And the King of glory entered in like a man, and all the dark places of Hades were illumined." (V,3) Then Jesus manhandles Satan and turns him over to Hades for torture: "Bind with iron fetters his hands and his feet and his neck and his mouth." Hades accuses Satan of losing what he gained from the Tree of Knowledge to the tree of the cross. So human independence gained through knowledge—for the Gnostics the chief virtue—is lost when God's own agent, Jesus, comes to reestablish human obedience to God (and dispel the heresy of knowledge) through his death on the cross. Jesus raises the dead—Adam the forefather, the prophets, the patriarchs, and martyrs. He offers hope of salvation and entry into heaven.

In the *Paradosis* (Pilate's surrender of Jesus to the Jews), Pilate is accused by Caesar of not recognizing Jesus as a man of good deeds and miracles, of not understanding him as the Christ (the Messiah) and as the true God. He has Pilate arrested. Pilate shifts the blame to the Jews, so Caesar orders the complete destruction of the whole Jewish nation. Then he orders Pilate to be beheaded for his acts "against this righteous man called Christ." By implication, Caesar the Roman is also at heart one of the Christian fold. As for Pilate, the Lord sends an angel to receive Pilate's head as it falls from the block. With this last event Pilate became, in the eyes of the Eastern Church, a saint and martyr.

Texts of the *Gospel of Nicodemus* exist in Latin and Greek on the basis of which this translation into English by R. McL. Wilson from the German of Wilhelm Schneemelcher was originally done. Versions of the gospel also exist in Syriac, Coptic, and Armenian.

Notes

1. Ron Cameron, *The Other Gospels* (Philadelphia: Westminster Press, 1982), p. 163.
2. Cameron, *The Other Gospels*, p. 164.

ACTS OF PILATE*

records in the Hebrew language—runs approximately as follows:

Prologue

I, Ananias, an officer of the guard, being learned in the law, came to know our Lord Jesus Christ from the sacred scriptures, which I approached with faith, and was accounted worthy of holy baptism. And having searched for the reports made at that period in the time of our Lord Jesus Christ which the Jews committed to writing under Pontius Pilate, I found these acts in the Hebrew language and according to God's good pleasure I translated them into Greek for the information of all those who call upon the name of our Lord Jesus Christ, in the eighteenth year of the reign of our Emperor Flavius Theodosius and in the fifth year of the "Nobility" of Flavius Valentinianus, in the ninth indiction.

Therefore all you who read this and copy it out, remember me and pray for me that God may be gracious to me and forgive my sins which I have sinned against him. Peace be to those who read and hear it, and to their servants. Amen.

In the nineteenth year of the reign of the Roman Emperor Tiberius, when Herod was king of Galilee, in the nineteenth year of his rule, on the eighth day before the Kalends of April, that is, the 25th of March, in the consulate of Rufus and Rubellio, in the fourth year of the two hundred and second Olympiad, when Joseph Caiaphas was high priest of the Jews.

What Nicodemus after the passion of the Lord upon the cross recorded and delivered concerning the conduct of the chief priests and the rest of the Jews— and the same Nicodemus drew up his

I

The chief priests and scribes assembled in council, Annas and Caiaphas, Semes, Dathaes and Gamaliel, Judas, Levi and Nephthalim, Alexander and Jairus, and the rest of the Jews, and came to Pilate accusing Jesus of many deeds. They said: "We know that this man is the son of Joseph the carpenter and was born of Mary; but he says he is the Son of God and a king. Moreover he pollutes the Sabbath and wishes to destroy the law of our fathers." Pilate said: "And what things does he do that he wishes to destroy it?" The Jews say: "We have a law that we should not heal anyone on the Sabbath. But this man with his evil deeds has healed on the Sabbath the lame, the bent, the withered, the blind, the paralytic, and the possessed." Pilate asked them: "With what evil deeds?" They answered him: "He is a sorcerer, and by Beelzebub the prince of the devils he casts out evil spirits, and all are subject to him." Pilate said to them: "This is not to cast out demons by an unclean spirit, but by the god Asclepius."

The Jews said to Pilate: "We beseech your excellency to place him before your judgment seat and to try him." And Pilate called them to him and said: "Tell me! How can I, a governor, examine a king?" They answered: "We do not say that he is a king, but he says he is." And Pilate summoned his messenger and said to him: "Let Jesus be brought with gentleness." So the messenger went out, and when he perceived him, he did him reverence, and taking the kerchief which was in his hand, he spread it upon the ground, and said to him: "Lord, walk on this and go in, for the governor calls you." But when the Jews saw what the messenger had done, they cried out against Pilate and said: "Why did you not order him to come in by a herald, but by a messenger? For as soon as he saw

*All selections in this chapter are from Edgar Hennecke and Wilhelm Schneemelcher, eds., R. McL. Wilson, trans., *New Testament Apocrypha*, vol. 1 (Philadelphia: Westminster Press, 1963), pp. 449–476, 482–484, 403.

him the messenger reverenced him, and spread out his kerchief on the ground, and made him walk on it like a king."

Then Pilate called for the messenger and said to him: "Why have you done this, and spread your kerchief on the ground and made Jesus walk on it?" The messenger answered him: "Lord governor, when you sent me to Jerusalem to Alexander, I saw him sitting on an ass, and the children of the Hebrews held branches in their hands and cried out; and others spread their garments before him, saying: 'Save now, you who are in the highest! Blessed is he that comes in the name of the Lord!' "

The Jews cried out to the messenger: "The children of the Hebrews cried out in Hebrew; how do you know it in Greek?" The messenger replied: "I asked one of the Jews, and said: What is it that they cry out in Hebrew? And he interpreted it to me." Pilate said to them: "And what did they cry out in Hebrew?" The Jews answered: "Hosanna membrome baruchamma adonai." Pilate asked again: "And the Hosanna and the rest, how is it translated?" The Jews replied: "Save now, you who are in the highest. Blessed is he that comes in the name of the Lord." Pilate said to them: "If you testify to the words of the children, what sin has the messenger committed?" And they were silent. The governor said to the messenger: "Go out and bring him in in whatever way you wish." And the messenger went out and did as before and said to Jesus: "Enter, the governor calls you."

Now when Jesus entered in, and the standard-bearers were holding the standards, the images of the emperor on the standards bowed and did reverence to Jesus. And when the Jews saw the behavior of the standards, how they bowed down and did reverence to Jesus, they cried out loudly against the standard-bearers. But Pilate said to them: "Do you not marvel how the images bowed and did reverence to Jesus?" The Jews said to Pilate: "We saw how the standard-bear-

ers lowered them and reverenced him." And the governor summoned the standard-bearers and asked them: "Why did you do this?" They answered: "We are Greeks and servers of temples, and how could we reverence him? We held the images; but they bowed down of their own accord and reverenced him."

Then Pilate said to the rulers of the synagogue and the elders of the people: "Choose strong men to carry the standards, and let us see whether the images bow by themselves." So the elders of the Jews took twelve strong men and made them carry the standards by sixes, and they were placed before the judgment seat of the governor. And Pilate said to the messenger: "Take him out of the praetorium and bring him in again in whatever way you wish." And Jesus left the praetorium with the messenger. And Pilate summoned those who before carried the images, and said to them: "I have sworn by the safety of Caesar that, if the standards do not bow down when Jesus enters, I will cut off your heads." And the governor commanded Jesus to enter in the second time. And the messenger did as before and besought Jesus to walk upon his kerchief. He walked upon it and entered in. And when he had entered in, the standards bowed down again and did reverence to Jesus.

II

When Pilate saw this he was afraid, and sought to rise from the judgment seat. And while he was still thinking of rising up, his wife sent to him saying: Have nothing to do with this righteous man. For I have suffered many things because of him by night [Matt. 27:19]. And Pilate summoned all the Jews, and stood up and said to them: "You know that my wife fears God and favors rather the customs of the Jews, with you." They answered him: "Yes, we know it." Pilate said to them: "See, my wife sent to me saying: Have nothing to do with this righteous man. For I have suffered many things because of him by night." The Jews answered Pilate: "Did we not tell you that he is a sorcerer? Behold, he has sent a dream to your wife." And Pilate called Jesus to him and said to him: "What do these men testify against you? Do you say nothing?" Jesus answered: "If they had no power, they would say nothing; for each man has power over his own mouth, to speak good and evil. They shall see to it."

Then the elders of the Jews answered and said to Jesus: "What should we see? Firstly, that you were born of fornication; secondly, that your birth meant the death of the children in Bethlehem; thirdly, that your father Joseph and your mother Mary fled into Egypt because they counted for nothing among the people." Then some of the Jews that stood by, devout men, declared: "We deny that he came of fornication, for we know that Joseph was betrothed to Mary, and he was not born of fornication." Pilate then said to the Jews who said that he came of fornication: "Your statement is not true; for there was a betrothal, as your own fellow countrymen say." Annas and Caiaphas say to Pilate: "We, the whole multitude, cry out that he was born of fornication, and we are not believed; these are proselytes and disciples of his." And Pilate called Annas and Caiaphas and said to them: "What are proselytes?" They answered: "They were born children of Greeks, and now have become Jews." Then those who said that he was not born of fornication, namely Lazarus, Asterius, Antonius, Jacob, Amnes, Zeras, Samuel, Isaac, Phinees, Crispus, Agrippa, and Judas said: "We are not proselytes, but are children of Jews and speak the truth; for we were present at the betrothal of Joseph and Mary."

And Pilate called to him these twelve men who denied that he was born of fornication, and said to them: "I put you on your oath, by the safety of Caesar, that your statement is true, that he was not born of fornication." They said to Pilate: "We have a law not to swear because it is a sin. But let *them* swear by the safety of Caesar that it is not as we have said, and we will be worthy of death." Pilate said to Annas and Caiaphas: "Do you not answer these things?" And Annas and Caiaphas said to Pilate: "These twelve men who say that he was not born of fornication are believed. But we, the whole multitude, cry out that he was born of fornication and is a sorcerer, and claims to be the Son of God and a king, and we are not believed." And Pilate sent out the whole multitude, except the twelve men who denied that he was born of fornication, and commanded Jesus to be set apart. And he asked them: "For what cause do they wish to kill him?" They answered Pilate: "They are incensed because he heals on the Sabbath." Pilate said: "For a good work do they wish to kill him?" They answered him: "Yes."

III

And Pilate was filled with anger and went out of the praetorium and said to them: "I call the sun to witness that I find no fault in this man." The Jews answered and said to the governor: "If this man were not an evildoer, we would not have handed him over to you" [John 18: 30]. And Pilate said: "Take him yourselves and judge him by your own law." The Jews said to Pilate: "It is not lawful for us to put any man to death" [John 18:31]. Pilate said: "Has God forbidden you to slay, but allowed me?"

And Pilate entered the praetorium again and called Jesus apart and asked him: "Are you the king of the Jews?" Jesus answered Pilate: "Do you say this of your own accord, or did others say it to you about me?" Pilate answered Jesus: "Am I a Jew? Your own nation and the chief priests have handed you over to me. What have you done?" Jesus answered: "My kingship is not of this world; for if my kingship were of this world, my servants would fight, that I might not be handed over to the Jews. But now is my kingship not from here." Pilate said to him: "So you are a king?" Jesus answered him: "You say that I am a king. For this cause I was born and have come, that everyone who is of the truth should hear my voice." Pilate said to him: "What is truth?" [John 18:33–38]. Jesus answered him: "Truth is from Heaven." Pilate said: "Is there not truth upon earth?" Jesus said to Pilate: "You see how those who speak the truth are judged by those who have authority on earth."

IV

And Pilate left Jesus in the praetorium and went out to the Jews and said to them: "I find no fault in him" [John 18:38]. The Jews said to him: "He said, 'I am able to destroy this temple and build it in three days'" [Matt. 26:61]. Pilate said: "What temple?" The Jews said: "That which Solomon built in forty-six years; but this man says he will destroy it and build it in three days." Pilate said to them: "I am innocent of the blood of this righteous man; see to it yourselves." The Jews replied "His blood be on us and on our children" [Matt. 27:24f.]. And Pilate called to him the elders and the priests and the Levites and said to them secretly: "Do not act thus; for nothing of which you have accused him deserves death. For your accusation concerns healing and profanation of the Sabbath." The elders and the priests and the Levites answered: "If a man blasphemes against Caesar, is he worthy of death or not?" Pilate said: "He is worthy of death." The Jews said to Pilate: "If a man blasphemes against Caesar, he is worthy of death, but this man has blasphemed against God."

Then the governor commanded the Jews to go out from the praetorium, and he called Jesus to him and said to him: "What shall I do with you?" Jesus answered Pilate: "As it was given to you."

Pilate said: "How was it given?" Jesus said: "Moses and the prophets foretold my death and resurrection." The Jews had been eavesdropping and heard, and they said to Pilate: "What further need have you to hear of this blasphemy?" Pilate said to the Jews: "If this word is blasphemy, take him, bring him into your synagogue and judge him according to your law" [John 18:31]. The Jews answered Pilate: "It is contained in our law, that if a man sins against a man, he must receive forty strokes save one, but he who blasphemes against God must be stoned."

Pilate said to them: "Take him yourselves and punish him as you wish." The Jews said to Pilate: "We wish him to be crucified." Pilate said: "He does not deserve to be crucified." The governor looked at the multitudes of the Jews standing around, and when he saw many of the Jews weeping, he said: "Not all the multitude wishes him to die." But the elders of the Jews said: "For this purpose has the whole multitude of us come, that he should die." Pilate said to the Jews: "Why should he die?" The Jews said: "Because he called himself the Son of God and a king."

V

Now Nicodemus, a Jew, stood before the governor, and said: "I beseech you, honorable governor, to allow me a few words." Pilate said: "Speak." Nicodemus said: "I said to the elders and the priests and the Levites and to all the multitude in the synagogue: What do you intend to do with this man? This man does many signs and wonders, which no one has done nor will do. Let him alone and contrive no evil against him. If the signs which he does are from God, they will stand; if they are from men, they will come to nothing [Acts 5:38f.]. For Moses also, when he was sent by God into Egypt, did many signs which God commanded him to do before Pharaoh, king of Egypt. And there were there servants of Pharaoh, Jannes and Jambres, and they also did signs not a few which Moses did, and the Egyptians held them as gods, Jannes and Jambres. And since the signs which they did were not from God, they perished as well as those who believed them. And now let this man go, for he does not deserve death."

The Jews said to Nicodemus: "You became his disciple and speak on his behalf." Nicodemus answered them: "Has the governor also become his disciple, and speaks on his behalf? Did not Caesar appoint him to this high office?" Then the Jews raged and gnashed their teeth against Nicodemus. Pilate said to them: "Why do you gnash your teeth against him, when you hear the truth?" The Jews said to Nicodemus: "Receive his truth and his portion." Nicodemus said: "Amen, may it be as you have said."

VI

Then one of the Jews hastened forward and asked the governor that he might speak a word. The governor said: "If you wish to say anything, say it." And the Jew said: "For thirty-eight years I lay on a bed in anguish of pains, and when Jesus came many demoniacs and those lying sick of diverse diseases were healed by him. And certain young men took pity on me and carried me with my bed and brought me to him. And when Jesus saw me he had compassion, and spoke a word to me: Take up your bed and walk. And I took up my bed and walked" [Mark 2:1ff.; John 5:1ff.]. The Jews said to Pilate: "Ask him what day it was on which he was healed." He that was healed said "On a Sabbath." The Jews said: "Did we not inform you so, that on the Sabbath he heals and casts out demons?"

And another Jew hastened forward and said: "I was born blind; I heard any man's voice, but did not see his face. And as Jesus passed by I cried with a loud voice: Have mercy on me, Son of David. And he took pity on me and put his hands on my eyes and I saw immediately" [Mark 10:46ff.]. And another Jew hastened forward and said "I was bowed, and he made me straight with a word." And another said: "I was a leper, and he healed me with a word."

VII

And a woman called Bernice, crying out from a distance, said: "I had an issue of blood and I touched the hem of his garment, and the issue of blood, which had lasted twelve years, ceased" [Mark 5:25ff.]. The Jews said "We have a law not to permit a woman to give testimony."

VIII

And others, a multitude of men and women, cried out: "This man is a prophet, and the demons are subject to him." Pilate said to those who said the demons were subject to him: "Why are your teachers also not subject to him?" They said to Pilate: "We do not know." Others said: "Lazarus who was dead he raised up out of the tomb after four days." Then the governor began to tremble and said to all the multitude of the Jews: "Why do you wish to shed innocent blood?"

IX

And he called to him Nicodemus and the twelve men who said he was not born of fornication and said to them: "What shall I do? The people are becoming rebellious." They answered him: "We do not know. Let them see to it." Again Pilate called all the multitude of the Jews and said: "You know the custom that at the feast of unleavened bread a prisoner is released to you. I have in the prison one condemned for murder, called Barabbas, and this Jesus who stands before you, in whom I find no fault. Whom do you wish me to release to you?" They cried out: "Barabbas." Pilate said: "Then what shall I do with Jesus who is called Christ?" The Jews cried out: "Let him be crucified" [Matt. 27:15ff.]. But some of the Jews answered: "You are not Caesar's friend if you release this man [John 19:12], for he called himself the Son of God and a king. You wish him therefore to be king and not Caesar."

And Pilate was angry and said to the Jews: "Your nation is always seditious and in rebellion against your benefactors." The Jews asked: "What benefactors?" Pilate answered: "As I have heard, your God brought you out of Egypt out of hard slavery, and led you safe through the sea as if it had been dry land, and in the wilderness nourished you and gave you manna and quails, and gave you water to drink from a rock, and gave you the law. And despite all this you provoked the anger of your God: you wanted a molten calf and angered your God, and he wished to destroy you; and Moses made supplication for you, and you were not put to death. And now you accuse me of hating the emperor."

And he rose up from the judgment seat and sought to go out. And the Jews cried out: "We recognize as king Caesar alone and not Jesus. For indeed the wise men brought him gifts from the east, as if he were a king. And when Herod heard from the wise men that a king was born, he sought to slay him. But when his father Joseph knew that, he took him and his mother, and they fled into Egypt. And when Herod heard it, he destroyed the children of the Hebrews who were born in Bethlehem."

When Pilate heard these words, he was afraid. And he silenced the multitudes, because they were crying out, and said to them: "So this is he whom Herod sought?" The Jews replied: "Yes, this is he." And Pilate took water and washed his hands before the sun and said: "I am innocent of the blood of this righteous man. You see to it." Again the Jews cried out: "His blood be on us and on our children" [Matt. 27:24f.].

Then Pilate commanded the curtain to be drawn[1] before the judgment seat on which he sat, and said to Jesus: "Your nation has convicted you of claiming to be a king. Therefore I have decreed that you should first be scourged according to the law of the pious emperors, and then hanged on the cross in the garden where you were seized. And let Dysmas and Gestas, the two malefactors, be crucified with you."

X

And Jesus went out from the praetorium, the two malefactors with him. And when they came to the appointed place, they stripped him and girded him with a linen cloth and put a crown of thorns on his head. Likewise they hanged up also the two malefactors. But Jesus said: "Father, forgive them, for they know not what they do" [Luke 23:34]. And the soldiers parted his garments among them. And the people stood looking at him. And the chief priests and the rulers with them scoffed at him, saying: "He saved others, let him save himself. If he is the Son of God, let him come down from the cross." And the soldiers also mocked him, coming and offering him vinegar with gall, and they said: "If you are the king of the Jews, save yourself" [Luke 23:35ff.]. And after the sentence Pilate commanded the crime brought against him to be written as a title in Greek, Latin, and Hebrew, according to the accusation of the Jews that he claimed to be king of the Jews [John 19:19f.].

One of the malefactors who were crucified said to him: "If you are the Christ, save yourself and us." But Dysmas rebuked him: "Do you not at all fear God, since you are in the same condemnation? And justly so. For we are receiving the due reward of our deeds. But this man has done nothing wrong." And he said to Jesus: "Lord, remember me in your kingdom." And Jesus said to him: "Truly, I say to you, today you will be with me in Paradise" [Luke 23:39ff.].

367

XI

And it was about the sixth hour, and there was darkness over the land until the ninth hour, for the sun was darkened. And the curtain of the temple was torn in two. And Jesus cried with a loud voice: "Father, baddach ephkid rouel," which means: "Into thy hands I commit my spirit." And having said this he gave up the ghost. And when the centurion saw what had happened, he praised God, saying: "This man was righteous." And all the multitudes who had come to this sight, when they saw what had taken place, beat their breasts and returned [Luke 23:44–48].

But the centurion reported to the governor what had happened. And when the governor and his wife heard, they were greatly grieved, and they neither ate nor drank on that day. And Pilate sent for the Jews and said to them: "Did you see what happened?" But they answered: "There was an eclipse of the sun in the usual way." And his acquaintances had stood far off and the women who had come with him from Galilee, and saw these things. But a certain man named Joseph, a member of the council, from the town of Arimathaea, who also was waiting for the kingdom of God, this man went to Pilate and asked for the body of Jesus. And he took it down, and wrapped it in a clean linen cloth, and placed it in a rock-hewn tomb, in which no one had ever yet been laid [Luke 23: 50–53].

XII

When the Jews heard that Joseph had asked for the body, they sought him and the twelve men who said that Jesus was not born of fornication, and Nicodemus and many others, who had come forward before Pilate and made known his good works. But they all hid themselves, and only Nicodemus was seen by them, because he was a ruler of the Jews. And Nicodemus said to them: "How did you enter the synagogue?" The Jews answered him: "How did you enter the synagogue? You are an accomplice of his, and his portion shall be with you in the world to come." Nicodemus said: "Amen, amen." Likewise also Joseph came forth from his concealment and said to them: "Why are you angry with me because I asked for the body of Jesus? See, I have placed it in my new tomb, having wrapped it in clean linen, and I rolled a stone before the door of the cave. And you have not done well with the righteous one, for you did not repent of having crucified him, but also pierced him with a spear."

Then the Jews seized Joseph and commanded him to be secured until the first day of the week. They said to him: "Know that the hour forbids us to do anything against you, because the Sabbath dawns. But know also that you will not even be counted worthy of burial, but we shall give your flesh to the birds of the heaven." Joseph answered: "This word is like that of the boastful Goliath who insulted the living God and the holy David. For God said by the prophet: Vengeance is mine, I will repay, says the Lord [Rom. 12:19; cf. Deut. 32:35]. And now he who is uncircumcised in the flesh, but circumcised in heart, took water and washed his hands before the sun, saying, I am innocent of the blood of this righteous man. You see to it. And you answered Pilate: His blood be on us and on our children [Matt. 27:25]. And now I fear lest the wrath of God come upon you and your children, as you said." When the Jews heard these words, they were embittered in their hearts, and laid hold of Joseph and seized him and shut him in a building without a window, and guards remained at the door. And they sealed the door of the place where Joseph was shut up.

And on the Sabbath the rulers of the synagogue and the priests and the Levites ordered that all should present themselves in the synagogue on the first day of the week. And the whole multitude rose up early and took counsel in the synagogue concerning how he should be killed. And when the council was in session they commanded him to be brought with great dishonor. And when they opened the door they did not find him. And all the people were astonished and filled with consternation because they found the seals undamaged, and Caiaphas had the key. And they dared no longer lay hands on those who had spoken before Pilate on behalf of Jesus.

XIII

And while they still sat in the synagogue and marveled because of Joseph, there came some of the guard which the Jews had asked from Pilate to guard the tomb of Jesus, lest his disciples should come and steal him. And they told the rulers of the synagogue and the priests and the Levites what had happened, how there was a great earthquake. "And we saw an angel descend from heaven, and he rolled away the stone from the mouth of the cave, and sat upon it, and he shone like snow and like lightning. And we were in great fear, and lay like dead men [Matt. 28:2–4]. And we heard the voice of the angel speaking to the women who waited at the tomb: Do not be afraid. I know that you seek Jesus who was crucified. He is not here. He has risen, as he said. Come and see the place where the Lord lay. And go quickly and tell his disciples that he has risen from the dead and is in Galilee" [Matt. 28:5–7].

The Jews asked: "To what women did he speak?" The members of the guard answered: "We do not know who they were." The Jews said: "At what hour was it?" The members of the guard answered: "At midnight." The Jews said: "And why did you not seize the women?" The members of the guard said: "We were like dead men through fear, and gave up hope of seeing the light of day; how could we then have seized them?" The Jews said: "As the Lord lives, we do not believe you." The members of the guard said to the Jews: "So many signs you saw in that man and you did not believe; and how can you believe us? You rightly swore: As the Lord lives. For he *does* live." Again the members of the guard said: "We have heard that you shut up him who asked for the body of Jesus, and sealed the door, and that when you opened it you did not find him. Therefore give us Joseph and we will give you Jesus." The Jews said: "Joseph has gone to his own city." And the members of the guard said to the Jews: "And Jesus has risen, as we heard from the angel, and is in Galilee."

And when the Jews heard these words, they feared greatly and said: "Take heed lest this report be heard and all incline to Jesus." And the Jews took counsel, and offered much money and gave it to the soldiers of the guard, saying: "Say that when you were sleeping his disciples came by night and stole him. And if this is heard by the governor, we will persuade him and keep you out of trouble" [Matt. 28:12–14].

XIV

Now Phinees, a priest, and Adas, a teacher, and Angaeus, a Levite, came from Galilee to Jerusalem, and told the rulers of the synagogue and the priests and the Levites: "We saw Jesus and his disciples sitting upon the mountain which is called Mamilch. And he said to his disciples: Go into all the world and preach the gospel to the whole creation. He who believes and is baptized will be saved; but he who does not believe will be condemned. And these signs will accompany those who believe: in my name they will cast out demons; they will speak in new tongues; they will pick up serpents; and if they drink any deadly thing, it will not hurt them; they will lay their hands on the sick, and they will recover [Mark 16:15–18]. And while Jesus was still speaking to his disciples, we saw him taken up into Heaven."

369

Then the elders and the priests and the Levites said: "Give glory to the God of Israel, and confess before him if you indeed heard and saw what you have described." Those who told them said: "As the Lord God of our fathers Abraham, Isaac, and Jacob lives, we heard these things and saw him taken up to Heaven." The elders and the priests and the Levites said to them: "Did you come to tell us this, or did you come to offer prayer to God?" They answered: "To offer prayer to God." The elders and the chief priests and the Levites said to them: "If you came to offer prayer to God, to what purpose is this idle tale which you have babbled before all the people?" Phinees, the priest, and Adas, the teacher, and Angaeus, the Levite, said to the rulers of the synagogue and priests and Levites: "If the words which we spoke concerning what we heard and saw are sin, see, we stand before you. Do with us as it seems good in your eyes." And they took the law and adjured them to tell this no more to any one. And they gave them to eat and drink, and sent them out of the city, having given them money and three men to accompany them, and ordered them to depart as far as Galilee; and they went away in peace.

But when those men had departed to Galilee, the chief priests and the rulers of the synagogue and the elders assembled in the synagogue, and shut the gate, and raised a great lamentation, saying: "Why has this sign happened in Israel?" But Annas and Caiaphas said: "Why are you troubled? Why do you weep? Do you not know that his disciples gave much money to the guards of the tomb, took away his body, and taught them to say that an angel descended from Heaven and rolled away the stone from the door of the tomb?" But the priests and the elders replied: "Let it be that his disciples stole his body. But how did the soul enter again into the body, so that Jesus now waits in Galilee?" But they, unable to give an answer, came with difficulty to say: "It is not lawful for us to believe the uncircumcised."

XV

And Nicodemus stood up and stood before the council and said: "What you say is right. You know, people of the Lord, that the men who came from Galilee fear God and are men of substance, that they hate covetousness,[2] and are men of peace. And they have declared on oath: We saw Jesus on the mountain Mamilch with his disciples. He taught them what you have heard from them. And we saw him taken up into Heaven. And no one asked them in what manner he was taken up. Just as the holy Scriptures tell us that Elijah also was taken up into Heaven, and Elisha cried with a loud voice, and Elijah cast his sheepskin cloak upon Elisha, and Elisha cast his cloak upon the Jordan, and crossed over and went to Jericho. And the sons of the prophets met him and said: 'Elisha, where is your master Elijah?' And he said that he was taken up into Heaven. But they said to Elisha: 'Has perhaps a spirit caught him up and cast him on one of the mountains? But let us take our servants with us and search for him.' And they persuaded Elisha, and he went with them. And they searched for him for three days and did not find him, and they knew that he had been taken up [2 Kings 2]. And now listen to me, and let us send to every mountain of Israel and see whether the Christ was taken up by a spirit and cast upon a mountain." And this proposal pleased them all. And they sent to every mountain of Israel, and searched for Jesus and did not find him. But they found Joseph in Arimathaea and no one dared to seize him.

And they told the elders and the priests and the Levites: "We went about to every mountain of Israel, and did not find Jesus. But Joseph we found in Arimathaea." And when they heard about Joseph, they rejoiced and gave glory to the God of Israel. And the rulers of the synagogue and the priests and the Levites took counsel how they should meet with Joseph, and they took a roll of papyrus and wrote to Joseph these words. "Peace be with you. We know that we have sinned against God and against you, and we have prayed to the God of Israel that you should condescend to come to your fathers and your children, because we are all troubled. For when we opened the door we did not find you. We know that we devised an evil plan against you; but the Lord helped you, and the Lord himself has brought to nothing our plan against you, honored father Joseph."

And they chose from all Israel seven men who were friends of Joseph, whom also Joseph himself acknowledged as friends, and the rulers of the synagogue and the priests and the Levites said to them: "See! If he receives our letter and reads it, know that he will come with you to us. But if he does not read it, know that he is angry with us, and salute him in peace and return to us." And they blessed the men and dismissed them. And the men came to Joseph and greeted him with reverence, and said to him: "Peace be with you!" He replied: "Peace be with you and all Israel!" And they gave him the roll of the letter. Joseph took it and read it and kissed the letter, and blessed God and said: "Blessed be God who has delivered the Israelites from shedding innocent blood. And blessed be the Lord, who sent his angel and sheltered me under his wings." And he set a table before them, and they ate and drank and lay down there.

And they rose up early in the morning and prayed. And Joseph saddled his she-ass and went with the men, and they came to the holy city Jerusalem. And all the people met Joseph and cried: "Peace be to your entering in!" And he said to all the people: "Peace be with you!" And all kissed him, and prayed with Joseph, and were beside themselves with joy at seeing him. And Nicodemus received

him into his house and made a great feast, and called the elders and the priests and the Levites to his house, and they made merry, eating and drinking with Joseph. And after singing a hymn each one went to his house; but Joseph remained in the house of Nicodemus.

And on the next day, which was the preparation, the rulers of the synagogue and the priests and the Levites rose up early and came to the house of Nicodemus. Nicodemus met them and said: "Peace be with you!" They answered: "Peace be with you and with Joseph and with all your house and with all the house of Joseph!" And he brought them into his house. And the whole council sat down, and Joseph sat between Annas and Caiaphas. And no one dared to speak a word to him. And Joseph said: "Why have you called me?" And they beckoned to Nicodemus to speak to Joseph. Nicodemus opened his mouth and said to Joseph: "Father, you know that the honorable teachers and the priests and the Levites wish information from you." Joseph answered: "Ask me." And Annas and Caiaphas took the law and adjured Joseph, saying: "Give glory to the God of Israel and make confession to him. For Achan also, when adjured by the prophet Joshua, did not commit perjury, but told him everything and concealed nothing from him [Joshua 7]. So do you also not conceal from us a single word." Joseph answered: "I will not conceal anything from you." And they said to him: "We were very angry because you asked for the body of Jesus, and wrapped it in a clean linen cloth, and placed it in a tomb. And for this reason we secured you in a house with no window, and locked and sealed the door, and guards watched where you were shut up. And on the first day of the week we opened it, and did not find you, and were much troubled, and all the people of God were amazed until yesterday. And now tell us what happened to you."

And Joseph said: "On the day of preparation about the tenth hour you shut me in, and I remained the whole Sabbath. And at midnight as I stood and prayed, the house where you shut me in was raised up by the four corners, and I saw as it were a lightning flash in my eyes. Full of fear, I fell to the ground. And someone took me by the hand and raised me up from the place where I had fallen, and something moist like water flowed from my head to my feet, and the smell of fragrant oil reached my nostrils. And he wiped my face and kissed me and said to me: 'Do not fear, Joseph. Open your eyes and see who it is who speaks with you.' I looked up and saw Jesus. Trembling, I thought it was a phantom, and I said the ten commandments. And he said them with me. Now as you well know, a phantom immediately flees if it meets anyone and hears the commandments. And when I saw that he said them with me, I said to him: 'Rabbi Elijah!' He said: 'I am not Elijah.' And I said to him: 'Who are you, Lord?' He replied: 'I am Jesus, whose body you asked for from Pilate, whom you clothed in clean linen, on whose face you placed a cloth, and whom you placed in your new cave, and you rolled a great stone to the door of the cave.' And I asked him who spoke to me; 'Show me the place where I laid you.' And he took me and showed me the place where I laid him. And the linen cloth lay there, and the cloth that was upon his face. Then I recognized that it was Jesus. And he took me by the hand and placed me in the middle of my house, with the doors shut, and led me to my bed and said to me: 'Peace be with you!' Then he kissed me and said to me: 'Do not go out of your house for forty days. For see, I go to my brethren in Galilee.' "

XVI

And when the rulers of the synagogue and the priests and the Levites heard these words from Joseph, they became as dead men and fell to the ground and fasted until the ninth hour. And Nicode-mus and Joseph comforted Annas and Caiaphas and the priests and Levites, saying: "Get up and stand on your feet, and taste bread and strengthen your souls. For tomorrow is the Sabbath of the Lord." And they rose up and prayed to God, and ate and drank, and went each to his own house.

And on the Sabbath our teachers and the priests and the Levites sat and questioned one another, saying: "What is this wrath which has come upon us? For we know his father and his mother." Levi the teacher said: "I know that his parents fear God and do not withhold their prayers and pay tithes three times a year. And when Jesus was born, his parents brought him to this place, and gave God sacrifices and burnt offerings. And the great teacher Symeon took him in his arms and said: Lord, now let your servant depart in peace, according to your word; for my eyes have seen your salvation which you have prepared in the presence of all peoples, a light for revelation to the Gentiles, and for glory to your people of Israel. And Symeon blessed them and said to Mary, his mother: I give you good tidings concerning this child. And Mary said: Good, my lord? And Symeon said to her: Good. Behold, this child is set for the fall and rising of many in Israel, and for a sign that is spoken against and a sword will pierce through your own soul also, that thoughts out of many hearts may be revealed" [Luke 2:28–35].

They said to Levi, the teacher: "How do you know this?" Levi answered them: "Do you not know that I learned the law from him?" The council said to him: "We wish to see your father." And they sent for his father. And when they questioned him, he said to them: "Why did you not believe my son? The blessed and righteous Symeon taught him the law." The council said: "Rabbi Levi, is the word true which you have spoken?" He answered: "It is true." Then the rulers of the synagogue and the priests and the Levites said among themselves: "Come, let us send to Galilee to the three men who came and told us of his teaching and of his being taken up, and let them tell us how they saw him taken up." And this word pleased them all. And they sent the three men who before had gone to Galilee with them, and said to them: "Say to Rabbi Adas and Rabbi Phinees and Rabbi Angaeus: Peace be with you and all who are with you. Since an important inquiry is taking place in the council, we were sent to you to call you to this holy place Jerusalem."

And the men went to Galilee and found them sitting and studying the law, and greeted them in peace. And the men who were in Galilee said to those who had come to them: "Peace be to all Israel." They answered: "Peace be with you." And again they said to them: "Why have you come?" Those who had been sent replied: "The council calls you to the holy city Jerusalem." When the men heard that they were sought by the council, they prayed to God and sat down at table with the men and ate and drank, and then arose and came in peace to Jerusalem.

And on the next day the council sat in the synagogue and questioned them, saying: "Did you indeed see Jesus sitting on the mountain Mamilch, teaching his eleven disciples? And did you see him taken up?" And the men answered them and said: "As we saw him taken up, so we have told you." Annas said: "Separate them from one another, and let us see if their accounts agree." And they separated them from one another. And they called Adas first and asked him: "How did you see Jesus taken up?" Adas answered: "As he sat on the mountain Mamilch and taught his disciples, we saw that a cloud overshadowed him and his disciples. And the cloud carried him up to Heaven, and his disciples lay on their faces on the ground." Then they called Phinees the priest and asked him also: "How did you see Jesus taken up?" And he said the same thing. And again they asked Angaeus, and he said the

same thing. Then the members of the council said: "At the mouth of two or three witnesses shall every matter be established" [Deut. 19:15]. Abuthem, the teacher, said: "It is written in the law: Enoch walked with God, and was not, for God took him" [Gen. 5:24]. Jairus, the teacher, said: "Also we have heard of the death of the holy Moses, and we do not know how he died. For it is written in the law of the Lord: And Moses died as the mouth of the Lord determined, and no man knew of his sepulcher to this day" [Deut. 34:5f.]. And Rabbi Levi said: "Why did Rabbi Symeon say, when he saw Jesus: Behold, this child is set for the fall and rising of many in Israel, and for a sign that is spoken against? [Luke 2:34]. And Rabbi Isaac said: "It is written in the law: Behold, I send my messenger before your face. He will go before you to guard you in every good way. In him my name is named" [Exod. 23:20f.].

Then Annas and Caiaphas said: "You have rightly said what is written in the law of Moses, that no one knows the death of Enoch and no one has named the death of Moses. But Jesus had to give account before Pilate; we saw how he received blows and spitting on his face, that the soldiers put a crown of thorns upon him, that he was scourged and condemned by Pilate and then was crucified at the place of a skull; he was given vinegar and gall to drink, and Longinus the soldier pierced his side with a spear. Our honorable father Joseph asked for his body; and, he says, he rose again. And the three teachers declare: We saw him taken up into Heaven. And Rabbi Levi spoke and testified to the words of Rabbi Symeon: Behold, this child is set for the fall and rising of many in Israel, and for a sign that is spoken against [Luke 2:34]." And all the teachers said to all the people of the Lord: "If this is from the Lord, and it is marvelous in your eyes, you shall surely know, O house of Jacob, that it is written: Cursed is everyone who hangs on a tree [Deut. 21:23]. And another passage of scripture teaches: The gods who did not make the Heaven and the earth shall perish [Jer. 10:11]." And the priests and the Levites said to one another: "If Jesus is remembered after fifty years,[3] he will reign forever and create for himself a new people." Then the rulers of the synagogue and the priests and the Levites admonished all Israel: "Cursed is the man who shall worship the work of man's hand, and cursed is the man who shall worship created things alongside the creator." And the people answered: "Amen, amen."

And all the people praised the Lord God and sang: "Blessed be the Lord who has given rest to the people of Israel according to all his promises. Not one word remains unfulfilled of all the good which he promised to his servant Moses. May the Lord our God be with us as he was with our fathers. May he not forsake us. May he not let the will die in us, to turn our heart to him, and walk in all his ways, and keep his commandments and laws which he gave to our fathers. And the Lord shall be king over all the earth on that day. And there shall be one God and his name shall be one, our Lord and king. He shall save us. There is none like you, O Lord. Great art you, O Lord, and great is your name. Heal us, O Lord, in your power, and we shall be healed. Save us, Lord, and we shall be saved. For we are your portion and inheritance. The Lord will not forsake his people for his great name's sake, for the Lord has begun to make us his people." After this hymn of praise they all departed, every man to his house, glorifying God. For his is the glory forever and ever. Amen.

CHRIST'S DESCENT INTO HELL

I

Joseph said: "Why then do you marvel at the resurrection of Jesus? It is not this that is marvelous, but rather that he was not raised alone, but raised up many other dead men who appeared to many in Jerusalem. And if you do not know the others, yet Symeon, who took Jesus in his arms, and his two sons, whom he raised up, you do know. For we buried them a little while ago. And now their sepulchers are to be seen opened and empty, but they themselves are alive and dwelling in Arimathaea." They therefore sent men, and they found their tombs opened and empty. Joseph said: "Let us go to Arimathaea and find them."

Then arose the chief priests Annas and Caiaphas, and Joseph and Nicodemus and Gamaliel and others with them, and went to Arimathaea and found the men of whom Joseph spoke. So they offered prayer, and greeted one another. They then went with them to Jerusalem, and they brought them into the synagogue, and secured the doors, and the chief priests placed the Old Testament of the Jews in the midst and said to them: "We wish you to swear by the God of Israel and by Adonai and so speak the truth, how you arose and who raised you from the dead." When the men who had arisen heard that, they signed their faces with the sign of the cross, and said to the chief priests: "Give us paper and ink and pen." So they brought these things. And they sat down and wrote as follows:

II

"O Lord Jesus Christ, the resurrection and the life of the world, give us grace that we may tell of your resurrection and of your miracles which you performed in Hades. We, then, were in Hades with all who have died since the beginning of the world. And at the hour of midnight there rose upon the darkness there something like the light of the sun and shone, and light fell upon us all, and we saw one another. And immediately our father, Abraham, along with the patriarchs and the prophets, was filled with joy, and they said to one another: "This shining comes from a great light." The prophet

Isaiah, who was present there, said: "This shining comes from the Father and the Son and the Holy Spirit. This I prophesied when I was still living: The land of Zabulon and the land of Nephthalim, the people that sit in darkness saw a great light."

Then there came into the midst another, an anchorite from the wilderness. The patriarchs asked him: "Who are you?" He replied: "I am John, the last of the prophets, who made straight the ways of the Son of God, and preached repentance to the people for the forgiveness of sins. And the Son of God came to me, and when I saw him afar off, I said to the people: Behold, the Lamb of God, who takes away the sin of the world [John 1:29]. And with my hand I baptized him in the river Jordan, and I saw the Holy Spirit like a dove coming upon him, and heard also the voice of God the Father speaking thus: This is my beloved Son, in whom I am well pleased [Matt. 3:16f.]. And for this reason he sent me to you, to preach that the only begotten Son of God comes here, in order that whoever believes in him should be saved, and whoever does not believe in him should be condemned. Therefore I say to you all: When you see him, all of you worship him. For now only have you opportunity for repentance because you worshiped idols in the vain world above and sinned. At another time it is impossible."

III

Now when John was thus teaching those who were in Hades, the first-created, the first father Adam heard, and said to his son Seth: My son, I wish you to tell the forefathers of the race of men and the prophets where I sent you when I fell into mortal sickness." And Seth said: "Prophets and patriarchs, listen. My father Adam, the first-created, when he fell into mortal sickness, sent me to the very gate of Paradise to pray to God that he might lead me by an angel to the tree of mercy, that I might take oil and anoint my father, and he arise from his sickness. This also I did. And after my prayer an angel of the Lord came and asked me: 'What do you desire, Seth? Do you desire, because of the sickness of your father, the oil that raises up the sick, or the tree from which flows such oil? This cannot be found now. Therefore go and tell your father that after the completion of fifty-five hundred years from the creation of the world, the only-begotten Son of God shall become man and shall descend below the earth. And he shall anoint him with that oil. And he shall arise and wash him and his descendants with water and the Holy Spirit. And then he shall be healed of every disease. But this is impossible now.'" When the patriarchs and prophets heard this, they rejoiced greatly.

IV

And while they were all so joyful, Satan the heir of darkness came and said to Hades: "O insatiable devourer of all, listen to my words. There is one of the race of the Jews, Jesus by name, who calls himself the Son of God. But he is only a man, and at our instigation the Jews crucified him. And now that he is dead, be prepared that we may secure him here. For I know that he is only a man, and I heard him saying: My soul is very sorrowful, even to death [Matt. 26:38]. He did me much mischief in the world above while he lived among mortal men. For wherever he found my servants, he cast them out, and all those whom I had made to be maimed or blind or lame or leprous or the like, he healed with only a word, and many whom I had made ready to be buried he also with only a word made alive again."

Hades said: "Is he so powerful that he does such things with only a word? And if he is of such power, are you able to withstand him? It seems to me that no one will be able to withstand such as he is. But whereas you say that you heard how he feared death, he said this to mock and laugh at you, being determined to seize you with a strong hand. And woe, woe to you for all eternity." Satan answered: "O all-devouring and insatiable Hades, did you fear so greatly when you heard about our common enemy? I did not fear him, but worked upon the Jews, and they crucified him and gave him gall and vinegar to drink. Therefore prepare yourself to get him firmly into your power when he comes."

Hades answered: "O heir of darkness, son of perdition, devil, you have just told me that many whom you made ready to be buried he made alive again with only a word. If then he freed others from the grave, how and with what power will he be overcome by us? I a short time ago swallowed up a certain dead man called Lazarus, and soon afterwards one of the living snatched him up forcibly from my entrails with only a word. And I think it is the one of whom you speak. If, therefore, we receive him here, I fear lest we run the risk of losing the others also. For, behold, I see that all those whom I have swallowed up from the beginning of the world are disquieted. I have pain in the stomach. Lazarus who was snatched from me before seems to me no good sign. For not like a dead man, but like an eagle he flew away from me, so quickly did the earth cast him out. Therefore I adjure you by your gifts and mine, do not bring him here. For I believe that he comes here to raise all the dead. And I tell you this: By the darkness which surrounds us, if you bring him here, none of the dead will be left for me."

V

While Satan and Hades were speaking thus to one another, a loud voice like thunder sounded: "Lift up your gates, O rulers, and be lifted up, O everlasting doors, and the King of glory shall come in" [Ps. 23:7 LXX]. When Hades heard this, he said to Satan: "Go out, if you can, and withstand him." So Satan went out. Then Hades said to his demons: "Make fast well and strongly the gates of brass and the bars of iron, and hold my locks, and stand upright and watch every point. For if he comes in, woe will seize us."

When the forefathers heard that, they all began to mock him, saying: "O all-devouring and insatiable one, open, that the King of glory may come in." The prophet David said: "Do you not know, blind one, that when I lived in the world, I prophesied that word: 'Lift up your gates, O rulers?'" [Ps. 23:7]. Isaiah said: "I foresaw this by the Holy Spirit and wrote: 'The dead shall arise, and those who are in the tombs shall be raised up, and those who are under the earth shall rejoice [Ps. 26:19]. O death, where is your sting? O Hades, where is your victory?'" [1 Cor. 15:55, taken as referring to Isa. 25:8]. Again the voice sounded: "Lift up the gates." When Hades heard the voice the second time, he answered as if he did not know it and said: "Who is this King of glory?" The angels of the Lord said: "The Lord strong and mighty, the Lord mighty in battle" [Ps. 23:8 LXX]. And immediately at this answer the gates of brass were broken in pieces and the bars of iron were crushed and all the dead who were bound were loosed from their chains, and we with them. And the King of glory entered in like a man, and all the dark places of Hades were illumined.

VI

Hades at once cried out: "We are defeated, woe to us. But who are you, who have such authority and power? And who are you, who without sin have come here, you who appear small and can do great things, who are humble and exalted, slave and master, soldier and king, and have authority over the dead and the living? You were nailed to the cross, and laid in the sepulcher, and now you have become free and have destroyed all our power. Are you Jesus, of whom the chief ruler Satan said to us that through the cross and death you would inherit the whole world?"

Then the King of glory seized the chief ruler Satan by the head and handed him over to the angels, saying: "Bind with iron fetters his hands and his feet and his neck and his mouth." Then he gave him to Hades and said: "Take him and hold him fast until my second coming."

VII

And Hades took Satan and said to him: "O Beelzebub, heir of fire and torment, enemy of the saints, through what necessity did you contrive that the King of glory should be crucified, so that he should come here and strip us naked? Turn and see that not one dead man is left in me, but that all which you gained through the Tree of Knowledge you have lost through the tree of the cross. All your joy is changed into sorrow. You wished to kill the King of glory, but have killed yourself. For since I have received you to hold you fast, you shall learn by experience what evils I shall inflict upon you. O Arch-Devil, the beginning of death, the root of sin, the summit of all evil, what evil did you find in Jesus that you went about to destroy him? How did you dare to commit such great wickedness? How were you bent on bringing down such a man into this darkness, through whom you have been deprived of all who have died since the beginning?"

VIII

While Hades was thus speaking with Satan, the King of glory stretched out his right hand, and took hold of our forefather Adam and raised him up. Then he turned also to the rest and said: "Come with me, all you who have suffered death through the tree which this man touched. For behold, I raise you all up again through the tree of the cross."

With that he put them all out. And our forefather Adam was seen to be full of joy, and said: 'I give thanks to your majesty, O Lord, because you have brought me up from the lowest depth of Hades." Likewise also all the prophets and the saints said: "We give you thanks, O Christ, Savior of the world, because you have brought up our life from destruction."

When they had said this, the Savior blessed Adam with the sign of the cross on his forehead. And he did this also to the patriarchs and prophets and martyrs and forefathers, and he took them and leaped up out of Hades. And as he went the holy fathers sang praises, following him and saying: "Blessed be he who comes in the name of the Lord. Alleluia [Ps. 118:26]. To him be the glory of all the saints."

IX

Thus he went into Paradise holding our forefather Adam by the hand, and he handed him over and all the righteous to Michael the archangel. And as they were entering the gate of Paradise, two old men met them. The holy fathers asked them: "Who are you, who have not seen death nor gone down into Hades, but dwell in Paradise with your bodies and souls?" One of them answered: "I am Enoch, who pleased God and was removed here by him. And this is Elijah the Tishbite. We shall live until the end of the world. But then we shall be sent by God to withstand Antichrist and to be killed by him. And after three days we shall rise again and be caught up in clouds to meet the Lord."

X

While they were saying this there came another, a humble man, carrying a cross on his shoulder. The holy fathers asked him: "Who are you, who have the appearance of a robber, and what is the cross you carry on your shoulder?" He answered: "I was, as you say, a robber and a thief in the world, and therefore the Jews took me and delivered me to the death of the cross together with our Lord Jesus Christ. When, therefore, he hung on the cross, I saw the wonders which happened and believed in him. And I appealed to him and said: 'Lord, when you reign as king, do not forget me.' And immediately he said to me: 'Truly, truly, today, I say to you, you shall be with me in Paradise' [Luke 23: 43]. So I came into Paradise carrying my cross, and found Michael the archangel, and said to him: 'Our Lord Jesus Christ, who was crucified, has sent me here. Lead me, therefore, to the gate of Eden.' And when the flaming sword saw the sign of the cross, it opened to me and I went in. Then the archangel said to me: 'Wait a short while. For Adam also, the forefather of the race of men, comes with the righteous, that they also may enter in. And now that I have seen you, I have come to meet you.' When the saints heard this, they all cried with a loud voice: 'Great is our Lord, and great is his power.' "

XI

"All this we saw and heard, we two brothers who also were sent by Michael the archangel and were appointed to preach the resurrection of the Lord, but first to go to the Jordan and be baptized. There also we went and were baptized with other dead who had risen again. Then we went to Jerusalem also and celebrated the passover of the resurrection. But now we depart, since we cannot remain here. And the love of God the Father and the grace of our Lord Jesus Christ and the fellowship of the Holy Spirit be with you all [2 Cor. 13:14]." When they had written this and had sealed the books, they gave half to the chief priests and half to Joseph and Nicodemus. And they immediately vanished. To the glory of our Lord Jesus Christ. Amen.

THE PARADOSIS

When the report of Pilate reached Rome and was read to Caesar, while not a few stood by, all were amazed that it was because of the lawless conduct of Pilate that the darkness and the earthquake had come upon the whole world; and Caesar, filled with anger, sent soldiers with orders to bring Pilate in chains.

And when he had been brought to Rome and Caesar heard that Pilate was there, he sat down in the temple of the gods in the presence of the whole senate and the whole army and all the great ones of his empire. And he commanded Pilate to come forward and said to him: "How could you dare to do such a thing, you most impious one, when you had seen such great signs concerning that man? By your wicked daring you have destroyed the whole world."

Pilate answered: "Almighty Caesar, I am innocent of these things; it is the multitude of the Jews who are the guilty instigators." Caesar asked: "Who are they?" Pilate said: "Herod, Archelaus, Philip, Annas, and Caiaphas, and all the multitude of the Jews." Caesar said: "Why did you follow their advice?" Pilate said: "This nation is rebellious and refractory, and does not submit to your power." Caesar said: "As soon as they handed him over to you, you should have kept him secure and sent him to me, and not have followed them and crucified such a man who was righteous and did such wonderful signs as you have mentioned in your report. For it is clear from these signs that Jesus was the Christ, the king of the Jews."

And when Caesar said this and named the name of Christ, all the gods fell down, where Caesar sat with the senate, and became as dust. And all the people who stood by Caesar trembled by reason of the naming of the name and the fall of their gods, and gripped by fear they all went away, each to his own house, marveling at what had taken place. And Caesar commanded that Pilate should be kept in custody, in order that he might learn the truth about Jesus.

On the next day Caesar sat in the Capitol with all the senate with the intention of questioning Pilate. And Caesar said: "Speak the truth, you most impious man, for through your godless behavior against Jesus, even here the working of your crime was shown in the overthrowing of the gods. Tell me now: Who is that crucified one, that his name destroyed all the gods?" Pilate answered: "Truly, the charges made against him are true. For I myself was convinced by his deeds that he is greater than all the gods whom we worship." Caesar said: "Why then did you treat him with such wickedness, although you knew him? In doing this you must have wished to harm my kingdom." Pilate answered: "I did it because of the unlawful insubordination of the lawless and godless Jews."

Then Caesar, filled with anger, took counsel with all the senate and his forces, and ordered the following decree to be recorded against the Jews: "To Licianus, chief governor of the east, greeting! At the present time the Jews who live in Jerusalem and the neighbouring towns have committed a lawless crime in forcing Pilate to crucify Jesus who was acknowledged as God. Because of this crime of theirs the world was darkened and dragged down to ruin. Therefore by this decree proceed there with all speed with a strong body of troops and take them prisoner. Obey, and advance against them, and dispersing them among all the nations enslave them, and expel them from Judaea, making the nation so insignificant that it is no longer to be seen anywhere, since they are men full of evil."

When this decree arrived in the east, Licianus carried out its terrible instructions and destroyed the whole Jewish nation, and those who were left in Judaea he scattered as slaves among the nations, so that Caesar was pleased when he learned of the actions of Licianus against the Jews in the east.

And again Caesar questioned Pilate, and commanded an officer called Albius to behead him, saying: "As this man raised his hand against the righteous man called Christ, so shall he fall in the same way, and find no deliverance." And when Pilate came to the place of execution, he prayed silently: "Lord, do not destroy me with the wicked Hebrews, for it was through the lawless nation of the Jews that I raised my hand against you, because they plotted a revolt against me. You know that I acted in ignorance. Therefore do not condemn me because of this sin, but pardon me, Lord, and your servant Procla, who stands with me in this hour of my death, whom you made to prophesy that you must be nailed to the cross. Do not condemn her also because of my sin, but pardon us and number us among your righteous ones."

And behold, when Pilate had finished his prayer, there sounded a voice from Heaven: "All generations and families of the Gentiles shall call you blessed, because in your governorship all was fulfilled which the prophets foretold about me. And you yourself shall appear as my witness at my second coming, when I shall judge the twelve tribes of Israel and those who have not confessed my name." And the prefect cut off Pilate's head, and behold, an angel of the Lord received it. And when Procla his wife saw the angel coming and receiving his head, she was filled with joy, and immediately gave up the ghost, and was buried with her husband.

THE PISTIS SOPHIA: CONCERNING THE UNION OF THE CHILD JESUS WITH THE SPIRIT (GNOSTIC)

Mary declares to the risen Jesus: "When you were small, before the Spirit had come upon you, while you were with Joseph in a vineyard, the Spirit came from on high and came to me in my house, resembling you, and I did not recognize him, and I thought that it was you. And the Spirit said to me: 'Where is Jesus, my brother, that I may meet him?' When he said this to me, I was perplexed and thought that it was a ghost come to tempt me. And I seized him and bound him to the foot of the bed which is in my house, until I went out to you both, to you and Joseph in the field and found you in the vineyard, while Joseph was fencing in the vineyard. Now it came to pass that, when you heard me speak the word to Joseph, you understood the word, and were glad and said: 'Where is he, that I may see him? for I await him in this place.' And it came to pass that, when Joseph heard you say these words, he was perplexed, and we went up together, entered the house, and found the Spirit bound to the bed. And we looked at you and him and found that you resembled him, and when he who was bound to the bed was freed, he embraced you and kissed you, and you kissed him and you both became one."

Notes

1. The author has no knowledge of how trials were actually conducted. For him the tribunal (judgment seat) was in the praetorium; in actual fact it was never set up there, but "under the open sky or in a covered space accessible to the public," which the praetorium is not (except in the *Acts of Pilate*). Correctly, John 19:13. A curtain was drawn only at non-public trials; when the public was admitted, as at the pronouncement of the verdict, it was removed. Here also the opposite takes place: the tribunal is visible during the trial, and the curtain is drawn before it for the pronouncement of sentence.

2. As men of substance and hating covetousness, they could not be bribed by the disciples of Jesus.

3. With "ascendentem in coelum," that is, at this point, one of the two recensions of the Latin translation ends, followed by the Latin recension A of the Decensus. The other follows the Greek text a little further, taking over Levi's quotation of the words of Symeon, but remolding the rest in a way impossible to the spirit of the *Acts of Pilate:* "Then the teacher Didas said to all the congregation: 'If everything which these men have testified came to pass in Jesus, it is of God, and let it not be marvelous in your eyes.' The rulers of the synagogue and the priests and the Levites said one to another: 'It is contained in our law: His name shall be blessed forever. His place endures before the sun and his seat before the moon, and in him shall all the tribes of the earth be blessed, and all nations shall serve him; and kings shall come from afar to worship and magnify him' " (after Ps. 71 LXX).

5
INFANCY GOSPELS

The Infancy Gospel of James (The Birth of Mary)

(Christian Apocrypha)

Although the New Testament gospels say little of Jesus' childhood—Mark and John say nothing at all—and the earliest theological interest was in Christ the teacher, the crucified, and the resurrected, by the second century infancy gospels were very popular. The sources were outside the synoptic gospels, for between the nativity scene and the story of Jesus at the age of twelve in the temple, there is only one reference to the young Jesus: "the child grew and became strong" (Luke 2:40). As for the formal observance of Christmas, this did not take place until the fourth century.

There was great human interest in Jesus' childhood and, in several infancy gospels, tales of children of gods are introduced. Jesus becomes a divine prankster. There were also theological and political reasons for the infancy gospels. A common "slander" of the time was that Jesus was the illegitimate son of a soldier called Panthera, and indeed that story (including the discovery of a gravestone in Germany with the name "Panthera") has never failed to interest historians and pseudohistorians. The problem of legitimacy was caused by the assertion on the one hand that Jesus was born of a virgin birth, and the genealogies in Matthew and Luke on the other to demonstrate Jesus' Davidic descent through Joseph. A solution was found in the infancy *Gospel of James* by making Mary descend from David. The infancy gospels also offered an answer to the perplexing problem of Mary's perpetual virginity, since the early scriptures speak of Jesus' brothers. Joseph is presented as a widower, with children by a previous marriage. But the gospels did not lack detracters, even as early as Jerome in the fifth century. Luther roundly condemned the apocryphal infancy gospels.

The two earliest gospels of Jesus' childhood are the *Gospel of James*, also called the *Protevangelium Jacobi*, and the *Gospel of Thomas*. The former deals with the birth, childhood, and motherhood of Mary, and the latter describes the miracles of the child Jesus. The *Gospel of Thomas* is a mutilated text, from which the teachings have been removed. In its existing form, it presents the young Jesus as a fearsome, and indeed ferocious, miracle worker.

The *Gospel of James* was attributed to Jesus' brother James. James (Jacob) was thought to be Jesus' younger brother by Mary, or, by those who maintained Mary's perpetual virginity, Joseph's son by a previous marriage. In any case, the *Gospel* could not have been written before A.D. 150, which eliminates James as the author. It was probably written, scholars agree, not by a Jewish Christian but a Gentile. This poetic and gentle narrative of Mary's birth, childhood, and betrothal to Joseph was the source of much of the iconographic tradition of Christian artists in portraying the birth of Jesus. In the narrative Mary is twelve when she is betrothed to Joseph; from twelve to seventeen, depending on the manuscript, when she conceives. In Mariology and in graphic depictions, a somewhat older woman emerges.

The infancy gospel brings up one of the most disputed aspects of Christian doctrine: the virgin birth. Joseph at first does not believe that his wife has been faithful to him. He throws himself to the ground and weeps bitterly, asking, "Who is he who has deceived me? Who did this evil thing in my house and defiled her?" Then Mary weeps and says that she is pure. Joseph wonders whether he should hide her sin or expose her and have her killed, but that night in a dream an angel of the Lord comes to him and tells him that the child is from the Holy Spirit. Joseph rises and blesses the God of Israel and decides to keep the child. But neither Joseph's nor Mary's problems are over. The priests remain skeptical. On the way to Bethlehem where they are going to be "enrolled," that is, registered, Mary comes down from her donkey, knowing that her time has come. Joseph takes her into a cave and while the heaven stands still and the birds of heaven rest, while time itself throughout nature and humanity comes to a stop, Mary gives birth to Jesus. A great light appears in the cave as the baby appears. The drama continues with the star in the east and Herod's attempt to kill all babies two years old and under. Elizabeth then takes John to the mountains to hide, and the mountain opens to receive her. The murder of the good Zaharias ends the drama, although this episode is considered a later addition to the story. When Zaharias is murdered the panels of the Temple cry aloud. Miracles come from every quarter to glorify the birth of Jesus.

Although Mary is not described in any detail—she is referred to as an innocent child—her situation is compelling and wondrous. The very delicate treatment of the figure of Mary has probably contributed to her warm and mysterious presence in later Mariology.

Early manuscripts of the *Gospel* exist in Greek, Syriac, Armenian, and later in many languages, including Ethiopic, Georgian, and Slavonic. No Latin manuscript survived the early condemnation of the book in the west. Ron Cameron makes important observations about the oral and written sources of the more than 130 extant Greek manuscripts of the *Gospel*. Stylistically, he writes, "the entirety of the *Protevangelian of James* is steeped in the language of the Septuagint, the Greek translation of the Jewish scriptures."[1] The two main thematic sources are Matthew and Luke, whose infancy stories are conflated. Cameron suggests that the new "harmony" based on the synoptic infancy stories, like Matthew and Luke themselves, whose sources are not preserved, form part of the " 'midrashic' exetetical tradition."[2]

Notes

1. Ron Cameron, *The Other Gospels* (Philadelphia: Westminster Press, 1982), p. 108.
2. Cameron, *The Other Gospels*, p. 108.

THE INFANCY GOSPEL OF JAMES (PROTEVANGELIUM JACOBI) (THE BIRTH OF MARY)*

According to the histories of the twelve tribes of Israel, Joachim was a very wealthy man. He brought his offerings twofold to the Lord, saying to himself, "This from my abundance will be for all the people, and this which I owe as a sin offering will be for the Lord God as a propitiation for me."

Now the great day of the Lord drew near, and the children of Israel brought their offerings. Reuben stood up against Joachim, saying, "It is not permissible for you to bring your offerings first, for you did not produce offspring in Israel."

Joachim was greatly distressed, and he went to the book of the twelve tribes of Israel, saying to himself, "I will look at the records of the twelve tribes of Israel to determine whether I alone did not produce offspring in Israel." He searched, and he found that all the righteous had raised up offspring in Israel. Further, he remembered the patriarch Abraham, that near his last day the Lord God gave to him a son, Isaac.

*From David R. Cartlidge and David L. Dungan, eds. and trans., *Documents for the Study of the Gospels* (Philadelpha: Fortress Press, 1980), pp. 107–116.

Joachim was very sorrowful; he did not appear to his wife, but betook himself into the desert and pitched his tent there. Then he fasted for forty days and forty nights, saying to himself, "I will not return, either for food or drink, until the Lord my God considers me. Prayer will be my food and drink."

Now his wife, Anna, sang two dirges and beat her breast in a twofold lament, saying, "I will mourn my widowhood, and I will mourn my barrenness."

The great day of the Lord drew near and Euthine, her maid, said to her, "How long will you humble your soul? Behold, the great day of the Lord has come, and it is not proper for you to mourn. Rather, take this headband which the mistress of work gave to me; it is not permissible for me to wear it, because I am your servant-girl and it has a mark of royalty." Then Anna said, "Get away from me! I have not done these things; the Lord God has humbled me greatly. Perhaps someone gave this to you deceitfully, and now you have come to make me a partner in your sin." Euthine, her maid, said, "What am I to you, since you do not listen to my voice? The Lord God closed your womb in order not to grant you fruit in Israel."

Anna was very grieved, and she took off her mourning garments and cleansed her head and put on her bridal garments.

About the ninth hour she went down into her garden to walk and she saw a laurel tree and sat down beneath it; and she entreated the Lord, saying, "O God of my fathers, bless me and hear my prayer, even as you blessed the womb of Sarah and gave to her a son, Isaac."

Anna looked up toward Heaven and saw a nest of sparrows in the laurel tree; and she sang a dirge to herself, saying, "Woe is me! Who gave me birth? What sort of womb brought me forth? For I was born a curse among the children of Israel. I was made a reproach, and they derided me and banished me out of the Temple of the Lord my God. "Woe is me! To what am I likened? I am not likened to the birds of heaven, for even the birds of heaven are fruitful before you, O Lord. Woe is me! To what am I likened? I am not likened to the wild beasts of the earth, for even the wild beasts of the earth are fruitful before you, O Lord. Woe is me! To what am I likened? I am not likened to the voiceless creatures, for even the voiceless creatures are fruitful before you, O Lord. Woe is me! To what am I likened? I am not likened to these waters, for even these waters are fruitful before you, O Lord. Woe is me! To what am I likened? I am not likened to this earth, for even the earth brings forth her fruit in its season and blesses you, O Lord."

And behold, an angel of the Lord appeared, saying, "Anna, Anna, the Lord God heard your prayer, and you will conceive and give birth, and your offspring shall be spoken of in the whole inhabited world." Anna said, "As the Lord my God lives, if I give birth, whether male or female, I will present it as a gift to the Lord my God, and it shall be a ministering servant to him all the days of its life." And behold, two angels came, saying to her, "Behold, your husband Joachim is coming with his flocks."

Now an angel of the Lord had come down to Joachim, saying, "Joachim, Joachim, the Lord God heard your prayer. Go down from here; for behold, your wife Anna is pregnant." Joachim went down, and he summoned his shepherds, saying, "Bring here to me ten female lambs, spotless and without blemish, and the ten lambs shall be for the Lord my God; and bring to me twelve choice calves, and the twelve calves shall be for the priests and the council of elders; and a hundred year-old he goats, and the hundred he goats shall be for all the people."

And behold, Joachim came with his flocks, and Anna stood at the door and saw Joachim coming with his flocks. Anna ran and threw her arms around his neck, saying, "Now I know that the Lord God has blessed me very greatly, for behold, the widow is no longer a widow, and she who was barren has conceived!" Then Joachim remained in his house for the first day.

On the next day he brought his offerings, saying to himself, "If the Lord God has had mercy on me, the golden plate of the priest's headdress will make it apparent to me." Joachim brought his offerings, and he observed the priest's golden plate intently as he went up to the altar of the Lord; and he did not see sin in himself. Joachim said, "Now I know that the Lord God has had mercy on me and forgiven me all my sins." Then he went down from the Temple of the Lord, justified, and came into his house.

Now her time was fulfilled, and in the ninth month Anna gave birth. She said to the midwife, "What have I borne?" The midwife said, "A girl." Then Anna said, "My soul is exalted this day"; and she laid herself down.

When the required days were completed, Anna cleansed herself of the impurity of childbirth, and gave her breast to the child. She called her name Mary.

Day by day the child grew strong. When she was six months old her mother stood her on the ground to see if she could stand. Walking seven steps, she came to her mother's bosom. Her mother caught her up, saying, "As the Lord my God lives, you shall not walk on this earth until I bring you into the Temple of the Lord." Then she made a sanctuary in her bedroom, and prohibited everything common and unclean from passing through it; and she summoned the undefiled daughters of the Hebrews, and they served her.

Now the child came to be a year old, and Joachim gave a great feast; he invited the high priests, the priests, the scribes, the elders of the council, and all the people of Israel. Joachim brought the child to the priests and they blessed her saying, "O God of our fathers, bless this child, and give to her a name famous forever in all generations." All the people responded, "So let it be. Amen." Then he brought her to the high priests and they blessed her, saying, "O God of the high places, look upon this child, and bless her with the highest blessing which has no successor."

Her mother picked her up and brought her into the sanctuary of her bedroom, and gave her breast to the child. Then Anna sang a hymn to the Lord God, saying, "I will sing a sacred song to the Lord my God, because he considered me and took away from me the reproach of my enemies; and the Lord my God gave me a fruit of his righteousness, one yet manifold before him. Who will report to the sons of Reuben that Anna gives suck?"

She laid the child to rest in the bedroom, in her sanctuary, and she went out and served them at the feast. When the meal was finished, they went down rejoicing and they glorified the God of Israel.

Months passed. The child became two years old, and Joachim said, "Let us take her up into the Temple of the Lord, in order that we may fulfill the pledge which we have made; lest the Lord send to us for it and our gift be unacceptable." Anna said, "Let us await the third year, lest the child long for her father and mother." And Joachim said, "So let it be."

When the child was three years old,

Joachim said, "Let us call the undefiled daughters of the Hebrews, and let each one take a torch, and let them be burning, in order that the child not turn back and her heart be misled out of the Temple of the Lord." Thus they did, until they had gone up into the Temple.

The priest received her, and kissing her he blessed her and said, "The Lord God has magnified your name in all generations; in you, at the end of days, will the Lord God manifest his deliverance to the children of Israel." He set her on the third step of the altar, and the Lord God gave grace to her; and she danced with her feet, and all the house of Israel loved her.

Her parents returned, marveling and giving praise and glorifying the Lord God that the child did not turn back.

Now Mary was in the Temple of the Lord like a dove being fed, and she received food from the hand of an angel.

When she was twelve years old there took place a conference of the priests, saying, "Behold, Mary has become twelve years old in the Temple of the Lord our God. What, therefore, shall we do with her, lest she defile the sanctuary of the Lord?" The high priests said to Zacharias, "You stand at the altar of the Lord. Enter and pray concerning her; and whatever the Lord God may reveal to you, this let us do."

The priest entered the Holy of Holies, taking the vestment with the twelve bells, and he prayed concerning her. And behold, an angel of the Lord appeared, saying, "Zacharias, Zacharias, go out and call together the widowers of the people, and let each of them bring a rod; and to whomever the Lord God shows a sign, to this one shall she be wife." The heralds therefore went forth through the whole Jewish countryside and sounded the trumpet of the Lord, and all came running.

Now Joseph, casting down his adze, came himself into their meeting. When they all were gathered together, they came to the priest, taking the rods. He,

387

having received the rods of all of them, went into the Temple and prayed. When he finished the prayer he took the rods and came out and returned them; and there was no sign on them. Joseph received the last rod, and behold, a dove came forth from the rod and settled on Joseph's head. Then the priest said, "Joseph, Joseph, you have been designated by lot to receive the virgin of the Lord as your ward."

Joseph refused, saying, "I have sons, and I am an old man, but she is a young maiden—lest I be a laughing stock to the children of Israel." The priest said, "Joseph, fear the Lord your God! Remember what God did to Dathan and Abiram and Korah, how the earth was split in two and they were all swallowed up on account of their disputing. And now, Joseph, beware lest these things be also in your house."

Joseph, frightened, received her as his ward; and Joseph said to her, "Mary, I have received you from the Temple of the Lord. Now I am leaving you behind in my house, and I am going away to build houses; later I will return to you. The Lord will guard you."

There took place a council of the priests, saying, "Let us make a veil for the Temple of the Lord." The priest said, "Call the undefiled virgins from the tribe of David." The attendants went out and sought them, and they found seven. Then the priest remembered the child Mary, that she was of the tribe of David and was pure before God; and the attendants went forth and brought her.

They brought them into the Temple of the Lord, and the priest said, "Assign by lot for me here someone who will spin the gold thread and the white and the linen and the silk and the hyacinth-blue and the scarlet and the genuine purple." The genuine purple and the scarlet were assigned by lot to Mary, and taking them she went into her house. Now at that time Zacharias was dumb, and Samuel replaced him until the time when Zacharias spoke. Mary, taking the scarlet, spun

it. She took her pitcher and went out to fill it full of water; and behold, there came a voice saying, "Hail, highly favored one! The Lord is with you; you are blessed among women." Mary looked about, to the right and to the left, to see whence this voice might be coming to her. Filled with trembling she went into her house; and putting down the pitcher, she took the purple and sat down on a chair and drew out the purple thread.

Behold, an angel of the Lord stood before her, saying, "Do not fear, Mary, for you have found favor before the Lord of all, and you will conceive by his Word." Mary, having heard this, considered to herself, saying, "Shall I conceive by the Lord, the living God? As all women do, shall I give birth?" And behold, the angel appeared, saying to her, "Not thus, Mary, for the power of God will overshadow you; therefore also that holy thing which is born shall be called Son of the Most High. You shall call his name Jesus, for he shall save the people from their sins." Then Mary said, "Behold the servant-girl of the Lord is before him. Let it be to me according to your word."

She worked the purple and the scarlet and brought them to the priest; and the priest blessed her and said, "Mary, the Lord God has blessed your name, and you will be blessed among all the families of the earth."

Mary, full of joy, went to her kinswoman Elisabeth and knocked on the door. Elisabeth, hearing her, put down the scarlet and ran to the door and opened it to her; and she blessed her and said, "How is it that the mother of the Lord should come to me? For behold, that which is in me leapt and blessed you." But Mary forgot the mysteries of which the angel Gabriel spoke; and she looked up toward Heaven and said, "Who am I that, behold, all the families of the earth bless me?" She remained three months with Elisabeth. Day by day her womb became larger; Mary, becoming fearful, came to her house and hid herself from the children of Israel. Now she was sixteen[1] years old when these strange events happened to her.

It came to be the sixth month for her, and behold, Joseph came from his buildings; and he came into his house and found her pregnant. He struck his face and threw himself to the ground on the sackcloth and wept bitterly, saying, "With what sort of countenance shall I look to the Lord God? What shall I pray concerning this maiden? For I received her a virgin from the Temple of the Lord God, and I did not guard her. Who is he who has deceived me? Who did this evil thing in my house and defiled her? Is not the story of Adam summed up in me? For just as Adam was in the hour of his giving glory to God and the serpent came and found Eve alone and deceived her, thus it has also come about for me."

Joseph arose from the sackcloth and called Mary and said to her, "Having been cared for by God, why did you do this, forgetting the Lord your God? Why have you humbled your soul, you who were nurtured in the Holy of Holies and who received food from the hand of an angel?"

She wept bitterly, saying, "I am pure, and I do not know a man." Joseph said to her, "Whence then is this which is in your womb?" She said, "As the Lord my God lives, I do not know whence it came to me."

Then Joseph feared greatly and stopped talking with her, considering what he would do with her. Joseph said, "If I should hide her sin, I will be found disputing with the law of the Lord; if I show her to the children of Israel, I am afraid lest that which is in her is angelic and I shall be found delivering innocent blood to the judgment of death. What therefore shall I do with her? Shall I put her away secretly from me?"

Night came upon him; behold an angel of the Lord appeared to him in a dream, saying, "Do not fear this child, for that which is in her is from the Holy Spirit. She will bear a son, and you shall call his name Jesus, for he will save his people

from their sins." Then Joseph arose from his sleep and glorified the God of Israel who had given to him this favor; he guarded the child.

Now Annas, the scribe, came to Joseph and said to him, "Joseph, why have you not appeared in our assembly?" Joseph said to him, "Because I was weary from my journey, and I rested the first day."

Annas turned and saw Mary pregnant; and he came running to the priest and said to him, "Joseph, to whom you have borne witness, has acted very lawlessly." The priest said, "What is this?" Annas answered, "The virgin whom Joseph received from the Temple of the Lord he has defiled; he married her secretly and did not reveal it to the childen of Israel." The priest said to him, "Joseph did these things?" Annas responded, "Send attendants, and you will find the virgin pregnant."

The attendants went forth and found her as he said; and they brought her into the sanctuary, and she stood at the tribunal. The priest said to her, "Mary, why did you do this? Why did you humble your soul, forgetting the Lord your God? You who were nurtured in the Holy of Holies, and received food from the hand of an angel, and heard their hymns, and danced before the Lord—why did you do this?" But Joseph said, "As the Lord God lives, I am pure regarding her." Then the priest said, "Do not bear false witness, but tell the truth. You married her secretly and did not reveal it to the children of Israel; you did not incline your head beneath the Mighty Hand so that your seed might be blessed." And Joseph was silent.

The priest then said, "Give back the virgin whom you received from the Temple of the Lord." Joseph began to weep. The priest went on, "I will give you to drink the water of the Lord's testing, and it will make your sins manifest in your eyes." Taking it, the priest gave Joseph to drink and sent him into the desert; and he came back whole. He also gave the child to drink and sent her into the desert; she also returned whole. And all the people wondered, since their sin did not appear in them.

The priest said, "If the Lord God did not make your sin manifest, neither will I judge you"; and he released them. Then Joseph took Mary and went into his house, rejoicing and glorifying the God of Israel.

Now there came an order from Augustus the emperor for all who were in Bethlehem of Judea to be enrolled. Joseph said, "I will enroll my sons, but this child —what shall I do with her? How shall I enroll her? As my wife? I am ashamed to do so. As my daughter? The children of Israel know that she is not my daughter. This day of the Lord he will do as he wishes."

He saddled his donkey and set her upon it; his son led, and Samuel followed. They drew near to Bethlehem— they were three miles distant—and Joseph turned and saw Mary looking gloomy, and he said, "Probably that which is in her is distressing her." Once again Joseph turned and saw her laughing, and he said, "Mary, how is it that I see your face at one moment laughing and at another time gloomy?" She said to Joseph, "It is because I see two peoples with my eyes, the one weeping and mourning, the other rejoicing and glad."

They were in the midst of the journey, and Mary said to him, "Joseph, take me down from the donkey, for that which is in me is ready to be born." He took her down from the donkey and said to her, "Where shall I take you to shelter your shame? For the place is desolate."

He found there a cave, and he brought her in and placed his sons beside her. Then he went out to seek a Hebrew midwife in the country of Bethlehem.

Now I, Joseph, was walking about, and I looked up and saw the Heaven standing still, and I observed the air in amazement, and the birds of Heaven at rest. Then I looked down at the earth, and I saw a vessel lying there, and work-men reclining, and their hands were in the vessel. Those who were chewing did not chew, and those who were lifting did not lift up, and those who were carrying to their mouths did not carry, but all faces were looking upward. I saw sheep standing still, and the shepherd raised his hand to strike them, and his hand remained up. I observed the streaming river; and I saw the mouths of the kids at the water, but they were not drinking. Then suddenly all things were driven in their course.

Finding a midwife, he brought her. They came down from the mountain, and Joseph said to the midwife, "Mary is the one who was betrothed to me, but she, having been brought up in the Temple of the Lord, has conceived by the Holy Spirit." And she went with him.

They stood in the place of the cave, and a dark cloud was overshadowing the cave. The midwife said, "My soul is magnified today, for my eyes have seen a mystery: a Savior has been born to Israel!" And immediately the cloud withdrew from the cave, and a great light appeared in the cave so that their eyes could not bear it. After a while the light withdrew, until the baby appeared. It came and took the breast of its mother Mary; and the midwife cried out, "How great is this day, for I have seen this new wonder!"

The midwife went in and placed Mary in position, and Salome examined her virginal nature; and Salome cried aloud that she had tempted the living God— "and behold, my hand falls away from me in fire." Then she prayed to the Lord.

Behold, an angel of the Lord appeared, saying to Salome, "Your prayer has been heard before the Lord God. Come near and take up the child, and this will save you." She did so; and Salome was healed as she worshiped. Then she came out of the cave. Behold, an angel of the Lord spoke, saying, "Salome, Salome, do not report what marvels yu have seen until the child has come into Jerusalem."[3]

And behold, Joseph was prepared to

go into Judea. Now there arose a tumult in Bethlehem of Judea, for Magi came saying, "Where is the king of the Jews? For we saw his star in the east, and we have come to worship him." Herod, hearing this, was terrified. He sent attendants and summoned them, and they explained clearly to him concerning the star.

The Magi departed, and behold, they saw a star in the east, and it preceded them until they came into the cave and stood at the head of the child. Then the Magi, seeing the child with its mother Mary, brought forth gifts from their leather pouches: gold, frankincense, and myrrh. But having been warned by an angel, they went away by a different route into their own land.

When Herod realized that he had been deceived by the Magi, in his wrath he sent his murderers, telling them to kill all the babies two years old and under. Mary, hearing that they were killing the babies, was frightened, and she took the child and wrapped him and placed him in a cow stable.

Now Elisabeth, hearing that Herod sought John, took him and went up into the mountain. She looked around for a place where she might hide him, but there was no place. Then Elisabeth groaned, saying in a loud voice, "Mountain of God, receive a mother with her child"—for Elisabeth was unable to ascend. And immediately the mountain opened up and it received her. That mountain appeared to her as a light, for an angel of the Lord was with them, protecting them.

Herod sought John, and he dispatched attendants to the altar to Zacharias, saying to him, "Where have you hidden your son?" He answered, saying to them, "I am a ministering servant of God, and I serve in the Temple. How do I know where my son is?" The attendants went away and reported all these things to Herod.

Angered, Herod said, "His son is going to be king in Israel." Again he sent the attendants, saying to him, "Tell me the truth! Where is your son? You know that you are at my mercy." The attendants went forth and reported these things to Zacharias. In answer he said, "I am a witness of God; pour out my blood. The Lord will receive my spirit, for it is innocent blood you are shedding at the doorway of the Temple of the Lord." About daybreak Zacharias was murdered, and the children of Israel did not know how he was murdered.

But at the hour of the salutation, the priests went in, and the blessing of Zacharias did not meet them as was customary. The priests stood waiting for Zacharias to greet them in prayer and to glorify the most high God. When he failed to come they were all afraid. But a certain one of them, getting up his courage, went into the sanctuary and saw by the altar of the Lord dried blood; and a voice said, "Zacharias has been murdered, and his blood will not be wiped away until his avenger comes."

When he heard these words he was afraid, and he came out and reported to the priests what he had seen and heard. They took courage and went in, and they saw what had taken place; and the wall panels of the Temple cried aloud, and they split in two from top to bottom. They did not find his corpse, but they found his blood, which had become like stone.

They were filled with fear, and they went out and reported that Zacharias had been murdered. All the tribes of the people heard it, and they mourned and lamented him three days and three nights.

Now after the three days, the priests deliberated on whom they would set up in the place of Zacharias, and the lot fell on Simeon. This was the one to whom it had been revealed by the Holy Spirit that he would not see death until he saw Christ in the flesh.

Now I, James, who wrote this history in Jerusalem, there having arisen a clamor when Herod died, withdrew myself into the desert until the tumult in Jerusalem ceased. Now I glorify the Lord who gave me the wisdom to write this history. And grace will be with all who fear the Lord. Amen.

Notes

1. The manuscript gives Mary's age variously from twelve to seventeen years. The oldest, as well as the largest number, of the manuscripts have sixteen.

2. See Numbers 5:11–31.

3. There is also a more elaborate version of this section (chapter 20), which is found in most of the later manuscripts:

> The midwife went in and said, "Mary, get yourself in position, for a great deal of controversy surrounds you." Then Salome tested her virginal nature with her finger; and Salome cried out and said, "Woe is my lawlessness and my faithlessness, for I have tempted the living God. And behold, my hand falls away from me in fire."
>
> Then she bowed her knees before the Lord, saying, "God of my fathers, remember me, for I am seed of Abraham and Isaac and Jacob. Do not expose me to contempt to the children of Israel, but return me to the needy. For you know, O Lord, that I accomplished my healings in your name, and I received my pay from you."
>
> And behold, an angel of the Lord appeared, saying to Salome, "The Lord heard your prayer. Bring your hand near to the child and take him up, and it will be to you salvation and joy." Salome, overjoyed, came to the child, saying, "I will worship him, I will take him up, and I will be healed, for a great king is born to Israel." Immediately, Salome was healed; and she came out of the cave justified. And behold, there came a voice saying to her, "Salome, Salome, do not report what marvels you have seen in Bethlehem until the child comes to Jerusalem."

The Infancy Gospel of Pseudo-Matthew: The Book about the Origin of the Blessed Mary and the Childhood of the Savior

(Christian Apocrypha)

The *Infancy Gospel of Pseudo-Matthew* is a strangely poetic version of the *Infancy Gospel of James*. Joseph is accused of defiling Mary, but he exonerates himself. Then Mary is accused of deceiving Joseph, but she "drank the water of testing" to prove her innocence. Mary calls on her God, "Adonai of hosts" to declare that she has never known a man. Since infancy she has vowed to live without stain. Then Jesus is born in the cave and placed in the manger where he is worshiped by a donkey and an ox. So the prophecy of Habbakuk is fulfilled: "You will be known by these two animals."

Thereafter Jesus, who asks not to be considered a child but "a perfect man," charms dangerous dragons, lions, and leopards, and causes them to worship him. Thereupon lions join their caravan of oxen, donkeys and sheep and no harm came to any beast. Wolves join them. The prophecy is again fulfilled: "Wolves shall be pastured with lambs, the lion and the ox shall eat fodder together" (Ps. 148:7). The infant Jesus, still at his mother's breast in the third day of his life, hears that his mother is hungry and thirsty. He orders a palm tree to bend down, which it does, so his mother can gather fruit from it. Then he orders it to raise itself to be a companion of trees in Heaven, whereupon fountains of water pour out from its roots to refresh his family.

The child as divine man of miracles continues when Jesus orders an angel to take a branch from the tree and fly off with it to Heaven, and he shortens the thirty-day trip across the desert to Egypt into a single day. In Egypt when Mary and Jesus enter a religious temple, the three hundred and sixty-five idols immediately fall to the ground and shatter. The governor is so impressed that he and the entire city of Egyptians convert to the true Lord God. Finally, the angel brings Joseph the good news that those who sought the life of Jesus are now dead.

The prophecy fulfillment devices in the narrative were used in Matthew and hence the title, the *Infancy Gospel of Pseudo-Matthew*. The actual title of the *Gospel* is *The Book About the Origin of the Blessed Mary and the Childhood of the Savior*. The sources of the *Gospel* are the *Gospel of James* and also the *Infancy Gospel of Thomas*, insofar as Jesus is depicted as an infant miracle-maker. The text exists in Latin and was probably written and compiled in the eighth or ninth century.

THE INFANCY GOSPEL OF PSEUDO-MATTHEW*

Joseph was in Capernaum-by-the-Sea, on the job; he was a carpenter. He stayed there for nine months. When he returned home he found Mary pregnant. Totally gripped by anguish, he trembled and cried out, "Lord God, accept my spirit, because it is better for me to die than to live." The virgins with Mary said to him, "What are you saying, Lord Joseph? We know ourselves that no man has touched her; we know ourselves that, in her, innocence and virginity were preserved unspoiled. For she has been guarded by God; she always persists with us in prayer. Daily an angel of the Lord speaks with her; daily she accepts food from the hand of an angel. How is it possible that there should be any sin in her? For if you want us to voice our suspicion to you, this pregnancy was caused by none other than

*From David R. Cartlidge and David L. Dungan, eds. and trans., *Documents for the Study of the Gospels* (Philadelphia: Fortress Press, 1980), pp. 98–103.

God's angel." Joseph, however, said, "Would you try to have me believe that an angel of the Lord impregnated her? It is indeed possible that someone dressed up as an angel of the Lord and tricked her." As he said this, he wept and said, "With what aspect am I to go to God's Temple? With what pretext am I to visit the priests of God? What am I to do?" After he said this he made plans to hide her and set her aside.

When he planned to arise in the night and flee, so that he could live in hiding; behold, in that very night, an angel of the Lord appeared to him in a dream and said, "Joseph, son of David, do not fear to accept Mary as your wife, because that which is in her womb is from the Holy Spirit. She will bear a son who will be called Jesus; he will save his people from their sins." Joseph arose from his sleep, gave thanks to his God, and told his vision to Mary and the virgins with her. And after having been reassured by Mary, he said, "I have sinned because I was suspicious of you."

It so happened that after this a rumor went out that Mary was pregnant. Joseph was seized by the Temple's agents and led to the high priest who, together with the priests, began to reproach him, saying, "How have you been cheated of such a wedding and a virgin whom the angels of God nourished as a dove in the Temple, who wished never to see any man, who had excellent learning in the law of God? If you yourself had not violated her, she today would remain a virgin." Joseph, however, took an oath, swearing that he had never touched her. Abiathar, the high priest, said to him, "As God lives, therefore I will have you drink water of the Lord's testing, and at once he will demonstrate your sin."

All the multitude of Israel gathered together, so many that it was impossible to count them, and Mary was led to the Lord's Temple. Indeed, priests and neighbors and her parents cried out and said to Mary, "Confess your sin to the priests, you who were as a dove in the Temple of God and who accepted nourishment from the hand of an angel." Joseph also was called to the altar and given the water of the Lord's test- ing— which, if a man at fault should drink and then circle the altar seven times, God will cause his sin to show in the man's face. When therefore a cheerful Joseph drank and circled the altar, no sign of sin was revealed in him. Then all the priests and ministers and people sanctified him, saying, "Blessed are you because no guilt was discovered in you." Then they called Mary and said to her, "Now what excuse can you have? Or what sign will he manifest in you beyond that which your pregnancy reveals in your womb? This alone will we require from you that—because Joseph is clear in respect to you— you should confess who it is who deceived you. It is better indeed that your confession betray you than that the wrath of God give a sign in your face and expose you in the midst of the people."

Then Mary, standing firm and intrepid, said, "If there is in me any pollution or sin, or if there was in me any concupiscence or lewdness, may the Lord expose me in view of all the people, so that I may be an example for the correction of all." And she went to the altar of God confidently, drank the water of testing, went around the altar seven times, and no fault was found in her.

And while all the people marveled and stammered, seeing that she was pregnant and yet no sign of guilt appeared in her face, they began to be agitated and to murmur among themselves as crowds do. Some said a blessing, others through bad conscience accused her. Then, seeing the suspicions of the people, that they had not been purged by her integrity, with everybody listening, Mary spoke in a clear voice, "As God lives, Adonai of hosts, in whose view I stand, I have never known a man; I have never even considered to know a man, because from my infancy through my lifetime I have been of this mind. And this offering I made to God from my infancy so that I should continue in integrity with him who created me, to live in him alone with whom I confide, and, as long as I should live, to remain with him alone without stain."

Then they all kissed her, asking that she give forgiveness for their nasty suspicions. And all the people and the priests and all the virgins, with exultation and praise, led her to her house, shouting and saying, "Blessed be the name of the Lord, who has revealed your sanctity to all the masses of Israel.". . .

[The birth of Jesus. The story appears to be based on the *Gospel of James*, and it features Salome's gynecological inspection of Mary. This chapter also recapitulates the Lukan birth narrative.]

On the third day after the Lord's birth, Mary went out of the cave; she went into the stable and placed the child in a manger, and an ox and a donkey worshiped him. Then that which was spoken through Isaiah the prophet was fulfilled: "The ox knows his owner and the donkey his lord's manger." These animals, with him between them, unceasingly worshiped him. Thus that which was spoken through the prophet Habbakuk was fulfilled: "You will be known between the two animals." Joseph and Mary stayed there with the child three days. . . .

[They go to Bethlehem. Jesus is circumcised. The presentation at the Temple (see Luke 2). The coming of the Magi. The massacre of the Jewish children.]

When they came to a certain cave and wanted to rest in it, Mary got down from the pack mule, and, sitting down, held Jesus in her lap. There were three boys traveling with Joseph and a girl with Mary. And behold, suddenly, many dragons came out of the cave. When the boys saw them in front of them they shouted with great fear. Then Jesus got down from his mother's lap, and stood on his feet before the dragons. They, however, worshiped him, and, while they worshiped, they backed away. Then what was said through the prophet David was fulfilled: "You dragons of the earth, praise the Lord, you dragons and all creatures of the abyss." Then the infant Jesus walked before them and ordered them not to harm any man. But Mary and Joseph were very afraid lest the child should be harmed by the dragons. Jesus said to them, "Do not be afraid, nor consider me a child; I always have been a perfect man and am so now; it is necessary that all the wild beasts of the forest be tame before me."

Similarly, lions and leopards worshiped him and accompanied them in the desert. Wherever Mary and Joseph went, they preceded them; showing the way and inclining their heads, they worshiped Jesus. However, the first time that Mary saw the lions and other types of wild beasts around her, she was very frightened. The child Jesus, with cheerful face, looked back and said, "Do not be afraid, Mother, they did not rush here to hurt you but they rush to obey you." When he said this, he cut off the fear in her heart. The lions traveled with them and with the oxen and donkeys and the pack animals which carried their necessities, and they hurt none of them while

they remained. They were tame among the sheep and rams which they brought with them from Judea and had with them. They traveled among wolves and they were not frightened; there was no harm to the one from the other. Then that which was said by the prophet was fulfilled: "Wolves shall be pastured with lambs, the lion and the ox shall eat fodder together." There were two oxen and the wagon, in which they carried their necessities, which the lions guided on their journey.

It so happened that, on the third day after their departure, Mary was fatigued by the excessive heat of the sun in the desert and, seeing a palm tree, said to Joseph, "I want to rest a bit under its shadow." Joseph quickly led her to the palm and let her get down from the animal. While Mary sat, she looked at the top of the palm and saw it full of fruit. She said to Joseph, "I wish, if it is possible, that I have some fruit from this palm." Joseph said to her, "I am astonished that you say this, when you see how high this palm is, that you think to eat from the fruit of the palm. I think more of the lack of water, which already fails us in the water bags; we now have nothing by which we can refresh ourselves and the animals."

Then the infant Jesus, who was resting with smiling face at his mother's bosom, said to the palm, "Bend down, tree, and refresh my mother with your fruit." And immediately, at this voice, the palm bent down its head to the feet of Mary, and they gathered fruit from it by which all were refreshed. After they had gathered all its fruit, it remained bent down, waiting so that it should raise up at the command of him who had commanded it to bend. Then Jesus said to it, "Raise up, palm, and be strong, and be a companion of my trees which are in my Father's Paradise. Open a water course beneath your roots which is hidden in the earth, and from it let flow waters to satisfy us." And the palm raised itself at once, and fountains of water, very clear and cold and sweet, began to pour out through the roots. When they saw the fountains of water they rejoiced with great rejoicing, and they and the beasts of burden were all satisfied, and they gave thanks to God.

The next day they went on from there. At the time they began the journey, Jesus turned to the palm and said, "I give you this privilege, palm, that one of your branches be carried by my angels and planted in my Father's Paradise. I confer upon you this blessing, that all who win in any contest, it shall be said to them, 'You have attained the palm of victory.' " When he said this, behold an angel of the Lord appeared and stood above the palm tree. He took one of its branches and flew to Heaven with the branch in his hand. When they saw this they fell on their faces and were just as if they were dead. Jesus spoke to them, saying, "Why has fear gripped your hearts? Do you not know that this palm, which I have had carried into Paradise, will be ready for all the saints in the place of delight, just as it was ready for you in this desert place." They were all filled with joy and arose.

While they traveled on, Joseph said to him, "Lord, the excessive heat is cooking us; if it pleases you, let us go by the sea, so that we can travel, resting in the coastal towns." Jesus said to him, "Fear not, Joseph, I will shorten your journey, so that what you were going to travel across in the space of thirty days, you will finish in one day." While this was being said, behold, they began to see the mountains and cities of Egypt.

Rejoicing and exulting they came to the region of Hermopolis, and went into one of the Egyptian cities called Sotinen. Since they knew no one in it from whom they could ask for hospitality, they went into the temple which was called the "Capitolium of Egypt." There had been placed in this temple three hundred and sixty-five idols, to which, on appointed days, divine honor was given in sacrilegious ceremonies.

It happened that, when the most blessed Mary, with her child, had entered the temple, all the idols were thrown to the ground, so that all lay flat, convulsed and with their faces shattered. Thus they revealed openly that they were nothing. Then that which was said by the prophet Isaiah was fulfilled: "Behold, the Lord shall come on a swift cloud and enter Egypt, and all the idols made by Egyptians shall be moved from his face."

When this had been announced to Afrodosius, the governor of the city, he came to the temple with his whole army. When the priests of the temple saw that Afrodosius hastened to the temple with his whole army, they supposed to see his revenge on those because of whom the idols were overthrown. He entered the temple, and when he saw that all the idols lay prostrate on their faces, he went to Mary and worshiped the child whom she carried at her bosom, and while he worshiped him, he said to his whole army and his friends, "If he were not the God of our Gods, our Gods would certainly not have fallen before him on their faces, nor would they lie prostrate in his presence. They thus silently confess he is their Lord. If we all do not do with prudence what we see our Gods do, we shall possibly incur his indignation and all come into destruction, just as happened to Pharaoh, king of the Egyptians, who did not believe in such marvels and was drowned in the sea with his whole army." Then all the people of that city believed in the Lord God through Jesus Christ.

After a little time the angel said to Joseph, "Return to the land of Judah; they who sought the life of the boy are dead."

The Infancy Gospel of Thomas

(Christian Apocrypha)

The *Infancy Gospel of Thomas* is one of the earliest infancy gospels, written about A.D. 150, and was extremely popular in the first centuries. It appears in translation in many languages. The *Gospel* deals with the period between Jesus' birth and the incident of Jesus in the Temple, which is recounted in Luke 2:40. For modern apologists, the work is an ethical embarrassment, for the little Jesus is not only a child prodigy but a child terror, performing nasty miracles. The author was probably Gentile, since the work betrays no knowledge of Judaism. In keeping with other apocryphal scriptures, Jesus and his family are depicted as surrounded by unfriendly Jews but they themselves, somehow, are not Jews. Cartlidge and Dungan, the translators of this text from the Greek, speak of the gospel as "a classic example of the influence of the Hellenistic "divine man" concept on a Christian description of Jesus Christ."[1]

The book begins with the exciting narrative of Jesus at five modeling twelve sparrows out of clay by a rushing stream. It is the Sabbath, which he gladly profanes before "a certain Jew." With that act of Jesus at the beginning of the tale, the line is drawn between Judaism and Christianity. The child claps his hands like a magician and the clay becomes flesh, the sparrows fly off chirping. When another child, the son of the scribe Annas, disturbs the water with a willow branch, Jesus curses the "impious ignoramus" and withers him. Then another village child runs along and bangs into his shoulder. Angered, Jesus kills him on the spot. Only his father, Joseph, dares reprimand him, by pulling his ear hard. At this Jesus is angered and warns his "stupid" father. But Joseph thinks the young Jesus should learn to read and so he brings him to Zaccheus the teacher. Jesus outwits and humiliates Zaccheus, who begs Joseph to take him away. Then the holy child embarks on a series of dazzling miracles of a more positive nature. He raises a child to life (to prove he had not himself killed him), he repairs a broken pitcher with a word, he lengthens a beam of wood. The miracles are devoid of ethical content, being presented as magic tricks to convey the powers of the performer. When he is taken to a new teacher to learn to read Greek and Hebrew, he kills the teacher but quickly brings him back to life. The *Gospel* ends with Jesus at age twelve in the Temple, amazing the elders and teachers with his ability to solve the problems of the Law and the parables of the prophets.

The *Infancy Gospel of Thomas* is normally described as crude and without a moral dimension, and indeed such description is correct. Its immense popularity, however, cannot be denied. Although Jesus is portrayed as a superchild, there is little child in the figure. Vindictive but not wise, the young Jesus represents the later Jesus of the sword who damns the unfaithful, rather than the Jesus of love and "the other cheek."

THE INFANCY GOSPEL OF THOMAS*

I, Thomas the Israelite, announce and make known to all you brethren from the Gentiles the childhood and great deeds of our Lord Jesus Christ, which he did when he was born in our country. This is the beginning.

When this child Jesus was five years old, he was playing at the ford of a stream. He made pools of the rushing water and made it immediately pure; he ordered this by word alone. He made soft clay and modeled twelve sparrows from it. It was the Sabbath when he did this. There were many other children playing with him. A certain Jew saw what Jesus did while playing on the Sabbath; he immediately went and announced to his father Joseph, "See, your child is at the stream, and has taken clay and modeled twelve birds; he has profaned the Sabbath." Joseph came to the place, and seeing what Jesus did he cried out, "Why do you do on the Sabbath

*From David R. Cartlidge and David L. Dungan, eds. and trans., *Documents for the Study of the Gospels* (Philadelphia: Fortress Press, 1980), pp. 92–97.

what it is not lawful to do?" Jesus clapped his hands and cried to the sparrows, "Be gone." And the sparrows flew off chirping. The Jews saw this and were amazed. They went away and described to their leaders what they had seen Jesus do.

The son of Annas the scribe was standing there with Joseph. He took a branch of a willow and scattered the water which Jesus had arranged. Jesus saw what he did and became angry and said to him, "You unrighteous, impious ignoramus, what did the pools and the water do to harm you? Behold, you shall also wither as a tree, and you shall not bear leaves nor roots nor fruit." And immediately that child was all withered. Jesus left and went to the house of Joseph. The parents of the withered one bore him away, bemoaning his lost youth. They led him to Joseph and reproached him, "What kind of child do you have who does such things?"

Once again he was going through the village, and a child who was running banged into his shoulder. Jesus was angered and said to him, "You shall go no further on your way." And immediately the child fell down dead. Some people saw this happen and said, "From whence was this child begotten, for his every word is an act accomplished?" The parents of the dead boy went to Joseph and blamed him: "Because you have such a boy, you cannot live with us in the village; your alternative is to teach him to bless and not to curse, for he is killing our children."

Joseph took the child aside privately and warned him, saying, "Why do you do such things? These people are suffering and they hate us and are persecuting us!" Jesus said, "I know that these are not your words, but on account of you I will be silent. However, they shall bear their punishment."[1] Immediately, those who accused him were blinded. Those who saw were very frightened and puzzled, and they said about him, "Every word he speaks, whether good or evil, happens and is a miracle." When he saw what Jesus had done, Joseph arose and took hold of Jesus' ear and pulled it hard. The child was angry and said to him, "It is fitting for you to seek and not find. You have acted very stupidly. Do you not know I am yours? Do not vex me."

A man named Zaccheus, a teacher, was standing there and he heard, in part, Jesus saying these things to his father. He was greatly astonished that he said such things, since he was just a child. And after a few days he approached Joseph and said to him, "You have a smart child, and he has a mind. Come, hand him over to me so that he may learn writing. I will give him all understanding with the letters, and teach him to greet all the elders and to honor them as grandfathers and fathers and to love his peers." He told him all the letters from the Alpha to the Omega plainly, with much discussion. But Jesus looked at Zaccheus the teacher, and said to him, "You do not know the Alpha according to nature, how do you teach others the Beta? You hypocrite! First, if you know it, teach the Alpha, then we shall believe you about the Beta." Then he began to question the teacher about the first letter and he could not answer him.

Many heard as the child said to Zaccheus, "Listen, teacher, to the order of the first element, and pay attention to this, how it has lines, and a central mark which goes through the two lines you see, they converge, go up, again come to head, become the same three times, subordinate, and hypostatic, isometric . . . [the text is unreliable.] You now have the lines of Alpha."

When the teacher, Zaccheus, heard so many such allegories of the first letter spoken by the child, he was puzzled about such expoundings and his teaching. He said to those present, "Woe is me, I am wretched and puzzled; I have shamed myself trying to handle this child. I beg you, brother Joseph, take him away. I cannot bear the severity of his glance. I cannot understand his speech at all. This child is not earthborn; he is able to tame even fire. Perhaps he was begotten before the world's creation. What belly bore him, what womb nurtured him, I do not know. Woe is me, friend, he completely confuses me. I cannot follow his understanding. I have fooled myself; I am thrice wretched. I worked anxiously to have a disciple, and I found myself with a teacher. I consider my shame, friends; I am an old man and have been conquered by a child; for at this hour I cannot look into his gaze. When they all say that I have been conquered by a little child, what can I say? What can I discuss about the lines of the first element he spoke to me? I do not know, O friends, for I do not know its beginning and end. Therefore, I beg you, brother Joseph, take him into your house. He is something great: a God, an angel, or what I should say I do not know."

While the Jews were comforting Zaccheus, the child gave a great laugh, saying, "Now let what is yours bear fruit, and the blind in heart see. I am from above in order that I may curse them and call them into the things which are above, because he who sent me on your account ordered it." And as the child ceased talking, immediately all those who had fallen under his curse were saved (or, healed). And after that no one dared to anger him, lest he should curse him, and he should be crippled.

After some days Jesus was playing upstairs in a certain house, and one of the children playing with him fell from the house and died. And when the other children saw this they ran away, and Jesus remained alone. The parents of the dead child came and accused Jesus of throwing him down. Jesus replied, "I did not throw him down." But still they accused him. Then Jesus leaped down from the roof and stood by the body of the child and cried out in a great voice, saying "Zenon!"—that was his name— "rise up and tell me, did I throw you down?" He immediately rose up and said: "No, Lord, you did not throw me down, but you raised me." Those who saw this were astonished. The parents of the child glorified God because of this sign that happened, and they worshiped Jesus.

After a few days a young man was splitting wood in the vicinity; the axe fell and split the bottom of his foot, and he was bleeding to death. There was an outcry and people gathered. The child Jesus ran there. He pushed through the crowd, and seized the injured foot of the youth; immediately he was healed. He said to the youth, "Now get up, split your wood, and remember me." The crowd, seeing what had happened, worshiped the child, saying, "Truly, the Spirit of God lives in this child!"

When he was six, his mother sent him to draw water and to bring it into the house, giving him a pitcher. But in the crowd, he had a collision; the water jug was broken. Jesus spread out the garment he had on, filled it with water, and bore it to his mother. When his mother saw the miracle she kissed him, and she kept to herself the mysteries which she saw him do.

Again, during planting time the child went with his father to sow seed in their field. While they planted, his father sowed, and the child Jesus planted one grain of wheat. When he had reaped and threshed it, it yielded one hundred measures, and he called all the poor of the village to the threshing floor and gave them the grain. Joseph took the remainder of the grain. He was eight when he did this sign.

His father was a carpenter and at that time made ploughs and yokes. He received an order from a certain rich man to make a bed for him. One beam came out shorter than the other, and he did not know what to do. The child Jesus said to Joseph his father, "Lay the two pieces of wood alongside each other, and make them even at one end." Joseph did as the child told him. Jesus stood at the other end and grasped the shorter beam; he stretched it and made it equal with the other. His father Joseph saw and was astonished, and embracing the child he kissed him and said, "I am blessed because God has given this child to me."

When Joseph saw the mind and age of the child, that he was growing up, he again wished him not to be ignorant of letters. And he took him and gave him to another teacher. But the teacher said to Joseph, "First I will teach him Greek, and then Hebrew." For the teacher knew the child's learning and feared him. Nevertheless he wrote the alphabet and taught him for many hours, but Jesus did not answer him. Then Jesus said to him, "If you really are a teacher, and you know the letters well, tell me the power of Alpha and I will tell you that of Beta." The teacher was angered and hit Jesus on the head. The child was hurt and cursed him. Immediately the teacher fainted, falling to the ground upon his face. The child returned to the house of Joseph. But Joseph was grief-stricken and gave this order to his mother: "Do not let him go outside the door, because anyone who angers him dies."

After some time there was another teacher, a good friend of Joseph. He said to him, "Bring the child to me at school, maybe by flattery I can teach him letters." Joseph said, "If you dare, brother, take him with you." He took him with fear and much anxiety, but the child went with pleasure. Jesus went boldly into the school and found a book lying on the lectern, and taking it, did not read the letters in it, but opened his mouth and spoke by the Holy Spirit and taught the Law to those standing nearby. A great crowd gathered and stood listening to him. They were astonished at the beauty of his teaching and the eloquence of his words, that being a babe he could say such things. Joseph heard and was frightened. He ran into the school, wondering whether this teacher was also without skill, but the teacher said to Joseph, "Know, brother, that I took the child as a disciple, but he is full of much grace and wisdom, and I beg you brother, take him into your house." When the child heard this, immediately he smiled at him and said, "Since you spoke correctly and witnessed correctly, on account of you the one who was stricken shall be healed." And immediately the other teacher was healed. Joseph took the child and returned home.

Joseph sent his son James to gather wood and to bring it into the house. The child Jesus followed him. While James was gathering the sticks, a snake bit James's hand. As he lay dying, Jesus came near and breathed on the bite. Immediately James ceased suffering, the snake burst, and James was healed.

After this, in the neighborhood of Joseph a certain child took sick and died. His mother wept bitterly. Jesus, hearing the great mourning and clamor, ran quickly and found the child dead. He touched his breast and said, "I say to you, child, do not die, but live and be with your mother!" And immediately the child looked up and laughed. Jesus said to the woman, "Pick him up and give him milk, and remember me." The crowd standing around saw and was amazed, and they said, "Truly this child is a God or an angel of God, because his every word becomes a finished deed." And Jesus left there and played with the other children.

After some time a house was being built and there was a great clamor. Jesus arose and went there. Seeing a man lying dead he took his hand and said, "I say to you, man, arise, to your work!" And immediately he arose and worshiped him. Seeing this, the crowd was astonished and said, "This is a heavenly child, for he saved many souls from death, and can save them all his life."

When he was twelve his parents, according to custom, went to Jerusalem to the Passover with their traveling companions. After the Passover they returned to their house. While they were going home, the child Jesus went back to Jerusalem. His parents thought that he was in the caravan. After a day's travel, they sought him among their kinfolk and when they did not find him they were troubled. They returned again to the city to seek him. After three days they found him in the Temple, seated in the midst of the teachers, listening and questioning them. They all were attentive and amazed at how he, being a child, could argue with the elders and teachers of the people, solving the chief problems of the Law and the parables of the prophets. His mother, Mary, came up and said to him, "How can you have done this to us, child? Behold, we have looked everywhere for you, grieving." And Jesus said to them, "Why did you look for me? Do you not know that I must be in my Father's house?" The scribes and Pharisees said, "Are you the mother of this child?" She said, "I am." They said to her, "You are blessed among women, because God has blessed the fruit of your womb. We have never before seen or heard such glory or such excellence and wisdom." Jesus arose and followed his mother and was obedient to his parents. But his mother kept in her heart all that had happened. Jesus grew in wisdom and stature and grace. Glory be to him forever and ever. Amen.

Note

1. An interesting Syriac variant: "If these children had been born in wedlock they would not be cursed."

A Latin Infancy Gospel: The Birth of Jesus*

(Christian Apocrypha)

This is a medieval document that exists in two manuscripts. Most of this *Gospel* is based upon *Pseudo-Matthew* and the *Gospel of James*. However, there are passages that are unique to this gospel, which appear to use a source that is probably from the Church's early years, and which have a birth narrative unknown elsewhere. M. R. James, who first published the Arundel and Hereford manuscripts of the gospel, claims that the birth narrative may be from the second century. We have selected passages from the Arundel manuscript—it is more primitive than the Hereford version—which rely upon the unknown source.

———
*Introduction by David R. Cartlidge and David L. Dungan.

A LATIN INFANCY GOSPEL: THE BIRTH OF JESUS*

Behold a girl came with a chair which was customarily used to help women giving birth. She stopped. When they saw her they were amazed, and Joseph said to her, "Child, where are you going with that chair?" The girl responded, "My mistress sent me to this place because a youth came to her with great haste and said, 'Come quickly to help with an unusual birth; a girl will give birth for the first time.' When she heard this, my mistress sent me on before her; look, she herself is following."

Joseph looked back and saw her coming; he went to meet her and they greeted each other. The midwife said to Joseph, "Sir, where are you going?" He replied, "I seek a Hebrew midwife." The woman said to him, "Are you from Israel?" Joseph said, "I am from Israel." The woman said to him, "Who is the young woman who will give birth in this cave?" Joseph replied, "Mary, who was promised to me, who was raised in the Lord's Temple." The midwife said to him, "She is not your wife?" And Joseph said, "She was promised to me, but was made pregnant by the Holy Spirit." The midwife said to him, "What you say, is it true?" Joseph said to her, "Come and see."

They entered the cave. Joseph said to the midwife, "Come, see Mary." When she wished to enter to the interior of the cave, she was afraid, because a great light shone resplendent in the cave, the light did not wane in the day nor through the night as long as Mary stayed there . . . .

Joseph said, "Mary. Behold, I have brought to you a midwife, Zachel, who stands outside in front of the cave, who because of the brightness not only dares not enter the cave, but even cannot." When she heard this, Mary smiled. Joseph said to her, "Do not smile, but take care; she comes to examine you in case you need medicine." He ordered the midwife to enter to Mary and she stood before her. For hours Mary permitted herself to be watched, then the midwife cried with a loud voice and said, "Lord, great God, have mercy, because never has this been heard, nor seen, nor even dreamed of, until now, that the breasts should be full of milk and a male child, after birth, should make his mother known to be a virgin. There was no offering of blood in the birth, no pain occurred in the parturition. A virgin conceived, a virgin has given birth and after she gave birth, she remained a virgin."

[The midwife is asked to relate what she had seen to Symeon, Joseph's son. See Matt. 13:55; Mark 6:3. The following is, therefore, a flashback.]

"When I entered to the maiden, I found her face looking upward; she was inclined toward Heaven and speaking to herself. I truly believe that she prayed to and blessed the Most High. When I had come to her, I said to her, 'Daughter, tell me, do you not feel some pain, or is not some part of your body gripped with pain?' She, however, as if she heard nothing, remained immobile like solid rock, intent on Heaven.

"In that hour, everything ceased. There was total silence and fear. For even the winds stopped, they made no breeze; there was no motion of tree leaves; no sound of water was heard. The streams did not flow; there was no motion of the sea. All things produced in the water were quiet; there was no human voice sounding; there was a great silence. For the pole itself ceased its rapid course from that hour. Time almost stopped its measure. All, overwhelmed with great fear, kept silent; we were ex-

*This excerpt includes selections from the Arundel Manuscript, chapters 68–74. From David R. Cartlidge and David L. Dungan, eds. and trans., *Documents for the Study of the Gospels* (Philadelphia: Fortress Press, 1980), pp. 104–106.

405

pecting the advent of the most high God, the end of the world.

"As the time drew near, the power of God showed itself openly. The maiden stood looking intently into Heaven; she became as a grapevine [or, she became snow-white]. For now the end of good things was at hand. When the light had come forth, Mary worshiped him to whom she saw she had given birth. The child himself, like the sun, shone bright, beautiful, and was most delightful to see, because he alone appeared as peace, soothing the whole world. In that hour, when he was born, the voice of many invisible beings in one voice proclaimed "Amen." And the light, when it was born, multiplied, and it obscured the light of the sun itself by its shining rays. The cave was filled by the bright light together with a most sweet odor. The light was born just as the dew descends from Heaven to the earth. For its odor is fragrant beyond all the sweet smell of ointments.

"I, however, stood stupefied and amazed. Awe grasped me. I was gazing intently at the fantastically bright light which had been born. The light, however, after a while, shrank, imitated the shape of an infant, then immediately became outwardly an infant in the usual manner of born infants. I became bold and leaned over and touched him. I lifted him in my hands with great awe, and I was terrified because he had no weight like other babies who are born. I looked at him closely; there was no blemish on him, but he was in his body totally shining, just as the dew of the most high God. He was light to carry, splendid to see. For a while I was amazed at him because he did not cry as newborn children are supposed to. While I held him, looking into his face, he laughed at me with a most joyful laugh, and, opening his eyes, he looked intently at me. Suddenly a great light came forth from his eyes like a great flash of lightning."

The Arabic Infancy Gospel: The Children Who Were Changed into Goats

(Christian Apocrypha)

Among the popular infancy gospels is the *Arabic Infancy Gospel*, which deals with the birth of Jesus, miracles in Egypt by Jesus and Mary, and miracles by the child Jesus. The latter derive from the *Infancy Gospel of Thomas*. The work itself appears to be a translation from the Syriac. The fact that the work was translated into Arabic made it available to Mohammed (or whoever compiled the Koran), who in turn adopted its legends in the Koran. The stories entered Persian legends and reached India as well. *The Arabic Infancy Gospel* was first edited and translated into English by Henry Sike in 1697.

The pattern of the excerpt included here, "The Children Who were Changed into Goats," is typical of many morality miracles attributed to Jesus. The child Jesus causes a terrible event—he maims, blinds, or kills. Then, after the faithful offer prayers to the all-powerful, all-knowing child, he restores the victim to his or her previous condition. He heals or restores life. Presumably those who ignore or lack faith in the Lord Jesus are punished, while those who are strong in faith and praise and pray to Lord Jesus are saved.

THE ARABIC INFANCY GOSPEL: THE CHILDREN WHO WERE CHANGED INTO GOATS*

One day the Lord Jesus went out into the street and saw children who had come together to play. He followed them, but the children hid themselves from him. Now when the Lord Jesus came to the door of a house and saw women standing there, he asked them where those children had gone. They replied that no one was there; and the Lord Jesus said: "Who are those whom you see in the furnace?" "They are three-year-old goats," they answered. And the Lord Jesus said: "Come out to your shepherd, you goats." Then the children in the form of goats came out and began to skip round him. When those women saw this, they were seized with wonder and fear, and speedily fell down before the Lord Jesus and implored him, saying: "O our Lord Jesus, son of Mary, truly you are the good shepherd of Israel, have mercy on your handmaids who stand before you and have never doubted: for you have come, our Lord, to heal and not to destroy." The Lord Jesus answered and said: "The children of Israel are like the Ethiopians among the peoples." And the women said: "You, Lord, know everything, and nothing is hidden from you; but now we beg and implore you of your mercy to restore to their former state these children, your servants." So the Lord Jesus said: "Come, children, let us go and play." And immediately in the presence of these women the goats were changed into children.

---

*Translated by A. J. B. Higgins. From Edgar Hennecke and Wilhelm Schneemelcher, eds., *New Testament Apocrypha*, vol. 1 (Philadelphia: Westminster Press, 1963), p. 409.

6
ACTS

The Apocryphal Acts
of the Apostles and the
Acts of John

The New Testament Acts of the Apostles is attributed to Luke, author of the Gospel of Luke. Acts serves as a supplement to the synoptic gospels, and provides a history of early Christianity. Its theological mission was to offer Gentiles—from Jerusalem to Rome—word about the End, that is, the good news of salvation. Its aim was to inspire faith in the recent messianic speculation of a reformist Jewish sect, a sect known as Christians (messianists) after its crucified leader, Christ the Messiah.

The *Apocryphal Acts of the Apostles* consists of the five acts of John, Peter, Paul, Andrew, and Thomas, which date from the second and third centuries. They enter the world of Christendom with suspect credentials. Gathered by the Manichaeans into a corpus, they reveal many Gnostic as well as primitive Catholic notions. The *Acts of John*, the oldest of these documents, is the most clearly Gnostic work and it was widely condemned by early orthodox sources. In the late fifth century Leo the Great declared: "The apocryphal writings, however, which under the names of the Apostles contain a hotbed of manifold perversity, should not only be forbidden but altogether removed and burnt with fire" (Ep. 15.15). The Nicene Council of 787 also consigned the *Acts of John* to fire. While the attack on the *Apocryphal Acts* was harsh and many of the more flagrant Gnostic notions were undoubtedly excised, about seventy percent of the *Acts of John* has survived. Together with the other acts, the entire corpus represents a major document of early Christianity, comparable in size and scope to the New Testament itself. Of course, like the Lucan acts and Paul's acts

411

and epistles, the immediate frame of the *Apocryphal Acts* is the crucial period of evangelism following the crucifixion.

The *Apocryphal Acts* tells fabulous stories of the journeys'and deeds of the apostles. An essential feature of the message is sexual continence. This encratite strain reflects the Gnostic's almost furious separation of spirit from body, the latter a dark prison of error. So Peter prefers to keep his own virgin daughter a cripple rather than expose her to the ways of the flesh. He does cure her momentarily, however, to prove that he has the miraculous powers to do so. The ascetic fervor combines with the miraculous to give the *Acts* their special cast. Miracles occur much more frequently than in the New Testament and, to the embarrassment of many commentators, are bizarre and outrageously exaggerated. In a word, the traveling apostles are glorified as miracle-workers in these highly imaginative narrations, which were a form of popular literature and entertainment for the uneducated followers of Christianity. The practical aim was less theological than evangelical. The sheer wonder and excitement of the legends were intended to overwhelm, to convert, and to confirm belief in the powers of the new religion. One of the loveliest pieces is a purely Gnostic work, the *Hymn of the Pearl*, which was originally appended to the *Act of Thomas*. It is the jewel of the collection (see part 3, "Wisdom Literature and Poetry").

Traditionally, the five *Acts* were written by Leucius Charinus. Actually, the works were composed over a period of at least one hundred years in the second and third centuries. Leucius seems to be the pen name of the author of the *Acts of John*. Texts and fragments of texts survive from Syriac, Greek, and Latin. There were soon after translations in Armenian, Coptic, Ethiopic, Arabic, and other languages of the first Christian peoples.

The Acts of John

(Christian Apocrypha)

The *Acts of John* contains numerous episodes in which John preaches, converts, saves by miracles, and forgives in exchange for faith. So he heals a sick woman, raises another from the dead, forgives a parricide and adulterer. He cheerfully destroys a pagan temple to Artemis at Ephesus and also orders bedbugs to cease disturbing his sleep and that of other servants of God (the bugs obey). By far the most spiritual passages concern the description of Christ's earthly appearance. The "Revelation of the Mystery of the Cross" seems to be a Valentinian Gnostic revelation of the passion of Jesus. We have already seen in "Christ's Earthly Appearance" that Jesus is at one moment of flesh and blood and the next incorporeal. John touches him but there is nothing there. Herein we see the dualism typical of the Gnostic world view. Similarly, Christ informs him that he is not as he appears to be. He suffers yet does not suffer. "Nor am I the man who is on the Cross," he tells us. This conforms to the Gnostic and Docetic notion that a phantom Jesus was crucified. To the orthodox Christian the idea of a nonsuffering Christ was most repugnant and heretical. The passages concerning Jesus are mysterious and of consummate theological and poetic interest.

FROM MILETUS TO EPHESUS*

Now John was hastening to Ephesus, prompted by a vision; so that Demonicus and his kinsman, Aristodemus, and a very wealthy man named Cleobius and the wife of Marcellus prevailed upon him with some difficulty to remain for one day at Miletus and rested with him. And when they departed very early in the morning and some four miles of their journey were already accomplished, a voice came from Heaven in the hearing of us all, saying "John, you shall give glory to your Lord in Ephesus, glory of which you shall know, both you and all your brothers that are with you and some of those in that place who shall believe through you." Then John joyfully considered what was to happen at Ephesus, saying, "Lord, behold, I go according to your will. Your will be done."

FIRST STAY IN EPHESUS**

And as we approached the city we were met by Lycomedes, a wealthy man who was praetor of the Ephesians; and he fell at John's feet and entreated him, saying "Is your name John? The God whom you preach has sent you to help my wife who has been paralyzed for the past seven days and is lying there unable to be cured. But glorify your God by healing her, and have pity upon us. For while I was considering what conclusion to draw from this, someone came to me and said, 'Lycomedes, enough of this thought which besets you, for it is harm-

*Chapter 18. All selections from the *Acts of John* are translated by G. C. Stead and are from Edgar Hennecke and Wilhelm Schneemelcher, eds., *New Testament Apocrypha*, vol. 2 (Philadelphia: Westminster Press, 1963), pp. 215–221, 225–227, 232–241, 243–244, 256–258.
**Chapters 19–25.

ful. Do not submit to it! For I have had compassion on my servant, Cleopatra, and have sent from Miletus a man named John, who will raise her up and restore her to you in good health.' Do not delay then, servant of God, who has revealed himself to me; come quickly to my wife, who is only just breathing." Then John went at once, and the brothers who were with him, and Lycomedes, from the gate to that man's house. But Cleobius said to his servants, "Go to my kinsman, Callippus, and let him give you a comfortable lodging—for I am coming there with his son—so that we may find everything convenient."

But when Lycomedes came with John into the house in which the woman was lying, he grasped his feet again and said "See, my Lord, this faded beauty; look at her youth; look at the famous flower-like grace of my poor wife, at which all Ephesus was amazed! Wretched man, I am the victim of envy; I am humbled; my enemies' eye has fallen upon me! I have never wronged anyone, although I was able to injure many, for I had just this in view and was on my guard, so as not to see any evil or misfortune like this. What use then, Cleopatra, was my care? What have I gained by being known as a pious man until today? I suffer worse than a heathen seeing you, Cleopatra, lying there so. The sun in its course shall no more see me, if you cease to be my companion. I will go before you, Cleopatra, and despatch myself from life. I will not spare my vigorous health, though it be still youthful. I will defend myself before Justice, as one that has served her justly, though I might indict her for judging unjustly. I will call her to account when I come before her a mere phantom of life. I will say to her 'You have forced me to leave the light[1] by tearing away Cleopatra; you have made me a dead man by bringing this upon me; you have forced me to anger Providence by cutting off my joy.' "

And Lycomedes, still speaking to

Cleopatra, approached her bed and lamented with a loud voice.

But John pulled him away and said, "Cease from these lamentations and from these unfitting words of yours. It is not proper for you who saw the vision to be unbelieving; for you shall receive your consort again. Stand then with us, who have come on her behalf, and pray to the God whom you saw as he manifested himself to you in dreams. What is it, then, Lycomedes? You too must wake up and open your soul. Cast off this heavy sleep of yours! Call on the Lord; entreat him for your consort and he shall revive her." But he fell upon the ground and lamented with all his soul.

John therefore said with tears, "Alas for the fresh betrayal of my vision! Alas for the fresh temptation that is prepared for me! Alas for the fresh contrivance of him that is contriving against me! The voice from Heaven that came to me on the way, did it intend this for me? Did it forewarn me of this that must happen here, betraying me to this great crowd of citizens because of Lycomedes? The man lies there lifeless, and I know very well that they will not let me leave the house alive. Why do you tarry, Lord? Why have you withdrawn from us your gracious promise? No, Lord, I pray you; do not let him exult who delights in the misfortunes of others; do not let him dance who is always deriding us! But let your holy name and your mercy make haste! Raise up the two dead who have brought enmity against me!"

And while John was crying aloud, crowds from the city of the Ephesians came running to the house of Lycomedes, supposing him dead. But John, seeing the great crowd that had come, said to the Lord, "Now is the time of refreshment and of confidence in you, O Christ. Now is the time for us who are sick to have help from you, O physician, who heals freely. Keep my entrance to this place free from derision. I pray you Jesus, help this great multitude come to you who are Lord of the universe. Look at the affliction, look at those who lie here! Do prepare, even from those gathered here, holy vessels for your service, when they have seen your gracious gift. For you yourself have said, O Christ, 'Ask, and it shall be given you.' We therefore ask of you, O King, not gold or silver, not substance or possessions, nor any of the perishable things upon earth, but two souls, through whom you shall convert those who are present to your way and to your teaching, to your confidence, to your excellent promise; for some of them shall be saved when they learn your power through the resurrection of these who are lifeless. So now, grant us hope in you. I am going, then, to Cleopatra and say, 'Arise in the name of Jesus Christ.'"

And he went to her and touched her face and said, "Cleopatra, He speaks, whom every ruler fears, and every creature, power, abyss and all darkness, and unsmiling death, the height of heaven and the circles of Hell, the resurrection of the dead and the sight of the blind, the whole power of the prince of this world and the pride of its ruler. Arise, he says, and be not an excuse for many who wish to disbelieve, and an affliction to souls who are able to hope and be saved." And Cleopatra cried out at once with a loud voice, "I arise, Master, save your handmaid."

And when she had arisen after seven days of mortal sickness, the city of the Ephesians was stirred at that amazing sight.

But Cleopatra asked after her husband, Lycomedes. But John said to her, "Cleopatra, keep your soul unmoved and unwavering, and then you shall have your husband standing here with you; if you are not disturbed nor shaken by what has happened, but have come to believe in my God, then through me he shall be given back to you alive. Come then with me to your other bedroom, and you shall see him dead indeed, but rising again through the power of my God." And when Cleopatra came with John into her bedroom and saw Lycomedes, dead on her account, she lost her voice, and ground her teeth and bit her tongue, and closed her eyes, raining down tears; and she quietly attended to the apostle.

But John had pity upon Cleopatra when he saw her neither raging nor distraught, and called upon the perfect and condescending mercy, and said, "Lord Jesus Christ, you see her distress, you see her need, you see Cleopatra crying out her soul in silence for she contains within her the intolerable raging of her sorrow; and I know that for Lycomedes' sake she will follow him to death." And she quietly said to John, "That is in my mind, Master, and nothing else." Then the apostle went up to the couch on which Lycomedes lay, and, taking Cleopatra's hand, he said, "Cleopatra, because of the crowd that is present, and because of your relatives who have come here also, speak with a loud voice to your husband and say, 'Rise up and glorify the name of God, since to the dead he gives back the dead.'" And she went near and spoke to her husband as she was instructed, and immediately raised him up. And he arose and fell to the ground and kissed John's feet; but he lifted him up and said, "It is not my feet, man, that you should kiss, but those of God in whose power you both have been raised up."

But Lycomedes said to John, "I beg and entreat you in God's name through whom you raised us up, to stay with us, both you and your companions." Likewise Cleopatra grasped his feet and said the same. But John said to them, "For tomorrow I will be with you." And they said to him again, "There is no hope for us in your God, but we shall have been raised in vain, if you do not stay with us." And Cleobius together with Aristodemus and also Demonicus, in distress of soul, said to John, "Let us stay with them, that they may stay free of offence before the Lord." And he remained there with the brethren.

THE PORTRAIT OF JOHN*

Then there came together a great gathering of people because of John. And while he was addressing those who were present Lycomedes, who had a friend who was a skillful painter, went running to him and said, "You see how I have hurried to come to you. Come quickly to my house and paint the man whom I show you without his knowing it." And the painter, giving someone the necessary implements and colors, said to Lycomedes, "Show me the man and for the rest have no anxiety." Then Lycomedes pointed out John to the painter, and brought him near and shut him up in a room from which the apostle of Christ could be seen. And Lycomedes was with the blessed man, feasting upon the faith and the knowledge of our God, and rejoiced even more because he was going to have him in a portrait.

So on the first day the painter drew his outline and went away; but on the next day he painted him in with his colors, and so delivered the portrait to Lycomedes, to his great joy; and he took it and put it in his bedroom and put garlands on it; so that when John saw it afterwards, he said to him, "My dear child, what is it you are doing when you come from the bath into your bedroom alone? Am I not to pray with you and with the other brethren? Or are you hiding something from us?" And saying this and joking with him he went into the bedroom; and he saw there a portrait of an old man crowned with garlands, and lamps and an altar set before it. And he called him and said, "Lycomedes, what

*Chapters 26–29.

is it that you have done with this portrait? Is it one of your gods that is painted here? Why, I see you are still living as a pagan!" And Lycomedes answered him, "He alone is my God who raised me up from death with my wife. But if besides that God we may call our earthly benefactors gods, it is you, my father, whose portrait I possess, whom I crown and love and reverence, as having become a good guide to me." Then John, who had never beheld his own face, said to him, "You are teasing me, child; am I so gracious in form as your Lord? How can you persuade me that the portrait is like me?" And Lycomedes brought him a looking-glass, and when he had seen himself in the glass and gazed at the portrait, he said, "As the Lord Jesus Christ lives, the portrait is like me; yet not like me, my child, but like my image in the flesh; for if the painter who has copied my face here wants to put me in a portrait, then he needs the colors that were given you and boards and the shape of my figure, and age and youth and all such visible things.

"But do you be a good painter for me, Lycomedes. You have colors which he gives you through me, that is, Jesus, who paints us all from life for himself, who knows the shapes and forms and figures and dispositions and types of our souls. And these are the colors which I tell you to paint with: faith in God, knowledge, reverence, kindness, fellowship, mildness, goodness, brotherly love, purity, sincerity, tranquility, fearlessness, cheerfulness, dignity, and the whole band of colors which portray your soul and already raise up your members that were cast down and level those that were lifted up, which cure your bruises and heal your wounds and arrange your tangled hair and wash your face and instruct your eyes and cleanse your heart and purge your belly and cut off that which is below it; in brief, when a full set and mixture of such colors has come together into your soul, it will present it to

our Lord Jesus Christ, undismayed and undaunted and rounded in form. But what you have now done is childish and imperfect; you have drawn a dead likeness of what is dead."

CHRIST'S EARTHLY APPEARANCE*

For when he had chosen Peter and Andrew, who were brothers, he came to me and to my brother James, saying, "I need you; come with me!" And my brother said this to me, "John, what does he want, this child on the shore who called us?" And I said, "Which child?" And he answered me, "The one who is beckoning to us." And I said "This is because of the long watch we have kept at sea. You are not seeing straight, brother James. Do you not see the man standing there who is handsome, fair, and cheerful-looking?" But he said to me, "I do not see that man, my brother. But let us go, and we will see what this means."

And when we had brought the boat to land, we saw how he also helped us to beach the boat. And as we left the place, wishing to follow him, he appeared to me again as rather bald-headed but with a thick flowing beard, but to James as a young man whose beard was just beginning. So we wondered, both of us, about the meaning of the vision we had seen. Then, as we both followed him we became gradually more perplexed about this matter.

But then there appeared to me a yet more amazing sight; I tried to see him as he was, and I never saw his eyes closing, but always open. But he sometimes appeared to me as a small man with no good looks, and then again as looking up to Heaven. And he had another strange property; when I reclined at table he would take me to his own breast, and I

*Chapters 88–93.

417

held him fast; and sometimes his breast felt to me smooth and soft, but sometimes hard like rock so that I was perplexed in my mind and said, "Why do I find it so?"

Another time he took me and James and Peter to the mountain where he used to pray, and we saw on him a light such that a man, who uses mortal speech, cannot describe what it was like. Again he took us three likewise up the mountain, saying "Come with me." And again we went; and we saw him at a distance praying. Then I, since he loved me, went quietly up to him, as if he could not see, and stood looking at his hinder parts; and I saw him not dressed in clothes at all, but stripped of those that we usually saw upon him, and not like a man at all. And I saw that his feet were whiter than snow, so that the ground there was lit up by his feet; and that his head stretched up to Heaven, so that I was afraid and cried out; and he, turning about, appeared as a small man, and caught hold of my beard and pulled it and said to me, "John, do not be faithless, but believing, and not inquisitive." And I said to him, "Why, Lord, what have I done?" But I tell you, my brethren, that I suffered such pain for thirty days in the place where he touched my beard, that I said to him, "Lord, if your playful tug has caused such pain, what would it be if you had dealt me a blow?" And he said to me, "Let it be your concern from now on not to tempt him that cannot be tempted."

But Peter and James were vexed as I spoke with the Lord, and beckoned me to come to them and leave the Lord alone. And I went, and they both said to me, "Who was it who spoke with the Lord when he was on the mountain top? For we heard them both speaking." And when I considered his abundant grace and his unity within many faces and his unceasing wisdom that looks after us, I said, "You shall learn this from him if you ask him."

And again when we—that is, all his disciples—were sleeping in one house at Gennesaret, I wrapped myself in my cloak and watched by myself to see what he was doing. And first I heard him say, "John, go to sleep." Then I pretended to sleep; and I saw another like him coming down, and I heard him also saying to my Lord, "Jesus, the men you have chosen still disbelieve you." And my Lord said to him, "You are right; for they are men."

I will tell you another glory, brethren; sometimes when I meant to touch him I encountered a material, solid body; but at other times again when I felt him, his substance was immaterial and incorporeal, and as if it did not exist at all.

And if ever he were invited by one of the Pharisees and went where he was invited, we went with him; and one loaf was laid before each one of us by those who had invited us, and so he also would take one; but he would bless his and divide it among us; and every man was satisfied by that little piece, and our own loaves were kept intact, so that those who had invited him were amazed.

And I often wished, as I walked with him, to see his footprint in the earth, whether it appeared—for I saw him raising himself from the earth—and I never saw it. And I tell you this much, my brethren, so as to encourage your faith in him: for his miracles and wonderful works must not be told for the moment, for they are unspeakable and, perhaps, can neither be uttered nor heard.

REVELATION OF THE MYSTERY OF THE CROSS*

After the Lord had so danced with us, my beloved, he went out. And we were

*Chapters 97–102.

like men amazed or fast asleep, and we fled this way and that. And so I saw him suffer, and did not wait by his suffering, but fled to the Mount of Olives and wept at what had come to pass. And when he was hung upon the cross on Friday, at the sixth hour of the day there came a darkness over the whole earth. And my Lord stood in the middle of the cave and gave light to it and said, "John, for the people below in Jerusalem I am being crucified and pierced with lances and reeds and given vinegar and gall to drink. But to you I am speaking, and listen to what I speak. I put into your mind to come up to this mountain so that you may hear what a disciple should learn from his teacher and a man from God."

And when he had said this he showed me a cross of light firmly fixed, and around the cross a great crowd, which had no single form; and in the cross was one form and the same likeness. And I saw the Lord himself above the cross, having no shape but only a kind of voice; yet not that voice which we knew, but one that was sweet and gentle and truly the voice of God, which said to me, "John, there must be one man to hear these things from me, for I need one who is ready to hear. This cross of light is sometimes called logos by me for your sakes, sometimes mind, sometimes Jesus, sometimes Christ, sometimes a door, sometimes a way, sometimes bread, sometimes seed, sometimes resurrection, sometimes Son, sometimes Father, sometimes Spirit, sometimes life, sometimes truth, sometimes faith, sometimes grace; and so it is called for men's sake.

"But what it truly is, as known in itself and spoken to us, is this: it is the distinction of all things, and the strong uplifting of what is firmly fixed out of what is unstable, and the harmony of wisdom, being wisdom in harmony. But there are places on the right and on the left, powers, authorities, principalities and demons, activities, threatenings, passions, devils, Satan, and the inferior root from which the nature of transient things proceeded.

"This cross then is that which has united all things by the word and which has separated off what is transitory and inferior, which has also compacted all things into one. But this is not that wooden cross which you shall see when you go down from here; nor am I the man who is on the cross, I whom now you do not see but only hear my voice. I was taken to be what I am not, I who am not what for many others I was; but what they will say of me is mean and unworthy of me. Since then the place of my rest is neither to be seen nor told, much more shall I, the Lord of this place, be neither seen nor told.

"The multitude around the cross that is not of one form is the inferior nature. And those whom you saw in the cross, even if they have not yet one form—not every member of him who has come down has yet been gathered together. But when human nature is taken up, and the race that comes to me and obeys my voice, then he who now hears me shall be united with this race and shall no longer be what he now is, but shall be above them as I am now. For so long as you do not call yourself mine, I am not what I am; but if you hear me, you also as hearer shall be as I am, and I shall be what I was, when you are as I am with myself; for from me you are what I am. Therefore ignore the many and despise those who are outside the mystery; for you must know that I am wholly with the Father, and the Father with me.

"So then I have suffered none of those things which they will say of me; even that suffering which I showed to you and to the rest in my dance, I will that it be called a mystery. For what you are, that I have shown you, as you see; but what I am is known to me alone, and no one else. Let me have what is mine; what is yours you must see through me; but me you must see truly—not that which I am, as I said, but that which you, as my kinsman, are able to know. You hear that I suffered, yet I suffered not; and that I suffered not, yet I did suffer; and that I was pierced, yet I was not wounded; that I was hanged, yet I was not hanged; that blood flowed from me, yet it did not flow, and, in a word, that what they say of me, I did not endure, but what they do not say, those things I did suffer. Now what these are, I secretly show you; for I know that you will understand. You must know me, then, as the torment of the logos, the piercing of the logos, the blood of the logos, the wounding of the logos, the fastening of the logos, the death of the logos. And so I speak, discarding the manhood. The first then that you must know is the logos, then you shall know the Lord; and thirdly the man, and what he has suffered."

When he had said these things to me, and others which I know not how to say as he wills, he was taken up, without any of the multitude seeing him. And going down I laughed at them all, since he had told me what they had said about him; and I held this one thing fast in my mind, that the Lord had performed everything as a symbol and a dispensation for the conversion and salvation of man.

THE DESTRUCTION OF THE TEMPLE OF ARTEMIS*

Now the brothers from Miletus said to John, "We have remained a long time in Ephesus; if you agree, let us go to Smyrna. For already we hear that the great works of God have arrived there also." And Andronicus said to them, "When our teacher wishes, then let us go." But John said, "Let us first go into the Temple of Artemis; for perhaps if we are seen

_____
*Chapters 37–45.

there, the servants of the Lord will be found there also."

Now two days later, there was the dedication festival of the idol temple. So while everyone was wearing white, John alone put on black clothing and went up to the temple; and they seized him and tried to kill him. But John said, "You are mad to lay hands on me, a man who serves the one true God." And he went up on a high platform, and said to them,

"Men of Ephesus, you are liable to behave like the sea; every river at its outfall, every spring that flows down, the rains and incessant waves and stony torrents, are all made salt by the bitter brine that is in it. You, likewise, have remained to this day unchanged in your attitude towards the true religion, and are being corrupted by your ancient rituals. How many miracles and cures of diseases have you seen performed through me? And yet you are blinded in your hearts, and cannot recover your sight. What is it then, men of Ephesus? I have ventured to come up now into this very idol temple of yours. I will convict you of being utterly godless and dead through human reasoning. See, here I stand. You all say that you have Artemis as your goddess; so pray in her name that I, and I alone, may die; or if you cannot do this, then I alone will call upon my own God and because of your unbelief I will put you all to death."

But since they had long experience of him and had seen dead men raised by him, they cried out, "Do not destroy us like that, we implore you, John; we know that you can do it!" And John said to them, "If you do not wish to die, then your religion must be convicted. And why convicted? So that you may abandon your ancient error. For now is the time! Either you must be converted by my God, or I myself will die at the hands of your goddess; for I will pray in your presence and entreat my God that you may find mercy."

So saying, he uttered this prayer: "O God, who are God, above all that are called gods; yet rejected till this day in the city of the Ephesians; who put me in mind to come to this place, of which I never thought; who convicts every form of worship, by converting men to you; at whose name every idol takes flight, and every demon and every unclean power. Now let the demon that is here take flight at your name, the deceiver of this great multitude and show your mercy in this place, for they have been led astray."

And while John was saying this, of a sudden the altar of Artemis split into many pieces, and all the offerings laid up in the temple suddenly fell to the floor and its goodness was broken, and so were more than seven images; and half the temple fell down, so that the priest was killed at one stroke as the roof came down. Then the assembled Ephesians cried out, "There is but one God, the God of John! There is but one God who has mercy upon us; for you alone are God! We are converted, now that we have seen your marvelous works! Have mercy upon us, O God, according to your will, and save us from our great error!" And some of them lay on their faces and made supplication; others bent their knees and prayed; some tore their clothes and wept, and others tried to take flight.

But John stretched out his hands and with uplifted heart said to the Lord, "Glory be to you, my Jesus, the only God of truth, for you gain your servants by elaborate means." And having said this he said to the people, "Rise up from the ground, men of Ephesus, and pray to my God, and acknowledge his invisible power that is openly seen, and the wonderful works that were done before your eyes. Artemis should have helped herself; her servant should have been helped by her, and not have died. Where is the power of the demon [i.e., the goddess]? Where are her sacrifices? Where are her dedication festivals, her feasts, her garlands? Where is all that sorcery and the poisoner's art that is sister to it?"

And the people, rising from the ground, went running and threw down the rest of the idol temple, crying out, "The God of John is the only God we know; from now on we worship him, since he has had mercy upon us!" And as John came down from that place a great crowd took hold of him, saying, "Help us, John; stand by us, for we perish in vain. You see our purpose; you see the people following after you, hanging in hope upon your God. We have seen the way which we followed in error when we lost him; we have seen that our gods were set up in vain; we have seen their great and shameful derision. But let us, we beg you, come to your house and receive help without hindrance. Accept us, for we are desperate!"

But John said to them, "Friends, you must believe that it was on your account that I remained at Ephesus, although I was eager to go to Smyrna and the other cities, that the servants of Christ who are there may be converted to him. But since I was about to depart without being fully at ease about you, I have waited, praying to my God, and asked him that I should leave Ephesus only when I have confirmed you in the faith; and now that I see this has come and is still increasing, I will not leave you until I have weaned you like children from the nurse's milk and set you upon a solid rock."

RESURRECTION OF THE PRIEST OF ARTEMIS*

So John remained with them and received them in the house of Andronicus. And one of those who were assembled there laid down the dead body of the priest of Artemis before the door, for he was his kinsman, and came in quickly with the rest, telling no one. Therefore John, after he had addressed the breth-

*Chapters 46–47.

ren, and after the prayer and the thanksgiving eucharist, and after he had laid hands on each of those who were assembled, said in the Spirit, "There is one of those present who is moved by faith in God, who has laid down the priest of Artemis before the door and has come in; and in the longing of his soul he has put the concern for himself first, reasoning thus with himself; 'It is better that I should take thought for the living than for my dead kinsman; for I know that if I turn to the Lord and save my own soul, John will not refuse even to raise up the dead.' " And John, rising from his place, went where the priest's kinsman, who had thought this, came in; and he took him by the hand, and said, "Had you these thoughts when you came in to me, my son?" And he, overcome with trembling and fright, said, "Yes, my Lord," and threw himself at his feet. And John said, "Our Lord is Jesus Christ, and he will show his power on your dead kinsman by raising him again."

And he made the young man rise and took his hand and said, "It is no great matter for a man who has power over great mysteries to be still concerned with small things. Or is it any great matter if bodily sicknesses are cured?" And still holding the young man by the hand he said, "I tell you, my son, go and raise up the dead man yourself, saying nothing but only this: 'John, the servant of God, says to you, Arise!' " And the young man went to his kinsman and said just this, while a great crowd of people were with him, and came in to John bringing him alive.

And when John saw the man who was raised up, he said, "Now that you have risen, you are not really living, nor are you a partner and heir to the true life; will you belong to him by whose name and power you were raised up? So now, believe, and you shall live for all eternity." And then and there he believed the Lord Jesus, and from that time kept company with John.

ENCOUNTER WITH A PARRICIDE*

On the next day John saw in a dream that he was to walk three miles outside the gates, and he did not ignore it, but rose up at dawn and started with the brothers along the road. And there was a countryman who was warned by his father not to possess himself of the wife of his fellow laborer, while he threatened to kill him; but the young man could not put up with his father's warning, but kicked him and left him speechless. But when John saw what had happened, he said to the Lord, "Lord, was it because of this that you told me to come here today?"

But the young man, seeing his sudden death and fearing arrest, took out the sickle that was in his belt and began running towards his cottage; but John met him and said, "Stand still, you ruthless demon, and tell me where you are running with that bloodthirsty sickle." And the young man in his confusion let his weapon fall to the ground and said to him, "I have committed a monstrous and inhuman act, and I know it, so I resolved to do something worse and more cruel to myself, and to die at once. My father was always urging me to live a chaste and honorable life, yet I could not put up with his reproofs, but kicked him to death. And when I saw what had happened, I was hurrying to the woman for whom I murdered my father, and I meant to kill her and her husband and last of all myself. I could not bear the woman's husband to see me suffer the death penalty."

Then John said to him, "I will not go away and leave you in danger, or I shall give place to him who would laugh and scoff at you. No, come with me and show me where your father is lying. And

---

*Chapters 48–54.

if I raise him up for you, shall I keep you apart from the woman who has become so dangerous to you?" And the young man said, "If you raise me up my father himself alive and I see him whole and continuing in life, I will keep away from her in future."

And as he said this, while they talked they came to the place where the old man lay dead, and there were a number of passersby standing by the place. And John said to the young man, "You wretch, did you not even spare your father's old age?" But he wept and tore his hair and said he was sorry for it. And John, the servant of the Lord, said, "Lord, who showed me today that I was to come to this place, who knew that this would happen, since nothing that is done in this life can escape you, who grant me every kind of cure and healing by your will; grant even now that this old man may live, seeing that his murderer has become his own judge. Spare him, you who are Lord alone, though he did not spare his father, because he gave him counsel for the best."

With these words he went to the old man and said, "My Lord will not be slack to extend his good pity and his condescending heart even to you; rise up and give glory to God for the work that has been revealed." And the old man said, "I arise, my Lord." And he arose. And seating himself he said, "I was released from a terrible life in which I suffered many grievous insults from my son, and his lack of affection, and you called me back, servant of the living God—for what purpose?" And John answered him, "If you are arising to this same life, you should rather be dead; but rouse yourself to a better one!" And he took him and brought him into the city and proclaimed the grace of God to him, so that before they reached the gate the old man believed.

But when the young man saw the marvelous resurrection of his father and his own deliverance, he took the sickle and took off his private parts; and he ran to the house where he kept his adulteress and threw them down before her, and said, "For your sake I became my father's murderer, and of you two, and of myself. There you have the pattern and cause of all this! As for me, God has had mercy on me and shown me his power." And he went and told John before the brethren what he had done.

But John said to him, "Young man, the one who tempted you to kill your father and commit adultery with another man's wife, he has also made you take off the unruly members as if this were a virtuous act. But you should not have destroyed the place of your temptation, but the thought which showed its temper through those members; for it is not those organs whch are harmful to man, but the unseen springs through which every shameful emotion is stirred up and comes to light. So, my son, if you repent of this fault and recognize the devices of Satan, you have God to help you in everything that your soul requires." And the young man kept quiet, repenting of his former sins to obtain pardon from the goodness of God; and he would not separate from John.

THE OBEDIENT BUGS*

And on the first day we arrived at a lonely inn; and while we were trying to find a bed for John we saw a curious thing. There was one bed there lying somewhere not made up; so we spread the cloaks which we were wearing over it, and begged him to lie down on it and take his ease, while all the rest of us slept on the floor. But when he lay down he was troubled by the bugs; and as they became more and more troublesome to him, and it was already midnight, he said to them in the hearing of us all, "I

_____

*Chapters 60–61.

tell you, you bugs, to behave yourselves, one and all; you must leave your home for tonight and be quiet in one place and keep your distance from the servants of God." And while we laughed and went on talking, John went to sleep; but we talked quietly and thanks to him were not disturbed.

Now as the day was breaking I got up first, and Verus and Andronicus with me; and we saw by the door of the room which we had taken a mass of bugs collected; and as we were astounded at the great number of them, and all the brethren had woken up because of them, John went on sleeping. And when he woke up we explained to him what we had seen. And he sat up in bed and looked at them and said, "Since you have behaved yourselves and listened to my correction, go back to your own place." And when he had said this and had got up from the bed, the bugs came running from the door towards the bed and climbed up its legs and disappeared into the joints. Then John said again, "This creature listened to a man's voice and kept to itself and was quiet and obedient; but we who hear the voice of God disobey his commandments and are irresponsible; how long will this go on?"

THE DEATH OF JOHN**

After this he said to Verus, "Take some men with you, with two baskets and shovels, and follow me." And Verus, without delay, did what was ordered by John, the servant of God. So the blessed John came out of the house and walked outside the gates, having told the greater number that they should leave him; and when he came to a tomb of a brother of ours, he said to the young men, "Dig, my sons." And they dug. And he was more insistent with them, and said, "The

**Chapters 111–115.

digging must go deeper." And while they were digging he spoke to them the word of God and encouraged those that had come from the house with him, edifying them and preparing them for the greatness of God and praying for each one of us.

And when the young men had finished the trench as he desired, while we knew nothing of his intention he took off the outer clothes which he had on and laid them like a mattress in the bottom of the trench; and standing in his vest only he lifted up his hands and prayed, saying, "O you who chose us for the apostolate among the Gentiles; O God who has sent us into all the world; who has shown yourself through the law and the prophets; who has never rested, but from the foundation of the world always saves those who can be saved; who has revealed yourself through all nature; who has proclaimed yourself even among beasts; who has made even the lonely and embittered soul grow tame and quiet; who has given yourself to it when it thirsted for your words; who has speedily appeared to it when it was dying, who has shown yourself to it as a law when sunk into lawlessness; who has revealed yourself to it when overcome by Satan; who has overcome its adversary when it took refuge with you; who has given to it your hand and aroused it from the works of Hades; who has not suffered it to conform to the body; who has shown it its own enemy; who has made for it a pure knowledge of you, O God Jesu, Father of beings beyond the heavens, Lord of those that are in the heavens, Law of the ethereal beings and Path of those in the air, Guardian of beings upon earth, Terror of those beneath the earth, and Grace of those that are yours; receive also the soul of your John which, it may be, is approved by you.

"You who have kept me also till this present hour pure for yourself and untouched by union with a woman; who, when I wished to marry in my youth, appeared to me and said, 'John, I need you'; who prepared for me also an infirmity of the body; who on the third occasion when I wished to marry prevented me at once, and then at the third hour of the day said to me upon the sea, 'John, if you were not mine, I should have allowed you to marry'; who blinded me for two years, letting me be grieved and entreat you; who in the third year opened the eyes of my understanding and gave me back my eyes that are seen; who when I regained my sight disclosed to me the repugnance even of looking closely at a woman; who saved me from the illusion of the present and guided me into that life which endures forever; who rid me of the foul madness that is in the flesh; who snatched me from a bitter death and presented me only to you; who silenced the secret disease of my soul and cut off the open deed; who weakened and expelled the rebellious enemy within me; who made my love for you unsullied; who ruled my course to you unbroken; who gave me undoubting faith in you; who instructed my knowledge of you with purity; who gives to each man's works their due reward; who inspired my soul to have no possession but you alone—for what is more precious than you? So, Lord, now that I have fulfilled the charge which I was entrusted by you, count me worthy of thy rest and grant me my end in you, which is inexpressible and unutterable salvation.

"And as I come to you let the fire retreat and the darkness yield; let chaos be enfeebled, the furnace grow dim and Gehenna be quenched; let angels follow and demons be afraid; let the rulers be shattered and the powers fall; let the places on the right hand stand fast and those on the left be removed; let the devil be silenced; let Satan be derided; let his wrath be burned out; let his madness be calmed; let his vengeance be disgraced; let his assault be distressed; let his children be wounded and all his root be uprooted. And grant me to finish my way to you preserved from violence and insult, receiving what you have promised to them that live purely and love you alone."

And having sealed himself in every part, standing thus, he said "Be with me, Lord Jesus Christ"; and he lay down in the trench where he had spread out his clothes; and he said to us, "Peace be with you, my brethren," and gave up his spirit rejoicing.

Note

1. Or: "You have robbed me of my light."

The Acts of Peter

(Christian Apocrypha)

The *Acts of Peter* appear to be of Eastern origin, recorded some time in the second century. Peter is a miracle-maker and he uses his powers to instill faith in the Roman public. His enemies are the Pagans, who will eventually have him crucified for his having converted Pagan wives to Christianity and chastity. But the enemy who elicits Peter's hatred is Simon Magus, a rival Christian Gnostic. Their encounters in Rome, their attacks and counterattacks through the common weapon of miracles, are among the dramatic adventures of early Christian legend.

The *Acts* begins with the story of Peter's daughter, an episode preserved in a Coptic manuscript. Peter's virgin daughter is paralyzed, lying in the corner, helpless. The people ask him why he does not heal his own daughter. Peter then causes his daughter to rise, her health restored. But once having proved the powers of Jesus, he orders her to lie down and resume her infirmity, "for this is profitable for you and for me." Peter has safeguarded her virginity, saved her from corruption and pollution. The message is encratite, that is, the ascetic view that sexual continence leads to salvation. The Gnostics, particularly the Manichaeans, despised the body (though one group, the Carpocrates, thoroughly condemned by Augustine and others, abused the body through orgies as a way of showing its little worth); this tractate advocating self-control and continence is not alien to Gnostic thought. It is the victory of mind over mere flesh, the victory of faith over death and worldly temptations.

The real melodrama of the *Acts of Peter* is Peter's conflict with Simon. In the story of Eubula we have an introduction to Simon's magical arts to create delusion. Then in the famous contest in the Forum, Peter matches Simon miracle for miracle. We first hear talking dogs; then the dead are raised. But the climax comes when Simon vows to fly into the sky up to God. The next day the crowd assembles in the Sacred Way and all over Rome the crowd sees him passing over the temples and hills. Peter cries out to the Lord Jesus Christ and prays for Simon to fall and cripple himself by breaking his leg in three places. Simon falls and, as a result, the crowd favors Peter's faith and stones Simon. The angel of the Devil later kills the sorcerer Simon Magus, which leads Peter and his brethren to rejoice in the Lord.

Peter's last adventure is his martyrdom—a practice thoroughly condemned by the Gnostics. Peter is converting Roman wives, and when the angry husbands complain to Agrippa, Peter's death is ordered. Then follows the famous Quo Vadis scene. As Peter, disguised, reluctantly flees Rome through the gate, he sees the Lord entering Rome. "Lord, where are you going? (Quo Vadis?)," he asks. The Lord replies: "I am coming to Rome to be crucified." With this epiphany, Peter returns to Rome, happy in the knowledge that he will be crucified. He asks to be crucified upside down. Christ is the Word and "the Word is this upright tree on which I am crucified."

Peter's tales form an aretology, a treatise on virtue and continence. With the full characterization of the participants, this *Act*, in particular, has been characterized as an apostle's novel. In the end all the literary devices, the memorable dialogues, the miraculous dimension, and the visions and deaths have but one purpose: instruction to reinforce Christian faith.

PETER'S DAUGHTER*

But on the first day of the week, which is the Lord's day, a crowd collected, and they brought many sick people to Peter for him to heal them. But one of the crowd ventured to say to Peter, "Look, Peter, before our eyes you have made many who were blind to see, and the deaf to hear and the lame to walk, and you have helped the weak and given them strength. Why have you not helped your virgin daughter, who has grown up beautiful and has believed on the name of God? For she is quite paralyzed on one side, and she lies there stretched out in the corner helpless. We see the people you have healed; but your own daughter you have neglected."

But Peter smiled and said to him, "My son, it is evident to God alone why her

*Pages 128–141. All selections from the *Acts of Peter* are translated by G. C. Stead and are from Edgar Hennecke and Wilhelm Schneemelcher, eds. and trans., *New Testament Apocrypha*, vol. 2 (Philadelphia: Westminster Press, 1963), pp. 276–278, 289–301, 306–322.

body is not well. You must know, then, that God is not weak or powerless to grant his gift to my daughter. But to convince your soul and increase the faith of those who are here"—he looked then towards his daughter, and spoke to her: "Rise up from your place without any man's help but Jesus' alone and walk naturally before them all and come to me." And she rose up and went to him; but the crowd rejoiced at what had happened. Then Peter said to them, "Look, your heart is convinced that God is not powerless in all the things which we ask of him." Then they rejoiced even more and praised God. Then said Peter to his daughter, "Go to your place, lie down and return to your infirmity, for this is profitable for you and for me." And the girl went back, lay down in her place, and became as she was before. The whole crowd lamented and entreated Peter to make her well.

Peter said to them: "As the Lord lives, this is profitable for her and for me. For on the day when she was born to me I saw a vision, and the Lord said to me, 'Peter, today there is born for you a great trial; for this daughter will do harm to many souls if her body remains healthy.' But I thought that the vision mocked me.

"When the girl was ten years old she became a temptation to many. And a rich man named Ptolemaeus, who had seen the girl with her mother bathing, sent for her to take her as his wife; but her mother would not agree. He sent many times for her, he could not wait.

"The servants of Ptolemaeus brought the girl and laid her down before the door of the house and went away. But when I and her mother perceived it, we went down and found the girl, and that all one side of her body from her toes to her head was paralyzed and wasted; and we carried her away, praising the Lord who had preserved his servant from uncleanness and shame. This is the cause of the matter, why the girl continues in this state until this day.

"Now then it is right that you should know the fate of Ptolemaeus. He went home and grieved night and day over what had happened to him; and because of the many tears which he shed, he became blind; and he resolved to go up and hang himself. And lo, about the ninth hour of that day, when he was alone in his bedroom, he saw a great light which lit up the whole house, and heard a voice which said to him: 'Ptolemaeus, God has not given the vessels for corruption and shame; nor is it right for you, a believer in me, to defile my virgin, one whom you are to know as your sister, as if I were for both of you one spirit. But get up and go quickly to the house of the Apostle Peter, and you shall behold my glory; he will explain this matter to you.' But Ptolemaeus made no delay, and told his servants to show him the way and bring him to me. And coming to me he told me all that had happened to him in the power of our Lord Jesus Christ. Then he did see with the eyes of his flesh and with the eyes of his soul, and many people set their hopes on Christ. He did good to them and gave them the gift of God.

"After this Ptolemaeus died; he departed this life and went to his Lord. And when he made his will, he bequeathed a piece of land in the name of my daughter, because it was through her that he had believed in God and had been made whole. But I, being given this trust executed it with care. I sold the land, and God alone knows—neither I nor my daughter received the price—I sold the land, and kept back none of the price of the land but gave all the money to the poor.

"Know then, O servant of Jesus Christ, that God cares for his own and prepares good for every one of them, although we think that God has forgotten us. But now, brethren, let us be sorrowful and watch and pray, and God's goodness shall look upon us, and we wait for it." And Peter continued speaking before them all, and praising the name of the Lord Christ, he gave of the bread to them all; and when he had distributed it he rose up and went to his house.

THE GARDENER'S DAUGHTER

Consider and take note of the happening about which the following account informs us:

A peasant had a girl who was a virgin. She was also his only daughter, and therefore he besought Peter to offer a prayer for her. After he had prayed, the apostle said to the father that the Lord would bestow upon her what was expedient for her soul. Immediately, the girl fell down dead.

O reward, worthy and ever pleasing to God, to escape the shamelessness of the flesh and to break the pride of the blood!

But this distrustful old man, failing to recognize the worth of the heavenly grace, i.e., the divine blessing, besought Peter again that his only daughter be raised from the dead. And some days later, after she had been raised, a man who passed himself off as a believer came into the house of the old man to stay with him, and seduced the girl, and the two of them never appeared again.

MARCELLUS*

But the brethren repented and entreated Peter to overthrow Simon, who said that he was the power of God; now he was staying at the house of the Senator Marcellus, who was persuaded by his charms. And they said, "Believe us, brother Peter; no one was so wise among men as this Marcellus. All the widows who hoped in Christ found refuge with him; all the orphans were fed by him. And what more, brother? All the poor called Marcellus their patron, and his house was called the house of pilgrims and of the poor. The emperor said to him, 'I am keeping you out of every office, or you will plunder the provinces to benefit the Christians'; and Marcellus replied, 'All my goods are yours'; but Caesar said to him, 'They would be mine, if you kept them for me; but now they are not mine, because you give them to whom you will and to I know not what wretches.' We have this in view, brother Peter, and warn you that all that man's great charity has turned to blasphemy; for if he had not been won over, we in turn should not have deserted the holy faith in our Lord God. This Marcellus is now enraged and repents of his good deeds, and says, 'All this wealth I have spent in all this time, vainly believing that I paid it for the knowledge of God.' So much so, that if one of the strangers comes to his house door, he strikes him with his staff and orders him to be driven away, saying, 'If only I had not spent so much money on these impostors!'—and yet more blasphemous

_____
*Chapters 8–11.

words. But if there remains in you any of our Lord's mercy or of the goodness of his commandments, give help to this man's error who has so abundantly given alms to the servants of God."

But Peter, perceiving this, was struck with sorrow and uttered this reproach: "O what manifold arts and temptations of the devil! O what contrivances and inventions of evil! He prepares for himself a great fire in the day of wrath, the destruction of simple men, the ravening wolf, the devourer and waster of eternal life! You have ensnared the first man in lustful desire and bound him by your ancient wickedness and with the chain of the body; you are the fruit of the tree of bitterness, which is all most bitter, inducing lusts of every kind. You have made Judas, who was a disciple and apostle together with me, do wickedly and betray our Lord Jesus Christ, who must punish you. You hardened the heart of Herod and provoked Pharaoh, making him fight against Moses, the holy servant of God; you gave Caiaphas the boldness to hand over our Lord Jesus Christ to the cruel throng, and even now you shoot at innocent souls with your poisoned arrows. You wicked enemy of all, accursed shall you be from the Church of the Son of holy and almighty God, and like a firebrand thrust out from the hearth you shall be quenched by the servants of our Lord Jesus Christ. Upon you may your blackness be turned and upon your sons, that most wicked seed; upon you be turned your misdeeds, upon you your threats, and upon you and your angels, your temptations, you, source of wickedness and abyss of darkness! May your darkness be with you and with your vessels whom you possess. Depart therefore from these who shall believe in God; depart from the servants of Christ and from them who would fight for him. Keep for yourself your gates of darkness; in vain you knock at the doors of others, which belong not to you but to Christ Jesus who keeps them. For you, devouring wolf, would carry off sheep which are not yours, but belong to Christ Jesus, who keeps them with the most careful care."

While Peter said this in great distress of mind, many more were added as believers in the Lord. And the brethren entreated Peter to join battle with Simon and not allow him to vex the people any longer. And without delay, Peter left the assembly and went to the house of Marcellus, where Simon was staying; and great crowds followed him. And when he came to the door, he called the doorkeeper and said to him, "Go and tell Simon: 'Peter, on whose account you fled from Judaea, is waiting for you at the door.'" The doorkeeper answered Peter, "I do not know, Sir, whether you are Peter; but I have an order; for Simon found out that you came into the city yesterday, and he said to me, 'Whether it be by day or by night, at whatever time he comes, tell him that I am not in the house.'" But Peter said to the young man, "You were right to say this, and explain what he made you say"; and Peter turned to the people who followed him, and said, "You shall see a great and marvelous wonder." And Peter, seeing a great dog tied fast with a massive chain, went up to him and let him loose. And when the dog was let loose he acquired a human voice and said to Peter, "What do you bid me do, you servant of the ineffable living God?" And Peter said to him, "Go in and tell Simon in the presence of his company, 'Peter says to you, Come out in public; for on your account I have come to Rome, you wicked man and troubler of simple souls.'" And immediately the dog ran and went in and rushed into the middle of Simon's companions and lifting his forefeet called out with a loud voice, "I tell you Simon, Peter, the servant of Christ, is standing at the door, and says to you, 'Come out in public; for on your account I have come to Rome, you most wicked deceiver of simple souls.'" And when Simon heard it and saw the incredible sight, he lost the words with which he was deceiving

those who stood by, and all were amazed.

But when Marcellus saw it he went to the door and threw himself down at Peter's feet and said, "Peter, I clasp your feet, you holy servant of the holy God; I have sinned greatly; but do not punish my sins, if you have any true faith in the Christ whom you preach, if you remember his commandments, not to hate anyone, not to be angry with anyone, as I have learnt from Paul, your fellow apostle. Do not consider my faults, but pray for me to the Lord, the holy Son of God, whom I provoked to anger by persecuting his servants. Pray therefore for me like a good steward of God, that I be not consigned—with the sins of Simon—to eternal fire; for he even persuaded me to set up a statue to him with this inscription, 'To Simon the young God.' If I knew, Peter, that you could be won over with money, I would give my whole fortune; I would have given it to you and despised it, in order to regain my soul. If I had sons, I would have thought nothing of them, if only I could believe in the living God. But I protest that he would not have deceived me except by saying that he was the power of God. Yet I will tell you, dearest Peter, I was not worthy to hear you, servant of God, nor was I firmly grounded in the faith of God which is in Christ; and for this reason I was overthrown. So I beg you, do not resent what I am about to say: that Christ our Lord, whom you preach in truth, said to your fellow apostles in your presence, 'If you have faith like a grain of mustard-seed, you shall say to this mountain, Remove yourself, and at once it will remove.' But, Peter, this Simon called you an unbeliever, since you lost faith when upon the water; indeed I heard that he also had said, 'Those who are with me have not understood me.' Therefore if you lost faith, you on whom he laid his hands, whom he also chose, and with whom he worked miracles, then since I have this assurance, I repent and resort to your prayers. Receive my soul, though I have fallen away from our Lord and from his promise. But I believe that he will have mercy on me, since I repent. For the Almighty is faithful to forgive me my sins."

But Peter said with a loud voice, "To you, our Lord, be glory and splendor, almighty God, Father of our Lord Jesus Christ. To you be praise and glory and honor, forever and ever, Amen. As you have fully encouraged and established us now in you, in the sight of all beholders, holy Lord, so strengthen Marcellus and send your peace to him and his house today; but whatever is lost or astray, you alone can restore. We all beseech you, O Lord, the shepherd of sheep that once were scattered, but now shall be gathered in one through thee: receive Marcellus again as one of your lambs and suffer him no longer to riot in error or in ignorance; but accept him among the number of your sheep. Even so, Lord, receive him, that with sorrow and tears we entreat you."

So saying, Peter embraced Marcellus. Then Peter turned to the crowd who stood by him, and saw in the crowd a man half laughing, in whom was a most wicked demon. And Peter said to him, "Whoever you are that laughed, show yourself openly to all who stand by." And hearing this, the young man ran into the courtyard of the house, and he shouted aloud and threw himself against the wall and said, "Peter, there is a huge contest between Simon and the dog which you sent; for Simon says to the dog, 'Say that I am not here'—but the dog says more to him than the message you gave; and when he has finished the mysterious work which you gave him, he shall die at your feet." But Peter said, "You too, then, whatever demon you may be, in the name of our Lord Jesus Christ, come out of the young man and do him no harm; show yourself to all who stand by!" And hearing this, he left the young man, and caught hold of a great marble statue, which stood in the courtyard of the house, and kicked it to pieces. Now it was a statue of Caesar. And when Marcellus saw that he beat his forehead, and he said to Peter, "A great crime has been committed; if Caesar hears of this through some busybody, he will punish us severely." But Peter answered him, "I see you are not the man you were just now; for you said you were ready to spend your whole fortune to save your soul. But if you are truly repentant and believe in Christ with all your heart, take some running water in your hands and pray to the Lord; then sprinkle it in his name over the broken pieces of the statue, and it will be restored as before." And Marcellus did not doubt, but believed with his whole heart, and before taking the water in his hands he looked upwards and said, "I believe in you, Lord Jesus Christ, for I am being tested by your apostle, Peter, whether I truly believe in your holy name. Therefore I take water in my hands, and in your name I sprinkle those stones, that the statue may be restored as it was before. So, Lord, if it be your will that I remain in the body and suffer nothing at Caesar's hand, let this stone be restored as it was before." And he sprinkled the water upon the stones, and the statue was restored. So Peter exulted because he had not doubted when he prayed to the Lord, and Marcellus also was uplifted in spirit, because this first miracle was done by his hands; and he therefore believed with his whole heart in the name of Jesus Christ, the Son of God, through whom all things impossible are made possible.

PETER'S MIRACLES AND FIRST ATTACKS ON SIMON*

But Simon was in the house and said to the dog, "Tell Peter that I am not in the

_____

*Chapters 12–15.

house." And the dog answered him in the presence of Marcellus, "You most wicked and shameless man, you enemy of all that live and believe in Christ Jesus. Here is a dumb animal sent to you, taking a human voice to convict you and prove you a cheat and a deceiver. Have you thought for all these hours only to say, 'Say that I am not here'? Were you not ashamed to raise your feeble and useless voice against Peter, the servant and apostle of Christ, as if you could hide from him who commanded me to speak against you to your face? And this is not for your sake, but for those whom you were perverting and sending to destruction. Cursed therefore you shall be, your enemy and corruptor of the way to the truth of Christ, who shall prove your iniquities which you have done with undying fire, and exile you in outer darkness." Having said these words, the dog ran off; and the people followed, leaving Simon alone. So the dog came to Peter, who was sitting with the crowd which had come to see the face of Peter; and the dog reported his dealings with Simon. So the dog said, "Messenger and apostle of the true God, Peter, you shall have a great contest with Simon, the enemy of Christ, and with his servants; and you shall convert many to the faith that were deceived by him. Therefore you shall receive from God a reward for your work." And when the dog had said this, he fell down at the apostle Peter's feet and gave up his spirit. And when the crowd with great amazement saw the dog speaking, some began to throw themselves down at Peter's feet, but others said, "Show us another sign, that we may believe in you as the servant of the living God; for Simon too did many signs in our presence, and therefore we followed him."

But Peter turned round and saw a smoked tunny-fish hanging in a window; and he took it and said to the people, "If you now see this swimming in the water like a fish, will you be able to believe in him whom I preach?" And they all said with one accord, "Indeed, we will believe you!" Now there was a fishpond near by; so he said, "In your name, Jesus Christ, in which they still fail to believe," he said to the tunny, "in the presence of all these, be alive and swim like a fish!" And he threw the tunny into the pond, and it came alive and began to swim. And the people saw the fish swimming; and he made it do so not merely for that hour, or it might have been called a delusion; but he made it go on swimming, so that it attracted crowds from all sides and showed that the tunny had become a live fish so much so that some of the people threw in bread for it, and it ate it all up. And when they saw this, a great number followed him and believed in the Lord, and they assembled by day and by night in the house of Narcissus, the presbyter. And Peter expounded to them the writings of the prophets and what our Lord Jesus Christ had enacted both in word and in deeds.

Now Marcellus was being, day by day, more firmly established through the signs which he saw performed by Peter through the grace of Jesus Christ which he had granted him. And Marcellus ran in on Simon as he sat in his house in the dining room, and he cursed him, saying: "Most hateful and foulest of men, corrupter of my soul and of my house, who would have had me abandon Christ, my Lord and Savior!" And he laid hands on him and ordered him to be driven from the house. And now the slaves had him in their power, and rained insults upon him, some boxing his face, some using the stick and some the stone, while others emptied pots full of filth over his head, those who had offended their master on his account and had long been in chains; and other fellow slaves of theirs whom he had maligned before their master abused him and said to him: "Now we are repaying you a just reward, through the will of God, who has had mercy on us and on our master." So Simon was soundly beaten and thrown out of the house; and he ran to the house where Peter was staying; and he stood at the door of the house of Narcissus, the presbyter, and called out, "Here am I, Simon; so come down, Peter, and I will convict you of having believed in a mere man, a Jew and the son of a carpenter."

Now Peter was told that Simon had said this; and Peter sent to him a woman who had a child at the breast, saying to her, "Go down quickly, and you will see someone looking for me. And you are not to answer him; but keep silent and hear what the child you are holding will say to him." So the woman went down. Now the child whom she suckled was seven months old; and it took the voice of a man and said to Simon: "You abomination of God and men, you destruction of the truth and most wicked seed of corruption, you fruitless one of nature's fruits! But you appear but briefly and for a minute, and after this everlasting punishment awaits you. Son of a shameless father, striking no roots for good but only for poison, unfaithful creature, devoid of any hope! A dog reproved you, yet you were not shaken; now I, an infant, am compelled by God to speak, and yet you do not blush for shame! But even though you refuse, on the coming sabbath another shall bring you to the forum of Julius to prove what kind of man you are. So get away from the door which the feet of the saints are using; for no longer shall you corrupt the innocent souls whom you used to pervert and made them offended at Christ. So now your most evil nature shall be exposed and your contrivance destroyed. This last word I am telling you now: Jesus Christ says to you, 'Be struck dumb by the power of my name and depart from Rome until the coming sabbath.'" And immediately he became dumb and could not resist, but left Rome until the sabbath and lodged in a stable. The woman went back with her child to Peter, and told him and the other brethren what the child had said to Simon; and they glorified the Lord who had shown these things to men.

PETER'S VISION AND NARRATIVE ABOUT SIMON*

But when night came on Peter saw Jesus clothed in a robe of splendor, smiling and saying to him while he was still awake, "Already the great mass of the brethren have turned back to me through you and through the signs which you have done in my name. But you shall have a trial of faith on the coming sabbath, and many more of the Gentiles and of the Jews shall be converted in my name to me, who was insulted, mocked and spat upon. For I will show myself to you when you ask for signs and miracles, and you shall convert many; but you will have Simon opposing you with the works of his father. But all his actions shall be exposed as charms and illusions of magic. But now do not delay, and you shall establish in my name all those whom I send you." And when it was light he told the brethren that the Lord had appeared to him and what he had commanded.

"But believe me, men and brethen, I drove this Simon out of Judaea, where he did much harm by his incantations. He stayed in Judaea with a woman named Eubula, a woman of some distinction in this world, who possessed much gold and pearls of no little value. Simon stole into her house with two others like himself; though none of the household saw these two, but only Simon; and by means of a spell they took away all the woman's gold and disappeared. But Eubula, discovering this crime, began to torture her household, saying, 'You took advantage of the visit of this godly man and have robbed me, because you saw

---

*Chapters 16–18.

him coming in to me to do honor to a simple woman; but his name is "the power of the Lord." '

"Now as I fasted for three days and prayed that this crime should come to light, I saw in a vision Italicus and Antulus, whom I had instructed in the name of the Lord, and a boy who was naked and bound, who gave me a wheaten loaf and said to me, 'Peter, hold out for two days and you shall see the wonderful works of God. For the things which are lost from Eubula's house were stolen by Simon and two others, using magical arts and creating a delusion. And you shall see them on the third day at the ninth hour by the gate which leads towards Naples, selling to a goldsmith named Agrippinus a young satyr made of gold, of two pounds weight, and having a precious stone set in it. Now you are not to touch it, to avoid pollution; but have with you some of the lady's servants; then show them the goldsmith's shop and leave them. For this event will cause many to believe in the name of the Lord. For the things which they have constantly stolen by their cunning and wickedness shall be brought to light.'

"When I heard this, I came to Eubula and found her sitting and lamenting with her clothes torn and her hair in disorder; and I said to her, 'Eubula, rise up from your bed and compose your face, put up your hair and put on a dress that becomes you, and pray to the Lord Jesus Christ who judges every soul. For he is the Son of the invisible God; in him you must be saved, if indeed you repent with all your heart of your former sins. And receive power from him; for now the Lord says to you through me, "All that you have lost you shall find." And when you have received them, be sure that you find yourself, so as to renounce this present world and seek for everlasting refreshment. Listen then to this: let some of your people keep watch by the gate that leads towards Naples. On the day after tomorrow, about the ninth hour, they will see two young men with a

young satyr in gold of two pounds weight set with stones, as a vision has shown me, and they will offer it for sale to a certain Agrippinus, who is familiar with the godly life and the faith in our Lord Jesus Christ. And through Christ it will be shown you that you must believe in the living God and not in Simon the sorcerer, that inconstant demon, who would have you remain in mourning and your innocent household be tortured, who with his soothing eloquence perverted you with empty words and spoke of devotion to God with his lips alone, while he himself is wholly filled with wickedness. For when you meant to celebrate a festival and put up your idol and veiled it and put out all the ornaments upon a stand, he had brought in two young men whom none of you saw; and they made an incantation and stole your ornaments and disappeared. But his plan miscarried; for my God disclosed it to me, so that you should not be deceived nor perish in Hell, whatever wickedness and perversity you have shown towards God, who is full of all truth and a just judge of the living and the dead. And there is no other hope of life for man, except through him, through whom your lost possessions are preserved for you. And now you must regain your own soul!' But she threw herself at my feet, saying, 'Sir, who you are I do not know; but I received him as a servant of God, and I gave by his hands whatever he asked of me for the care of the poor, a great deal, and made him large presents besides. What harm has he suffered from me, that he should cause such trouble to my house?' Peter answered her, 'We must put no faith in words, but in actions and deeds. So we must go on with what we have begun.'

"So I left her and went with two stewards of Eubula, and came to Agrippinus and said to him, 'Make sure that you take note of these men. For tomorrow two young men will come to you, wishing to sell you a young satyr in gold set with stones, which belongs to these men's mistress. So you are to take it as if to inspect it and to admire its workmanship. Afterwards, these men will come in; then God shall bring the rest to the proof.' And on the next day the lady's stewards came about the ninth hour, and also those young men, wishing to sell Agrippinus the golden satyr; and at once they were seized, and word was sent to the lady. But she in great distress of mind went to the magistrate, and loudly declared what had happened to her. And when the magistrate, Pompeius, saw her so distressed, whereas she had never before come out in public, he immediately rose up from the bench and went to the guardroom and ordered them to be produced and examined. And under torture they confessed that they were acting as Simon's agents—'who gave us money to do it.' And when tortured further, they confessed that all that Eubula had lost had been put underground in a cave outside the gate, and more besides. When Pompeius heard this, he got up to go to the gate, having those two men bound with two chains each. And there!—Simon came in at the gate, looking for them because they had been so long; and he saw a great crowd coming, and those men held fast in chains. At once he realized what had happened and took to flight, and has not been seen in Judaea until this day. But Eubula, having recovered all her property, gave it for the care of the poor; she believed in the Lord Jesus Christ and was strengthened in the faith; and despising and renouncing this world, she gave alms to the widows and orphans and clothed the poor; and after a long time she gained her repose. Now these things, my dearest brethren, were done in Judaea; and so he came to be expelled from there, who is called the messenger of Satan.

"Brethren, most dear and beloved, let us fast together and pray to the Lord. He who expelled him from there is able to uproot him from this place also. May he give us power to resist him and his incantations and to expose him as the messenger of Satan. For on the sabbath our Lord shall bring him, even if he refuses to come, to the forum of Julius. So let us bow our knees to Christ, who hears us even if we have not called upon him; it is he who sees us, even if he is not seen with these eyes, but is within us; if we are willing he will forsake us. Let us therefore cleanse our souls of every wicked temptation, and God will not depart from us; and if we only wink with our eyes, he is present with us."

THE CONTEST WITH SIMON IN THE FORUM*

Now the brethren assembled and all those that were in Rome, taking their places and paying a piece of gold for each; and the senators, prefects, and officers also collected together. Then Peter came in and took his place in the center. They all cried out, "Show us, Peter, who is your god, or what is his greatness, which has given you such confidence. Do not be ungenerous to the Romans; they are lovers of the gods. We have had evidence from Simon, now let us have yours; convince us, both of you, whom we should truly believe." And while they said this, Simon also came in; and he stood in confusion at Peter's side and gazed at him closely.

After a long silence Peter said, "You men of Rome, you must be our true judges. Now I say that I have believed in the living and true God, and I promise you to give evidence of him, such as I have known already, as many among you bear witness. For you see that this man is completely silent, since he has been convicted and I drove him from Judaea because of the impostures which he practiced on Eubula, an honorable and most simple woman, using his magic arts. Expelled from there by me, he has

---

*Chapters 23–29.

come to this place, believing he could hide himself among you; and there he stands face to face with me. Tell me now, Simon, did you not fall at my feet and Paul's in Jerusalem when you saw the healings which were done by our hands? —and you said, 'I beg you, take payment from me as much as you will, so that I can lay hands on men and work such benefits.' When we heard these words of yours we cursed you saying, 'Do you think you can tempt us to wish for possession of money?' And now are you not afraid? My name is Peter, because the Lord Christ thought fit to call me 'prepared for all things.' For I believe in the living God, through whom I shall destroy your sorceries. Now let Simon do the marvelous things he used to do, here in your presence. And what I have just told you of him, will you not believe me?"

But Simon said, "You presume to talk of Jesus the Nazarene, the son of a carpenter and a carpenter himself, whose family comes from Judaea. Listen, Peter, the Romans have sense; they are not fools." And he turned to the people and said, "You men of Rome, is God born? Is he crucified? He who owns a Lord is no God!" And as he said this, many answered, "Well said, Simon!"

But Peter said, "A curse on your words against Christ! Did you presume to speak in these terms, while the prophet says of him, 'His generation, who shall declare it?' And another prophet says, 'And we saw him and he had no grace nor beauty.' And: 'In the last times a boy is born of the Holy Spirit; his mother knows not a man, nor does anyone claim to be his father.' And again he says, 'She has given birth and has not given birth.' And again, 'Is it a small thing for you to make trouble . . . ?' And again: 'Behold, a virgin shall conceive in the womb.' And another prophet says in the Father's honor, 'We have neither heard her voice, nor is a midwife come in.' Another prophet says, 'He was not born from the womb of a woman, but

came down from a heavenly place'; and, 'A stone is cut out without hands and has broken all the kingdoms'; and, 'The stone which the builders rejected is become the head of the corner'; and he calls him a stone 'elect and precious.' And again the prophet says of him, 'And behold I saw one coming upon a cloud like a son of man.' And what more need be said? You men of Rome, if you were versed in the prophetic writings, I would explain all this to you; for through them it had to be told in secret and the kingdom of God be fulfilled. But these things shall be disclosed to you hereafter.

"Now, as for you, Simon; do one of those things with which you used to deceive them, and I will undo it through my Lord Jesus Christ." Simon put on a bold front and said, "If the prefect permits."

But the prefect wished to show impartiality towards both, so as not to appear to act unjustly. And the prefect put forward one of his young men, and said to Simon, "Take this man and put him to death." And he said to Peter, "And you, restore him to life." And the prefect addressed the people saying, "It is now for you to judge which of these men is acceptable to God, the one who kills or the one who gives life."

And immediately Simon spoke in the boy's ear, and made him speechless, and he died. And as a murmuring arose among the people, out of the widows who rested at Marcellus' house cried out from behind the crowd, "Peter, servant of God, my son is dead, the only one that I had." And the people made room for her and led her to Peter. But she threw herself down at his feet and said, "I had only one son; he provided my food with his hands, he lifted me up, he carried me. Now he is dead, who will lend me a hand?" Peter said to her, "Take these men for witnesses and go and bring your son, so that these may see, and be enabled to believe that by the power of God he is raised up." But when she heard this, she fell down. Then Peter said to the young men, "Now we need some young men, who are also willing to believe." And immediately thirty young men stood up, who were ready to carry her or to bring her dead son. And when the widow had hardly recovered herself, the young men lifted her up. But she was crying out and saying, "Look, my son, the servant of Christ has sent for you," and tearing her hair and her face. Now the young men who came examined the boy's nostrils, to see whether he were really dead. And seeing that he was dead, they comforted his mother and said, "If you truly believe in Peter's God, we will lift him up and bring him to Peter, that he may revive him and restore him to you."

While the young men were saying these things the prefect in the forum looked at Peter and said, "What say you, Peter? See, the boy lies there dead—of whom even the emperor thinks kindly—and I have not spared him. Certainly I had many other young men, but I trusted in you, and in your Lord whom you preach, if indeed you are sure and truthful; therefore I allowed him to die." Then Peter said, "God is not tested or weighed in the balance; but he is to be worshiped by those whom he loves with all their heart, and he will listen to those who are worthy. But now that God and my Lord Jesus Christ is tested among you, he is doing such signs and wonders through me for the conversion of his sinners. And now in the sight of them all, O Lord, in your power raise up through my voice the man whom Simon killed with his touch!" And Peter said to the boy's master, "Come, take his right hand, and you shall have him alive and able to walk with you." And Agrippa, the prefect, ran and came to the boy and, taking his hand, restored him to life. And when the crowds saw it they all cried out, "There is but one God, the one God of Peter!"

Meanwhile, the widow's son also was brought in on a stretcher by the young men; and the people made way for them and brought them to Peter. And Peter lifted up his eyes towards heaven and held out his hands and said, "Holy Father of your Son Jesus Christ, who has given us your power, that through you we may ask and obtain, and despise all that is in this world, and follow you alone; you who are seen by few, and would be known by many; shine about us, Lord, give light, appear, and raise up the son of this aged widow who cannot help herself without her son. Now I take up the word of Christ, my master, and say to you, young man, arise and walk with your mother, so long as you are useful to her. But afterwards, you shall offer yourself to me in a higher service, in the office of deacon and bishop." And immediately the dead man stood up, and the crowds were astonished at the sight, and the people shouted, "You are God the Savior, you, the God of Peter, the invisible God, the Savior!" And they spoke among themselves, being truly astonished at the power of a man that called upon his Lord by his word; and they accepted it to their sanctification.

So while the news spread round the whole city, the mother of a senator approached and, pressing through the middle of the crowd, she threw herself at Peter's feet, saying, "I have heard from my household that you are a servant of the merciful God, bestowing his grace to all who desire this light. Bestow then this light on my son, for I have heard that you are not ungenerous towards anyone; if even a lady entreats you, do not turn away!" Peter said to her, "Do you believe my God, by whom your son shall be restored to life?" But his mother cried aloud and said with tears, "I believe, Peter, I believe." All the people shouted, "Grant the mother her son!" Then Peter said, "Let him be brought here before all these." And Peter turned to the people and said, "You men of Rome, seeing that I too am one of you, wearing human flesh, and a sinner, but have obtained mercy, do not look at me, as though by my own power I were doing what I do; the power is my Lord Jesus Christ's, who is the judge of the living and of the dead. Believing in him and sent by him, I dare to entreat him to raise the dead. Go then, lady, let your son be brought here and restored to life."

Then the woman made her way through the crowd and went out into the street with haste and great joy, and believing in her heart she reached her house and made her young men carry him and came to the forum. And she told her young men to put their caps on their heads and walk in front of the bier, and all that was to be used for the body of her son for the funeral should be carried in front of the bier so that Peter should see it and have pity on the dead man and on herself. So with them all as mourners she came to the assembly; and a crowd of senators and ladies followed her to see the wonderful works of God. Now Nicostratus, the dead man, was much respected and liked among the senate; so they brought him in and laid him down before Peter. Then Peter called for silence and said with a loud voice, "Men of Rome, let there now be a just judgment between me and Simon, and consider which of us believes in the living God, he or I. Let him revive the body which lies here; then you may believe in him as an angel of God. But if he cannot, then I will call upon my God; I will restore her son alive to his mother, and then you shall believe that this is a sorcerer and a cheat, this guest of yours!"

And they all heard this and accepted Peter's challenge as just; and they encouraged Simon, saying, "Now, if there is anything in you, bring it out! Spite him, or be spited! Why are you waiting? Go on, begin!" But Simon, seeing them all pressing him, stood there silent; however, when he saw that the people had become silent and were looking at him, Simon raised his voice and said, "Men of Rome, if you see the dead man restored to life, will you throw Peter out of the city?" And all the people said, "We will

not only throw him out, but that self-same hour we will burn him with fire."

Then Simon went to the dead man's head, and stooped down three times and stood up three times, and showed the people that the dead man had raised his head and was moving, opening his eyes and bowing towards Simon. And at once they began to look for wood and kindling, in order to burn Peter. But Peter, gaining the strength of Christ, raised his voice and said to the men who were shouting against him, "Now I see, people of Rome, that I must not call you foolish and empty-headed, so long as your eyes and ears and hearts are blinded. So long as your sense is darkened, you do not see that you are bewitched, since you believe that a dead man has been revived when he has not stood up. I would have been content, you men of Rome, to keep silent and die without a word and leave you among the illusions of this world. But I have before my eyes the punishment of unquenchable fire. If you agree, then, let the dead man speak, let him get up if he is alive, let him free his jaw of its wrappings with his own hands, let him call for his mother, and when you call out, let him say, 'What is it you are calling?' Let him beckon to you with his hand. Now if you wish to see that he is dead and you are spellbound, let this man withdraw from the bier—this man who has persuaded you to withdraw from Christ—and you will see that the young man is still in the same state as when you saw him brought in."

But Agrippa, the prefect, could not contain himself, but got up and pushed Simon away with his own hands. And so the dead man lay there again as he was before. And the people were enraged and turned away from Simon's sorcery, and began to call out, "Hear us, Caesar! If the dead man does not stand up, let Simon be burnt instead of Peter, for he has truly blinded us." But Peter held out his hand and said, "Men of Rome, have patience! I am not telling you that Simon should be burnt when the boy is restored; for if I tell you, you will do it." The people shouted, "Even if you will not have it, Peter, we will do it!" Peter said to them, "If you are determined on this, the boy shall not return to life. For we have not learnt to repay evil with evil; but we have learnt to love our enemies and pray for our persecutors. For if even this man can repent, that is better; for God will not remember evil deeds. So let him come into the light of Christ. But if he cannot, let him possess the inheritance of his father, the Devil; but your hands shall not be stained."

And when he had said this to the people, he went up to the boy, and before he revived him he said to his mother, "Those young men whom you set free in honor of your son, are they to do service to their master as free men, when he is alive? For I know that some will feel injured on seeing your son restored to life, because these men will become his slaves once again. But let them all keep their freedom and draw their provisions as they drew them before, for your son shall be raised up, and they must be with him." And Peter went on looking at her, to see what she thought. And the boy's mother said, "What else can I do? So I will declare in the presence of the prefect: all that I meant to lay out for my son's funeral shall be their property." And Peter said to her, "Let the remainder be distributed to the widows." But Peter rejoiced in his heart, and said in the spirit, "Lord who is merciful, Jesus Christ, appear to your servant, Peter, who calls upon you, as you have always shown mercy and goodness; in the presence of all these men, who have obtained their freedom so as to do service, let Nicostratus now arise!" And Peter touched the boy's side and said, "Stand up." And the boy stood up and gathered up his clothes and sat down and untied his jaw and asked for other clothes; and he came down from the bier and said to Peter, "I beg you, sir,

let us go to our Lord Jesus Christ whom I saw talking with you; who said to you, as he showed me to you, 'Bring him here to me, for he is mine.'" When Peter heard this from the boy, he was yet more strengthened in mind by the help of the Lord; and Peter said to the people, "Men of Rome, this is how the dead are restored to life, this is how they speak, this is how they walk when they are raised up, and live for so long as God wills. Now therefore, you people who have gathered to see the show, if you turn now from these wicked ways of yours and from all your manmade gods and from every kind of uncleanness and lust, you shall receive the fellowship with Christ through faith, so that you may come to everlasting life."

From that same hour they venerated him as a god, and laid at his feet such sick people as they had at home, so that he might heal them. But the prefect, seeing that such a great number were waiting upon Peter, made signs to him that he should withdraw. But Peter invited the people to come to Marcellus' house. The boy's mother entreated Peter to set foot in her house but Peter had arranged to go to Marcellus on the Lord's day, to see the widows as Marcellus had promised, so that they should be cared for by his own hands. So the boy who had returned to life said, "I will not leave Peter." And his mother went joyfully and gladly to her own house. And on the next day after the sabbath she came to Marcellus' house bringing Peter two thousand pieces of gold and saying to Peter, "Divide these among the virgins of Christ who serve him." But when the boy who had risen from the dead saw that he had given nothing to anyone, he went home and opened the chest and himself brought four thousand gold pieces, saying to Peter, "Look, I myself, who am restored to life, am bringing a double offering, and present myself as a speaking sacrifice to God from this day on."

MARTYRDOM OF THE HOLY APOSTLE PETER*

Now on the Lord's day Peter was preaching to the brethren and encouraging their faith in Christ. Many of the senators were present and a number of knights and wealthy women and matrons, and they were strengthened in the faith. But there was present a very wealthy woman who bore the name of Chryse, the golden, because every utensil of hers was made of gold—for since her birth she had never used a silver or glass vessel, but only golden ones; she said to Peter, "Peter, servant of God, there came to me in a dream the one you say is God; and he said to me, 'Chryse, bring my servant, Peter, ten thousand pieces of gold; for you owe them to him.' So I have brought them, for fear lest I should suffer some harm from him who appeared to me, who has gone away into Heaven." So saying, she laid down the money and departed. But Peter, when he saw it, gave praise to the Lord, because the afflicted could now be relieved. Now some of those who were present said to him, "Peter, you were wrong to accept this money from her; for she is notorious all over Rome for fornication and they say that she does not consort with one man only; indeed, she even goes in to her own house boys. So have no dealings with the 'golden' table—Chryse's table—but let her money be returned to her." But Peter, when he heard this, laughed and said to the brethren, "I do not know what this woman is as regards her usual way of life; but in taking this money I did not take it without reason; for she was bringing it as a debtor to Christ, and is giving it to Christ's servants; for he himself has provided for them."

And they brought the sick people also to him on the sabbath, entreating him

*Chapters 30–41.

that they might be cured of their diseases. And many paralytics were healed, and many sufferers from dropsy and from two- and four-day fevers, and they were cured of every bodily disease, such as believed in the name of Jesus Christ, and very many were added every day to the grace of the Lord.

But after a few days had elapsed Simon, the magician, promised the rabble that he would show Peter that he had not put his faith in the true God but in a deception. Now while he performed many false miracles, he was laughed to scorn by those disciples who were already firm in the faith. For in their living rooms he caused certain spirits to be brought in to them, which were only appearances without real existence. And what more is there to say? Although he had often been convicted for his magic art, he made the lame apear to be sound for a short time, and the blind likewise, and once he appeared to make many who were dead come alive and move, as he did with Nicostratus. But all the while Peter followed him and exposed him to the onlookers. And as he was now always out of favor and derided by the people of Rome and discredited, as not succeeding in what he promised to do, it came to such a point that he said to them, "Men of Rome, at present you think that Peter has mastered me, as having greater power, and you attend to him rather than me. But you are deceived. For tomorrow I shall leave you, who are utterly profane and impious, and fly up to God, whose power I am, although enfeebled. If then you have fallen, behold I am he who stands. And I am going up to my Father and shall say to him, 'Even me, your son who stands, they desired to bring down; but I did not give consent, and am returned to myself.' "

And by the following day a large crowd had assembled on the Sacred Way to see him fly. And Peter, having seen a vision, came to the place, in order to convict him again this time; for when Simon made his entry into Rome, he astonished the crowds by flying; but Peter, who exposed him, was not yet staying in Rome, the city which he so carried away by his deceptions that people lost their senses through him.

So this man stood on a high place, and seeing Peter, he began to say: "Peter, now of all times, when I am making my ascent before all these onlookers, I tell you: If your god has power enough—he whom the Jews destroyed, and they stoned you who were chosen by him—let him show that faith in him is of God; let it be shown at this time whether it be worthy of God. For I, by ascending, will show to all this crowd what manner of being I am." And lo and behold, he was carried up into the air, and everyone saw him all over Rome, passing over its temples and its hills while the faithful looked towards Peter. And Peter, seeing the incredible sight, cried out to the Lord Jesus Christ, "Let this man do what he undertook, and all who have believed in you shall now be overthrown, and the signs and wonders which you gave them through me shall be disbelieved. Make haste, Lord, with your grace; and let him fall down from this height, and be crippled, but not die; but let him be disabled and break his leg in three places!" And he fell down from that height and broke his leg in three places. Then they stoned him and went to their own homes; but from that time they all believed in Peter.

But one of Simon's friends named Gemellus, from whom Simon had received much support, who was married to a Greek woman, came along the road shortly afterwards and seeing him with his leg broken said, "Simon, if the power of God is broken, shall not the God himself, whose power you are, be proved an illusion?" So Gemellus also ran and followed Peter, saying to him, "I too desire to be one of those who believes in Christ." But Peter said, "Then what objection can there be, my brother? Come and stay with us." But Simon in his misfortune found some helpers who carried him on a stretcher by night from Rome to Aricia; and after staying there he was taken to a man named Castor, who had been banished from Rome to Terracina on a charge of sorcery; and there he underwent an operation; and thus Simon, the angel of the Devil, ended his life.

But Peter stayed in Rome and rejoiced with the brethren in the Lord and gave thanks night and day for the mass of people who were daily added to the holy name by the grace of the Lord. And the concubines of the prefect Agrippa also came to Peter, being four in number, Agrippina and Nicaria and Euphemia and Doris. And hearing the preaching of purity and all the words of the Lord, they were cut to the heart and agreed with each other to remain in purity, renouncing intercourse with Agrippa; and they were molested by him. Now when Agrippa was perplexed and distressed about them—for he loved them passionately—he made inquiries, and when he sent to find out where they had gone, he discovered that they had gone to Peter. And when they came back he said to them, "That Christian has taught you not to consort with me; I tell you, I will both destroy you and burn him alive." They therefore took courage to suffer every injury from Agrippa, wishing only to be vexed by passion no longer, being strengthened by the power of Jesus.

But one woman who was especially beautiful, the wife of Albinus the friend of Caesar, Xanthippe by name, came with the other ladies to Peter, and she too separated from Albinus. He therefore, filled with fury and passionate love for Xanthippe, and amazed that she would not even sleep in the same bed with him, was raging like a wild beast and wished to do away with Peter; for he knew that he was responsible for her leaving his bed. And many other women besides fell in love with the doctrine of purity and separated from their husbands, and men too ceased to sleep with their own wives since they wished to worship God in sobriety and purity. So there was the greatest disquiet in Rome; and Albinus put his case to Agrippa, and said to him, "Either you must get me satisfaction from Peter, who caused my wife's separation, or I shall do so myself"; and Agrippa said that he had been treated in the same way by him, by the separation of his concubines. And Albinus said to him, "Why then do you delay, Agrippa? Let us find him and execute him as a troublemaker so that we may recover our wives, and in order to give satisfaction to those who cannot execute him, who have themselves been deprived of their wives by him."

But while they made these plans, Xanthippe discovered her husband's conspiracy with Agrippa and sent and told Peter, so that he might withdraw from Rome. And the rest of the brethren together with Marcellus entreated him to withdraw. But Peter said to them, "Shall we act like deserters, brethren?" But they said to him, "No, it is so that you can go on serving the Lord." So he assented to the brethren and withdrew by himself, saying, "Let none of you retire with me, but I shall retire by myself in disguise." And as he went out of the gate he saw the Lord entering Rome; and when he saw him he said, "Lord, where are you going?" And the Lord said to him, "I am coming to Rome to be crucified." And Peter said to him, "Lord, are you being crucified again?" He said to him, "Yes, Peter, I am being crucified again." And Peter came to himself; and he saw the Lord ascending into Heaven; then he returned to Rome, rejoicing and giving praise to the Lord, because he said, "I am being crucified"; since this was to happen to Peter.

So he returned to the brethren and told them what had been seen by him; and they were grieved at heart, and said with tears, "We entreat you, Peter, take thought for us that are young." And Peter said to them, "If it is the Lord's will, it will come to pass even if we will not have it so. But the Lord is able to establish you in your faith in him, and he will lay your foundation on him and enlarge you in him, you whom he himself has planted, so that you may plant others through him. But as for me, so long as the Lord wills me to be in the flesh, I do not demur; again, if he will take me, I rejoice and am glad."

And while Peter was saying this and all the brethren were in tears, four soldiers arrested him and took him to Agrippa. And he, in his distemper, ordered that he be charged with irreligion and be crucified.

So the whole mass of the brethren came together, rich and poor, orphans and widows, capable and helpless, wishing to see Peter and to rescue him; and the people cried out irrepressibly with a single voice, "What harm has Peter done, Agrippa? How has he injured you? Answer the Romans!" And others said, "If this man dies, we must fear that the Lord will destroy us too."

And when Peter came to the place of execution, he quietened the people and said, "You men, who are soldiers of Christ, men who set their hopes on Christ, remember the signs and wonders which you saw through me, remember the compassion of God, how many healings he has performed for you. Wait for him who shall come and reward everyone according to his deeds. And now, do not be angry with Agrippa; for he is the servant of his father's influence; and this is to happen in any event, because the Lord has showed me what is coming. But why do I delay and not go to the cross?"

Then when he had approached and stood by the cross he began to say, "O name of the cross, mystery that is concealed! O grace ineffable that is spoken in the name of the cross! O nature of man that cannot be parted from God! O love, unspeakable and inseparable, that cannot be disclosed through unclean lips! I seize you now, being come to the end of my release from here. I will declare you, what you are; I will not conceal the mystery of the cross that has long been enclosed and hidden from my soul. You who hope in Christ, for you the cross must not be this thing that is visible; for this passion, like the passion of Christ, is something other than this which is visible. And now above all, since you who can hear, can hear it from me, who am at the last closing hour of my life, give ear; withdraw your souls from every outward sense and from all that appears but is not truly real; close these eyes of yours, close your ears, withdraw from actions that are outwardly seen; and you shall know the facts about Christ and the whole secret of your salvation. Let so much be said to you who hear as though it were unspoken. But it is time for you, Peter, to surrender your body to those who are taking it. Take it, then, you whose duty this is. I request you therefore, executioners, to crucify me head downwards—in this way and no other. And the reason, I will tell to those who hear."

And when they had hanged him up in the way which he had requested, he began to speak again, saying, "Men whose duty it is to hear, pay attention to what I shall tell you at this very moment that I am hanged up. You must know the mystery of all nature, and the beginning of all things, how it came about. For the first man, whose likeness I have in my appearance, in falling head downwards, showed a manner of birth that was not so before; for it was dead, having no movement. He therefore, being drawn down—he who also cast his first beginning down to the earth—established the whole of this cosmic system, being hung up as an image of the calling, in which he showed what is on the right hand as on the left, and those on the left as on the right, and changed all the signs of their nature, so as to consider fair those things that were not fair, and take those that were really evil to be good. Concerning this the Lord says in a mystery, 'Unless you make what is on the right hand as what is on the left and what is on the left hand as what is on the right and

what is above as what is below and what is behind as what is before, you will not recognize the Kingdom.' This conception, then, I have declared to you, and the form in which you see me hanging is a representation of that man who first came to birth. You then, my beloved, both those who hear me now and those that shall hear in time, must leave your former error and turn back again; for you should come up to the cross of Christ, who is the Word stretched out, the one and only, of whom the Spirit says, 'For what else is Christ but the Word, the sound of God?' So that the Word is this upright tree on which I am crucified; but the sound is the cross-piece, the nature of man; and the nail that holds the cross-piece to the upright in the middle is the conversion (or turning point) and repentance of man.

"Since then you have made known and revealed these things to me, O word of life, which name I have just given to the tree. I give you thanks, not with these lips that are nailed fast, nor with the tongue, through which truth and falsehood issues forth, nor with this word that comes forth by the skill of physical nature; but I give you thanks, O King, with that voice which is known in silence, which is not heard aloud, which does not come forth through the bodily organs, which does not enter the ears of the flesh, that is not heard by corruptible substance, that is not in the world or uttered upon earth, nor is written in books, nor belongs to one but not to another; but with this voice, Jesu Christ, I thank you, with silence of the voice, with which the spirit within me, that loves you and speaks to you and sees you, makes intercession. You are known to the spirit only. You are my father; you are my mother. You are my brother. You are friend. You are servant. You are housekeeper. You are the All, and the All is in you. You are Being, and there is nothing that is, except you.

"With him then do you also take refuge, brethren, and learning that in him alone is your real being, you shall obtain those things of which he says to you, 'What eye has not seen nor ear heard, nor has it entered the heart of man.' We ask then, for that which you have promised to give us, O Jesus undefiled; we praise you, we give thanks to you and confess you, and being yet men without strength we glorify you; for you are God alone and no other, to whom be glory both now and for all eternity, Amen."

But as the crowd that stood by shouted Amen with a resounding cry, at that very Amen, Peter gave up his spirit to the Lord.

But when Marcellus saw that the blessed Peter had given up his spirit, without taking anyone's advice, since it was not allowed, he took him down from the cross with his own hands and washed him in milk and wine; and he ground up seven pounds of mastic, and also fifty pounds of myrrh and aloe and spice and embalmed his body, and filled a trough of stone of great value with Attic honey and laid it in his own burial-vault.

But Peter visited Marcellus by night and said, "Marcellus, you heard the Lord saying, 'Let the dead be buried by their own dead'?" And when Marcellus said, "Yes," Peter said to him, "The things which you laid out for the dead, you have lost; for you who are alive were like a dead man caring for the dead." And Marcellus awoke and told the brethren of Peter's appearing; and he remained with those whom Peter had strengthened in the faith of Christ, gaining strength himself yet more until the coming of Paul to Rome.

But when Nero later discovered that Peter had departed this life, he censured the prefect Agrippa because he had been put to death without his knowledge; for he would have liked to punish him more cruelly and with extra severity; for Peter had made disciples of some of his servants and caused them to leave him; so that he was greatly incensed and for some time would not speak to Agrippa; for he sought to destroy all those brethren who had been made disciples by Peter. And one night he saw a figure scourging him and saying, "Nero, you cannot now persecute or destroy the servants of Christ. Keep your hands from them!" And so Nero, being greatly alarmed because of this vision, kept away from the disciples from the time that Peter departed this life.

And thereafter the brethren kept together with one accord, rejoicing and exulting in the Lord, and glorifying the God and Savior of our Lord Jesus Christ with the Holy Spirit, to whom be the glory forever and ever. Amen.

The Acts of Paul

(Christian Apocrypha)

The *Acts of Paul* was composed around A.D. 185–195 by a presbyter in Asia Minor, who was rewarded for his work by expulsion from the Church. Such is the attestation of Tertullian in *De baptismo 17*. Tertullian disapproved of the *Acts of Paul* because Thecla, the heroine and major figure of the tract, not only baptizes herself, but also preaches and baptizes others. This daring act by a woman—which has no parallel in the canonical *Acts of the Apostles*—was not to be condoned by the Church. As in the other apocryphal *Acts*, the motif of the *Acts of Paul* is continence and salvation. The demand by the apostle for sexual continence on the part of officials' wives, here and in other Acts, brings about persecution and martyrdom. Such a denouement illustrates the worthlessness of this world and the wonder of the world to come. Sexual purity is a key to the salvation of the immortal soul.

Thecla is apparently a saintly figure worshiped in Seleucia. In his study of the *Acts* Wilhelm Schneemelcher suggests that the author of the *Acts* gave his own stamp to traditional material about Thecla, which had been part of oral tradition for a century.[1] Thecla is depicted as an elegant, braceleted virgin, whose Christian rebuff of her fiancé Thamyris leads Thamyris to murderous jealousy. Thecla secretly goes to Paul's prison cell at night, and kisses Paul's fetters. She is denounced for her visit, and then "with joy exulting" she is brought to the governor for punishment. There follow an episode of sensual melodrama and miracle, comparable to the tale of Perpetua and Felicity. Thecla is condemned to be burned. She is brought in naked and the governor weeps and marvels at her powers as she mounts the pyre. When the fire is kindled, God quenches the flame with sudden rain and hail. Then follows a joyful and loving reunion with Paul, who praises Thecla's beauty and tells her she can endure temptation.

Thecla's next adventure involves Alexander, another would-be lover, whom Thecla spurns, for which she is condemned by the governor to be torn apart by beasts. Thecla is again taken naked into the stadium. A bear and lioness charge her, but a protective lion kills them. After Thecla baptizes herself, she dives into a pit of water with killer seals. But lightning causes the seals to float up to the surface dead. Then, as more terrible beasts are loosed upon her, God sends in a cloud of fire to keep the beasts away and to conceal her nakedness. Other women throw flowers and perfumes into the ring, which overpowers the beasts in sleep. Finally, the governor releases her. Thecla says: "He who clothed me when I was naked among the beasts shall clothe me with salvation in the day of judgment."

Thecla yearns for Paul, however, and seeks him everywhere. The crowd wonders "whether another temptation was not upon her." Paul takes her by the hand, marvels at her tales, and sees her depart. Then Thecla begins a career of preaching and enlightening in Seleucia until she "sleeps a noble sleep." So ends one of the beautiful romances of apocryphal literature.

We next find Paul in Ephesus, where he is condemned to be killed by beasts for preaching chastity to wives of local officials. In the stadium Paul has a remarkable conversation with a fierce lion whom he had earlier baptized. God saves both Paul and the baptized lion by causing sudden hail to fall on the stadium, which kills many people and beasts, and tears off the ear of Hieronymous, one of the spurned husbands. Paul and the lion escape. Paul's martyrdom takes place in Rome. His witnesses are the Roman prefect Longus and the centurion Cestus. The apostle converts them by a miraculous occurrence at his beheading. "But when the executioner struck off his head, milk spurted upon the soldier's clothing. And when they saw it, the soldier and those who stood by were amazed, and glorified God who had given Paul such glory." Paul returns again before Caesar as "God's soldier" to haunt the bloody tyrant.

In the appendix to the *Acts*, based on a Coptic text, we read more details of Paul's baptism of the lion. After Paul immersed the lion three times in the water, the lion runs off to the country, rejoicing. Now, fortified by faith, the lion's sexual self-control before temptation is shown. "A lioness met him, and he did not yield himself to her but . . . ran off."

The apocryphal *Acts of Paul* is a religious tract, composed for edification and entertainment. Although Paul's preaching leads Thecla to break off her engagement and miracles save her from martyrdom, the extreme ascetic message is conveyed in colorful, effective, and truly sensual language. The legend of Paul's martyrdom is well known and ordinary among saints' tales. Ordinary also is the depiction of Thecla as a woman. At first it appears that she will be considered for no other human traits than her womanhood—her comeliness, her bracelets and nakedness, her temptation to sin carnally and her power, through faith in Jesus, to abstain. Typically, she is stereotyped as merely a feminine body. Then a heretical notion is introduced. She is treated as a human being, not merely as a woman. She is allowed to baptize and to preach. This breach in the code did not go undenounced then, as it would not today. Thecla's professional role is a rare example in Christian scriptures of a woman's right to officiate in Church ceremonies. In an unguarded and unrepeated moment, a woman, in an inevitable and natural way, has an important position in the religious society. She is teacher and priest. She is not confined to her highly prescribed roles.

Note

1. *Acts of Paul*, from Edgar Hennecke and Wilhelm Schneemelcher, eds. and trans., *New Testament Apocrypha*, vol. 2 (Philadelphia: Westminster Press, 1963), p. 332.

ACTS OF PAUL AND THECLA*

As Paul went up to Iconium after his flight from Antioch, his traveling companions were Demas and Hermogenes, the coppersmith, who were full of hypocrisy and flattered Paul as if they loved him. But Paul, who had eyes only for the goodness of Christ, did them no evil, but loved them greatly, so that he sought to make sweet to them all the words of the Lord, of the doctrine and of the interpretation of the Gospel, both of the birth and of the resurrection of the Beloved, and he related to them word for word the great acts of Christ as they had been revealed to him.

And a man named Onesiphorus, who had heard that Paul was come to Iconium, went out with his children, Simmias and Zeno, and his wife, Lectra, to meet

*Chapters 1–43. All selections from the *Acts of Paul* are translated by Wilhelm Schneemelcher and are from Edgar Hennecke and Wilhelm Schneemelcher, eds. and trans., *New Testament Apocrypha*, vol. 2 (Philadelphia: Westminster Press, 1963), pp. 353–364, 370–373, 383–387, 388–390.

Paul that he might receive him to his house. Titus had told him what Paul looked like for hitherto he had not seen him in the flesh, but only in the spirit. And he went along the royal road which leads to Lystra, and stood there waiting for him, and looked at all who came, according to Titus' description. And he saw Paul coming, a man small of stature, with a bald head and crooked legs, in a good state of body, with eyebrows meeting and nose somewhat hooked, full of friendliness; for now he appeared like a man, and now he had the face of an angel.

And when Paul saw Onesiphorus he smiled and Onesiphorus said: "Greeting, servant of the blessed God!" And he replied: "Grace be with you and your house!" But Demas and Hermogenes grew jealous, and went even further in their hypocrisy so that Demas said: "Are we then not servants of the Blessed, that you did not greet us thus?"And Onesiphorus said: "I do not see in you any fruit of righteousness; but if you are anything, come also into my house and rest yourselves!" And when Paul entered into the house of Onesiphorus there was great joy, and bowing of knees and breaking of bread, and the word of God concerning continence and the resurrection, as Paul said:

447

"Blessed are the pure in heart, for they shall see God.

"Blessed are they who have kept the flesh pure, for they shall become a temple of God.

"Blessed are the continent, for to them will God speak.

"Blessed are they who have renounced this world, for they shall be well pleasing unto God.

"Blessed are they who have wives as if they had them not, for they shall inherit God.

"Blessed are they who have fear of God, for they shall become angels of God.

"Blessed are they who tremble at the words of God, for they shall be comforted.

"Blessed are they who have received the wisdom of Jesus Christ, for they shall be called sons of the Most High.

"Blessed are they who have kept their baptism secure, for they shall rest with the Father and the Son.

"Blessed are they who have laid hold upon the understanding of Jesus Christ, for they shall be in light.

"Blessed are they who through love of God have departed from the form of this world, for they shall judge angels and at the right hand of the Father they shall be blessed.

"Blessed are the merciful, for they shall obtain mercy, and shall not see the bitter day of judgment.

"Blessed are the bodies of the virgins, for they shall be well pleasing to God, and shall not lose the reward of their purity.

"For the word of the Father shall be for them a work of salvation in the day of his Son, and they shall have rest forever and ever."

And while Paul was thus speaking in the midst of the assembly in the house of Onesiphorus, a virgin named Thecla—her mother was Theocleia—who was betrothed to a man named Thamyris, sat at a nearby window and listened night and day to the word of the virgin life as it was spoken by Paul; and she did not turn away from the window, but pressed on in the faith rejoicing exeedingly. Moreover, when she saw many women and virgins going in to Paul she desired to be counted worthy herself to stand in Paul's presence and hear the word of Christ; for she had not yet seen Paul in person, but only heard his word. Since, however, she did not move from the window, her mother sent to Thamyris. He came in great joy as if he were already taking her in marriage. So Thamyris said to Theocleia: "Where is my Thecla, that I may see her?" And Theocleia said: "I have a new tale to tell you, Thamyris. For indeed for three days and three nights Thecla has not risen from the window either to eat or to drink, but gazing steadily as if on some joyful spectacle she so devotes herself to a strange man who teaches deceptive and subtle words that I wonder how a maiden of such modesty as she is can be so sorely troubled. Thamyris, this man is upsetting the city of the Iconians, and thy Thecla in addition; for all the women and young people go in to him, and are taught by him. 'You must,' he says, 'fear one single God only, and live chastely.' And my daughter also, like a spider at the window bound by his words, is dominated by a new desire and a fearful passion; for the maiden hangs upon the things he says, and is taken captive. But go to her and speak to her, for she is betrothed to you."

And Thamyris went to her, at one and the same time loving her and yet afraid of her distraction, and said: "Thecla, my betrothed, why do you sit thus? And what is this passion that holds you distracted? Turn to your Thamyris and be ashamed." And her mother also said the same: "Child, why do you sit thus looking down and making no answer, but like one stricken?" And those who were in the house wept bitterly, Thamyris for the loss of a wife, Theocleia for that of a daughter, the maidservants for that of a mistress. So there was a great confusion of mourning in the house. And while this was going on all around her, Thecla did not turn away, but gave her whole attention to Paul's word.

But Thamyris sprang up and went out into the street, and closely watched all who went in to Paul and came out. And he saw two men quarrelling bitterly with one another, and said to them: "You men, who are you, tell me, and who is he that is inside with you, the false teacher who deceives the souls of young men and maidens, that they should not marry but remain as they are? I promise now to give you much money if you will tell me about him; for I am the first man of this city."

And Demas and Hermogenes said to him: "Who this man is, we do not know. But he deprives young men of wives and maidens of husbands, saying: 'Otherwise there is no resurrection for you, except you remain chaste and do not defile the flesh, but keep it pure.'"

And Thamyris said to them: "Come into my house, you men, and rest with me." And they went off to a sumptuous banquet, with much wine, great wealth and a splendid table. And Thamyris gave them drink, for he loved Thecla and wished to have her for his wife. And during the dinner Thamyris said: "Tell me, you men, what is his teaching, that I also may know it; for I am greatly distressed about Thecla because she so loves the stranger, and I am deprived of my marriage."

But Demas and Hermogenes said:

"Bring him before the governor Castellius, on the ground that he is seducing the crowds to the new doctrine of the Christians, and so he will have him executed and you shall have your wife, Thecla. And we shall teach you concerning the resurrection which he says is to come, that it has already taken place in the children whom we have, and that we are risen again in that we have come to know the true God."

When Thamyris had heard this from them, he rose up early in the morning full of jealousy and wrath and went to the house of Onesiphorus with the rulers and officers and a great crowd with cudgels, and said to Paul: "You have destroyed the city of the Iconians, and my betrothed, so that she will not have me. Let us go to the governor Castellius!" And the whole crowd shouted: "Away with the sorcerer! For he has corrupted all our wives." And the multitude let themselves be persuaded.

And Thamyris stood before the judgment seat and cried aloud: "Proconsul, this man—we know not whence he is—who does not allow maidens to marry, let him declare before you for what cause he teaches these things." And Demas and Hermogenes said to Thamyris: "Say that he is a Christian, and so you will destroy him." But the governor was not easily swayed, and he called Paul, saying to him: "Who are you, and what do you teach? For it is no light accusation that they bring against you."

And Paul lifted up his voice and said: "If I today am examined as to what I teach, then listen, Proconsul. The living God, the God of vengeance, the jealous God, the God who has need of nothing, has sent me since he desires the salvation of men, that I may draw them away from corruption and impurity, all pleasure and death, that they may sin no more. For this cause God sent his own Son, whom I preach and teach that in him men have hope, who alone had compassion upon a world in error; that men may no longer be under judgment but have faith, and fear of God, and knowledge of propriety, and love of truth. If then I teach the things revealed to me by God, what wrong do I do, Proconsul?" When the governor heard this he commanded Paul to be bound and led off to prison until he should find leisure to give him a more attentive hearing.

But Thecla in the night took off her bracelets and gave them to the doorkeeper, and when the door was opened for her she went off to the prison. To the jailer she gave a silver mirror, and so went in to Paul and sat at his feet and heard him proclaim the mighty acts of God. And Paul feared nothing, but comported himself with full confidence in God; and her faith also was increased, as she kissed his fetters. But when Thecla was sought for by her own people and by Thamyris, they hunted her through the streets as one lost; and one of the doorkeeper's fellow slaves betrayed that she had gone out by night. And they questioned the doorkeeper and he told them: "She has gone to the stranger in the prison." And they went as he had told them and found her, so to speak, bound with him in affection. And they went out thence, rallied the crowd about them, and disclosed to the governor what had happened.

He commanded Paul to be brought to the judgment seat; but Thecla rolled herself upon the place where Paul taught as he sat in the prison. The governor commanded her also to be brought to the judgment seat, and she went off with joy exulting. But when Paul was brought forward again, the crowd shouted out even louder: "He is a sorcerer! Away with him!" But the governor heard Paul gladly concerning the holy works of Christ; and when he had taken counsel he called Thecla and said: "Why do you not marry Thamyris according to the law of the Iconians?" But she stood there looking steadily at Paul. And when she did not answer, Theocleia, her mother, cried out, saying: "Burn the lawless one! Burn

her that is no bride in the midst of the theater, that all the women who have been taught by this man may be afraid!"

And the governor was greatly affected. He had Paul scourged and drove him out of the city, but Thecla he condemned to be burned. And forthwith the governor arose and went off to the theater, and all the crowd went out to the unavoidable spectacle. But Thecla sought Paul, as a lamb in the wilderness looks about for the shepherd. And when she looked upon the crowd, she saw the Lord sitting in the form of Paul and said: "As if I were not able to endure, Paul has come to look after me." And she looked steadily at him; but he departed into the heavens.

Now the young men and maidens brought wood and straw that Thecla might be burned. And as she was brought in naked, the governor wept and marveled at the power that was in her. The executioners laid out the wood and bade her mount the pyre; and making the sign of the cross [i.e., stretching out her arms] she climbed up on the wood. They kindled it and although a great fire blazed up, the fire did not touch her. For God in compassion caused a noise beneath the earth and a cloud above, full of rain and hail, overshadowed the theater and its whole content poured out, so that many were in danger and died, and the fire was quenched and Thecla saved.

At this time, Paul was fasting with Onesiphorus and his wife and the children in an open tomb on the way by which they go from Iconium to Daphne. And when many days were past, as they were fasting the boys said to Paul: "We are hungry." And they had nothing with which to buy bread, for Onesiphorus had left the things of the world and followed Paul with all his house. But Paul took off his outer garment and said: "Go, my child, sell this and buy several loaves and bring them here." But while the boy was buying the bread, he saw his neighbor Thecla, and was astonished and said:

"Thecla, where are you going?" And she said: "I am seeking Paul, for I was saved from the fire." And the boy said: "Come, I will take you to him, for he has been mourning for you and praying and fasting six days already."

But when she came to the tomb, Paul had bent his knees and was praying and saying: "Father of Christ, let not the fire touch Thecla, but be merciful to her, for she is yours!" But she standing behind him cried out: "Father, who made Heaven and earth, the Father of your beloved Son Jesus Christ, I praise you that you saved me from the fire, that I might see Paul!" And as Paul arose he saw her and said: "O God the knower of hearts, Father of our Lord Jesus Christ, I praise you that you have so speedily accomplished what I asked, and have hearkened unto me." And within the tomb there was much love, Paul rejoicing, and Onesiphorus and all of them. But they had five loaves, and vegetables, and water, and they were joyful over the holy works of Christ. And Thecla said to Paul: "I will cut my hair short and follow you wherever you go." But he said: "The season is unfavorable, and you are comely. May no other temptation come upon you, worse than the first, and you endure not and play the coward!" And Thecla said: "Only give me the seal in Christ, and temptation shall not touch me." And Paul said: "Have patience, Thecla, and you shall receive the water."

And Paul sent away Onesiphorus with all his family to Iconium and so taking Thecla, came into Antioch. But immediately as they entered, a Syrian by the name of Alexander, one of the first of the Antiochenes, seeing Thecla fell in love with her, and sought to win over Paul with money and gifts. But Paul said: "I do not know the woman of whom you speak, nor is she mine." But he, being a powerful man, embraced her on the open street; she, however, would not endure it, but looked about for Paul and cried out bitterly, saying: "Force not the stranger, force not the handmaid of God!

Among the Iconians I am one of the first, and because I did not wish to marry Thamyris I have been cast out of the city." And taking hold of Alexander she ripped his cloak, took off the crown from his head, and made him a laughingstock.

But he, partly out of love for her and partly in shame at what had befallen him, brought her before the governor; and when she confessed that she had done these things, he condemned her to the beasts, since Alexander was arranging games. But the women were panic-stricken, and cried out before the judgment seat: "An evil judgment! A godless judgment!" But Thecla asked of the governor that she might remain pure until she was to fight with the beasts. And a rich woman named Tryphaena, whose daughter had died, took her under her protection and found comfort in her.

When the beasts were led in procession, they bound her to a fierce lioness, and the queen Tryphaena followed her. And as Thecla sat upon her back, the lioness licked her feet, and all the crowd was amazed. Now the charge upon her superscription was: guilty of sacrilege. But the women with their children cried out from above, saying: "O God, an impious judgment is come to pass in this city!" And after the procession Tryphaena took her again; for her daughter who was dead had spoken to her in a dream: "Mother, you shall have in my place the stranger, the desolate Thecla, that she may pray for me and I be translated to the place of the just." So when Tryphaena received her back from the procession she was at once sorrowful, because she was to fight with the beasts on the following day, but at the same time loved her dearly like her own daughter Falconilla; and she said: "Thecla, my second child, come and pray for my child, that she may live; for this I saw in my dream." And she without delay lifted up her voice and said: "God of heaven, Son of the Most High, grant to her according to her wish, that her daughter Falconilla may live for ever!"

And when Thecla said this, Tryphaena mourned, considering that such beauty was to be thrown to the beasts.

And when it was dawn, Alexander came to take her away—for he himself was arranging the games—and he said: "The governor has taken his place, and the crowd is clamoring for us. Give me her that is to fight the beasts, that I may take her away." But Tryphaena cried out so that he fled, saying: "A second mourning for my Falconilla is come upon my house, and there is none to help; neither child, for she is dead, nor kinsman, for I am a widow. O God of Thecla my child, help Thecla." And the governor sent soldiers to fetch Thecla. Tryphaena, however, did not stand aloof, but taking her hand herself led her up, saying: "My daughter Falconilla I brought to the tomb; but you, Thecla, I bring to fight the beasts." And Thecla wept bitterly and sighed to the Lord, saying: "Lord God, in whom I trust, with whom I have taken refuge, who delivered me from the fire, reward Tryphaena, who had compassion upon your handmaid, and because she preserved me pure." Then there was a tumult, and roaring of the beasts, and a shouting of the people and of the women who sat together, some saying: "Bring in the sacrilegious one!" but the women said: "May the city perish for this lawlessness!" Slay us all Proconsul! A bitter sight, an evil judgment!"

But Thecla was taken out of Tryphaena's hands and stripped, and was given a girdle and flung into the stadium. And lions and bears were set upon her, and a fierce lioness ran to her and lay down at her feet. And the crowd of the women raised a great shout. And a bear ran upon her, but the lioness ran and met it, and tore the bear asunder. And again a lion trained against men, which belonged to Alexander, ran upon her; and the lioness grappled with the lion, and perished with it. And the women mourned the more, since the lioness which helped her was dead.

Then they sent in many beasts, while she stood and stretched out her hands and prayed. And when she had finished her prayer, she turned and saw a great pit full of water, and said: "Now is the time for me to wash." And she threw herself in, saying: "In the name of Jesus Christ I baptize myself on the last day!" And when they saw it, the women and all the people wept, saying: "Do not cast yourself into the water!"; so that even the governor wept that such beauty should be devoured by seals. So, then, she threw herself into the water in the name of Jesus Christ; but the seals, seeing the light of a lightning flash, floated dead on the surface. And there was about her a cloud of fire, so that neither could the beasts touch her nor could she be seen naked.

But as other more terrible beasts were let loose, the women cried aloud, and some threw petals, others nard, others cassia, others amomum, so that there was an abundance of perfumes. And all the beasts let loose were overpowered as if by sleep, and did not touch her. So Alexander said to the governor: "I have some very fearsome bulls—let us tie her to them." The governor, frowning, gave his consent, saying: "Do what you wish." And they bound her by the feet between the bulls, and set red-hot irons beneath their bellies, that being the more enraged they might kill her. The bulls indeed leaped forward, but the flame that blazed around her burned through the ropes, and she was as if she were not bound. But Tryphaena fainted as she stood beside the arena, so that her handmaids said: "The queen Tryphaena is dead!" And the governor took note of it, and the whole city was alarmed. And Alexander fell down at the governor's feet and said: "Have mercy upon me, and on the city, and set the prisoner free, lest the city also perish with her. For if Caesar should hear this, he will probably destroy both us and the city as well because his kinswoman Tryphaena has died at the circus gates."

And the governor summoned Thecla from among the beasts, and said to her: "Who are you? And what do you have about you, that not one of the beasts touched you?" She answered: "I am a handmaid of the living God. As to what I have about me, I have believed in him in whom God is well pleased, his Son. For his sake not one of the beasts touched me. For he alone is the goal of salvation and the foundation of immortal life. To the storm-tossed, he is a refuge; to the oppressed, relief; to the despairing, shelter; in a word, whoever does not believe in him shall not live, but die forever." When the governor heard this, he commanded garments to be brought, and said: "Put on these garments." But she said: "He who clothed me when I was naked among the beasts shall clothe me with salvation in the day of judgment." And taking the garments she put them on.

And straightway the governor issued a decree, saying: "I release to you Thecla, the pious handmaid of God." But all the women cried out with a loud voice, and as with one mouth gave praise to God, saying: "One is God, who has delivered Thecla!" so that all the city was shaken by the sound. And Tryphaena, when she was told the good news, came to meet her with a crowd, and embraced Thecla and said: "Now I believe that the dead are raised up! Now I believe that my child lives! Come inside, and I will assign to you all that is mine." So Thecla went in with her and rested in her house for eight days, instructing her in the word of God, so that the majority of the maidservants also believed; and there was great joy in the house.

But Thecla yearned for Paul and sought him, sending in every direction. And it was reported to her that he was in Myra. So she took young men and maidservants and girded herself, and sewed her mantle into a cloak after the fashion of men, and went off to Myra, and found Paul speaking the word of God and went to him. But he was astonished when he saw her and the crowd that was with her, pondering whether another temptation was not upon her. But observing this she said to him: "I have taken the bath, Paul; for he who worked with you for the Gospel has also worked with me for my baptism." And taking her by the hand, Paul led her into the house of Hermias, and heard from her everything that had happened, so that Paul marveled greatly and the hearers were confirmed and prayed for Tryphaena. And Thecla arose and said to Paul: "I am going to Iconium." But Paul said: "Go and teach the word of God!" Now Tryphaena sent her much clothing and gold, so that she could leave some of it for the service of the poor. But she herself went away to Iconium and went into the house of Onesiphorus, and threw herself down on the floor where Paul had sat and taught the oracles of God, and wept, saying: "My God, and God of this house where the light shone upon me, Christ Jesus, the Son of God, my helper in prison, my helper before governors, my helper in the fire, my helper among the beasts, you are God, and to you be the glory forever. Amen."

And she found Thamyris dead, but her mother still alive; and calling her mother to her she said to her: "Theocleia, my mother, can you believe that the Lord lives in Heaven? For if you desire money, the Lord will give it to you through me; or your child, see, I stand beside you."

And when she had borne this witness she went away to Seleucia; and after enlightening many with the word of God she slept with a noble sleep.

PAUL IN EPHESUS

". . . For your gods are of . . . and stone and wood and can neither take food nor see nor hear nor even stand. Form a good resolve, and be saved, lest God be angry and burn you with unquenchable fire, and the memory of you perish." And when the governor heard this in the theater with the people, he said: "You men of Ephesus, that this man has spoken well I know, but also that is no time for you to learn these things. Decide now what you wish!" Some said he should be burned, but the goldsmiths said: "To the beasts with the man!" And since a great tumult broke out, Hieronymus condemned him to the beasts, after having him scourged. Now the brethren, since it was Pentecost, did not mourn or bow their knees, but rejoiced and prayed, standing. But after six days, all who saw it were astonished at the size of the beasts.

[The first lines are imperfect. Paul sits a prisoner, and hears the preparations for the fight with the beasts.]

And when the lion came to the side door of the stadium where Paul was imprisoned, it roared loudly, so that all cried out: "The lion!" For it roared fiercely and angrily, so that even Paul broke off his prayer in terror. There was Diophantes, a freedman of Hieronymus, whose wife was a disciple of Paul and sat beside him night and day, so that Diophantes became jealous and hastened on the conflict. And Artemilla, the wife of Hieronymus, wished to hear Paul praying. And she went and told Paul, and Paul full of joy said: "Bring her." She put on darker clothes, and came to him with Eubula. But when Paul saw her, he groaned and said: "Woman, ruler of this world, mistress of much gold, citizen of great luxury, splendid in your raiment, sit down on the floor and forget your riches and your beauty and finery. For these will bring you no profit if you pray not to God who regards as dross all that here is imposing, but graciously bestows what there is wonderful. Gold perishes, riches are consumed, clothes become worn out. Beauty grows old, and great cities are changed, and the world will be destroyed in fire because of the lawlessness of men. God alone abides, and the sonship that is given through him in

whom men must be saved. And now, Artemilla, hope in God and he will deliver you, hope in Christ and he will give you forgiveness of sins and will bestow upon you a crown of freedom, that you may no longer serve idols and the steam of sacrifice but the living God and Father of Christ, whose is the glory forever and ever. Amen." And when Artemilla heard this, she with Eubula entreated Paul to baptize her in God. And the fight with the beasts was arranged for the next day.

And Hieronymus heard from Diophantes that the women sat night and day with Paul, and he was not a little angry with Artemilla and the freedwoman Eubula. And when he had dined, Hieronymus withdrew early that he might quickly carry through the beast hunt. But the women said to Paul: "Do you wish us to bring a smith, that you may baptize us in the sea as a free man?" And Paul said: "I do not wish it, for I have faith in God, who delivered the whole world from its bonds." And Paul cried out to God on the Sabbath as the Lord's day drew near, the day on which Paul was to fight with the beasts, and he said: "My God, Jesus Christ, who redeemed me from so many evils, grant me that before the eyes of Artemilla and Eubula, who are yours, the fetters may be broken from my hands." And as Paul thus testified, there came a youth very comely in grace who loosed Paul's bonds, the youth smiling as he did so. And straightway he departed. But because of the vision which was granted to Paul, and the eminent sign relating to his fetters, his grief over the fight with the beasts departed and, rejoicing, he leaped as if in Paradise. And taking Artemilla, he went out from the narrow and dark place where the prisoners were kept.

[In the following there are considerable gaps, which Schmidt has meaningfully restored. The subject is Artemilla's baptism at the sea. As Artemilla swoons at the sight of the surging sea, Paul prays:]

"O you who give light and shine, help, that the heathen may not say that Paul, the prisoner, fled after killing Artemilla." And again the youth smiled, and the matron, Artemilla, breathed again, and she went into the house as dawn was already breaking. But as he went in, the guards being asleep, he broke bread and brought water, gave her to drink of the word, and dismissed her to her husband Hieronymus. But he himself prayed.

At dawn there was a cry from the citizens: "Let us go to the spectacle! Come, let us see the man who possesses God fighting with the beasts!" Hieronymus himself joined them, partly because of his suspicion against his wife, partly because Paul had not fled; he commanded Diophantes and the other slaves to bring Paul into the stadium. Paul was dragged in, saying nothing but bowed down and groaning because he was led in triumph by the city. And when he was brought out he was immediately flung into the stadium, so that all were vexed at Paul's dignity. But since Artemilla and Eubula fell into a sickness and were in extreme danger because of Paul's impending destruction, Hieronymus was not a little grieved over his wife, but also because the rumor was already abroad in the city and he did not have his wife with him. Hieronymus ordered a very fierce lion, which had but recently been captured, to be set loose against him.

[The following text is very imperfect. It deals with the lion's prayer and its conversation with Paul. The people thereupon cry out:]

"Away with the sorcerer! Away with the poisoner!" But the lion looked at Paul and Paul at the lion. Then Paul recognized that this was the lion which had come and been baptized. And borne along by faith, Paul said: "Lion, was it you whom I baptized?" And the lion in answer said to Paul: "Yes." Paul spoke to it again and said: "And how were you captured?" The lion said with one voice: "Even as you, Paul."

As Hieronymus sent many beasts, that Paul might be slain, and against the lion archers, that it too might be killed, a violent and exceedingly heavy hailstorm fell from Heaven, although the sky was clear, so that many died and all the rest took to flight. But it did not touch Paul or the lion, although the other beasts perished under the weight of the hail, which was so severe that Hieronymus' ear was smitten and torn off, and the people cried out as they fled: "Save us, O God, save us, O God of the man who fought with the beasts!" And Paul took leave of the lion and went out of the stadium and down to the harbor and embarked on the ship which was sailing for Macedonia; for there were many who were sailing, as if the city were about to perish. So he embarked too like one of the fugitives, but the lion went away into the mountains, as was customary for it.

MARTYRDOM OF THE HOLY APOSTLE PAUL*

There were awaiting Paul at Rome Luke from Gaul and Titus from Dalmatia. When Paul saw them he was glad, so that he hired a barn outside Rome, where with the brethren he taught the word of truth. The news was spread abroad, and many souls were added to the Lord, so that there was a rumor throughout Rome, and a great number of believers came to him from the house of Caesar, and there was great joy.

But a certain Patroclus, Caesar's cupbearer, came late to the barn and, being unable because of the crowd to go in to Paul, sat at a high window and listened to him teaching the word of God. But since the wicked Devil was envious of the love of the brethren, Patroclus fell

_____
*Chapters 1–7.

from the window and died, and the news was quickly brought to Nero. But Paul, perceiving it in the spirit, said: "Brethren, the evil one has gained an opportunity to tempt you. Go out, and you will find a youth fallen from a height and already on the point of death. Lift him up, and bring him here to me!" So they went out and brought him. And when the crowd saw him, they were troubled. Paul said to them: "Now, brethren, let your faith be manifest. Come, all of you, let us mourn to our Lord Jesus Christ, that this youth may live and we remain unmolested." But as they all lamented, the youth drew breath again, and setting him upon a beast they sent him back alive with the others who were of Caesar's house.

When Nero heard of Patroclus' death, he was greatly distressed, and when he came out from the bath he commanded that another be appointed for the wine. But his servants told him the news, saying: "Caesar, Patroclus is alive and standing at the table." And when Caesar heard that Patroclus was alive he was afraid, and did not want to go in. But when he had entered, he saw Patroclus and, beside himself, cried out: "Patroclus, are you alive?" And he said: "I am alive, Caesar." But he said: "Who is he who made you live?" And the youth, borne by the conviction of faith, said: "Christ Jesus, the king of the ages." But Caesar in perplexity said: "So he is to be king of the ages, and destroy all the kingdoms?" Patroclus said to him: "Yes, all the kingdoms under Heaven he destroys, and he alone shall be forever, and there shall be no kingdom which shall escape him." But he struck him on the face and said: "Patroclus, do you also serve in that king's army?" And he said: "Yes, lord Caesar, for indeed he raised me up when I was dead." And Barsabas Justus of the flat feet, and Urion the Cappadocian, and Festus the Galatian, Nero's chief men, said: "We also are in the army of that king of the ages." But he

shut them up in prison, after torturing dreadfully men whom he greatly loved, and commanded that the soldiers of the great king be sought out, and he issued a decree to this effect, that all who were found to be Christians and soldiers of Christ should be put to death.

And among the many Paul also was brought bound; to him all his fellow prisoners gave heed, so that Caesar observed that he was the man in command. And he said to him: "Man of the great king, but now my prisoner, why did it seem good to you to come secretly into the empire of the Romans and enlist soldiers from my province?" But Paul, filled with the Holy Spirit, said before them all: "Caesar, not only from your province do we enlist soldiers, but from the whole world. For this charge has been laid upon us, that no man be excluded who wishes to serve my king. If you also think it good, do him service! For neither riches nor the splendor of this present life will save you, but if you submit and entreat him, then you shall be saved. For in one day he will destroy the world with fire."

When Caesar heard this, he commanded all the prisoners to be burned with fire, but Paul to be beheaded according to the law of the Romans. But Paul did not keep silence concerning the word, but communicated it to the prefect Longus and the centurion Cestus.

In Rome, then, Nero was raging at the instigation of the evil one, many Christians being put to death without trial, so that the Romans took their stand at the palace and cried: "It is enough, Caesar! For these men are ours. You are destroying the power of the Romans!" Then he made an end of the persecution, whereupon none of the Christians was to be touched until he had himself investigated his case.

Then Paul was brought before him in accordance with the decree, and he adhered to the decision that he should be beheaded. But Paul said: "Caesar, it is not for a short time that I live for my king. And if you behead me, this will I do: I will arise and appear to you in proof that I am not dead, but alive to my Lord Christ Jesus, who is coming to judge the world."

But Longus and Cestus said to Paul: "Whence have you this king, that you believe in him without change of heart, even unto death?" Paul communicated the word to them and said: "You men who are in this ignorance and error, change your mind and be saved from the fire that is coming upon the whole world. For we do not march, as you suppose, with a king who comes from earth, but one from Heaven, the living God, who comes as judge because of the lawless deeds that are done in this world. And blessed is that man who shall believe in him, and live forever, when he comes to burn the world till it is pure." So they besought him and said: "We entreat you, help us and we will let you go." But he answered and said: "I am no deserter from Christ, but a lawful soldier of the living God. Had I known that I was to die, I would have done it, Longus and Cestus. But since I live for God and love myself, I go to the Lord that I may come again with him in the glory of his Father." They said to him: "How then shall we live, when you are beheaded?"

While they were still saying this, Nero sent a certain Parthenius and Pheretas to see if Paul had already been beheaded; and they found him still alive. But he called them to him and said: "Believe in the living God, who raises up from the dead both me and all who believe in him!" But they said: "We are going now to Nero; but when you die and rise again, then will we believe in your God." But when Longus and Cestus questioned him further about salvation, he said to them: "Come quickly here to my grave at dawn, and you will find two men praying, Titus and Luke. They will give you the seal in the Lord."

Then Paul stood with his face to the east, and lifting up his hands to Heaven prayed at length; and after communing in prayer in Hebrew with the fathers, he stretched out his neck without speaking further. But when the executioner struck off his head, milk spurted upon the soldier's clothing. And when they saw it, the soldier and all who stood by were amazed, and glorified God who had given Paul such glory. And they went off and reported to Caesar what had happened.

When he heard it, he marveled greatly and was at a loss. Then Paul came about the ninth hour, when many philosophers and the centurion were standing with Caesar, and he stood before them all and said: "Caesar, here I am—Paul, God's soldier. I am not dead, but alive in my God. But for you, unhappy man, there shall be many evils and great punishment, because you unjustly shed the blood of the righteous, and that not many days hence!" And when he had said this, Paul departed from him. But when Nero heard it he was greatly troubled, and commanded the prisoners to be set free, including Patroclus and Barsabas and his companions.

As Paul directed, Longus and Cestus went at dawn and with fear approached Paul's tomb. But as they drew near they saw two men praying, and Paul between them, so that at the sight of this unexpected wonder they were astounded, while Titus and Luke were seized with human fear when they saw Longus and Cestus coming towards them, and turned to flight. But they followed after them, saying: "We are not pursuing you to kill you, as you imagine, blessed men of God, but for life, that you may give it to us as Paul promised us, whom we saw but now standing between you and praying." And when Titus and Luke heard this from them, with great joy they gave them the seal in the Lord, glorifying the God and Father of our Lord Jesus Christ, unto whom be the glory forever and ever. Amen.

457

THE BEGINNING OF THE STAY IN EPHESUS

"I was walking in the night, meaning to go to Jericho in Phoenicia, and we covered great distances. But when morning came, Lemma and Ammia were behind me, they who gave the *agape*, for I was dear to their hearts, so that they were not far from me. There came a great and terrible lion out of the valley of the burying ground. But we were praying, so that through the prayer Lemma and Ammia did not come upon the beast. But when I finished praying, the beast had cast himself at my feet. I was filled with the Spirit and looked upon him, and said to him: "Lion, what do you want?" But he said: 'I wish to be baptized.'

"I glorified God, who had given speech to the beast and salvation to his servant. Now there was a great river in that place, and I went down into it. Then, men and brethren, I cried out, saying: 'You who dwell in the heights, who looked upon the humble, who gave rest to the afflicted, who with Daniel shut the mouths of the lions, who sent to me our Lord Jesus Christ, accomplish your plan which you have appointed for me.' When I had prayed thus, I took the lion by his mane and in the name of Jesus Christ immersed him three times. But when he came up out of the water he shook out his mane and said to me: 'Grace be with you!' And I said to him: 'And likewise with you.'

"The lion ran off to the country rejoicing (for this was revealed to me in my heart). A lioness met him, and he did not yield himself to her but ran off."

The Acts of Andrew

(Christian Apocrypha)

The *Acts of Andrew* is a drama of martyrdom. Andrew is condemned by the proconsul Aegeates to be crucified. He is to hang so the dogs will tear him apart. The crime of "the slave of Christ" was to corrupt Aegeates' wife in the ways of Christianity so that she would no longer satisfy him sexually. Andrew also corrupted the proconsul's brother, Stratocles, who is an ally of Andrew. Twice Andrew has a chance to escape. Stratocles personally strongarms the guards who were taking Andrew to the cross. But Andrew, after an impassioned address to the cross, insists on being killed. The people protest and out of fear Aegeates reverses his orders. But again Andrew insists on his martyrdom. When he dies, the unjust proconsul is maddened and one night throws himself to his death from a great height. His wife and brother rejoice at the death of the wicked ruler.

The *Acts of Andrew* reveals the early Christian passion for death, which the Gnostics mocked although they too believed that life on the earth was an error, but one which must be endured. The desire for fellowship with Christ and God, the desire to emulate Christ, and the disparagement of earthly existence endow martyrs with detachment and fearlessness. Not only do martyrs not dread the worst human punishments, they welcome them. The more excruciating the torture, the greater the proof of their power and sacrifice. Although the people weep for martyrs, martyrs do not weep, for they are fulfilled. The desirability of death puts into question the possibility of a truly Christian drama, since the source of the drama, death, is a good rather than a tragic action. Can pity and fear be aroused for a death that is welcomed? It would seem, as with the crucifixion of Jesus himself, that compassion for the victim is not possible when the victim triumphs. Although in most narratives of martyrdom there is a dramatic attempt to have it both ways, the victory of the martyr deprives him or her of a tragic element. As the Gnostics insisted that Jesus was not a man and only appeared to suffer, for which reason compassion for a human victim is impossible, so the actual suffering of human martyrs was similarly undermined by the psychological inversion of their emotions: their passionate yearning for suffering and death.

RECONSTRUCTED TEXT OF THE MARTYRDOM*

And Andrew conversed all night with the brethren and prayed with them and committed them to the Lord; afterwards, early in the morning, the proconsul Aegeates had the prisoner Andrew brought to him and said to him:

"The end of the proceedings against you has come, you stranger, opponent of this present life, and enemy of all my house. For why did you think it good to force your way into places which were no concern of yours and to corrupt a wife who, prior to that, satisfied me? Why have you done this to me and all Achaea? Therefore receive gifts from me as retaliation for what you have done to me."

And he gave orders for him to be beaten with seven scourges. After that he ordered him to be crucified. And he instructed the executioners not to break his legs, intending in that way to make his punishment more severe.

The news now spread abroad throughout all Patrae that the stranger, the righteous man, the slave of Christ, whom Aegeates held prisoner, was being crucified, although he had done nothing wrong; and with one accord they all ran together to the spectacle, angered by the proconsul's impious judgment.

And as the executioners led him to the spot and wished to carry out what they had been ordered, Stratocles, who had learned what was happening, came running and saw the blessed Andrew being dragged along by the executioners like a criminal. And he did not spare them but beat every one of them soundly, ripping their coats from top to bottom, and he tore Andrew from them, crying to them: "You may thank this blessed man that he trained me and taught me to restrain the strength of my anger. Otherwise I would have shown you of what Stratocles and the foul Aegeates are capable. For we have learned to endure what other inflict on us." And taking the apostle by the hand he went with him to the place beside the sea where he was to be crucified.

But the soldiers to whom the proconsul had handed him over left him with Stratocles and, returning, reported to Aegeates: "As we were marching along with Andrew, Stratocles sprang on us, ripped our coats, seized him from us and took him with him; and now as you see here we are." And Aegeates answered them: "Put on other clothes and go and do and carry out what I have commanded you in regard to Andrew who has been condemned. Do not let Stratocles see you and do not gainsay him if he should ask anything from you. For I know his rash nature. He would not even spare me if he were provoked to anger."

And these did just as Aegeates had told them. Stratocles, however, came with the Apostle to the predetermined place. When Andrew now noticed that Stratocles was embittered against Aegeates and was reviling him in a low voice, he said to him: "My child, Stratocles, I wish that for the future you would possess your soul unmoved and would reject such a thing so that you neither inwardly respond to the wicked intentions

---

*Translated by E. Best. From Edgar Hennecke and Wilhelm Schneemelcher, eds. and trans., *New Testament Apocrypha*, vol. 2 (Philadelphia: Westminster Press, 1963), pp. 416–423.

of men nor outwardly be inflamed. For it is becoming that the slave of Jesus should be worthy of Jesus. And there is another thing that I would say to you and the brethren walking with me: Whenever the enemy dares something and finds no one who agrees with him, then he is struck and beaten and completely brought to death because he did not accomplish what he set out to do. Let us, little children, therefore, always hold him before our eyes so that we do not fall asleep and our adversary slay us."

He said these and many other things to Stratocles and to those who were going along with them. Then he came to the place where he was to be crucified. And when he saw the cross set in the sand at the seashore, he left them all and went to the cross and with a strong voice addressed it as if it were a living creature:

"Hail, O cross; indeed may you rejoice. I know well that you will rest in the future because for a long time you have been weary set up awaiting me. I am come to you whom I recognize as mine own; I am come to you, who long for me. I know the mystery for which you have indeed been set up. For you are set up in the cosmos to establish the unstable. And one part of you stretches up to heaven so that you may point out the heavenly logos, the head of all things. Another part of you is stretched out to right and left that you may put to flight the fearful and inimical power and draw the cosmos into unity. And another part of you is set on the earth, rooted in the depths, that you may bring what is on earth and under the earth into contact with what is in Heaven. O cross, tool of salvation of the Most High! O cross, trophy of the victory of Christ over his enemies! O cross, planted on earth and bearing your fruit in Heaven! O name of the cross, filled with all things! Well done, O cross, that you have bound the circumference of the world! Well done, form of understanding, that you have given a form to your own formlessness! Well

done, invisible discipline, that you discipline severely the substance of the knowledge of many gods and drive out from humanity its discoverer! Well done, O cross, that you have clothed yourself with the Lord, and borne as fruit the robber, and called the apostle to repentance, and not thought it beneath you to receive us! But for how long shall I say these things and not be embraced by the cross, that in the cross I may be made to live and through the cross I may go out of this life into common death? Approach, ministers of my joy and servants of Aegeates, and fulfill the desire we both have and bind the lamb to the suffering, the man to the Creator, the soul to the Savior."

The blessed Andrew said this standing on the ground and staring steadfastly towards the cross. Then he besought the brethren that the executioners should come and carry out what they had been commanded. For they were standing at a distance.

And they came and bound his hands and his feet and did not nail him; for they had been so instructed by Aegeates. He wished in this way to torture him as he hung in that he would be eaten alive by dogs. And they left him hanging and departed from him.

And when the crowds that stood around who had been made disciples in Christ by him saw that they did none of these things which were usual in the case of crucifixions, they hoped to hear again something from him. For as he hung he moved his head and smiled. And Stratocles asked him: "Why do you smile, slave of God? Your laughter makes us mourn and weep because we are being deprived of you." And the blessed Andrew answered him: "Shall I not laugh, my child Stratocles, at the vain plot of Aegeates by which he intends to avenge himself on us? We are strangers to him and his designs. He is not capable of hearing. For if he had been capable he would have heard that a man who belongs to Jesus, because he is

461

known to him, is immune from revenge for the future."

Then he spoke a word to them all together—for even the heathen had come running up to join them, complaining about the iniquitous judgment of Aegeates: "You men who are present, and women and children and old people, slaves and free, and all who wish to hear, pay no heed to the vain illusion of this temporal life. Rather, pay heed to us who hang here for the Lord's sake and soon forsake this body; renounce every worldly desire, and scorn the cult of abominable idols; hasten to the true worship of our God who does not lie, and make of yourselves a holy temple ready for the reception of the word."

And the crowds who heard his words did not leave the spot; and Andrew continued speaking further to them for a day and a night. And when on the following day they saw his constancy and steadfastness of soul, his wisdom of spirit and strength of mind, they burned with indignation and rushed with one accord to the judgment seat of Aegeates and cried out: "What, O proconsul, is this judgment of yours? You have condemned wrongly! You have judged unjustly! What wrong has this man done? What transgression has he committed? The whole city is in uproar! You wrong us all! Do not destroy Caesar's city! Hand over to us the righteous man! Give us the holy man! Do not kill a man who is dear to God! Do not destroy a man so gentle and pious! He has hung there for two days and he is still alive. He has eaten nothing but has nourished all of us with his words. And behold, we believe in the God whom he preaches. Take down the righteous man and we will all become philosophers. Set free the ascetic and all of Patrae will have peace. Release the wise man and all Achaea will be freed through him."

When Aegeates at first would not listen and with a wave of his hand commanded the crowd to go away, they were filled with anger and determined to take some action against him. They were about two thousand in number.

When the proconsul saw that they were in some way maddened, he was afraid that he would suffer some terrible misfortune and he got up from the judge's bench and went with them, promising to set Andrew free. Some ran on ahead and told the apostle and the rest of the crowd with him why the proconsul was coming. And the crowd of disciples, among whom were Maximilla, Iphidamia, and Stratocles, rejoiced.

But when Andrew heard it he began to speak: "O the dullness and unbelief and simplicity of those whom I have instructed! How much have we said up to now and yet we have not persuaded our own to flee from the love of earthly things! But they are still bound to them and abide in them and do not wish to leave them. What kind of a friendship and love and habituation to the flesh is this? How long will you be taken up with earthly and temporal things? How long will you fail to understand what is higher than yourselves and not press forward to lay hold of what is there? Leave me now to be put to death in the manner you see, and let no one release me in any way from these bonds. For there has been allotted me this destiny: to depart out of the body and to live with the Lord, with whom I am even being crucified."

And Andrew turned to Aegeates and said to him: "Why have you come, Aegeates, to him who is by nature alien to you? What do you wish again to dare, to contrive, to fetch? What do you want to say to us? That you are come as a penitent to set us free? Even if you were truly repentant I would not come to terms with you. Even if you were to promise me all your possessions I would not stand aloof from myself. Even if you were to say that you yourself were my disciple I would not trust you. Do you set free him who is bound? Or do you rather not set free him that has been set free? Do you not set free him who was known by God who is, in nature, akin to him? Who has received mercy from him and been loved by him? Who is an alien and a stranger to you? Who appeared only to you? I have him with whom I shall be forever. I have him with whom I shall converse through countless ages. To him I depart; to him I hasten, even to him who caused me to recognize you, who said to me: 'Understand Aegeates and his gifts. Do not let that fearful man terrify you, nor let him think that he can get into his power, you who belong to me. He is your enemy—a corrupter, deceiver, destroyer, a madman, a magician, a cheat, a murderer, wrathful, without compassion.' Leave me now, you worker of all iniquity. I, however, and those who are akin in nature to me, hasten towards what is ours, and we leave you to be what you were, although you do not know what you are."

And the proconsul stood there speechless and, as it were, out of his mind. When now the whole city noisily demanded that he free Andrew, and he ventured to approach the cross to unloose him and take him down, Andrew cried out loudly: "Do not permit, Lord, that Andrew who has been bound to your cross, should be set free. Do not give me up, who am on your cross, to the shameless Devil. O Jesus Christ, let not your adversary loose me who hang on your cross. Father, let this little one no longer humiliate him who has known your greatness. Jesus Christ, whom I have seen, whom I have, whom I love, in whom I am and will be, receive me in peace into your eternal tabernacles, that

through my exodus the many who are akin in nature to me may enter to you and may rest in your majesty."

And when he had said these things and had glorified the Lord even more, he gave up the ghost, while all wept and lamented at his departure.

And after the death of the blessed Andrew, Maximilla came with Stratocles without a thought of those who were standing around and took down the body of Andrew. And when the evening came she buried him, after she had given the body the customary attention. And she lived apart from Aegeates because of his savage nature and his wicked manner of life; she chose a holy and retired life which she, full of the love of Christ, spent among the brethren. Aegeates urged her strongly, promising her that she would have control over his affairs, but he was not able to persuade her. Then he got up one night exceptionally early and without any of his household knowing it threw himself down from a great height and died.

But Stratocles, his brother, according to the flesh, was not willing to touch any of his belongings—for the wretched man had died childless—but he said: "May your possessions go with you, Aegeates. For I am satisfied with the Lord Jesus whom I have known through his servant, Andrew." And so the riot of the crowd came to an end, because they rejoiced at the extraordinary and untimely and sudden fall of the impious and lawless Aegeates.

The Acts of Thomas

(Christian-Gnostic Apocrypha)

The *Acts of Thomas* is the only complete version we have of the five romances of the apostles. Early texts exist, both in Greek and Syriac, but the original version was probably written in Syriac, in Edessa, early in the third century A.D.

The *acts* show how the apostles divided the world into five parts. Judas Thomas the Twin was selected to go to India, where he converted King Gundaphar as well as his wife. As a good carpenter Thomas was given funds to build a great palace for the king, but he gave the money away to the poor, built nothing, and spent his time converting the absent king's wife to chastity. When the king returned, he was furious and ordered the apostle to be executed; but when the king's brother returned from death with word that Thomas had built the king "a palace for eternity" in Heaven, he not only spared the apostle's life but converted to Christianity and, like his wife, chose to practice chastity. Characteristic of Syrian Christianity, Thomas preached virginity as a primary virture.

The *Acts of Thomas* bears some similarity to the Gnostic *Gospel of Thomas* from the Nag Hammadi Egyptian texts, which also tells the story of Thomas, Twin of the Messiah. The Acts reflects Gnosticism of Syria in this period, and was evidently known to Mani and his followers, the Manichaeans; as Günther Bornkamm writes, out of its "elements Mani shaped his own doctrine." The narrations are interspersed with sermons, and contain two famous hymns, the "Song of the Bride" in the first Act and the "Hymn of the Pearl" in the ninth. Both poems are overtly Gnostic in their meaning and lexicon. (The "Hymn of the Pearl" is included in the "Wisdom Literature and Poetry" section.) The other narratives are largely Gnostic in character, although some have been more Catholicized as they passed from editor to editor of succeeding manuscripts. Bornkamm very well summarizes the literary character of the *Acts of Thomas (ATh)*:

> The *ATh* are a Christian-Gnostic variety of the Hellenistic-Oriental romance. The elements abundantly employed in this literature may be recognized in a body in the *ATh*, although frequently in a popular and coarser form; the journey of a hero into a foreign wonderland, the linking of his story with that of historical figures, the description of fantastic works of power by the hero and of astonishing prodigies, the partiality for erotic scenes and the developed inclination towards the tendentious, and in addition the stylistic methods of the novel and of the narrative art of fiction.[1]

The most obvious Gnostic feature that distinguishes the *Acts of Thomas* from the other four apocryphal *Praxeis (Acts)* is its heavenly Redeemer myth. The faithful on earth are alien to their world but are intimate with the Redeemer, the physician, the man of light, who works to save light-souls from the darkness. Many of these Gnostic images have parallels in Indian religions, such as the eagle representing the Redeemer. In Indian myth the Garuda eagle, Vishnu's bird, steals the food of immortality. The beautiful "Song of the Bride" introduces the Father of Truth, the Mother of Wisdom (Sophia), and the Living Spirit, thus giving us the Gnostic trinity.

Note

1. Edgar Hennecke, *New Testament Apocrypha*, ed. Wilhelm Schneemelcher, trans. R. McL. Wilson (Philadelphia: Westminster Press, 1966), vol. 2, p. 440.

HOW THE LORD SOLD HIM TO THE MERCHANT ABBAN*

At that time we apostles were all in Jerusalem, Simon called Peter and Andrew, his brother; James, the son of Zebedee, and John, his brother; Philip and Bartholomew; Thomas and Matthew, the publican; James, the son of Alphaeus; Simon the Cananaean; and Judas, the brother of James; and we divided the regions of the world, that each one of us might go to the region which fell to his

---

*Chapters 1–16. All selections from the *Acts of Thomas* are translated by R. McL. Wilson and are from Edgar Hennecke and Wilhelm Schneemelcher, eds. and trans., *New Testament Apocrypha*, vol. 2 (Philadelphia: Westminster Press), pp. 442–461, 471–475, 526–531.

lot, and to the nation to which the Lord sent him. According to lot, India fell to Judas Thomas, who is also called Didymus; but he did not wish to go, saying that through weakness of the flesh he could not travel, and: "How can I, who am a Hebrew, go and preach the truth among the Indians?" And as he considered and said this, the Savior appeared to him by night and said to him: "Fear not, Thomas, go to India and preach the word there, for my grace is with you." But he would not obey and said: "Send me where you will—but somewhere else! For I am not going to the Indians."

And as he thus spoke and thought, it happened that a certain merchant was there who had come from India. His name was Abban and he had been sent by king Gundaphorus, and had received

465

orders from him to buy a carpenter and bring him back to him. Now the Lord saw him walking in the marketplace at noon, and said to him: "Do you wish to buy a carpenter?" He said to him: "Yes." And the Lord said to him: "I have a slave who is a carpenter, and wish to sell him." And when he had said this he showed him Thomas from a distance, and agreed with him for three pounds of uncoined silver, and wrote a deed of sale saying: I, Jesus, the son of Joseph, the carpenter, confirm that I have sold my slave, Judas by name, to you Abban, a merchant of Gundaphorus, the king of the Indians. And when the deed of sale was completed, the Savior took Judas, who is also called Thomas, and led him to the merchant Abban. And when Abban saw him, he said to him: "Is this your master?" And the apostle said: "Yes he is, my Lord." But he said: "I have bought you from him." And the apostle was silent.

On the following morning the apostle prayed and besought the Lord, and said: "I go wherever you command, Lord Jesus; your will be done!" And he went off to Abban, the merchant, carrying with him nothing at all, save only his price. For the Lord had given it to him, saying: "Let your price also be with you, with my grace, wherever you go!" But the apostle found Abban carrying his baggage aboard the ship, and he too began to carry it with him. And when they had embarked on the ship and sat down, Abban questioned the apostle, saying: "What manner of trade do you know?" And he said: "In wood I can make ploughs and yokes and balances, goads and ships and oars for ships, and masts and pulleys; and in stone, pillars and temples and royal palaces." And Abban the merchant said to him: "It is good, for of such a craftsman are we in need." So they began their voyage. They had a favorable wind, and sailed prosperously until they arrived at Andrapolis, a royal city.

Leaving the ship, they went into the city. And lo, sounds of flutes and water-organs and trumpets echoed round about them; and the apostle inquired, saying: "What is this feast which is being celebrated in this city?" The people there said to him: "You too have the gods brought to keep festival in this city. For the king has an only daughter, and now he is giving her to a man in marriage. So it is for the wedding, this rejoicing and this assembly for the feast today which you have seen. And the king has sent out heralds to proclaim everywhere that all should come to the wedding, rich and poor, bond and free, strangers and citizens; but if any man refuse, and come not to the marriage, he shall be accountable to the king." When Abban heard it, he said to the apostle:"Let us also go, then, that we may not give offence to the king, especially since we are strangers." And he said: "Let us go." And after taking quarters at the inn and resting a little they went to the wedding. And the apostle, seeing them all reclining, himself lay down in the midst; and they all looked at him, as at a stranger and one come from a foreign land. But Abban the merchant, as being the master, lay down at another place.

But while they dined and drank, the apostle tasted nothing; so those who were round about him said: "Why did you come here neither eating nor drinking?" But he answered and said to them: "For something greater than food or drink am I come here, for the king's rest and that I may accomplish the king's will. For the heralds proclaim the king's commands and whoever does not listen to the heralds shall be liable to the king's judgment." And when they had dined and drunk, and crowns and scented oils were brought, each one took of the oil, and one anointed his face, another his chin and his beard, another again other parts of his body; but the apostle anointed the crown of his head and smeared a little upon his nostrils, dropped some also into his ears, touched his teeth with it, and carefully anointed the parts about his heart; and the crown that was brought to him, woven of myrtle and other flowers, he took and set upon his head; and he took a branch of a reed in his hand and held it. Now the flute-girl, holding her flute in her hand, was going round all the company and playing; but when she came to the place where the apostle was, she stood over him and played at his head for a long time. Now that flute-girl was by race a Hebrew.

While the apostle was looking at the ground, one of the cup-bearers stretched out his hand and slapped him. But the apostle lifted up his eyes, directed his gaze at the man who had struck him, and said: "My God will forgive you this injury in the world to come, but in this world he will show forth his wonders, and I shall even now see that hand that smote me dragged by dogs." And when he had said this he began to sing this song and to say:

The maiden is the daughter of light.
Upon her stands and rests the majestic effulgence of kings.
Delightful is the sight of her,
radiant with shining beauty.
Her garments are like spring flowers,
and a scent of sweet fragrance is diffused from them.
In the crown of her head the king is established,
feeding with his own ambrosia those who are set under him.
Truth rests upon her head.
By the movement of her feet she shows forth joy.
Her mouth is open, and that becomingly,
for with it she sings loud songs of praise.
Thirty and two are they that sing her praises.   32
Her tongue is like the curtain of the door,
which is flung back for those who enter in.
Like steps her neck,
which the first craftsman wrought, mounts up.
Her two hands make signs and secret patterns, proclaiming the dance of the
    blessed Aeons.
Her fingers open the gates of the city.
Her chamber is full of light,
breathing a scent of balsam and all sweet herbs,
and giving out a sweet smell of myrrh and aromatic leaves.
Within are strewn myrtle branches and all manner of sweet-smelling flowers,
and the portals are adorned with reeds.
Her groomsmen keep her compassed about, whose number is seven,   7
whom she herself has chosen;
and her bridesmaids are seven,
Who dance before her.
Twelve are they in number who serve before her   12
and are subject to her,
having their gaze and look toward the bridegroom,
that by the sight of him they may be enlightened;
and forever shall they be with him in that eternal joy,
and they shall be at that marriage
for which the princes assemble together,
and shall linger over the feasting
of which the eternal ones are accounted worthy;

And they shall put on royal robes
and be arrayed in splendid raiment,
and both shall be in joy and exultation
and they shall glorify the Father of all,
whose proud light they received
and were enlightened by the vision of their Lord,
whose ambrosial food they received,
which has no deficiency at all;
and they drank too of his wine
which gives them neither thirst nor desire;
and they glorified and praised, with the living spirit,
the Father of Truth and the Mother of Wisdom.

And when he had sung and ended this song, all who were present gazed upon him; and he was silent. They saw also his appearance changed, but they did not understand what he said, since he was a Hebrew and what he said was spoken in the Hebrew tongue. The flute-girl alone heard it all, for she was a Hebrew by race; and moving away from him she played to the others, but often looked back and gazed on him. For she loved him greatly, as a man of her own race; moreover, in appearance he was comely above all that were present. And when the flute-girl had quite finished her playing, she sat down opposite him and looked steadily at him. But he looked at no one at all, nor did he pay attention to anyone, but kept his eyes only on the ground, waiting for the time when he might take his departure. But the cup-bearer who had slapped him went down to the well to draw water. And it happened that there was a lion there, and it slew him and left him to lie on the spot, after tearing his limbs to pieces. And immediately dogs seized his limbs, and among them a black dog grasped his right hand in its mouth and carried it into the place where the feast was.

But when they saw it, they were all amazed and inquired which of them was absent. But when it became evident that it was the hand of the cup-bearer who had struck the apostle, the flute-girl smashed her flute and threw it away, and went to the apostle's feet and sat down, saying: "This man is either a god or an apostle of God; for I heard him say to the cup-bearer in Hebrew: 'Even now shall I see the hand that smote me dragged by dogs'—which you also have now seen; for as he said, so did it come to pass." And some believed her, but some did not. But when the king heard it, he came and said to the apostle: "Arise and come with me, and pray for my daughter! For she is my only child, and today I give her in marriage." But the apostle would not go with him, for the Lord was not yet revealed to him there. But the king led him away against his will into the bridal chamber, that he might pray for the bridal pair.

And the apostle, standing, began to pray and to speak thus: "My Lord and my God, the companion of his servants, who guides and directs those who believe in him, the refuge and rest of the oppressed, the hope of the poor and redeemer of the captives, the physician of the souls laid low in sickness and Savior of all creation, who quickens the world to life and strengthens the souls, you know what is to be and also can accomplish it through us; you, Lord, who reveals hidden mysteries and makes manifest words that are secret; you, Lord, who are the planter of the good tree, and by your hands are all good works engendered; you, Lord, are he who is in all and passes through all and dwells in all your works, and manifests in the working of them all; Jesus Christ, son of compassion and perfect Savior; Christ, Son of the living God, the undaunted power which overthrew the enemy, the voice that was heard by the Archons, which shook all their powers; ambassador sent from the height who did descend even to Hell, who having opened the doors did bring up thence those who for many ages had been shut up in the treasury of darkness, and show them the way that leads up to the height; I pray you, Lord Jesus, as I bring to you my supplication for these young people, that you do for them the things that help and are useful and profitable." And after laying his hands upon them and saying: "The Lord shall be with you," he left them in that place and departed.

The king required the attendants to go out of the bridal chamber. And when all had gone out and the doors were shut, the bridegroom lifted up the veil of the bridal chamber, that he might bring the bride to him. And he saw the Lord Jesus in the likeness of the apostle Judas Thomas, who shortly before had blessed them and departed from them, conversing with the bride, and he said to him: "Did you not go out before them all? How can you now be found here?" But the Lord said to him: "I am not Judas who is also Thomas; I am his brother."

And the Lord sat down upon the bed and bade them also sit on the chairs, and began to say to them: "Remember, my children, what my brother said to you, and to whom he commended you; and know this, that if you abandon this filthy intercourse you become holy temples, pure and free from afflictions and pains both manifest and hidden, and you will not be girt about with cares for life and for children, the end of which is destruction. But if you get many children, then for their sakes you become robbers and avaricious, people who flay orphans and defraud widows, and by so doing you subject yourselves to the most grievous punishments. For the majority of children become unprofitable, possessed by demons, some openly and some in secret; for they become either lunatic or half-withered, consumptive or crippled or deaf or dumb or paralytic or stupid. Even if they are healthy, again will they be unserviceable, performing useless and abominable deeds; for they are caught either in adultery or in murder or in theft or in unchastity, and by all these you will be afflicted. But if you obey, and keep your souls pure unto God, you shall have living children whom these hurts do not touch, and shall be without care, leading an undisturbed life without grief or anxiety, waiting to receive that incorruptible and true marriage as is befitting for you, and in it you shall be groomsmen entering into that bridal chamber which is full of immortality and light."

But when the young people heard this, they believed the Lord and gave themselves entirely to him, and refrained from the filthy passion, and so remained throughout the night in that place. And the Lord departed from them, saying: "The grace of the Lord shall be with you!" When morning broke, the king came to meet them, and after furnishing the table brought it in before the bridegroom and the bride; and he found them sitting opposite one another, the bride with her face unveiled and the bridegroom very cheerful. But her mother came in and said to the bride: "Why do you sit thus, child, and are not ashamed, but behave as if you had lived a long time with thine own husband?" And her father said: "Is it because of your great love for your husband that you do not even veil yourself?"

The bride in answer said: "Truly, father, I am in great love, and I pray to my Lord that the love which I experienced this night may remain with me, and I will ask for the husband of whom I have learned today. But I do not veil myself because the mirror of shame is taken from me; and I am no longer ashamed or abashed, because the work of shame and bashfulness has been removed far from me. And the reason that I am not alarmed is because alarm did not remain with me. And I am cheerful and filled with joy because the day of joy was not disturbed. And the reason that I have set at naught this man, and this marriage which passes away from before my eyes is because I am bound in another marriage. And that I have had no intercourse with a short-lived husband, the end of which is remorse and bitterness of soul, is because I am yoked with the true man."

And while the bride was saying yet more than this, the bridegroom answered and said: "I thank you, Lord, who through the stranger was proclaimed and found in us; who has removed me from corruption and sown in me life; who freed me from this sickness, hard to heal and hard to cure and abiding forever, and implanted in me sober health; who showed yourself to me and revealed to me all my condition in which I am; who redeemed me from the fall and led me to the better, and freed me from things transitory but counted me worthy of those that are immortal and everlasting; who humbled yourself to me and my smallness, that setting me beside your greatness you might unite me with you; who did not withhold your mercy from me that was ready to perish, but showed me to seek myself and to recognize who I was and who and how I now am, that I may become again what I was; whom I did not know, but you yourself did seek me out; of whom I was unaware, but you yourself took me to you; whom I have perceived, and now cannot forget; whose love ferments within me, and of whom I cannot speak as I ought, but what I can say about him is short and very little and does not correspond to his glory; but he does not blame me when I make bold to say to him even what I do not know; for it is for love of him that I say this."

But when the king heard this from the bridegroom and the bride he rent his garments and said to those who stood near

him: "Go out quickly and go through all the city, and seize and bring to me that man, the sorcerer who by an evil chance is in this city. For I brought him with my own hands into my house, and told him to pray over my most unfortunate daughter. And whosoever finds and brings him to me, to him do I give all that he may ask of me." So they departed and went about in search of him, and did not find him; for he had set sail. They went also into the inn where he had lodged, and there they found the flute-girl weeping and distressed, because he had not taken her with him. But when they told her what had happened in the case of the young people, she was very glad when she heard it, and setting aside her grief she said: "Now have I too found rest here!" And rising up, she went to them, and stayed with them a long time, until they had taught the king also. And many of the brethren also gathered there, until they heard a report about the apostle, that he had landed in the cities of India and was teaching there. And they went off and joined him.

CONCERNING HIS COMING TO KING GUNDAPHORUS*

But when the apostle came to the cities of India with Abban the merchant, Abban went off to salute King Gundaphorus, and reported to him concerning the carpenter whom he had brought with him. The king was glad, and commanded that he should come to him. So when he came the king said to him: "What kind of trade do you understand?" The apostle said to him: "Carpentry and building." The king said to him: "What craftsmanship, then, do you know in wood, and what in stone?" The

_____

*Chapters 17–29.

470

apostle said: "In wood, ploughs, yokes, balances, pulleys, and ships and oars and masts; and in stone, pillars, temples and royal palaces." And the king said: "Will you build me a palace?" And he answered: "Yes, I will build and finish it; for this is why I came, to build and work as a carpenter."

And the king took him and went out of the gates of the city, and began to discuss with him on the way the building of the palace and how the foundations should be laid, until they came to the place where he wanted the building to be. And he said: "I wish the building to be here." And the apostle said: "Yes, for this place is suitable for the building." But the place was wooded, and there was much water there. So the king said: "Begin to build." But he said: "I cannot begin to build now at this season." And the king said: "When can you?" And he said: "I will begin in November and finish in April." But the king said in astonishment: "Every building is built in summer, but you can build and establish a palace even in winter?" And the apostle said: "So it ought to be, and there is no other way." And the king said: "Well then, if this is your resolve, draw me a plan how the work is to be, since I shall come back here only after some time." And the apostle took a reed and drew, measuring the place; and the doors he set toward the east, to face the light, and the windows to the west towards the winds, and the bakehouse he made to be to the south, and the aqueduct for the service to the north. But when the king saw it, he said to the apostle: "Truly, you are a craftsman, and it is fitting for you to serve kings." And leaving much money with him, he departed.

And, at appointed times, he used to send him money and what was necessary, both for his own sustenance and for that of the other workmen. But he took it all and dispensed it, going about the towns and the villages round about, distributing it and bestowing alms on the poor and afflicted, and he gave them re-lief, saying: "The king knows that he will receive a royal recompense, but the poor must for the present be refreshed." After this the king sent an ambassador to the apostle, writing to him thus: "Show me what you have done, or what I should send you, or what you require." The apostle sent to him, saying: "The palace is built, and only the roof remains." When the king heard this, he sent him again gold and uncoined silver, writing: "If the palace is built, let it be roofed!" But the apostle said to the Lord: "I thank you, Lord, in every respect, that you for a short time did die that I might live eternally in you, and that you did sell me in order to deliver many through me." And he did not cease from teaching and re-freshing the afflicted, saying: "The Lord has dispensed this to you, and himself provides to each his food. For he is the nourisher of the orphans and supporter of the widows, and to all that are afflicted he is relief and rest."

But when the king came to the city he inquired of his friends concerning the palace which Judas who is also Thomas was building for him. But they said to him: "Neither has he built a palace, nor has he done anything else of what he promised to do, but he goes about the towns and villages, and if he has anything he gives it all to the poor, and he teaches a new God and heals the sick and drives out demons and does many other wonderful things; and we think he is a magician. But his works of compassion, and the healings which are wrought by him without reward, and moreover his simplicity and kindness and the quality of his faith, show that he is righteous or an apostle of the new God whom he preaches. For continually he fasts and prays, and eats only bread with salt, and his drink is water, and he wears one garment whether in fine weather or in foul winter, and takes nothing from anyone, and what he has he gives to others." When he heard this, the king smote his face with his hands, shaking his head for a long time.

And he sent for the merchant who had brought him, and for the apostle, and said to him: "Have you built me the palace?" And he said: "Yes, I have built it." The king said: "Then when shall we go and see it?" But he answered him and said: "Now you cannot see it, but when you depart this life, you shall see it." But the king, in great wrath, commanded both the merchant and Judas to be put in bonds and cast into prison until he should investigate and learn to whom the king's money had been given, and so destroy him together with the merchant. But the apostle went rejoicing into the prison, and said to the merchant: "Fear nothing, but only believe in the God who is preached by me, and you shall be freed from this world but from the age to come shall obtain life."

Now the king was considering with what manner of death he should destroy them. But when he had resolved to flay them alive and then burn them with fire, in the same night Gad, the king's brother, fell sick, and because of the pain and disappointment which the king had suffered he was greatly depressed. And he sent for the king and said to him: "My brother, the king, my house and my children I commend to you. For I have been grieved on account of the despiteful usage that has befallen you and behold, I am dying, and if you do not come down with vengeance upon the head of that magician, you will give my soul no rest in Hades." But the king said to his brother: "The whole night through I was considering how I should put him to death; and this have I resolved, to flay him live and then burn him with fire, both him and with him the merchant who brought him."

And as they conversed, the soul of Gad his brother departed. The king mourned Gad deeply, for he loved him greatly, and commanded him to be buried in royal and costly apparel. But when this happened, angels took the soul of Gad, the king's brother, and carried it up into Heaven, showing him the places there and the dwellings and asking him: "In what kind of place would you live?" But when they drew near to the building of Thomas the apostle, which he built for the king, Gad, when he saw it, said to the angels: "I pray you, sirs, allow me to live in one of these lower apartments." But they said to him: "You cannot live in this building." And he said: "Why?" They said to him: "This palace is the one which that Christian built for your brother." But he said: "I pray you, sirs, allow me to go to my brother, that I may buy this palace from him. For my brother does not know of what kind it is, and will sell it to me."

Then the angels let Gad's soul go. And while they were putting the grave clothes on him, his soul entered into him; and he said to those who stood around him: "Call to me my brother, that I may ask of him one request." So at once they brought the good news to the king, saying: "Your brother is alive again!" The king sprang up and came with a great crowd to his brother, and going in he stood by his bed as if stupefied, unable to speak to him. But his brother said: "I know and am persuaded, brother, that if anyone asked of you the half of your kingdom, you would have given it for my sake. Therefore, I beseech you to grant me one favor, that you sell me what I ask from you." But the king said in answer: "And what is it that you ask me to sell you?" But he said: "Convince me by an oath that you will grant it me." And the king swore to him: "Whatever of my possessions you ask for thyself, I give you." And he said to him: "Sell me that palace which you have in Heaven." And the king said: "Whence should I have a palace in Heaven?" But he said: "The one that Christian built for you, who is now in prison—the man the merchant brought you after buying him from one Jesus. I mean that Hebrew slave whom you wished to punish, as having suffered some deception at his hand—against whom I too was vexed, and died, and now I am alive again."

Then the king, considering the matter, understood his words concerning the eternal goods which were more excellent for him and which he was to receive, and said: "That palace I cannot sell you, but I pray that I may enter it and live in it, and be counted worthy to belong to its inhabitants. But if you truly wish to buy such a palace, behold, the man is alive, and will build you one better than that." And immediately he sent and brought the apostle out of the prison, and the merchant who had been shut up with him, saying: "I entreat you, as a man entreating the servant of God, to pray for me and beseech him whose servant you are, that he forgive me and overlook the things that I have done against you, or thought to do, and that I may become a worthy inhabitant of that dwelling for which I did not labor at all, but you built it for me laboring alone, the grace of your God working with you, and that I too may become a servant, and serve this God whom you proclaim." And his brother also fell down at the apostle's feet and said: "I pray you and implore before your God, that I may become worthy of this ministry and service, and that it may be my lot to be worthy of the things shown to me by his angels."

But the apostle, possessed with joy, said: "I praise you, Lord Jesus, that you have revealed your truth in these men. For you alone are the God of truth, and no other; and you are he who knows all that is unknown to the many; you, Lord, are he who in all things shows mercy and forbearance to men. For men, because of the error that is in them, forsook you, but you did not forsake them. And now, as I beseech and supplicate you, receive the king and his brother and unite them with your flock, cleansing them with your washing and anointing them with your oil from the error which surrounds them. Preserve them also from the wolves, leading them in your pas-

tures. Give them drink from your ambrosial spring which neither is turbid nor dries up. For they pray to you and implore and desire to become your ministers and servants, and for this cause they are content even to be persecuted by your enemies, and for your sake to be hated by them and be despitefully used and put to death, even as you, for our sakes, suffered all these things that you might preserve us, who are Lord and truly a good shepherd. But do grant them that they may have confidence in you alone, and obtain the help which comes from you and hope of their salvation, which they expect from you alone, and that they may be established in your mysteries and receive of your graces and gifts the perfect good, and may flourish in your service, and bring forth fruit to perfection in your Father."

Being now well disposed to the apostle, King Gundaphorus and his brother Gad followed him, departing from him not at all and themselves supplying those who were in need, giving to all and refreshing all. And they besought him that they also might now receive the seal of the word, saying to him: "Since our souls are at leisure and we are zealous for God, give us the seal! For we have heard you say that the God whom you preach knows his own sheep by his seal." But the apostle said to them: "I also rejoice and pray you to receive this seal, and to share with me in this eucharist and feast of blessing of the Lord, and be made perfect in it. For this is the Lord and God of all, Jesus Christ whom I preach, and he is the Father of truth in whom I have taught you to believe." And he commanded them to bring oil, that through the oil they might receive the seal. So they brought the oil, and lit many lamps; for it was night.

And the apostle rose up and sealed them. But the Lord was revealed to them by a voice, saying: "Peace be with you, brethren!" But they only heard his voice, but his form they did not see; for they had not yet received the additional sealing of the seal. And the apostle took the oil and, pouring it on their heads, anointed and chrismed them, and began to say:

Come, holy name of Christ that is above every name;
Come, power of the most high and perfect compassion;
Come, highest gift;
Come, compassionate mother;
Come, fellowship of the male;
Come, you that reveals the hidden mysteries;
Come, mother of the seven houses, that your rest may be in the eighth house;
Come, elder messenger of the five members—understanding, thought, prudence, consideration, reasoning,
Communicate with these young men!
Come, Holy Spirit, and purify their reins and their heart
And give them the added seal in the name of Father and Son and Holy Spirit.

And when they had been sealed, there appeared to them a young man carrying a blazing torch, so that the very lamps were darkened at the onset of its light. And going out, he vanished from their sight. But the apostle said to the Lord: "Beyond our comprehension, Lord, is your light, and we are not able to bear it; for it is greater than our sight." But when dawn came and it was light, he broke bread and made them partakers in the eucharist of Christ. And they rejoiced and were glad. And many others also, believing, were added to the faithful and came into the refuge of the Savior.

But the apostle did not cease preaching and saying to them: "Men and women, boys and girls, youths and maids, vigorous and aged, whether you are slaves or free, abstain from fornication and avarice and the service of the belly; for in these three heads all lawlessness is comprised. For fornication blinds the mind and darkens the eyes of the soul, and is a hindrance to the right ordering of the body, turning the whole man to weakness and throwing the whole body into sickness. Insatiate desire brings the soul into fear and shame, since it is within the body and plunders the goods of others, and harbors this suspicion, that if it restore the goods of others to the owners it will be put to shame. And the service of the belly plunges the soul into cares and anxieties and sorrows, since it becomes anxious lest it come to be in want, and reaches out for what is far from it. If then you escape from these, you become free from care and sorrow and fear, and there remains with you that which was said by the Savior: Be not anxious for the morrow, for the morrow will take care of itself. Remember also that word which was spoken before: Look at the ravens and consider the birds of the heaven, that they neither sow nor reap nor gather into barns, and God provides for them. How much more for you, O you of little faith? But wait for his coming, and set your hope in him, and believe in his name. For he is the judge of living and dead, and he gives to each one according to his works. And at his coming and later appearance no man has any word of excuse when he is about to be judged by him, as if he had not heard. For his heralds are proclaiming to the four regions of the world. Repent, then, and believe the gospel, and receive a yoke of meekness and a light burden, that you may live and not die! These things obtain, these keep. Come out from the darkness, that the light may receive you! Come to him who is truly good, that you

474

may receive grace from him and lay up his sign in your souls."

When he had said this, some of the bystanders said to him: "It is time for the creditor to receive the debt." But he said to them: "The creditor always wishes to receive more than enough, but let us give him what is needful." And when he had blessed them he took bread and oil and herbs and salt, and blessed and gave to them; but he himself continued in his fasting, for the Lord's day was about to dawn. As he slept in the following night, the Lord came and stood at his head and said: "Thomas, rise up early and bless them all, and after the prayer and service go down the eastern road two miles, and there I will show in you my glory. For because of your going many will take refuge in me, and you shall demonstrate the nature and power of the enemy." And rising up from sleep, he said to the brethren who were with him: "Children and brethren, the Lord wishes to accomplish something through me today. But let us pray and entreat him, that nothing may become a hindrance for us towards him, but that as at all times so now it may come to pass through us according to his will and desire." And when he had said this, he laid his hands upon them and blessed them. And breaking the bread of the eucharist, he gave it to them, saying: "This eucharist shall be to you for compassion and mercy, and not for judgment and requital." And they said: "Amen."

CONCERNING THE SERPENT*

And the apostle went out to go where the Lord had commanded him; and when he was near the second milestone and had turned aside a little from the road, he saw lying there the body of a

*Chapters 30–33.

comely youth, and said: "Lord, was it for this that you brought me out here, that I might see this temptation? Your will be done, then, as you will." And he began to pray and say: "O Lord, judge of living and dead (Acts 10:42), of the living who stand by and the dead who lie here, Lord of all and Father—but Father not of the souls that are in bodies, but of those that are gone out; for of the souls that are in pollutions you are Lord and judge—come in this hour in which I call upon you, and show your glory toward this man who lies here." And turning to those who followed him, he said: "This thing has not happened to no purpose, but the enemy has been at work, and has wrought this that he may make an attack thereby; and you see that he has made use of no other form and wrought through no other creature than that which is his subject."

And when he had said this a great serpent came out of a hole, darting his head and lashing his tail on the ground, and said with a loud voice to the apostle: "I will say before you for what reason I slew him, for to this end have you come, to put my works to shame." And the apostle said: "Yes, speak on." And the serpent: "There is a certain beautiful woman in this village over against us. And as she once passed by my place, I saw her and fell in love with her, and following her I kept watch on her. And I found this young man kissing her, and he had intercourse with her and did other shameful things with her. Now it would be easy for me to disclose them before you, but I dare not do it. For I know that you are the twin brother of Christ, and do ever abolish our nature. But not wishing to disquiet her, I did not kill him in that very hour, but watched for him, and as he came by in the evening I smote and slew him, the more especially since he dared to do this on the Lord's day." But the apostle questioned him, saying: "Tell me of what seed and what race you are."

And he said to him: "I am a reptile of

reptile nature, the baleful son of a baleful father; I am son of him who hurt and smote the four standing brothers; I am son of him who sits upon the throne and has power over the creation which is under Heaven, who takes his own from those who borrow; I am son of him who girds the sphere about; and I am a kinsman of him who is outside the ocean, whose tail is set in his own mouth; I am he who entered through the fence into Paradise and said to Eve all the things my father charged me to say to her; I am he who kindled and inflamed Cain to slay his own brother, and because of me thorns and thistles sprang up on the earth; I am he who hurled the angels down from above, and bound them in lusts for women, that earthborn children might come from them and I fulfill my will in them; I am he who hardened Pharaoh's heart, that he might slay the children of Israel and enslave them in a yoke of cruelty; I am he who led the multitude astray in the wilderness, when they made the calf; I am he who inflamed Herod and kindled Caiaphas to the false accusation of the lie before Pilate; for this was fitting for me; I am he who kindled Judas and bribed him to betray Christ to death; I am he who inhabits and possesses the abyss of Tartarus, but the Son of God did me wrong against my will, and chose out his own from me; I am a kinsman of him who is to come from the east, to whom also is given power to do what he will on the earth."

When the serpent had said this, in the hearing of all the crowd,[1] the apostle lifted up his voice on high and said: "Cease now, most shameless one, and be put to shame and entirely done to death! For your end, destruction, is come. And do not dare to say what you have wrought through those who have become subject to you. I command you in the name of that Jesus who contends with you until now for the men who are his own, that you suck out your poison which you put into this man, and draw it out and take it from him." But the serpent said: "Not yet is the time of our end come, as you have said. Why do you compel me to take what I have put into this man and die before the time? For indeed, if my father draw forth and suck out what he cast into the creation, then is his end." But the apostle said to him: "Show now the nature of your father!" And the serpent came forward and set his mouth against the young man's wound and sucked the gall out of it. And, little by little, the young man's color, which was as purple, became white, but the serpent swelled up. But when the serpent had drawn up all the gall into himself, the young man sprang up and stood, then ran and fell at the apostle's feet. But the serpent, being swollen, burst and died, and his poison and gall poured out; and in the place where his poison poured out there came a great chasm, and that serpent was swallowed up. And the apostle said to the king and his brother: "Send workmen and fill up that place, and lay foundations and build houses on top, that it may become a dwelling place for the strangers."

CONCERNING THE YOUTH WHO HAD MURDERED THE MAIDEN*

Now there was a certain young man who had wrought a lawless deed. As he came forward and took the Eucharist with his mouth, his two hands withered up, so that he could no longer put them to his mouth. When those who were present saw him, they informed the apostle of what had happened, and calling him the apostle said to him: "Tell me, child, and be not ashamed: what was it that you did? For the Lord's Eucharist has convicted you of an evil deed. For this gift, passing into many, brings healing, especially to those who approach in faith and love, but you it has withered away, and what

_____

*Chapters 51–57.

476

has happened has not taken place without some action on your part." But the young man, convicted by the Lord's Eucharist, came and fell at the apostle's feet and besought him, saying: "An evil deed has been wrought by me, although I thought to do something good. I loved a woman who lives outside the city in an inn, and she also loved me. But when I heard the sermon from you and believed that you proclaim the living God, I came forward and received the seal from you with the others. But you said: 'Whoever shall unite in the impure union, and especially in adultery, he shall not have life with the God whom I preach.' Since, then, I loved her greatly, I besought her and tried to persuade her to become my consort in chastity and pure conduct, which you yourself teach; but she would not. Since she was unwilling, then, I took a sword and slew her; for I could not see her commit adultery with another."

When the apostle heard this, he said: "O insensate union, how do you run to shamelessness! O desire not to be checked, how did you move this man to do this! O work of the serpent, how do you rage in your own!" But the apostle commanded water to be brought to him in a basin. And when the water was brought, he said: "Come, waters from the living waters, the existent from the existent and sent to us; rest that was sent to us from the Rest; power of salvation that comes from that power which conquers all things and subjects them to its own will—come and dwell in these waters, that the gift of the Holy Spirit may be perfectly fulfilled in them!" And he said to the young man: "Go, wash your hands in these waters!" And when he had washed, they were restored, and the apostle said to him: "Do you believe in our Lord Jesus, that he is able to do all things?" And he said: "Though I be but the least, I believe. But I wrought this deed thinking to do something good; for I besought her, as I told you, to keep herself chaste, but she would not obey me."

But the apostle said to him: "Come, let us go to the inn where you committed this deed, and let us see what has come to pass!" And the young man went before the apostle on the way; and when they arrived in the inn they found her lying. And seeing her the apostle was despondent, for she was a comely girl. And he commanded her to be brought into the middle of the inn. And they laid her on a bed, carried her out, and laid her in the middle of the court of the inn. And the apostle laid his hand upon her, and began to say: "Jesus, who appears to us at all times—for this is your will, that we should ever seek you, and you yourself have given us this right to ask and to receive, and not only did you grant this, but also you taught us to pray, you who are not seen with our bodily eyes, but are never hidden at all from those of our soul; your form indeed is hidden, but your works are manifest to us; and by your many works we have come to know you, as we are able, but you yourself have given to us your gifts without measure, saying: Ask, and it shall be given you, seek and you shall find, knock and it shall be opened unto you. We pray now, since we have a fear because of our sins. But we ask you not for wealth, neither gold nor silver nor possessions nor any other of the things which come of the earth and return again to the earth, but this we beseech of you and entreat, that in your holy name you raise up her who lies here by your power, to your glory and the confirmation of the faith of them that stand by."

And he said to the young man, after sealing him: "Go, take her hand and say to her: I with my hands did slay you with iron, and with my hands by faith in Jesus I raise you up." So the young man went and stood beside her, saying: "I have believed in you, Christ Jesus." And looking at Judas Thomas the apostle, he said to him: "Pray for me, that my Lord, upon whom I call, may come to my help." And laying his hand upon her hand he said: "Come, Lord Jesus Christ; unto her grant life, and to me the earnest of your faith!'' And immediately when he drew on her hand she sprang up and sat, looking on the great crowd that stood by. She saw also the apostle standing opposite her, and leaving the bed and springing up she fell at his feet and caught hold of his garments, saying: ''I pray you, my Lord, where is that other who was with you, who did not leave me to remain in that dreadful and cruel place, but delivered me to you, saying: Take this woman, that she may be made perfect, and hereafter be gathered to her place?''

But the apostle said to her: ''Relate to us where you have been.'' And she answered: ''You who were with me, to whom also I was delivered, do you wish to hear?'' And she began to say: ''A man received me, hateful of countenance, entirely black, and his clothing exceedingly dirty. And he led me to a place in which there were many chasms, and much ill odor and a hateful vapor was given off. And he made me look down into each chasm, and I saw in the first chasm a flaming fire, and wheels of fire were running hither and thither, and souls were hung upon those wheels, dashed against each other. And there was a cry there and a very great lamentation, but there was none to deliver. And that man said to me: 'These souls are kindred to you, and in the days of reckoning they were delivered for punishment and destruction. And then, when the chastisement of each is ended, others are brought in their stead, and likewise these again to another chasm. These are they who perverted the intercourse of man and woman.' And when I looked, I saw newborn infants heaped one upon another and struggling with one another as they lay upon them. And he answered and said to me: 'These are their children, and therefore are they set here for a testimony against them.'

And he led me to another chasm, and looking in I saw mire, and worms welling up, and souls wallowing there, and heard a great gnashing break out thence from among them. And that man said to me: 'These are the souls of women who forsook their husbands and men who left their wives and committed adultery with others, and have been brought to this torment.' Another chasm he showed me, and when I looked into it I saw souls, some hanging by the tongue, some by the hair, some by the hands, some by the feet head downwards, and all reeking with smoke and brimstone. Concerning these, that man who was with me answered me: 'These souls which are hung by the tongue are slanderers, and such as utter lying and infamous words and are not ashamed. And those that are hung by the hair are the shameless who have no modesty at all and go about in the world bareheaded. And those which are hung by the hands, these are they who took away and stole the goods of others, and never gave anything to the needy or gave help to the afflicted, and did this because they wished to take everything, and paid no heed whatever to justice and to the law. And those who hang upside down by the feet, these are they who lightly and eagerly run upon evil ways and disorderly paths, not visiting the sick and not escorting them that depart this life. And for this cause each soul receives what was done by it.'

Leading me away again he showed me a cave, very dark and breathing out a great stench, and many souls looked out thence, wishing to get something of the air; but their guards did not allow them to look out. And he who was with me said: 'This is the prison of those souls which you did see. For when they have fulfilled their punishments for what each one did, others later succeed them. And some are entirely consumed, and some are handed over to other punishments. Now those who guarded the souls that were in the dark cave said to the man who had received me: 'Give her to us that we may take her in to the others until the time comes for her to be handed over for punishment.' But he answered them: 'I do not give her to you, for I fear him who delivered her to me; for I was not commanded to leave her here. I am taking her back with me until I receive an order concerning her.' And he took me and led me to another place where there were men being tortured cruelly. But he who is like you delivered me to you, saying to you: 'Take her, for she is one of the sheep that have gone astray.' And received by you I am now before you. I beseech you, therefore, and entreat that I may not depart into those places of punishment which I saw."

MARTYRDOM OF THE HOLY AND ESTEEMED APOSTLE THOMAS*

And after these things Judas went away to be imprisoned. And not only so, but Tertia and Mygdonia and Marcia went away to be imprisoned. And Judas said to them:

"My daughters, handmaids of Jesus Christ, hear me in this my last day on which I shall accomplish my word among you, to speak no more with you in the body. For behold, I am taken up to my Lord Jesus who had mercy on me, who humbled himself even to my littleness and led me to a service of majesty, and counted me worthy to become his servant. But I rejoice that the time is near for my release from hence, that I may go and receive my reward in the end. For righteous is my requiter; he knows how recompense must be made. For he is not grudging, but he is lavish with his goods, since he is confident that his possessions are unfailing. I am not Jesus, but a servant of Jesus. I am not Christ, but I am a minister of Christ. I am not the Son of God, but I pray to be counted worthy with him. But abide in the faith of Jesus Christ! Wait for the hope of the Son of God! Do not shrink in afflictions,

*Chapters 159–170.

neither be doubtful when you see me insulted and imprisoned and dying. For in these I fulfill what has been appointed for me by the Lord. For if I wished not to die, you know that I am able. But this apparent death is not death, but deliverance and release from the body.

"And this I shall await gladly, that I may go and receive that fair one, the merciful. For I am altogether worn out in his service, and what I have done by his grace, and now he will certainly not forsake me. But see to it that that one come not upon you, who comes in by stealth and divides the thoughts and casts into doubt; for stronger is he whom you have received. Look then for his coming, that when he comes he may receive you; for you shall see him when you depart."

But when he had completed his word to them, he went into the dark house, and said: "My Savior, who endured much for our sakes, let these doors become as they were, and let them be sealed with their seals!' And leaving the women, he went away to be shut up. But they were grieved and wept, since they knew that king Misdaeus would destroy him.

But Judas, when he returned, found the guards fighting and saying: "What sin have we committed against that sorcerer, that by magic art he opened the doors of the prison, and wishes all the prisoners to escape? But let us go and inform the king, and let us tell him also about his wife and son!" But while the jailers were saying this, Judas was listening in silence. And as soon as day broke they arose and went off to king Misdaeus, and said: "Lord, release that sorcerer, or command him to be kept in custody somewhere else. For twice has your good fortune kept the prisoners together. Though we shut the doors at the proper time, yet when we awake we find them open. And moreover, your wife and your son, together with those others, do not stay away from the man." When he heard this, the king went to inspect the seals which he had set upon the doors; and he found the seals as they were before. And he said to the jailers: "Why do you lie? For indeed these seals are still intact. And how say you, that Tertia and Mygdonia went into the prison?" And the guards said: "We told you the truth."

After this the king went into the judgment hall and sent for Judas. But when he came, they stripped him and girded him with a girdle, and set him before the king. And Misdaeus said to him: "Are you a slave or a free man?" And Judas said: "I am a slave, but you have no authority over me at all." And Misdaeus said: "How did you come as a runaway to this country?" And Judas said: "I came here to save many, and that I might at your hands depart from this body." Misdaeus says to him: "Who is your master? And what is his name? And of what country?" "My Lord," says Thomas, "is my master and yours, since he is Lord of Heaven and earth." And Misdaeus said: "What is his name?" Judas said: "You cannot hear his true name at this time, but the name which was bestowed upon him for a season is Jesus, the Christ." And Misdaeus said: "I have not hastened to destroy you, but have restrained myself. But you have made addition to your deeds, so that thy sorceries are reported in all the land. But now I will so deal with you that your sorceries may perish with you, and our nation be cleansed from them." And Judas said: "These sorceries, as you call them, shall never depart from hence."

During these words Misdaeus was considering in what manner he should put him to death; for he was afraid of the crowd which stood around, since many believed him, even some of the leading people. And rising up, he took Judas with him outside the city; and a few armed soldiers followed him. But the crowds supposed that the king wished to learn something from him; and they stood and observed him. But when they had advanced three stadia, he handed him over to four soldiers and one of the officers, commanding them to take him to the mountain and despatch him with spears. And he himself returned to the city.

The bystanders ran to Judas, eager to snatch him away. But he was led away, the soldiers escorting him two on either side, holding their spears, and the officer holding his hand fast and leading him. And as they went, Judas said: "O your hidden mysteries, which even to life's end are fulfilled in us! O riches of your grace, who do not allow that we should feel the sufferings of the body! For behold, how four have laid hold of me, since from the four elements I came into being! And one leads me, since I belong to one, to whom I depart. But now I learn that my Lord, since he was of one, to whom I depart and who is ever invisibly with me, was smitten by one; but I, since I am of four, am smitten by four."

But when they came to the place where they were to slay him, Judas said to those who held him: "Listen to me now at least, because I stand at the point of departure from the body! And let not the eyes of your understanding be darkened, nor your ears stopped that they do not hear! Believe in the God whom I preach! Released from the arrogance of the heart, conduct yourselves in a manner of life befitting free men, and in esteem among men and in life with God!"

But to Vazan he said: "Son of the earthly king, but servant of Jesus Christ, give to those who attend on the command of king Misdaeus what is due, that I may be released by them and go and pray." And when Vazan had persuaded the soldiers, Judas turned to prayer; and it was this: "My Lord and my God, and hope and redeemer and leader and guide in all the lands, be with all who serve you, and lead me today, since I come to you! Let none take my soul, which I have committed unto you. Let not the tax collectors see me, and let not the exactors lay false charge against me! Let not the serpent see me, and let not the children of the dragon hiss me! Behold, Lord, I have fulfilled your work and accomplished your command. I have become a slave; therefore, today do I receive freedom. Do you now give it to me completely! But this I say not as one doubting, but that they may hear who ought to hear."

And when he had prayed, he said to the soldiers: "Come and fulfill the command of him who sent you!" And at once the four smote him and slew him. But all the brethren wept. And wrapping him in fine robes and many fine linen cloths, they laid him in the tomb in which the kings of old were buried.

But Siphor and Vazan were unwilling to go down into the city, and after spending the whole day there they passed the night there also. And Judas appeared to them, and said: "I am not here. Why do you sit here and watch over me? For I have gone up and received what was hoped for. But arise and walk, and after no great time you shall be gathered to me." But Misdaeus and Charisius brought great pressure to bear on Tertia and Mygdonia, but did not persuade them to depart from their belief. And Judas appeared and said to them: "Forget not the former things! For Jesus the holy and living will himself help you." And those about Misdaeus and Charisius, being unable to persuade them, allowed them to live according to their own will. And all the brethren there used to assemble together; for Judas on the mountain had made Siphor a presbyter and Vazan a deacon, when he was being led off to die. But the Lord helped them, and increased the faith through them.

But after a long time had passed it befell that one of Misdaeus' sons was possessed by a demon; and since the demon was stubborn, no one was able to heal him. But Misdaeus pondered and said: "I will go and open the tomb, and take one of the bones of the apostle of God, and fasten it upon my son, and I know that he will be healed." And he went away to do what he had in mind. And Judas appeared to him and said: "Since you did not believe in the living, how do you wish to believe in the dead? But fear not! Jesus the Christ, because of his great goodness, acts humanely towards you." But Misdaeus did not find the bones; for one of the brethren had stolen them away, and carried them to the regions of the west. But taking dust from the place where the bones of the apostle had lain, he attached it to his son and said: "I believe in you, Jesus, now when he has left me, whoever confuses men that they may not look upon your rational light." And when his son was in this manner restored to health, Misdaeus came together with the other brethren, becoming submissive to Siphor. And he besought all the brethren to pray for him, that he might find mercy from our Lord Jesus Christ.

The acts of Judas Thomas the apostle are completed, which he wrought in the land of the Indians, fulfilling the command of him who sent him; to whom be glory forever and ever. Amen.

Note

1. Here, according to the Syriac, the crowd says: "One is (God), the God of this man, who has taught us about his God and through his word has commanded this fearful beast to reveal its nature to us." Then the narrative continues: And they prayed him that, as he by his word had commanded it to speak like a man, he would also kill it by his word.

7
APOCALYPSES

The Book of Enoch (1 Enoch)

(Jewish Pseudepigrapha)

The *Book of Enoch (1 Enoch)* is perhaps the best example of an intertestamental apocalypse—a work of prophecy and visionary revelation, giving divine secrets and fantastic information about creation, salvation, Heaven, and Hell. With sources in Old Testament scriptures, the apocalypses of the pseudepigrapha span a period from 200 B.C. to at least A.D. 100, and give rise to the New Testament Book of Revelation and the many apocalypses of the Gnostics. In their wondrous and transcendent poetic vision, these documents contain universal stories and preoccupations which relate them to other great myths of the ancient world.

The text of *1 Enoch* is based on the predeluvian patriarch, Enoch, who is mentioned in Genesis (5:18–24). Only Enoch and Noah "walked with God." Enoch, who lived 365 years, is one of two men who were taken up bodily into the presence of God without dying. (The prophet Elijah (2 Kings 2:1–11) is the other.) Because Enoch was enraptured or translated bodily into Heaven, he became the center of the apocalyptic tradition. Three books of the pseudepigrapha bear his name; a passage in *1 Enoch* 1:9 appears in the New Testament Epistle of Jude. The basis for nearly all the later voluminous literature on Enoch are two brief lines in Genesis (5:24): "Enoch walked with God. Then he vanished because God took him."

The *Book of Enoch* is a very large volume, divided into five sections and 108 chapters. It is a composite work, composed at different times during the last two centuries B.C. The oldest sections, according to C. C. Torrey and R. H. Charles, go back at least to the Maccabean period. George Nickelsburg suggests that chapters 1 through 36 were known before the death of Judas Maccabeus in 160 B.C., and hence they probably date before 175 B.C. The many subjects treated are, in the first division, the judgment of the world, an elaborate angelology, and the fall of the rebellious angels.

The second division is a section of parables, giving messianic hope to the good; it speaks of the Son of man, the conversion of the Gentiles, and the salvation and immortality of the soul. The third is an astronomical book. The fourth consists of two dream visions, one about the flood and the other about the history of the world until the coming of the messiah. The last section has more dream visions, and the *Apocalypse of Ten Weeks*, a short poem (chapters 91–93) that tells the history of a good man, from birth to apocalyptic salvation. In the concluding chapters we are told of the birth of Noah, miracles, and Enoch's exhortation to his son Methuselah to spread the word of salvation.

The pseudepigrapha were favorite reading of the early Christians and, as R. H. Charles writes in his introduction to his edition of *1 Enoch*, represent "the development of that side of Judaism, to which historically Christendom in large measure owes its existence."[1] Notions such as the conversion of the Gentiles and the coming of the messiah, the "Son of man," are obvious examples of the continuation in the New Testament of intertestamental Jewish notions, even though these terms, in their new context, may have other meanings. For later Jewish literature, particularly the Kabbalah and mystical documents, the pseudepigraphical elaboration of God's throne, chariot, and heavenly voyages provided a frequent model. The extraordinary literary value of the Enoch books is seen in the first passages excerpted in this volume:

> The vision clouds invited me and a mist summoned me, the course of the stars and lightning sped me, and the winds in the vision caused me to fly, lifting me upward and bearing me into heaven. I went in till I came near a wall built of crystals and surrounded by tongues of fire. It began to frighten me. I went into the tongues of fire and came near a large house built of hailstone crystals.

If the vision seems to resemble a passage from William Blake, it should be remembered that this Romantic rebel knew the *Book of Enoch* and, as one who rejected orthodox Christianity, he saw in it a vision of Heaven and Hell which enforced his *other* view of religious scriptures.

The *Book of Enoch* is preserved in its entirety only in Ethiopic; fragments also exist in Greek and Latin. The Greek translation goes back to originals in Hebrew and Aramaic. Among the Dead Sea Scrolls discovered at Qumran are fragments of ten Aramaic manuscripts.

Note

1. R. H. Charles, *The Apocrypha and Pseudepigrapha of the Old Testament*, vol. 2 (Oxford: Clarendon Press, 1913), p. 197.

ENOCH'S DREAM VISION OF HEAVEN, THE WATCHERS, AND THE GIANTS*

This vision was shown to me. The vision clouds invited me and a mist summoned me, the course of the stars and lightning sped me, and the winds in the vision caused me to fly, lifting me upward and bearing me into Heaven. I went in till I came near a wall built of crystals and surrounded by tongues of fire. It began to frighten me. I went into the tongues of fire and came near a large house built of hailstone crystals. The walls of the house were like a tesselated floor of crystals, its floor also was crystal. Its ceiling was the path of stars and lightning. Between them were fiery cherubim. Their heaven was clear as water. A fire surrounded the walls and its portals blazed. I entered that house and it was hot as fire, cold as ice. There were no delights of life therein. Fear covered me, and trembling seized me. I quaked, fell on my face, and beheld a vision! There was a second house, greater than the former, and its entire portal stood open before me. Made of fire, it excelled in indescribable splendor and magnificence. Its floor was fire, and above it stars and lightning. Its ceiling also was fire. And I looked and saw a lofty throne. Its appearance was transparent hailstone, its wheels like the sun, and then the sight of the cherubim. From underneath the throne came streams of fire so that I could not look directly at it. The great Glory sat there. His raiment shone more brightly than sun and was whiter than snow. No angel could enter and behold his face because of his magnificence and glory, nor could any flesh behold him. Fire was around

and before him, and no one could come near. Ten thousand times ten thousand stood before him, yet he needed no counselor. The holiest ones near him were by him night and day. All this time I was prostrate on my face and trembling. The Lord called me with his own mouth, saying: "Come here, Enoch, and hear my word." Then one of the holy ones came to me and waked me. He made me rise and approach the door. I bowed my face.

The Lord spoke: "Have no fear, Enoch, good man and scribe of goodness. Come hear my voice. Go speak to the Watchers of Heaven, who have sent you to intercede for them. Tell them, You should intercede for men, and not men for you. Why did you leave lofty, holy Heaven to sleep with women, to defile yourselves with the daughters of men and take them as your wives, and like the children of the earth to beget sons, in your case giants?[1] Though you were holy and spiritual, living the eternal life, you defiled yourself with the blood of women, you begot children with the blood of flesh, and like the others you have lusted after flesh and blood as do those who die and perish. Because they perish I gave them wives so they might impregnate them, have children, and nothing be lacking on the earth. But you were spiritual and immortal for all generations of the world. So I gave you no wives, for Heaven is your proper dwelling place. And now the giants, offspring of spirit and flesh, will be called spirits[2] on the earth, and earth shall be their dwelling. Their bodies emitted evil spirits because they were born from human women and the holy Watchers. The giants afflict, oppress, destroy, attack over the earth. Although they hunger and thirst, they do not eat. They offend. These spirits will rise up against men and women because they proceed from them.

"The giants will slaughter, unpunished, until the day of the great judgment. Then the age, the Watchers, and

---

*Chapters 14–16. The selections in this chapter are revisions of a translation in R. H. Charles, *The Apocrypha and Pseudepigrapha of the Old Testament*, vol. 2 (Oxford: Clarendon Press, 1913), pp. 197–199, 199–201, 204–205, 214–217, 218–219, 235–237, 259–260.

the godless will be wholly consummated. As for the Watcher who sent you to intercede for them, tell them: 'You were in Heaven but the mysteries were not revealed to you. You knew worthless ones, and in the hardness of your hearts you revealed these to women, and through these secrets women and men work much evil earth.' Say to them, 'You have no peace.' "

ENOCH'S JOURNEYS THROUGH SHEOL (HELL) AND HEAVEN*

And they brought me to a place in which people were like flaming fire. When they wished, they appeared as men. And then they brought me to the place of darkness, and to a mountain whose summit reached to Heaven. And I saw the places of the luminaries, the treasuries of the stars and the thunder, and, in the uttermost depths, a fiery bow,[3] arrows, their quiver, a fiery sword, and all lightnings. They took me to a river of fire[4] in which the fire flows like water and discharges into the great sea toward the west. I saw the great rivers[5] and came to the mighty river and immense darkness, and went to the place where no flesh walks. I saw the mountains of the darkness of winter and the place from which all waters of the deep flow. I saw the mouths[6] of all the rivers of the earth and the mouth of the deep.

I saw the treasuries of all the winds. I saw how God had furnished the whole creation and the firm foundations of the earth. And I saw the cornerstone of the earth. Then I observed the four winds which bear the earth and the firmament of heaven. And I saw how the winds stretch out the vaults of Heaven and

have their station between heaven and earth. These are Heaven's pillars. I saw columns of heavenly fire and among them I saw columns of fire fall, beyond all measure of height and depth. And beyond that abyss I saw a place which had no firmament of the heaven above and no firmly founded earth beneath it. There was no water on it and no birds; it was a horrible wasteland. There I saw seven stars like great burning mountains, and when I asked about them the angel told me: "This place is the end of Heaven and earth. It has become a prison for the stars and the host of Heaven." And the stars which roll over the fire have transgressed the Lord's commandment in the beginning of their rising, for they did not appear at their appointed times. And God was angry with them and bound them for ten thousand years until their guilt was appeased.

And the archangel Uriel said to me, "Here shall stand the angels who have been attached to women. Their spirits, assuming many different forms, are defiling mankind and will lead them astray into sacrificing to demons as gods. Here they shall stand till the day of the the winds of Heaven which turn and bring the circumference of the sun and all the stars to their setting. I saw the winds on the earth carrying clouds. I saw the paths of the angels. I saw at the end of the earth the firmament of the Heaven above. And I proceeded and saw a place which burns day and night, where there are seven mountains of magnificent stones, three toward the east and three toward the south. And as for those toward the east, one was of colored stone, one of pearl, one jacinth, and those toward the south of red stone. But the middle mountain was alabaster and reached to Heaven as the throne of God, and the summit of the throne was sapphire. And I saw a flaming fire. Beyond these mountains is a region at the end of the great earth. There the heavens were completed. And I saw a steep abyss with

---

*Chapters 17–19, 24–25, 46, 48, 51, 71, 90, 105.

great judgment when they shall be destroyed. And the women of the angels who went astray shall become sirens." Only I, Enoch, saw the vision of the ends of all things, and no one will see as I have seen.

The Seven Mountains in the Northwest and the Tree of Life

And from there I went to another place of the earth where my escort angel, Raguel, showed me a mountain range of fire that burnt day and night. I went beyond it and saw seven magnificent mountains, each different, whose stones were magnificent and beautiful. Three were toward the east and three toward the south. These mountains had deep rough ravines; none of the ravines were joined. The seventh mountain was in the midst of them and it excelled in height, resembling the seat of a throne. Fragrant trees encircled the throne. Among them was a tree like no other. Its fragrance was beyond all fragrance, and its leaves and blooms and wood never withered. Its fruit was beautiful, resembling the dates of the palm. Then I said, "How beautiful this tree is! Its leaves are fair, and its blooms delightful in appearance." Michael,[7] the leader of the holy and honored angels with me, answered, "Enoch, why do you ask me about the fragrance of the tree and why do you want to learn its truth?"

I replied, "I wish to know about everything, especially about this tree."

Michael answered: "This high mountain which you have seen, whose summit is like the throne of God, is the throne of God. It is where the holy great one, the Lord of glory, the eternal king, will sit when he comes to visit the earth with goodness. As for this fragrant tree, no mortal is permitted to touch it till the great judgment when God's justice redresses all and brings everything to its ultimate consummation. The tree shall then be given to the good and holy. Its food shall be food for the elect. It shall be transplanted to the holy temple of the Lord, the eternal king.

They will be joyful and glad
and enter the holy place.
Its fragrance will be in their bones
and they will live a long life on earth
as your fathers lived.
Nor sorrow nor plague nor torment of calamity
will ever touch them in all their days."

Then I blessed the God of glory, the eternal king, who prepared such things for the good, who created them and promised their gift.

The Head of Days and the Son of Man[8]

There I saw one who had a head of days
and his head was white like wool
and with him was another being whose countenance
had the appearance of a man.
His face was filled with graciousness
like a holy angel.

489

And I asked the angel with me to show me the hidden things concerning the Son of man. Who was he, where did he come from and why did he go with the Head of Days? And he answered:

"This is the Son of man who is filled with goodness,
with whom goodness lives
and who reveals all treasures that are concealed,
for the Lord of Spirits chose him.
Whose lot is preeminent before the Lord of spirits in goodness forever?
This Son of man whom you have seen
will raise up kings and the mighty from their seats,
the strong from their thrones.
He will loosen the reins of the strong
and break the teeth of sinners.
He will throw down kings from their thrones and their kingdoms
because they do not extol and praise him,
nor humbly acknowledge how their kingdom was given them.
He will humble the countenance of the strong,
fill them with shame,
and darkness will be their dwelling
and worms their bed.
They will have no hope of rising from their beds,
for they do not extol the name of the Lord of Spirits."

Fountain of Goodness and the Son of Man

There I saw the fountain of goodness
which was inexhaustible.
Around it were many fountains of wisdom.
All the thirsty drank from them
and were filled with wisdom
and they lived with the good, the holy, and the elect.
At that hour the Son of man was named
before the Lord of Spirits,
and his name was the Head of Days.

Yes, before the sun and the signs were created,
before the stars of Heaven were made
his name was named before the Lord of Spirits.

He will be a staff to the good to stay themselves and not fall,
he will be the light of the Gentiles,[9]
and the hope of those who are troubled of heart.

All who live on earth will fall down and worship him,
will praise and bless and celebrate the Lord of Spirits with song.

And so he has been chosen and hidden before God,
before the creation of the world and for eternity.

The wisdom of the Lord of Spirits has revealed him to the holy and the good,
for he preserved the good

because they have despised the world of evil,
hated all its works and ways in the name of the Lord of Spirits.
In his name they are saved
according to his good pleasure.

In these days the kings of the earth
and the strong who possess the land because of the works of their hands
are all downcast
for they know that on the day of their anguish they will not be able to save
   themselves.
I will turn them over into the hands of my elected ones.
Like straw in fire they will burn before the face of the holy,
like lead in water they will sink before the face of the good,
and no trace of them will ever be found.

On the day of their anguish there will be rest on earth.
They will fall but not rise again.

No one will take them with his hands and raise them,
for they have denied the Lord of Spirits and his Anointed.
The name of the Lord of Spirits be blessed.

The Resurrection of the Dead

In those days the earth will give back what was entrusted to it,
Sheol will return what it has received
and Hell will give back what it owes.
For in those days the Elected One will arise
and choose the good and holy from those who died.
The day has come when they are to be saved.
The Elected One in those days will sit on my throne
and his mouth pour forth secrets of wisdom and counsel.
The Lord of Spirits gave them to him and glorified him.

And in those days the mountains will leap like rams,
the hills will skip like lambs satisfied with milk,
and the faces of all angels in Heaven will glow with joy.

The earth will rejoice,
the good will live on it
and the elect walk there

and the Lord of Spirits will rule over them.
They will eat with the Son of man
and lie down and rise up forever and ever.
The good and the elect will rise from the earth
and cease to be of downcast countenance.

They will be clothed with garments of glory,
the garments of life from the Lord of Spirits.
Your garments will not grow old,
nor your glory pass away before the Lord of Spirits.

Two Visions of Enoch

And so my spirit was translated
and it ascended into the heavens
and I saw the holy sons of God.

They were stepping on flames of fire.
Their garments were white
and their faces shone like snow.

I saw two streams of fire
and the light of that fire shone like hyacinths.
I fell on my face before the Lord of Spirits.

The angel Michael seized me by my right hand
and lifted me up and let me into all secrets.
He showed me the secrets of goodness.

He showed me the mysteries of the ends of the Heaven,
all the chambers of the stars and all the luminaries
where they walk before the faces of the holy.

And he translated my spirit into the Heaven of Heavens,
and there I saw a structure built of crystals,
and tongues of living fire between those crystals.

My spirit saw the girdle which circled that house of fire,
and on its four sides were streams of living fire
and they circled that house.

There were seraphim, cherubim, and ophannim,
who do not sleep.
They guard the throne of his glory.

I saw angels beyond count,
a thousand thousand, ten thousand times ten thousand,
circling that house.

Michael and Gabriel and Phanuel,
and holy angels who are above the heavens,
go in and out of that house.

They go out—
Michael, Gabriel, Raphael and Phanuel,
and holy angels beyond count.

With them the Head of Days,
his head white and pure as wool,
his raiment indescribable.

I fell on my face
and my whole body surrendered to calm
and my spirit was transfigured.

I cried out with a loud voice,
with the soul of power,
and blessed and glorified and extolled.

The New Jerusalem, Conversion,
Resurrection of the Good, the Messiah

I stood up to look while they folded up that old house and carried off all the pillars. The beams and ornaments were also folded up and taken to a place in the south of the land. I watched until the Lord of the sheep brought a new house greater and loftier than the first and set it up in the place of the first which had been folded up. All its pillars were new, its ornaments new and larger than the first. Sheep were inside it.

I saw all the sheep which had been left, all the beasts of the earth, all the birds of heaven, falling down and doing homage to those sheep and entreating them and obeying them in everything. Thereafter those three clothed in white seized my hand (those who had taken up before) and the ram also seized my hand and they took me up and set me down in the midst of those sheep before the judgment took place. The sheep were white, their wool abundant and clean. And there assembled in that house all that had previously been dispersed and destroyed, all the beasts of the field and all the birds of heaven. The Lord of the sheep rejoiced because they were good and had returned to his house. I saw them lay down the sword which had been given to the sheep. They carried it back to the house, and it was sealed in the presence of the Lord. All the sheep were invited into that house. Their eyes were opened and they saw the good and not one of them did not see. I observed that the house was broad and long and very full.

Then I saw that a white bull[10] was born with large horns, and all the beasts of the field and all the birds of the air feared him and entreated him constantly. I watched until all generations were transformed into white bulls. The first among them became a lamb, and that lamb became a great animal and had great black horns on its head. The Lord of the sheep rejoiced over it and over all the oxen. I slept among them and woke and saw everything. This is the vision I saw while I was sleeping, and I woke and blessed the Lord of goodness and glorified him. Then I wept and my tears were so abundant I could scarcely endure it. When I looked they flowed because of what I saw. I saw how all will come, be fulfilled, all the deeds of humanity will be fulfilled. On that night I remembered the first dream. Because of it I wept and was troubled, because I had seen the vision.

God and the Messiah to Live with
Humanity

In those days the Lord summoned them to testify to the children of the earth concerning their wisdom. Then he said, "Reveal it to them, for you are their guides and a consolation over the whole earth. My Son and I will be united with them forever in the ways of goodness in their lives, and you will have peace.[11] Be happy, children of goodness."

Notes

1. Men and women marry to continue the race. For immortal angels, copulation with humans is a corruption. As is written in Matthew 22:30, there is no marriage in Heaven.

2. evil spirits. When the giants die, evil spirits—that is, demons—will remain living on earth.

3. fiery bow. Lightning is shot with a fiery bow.

4. river of fire. The Pyriphlegethon. This section has many Greek elements.

5. the great rivers. Probably the Styx, Acheron, and Cocytus.

6. mouths of all the rivers. Oceanus.

7. Michael. Patron angel of Israel.

8. Son of man. The messiah. The designation "Son of man," frequently found in the pseudepigrapha, in *1 Enoch, 4 Ezra,* and the *Psalms of Solomon,* is one of the many connections between intertestamental literature and New Testament thought and language. The messiah, meaning "the anointed one" in Hebrew, in Greek is *Christos,* in English Christ. *Jesus Christ* is a Greek version from Hebrew which is more properly translated into English as *Joshua the Messiah* or *Jeshua the Anointed* or any combination thereof. *Son of man* also appears in the Old Testament. This passage is derived from Daniel 7:8.

9. the light of the Gentiles. In Isaiah 56:3–8, Isaiah welcomes the Gentiles to convert and love God. No one, neither outcast nor eunuch, will be excluded when God brings the Gentiles into the covenant, to his holy mountain. Conversion is emphasized in the pseudepigrapha and is another link to New Testament emphases of Jewish thought.

10. white bull. The white bull and the sheep represent, according to Nickelsburg, the messiah and the righteous of Israel or conflicting figures and groups in the time of the Maccabeans. The symbolism of bulls, sheep, lamb, and rams is reminiscent of Daniel 7.

11. you will have peace. In contrast to earlier, 16, "you have no peace."

The Book of the Secrets of Enoch (2 Enoch)

(Jewish Pseudepigrapha)

The *Book of the Secrets of Enoch* or *2 Enoch*, the so-called Slavonic as opposed to the Ethiopic Enoch, is discussed earlier in *Creation Myths*, where excerpts dealing with creation and Adam are included. The excerpts below treat Enoch's journey through the seven or ten heavens. In this first of Enoch's two cosmic tours, much information is given on the fate of the Watchers, the fallen rebellious angels, as well as the hopes of the good man or woman. The tone is noble, reminiscent of the teaching in Ecclesiastes. In the final section Enoch is commanded to write 366 books for all the souls of humanity, who existed before the formation of the world. This Platonic notion of the preexistence of the soul appears in Philo and other texts of the time. In later Judaism the notion became a prevailing dogma.

ENOCH'S LIFE AND DREAM*

There was a wise man, a great artificer, and the Lord conceived love for him and received him so that he could see the uppermost dwellings and personally see the wise, great, inconceivable, and immutable realm of almighty God, of the wonderful, glorious, bright, and many-eyed station of the Lord's servants, of the inaccessible throne of the Lord, of the degrees and manifestations of the incorporeal hosts, of the ineffable ministration of the multitude of the elements, of the various apparitions and inexpressible singing of the ghost of cherubim, and of the boundless light.

*The selections in this chapter are modern revisions of the translation in R. H. Charles and W. R. Morfill, *The Book of the Secrets of Enoch* (Oxford: Clarendon Press, 1896), pp. A, 1B, 2–7A, 8–10, 11A, 12, 17B, 18B–A, 19A–20, 21, 22, 23.

The Revelations of Enoch

When I was three hundred and sixty-five years old, one day of the second month I was alone in my house. I was in great trouble, weeping asleep on my couch, and there appeared to me two very big men, such as I have never seen on earth —their faces shone like the sun, their eyes were burning candles, out of their mouths came fire, their clothes and singing were various, and their arms like golden wings. They stood at the head of my couch, and called me by my name.

Having wakened from my sleep, I stood up, bowed down to them, and covered my face from terror. And the two men spoke to me: "Have courage, Enoch, do not fear. The Eternal Lord sent us to you. Behold, today you shall go up with us on to the heavens. Tell your sons and your household all that they must do in your house, and let no one seek you till the Lord return you to them."

And I listened and went out, summoned my sons Mefusailom[1] and Regim, and told them all that those two men had spoken to me.

And behold, my children, I do not know where I am going nor what will befall me. Now, my children, do not turn from God, walk before the Lord's face and observe his judgments, and do not bow down to vain gods, to gods who made neither Heaven nor earth. They shall perish.

Keep your hearts true to the terror of the Lord and, sons, let no one seek me till the Lord returns me to you.

ASCENSION INTO THE HEAVENS

Enoch's Ascent to the First Heaven

And it happened when I had spoken to my sons, and the two men summoned me, and took me on to their wings and carried me up on to the first heaven and set me down there, and brought me before the face of the elder, the ruler of the stellar orders, and he showed me all their courses, and their passages from year to year, and he showed me two hundred angels, and he showed me there a very great sea, greater than the earthly sea, and angels were flying with their wings.

He showed me the storehouse of cloud, from which it goes up and out, and showed me all the treasure houses of snow and cold, and terrible angels guarding the treasure houses, and he showed me the treasure houses of the dew, like olive oil, and angels guarding their treasure houses, and their clothing like all the flowers of the earth.

How Enoch Was Taken to the Second Heaven

And those men took me and let me up to the second heaven, and showed me darkness, greater than earthly darkness, and there I saw prisoners hanging, guarded, waiting the great and boundless judgment, and these angels were dark-looking, more than earthly darkness, and incessantly weeping, and I said to the men who were with me, "Why are they incessantly tortured?" They answered me, "These are God's apostates, who did not obey God's commands, but took counsel with their own will, and turned away with their prince, who also is fastened on the fifth heaven. And I felt great pity for them, and they saluted me, and said to me, "Man of God, pray for us to the Lord." And I answered them, "Who am I, a mortal man, to pray for angels? Who knows where I am going, or what will befall me? Who will pray for me?"

Of the Assumption of Enoch to the Third Heaven

And those men led me up to the third heaven, and placed me there; and I looked downward and saw the produce of these places, like no other goodness.

And I saw all the sweet-flowering trees and beheld their fruits, which were sweet-smelling, and all the foods borne by them bubbling with fragrance. And in the midst of the trees is the Tree of Life, that place where the Lord rests when he goes up into Paradise. And this tree is of ineffable goodness and fragrance, and adorned more than any existing thing. And on all sides its form is gold and vermilion and fire-like. It covers all, and has produce from all fruits. Its root is in the garden at the earth's end. And Paradise is between corruptibility and incorruptibility. Two springs come out which send forth honey and milk, and their springs send forth oil and wine, and they separate into four parts, go round quietly, and go down into the Paradise of Eden, between corruptibility and incorruptibility. And then they go forth along the earth, which revolves like the elements. Here there is no unfruitful tree, and every place is blessed. And there are three hundred bright angels who keep the garden, and with sweet singing and never-silent voices serve the Lord throughout all days and hours.

Showing Enoch the Place of the Righteous and Compassionate

And I said, "How very sweet is this place," and those men said to me, "This place, Enoch, is prepared for the righteous, who endure all manner of offence from those that exasperate their souls, who avert their eyes from iniquity and make righteous judgment, who give bread to the hungering, cover the naked with clothing, raise up the fallen, help injured orphans, who walk without fault before the face of the Lord and serve him alone, and this place is prepared for their eternal inheritance."

Here They Showed Enoch the Terrible Place and Various Tortures

And those two men led me up onto the northern side, and showed me a very terrible place.[2] It had all manner of tortures: cruel darkness and unillumined gloom. There was no light there, but murky fire constantly flaming up. It had a fiery river and the whole place is everywhere fire, everywhere frost and ice, thirst and shivering, while the bonds are very cruel, and the angels fearful and merciless, bearing angry weapons and merciless torture. I said, "How terrible is this place," and those men said to me, "This place, Enoch, is prepared for those who dishonor God, who on earth practice sin against nature, which is enchantments and devilish witchcrafts. It is for those who boast of their wicked deeds—stealing, lies, calumnies, envy, rancor, fornication, murder—and those accursed ones who steal the souls of men, who take away goods from the poor and make themselves rich, injuring them for their own good. It is for those who corrupt children through sodomy, who perform magic; for those who, able to satisfy the needy, made the hungering die; for those who could clothe but stripped the naked; and those who knew not their Creator, and bowed down to soulless Gods, who are deceived by vain gods, who also built hewn images and bowed down to unclean handiwork. For all these is prepared this place for eternal inheritance."

Here They Took Enoch Up to the Fourth Heaven, the Course of Sun and Moon

Those men took me, and led me up on to the fourth heaven, and showed me all the successive goings, and all the rays of the light of sun and moon. And I measured their goings, and compared to their light, and saw that the sun's light is greater than the moon's. Its circle and the wheels on which it goes always, like a wind going past with marvelous speed, and day and night it has no rest. Its passage and return are accompanied by four great stars, and each star has under it a thousand stars, to the right of the sun's wheel, and by four to the left, each having under it a thousand stars, altogether eight thousand, issuing with the sun continually. And by day fifteen myriads of angels attend it, and by night a thousand. And six-winged ones issue with the angels before the sun's wheel into the fiery flames, and a hundred angels kindle the sun and set it on fire.

Of the Marvelous Elements of the Sun

And I looked and saw other flying elements of the sun, whose names are Phoenixes and Chalkydri,[3] marvelous, with feet and tails in the form of a lion, and a crocodile's head. They are purple like the rainbow. Their size is nine hundred measures, their wings are like those of angels, each has twelve, and they attend and accompany the sun, bearing heat and dew, as it is ordered by God. Thus the sun revolves and rises under the heaven, and its course goes under the earth with the light of its rays incessantly.

This Is the Lunar Disposition

And in the midst of the heaven I saw armed troops serving the Lord on cymbals and organs, and I was delighted listening.

Enoch's Ascent to the Fifth Heaven

And the men carried me up on to the fifth heaven, and I saw there many troops, Grigori,[4] and their appearance was human and their size greater than that of great giants and their faces withered, and the silence of their mouths perpetual, and there was no service on the fifth heaven, and I said to the men who were with me, "Why are their faces melancholy and withered, their mouths silent, and why is there no service on this heaven?" And they said to me, "These are the Grigori, who with their prince, Satanail, rejected the Lord of light, and after them are those who are held in great darkness on the second heaven,

and three of them went down to earth from the Lord's throne to the place Ermon,[5] and broke through their vows on the shoulder of the hill Ermon and saw how good are the daughters of men. They took them as their wives, and befouled the earth with their deeds, and in all times of their age were lawless and promiscuous. Giants were born and marvelous big men and great enmity. And therefore God judged them with great punishment, and they weep for their brethren and they will be punished on the Lord's great day." And I said to the Grigori, "I saw your brethren and their works, and their great torments, and I prayed for them, but the Lord has condemned them to be under earth till heaven and earth shall end forever." And I said, "Why do you wait, brethren, and not serve before the Lord's face? Why have you not put your services before the Lord's face, lest you anger your Lord utterly?"

And they listened to my admonition, and spoke to the four ranks in heaven, and lo! as I stood with those two men four trumpets trumpeted together with great voice, and the Grigori broke into song with one voice, and their voice went up before the Lord pitifully and affectingly.

Of the Taking of Enoch on to the Sixth Heaven

And then those men took me and bore me up to the sixth heaven, and there I saw seven bands of angels, very bright and very glorious, and their faces shining more than the sun's shining, glistening, and there is no difference in their faces, or behavior, or manner of dress; and these make the orders, and learn the goings of the stars, and the alteration of the moon, or revolution of the sun, and the good government of the world. And when they see evildoing they make commandments and instruction, and sweet and loud singing, and all songs of praise. These are the archangels who are above angels, measure all life in Heaven and on earth, who are appointed over seasons and years, the angels who are over rivers and sea, over the fruits of the earth, and the angels who are over every grass, giving food to all, to every living thing, and the angels who write all the souls of men, all their deeds, and their lives before the Lord's face; in their midst are six phoenixes and six cherubim and six six-winged ones continually with one voice singing one voice, and it is not possible to describe their singing, and they rejoice before the Lord at his footstool.

Enoch in the Seventh Heaven

And those two men lifted me up then on to the seventh heaven, and I saw there a very great light, and fiery troops of great archangels, incorporeal forces, and dominions, orders and governments, cherubim and seraphim, thrones and many-eyed ones, nine regiments, the Ioanit[6] stations of light, and I became afraid, and began to tremble with great terror, and those men took me, and led me after them, and said to me: "Have courage, Enoch, do not fear," and showed me the Lord from afar, sitting on his very high throne. For what is there on the tenth heaven,[7] since the Lord dwells here? On the tenth heaven is God, in the Hebrew tongue he is called Aravat.[8] And all the heavenly troops would come and stand on the ten steps according to their rank, and would bow down to the Lord, and would again go to their places in joy and felicity, singing songs in the boundless light with small and tender voices, gloriously serving him.

How the Angels Left Enoch at the End of the Seventh Heaven

The cherubim and seraphim standing around the throne, the six-winged and many-eyed ones do not depart, standing before the Lord's face, doing his will. They cover his whole throne, singing with gentle voices before the Lord's face:

"Holy, holy, holy, Lord Ruler of Sabbath, Heavens and earth are full of your glory." When I saw all these things, those men said to me, "Enoch, we are commanded to journey with you only this far," and they went away, and I saw them no more. I remained alone at the end of the seventh heaven and became afraid, and fell on my face and said to myself: "How dreadful, what has happened to me?" And the Lord sent one of his glorious ones, the archangel Gabriel, and he said to me, "Have courage, Enoch, do not fear, arise before the Lord's face, eternity, arise and follow me." And I answered him, saying to myself, "My Lord, my soul is departed from me, because of terror and trembling." I called to the men who had led me up to this place, on whom I relied, for it was with them I was to go before the Lord's face. And Gabriel caught hold of me like a leaf caught in the wind, and placed me before the Lord's face.

And I saw the eighth heaven, which is called in Hebrew Muzaloth,[9] changer of the seasons, of drought, wet, and the twelve signs of the zodiac which are above the seventh heaven. Then I saw the ninth heaven, which is called in Hebrew Kuchavim,[10] which are the stars, the heavenly homes of the twelve signs of the zodiac.

Enoch in the Tenth Heaven

In the Tenth Heaven the Archangel Michael Led Enoch Before God's Face

On the tenth heaven, Aravoth,[11] I saw the appearance of the Lord's face, like iron glowing in fire, emitting sparks, and burning. Thus I saw the Lord's face, but the Lord's face is ineffable, marvelous, awful, and very, very terrible. And who am I to tell of the Lord's unspeakable being, of his wondrous face? I cannot tell the quantity of his many instructions, his various voices. I cannot tell of the Lord's throne, great and not made by hands, nor of how many are standing around him, how many troops of cherubim and seraphim, nor of their incessant singing, nor of his immutable beauty. Who can tell of the ineffable greatness of his glory?

And I fell prone and bowed before the Lord, and the Lord with his lips said to me: "Have courage, Enoch, do not fear, arise and stand before my face into eternity."

And the archistratege Michael lifted me up, and led me before the Lord's face.

And the Lord said to his servants, tempting them, "Let Enoch stand before my face into eternity," and the glorious ones bowed down to the Lord, and said, "Let Enoch go according to your word." Then the Lord said to Michael, "Go and remove Enoch's earthly garments, and anoint him with my sweet ointment, and put him in the garments of my glory."

And Michael did as the Lord told him. He anointed me, and dressed me, and the appearance of that ointment is more than the great light, and his ointment is like sweet dew, and its smell mild, shining like a sunray, and I looked at myself and was like his glorious ones.

And the Lord summoned his archangel Pravuil.[12] "Bring out the books from my storehouses, and a quick-writing reed, and give it to Enoch. Bring him the choice and comforting books in your own hand."

How Enoch Wrote Three Hundred and Sixty-Six Books

And he was telling me all the works of Heaven, earth, and sea, all the elements, their passages and goings, and the thunderings of the thunders, the sun and moon, the goings and changes of the stars, the seasons, years, days and hours, the risings of the wind, the numbers of the angels, and the formation of their songs, and all human things, the tongue of every human song and life, the commandments, instructions, sweet-voiced song, and all things fitting to learn. And Pravuil told me, "All these things I have told you we have written. Sit and write for all souls of humanity, however many are born, and address the places prepared for them for eternity, for all souls are prepared for eternity, even before the formation of the world."[13] For two months I wrote out all things, exactly, in three hundred and sixty-six books.

Notes

1. Mefusailom. Methuselah, son of Enoch. Regim is of the brethren of Methuselah.

2. The idea of torture and evil in Heaven is surprising, but we find Satan in Heaven in Job 1:7–8.

3. Chalkydri. Winged dragons or serpents.

4. Grigori. Giant angels, also called Watchers, who revolted in Heaven and sinned with the daughters of men. In Genesis 6:2, "the sons of God (angels), looking at the daughters of men, saw that they were pleasing and married as many as they chose." The intercourse of God's own sons with humans enraged God. In Genesis 6:3, we read God's words: "My spirit must not be disgraced in man, for he is but flesh." As punishment "his life shall last for no more than a hundred and twenty years." For all this wickedness and corruption, in the next lines, God introduces Noah and the Flood.

5. Ermon. Mount Hermon in upper Galilee.

6. Ioanit. John. Apparently a reference to the *Apocalypse of John*.

7. tenth heaven. Perhaps seventh heaven.

8. Aravat. Aravat is not a name of God but probably tenth heaven. It is also translated elsewhere as seventh heaven.

9. Muzaloth. The Hebrew name for the twelve signs of the Zodiac.

10. Kuchavim. Ninth heaven, the path of the stars.

11. Aravoth. Same as Aravat. See note 8.

12. Pravuil. Unidentified archangel.

13. souls. "All souls are prepared before the existence of the world." This Platonic doctrine of the preexistence of the soul is taught here. The notion exists in Jewish thought in Philo, the *Wisdom of Solomon*, and Josephus. It became a prevailing dogma in later Judaism. All souls existed before the creation of the world.

The Sibylline Oracles

(Jewish Pseudepigrapha)

The *Sibylline Oracles* give voice to the sibyl, a woman of wisdom, mystery, knowledge of past and future, and of the ways of God. She is traditionally exempt from ordinary mortality and may be centuries old. Speaking from a state of ecstasy, she is a holy prophetess whose word reveals divinity to humanity. Her comments on human behavior are a guide to salvation. In her Greek form, she was the main female oracular figure in the Greek tradition. The invention of a Jewish sibyl by an Alexandrian Jew of the second century B.C. represents the typical Hellenistic blend of Greek and biblical qualities found in the Jewish Diaspora.

In the Greek tradition the sibyl was originally supposed to have lived in Erythrae in Ionia or in Marpessos. Clement of Alexandria gives her date as prior to the legendary Orpheus, while Augustine makes her a contemporary of Achilles. Suidas puts her five centuries after Troy. She is said to be the offspring of a shepherd and a nymph, and her powers were derived from Apollo. Over the centuries she multiplied and became thirty or forty sibyls from diverse places such as Samos, Rhodes, Colophon, Ephesus, Sicily, Lybia, Babylonia, and Egypt. She became a figure of divine authority for Pagan, Jew, and Christian, and as she grew in number so too multiplied the books ascribed to her.

The Jewish oracular literature was composed in Egypt, in Greek hexameters, in the middle of the second century B.C. Of the original fifteen books, twelve survive. They are thought to have been composed by a cultivated Jew whose purpose was to spread the sibyl's words to Jew and Gentile alike. "Her" words glorify the history of the Jews, denounce animal sacrifice, sexual immorality, and worship of idols, and proclaim the truth of monotheism and the absolute sovereignty of its self-sprung, invisible God. The Jewish *Sibyllines* contain strong apocalyptic elements—a vision of God's cosmic fire on the day of judgment and a vision of felicity and peace on earth for the faithful. The most unusual quality of the work lies in its missionary zeal, rare in Jewish literature, which normally shuns all forms of proselytizing. While Diaspora Judaism of Alexandria was both sophisticated and enthusiastic about its own achievements in the Pagan world (Aristobulus went so far as to try to prove that the Bible was the primary source of the best works in the Greek literature), it was at the same time obsessed with eschatological concerns, specifically, with the coming of the messiah. The description of the messiah in oracular literature gave hope to Diaspora Jews and became, through Christian revision and interpolation, a popular Christian document and a source for later Christian Sibylline books.

THE SIBYLLINE ORACLES*

*From Book 3***

In the city of Camarina down in the land of Ur came the most virtuous race of men who devoted themselves to sound counsel and fair deeds. They do not seek the circling course of the sun or moon, nor monstrosities below the earth, nor the depth of the ocean's shimmering sea, nor portents of sneezes, nor birds of augurers, nor wizards, magicians, nor enchanters, nor the deceits of ventriloquists, nor foolish words, nor do they study the predictions of Chaldaean astrology, nor do they astronomize: for all these things are in their nature prone to deceive. For such things witless men search night and day, exercising their souls for a valueless work. Moreover, they have taught these deceptions to ill-starred people. From these mistakes evils come to mortals on the earth and they are led from good paths and righteous deeds. But these people ordinarily keenly practice justice and virtue rather than greed, which is the source of myriad ills to mortals, of war and desperate famine.

Good people have just measures in country and city. They do not rob each other at night, nor drive off herds of oxen and sheep and goats, nor does a neighbor remove his neighbor's landmarks, nor does a rich person offend his lesser brother, nor does anyone afflict widows. Rather, they help widows and are always ready to supply them with corn and wine and oil. The rich man always sends a portion of his harvest to those who have nothing and are in want, fulfilling the command of mighty God, which is that Heaven has wrought the earth for all alike.

When the people of the twelve tribes with their God-sent leaders[1] are to leave Egypt and pursue their road, journeying with a fiery pillar at night and inside a pillar of clouds when dawn turns to day, over them he will set up as their leader Moses, the mighty man whom the princess found as a child and took home from a marsh and brought up as her son. When he leads the people whom God delivers from Egypt to Mount Sinai, God will give them the law from Heaven, writing all its ordinances on two tablets, and he commands them to keep the law. If any disobey, they should pay the penalty according to mortal law or if they escape mortal hands they should perish by divine justice.

To the good people alone does the fruitful field yield its fruit, and up to a

---

*A revision of the text translated from Greek in R. H. Charles, *The Apocrypha and Pseudepigrapha of the Old Testament*, vol. 2 (Oxford: Clarendon Press, 1913).
**Chapters 218, 237, 248, 263, 286, 813; pp. 382–384, 393–394, 404–406.

hundredfold from one seed, and so are distributed God's measures.

But this people will also have evil, and not escape pestilence. They will leave their lovely shrine and flee, since it was their fate to leave their holy soil. They will be carried off to the Assyrians and see their infant children and wives enslaved to hostile men, and their livelihood and wealth perish. Every land and every sea will be populated with their wives and all will be incensed against their customs. Their whole land will be emptied. They will be taken away and their altar fenced off, and the temple of the mighty God and its long walls will all fall to the ground, because in their minds they did not obey the holy law of the immortal God. They went astray and served miserable idols, and did not fear the immortal Father of gods and of all people. They would not honor him but rather honored the idols of mortals. So for seven decades their fruitful land will be empty and so too their wondrous shrine. But at the end good things and exceedingly great glory await them, for the immortal God has selected them. But they must not delay. Trusting in the holy laws of the mighty God they bow their knee and pray toward the light of dawn.

And then the God of Heaven will send a king,[2] and will judge each man or woman with blood and flame of fire. There is a royal tribe[3] whose family will never stumble. In the circuit of time they will have dominion and begin to raise up a new shrine to God. And all the kings of Persia will succor it with gold and brass as well as wrought iron. God himself at night will give away his holy dream. Then the temple will be as it was before.

And mortals throughout Greece will call me a stranger of another land, born of Erythrae[4] and shameless. Others will call me born of my mother, Circe, and my father, Gnostos, the sibyl, a crazy imposter. But when all things come to pass, you will know me and no one will any more call me crazy but rather the proph-etess of the mighty God. God did not reveal to me all the first things of the world which he revealed to my parents, but God did give me understanding of later things so that I might proclaim the things that will be and that were before and tell them to mortal men. When the world was being swallowed up by the waters, and one man alone found favor, floating on the waters in a dwelling of hewn wood, with beasts and birds that the world might be replenished again, I was his daughter-in-law and I came of his blood, and the first things happened to me. Now the later things have all been told. So let all these things be accounted true that are spoken from my mouth.

*From Book 4**

Hear, O people of vaunting Asia and Europe, the prophetic strains of truth which, here from our shrine, I intend to pour forth through the honeyed speech of my mouth. I am no oracle monger of a false Phoebus, whom vain men have called a god and falsely termed a seer. Rather, I am the prophetess of the mighty God who was not fashioned by men's hands like dumb idols of polished stones. He has not made his habitation a stone set up in a temple, dumb and helpless, a bugbear of miseries to mortals. He is one whom none can see from earth, nor measure with mortal eyes, since he was not fashioned by mortal hand. With all-embracing vision, he sees all but is himself unseen. His is the murky night and day, the sun, the stars and moon, and sea, the haunt of fish; and land and rivers and the source of perennial streams, creatures ordained for sustaining life and showers that cause the wheat-field fruit to grow, and trees and vines and olive trees. He has driven a goad right through my heart so I will proclaim exactly and all that is happening to human beings and that is to hap-

_____

*Chapters 1 and 24.

pen, from the first to the tenth generation. He will vindicate all by causing it to happen. O people, listen to the Sibyl in all things as she pours forth true speech from her holy mouth.

Those people will be happy everywhere on earth who will truly love the mighty God, blessing him before eating and drinking,[5] staunch in their godliness. When they see temples and altars, vain erections of senseless stones befouled with constant blood of living things and sacrifices of four-footed beasts, they will disown all these. But they will look to the great glory of the one God, who does not commit dreadful murder, nor barter for dishonest gain, which are altogether evil things. Nor do his people place foul affection in another's bed, nor do they spend their affection on the hateful and hideous abuse of males.

*From Book 5**

From the blessed plains of Heaven a blessed man has come with the scepter in his hand which God committed to his clasp, and he has won fair dominion over all, and has restored to all good people the wealth taken earlier by others. And he has destroyed every city from its foundations with sheets of fire, and burnt up the families of men who before wrought evil. The city which God loved he made more radiant than the stars and the sun and the moon, and he set it as the jewel of the world, and made an extraordinarily beautiful temple in its beautiful sanctuary. He built it many furlongs long with a giant tower touching the very clouds and seen by all so that the faithful and the virtuous may see the glory of the invisible God, may have the vision of delight. East and west have hymned the glory of God. No longer are wretched mortals beset with deeds of shame, with adulteries and unnatural

_____
*Chapters 14, 64, and 12.

passions for boys, with murder and tumult. Rivalry is fair among all. It is the time of the saints and God accomplishes all these things—God the sender of thunder, the creator of the great temple.

When a wintry blast distills into snow, when a great river of the largest lakes is frozen, a barbarian horde will then make its way to the land of Asia and destroy the race of the dreaded Thracians as if it were feeble. Then mortals in desperation, in the last stages of famine, will devour their own parents, will consume them greedily as food. And in every house beasts will devour what is on the table and even birds will devour mortals. As a result of grievous wars the bloodstained ocean will be filled with flesh and blood of insensate men. There will be such faintness on the earth that one will be able to count the number of men and the measure of women. There will be myriad lamentations of the wretched generation when the sun sets never to rise again, waiting to be bathed in the waters of the ocean. For it has seen the unholy villainies of many men. There will be a moonless darkness even around great Heaven, and enormous mist will envelop the folds of the earth a second time. But then God's light will guide all those good people who have raised their hymns to God.

I saw the threatening of the gleaming sun among the stars and the moon's grievous wrath among the lightning flashes. The stars travailed with war and God suffered them to fight. In place of the sun, long flames rose in revolt, and the two-horned revolution of the moon was changed. Mounted on Leo's back, Lucifer waged battle. Capricorn smote the heel of the young Taurus, and Taurus snatched the day of return from Capricorn. Orion removed the scales so they disappeared. Virgo changed her sphere with the Twins in Aries. The Pleiades no longer appeared and the Dragon disowned the belt. Pisces entered into Leo's girdle. Cancer did not stay for he feared Orion. Scorpio drew up his tail, because of savage Leo, and the dogstar perished from the sun's flame. The might of brave Lucifer burned up Aquarius. Heaven itself was stirred till it shook the warriors, and in anger cast them headlong down to the earth. Smitten swiftly by the waters of the ocean, they kindled the whole earth and the sky remained starless.

Notes

1. Moses and Aaron, or angels.

2. The Persian king Cyrus who defeated the Babylonians, thus ending the Babylonian captivity of the Jews. Some have seen the savior king as the messiah.

3. The royal tribe is Judah

4. The sibyl claims she, not the legendary Greek imposter, is the true sibyl. While the sibyl rejects the Greek sibyl, the entire work is a mixture of Hellenistic style and thought and Jewish theology; while it rejects idolatry and polytheism, it invites the Gentile to worship the true God.

5. The custom of saying grace before meals is Essene. The abhorrence of temples and animal sacrifice is also particularly Essene.

The Apocalypse of Baruch (2 Baruch)

(Jewish Pseudepigrapha)

The *Apocalypse of Baruch* is a dialogue between a prophet and God. The prophet is Baruch, in the Bible a scribe to Jeremiah but here a prophet and more powerful than Jeremiah. God is ultimately the judge who decrees the final disposition of reward on earth and in Heaven, but for the most part he is also the defendant in a dialogue in which Baruch is an insistent interrogator. Why has God allowed Jerusalem to be captured, its Temple destroyed, its people dispersed? What reason is there for human corruptibility, the decay of human life? God answers that Israel's suffering is because of her own sins, her failure to heed the Torah, yet present distress is temporary and will give way to future glory and the punishment of her aggressors. Human woes will fade with the coming of the messiah who will make the earth blossom like Paradise. The dead will rise and mortality and corruptibility end. The *Apocalypse* was written in the latter part of the first century A.D., after Titus had burned the Temple of Jerusalem in A.D. 70, and these gloomy times gave rise to fearful questions and revelational answers. The notion of a severe dialogue between a human being and God goes back to Job and even continued in Auschwitz, where rabbis put God on trial and judged him guilty of condoning evil, while maintaining belief in his divine existence.

The text of *2 Baruch* begins with a pessimistic lament. We are told that the sin of Adam is the foundation of the original woes of the world. "Blessed is one who was not born/or, having been born, has died" (10:6–7). We hear the same despairing tone in poems by contemporary Greeks in the Palatine Anthology. The lamentation tells the priests to take "the keys of the sanctuary and hurl them at the heavens." In the dialogue with God, the poem admonishes the deity to take the responsibility himself, since his stewards have failed: "Guard your own house," it declares. Baruch evokes Babylon as the prospering power which has caused Zion's infinite misery. But Babylon and its sixth century B.C. destruction of the Temple and the subsequent exile in Mesopotamia is a symbol of first century Rome, its aggression, and the forced Diaspora of the Jews to other states.

The second selection (chapters 36–40) is "The Vision of the Forest, the Vine, the Fountain, and the Cedar." This is pure apocalyptic vision. Baruch asks God to interpret the vision, and God does so, with full authority over future events. The major event will be the appearance of the messiah who will be a consolation for every hardship. As desolation characterizes the present, joy will command the future. Our selection ends with the angel Ramiel's announcement of the coming of the messiah. Then

> Healing will descend in dew,
> disease will withdraw,
> and worry and pain and lamentation will be unknown to men
> and felicity will cover the earth.

The terrible conditions in the latter first century, when "the earth was bad," led Jew and Christian to look for the messiah. According to Robert M. Grant the failure of Jewish apocalyptic literature—that is, the failure of the messiah to materialize, and the disappointment of orthodox Christians in their creed—led Jew and Christian to seek the Gnostic Redeemer, to create their own mythology, and to turn away from tribal solutions in order to find light and salvation within themselves.

Thus 2 Baruch is an eloquent statement of worldly sorrows and the joy of anticipated redemption. With great literary means it depicts that confused period of the early Diaspora when pessimism reigned, when night once again covered the waters and desert. Its dark outlook is interrupted by an almost forced vision of salvific triumph and glory.

BARUCH'S LAMENT OVER ZION*

Blessed is one who was not born
or, having been born, has died.
But as for us who are alive
we ache because we see the afflictions of Zion
and Jerusalem's fate.

---

*Chapters 10:6–19; 11:1–7, 36–40, and 73–74. 2 Baruch was composed in Hebrew, then translated into Greek, and later into Syriac. A text in Syriac, dating from the sixth century A.D., is preserved in its entirety. The Hebrew original is lost and only a few fragments remain from the Greek. All sections in this chapter are revisions by Willis Barnstone based on R. H. Charles's translation in R. H. Charles, The Apocrypha and Pseudepigrapha of the Old Testament, vol. 2 (Oxford: Clarendon Press, 1913), pp. 485–487, 500–501, 518.

I shall call the Sirens from the sea
(those wives of angels gone astray),
and you, Lilin,[1] night demons, come from the desert,
and you, Shedim[2] and dragons of the forests,
wake and gird your loins for mourning,
sing dirges with me,
sing lamentations with me.

Farmers, do not sow again.
Earth, why bother to give your harvest fruits?
Keep your sweet foods under the earth.
Vine, why bother to give wine?
For in Zion offerings will not be made again,
no fruit be forthcoming.

Heavens, hold back your dew,
keep sealed the treasuries of rain.
Sun, hold back the light of your rays.
Moon, extinguish the multitude of your light.
Why should light rise again
when the light of Zion is shadow?

Grooms, do not come near,
nor let brides loop their hair with flowers.
Women, pray for barrenness,
for barren will be the happiest,
the sonless be glad
and those with sons will grieve.

Why should a woman bear children in pain
only to bury them in grief?
Why should we have sons?
Why should we give names to our seed
when the mother Jerusalem is desolate
and her sons captive?

From now on let us not speak of beauty
or grace.

Priests, take the keys of the sanctuary
and hurl them at the heavens.
Give them back to the Lord, saying:
"Guard your own house.
We are false stewards."

And virgins, who weave gold of Ophir
into delicate linen and silks,
quickly
cast them in the fire
that fire may carry them to him their creator
lest the enemy seize them.

And Babylon,[3] against you, I, Baruch, say:
"Had you prospered
and Zion dwelled in her glory

we would still grieve
to find you equal to Zion.
But now our misery is infinite,
our lamentation unending,
for you prosper
while Zion is desolate.

"Who will judge these things?
To whom shall we complain?
O Lord, how do you bear this?
Our fathers died peacefully
and the righteous sleep in the earth serenely.
They didn't know this anguish
or our fate.
O earth, if only you had tears,
O dust, if only you had a heart,
you would announce in Sheol,
addressing the dead,
'You are more blessed than we who are alive.' "

THE VISION OF THE FOREST, THE VINE, THE FOUNTAIN, AND THE CEDAR

And when I had said these things I fell asleep there, and I saw a vision in the night. And behold, a forest of trees planted on the plain, and lofty and rugged rocky mountains surrounded it, and that forest was huge. And behold, over it a vine rose, and from under it a peaceful fountain flowed. Now the fountain stream reached the forest and became great waves, and those waves sank the forest, and suddenly they rooted out most of the forest, and overthrew the mountains circling it. The high forest was made low, the mountain summits were made low, and that fountain prevailed so that nothing was left of the forest except for one cedar. When the waves had destroyed and rooted everything from the earth, nothing was left and the place was unrecognizable; the vine began to come from the fountain in peace, and came near the cedar. And I saw that the vine opened its mouth and spoke and said to that cedar:

"Are you not that cedar which was left from the forest of wickedness, by whose means wickedness persisted for so many years, never allowing goodness to survive? And you kept conquering what was not yours, and you showed no compassion, and you kept extending your power over those who were far away. Those who drew near you you held in the net of your wickedness, and you hovered over everything as one who could not be rooted out! But now your time has sped away and your hour has come. Cedar, leave, following the forest which left before you, and become dust with it and let your ashes be mingled together. And now recline in anguish, rest in torment till your last time comes, when you will come again, and be tormented even more."

Interpretation of the Vision
And I prayed and said: "O Lord, my Lord, you always enlighten those who are led by understanding. Your law is life, and your wisdom is guidance. Make known to me the interpretation of this vision. You know that my soul has al-

509

ways walked in your law and from youngest days I have not strayed from your wisdom."

And he answered, saying to me: "Baruch, this is the interpretation of the vision which you have seen. The great forest surrounded by lofty and rugged mountains is the word. Behold! the days come, and the kingdom which once destroyed Zion will be destroyed, and a third will arise and that also will have dominion for a time and it will be destroyed. And after these a fourth kingdom[4] will arise whose power will be harsh and evil far beyond those before it, and like the forests on the plain it will rule many times, and it will hold on for periods of time, and exalt itself more than cedars of Lebanon. It will hide the truth, and all those who are polluted with iniquity will flee to it, since evil beasts flee and creep into the forest. And it will come to pass when the time of its

fall has come, that the principiate of my messiah will be revealed, which is like the fountain and the vine, and when it is revealed it will root out the multitude of its host. And touching what you have seen, the lofty cedar, the sole tree left of that forest, will have converse with the vine. You heard the words that the vine spoke. It is the word.

"The last leader[5] of that time will be left alive when the multitude of his hosts will be put to the sword, and he will be bound, and they will take him up Mount Zion, and my messiah will convict him of all his impieties, and will gather and set before him all the work of his hosts. Later he will put him to death, and protect the rest of my people who will be found in the place I have chosen. And his principiate will stand forever, until the world of corruption is at an end, and until all the aforesaid is fulfilled. This is my vision, and this is its interpretation."

THE ANGEL RAMIEL SPEAKS OF THE COMING OF THE BRIGHT LIGHTNING, THE MESSIAH

When he has brought low everything in the world
and on the throne of his kingdom, for that whole age, sits down in peace,
then joy will be revealed
and also rest.

Healing will descend in dew,
disease will withdraw,
and worry and pain and lamentation will be unknown to men
and felicity will cover the earth.

No one will die untimely
nor will adversity strike.

Judgments, reviling, contention, revenge,
blood, passion, envy, hatred
will all be condemned and removed.

For those are the evils that fill the world
and trouble man.

Wild beasts will leave the forest and minister to men,
and asps and dragons will come out of their holes and serve a little child.

Women will no longer feel pain when they bear
nor suffer torment when they yield the fruit of the womb.

And in those days reapers will not grow weary
nor builders feel toil
and their labors will advance swiftly
and serenely,
for in that time the corruptible will vanish
and the incorruptible will have its beginning,
to which good things belong,
far from evil and near the immortal.
This is bright lightning who came after the last dark waters.

Notes

1. Lilin. Night demons in Assyrian and Babylonian demonology.

2. Shedim. Male demons in Assyrian and Babylonian demonology.

3. Babylon stands for Rome as in Revelations 14:8.

4. The four empires are probably Babylon, Persia, Diadochi, and Rome.

5. Probably Pompey.

The Apocalypse of Ezra (4 Ezra)

(Jewish Pseudepigrapha)

Before speaking of the contents of the *Apocalypse of Ezra*, a Jewish text of the late first century A.D., we should make clear its curious relation to *2 Esdras*, a Christian writing and a standard book of the Apocrypha.[1] The *Apocalypse of Ezra* appears as chapters 3 through 14 of *2 Esdras*. (Esdras is the Greek form of the Hebrew name Ezra.) While *4 Ezra* raises the disturbing question of theodicy—how could a just God allow the defeat and destruction of his people—*2 Esdras* resolves the question by saying that God has forsaken Israel in order to give his name to other nations and to the new mother church. Like the Gospel according to Matthew, *2 Esdras* is a reinterpretation of a Jewish document concerning the Son of man, that complex figure first spoken of in Daniel 7, who is also called the messiah. The original apocalypse was probably composed in Hebrew. By the second century, a Christian editor added chapters to the Greek translation of the Jewish text and brought it into line with the notion that God abandoned the children of Israel in order to have the "Son of man" save his new people.

The original apocalypse of Ezra reflects that pessimism, found in *2 Baruch*, caused by the destruction of the Temple in A.D. 70. For the seer, who is called "Ezra," Israel's punishment at the hands of the Gentiles is almost an indictment of God's ways. How could God betray the covenant and abandon his people? To dramatize the scene, the setting is in Babylonia, thirty years after the destruction of Jerusalem in 557 B.C. The parallel between these two disastrous periods is obvious. To answer Ezra's accusatory questions, the angel Uriel gives the traditional answer of other apocalypses. The fall of Jerusalem came about because of evil, beginning with Adam's transgression and then Israel's sins. But the Son of man, the messiah, will come. Ezra is not satisfied, for the wait is long, the number saved will be few, and he is less than happy with his disputations, each of which ends with his fasting in preparation for another revelation. Finally, Ezra addresses God and, as in the book of Job, God has basically no answer other than to demand faith and obedience to the Torah while awaiting the new Jerusalem in heaven. As George Nickelsburg writes, "God simply pulls rank, maintaining that no human can hope to understand his ways."[2]

Ezra has four visions in the second part of the book, which, in contrast to the grief of the earlier chapters, offers consolation and hope. In the vision of the three heads of the eagle, the heads represent the Roman emperors Vespasian, Titus, and Domitian. Imperial Rome is wickedness, as is the "beast" in the New Testament Apocalypse of John. But that Rome will be overthrown by the Lion of Judah, "the Messiah . . . who will spring from the seed of David" (12:32), and the rule of God will be a reality on earth. What is clear, however, is that the new Jerusalem will not be on earth but in Heaven. We are to look forward to the heavenly city in a future incorruptible age. From a theological point of view, 4 Ezra is essentially otherworldly in its eschatology. The body is the mere prison of the soul, a "corruptible vessel" (7:88), and only the soul is immortal. The soul, not the body, will be resurrected on the day of the "fruit of immortality" (7:13). The writer's dualism is absolute.

The Apocalypse of Ezra is a gloomy and visionary work, offering hope for the few in another spiritual realm. The messiah will be the instrument of salvation. The final vision of this ascetic book is that of the "Man from the Sea." The Man from the Sea is the preexistent messiah, who will use the weapons of fire to destroy enemies and bring the tribes of Israel back to a messianic kingdom of peace. In its primordial qualities the myth goes beyond allegiance to one people. The salvific figure of extraordinary powers is a universal type commonly found in the legends of virtually every people. His appearance in 4 Ezra brings to a climax the literary qualities and theological statements of the apocalypse.

Notes

1. The Apocryphal books, which Jerome included in his Latin translation of the Bible called the Vulgate, are all translated from the Greek Septuagint with the exception of 2 Esdras.

2. George W. E. Nickelsburg, *Jewish Literature between the Bible and the Mishnah* (Philadelphia: Fortress Press, 1981), p. 293.

THE SEER SPEAKS OF THE SIGNS
WHICH PRECEDE THE END*

Days come when the inhabitants of the earth are seized with great panic
and the way of truth hidden
and the land[1] will be barren of faith.

Then the sun will suddenly shine by night
and the moon by day.
Blood will trickle forth from wood
and stone speak its voice.
People will be confounded
and stars change course.

An unknown force will wield sovereignty
and birds take general flight
and the sea hurl up its fish
An unknown voice will be heard by night
and all will hear,
and the earth will break open over vast regions
and fire explode interminably.
Wild beasts will desert their haunts, and women bear monsters.

One-year-old children will speak,
pregnant women will bring forth at three or four months,
and these will live and dance.
Sown fields will dry up, full storehouses be empty,
salt waters turn sweet,
friends attack each other fiercely.
Then intelligence will hide
and wisdom withdraw to its chamber
where none can find it.
Unrighteousness and lust will cloud the earth
and lands will ask each other:
"Has righteousness come your way?"
And the answer will be No.
In that time all hope will fail,
all labor fail.
These signs I tell you, but if you pray, weep, and fast seven days,
you will hear wondrous things.

---

*Chapters 5:1, 5:4–13. All selections in this
chapter are revisions of selections from the
translation in R. H. Charles, *The Apocrypha and
Pseudepigrapha of the Old Testament*, vol. 2 (Oxford: Clarendon Press, 1913), pp. 569–570.

THE ANGEL SPEAKS*

For you Paradise is opened,
the Tree of Life planted,
the future age and abundance
are prepared,
a city is built[2]
and rest appointed,
good words established,
wisdom defined.
Evil roots are sealed up from you,
sickness extinguished from your path.
Death is concealed,
Hades fled,
corruption sinks in oblivion,
sorrow is gone,
and in the end
the gold of immortality is manifest.

THE MAN FROM THE SEA[3]
(SIXTH VISION)*

And it came to pass that after seven days I dreamt a dream at night. There arose a violent wind from the sea and it stirred all its waves. Out of the heart of the seas the wind caused the form of a man to come up. I looked and this man flew with the clouds of Heaven. Wherever he turned his countenance, everything he saw trembled. Wherever the voice went out of his mouth, all that heard his voice melted away as wax melts when it feels fire. After this I saw that from the four winds of Heaven was gathered together an innumerable multitude[4] of men to make war against the Man who came up out of the sea. But he cut out a great mountain and flew up upon it. I tried to see the region or place from which the mountain had been cut out but I could not. And then I saw all who were gathered together against him to wage war.

They were seized with a great fear but they dared to fight. When he saw the assault of the multitude coming near him, he neither lifted his hand nor held a spear or any weapon. But out of his mouth he sent a fiery stream and from his lips a flaming breath, and from his tongue he shot forth a storm of sparks. And these were all mingled together—the fiery stream, the flaming breath, and the storm. It all fell on the assault of the multitude which was preparing to fight and it burned them all up, so that suddenly the innumerable multitude was nothing but dust of ashes and smell of smoke. When I saw this I was amazed. Later I saw the same Man come down from the mountain, and call another multitude to him—which was peaceful. The faces of many men drew near him, some of them glad, some sorrowful. Some were in bonds,[5] some brought others who should be offered in oblation.

The Interpretation of the Vision
"These are the interpretations of the vision. Since you saw a Man coming up from the heart of the sea, it is he whom the Highest One is keeping for many ages (and through whom he will deliver his creation).[6] He will determine the survivors. Since you saw that wind, fire, and storm came out of his mouth, that he held neither spear nor weapon, but destroyed the assaulting multitude who had come to fight against him, here is the interpretation:

"Behold, the days come when the Highest One is about to deliver those who are on the earth. And these earth dwellers will be astonished. They will plan to war against each other, city against city, place against place, people against people, and kingdom against kingdom. And when these things come to pass and the signs happen that I showed you, then will my Son be revealed as the Man you saw ascending. When all nations hear my voice, every man will leave his own land and the war-

---

*Chapter 8:52, pp. 597–598.
*Chapters 13:1–13, 25–52; pp. 616–617, 618 –619.

fare of one against the other, and an innumerable multitude will be gathered together, as you saw, desiring to come and to fight against him. But he will stand upon the summit of Mount Zion. And Zion will come[7] and will be made manifest to all men, prepared and built, as you saw the mountain cut out without hands. But he, my Son, will reprove the nations that have come for their ungodliness, and the rebukes are like a storm and will reproach them to their face with their evil thoughts and with tortures with which they are destined to be tortured—like flame. Then he will destroy them without labor by the Law, which is like fire.

"And since you saw that he also summoned and gathered to himself another peaceful multitude—the ten tribes that were led away captive out of their own land in the days of Josiah the king,[8] tribes that Salmanassar, king of the Assyrians, led away captive. He took them across the river and transported them into another land. But they took counsel among themselves that they should leave the multitude of the heathen and go forth into a still more distant land where the human race had never dwelt, and there at least keep their statutes which they had not kept in their own land. They entered by the narrow passages of the Euphrates river. Then the Highest One wrought wonders for them, and stayed the springs of the river until they passed over it. And through that country there was a great way to go, a journey of a year and a half, and that region was called Arzareth. There they have dwelt until the last times, and now, when they are about to come again, the Highest One will again stay the springs of the river so that they may pass over it. So you see a multitude gathered together in peace. The survivors of your people, even those who are found within my holy borders, will be saved. Then he will destroy the multitude of nations gathered together, and will defend the people who remain. And he will show them many wonders."

And I said: "O Lord my Lord, show me this. Why have I seen the Man coming up from the heart of the sea?" And he said to me, "Just as one can neither seek out nor know what is in the deep of the sea, so no one on earth can see my Son or those who are with him but in the time of his day. Such is the interpretation of the dream you have seen."

Notes

1. The Roman Empire.
2. Heavenly Jerusalem, which will compensate for the loss of Jerusalem on earth.
3. The messiah.
4. The innumerable multitude, like the nations of the world, is the enemy of the messiah. They are all heathen nations against the people of God.
5. Jews in captivity.
6. The messiah is preexistent to the creation.
7. Zion here is the heavenly city which will descend from Heaven at the end of the messianic age.
8. Josiah is an error. The name of the king in whose reign the captivity took place is Hosea. See 2 Kings 17.

The Ascension of Isaiah

(Christian Apocrypha)

When in the *Commedia* we follow Dante's journey into Hell and discover the horrible punishments, the grotesque tortures of its inhabitants, or rise with the poet into Paradise and witness the white rose of love and hear the singing of God's angels, we have traveled the same route as in an early Christian apocalypse. Virgil accompanies Dante instead of an "interpreting angel," but the vision and prophecy of the End are the same.

The Christian apocalypse is an eschatological genre of writing in which knowledge of the End is the author's main aim. This knowledge, serving as a universal warning and hope, is conveyed through a journey to Hell and to Heaven, resulting in the disclosure of otherworldly secrets. Usually the author recounts his vision as a rapture, that is, an ecstatic ascent, outside of time, to other realms. To give authority to the vision, the apocalyptist (the author of the apocalypse) takes on the name of a great figure of the past, either an apostle or a patriarch of the Old Testament. To increase its prophetic value, the work is usually placed in the past; thus the prophecy of future history can be proved correct (because in fact these earlier events have already occurred). An important reason for this intent to deceive the reader is to prove God's power to determine all events in the world. God who created the world foreordained its course. The apocalypse, like the Sibylline oracles, used a symbolic or allegorical language to convey the message about the imminent End.

In every regard the Christian apocalypses used the method and themes of earlier Jewish apocalypse as well as Jewish Sibylline prophetic texts. Frequently, the Christian writers took Jewish scriptures, reworked them, Christianized them, substituted Christ for the Jewish messiah or for the Son of man, the frequent messianic figure of inter-

517

testamental scriptures. As in Jewish works, they often inserted a prayer between the vision and its interpretation. They retained the basic dualism of a Two-Ages division of the temporary and perishable Age as opposed to the future imperishable and eternal Age. The depreciation of the present Age results in an extreme pessimism for all worldly things.

Martin Buber carefully distinguished between the prophetic and the apocalyptic traditions in *Kampf um Israel* (1933). In the prophetic tradition evil forces are warned and are given the option to repent and be saved; the good will be saved if they do not convert. In the apocalyptic tradition, which Buber traces to Islamic dualism of good and evil, evil is totally destroyed by good. While the prophets saw Nature as a good force and the earth as redeemable, in the apocalyptic tradition this world, all of Nature, is doomed to make way for otherworldly places. The utter rejection of the world is but one step away from the Gnostics, who used this notion as a basic principle to reject not only this world but its Creator God.

Apocalypses have also been found among the Nag Hammadi Gnostic texts. In general they place more emphasis on a visionary view of creation and salvation rather than on an apocalyptic gaze into Hell and Heaven. In any case they show the same visionary impulse developed within the Gnostic tradition. Some scholars think that the Gnostics themselves came about specifically because of the failure of Jewish apocalyptic hopes. (See Robert M. Grant's *Gnosticism and Early Christianity.*)

The word apocalypse in Greek means an "uncovering," a "revelation," and it is used to designate knowledge of the end of the world, of the secrets of other worlds. Only the Apocalypse of John, the Book of Revelation, uses the presumed name of its author. The others, as said, are pseudepigraphical, borrowing names of earlier great personages. The Christian apocalypses are thoroughly frightening for the sadistic punishments inflicted on the inhabitants of Hell, for the inventions of extreme torture and dismemberment. The descriptions of Heaven are scarcely less awesome, with pictures of angel servants in the Heavens, singing eternal hymns of praise to a bejeweled Lord whose face is too bright to be perceived.

To return to Dante, the spectacle of the End is not pleasant nor ordinary; it is extraordinary, overwhelming. Although these apocalypses use stock material of the genre, in their preset and predetermined vision they contain a fiery ecstatic glimpse into "the beyond." The vision is a highmark of literary and religious expression.

The *Ascension of Isaiah* is an uneven work, with lyrical passages describing the life of prophets exiled in the mountains and instructional passages on the virtue of Isaiah and the rewards of Heaven. The book is divided into two parts: the familiar story of Isaiah's betrayal and martyrdom and the prophet's vision of his heavenly journey. Most scholars contend that the two parts are entirely separate, and the sense as well as the manuscript tradition seems to bear this out. The book or parts of it are available in Greek, Old Slavonic, and Coptic. The entire work exists in Ethiopic translation.

The martyrdom of Isaiah is also said to be originally a Jewish pseudepigraphical work from no later than the first century A.D. The visionary section is a Christian apocalypse from about the middle of the second century. But if the first part is Jewish in origin, it is, in its present form, thoroughly interpolated with Christian thought. The references to the "Beloved" bring in Jesus Christ on the very first page. Other references to the twelve apostles, and to the death and resurrection of the Beloved, are an appropriate parallel to Isaiah's company of surrounding prophets, his prophecy of his death, and his ascension to the seventh heaven. In the present redaction Isaiah actually claims that when he rose to Heaven he saw Jesus Christ waiting to descend to earth. Further, Isaiah himself believes in the divinity of Jesus Christ crucified. The Christianization of indispensable Jewish prophets was one of the common elements of early Christian apocrypha.

As Isaiah rises from one heaven to another, there appears to be great rivalry between the competing rungs, with the seventh heaven triumphant and superior. Some of Heaven's famous inhabitants—Adam, Abel, Enoch—are in their glory, but are without their crowns and thrones. They are waiting for Christ to descend and rise again, after which they will be granted emblems of their own rank. Heaven also has books on everything that happens in the world. Nothing is "hidden" from Heaven. The image of books implies God's determination of all events, through all time.

In Heaven the main occupation is worshiping and saying praise to the Lord and rejoicing at the splendor of the ruling figures. Failure to sing praise means a fall from Heaven. Heaven is not described with the fascinating detail of descriptions applied to Hell in other apocalypses. As for truly heavenly joy, that is usually reserved for Eden, though even in Eden joy is brief and clouded by paternal taboos and impending doom.

The *Ascension of Isaiah* is a Christian apocalypse with strong didactic elements. The two main messages tell us that Isaiah was a proto-Christian, who actually saw Christ when he rose to Heaven; and that Heaven is the reward of virtue while Hell is the destiny of sinners who will be struck by fire from the mouth of Jesus Christ when he descends into Hell.

THE ASCENSION OF ISAIAH*

It came to pass in the twenty-sixth year of the reign of Hezekiah, king of Judah, that he called Manasseh his son who was the only son he had. And he called him into the presence of the prophet Isaiah, the son of Amoz, and into the presence of Jasub, the son of Isaiah, in order to deliver to him the words of righteousness which he, the king, himself had seen, and the eternal judgments and the punishments of Hell and of the prince of this world, and of his angels, authorities and powers; and the words of the faith concerning the Beloved which he himself had seen in the fifteenth year of his reign

*Chapters 1–5. All selections in this chapter are from Edgar Hennecke and Wilhelm Schneemelcher, eds. and trans., *New Testament Apocrypha*, vol. 2 (Philadelphia: Westminster Press, 1963), pp. 644–663.

during his illness. And he delivered to him the recorded words which Sebna, the scribe, had written and that which Isaiah the son of Amoz had given to him together with the prophets, that they might write down and store with him what he himself had seen in the king's house concerning the judgments of the angels and the destruction of this world, concerning the garments of the righteous, and concerning the going forth, the transformation, the persecution, and ascension of the Beloved.

And in the twentieth year of the reign of Hezekiah, Isaiah had seen the words of this prophecy and had delivered them to his son Jasub. And whilst the former gave commands, with Jasub the son of Isaiah present, Isaiah said to king Hezekiah, but not in the presence of Manasseh alone did he say it to him, "As truly as the Lord liveth, whose name has not been sent into this world, and as truly as the Beloved of my Lord liveth, and the spirit which speaketh in me liveth, all these commands and these words will have no value for thy son Manasseh, and by the outrage of his hands I shall depart amid the torture of my body. And Sammael Malkira will serve Manasseh and execute all his desires, and he will be a follower of Beliar rather than of me. And many in Jerusalem and in Judah will he cause to depart from the true faith, and Beliar will dwell in Manasseh, and by his hand shall I be sawn asunder."

And when Hezekiah heard these words, he wept very bitterly, rent his clothes, cast dust upon his head and fell on his face. And Isaiah said to him, "The design of Sammael against Manasseh is already settled: nothing will help you." On that day Hezekiah resolved within himself to kill his son. But Isaiah said to Hezekiah, "The Beloved will make your purpose fruitless and the thought of your heart will not be accomplished, for with this calling have I been called, and I must have my portion with the inheritance of the Beloved."

And after Hezekiah died and Manasseh became king, he remembered no more the commands of his father Hezekiah, but forgot them, and Sammael settled upon Manasseh and clung fast to him. And Manasseh ceased from serving the God of his father and served Satan and his angels and powers. And he caused the house of his father, which had been under the eye of Hezekiah, to depart from the words of wisdom and from the service of God. And Manasseh altered his purpose and became a servant of Beliar, whose name is Matanbukus. Now this Beliar rejoiced in Jerusalem over Manasseh and strengthened him in his leading to apostasy and in the lawlessness which was spread abroad in Jerusalem. Witchcraft and the practice of magic increased, and predictions from the flight of birds, divination, fornication, [adultery], the persecution of the righteous by Manasseh, [Belchira], Tobia the Canaanite, John of Anathoth, and Zadok, the overseer of works. The rest of the narrative is recorded in the book of the kings of Judah and Israel.

And when Isaiah the son of Amoz saw the evil which was taking place in Jerusalem, the worship of Satan and its wantonness, he withdrew from Jerusalem and settled in Bethlehem-Judah. But there was much lawlessness there also; so he withdrew from Bethlehem and settled on a mountain in desert country. And Micaiah the prophet and Ananias the aged, and Joel, Habakkuk and Jasub his son, and many of the faithful who believed in the ascension to Heaven withdrew and settled on the mountain.

And they all put on sackcloth and all were prophets; they had nothing with them, but were naked and they bitterly lamented the apostasy of Israel. And they had nothing to eat except wild herbs which they gathered on the mountains, and after they had cooked them, they ate them in the company of the prophet Isaiah. And thus they spent two years on the mountains and hills.

And after this, while they were in the

desert, a man appeared in Samaria named Belchira, of the family of Zedekiah, the son of Chenaan, a false prophet who had his dwelling place in Bethlehem; now Hezekiah, the son of Chanani, his father's brother, was in the days of Ahab king of Israel the teacher of the four hundred prophets of Baal, and Zedekiah smote and abused the prophet Micaiah, the son of Imlah. And Micaiah was also abused by Ahab and was thrown into prison. And he was with the false prophet Zedekiah; they were with Ahaziah the son of Ahab in Samaria. But Elijah the prophet from Thisbe in Gilead rebuked Ahaziah and Samaria, and prophesied concerning Ahaziah that he would die on his bed of a sickness, and that Samaria would be delivered into the hand of Salmanasser, because he had slain the prophets of God. And when the false prophets who were with Ahaziah, the son of Ahab and their teacher Jallarias from Mount Joel heard—now Belchira was a brother of Zedekiah—when they heard, they prevailed upon Ahaziah, king of Gomorrah, and slew Micaiah.

But Belchira found and saw the whereabouts of Isaiah and the prophets who were with him, for he lived in the region of Bethlehem and was an adherent of Manasseh. And he appeared as a false prophet in Jerusalem and many in Jerusalem joined with him, although he was from Samaria. And it came to pass when Salmanasser, king of Assyria, came and captured Samaria and led the nine and a half tribes into captivity, and dragged them off to the mountains of the Medes and to the river Gozan, this man, while still a youth, escaped and reached Jerusalem in the days of Hezekiah, king of Judah; but he walked not in the ways of his father of Samaria, for he feared Hezekiah. And he was found in the days of Hezekiah delivering impious speeches in Jerusalem. And the servants of Hezekiah accused him and he fled to the region of Bethlehem, and they persuaded. [. . .] Now Belchira accused Isaiah and the prophets who were with him in these words,

"Isaiah and his companions prophesy against Jerusalem and against the cities of Judah that they shall be laid waste, and against the children of Judah and Benjamin, that they shall go into captivity, and against you also, O lord my king, that you shall go bound with hooks and iron chains; but they prophesy falsely concerning Israel and Judah. And Isaiah himself has said, 'I see more than the prophet Moses.' Now Moses said, 'There is no man who can see God and live,' but Isaiah has said, 'I have seen God and behold, I live.' Know therefore, O king, that he is a liar. Moreover he has called Jerusalem Sodom and the princes of Judah and Jerusalem he has declared to be the people of Gomorrah." And he brought many accusations against Isaiah and the prophets before Manasseh. But Beliar abode in the heart of Manasseh and in the hearts of the princes of Judah and Benjamin, of the eunuchs and councillors of the king. And the speech of Belchira pleased him exceedingly and he sent and seized Isaiah.

For Beliar harbored great wrath against Isaiah on account of the vision and of the exposure with which he had exposed Sammael, and because through him the coming forth of the Beloved from the seventh heaven had been revealed, and his transformation, his descent and the likeness into which he was to be transformed, namely, the likeness of a man, and the persecution which he was to suffer, and the tortures with which the children of Israel were to afflict him, and the coming of the twelve disciples and the instruction, and that he should before the Sabbath be crucified on the tree and that he was to be crucified together with criminals, and that he would be buried in a sepulcher, and that the twelve who were with him would be offended because of him, and the watch of the guards of the grave, and the descent of the angel of the church which is in the heavens, whom he will summon in the last days; and that the angel of the Holy Spirit and Michael, the chief of the holy angels, would open his grave on the third day, and that the Beloved, sitting on their shoulders, will come forth and send out his twelve disciples, and that they will teach to all the nations and every tongue the resurrection of the Beloved, and that those who believe on his cross will be saved, and in his ascension to the seventh heaven, whence he came; and that many who believe in him will speak in the power of the Holy Spirit, and that many signs and wonders will take place in those days; and afterwards, when he is at hand, his disciples will forsake the teaching of the twelve apostles and their faith, their love and their purity, and there will arise much contention about his coming and his appearing. And in those days there will be many who will love office though they are devoid of wisdom, and many elders will be lawless and violent shepherds to their sheep and will become ravagers of the sheep, since they have no holy shepherds. And many will exchange the glory of the garment of the saints for the garment of the covetous, and respect for persons will be common in those days, and such as love the honor of this world. And there will be much slandering and boasting at the approach of the Lord and the Holy Spirit will depart from many. And in those days there will not be many prophets nor such as speak reliable words, except a few here and there, on account of the spirit of error, of fornication, of boasting, and of covetousness which shall be in those who yet will be called his servants and who receive him. Great discord will arise among them, between shepherds and elders. For great jealousy will prevail in the last days, for each will say what seems pleasing in his own eyes. And they will set aside the prophecies of the prophets which were before me and also pay no attention to these my visions, in order to speak forth from the torrent of their heart.

And now, Hezekiah and Jasub, my son, these are the days of the completion of the world. And after it has come to its consummation, Beliar, the great prince, the king of this world who has ruled it since it came into being, shall descend; he will come down from his firmament in the form of a man, a lawless king, a slayer of his mother, who himself even this king will persecute the plant which the twelve apostles of the Beloved have planted; and one of the twelve will be delivered into his hand. This ruler will thus come in the likeness of that king and there will come with him all the powers of this world and they will hearken to him in all that he desires. And at his word the sun will rise in the night and he will cause the moon to shine at the sixth hour. All that he desires he will do in the world; and he will act and speak in the name of the Beloved and say, "I am God and before me there has been none else." And all the people in the world will believe in him, and will sacrifice to him and serve him saying, "This is God and beside him there is none other." And the majority of those who have united to receive the Beloved will turn aside to him, and the power of his miracles will be manifest in every city and region, and he will set up his image before him in every city, and he shall rule three years, seven months, and twenty-seven days. And many believers and saints, after they have seen him for whom they hoped, Jesus Christ the crucified—after I, Isaiah, have seen him who was crucified and ascended—who thus believed in him, of these only a few will remain as his servants, fleeing from desert to desert and awaiting his coming.

And after one thousand three hundred and thirty-two days the Lord will come with his angels and with the hosts of the saints from the seventh heaven with the glory of the seventh heaven, and will drag Beliar with his hosts into Gehenna, and he will bring rest to the pious who shall be found alive in the body in this world and the sun shall grow red with shame, and to all who through faith in him have cursed Beliar and his kings. But the saints will come with the Lord in their garments which are stored on high in the seventh heaven; with the Lord they will come, whose spirits are clothed, they will descend and be present in the world, and those who are found in the body will be strengthened by the image of the saints in the garments of the saints, and the Lord will minister to those who were watchful in the world. And afterwards they will turn themselves upwards in their garments but their body will remain in the world. Then the voice of the Beloved will in wrath rebuke this Heaven and this dry place (the earth) and the mountains and hills, the cities, the desert, and the forests, the angels of the sun and of the moon and all things wherein Beliar manifests himself and acts openly in this world, and resurrection and judgment will take place in their midst in those days, and the Beloved will cause fire to go forth from himself, and it will consume all the impious and they will be as if they had not been created.

The remainder of the words of the vision is recorded in the vision concerning Babylon. And the rest of the vision of the Lord, behold, it is recorded in parables in my words which are written in the book which I openly proclaimed. Moreover the descent of the Beloved into the realm of the dead is recorded in the section where the Lord says, "Behold, my servant is prudent." And behold, all these things are written in the Psalms in the poems of David, the son of Jesse, in the sayings of his son Solomon, in the words of Korah and Ethan, the Israelite, and in the words of Asaph, and in the remaining Psalms which the angel of the spirit caused to be written by those whose name is not recorded, and in the words of Amoz, my father, and of the prophets Hosea and Micah, Joel, Nahum, Jonah, Obadiah, Habakkuk, Haggai, Zepha-

niah, Zechariah, and Malachi, and in the words of Joseph the Just, and in the words of Daniel.

On account of this vision, therefore, Beliar grew angry with Isaiah and he dwelt in the heart of Manasseh, and Isaiah was sawn asunder with a treesaw. And when Isaiah was being sawn asunder, Belchira, his accuser, and all the false prophets stood there, laughing and expressing their malicious joy over Isaiah. And Belchira, at the instigation of Mekembukus, stood before Isaiah, mocking him. And Belchira said to Isaiah: "Say 'In all that I have spoken, I have lied: the ways of Manasseh are good and right, also the ways of Belchira and his companions are right.' " This he said to him when they were beginning to saw him asunder. But Isaiah was absorbed in a vision of the Lord, and although his eyes were open, he did not see them. And Belchira spoke thus to Isaiah, "Say what I say to you and I will alter their purpose, and I will prevail upon Manasseh and the princes of Judah and the people and all Jerusalem to reverence you, upon their knees." And Isaiah answered and said, "So far as I am concerned, so to speak, damned and cursed be you, all your powers, and your whole house, for you can take no more than the skin of my flesh." So they seized and sawed asunder Isaiah the son of Amoz, with a saw. And Manasseh, Belchira, the false prophets, and the princes, and the people all stood and looked on. And to the prophets who were with him he said before he was sawn asunder: "Go to the region of Tyre and Sidon; for me alone has God mingled the cup." But while he was being sawn asunder Isaiah neither cried out nor wept, but his mouth conversed with the Holy Spirit until he had been sawn apart.

This did Beliar to Isaiah through Belchira and Manasseh, for Sammael cherished fierce anger against Isaiah from the days of Hezekiah king of Judah, on account of the things which he had seen concerning the Beloved, and because of the destruction of Sammael, which he had seen through the Lord, while his father Hezekiah was still king. And he acted according to the will of Satan.

THE VISION WHICH ISAIAH THE SON OF AMOZ SAW*

In the twentieth year of the reign of Hezekiah, king of Judah, Isaiah the son of Amoz and Jasub the son of Isaiah came from Gilgal to Jerusalem to Hezekiah. And after Isaiah had entered he sat down on the king's couch and, although they brought him a chair, he refused to sit on it. So Isaiah began to speak words of faith and righteousness with Hezekiah, while all the princes of Israel sat around with the eunuchs and the king's councillors. And there were there forty prophets and sons of the prophets who had come from the neighboring districts, from the mountains and from the plains, when they heard that Isaiah had come from Gilgal to Hezekiah. They had come to greet him and to hear his words, and that he might lay his hands upon them and that they might prophesy and that he might hear their prophecy; and they were all before Isaiah. When Isaiah was speaking to Hezekiah the words of truth and faith, they all heard the door which someone had opened, and the voice of the spirit. Then the king called all the prophets and the entire people who were found there, and they came in, and Micaiah and the aged Ananias, and Joel and Jasub sat on his right hand and on his left. And it came to pass when they all heard the voice of the Holy Spirit they all fell upon their knees in worship and glorified the God of righteousness, the Most High in the highest world who as the Holy One has his seat on high and rests among his saints, and they gave honor to him who had granted such a door in the alien world, and had granted it to a man.

And while he was speaking by the Holy Spirit in the hearing of all, he suddenly became silent and his consciousness was taken from him and he saw no more the men who were standing before him: his eyes were open, but his mouth was silent and the consciousness in his body was taken from him; but his breath was still in him, for he saw a vision. And the angel who was sent to make him behold it belonged neither to his firmament nor to the angels of the glory of this world, but had come from the seventh heaven. And the people who were standing around, with the exception of the circle of prophets, did not think that the holy Isaiah had been taken up. And the vision which he saw was not of this world, but from the world which is hidden from all flesh. And after Isaiah had beheld this vision, he imparted it to Hezekiah, his son Jasub, and the remaining prophets. But the leaders, the eunuchs, and the people did not hear, with the exception of Sebna the scribe, Joachim, and Asaph the chronicler, for they were doers of righteousness and the sweet fragrance of the spirit was upon them. But the people did not hear, for Micaiah and Jasub his son had caused them to go forth, when the knowledge of this world was taken from him and he became as a dead man.

Now the vision which he had seen Isaiah narrated to Hezekiah, his son Jasub, Micaiah and the rest of the prophets saying, "In that moment when I was prophesying according to things heard by you, I saw a sublime angel and he was not like the glory of the angels which I was accustomed already to see, but he possessed great glory and honor, so that I cannot describe the glory of this angel. And he took hold of me by my hand and then I saw; and I said to him, 'Who are you, and what is your name,

---

*Chapters 6–11.

and why do you lead me on high?' for strength was granted to me to speak with him. And he said to me: 'When I have led you on high by degrees and have shown you the vision for which I have been sent to you, then will you know who I am, but my name you shall not find out, since you must return to this, your body. But whither I would raise you on high, you shall see, since for this purpose I have been sent.' And I rejoiced because he spoke amiably with me. And he said to me: 'Do you rejoice because I have spoken amiably to you?'; and he went on, 'You will see one who is greater than I, who will speak amiably and peaceably with you; and his Father also who is greater you will see, because for this purpose have I been sent from the seventh heaven to explain all these things for you.' And we ascended to the firmament, I and he, and there I saw Sammael and his hosts, and a great struggle was taking place there, and the angels of Satan were envious of one another. And as it is above, so is it also on the earth, for the likeness of that which is in the firmament is also on the earth. And I said to the angel, 'What is this struggle and what is this envy?' And he said to me, 'So it has been, since this world began until now, and this struggle will continue till he whom you shall see shall come and destroy Satan.'

"And after this he brought me up above the firmament, which is the first heaven. And there I saw a throne in the midst, and on the right and on the left of it were angels. But the angels on the left were not like the angels who stood on the right, for those on the right possessed a greater glory, and they all praised with one voice; and there was a throne in the midst; and likewise those on the left sang praises after them, but their voice was not such as the voice of those on the right, nor their praise like their praise. And I asked the angel who led me and said unto him, 'To whom is this praise given?' And he said to me, 'It is for the praise of him who is in the seventh heaven, for him who rests in eternity among his saints, and for his Beloved, whence I have been sent unto you.' And again he caused me to ascend to the second heaven, and the height of that heaven is the same as from heaven to earth and to the firmament. And I saw there as in the first heaven, angels on the right and on the left and a throne in the midst and the praise of the angels in the second heaven; and he who sat on the throne in the second heaven had a greater glory than all the rest. And there was much more glory in the second heaven, and their praise was not like the praise of those in the first heaven. And I fell on my face to worship him, and the angel who conducted me did not allow me, but said to me, 'Worship neither angel nor throne which belongs to the six heavens—for this reason was I sent to conduct you—till I tell you in the seventh heaven. For above all the heavens and their angels is your throne set, and your garments and your crown which you shall see.' And I rejoiced greatly that those who love the Most High and his Beloved will at their end ascend thither by the angel of the Holy Spirit.

"And he brought me up to the third heaven, and in like manner I saw those on the right and on the left, and there stood there also a throne in the midst but the remembrance of this world is not known there. And I said to the angel who was with me, for the glory of my countenance was being transformed as I ascended from heaven to heaven, 'Nothing of the vanity of that world is here named.' And he answered and said to me, 'Nothing is named by reason of its weakness, and nothing is hidden here of what took place.' And I desired to find out how it is known, but he answered and said to me, 'When I have brought you to the seventh heaven whence I was sent, high above these, then shall you know that nothing is hidden from the thrones and from those who dwell in the heavens and from the angels.' And great were the praises they sang and the glory of him who sat on the throne, and the angels on the right and on the left possessed a greater glory than those in the heaven beneath them.

"And again he carried me upwards to the fourth heaven, and the distance from the third heaven to the fourth is greater than that from earth to the firmament. And there once more I saw those on the right and on the left, and he who sat on the throne was in the midst, and here also they sang their praises. And the praise and glory of the angels on the right was greater than that of those on' the left, and again the glory of him who sat on the throne was greater than that of the angels on the right, and their glory was greater than that of those who were below.

"And he brought me up to the fifth heaven. And again I saw those on the right and those on the left and him who sat on the throne, possessing greater glory than those in the fourth heaven. And the glory of those on the right surpassed that of those on the left. And the glory of him who sat on the throne was greater than the glory of the angels on the right, and their praises were more glorious than those in the fourth heaven. And I praised the unnamed one and the only one, who dwells in the heavens, whose name is unfathomable for all flesh, who has bestowed such a glory from heaven to heaven, who makes great the glory of the angels and makes greater the glory of him who sits on the throne.

"And again he raised me up into the air of the sixth heaven, and I saw there a glory such as I had not seen in the fifth heaven, as I ascended, namely, angels in greater glory; and there was a holy and wonderful song of praise there. And I said to the angel who conducted me 'What is this that I see, my Lord?' And he said, 'I am not your Lord, but your companion.' And once more I asked him saying, 'Why are the angels not any longer in two groups?' And he said, 'From the sixth heaven and upwards there are no longer any angels on the left, nor is there a throne in the midst, but they receive their arrangement from the power of the seventh heaven, where the unnamed one dwells and his Elect one whose name is unfathomable and cannot be known by the whole heaven, for it is he alone to whose voice all the heavens and thrones give answer. Thus I have been empowered and sent to bring you up here to see the glory, and to see the Lord of all those heavens and these thrones being transformed till he comes to your image and likeness. But I say to you, Isaiah, that no one who has to return to a body in this world has ascended or seen or perceived what you have perceived and what you shall yet see; for it is appointed unto you in the lot of the Lord, the lot of the cross of wood, to come hither and from hence comes the power of the sixth heaven and the air.'

"And I extolled my Lord with praise that I through his lot should come hither. And he said, 'Hear then this from your companion: when you by the will of God have ascended here from the body, then shall you receive the garment which you shall see, and the other garments as well, numbered and stored up, you shall see; and then shall you resemble the angels in the seventh heaven.'

"And he brought me up into the sixth heaven and there was no one on the left and no throne in the midst, but all had one appearance and their song of praise was the same. And power was given to me and I sang praise with them, and that angel also, and our praise was like theirs. And there they all named the primal Father and his Beloved, Christ, and the Holy Spirit, all with one voice, but it was not like the voice of the angels in the fifth heaven, nor like their speech, but another voice resounded there, and there was much light there. And then, when I was in the sixth heaven, I considered that light which I had seen in the five heavens as darkness. And I rejoiced and praised him who has bestowed such light on those who wait for his promise. And I besought the angel who conducted me that he would no more take me back to the world of the flesh. I say to you, Hezekiah, and Jasub, my son, and Micaiah, that there is much darkness here. And the angel who conducted me perceived what I thought and said, 'If you rejoice already in this light, how much will you rejoice when, in the seventh heaven, you see that light where God and his Beloved are, whence I have been sent, who in the world will be called "Son." Not yet is he revealed who shall be in this corrupted world and the garments, thrones, and crowns which are laid up for the righteous, for those who believe in that Lord who shall descend in your form. For the light there is great and wonderful. As far as your wish not to return to the flesh is concerned, your days are not yet fulfilled that you may come here.' When I heard that I was sad; but he said, 'Do not be sad.'

"And he conveyed me into the air of the seventh heaven and I heard again a voice saying, 'How far shall he ascend who dwells among aliens?' And I was afraid and began to tremble. And when I trembled, behold, there came another voice, sent forth thence, and said, 'It is permitted to the holy Isaiah to ascend hither, for his garment is here.' And I asked the angel who was with me and said, 'Who is he who forbade me, and who is this who has permitted me to ascend?' And he said unto me, 'He who forbade you is he who is placed over the praise of the sixth heaven, and he who gave permission is your Lord, God, the Lord Christ, who will be called Jesus on earth, but his name you cannot hear till you have ascended out of your body.'

"And he caused me to ascend into the seventh heaven and I saw there a wonderful light and angels without number. And there I saw all the righteous from Adam. And I saw there the holy Abel and all the righteous. And there I saw Enoch and all who were with him, stripped of the garment of the flesh, and I saw them in their higher garments, and they were like the angels who stand there in great glory. But they did not sit on their thrones, nor were their crowns of glory on their heads. And I asked the angel who was with me, 'How is it that they have received their garments, but are without their thrones and their crowns?' And he said to me, 'Crowns and thrones of glory have they not yet received, but first the Beloved will descend in the form in which you will see him descend; that is to say, in the last days the Lord, who will be called Christ, will descend into the world. Nevertheless, they see the thrones and know to whom they shall belong and to whom the crowns shall belong after he has descended and become like you in appearance, and they will think that he is flesh and a man. And the god of that world will stretch forth his hand against the Son, and they will lay hands on him and crucify him on a tree, without knowing who he is. So his descent, as you will see, is hidden from the heavens so that it remains unperceived who he is. And when he has made spoil of the angel of death, he will arise on the third day and will remain in that world five hundred and forty-five days; and then many of the righteous will ascend with him, whose spirits do not receive their garments till the Lord Christ ascends and they ascend with him. Then indeed will they receive their garments and thrones and crowns when he shall have ascended into the seventh heaven.'

"And I said unto him, 'As I asked you in the third heaven, show me how what happens in the world becomes known here.' And while I was still talking with him, behold, there came one of the angels who stood by, more glorious than the glory of that angel who had brought me up from the world, and he showed me books, but not like books of this world, and he opened them and the books were written, but not like books of this world. And he gave them to me and I read them and behold, the deeds of the children of Israel were recorded therein, and the deeds of those whom I know not, my son Jasub. And I said, 'Truly there is nothing hidden in the seventh heaven of that which happens in the world.' And I saw there many garments stored up, and many thrones, and many crowns, and I said to the angel who conducted me, 'To whom do these garments and thrones and crowns belong?' And he said to me, 'These garments shall many from that world receive, if they believe on the words of that one who, as I have told you, shall be named, and observe them and believe therein, and believe in his cross. For them are these laid up.' And I saw one standing whose glory surpassed that of all, and his glory was great and wonderful. And after I had beheld him, all the righteous whom I had seen and all the angels whom I had seen came unto him, and Adam, Abel, and Seth and all the righteous approached first, worshiped him and praised him, all with one voice, and I also sang praise with them, and my song of praise was like theirs. Then all the angels drew near and worshiped and sang praise. And again I was transformed and became like an angel. Then the angel who conducted me said to me, 'Worship this one'; so I worshiped and praised. And the angel said to me, 'This is the Lord of all glory whom you have seen.'

"And while the angel was still speaking, I saw another glorious one, like to him, and the righteous drew near to him, worshiped, and sang praise, and I too sang praise with them, but my glory was not transformed in accordance with their appearance. And thereupon the angels approached and worshiped. And I saw the Lord and the second angel, and they were standing; but the second one whom I saw was on the left of my Lord. And I asked, 'Who is this?' and he said

to me, 'Worship him, for this is the angel of the Holy Spirit, who speaks through you and the rest of the righteous.' And I beheld the great glory, for the eyes of my spirit were open, and I was not thereafter able to see, nor the angel who was with me, nor all the angels whom I had seen worshiping my Lord. But I saw the righteous beholding with great power the glory of that One. So my Lord drew near to me, and the angel of the Spirit, and said, 'Behold, now it is granted to you to behold God, and on your account is power given to the angel with you.' And I saw how my Lord worshiped, and the *angel of the Holy Spirit,* and how both together praised God. Thereupon all the righteous drew near and worshiped, and the angels approached and worshiped, and all the angels sang praise.

"And thereupon I heard the voices and the hymns of praise which I had heard ascending in each of the six heavens and they were audible here. And they were all directed to the glorious One whose glory I could not see. And I myself heard and saw the praise for him. And the Lord and the angel of the spirit beheld all and heard all; and all the praises, which are sent forth from the six heavens, are not only heard, but are seen also. And I heard the angel who led me, how he said, This is the Most High of the High ones, who dwells in the holy world and rests with the holy ones, who will be called by the Holy Spirit, through the mouth of the righteous, the Father of the Lord.' And I heard the words of the Most High, the Father of my Lord, as he spoke to my Lord Christ who shall be called Jesus: 'Go and descend through all the heavens; descend to the firmament and to that world, even to the angel in the realm of the dead; but to Hell you shall not go. And you shall become like to the form of all who are in the five heavens; and with carefulness you shall resemble the form of the angels of the firmament and the angels also who are in the realm of the dead. And none of the angels of this world will know that you, along with me, are the Lord of the seven heavens and of their angels. And they will not know that you are mine till with the voice of Heaven I have summoned their angels and their lights, and the mighty voice be made to resound to the sixth heaven, that you may judge and destroy the prince and his angels and the gods of this world and the world which is ruled by them, for they have denied me and said "We alone are, and there is none beside us." And afterwards you will ascend from the angels of death to your place, and you will not be transformed in each heaven, but in glory you will ascend and sit on my right hand. And the princes and powers of this world will worship you.' Thus I heard the great glory give command to my Lord.

"Then I saw that my Lord went forth from the seventh heaven to the sixth heaven. And the angel who conducted me from this world was with me and said, 'Attend, Isaiah, and behold, that you may see the transformation of the Lord and his descent.' And I beheld and when the angels who are in the sixth heaven saw him they praised and extolled him, for he had not yet been transformed into the form of the angels there, and they praised him, and I also praised with them. And I saw how he descended into the fifth heaven, and in the fifth heaven took the appearance of the angels there, and they did not praise him, for his appearance was like theirs. And immediately he descended into the fourth heaven and took the form of the angels there; and when they saw him, they did not praise and laud him, for his appearance was as theirs. And again I beheld when he descended into the third heaven and took the form of the angels of the third heaven. And the guardians of the gate of this heaven demanded the password and the Lord gave it to them in order that he should not be recognized, and when they saw him they did not

praise and extol him, for his appearance was as theirs. And again I beheld when he descended into the second heaven, and again he gave the password there, for the doorkeepers demanded it and the Lord gave it. And I saw when he took the form of the angels in the second heaven; they saw him but did not praise him, since his form was like theirs. And again I beheld when he descended into the first heaven and also gave the password to the doorkeepers there, and took the form of the angels who are on the left of that throne; and they did not praise or laud him, for his appearance was as theirs. But no one asked me, on account of the angel who conducted me. And again he descended into the firmament where the prince of this world dwells, and he gave the password to those on the left, and his form was like theirs, and they did not praise him there, but struggled with one another in envy, for there the power of evil rules, and envying about trifles. And I beheld, when he descended and became like the angels of the air and was like one of them. And he gave no password for they were plundering and doing violence to one another.

"And after this, I beheld, and the angel who talked with me and conducted me said to me, 'Attend, Isaiah, son of Amoz, because for this purpose have I been sent from God.' And I saw of the family of David the prophet a woman named Mary, who was a virgin, and betrothed to a man called Joseph, a carpenter, and he also was of the seed and family of the righteous David, of Bethlehem in Judah. And he came to his portion. And when she was betrothed, it was found that she was with child, and Joseph, the carpenter, wished to put her away. But the angel of the Spirit appeared in this world, and after that Joseph did not put Mary away, but kept her; but he did not reveal the matter to anyone. And he did not approach Mary, but kept her as a holy virgin, although she was with child. And he did not yet live with her for two months. And after two months, when Joseph was in his house, and his wife Mary, but both alone, it came to pass, while they were alone, that Mary straightway beheld with her eyes and saw a small child, and she was amazed. And when her amazement wore off, her womb was found as it was before she was with child. And when her husband Joseph said to her, 'What made you amazed?' his eyes were opened and he saw the child and praised God, that the Lord had come to his portion. And a voice came to them: 'Tell this vision to no one.' But the report concerning the child was noised abroad in Bethlehem. Some said, 'The virgin Mary has given birth before she was married two months,' and many said 'She has not given birth: the midwife has not gone up to her and we have heard no cries of pain.' And they were all in the dark concerning him, and they all knew of him, but no one knew whence he was. And they took him and came to Nazareth in Galilee.

"And I saw, O Hezekiah and Jasub, my son, and declare before the other prophets who stand here that this was hidden from all the heavens and all the princes and every god of this world. And I saw: in Nazareth he sucked the breast like a baby, as was customary, so that he would not be recognized. And when he grew up he performed great signs and wonders in the land of Israel and in Jerusalem. And after this the adversary envied him and roused the children of Israel against him, not knowing who he was, and they delivered him to the king and crucified him, and he descended to the angel of the underworld. In Jerusalem indeed I saw how he was crucified on the tree, and how he was raised after three days and remained still many days. And the angel who conducted me said to me, 'Attend, Isaiah.' And I saw when he sent out his twelve apostles and ascended. And I saw him and he was in the firmament, but he had not changed to their form, and all the angels of the firmament and the Satan saw him, and they worshiped him. And great sorrow was occasioned there, while they said, 'How did our Lord descend in our midst and we perceived not the glory which was upon him which, as we see, was found on him from the sixth heaven?' And he ascended into the second heaven and was not changed, but all the angels on the right and on the left and the throne in the midst worshiped him and praised him saying, 'How did our Lord remain hidden from us when he descended, and we perceived not?' And in like manner he ascended to the third heaven and they sang praise and spoke in the same way. And in the fourth and the fifth heavens they spoke exactly in the same manner; there was rather one song of praise and also after that he was not changed. And I saw when he ascended to the sixth heaven, and they worshiped him and praised him, but in all the heavens the song of praise increased. And I saw how he ascended into the seventh heaven, and all the righteous and all the angels praised him. And then I saw how he sat down on the right hand of that great glory, whose glory, as I told you, I was not able to behold. And also I saw the angel of the Holy Spirit sitting on the left. And this angel said to me, 'Isaiah, son of Amoz, it is enough for you, for these are great things; for you have seen what none born of flesh has yet seen, and you will return into your garment till your days are fulfilled: then you will come hither.' This have I seen."

And Isaiah told it to all who stood before him, and they sang praise. And he spoke to king Hezekiah and said, "Such things have I spoken, and the end of this world and all this vision will be consummated in the last generation." And Isaiah made him swear that he would not tell this to the people of Israel, nor permit any man to write down the words. As far as you understand from the king what is

530

said in the prophets, so far shall you read. And you shall be in the Holy Spirit so that you may receive your garments and the thrones and crowns of glory which are preserved in the seventh heaven.

On account of these visions and prophecies Sammael Satan sawed asunder the prophet Isaiah the son of Amoz, by the hand of Manasseh. And all these things Hezekiah delivered to Manasseh in the twenty-sixth year. But Manasseh did not remember them nor take them to heart, but after becoming the servant of Satan, he went to ruin.

Here ends the vision of the prophet Isaiah with his ascension.

Apocalypse of Peter

(Christian Apocrypha)

In the *Apocalypse of Peter* God, for whom all is possible, opens Hell's bars of steel so that the damned may present themselves at the day of judgment. On that day cataracts of fire destroy the earth and the stars. Peter is the privileged spectator of heavenly thrones and clouds shining with angels as well as the other place, the pit where the sinners are tormented. In contrast to the Apocalypse of John (The Book of Revelation) which concerns the struggle and triumph of Jesus the Redeemer, the *Apocalypse of Peter* takes the reader to the afterlife and startles him or her with its glory or infamy.

Insofar as drama is more interesting than tedium, the tortured are more interesting than the blessed. And the drama is savage, like details of lurid journalism. So one reads "And again two women: they are hung up by their neck and by their hair and are cast into the pit. These are they who plaited their hair, not to create beauty, but to turn to fornication. . . . And the men who lay with them in fornication are hung by their thighs in that burning place, and they say to one another, 'We did not know that we would come into everlasting torture.' " For other sexual adventures women sit in lakes of excrement, their eyes smote with rays of fire, their entrails consumed by worms. Others have their lips cut off, are tormented with red-hot irons. The message of death and pain for those who "misuse" their bodies or transgress religious law is fearfully plain.

When we ascend the holy mountain, the glory, the shining raiments, the never-fading flowers, and the beauty are overwhelming. Peter trembles, fearful before such wondrous revelations. He sees with amazement the princes of the Scriptures, Moses and Elias in the flesh, entering the gate of Heaven.

The *Apocalypse of Peter* is a primitive form of didactic literature for a closed, authoritarian society. It rules by reward and dread. It reveals psychological excursions into sadism, dream, nightmare. The unconscious myths of ultimate pleasure and pain are given naked expression in these fiery visions of the apocalypse in which there is neither love, measure, meditation, nor reason. The ambience is war and its eternal wages.

THE DAY OF JUDGMENT*

Behold now what they shall experience in the last days, when the day of God comes. On the day of the decision of the judgment of God, all the children of men from the east unto the west shall be gathered before my Father who ever lives, and he will command Hell to open its bars of steel and to give up all that is in it. And the beasts and the fowls shall he command to give back all flesh that they have devoured, since he desires that men should appear again; for nothing perishes for God, and nothing is impossible with him, since all things are his. For all things come to pass on the day of decision, on the day of judgment, at the word of God, and as all things came to pass when he created the world and commanded all that is therein, and it was all done—so shall it be in the last days, for everything is possible with God and he says in the Scripture: "Son of man, prophesy upon the several bones, and say to the bones—bone unto bone in joints, sinews, nerves, flesh and skin and hair thereon." And soul and spirit shall the great Uriel give at the command of God. For him God has appointed over the resurrection of the dead on the day of judgment. Behold and consider the

*Chapters 4–6. The earliest text of the *Apocalypse of Peter* is a Greek text from Akhmin in Upper Egypt. The apocalypse probably dates from the first half of the second century. There is also a longer text translated into Ethiopic which dates from the seventh-eighth century. The present text combines fragments, found in Schneemelcher, from both the Greek and Ethiopic. All selections in this chapter are from Edgar Hennecke and Wilhelm Schneemelcher, eds. and trans., *New Testament Apocrypha*, vol. 2 (Philadelphia: Westminster Press, 1963), pp. 671–681.

corns of wheat which are sown in the earth. As something dry and without a soul does a man sow them in the earth; and they live again, bear fruit, and the earth gives them back again as a pledge entrusted to it. And this which dies, which is sown as seed in the earth and shall become alive and be restored to life, is man. How much more shall God raise up on the day of decision those who believe in him and are chosen by him and for whom he made the earth; and all this shall the earth give back on the day of decision, since it shall also be judged with them, and the Heaven with it.

And these things shall come to pass in the day of judgment of those who have fallen away from faith in God and have committed sin: cataracts of fire shall be let loose; and obscurity and darkness shall come up and cover and veil the entire world, and the waters shall be changed and transformed into coals of fire, and all that is in it shall burn and the sea shall become fire; under the heaven there shall be a fierce fire that shall not be put out and it flows for the judgment of wrath. And the stars shall be melted by flames of fire, as if they had not been created, and the fastnesses of Heaven shall pass away for want of water and become as though they had not been created. And the lightnings of Heaven shall be no more and, by their enchantment, they shall alarm the world. And the spirits of the dead bodies shall be like to them and at the command of God will become fire. And as soon as the whole creation is dissolved, the men who are in the east shall flee to the west and those in the west to the east; those that are in the south shall flee to the north and those in the north to the south, and everywhere will the wrath of the fearful fire overtake them; and an unquenchable flame shall drive them and bring them to the judgment of wrath in the stream of unquenchable fire which flows, flaming with fire, and when its waves separate one from another, seething, there shall be much gnashing of teeth among the children of men.

And all will see how I come upon an eternal shining cloud, and the angels of God who will sit with me on the throne of my glory at the right hand of my heavenly Father. He will set a crown upon my head. As soon as the nations see it, they will weep, each nation for itself. And he shall command them to go into the river of fire, while the deeds of each individual one of them stand before them. Recompense shall be given to each according to his work. As for the elect who have done good, they will come to me and will not see death by devouring fire. But the evil creatures, the sinners and the hypocrites, will stand in the depths of the darkness that passes not away, and their punishment is the fire, and angels bring forward their sins and prepare for them a place wherein they shall be punished for ever, each according to his offence. The angel of God, Uriel, brings the souls of those sinners who perished in the flood, and of all who dwell in all idols, in every molten image, in every love and in paintings, and of them that dwell on all hills and in stones and by the wayside, whom men call gods: they shall be burned with them [i.e., the objects in which they lodge] in eternal fire. After all of them, with their dwelling places, have been destroyed, they will be punished eternally.

AKHMIM

But I saw also another place, opposite that one, very gloomy; and this was the place of punishment, and those who were punished there and the angels who punished had dark raiment, clothed according to the air of the place.

And some there were there hanging by their tongues: these were those who had blasphemed the way of righteousness; and under them was laid fire, blazing and tormenting them. And there was a great lake full of burning mire in which were fixed certain men who had turned away from righteousness, and tormenting angels were placed over them.

And I saw the murderers and their accessaries cast into a gorge full of venomous reptiles and tormented by those beasts, and thus writhing in that torture, and worms oppressed them like dark clouds. But the souls of those who had been murdered stood and watched the punishment of those murderers and said, "O God, righteous is your judgment."

And behold again another place: this is a great pit filled, in which are those who have denied righteousness; and angels of punishment visit them and here do they kindle upon them the fire of their punishment. And again two women: they are hung up by their neck and by their hair and are cast into the pit. These are they who plaited their hair, not to create beauty, but to turn to fornication, and that they might ensnare the souls of men to destruction. And the men who lay with them in fornication are hung by their thighs in that burning place, and they say to one another, "We did not know that we would come into everlasting torture."

Other men and women stand above them naked. And their children stand opposite to them in a place of delight. And they sigh and cry to God because of their parents, "These are they who neglected and cursed and transgressed thy commandment. They killed us and cursed the angel who created us and hung us up. And they withheld from us the light which you have appointed for all." And the milk of the mothers flows from their breasts and congeals and smells foul, and from it come forth beasts that devour flesh, which turn and torture them for ever with their husbands, because they forsook the commandment of God and killed their children. And the children shall be given to the angel Temlakos. And those who slew them will be tortured forever, for God wills it to be so.

And near that place I saw another gorge in which the discharge and the excrement of the tortured ran down and became like a lake. And there sat women, and the discharge came up to their throats; and opposite them sat many children, who were born prematurely, weeping. And from them went forth rays of fire and smote the women on the eyes. And these were those who produced children outside marriage and who procured abortions.

And other men and women stood in flames up to the middle of their bodies and were cast into a dark place and were scourged by evil spirits and had their entrails consumed by worms which never wearied. These were those who persecuted the righteous and handed them over.

And near to those who live thus were other men and women who chew their tongues, and they are tormented with red-hot irons and have their eyes burned. These are the slanderers and those who doubt my righteousness.

Other men and women—whose deeds were done in deception—have their lips cut off and fire enters into their mouths and into their entrails. These are those who slew the martyrs by their lying.

And in another place were glowing pebbles, sharper than swords or any spit, and men and women, clad in filthy rags, rolled upon them in torment. These were they who were rich and trusted in their riches and had no mercy upon orphans and widows, but despised the commandment of God.

And in another great lake, full of discharge and blood and boiling mire, stood men and women up to their knees. These were those who lent money and demanded compound interest.

Other men and women who cast themselves down from a high slope came to the bottom and were driven by their torturers to go up the precipice and were then thrown down again, and had no rest from this torture. These were those who defiled their bodies, behaving like women. And the women with them, these were those who behaved with one another as men with a woman.

And near that precipice was a place filled with powerful fire. And there stood men who, with their own hands, had fashioned images in place of God.

And beside them were other men and women who had glowing rods and smote one another and had no rest from this torture.

And near to them still other men and women who were burned and turned in the fire and were baked. These were those who forsook the way of God.

And my Lord Jesus Christ, our King, said to me, "Let us go into the holy mountain." And his disciples went with him, praying.

And behold, there were two men, and we could not look on their faces, for a light came from them which shone more than the sun, and their raiment also was glistening and cannot be described, and there is nothing sufficient to be compared to them in this world. And its gentleness . . . that no mouth is able to express the beauty of their form. For their aspect was astonishing and wonderful. And the other, great, I say, shines in his appearance more than hail [crystal]. Flowers of roses is the likeness of the color of his appearance and his body . . . his head. And upon his shoulders and on their foreheads was a crown of nard, a work woven from beautiful flowers; like the rainbow in water was his hair. This was the comeliness of his countenance, and he was adorned with all kinds of ornament. And when we suddenly saw them, we marveled.

And I approached the Lord and said, "Who are these?" He said to me, "These are your righteous brethren whose form you did desire to see." And I said to him, "And where are all the righteous, and what is the nature of that world in which these are who possess such glory?" And the Lord showed me a widely extensive place outside this world, all gleaming with light, and the air there flooded by the rays of the sun, and the earth itself budding with flowers which fade not, and full of spices and plants which blossom gloriously and fade not and bear blessed fruit. So great was the fragrance of the flowers that it was borne thence even to us. The inhabitants of that place were clad with the shining raiment of angels and their raiment was suitable to their place of habitation. Angels walked there amongst them. All who dwell there had an equal glory, and with one voice they praised God the Lord, rejoicing in that place. The Lord said unto us, "This is the place of your high priests, the righteous men."

And I was joyful and believed and understood that which is written in the book of my Lord Jesus Christ. And I said to him, "My Lord, do you wish me to make here three tabernacles, one for you, one for Moses, and one for Elias?" And he said to me in wrath, "Satan makes war against you, and has veiled your understanding, and the good things of this world conquer you. Your eyes must be opened and your ears unstopped that . . . a tabernacle, which the hand of man has not made, but which my heavenly Father has made for me and for the elect." And we saw it full of joy.

And behold there came suddenly a voice from heaven saying, "This is my Son, whom I love and in whom I have pleasure, and my commandments . . ." And there came a great and exceeding white cloud over our heads and bore away our Lord and Moses and Elias. And I trembled and was afraid, and we looked up and the heavens opened and we saw men in the flesh, and they came and greeted our Lord and Moses and Elias, and went into the second heaven. And the word of Scripture was fulfilled: This generation seeks him and seeks the face of the God of Jacob. And great fear and great amazement took place in Heaven; the angels flocked together that the word of Scripture might be fulfilled which says: Open the gates, you princes! After that the Heaven was shut, that had been opened. And we prayed, and went down from the mountain, and we praised God who has written the names of the righteous in Heaven in the book of life.

Apocalypse of Paul

(Christian Apocrypha)

The *Apocalypse of Paul* was purportedly written by the apostle Paul, and a rather elaborate scheme was devised to prove its authenticity and to justify its appearance centuries after Paul's death: the revelation was stored in a sealed marble box, along with Paul's shoes. The details of the discovered scriptures calls to mind the detailed evidence associated with the discovery of Mormon scriptures in New York state. The *Apocalypse of Paul* was found in Tarsus, in the foundations of Paul's own house, during the consulate of Cynegius (A.D. 388), suggesting that the Latin version of the *Apocalypse* was written no later than this date. The original *Apocalypse* was in Greek, and it contains Greek ideas of the afterlife, such as the voyage to Heaven on Lake Acherusia, whiter than milk. The journey of a gold ship to a holy precinct recalls the Greek myth of the voyage of the gold ship *Parabola* to the holy island of Delos. It is also clear that the author of the *Apocalypse*, in addition to using stock imagery, was familiar with the *Apocalypse of Peter*. Thomas Silverstein, the editor of *Visio Pauli* (1935), the best edition of the texts, wrote an article suggesting that Dante was familiar with the *Apocalypse* ("Did Dante know the Vision of St. Paul?" for *Harvard Studies and Notes in Philology and Literature*, 1937). What is certain is that, whether or not Dante knew this particular work, he used the apocalyptic tradition as a primary source for the *Inferno*. With its borrowings from Greek myth, its repetition of Judeo-Christian apocalyptic stock images, and its feeding of the medieval Christian tradition culminating with Dante, the *Apocalypse of Paul* evidences these eclectic and syncretic tendencies of early Christian scriptures.

The particular reason for putting this visionary work in Paul's name stems from 2 Corinthians 12, in which Paul speaks of his rapture into Paradise. Paul calls the experience ineffable, as mystics commonly refer to their transport. The author of the *Apocalypse*, however, ignores Paul's declaration of his vision's ineffability. When the narrator of the vision rises to the city of Christ, he finds a city fortified with twelve walls and twelve thousand towers. It is circled by four rivers—of honey, milk, wine, and oil. God is briefed by angels each morning and evening about the deeds of humans, and on this basis determines where they will spend eternity. Those in the city of Christ have the benefit of abundant fruit trees and song. David sits near God and sings psalms to him in Hebrew, the language of God and angels. Paul meets patriarchs, saints, and prophets in Heaven. The names of very important figures are inscribed on golden tablets on Heaven's gates.

From Heaven the space traveler goes down to the river of boiling fire where the sinners live with less comfort than the blessed above. Guardian angels form a *guardia civil* in Hell, inflicting punishments on its victims. As in Federico García Lorca's "Ballads of the Civil Guard" from the *Romancero gitano*, with its sado-sexual tone, the guardian angels cut breasts off women; they also strangle clergymen who did not carry out their duties properly, use pronged instruments to pierce intestines, and razors to cut off lips. Worms and wild animals also contribute to the dismemberment of the fallen. For Paul's sake Christ is persuaded not to have sinners tortured on Sunday. The *Apocalypse of Paul* is a promise and a warning.

APOCALYPSE OF PAUL*

The revelation of the holy apostle Paul: the things which were revealed to him when he went up even to the third heaven and was caught up into Paradise and heard unspeakable words.

In the consulate of Theodosius Augustus the Younger and of Cynegius a certain respected man was living in Tarsus in the house which had once belonged to St. Paul; during the night an angel appeared to him and gave him a revelation telling him to break up the foundations of the house and to make public what he

_____

*Chapters 1–2, 12, 22–50. Texts of the *Apocalypse* exist in Greek, Latin, Syrian, Armenian, Slavonic, Ethiopic, and Coptic. The Latin is the best preserved. The Greek is only a summary. The Latin text is followed below, except for a few sentences from the Coptic, where the Latin is missing or unreadable. (The recently discovered Coptic *Apocalypse of Paul* in the Nag Hammadi Library has nothing to do with this *Apocalypse of Paul*.) From Edgar Hennecke and Wilhelm Schneemelcher, *New Testament Apocrypha*, vol. 2 (Philadelphia: Westminster Press, 1963), pp. 759–760, 764, 773–794, 795, 798.

found. But he thought this was a delusion.

However, the angel came the third time and scourged him and compelled him to break up the foundations. And when he had dug he discovered a marble box which was inscribed on the sides; in it was the revelation of Saint Paul and the shoes in which he used to walk when he was teaching the word of God. But he was afraid to open the box and brought it to a judge; the judge accepted it and sent it as it was, sealed with lead, to the emperor Theodosius; for he was afraid it might be something else. And when the emperor received it he opened it and found the revelation of Saint Paul. After a copy had been made he sent the original manuscript to Jerusalem. And it was written in it as follows:

And I looked into the height and I saw other angels with faces shining like the sun; their loins were girt with golden girdles and they had palms in their hands, and the sign of God; and they were clothed in raiment on which was written the name of the Son of God; and they were filled with all gentleness and pity.

And I asked the angel and said: "Who are these, sir, who have so much beauty and pity?" And the angel answered and said to me: "These are the angels of righteousness; they are sent to lead in the hour of their need the souls of the righteous who believed God was their helper." And I said to him: "Must the righteous and the sinners meet the witnesses when they are dead?" And the angel answered and said to me: "There is one way by which all pass over to God, but the righteous, because they have a holy helper with them, are not troubled when they go to appear before God."

And I looked round that land and I saw a river flowing with milk and honey; and at the edge of the river were planted trees full of fruit. And each tree was bearing twelve times twelve fruits in the year, various and different. And I saw the creation of that place and all the work of God. And I saw there palm trees, some of twenty cubits and others of ten cubits. Now that land was seven times brighter than silver. And the trees were full of fruit from root up to treetop. (L[1] is incomprehensible here and we replace with C:) From the root of each tree up to its heart there were ten thousand branches with tens of thousands of clusters and there were ten thousand clusters on each branch and there were ten thousand dates in each cluster. And it was the same with the vines. Each vine had ten thousand branches, and each branch had on it ten thousand bunches of grapes, and each bunch had ten thousand grapes. And there were other trees there, myriads of myriads of them, and their fruit was in the same proportion. And I said to the angel: "Why does each single tree yield thousands of fruits?" And the angel answered and said to me: "Because the Lord God of his abundance gives gifts profusely to the worthy, for they, while they were in the world, afflicted themselves of their own will and did everything for his holy name's sake."

And again I said to the angel: "Sir, are these the only promises which the Lord God has promised to his saints?" And the angel replied and said: "No! for there are those which are seven times greater."

I tell you, however, that when the righteous have come forth from the body and see the promises and good things which God has prepared for them, they will sigh and weep yet again, saying: "Why did we utter a word from our mouth to irritate our neighbor even for a single day?" I, however, asked and said again: "Are these the only promises of God?" And the angel answered and said to me: "What you now see is for the married who have kept the purity of their marriages in acting chastely. But to virgins and to those who hunger and thirst after righteousness and afflict themselves for the name of the Lord, God will give things seven times greater than what I shall now show you."

And after that he took me up away from that place where I had seen these things and, behold, a river whose waters were very white, whiter than milk. And I said to the angel: "What is this?" And he said to me: "This is Lake Acherusia where the city of Christ is, but not every man is allowed to enter into that city. For this is the way which leads to God; and if there is anyone who is a fornicator and ungodly and who turns and repents and brings forth fruit worthy of repentance, first when he has come forth from the body he is brought and worships God and is handed over from there at the command of God to the angel Michael and he baptizes him in Lake Acherusia. Thus he leads him into the city of Christ with those who have not sinned." And I marveled and blessed the Lord God because of all I had seen.

And the angel answered and said to me: "Follow me and I shall lead you into the city of Christ." And he stood by Lake Acherusia and put me in a golden boat and about three thousand angels were singing a hymn before me until I reached the city of Christ. Now the inhabitants of the city of Christ rejoiced greatly over me as I came to them, and I entered and saw the city of Christ; and it was completely golden and there were twelve walls around it and twelve towers in it, and the individual walls as they encircled were distant from one another a stadium. And I said to the angel: "Sir, how much is one stadium?" The angel answered and said to me: "It is as great as between the Lord God and men on earth, for indeed the city of Christ is uniquely great." And in the circuit of the city there were twelve gates of great beauty, and four rivers which encircled it. Now there was a river of honey and a river of milk and a river of wine and a river of oil. And I said to the angel: "What are these rivers which encircle this city?" And he said to me: "These are the four rivers which flow abundantly for those who are in this land of promise; as for their names: the river of honey is called Phison, and the river of milk Euphrates, and the river of oil Gihon and the river of wine Tigris. As therefore the righteous when they were in the world did not use their power over these things but went hungry without them and afflicted themselves for the name of the Lord God, therefore when they enter into this city the Lord will give them these above number or measure."

And when I entered in through the gate I saw before the doors of the city trees which were big and very high and which had no fruit but only leaves. And I saw a few men scattered about among the trees and they wept greatly when they saw anyone enter into the city. And the trees did penance for them by abasing themselves and bowing down and by raising themselves up again. And I saw it and wept with them and asked the angel and said: "Sir, who are these who are not allowed to enter into the city of Christ?" And he said to me: "These are those who fasting day and night have zealously practised renunciation, but they have had a heart proud beyond that of other men in that they have glorified and praised themselves and done nothing for their neighbors. For some they greeted in a friendly way, but to others they did not even say 'Greetings': and to whom they wished they opened the doors of the monastery, and if they did some small good to their neighbor they became puffed up." And I said: "What then, sir? Has their pride prevented them from entering into the city of Christ?" And the angel answered and said to me: "Pride is the root of all wickedness."

And with the angel leading me I went on, and he brought me to the river of honey; and I saw there Isaiah and Jeremiah and Ezekiel and Amos and Micah and Zechariah, the major and minor prophets, and they greeted me in the city. I said to the angel: "What is this way?" And he said to me: "This is the way of the prophets. Everyone who has grieved his own soul and on account of God has not done his own will, when he has come forth from the world and been led to the Lord God and has worshiped him, then at God's command he is handed over to Michael who leads him into the city to this place of the prophets; and they greet him as their friend and neighbor because he did the will of God."

Again he led me where the river of milk was; and there I saw in that place all the infants whom king Herod had slain for the name of Christ, and they greeted me. And the angel said to me: "All who preserve their chastity and purity, when they come forth from their bodies, are handed over to Michael after they have worshiped the Lord God, and they are brought to the children and they greet them saying, 'You are our brothers and friends and associates.' Among them they will inherit the promises of God."

Again he took me up and brought me to the north of the city and he led me where the river of wine was, and I saw there Abraham, Isaac, and Jacob, Lot and Job and other saints; and they greeted me. And I asked and said: "What is this place, sir?" The angel answered and said to me: "All those who have given hospitality to strangers, when they come forth from the world, first worship the Lord God and are handed over to Michael and by this route are led into the city, and all the righteous greet them as sons and brothers and say to them, 'Because you have kept humanity and hospitality for strangers, come, receive an inheritance in the city of our God.' And each righteous man will receive the good gifts of God in the city in accordance with his own behavior."

And again he brought me to the river of oil to the east of the city. And I saw there men who rejoiced and sang psalms, and I said: "Who are these, sir?" And the angel said to me: "These are those who dedicated themselves to God with the whole heart and had no pride in themselves. For all who rejoice in the Lord God and sing praises to him with the whole heart are brought here into this city."

And he brought me into the middle of the city close to the twelfth wall. Now at this place it was higher than the others. And I asked and said: "Is there a wall in the city of Christ surpassing this spot in honor?" And the angel answered and said to me: "The second is better than the first and similarly the third than the second because each one surpasses the other right up to the twelfth wall." And I said: "Why, sir, does one surpass another in glory? Explain to me." And the angel answered and said to me: "From all who in themselves have only a little slander or envy or pride something is taken away from their glory, although they appear to be in the city of Christ. Look behind you."

And I turned and saw golden thrones which were set at the several gates, with men on them who had golden diadems and gems. And I looked and saw within, between the twelve men, thrones set in another rank which appeared to be of greater glory, so that no one was able to declare their praise. And I asked the angel and said: "Sir, who are those who shall sit on the thrones?" And the angel answered and said to me: "These are the thrones of those who had goodness and understanding of heart and yet made themselves fools for the Lord God's sake in that they neither knew the Scriptures nor many Psalms but paid heed to one chapter concerning the commandments of God and hearing them acted with great carefulness in conformity to these commandments and have thereby shown a true zealousness before the Lord God. And admiration of these lays hold on all the saints before the Lord God, for they discuss with one another and say: Wait and see these unlearned men who understand nothing more, how they have merited such a great and beautiful robe and such glory because of their innocence."

And I saw in the midst of the city a great and very high altar; and there was standing alongside the altar one whose face shone like the sun and who held in his hands a psaltery and a harp and who sang saying, "Hallelujah!" And his voice filled all the city. And as soon as all who were on the towers and at the gates heard him they replied, "Hallelujah!" so that the foundations of the city were shaken. And I asked the angel and said: "Who, sir, is this here with such great power?" And the angel said to me: "This is David; this is the city of Jerusalem. But when Christ, the king of eternity, shall have come with the confidence of his kingdom, then he will again step forward to sing and all the righteous will sing in reply at the same time, 'Hallelujah.' " And I said: "Sir, why is it that David alone begins the singing before all the other saints?" And the angel answered and said to me: "Because Christ, the Son of God, sits at the right hand of his Father, this David will sing psalms before him in the seventh heaven; and just as it is done in the Heavens, so it is done below, because it is not permitted to offer to God a sacrifice without David, but it is necessary for David to sing psalms at the time of the offering of the body and blood of Christ; as it is carried out in the Heavens, so also on earth."

And I said to the angel: "Sir, what is 'Hallelujah'?" And he answered and said to me: "You search and inquire into everything." And he said to me: "Hallelujah is a word in Hebrew, the language of God and angels. And the meaning of Hallelujah is this: tecel. cat. marith. macha." And I said: "Sir, what is tecel. cat. marith. macha?" And the angel answered and said to me: "Tecel. cat. marith. macha is this: 'Let us bless him all together.'" I asked the angel and said: "Sir, do all who say 'Hallelujah' bless the Lord?" And the angel answered and said to me: "That is so; and again, if anyone should sing Hallelujah and there are some present who do not sing it at the same time, they commit sin because they do not join in the singing." And I said: "Sir, does someone who is doting or very old sin in the same way?" And the angel answered and said to me: "No, but whoever is able, and does not join in the singing, you know that he is a despiser of the word. And it would be proud and discreditable that he should not bless the Lord God his maker."

And when he had ceased speaking to me, he led me forth out of the city through the midst of the trees and back from the sites of the land of good things, and he set me above the river of milk and honey. And then he led me to the ocean that bears the foundations of the Heavens. And the angel answered and said to me: "Do you understand that you are going away from here?" And I said: "Yes, sir." And he said to me: "Come, follow me, and I shall show you the souls of the godless and sinners that you may know what the place is like." And I set out with the angel and he brought me towards the setting of the sun, and I saw the beginning of Heaven, founded on a great river of water, and I asked: "What is this river of water?" And he said to me: "This is the ocean which encircles the whole earth." And when I was beyond the ocean I looked and there was no light in that place, but darkness and sorrow and distress; and I sighed.

And there I saw a river boiling with fire, and in it was a multitude of men and women immersed up to their knees, and other men up to the navel, others up to the lips, and others up to the hair. And I asked the angel and said: "Sir, who are these in the river of fire?" And the angel answered and said to me: "They are those who are neither hot nor cold because they were found neither among the number of the righteous nor among the number of the godless. For these spent the period of their life on earth in passing some days in prayers but other days in sins and fornications right up to their death." And I asked and said: "Who are these, sir, who are immersed up to the knees in fire?" And he answered and said to me: "These are those who when they have come out of church occupy themselves in discussing in strange discourses. Those, however, who are immersed up to the navel are those who when they have received the body and blood of Christ go away and fornicate and do not cease from their sins until they die. And those who are immersed up to the lips are those who when they meet in the church of God slander one another. Those immersed up to the eyebrows are those who give the nod to one another and in that way secretly prepare evil against their neighbor."

And I saw to the north a place of varied and different punishments which was full of men and women, and a river of fire poured over them. And I looked and saw very deep pits and in them there were very many souls together; and the depth of that place was about three thousand cubits, and I saw them sighing and weeping and saying: "Lord, have mercy on us." But no one had mercy on them. And I asked the angel and said: "Who are these, sir?" And the angel answered and said to me: "These are those who did not hope in the Lord that they would be able to have him for a helper." And I asked and said: "Sir, if these souls remain through thirty or forty generations thus one above another, I believe the pits will not hold them unless they are made to go deeper." And he said to me: "The abyss has no measure; moreover there also follows on it the gulf which is below it. And it is as if perhaps someone takes a stone and throws it into a very deep well and after many hours it reaches the ground; so is the abyss. For when these souls are thrown in they have scarcely reached the bottom after five hundred years."

Now when I had heard that, I wept and sighed for the race of men. The angel answered and said to me: "Why do you weep? Are you more compassionate than God? For since God is good and knows that there are punishments, he bears patiently the race of men, permitting each one to do his own will for the time that he lives on earth."

And I looked yet again at the river of fire and I saw there a man being strangled by angels, the guardians of Tartarus, who had in their hands an iron instrument with three prongs with which they pierced the intestines of that old man. And I asked the angel and said: "Sir, who is that old man on whom such torments are inflicted?" And the angel answered and said to me: "He whom you see was a presbyter who did not execute his ministry properly. While he ate and drank and fornicated he offered to the Lord the sacrifice on his holy altar."

And not far away I saw another old man whom four evil angels brought running in haste and they immersed him up to his knees in the river of fire and they struck him with stones and they wounded his face like a storm and they did not allow him to say: "Have mercy on me." And I asked the angel and he said to me: "He whom you see was a bishop but he did not execute his episcopal office properly; he did indeed receive a great name but he did not enter into the holiness of him who gave to him that name all his

life, for he did not give righteous judgments and he had no compassion on the widows and orphans. But now he is being requited according to his iniquity and his deeds."

And I saw another man up to his knees in the river of fire. And his hands were stretched out and bloody, and worms came out of his mouth and from his nostrils and he was groaning and weeping and crying, and he said: "Have mercy on me, for I suffer more than the rest who are in this punishment." And I asked: "Who is this, sir?" And he said to me: "He whom you see was a deacon who ate up the offerings and committed fornication and did not do right in the sight of God. Therefore unceasingly he pays this penalty."

And I looked and saw at his side another man who was brought with haste and thrown into the river of fire, and he was in it up to the knees. And the angel came who was appointed over the punishments and he had a great blazing razor with which he lacerated the lips of that man and in the same way his tongue. And sighing I wept and asked: "Who is that, sir?" And he said to me: "He whom you see was a reader and he read to the people; but he himself did not keep the commandments of God. Now he also pays his own penalty."

And in that place I saw another set of pits and in the middle of it a river full of a multitude of men and women whom worms were devouring. I then wept, and with a sigh I asked the angel and said: "Sir, who are these?" And he said to me: "They are those who exacted usury at compound interest and trusted in their riches and did not hope in God that he would be a helper to them."

And then I looked and I saw another place which was very confined, and there was as it were a wall and fire in its bounds. And in it I saw men and women chewing at their tongues. And I asked: "Who are these, sir?" And he said to me: "They are those who reviled the Word of God in church, paying no attention to it, but counting God and his angels as nothing. Therefore in the same way they now pay their own special penalty."

And I looked and I saw another hole below in the pit, and it had the appearance of blood. And I asked and said: "Sir, what is this place?" And he said to me: "All the punishments flow together into this pit." And I saw men and women submerged up to their lips and I asked: "Who are these, sir?" And he said to me: "These are magicians who dispensed magical charms to men and women and made it impossible for them to find peace until they died." And again I saw men and women with very black faces in the pit of fire; and sighing and weeping I asked: "Who are these, sir?" And he said to me: "These are fornicators and adulterers who although they had their own wives committed adultery; and similarly the women committed adultery in the same way, though they had their own husbands. Therefore unceasingly they pay the penalty."

And there I saw girls wearing black clothing and four dreadful angels who had blazing chains in their hands. And they set the chains on their necks and led them into darkness. And again weeping I asked the angel: "Who are these, sir?" And he said to me: "They are those who although they were appointed as virgins defiled their virginity unknown to their parents. For that reason they pay their own particular penalty unceasingly."

And again I saw there men and women set with lacerated hands and feet and naked in a place of ice and snow, and worms consumed them. And when I saw it I wept and asked: "Who are these, sir?" And he said to me: "They are those who harmed orphans and widows and the poor, and did not hope in the Lord; therefore they pay their own particular penalty unceasingly."

And I looked and saw others hanging over a channel of water and their tongues were very dry and much fruit was placed within their sight and they were not allowed to take of it; and I

asked: "Who are these, sir?" And he said to me: "They are those who broke their fast before the appointed hour; therefore they pay these penalties unceasingly."

And I saw other men and women suspended by their eyebrows and hair, and a river of fire drew them; and I said: "Who are these, sir?" And he said to me: "They are those who did not give themselves to their own husbands and wives but to adulterers, and therefore they pay their own particular penalty unceasingly."

And I saw other men and women covered in dust, and their faces were like blood, and they were in a pit of tar and brimstone, and they were running in a river of fire. And I asked: "Who are these, sir?" And he said to me: "They are those who have committed the iniquity of Sodom and Gomorrah, men with men. Therefore they pay the penalty unceasingly."

And I looked and saw men and women clothed in bright clothing, whose eyes were blind, and they were set in a pit of fire; and I asked: "Who are these, sir?" And he said to me: "They are the heathen who gave alms and did not know the Lord God; therefore they pay unceasingly their own particular penalty."

And I looked and saw other men and women on a fiery pyramid and wild animals were tearing them to pieces, and they were not allowed to say: "Lord have mercy on us." And I saw the angel of punishments laying punishments most vigorously on them and saying: "Acknowledge the judgment of the Son of God! For you were forewarned; when the divine Scriptures were read to you, you did not pay attention; therefore God's judgment is just; for your evil deeds laid hold on you and have led you into these punishments." But I sighed and wept; and I asked and said: "Who are these men and women who are strangled in the fire and pay the penalty?" And he answered me: "They are the women who defiled what God had fashioned in that they gave birth to children from the womb and they are the men who went to bed with them." However, their children appealed to the Lord God and the angels who are set over the punishments, saying: "Defend us from our parents, for they have defiled what is fashioned by God; they have the name of God but they do not keep his commandments, and they gave us for food to dogs and to be trampled by pigs; and they threw others into the river." But those children were handed over to the angels of Tartarus, who were over the punishments, so that they should lead them into a spacious place of mercy. However their fathers and mothers were strangled in an everlasting punishment. And after this I saw men and women clothed in rags full of tar and sulphurous fire, and dragons were wound about their necks and shoulders and feet; and angels with fiery horns confined them and struck them and closed up their nostrils, saying to them: "Why did you not know the time in which it was right for you to repent and to serve God, and did not do it?"

And I sighed and wept and said: "Woe to men! woe to sinners! Why were you born?" And the angel answered and said to me: "Why are you weeping? Are you more compassionate than the Lord God, who is blessed forever, who has appointed judgment and allowed every man to choose good or evil and act as he wishes?" Again I wept even very vehemently, and he said to me: "Are you weeping, when you have not yet seen the greater punishments? Follow me and you will see those that are seven times greater than these."

And he brought me to the north, to the place of all punishments, and he placed me above a well and I found it sealed with seven seals. And the angel who was with me answered and spoke to the angel of that place: "Open the mouth of the well that Paul, God's dearly beloved, may look in, because power has been given him to see all the punish-ments of the underworld." And the angel said to me: "Stand at a distance, for you will not be able to bear the stench of this place." Then when the well was opened there came up immediately a disagreeable and very evil smell which surpassed all the punishments. And I looked into the well and saw fiery masses burning on all sides, and the narrowness of the well at its mouth was such that it was only able to take a single man. And the angel answered and said to me: "If someone is sent into this well of the abyss and it is sealed above him, reference is never made to him before the Father and the Son and the Holy Spirit and the holy angels." And I said: "Who are these, sir, who are sent into this well?" And he said to me: "They are those who have not confessed that Christ came in the flesh and that the Virgin Mary bore him, and who say that the bread of the Eucharist and the cup of blessing are not the body and blood of Christ."

And I looked from the north towards the west and I saw there the worm that never rests, and in that place there was gnashing of teeth. Now the worm was a cubit in size and it had two heads. And I saw there men and women in the cold and gnashing of teeth. And I asked and said: "Sir, who are these in this place?" And he said to me: "They are those who say that Christ has not risen from the dead and that this flesh does not rise." And I asked and said: "Sir, is there neither fire nor heat in this place? And he said to me: "In this place there is nothing other than cold and snow." And again he said to me: "Even if the sun were to rise over them they would not become warm because of the excessive coldness of the place and the snow."

When I heard this, I stretched out my hands and wept and with a sigh I said again: "It would be better for us if we who are all sinners had not been born."

However, when those who were in this very place saw me weeping with the angel, they cried out and themselves wept, saying: "O Lord God, have mercy on us!" And after that I saw Heaven opened and the archangel Michael coming down from heaven, and with him the whole host of angels, and they came to those who were placed in the punishments. And seeing him they cried out again with tears, and said: "Have mercy on us, archangel Michael, have mercy on us and on the human race, for because of your prayers the earth continues. We have now seen the judgment and known the Son of God. It was impossible for us to pray for this previously before we came to this place. For we did hear that there was a judgment before we came forth from the world, but tribulations and a worldy minded life did not allow us to repent." And Michael answered and said: "Listen when Michael speaks: It is I who stand in the presence of God every hour. As the Lord lives, in whose presence I stand, for one day or one night I do not cease from praying continually for the human race, and I pray for those who are still on earth. They, however, do not stop committing iniquity and fornication and they do not help me in what is good while they are placed on earth. And the time during which you ought to have repented you used up in vanity. But I have always thus prayed and now I beseech that God may send dew and that rain may be appointed over the earth, and I continue to pray until the earth bring forth its fruit; and I say that if anyone has done even only a little good I will strive for him and protect him until he escapes the judgment of punishments. Where are your prayers? Where is your repentence? You have squandered time contemptibly. But now weep, and I will weep with you, and the angels who are with me together with the dearly beloved Paul, if perchance the merciful God will show mercy and give you ease." And when they heard these words they cried out and wept much and said all together: "Have mercy on us, Son of God." And I, Paul, sighed and said: "Lord God, have mercy on what

you have fashioned, have mercy on the children of men, have mercy on your own image."

And I looked and I saw Heaven move as a tree shaken by the wind. And they suddenly threw themselves on their faces before the throne; and I saw the twenty-four elders and the four beasts worshiping God, and I saw the altar and the veil and the throne, and all were rejoicing; and the smoke of a good odor rose up beside the altar of the throne of God, and I heard the voice of one who said: "For what reason do you pray, angels and ministers of ours?" And they cried out and said: "We pray because we see thy great goodness to the race of men." And after that I saw the Son of God coming down from Heaven, and a diadem was on his head. And when those who were placed in the punishments saw him, they all cried out together: "Have mercy on us, Son of the most High God; it is you who have granted ease to all in heaven and on earth; have mercy likewise on us; for since we have seen you, we have had ease." And a voice went forth from the Son of God throughout all the punishments, saying: "What work have you done, that you ask me for ease? My blood was poured out for your sakes and even so you did not repent. For your sakes I bore the crown of thorns on my head; for you I was slapped on the cheeks, and even so you did not repent. Hanging on the cross I begged for water, and they gave me vinegar mingled with gall; with a spear they laid open my right side. For my name's sake they killed my servants, the prophets and the righteous, and in all these things I gave you the opportunity for repentance, and you were not willing. Now, however, for the sake of Michael, the archangel of my covenant, and the angels who are with him, and for the sake of Paul, my dearly beloved, whom I would not sadden, and for the sake of your brethren who are in the world and present offerings, and for the sake of your children, because my commandments are in them, and even more for my own goodness—on the very day on which I rose from the dead I grant to you all who are being punished a day and a night of ease forever." And they all cried out and said: "We bless you, Son of God, because you have granted to us ease for a day and a night. For one day's ease is better for us than all the time of our life which we were on earth: and if we had clearly known that this place was appointed for those who sin we would have done no other work at all, have practiced nothing, and have committed no evil. What need was there for us to be born into the world? For here is our pride comprehended, which rose up out of our mouth against our neighbors. Discomfort and our exceptionally great anguish and tears and the worms which are under us, these are worse for us than the punishments which [. . .] us." When they said this, the wicked angels and those in charge of the punishments were angry with them and said: "How long have you wept and sighed? For you have shown no mercy. This indeed is the judgment of God on him who has shown no mercy. However you have received this great grace—ease for the day and night of the Lord's day for the sake of Paul, the dearly beloved of God, who has come down to you."

And after this the angel said to me: "Have you seen everything?" And I said: "Yes, sir." And he said to me: "Follow me and I will lead you into Paradise, and the righteous who are there will see you: for behold, they hope to see you and are ready to come to meet you with joy and exultation." Impelled by the Holy Spirit I followed the angel and he transferred me to Paradise, and said to me: "This is Paradise where Adam and his wife sinned." And I entered into Paradise and I saw the origin of the waters; and the angel beckoned to me and said to me: "See," he said, "the waters; for this is the river Pison which encircles the whole land of Evila, and this other is the Gihon which encircles the whole land of Egypt

and Ethiopia, and this other is the Tigris which is opposite Assyria, and this other is the Euphrates which waters the land of Mesopotamia." And going in further I saw a tree planted out of whose roots waters flowed, and the source of the four rivers was in it. And the Spirit of God rested over that tree and when the Spirit breathed the waters flowed. And I said: "Sir, is it this tree itself which makes the waters flow?" And he said to me: "Because in the beginning before Heaven and earth appeared everything was invisible, the Spirit of God hovered over the waters; but since the commandment of God brought to light Heaven and earth, the Spirit rests over this tree. Therefore when the Spirit has breathed, the waters flow from the tree." And he took me by the hand and led me to the Tree of the Knowledge of good and evil and said: "This is the tree through which death entered into the world, and Adam receiving from his wife ate of it and death came into the world." And he showed to me another tree in the middle of Paradise, and he said to me: "This is the Tree of Life."

While I still considered the tree, I saw a virgin coming from a distance, and two hundred angels singing hymns before her. And I asked and said: "Sir, who is this who comes in such great glory?" And he said to me: "This is the Virgin Mary, the Mother of the Lord." And when she had come near, she greeted me and said: "Greetings, Paul, of God and angels and men dearly beloved. For all the saints have implored my son Jesus, who is my Lord, that you might come here in the body so that they might see you before you depart out of the world; and the Lord said to them: 'Wait and be patient. Just a short time and you will see him and he will be with you forever.' And again all together they said to him: 'Do not sadden us for we wish to see him while he is in the flesh; through him your name has been greatly glorified in the world, and we have seen that he has taken on himself all the works both of little and great. From those who come here we inquire saying: "Who is it who guided you in the world?" And they answer us: "There is a man in the world whose name is Paul; he in his preaching proclaims Christ, and we believe that because of the power and sweetness of his speech many have entered into the Kingdom." ' Behold, all the righteous are behind me coming to meet you. But I say to you, Paul, that I come first to meet those who have done the will of my Son and Lord Jesus Christ, I go first to meet them and I do not leave them to be as strangers until they meet my beloved Son in peace."

While she was still speaking I saw coming from a distance three very beautiful men, in appearance like Christ, with shining forms, and their angels; and I asked: "Who are these, sir?" And he said to me: "Do you not know them?" And I said: "I do not, sir." And he answered: "These are the fathers of the people, Abraham, Isaac, and Jacob." And when they had come near to me they greeted me and said: "Greetings, Paul, dearly beloved of God and men; blessed is he who endured violence for the sake of the Lord." And Abraham answered me and said: "This is my son Isaac, and Jacob, my dearly beloved. And we knew the Lord and followed him. Blessed are all those who believed your word, that they might inherit the kingdom of God through work, renunciation and holiness and humility and love and gentleness and right faith in the Lord. And we also have devoted ourselves to the Lord whom you preach, covenanting that we will assist and serve all the souls that believe in him, just as fathers serve their sons."

While they were still speaking I saw twelve others coming in honor from a distance, and I asked: "Who are these, sir?" And he said: "These are the patriarchs." And they stepped up and greeted me and said: "Greetings, Paul, dearly beloved of God and men. The Lord has not saddened us, so that we see

you while you are still in the body before you leave the world." And in accordance with their order each of them gave me his name, from Reuben to Benjamin; and Joseph said to me: "I am the one who was sold; and I tell you, Paul, that for all that my brothers did against me, I have not behaved in any way badly towards them, not even in all the labor that they laid on me, nor have I hurt them in any thing for that reason from morning until evening. Blessed is he who for the Lord's sake has been injured in something and has endured, for the Lord will repay him many times when he has come forth from the world."

While he was still speaking I saw another beautiful one coming from a distance and his angels were singing hymns, and I asked: "Who is this, sir, who is beautiful of face?" And he said to me: "Do you not know him?" And I said: "No, sir." And he said to me: "This is Moses the lawgiver, to whom God gave the law." And when he had come near me he immediately began to weep, and then he greeted me. And I said to him: "Why are you weeping? for I have heard that you excell all men in meekness." And he answered and said: "I weep over those whom with trouble I planted, because they have borne no fruit and none of them has made progress. And I saw that all the sheep whom I pastured were scattered and become as those who had no shepherd and that all the labors which I endured for the children of Israel were considered of no value and how many mighty deeds I had done among them and they had not understood; and I am amazed that aliens and uncircumcised and idol-worshipers are converted and have entered into the promises of God, but Israel has not entered. And I tell you, brother Paul, that at that hour when the people hanged Jesus, whom you preach, that the Father, the God of all, who gave me the law, and Michael and all the angels and archangels and Abraham and Isaac and Jacob and all the righteous wept for the Son of God as he hung on the cross. And all the saints turned their attention to me at that time, looking at me and saying: 'See, Moses, what those of your people have done to the Son of God.' Therefore you are blessed, Paul, and blessed is the generation and people who have believed your word."

While he was still speaking twelve others came, and when they saw me they said: "Are you Paul, who are extolled in Heaven and on earth?" And I answered and said: "Who are you?" The first answered and said: "I am Isaiah, whose head Manasseh cut off with a wooden saw." And the second likewise said: "I am Jeremiah, who was stoned by the children of Israel and killed." And the third said: "I am Ezekiel, whom the children of Israel dragged by the feet over the rocks on the mountain until they dashed out my brains. And we bore all these trials because we wished to save the children of Israel. And I tell you that after the trials which they inflicted on me, I threw myself on my face before the Lord, praying for them, bending my knees until the second hour of the Lord's Day, until Michael came and lifted me up from the earth. Blessed are you, Paul, and blessed the people who have believed through you."

When these had passed on I saw another with a beautiful face and I asked: "Who is this, sir?" When he had seen me he rejoiced. And he said to me: "This is Lot who was found righteous in Sodom." When he had seen me he rejoiced, and coming up to me he greeted me and said: "Blessed are you, Paul, and blessed the generation which you have served." And I answered and said to him: "Are you Lot, who was found righteous in Sodom?" And he said: "I received angels into my house as strangers, and when the men of the city wished to violate them, I offered to them my two virgin daughters who had never known men, and gave to them saying: 'Use them as you wish, so long as you do nothing evil to these men; for this reason

they have entered under the roof of my house.' We ought therefore to have confidence and understand that whatever anyone has done God will repay it to him many times over when they come to him. Blessed are you, Paul, and blessed the race which has believed your word."

When then he had ceased speaking to me I saw coming from a distance another man with a very beautiful face and he was smiling, and his angels were singing hymns; and I said to the angel who was with me: "Does then each of the righteous have an angel as his companion?"

And he said to me: "Each of the saints has his own angel who helps him and sings a hymn, and the one does not leave the other." And I said: "Who is this, sir?" And he said: "This is Job." And he approached and greeted me and said: "Brother Paul, you have great honor with God and men. For I am Job who suffered much through thirty years from the suppuration of a wound. And at the beginning the sores that came out from my body were like grains of wheat; on the third day, however, they became like an ass's foot; and the worms which fell were four fingers long. And the Devil appeared to me for the third time and said to me: 'Speak a word against the Lord and die.' I said to him: 'If it is the will of God that I continue in affliction all the time I live until I die, I shall not cease to praise the Lord God and shall receive greater reward. For I know that the trials of this world are nothing in comparison to the consolation that comes afterwards.' Therefore, Paul, you are blessed, and blessed is the race which has believed through your agency."

While he was still speaking another man came from a distance crying and saying: "You are blessed, Paul, and I am blessed because I have seen you, the beloved of the Lord." And I asked the angel: "Who is this, sir?" And he answered and said to me: "This is Noah from the time of the flood." And immediately we greeted one another. And with great joy he said to me: "You are Paul, the dearly beloved of God." And I asked him: "Who are you?" And he said: "I am Noah, who lived in the time of the flood. And I tell you, Paul, that I spent a hundred years making the ark when I did not take off the shirt I wore nor cut the hair of my head. Moreover, I strove after continence, not coming near my wife; and in those hundred years the hair of my head did not grow in length nor were my clothes dirty. And I implored the men of that time, saying: 'Repent, for a flood of water will come upon you.' But they ridiculed me and mocked at my words. And again they said to me: 'This time is rather for those who can play and would sin as they please, for him to whom it is possible to commit fornication not a little; for God does not see and does not know what is done by us all, and a flood of water will certainly not come on this world.' And they did not cease from their sins until God destroyed all flesh which had the spirit of life in itself. But know, God cares more for one righteous man than for a whole generation of the ungodly. Therefore you, Paul, are blessed, and blessed is the people who believed through your agency."

And I looked and saw another who surpassed them all, very beautiful. And I said to the angel: "Who is this, my lord?" He said to me: "This is Adam, the father of you all." When he came up to me, he greeted me with joy. He said to me: "Courage, Paul, beloved of God, you who have brought a multitude to faith in God and to repentance, as I myself have repented and received my praise from the Compassionate and Merciful One."

I, Paul, however, came to myself and I knew and understood what I had seen and I wrote it in a roll. And while I lived, I did not have rest to reveal this mystery, but I wrote it down and deposited it under the wall of a house of that believer with whom I was in Tarsus, a city of Cilicia. And when I was released from this temporal life and stood before my Lord, he spoke thus to me: "Paul, have I shown everything to you so that you should put it under the wall of a house? Rather send and reveal it for its sake so that men may read it and turn to the way of truth that they may not come into these bitter torments."

And thus this revelation was discovered.

Apocalypse of Thomas

(Christian Apocrypha)

The brief *Apocalypse of Thomas* describes the seven days of the End. Dating from the fifth century, or perhaps earlier, it follows the Revelation of John in certain imagery and is the only apocryphal apocalypse to assign seven days to the destruction of the End. The Book of Revelation has its own interest in seven—seven seals, seven trumpets, seven bowls. In its present version, undoubtedly subject to orthodox and heretic revisions, the most interesting aspect of the *Apocalypse of Thomas* is its Gnostic tendencies. After the "rain of blood" of earlier days, on the sixth day everything is permeated with light, a Gnostic light. We read: "Then they will put on the garment of eternal life; the garment from the clouds of light which has never been seen in the world." The garment as a symbol of spirit was found much earlier in the beautiful Gnostic "Hymn of the Pearl." In the end the "elect" rise to their salvation. The notion of the elect as such, as those who will be saved, is specifically Gnostic. When the elect rejoice that the destruction of the world has come, one recalls the Gnostic desire to leave the prison of the world to return to the realm of light.

APOCALYPSE OF THOMAS*

Hearken, Thomas, for I am the Son of God the Father and I am the father of all spirits. Hear from me the signs which

---

*The original text is thought to have been written in Greek. This version is based on the Latin manuscript. From Edgar Hennecke and Wilhelm Schneemelcher, eds. and trans., *New Testament Apocrypha*, vol. 2 (Philadelphia: Westminster Press, 1963), pp. 799–803.

will be at the end of this world, when the end of the world will be fulfilled before my elect come forth from the world.

I tell you openly what now is about to happen to men. When these are to take place the princes of the angels do not know, for they are now hidden from them. Then the kings will divide the world among themselves; there will be great hunger, great pestilences, and much distress on the earth. The sons of men will be enslaved in every nation and

551

will perish by the sword. There will be great disorder on earth. Thereafter when the hour of the end draws near there will be great signs in the sky for seven days and the powers of the heavens will be set in motion. Then at the beginning of the third hour of the first day there will be a mighty and strong voice in the firmament of the heaven; a cloud of blood will go up from the north and there will follow it great rolls of thunder and powerful flashes of lightning and it will cover the whole heaven. Then it will rain blood on all the earth. These are the signs of the first day.

And on the second day a great voice will resound in the firmament of heaven and the earth will be moved from its place. The gates of Heaven will be opened in the firmament of heaven from the east. The smoke of a great fire will burst forth through the gates of Heaven and will cover the whole heaven as far as the west. In that day there will be fears and great terrors in the world. These are the signs of the second day.

And on the third day at about the third hour there will be a great voice in heaven and the depths of the earth will roar out from the four corners of the world. The pinnacles of the firmament of heaven will be laid open and all the air will be filled with pillars of smoke. An exceedingly evil stench of sulphur will last until the tenth hour. Men will say: We think the end is upon us so that we perish. These are the signs of the third day.

And at the first hour of the fourth day the abyss will melt and rumble from the land of the east; then the whole earth will shake before the force of the earthquake. In that day the idols of the heathen will fall as well as all the buildings of the earth before the force of the earthquake. These are the signs of the fourth day.

But on the fifth day at the sixth hour suddenly there will be great thunderings in the heaven and the powers of the light will flash and the sphere of the sun will be burst and great darkness will be in the whole world as far as the west. The air will be sorrowful without sun and moon. The stars will cease their work. In that day all nations will so see as if they were enclosed in a sack, and they will despise the life of this world. These are the signs of the fifth day.

And at the fourth hour of the sixth day there will be a great voice in heaven. The firmament of heaven will be split from east to west and the angels of the heavens will look out on the earth through the rents in the heavens and all men who are on earth will see the angelic host looking out from Heaven. Then all men will flee into the tombs and hide themselves from before the righteous angels, and say, "Oh that the earth would open and swallow us." For such things will happen as never happened since this world was created. Then they will see me as I come down from above in the light of my Father with the power and honor of the holy angels. Then at my arrival the restraint on the fire of Paradise will be loosed, for Paradise is enclosed with fire. And this is the eternal fire which devours the earthly globe and all the elements of the world. Then the spirits and souls of the saints will come forth from Paradise and come into all the earth, and each go to its own body where it is laid up; and each of them will say, "Here my body is laid up." And when the great voice of those spirits is heard there will be an earthquake everywhere in the earth and by the force of that earthquake the mountains will be shattered above and the rocks beneath. Then each spirit will return to its own vessel and the bodies of the saints who sleep will rise. Then their bodies will be changed into the image and likeness and honor of the holy angels and into the power of the image of my holy Father. Then they will put on the garment of eternal life: the garment from the cloud of light which has never been seen in this world; for this cloud comes down from the upper kingdom of the heavens by the power of my Father, and will invest with its glory every spirit that has believed in me. Then they will be clothed and, as I said to you before, borne by the hands of the holy angels. Then they will be carried off in a cloud of light into the air, and rejoicing go with me into the heavens and remain in the light and honor of my Father. Then there will be great joy for them in the presence of my Father and in the presence of the holy angels. These are the signs of the sixth day.

And at the eighth hour of the seventh day there will be voices in the four corners of Heaven. All the air will be set in motion and filled with holy angels. These will make war among themselves for the whole day. In that day the elect will be delivered by the holy angels from the destruction of the world. Then all men will see that the hour of their destruction is come near. These are the signs of the seventh day.

And when the seven days are finished, on the eighth day at the sixth hour there will be a gentle and pleasant voice in Heaven from the east. Then that angel who has power over the holy angels will be made manifest. And there will go forth with him all the angels sitting on my holy Father's chariots of clouds, rejoicing and flying around in the air under Heaven, to deliver the elect who believed in me; and they will rejoice that the destruction of the world has come.

The words of the Savior to Thomas about the end of this world are finished.

Christian Sibyllines

(Christian Apocrypha)

The Christian Sibyllines are a continuation of the apocalyptic prophecy in the Jewish Sibyllines. The earliest Christian Sibyllines are thought to date from the middle of the second century. For a more complete description of the genre, see introduction to the Sibylline Oracles. The sibyls in Greek antiquity were women who proclaimed future events in a state of ecstasy. Usually, their prophecies were placed in a period much earlier than that of their authors, so that the events prophesied had already taken place. By this device the historical accuracy of the "prophecy" was guaranteed and the reputation of the sibyl was enhanced. The prophecy tradition is thought to have come to Greece from the east, from Iran and the Zoroastrians.

The best-known Greek sibyls were from Marpessos, Erythraia, and Cumae. The Erythraian Sibyl went to Delphi, where she entered Greek mythology. The Cumean Sibyl lived in a cave at the citadel at Cumae. Virgil described her. In his Fourth Ecologue he has her foretell the coming of a savior, which Christian writers later drew upon both to prove Pagan intuition of the coming of Christ as well as to establish grounds for Virgil's own Christian redemption.

While the Jewish Sibyllines were written in Alexandria and were, unlike most Jewish writing, candidly proselytizing, the Christian Sibyllines—largely Jewish Sibylline writing revised and with Christian interpolations—proclaimed not only the history of the End but the glory of Christ. They were markedly anti-Jewish and anti-Pagan. Some Sibylline texts—Book 7 of these selections—reveal clear Gnosticizing tendencies. The sibylline tradition continued into the Middle Ages, in Byzantium and in the west. One of the finest literary passages occurs in the last section below in which, in the style of Job, the magnificent achievements of God are described.

END OF BOOK I*

When the maid shall give birth to the logos of God Most High,
But as wedded wife shall give to the logos a name,
Then from the east shall a star shine forth in the midst of the day
Radiant and gleaming down from the heaven above,
Proclaiming a great sign to poor mortal men.
Yea, then shall the Son of the great God come to men,
Clothed in flesh, like unto mortals on earth.
Four vowels he has, twofold the consonants in him,
And now will I declare to you also the whole number:
Eight monads, and to these as many decads,
And eight hundreds also his name will show
To unbelieving men; but think in your heart
Of Christ, the Son of the immortal, most high God.
He will fulfill God's law, and not destroy,
Offering a pattern for imitation, and will teach all things.
To him shall priests bring and offer gold
And myrrh and frankincense; for indeed all these he will make.
But when a voice shall come through a desert place
Bringing tidings to men, and shall call upon all
To make straight the ways and to cast out
All evil from the heart, and that every body among men
Be illumined by the waters, that born anew
They may no more in any way at all forsake the paths of right,
Then one of barbarous mind, ensnared by the dancer's art,
Shall give in reward the head of him that cried, and a sudden portent
Shall be to men, when from the land of Egypt
Shall come, safeguarded, a precious stone; upon it
The people of the Hebrews shall stumble, but Gentiles shall gather
By his guidance; for indeed God who rules on high
They shall come to know through him, and a path in a common light.
For he shall show eternal life to men
Elect, but on the lawless he will bring the inextinguishable fire.
Then shall he heal the sick and all the afflicted,
As many as put their trust in him.
And the blind shall see, and the lame walk,
And the deaf shall hear, and they that speak not shall speak;
Demons he shall drive out, and there shall be resurrection of the dead;
On the waves he shall walk, and in a desert place
From five loaves and fish from the sea
Shall feed five thousand; and the remains of these
Shall fill twelve baskets for the holy maiden.

---

*All selections in this chapter are from Edgar Hennecke and Wilhelm Schneemelcher, eds. and trans., *New Testament Apocrypha*, vol. 2 (Philadelphia: Westminster Press, 1963), pp. 709–720, 732–739, 741, 744–745.

Then Israel in her intoxication shall not perceive,
Nor yet, weighed down, shall she hear with delicate ears.
But when the wrath of the Most High comes on the Hebrews
In raging fury and takes away faith from them,
Because they ill-used the heavenly Son of God,
And then indeed blows and poisonous spitting
Shall Israel give him with their polluted lips,
And for food gall, and for drink unmixed vinegar
They shall impiously give him, smitten they by evil frenzy
In breast and heart; but not seeing with their eyes,
Blinder than moles, more dreadful than creeping beasts
That shoot poison, shackled in deep slumber.
But when he stretches out his hands and measures all things,
And wears the crown of thorns, and his side
They pierce with spears for the sake of the law, three whole hours
There shall be night of monstrous darkness in the midst of the day.
And then shall Solomon's temple show to men
A mighty wonder, when to the house of Aidoneus
He goes down, proclaiming a resurrection to the dead.
But when in three days he comes again to the light,
And shows to mortals a token, and teaches all things,
Ascending in clouds will he journey to the house of Heaven,
Leaving to the world the ordinance of the Gospel.
Called by his name, a new shoot shall blossom forth
From the Gentiles guided by the law of the Mighty.
And moreover after this there shall be wise guides,
And then shall be thereafter a cessation of prophets.
    Then when the Hebrews reap the bitter harvest,
Much gold and silver shall a Roman king carry off
In plunder. And thereafter other kingdoms
Shall follow without remission, as kingdoms perish,
And shall afflict men. But there shall be to those men
A mighty fall, when they rule in unrighteous arrogance,
But when Solomon's temple falls to the holy earth,
Cast down by men of barbarian speech
And brazen breastplates, and the Hebrews are driven from the land
Wandering and plundered, and they mingle many tares
With the wheat, than shall there be an evil discord
For all men; and the cities despoiled on either side
Shall mourn each other, since they transgressed by an evil deed,
And received the wrath of great God to their bosoms.

BOOK II

And then shall God thereafter make a great sign.
For like a radiant crown a star shall shine,
Radiant and brightly beaming from the brilliant heaven
For not a few days; for then he will show from Heaven

A victor's crown for men who contend in the contest.
And then shall come the time of the great triumphal entry
Into the heavenly city, and it shall be universal
For all men, and have the renown of immortality.
And then shall every people in immortal contests
Contend for glorious victory; for there shall none
Be able shamelessly to purchase a crown for silver.
For Christ the holy shall adjudge to them just rewards,
And crown the excellent, and a prize immortal he will give
To martyrs who endure the contest even unto death.
And to virgins who run their course well a prize incorruptible
He will give, and to all among men who deal justly
And to nations from far-distant lands
Who live holy lives and recognize one God.
And those who love marriage and abstain from stolen unions,
Rich gifts will he give to them also, and eternal hope.
For every soul of men is a gift of God,
And it is not lawful for men to defile it with all manner of shame.

This is the contest, these the prizes, these the awards;
This is the gate of life and entry to immortality
Which the heavenly God appointed for righteous men
As guerdon of victory. They who receive
The crown nobly shall enter in by it.
   But when this sign appears throughout all the world,
Children grown grey at the temples from birth,
And afflictions of men, famines and plagues and wars,
And change of seasons, lamentations, many tears—
Ah, how many children in all lands, bitterly wailing,
Shall devour their parents, wrapping the flesh
In shrouds, and foul with blood and dust
Bury them in earth, the mother of peoples! Poor wretches,
Men of the last generation, dreadful transgressors,
Children who do not understand that, when the race of women
Do not give birth, the harvest of mortal men is come!
Near is the end, when instead of prophets
False deceivers approach, spreading reports on earth.
And Beliar too shall come and do many signs
For men. Then indeed a confusion among holy men,
Elect and faithful, and there shall be a plundering
Of them and the Hebrews. Dread wrath shall come upon them,
When a twelve-tribe people shall come from the east
Seeking a people which Assyria's shoot destroyed,
Their kindred Hebrews; thereupon nations shall perish.
Later again shall rule over men exceeding mighty
Elect and faithful Hebrews, when they have brought them
To slavery as of old, for power shall never leave them.
And the Most High, the all-surveying who dwells in the ether,
Shall send sleep upon men, veiling their eyelids.
O blessed servants, whom the master when he comes
Shall find wakeful, who all kept watch,

Ever expectant with sleepless eyes.
Come he at dawn or dusk, or in the midst of the day,
Yet come he will for certain, and it shall be as I declare.
He shall appear to the sleepers, when from the starry heaven
All the stars shall be seen of all in the midst of the day,
With the two great lights as time presses on.
   And then the Tishbite, speeding the heavenly chariot
From Heaven and descending to earth, shall show three signs
To all the world, signs of a life that is perishing.
Woe to all those who in that day are found to be
Great with child, all those who give milk
To infant children, all those who dwell upon the wave;
Woe to all those who look upon that day!
For a murky cloud shall cover the boundless earth,
From east and west and north and south.
And then a great river of burning fire
Shall flow down from heaven and consume every place,
Earth and great ocean and the grey-blue sea,
Lakes and rivers, springs and relentless Hades
And the heavenly sphere. And the lights of Heaven
Shall be dashed together into a form all-desolate;
For the stars shall all fall from Heaven into the sea.
And all souls of men shall gnash with their teeth,
Burning in the river of pitch and the raging fire
On a glowing plain, and ashes shall cover all things.
And then shall all the elements of the world be desolate,
Air, earth and sea, light, Heaven, days and nights.
No more shall unnumbered birds fly in the air,
No more the swimming creatures swim the sea,
Nor laden ship voyage upon the waves,
Nor guided cattle plough the earth;
No sound of trees beneath the wind. But in an instant all
Shall fuse together, and be separated into purity.
   But when the undying messengers of the immortal God,
Michael and Gabriel, Raphael and Uriel, shall come,
Who know full well what evils a man did before,
They shall bring the souls of men from the cloudy darkness
To judgment all, at the seat of God
Great and immortal; for one only is undying,
The Almighty himself, who shall be the judge of mortals.
And then to those beneath shall the heavenly give souls
And breath and speech, bones fitted together
With all manner of joints, flesh, and nerves,
And veins and skin about the flesh, and hair of the head.
Divinely compacted, breathing and set in motion,
Bodies of earthly men shall rise on one day.
Cruel, unbreakable, and inflexible are the monstrous bars
Of the gates of Hades, not forged of metal;
Yet Uriel, the great angel, shall burst and fling them open,
And shall bring all the shapes deeply mourning unto judgment:
The phantoms especially of Titans, born long ago,

And giants too, and all whom the Flood carried off,
And whom on the deep the wave of the sea destroyed,
And all whom beasts and creeping things and birds
Devoured, all these shall he call to the judgment seat;
And again, whom the flesh-devouring fire destroyed in flame,
These too shall he gather and set before God's judgment seat.
But when he raises the dead, loosing the bond of destiny,
And Sabaoth Adonai the high-thundering shall sit
On a heavenly throne and establish a great pillar,
There shall come on a cloud to the eternal, eternal himself,
Supplying in their turn; and those who did not obey,
But answered savage words to them that begat them;
And all who receiving pledges denied it,
And all servants who turned against their masters,
And again those who defiled their flesh with lewdness,
And all who loosed the maiden girdle
In stealthy union, and women who slay the burden
Of the womb, and all who lawlessly cast out their offspring;
Wizards and witches with them, them also
The wrath of the heavenly and incorruptible God
Shall bring to the pillory, where in circle all about
Flows unwearied the fiery stream, and all of them together
The angels of the immortal, everlasting God
Shall punish fearfully with flaming whips,
Binding them tightly about with fiery chains
And unbreakable fetters; then in the dead of night
Shall they be flung into Gehenna among the beasts of Tartarus,
Many and fearful, where darkness has no measure.
But when they have laid many torments upon all
Whose heart was evil, later again the fiery wheel
From the great river shall close in upon them,
Because wicked works were all their concern.
Then shall they lament, one here, one there, from afar
At their piteous lot, fathers and infant children,
Mothers too, and little ones weeping at the breast.
Neither shall there be for them surfeit of tears, nor shall the voice
Of them that wail bitterly, now here, now there, be hearkened to,
But far beneath Tartarus dark and dank
Afflicted they shall howl; in places unhallowed
They shall pay threefold for every evil deed they wrought,
Burning in a mighty fire. They shall gnash with their teeth,
All wasting away with violent and consuming thirst,
And shall call death fair, and it shall flee from them.
For neither death nor night shall give them rest any more.
Many an appeal, but in vain, shall they make to God who rules on high,
And then will he openly turn away his face from them.
For seven age-long days of repentance did he give
To erring men, by the hand of a holy virgin.
But the others, all who took thought for justice and noble works,
And piety and righteous ways of thinking,
Angels shall bear them through the burning river

And bring them to light and to a carefree life,
Where runs the immortal path of great God
And there are threefold springs of wine and milk and honey.
Earth the same for all, not divided by walls   )
And fences, will then bear fruits more abundant
Of its own accord; livelihood held in common, wealth unapportioned!
No pauper is there, no rich man, nor any tyrant,
No slave, nor again any great, nor shall any be small,
No kings, no rulers; but all share in common.
No longer shall any say "Night fell," nor again "Tomorrow"
Nor "It happened yesterday," nor be concerned with many days,
Nor spring nor harvest, nor winter nor autumn,
Nor marriage nor death, nor buying nor selling,
Nor sunset and sunrise; for all is one long day.
And for them will almighty, eternal God provide yet more.
To the pious, when they ask eternal God,
He will grant them to save men out of the devouring fire
And from everlasting torments. This also he will do.
For having gathered them again from the unwearying flame
And set them elsewhere, he will send them for his people's sake
Into another life and eternal with the immortals,
In the Elysian plain, where are the long waves
Of the ever-flowing, deep-bosomed Acherusian lake.
Ah, unhappy me, what will become of me in that day!
For that in my folly, laboring more than all,
I sinned, taking thought neither for marriage nor for reason;
Yea more, in my house I shut out the inferiors
Of a wealthy man; and lawless things I did aforetime
Knowingly. But you, Savior, deliver me the shameless
From my scourgers, though I have wrought unspeakable things!
And I pray you, let me rest a little from my song,
Holy Giver of manna, king of a great kingdom.

BOOK VI: HYMN TO CHRIST

I sing from the heart the great son and famous of the Immortal,
To whom the Most High, his begetter, gave a throne to take
Ere he was born; for according to the flesh he was raised up
The second time, after he had washed in the stream of the river
Jordan, which is borne along on silvery foot, drawing its waves.
Who first, escaping from fire, shall see God
Coming in sweet spirit, on the white wings of a dove.
And a pure flower shall blossom, and springs gush forth.
He shall show ways to men, he shall show heavenly paths;
And he shall teach all with wise speeches.
He shall bring to judgment and persuade a disobedient people,
Proudly declaring the praiseworthy race of his heavenly Father.
He shall walk the waves, and deliver man from sickness,

He shall raise up the dead, and banish many pains.
And from one wallet there shall be sufficiency of bread for men
When David's house puts forth its shoot. In his hand
Is all the world, and earth and Heaven and sea.
He shall flash like lightning on the earth, as at his first appearance
Two saw him, begotten from each other's side.
It shall be, when earth shall rejoice in the hope of a Son.
　But for you alone, land of Sodom, evil woe lies waiting;
For you in your folly did not perceive your God
When he came in the eyes of men. But from the thorn
You wove a crown, and bitter gall you mingled
For an insulting drink. This will bring you evil woe.
　O tree most blessed, on which God was stretched out,
Earth shall not have you, but you shall see a heavenly home,
When your fiery eye, O God, shall flash like lightning.

JESUS CHRIST, SON OF GOD, REDEEMER, CROSS

Earth shall sweat, when the sign of judgment shall appear.
From Heaven shall come the eternal king who is to be;
When he comes, he shall judge all flesh and the whole world.
And mortals, faithful and faithless, shall see God
Most High with the saints at the end of time.
He shall judge on his throne the souls of flesh-clothed men
When all the world becomes dry land and thorns.
Men shall cast down their idols and all their wealth.
And the fire shall burn up earth, Heaven, and sea,
Ranging abroad, and shall break the gates of Hades' prison.
Then shall all flesh of the dead come to the light of freedom,
That is, the saints; the lawless the fire shall torment for ages.
Whatever a man wrought secretly, then shall he speak all openly;
For God will open dark breasts with his lights.
There shall be wailing from all, and gnashing of teeth.
The light of the sun shall be eclipsed, the dances of the stars;
Heaven he will roll up; and the light of the moon shall perish.
He will raise aloft the chasms, lay low the high places of the hills;
No more shall baneful height be seen among men.
Mountains shall be level with plains, and all the sea
Shall no more have voyages. For earth shall then be parched
With its springs, and the foaming rivers run dry.
A trumpet from Heaven shall send forth a sound of great lamentation,
Mourning defilement of limbs and a world's calamity.
Then shall a gaping earth display the abyss of Tartarus.
All kings shall come to God's judgment seat.
From Heaven shall flow a river of fire and brimstone.
Then shall be a sign for all mortals, a notable seal,
The wood among the faithful, the horn long desired,

561

Life for pious men, but a stumbling block for the world,
With its waters enlightening the elect in twelve springs;
A staff of iron, shepherding, shall hold sway.
This is our God now proclaimed in acrostics,
Savior, immortal King, who suffered for our sakes.
Whom Moses typified, extending holy arms,
Conquering Amalek by faith, that the people might know
That with God the Father elect and precious is
The staff of David, and the stone which he promised,
He who believes on which shall have eternal life.
For not in glory but as a mortal shall he come into the world,
Pitiable, dishonored, unsightly, to give hope to the pitiable.
And to corruptible flesh he will give form, and heavenly faith
To the faithless, and he will give shape to the man
Molded in the beginning by God's holy hands,
Whom the serpent led astray by guile, to go to a destiny
Of death and receive knowledge of good and of evil,
So that forsaking God he was subject to mortal customs.
For him first of all did the Almighty take as counselor
In the beginning, and say: "My child, let us two make
The tribes of mortals, modeling them from our image!
Now I with my hands, and you thereafter with the logos,
Shall tend our figure, that we may produce a common creation!"
Mindful of this resolve, then, will he come into the world
Bringing a corresponding copy to a holy virgin,
At the same time enlightening with water by older hands,
Doing all with a word and healing every disease.
With a word shall he make the winds to cease, and calm the sea
While it rages walking on it with feet of peace and in faith.
And from five loaves and fish of the sea
He shall feed five thousand men in the desert,
And then taking all the fragments left over
He will fill twelve baskets for a hope of the people.
He shall call the souls of the blessed, and love the pitiable,
Who when scoffed at return good for evil,
Beaten and scourged and yearning for poverty.
Perceiving all and seeing all and hearing all
He shall spy out the inmost parts and lay them bare for scrutiny;
For himself of all is hearing and understanding and vision.
And the Word that creates forms, whom all obey,
Saving the dead and healing every disease,
Shall come at the last into the hands of lawless and unbelieving men,
They shall give to God blows with their unclean hands
And with their polluted mouths poisonous spitting.
Then shall he expose his back and submit it to the whips,
And buffeted shall keep silence, lest any should know
Who and of whom he is and whence he came to speak to the dying.
And he shall wear the crown of thorns; for of thorns
Is the crown of the elect, their eternal glory.
They shall pierce his sides with a reed because of their law . . .
But when all these things are accomplished which I have spoken,

Then in him shall all the law be dissolved, which from the beginning
Was given to men in ordinances because of a disobedient people.
He shall stretch out his hands and measure the whole world.
But for food they gave him gall, and to drink, sour wine;
The table of inhospitality will they display.
But the veil of the temple was rent, and in the midst of day
There shall be night dark and monstrous for three hours.
For no longer by secret law and in hidden temple to serve
The phantoms of the world, the hidden truth was again revealed
When the eternal Master came down upon earth.
But he shall come to Hades, announcing hope to all
The saints, the end of ages and the final day,
And shall fulfill death's destiny when he has slept the third day;
And then returning from the dead he shall come to the light,
The first to show them that are called the beginning of resurrection,
Having washed away the former iniquities in the waters
Of an immortal spring, that born from above
They may no more be in thrall to the lawless customs of the world.
First to his own did the Lord then openly appear
In flesh, as he was before, and show in his hands and feet
Four nail prints pierced in his own limbs,
East and west and south and north;
So many kingdoms of the world shall accomplish
The lawless, blameworthy deed as our example.
Rejoice, holy daughter of Sion, you have suffered so much!
Your king himself shall come, mounted on a gentle colt.
Meek, behold, he will come to take away our yoke
Of slavery, hard to bear, that rests upon our neck,
And godless ordinances will he dissolve, and oppressive fetters.

Then shall all the elements of the world be desolate,
Air, earth and sea, and the light of blazing fire;
And the heavenly sphere, and night, and all the days
Shall be dashed together into one, into a form all-desolate.
For the stars of the luminaries shall all fall from Heaven.
No more shall the plumed birds fly on the air
Nor is there step on earth; for the wild beasts shall all perish.
No sounds of men or beasts or winged things.
A world in disorder shall hear no useful echo;
But the deep sea shall ring forth a great sound of menace
And the swimming creatures of the sea shall all trembling die;
And ship bearing cargo shall no more sail upon the waves.
But earth shall bellow, bloodstained by wars,
And all souls of men shall gnash with their teeth,
Consumed with thirst and hunger, pestilence and slaughters,
And they shall call death fair, and it shall flee from them;
For no more shall death give them rest, nor night.
Many an appeal, but in vain, shall they make to God who rules on high,
And then will he openly turn away his face from them.
For seven age-long days of repentance did he give
To erring men, by the hand of a holy virgin.

God himself has made known to me all these things in my mind,
And he will accomplish all that is spoken by my mouth:
"I know the number of the sand and the measures of the sea,
I know the inmost parts of earth, and murky Tartarus,
I know the numbers of the stars, the trees, and how many tribes
Of things four-footed and swimming and of winged birds,
And of men, that are and shall be, and of the dead.
Myself I molded the forms and the mind of men,
And gave them right reason, and taught them knowledge;
I who formed eyes and ears, seeing and hearing
And perceiving every thought, and privy to all,
Lurking within I keep silence, and later myself will convict them.

The dumb I understand, he that speaks not I hear,
And how great is the whole height from earth to Heaven,
Beginning and End I know, I who made Heaven and earth.
For I alone am God, and other god there is none.
They seek oracles of my image, wrought from wood,
And shaping with their hands a speechless idol
They honor it with prayers and unholy ritual.
Forsaking the Creator, they render service to wantonness;
Worthless the gifts men have, to useless beings they give them,
And as it were for my honor they think all these useful,
Celebrating a steaming banquet, as for their own dead.
For they burn flesh, and bones full of marrow,
Sacrificing on their altars, and to the demons pour out blood;
And lights they kindle for me, the giver of light,
And as if God were athirst men pour libations of wine
On their useless idols, getting drunk to no purpose.
I need no sacrifice or libation at your hand,
No foul reek of fat, no hateful blood.
For these things will they do in memory of kings
And tyrants, for dead demons, as if they were heavenly,
Performing a ritual godless and destructive.
And gods do the godless call their images,
Forsaking the Creator, thinking that from them they have
All hope and life, trusting to their hurt
In the dumb and speechless, that know not the good end.
I myself set forth two ways, of life and death,
And I set it in their mind to choose the good life;
But they turned eagerly to death and eternal fire.
Man is my image, possessed of right reason.
For him set a pure and bloodless table,
Filling it with good things, and give to the hungry bread
And to the thirsty drink, and to the naked body clothing,
Of your own labors providing it with holy hands!
Receive the afflicted, come to the aid of the weary,
And present this living sacrifice to the living God,
Sowing now on the water, that I one day may give you
Immortal fruits, and you shall have light eternal
And life unfading, when I bring all men to proof by fire.

For I shall smelt all things, and separate them into purity.
Heaven I shall roll up, earth's crannies I shall open,
And then shall I raise up the dead, destroying fate
And death's sting, and later shall I come to judgment,
Judging the life of pious and of impious men;
And I will set ram with ram, shepherd with shepherd,
And calf with calf, hard by one another for the testing.
All who were exalted, convicted in the trial,
And stopped the mouth of every man, that they full of envy
Might enslave all alike those who act in holy fashion,
Bidding them keep silence, eager for gain,
All these shall then depart, as not approved in my presence.
No more thereafter shall you say in sorrow 'Will it be tomorrow?'
Nor 'It happened yesterday'; you are not concerned for many days,
Nor spring nor winter, nor harvest nor autumn,
Nor sunset and sunrise; for I will make day long.
But the light of Majesty shall be desired forever."

PROPHETIA SIBILLAE MAGAE
(FOURTH OR FIFTH CENTURY)
(MUNDUS ORIGO MEA EST)

The world is my origin, but soul have I drawn from the stars.
My body inviolate God makes to tremble altogether.
What God sets in my heart, that will I proclaim to men,
If abundant faith adjudge truly devout.
Many a song have my songs uttered aforetime,
But the songs which now I write, these God knows.
The heavenly homeland's citadel first God created with a word
As a divine and perfect work and a great service,
At the beginning of light, before chaos, God himself.
Beginning without end is God, God author of all.
He set chaos aside, separate from kindly night,
Commanded the day to stand, and night and day
To exchange in succession with their lights and move with the stars
By which the ages of all things are renewed in cycle.
Thus he addresses you, you saints, with a gracious heart:
"Lo, I am he who made the frame of heaven and the stars,
Who commanded the world to shine with a twofold light,
Who founded earth and the seas, and poured forth souls,
Who with my hands led limbs through the members,
Added body to bones, and in the bones marrow,
Made firm the sinews, and veins filled with blood,
Who formed the gleaming skin from glutinous mud
And inserted souls and added senses to minds,
Who gave nourishment to souls and food for the body,
And riches I gave to the streams, and to the fields metals,
And pure springs, and waters meet for fountains,

And cattle, the race of flocks, the natures of birds,
Who shut up milk in the udders, separating the blood,
Who willed the grass to grow green in the furrows on the dry ground,
Who enclosed the fragile grain in spiked seed,
Who painted the earth with flowers in varied bud,
Who cared for the sweet souls of bees and their homes,
Who commanded the globes on the fruit trees to swell with moisture,
Who gave vineyards, and made veins in the body.
These I provided and gave to man, nor denied him invention.
If I be worthy, snatch them away, and let it set my soul in Heaven.
Short is man's life, and when ended dissolves with the years.

Hermes Trismegistus: Poimandres

(Pagan Gnostic)

The *Poimandres* is a Pagan Gnostic treatise attributed to Hermes Trismegistus, the "Thrice-greatest Hermes." The *Poimandres*, meaning "shepherd of man" in Greek, or possibly "knowledge of the Sun-God Ra" in Coptic, comes from a large collection of writings known as the *Corpus Hermeticum* because they are concerned with the God Hermes. Although the author (or authors) of the *Poimandres* is aware of Judaism and Christianity, this syncretic work is basically Pagan, deriving from Egyptian Hellenistic Platonism. By ancient tradition, however, and confirmed by Lactanius in the fourth century, these ecstatic tracts derive from the occult books of an ancient Egyptian sage who lived shortly after Moses. Hermes is the common translation of the Egyptian god Thoth and is identified with his attributes. The notion that the "mysterious, hermetic" writings of the *Corpus Hermeticum* were the work of a secret Egyptian seer persisted from before Augustine, who took this to be a fact, to Giordano Bruno in the Renaissance. The Hermetic writings, including the *Poimandres*, were probably composed and compiled at the end of the second century A.D.

False attribution in order to lend authority to a text was a common practice in antiquity—we have many poems incorrectly attributed to Sappho, Plato, Anacreon, and Theognis—as it also was among European bookprinters until very recently. As for religious texts, the practice was the rule. Most of the apocryphal works of the intertestamental period as well as those of the Christian *acta* carried the names of venerated figures: Enoch, Daniel, Abraham, Paul, Thomas, Peter. With the names of these Jewish prophets and early Christian apostles these scriptures took on the importance of sacred works. The matter of false attributions underscores the importance of a favorable context for a sacred scripture or indeed any literary work from the Songs of Solomon and the Psalms of David (by neither Solomon nor David) to MacPherson's forgery, *The Poems of Ossian*. Today, bookjacket blurbs by famous critics perform the contextual deed of ancient false attributions.

Hermes Trismegistus, then, represents a tradition rather than a single man, and, as such, the *Poimandres* is a prime source of Gnostic speculation. The speaker in the Socratic dialogue, Poimandres, proposes a severely dualistic view of life in which the body represents everything dark, deceptive, temporal, and mortal while the mind (*nous*) represents light, truth, timelessness, and eternal salvation. The purpose of life is to free the soul from the prison of the body through gnosis (knowledge and enlightenment) and to return to the heavenly realm of light. So one leaves the physical universe by embarking on a celestial journey, through seven levels of spirituality, until one comes to the Father of All. There one becomes God. For the Hermeticists, God is, despite the title "Father of All," androgynous, containing both sexes. In *Asclepius*, the Hermetic fragment included here, God is defined as bisexual.

The *Poimandres* has three sections: the creation of the world and human life; the soul's escape from the world, its ascent to Heaven and mystical union with God; and instructions for proselytizing the gospel of gnosis. The work ends with a prayer. Part one is a major Gnostic cosmogony and anthropogony, revealed to the speaker as a visionary experience. Poimandres serves as a rather severe mentor to the speaker in the dialogue, explaining, reproaching, "ordering" redemption. We soon understand that Poimandres is the *nous*, the highest godhead. The creations or divine emanations of the Father of All are the logos (Word), the Mind-Demiurge (who in turn creates the planetary system and the physical world in which humanity is trapped), and *anthropos*, humanity. *Anthropos* appears in God's image, since he and she are begotten by himself as an androgynous generative principle and contains a divine soul, a spark of light.

In other Gnostic works the soul (*psyche*) is of a lower order than spirit (*pneuma*), and soul is associated with earthbound entities, particularly with the biblical Creator God. But in the *Poimandres* soul, rather than spirit, is the highest divine quality of *Anthropos*, and both *nous* and *psyche* contain this meaning. As in other Gnostic texts, Primal Man descends through the cosmos to the Earth where he mingles with darkness and matter; that is, he becomes trapped in nature. To be free of that darkness, one must abhor the senses, the body, all matter. After death, the soul's ascent back through the sphere is a privilege of the select. After Primal Man's cosmic fall, a human being returns to become one with God. Hans Jonas points out that long after the particular myth of cosmic return had disappeared, the technique of spiritual ascent, while alive and in the body, lived on as a later development of Neoplatonic and Judeo-Christian mysticism. We see this phenomenon, of course, in Plotinus, the last original Neoplatonist, and in the practices of shamans and mystics, east and west, whose principal aim is ecstatic transcendence. Jonas summarizes brilliantly:

In a later stage of "gnostic" development (though no longer passing under the name of Gnosticism) the external topology of the ascent through the spheres, with the successive divesting of the soul of its worldly envelopments and the regaining of its original acosmic nature, could be "internalized" and find its analogue in a psychological technique of inner transformations by which the self, *while still in the body*, might attain the Absolute as an immanent, if temporary, condition: an ascending scale of mental states replaces the stations of the mythical itinerary: the dynamics of progressive spiritual self-transformations, the spatial thrust through the heavenly spheres. Thus could transcendence itself be turned into immanence, the whole process become spiritualized and put within the power and the orbit of the subject. With this transposition of a mythological scheme into the inwardness of the person, with the translation of its objective stages into subjective phases of self-performable experience whose culmination has the form of ecstasis, gnostic myth has passed into mysticism (Neoplatonic and monastic), and in this new medium it lives on long after the disappearance of the original mythological beliefs.[1]

The writing attributed to Hermes Trismegistus, and of Plotinus and Dionysius the Areopagite have been a prime source for the occult as well as orthodox religious mysticism in the west. Plotinus was a historical Greek from Egypt, Dionysius a Christian—probably a fifth-century Syrian monk; but Hermes Trismegistus, the Thrice-greatest, has the aura of a mysterious visionary, a lunatic in the eyes of skeptics, a demigod to the faithful. All these human and divine attributes are intriguing and peculiar since, in all probability, Hermes Trismegistus was nobody at all; that is, he was a resonant name to replace a major Hellenistic religious tradition.

Note

1. Hans Jonas, *The Gnostic Religion*, 2d ed., rev. (1958; reprint, Boston: Beacon Press, 1970), pp. 165–66.

HERMES TRISMEGISTUS: POIMANDRES*

Once when I began to think about the things that are, and my thoughts soared exceedingly high, and my bodily senses were held down by sleep like people weighed down by overeating and weari-

ness, I thought I saw a being of vast and boundless magnitude coming toward me, who called me by name, and said, "What do you wish to hear and see, to learn and know?"

"Who are you?" I said.

"I am Poimandres," he said, "the Mind (*nous*) of absolute power. I know what you want and I am with you everywhere."

"I want to learn about the things that are, their nature, and to know God," I replied.

*"Poimandres, the Shepherd of Man," Book 1 from the *Corpus Hermeticum*. Translated from Greek by Willis Barnstone.

"I know what you wish, for I am with you everywhere. Keep in mind what you wish to learn and I will teach you."

With these words he changed his form, and in a flash everything opened before me and I saw an unbounded vista. All was Light, a soothing and happy Light. And as I gazed I was entranced. But soon a stark and terrifying Darkness descended gradually like a coiled snake, and I saw the Darkness turn into a watery substance,[1] unspeakably agitated, giving off smoke as from fire, emitting an indescribable sound of lamentation. And after that an inarticulate cry like the voice of fire.

Out of the Light a holy Word (logos) descended upon the watery substance, and I thought this Word the voice of Light, and unmingled fire leapt out of the watery substance and soared upward. The fire was quick and violent, and the air, being light, followed the Breath (*pneuma*)[2] as it rose from earth and water to the fire, so that the Breath seemed suspended from the fire. But the earth and water remained intermingled and the earth could not be seen apart from the water. All these elements were kept in audible motion by the Breath of the Word hovering above them.

Then Poimandres asked me, "Do you understand what that vision means?"

"I will understand," I said.

"I am that Light," he said, "and I am the Mind, the first God, who existed before the watery substance appeared out of the Darkness. And the luminous Word that issued from the Mind is the son of God."

"In what way?"

"Understand that what sees and hears inside you is the Word of the Lord, its son, but the Mind is God the Father. And they are not divided one from the other, for they are united by Life."

"Thank you," I said.

"But think about the Light, and understand it."

Having said this he gazed intently at me for a long time and I trembled at his aspect. When I raised my head I saw in my mind the Light, consisting of innumerable powers, which had become a limitless cosmos, and the fire, contained by a mighty power, was held in place. This is what I saw and understood from the words of Poimandres.

I was amazed, and he spoke to me again, "You have seen in your mind the archetypal form, infinite and prior to the beginning."

"But where do the elements of Nature come from?" I asked.

"From God's Will, which received the Word, and saw and imitated the beautiful world. The watery substance of Nature received the Word and made itself into an orderly world from its diverse elements, and a brood of living creatures came forth.

"And the first Mind, being both male and female, both Life and Light, generated through the Word another Mind, the Demiurge (Maker of Things), and this second Mind of fire and breath fashioned seven Rulers, who encompass within their orbits the world perceived by the senses. Their government is called Destiny (*heimarmene*).

"Suddenly, the Word of God leapt out of the downward moving elements of Nature to the pure body of Heaven and was united with the Mind of the Demiurge. For the Word was of one substance with the Mind. And the lower elements of Nature were left Wordless (*alogos*), that is, without reason, and became mere matter.

"Now the Demiurge-Mind worked together with the Word to encompass the spheres of the Rulers and to whirl them with thunderous speed, with no fixed beginning or determined end, since their revolutions begin where they end. And according to the Mind's will, the lower elements of Nature became animals devoid of reason, for they did not have the Word. And the air brought forth winged creatures and water fish, and by then earth and water were separated from each other according to the will of the Mind. And earth brought forth four-footed creatures and creeping things and wild and tame beasts.

"But Mind, the Father of All, who is Life and Light, gave birth to a being like himself. And he loved him as his own child, for he was very beautiful, bearing the likeness of his father. And God was very pleased with his own beauty in Primal Man (*anthropos*) and delivered to him all that he had created.

"And Primal Man took station in the highest sphere of Heaven and observed the things made by its author, his brother the Demiurge, who ruled over the region of fire. Now that Man had seen those things made in fire, he wished to create things of his own. And his father permitted him to do so. And since the Rulers loved him too, each gave him a share of his own nature.

"When Man learned their characteristics, he wished to break through the bounding orbits of the Rulers and to share the power of him who rules over the fire.

"Then Primal Man, who possessed all authority over the world of mortal creatures and irrational animals, leaned down through the Harmony (the world of the spheres) and, having broken the vault, showed lower Nature the beautiful form of God. When Nature saw the beautiful form of God, it smiled on Man with love, for it had seen the wondrous beauty of Man reflected in the water and its shadow on the earth. And Man too, on seeing this form, a form similar to his own reflected in the water, loved it and wanted to live in it. And his wish was immediately realized and he began to inhabit a form devoid of reason. And Nature received its loved one, embraced him, and they mingled, for they were lovers.

"And this is why Man, of all creatures on the earth, is twofold: mortal in his body but immortal through the eternal Man. Though he is immortal and has power over all things, he also suffers mortality, since he is subject to Destiny (*heimarmene*). Though above the world of the spheres (Harmony), he is a slave of Destiny. Though he is male and female (androgynous), being born of a Father who contains male and female and is sleepless as his Father is sleepless, he is vanquished by love and oblivion."

And after this I said, "O Mind, tell me the rest. I too love your teaching."

And Poimandres answered, "Here is the mystery which has been hidden until this day. Nature, intimately mingled with Primal Man, produced a most wondrous miracle. Man had in himself the world of spheres of the seven Rulers, which, as I told you, was made of fire and air. Nature immediately made seven Men corresponding to the natures of the seven Rulers, and they were androgynous and sublime."

Then I said, "O Poimandres, a powerful desire has seized me and I want to hear more. Do not stop."

"Silence," Poimandres replied. "I have not yet finished with the first discourse."

"See, I am silent," I said.

"These seven Men were born as follows: Nature brought forth their bodies. Earth was the female element, water the generative male element; from fire came their nature, from ether their spirit (*pneuma*). Nature brought forth their bodies in the likeness of Man. And Man, who was formed of Life and Light, became soul (*psyche*) and mind (*nous*): soul from Life and mind from Light. And all creatures in the world of senses remained that way until the end of an era.

"Now I will tell you what you long to hear. When that era was completed, the bond uniting all things was loosened by God's will. All living creatures, being androgynous, were suddenly divided into two, and Primal Man (*anthropos*) became at once male and female. God immediately spoke a holy word, 'Increase and multiply, all you creatures and creations.

And let Man, being a Man with a Mind, recognize himself as immortal and know that the cause of death is Eros.'

"And when God said this, his Providence (*pronoia*), by means of Destiny and the world of spheres, brought male and female into union and established generations. And all creatures multiplied according to their kind. And he who recognized himself attained that Good which is supreme, while he who was led astray by desire, by love for the body, will wander in the darkness of the world of senses, and suffer death."

"But what kind of sin do the ignorant commit that they should be deprived of immortality?" I asked.

"You do not seem to have thought about what I told you. Did I not tell you to pay attention?"

"I understand and remember, and thank you at the same time."

"If you understand, tell me why those who are ignorant deserve death?"

"Because the material body has its source in the abhorrent Darkness, from which came the watery substance of which the body is composed in the sensible world, and from this body death slakes its thirst."

"You have understood correctly. But why is it, as the Word of God has it, that he who recognizes and knows himself enters into the Good?"

I answered: "Because the Father of All consists of Light and Life, and from him Man was born."

"You are right. Light and Life are God and Father out of which Man came. And if you learn that you are also made of Light and Life, you will return to Light and Life." These things Poimandres said.

"But tell me," I said, "how I shall come into Life, for God told me 'Let the thinking Man know himself.' Do not all people have a Mind?"

"Do not speak that way, for I, Mind, am present to the holy and good and pure and merciful, and my presence is a help to them, and all at once they recognize everything and win the mercy of loving God, and thank him and praise him and sing hymns to him, and turn to him with devotion. And before they abandon the body to death, they loathe the bodily senses, since they know how they work. I, the Mind, will not allow the workings of the body to attain their purpose. As a guardian of the gates, I bar the way to evil and shameful energies. I cut off their strategies.

"And I am far removed from those who are foolish and evil and sly and envious and covetous and murderous and godless. I yield place to the avenging Daimon who visits such a man with the sharpness of fire, piercing his senses and driving him to further lawlessness so that he may incur greater punishment. Never ceasing his dark struggle, and giving in to boundless appetite, he inflicts upon himself greater torment and hotter fire."

"Mind, you have instructed me well in all things. But tell me more about the ascent. How shall I come to Life?"

At this Poimandres said, "First, with the dissolution of your material body, you yield your character to the Daimon. Your image vanishes. The bodily senses return to their own sources, becoming part of the cosmos, and, combined in new ways, do other work. And anger and desire enter thoughtless Nature.

"And then man rises into the Harmony, the world of the spheres. In the first zone he leaves behind the force to grow and decrease, in the second the machinations of evil, in the third the guile of lust, in the fourth his domineering arrogance, in the fifth his unholy daring and rashness, in the sixth his striving for wealth by evil means, and in the seventh zone the malicious lie—all rendered powerless.

"Then, stripped naked by the force of the Harmony, he enters the eighth sphere of the fixed star, Ogdoas, and possessing his own energy he remains there with others, singing hymns to the Father. And the others are happy at his coming. Resembling those who live there, he hears the Powers who have their place in the substance of the eighth sphere and who sing to God with a special voice. They move in order up to the Father. They surrender to the Powers, and become the Powers, and are in God. This is the Good, the aim of those who have Gnosis: *to become God.*

"Why then do you hesitate? Now that you have received everything from me, why not make yourself a guide to the worthy so that humanity may be saved by God through you?" And, having said these things, Poimandres before my eyes mingled with the Powers.

I thanked and blessed the Father of All, and was sent forth, empowered and instructed concerning the Nature of All and with a supreme vision. And I began to preach to the people of beauty, of piety and Gnosis: "O people born of the Earth, given over to drunkenness and sleep and ignorance of God, end your drunkenness and unreasoning sleep."

When they heard this, they gathered around me. I said, "Why have you accepted death when you have been given the power to enjoy immortality? Change your ways, you who walk with error and keep company with ignorance. Free yourself of Darkness and seize the Light. Abandon corruption and receive immortality."

And some of them mocked me and left me, for they had given themselves to death. But others begged me to teach them and they threw themselves at my feet. I raised them up and became a guide to humanity, teaching them the Word and how they might be saved. And I sowed words of wisdom in them and they were nourished with ambrosial water. When evening came and the rays of sun began to fade, I called on them to thank God. And when they completed the thanksgiving, each sought his or her own bed.

I recorded the beneficence of Poimandres, and how my hopes had been fulfilled. For the body's sleep became the soul's awakening, the closing of my eyes became the true vision; my silence pregnant with the Good, and my words the expression of good things. And all this happened to me, since I had received it from my Mind, that is, from Poimandres, the Word and Mind of Absolute Sovereignty. I became God-inspired, God-Minded, and came with the Truth.

So with all my soul and strength I praise the God the Father:
Holy is God the Father of All, who precedes all beginnings.
Holy is God whose Will is accomplished by his own Powers.
Holy is God who wishes to be known and is known to those who are his own.
You are holy who by your Word made all things that are.
You are holy who did not blacken Nature.
You are holy who has become the image of all Nature.
You are holy who are stronger than all domination.
You are holy who are greater than all eminence.
You are holy who are superior to all praise.
Accept the pure offering of words from a soul and heart which rise to you,
    Unnameable, Ineffable, whom only Silence calls!

I beg you, let me not be removed from Gnosis, which is our nature. Fill me with strength, and with your grace let me bring Light to those of my race who are in ignorance, to my brothers and sisters, sons and daughters.

Therefore I believe and bear witness. I go to Life and to Light.

Father, bless you. Your child wishes to share the holy salvation you confer through your total authority.

Note

1. physis. Nature

Hermes Trismegistus: Asclepius

(Pagan Gnostic)*

A Hermetic tractate, the Coptic *Asclepius* 21–29 was previously known from a Latin version and some brief quotations from the original Greek. Only a portion of the entire *Asclepius* is to be found in Codex VI, and this excerpt may very well have been meant to be juxtaposed with the Hermetic *Discourse on the Eighth and Ninth* (VI, 6).

Asclepius 21–29 is a dialogue between the mystagogue, Hermes Trismegistus, and an initiate, Asclepius. The tractate opens with a comparison of the mystery and sexual intercourse: both are accomplished in secret and involve intimate interaction. There follows a discussion of piety as knowledge and impiety as ignorance. With the acquisition of knowledge human beings become better than the gods, for then they are both mortal and immortal. Hermes Trismegistus next suggests that just as the Lord of the universe creates gods, so also humanity creates gods according to human likeness. In an apocalyptic section, with significant Egyptian and Jewish parallels, the speaker predicts that woes will come upon Egypt, but also promises that finally God the Creator will restore order again. The tractate closes with a discussion of individual eschatology; after death the soul is judged, and rewarded or punished accordingly.

This Coptic excerpt from *Asclepius* shows both Hermetic and Gnostic traits. On the one hand, certain passages seem to be quite pantheistic: God is in every place, and beholds every place. Yet dualistic emphases also occur, as in the discussion of the two human natures. This dualism, together with the theme of the importance of knowledge for salvation, may suggest that the tractate has certain Gnostic characteristics.

*Introduction by James Brashler, Peter A. Dirkse, and Douglas M. Parrott.

HERMES TRISMEGISTUS:
ASCLEPIUS 21–29*

"And if you wish to see the reality of this mystery, then you should see the wonderful representation of the intercourse that takes place between the male and the female. For when the semen reaches the climax, it leaps forth. In that moment the female receives the strength of the male; the male for his part receives the strength of the female, while the semen does this.

"Therefore the mystery of intercourse is performed in secret, in order that the two sexes might not disgrace themselves in front of many who do not experience that reality. For each of the sexes contributes its own part in begetting. For if it happens in the presence of those who do not understand the reality, it is laughable and unbelievable. And, moreover, they are holy mysteries, of both words and deeds, because not only are they not heard, but also they are not seen.

"Therefore such people—the unbelievers—are blasphemers. They are atheistic and impious. But the others are not many; rather, the pious who are counted are few. Therefore wickedness remains among the many, since learning concerning the things which are ordained does not exist among them. For the knowledge of the things which are ordained is truly the healing of the passions of matter. Therefore learning is something derived from knowledge.

"But if there is ignorance, and learning does not exist in the soul of man, then the incurable passions persist in the soul. And additional evil comes with the passions in the form of an incurable sore. And the sore constantly gnaws at the soul, and through it the soul produces

worms from the evil and stinks. But God is not the cause of these things, since he sent to men knowledge and learning."

"O Trismegistus, did he send them to men alone?"

"Yes, O Asclepius, he sent them to men alone. And it is fitting that we tell you why to men alone he granted knowledge and learning, the allotment of his good.

"And now listen! God and the Father, even the Lord, created man subsequent to the gods, and he took him from the region of matter. Since matter is involved in the creation of man of [. . .], the passions are in it. Therefore they continually flow over his body, for this living creature would not exist in any other way except that he take this food, since he is mortal. It is also inevitable that inopportune desires which are harmful dwell in him. For the gods, since they came into being out of a pure matter, do not need learning and knowledge. For the immortality of the gods is learning and knowledge, since they came into being out of pure matter. Immortality assumed for them the position of knowledge and learning. By necessity God set a boundary for man; he placed him in learning and knowledge.

"Concerning learning and knowledge, which we have mentioned from the beginning, he perfected them in order that by means of these things he might restrain passions and evils, according to his will. He brought man's mortal existence into immortality; man became good and immortal, just as I have said. For God created a twofold nature for him: the immortal and the mortal.

"And it happened this way because of the will of God that men be better than the gods, since indeed the gods are immortal, but men alone are both immortal and mortal. Therefore man has become akin to the gods, and they know the affairs of each other with certainty; the gods know the things of men, and men know the things of the gods. And I am speaking about men, O Asclepius, who

*VI 65, 15–78, 43. Translated by James Brashler, Peter A. Dirkse, and Douglas M. Parrott. From James M. Robinson, ed., *The Nag Hammadi Library* (San Francisco: Harper & Row, 1977), pp. 300–307.

have attained learning and knowledge. But about those who are more vain than these, it is not fitting that we say anything base, since we are divine and are introducing holy matters.

"Since we have entered the matter of the communion between the gods and men, know, O Asclepius, that in which man can be strong! For just as the Father, the Lord of the universe, creates gods, in this very way man too, this mortal, earthly, living creature, the one who is not like God, also himself creates gods. Not only does he strengthen, but he is also strengthened. Not only is he god, but he also creates gods. Are you astonished, O Asclepius? Are you yourself another disbeliever like the many?"

"O Trismegistus, I agree with the words spoken to me. And I believe these things you speak. But I have also been astonished at the discourse about this. And I have decided that man is blessed, since he has enjoyed this great power."

"And that which is greater than all these things, O Asclepius, is worthy of admiration. Now it is revealed to us concerning the race of the gods, and we confess along with everyone else, that the race of the gods has come into being out of pure matter. And their bodies are heads only. But that which men create is the likeness of the gods. The gods are from the farthest part of matter, and the object created by men is from the outer part of the being of men. Not only are what men create heads, but they are also all the other members of the body and according to their likeness. Just as God has willed that the inner man be created according to his image, in the very same way man on earth creates gods according to his likeness."

"O Trismegistus, you are not talking about idols, are you?"

"O Asclepius, you yourself are talking about idols. You see that again you yourself, O Asclepius, are also a disbeliever of the discourse. You say about those who have soul and breath, that they are idols—these who bring about these great

events. You are saying about these who give prophecies that they are idols—these who give men sickness and healing.

"Or are you ignorant, O Asclepius, that Egypt is the image of Heaven? Moreover, it is the dwelling place of Heaven and all the forces that are in Heaven. If it is proper for us to speak the truth, our land is the Temple of the world. And it is proper for you not to be ignorant that a time will come in our land when Egyptians will seem to have served the divinity in vain, and all their activity in their religion will be despised. For all divinity will leave Egypt and will flee upward to Heaven. And Egypt will be widowed; it will be abandoned by the gods. For foreigners will come into Egypt, and they will rule it. Egypt! Moreover, Egyptians will be prohibited from worshiping God. Furthermore, they will come into the ultimate punishment, especially whoever among them is found worshiping and honoring God.

"And in that day the country that was more pious than all countries will become impious. No longer will it be full of temples, but it will be full of tombs. Neither will it be full of gods, but it will be full of corpses. O Egypt! Even Egypt will become like the fables. And [. . .] the barbarian will be better than you, O Egyptian, in his religion, whether he is a Scythian, or Hindu, or some other of this sort.

"And what is this that I say about the Egyptian? For they will not abandon Egypt. For in the time when the gods have abandoned the land of Egypt, and have fled upward to Heaven, then all Egyptians will die. And Egypt will be made a desert by the gods and the Egyptians. And as for you, O river, there will be a day when you will flow with blood more than water. And dead bodies will be stacked higher than the dams. And he who is dead will not be mourned as much as he who is alive. Indeed, the latter will be known as an Egyptian on account of his language in the second period of time. O Asclepius, why are you weeping? He will seem like a foreigner in regard to his customs. Divine Egypt will suffer evils greater than these. Egypt, lover of God, and the dwelling place of the gods, school of religion, will become an example of impiousness.

"And in that day the world will not be marveled at [. . .] immortality, nor will it be worshiped [. . .] since we say that it is not good [. . .]. It has become neither a single thing nor a vision. But it is in danger of becoming a burden to all men. Therefore it will be despised—the beautiful world of God, the incomparable work, the energy that possesses goodness, the many-formed vision, the abundance that does not envy, that is full of every vision. Darkness will be preferred to light and death will be preferred to life. No one will gaze into Heaven. And the pious man will be counted as insane, and the impious man will be honored as wise. The man who is afraid will be considered as strong. And the good man will be punished like a criminal.

"And concerning the soul and the things of the soul and the things of immortality, along with the rest of what I have said to you, O Tat, Asclepius, and Ammon, not only will they be considered ridiculous, but they will also be thought of as a vanity. But believe me when I say that people of this kind will be endangered by the ultimate danger to their soul. And a new law will be established. [. . .] The wicked angels will remain among men, and be with them and lead them into wicked things recklessly, as well as into atheisms, wars, and plunderings, by teaching them things contrary to nature.

"In those days the earth will not be stable, and men will not sail the sea, nor will they know the stars in heaven. Every sacred voice of the word of God will be silenced, and the air will be diseased. Such is the senility of the world: atheism, dishonor, and the disregard of noble words.

"And when these things had happened, O Asclepius, then the Lord, the Father and only primal God, God the Creator, when he looked upon the things that happened, established his design, which is good, against the disorder. He took away error, and cut off evil. Sometimes he submerged it in a great flood, at other times he burned it in a searing fire, and at still other times he crushed it in wars and pestilence [. . .]. And this is the birth of the world.

"The restoration of the nature of the pious ones who are good will take place in a period of time that never had a beginning. For the will of God has no beginning, even as his nature, which is his will, has no beginning. For the nature of God is will. And his will is the good."

"O Trismegistus, is purpose, then, will?"

"Yes, O Asclepius, since will is included in counsel. For what is the case with what he has? He does not will it from deficiency. Since he is complete in every part, he wills what he already fully has. And he has every good. And what he wills, he wills. And he has the good that he wills. Therefore he has everything. And God wills what he wills. And the good world is an image of the good one."

"O Trismegistus, is the world good?"

"O Asclepius, it is good, as I shall teach you. For just as the soul and life comes forth in the world in matter, those that are good are like the beauty and the ripening of the fruits, and the things similar to all these. Because of this, God has control over the heights of Heaven. He is in every place and he looks out over every place. And in his place there is neither Heaven nor star. And he is free from the body.

"Now the creator has control in the place that is between the earth and Heaven. He is called Zeus, that is, life. Plutonius Zeus is lord over the earth and sea. And he does not possess the nourishment for all mortal living creatures, for it is Kore who bears the fruit. These forces always are powerful in the circle of the earth, but those of others are always from him Who Is.

"And the lords of the earth will withdraw themselves. And they will establish themselves in a city that is in a corner of Egypt and that will be built toward the setting of the sun. Every man will go into it, whether they come on the sea or on the shore."

"O Trismegistus, where will these be settled now?"

"O Asclepius, in the great city that is on the Libyan mountain . . . it frightens . . . as a great evil, in ignorance of the matter. For death occurs, which is the dissolution of the labors of the body and the dissolution of the number of the body, when death completes the number of the body. For the number is the union of the body. Now the body dies when it is not able to support the man. And this is death: the dissolution of the body and the destruction of the sensation of the body. And it is not necessary to be afraid of this, nor because of this, but because of what is not known and is disbelieved one is afraid."

"But what is not known or is disbelieved?"

"Listen, O Asclepius! There is a great demon. The great God has appointed him to be overseer or judge over the souls of men. And God has placed him in the middle of the air between the earth and Heaven. Now, when the soul comes forth from the body, it is necessary that it meet this demon. Immediately, the demon will surround this one and examine him in regard to the character that he has developed in his life. And if he finds that he piously performed all of his actions for which he came into the world, this demon will allow [. . .]. But if [. . .] he brought his life into evil deeds, he grasps him, as he flees upward and throws him down so that he is suspended between Heaven and earth and is punished with a great punishment. And he will be deprived of his hope, and be in great pain.

"And that soul has been put neither on the earth nor in Heaven. But it has come into the open sea of the air of the world, the place where there is a great fire and crystal water and furrows of fire and a great upheaval. The bodies are tormented in various ways. Sometimes they are cast upon raging waters; at other times they are cast down into the fire in order that it may destroy them. Now, I will not say that this is the death of the soul, for it has been delivered from evil, but it is a death sentence.

"O Asclepius, it is necessary to believe these things and to fear them in order that we might not encounter them. For unbelievers are impious and commit sin. Afterwards, they will be compelled to believe, and they will not hear by word of mouth only, but will experience the reality itself. For they kept believing that they would not endure these things. First, O Asclepius, all those of the earth die and those who are of the body cease [. . .] of evil [. . .] with these of this sort. For those who are here are not like those who are there. So with the demons who [. . .] men, they despise [. . .] there. Thus it is not the same. But truly the gods who are here will punish more whoever has hidden it here every day."

"O Trismegistus, what is the character of the iniquity that is there?"

"Now you think, O Asclepius, that when one takes something in a temple, he is impious. For that kind of a person is a thief and a bandit. And this matter concerns gods and men. But do not compare those here with those of the other place. Now I want to speak this discourse to you confidentially; no part of it will be believed. For the souls that are filled with much evil will not come and go in the air, but they will be put in the places of the demons, which are filled with pain, and are always filled with blood and slaughter. And their food is weeping, mourning, and groaning."

"O Trismegistus, who are these demons?"

"O Asclepius, they are the ones who

are called stranglers, and those who roll souls down on the dirt, and those who scourge them, and those who cast into the water, and those who cast into the fire, and those who bring about the pains and calamities of men. For such as these are not from a divine soul, nor from a rational soul of man. Rather, they are from the terrible evil."

Hermes Trismegistus: On God's Bisexuality

(Pagan Gnostic)*

The two preceding passages from the Hermes Trismegistus tradition are translations from the Greek original (the *Poimandres*) and from a Coptic version of the Greek (*Asclepius*). This fragment is from the Latin tradition. The notion of God's bisexuality is a common Gnostic notion: God is androgynous: male in its mind (*nous*), female in its thought (*epinoia* and *ennoia*); the substance is male, the process female. Of great interest is the declaration that God's bisexuality extends to all beings, whether endowed with soul or soulless. Later mystics of western Christianity often used physical love as their metaphor for union with God. In this passage "the conjunction of the two sexes," their "fusion," becomes a sacrament reflecting heavenly love in all beings.

HERMES TRISMEGISTUS: ON GOD'S BISEXUALITY

Ascl. You say then, Trismegistus, that God is bisexual? *Trism.* Yes, Asclepius; and not God alone, but all kinds of beings, whether endowed with soul or soulless. Nothing that exists can be barren; for if all things that now exist are deprived of fertility, it will be impossible for the now existing races to endure for ever. I tell you that God eternally generates the Cosmos, and that the Cosmos possesses generative power, and thereby maintains all races that have come into being. For either sex is filled with procreative force; and in that conjunction of the two sexes, or, to speak more truly, that fusion of them into one, which may be rightly named Eros, or Aphrodite, or both at once, there is a deeper meaning than man can comprehend. It is a truth to be accepted as sure and evident above all other truths, that by God, the Master of all generative power, has been devised and bestowed upon all creatures this sacrament of eternal reproduction, with all the affection, all the joy and gladness, all the yearning and the heavenly love that are inherent in its being.

------

*Introduction by Willis Barnstone.

The Book of Thomas the Contender

(Gnostic)*

The *Book of Thomas the Contender* is a dialogue between the resurrected Jesus and his brother Judas Thomas, and is allegedly recorded by a certain Mathaias (the apostle Matthew?) as he heard them speaking together. The literary genre of the tractate—a genre also represented in several other tractates from the Nag Hammadi library—is the Gnostic revelation dialogue, typically occurring between the resurrected Savior and a trusted apostle or apostles during the time between the Savior's resurrection and ascension. Here the trusted individual with whom the resurrected Jesus converses is none other than Thomas, the Savior's twin who was thought to have direct insight into the nature of the Savior and his teaching. By "knowing himself" Thomas could also know the "depth of the All" from which the Savior came and to which he was going to return; and thus Thomas could become a missionary proclaiming the true (here, the ascetic and somewhat Gnostic) teaching of the exalted Jesus. Hence, like the *Gospel of Thomas* (II, 2) and the *Acts of Thomas*, the *Book of Thomas the Contender* presents traditions about the apostle Thomas such as were prevalent within the ascetic Christianity of Syrian Edessa; the *Book of Thomas the Contender* was probably composed in Syria during the first half of the third century.

Following the introductory lines of the tractate, the text of the *Book of Thomas the Contender* can be divided into two major sections. The first section (138:4–142, 26) consists of a revelation dialogue between Jesus and Thomas, while the second section (142:26–145, 16) is a monologue, a homily delivered by the Savior. At the end of the tractate are added the title and a final colophon written by the scribe.

---

*Introduction by John D. Turner.

Consistently and intensely ascetic in doctrine, the tractate warns against fire—the fire of sexual passions and the fire of hellish punishment. The tractate stresses the true and divine light of the Savior, who as the emissary of the light descends to illumine the eyes and the minds of those living in a darkened world.

THE BOOK OF THOMAS THE CONTENDER*

The secret words that the Savior spoke to Judas Thomas which I, even I Mathaias, wrote down—I was walking, listening to them speak with one another.

The Savior said, "Brother Thomas, while you have time in the world, listen to me and I will reveal to you the things you have pondered in your mind.

"Now since it has been said that you are my twin and true companion, examine yourself that you may understand who you are, in what way you exist, and how you will come to be. Since you are called my brother, it is not fitting that you be ignorant of yourself. And I know that you have understood, because you had already understood that I am the knowledge of the truth. So while you accompany me, although you are uncomprehending, you have in fact already come to know, and you will be called 'the one who knows himself.' For he who has not known himself has known nothing, but he who has known himself has at the same time already achieved knowledge about the depth of the All. So then, you, my brother Thomas, have beheld what is obscure to men, that is, that against which they ignorantly stumble."

Now Thomas said to the Lord, "Therefore I beg you to tell me what I ask before your Ascension, and when I hear from you about the hidden things, then I can speak about them. And it is obvious to

*II 138:1–45, 19; 145:20–23. Translated by John D. Turner. From James M. Robinson, ed., *The Nag Hammadi Library* (San Francisco: Harper & Row, 1977), pp. 188–194.

me that the truth is difficult to perform before men."

The Savior answered, saying, "If the things that are visible to you are obscure to you, how can you hear about the things that are not visible? If the deeds of the truth that are visible in the world are difficult for you to perform, how indeed, then, shall you perform those that pertain to the exalted height and to the Pleroma which are not visible? And how shall you be call 'laborers'? In this respect you are apprentices, and have not yet received the height of perfection."

Now Thomas answered and said to the Savior, "Tell us about these things that you say are not visible, but are hidden from us."

The Savior said, "All bodies of men and beasts are begotten irrational. . . . Those, however, that are above are not visible among things that are visible, but are visible in their own root, and it is their fruit that nourishes them. But these visible bodies eat of creatures similar to them with the result that the bodies change. Now that which changes will decay and perish, and has no hope of life from then on, since that body is bestial. So just as the body of the beasts perishes, so also will these formations perish. Do they not derive from intercourse like that of the beasts? If the body too derives from intercourse, how will it beget anything different from beasts? So, therefore, you are babes until you become perfect."

And Thomas answered, "Therefore I say to you, Lord, that those who speak about things that are invisible and difficult to explain are like those who shoot their arrows at a target at night. To be sure, they shoot their arrows as anyone would—since they shoot at the target—but it is not visible. Yet when the light comes forth and hides the darkness, then the work of each will appear. And you, our light, enlighten, Lord."

Jesus said, "It is in light that light exists."

Thomas spoke, saying, "Lord, why does this visible light that shines on behalf of men rise and set?"

The Savior said, "O blessed Thomas, of course this visible light shone on your behalf—not in order that you remain here, but rather that you come forth—and whenever all the elect abandon bestiality, then this light will withdraw up to its essence, and its essence will welcome it, since it is a good servant."

Then the Savior continued and said, "O unsearchable love of the light! O bitterness of the fire that burns in the bodies of men and in their marrow, burning in them night and day, burning in the limbs of men and making their minds drunk and their souls deranged and moving them within males and females by day and night and moving them with a movement that moves secretly and visibly. For the males move; they move upon the females and the females upon the males. Therefore it is said, 'Everyone who seeks the truth from true wisdom will make himself wings so as to fly, fleeing the lust that scorches the spirits of men.' And he will make himself wings to flee every visible spirit."

And Thomas answered, saying, "Lord, this indeed is what I am asking you about, since I have understood that you are the one who is good for us, as you say."

Again the Savior answered and said, "Therefore it is necessary for us to speak to you, since this is the doctrine for the perfect. If, now, you desire to become perfect, you shall observe these things; if not, your name is 'Ignorant,' since it is impossible for a wise man to dwell with a fool, for the wise man is perfect in all wisdom. To the fool, however, the good and bad are the same—for 'the wise man

will be nourished by the truth' and 'will be like a tree growing by the meandering stream'—seeing that there are some who, although having wings, rush upon the visible things, things that are far from the truth. For that which guides them, the fire, will give them an illusion of truth, and will shine on them with a perishable beauty, and it will imprison them in a dark sweetness and captivate them with fragrant pleasure. And it will blind them with insatiable lust and burn their souls and become for them like a stake stuck in their heart which they can never dislodge. And like a bit in the mouth it leads them according to its own desire.

"It has fettered them with its chains and bound all their limbs with the bitter bond of lust for those visible things that will decay and change and swerve by impulse. They have always been attracted downwards: as they are killed, they are assimilated to all the beasts of the perishable realm."

Thomas answered and said, "It is obvious and has been said, 'Many are the things revealed to those who do not know that they will forfeit their soul.'"

And the Savior answered, saying, "Blessed is the wise man who sought after the truth, and when he found it, he rested upon it for ever and was unafraid of those who wanted to disturb him."

Thomas answered and said, "Is it good for us, Lord, to rest among our own?"

The Savior said, "Yes, it is useful. And it is good for you since things visible among men will dissolve—for the vessel of their flesh will dissolve, and when it is brought to naught it will come to be among visible things, among things that are seen. And then the fire which they see gives them pain on account of love for the faith they formerly possessed. They will be gathered back to that which is visible. Moreover, those who see among things that are not visible, without the first love they will perish in the concern for this life and the scorching in the fire. Only a little time until that which is visible dissolves; then shapeless shades will emerge and in the midst of tombs they will forever dwell upon the corpses in pain and corruption of soul."

Thomas answered and said, "What have we to say in the face of these things? What shall we say to blind men? What doctrine should we express to these miserable mortals who say, 'We came to do good and not to curse,' and yet claim, 'Had we not been begotten in the flesh, we would not have known iniquity'?"

The Savior said, "Truly, as for those, do not esteem them as men, but regard them as beasts, for just as beasts devour one another, so also men of this sort devour one another. On the contrary, they are deprived of the kingdom since they love the sweetness of the fire and are servants of death and rush to the works of corruption. They fulfill the lust of their fathers. They will be thrown down to the abyss and be afflicted by the torment of the bitterness of their evil nature. For they will be scourged so as to make them rush headlong to the place that they do not know, and they will not recede from their limbs patiently, but with despair. And they rejoice over the concern for this life with madness and derangement! Some pursue this derangement without realizing their madness, thinking that they are wise. They are beguiled by the beauty of their body as if it would not perish. And they are frenetic; their thought is occupied with their deeds. But it is the fire that will burn them!"

And Thomas answered and said, "Lord, what will the one thrown down to them do? For I am most anxious about them; many are those who fight them."

The Savior answered and said, "Do you possess that which is visible?"

Judas—the one called Thomas—said, "It is you, Lord, whom it befits to speak, and me to listen."

The Savior replied, "Listen to what I am going to tell you and believe in the truth. That which sows and that which is sown will dissolve in their fire—within

the fire and the water—and they will hide in tombs of darkness. And after a long time they shall appear as the fruit of the evil trees, being punished, being slain in the mouth of beasts and men at the instigation of the rains and winds and air and the light that shines above."

Thomas replied, "You have certainly persuaded us, Lord. We realize in our heart and it is obvious that this is so, and that your word is sufficient. But these words that you speak to us are ridiculous and contemptible to the world since they are misunderstood. So how can we go preach them, since we are not esteemed in the world?"

The Savior answered and said, "Truly I tell you that he who will listen to your word and turn away his face or sneer at it or smirk at these things, truly I tell you that he will be handed over to the Ruler above who rules over all the powers as their king, and he will turn that one around and cast him from heaven down to the abyss, and he will be imprisoned in a narrow dark place. Moreover, he can neither turn nor move on account of the great depth of Tartaros and the heavy bitterness of Hades that besets him. They are imprisoned in it in order that they might not escape—their madness will not be forgiven. And the Rulers who will pursue you will deliver them over to the angel Tartarouchos and he will take whips of fire, pursuing them with fiery scourges that cast a shower of sparks into the face of the one who is pursued. If he flees westward, he finds the fire. If he turns southward, he finds it there as well. If he turns northward, the threat of seething fire meets him again. Nor does he find the way to the east so as to flee there and be saved, for he did not find it in the day he was in the body, so that he will find it in the day of Judgment."

Then the Savior continued, saying, "Woe to you, godless ones, who have no hope, who rely on things that will not happen!

"Woe to you who hope in the flesh and in the prison that will perish! How long will you be oblivious? And the imperishables, do you think that they will perish too? Your hope is set upon the world and your god is this life! You are corrupting your souls!

"Woe to you for the fire that burns in you, for it is insatiable!

"Woe to you because of the wheel that turns in your minds!

"Woe to you because of the burning that is in you, for it will devour your flesh openly and rend your souls secretly, and prepare you for your companions!

"Woe to you, captives, for you are bound in caverns! You laugh! In mad laughter you rejoice! You neither realize your perdition, nor do you reflect on your circumstances, nor have you understood that you dwell in darkness and death! On the contrary, you are drunk with the fire and full of bitterness. Your mind is deranged on account of the burning that is in you, and sweet to you is the crown of your enemies' blows! And the darkness rose for you like the light, for you surrendered your freedom for servitude! You darkened your hearts and surrendered your thoughts to folly, and you filled your thoughts with the smoke of the fire that is in you! And your light has hidden in the cloud of darkness and the garment that is put upon you, you pursued deceitfully and you were seized by the hope that does not exist. And whom is it you have believed? Do you not know that you all dwell among those who want you to curse yourselves as if your hope were nonexistent? You baptized your souls in the water of darkness! You walked by your own whims!

"Woe to you who dwell in error, heedless that the sun which judges and looks down upon the All will circle around all things so as to enslave the enemies. You do not even notice the moon, how by night and day it looks down, looking at the bodies of your corpses!

"Woe to you who love intimacy with womankind and polluted intercourse with it!

"And woe to you because of the powers of your body, for those will afflict you!

"Woe to you because of the forces of the evil demons!

"Woe to you who beguile your limbs with the fire! Who is it that will rain a refreshing dew on you to extinguish the mass of fire from you along with your burning? Who is it that will cause the sun to shine upon you to disperse the darkness in you and hide the darkness and polluted water?

"The sun and the moon will give a fragrance to you, together with the air and the spirit and the earth and the water. For if the sun does not shine upon these bodies, they will wither and perish just like weeds or grass. If the sun shines on the weeds, it prevails and chokes the grapevine; but if the grapevine prevails and shades those weeds and all that other brush growing alongside and spreads and flourishes, it alone inherits the land in which it grows and dominates every place it shaded. And then when it grows up, it dominates all the land and is bountiful for its master, and it pleases him even more, for he would have suffered great pains on account of these plants until he uprooted them. But the grapevine alone removed them and choked them, and they died and became like the soil."

Then Jesus continued and said, "Woe to you, for you did not receive the doctrine, and those who are ignorant will labor at preaching instead of you, and you are rushing into profligacy. Yet there are some who have been sent down to rescue all those whom you killed daily in order that they might rise from death.

"Blessed are you who have prior knowledge of the stumbling blocks and who flee alien things.

"Blessed are you who are reviled and not esteemed on account of the love their Lord has for them.

"Blessed are you who weep and are oppressed by those without hope, for you will be released from every bondage.

"Watch and pray that you not come to be in the flesh, but rather that you come forth from the bondage of the bitterness of this life. And as you pray, you will find rest, for you have left behind the suffering and the disgrace. For when you come forth from the sufferings and passion of the body, you will receive rest from the Good One, and you will reign with the King, you joined with him and he with you, from now on, forever and ever. Amen."

The Book of Thomas
the Contender writing
to the Perfect.

Remember me also, my brethren,
in your prayers:
Peace to the Saints
and the Spiritual.

Trimorphic Protennoia

(Gnostic)*

The tractate *Trimorphic Protennoia* appears to be, in its final form, a Barbeloite treatise with Sethian influences. Presumably having a rather complex compositional history, the tractate may have attained to this final form around or shortly after A.D. 200 Thus it may be considered as roughly contemporaneous with the *Apocryphon of John,* which it resembles in certain interesting ways. The *Trimorphic Protennoia* probably survived for some time in Greek, but it was eventually translated into Coptic, and found its way into Codex XIII of the Nag Hammadi library.

The *Trimorphic Protennoia* offers philosophical and apocalyptic speculation on the nature of history and the universe. The tractate proclaims three descents of the Gnostic heavenly redeemer Protennoia, who is actually Barbelo, the First Thought of the Father. The *Trimorphic Protennoia* itself is divided into three sections, each with individual subtitles and each describing one of the descents of the heavenly redeemer. First she appears as Father, or Voice; second, as Mother, or Sound; and third, as Son, or Word (logos). Each of these three sections, in turn, is capable of being subdivided into three parts: first, an aretalogy ("I am . . . "); second, a doctrinal presentation (on cosmogony, eschatology, and soteriology, respectively); and third, a concluding revelation. As the tractate proclaims, Protennoia is the Thought of the Father, the one born first of all beings, the one who has three names and yet exists alone, as one. She dwells at all levels of the universe; she is the revealer who awakens those that sleep, who utters a call to remember, who saves. In three descents from the realm of Life and Light, the divine Protennoia brings to the fallen world of mortality a salvation through knowledge and the "Five Seals."

The question of the Christian or non-Christian character of *Trimorphic Protennoia* deserves special mention. The name "Christ" appears a

---

*Introduction by John D. Turner.

588

few times; and the similarities between the second subtractate (on eschatology) and the synoptic apocalypse (Mark 13 and parallels) and 1 Corinthians 15, and especially between the third subtractate (on the Son or logos) and the Gospel of John, are extremely interesting. *Trimorphic Protennoia* may in part reflect these New Testament sources. Yet it is quite probable that the tractate has been secondarily Christianized.

TRIMORPHIC PROTENNOIA*

"I am Protennoia, the Thought that dwells in the Light. I am the movement that dwells in the All, she in whom the All takes the Son of God! It is he who is! The Aeon of Aeons! He beholds the Aeons which he begot. For it is you who has begotten by your own desire! Therefore we glorify you: ma mo o o o eia ei on ei! The Aeon of Aeons! The Aeon which he gave!"

Then, moreover, the God who was begotten gave the Aeons a power of life for them to rely on and he established them. The first Aeon he established over the first: Armedon, Nousanios, Armoze; the second he established over the second Aeon. Phaionios, Ainios, Oroiael; the third over the third Aeon: Mellephaneus, Loios, Daveithai; the fourth over the fourth: Mousanios, Amethes, Eleleth. Now those Aeons are the ones begotten by the God who was begotten—the Christ—and these Aeons received as well as gave glory. They were the first to appear, exalted in their thought, and each of the Aeons gave ten thousand glories within great unsearchable lights and they all together blessed the perfect Son, the God who was begotten.

Then there came forth a word from the great Light, Eleleth, and said, "I am King! Who belongs to chaos and who belongs to the underworld?" And at that instant his Light appeared, shining forth, endowed with the Epinoia. The Powers of the Powers did not entreat him and immediately there appeared the great Demon who rules over the lowest part of the underworld and chaos. He has neither form nor perfection, but, on the contrary, possesses the form of the glory of those begotten in the darkness. Now he is called "Saclas," that is, "Samael," "Ialdabaoth," he who had taken power; who had snatched it away from the guileless one, Sophia; who had at first overpowered her who is the Light's Epinoia who had descended, her from whom the great Demon had come forth from the first.

Now the Epinoia of the Light knew that she had begged him, Eleleth, for another order different from hers, and she said, "Give me another order so that you may become for me a dwelling place lest I become disorderly forever." And the order of the entire house of glory was agreed upon her word. A blessing was conveyed to her and the higher order yielded to her.

And the great Demon began to produce aeons in the likeness of the real Aeons, except that he produced them out of his own power.

Then I too revealed my Voice secretly, saying, "Cease! Desist, you who tread on matter, for behold! I am coming down to the world of mortals for the sake of my portion that was in that place from the time when the guileless Sophia was conquered, she who descended, so that I might thwart their aim which the one who reveals himself through her appoints." And everyone who dwelt in the

*Translated by John D. Turner. From James M. Robinson, ed., *The Nag Hammadi Library* (San Francisco: Harper & Row, 1977), pp. 461–470.

house of the unknowable Light was disturbed, and the abyss trembled. And the Archigenetor of ignorance reigned over Chaos and the underworld and produced a man in my likeness. But he neither knew that that one would become for him a decree of annulment nor does he recognize the power in him.

But now I have come down and reached down to chaos. And I was with my own who were in that place. I am hidden within them, empowering them, giving them shape. And from this day until the day when I will grant mighty glory to those who are mine, I will reveal myself to those who have heard my mysteries, that is, the sons of the Light.

I am their Father and I shall tell you an ineffable and indivulgeable mystery from my Forethought: Every bond I loosed from you, and the chains of the demons of the underworld I broke, these things which are bound on my members as restraints. And the high walls of darkness I overthrew, and the secure gates of those pitiless ones I broke, and I smashed their bars. And as for the evil force and the one who beats you, and the one who hinders you, and the tyrant, and the adversary, and the one who is King, and the real enemy, indeed all these I explained to those who are mine, who are the sons of the Light, in order that they might nullify them all and be saved from all those bonds and enter into the place where they were at first.

I am the first one who descended on account of my portion which is left behind, that is, the spirit that now dwells in the soul, but which originated from the water of life. And out of the immersion of the mysteries I spoke, I, together with the archons and Authorities. For I went down below their language and I spoke my mysteries to my own—a hidden mystery—and the bounds and eternal oblivion were nullified. And I bore fruit in them, that is, the Thought of the unchanging Aeon, and my house, and their Father. And I went down to those who were mine from the first and I reached them and broke the first strand that enslaved them. Then everyone within me shone, and I constructed a pattern for those Lights that are ineffably within me. Amen.

The Discourse of Protennoia

I am the Voice that appeared through my Thought, for I am "He who is syzygetic," since I am called "the Thought of the Invisible One." Since I am called the "the Unchanging Sound," I am called "She who is syzygetic."

I am a single one since I am undefiled. I am the Mother of the Voice, speaking in many ways, completing the All. It is in me that knowledge dwells, the knowledge of things everlasting. It is I who speak within every creature and I was known by the All. It is I who lift up the Sound of the Voice to the ears of those who have known me, that is, the Sons of the Light.

Now I have come the second time in the likeness of a female and have spoken with them. And I shall tell them of the coming end of this Aeon and teach them of the beginning of the Aeon to come, the one without change, the one in which our appearance will be changed. We shall be purified within those Aeons from which I revealed myself in the Thought of the likeness of my masculinity. I settled among those who are worthy in the Thought of my changeless Aeon.

For I shall tell you a mystery of this Aeon that is, and tell you about the forces that are in it. The birth cries out; hour begets hour, and day begets day. The months made known the month. Time has gone round succeeding time. This Aeon that is was completed in this fashion, and it was estimated, and it was short, for it was a finger that released a finger and a joint that was separated from a joint. Then when the great Authorities knew that the time of fulfillment had appeared—just as in the pangs of the parturient it the time has drawn nigh, so also had the destruction approached—all together the elements trembled, and the foundations of the underworld and the ceilings of Chaos shook and a great fire shone within their midst, and the rocks and the earth were shaken like a reed shaken by the wind. And the lots of Fate and those who apportion the domiciles were greatly disturbed over a great thunder. And the thrones of the Powers were disturbed since they were overturned, and their King as afraid. And those who pursue Fate paid their allotment of visits to the path, and they said to the Powers, "What is this disturbance and this shaking that has come upon us through a Voice belonging to the exalted Sound? And our entire habitation has been shaken, and the entire circuit of our path of ascent has met with destruction, and the path upon which we go, which takes us up to the Archigenetor of our birth, has ceased to be established for us." Then the Powers answered, saying, "We too are at a loss about it since we did not know what was responsible for it. But arise, let us go up to the Archigenetor and ask him." And the Powers all gathered and went up to the Archigenetor. They said to him, "Where is your boasting in which you boast? Did we not hear you say, 'I am God and I am your Father and it is I who begot you and there is no other beside me'? Now behold, there has appeared a Voice belonging to that invisible Sound of the Aeon that we know not. And we ourselves did not recognize to whom we belong, for that Voice which we heard is foreign to us, and we do not recognize it; we did not know whence it was. It came and put fear in our midst and weakening in the members of our arms. So now let us weep and mourn most bitterly! As for the future, let us make our entire flight before we are imprisoned perforce and taken down to the bosom of the underworld. For already the slackening of our bondage has approached, and the times are cut short and the days have shortened and our time has been fulfilled, and the weeping of our destruction has ap-

proached us so that we may be taken to the place we recognize. For as for our tree from which we grew, a fruit of ignorance is what it has, and also its leaves, it is death that dwells in them, and darkness dwells under the shadow of its boughs. And it was in deceit and lust that we harvested it, this tree through which ignorant Chaos became for us a dwelling place. For behold, even he, the Archigenetor of our birth, about whom we boast, even he did not know this Sound."

So now, O Sons of the Thought, listen to me, to the Sound of the Mother of your mercy, for you have become worthy of the mystery hidden from the Aeons, so that you might be perfect. And the consummation of this Aeon that is and of the life of injustice has approached, and there dawns the beginning of the Aeon to come which has no change forever.

I am androgynous. I am both Mother and Father since I copulate with myself. I copulate with myself and with those who love me, and it is through me alone that the All stands firm. I am the Womb that gives shape to the All by giving birth to the Light that shines in splendor. I am the Aeon to come. I am the fulfillment of the All, that is, Meirothea, the glory of the Mother. I cast a Sound of the Voice into the ears of those who know me.

And I am inviting you into the exalted, perfect Light. Moreover as for this Light, when you enter it you will be glorified by those who give glory, and those who enthrone will enthrone you. You will receive robes from those who give robes and the baptizers will baptize you and you will become gloriously glorious, the way you first were when you were Light.

And I hid myself in everyone and revealed myself within them, and every mind seeking me longed for me, for it is I who gave shape to the All when it had no form. And I transformed their forms into other forms until the time when a form will be given to the All. It is through me that the Voice originated and it is I who put the breath within my own.

And I cast into them the eternally Holy Spirit and I ascended and entered my Light. I went up upon my branch and sat there among the sons of the holy Light. And I withdrew to their dwelling place which become glorious. Amen.

On the Heimarmene

I am the Word who dwells in ineffable Silence. I dwell in undefiled Light and a Thought revealed itself perceptibly through the great Sound of the Mother, although it is a male offspring that supports me as my foundation. And the Sound exists from the beginning in the foundations of the All.

But there is a Light that dwells hidden in Silence and it was first to come forth. Whereas the Mother alone exists as Silence, I alone am the Word, ineffable, incorruptible, immeasurable, inconceivable. The Word is a hidden Light, bearing a fruit of life, pouring forth living water from the invisible, unpolluted, immeasurable spring, that is, the unreproducible Voice of the glory of the Mother, the glory of the offspring of God; a male virgin by virtue of a hidden Intellect, that is, the Silence hidden from the All, being unreproducible, an immeasurable Light, the source of the All, the root of the entire Aeon. It is the foundation that supports every movement of the Aeons that belong to the mighty glory. It is the founding of every foundation. It is the breath of the powers. It is the eye of the three permanences, which exist as a Voice by virtue of Thought. And it is a Word by virtue of the Sound: it was sent to illumine those who dwell in the darkness.

Now behold! I will reveal to you my mysteries since you are my fellow brethren, and you shall know them all. I told them all about my mysteries that exist in the ineffable, inexpressible Aeons. I taught them the mysteries through the Voice that exists within a perfect Intellect and I became a foundation for the All, and I empowered them.

The second time I came in the Sound of my Voice. I gave shape to those who took shape until their consummation.

The third time I revealed myself to them in their tents as the Word and I revealed myself in the likeness of their shape. And I wore everyone's garment and I hid myself within them, and they did not know the one who empowers me. For I dwell within all the sovereignties and Powers and within the angels and in every movement that exists in all matter. And I hid myself within them until I revealed myself to my brethren. And none of them the Powers knew me, although it is I who work in them. Rather, they thought that the All was created by them since they are ignorant, not knowing their root, the place in which they grew.

I am the Light that illumines the All. I am the Light that rejoices in my brethren, for I came down to the world of mortals on account of the Spirit that remains in that which descended and came forth from the guileless Sophia. I came and I went to [. . .] which he had formerly and I gave to him from the living water, which strips him of the chaos that dwells in the uttermost darkness existing inside the entire abyss, that is, the corporeal and the psychic thought. All these I put on. And I stripped him of the inferior thought and I put upon him a shining light, that is, the knowledge of the Thought of the Fatherhood.

And I delivered him to those who give robes—Yammon, Elasso, Amenai—and they covered him with a robe from the robes of the light; and I delivered him to the baptizers and they baptized him—Micheus, Michar, Mnesinous—and they immersed him in the spring of the water of life. And I delivered him to those who enthrone—Bariel, Nouthan, Sabenai—and they enthroned him from the throne of glory. And I delivered him to those who glorify—Ariom, Elien, Phariel—and they glorified him with the glory of the Fatherhood. And those who snatch away snatched away—Kamaliel, Sambio, the servants of the great holy luminaries—and they took him into the light-place of his Fatherhood. And he received the five seals from the Light of the Mother, Protennoia, and it was granted him to partake of the mystery of knowledge, and he became a Light in Light.

So, now, I was dwelling in them in the form of each one. The Archons thought that I was their Christ. Actually, I am the Father of everyone. Indeed, within those in whom I revealed myself as Light, I eluded the Archons. I am their beloved, for in that place I clothed myself as the son of the Archigenetor, and I was like him until the end of his regime, which is the ignorance of Chaos. And among the angels I revealed myself in their likeness, and among the Powers as if I were one of them, but among the sons of Man as if I were a son of Man, even though I am Father of everyone.

I hid myself within them all until I revealed myself among my members, which are mine, and I taught them about the ineffable ordinances, and about the brethren. But they are inexpressible to every sovereignty and every ruling Power except to the sons of the Light alone, that is, the ordinances of the Father. These are the glories that are higher than every glory, that is, the five seals,

complete by virtue of Intellect. He who possesses the five seals of these particular names has stripped off the garments of ignorance and put on a shining Light. And nothing will appear to him that belongs to the Powers of the Archons. Within those of this sort, darkness will dissolve and ignorance will die. And the thought of the creature which is scattered will present a single appearance and dark chaos will dissolve . . . until I reveal myself to my fellow brethren and until I gather together all my fellow brethren within my eternal kingdom. And I proclaimed to them the ineffable five seals in order that I might abide in them and they also might abide in me.

As for me, I put on Jesus. I bore him from the cursed wood, and established him in the dwelling places of his Father. And those who watch over their dwelling places did not recognize me. For I, I am unrestrained together with my seed, and my seed, which is mine, I shall place into the holy Light within an intangible Silence. Amen.

The Discourse of the Appearance

Trimorphic Protennoia, in 3 parts

A Sacred Scripture written by the Father with perfect Knowledge

The Thunder, Perfect Mind

*(Gnostic)**

The short tractate entitled *The Thunder, Perfect Mind* is a revelation discourse delivered by a female revealer in the first person. It is characteristic of the revelation imparted that the self-proclamation ("I am . . . ") is of an antithetical or paradoxical sort: "I am the whore and the holy one. I am the wife and the virgin." In addition there are added various exhortations to hear and reflect, and reproaches for failing to do so.

In terms of religious tradition *Thunder, Perfect Mind* is difficult to classify. It presents no distinctively Jewish, Christian, or Gnostic themes, nor does it seem to presuppose a particular Gnostic myth. While the Jewish wisdom literature and the Isis aretalogies provide texts which are parallel in tone and style, the particular significance of the self-proclamations of *Thunder, Perfect Mind* may be found in their antithetical character. Antithesis and paradox may be used to proclaim the absolute transcendence of the revealer, whose greatness is incomprehensible and whose being is unfathomable.

---

*Introduction by George W. MacRae.

THE THUNDER, PERFECT MIND*

I was sent forth from the power,
  and I have come to those who reflect upon me,
  and I have been found among those who seek after me.
Look upon me, you who reflect upon me,
  and you hearers, hear me.
  You who are waiting for me, take me to yourselves.
And do not banish me from your sight.
  And do not make your voice hate me, nor your hearing.
  Do not be ignorant of me anywhere or any time. Be on your guard!
  Do not be ignorant of me.

For I am the first and the last.
I am the honored one and the scorned one.
I am the whore and the holy one.
I am the wife and the virgin.
I am the mother and the daughter.
I am the members of my mother.
I am the barren one
  and many are her sons.
I am she whose wedding is great,
  and I have not taken a husband.
I am the midwife and she who does not bear.
I am the solace of my labor pains.
I am the bride and the bridegroom,
  and it is my husband who begot me.
I am the mother of my father
  and the sister of my husband,
  and he is my offspring.
I am the slave of him who prepared me.
I am the ruler of my offspring.
  But he is the one who begot me before the time on a birthday.
  And he is my offspring in due time, and my power is from him.
I am the staff of his power in his youth,
  and he is the rod of my old age.
  And whatever he wills happens to me.
I am the silence that is incomprehensible
  and the idea whose remembrance is frequent.
I am the voice whose sound is manifold
  and the word whose appearance is multiple.
I am the utterance of my name.

Why, you who hate me, do you love me,
  and you hate those who love me?
You who deny me, confess me,
  and you who confess me, deny me.

---

*Translated by George W. MacRae; edited by Douglas M. Parrott. From
James M. Robinson, ed., *The Nag Hammadi Library* (San Francisco: Harper &
Row, 1977), pp. 271–277.

You who tell the truth about me, lie about me,
　and you who have lied about me, tell the truth about me.
You who know me, be ignorant of me,
　and those who have not known me, let them know me.

For I am knowledge and ignorance.
I am shame and boldness.
I am shameless; I am ashamed.
I am strength and I am fear.
I am war and peace.
Give heed to me.
I am the one who is disgraced and the great one.

Give heed to my poverty and my wealth.
Do not be arrogant to me when I am cast out upon the earth,
　and you will find me in those that are to come.
And do not look upon me on the dung-heap
　nor go and leave me cast out,
　and you will find me in the kingdoms.
And do not look upon me when I am cast out among those who
　are disgraced and in the least places,
　nor laugh at me.
And do not cast me out among those who are slain in violence.
But I, I am compassionate and I am cruel.

Be on your guard!
Do not hate my obedience
　and do not love my self-control.
In my weakness, do not forsake me,
　and do not be afraid of my power.
For why do you despise my fear
　and curse my pride?
But I am she who exists in all fears
　and strength in trembling.
I am she who is weak,
　and I am well in a pleasant place.
I am senseless and I am wise.

Why have you hated me in your counsels?
For I shall be silent among those who are silent,
　and I shall appear and speak,
Why then have you hated me, you Greeks?
　Because I am a barbarian among the barbarians?
For I am the wisdom of the Greeks
　and the knowledge of the barbarians.
I am the judgment of the Greeks and of the barbarians.
I am the one whose image is great in Egypt
　and the one who has no image among the barbarians.
I am the one who has been hated everywhere
　and who has been loved everywhere.
I am the one whom they call life,
　and you have called death.

I am the one whom they call law,
   and you have called lawlessness.
I am the one whom you have pursued,
   and I am the one whom you have seized.
I am the one whom you have scattered,
   and you have gathered me together.
I am the one before whom you have been ashamed,
   and you have been shameless to me.
I am she who does not keep festival,
   and I am she whose festivals are many.
I, I am godless,
   and I am the one whose God is great.
I am the one whom you have reflected upon,
   and you have scorned me.
I am unlearned,
   and they learn from me.
I am the one whom you have despised,
   and you reflect upon me.
I am the one whom you have hidden from,
   and you appear to me.
But whenever you hide yourselves,
   I myself will appear.
For whenever you appear,
   I myself will hide from you.

Take me to yourselves from understanding and grief.
And take me to yourselves from places that are ugly and in ruin,
   and rob from those which are good even though in ugliness.
Out of shame, take me to yourselves shamelessly;
   and out of shamelessness and shame, upbraid my members in yourselves.
And come forward to me, you who know me and you who know my members,
   and establish the great ones among the small first creatures.
Come forward to childhood,
   and do not despise it because it is small and it is little.
And do not turn away greatnesses in some part from the smallnesses,
   for the smallnesses are known from the greatnesses.

Why do you curse me and honor me?
You have wounded and you have had mercy.
Do not separate me from the first ones whom you have known.
And do not cast anyone out nor turn anyone away
I know the first ones and those after them know me.

I am the knowledge of my inquiry,
   and the finding of those who seek after me,
   and the command of those who ask of me,
   and the power of the powers in my knowledge
     of the angels, who have been sent at my word,
     and of gods in their seasons by my counsel,
    and of spirits of every man who exists with me, and of women who dwell
within me.

I am the one who is honored, and who is praised,
  and who is despised scornfully.
I am peace,
  and war has come because of me.
And I am an alien and a citizen.
I am the substance and the one who has no substance.

Those who are without association with me are ignorant of me,
  and those who are in my substance are the ones who know me.
Those who are close to me have been ignorant of me,
  and those who are far away from me are the ones who have known me.
On the day when I am close to you,
    you are far away from me,
  and on the day when I am far away from you,
    I am close to you.

I am . . . within.
I am . . . of the natures.
I am of the creation of the spirits.
I am control and the uncontrollable.
I am the union and the dissolution.
I am the abiding and I am the dissolving.
I am the one below,
  and they come up to me.
I am the judgment and the acquittal.
I, I am sinless,
  and the root of sin derives from me.
I am lust in outward appearance,
  and interior self-control exists within me.
I am the hearing which is attainable to everyone
  and the speech which cannot be grasped.
I am a mute who does not speak,
  and great is my multitude of words.

Hear me in gentleness, and learn of me in roughness.
I am she who cries out,
  and I am cast forth upon the face of the earth.
I prepare the bread and my mind within.
I am the knowledge of my name.
I am the one who cries out,
  and I listen.
I am the one who is called Truth
  and iniquity.

You honor me and you whisper against me.
Judge them before they give judgment against you,
  because the judge and partiality exist in you.
If you are condemned by this one, who will acquit you?
  Or, if you are acquitted by him, who will be able to detain you?
For what is inside of you is what is outside of you,
  and the one who fashions you on the outside
    is the one who shaped the inside of you.

And what you see outside of you,
  you see inside of you;
  it is visible and it is your garment.
Hear me, you hearers,
  and learn of my words, you who know me.
I am the hearing that is attainable to everything;
  I am the speech that cannot be grasped.
I am the name of the sound
  and the sound of the name.
I am the sign of the letter
  and the designation of the division.
  And I will speak his name.

Look then at his words
  and all the writings which have been completed.
Give heed then, you hearers
  and you also, the angels and those who have been sent,
  and you spirits who have arisen from the dead.
For I am the one who alone exists,
  and I have no one who will judge me.

For many are the pleasant forms which exist in
  numerous sins,
  and incontinencies,
  and disgraceful passions,
  and fleeting pleasures,
    which men embrace until they become sober
    and go up to their resting place.
And they will find me there,
  and they will live,
  and they will not die again.

8
DIVERSE GNOSTIC TEXTS

Simon Magus

We have no writings by Simon Magus, whom the Fathers of the Church credited with being the father of heresy. Simon was also accursed of being the founder of Gnosticism, and the source of all Gnostic doctrines. But while the Simonian texts have disappeared, the theology of this early heresiarch has been preserved in other writers—by Irenaeus, Hippolytus, Tertullian, Epiphanius, Justin Martyr, and in the pseudo-Clementines. These were Simon's enemies, but they have provided us with an outline of the main tenets of the Simonian speculation. A principal source is Irenaeus, the Christian bishop of Lyons, who around A.D. 180 wrote *Adversus haereses* (Against Heresies). Simon was accused by Irenaeus of being the bridge between Christian heresy (though Werner Foerster argues that "Simon shows no relationship with Christianity"[1]) and libertarian practices. Irenaeus also accused him of defaming the Old Testament with the notion that its laws were ordained by wicked angels.

The first mention of Simon Magus is in the Acts of the New Testament. Yet it is not at all certain that Simon of the Acts is the same as the Simon we find described in Irenaeus and Justin or in the *pseudo-Clementine Homilies*. In fact, Robert M. Grant considers that there were three Simons. In any case the Simon Magus of the Acts is scarcely more than a symbol of heresy and the initiator of "simony," the act of buying spiritual favor with money. What is certain is that Simon Magus was an originator of the Syrian school of Gnosticism and that his thought was immediately carried on by his successors, Menander and Saturninus. The very fury against Simon and his followers by orthodox Christians proves the importance of this supposed contemporary of the apostles. In addition to the "historical" descriptions of Simon and his thought, we have the more colorful myths in several apocryphal accounts, such as the wondrous and tragicomic tale of Simon flying over Rome to prove his divinity, only to be prayed into crashing by the apostle Peter. In the account in the apocryphal Acts of

Peter, there is no question that Simon had the magical powers to fly into the sky. The orthodox presentation made clear, rather, that Peter's powers, derived from God, were even greater.

As an early Gnostic, Simon differed from most of the later leaders in that he was not a dissident Christian or, as Gershom Scholem might say, a radical Jew reacting against orthodoxy. His message was a "rival message of obviously independent origin,"[2] Jonas states. Simonism did not accept Jesus except as a precursor of Simon himself, who was the messiah, who was indeed God descended to redeem the world. Celsus quotes a sermon by Simon:

> I am God (or a son of God, or a divine Spirit). And I have come. Already the world is being destroyed. And you, O men, are to perish because of your iniquities. But I wish to save you. And you see me returning again with heavenly power. Blessed is he who has worshipped me now! But I will cast everlasting fire upon all the rest, both on cities and on country places. And men who fail to realize the penalties in store for them will in vain repent and groan. But I will preserve for ever those who have been convinced by me.[3]

As for messiahs, Celsus observes that pseudo-messiahs were swarming in Phoenicia and Palestine in the middle of the second century. If we assume, as most scholars do, that the Gnostic Simon lived a generation or two after the Simon Magus of the Acts, Celsus's observation would pertain to the Simon who declared himself God.

What is the nature of the Simonian God? In Hippolytus we read that God is one Power, divided into upper and lower divisions, begetting itself, being its own mother, its own father . . . its own daughter, its own son. God contains all sexes, is unbegotten. The lower division is the world of matter, the upper of spirit. Thus the dualism of spirit and matter is contained in himself, which is characteristic of Syrian and Alexandrian *gnosis* as opposed to Iranian Gnosticism (Manichaeism), in which the powers of darkness, ignorance, matter represent another principle, external and opposed to the primal being.

The infinite, undifferentiated Power, the "one root," lies in "unfathomable Silence." It takes on form when it becomes Mind (*nous*) and Thought (*Epinoia* or *Ennoia*). The former is male (following the Greek gender) while the latter is female. While the male Mind, the higher element of creation, remains in the female Thought, the lower element, the female principle, brings forth everything. She is the Mother of All. Thus Thought has absorbed into herself the generative power of the Father and so, working as an androgynous unit of Mind and Thought, she creates the world. In Irenaeus we read, "For this Ennoia had come out of him, and knowing what her Father willed, descended into the lower regions and generated angels and powers by whom, according to his doctrine, this world too was made." But as frequently happens when new entities are created, the original power soon loses control of the offspring. In the case of Ennoia, she "was held in bondage by the powers and angels emitted by her; and they subjected her to every form of humiliation to prevent her from hastening back to her Father. In other Gnostic speculations the creations are ultimately alienated from their source, and as the process of degradation goes on, the forces of darkness, ignorance, and suffering take over. Redemption lies in the return of the creations to the original source of light.

To continue with the adventures of Ennoia, the Mother of All fell from Heaven into the cosmos, down to earth, and was enclosed in human female flesh, where she was abused as Helena (Helen), the whore of Tyre. The Trojan War was fought over her, although she was only a phantasm of the suffering Helen. Now Simon appears. Because of these sorry matters, of the badly governing angels and the humiliation of Ennoia imprisoned in female flesh, Simon descended from Heaven "to raise her up and free her from her bonds, but also to bring men salvation from the fact of recognizing him." Simon must rescue Thought from those evil angels who created the world, and so he appears in various forms. Epiphanius informs us:

> In every heaven I took on a different form, according to the form of the beings in each heaven, that I might remain concealed from the ruling angels and descend to the Ennoia, who is called also Prunikos and Holy Spirit, through whom I created the angels, who then created the world and man. (*Haer*. 212.4)

Simon tells us further, according to Irenaeus, that he, Simon, appears in Judaea as Son, in Samaria as Father, and in other nations as the Holy Spirit. Jesus is notably missing from this catalogue, for Simon takes on his messianic role. But as for the messiah's suffering, here Simon conforms to the common Gnostic notion that the messiah's suffering was not real, for on the cross a simulacrum appeared, a ghost rather than a suffering human being. Irenaeus writes of Simon, "And he was thought to have suffered in Judaea, whereas he did not suffer."

Simon's consort Helen, whom he has come to save, has multiple associations. Apart from being identified with the whore of Tyre (which Gilles Quispal speaks of as slander, thus robbing the Mother of All of her human humiliation), she is also Selene, the Moon, and Sophia, the last Aeon of the Gnostic Pleroma. While the "Magician Simon" outraged orthodox Christians for innumerable heresies, the foremost of which was his claim to be the descended godhead, not low among his trespasses was taking as his consort a whore of Tyre whom he claimed was the Mother of All. While he himself as the Son in Judaea does not suffer, his consort does, and he emphasizes her humiliation and imprisonment in human flesh and her many transformations. So our compassion is directed to her, for her situation, for her suffering, for her goodness. She made the world and now must be saved.

Unlike other Gnostics (even Mani, who, like Simon, declared himself the messiah), Simon Magus has come down to us as the most villainous heretic, the archheretic. He was surely what other prophets of his time were—an itinerant magician (or miracle-worker, for the faithful), and if the flamboyant story from the Apocrypha of his contest with Peter at Rome reflects any truth, then he was a most extravagant showman. Of more importance than the legends and fame is the Gnostic theology which, because of its probable early origin, makes it of supreme value in the history of religious thought. As for his latter legendary reputation, we have inherited from him a most important figure of medieval and renaissance stories: Faust. In Latin Simon was referred to as *Faustus* (the favored one). So Marlowe and Goethe, who elaborated the figure of an irreverent scholar and magician, envisioning Helen of Troy as his consort, were using as their source the very old Gnostic Samaritan, Simon Magus.

Notes

1. Werner Foerster, *Gnosis: A Selection of Gnostic Tests*, vol. 1, trans. R. McL. Wilson (Oxford: Oxford University Press, 1972), p. 29.

2. Hans Jonas, *The Gnostic Religion*, 2d ed. rev., with preface for 3rd printing (1958; reprint, Boston: Beacon Press, 1970), p. 103.

3. Origen, *Contra Celsum*, trans. H. Chadwick (Cambridge University Press, 1953), VII, 9, pp. 402–3.

CONVERSION OF SIMON THE SORCERER*

But there was a man named Simon who had previously practiced magic in the city and amazed the nation of Samaria, saying that he himself was somebody great. They all gave heed to him, from the least to the greatest, saying, "This man is that power of God which is called Great." And they gave heed to him, because for a long time he had amazed them with his magic. But when they believed Philip as he preached good news about the kingdom of God and the name of Jesus Christ, they were baptized, both men and women. Even Simon himself believed, and after being baptized he continued with Philip. And seeing signs and great miracles performed, he was amazed.

Now when the apostles at Jerusalem heard that Samaria had received the word of God, they sent to them Peter and John, who came down and prayed for them that they might receive the Holy Spirit; for it had not yet fallen on any of them, but they had only been baptized in the name of the Lord Jesus. Then they laid their hands on them and they received the Holy Spirit. Now when Simon saw that the Spirit was given through the laying on of the apostles' hands, he offered them money, saying, "Give me also this power, that any one on whom I lay my hands may receive the Holy Spirit." But Peter said to him, "Your silver perish with you, because you thought you could obtain the gift of God with money! You have neither part nor lot in this matter, for your heart is not right before God. Repent therefore of this wickedness of yours, and pray to the Lord that, if possible, the intent of your heart may be forgiven you. For I see that you are in the gall of bitterness and in the bond of iniquity." And Simon answered, "Pray for me to the Lord, that nothing of what you have said may come upon me."

Now when they had testified and spoken the word of the Lord, they returned to Jerusalem, preaching the gospel to many villages of the Samaritans.

*From Acts 8:9–25, RSV.

COMMENTARIES*

Irenaeus (Adv. Haer. I 23, 2–4)

The Samaritan Simon, from whom all the heresies take their origin, has the basic ideas of the following heresy. He led about with him a certain Helena, whom he had redeemed as a harlot in Tyre, a city of Phoenicia, and said that she was his first "thought," the mother of all, through whom in the beginning he had conceived the idea of making angels and archangels. This Ennoia, leaping forth[1] from him and knowing what her father willed, descended to the lower regions and gave birth to angels and powers, by whom he said this world was made. But after she had given birth to them, she was detained by them out of envy, because they did not wish to be considered the progeny of any other. For he himself had remained entirely unknown to them; but his Ennoia was detained by the powers and angels which had been emitted by her, and suffered every contumely from them, that she might not return again to her father, even to the point that she was shut up in a human body and through the centuries, as from one vessel to another, migrated into ever different female bodies. She was also in that Helen for whose sake the Trojan War was joined; hence Stesichorus, who had defamed her in a poem, was deprived of his eyesight, but then afterwards he repented and wrote the so-called *Palinodes*, in which he glorified her, and saw again. In her wandering from body to body, in which she continually endured ignominy, she finally prostituted herself in a brothel—and this was the lost sheep [Matt. 18:19 par.].

Hence he himself came, that he might take her first to himself and free her from the fetters; but to men he accorded re-

demption through the recognition of him. For since the angels were governing the world badly, because each one of them desired the supremacy, he came to bring things to order. He descended in transfigured form, made like to the powers and authorities and angels, so that he might appear to men as a man, although he was not a man; he was thought to have suffered in Judaea, although he did not suffer.[2] The prophets spoke their prophecies inspired by the angels who created the world, hence those who have their hope in him and in his Helena trouble themselves no further with them, and as free men do what they wish. For through his grace are men saved, and not through righteous works. Nor are works just by nature, but by convention, as the angels who made the world ordained, in order to enslave men by such precepts. Hence he promised that the world will be dissolved, and those who are his liberated from the dominion of those who made the world.

Therefore their mystery priests live licentiously, and perform sorceries, as each one is able. They practise exorcisms and incantations, love potions and erotic magic; the so-called familiar spirits and dream-inducers, and whatever other occult things exist, are zealously cultivated among them. They have an image also of Simon, made in the form of Zeus, of Helena in the form of Athena, and these they worship. They have their name from Simon, the founder of their impious opinion being called Simonians, and from them the falsely so-called Gnosis took its beginnings, as one may learn from their own assertions.

Hippolytus (Ref. VI 19, 5)

These became imitators of error and of Simon Magus and do the same things, saying that one must engage in intercourse without consideration, affirming: "All earth is earth, and it makes no difference where a man sows, if only he sows." Indeed, they count themselves

*From Werner Foerster, *Gnosis: A Selection of Gnostic Texts*, trans. R. McL. Wilson, 2d ed., rev. (Oxford: Oxford University Press, 1972), pp. 31–33.

blessed because of this union, and say that this is perfect love and the holy of holies.

Hippolytus (Ref. VI 20, 2–3)

Peter resisted Simon at length, since he deceived many by his magic. Finally . . . he sat down under a plane tree and taught.

And when at last he was near to being refuted because of the passing of time, he said that if he were buried alive he would rise again on the third day. Commanding a grave to be dug, he ordered his disciples to heap earth upon him. They did as he commanded, but he remained in it until this day. For he was not the Christ.

Clem Alex., Strom. (II 11 = §52, 2)

The adherents of Simon want to be like in conduct to the "standing one" whom they worship.

Origen (Contra Celsum I 57)

The magician Simon also, the Samaritan, wanted to win some through magic, and he deceived them at that time. But now one cannot find thirty all told in the world, and perhaps this number is too high. Even in Palestine they are very few, and nowhere in the rest of the world is his name to be found. . . .

Dositheus

On Simon's predecessors and disciples not very many reports, and these not very accurate, have been preserved.

According to the Clementine Recognitions and Homilies both Dositheus and Simon were disciples of John the Baptist. Since on John's death Simon was in Egypt, Dositheus took over the position of leader. On his return Simon did not venture to displace him directly from his station, but through a miracle brought it about that Dositheus worshiped him, Simon, as the "standing one"; shortly afterwards Dositheus died. Among the Church Fathers only Origen has preserved a report about him, that Dositheus gave himself out to be the Messiah or Christ. It is characteristic, and gives the impression of sound information, that it is reported of his followers that they both possessed writings from him and were of the belief that he did not taste of death.

Origen (In Joh. XIII 27 [on John 4:25])

Thus a certain Dositheus of the Samaritans came forward and said that he was the prophesied Christ; from that day until now there are Dositheans, who both produce writings of Dositheus and also relate some tales about him, as that he did not taste of death, but is still alive.[3]

Menander

Menander from Kapparetaia in Samaria worked in Antioch. He affirmed that his adherents would not die, and that through the baptism which he gave them. Whether in this there is any influence of Christian or Jewish ideas at work remains uncertain.

The adherents of Simon and Menander evidently did not long continue. This is readily comprehensible, since each linked his activity with his own person and for that reason its effectiveness was subsequently bound to go into decline.

Justin (Apol. I 26, 1, 4)

Thirdly, I adduce the fact that even after the taking-up of Christ into Heaven the demons put forward some men who said that they were gods. . . .

Concerning one Menander, likewise a Samaritan from the village of Kapparetaia, a disciple of Simon, who likewise obtained power from the demons, we know that he came to Antioch and deceived many through magic arts, and that he alleged to his disciples that they would not die. And even now there are some of them who affirm this.

Irenaeus (Adv. Haer. I 23, 5)

Simon's successor was Menander, a Samaritan by race, who himself attained to the highest point of magic. He said that the first Power was unknown to all, but that he himself was the one who was sent by the invisible as a savior for the salvation of men. The world was made by angels, whom he too—like Simon— said had been brought forth by Ennoia. He added that he brought it about through the magic knowledge that was taught by him that he conquered the angels who created the world. His disciples received resurrection through baptism into him, and they can no longer die, but remain without growing old and immortal.

Notes

1. The same image of "springing forth" also in Iren. I.2.2 (Valentinism) and 29.4 (Barbelognosis).

2. This last point is certainly Christian, but probably also what Irenaeus says about his descent.

3. According to Origen (*De princ.* IV 3.2), Dositheus affirmed that one ought to remain in the garment and in the position in which he was overtaken on the Sabbath, until the Sabbath is past. Whether this refers to the Gnostic Dositheus is questionable.

Valentinus and the Valentinian System of Ptolemaeus

Valentinus was in many ways more compatible with Christian orthodoxy than any leader of a Gnostic sect. Evidence of this is suggested by the fact that in the middle of the second century this educated Egyptian was a candidate for election as the new Bishop of Rome. It is always fascinating to speculate what would have been the history of Christianity, indeed of western culture, had Valentinus won that election and become a Gnostic pope. Saint Augustine two centuries later also had a Gnostic past, having been a Manichaean for nine years, but his conversion like that of Paul was accompanied by ardent opposition to, rather than compatibility with, his past.

One document is attributed to Valentinus himself, the *Gospel of Truth*, a work in Coptic translation found among the Nag Hammadi texts. It is a Gnostic text, yet several standard Gnostic figures are missing, such as the Aeons, the two Gods (the Good Father and the Evil Creator God), and Sophia. Some scholars speculate that at the beginning of his career Valentinus saw the possibility of reconciliation between his ideas and those of the Church. He was not yet the heretic against whom so many Christian fathers were to write and provide us with so much valuable, if colored, information. This "tentative" Gnostic is also clearly seen in the *Letter to Flora* by Ptolemaeus, Valentinus' main disciple in Italy. In this subtle and intelligent letter Ptolemaeus gently attempts to instill Gnostic ideas into the mind of a good Christian woman. The same Ptolemaeus, however, is also the author of a fully elaborate Valentinian system, with its mythical creation of gods, heavens, and world. Like Basilides, he was one of the great systemizers. For further information about the system and Valentinus, see the introduction to the *Gospel of Truth*.

THE VALENTINIAN SYSTEM OF PTOLEMAEUS*

The Pleroma

There is a perfect preexistent Aeon, dwelling in the invisible and unnameable elevations; this is Pre-Beginning and Forefather and Depth. He is uncontainable and invisible, eternal and ungenerated, in quiet and in deep solitude for infinite aeons. With him is Thought, which is also called Grace and Silence. Once upon a time, Depth thought of emitting from himself a Beginning of all, like a seed, and he deposited this projected emission, as in a womb, in that Silence who is with him. Silence received this seed and became pregnant and bore Mind, which resembled and was equal to him who emitted him. Mind alone comprehends the magnitude of his Father; he is called Only-Begotten and Father and Beginning of all. Along with him, Truth was emitted; this makes the first Four, the root of all: Depth and Silence, then Mind and Truth.

When Only-Begotten perceived why he had been emitted, he too emitted Logos and Life, since he was the Father of all who were to come after him and was the beginning and form of the whole Pleroma. From the union of Logos and Life were emitted Man and Church. This is the originative Eight, the root and substance of all, called by four names: Depth and Mind and Logos and Man. Each of them is male-female, as follows: first the Forefather was united with his own Thought; then Only-Begotten Mind with Truth; then Logos with Life and Man with Church.

When these Aeons, which had been emitted to the glory of the Father, themselves desired to glorify the Father through their own products, they emitted emanations by uniting. After emit-

*From Robert M. Grant, *Gnosticism* (New York: Harper & Brothers, 1961), pp. 163–181.

ting Man and Church, Logos and Life emitted ten other Aeons, whose names are as follows: Deep and Mingling, Un-ageing and Union, Self-Produced and Pleasure, Immovable and Mixture, Only-Begotten and Blessing. Man with Church emitted twelve Aeons, whose names are as follows: Paraclete and Faith, Paternal and Hope, Maternal and Love, Everlasting and Intelligence, Ecclesiastical and Blessedness, Willed and Sophia. These are the thirty Aeons which are kept in silence and are not known. This is the invisible and spiritual Pleroma, triply divided into an Eight, a Ten, and a Twelve.

Proofs from Scripture

For this reason the Savior[1] did nothing openly for thirty years [cf. Luke 3:23], in order to set forth the mystery of these Aeons. In the parable of the laborers in the vineyard [Matt. 20:1–16] there is a very clear indication of these thirty Aeons, for laborers are sent about the first hour, others about the third, others about the sixth, others about the ninth, and others about the eleventh; and when these hours are added together they make the sum of thirty—for $1 + 3 + 6 + 9 + 11 = 30$. The hours mean Aeons. These are the great and marvelous and ineffable mysteries which we bear as fruit.

Disturbance and Restoration in the Pleroma

The Forefather was known only to Only-Begotten Mind, who came into existence from him, while to all the rest he is invisible and incomprehensible. Only Mind took pleasure in beholding the Father and rejoiced in understanding his immeasurable magnitude. Mind intended to impart to the other Aeons the magnitude of the Father, to tell them his greatness and his size and how he was without beginning and uncontainable and incapable of being seen; but Silence, by the Father's will, restrained him because she wished to lead all of them to the thought and longing of seeking for their Forefather. Likewise the other Aeons silently longed to see the one who had

611

emitted their seed and to learn of the root without beginning.

It was the very last and youngest of the twelve derived from Man and Church, the Aeon Sophia, which leaped forth [cf. Wisd. 18:15] and experienced passion apart from the embrace of her consort, Willed. That longing which started at those about Mind and Truth fell suddenly on this erring Aeon, on the pretext of love but actually because of audacity, because she did not have fellowship with the perfect Father such as Mind enjoyed. Her passion was the search for the Father; for she wished to comprehend his magnitude. When she was unable to do so, because she had undertaken an impossible task and was in great agony because of the greatness of the depth and the inscrutability of the Father [cf. Rom. 11:33] and her love for him, she was ever extended forward, so that she would finally have been swallowed up by his sweetness and dissolved into the substance of the whole Pleroma if she had not encountered the power which consolidates all the Aeons and keeps them outside the Ineffable Magnitude. This power is called Limit. By it Sophia was stopped and consolidated and—with difficulty—made to return to herself [cf. Luke 15:17]; and since she was persuaded that the Father is incomprehensible, she put off her former Desire along with the passion which had come upon her when she was struck by wonder.

Another Valentinian Version

Since Sophia had undertaken an impossible and unattainable task, she brought forth a shapeless being, a thing such as a female by herself can bear. When she looked at it, she first grieved because of the imperfection of the creature; then she was afraid that it would cease to be; then she was amazed and at a loss, as she sought for its cause and wondered how to hide what had come into existence. While she was concerned with her passions, she obtained conversion and tried to run upwards to the Father; she came

to such a point of daring that she became exhausted and became a suppliant of the Father. The other Aeons, especially Mind, also made petition with her. From this the substance of matter had its primal origin, from her ignorance and grief and fear and consternation.

In addition to the others, the Father, through Only-Begotten, emitted Limit in his own image [cf. Gen. 1:26], without companion, without female.[2]

The Work of Limit: The Restoration of Sophia

Limit is also called Cross and Redeemer and Emancipator and Definer and Guide. Through Limit Sophia was purified and consolidated and restored to union with her partner. For when Desire had been separated from her, along with the passion which had come upon her, she herself remained within the Pleroma, but her Desire, with the passion, was separated and crucified [cf. Gal. 6:14][3] by Limit. When Desire was outside Limit, it was a spiritual substance, like some natural desire of an Aeon, but it was shapeless and ugly because it comprehended nothing. Therefore it was a weak female fruit.

After Desire had been banished outside the Pleroma of the Aeons, her Mother was restored to her own partner, while Only-Begotten again emitted another pair in accordance with the Father's foreknowledge so that none of the Aeons might experience passion as Sophia did. This pair was Christ and Holy Spirit, emitted from the fixity and consolidation of the Pleroma; by these the Aeons were made perfect. For Christ taught them the nature of pairs [cf. Matt. 19:6] and that they were capable of comprehending the ungenerated one, and he proclaimed among them the knowledge of the Father—how he is uncontainable and incomprehensible and cannot be seen or heard, but is known only through Only-Begotten [John 1:18]. The cause of the eternal permanence of the other Aeons is what in the Father is incomprehensible; that of the origin and formation is what in the Father is comprehensible, his Son. The Christ, who had just been emitted, effected these things in them.

When they had all been made equal, Holy Spirit taught them to give thanks and explained what the true "rest" [cf. Gen. 2:2; Heb. 4:10] was. Thus the Aeons became equal in form and in mind, becoming all Minds, all Logoi, all Men, all Christs; similarly all the female Aeons became Truths and Lives and Spirits and Churches.[4] After this, all things were consolidated and given perfect rest; with great joy they praised the Forefather and shared in much gladness. And because of this beneficence, the whole Pleroma of the Aeons with one counsel and mind, while Christ and Spirit consented and their Father ratified the decision—each one of the Aeons gave and contributed what it had that was most beautiful and bright—wove together and united their contributions harmoniously, and emitted an emanation to the honor and glory of Depth. This was the most perfect beauty and the star of the Pleroma, its perfect fruit, Jesus, who is also called Savior and Christ and Logos, after his origin, and All, because he is from all [cf. Col 2:9]. As guards for him they emitted angels of the same kind as themselves.

Proofs from Scripture

These matters were not described openly because not all hold this knowledge [gnosis] [Matt. 19:11], but were all spoken mysteriously through parables by the Savior to those who were able to understand in this way [Matt. 13:10–11]. . . . Paul very clearly names these Aeons at many points and also preserves their order, for he says, "To all the generations of the Aeons of the Aeon" [Eph. 3:21]. When members of the psychic Church end prayers of thanksgiving with "to the Aeons of the Aeons," they are referring to those Aeons above.

The emanation of the Twelve of Aeons is signified by the Savior's discourse with the scribes at the age of twelve [Luke 2: 42] and by his choice of the apostles; for there were twelve apostles. The other eighteen Aeons are indicated in his eighteen months' stay with the disciples after the resurrection of the dead, as well as through the first two letters of his name, iota [10] and eta [8]. The ten Aeons are signified by the first letter of his name, (iota); therefore the Savior said, "One iota or one apex shall not pass away until everything takes place" [Matt. 5:18].

The passion which was experienced in relation to the twelfth Aeon is indicated through the apostasy of Judas, who was the twelfth of the apostles [cf. Mark 3:19, etc.], and through the fact that the Savior suffered in the twelfth month; for he proclaimed the gospel for one year after his baptism. Furthermore, this is most clearly revealed in the case of the woman with an issue of blood [Matt. 9:20–22, etc.]. She had suffered for twelve years before she was healed by the coming of the Savior, when she touched the hem of his garment, and therefore the Savior said, "Who touched me?"—teaching the disciples the mystery which had taken place among the Aeons and the healing of the Aeon which had experienced passion. For the one who suffered for twelve years is that power which would have been extended and whose substance would have flown into the boundless [cf. Luke 8:43 var., "had spent all her living"], unless she had touched the garment of the Son, that is, of the Truth of the first Four [indicated through the "hem"] and she would have been dissolved into the general substance. But she stayed there and stopped experiencing passion, for the power of the Son which came forth [i.e., Limit] healed her and separated the passion from her.

The Savior, who is from all, is the All because of the expression, "All, a male, which open the womb" [Luke 2:23]; he, being the All, opened the womb of the Desire of the suffering Sophia and banished Desire outside the Pleroma; this Desire is the second Eight. For this reason Paul plainly said, "And he is the All" [Col. 3:11], and again, "All is to him and from him is All" [Rom. 11:36], and again, "In him dwells All, the Pleroma of deity" [Col. 2:9], and "All is recapitulated in Christ through God" [Eph. 1:10].

Limit has two modes of operation, confirming and dividing. As he confirms and strengthens, he is Cross; so when he divides and delimits, he is Limit. The Savior thus inducated his modes of operation: first the confirming, when he said, "Whoever does not bear his Cross and follow me cannot be my disciple" [Luke 14:27; Mark 10:38], and again, "Take up the Cross and follow me" [Mark 8:34]; the delimiting, when he said, "I came not to cast peace but a sword" [Matt. 10:-34]. And John indicated the same thing when he said, "The fan is in his hand; he will purify the threshing-floor and will gather the wheat into his barn; but he will burn up the chaff in unquenchable fire" [Luke 3:17]. In this saying he indicated the operation of Limit; for that "fan" is the Cross, which is actually consuming all the material elements as fire consumes chaff but is purifying those who are saved as the fan purifies wheat. Paul the apostle himself referred to this Cross in the following words: "The message of the Cross is folly to those who are perishing but the power of God to those who are saved" [1 Cor. 1:18], and again, "Far be it from me to boast of anything except the Cross of Christ, through which the world has been crucified to me and I to the world" [Gal. 6:14].

Desire (Achamoth) and the Demiurge
Outside the Pleroma
When the Desire of the Sophia above, also called Achamoth,[6] had been banished from the Pleroma above, by necessity she was cast with her passion in places of Shadow and the Void. She was outside the Light and the Pleroma; she was shapeless and ugly, like an abortion, because she had comprehended nothing.

The Christ above took pity on her and was extended through the Cross to form her shape by his own power, a shape which was in substance only, not in knowledge. When he had done this, he returned above, withdrawing his power, and left her, so that she might sense the passion related to her because of her departure from the Pleroma and might strive for better things, since she had a certain aroma of imperishability which had been left her by Christ and the Holy Spirit. For this reason she is called by both names, Sophia after her mother[7] and Holy Spirit from the Spirit with Christ.

When she received shape and became intelligent, and was immediately deprived of the Logos which had invisibly been with her [i.e., Christ], she strove to seek for the light which had left her, but she was unable to comprehend it [cf. John 1:5] because she was hindered by Limit. Then the Limit which was hindering her in her forward striving said, "Iao." This is the origin of the name Iao.

Since she was unable to pass through Limit because she was entangled with passion and had been abandoned outside, she was weighed down by every part of passion, (which was multipartite and manifold). She suffered grief, because she did not comprehend; fear, lest life abandon her as light had done; in addition to these, perplexity; all these, in ignorance. She was not like her mother, the First Sophia Aeon, who had degeneration in her passions; on the contrary, another disposition came upon her, that of conversion to the Life-Giver.

This was the composition and substance of the matter of which the universe consists. From the conversion of Achamoth the whole soul of the universe and of the Demiurge orginated; from her fear and grief the rest took their origin.

For from her tears comes every humid substance, from her laughter that which shines with light; from her grief and consternation come the corporeal elements of the universe.

Sometimes she mourned and grieved,
  For she was left alone in darkness and the void;
Sometimes she reached a thought of the light which
  had left her,
  And she was cheered and laughed;
Sometimes she feared;
  At other times she was perplexed and astonished.

Our Mother passed through every passion and barely emerged from them, she turned to supplicate the light which had left her, i.e., Christ. When he had ascended to the Pleroma, he sent the Paraclete to her, i.e., the Savior, having given him all the power of the Father [cf. Matt. 28:18] and having delivered everything under his authority. The Aeons similarly so that "in him all things might be created, visible and invisible, thrones, deities, dominions" [cf. Col 1:16]. He was sent out to her along with the angels who were his peers.

When Achamoth turned towards him she was at first ashamed and put on a veil, but then when she saw him with his whole harvest of angels she ran to him and received power from his appearing.

He gave her the formation which is in accordance with knowledge and providing healing for her passions; he separated them from her but did not neglect them, for it was not possible for them to vanish as the passions of the prior Sophia did, since they were habitual and powerful. After separating them he mixed them together and solidified them and changed them from incorporeal passion into incorporeal matter. Then he provided them with an aptitude and a nature so that they could become compounds and bodies, so that there might be two natures, the one from the passions evil, the other from the conversion in a state of emotion. In this way the Savior practically effected a work of creation.

When Achamoth was relieved of passion, and joyfully conceived the vision of the angels with him and in her longing became pregnant with fruits after their image, a spiritual embryo after the likeness of the guards of the Savior.

When these three kinds of materials existed—matter from passion, the psychic from conversion, the spiritual which she conceived—she turned to shaping them. But she was unable to shape the spiritual since it was of the same nature as she was. She turned then to shaping the psychic nature which had come into existence from her conversion and projected the teachings of the Savior. First, from the psychic nature she formed the Father and King of all who are of the same nature as he is [i.e., the psychics]—which are on the right hand—and of those who come from passion and matter—which are on the left hand. He shaped all the beings after himself, secretly moved by the Mother; hence he is called Mother-Father and Fatherless and Demiurge and Father. He is Father of those on the right [i.e., the psychics], he is Demiurge of those on the left [i.e., material beings]; and he is King of them all. Desire [Achamoth] wanted to make all things in honor of the Aeons and she made images of them—or rather the Savior did so through her. And she preserved the image of the invisible Father, which was not known by the Demiurge; the Demiurge preserved that of the Only-Begotten Son; the archangels and angels made by him preserved the images of the other Aeons.

The Demiurge was the Father and God of the beings outside the Pleroma, the maker of all psychic and material beings. For he separated the two mixed natures, and made bodies out of the incorporeal, and thus created heavenly and earthly beings, and became the Demiurge of material and psychic beings, the right and the left, the light and the heavy, those borne above and those borne below. He fashioned seven heavens and dwells above them. For this reason he is called Seven, and the Mother Achamoth is called Eight; she preserves the number of the first-generated Eight; the first in the Pleroma. The seven heavens are intelligent; they are angels, and the Demiurge himself is an angel, like God. Paradise, which is above the third heaven [cf. 2 Cor. 12:2, 4] is practically an archangel, and from him Adam received something when he lived in him.

The Demiurge supposed that he made these things of himself, but he made them after Achamoth projected them. He made Heaven without knowing Heaven; he formed man in ignorance of man; he brought earth to light without understanding earth. In every case he was ignorant of the ideas of the things he made, as well as of the Mother; and he thought he was entirely alone. But the Mother was the cause of his creating; she wanted to bring him forth as the head and beginning of her own nature and as lord of the whole operation. The Mother is called Eight and Sophia and Earth and Jerusalem and Holy Spirit and Lord, in her masculine aspect; she has the place of the Middle and is above the Demiurge but below or outside the Pleroma, until the end.

Since, then, the material nature is derived from the three passions, fear and grief and perplexity, psychic beings consist of fear and conversion; the Demiurge originated from conversion, and all the rest of the psychic creation—souls of irrational animals and beasts and men—comes from fear. For this reason the Demiurge, who is impotent to know spiritual beings, thought that he was the only God and said through the prophets, "I am God and apart from me there is no one" [Isa. 45:5, 46:9]. From grief came "the spiritual beings of wickedness" [Eph. 6:12], as well as the Devil, also called World-Ruler, and the demons and the angels and all the spiritual substance of wickedness. The Demiurge is the psychic son of our Mother, while the World-Ruler is the creation of the Demiurge. The World-Ruler knows the beings above him, for he is a spirit of wickedness, but the Demiurge does not know them since he is merely psychic. Our Mother dwells in the superheavenly place, i.e., in the Middle, while the Demiurge dwells in the heavenly place, i.e., in the Seven, and the World-Ruler in our universe.

From perplexity and anguish, as from a very ignoble source, came the corporeal elements of the universe—earth related to the stability of consternation, water related to the motion of fear, air related to the congelation of grief. Fire is immanent in all of them as death and decay, just as ignorance is hidden in the three passions.

When he had fashioned the universe, he made the earthly man, not out of this dry land but out of the invisible substance, taking him from the liquid and flowing part of matter; and into him was breathed the psychic man. This is the man who came into being "after the image and likeness" [Gen. 1:26]; "after the image" is the material, who is similar to God but not of the same substance; "after the likeness" is the psychic, and his substance is therefore called "spirit of life" [Gen. 2:7], since it is from spiritual emanation. Finally, he was clothed with the "coat of skin" [Gen. 3:21]; this is his flesh which is subject to sense-perception.

The embryo of our Mother Achamoth, which she conceived in accordance with the vision of the angels about the Savior [it is of the same spiritual substance as that of the Mother], was unknown to the Demiurge and was secretly inserted into him while he remained ignorant, so that through him it might be sown into the soul created by him and into the material body, might grow and increase in them, and might become ready for the reception of the perfect Logos. The Demiurge was unaware of the spiritual man who was sown, in his "inbreathing" [Gen. 2:7], by Sophia with ineffable power and foreknowledge. As he did not know the Mother, so he does not know her seed. This seed is the Church, which corresponds to the [Aeon] Church above. Man thus has his soul from the Demiurge, his body from liquid and his flesh from matter, but his "spiritual man" from the Mother Achamoth.

Salvation

There are these three elements in man: the material, also called "left," which necessarily perishes since it cannot possibly receive the breath of imperishability; the psychic, also called "right," which lies between the spiritual and the material and extends to either one as it has the inclination; the spiritual, which was sent forth to be shaped in union with the psychic and to be instructed with it in its conduct. This last element is the "salt" and the "light of the world" [Matt. 5:13–14]; for it needed psychic and perceptible instructions; for this reasion the universe was constructed. And the Savior came to this psychic element, since it has free will, in order to save it. He assumed the primary elements of those beings which he was going to save. From Achamoth he took the spiritual, from the Demiurge he put on the psychic Christ, and from the constitution of the universe he acquired a body which had psychic substance and was constructed by ineffable art so to be visible, tangible, and subject to passion. He acquired nothing material at all, for matter is not capable of being saved. The end will come when all that is spiritual is shaped and perfected in knowledge. All that is spiritual means the spiritual men who have perfect knowledge about God and have been initiated in the mysteries of Achamoth.

The psychic men have been instructed in psychic matters; they are strengthened by works and mere faith and do not have the perfect knowledge; they belong to the earthly church. Good conduct is necessary for them, for otherwise they cannot be saved; but we spirituals shall certainly be saved not by conduct but simply because we are by nature spiritual. Just as the earthly cannot participate in salvation, for it is not capable of receiving it [cf. 1 Cor. 15:50], so in turn the spiritual cannot accept decay, no matter what actions it undertakes. Just as gold placed in mud does not lose its beauty but retains its own nature, and the mud cannot harm the gold, so we cannot damage or lose our spiritual nature, even if we engage in various material actions.[8]

Those of the church receive grace as a loan, and therefore will be deprived of it; but we have it as our own possession after it has come down from above from the ineffable and unnameable Pair. For this reason it will be "bestowed" on us [cf. Matt. 6:33; Luke 19:26], and we must always meditate on the mystery of union in every way. Whoever is "in the world" and does not love a women so that he unites with her is not "of the truth" and will not attain the truth; but he who is from the world and unites with a woman will not attain the truth because he lustfully unites with the woman. For this reason the psychics, who are "of the world," [John 17:11, 14–16; 18:37] must practice continence and good conduct, so that through it they may come to the place of the Middle; for us, who are spiritual and perfect, this is not necessary at all. It is not conduct which leads one to the Pleroma, but the seed sent out from there as an infant and made mature (perfect) there.

When the whole seed is perfected, then our Mother Achamoth will depart from the place of the Middle and will enter into the Pleroma and will receive the Savior, made from all the Aeons, as her bridegroom so that there will be a union of the Savior and the Sophia who is Achamoth. These are the bridegroom and the bride [cf. John 3:29], and the bridechamber is the whole Pleroma.

The spirituals will put off their souls and will become intelligent spirits, entering without hindrance, and invisibly, into the Pleroma, and they will be given as brides to the angels about the Savior. The Demiurge himself will depart to the place of the Mother Sophia, in the Middle, and the souls of the righteous too will be refreshed in the place of the Middle, for nothing psychic can come within the Pleroma. When these events take place, then the fire hidden in the universe will shine forth and ignite and become effective in consuming all matter along with itself and finally will become nonexistent. The Demiurge knew none of these things before the coming of the Savior.

The Demiurge, some say, emitted Christ, his own son, a psychic being like him, and spoke concerning him through the prophets. He passed through Mary as water passes through a pipe. On him at the baptism there descended that Savior from the Pleroma, from all the Aeons, in the form of a dove. The Savior was a composite being consisting of these four elements and thus preserving the model of the primal and original Four—from the spiritual, what was from Achamoth; from the psychic, what was from the Demiurge; and the constitution of the universe, what was constructed by ineffable art; and from the Savior, what was the dove which came down into him. It, the Savior, remained impassible—for it could not experience passion, since it was unconquerable and invisible—therefore when Christ was led before Pilate, that Spirit of Christ set in him was taken away. But the seed which was from the Mother also did not experience passion, for it too was impassible because it was spiritual and invisible, even to the Demiurge. What suffered was the psychic Christ, the one constructed from the constitution of the universe, in a mysterious fashion, so that through him the Mother might set forth the model of the Christ above, when he was extended on the cross and had shaped the essential form of Achamoth.[9]

Revelation

The souls which have the seed of Achamoth are better than the others, and therefore are loved more by the Demiurge, who does not know why he loves them but supposes that they are what they are because they come from him. For this reason he appointed them as prophets, priests, and kings. Many statements were made by this seed through the prophets . . . since its nature is highly exalted; and the Mother spoke of many things concerning things above, but she did so through the seed and the souls originating from it. The prophecies contain three kinds of statements: those which stem from the Mother; those which stem from the seed; those which stem from the Demiurge. Similarly, the sayings of Jesus were derived partly from the Savior, partly from the Mother, and partly from the Demiurge.

Since the Demiurge was ignorant of what was above him, he was moved by what was said but thought little of it, attributing various causes to it, such as the prophetic spirit, which has some movement of its own, or the man who was speaking, or his involvement in inferior matters. Thus he continued in ignorance until the coming of the Savior; but when the Savior came he learned everything from him and gladly joined him, with all his power. He is the centurion in the Gospel [Matt. 8:9; Luke 7:8], who said to the Savior, "I too have under my authority soldiers and slaves, and they do whatever I command"; he will govern the structure of the universe until the appointed time, especially because of his care for the Church and his knowledge of the reward prepared for him, his going to the place of the Mother.

There are three classes of men: spiritual, material, psychic, corresponding to Cain, Abel, and Seth, who reflect these three natures not as individuals but generically. The material ends in decay; and the psychic, if it chooses what is better, will rest in the place of the Middle; if it chooses what is worse, it too will end in a destiny like its choice. Whatever spiritual beings Achamoth inseminates in righteous souls, even until now, trained and brought up here on earth, because they were sent forth as infants, were later accounted worthy of maturity [perfection] and will be given as brides to the angels of the Savior, while their souls will be forced to rest forever in the Middle with the Demiurge. These souls themselves are divided into those by nature good and those by nature evil; the good are those which are capable of receiving the seed; those by nature evil can never receive that seed.

Biblical Proofs

In the last times of the universe the Savior came to his passion for this reason: to set forth the passion which took place in regard to the last of the Aeons, and through this end of life to show the goal of the operation of the Aeons. That twelve-year-old girl, the daughter of the head of the synagogue [Luke 8:41], whom the Savior stood by and raised from the dead, corresponds to Achamoth, whom the extended Christ shaped and led to perception of the light which had left her. Because the Savior manifested himself to her when she was outside the Pleroma, as was right for an abortion, Paul said in 1 Corinthians [15:-8], "Last of all he appeared also to me as to the abortion." The coming of the Savior and his angels to Achamoth was also revealed by Paul in the same epistle [11: 10] when he said, "The woman must have a veil on her head because of the angels." The fact that, when the Savior came to her, Achamoth placed a veil over her face for shame, was also made manifest by Moses when he placed a veil over his face [cf. 2 Cor. 3:13].

The passions of Achamoth were indicated by the Savior on the cross. When he said, "My God, why have you abandoned me?" [Matt. 27:46; Mark 15:34] he indicated that Sophia had been abandoned by the light and kept by Limit from moving forward. Her grief was shown by "My soul is grieved" [Matt. 26:38]; her fear in the saying, "Father, if it be possible, let the cup pass from me" [Matt. 26:39]; and her perplexity in the statement, "And I do not know what to say" [John 12:27].

He also pointed out the three kinds of men: (1) the material, when he answered the one who said he would follow him by saying, "The Son of Man has nowhere to lay his head" [Matt. 8:20; Luke 9:58]; (2) the psychic, when he answered the one who said he would follow him but first had to arrange his affairs, "No one who lays his hand on the plough and then looks back is ready for use in the kingdom of heaven" [Luke 9:62]— this person is one of those of the Middle, and he has acted like the one who has acknowledged most parts of righteousness but then does not wish to follow but has been overcome by riches so that he does not become perfect [Matt. 19:16], and he has become one of the psychic class; and (3) the spiritual, when he said, "Let the dead bury their own dead" [Matt. 8:22; Luke 9:60], and, in the case of Zacchaeus the tax collector, "Descend quickly, for I must stay in your house today" [Luke 19:5]—these were men of the spiritual class. And the parable of the leaven, which the woman is said to have hidden in three measures of meal [Luke 13:21], refers to the three classes; the woman is Sophia, the three measures of meal are the three classes of men [spiritual, psychic, earthly]; the leaven is the Savior himself. And Paul explicitly spoke of earthly, psychic, and spiritual, in passages where he says, "as is the earthly man, so are the earthly men" [1 Cor. 15:

48], "the psychic man does not accept the things of the Spirit" [1 Cor. 2:14], and "the spiritual man judges everything" [1 Cor. 2:15]. The passage, "The psychic man does not accept the things of the Spirit" was spoken in regard to the Demiurge, who, since he is psychic, did not know the Mother, since she is spiritual, or her seed, or the Aeons in the Pleroma. But Paul said that the Savior received the first fruits of those whom he was about to save: "If the first fruit is holy, so is the lump" [Rom. 11:16]. By "first fruit" he meant the spiritual, and by "lump" he meant members of the psychic church, the "lump" of which he took up and raised up with himself, since he himself was "leaven."

And that Achamoth wandered outside the Pleroma and was formed by Christ and was sought by the Savior, he indicated when he said he came for the lost sheep [Matt. 18:12; Luke 15:3]. For the wandering sheep is our Mother from whom the church here was sown; her wandering is her life outside the Pleroma in all the passions from which matter came. The woman who cleans her house and finds the drachma [Luke 15:8–9] is the Sophia above, who lost her Desire [Achamoth], and later finds it, when everything has been cleaned through the coming of the Savior. For this reason she is restored within the Pleroma. And Simeon, who took the Christ in his arms and gave thanks to God, and said "Lord, now let your servant depart in peace, according to your word" [Luke 2:28–29], is a figure of the Demiurge, who, when the Savior came, learned of his change of place and gave thanks to Depth. And through Anna, the prophetess, who is proclaimed in the gospel, and had lived seven years with her husband, and for the remaining time had remained a widow, until she saw the Savior and recognized him and spoke about him to all [Luke 2:36–38]—she is very obviously Achamoth, who for a short time saw the Savior with his peers, the angels, but during the remaining interval waited in the Middle and "expected" his return, when he would restore her to her consort [Luke 2:38]. And her name was indicated by the Savior when he said, "And Sophia has been made righteous by her children" [Luke 7:35], and by Paul thus: "We speak of Sophia among the perfect" [1 Cor. 2:6]. And Paul spoke of the unions within the Pleroma, mentioning one example; for in writing of a human union he said, "This mystery is great, but I refer to Christ and the Church" [Eph. 5:32].

Notes

1. Irenaeus adds that the Valentinians do not wish to call the Savior "Lord."
2. Irenaeus adds that "sometimes the Father is said to be accompanied by Silence and sometimes the Valentinians say he is beyond male and beyond female."
3. Cf. also Ignatius *fom* vii.2: "my *eros* has been crucified."
4. So Irenaeus; the system requires the order "Churches and Spirits."
5. The same exegesis of *iota* and *eta* is found in Barnabas ix.8 and elsewhere in early Christian literature, but without reference to the Aeons.
6. The lower Sophia thus bears a name like the Hebrew word for "wisdom."
7. Irenaeus says "father," ironically.
8. At this point Irenaeus criticizes the Valentinians for eating meat consecrated to Pagan gods, for attending Pagan festivals and gladiatorial shows, and for seducing women. (6, 4) They also despise ordinary Christians for their ignorance, while regarding themselves as "perfect" and "seeds of election."
9. This paragraph is from another system, as Irenaeus indicated.

Ptolemaeus' Letter to Flora

Ptolemaeus was the head of the Valentinian school in Italy and apparently succeeded Valentinus himself, perhaps about A.D. 160. Nothing is known of his life, but it is evident from his work that he was the greatest systematic theologian of the school. Irenaeus' refutation of Valentinianism is directed primarily against that form of it created by Ptolemaeus, and our description of the system is translated from Irenaeus, *Adv. haer.* i. 1-8 (I, 8–71 Harvey).*

He was also an exegete, indeed the first exegete of the Fourth Gospel known to us. In the selection provided, once more, by Irenaeus (*Adv. haer.* i. 8. 5; I, 75–80 Harvey), he tried to prove that John, the Lord's disciple, knew and allegorically described the first Ogdoad in the prologue to his gospel.

And he was an apologist for Valentinianism. In his "Letter to Flora" he set forth the answers to some theological difficulties encountered by a Christian woman named Flora, carefully leading her along a seemingly orthodox path to the point where she will recognize that the Valentinians share in the apostolic tradition and that the truth of their teaching is guaranteed by the words of the Savior. This letter is preserved by Epiphanius, *Pan. haer.* xxxiii. 3–7; we translate the text of G. Quispel, *Ptolémée: Lettre à Flora* (Paris, 1949). *Flora* may be the Roman Church; see "Vigiliae Christianae" II (1957), 147–48.

---

*Introduction by Robert M. Grant.

PTOLEMAEUS' LETTER TO FLORA*

The Law ordained through Moses, my dear sister Flora, has not been understood by many persons, who have accurate knowledge neither of him who ordained it nor of its commandments. I think that this will be perfectly clear to you when you have learned the contradictory opinions about it.

Some say that it is legislation given by God the Father; others, taking the contrary course, maintain stubbornly that it was ordained by the opposite, the Devil who causes destruction, just as they attribute the fashioning of the world to him, saying that he is the Father and Maker of this universe. Both are completely in error; they refute each other and neither has reached the truth of the matter.

For it is evident that the Law was not ordained by the perfect God the Father, for it is secondary, being imperfect and in need of completion by another, containing commandments alien to the nature and thought of such a God. On the other hand, one cannot impute the Law to the injustice of the opposite, God, for it is opposed to injustice. Such persons do not comprehend what was said by the Savior. "For a house or city divided against itself cannot stand" [Matt. 12:25], declared our Savior.

Furthermore, the apostle says that the creation of the world is due to him, for "everything was made through him and apart from him nothing was made" [John 1:3]. Thus he takes away in advance the baseless wisdom of the false accusers, and shows that the creation is not due to a God who corrupts but to the one who is just and hates evil. Only unintelligent men have this idea, men who do not

*Epiphanius, *Pan.* xxxiii 3–7. From Robert M. Grant, *Gnosticism* (New York: Harper & Brothers, 1961), pp. 184–190.

recognize the providence of the creator and have blinded not only the eye of the soul but also the eye of the body.

From what has been said, it is evident that these persons entirely miss the truth; each of the two groups has experienced this, the first because they do not know the God of justice, the second because they do not know the Father of all, who alone was revealed by him who alone came.

It remains for us who have been counted worthy of the knowledge of both of these to provide you with an accurate explanation of the nature of the Law and of the legislator by whom it was ordained. We shall draw the proofs of what we say from the words of the Savior, which alone can lead us without error to the comprehension of reality.

First, you must learn that the entire Law contained in the Pentateuch of Moses was not ordained by one legislator —I mean, not by God alone; some commandments are Moses', and some were given by men. The words of the Savior teach us this triple division. The first part must be attributed to God himself and his legislating; the second to Moses—not in the sense that God legislates through him, but in the sense that Moses gave some legislation under the influence of his own ideas; and the third to the elders of the people, who seem to have ordained some commandments of their own at the beginning. You will now learn how the truth of this theory is proved by the words of the Savior.

In some discussion with those who disputed with the Savior about divorce, which was permitted in the Law, he said, "Because of your hard-heartedness Moses permitted a man to divorce his wife; from the beginning it was not so; for God made this marriage, and what the Lord joined together, man must not separate" [Matt. 19:8, 6]. In this way he shows that there is a Law of God, which prohibits the divorce of a wife from her husband, and another law, that of Moses, which permits the breaking of this yoke because of hard-heartedness. In fact, Moses lays down legislation contrary to that of God; for joining is contrary to not joining. But if we examine the intention of Moses in giving this legislation, it will be seen that he did not give it arbitrarily or of his own accord, but by necessity because of the weakness of those for whom the legislation was given. Since they were unable to keep the intention of God, according to which it was not lawful for them to reject their wives, with whom some of them disliked to live, and therefore were in danger of turning to greater injustice and thence to destruction, Moses wanted to remove the cause of dislike, which was placing them in jeopardy of destruction. Therefore because of the critical circumstances, choosing a lesser evil in place of a greater, he ordained, of his own accord, a second law, that of divorce, so that if they could not observe the first, they might keep this and not turn to unjust and evil actions, through which complete destruction would be the result for them. This was his intention when he gave legislation contrary to that of God. Therefore it is indisputable that here the law of Moses is different from the Law of God, even if we have demonstrated the fact from only one example.

The Savior also makes plain the fact that there are some traditions of the elders interwoven with the Law. "For God," he says, "said, Honor your father and your mother, that it may be well with you. But you," he says, addressing the elders, "have declared as a gift to God, that by which you might have been aided by me; and you have nullified the Law of God through the tradition of your elders." Isaiah also proclaimed this, saying, "This people honors me with their lips, but their heart is far from me, teaching precepts which are the commandments of men" [Matt. 15:4–9].

Therefore it is obvious that the whole Law is divided into three parts; we find in it the legislation of Moses, of the elders, and of God himself. This division

of the entire Law, as made by us, has brought to light what is true in it. This part, the Law of God himself, is in turn divided into three parts: the pure legislation not mixed with evil, which is properly called "law," which the Savior came not to destroy but to complete [Matt. 5: 17]—for what he completed was not alien to him but needed completion, for it did not possess perfection; next the legislation interwoven with inferiority and injustice, which the Savior destroyed because it was alien to his nature; and finally, the legislation which is exemplary and symbolic, an image of what is spiritual and transcendent, which the Saviour transferred from the perceptible and phenomenal to the spiritual and invisible.

The Law of God, pure and not mixed with inferiority, is the Decalogue, those ten sayings engraved on two tables, forbidding things not to be done and enjoining things to be done. These contain pure but imperfect legislation and required the completion made by the Savior.

There is also the law interwoven with injustice, laid down for vengeance and the requital of previous injuries, ordaining that an eye should be cut out for an eye and a tooth for a tooth, and that a murder should be avenged by a murder. The person who is the second one to be unjust is no less unjust than the first; he simply changes the order of events while performing the same action. Admittedly, this commandment was a just one and still is just, because of the weakness of those for whom the legislation was made so that they would not transgress the pure law. But it is alien to the nature and goodness of the Father of all. No doubt it was appropriate to the circumstances, or even necessary; for he who does not want one murder committed, saying, "You shall not kill," and then commanded a murder to be repaid by another murder, has given a second law which enjoins two murders although he had forbidden one. This fact proves that

623

he was unsuspectingly the victim of necessity. This is why, when his son came, he destroyed this part of the law while admitting that it came from God. He counts this part of the law as in the old religion, not only in other passages but also where he said, "God said, He who curses father or mother shall surely die" [Matt. 15:4].

Finally, there is the exemplary part, ordained in the image of spiritual and transcendent matters, I mean the part dealing with offerings and circumcision and the Sabbath and fasting and Passover and unleavened bread and other similar matters. Since all these things are images and symbols, when the truth was made manifest they were translated to another meaning. In their phenomenal appearance and their literal application they were destroyed, but in their spiritual meaning they were restored; the names remained the same but the content was changed. Thus the Savior commanded us to make offerings not of irrational animals or of incense of this worldly sort, but of spiritual praise and glorification and thanksgiving and of sharing and well-doing with our neighbors. He wanted us to be circumcised, not in regard to our physical foreskin but in regard to our spiritual heart; to keep the Sabbath, for he wishes us to be idle in regard to evil works; to fast, not in physical fasting but in spiritual, in which there is abstinence from everything evil. Among us external fasting is also observed, since it can be advantageous to the soul if it is done reasonably, not for imitating others or from habit or because of a special day appointed for this purpose. It is also observed so that those who are not yet able to keep the true fast may have a reminder of it from the external fast. Similarly, Paul the apostle shows that the Passover and the unleavened bread are images when he says, "Christ our Passover has been sacrificed, in order that you may be unleavened bread, not containing leaven" [by leaven he here means evil] "but may be a new lump" [1 Cor. 5:7].

Thus the Law of God itself is obviously divided into three parts. The first was completed by the Savior, for the commandments, "You shall not kill, you shall not commit adultery, you shall not swear falsely," are included in the forbidding of anger, desire, and swearing. The second part was entirely destroyed. For "an eye for an eye and a tooth for a tooth," interwoven with injustice and itself a work of injustice, was destroyed by the Savior through its opposite. Opposites cancel out. "For I say to you, do not resist the evil man, but if anyone strikes you, turn the other cheek to him." Finally, there is the part translated and changed from the literal to the spiritual, this symbolic legislation which is an image of transcendent things. For the images and symbols which represent other things were good as long as the Truth had not come; but since the Truth has come, we must perform the actions of the Truth, not those of the image.

The disciples of the Savior and the apostle Paul showed that this theory is true, speaking of the part dealing with images, as we have already said, in mentioning "the Passover for us" and the "unleavened bread"; of the law interwoven with injustice when he says that "the law of commandments in ordinances was destroyed" [Eph. 2:15]; and of that not mixed with anything inferior when he says that "the Law is holy, and the commandment is holy and just and good" [Rom. 7:12].

I think I have shown you sufficiently, as well as one can in brief compass, the addition of human legislation in the Law and the triple division of the Law of God itself.

It remains for us to say who this God is who ordained the Law; but I think this too has been shown you in what we have already said, if you have listened to it attentively. For if the Law was not ordained by the perfect God himself, as we have already taught you, nor by the devil, a statement one cannot possibly make, the legislator must be someone other than these two. In fact, he is the Demiurge and maker of this universe and everything in it; and because he is essentially different from these two and is between them, he is rightly given the name "Intermediate."

And if the perfect God is good by nature, as in fact he is, for our Savior declared that there is only a single good God, his Father whom he manifested; and if the one who is of the opposite nature is evil and wicked, characterized by injustice; then the one situated between the two, neither good nor evil and unjust, can properly be called just, since he is the arbitrator of the justice which depends on him. On the one hand, this god will be inferior to the perfect God and lower than his justice, since he is generated and not ungenerated—there is only one ungenerated Father, from whom are all things [cf. 1 Cor. 8:6], since all things depend on him in their own ways. On the other hand, he will be greater and more powerful than the adversary, by nature, since he has a substance and nature different from the substance of either of them. The substance of the adversary is corruption and darkness, for he is material and complex, while the substance of the ungenerated Father of all is incorruption and self-existent light, simple and homogeneous. The substance of the latter produced a double power, while the Savior is an image of the greater one.

Do not let this trouble you for the present in your desire to learn how from one first principle of all, simple, and acknowledged by us and believed by us, ungenerated and incorruptible and good, were constituted these natures of corruption and the Middle, which are of different substances, although it is characteristic of the good to generate and produce things which are like itself and have the same substance. For, if God permit, you will later learn about their origin and generation, when you are judged worthy of the apostolic tradition which we too have received by succession. We too are able to prove all our points by the teaching of the Savior.

In making these brief statements to you, my sister Flora, I have not grown weary; and while I have treated the subject with brevity, I have also discussed it sufficiently. These points will be of great benefit to you in the future, if like fair and good ground you have received fertile seeds and go on to show forth their fruit.

Basilides

In the second century Irenaeus, deriding the Gnostics, observed: "Every day every one of them invents something new" (*Adv. haer.* I.18.1). Basilides was a special target, for, with Mani and Ptolemaeus, he was a great system builder. Apart from producing a complex creation myth, as did other leading Gnostic thinkers, Basilides devised a universe with 365 heavens, each one derived from the other. He developed his speculation in Egypt, in the middle of the second century A.D., and with Valentinus is a major representative of Syrian-Egyptian Gnosticism.

There are two genuinely conflicting descriptions of Basilides' system. In Irenaeus we read of a theogony and cosmogony which begin with the ungenerated Father from whom all else emanates. In Hippolytus, however, there was nothing in the beginning, absolutely nothing, and somehow the nonexistent God made a nonexistent universe, with one seed in it that contained the other universe, the existing one. The latter cosmogony given by Hippolytus is more original and is generally considered to be Basilides' authentic contribution to Gnostic thought.

The system described in Irenaeus has the following hierarchy of divine emanations. From the ungenerated Father came Mind (*nous*); from Mind came the Word (*logos*), then Understanding (*phronesis*), Wisdom (*Sophia*) and Power (*dynamis*), and from Wisdom and Power came the Archons and angels who made the first heaven. Each heaven in turn made another heaven with Archons and angels who formed again another until there were 365 heavens. The year was given 365 days after the number of heavens. The angels of the last heaven created the world and its nations. The last Maker was the God of the Jews. This God of the Bible, who created our world, put his chosen people in control of other nations. Then the Father of All sent down his firstborn, Mind (Christ), as a man to free the subjected nations and to work miracles on earth. At the time of the crucifixion, there was much confusion, and when they were about to crucify Simon of Cyrene instead of Jesus, Jesus assumed Simon's form and was crucified. Of course, being incorporeal he did not suffer. In fact, he stood by and laughed at his executioners, at their blindness and ignorance in thinking they were hurting an ordinary man.

The notion of a laughing Jesus appears in Irenaeus and Epiphanius, but scholars suggest that this idea was held by Gnostics even before Basilides. The New Testament is notably devoid of laughter, sympathetic or scornful, but in Psalm 2:4 of the Old Testament we have: "He that sits in the heavens shall laugh: the Lord shall have them in derision." Robert M. Grant speculates that Psalm 2 may be the source of the laughing Savior among the Gnostics. Now with the discovery of the Nag Hammadi library in Egypt, we find not only examples of a Jesus laughing from the cross (in *The Second Treatise of the Great Seth* and in *The Apocalypse of Peter)*, but also several other instances of the laughing Savior. In a larger sense this "docetic" view, of an unsuffering Jesus amused by assailants who are crucifying a phantom, represents the general Gnostic tendency to reverse orthodox Christian and Jewish doctrine and to deride unenlightened practices. In *The Gnostic Gospels* Elaine Pagels speaks of the Gnostic derision of Christian martyrs, including Irenaeus, who longed for martrydom. Finally, the Gnostic view of the crucifixion also signifies the importance the Gnostics gave to spirit as opposed to body. Those who believe that Christ suffered bodily are slaves to the body, Basilides said. Salvation is for the soul alone.

The Basilides system as given by Hippolytus begins with a cosmogony where there is nothing, neither spirit nor matter. But there is a nonexistent God who "wished" (without desire) to make a universe and so he created a nonexistent universe. This was the first universe. But a second universe came about because the nonexistent universe contained a seed out of which our universe came. The seed contained all things.

From the seed came the ineffable great Archon, the Head of the universe, also called the Demiurge. Characteristic of Gnostic speculation, this great Archon, as with each new divine power, is unaware of his ancestors. So the biblical Creator God is arrogantly ignorant of his low position in the hierarchy of divinities. The first great Archon then created parts of the universe and a Son wiser and better than himself, who ruled the eighth realm, the Ogdoas. Then another Archon arose in the seventh realm, the Hebdomas, and he made everything below; he was the one who said to Moses, "I am the God of Abraham and Isaac and Jacob." And this Archon of the seventh realm also had a Son (Christ), but none of these entities knew that they were below the original Triple Sonship, which had been created by the nonexistent God.

The passage quoted by Hippolytus ends with a difficult section on the role of Jesus. The human goal is to know the Gospel, which is knowledge (*gnosis*), and so find one's way back across the dividing line to Spirit (*Pneuma*), to the Triple Sonship and the nonexistent God. It is not clear from the fragments we have where the realm of human redemption lies. But Jesus has come to clarify things, to separate commingled things into their original species in order to restore all to their origin above.

The followers of Basilides, living in Egypt, proclaimed themselves a group apart, "no longer Jews but . . . not yet Christians." There follows the mysterious line: "One may not speak of their mysteries aloud, but must preserve them in silence." (Iren. I, 24; 6) "What cannot be expressed in words," Wittgenstein says at the end of his *Tractatus*, "must be consigned to silence." Such is the formula for dealing with the ineffable, the mystical, or simply what goes beyond our language abilities. In actuality, Basilides was one of the most articulate and systematic thinkers of the Gnostic mysteries, and when he is speaking of unbeing and nonexistent universes, he writes with the concentrated rigor, if not thought, of the Presocratics. We are lucky to have these few pages of insight into his world.

BASILIDES*

But Basilides, in order to seem to have discovered something more exalted and more convincing, extended the teaching of his doctrine into the immeasurable, setting forth Mind, first born from the ungenerated Father; from it was generated Logos; then from Logos, Understanding, from Understanding, Sophia and Power [cf. 1 Cor. 1:24]; from Power and Sophia the powers and principalities and angels, which he calls "first," by whom the first heaven was made. Then, deriving their origin from these, others were made; and these made another heaven like the first; and similarly, when still others were made, derived from these, antitypes of those above them, they formed a third heaven. From the third of them, starting down from above, a fourth came into existence, and subsequently in this way still further principalities and angels were made, they say, and a total of three hundred and sixty-five heavens. For this reason the year has this many days, in accordance with the number of the heavens.

The angels who control the last

heaven, which is visible to us, fashioned everything in the world and made the various parts of the earth and of the nations on it. Their chief is the one who is thought to be the God of the Jews. Since he wanted to subjugate the other nations to his people, the Jews, all the rest of the principalities stood up and resisted him [Ps. 2:2]; therefore the rest of the nations resisted his nation. The unbegotten and unnamed Father, seeing their destruction, sent his firstborn Mind [Christ] to free those who believe him from the power of those who fashioned the world. And to their nations he appeared on earth as a man and worked miracles. Therefore, because he was Mind, he did not suffer, but a certain Simon of Cyrene was impressed to carry his cross for him, and because of ignorance and error he was crucified [cf. Mark 15:21–24], transfigured by him so that he might be thought to be Jesus: and Jesus himself assumed the form of Simon and, standing by, laughed at them [cf. Ps. 2:4]. Since he was incorporeal Power and the Mind of the unbegotten Father, he was transfigured in whatever way he wished and thus ascended to him who had sent him, deriding them because he could not be held [cf. Ps. 2:3] and was invisible to all.

Therefore those who know these things are freed from the world-making principalities. They should not confess

---

*Hippolytus, *Ref.* vii. 20–27. From Robert M. Grant, *Gnosticism* (New York: Harper & Row, 1961), pp. 33–34, 125–134.

the one who was crucified, but him who came in the form of man [cf. Phil. 2:7] and was thought to be crucified and was called Jesus and was sent by the Father, so that by means of this divine plan he might destroy the works of the world-makers. If anyone confesses the Crucified, he is still a slave and is under the power of those who made bodies. He who denies has been freed from them and knows the plan of the unbegotten Father. There is salvation for the soul alone, since the body is by nature perishable.

The prophecies were spoken by the world-making principalities, and the law by their chief, the one who led the people out of the land of Egypt. They despise meats sacrificed to idols and regard them as nothing [cf. 1 Cor. 10:19] and use them without any hesitation; they have an "indifferent" use of other actions and of universal lust. They use magic and images and incantations and invocations and all the other things which accompany these.

After inventing certain names as if they belonged to angels, they proclaim that some are in the first heaven, others in the second; then they try to set forth the names, principalities, angels, and powers of the three hundred and sixty-five fictitious heavens. The name in which they say the Savior descended and ascended is Caulacau [Isa. 28:10]. Therefore he who has learned these things and knows all the angels and their sources becomes invisible and incomprehensible to the angels and powers, just as Caulacau was. And as the Son is unknown to all [Matt. 11:27], so they should be known to no one; but since they all know [cf. 1 Cor. 8:1] and pass through all, they are invisible and unknown to all. For "you must know everyone, but no one should know you." Therefore men of such a kind are ready to deny and cannot "suffer for the name" [cf. 1 Pet. 4:14], since they resemble everyone else. "Not many can know these things—one out of a thousand and two out of myriads."

And they say that they are no longer Jews but are not yet Christians; it is not right to speak their mysteries at all; one must keep them hidden in silence.

They distribute the positions of the three hundred and sixty-five heavens as the astrologers do. Accepting their theorems, they have transferred them into their own form of teaching; their first principle is Abraxas, and therefore has the sum of three hundred and sixty-five in itself.

BASILIDES' SYSTEM

There was a time when there was nothing, but "nothing" was not anything existent. Simply and plainly, without any sophistry, there was absolutely nothing. When I say "was," I do not mean that anything "was," but I say it in order to signify what I want to show—I mean that there was absolutely nothing. What is called by a name is not absolutely ineffable; we may call it ineffable, but it is not ineffable, for the truly ineffable is not ineffable but "above every name which is named" [Eph. 1:21]. Names are not sufficient for designating all the objects in the world, because they are innumerable; names are inadequate. I do not undertake to find proper names for all. Instead, by understanding without speech one must receive the properties of the things named. Homonyms have produced trouble and error for those who hear.

Since, then, there was nothing—no matter, no substance, no nonsubstance, nothing simple, nothing complex, nothing not understood, nothing not sensed, no man, no angel, no god, not anything that is named or perceived through sense, not any intelligible things, and not anything which can be defined more subtly than anything else—the nonexistent God wished, without intelligence, without sense, without will, without choice, without passion, without desire, to make a universe [cosmos]. I say that he "wished" for the sake of saying something, but it was actually without wish, without intelligence, without sense; and I say "universe" in reference not to the one with breadth and divisibility which came into existence later and continued to exist, but to the seed of the universe. The seed of the universe had everything within it, just as the grain of mustard seed [Matt. 13:31–32], collecting everything in the smallest space, contains it all together—roots, stem, branches, innumerable leaves, seeds of the grains generated from the plant, and seeds of still other plants, when they are scattered.

Thus the nonexistent God made a nonexistent universe out of the nonexistent, establishing and giving substance to one certain seed which had within it the whole semination of the universe. It is like the egg of some variegated and many-colored bird, such as the peacock or some other bird which is even more multiform and many-colored, an egg which though one has within it many forms of multiform, many-colored, many-constituted substances. Thus the nonexistent seed, established by the nonexistent God as the semination of the universe, was at the same time polymorphous and many-substanced.

Everything, then, of which one can speak, and even of which one cannot speak because it does not exist; everything which was necessarily going to adapt itself to the universe which was to come from the seed and at proper times be given growth by such a God, so great that the creation cannot speak of him or contain him in thought; all these beings existed, deposited in the seed, just as we see in the case of the newborn child; we see the teeth which grow later, the paternal substance, intelligence, and all the things man does not have at first but gradually acquires as he grows up.

Why do we need "emanation" or why do we posit "matter" in order for God to make the universe, as if he were a spider making a web or a mortal man using bronze or wood or pieces of material? "He spoke and it was done" [Ps. 33:9]; this is what the expression of Moses means: "Let there be light; and there was light" [Gen. 1:3]. Whence came the light? From nothing; for we are told not what its source was but only that it came from the voice which spoke. He who speaks did not exist, nor did what came into existence. For the seed of the universe came into existence out of the nonexistent, i.e., the word which was spoken: "Let there be light." And this is what the gospels mean when they say, "It was true light, which illuminates every man coming into the universe" [John 1:9]. Man originates from that seed and is illuminated from it.

Do not ask about the origin of what I say came into existence after this. For the seed of the universe had all the seeds deposited and contained within itself, just as, though nonexistent, they were planned for by the nonexistent God. In this seed there was a Triple Sonship, in every respect having the same nature [homoousios] as that of the nonexistent God; it was generated out of the nonexistent. Of this Triple Sonship one part was subtle, another opaque, and the third in need of purification.

At the moment when the seed was first cast forth by the nonexistent God, the subtle part pulsated and ascended and ran upwards from below, as the poet says, "like a wing or like thought" [Odyss. vii:36], and came to the Nonexistent. For every being, each in its own way, is drawn by the extraordinary beauty and loveliness of him. The more opaque part, remaining in the seed, wanted to imitate the first, but could not run upwards because it was much less subtle than the Sonship which ran upwards by itself. So it was left behind. Then this more opaque Sonship winged itself with the Holy Spirit, which the Sonship puts on and benefits and from which it receives benefit. It benefits the Spirit, because a bird's wing, separated from the bird, could never by itself fly upwards on high; it is benefited, because a bird which has lost a wing could never fly upwards on high. This is the relation of the Sonship to the Holy Spirit and that of the Holy Spirit to the Sonship. The Sonship, borne upwards by the Spirit as by a wing, bears up the wing [i.e., the Spirit]. Coming close to the subtle Sonship and the nonexistent God who created out of the nonexistent, it was not able to keep the Spirit with itself; for the Spirit was not of the same substance or nature as the Sonship. As pure and dry air is unnatural and deadly for fish, so it was contrary to nature for the Holy Spirit to remain in that place more ineffable than what is ineffable and "above all names," the place of the nonexistent God and the Sonship. Then the Sonship left the Spirit near that blessed place, which cannot be conceived of or expressed in any word. It was not entirely deserted or abandoned by the Sonship; but as when a most odoriferous perfume is once put in a vase, one can most carefully empty the vase, but a certain odor of perfume still remains even if the vessel is emptied, and the vessel retains the odor if not the perfume—so the Holy Spirit, separated from the Sonship and deprived of it, still keeps the power of the perfume, the odor of the Sonship. This is what the psalmist means by saying, "Like perfume on Aaron's head which came down on his beard" [Ps. 133:2]. He means the perfume borne from above from the Holy Spirit down to the formless and distant place where we are, from which the Sonship began his ascent, borne as on the wings and back of an eagle [cf. Deut. 32: 11]. All beings desire to rise above from below, from the worse to the better; nothing is so unintelligent as to descend from the better.

The third Sonship, which needed purification, remained in the great Heap of the mixture of seeds, giving and receiving benefit. And after the first and second ascent of the Sonship(s), the Holy Spirit remained as described, set as a "firmament" [Gen. 1:6] between supermundane being and the universe. Existent beings are divided into two classes and categories: the first is called "universe" [cosmos], the second "supermundane" [hypercosmical]; the dividing line between the universe and the supermundane is the Spirit, which is holy and has the odor of the Sonship remaining in it. When the firmament above the heaven had come into existence, then from the cosmic Seed and the Heap of the mixture of seeds there pulsated and was begotten the great Archon, the Head of the universe, whose beauty and size and power cannot be expressed. For he is more ineffable than what is ineffable and more powerful than what is powerful and wiser than the wise and greater than any good things you might possibly mention. After being begotten, he raised himself and went upwards and the whole of him was borne above to the firmament, where he stood, regarding the firmament as the end of his ascent and exaltation and not imagining that there was anything at all beyond these things. He then became, of all the elements of the universe which were below, the wisest, the most powerful, the most excellent, the most luminous—in short, he surpassed everything remarkably good which you might possibly mention, save only the Sonship which still remained in the mixture of seeds; for he did not know that this Sonship was wiser, more powerful, and better than he. Regarding himself as lord and master and wise builder [cf. 1 Cor. 3:10], he turned to the creation of various parts of the universe. First he decided not to remain alone, and from the materials below he made for himself and begot a son much better and wiser than himself. All these things had been planned in advance by the nonexistent God when he established the mixture of seeds. When he saw his son, he marveled and loved him and was amazed—so great did the beauty of the son of the great Archon appear to him—and the Archon seated him at his right hand. This is the Eight where the great Archon is seated. For the great wise Demiurge made the whole heavenly creation; his son worked in him and advised him, since he was much wiser than the Demiurge.

When all these things had been fashioned, another Archon arose from the mixture of seeds; he was greater than everything below him except the Sonship which had been left below, but he was much inferior to the first Archon. This Archon too is called ineffable. His place is called the Seven, and he is the governor and fashioner of everything below. He too made a son for himself out of the mixture of seeds, and as in the case of the first Archon, the son was more intelligent and wiser than the father. In this space is the Heap and mixture of seeds, and the beings born there are born naturally. They hasten to be brought forth by the nonexistent God who tells what is to happen—when, what, and how it must occur. They have no governor or caretaker or Demiurge; what suffices for them is the thought which the Nonexistent thought when he made them.

When the whole universe and the supermundane were finished and lacked nothing more, there still remained in the mixture of seeds the third Sonship, which had been left in the seed to give and receive benefit. It was necessary for the abandoned Sonship to be revealed and to be restored above, above the dividing Spirit, to the subtle Sonship and to the one which imitated it and to the Nonexistent: as it is written, "The creation itself groans and suffers pangs, awaiting the revelation of the sons of God" [Rom. 8:19, 22]. We spiritual beings are sons, left down here to adorn and fashion and correct and perfect the souls below which have a nature such as to remain in this space. "From Adam to Moses sin reigned," as it is written [Rom. 5:13–14]; for the great Archon, who extends to the firmament, was reigning, thinking that he alone was God and that above him was nothing [Deut.

32:39; Isa. 45:5]; for everything was kept in secret silence. This is the "mystery which was not revealed to former generations" [Col. 1:26]. In those times the great Archon, the Eight, seemed to be King and Lord of all. The Seven was King and Lord of this space below, and while the Eight is ineffable, the Seven can be named. It was this Archon of the Seven who spoke to Moses and said, "I am the God of Abraham and Isaac and Jacob, and I did not reveal the name of God to them" [Exod. 6:2–3]²—the name of the ineffable Archon-god of the Eight. All the prophets before the Savior spoke from this source [cf. John 10:8].

When it was necessary for us to be revealed as the children of God, concerning whom "the creation groaned and was in pangs, awaiting the revelation," the Gospel came into the universe and passed through every principality and power and dominion and every name that is named [cf. Eph. 1:21]. It really came, even though nothing came down from above and though the blessed Sonship did not depart from that inconceivable and blessed nonexistent God. Just as Indian naphtha kindles fire even from a great distance, simply by appearing, so the powers reached upwards from the shapeless mass to the Sonship above. For like Indian naphtha, the Gospel kindles and seizes thoughts, just as even the son of the great Archon of the Eight is kindled from the blessed Sonship beyond the dividing line. For the power of the Sonship in the midst of the Holy Spirit in the dividing line transmitted the fluid and attracted thoughts of the Sonship to the son of the great Archon. Then the Gospel first came from the Sonship, through the son seated by the Archon, to the Archon. The Archon learned that he was not the God of all but had been begotten, and that he had his own treasure laid up, above the ineffable and unnameable Nonexistent and the Sonship. He was converted and was afraid, recognizing his previous state of ignorance. This is what is meant by, "The beginning of wisdom is the Lord's fear" [Ps. 111:10]. For he began to become wise, instructed by the Christ who sat by him. He learned who the Nonexistent is, who the Sonship is, what the Holy Spirit is, what the constitution of the universe is, and how the restoration will take place. This is the "wisdom spoken in a mystery" [1 Cor. 2:7], concerning which the Scripture says, "Not in words taught by human wisdom, but in those taught by the Spirit" [1 Cor. 2:13]. After being instructed, taught, and made to fear, the Archon made a confession of the sin which he had committed by magnifying himself. This is what is meant by, "I recognized my sin and I know my iniquity, which I will confess to the Aeon" [Ps. 32:5, 51:5]. When the great Archon had been instructed, the whole creation of the Eight was instructed and taught and the mystery was made known to the heavenly beings [cf. Eph. 3:9–10].

The Gospel still had to come to the Seven so that the Archon of the Seven might similarly be taught and evangelized. The son of the great Archon shone on the son of the Archon of the Seven with the light which he himself had, having kindled it from the Sonship. The son of the Archon of the Seven was illuminated and preached the Gospel to the Archon of the Seven and, as in the first case, this Archon was made to fear and made his confession. When everything in the Seven had been illuminated and the Gospel had been proclaimed among them—for in the spaces themselves there exist innumerable creatures and principalities and powers and authorities; then three hundred and sixty-five heavens, whose great Archon is Abrasax because his name contains the number three hundred and sixty-five; the number which this name represents contains everything and therefore the year consists of this number of days [cf. Irenaeus, *Adv haer*. i. 24]—it was still necessary to illuminate the formless space where we live, and to reveal the "mystery not known to former genera-

tions" to the Sonship which like an abortion had been abandoned in the formless space [cf. 1 Cor. 15:8; Gal. 1:16]—as it is written, "By revelation the mystery was made known to me" [Eph. 3:3] and "I heard ineffable words which it is not lawful for a man to utter" [2 Cor. 12:4].

Then the light came down from the Seven—it had come down from the Eight above to the son of the Seven—upon Jesus the son of Mary, and he was illuminated and set on fire by the light which shone upon him. This is what is meant by, "Holy Spirit will come upon you" [Luke 1:35]; it had come from the Sonship through the dividing Spirit upon the Eight and the Seven and as far as Mary. And "Power of the Most High will overshadow you": the power of judgment from the height above, through the Demiurge, down to the creation; this power belongs to the son.

The universe remains in this condition until the whole Sonship left below to benefit the souls, in their shapeless state, and to receive benefit by being refashioned, follows Jesus and ascends above and comes there after being purified. It becomes very tenuous so that it can ascend of its own accord as the first Sonship ascended. For it holds the whole power physically consolidated with it through the light which from above shone downward.

When the whole Sonship comes to be above the dividing line, the Spirit, then the creation will obtain mercy. To the present day it "groans and is tormented and awaits the revelation of the sons of God," in order that all the men of the Sonship may return thence. When this takes place, God will bring the great Ignorance upon the whole universe so that everything may remain in accordance with nature and nothing may desire anything contrary to nature. All the souls of this space which have a nature such as to remain immortal only in this space will remain; they will know nothing different from this space or better than it. There will be no report or knowledge [gnosis] of things above in things below, so that the souls below will not be tormented by the desire of what is impossible, like a fish desiring to graze on the mountains with sheep; for such a desire would mean destruction for them. Everything which remains in its place is imperishable; it is perishable only if it wants to pass beyond its natural limits. Thus the Archon of the Seven will know nothing of things above; the great Ignorance will overcome even him, so that "grief and pangs and groaning" [Isa. 35:10, 51:11] will depart from him; for he will desire nothing impossible and will not be grieved. Similarly, the same ignorance will overcome even the great Archon of the Eight and, to an equal extent, all the creatures lying below him, so that he will not desire anything contrary to nature or suffer grief.

Thus the restoration of all things will take place. In the beginning they were established in accordance with nature in the seed of the universe. At the proper seasons they will be restored [cf. 1 Tim. 6:15]. Each has its own proper season; this is proved by the Savior's saying, "My hour has not yet come" [John 2:4], as well as by the magi who saw the star [Matt. 2:1–2]. For the Savior himself was subject to the influence of the stars and had planned in advance, in the great Mass, the hour of restoration.

This is the "inner man" [Rom. 7:22, Eph. 3:16], the spiritual in the psychic. It is the Sonship leaving the soul there, not because it was mortal but because it remained there in accordance with its own nature, just as the first Sonship left the Holy Spirit, the dividing line, in its proper place above and then put on its own soul.

The Gospel is that knowledge [gnosis] of the supermundane things which the great Archon did not know. When it was made known to him that there is the Holy Spirit [the dividing line], and the Sonship, and the nonexistent God, the cause of all these, he rejoiced and was glad because of what was said.

After Jesus came into existence in the way we have described, everything took place as it is written in the gospels. These things happened so that Jesus might become the first fruits of the differentiation among confused beings. Since the universe is divided into an Eight— the head of the whole universe; the great Archon is the head of the whole universe —and into a Seven—the Demiurge of things below is the head of the Seven— and into this space where we live— where formlessness is—it was necessary for the confused beings to be differentiated through the differentiation which Jesus effected. The bodily part of his being suffered; since it came from formlessness it was restored to formlessness. The psychic part of his being rose again, since it belonged to the Seven, and was restored to the Seven. He raised the part which belonged to the height of the great Archon, and it remained with the great Archon. He bore above the part which belonged to the dividing Spirit, and it remained in the dividing Spirit. The Third Sonship was purified through him, the one abandoned to give and receive benefit, and it ascended to the blessed Sonship after passing through all these levels. Jesus, then, became the first fruits of the differentiation, and his suffering took place only for the differentiation of what was confused. In this way the whole Sonship left behind in the formless space in order to give and receive benefit must be differentiated as Jesus himself was differentiated.

The Naassene Psalm

The Naasenes probably wrote the hymn we have soon after Hadrian's reign (A.D. 117–138). Our information comes exclusively from Hippolytus, who identifies them with the Phrygians. They were a syncretic Gnostic group, using common Gnostic notions of Adam and Adamas as well as Greek mythological deities to trace the human soul. The god figure is represented by a preexistent Almond (the Father of All), the name given "to the being from which the invisible one came forth and was begotten"[1] and through whom everything came into existence. The Son born of the Almond is called the Flute-player, a harmonious spirit; this god was born from the perfect fruit within the Almond whose womb was sent down to produce the Child.

The Naasenes offer another theogony, of the *nous*, of Chaos, and the "soul clad in the shape of a hind." Jesus will come down to save the soul, and under the name of *gnosis* teach it the secrets of the holy way.

Note

1. Robert Haardt, *Gnosis* (Leiden: Brill, 1971), p. 97.

NAASSENE PSALM[1]*

The Law of Universal Genesis
was the firstborn *nous;* the second Chaos
shed by the firstborn. The third was received
by the soul. . . .[2] Clad in the shape of a hind
she is worn away in death's slavery.[3]
Now she has mastery and glimpses light:
now she is plunged in misery and weeps.
Now she is mourned, and herself rejoices.
Now she weeps and is finally condemned.
Now she is condemned and finally dies.
And now she even reaches the point where
hemmed in by evil, she knows no way out.
Misled, she has entered a labyrinth.
Then Jesus said: "Behold, Father,
she wanders the earth pursued by evil.
Far from thy Breath she is going astray.
She is trying to flee bitter Chaos,
and does not know how she is to escape.
Send me forth, o Father, therefore, and I,
bearing the seal shall descend and wander
all Aeons through, all mysteries reveal.
I shall manifest the forms of the gods
and teach the secrets of the holy way
which I call Gnosis."

Notes

1. The text of the psalm is in several places very corrupt.
2. Text corrupt.
3. The translation of the difficult and perhaps corrupt passage is uncertain.

*Hippolytus, *Ref.* v. 10.2. From Robert Haardt, *Gnosis* (Leiden: Brill, 1971), pp. 99–100.

Baruch by Justin*

All we know of Justin's system is contained in Hippolytus' *Refutation of All Heresies*, though it seems to be reflected in a late Marcionite system described by Eznik (Ch. 3). In this system the universe owes its origin to three principles. The first is the only Good, at one point identified with the cosmic Priapus; the second and third are Elohim and Eden, or the Demiurge and matter. From the union of Elohim and Eden are derived the world-making angels and thence the world. To the first human couple is given the primary law to "increase and multiply." Evil is the violation of this law. It originates when Elohim ascends to contemplate his creation and is captivated by the Good. In her frustration, Eden ordered her angels to bring about violations of the primary law, in order to torment Elohim's spirit within mankind. She worked especially through her angel Naas, the serpent in the garden. On the other hand, Elohim has sent his own angel Baruch ("blessed") to contend with Naas and to gain adherents for himself. Baruch came to Adam and Eve, to Moses, to the prophets, to Heracles, and finally to Jesus. Only Jesus remained faithful to Baruch and ascended to the Good.

This system is a combination of a philosophical or theological triad, common in second-century thought, with a psychological, almost Freudian, explanation of human and cosmic sin. Sin is violation of the propagation of the human species; it originates in frustration and results in frustration. Salvation comes through returning to the Good, the life-principle, Priapus.

---

*Introduction by Robert M. Grant

BARUCH BY JUSTIN*

The Oath of Secrecy

If you wish to know "what eye has not seen or ear heard, and what has not entered the heart of man" [1 Cor. 2:9], the One who is high above all good things, swear to keep secret the mysteries of the teaching; for our Father, having seen the Good and having been made perfect with him, kept secret the mysteries of silence, and he swore, as it is written, "The Lord swore and will not change his mind" [Ps. 110:4]. This is the oath: "I swear by the One above all, the Good, to keep these mysteries and to tell them to no one and not to return from the Good to the creation." When he takes this oath, he enters into the Good and sees "what eye has not seen or ear heard and what has not entered the heart of man," and he drinks from the living water, which is the washing, the spring of living water welling up [John 4:10, 14]. For there was a division between water and water [Gen. 1:6], and the water below the firmament belongs to the evil creation; in it are washed the earthly and psychical men. The water above the firmament belongs to the Good and is living; in it are washed the spiritual and living men, as Elohim was, when after washing he did not change his mind.

The Myth*

There were three unbegotten principles of the universe, two male, one female. One of the male principles is called Good, the only one so called [Luke 18:19], who takes forethought for the universe; the other is called Father of all begotten beings, without foreknowledge, without knowledge, invisible. The female one is without foreknowledge,

---

*Hippolytus, *Ref.* v. 24.1; 37.1–3. From R. M. Grant, *Gnosticism* (New York: Harper & Row, 1961), pp. 94–100.
*Hippolytus, *Ref.* v.26.1–37; 27.4.

wrathful, double-minded, double-bodied, a virgin above and a viper below. She is called Eden and Israel. These are the principles of the universe, the roots and springs from which everything came; there was nothing else.

When the Father, without foreknowledge, saw that half-virgin Eden, he came to a desire for her (this Father is called Elohim); Eden desired Elohim no less, and desire brought them into a single union of love. From such a union the father begot twelve angels for himself by Eden. The names of the paternal angels are these: Michael, Amen, Baruch, Gabriel, Esaddaeus . . . [seven names lost]. And, similarly, the names of the maternal angels which Eden made are listed; they are these: Babel, Achamoth, Naas, Bel, Belias, Satan, Sael, Adonaios, Kauithan, Pharaoth, Karkamenos, Lathen. Of these twenty-four angels, the paternal ones side with the Father and act entirely according to his will, the maternal ones with the mother, Eden. The total of all the angels together in Paradise, concerning which Moses says, "God planted Paradise in Eden to the east" [Gen. 2:8], that is, before the face of Eden, so that Eden might always see Paradise, that is, the angels. The angels of this Paradise are allegorically called trees, and the Tree of Life is the third of the paternal angels, Baruch, while the Tree of Knowledge of good and evil is the third of the material angels, Naas. Moses spoke these things covertly because not all hold the truth [cf. Matt. 19:11].

After Paradise came into existence from the mutual satisfaction of Elohim and Eden, the angels of Elohim took some of the most excellent earth, that is, not from the bestial part of Eden but from the upper, anthropoid parts, the civilized regions of earth, and made man [cf. Gen. 2:7]. From the bestial parts came wild beasts and the other animals. They made man, then, as a symbol of their unity and love and they gave him shares of their own powers; Eden provided the soul and Elohim the spirit.

And man, the Adam, became a kind of seal and memorial of their love and an eternal symbol of the marriage of Eden and Elohim. Similarly, as it was written by Moses, Eve became an image and a symbol, a seal of Eden to be kept forever; and similarly, the soul was set in the image, Eve, by Eden and the spirit by Elohim. And commandments were given them: "Increase and multiply and inherit the earth," that is, Eden. For Eden contributed all her power to Elohim, like a dowry in marriage. Therefore, in imitation of that first marriage, to this very day women present dowries to their husbands, in obedience to that divine and hereditary law which Eden obeyed in regard to Elohim.

When everything had been created, as it was written in the book of Moses, Heaven and earth and the things in them, the twelve angels of the mother were divided "into four principles" [Gen. 2:10], and each quadrant of these is called a river—Phison, Geon, Tigris, and Euphrates, as Moses says. These twelve angels, closely embraced in four parts, circle around and govern the universe, having a satrapic authority over the world derived from Eden. They do not always remain in the same places, but circle around as in a circular chorus, changing from place to place and at various times and intervals, giving up the places assigned them. When Phison is in control of places, then famine, distress, and tribulation occurs in that part of the earth; for the injunction of these angels is niggardly. Similarly, there are evil times and formations of diseases in each part of the four in accordance with the power and nature of each. This torrent of evil, in accordance with the rivers, that is, the control of the various quadrants, circles ceaselessly around the universe by the wish of Eden.

The necessity of evil is due to this cause. When Elohim had fashioned and framed the universe out of mutual satisfaction, he wished to ascend to the highest parts of Heaven and to see if anything was lacking in the creation. He took his own angels with him, for he was by nature borne upwards. He left Eden below, for being earth, she did not wish to follow her husband upwards. When Elohim came to the upper limit of Heaven and saw a light greater than the one he had fashioned, he said, "Open the gates for me so that I may enter and acknowledge the Lord [Ps. 118:19]; for I thought that I was the Lord." A voice from the light was given him; it said, "This is the gate of the Lord; the just enter through it" [Ps. 118:20]. The gate was immediately opened, and the Father—without his angels—went into the Good and saw "what eye has not seen or ear heard, and what has not entered the heart of man." Then the Good said to him, "Sit at my right hand" [Ps. 110:1]. The Father said to the Good, "Lord, let me destroy the universe which I made; for my spirit is imprisoned among men and I wish to take it back" [cf. Gen. 6:3]. Then the Good said to him, "Nothing which comes from me can be evil; you and Eden made the universe from mutual satisfaction; let Eden have the creation as long as she wants it; you stay with me" [cf. John 21:22]. Then Eden, knowing that she had been adandoned by Elohim, in grief set her angels about her and adorned herself attractively [cf. Gen. 2:1], so that somehow Elohim might come to desire her and return to her. Under the control of the Good, however, Elohim no longer descended to Eden. Then Eden commanded Babel [Aphrodite] to fashion adulteries and divorces among men, so that just as she herself was separated from Elohim, so the spirit of Elohim in men might be grieved and tormented and experience the same sufferings as did the abandoned Eden. And Eden gave great authority to her third angel, Naas, so that he could torture the spirit of Elohim in men with all possible torments, and so that through the spirit Elohim might be tortured, he who had abandoned his wife in violation of the covenant he had made with his wife.

When the Father Elohim saw these things he sent forth Baruch, his own third angel, to help the spirit which is in all men. When Baruch came, he stood in the midst of the angels of Eden, that is, in the midst of Paradise [Gen. 2:9]—Paradise means the angels, in whose midst he stood—and commanded men "to eat from every tree in Paradise, but not to eat from that of the knowledge of good and evil" [Gen. 2:16–17]. This tree is Naas. He could obey the other eleven angels of Eden, for they have passions but not transgression of the commandment; Naas had transgression, for he approached Eve and seduced her and debauched her and he also approached Adam and used him as a boy. This was the origin of adultery and pederasty. From this time, evil and good things have ruled over men. They originated from a single source, for when the Father ascended to the Good he showed the way for those who wish to ascend, and by departing from Eden he made the origin of evils for the spirit of the Father in men.

Baruch was sent to Moses, and through him spoke to the sons of Israel so that they would return to the Good; but the third angel of Eden, Naas, through the soul given by Eden and dwelling in Moses, as in all men, overshadowed the commandments of Baruch and made his own commandments heard. For this reason, the soul was set against the spirit and the spirit against the soul. For the soul is Eden, while the spirit is Elohim; and each is in all, both female and male.

After that Baruch was sent again to the prophets, so that through the prophets the spirit dwelling in men might hear and flee from Eden and the evil creation as the Father Elohim fled. And similarly, by the same idea, through the soul dwelling in man with the spirit of the Father, Naas beguiled the prophets, and they were all beguiled and did not follow the words of Baruch, which Elohim commanded.

Finally, Elohim chose a prophet from the uncircumcision, Heracles, and sent him to contend with the twelve angels of Eden and to free the spirit of the Father from the twelve evil angels of the creation. These are the twelve labors of Heracles in which Heracles contended in order, from the first to the last, the lion and the hydra and the boar and the rest; for these are the names of the nations which they were given from the power of the maternal angels. As he seemed to have been victorious, Omphale [Babel-Aphrodite] attacked him and seduced him and took off his power, the commandments of Baruch while Elohim commanded, and put on him her own robe, the power of Eden, which is the power from below. Thus the prophecy of Heracles and his works became ineffectual.

Finally "in the days of king Herod" [Luke 1:5], Baruch was sent again by Elohim, and he came to Nazareth [Luke 1:26] and found Jesus, the son of Joseph and Mary, feeding sheep, a boy of twelve years [Luke 2:42], and he told him everything which had taken place from the beginning, from Eden and Elohim and everything which will take place after this. He said, "All the prophets before you were seduced; but, Jesus, son of man, try not to be seduced but proclaim this message to men and tell them about the Father and about the Good and ascend to the Good and sit there with Elohim, the Father of us all." And Jesus obeyed the angel; he said, "Lord, I will do all things," and he made the proclamation. Naas wished to seduce him too, but he was not able to do so for Jesus remained faithful to Baruch. Then Naas became angry because he could not seduce him, and had him crucified. He left his body to Eden by the tree and ascended to the Good. For he said to Eden, "Woman, you have your son" [John 19: 26], that is, the psychical and earthly man, but he was "placing in the hands" the spirit of the Father [cf. Luke 23:46] and ascended to the Good.

The Good is Priapus, who created before there was anything; he is called Priapus because he prefabricated everything. For this reason he is erected in every temple, is honored by all creation, and before him on the roads carries fruits, that is, the fruits of creation, of which he was the cause, prefabricating the creation before there was any.

Therefore, when you hear men say that the swan came upon Leda and produced offspring from her, the swan is Elohim and Leda is Eden. When men say that the eagle came upon Ganymede, the eagle is Naas and Ganymede is Adam. And when they say that the gold came upon Danae and brought forth a child from her, the gold is Elohim and Danae is Eden.

When the prophets say, "Hear, Heaven, and give ear, earth; the Lord has spoken" [Isa. 1:2], Heaven means the spirit of Elohim in men, earth the soul in man with the spirit, the Lord Baruch, Israel Eden; for the wife of Elohim is called Eden and Israel. "Israel did not know me" [Isa. 1:3]; for if it had known that I am with the Good, it would not have tortured the spirit which is in men because of the Father's ignorance.

When the prophet says "to take for himself a woman of fornication because the earth has fornicated from behind the Lord" [Hos. 1:2], that is, Eden from Elohim, in these words the prophet clearly expressed the whole mystery, but he was not heard because of the wickedness of Naas.

Marcion

Marcion of Sinope in Pontus was even more troubling to the early Christians than Simon Magus. Simon was easily cast into the role of apostate, archheretic, and pseudomessiah, a magician who was neither Jew nor Christian. But Marcion, born near the Black Sea (Pontus) at the end of the first century, was the most Christian of the Gnostics, and, with uncompromising logic, considered himself the true Christian. In fact he was such a challenge to the new religion of Jesus Christ that, by reaction, he is said to have been the initial cause for the orthodox to establish, among their gospels and diverse letters and acts, a New Testament canon. He himself rejected the Old Testament and kept from the New Testament only an expurgated Luke and parts of the ten Pauline letters. Moreover, he was vigorously opposed to the early Christian practice of allegorical readings of the Old Testament to bring it into accord with Christian belief. Here he sided with those Jews who read the Scriptures literally, for the Old Testament was correct. It represented the work of the world-Creator and it was precisely this "just" God of "law," worshiped by Jew and Christian, whom he rejected.

It was Marcion's rejection of the biblical God in favor of the unknown, alien "Good God" that put him in the Gnostic camp. In other ways he was not at all a Gnostic. His belief derived, he claimed, from a literal reading of the Scriptures, a correct reading, and his belief was based on faith rather than understanding *(gnosis)*. In this recourse to faith he differed radically from other Gnostics. He offered his faithful no mystical illumination of the Spirit. Rather, he promised future bliss of the soul (and no hope for the body, which Irenaeus considered blasphemy) through the intervention of Jesus Christ, the son of the Alien God.

For Marcion the notion of alienation is total. While in other Gnostic speculations the Demiurge or biblical God who made the world has a geneaological connection with the Father of All, in Marcion's system the biblical God has nothing to do with the alien Good God. The former is a divinity in his own right and his messiah will come to bring earthly salvation to his people, but that salvation of the "just" God was restricted to the earth. Since the earth is not worth much—indeed, it is a prison—salvation here only strengthens the cause of the "just" God whom Marcion completely opposes. As for the earth's inhabitants, they are created by the biblical God without a spark of Spirit (*pneuma*), and so their eventual salvation by the Good God will not, as in other Gnostic beliefs, contribute to the eventual redemption of the biblical God.

What then does the Good God represent? First we should say what he is not. He is not concerned with anything on earth in a daily way; that is, he has not determined the events of the world, he is not an original cause, and so we have to discard the notion of divine determination or divine providence. The Alien God affected the cosmos in only one way: by sending down his son to redeem us and to save us from the Jewish-Christian God of creation:

> Man, this work of the creator-God, that better God chose to love, and for his sake he labored to descend from the third heaven into these miserable elements, and on his account he even was crucified in this puny cell of the creator. (Tertullian, *Contra Marc.* V.16)

Many of the fragments with Marcion's message are concerned with the two gods: the unknown God and the known biblical God from whom one must free oneself. Although Marcion was vehemently opposed to the biblical God, he was willing to let him have his way on earth, since things on earth have no importance. The body is worth nothing, nor is human life. His opposition to marriage and his ascetic morality are not based on opposition to sexual urges but rather a hostility to procreation. While the Christians condoned sexual intercourse only when its end was to produce another human being, Marcion was opposed not to the sexual act for itself, but precisely for its end of human procreation, which would further the work of the Creator God. Hans Jonas writes:

> Marcion here voices a genuine and typical *gnostic* argument, whose fullest elaboration we shall meet in Mani: that the reproductive scheme is an ingenious archontic device for the indefinite retention of souls in the world. Thus Marcion's asceticism, unlike that of the Essenes or later of Christian monasticism, was not conceived to further the sanctification of human existence, but was essentially negative in conception and part of the gnostic revolt against the cosmos.[1]

The anger of early Christians against rival Gnostics was multiple. Irenaeus was offended at Marcion because he had the arrogance to call himself an apostle as well as to discount the credentials of the other apostles apart from Paul. Not only did he reject most of the New Testament but, in effect, he authored his own gospel, although he would have denied that his writing constituted a gospel since only the Good God can author authentic scripture. Thus even the Gospel of

Luke is really not by Luke, since the authentic—as opposed to the spurious Luke—was written by God. But Marcion's main offensive gesture was his Gnostic belief in another, higher God. Ultimately he was excommunicated in Rome for his views in A.D. 144, the date Marcionites asserted for the foundation of their own church for which Marcion was condemned furiously. He succeeded in expanding it to the point that its theology spread through the Roman empire and Mesopotamia, Armenia, and the Orient, which caused Justin to place him with Simon Magus and Menander as among the dangerous heretics. He died about A.D. 160.

There is a fundamental irony in the Gnostics' ire against the Cosmocrator for having made the world, since their own contribution lies in part in the divine figures whom they created for the Gnostic hierarchy —at least thirty Aeons, to begin with, for the Pleroma. Marcion himself refrained from mythological creations. He proclaimed only one overriding, unknown divinity, the Good God, whom Cerdo had some years earlier also described:

> And a certain Cerdo, who got his inspiration from the Simonians, came to Rome under Hyginus . . . and taught that the God proclaimed by the law and the prophets is not the Father of Our Lord Jesus Christ. The God (of the Old Testament) is known, but the latter (the Father of Jesus Christ) is unknown. The one is just, but the other is good. (Iren. *Adv. haer.* I.27.1)

The Good God, whom Cerdo spoke of, did not have even an indirect hand in making the world or shaping our souls. Even in our souls we are the product of the "just" God. The reliable emblem of truth was, of course, Marcion himself. Among the Gnostics Marcion was a fundamentalist, a literalist, free of the syncretic views common to Gnosticism, and free of mystical fire. His view of the world was totally negative, for the world is the product of its Creator. He held out but one straw to the drowning: redemption through Jesus who intervened in human affairs for his father, the Alien God, whose generous gift of salvation derives solely from gratuitous goodness.

Note

1. Hans Jonas, *The Gnostic Religion*, 2d ed. rev., with Note on 3d printing (1958; reprint, Boston: Beacon Press, 1980), p. 145.

MARCION*

Marcion of Pontus succeeded Cerdo and developed his doctrine, shamelessly blaspheming him who was proclaimed God by the law and the prophets. He called himself the Author of Evil, desirous of war, shifty of purpose, and guilty of self-contradiction. Jesus came to Judaea from the Father, who is above the God who made the world, at the time of the governor Pontius Pilate, who was the prefect of the Emperor Tiberius, and revealed himself to the inhabitants of Judaea in the form of a man. He destroyed

*Irenaeus, *Adv. haer.* I.27.2–3. From Robert Haardt, *Gnosis* (Leiden: Brill, 1971), pp. 64–65.

the law and the prophets and all the works of that God who made the world, whom Marcion calls also "Cosmocrator." Furthermore, he pruned the Gospel according to Luke and removed everything relating to the origin of the Lord, as well as erasing a great deal concerning the teaching of the statements of the Lord, in which he clearly and openly acknowledges the Creator of this Universe as his Father, and in Scripture is called Lord. Marcion convinced his disciples that he himself was more deserving of belief than the apostles who handed down the Gospel, whereas he handed down not the Gospel, but a small section of it. In a similar way he abridged the epistles of the Apostle Paul, expurgating everything said by the apostle concerning the God who made the world—the latter being the Father of our Lord Jesus Christ—and also everything taught by the apostle by citation from the prophecies foretelling the coming of Our Lord.

Only souls which have learnt his doctrine will attain salvation, according to him: the body however cannot possibly participate in salvation, since it came from the earth. To this blasphemy against God, he adds the following story, in which he becomes the proper mouthpiece of the Devil and countermands the truth in every detail: Cain and his kin, the Sodomites, the Egyptians, and those like them, and in general all heathens who have walked in every aspect of evil, were saved by the Lord when he descended into Hades, and hastened to him, and were taken into his kingdom.

But Abel, Enoch, Noah, and the rest of the righteous, and those with the patriarch Abraham, along with all the prophets and those who pleased God, did not participate in salvation, as announced by the serpent in Marcion. For since they knew that their God was always testing and tempting them, he says, they suspected that he was also testing them at that time, and did not hasten to Jesus nor believe his proclamation; and therefore their souls remained in Hades, by his doctrine.

Carpocrates

Carpocrates was the scapegoat of the Gnostics because of his acceptance of promiscuity. This condolence of the flesh made him heinous to Christian orthodoxy and he was a favorite target of abuses directed against the Gnostics. In condemning Carpocrates' attitude toward the flesh, the orthodox distorted the philosophy and intention of the Carpocratians. It was not because they extolled the flesh, but rather because, in good Gnostic tradition, the body was so unimportant compared to the soul that it mattered little what one did with it. To be free of it, to transcend it, one must first experience it. In Hindu thought there is also the notion that to go beyond mere body one must abuse and control it. This universal notion also appears in Arthur Rimbaud's "derangement of the senses" to find God, not to mention standard Christian flagellation, a negative way to bypass awareness of the flesh.

Carpocrates, who is thought to have lived under Hadrian's reign (A.D. 117–38), countered Christian thought by saying that Joseph begat Jesus. (In other Gnostic sects where we have more information, we find that Jesus is initially considered an earthly man, with no divine qualities; and only later does the divine Christ, the Son of Man, that is the Son of the First Man, the Father of All, join with earthly Jesus either on the cross or at some other time.) To become greater than Jesus one must despise earthly things more than Jesus did. Yet, despite this advice, Carpocrates also suggested that people must experience every human experience (too terrible to mention, Irenaeus says) in order to free themselves of that experience and so they "will not be forced into another body, if something is still lacking in their freedom." Further, the Carpocratians say that the body is a prison and one must pay it its dues, its "last quadrant," in order to be saved. Souls which participate in all sins on earth will have paid their debts and will not be reincarnated in another body. Irenaeus then accuses the Carpocratians of imputing, through Mark, a secret language to Jesus and his disciples: "Jesus spoke in a mystery privately to his disciples and apostles (Mark 4:10–11)." To use a secret language for purposes of exegesis is a common linguistic practice, and is actually a characteristic embedded in virtually all religious texts. Conflict arises, as in the case of Irenaeus and the Carpocratians, in the matter of deciphering the secret language, of moving from a literal to an allegorical interpretation.

In the end Carpocrates said "nothing is evil by nature." Irenaeus connects this Gnostic sect with worldly Pagans such as Pythagoras, Plato, and Aristotle, clearly suggesting a Greek philosophical background to Gnostic ideas. He also speaks of a leader, Marcellina, who went to Rome to lead "many astray."

The second document we possess is by Epiphanes, Carpocrates' son. According to Clement's synopsis, God made all things in nature to be common property; the sun and stars shine on rich and poor alike, on male and female, on human beings and animals. Therefore we can share one woman, as the animals show us. Promiscuity is natural. He argues against the logic of God's interdictions, citing God himself as the source of our desire which preserves the race:

> With a view to the permanence of the race, he has implanted in males a strong and ardent desire which neither law nor custom nor any other restraint is able to destroy. For it is God's decree. . . . Consequently one must understand the saying "Thou shalt not desire" as if the lawgiver was making a jest, to which he added the even more comic words "thy neighbor's goods" [Exod. 20:17]. For he himself who gave the desire to sustain the race orders that it is to be suppressed, though he removes it from no other animals. And by the words "thy neighbor's wife" he says something even more ludicrous, since he forces what should be common property to be treated as a private possession.

There is no sect which more fully embodies, at its radical and logical extreme, the notions and values of the sharing of common property and of sexual freedom. It evokes the proclaimed ideals of pioneer communist tracts or the practices of other recent utopian communes. But for the Carpocratians, behind the sharing of material goods and sexual pleasures is the paradoxical philosophy of the utter worthlessness of such matter and the need to exhaust and transcend such things of this world. Not to do so, not to "despise and transgress all laws"[1] [of the biblical Creator God] is to make oneself subject to his powers, to suffer reincarnation, and to remove oneself from return to the true "unknown Father."

Note

1. Werner Foerster, *Gnosis: A Selection of Gnostic Texts*, vol. 1, trans. R. McL. Wilson (Oxford: Oxford University Press, 1972), p. 34.

CARPOCRATES*

Carpocrates says that the universe and its contents were made by angels much inferior to the unbegotten Father, but that Jesus was begotten by Joseph and, having come into existence like other men, became more righteous than the rest. When his soul became vigorous and pure it remembered what it had seen in its circuit [Plato, *Phaedrus* 248A] with the unbegotten God, and therefore power was sent it by him so that it could escape the world-creators by means of it and so that by passing through all, free among them all, it might come to him, similarly accepting what was like it. They say that the soul of Jesus was brought up lawfully in Jewish customs but despised them and therefore received powers through which it annihilated the passions which are attached to men and punish them. The soul which, like the soul of Christ, is able to despise the world-creating Archons will similarly receive power to do similar things. For this reason they have reached such a state of pride that they say they are like Jesus himself; but some say that they are even more powerful, and others say that they surpass his disciples, such as Peter and Paul and the rest of the apostles; they fall short of Jesus in no respect. Their souls, having come from the Authority above, and therefore similarly despising the world-creators, were deemed worthy of the same power and worthy to attain the same end. If anyone despises things below more than Jesus did, he can become greater than he was.

They practice magic arts and incantations, charms and spells, familiar spirits and dream-senders, and all other wicked activities, saying that they have power to rule over the rulers and makers of this world and also over all that they created. Like the Gentiles, they were driven by

*From Robert M. Grant, *Gnosticism* (New York: Harper & Brothers, 1961), pp. 36–40.

Satan to slander the divine name of the Church so that men who hear of their actions of one sort or another suppose that we are all of the same kind and turn their ears away from the proclamation of the truth. Seeing what they do, men blaspheme all of us, through we participate with them in nothing—doctrine, practice, daily life. But they lead a luxurious life and have an irreligious outlook; they misuse our name as a cloak for their wickedness [cf. 1 Pet. 2:16]; "their condemnation is just" [Rom. 3:8], and they receive from God a retribution worthy of their works.

They have reached such a pitch of madness that they say that it is in their power to do whatever is irreligious and impious, for they say that actions are good and bad only in accordance with human opinion. In the transmigrations into bodies, souls ought to experience every kind of life and action, if in a single life on earth any one of them has not first taken care to experience everything once for all and in equal completeness, actions such as it is not right for us to mention or to hear or even to have in mind, or to believe that any such thing is considered among men who live in the civilized world, so that, according to what their writings say, their souls, which have been involved in every experience, may not, when they depart, still suffer any lack. They must act in such a way that they will not be forced into another body if something is still lacking in their freedom.

For this reason, they say, Jesus told this parable: "When you are with your adversary on the way, act so that you may be freed from him, lest he deliver you to the judge and the judge to the officer and he cast you into prison; truly I say to you, you will not come out from there until you pay the last quadrant" [Luke 12:58–59; Matt. 5:25–26]. They say that the "adversary" is one of the angels who are in the world; they call him the Devil and they say that he was made in order to lead souls which have perished from the world to the "prince." They say that he is the first of the world-makers, and that he "delivers" such souls to another angel, who is his "officer," in order to enclose them in other bodies. They call the body a "prison" [cf. Plato, *Cratylus* 400C]. And the saying, "You will not come out from there until you pay the last quadrant," they explain as meaning that no one leaves the power of those angels who made the world; souls are always made reincarnate until they have completed all sins; when nothing is lacking, then the freed soul departs to [cf. Luke 12:58] the God above the world-creating angels, and thus all souls will be saved. The souls which in a single life on earth manage to participate in all sins will no longer become reincarnate but, having paid all their "debts," will be freed so that they no longer come to be in a body.

And if godless, unlawful, and unspeakable things are done by them, I should not believe them. But in their writings it is written, and they provide exegesis to prove, that Jesus spoke in a mystery privately to his disciples and apostles [Mark 4:10–11] and judged them worthy to transmit these things to those who were worthy and who believed them. For through faith and love [cf. Gal. 5:6] we are saved; all else is indifferent, after the opinion of men, and is sometimes considered good, sometimes bad. Nothing is evil by nature.

Some of them cauterize their disciples behind the lobe of the right ear. When Marcellina came to Rome under Anicetus, since she belonged to this school she led many astray. They call themselves Gnostics. They have images, some painted, some made of other materials, and they say that their picture of Christ was made by Pilate when Jesus was among men. They put crowns on these and place them with images of worldly philosophers like Pythagoras and Plato and Aristotle and the others; and the rest of their veneration of the images is like that of the Gentiles.

EPIPHANES, CONCERNING RIGHTEOUSNESS (JUSTICE)

The "righteousness" [justice] of God is a kind of sharing along with equality. There is equality in the heaven which is stretched out in all directions and contains the entire earth in its circle. The night reveals all the stars equally. The light of the sun, which is the cause of the daytime and the father of light, God pours out from above [cf. James 1:17] upon the earth in equal measure to all who have power to see. For all see alike, since here is no distinction between rich and poor, people and governor, stupid and clever, female and male, free men and slaves. Even the irrational animals are not accorded any different treatment; but in just the same way God pours out from above sunlight equally upon all the animals. He establishes his justice to both good and bad by seeing that none is able to get more than his share and to deprive his neighbor, so that he has twice the light his neighbor has. The sun causes food to grow for all living beings alike; the universal justice is given to all equally. In this respect there is no difference between the species of oxen and particular oxen, between the species of pigs and particular pigs, between the species of sheep and particular sheep, and so on with all the rest. In them universality is manifest as justice. Furthermore all plants "after their kind" are sown equally in the earth. Common nourishment grows for all beasts which feed on the earth's produce; to all it is alike. It is regulated by no law, but rather is harmoniously available to all through the gift of him who gave it and commanded it to grow [Gen. 1:11–12, 22].

And for birth there is no written law; otherwise it would have been transcribed. All beings beget and give birth alike, having received by justice an innate equality. The Creator and Father of all with his own justice appointed this, just as he gave equally the eye to all to enable them to see. He did not make a distinction between female and male, rational and irrational, nor between anything and anything else at all; rather he shared out sight equally and universally. It was given to all alike by a single command.

As the laws could not punish men who were ignorant of them, they taught men to transgress [cf. Gal. 4:19]. For particularity of the laws cut up and destroyed the universal equality of the divine law. . . .

The ideas of Mine and Thine crept in [cf. Gal. 2:4] through the laws which cause the earth, money, and even marriage no longer to bring forth fruit for common use. For God made vines for all to use in common, since they do not refuse the sparrow or the thief; and similarly wheat and the other fruits. But outlawed sharing and the vestiges of equality generated the thief of domestic animals and fruits.

For man God made all things to be common property. He brought the female to be with the male in common and in the same way united all the animals. He thus showed "righteousness" to be a universal sharing along with equality. But those who have been born in this way have denied the sharing which is the corollary of their origin and say, "Let him who has taken one woman keep her," whereas all can share her, just as the other animals show us.

With a view to the permanence of the race, he has implanted in males a strong and ardent desire which neither law nor custom nor any other restraint is able to destroy. For it is God's decree. . . . Consequently one must understand the saying "You shall not desire" as if the lawgiver was making a jest, to which he added the even more comic words "your neighbor's goods" [Exod. 20:17]. For he himself who gave the desire to sustain the race orders that it is to be suppressed, though he removes it from no other animals. And by the words "your neighbor's wife" he says something even more ludicrous, since he forces what should be common property to be treated as a private possession [Clement, *Strom.* iii. 6–9].

*The Cainites**

The picture of the Cainites, with their gallery of underdogs, outcasts, and "wicked" figures of the Old and New Testaments, suggests either slander on the part of Irenaeus, or, more likely, the depiction of a Gnostic sect whose very existence demanded a rejection of all conventional taboos. Although we do not possess their gospel and so have no record of most of their beliefs, the main reason for their rejections, as in other Gnostic sects, was their undermining the Creator God's works and particularly the sacred personages of his own book, the Bible. The Cainites even rejected Jesus in favor of Judas, claiming that Jesus came to distort the truth and Judas acted to avert that transgression. All these negations were presumably a premise to belief in the true Father of All. Following this line, Marcion went so far as to have Christ descend into Hell and leave there, unsaved, Abel, Enoch, Noah, Abraham, and the other prophets and patriarchs, and to raise the Sodomites, the Egyptians, and Cain. The "great" figures of the Bible had served the Creator God and therefore should remain in Hell. The Cainites were outrageous rebels against orthodoxy. They took their very name from their polemical opposition to established religious thought and practices.

THE CAINITES

Irenaeus, Adv. Haer. *I 31, 1–2*
1. Others again say that Cain was from the superior power, and confess Esau and (the tribe of) Korah and the Sodomites and all such as their kinsmen. They were attacked by the creator, but none of them suffered any ill. For Sophia snatched away from them to herself what belonged to her. This Judas the traitor knew very well, and he alone of

*From Werner Foerster, *Gnosis: A Selection of Gnostic Texts*, vol. 1, trans. R. McL. Wilson (Oxford: Oxford University Press, 1972), pp. 41–43.

all the apostles recognized the truth and accomplished the mystery of the betrayal, by which everything earthly and heavenly is dissolved, as they say. And they produce a fabrication, which they call the Gospel of Judas.

2. I have also collected writings of theirs, in which they urge the destruction of the works of Hystera (the womb); Hystera is the name they give to the fabricator of heaven and earth. And they say they cannot be saved in any other way, except they pass through all things, just as Carpocrates also said. And at every sinful and base action an angel is present and instils in him who ventures the deed audacity and impurity; what it is in act they say in the angel's name: "O thou angel, I make use of thy work; O thou power, I accomplish thy deed." And this is the perfect "knowledge," to enter without fear into such operations, which it is not lawful even to name.

Tertullian, Adv. Omn. Haer. 2
There also broke out another heresy, called that of the Cainites. For they glorify Cain, as if conceived by some potent power which operated in him. Abel was conceived and brought forth by an inferior power, and was therefore found to be inferior. Those who assert this also defend Judas the traitor, saying that he was admirable and great because of the benefits which he is claimed to have brought to the human race. For some of them think that thanksgiving should be rendered to Judas for this reason. "For

Judas," they say, "observing that Christ wanted to subvert the truth, betrayed him that the truth might not be overthrown." Others dispute this, saying: "Since the powers of this world did not wish Christ to suffer, that salvation might not be provided for the human race through his death, he betrayed Christ out of concern for the salvation of mankind, in order that the salvation which was being hindered by the powers opposed to the suffering of Christ might not be prevented altogether, and therefore through the passion of Christ the salvation of the human race might not be delayed."

Epiphanius, Panarion XXXVIII 2, 4f.
4. There came also into our hands a book in which they formulated certain things full of lawlessness, including the following: "This," he says, "is the angel who blinded Moses, and these are the angels who hid those about Korah and Dathan and Abiram (Num. 16) and brought them to another place."

5. Again they fabricate another little book in the name of Paul the Apostle, full of things unspeakable, which the so-called Gnostics use, which they call the Ascent of Paul; the pretext (for so calling it) they find in the fact that the Apostle says he ascended into the third heaven and heard ineffable words, which it is not permissible for a man to speak (2 Cor. 12:4). And these, they say, are the ineffable words.

The Sethians*

The words of the Sethians are among the most elusive and symbolic in the Gnostic creation stories. The Sethians, Hippolytus tells us, divided the universe into three principles, each with an infinite force: light, pneuma (spirit), and darkness. Each force was endowed with thought and reason. As the forces clashed, different organisms arose, each with a different image. Out of the first clash arose Heaven and earth, shaped like a maternal womb. To find the exact form of Heaven or earth, we are told to examine the womb of any pregnant creature. The pneuma (spirit) was spread among all creatures under Heaven. Then God, the perfect Father, sent down *nous* (mind) from light and pneuma into these creatures to give them strength to liberate themselves from the darkness and from human bodies, and to save the *nous* and the spirit from death and evil, from the Father below (the biblical Creator God) who is wind, a fierce, roaring, destructive wind. Finally, the Perfect Man, the logos, enters the repulsive mysteries of the Virgin's womb. The passage ends before we know whether the logos produces a redemptive Jesus, but we may assume this to be so. The fragment ends with a promise of salvation, for those who drink the sparkling water, who put off the form of a servant (servant of the biblical God), and choose a truly heavenly garment.

In Epiphanius we have a different account of the Sethians, although the triadic structures of Cain, Abel and Seth and light, darkness and pure spirit remain. This description deals with the Mother who gives birth to Seth, the perfect one. His seed must be preserved, amid the sin of preflood times and the cunning of conspiring angels, in order that Christ of the true Father appear.

---

*From Werner Foerster, *Gnosis: A Selection of Gnostic Texts*, vol. 1, trans. R. McL. Wilson (Oxford: Oxford University Press, 1972), pp. 296–298, 300–305.

THE SETHIANS

Hippolytus, v. 19, 1–22, I.

Let us now see what the Sethians say. They think that the universe has three clearly defined principles, and each principle has an infinite number of powers. When they speak of "powers" the listener may reckon that their meaning is this: everything that you conceive by thinking, or fail to conceive and ignore, is something that each principle is naturally able to become, as is the case in the human soul with every single art that is taught; for example, he says, this child will become a flute-player if he spends time with a flute-player, or a geometer, if he attends a geometer, a grammarian, if a grammarian, a mason, if a mason; and the like will happen with any of the other arts if he has contact with them. But the essential natures of the principles, he says, are light and darkness; and in between these is a pure spirit. But the spirit, which is placed in between the darkness which is below and the light which is above, is not a spirit like a puff of wind or a gentle breeze that can be observed, but it is like a scent of myrrh or of compounded incense, a subtle power which penetrates with inconceivable fragrance better than words can describe. But since the light is above and the darkness below, and between them, as I said, the spirit which is of this kind, and since the light, like a ray of the sun, was such as to shine from above on the darkness below, and again the fragrance of the spirit, which is situated between them, extends and diffuses everywhere, just as we have experienced the fragrance of incense-offerings on the fire diffusing everywhere—since this is the power of the elements divided into three, the power of the spirit and of the light is present together in the darkness that is situated below them. But the darkness is a dreadful water, into which the light, together with the spirit, is drawn down and transferred into this element. Now the darkness is not without intelligence, but cunning in all respects, and it knows that if the light is taken away from the darkness, the darkness remains deserted, dark, without light, without power, inert, and feeble. So it exerts itself with all its cunning and intelligence to keep in its possession the brilliance and the spark of light with the fragrance of the spirit.

A natural image of all this can be seen in the human face: the pupil of the eye, which is dark from the waters that underlie it, but illuminated by the spirit. So as the darkness seeks to possess the brilliant light, so that it may have the spark of light at its service and be able to see, in the same way the light and the spirit seek to possess their own power; and they hasten to remove and recover for themselves their own powers that have been mingled with the dark and dreadful water that lies beneath. And all the powers of the three principles, which are infinitely infinite in number, are each of them rational and intelligent as regards their own essential nature. And being innumerable in quantity and rational and intelligent, when they remain by themselves they all are at rest; but if one power approaches another, the unlikeness of the contact produces a movement and an energy which takes its form from the movement according to the impact of the converging powers. For the impact of the powers takes place like the stamp of a seal which is struck out by impact so as to resemble the man who (or, "stamp which") stamps out the substances presented. So since the powers of the three principles are infinite in number, and innumerable impacts result from the innumerable powers, there have necessarily come into being the images of innumerable seals. These images are the forms ("ideas") of the different living creatures. So from the first great impact of the three principles there has come a great form of a seal, namely that of heaven and earth. Heaven and earth are shaped like a womb having the navel in the middle. And, he says, if anyone wishes to visualize this shape, let him carefully examine a pregnant womb belonging to any animal he wishes, and he will find the design of heaven and earth and everything in between exactly laid out. Now the shape of heaven and earth came to resemble a womb at the first impact; but further, in between heaven and earth innumerable impacts of powers have occurred; and each impact produced and stamped out nothing else but the seal of heaven and earth resembling a womb; and in it there sprang to life, from the innumerable different seals, the innumerable multitudes of living creatures. And into all this infinite number which exists under heaven in the different living creatures there is inseminated and distributed, together with the light, the fragrance of the spirit.

Now from the water there has come, as a first derivative principle, a fierce and violent wind which is the cause of all generation. For by making a turbulence in the waters it raises swelling waves from them; and the generation of the waves, as if it were some urge to swell in pregnancy, is the origin of man or of the mind, whenever it is stirred to excitement by the urging of the spirit. But when this swelling wave, which is aroused from the water by the wind and made nature swell in pregnancy, receives in itself the offspring of a female being, it holds fast the light which is inseminated from above with the fragrance of the spirit; and this is the mind which takes form in its different patterns. And it is a perfect god, brought down from the unbegotten light above and from the spirit, and put into human nature as into a temple which is begotten from water by the impulse of nature and by the movement of the wind, and which is compounded and intermingled with bodies, being like salt among changing things and like light in darkness, which impatiently seeks to be freed from its bodies and cannot find its release or its

escape. For a tiny spark, a detached fragment from the ray of light from above, is intermingled in the variously compounded bodies, and calls out of many waters as—he says—it is said in the Psalms [29 (28):3]. So the whole thought and care of the light from above is, how and by what means the mind may be freed from the death of the wicked and benighted body, and from the father who is below, who is the wind which in roaring confusion stirred up swelling waves and begot perfect mind as his son, although it is not his own son in its essential nature. For there was a ray coming from above from that perfect light held fast in the dark, dreadful, bitter, filthy water, which is the spirit of light "rushing" over the water (Gen. 1:2) . . . as can be seen with all living creatures. But the violent and dreadful rush of wind sweeps along like a serpent, borne on wings. From this wind, that is, from the serpent, has come the beginning of generation in the aforesaid manner, when all beings received the beginning of their generation at the same time. Now since the light and the spirit, he says, are imprisoned in the unclean and hurtful womb of disorder, into which the serpent enters, the wind of darkness, the firstborn of the waters, and produces man, the unclean womb neither loves nor recognizes any other form.

So the perfect word of the light on high taking the likeness of that beast, the snake, entered into the unclean womb, deceiving it by his likeness with the beast, in order to undo the bonds which are laid upon the perfect mind which is begotten in the uncleanness of the womb by the firstborn of the water, by the serpent, the wind, the beast. This, he says, is the "form of a servant" [Phil. 2:7], and this is the reason that compelled the Word of God to come down into a virgin's womb. But, he says, it is not enough that the perfect man, the Word, entered a virgin's womb and "loosed the pangs" that were in that darkness; but after he entered into the foul mysteries of the womb he washed himself and drank the cup of living, springing water, which everyone must needs drink who is to put off the form of the servant and put on the heavenly apparel.

This, in brief, is what is said by the champions of the Sethian doctrines. . . . But they say that Moses too confirms their doctrine, when he speaks of "darkness and murk and storm" [Exod. 10:22; Deut. 5:22]—these, he says, are the three words; or when he says that there were three in paradise, Adam, Eve, and the serpent; or when he speaks of the three, Cain, Abel, and Seth, and again of three, Shem, Ham, Japheth [Gen. 6:10]; or when he speaks of three patriarchs, Abraham, Isaac, and Jacob; or when he says there were three days before the creation of the sun and moon [Gen. 1:5–13]; or when he speaks of three laws, the prohibitive, the permissive, and the punitive. A prohibitive law is "Of every tree in the garden Paradise you may freely eat, but of the Tree of Knowledge of Good and Evil you shall not eat" [Gen. 2:16f.]. When it says, "Go out from your land and from your family and come to a land which I will show you" [Gen. 12:1] this law, he says, is a permissive one; for the man who chooses can go out, the man who does not choose to, can remain. And a punitive law is the one which says, "Thou shalt not commit adultery, thou shalt not kill, thou shalt not steal" [Exod. 20:13–15]: for each of these misdeeds is assigned a penalty.

The whole content of their teaching comes from the ancient theologians, Musaeus, Linus, and Orpheus, who especially made known the rites and mysteries. . . . [In Phlius there is upon the gates an old man with wings, having his phallus erect, and a woman fleeing from him; the former is entitled *phaos rhyentes.*]

. . . They say that the name *phaos rhyentes* means the downward flow of light from above. . . . The threefold division seems to be confirmed by the poet, who says, "The whole is divided in three, each one partaking of honor" [Hom., *Il.* XV 189], meaning that each member of the threefold division has acquired power.

And the descent of the light into the underlying dark water here below, and the need to recover and take up from it the spark that was brought down, these things the ingenious Sethians seem to have borrowed from Homer, who says,

> Let earth be witness, and broad heaven above
> And the down-rushing stream of Styx, the oath
> Most great and dreadful for the blessed gods.
>
> (Hom., *Il.* XV 36-8.)

that is to say, the gods according to Homer think water to be something illomened and frightful, whereas the Sethians' doctrine says it is dreadful for *Nous*, the mind.

This and the like is what they say in innumerable books. And they persuade those who become their disciples to study the doctrine of infusion and mixture, which has been elaborated by many writers including Andronicus the Peripatetic. Now the Sethians say that the doctrine of infusion and mixture is constituted as follows: the ray of light has been infused from above and the tiny spark is finely intermixed with the dark waters below and united with them and turned into a single mass, like a single perfume arising from the many spices thrown upon the fire; and the expert, who has a keen sense of smell, must acutely distinguish from the single perfume each of the spices which are mixed together upon the fire, such as storax, myrrh, frankincense, or whatever else is mixed in. And they make use of other illustrations, saying that bronze is mixed with gold, and that a method has been invented for separating bronze from gold. Similarly if tin or bronze or the like is found to be mixed with silver, these too can be separated by a method which overcomes the mixture. Someone indeed actually separates water which is mixed with wine. In the same way, they say, everything that has been compounded is separated. Indeed, he says, you may realize this from animals. For when an animal is dead all its elements are separated, and at their parting the animal disappears. This, he says, is the saying, "I came not to bring peace on earth, but a sword" [Matt. 10:34], that is, to divide and put apart what is compounded. For everything that has been compounded is divided and separated, finding its own place. For just as there is a single place for all animals where they are compounded, so there is a single one fixed for their dissolution, which no one knows, he says, except only ourselves, the regenerate, who are spiritual, not carnal, whose "citizenship is in heaven" above [Phil. 3:20]. . . . For, he says, everything that is compounded, as aforesaid, has its own place and runs to its proper counterpart, as iron does to the magnet, or chaff that is near amber, or gold drawn by the sea-ray's sting. So the ray of light that is mixed with the water, when it receives its proper place by instruction and learning, presses towards the Word that came from above in the form of a servant, and with the Word becomes a Word in that place where the Word is, more than the iron does to the magnet. And to prove that this is so, and that all compounded things are separated in their proper places, attend to this: There is in Persia, in the city of Ampe on the Tigris, a well; and next to the well there is built up a cistern with three outlets from it. A man draws from the well with a bucket, raises what is drawn from the well, whatever it is, and pours it into the nearby cistern; and when what is poured in comes to the outlets, though it was drawn up in a single vessel, it is separated; and at one outlet rock-salt appears, at another outlet asphalt, and at the third oil. And the oil is black, as he says Herodotus reports, and gives off an acrid smell; and the Persians

call it rhadinace. This illustration of the well, say the Sethians, would suffice to prove their case better than anything that has been mentioned.

The Sethians' doctrine, we think, has been adequately explained. But if anyone wishes to acquaint himself with the whole of their system, let him read the book entitled *The Paraphrasis of Seth;* for there he will find all their secrets set down. . . .

THE SETHIANS

Epiphanius, Panarion *XXXIX, 1–5, 3*
The Sethians, again, are another sect, which goes by this name but is not to be found in every place. . . . I believe that I encountered this sect also in Egypt; I do not remember exactly in which country I met them. We have discovered some things about it by personal investigation with our own eyes, and have learnt some more from written accounts. The Sethians boast that they trace their descent from Seth the son of Adam, and glorify him and ascribe to him everything that seems virtuous and the proofs of virtue and justice and everything else of this kind. Indeed they even call him Christ and assert that he is Jesus. And their teaching is such as to say that the universe derives from angels and not from the power on high.

In this respect what they say agrees with the former heresy of the Cainites: that in the beginning two men first originated, and from these two were derived Cain and Abel, and over these two the angels fell out and made war on each other, and so caused Abel to be killed by Cain [Gen. 4:1–8]. For the quarrel among the angels who contended concerned the races of men and involved those two, the one who had begotten Cain and the one who had begotten Abel. But the power on high prevailed over them, the one they call the Mother, and Female; for they think that there are mothers in the higher world, and females and males—they almost talk of family relations and paternal authorities. Now when the one called Mother and Female prevailed, they say, since she knew that Abel had been killed she took thought and caused Seth to be born and put into him her own power, implanting in him a seed of the power from on high and the spark that was sent from on high for the first foundation of the seed and of the institution of the world. And this was the institution of justice and the election of the elect seed and race, so that through this institution and this seed destruction should come upon the powers of the angels who made the world and made the two men in the beginning. For this reason, then, the race of Seth is set apart and taken up from this world, since it is an elect race and separated from the other race.

For as the times went past, they say, and the two races were together, the race of Cain and that of Abel, and came together because of their great wickedness and were mixed with one another, the Mother of all took notice and resolved to purify the seed of men, as I said before, since Abel had been killed. And she chose this Seth and displayed him in purity and in him alone she put the seed of her power and purity.

But again, seeing the great confusion and the disorderly passion of angels and men, through which the two races intermingled, and uprisings of the races introduced by their disorder, the same Mother and female deity went and brought on a flood and destroyed every insurrection of all men of the opposing race [Gen. 6:9ff.], in order, of course, that the pure and just race deriving from Seth should alone remain in the world, for the institution of the higher race and of the spark of justice. But the angels again evaded her and brought Ham into the ark, who was of their seed. For when eight souls were saved in Noah's ark at that time, they say that seven belonged to the pure race, but one of them was Ham who belonged to the other power, who went in, evading the Mother on high. Now this plan contrived by the angels was effected in this way; when, as they say, the angels learnt that all their seed was to be wiped out in the flood, they cunningly introduced the aforesaid Ham to preserve the race of wickedness created by them. From this there arose forgetfulness and error among men and disorderly impulsions to sin and wicked promiscuity in the world; and so the world returned again to its original state of disorder and was filled with wickedness as it was in the beginning before the flood.

But from Seth, from his seed and descending from his race there came the Christ himself, Jesus, not by human birth but miraculously appearing in the world; and he is Seth himself, who both then and now visits the human race, being sent from the Mother on high.

They write certain books under the names of great men; they say there are seven books named after Seth, and some other different books they call Allogeneis; another which they call a Revelation (Apocalypse) takes its name from Abraham and is full of all manner of wickedness; others are named after Moses, others again after other men. And submitting their minds to great foolishness, they say that Seth had a wife named Horaea (Norea). For there are other heresies which say there is a power to which they give the name Norea; and this power which the others recognize and call Norea, is said by these men to be the wife of Seth.

The Sethian-Ophites

The Sethian-Ophites owe their name to Seth, the child of Adam and Eve from whom the Gnostics could seek their ancestors. Some of them said that the serpent, *ophis*, was really Sophia, the Mother of the Creator God, and like the Luminous Jesus in other Gnostic sects she gave Adam and Eve the fruit of knowledge, *gnosis*, to help them combat the tyranny of God.

The Sethian-Ophites had an elaborate theogony, similar to that of Valentinus. The Father of All is the First Light in the Depth. He is the First Man. His son, the Second Man, is the Son of Man, who was emitted by The First Man's Thought *(Ennoia)*. Below the First and Second Man is the Holy Spirit or Holy Ghost. She is the First Woman, also called the Mother of the Living. The child of both the First Man and Second Man and the First Woman (the Holy Spirit) is the Third Man, Christ. From the First Woman a Power overflowed producing Sophia, who was also called Prunicos, was male-female, and was the sister of Christ. Later, in this somewhat confusing family tree, there is reference to the upper Mother and the lower Mother, the upper Sophia and lower Sophia.

The Mother then produced a son who in turn produced another until there were seven. The first of them is Ialdabaoth, the Creator God. Ialdabaoth despised his Mother and struggled with her for primacy. He then had another son, Mind, in the form of a serpent *(ophis,* hence Ophites), from whom all worldy things came, including forgetfulness, wickedness, envy, and death. When Ialdabaoth drove him away, he proclaimed that he was the sole God: "I am Father and God, and above me is no one." The Mother reproached him for lying. Then Ialdabaoth created Man, but Sophia managed to deprive Ialdabaoth of the moist nature of light: when he breathed life into man and was secretly deprived of power. Then to deprive the man he had made of that light, Ialdabaoth created woman, Eve (whom Sophia deprived of power). Angels seduced her and generated sons from her. But Sophia planned to seduce Adam and Eve through a serpent so they would oppose Ialdabaoth. When they ate the fruit, they knew the Power of the Father of All, which is above that of Ialdabaoth, their maker, and they left. As the melodrama continues, Adam and Eve fall from Heaven into this world.

Sophia provided Adam and Eve with "moist light," that is, a soul, so they would know who they were and be aware of nakedness and their death. She also gave them knowledge that their body was a temporary vehicle toward a return to the imperishable light. Later, when Ialdabaoth sent the Flood, Sophia saved Noah in the ark. Then Ialdabaoth made a covenant with Noah's descendants, gave them a law, and made them Jews, and let them know that he was God.

Meanwhile, Sophia, moving about with no place to rest, spoke to her mother, the First Woman, who took pity on her and got the First Man to send down Christ, who was Sophia's brother. When Christ came down he put on his sister Sophia as a robe and they became the Bridegroom and the Bride. Then Christ combined with Jesus, who had been born of Mary, and so Jesus became Jesus Christ. Jesus then worked miracles and preached the word of the unknown Father, which enraged God (Ialdabaoth), who was the father of Jesus (as opposed to the unknown Father who was the father of Christ). Then angry God caused Jesus Christ to be crucified, at which point both Christ and Sophia (the Holy Spirit or Ghost) left Jesus alone on the cross to be crucified. But Christ did not forget who he had been and raised Jesus in a body that was both psychic and spiritual, but not physical. The apostles mistakenly thought Jesus had risen in a material body.

Now Christ sits next to Ialdabaoth, receiving souls with light, and will do so until all that light has been returned into the Aeon of Imperishability. This succinct and amazing history ends with the speculation that Sophia may have been the serpent who gave Adam knowledge to oppose his maker (Ialdabaoth). Our intestines, in the form of a serpent, show that the hidden Mother in the shape of a serpent is within us.

The Sethian-Ophite legend is one of the main Gnostic cosmogonies and theogonies, close to the Valentinian speculation which we find in the *Gospel of Truth*, the Coptic text from the Nag Hammadi library. Ophis, the serpent, indicates the important, ambiguous, but ultimately positive role played by the serpent in delivering knowledge, *gnosis*, to Adam and Eve, and consequently providing them with the means to combat God. By being free of their Creator God, they could find the light in their souls and return to the true Father.

THE SETHIAN-OPHITES*

There is a certain First Light in the Depth; this is the Father of All, who is called the First Man. The coming forth of his Thought is the emission of the Son of Man, the Second Man. Below these two is the Holy Spirit, and beneath her are the various elements—water, darkness, abyss, chaos [Gen. 1:2]—over which the Spirit was borne, the First Woman. Then the First Man with his Son rejoiced over the beauty of the female Spirit, and he illuminated her and from her generated an imperishable Light, the Third Man, who is called Christ, the Son of the First and Second Man and the Holy Spirit, the First Woman, when the Father and Son lay with the Woman, who is called the Mother of the Living [Gen. 3:20]. But when she was unable to carry or receive the greatness of the Light, it overflowed to the regions of the left side. Thus their only Son, Christ, is the right side and the ascension and was immediately drawn up to the imperishable Aeon, which is the true and holy Church, the calling and assembly and union of the Father of All, the First Man, with the Son, the Second Man, and with Christ, the Son of these two and the Woman.

The power which overflowed from the Woman and has the moist nature of light, fell from above, from its fathers. By its own will it has the moist nature of light, and is called left and Prunicos and Sophia and Male-Female. It came down directly upon the waters, when they were motionless, and set them in motion, moving boldly as far as the abysses; and it took a body for itself from them. Everything ran together and adhered to the moist nature of the power's light, and enclosed it; if everything had not possessed it, all things might have been completely absorbed and submerged by matter. When it was bound and weighed

down by the body of matter, it lay low, though it tried to escape from the waters and ascend to the Mother, though it could not do so because of the weight of the surrounding body. Since it was in such an unfortunate condition it tried to hide the light which had come from above, fearing that the light would be injured by the lower elements as it itself had been. And when it received power from the moist nature of the light which was with it, it leaped back and was borne upwards to the height. When it had ascended, it spread out and became a covering and formed the visible heaven out of its body; and it remained under the heaven which it made, retaining the form of a watery body. But when it acquired a desire for the light above, and was constantly gaining power, it put off its body and was freed from it. This body is called female, after the First Woman.

Her Son had in himself a certain aspiration towards the imperishable Aeon; this had been left in him by the Mother, who works through it. Becoming potent, he himself emitted from the waters a son without a mother; for he did now know the Mother. The second son emitted a son who was an imitation of his father; this third one generated a fourth, and the fourth himself generated a son; from the fifth a sixth son was generated, and the sixth generated a seventh. Thus the Seven was completed among them [cf. Gen. 2:1–2]; the Mother has the eighth place. Their dignities and powers correspond to their order of generation.

The one who is first from the Mother is Ialdabaoth; the next, Iao; the next, Sabaoth; the fourth, Adonaios [Adonai]; the fifth, Eloeus [Elohim]; the sixth, Oreus; the seventh and most recent of all, Astaphaeus. These heavens and excellences and powers and angels have places in heaven according to the order of their generation, and they invisibly reign over things celestial and terrestrial. The first of them, Iadabaoth, despised the Mother in that without her permission he made sons and grandsons—an-

---

*From Robert M. Grant, *Gnosticism* (New York: Harper & Brothers, 1961), pp. 52–59.

gels, archangels, excellences, powers, and dominions. When they had been made, his sons turned to a struggle against him for the primacy. Therefore, in grief and despair, Ialdabaoth looked down on the dregs of matter and solidified his desire into it and generated a son. This son is Mind, twisted in the form of a serpent [*ophis*, hence Ophites], and is also Spirit and Soul and everything worldly. From him were generated all forgetfulness and wickedness and jealousy and envy and death. Ialdabaoth drove out this serpent-shaped and twisted Mind [cf. Gen. 3:14] because of its crookedness, all the more because it had once been with his Father in Heaven and in Paradise. For this reason Ialdabaoth exulted, boasting because all these were beneath him, and said, "I am Father and God, and above me is no one" [cf. Isa. 44:6]. The Mother heard and cried out against him, "Do not speak falsely, Ialdabaoth; above you are the Father of All, the First Man, and the Man who is Son of Man." When all things were disturbed because of the new voice and the inconceivable address, and they were asking whence the call had come, Ialdabaoth said, in order to summon them and draw them to himself, "Come, let us make a man in our image" [Gen. 1:26].

The six powers heard these words, and when the Mother gave them the idea of man so that through him she might drive them out from the principal power, they came together and formed a man who was immeasurable in breadth and length. When he did nothing but writhe, they bore him to his Father, Ialdabaoth, while Sophia managed to deprive Ialdabaoth of the moist nature of light so that he could not be raised up against those who are above, by possessing power; Ialdabaoth breathed into man the breath of life [Gen. 2:7] and was thus secretly deprived of the power; hence man had mind and desire, and these are the parts of man which are saved. Immediately he gave thanks to the First Man, abandoning his makers.

The jealous Ialdabaoth wanted a plan for depriving man of the moist nature of Light through woman, and from his own desire he brought forth a woman whom Prunicos [Sophia] took and invisibly deprived of power. The others came and admired her beauty [Gen. 6:2] and called her Eve; they desired her and from her generated sons who are called angels. But their Mother, Sophia, planned to seduce Adan and Eve through a serpent so that they would transgress the commandment of Ialdabaoth. Eve, hearing this word as if it came directly from the Son of God, readily believed it and persuaded Adam to eat from the tree of which Ialdabaoth had said not to eat. When they ate, they knew the Power which is above all and they departed from those who had made them.

When Sophia saw that the powers were overcome by her creatures, she rejoiced greatly and again exclaimed that, since the Father was imperishable, Ialdabaoth spoke falsely when he called himself "Father"; and since the Man and the First Woman had already existed, Eve sinned when she committed adultery with angels. But Ialdabaoth, because of the forgetfulness which surrounded him, paid no attention to her exclamation but cast Adam and Eve out of Paradise, since they had transgressed his commandment. He had wanted to generate sons from Eve, but he did not succeed, since his Mother opposed him in every way and secretly deprived Adam and Eve of the moist nature of light, so that the Spirit from the Highest Power might not share in the curse or the disgrace. Thus they were emptied of divine substance, cursed by Ialdabaoth, and made to fall from Heaven into this world. The serpent, too, who had worked against his Father, was cast down into the lower world by him. The serpent brought the angels who are here under his power and generated six sons; he himself is the seventh, in imitation of the Seven which is about the Father. These are the seven wordly demons, forever opposing and resisting the human race; for their sake their father was cast down below.

At first Adam and Eve had light and bright bodies, "spiritual bodies," as they were formed originally. When they came to this place, they became darker and thicker and more sluggish. The soul, too, became lax and languid. And since they had received only a "worldly" breathing from their maker, Prunicos took pity on them and gave them the odor of the sweetness of the moist nature of light. Through this they came to remembrance of themselves; they recognized that they were naked and knew the material nature of the body [Gen. 3:7], and they knew that they bore the burden of death; but they were patient, recognizing that the body contained them only for a time. They found food to eat by the guidance of Sophia, and when they were filled they had sexual intercourse and generated Cain. Cain was immediately taken and overthrown by the serpent which was cast down, and by the serpent's six sons. The serpent filled him with worldly forgetfulness and brought him to stupidity and presumption so that when he killed his brother Abel he might be the first example of jealousy and death. After these, by the providence of Sophia, Seth was generated and then Norea.[1] All the rest of mankind was generated from them. By the lower Seven mankind was brought into all wickedness, and to apostasy from the holy Seven above, and to idolatry and to every kind of contempt. Since the Mother was always invisibly opposing the lower Seven, she saved what was her own, i.e., the moist nature of light.

The lower[2] Seven consists of the seven stars called planets, and the serpent who was cast down has two names, Michael and Samael.

Ialdabaoth was angry with men because they did not worship or honor him as Father and God; he sent a deluge upon them to destroy all of them at the same time. But Sophia withstood him at this point, too, and saved those who were with Noah in the ark because of the moist nature of that light which originated from her; through it the world was again filled with men. One of these, named Abraham, was chosen by Ialdabaoth himself, who gave him a covenant to the effect that if his seed persevered in serving him, he would give it the earth as an inheritance. Later through Moses he led the descendants of Abraham out of Egypt and gave them a law and made them Jews; from that time the seven days were chosen which make up the holy Seven [week]. And each one of the Seven chose his own herald to glorify and proclaim him as God, so that the others might hear the praises and serve the gods proclaimed through the prophets.

Thus Moses was the prophet of Ialdabaoth, as were Joshua, Amos and Habakkuk; Samuel, Nathan, Jonah, and Micah were prophets of Iao; Elijah, Joel, and Zechariah were prophets of Sabaoth; Isaiah, Ezekiel, Jeremiah, and Daniel were prophets of Adonai; Tobias and Haggai were prophets of Eloi; Micah and Nahum were prophets of Oreus; and Ezra and Zephaniah were prophets of Astanfeus.

Each one of these glorified his own Father and God, but Sophia spoke many things through them concerning the First Man and Imperishable Aeon and the Christ who is above, forewarning and preserving men for the imperishable Light and the First Man and the descent of Christ. When the Archons were terrified by these words and marveled at the novelty in what the prophets proclaimed, Prunicos effected through Ialdabaoth, who was ignorant of what he did the emission of two men, one from the sterile Elizabeth, the other from the virgin Mary. And since Sophia found no rest, either in Heaven or on earth [cf. Enoch 42], she was sorrowful and called for the help of her Mother. Her Mother, the First Woman, took pity on the repentance of her daughter, and asked the First Man to send Christ to her to help;

he was emitted and descended to his sister and to the moist nature of light.

When the Sophia below recognized that her brother descended to her, she proclaimed his coming through John and prepared the baptism of repentance and made Jesus suitable in advance so that the descending Christ might find a pure vessel, and so that through her son Ialdabaoth the Woman might be proclaimed by Christ. He descended through the seven heavens, and was made like their sons, and gradually deprived them of their power. All the moist nature of light ran together to him, and Christ, descending into this world, first put on his sister Sophia as a robe, and both rejoiced in mutual comfort; they are the Bridegroom and the Bride.

Jesus was generated from the virgin through the working of God [Ialdabaoth?]; he was wiser and purer and more righteous than all other men; Christ combined with Sophia descended into him and thus Jesus became Christ.

Many of his disciples did not recognize the descent of Christ into him; but when Christ descended into Jesus, then he began to work miracles and to heal and to proclaim the unknown Father and to confess himself openly as the Son of the First Man. Because of this the powers and the Father of Jesus were angry, and they took steps to kill him. When he was led to death, the Christ with Sophia departed to the Imperishable Aeon, while Jesus was crucified. Christ did not forget what was his own, but from above sent into him a certain power which raised him in a body which was both psychic and spiritual; the worldly elements remained in the world. When the disciples saw that the transformed Jesus had risen again, they did not recognize him [Luke 24:34], nor did they recognize the Christ[3] by whose grace he rose from the dead. And the greatest error of the disciples was this, that they thought he rose in a worldy [material] body, and did not know that "flesh and blood do not attain to the kingdom of God" [1 Cor. 15:50].

The descent and ascent of the Christ is confirmed by the fact that the disciples say that Jesus did nothing remarkable either before the baptism or after the resurrection. They are ignorant of the union of Jesus with the Christ and of the Imperishable Aeon with the Seven. [The "worldly body" is that which living beings have.] Jesus remained for eighteen months after the resurrection and from the perception which descended into him learned this teaching which is manifest. He taught these things to a few of his disciples who, he knew, could receive [Matt. 19:11] such great mysteries [Matt. 13:11], and thus was taken up into Heaven.

Christ sits at the right hand of the Father Ialdabaoth in order to receive to himself the souls of those who have known them, after they have put off the worldly flesh. Christ enriches himself, though his Father is ignorant of him and does not even see him, so that the more Jesus enriches himself with holy souls, the less his Father becomes deprived of his power through the souls. For Christ will not receive holy souls to send them back to the world; he will receive only those which are of substance, i.e., from the "breathing." The end will come when the whole moist nature of the spirit of light is collected and withdrawn into the Aeon of Imperishability.

Some of them say that the serpent was Sophia herself; for this reason it was opposed to the maker of Adam and gave knowledge to men, and therefore is called the wisest of all [Gen. 3:1]. And the position of our intestines through which food is taken in, and their shape, shows that the hidden Mother of the shape of the serpent is a substance within us.

Notes

1. For attempts to explain her existence cf. Epiphanius, *Pan.* 26.I.3–5.

2. Holy [text].

3. Irenaeus has "Jesus."

Ophite Diagrams*

In his "True Account," an attack on Christianity written between A.D. 177 and 180, a certain Celsus described a diagram apparently used by Ophites (whom he regarded as genuine Christians). Seventy years later, in his reply to Celsus, the Christian theologian Origen provided a fuller description of a similar diagram. Both descriptions are to be found in Origen's *Contra Celsum*, v. 24–38. The present translation has been revised in the light of that made by Henry Chadwick ("Origen Contra Celsum," Cambridge, 1953).

The Ophite Diagrams are interesting not only because of what they add to Gnostic theology, but because of the iconographic details in the description of the Ophite Diagrams. Celsus' description is replete with vivid, symbolically obscure images, which at times recall the apocalyptic vision and poetry of the Book of Revelation. *(WB)*

THE OPHITE DIAGRAMS*

Celsus' Description
Celsus says there is a diagram consisting of ten [or seven] separate circles, circumscribed by one circle which is said to be the world-soul and is called Leviathan. The diagram is divided by a thick black line, which is called Gehenna, i.e., Tar-

tarus. The "seal" is that of the one who imposes it, who is called Father; the one sealed is called Youth and Son, and he responds: "I have been anointed with white chrism from the Tree of Life." There are seven angels, who delivered the seal; they stand on both sides of the soul set free from the body; and there are other angels of light who are called Archontics. The Archon of the so-called Archontics is the accursed god of the Jews, who makes rain and thunder. He is the Demiurge of this world, the God of Moses described in his creation narra-

*Introduction by Robert M. Grant
*Origen, *Contra Celsum*, vi. 24–38. From Robert M. Grant, *Gnosticism* (New York: Harper & Brothers, 1961), pp. 52–59.

tive. Of the seven archontic demons, the first is lion-shaped; the second is a bull; the third is amphibious and hisses horribly; the fourth has the form of an eagle; the fifth has the appearance of a bear; the sixth, that of a dog; and the seventh, that of an ass named Thaphabaoth or Onoel. Some persons return to the archontic forms so that they become lions or bulls or serpents or eagles or bears or dogs. There is a square, and there are words said at the gates of Paradise.

They add still further matters: the sayings of prophets, and circles upon circles, and emanations of the earthly church and of circumcision, and the power emanating from a certain virgin Prunicos, and a living soul, and a Heaven slain that it may live, and earth slain with a sword, and many slain that they may live, and death stopped in Heaven, when the world's sin dies, and a narrow way back, and doors opening automatically. Everywhere there is the Tree of Life and a resurrection of flesh from the tree.

They say that some things are written within the two super-heavenly circles, the greater and lesser, those of the Son and the Father.

Origen's Description*

The first angel, lion-shaped, is called Michael; the second, bull-shaped, is called Souriel; the third, serpent-shaped, is called Raphael; the fourth, eagle-shaped, is called Gabriel; the fifth, bear-shaped, is called Thauthabaoth; the sixth, dog-shaped, is called Erathaoth; the seventh, ass-shaped, is called Onoel or Thartharaoth.

They are taught to say, after passing through the barrier of the Tree of Life and abandoned by the image after the likeness of the blameless one, "Let Grace be with me, Father, let it be with me."

In this diagram are the greater and the smaller circle. On their diameters is inscribed "Father" and "Son." Between the greater, in which the smaller lies, and another circle, consisting of two circles, the outer yellow and the inner dark blue, is the barrier, shaped like a two-edged axe. Above it is a small circle, smaller than the larger of those already mentioned, with "love" written on it. Below it is another with the word "life." In the second circle, combining and circumscribing the other two circles as well as another rhomboid shape, is written "Foreknowledge of Wisdom," and above their common intersection is a circle on which is written "Knowledge," and below, another in which is written "Understanding."

---

*From Origen, "Contra Celsum," vi. 24–38.

9
MANICHAEAN AND MANDAEAN GNOSTIC TEXTS

Mani and
Manichaeism

Manichaeism was the most developed, widespread, and enduring of the Gnostic ideologies. It persisted for nearly fifteen hundred years. Although most of the texts were destroyed, Mani and his followers generated many major scriptures, and great attention was paid to their preservation, their visual presentation, and even the materials used in their writing. The writings were at the heart of a highly organized institution, with an elaborate hierarchy of clergy, a supportive merchant class, and a community whose strictest command was unquestioning obedience to the religion. Kurt Rudolph observes that Manichaeism "can be regarded as one of the four world religions known to the history of religions. This means it shares a position with Buddhism, Christianity, and Islam." Robert Haardt characterizes it as "the final and logical systematization of the Gnosis of late antiquity as a universal religion of revelation with a missionary character."[1] Although in contrast to Rudolph's Buddhism, Christianity, and Islam (and why not Hinduism and Judaism as well?), Gnostic Manichaeism now lies in the past, there have been major discoveries of Manichaean literature in Iranian, Old Turkish, and Chinese (Turfan, 1898–1916) and in Coptic (Medinet Madi, Egypt, 1930), and enough of its theology and texts remain to produce a full picture. We have continued to ignore it for the same reasons that its scriptures and communities were destroyed: the Manichaeans were rivals. But to persist today in such parochial blindness is like ignoring the Roman Empire, which in fact did not last as long nor extend as far as this original syncretic religion born in the cities of Mesopotamia.

Mani, the founder of the religion, was born about 216 in Babylonia, near Seleucia-Ctesiphon on the Tigris. He was primarily a teacher, physician of the soul, and religious organizer in the Persian kingdom under Shapur I (241–272). After the ascension of Bahram I (274–277), his situation changed. The Magi, a priest caste of the Zoroastrian church, were reforming their religion and wished to eliminate this intruder. When he failed to alter the opinion of Gundeshapur, the Great King of Belapat, Mani was arrested and thrown into chains. There are conflicting accounts of his death. Some documents say that he was crucified (which Hans Jonas reports) or flayed alive because of his anti-Zoroastrian teachings. A Coptic psalm says that his body was mutilated and his head set high on the city gate. One document, however, the *Manichaean Homilies,* states that he died in prison at eleven o'clock on March 2, 276. His death is described "as a triumphant ascent to the realm of Light." In prison he was able to designate the religious succession of his order, appointing twelve teachers (apostles) and seventy-two Bishops.

During his life, Mani traveled as a missionary in India, Persia, Babylonia, and in the provinces of the Medes and Parthians. He made some converts, but he was also abused and expelled. "I seemed to be too heavy for these countries and their leaders," he is reported to have said.[2] But after his death, his fame as teacher, as messiah, as God, spread into the East and West. The Chinese Manichaeans called him the "Buddha of Light." Middle Iranian texts speak of him as the "life-giver" and "raiser of the dead." In other passages, he is simply referred to as "God." Mani's doctrine of two principles, of the antithesis between Light and Darkness, spread through Asia to Western China and North Africa and into Europe, from Armenia in Asia Minor to Rome and Spain, and was a powerful challenge to European Christianity. Only after the sixth century did his influence begin to wane in Europe, though it continued to appear as a threat in other guises as the Bogomils, the Paulicians, and the Catharists throughout the Middle Ages. After the public disappearance of Manichaeism in the West, its center became Central Asia, Eastern Iran, Turkestan, and especially western China in the Uigur empire, where in 762 it became the state religion and remained dominant until the thirteenth century when it became a victim of Mongolian hegemony. Its last manifestation in the West appeared in northern Italy and particularly among the Catharists (the Pure) or Albigensians in southern France, the "Albigensian heresy," which was annihilated—along with Provenal culture—in the thirteenth century. It lingered on in China. The emperors of the Ming dynasty in the fourteenth century were troubled by the influence of the followers of the religion of "venerable light," and the Portuguese spoke of Machinaean traditions in southern China as late as the seventeenth century.

Mani taught that Buddha, Zoroaster, and Jesus were his forerunners and that he was continuing their mission, perfecting it, surpassing the others with his own writings. He, Mani, would lead humanity from slavery to the King of Light. Although Mani's attitude of superiority may be criticized, his very acknowledgement of early religions as contributing to the formation of his own implies a tolerance unusual in religious movements. In descriptions of the leader, we find the title "Twin Spirit." The Twin Spirit apparently refers to a divine presence and authority that always accompanied Mani in his work and writings, a revelation from the King of Light. The title is also identified with Paraclete (comforter), one who reveals past and future. The founder is also depicted as a skillful physician and miracle worker. But above all, he was a writer of holy scriptures. Today Mani's writings exist mainly as fragments and partial quotations; originally they were at the core of his missionary intent, and he himself stated that the great failing of the founders of other religions was that they did not write and establish a canon of their books. Some of Mani's books were *The Great Gospel* or *Living Gospel, The Treasure of Life, Shabuhragan, Treatise, The Book of Secrets, The Book of Giants, Epistles, Psalms and Prayers,* and *The Drawings and the Commentary on the Drawings.* The latter contained the drawings of Mani the artist, who believed, evidently, that his work should also reach the readers pictorially.

Information about Mani and Manichaeism comes in part from Coptic hymns and from fragmentary texts in Persian, Middle Persian (Parthian), Greek, Arabic, and Chinese. Many of the main sources are the works of Mani's adversaries. These are an-Nadim (late tenth century) and Al-Biruni (eleventh century) in Arabic. In Syriac, the Christian father Ephraen (about 370) and Theodore bar Konai (about 790) wrote against the heresy of Mani. Greek Christian authors tended to regard Mani as a dangerous madman, making a pun on his name which resembles the Greek word for madness *(manía).* But around A.D. 300, shortly after Mani's death, Alexander Lycopolitanus, a philosopher of unknown religious attachment, wrote a sober piece in Greek about Mani. His work reveals that Mani's influence had already spread from Persia to southern Europe.

The main Christian author of the fourth and fifth centuries is Augustine (354–430). Born of a Christian mother and a non-Christian father, Augustine was a Manichaean for more than nine years (376–86). He was a "hearer," or "auditor," never actually leading the life of a Manichaean monk. It should also be remembered that he was a Manichaean as a young man and never achieved the position of authority and knowledge that he was to have as a Christian. When he converted to Christianity, he wrote more than a dozen documents against his former religion and coreligionists. The latter were themselves Christian intellectuals, for only Christian Gnostics were admitted to his Manichaean community in North Africa, which was removed from the syncretic Manichaeism of Asia, with its strong Zoroastrian and Buddhist ingredients. Augustine's books contained doctrinal and dogmatic essays and personal disputations *against* Manichaean opponents. Thus his works bear the title *Contra* as in *Contra Fortunatum, Contra Adimantum, Contra Faustum, Contra Felicem, Contra Secundinum* (against Fortunatus, Adimantus, Faustus, Felix, and Secundius). Ironically, those forces that wished to punish adherents to Manichaeism and burn their texts—the Persian rulers, Roman emperors, and Christian apologists—also contributed to preserving their memory. This was particularly true in the case of Augustine's reasoned refutations of Manichaean doctrine.

Augustine's *Synopsis of the Entire System* begins with the usual attack

671

on Mani's "insane" doctrine (punning on the Greek word for madness). He gives a summary of its dualism of good and evil, light and darkness. He also speaks of the Manichaeans' repulsive actions, such as the eating of the Eucharist sprayed with human semen. In particular, Augustine attacks the Catharists, who claim that divine forces are imprisoned in impure forms. Hence they eat horrifying nourishment, such as victuals containing human semen. They are also vegetarians, since there is no divine substance in animals and therefore no need to liberate the sparks of light from such matter. For similar reasons they do not consume eggs, milk, nor wine which they call "the bile of the Archon of Darkness."

There follows a description of the salvation of the souls of the elect and of reincarnation of others in higher or lower forms, much in keeping with the Buddhist cycle of rebirth. Because even plants and trees contain living things, however, it is wrong to pluck a thorn and agriculture is a form of murder. As for copulation, it is permissible as long as conception and procreation are avoided, for procreation brings another soul into bondage (and aids the work of the Creator God).

Christ is the Serpent to this Gnostic group, for he brings knowledge to Adam and Eve. In a later form Christ came to save souls, not bodies, and he did not really exist in the flesh. Therefore, his crucifixion was an illusion. God of the Bible was an Archon of Darkness, but the Holy Spirit of the Scriptures they interpret as their own Apostle Mani (Manicheaeus), whom Augustine refers to as Heresiarch (chief heretic). After some more details about their organization into bishops and presbyters and their opposition to baptism, the text ends with further references to their theology. They pray to the sun and the moon for the spirit. That spirit lives in the prison of the flesh. When the end of the world comes with a great conflagration and the spirit is freed, then the flesh will return to its original "lump" or "mass," a translation of *bolos* (a term used in Greek philosophy and meaning "lump of earth").

The preceding discussion by Augustine of Manichaeism is remarkably accurate although unfriendly. In the light of the discovery of Manichaean scriptures, however, we no longer have to depend almost exclusively on those who wrote against the religion. In his book, *Gnosis: the Nature and History of an Ancient Religion* (forthcoming in English translation), the German scholar Kurt Rudolph has given us the most succinct and cogent study of Manichaeism since Hans Jonas's monumental work. I am indebted to him for his ordering of some of the following information.

Manichaeism is based on the Gnostic dualism of spirit and body, light and darkness, good and evil. While this notion appears in Judaism and Christianity, it is a commonplace that it first appeared in Iranian Zoroastriansm, a direct source of Jewish dualism, and thus it is not surprising that Mani, of Iranian origin and living among Zoroastrians, should have developed a theology that radically emphasizes these antitheses. Since the original light of the Redeemer was caught in the matter of our earthly bodies and universe, salvation is the gift of our gradual liberation from darkness. Since the earth and material things are of negative value (in fact, a prison), the cosmology, in Mani's terms, is subservient to soteriology. To lose sight of salvation is to condemn oneself to endless rebirth in this world—an idea probably borrowed from Buddhism.

The leader of the realm of light, located in the North, is the King of Light or Father of Light. As opposed to the creator biblical God, he is the Redeemer. In Iranian texts, his name is Zurvan. His being is revealed in five spiritual attributes or hypostases or worlds. Also called his "aeons," these are reason, thinking, insight, speculation, and reflection. Darkness, in the South, also has five worlds: smoke, fire, sirocco, water, and darkness. In these worlds are demons under a commanding archon. These spheres of light and darkness are in battle: the darkness wants to trap light in its matter. The God of Light brings forth his own weapons. He creates the first invocation, Sophia (wisdom) who in turn brings forth "the Mother of the living," who gives birth to the Primal Man, called Ohrmazd in Persian. He is furnished with five elements, also referred to as garments or sons: fire, wind, water, light, and ether, which make up the "Living Soul." The Primal Man descends to find the darkness but is defeated, and his pentadic soul is taken into the underworld. The Manichaeans optimistically consider this defeat a means of actually capturing the darkness. Now the King of Light creates a second evocation, the "Living Spirit" or "Great Architect," called Mithra in Persian. He has, again, five sons (among them, the "Light-Adamas"). The Living Spirit begins his work of salvation by sending out an awakening call—the famous Manichaean call—to the Primal Man, to raise him back to light. "His salvation is the model," Rudolph writes, "for the salvation of Adam and of all men."[2] The actual cosmos comes into being now, however, as a result of the initial capture of Primal Man by the archons. The light that the archons swallow becomes the building material, the mixture of darkness and light, for stars, heaven, and earth. Ten firmaments and eight earthly spheres are created. The liberation of light is the next mission:

For the purpose of the actual salvation of the particles of light the cosmos must be set in motion. To this end the third "evocation" ensues, the main figure of which is the "third envoy" or the "God of the realm of light"; his abode is the sun, his female aspect, viz. his daughters, are the twelve virgins of light who represent the zodiac. He sets in motion the mechanism of the purification of light in the form of the three wheels of fire, water and wind. For the reception of the purified particles of light he creates the "pillar of glory" which is also called "perfect man". . . . It becomes visible in the Milky Way. On it the liberated particles of light ascend to the moon which gathers them up to its fullness (full moon), in order to pass them on afterwards, thus emptying itself (new moon), to the sun, whence they go to the "new aeon" which in the meantime was designed by the "great architect." In order to deprive the dark archons of the light that they had received, the "third envoy": . . . himself uncoveted in his male and female aspect, whereupon the lewd archons either defile themselves or abort. The semen falls, on the one hand, on dry land and brings forth the world of plants, on the other hand, it falls into the sea and produces a sea monster which is vanquished by the "light-adamas." The aborted embryons fall upon the earth, become demons and devour the fruit of the plants, *i.e.* the seed of darkness mixed with light, fertilize themselves and thus produce the animal kingdom.[3]

The archons, fearing the loss of the light, determine to create human beings. Two chosen demons, Saklas (the fool) and Nebroel create Adam and Eve. To counter this new imprisonment of light in the first humans, the King of Light sends the "Luminous Jesus," also called "Jesus Splendor," to enlighten Adam with knowledge, with *gnosis*. To awaken the soul many messengers are sent: Seth, Noah, Enosh, Enoch, Shem, Afraham, Buddha, Aurentes, Zoroaster, Jesus, and Paul. Mani is the last of these redeeming figures: he is the messiah. The earthly Jesus is not to be confused with the Luminous Jesus, who corresponds to Christ of the pleroma. As in other Docetic Gnostic sects, the Jesus of the crucifixion is merely a phantom and, as such, has no redemptive worth. In North Africa, Manichaeism incorporated a suffering Jesus, *Jesus patibilis*, into their speculation.

The earthly force to bring about the liberation of the soul is of course the Manichaean church. Its organization—and it was the most organized of the Gnostic cults (which accounts in large part for its long survival) included two main groups: the elect or perfect, and the hearers. The hierarchy was chosen from the elect and consisted of twelve apostles, seventy-two bishops, 360 elders and the plain elect. Women may be included in the elect, but they could not take office. While the hearers existed to serve the elect (who alone could achieve salvation without going through the ordeal of rebirth), the elect in turn were subject to severe ethical proscriptions. They were guided by the three "seals" of the mouth, the hand, and the sexual organs. They were not to consume meat or wine or to lie or to speak hypocritically (the mouth); they were not to damage their hands through manual labor (the hand); and they were not to damage themselves through intercourse (sexual organs). Their main work was producing and copying holy writings and making them known to the community. However, we also hear of many extreme duties of the elect: fasting for periods of thirty days at a stretch, and observing one hundred days of fasting a year. In their diet, they were careful to eat food that contained a high degree of light, such as cucumbers, melons, water, juices, and white bread. The role of the hearers was the physical and economic care of the elect. Their reward would be to be reborn among the elect. Along with their obsession to find light—that is, salvation—they also wished to avoid sin (in other Gnostic cults, the notion of sin is replaced by "error") and, to avoid a relapse into sin, they devised a form of confession and repentence. Probably modeled on a Buddhist prototype, confession (again in contrast to the more introspective speculation of other Gnostics for whom the clergy was of little importance) became an important Manichaean institution. Of course every personal act and public rite had but one end in view: escape from the trap of the body and the dark material world in order to rise through the spheres and merge one's divine luminous particles, the soul, redeemed and returned to the realm of light.

Notes

1. Kurt Rudolph, *Gnosis: The Nature and History of an Ancient Religion*, trans. Robert McLachlan Wilson (San Francisco: Harper & Row, 1984), pp. 326–27.
2. Rudolph, p. 337.
3. Rudolph, pp. 337–38.

SYNOPSIS OF THE ENTIRE SYSTEM ACCORDING TO AUGUSTINE*

The Manichaeans derive from a Persian, called Manes; his disciples, however, when his insane doctrine began to be proclaimed in Greece, perferred to call him "Manichaeus" and thus avoid the designation "Madness" [Gr. Mania]. This is why those amongst them who are, as it were, the scholars and thus the more mendacious, doubling the letter "N" call him "Mannichaeus," or one, who, as it were, scatters[1] Manna.

The latter introduced two principles which differ and are contrary to each other, eternal and in fact mutually eternal, in the sense that they have always existed. He assumed two natures and substances, that which is good and that which is evil, following other heretics of ancient times.

The Manichaeans dream up everything imaginable, asserting, persistently in their dogma, that these natures and substances at once combat each other and mingle with one another, and that the Good is purified of the Evil, and that the Good, which cannot be purified, falls prey to eternal damnation together with the Evil. It would take us too far were I to describe it all in this work.

Through these empty and sacrilegious fables of theirs, they are compelled to state that good souls must be freed of their admixture with the evil souls, which are of a contrary nature, and that these good souls are of the same nature as God. They furthermore acknowledge that while it is true that the world is made of the nature of God, it consists of an admixture of Good and Evil, which occurred when the two natures were struggling against each other. This purification and liberation of the Good from the Evil is brought about, according to their doctrine, not only by the forces of God throughout the world as a whole, and as regards all its elements, but also by their Elect, through the food which they take to themselves. For with this food, as with the world as a whole, is mixed, they maintain, God's substance.

This divine Substance, in their view, is purified in their Elect as a result of the way of life adopted by the Elect of the Manichaeans, holier, as it were, and more splendid than that of their congregations. For their church is composed of these two classes, i.e., that of the Elect and that of the congregation. In other people, even within their own congregations, this part of the good and divine substance, which is retained in a mixed and bound form in food and drink, and particularly in those people who procreate, lies in still more constricted and filthier bonds.

Everything of light, which is refined out from all directions, however, is given back to the Kingdom of God as the ultimate set of aspiration, by certain vessels, i.e., sun and moon. These vessels are similarly made of pure divine substance. And this physical light, which is accessible to the eyes of mortal creatures not

*From Augustine, *de haeresibus ad Quodvultdeum* 46 (Migne SL 42, col. 34–38). From Robert Haardt, *Gnosis* (Leiden: Brill, 1971), pp. 341-349.

only in these vessels, in which it is available to them in its purest form, but also in all other shining things, in which according to them it is mixed and must be purified: this light they term the Nature of God.

They ascribe five elements, which have produced their own Archons, to the Generation of Darkness: these elements are named by them as follows: Smoke, Darkness, Fire, Water, Wind. In Smoke two-footed creatures had their origin, and from them, they believe, men originated. In Darkness, crawling creatures came into being, in Fire the quadrupeds, in Water swimming creatures, in Wind flying creatures.

To combat these five evil elements, five other elements were sent out from the Kingdom and Substance of God, and in that battle mixed; Air with Smoke, Light with Darkness, the good Fire with the evil, the good Water with the evil, the good with the evil Wind. Those vessels, however, the two Lamps of Heaven, are distinguished by them as follows: the Moon is composed of the good Water, and the Sun of the good Fire. There are sacred Powers in those vessels, which transform themselves into male creatures in order to attract the female creatures of the enemy race, and conversely, into female creatures in order to attract the male creatures of the enemy race. And the light which they retained in mixed form in their limbs, escapes them whenever their desire is awakened by this attraction. And it is received by the angels of light for purification. Following purification it is loaded onto those vessels in order to be restored back to its own Kingdom.

For this reason, or rather, as a certain unavoidable consequence of their repulsive superstition, their Elect are forced to consume a Eucharist, so to speak, sprayed with human semen, so that by it, as by the other food which they consume, the divine substance may be purified. They deny doing so however, and state that it is others claiming to be Manichaeans who do so. Nevertheless, they were unmasked in the church in Carthage, as you know when you were appointed Deacon there, when some of them were presented at the instigation of the tribune Ursus, who at that time occupied a leading position in the Imperial Administration. A maiden named Margarita made public this vicious scandal, there, and said that she had been ravished as a result of this criminal mystery, although she was not twelve years of age. Thereupon Ursus managed, not without difficulty, to induce a certain Eusebia, an apparently chaste female Manichaean, to confess that she had suffered the same experience, for the same reasons, after first swearing that she was touched, and expressed the desire to be examined by a midwife. She was examined, and as was established as a result, she confessed that disgraceful crime, in the course of which meal was sprinkled underneath the copulating pair, so that the semen could be mixed and consumed; although she had not heard this, as she was absent when Margarita confessed it, she confessed it in similar fashion. Some of them were even discovered recently and taken to church, as is shown in the documents of the bishopric, which you have sent to us. Subjected to careful interrogation, they confessed this, which is not a "Sacrament" but that "Execrament."[2] One of them by the name of Viator admitted that those who do such things are really called Catharists, and that the other segments of the same Manichaean sect could be broken down into Mattars and Manichaeans in the narrower sense. He could not deny however that these three forms derived from one single founder, and that all in general were Manichaeans.

And they certainly all have in common, beyond any doubt, those Manichaean books in which these monstrosities are described concerning the transformation of male creatures into female, and female into male, in order to mislead the rulers of Darkness of both sexes and destroy them through desire, so that the divine substance imprisoned in them may be liberated, and escape. From this developed the abomination which each one of them denies having had anything to do with. For they believe that they are imitating the divine forces as far as they can, so that they purify a part of their God: they do indeed think that this part is imprisoned in impure form in all heavenly and earthly bodies and in the seed of all things just as it is in human semen. If follows therefrom that they have to purify the divine substance both from the human semen and from the other seeds which they consume in the form of victuals, by eating it. They are therefore also called "Catharists," or as it were, "Purifiers." They are so diligent in purifying the divine substance that they do not even shrink from such a horrifying and disgraceful act of nourishment.

Nevertheless, they eat no meat, since the divine substance has fled from dead or slain creatures. What remains, after the death of an animal, is of such quantity and quality that it is no longer worthy of being purified in the body of one of the Elect.

They do not even eat eggs, since these too died when they were broken, and no dead bodies must be eaten, and the only part of flesh that is living is what can be trapped in meal so that it does not die. Nor do they use milk as food, though it is milked or sucked from the body of the living animal. Not because they believe that nothing of the divine substance is mixed with it in this case, but because their error (i.e., erroneous doctrine) is not consistent. Nor do they drink any wine, but say that it is the bile of the Archons of Darkness, though on the other hand they do eat grapes. Nor do they drink any newly fermented wine, even when it is quite fresh.

They assume that the souls of their auditors pass into the Elect or—happily —into the food of their Elect, so that, purified of the foods they do not then return into any bodies. The remaining souls, however, return, they think, into animal bodies and into all that has a hold in the earth, through roots, and is so nourished.

They assume that plants and trees are in this way living, that the life which is in them feels and suffers when they are injured; and none of them could tear off or pluck anything of these without causing pain. They even consider it wrong, therefore, to cleanse a field of thorns. As a result they foolishly charge agriculture, the most innocent of all skills, as a still greater murderer.

And they think that this will be forgiven their auditors because they thereby provide nourishment for their Elect, so that the divine substance purified in their body obtains pardon for those by whom it is presented for purification. The Elect themselves do not work in the fields, therefore, pluck no fruit and do not even remove leaves, but expect these things to be brought to them by their auditors for their use; thus—regarded from the point of view of their own vain doctrine—they live by so many and such considerable murders by others. They therefore exhort their auditors not to kill animals themselves, if they eat meat, so as not to insult the Archons of Darkness who are fettered in the heavenly regions, from whom all flesh has it origin.

And when they copulate, they should avoid conception and procreation, so that the divine substance entering them through food and drink may not be fettered in fleshly bonds in succeeding generations. They believe that souls obtain entry to all flesh, and through food and drink. This is no doubt why they condemn marriage, and prevent it as far as they can; when they prohibit procreation, for the sake of which marriages are concluded, they assert that Adam and Eve were generated by the Archons of Smoke; when their father, called Saclas[3] had swallowed the offspring of all his colleagues, and had received all that was in them of admixed divine substance, he had, in sleeping with his wife, fettered in the flesh his descendants, as though with the most solid of bonds.

They assert, however, that Christ was the one called by our Scriptures the Serpent, and they assure us that they have been given insight into this in order to open the eyes of knowledge and to distinguish between Good and Evil. Christ came in the latter days to save souls, not bodies. He did not really exist in the flesh, but in mockery of the human senses proffered the simulated appearance of fleshly form, and thereby also produced the illusion not only of death, but also of resurrection. God, who issued the Law through Moses, and who spoke through the Hebrew prophets, was not the true God but one of the Archons of Darkness. Even the New Testament Scriptures, as though they had been falsified, are read by them so that they take from them what they want and reject what they do not want, and give preference to several apocryphal writings, as if they contained the whole truth. The promise of the Holy Ghost, of the Paraclete [cf. John 16:7] by our Lord Jesus Christ has been realized, they maintain, in the person of their Heresiarch, Manichaeus. For this reason he calls himself in his writings the apostle [i.e., "delegate"] of Jesus Christ, since Jesus Christ promised to send the Holy Ghost and has sent him in him [i.e., Mani].

This is the reason why Mani himself had twelve disciples, in approximation to the number of apostles, a number which the Manichaeans still observe. Among their Elect they have twelve whom they call teachers, and a thirteenth as their superior. They have seventy-two biships, who are ordained by the teachers, and in addition presbyters, who are ordained by the bishops. The bishops also have deacons; the remainder are simply called Elect. Yet they too are sent out, if they appear suitable, to maintain and propagate this erroneous doctrine, where it exists, or to disseminate it where it still has no foothold.

Baptism in water serves no useful purpose, they say, and do not believe that any of the people they deceive should be baptized.

They perform prayers to the sun in the daytime, according to its position in the sky, and to the moon at night, when it appears; should it fail to appear, they stand in a posture of prayer, facing the North, on the sun's path of return, following its setting, to the east. They ascribe the origin of sin not to free will but to the substance of the enemy race. This, in their doctrine, is mingled with man and all flesh is not the work of God, but of the evil spirit, which derives from the contrary principle and is eternal, together with God. Fleshly desire, through which the flesh desires against the spirit, is not a defect which dwells within us, as a result of the nature defiled with sin, in the first man, but the contrary substance, which so affects us that, once we are freed and purified, it is separated from us and lives on even in its own nature, forever. And those two souls, or two spirits, the one good and the other evil, are in conflict with one another in the same person, whenever the flesh desires in opposition to the spirit and the spirit in opposition to the flesh [cf. Gal. 5:17]. And this blemish—contrary to our view —will never be healed in us, but the substance of evil shall be separated from us and imprisoned in a lump when the end of the world has come[4] following the universal fire, and it shall live as in an eternal prison. Furthermore, they say, a covering and wrapping of souls shall be eternally linked to this lump, who are good by nature, and yet could not be cleansed of their contact with the evil nature.

Notes

1. Note the play on words: The name "Mannichaeus" is erroneously explained as

consisting of the words (Gr) *cheo* = (Lat.) *fundo* (pour, scatter).

2. Note the play on words "sacramentum" and "exsecramentum" ("exsecrari" = curse).

3. In the excerpts from Theodore bar Konai, the Son of the King of Darkness is called "Ashaklun."

4. "The Lump" or "the Mass" is an important concept in Manichaean eschatology.

679

Faust Concerning Good and Evil

In this discourse on God, Augustine contends that the notion of two Gods is senseless since the material principle is called Hyle (matter) or Demon, rather than God; just as good and evil are not two types of good, nor health and sickness two kinds of health, God is God, and not types of God. The letter is an exercise in linguistic (and scholastic) questions of naming, which began with Adam in the Garden when he assigned not only names to things but their hierarchical values.

FAUST CONCERNING GOOD AND EVIL*

Faust said: Is there one God, or two? Certainly, one. How is it then that you claim there are two? Never has there been any mention of two Gods, in our statements, but I should like to know where you gained the impression. Because you teach that there are two principles, one good and one evil. It is quite correct that we acknowledge two principles, but we call one of these God, the other Hyle (Matter) or, more generally and colloquially, Demon. If you consider that this means two Gods then you can also assume that when a doctor is engaged in discussing sickness and health, the matter at issue is two types of health. And if there is a discussion on good and evil, you could assume there are two types of good; or if you hear of abundance and scarcity, you will think there are two types of abundance. What? And if I talk of black and white, hot and cold, bitter and sweet, you may say that I am trying to prove that there are two kinds of white, two kinds of heat, and two kinds of sweetness; would it not then seem as if you had lost your reason and were insane? So if I teach that there are two principles, God and Hyle, you

*From Augustine, *Contra Faustum* XXI, 1. From Robert Haardt, *Gnosis* (Leiden, Brill, 1971), pp. 333–334.

should not have the impression that I am asserting the existence of two Gods. If we ascribe all of the evil power to Hyle and the beneficent power to God, as is proper, it is your opinion that this is the same thing as calling each of these principles God. If this were the case, then whenever you heard mention of poison and antidote, you might think it a matter of indifference whether one or the other was termed Antidote, since each of them possesses its powers, effect and strength. And if you heard of a doctor and a poisoner, would you not call the one a doctor as well as the other; and on mention of a just and an unjust man could you not call each of them a just man, since each of them produces an effect? And if this is a senseless procedure, how much more senseless is it to regard God and Hyle as two gods, because both of them produce an effect?

Augustine's Letters Against the Manichaeans

The Letters Against the Manichaeans are traditionally assigned to Augustine. They give a basic picture of Manichaean doctrine and recount Manichaean creation myths. Supposedly they quote Mani's *Epistula fundamenti*. In this short, seminal letter, we have key comments on Manichaean practices and thought; on the relation between the elect and the hearers (St. Augustine was a hearer or auditor); on the denial of Christ's virgin birth and his bodily death; and on God, whom they call the Prince of Darkness, who opposes the true God, the Father of Greatness. The emanation of the true God is the First Man, Ohrmizd, who came down to combat Darkness and was himself caught by the Darkness and mingled with the Prince of Darkness. The elect, by fasting, by purifying their souls, contribute to the purification of the true God's emissary, the First Man. Not mentioned here, but basic to Manichaean and Gnostic thought, is that the purification of one's soul also contributes to the liberation of the Creator God, the Prince of Darkness, from his own matter (*hyle*) and darkness.

EPISTULA 236.2*

The Hearers eat meat and cultivate lands, and, if they wish, have wives, none of which things is allowed to the Elect. The Hearers go on their knees before the Elect, humbly begging the imposition of their hands. They join them in adoring and praying to the sun and the moon. They fast with them on Sundays, and along with them they believe all the blasphemous tenets which make the Manichaean heresy so detestable. Thus they deny Christ's birth of a virgin, and say that his flesh was not true flesh, but false, that his passion accordingly was mere pretence, and his resurrection null. They speak evil of the partriarchs and the prophets. They say that the law, given by God's servant Moses, was not given by the true God, but by the Prince of Darkness. They consider all souls [i.e., here the Living Self, *viva anima*], not only of men, but even of beasts, to be of the substance of God, and altogether parts of God. Finally, they say that the good and true God [i.e., the Father of Greatness through the First Man, Ohrmizd] entered into conflict with the race of Darkness, which part is defiled all the world over, but is purified by the meals of the Elect and by the sun and moon; while any portion of deity which it has been found impossible thus to purify is bound with an everlasting bond of punishment at the end of the world. Thus God is believed to be not only liable to violation and contamination and corruption, seeing that a portion of him is reducible to such misery, but to be unable even at the end of the world to get himself wholly cleansed from the so great defilement and uncleanness and misery.

---

*From Jes P. Asmussen, *Manichaean Literature* (Del Mar, New York: Scholars' Facsmiles & Reprints, 1975), p. 15.

From Other Letters of Augustine on the Manichaeans

FROM *CONTRA EPISTULAM FUNDAMENTI*, 8, 12, 13, 15

At the time I was a Hearer among you I often asked why the Pascha of the Lord was generally kept with no solemnity at all, or if at all, quite coldly and by only a few, with no vigil, with no lengthy fast enjoined upon the Hearers, with no festal array, while your Bema, that is the day on which Manichaeus [Mani] was killed, you marked with great honors the setting up of a platform approached by five steps, covered with precious hangings, an open object of adoration to all. When I asked the question, I say, the answer given me was that the day of his passion should be kept who had truly suffered; but as for Christ, seeing he was not born of woman, nor had presented to human eyes any true, but only a pretended flesh, he had not suffered, but feigned his passion.*

You have turned to me, my dearest brother Patticius, to inform me that you wish to know in what manner Adam and Eve came into existence, whether they were brought forth through the Word or were begotten from a body. To this you shall receive an appropriate reply. This subject has been treated by most writers in various texts and revelations, when they came to speak of it, in varying ways. The true situation in this matter is therefore misunderstood by almost all peoples and by all who have discussed the subject at length and in detail. If they had attained a clear knowledge of the origin of Adam and Eve, they would never become subject to death and corruption. In order to penetrate to the heart of this mystery, however, beyond any ambiguity, one must of necessity set forth other facts in addition. In the first place, therefore, if you will, hearken to what was before the world came into existence, and how the struggle was conducted, so that you may be able to distinguish the nature of the Light and the Darkness.**

---

*Manichaean Literature Jes. T. Asmussen, (Delmar, N.Y.: Scholars' Facsimiles & Reprints, 1975), pp. 60–61.

**From Robert Haardt, *Gnosis* (Leiden: Brill, 1971), pp. 296–297.

These in the primeval beginning were the two substances separated from one another. God the Father ruled over the Light, eternal in his holy descendants, glorious in his power, by nature true, forever rejoicing over his eternity. In himself he contained wisdom and the living forces of the spirit[1] by which he also embraces the twelve members [i.e., Aeons] of his Light, which are the abounding riches of his rule. In each of his members, however, thousands of countless and immeasurable treasures are concealed. The Father himself, exalted in his glory and incomprehensible in his greatness, had joined with himself blessed and illustrious Aeons, whose number and extent cannot be estimated. The sacred and noble Father and Generator lives with them, and nothing is lacking to anyone in his splendid kingdoms, nor is anyone the lowest in rank. Thus his gleaming kingdoms are founded on a light and blessed earth, in such a way that they cannot be moved or shaken by anyone.*

Near the one section, but on one side of that elevated and holy land, was situated the Land of Darkness, deep and of immeasurable extent; in it resided fiery bodies, baneful breeds. Here, out of the same principle, came a boundless and incalculable darkness, together with its abortions. On the other side of the Darkness lay filthy whirling waters with their inhabitants; within the Darkness violent and terrifying storms with their Ruler and their Generators. Next follows another fiery Region a prey to destruction, with its leaders and peoples. In the same way there lived inside it a breed filled with dark and smoke, in which the horrible Ruler and Leader of all these worlds dwelt, who had congregated around himself innumerable Princes, the origin and spirit of all of whom was he himself. And these were the five Natures of the corruption-bearing Land.**

*Ibid., pp. 297–298.
**Ibid., pp. 298–300.

FROM *DE NATURA BONI*, 42 46

The Father of the Blessed Light, however, knew that a great devastation and destruction was rising from the darkness and menacing his sacred Aeons, unless he opposed to it an outstanding, brilliant, and powerful divinity, through which he would at once overcome the descendants of the Darkness and destroy them, and thus, following their destruction, ensure for the inhabitants of the Light eternal rest.

Then the Ruler of the Dark spoke in his wanton deceit to those who were with him: "What do you make of that powerful Light rising up over there? See, how it sets the heavens in motion and convulses most of the Powers. It is better therefore that you give over to me whatever Light you have in your Power. With it I shall make a picture of the Great One who appeared to us in glory.

"Through that image the glory will belong to us and we shall at last be freed of this sojourn in the Darkness."

When they had heard this and debated at length, they considered it best to render up what was desired. For they did not think that they would be able to keep back this light permanently. They therefore considered it better to offer it to their Ruler and hoped devoutly to exercise the power by this means. We must now consider the manner in which they transferred the Light which they possessed to the Ruler. Traces of this knowledge are also to be found in all divine writings and heavenly mysteries. For the wise, of course, a knowledge of the method of transfer is by no means difficult; for this becomes apparent and clearly recognized by him who truly and sincerely desires to know.

As the congregation of those who had assembled differed in sex, namely male and female, the Ruler commanded them to mate, whereby some in the act of coition ejected seed and the others became pregnant. The descendants were like their generators in appearance, and, as the firstborn, received the major part of their parents' powers. The Ruler received them and rejoiced over them as over an extraordinary gift. And just as we, even today, can observe that the principle of evil, which forms bodies, creates out of the bodies forces, in order to form new bodies, so the Ruler we have mentioned received the descendants of his companions, who possessed the sensual powers of their parents, their intelligence and also the Light which had been given to them at once, at the time of their generation, and consumed them. He drew a great deal of strength out of this food, in which there was not only strength but even more, cunning and the corrupted mind which derived from the savage mentality of their generators. He called on his female companion, who had issued from his sex. When he had united with her, he sowed in her, as the others had done beforehand, the surplus of evils which he had consumed, and added to these something of his thinking and his power, so that his own mind should shape and form all that he had brought forth. His female companion received it all, just as the best-tilled soil customarily receives the seed. For in her the images of all heavenly and earthly powers were shaped and interwoven, so that what took shape there, possessed a similarity to the entire Universe.

Note

1. "Sensus vitales": this is a question of five concepts, by which the essence of divine spirit is to be surrounded, but which Augustine here does not divulge. They correspond to the five dwelling places or Aeons of the godhead—Reason, Knowledge, Thought, Imagination, Reflection. Furthermore, of the three properties or aspects of the God—Light, Power, and Wisdom—in this context of the *Epistula fundamenti* only the last is mentioned.

Evodius, Against the Manichaeans

EVODIUS, AGAINST THE MANICHAEANS 28.5

The enemy, who hoped to have crucified that same Redeemer, the Father of the Righteous, was himself crucified: for at that time, appearance and real event were distinct.

. . . the souls which had allowed themselves to be seduced from their former Light-Nature by love of the world became enemies of the sacred Light; armed themselves openly for the destruction of the sacred elements, and gave themselves up obediently to the Spirit of Fire; and by their hostile persecution of the Holy Church and its Elect, did evil unto the adherents to the heavenly commandments; were shut out of the blessedness and glorified state of the sacred earth. And because they allowed themselves to be overcome by evil, they shall remain within that breed of evil and have no access to that peaceful earth and the regions of immortality. This will happen to them because they have become so entangled in evil works that they have become alienated from the life and freedom of the Sacred Light. Therefore they cannot be accepted into those peaceful kingdoms, but will be condensed into this terrible "mass" already mentioned, for which a guard must also be assigned. These souls therefore remain attached to what they have loved and stay behind in this "mass" of darkness. This they have brought upon themselves through their own misdeeds, because they made no effort to understand these teachings concerning the future, and when they were granted time to do so, distanced themselves from it.

The Kephalaia of the Teacher*

The work entitled *The Kephalaia [i.e., Chief Sections] of the Teacher*, deriving from the find at Medinet Madi, is a Coptic translation of a Greek copy which is unknown, and which probably is based, for its part, on a Syriac original. The volume, which is in the possession of the Berlin State Museum, and of which 122 chapters have been so far published (H. J. Polotsky and A. Böhlig, eds., *Kephalaia*, Stuttgart 1940. A. Böhlig, *Kephalaia*, 2d part, Stuttgart 1966), is a collection of doctrinal lectures by Mani, which was compiled, at his own wish on his death, to be added to his writings.

Further sections of the *Kephalaia of the Teacher* have been discovered in the Chester Beatty Collection, but their publication has not so far proved possible.

It may be said, in explanation of the text that follows, that, when at the end of the world the Great Fire has purified all the fragments of light which are still capable of salvation, the demons, together with those souls which are too closely bound up with Darkness to be saved, are isolated forever and separated out, the male demons being cast together in a heap (*bolos i.e.,* "lump" or "mass"), and the female imprisoned in the "grave." Thereupon the localities of the demons are sealed up forever by a stone of tremendous size.

---

*Introduction by Robert Haardt.

CONCERNING THE THREE BLOWS STRUCK AT THE ENEMY ON ACCOUNT OF THE LIGHT*

He turned again and said:

"The Darkness, the Enemy, on the other hand, received three hard blows and suffered three wars and menacing perils on the part of the Light in these three wars.

"The first blow: He was removed from the center and separated from his Land of Darkness, from whence he had come. He was vanquished in that first war and seized and bound by the Living Soul.

"The second blow: This is the time when he is dissolved and melted away in the great Fire and destroyed and annihilated, out of the images, which are all the things in which he exists, and gathered into the fetters corresponding to his first appearance, and so he shall become as he was at the very beginning.

"The third blow, which will strike the Enemy, is the setting in of the end, when everything is separated out, and the male is parted from the female. The male shall be chained up in the bolos (heap), but the female shall be cast into the grave. He shall be divided into pieces [lacuna] stone in their center for all generations and eternities.

"In this manner the Enemy shall be bound, in heavy and painful bondage, from which there is no way out, ever, but they have succeeded in binding him and have bound him in eternity, they have succeeded in separating him off and have separated him off for eternity.

"For this reason I say to my loved ones: Hearken to my words which I proclaim to thee. Hold fast to the works of life.

"Endure persecutions and temptations, which will come to you, fortify yourselves in these commandments which I gave you, that you may escape that second death and these last bonds, in which there is no hope of life, and that you may avoid the evil end of the deniers and blasphemers who have seen the truth with their own eyes and have turned away from it. They shall come unto the Place of Punishment at which there is no day of life. For the shining Light shall hide from them, and from that hour onward they shall not see it. The wind and the air shall be taken from them, and from them they shall receive no breath of life from that hour onward. Water and dew shall be removed from them and they shall never again taste of these.

"Hail to all those who escape the end of the sinners and deniers and avoid the ruin which confronts them in concealment for all eternity!"

---

*From Robert Haardt, *Gnosis* (Leiden: Brill, 1971), pp. 333–334.

Diverse Manichaean Documents

THE RELIGION THAT I, MANI, HAVE CHOSEN*

The religion that I, Mani, have chosen is in ten things above and better than the other, previous religions. Firstly: the primeval religions were in one country and one language. But my religion is of that kind that it will be manifest in every country and in all languages, and it will be taught in far away countries.

Secondly: the former religions existed as long as they had the pure leaders, but when the leaders had been led upwards [i.e., had died], then their religions fell into disorder and became negligent in commandments and works. . . . But my religion, because of the living books, of the Teachers, the Bishops, the Elect and the Hearers, and of wisdom and works will stay on until the End.

Thirdly: those previous souls that in their own religion have not accomplished the works, will come to my reli-

gion through metempsychosis, which certainly will be the door of redemption for them.

Fourthly: this revelation of mine of the two principles and my living books, my wisdom and knowledge are above and better than those of the previous religions.

MANI'S DEATH

Mani came to the audience of Bahram I, after he had summoned me, Nuhzadag the interpreter, Kushtai the scribe, and Abzakhya the Persian. The king was at his dinner table and had not yet washed his hands, not yet finished his meal. The courtiers entered and said: "Mani has come and is standing at the door." And the king sent the Lord the message: "Wait a moment until I can come to you myself." And the Lord again sat down to one side of the guard and waited there until the king should have finished his meal, when he was to go hunting. And he stood up from his meal; and, putting one arm round the queen of the Sakas and the other round Karder, the son of

---

*All selections in this chapter are from Jes P. Asmussen, *Manichaean Literature* (Delmar, New York: Scholars' Facsimiles, 1975), pp. 12, 54–58, 18–19, 20, 22, 48.

Ardavan, he came to the Lord. And his first words to the Lord were: "You are not welcome." And the Lord replied: "Why? What wrong have I done?" The King said: "I have sworn an oath not to let you come to this land!" And in anger he spoke thus to the Lord: "Ah, what need of you, since you go neither fighting nor hunting? But perhaps you are needed for this doctoring and this physicking? And you don't do even that!" And the Lord replied thus: "I have done you no evil. Always I have done good to you and your family. And many and numerous were your servants whom I have freed of demons and witches. And many were those whom I have caused to rise from their illness. And many were those from whom I have averted the numerous kinds of fever. And many were those who came unto death, and I have revived them. . . ."

Just like a sovereign who takes off armor and garment and puts on another royal garment, thus the Apostle of Light took off the warlike dress of the body and sat down in a ship of Light and received the divine garment, the diadem of Light, and the beautiful garland. And in great joy he flew together with the Light-gods that are going to the right and to the left of him, with harp-sound and song of joy, in divine miraculous power, like a swift lightning and a shooting star, to the Column of Glory, the path of the Light, and the Moon-Chariot, the meeting place of the gods. And he stayed there with god Ohrmizd the Father.

The ever Powerful One stood in prayer, he implored the Father with praise: "I have cleaned the earth and spread the seed, and the fruit full of life I have brought before you. I have built a palace and a quiet monstery for your *nous*. And the Holy Spirit I have sown in a green flower garden and brought a delightful garland to you. Brilliant trees I have made fruitful, and I showed the road leading to the sons on high. I have entirely accomplished your pious order

for the sake of which I was sent to this world. Take me then to the peace of salvation, where I shall not any longer see the figure of the enemies, nor hear their tyrannic voice. This time [viz., in distinction to the previous rebirths] give me the great garland of victory."

On the fourth of the month of Shahrevar, on the Monday and at the eleventh hour, when he had prayed, he shed the wonted garment of the body. Like the swift lightning he gleamed; brighter than the light of the sun the chariot glittered; and the Envoys spoke up and saluted the Righteous god. The house of the sky broke down to the outside; the earth trembled; a mighty voice was heard; and people that saw this sign were confused and fell on their faces. It was a day of pain and a time full of sorrow, when the Apostle of Light went into *Parinirvana* [i.e., died]. He left the leaders that guard the Church, and gave parting words of blessing to the whole great herd.

The Noble Prince, Mani, has fulfilled his promise that he spoke to us: "For your sake I will wait above, in the chariot of water [i.e., the moon, his resting place until the final salvation of the world] and always send you help."

And whoever strikes you, do not strike him again. And whoever hates you, do not hate him back. And whoever envies you, do not envy him again. And whoever brings forth anger towards you, always speak with kindness to him. And what you detest in another person, do not do that yourself. No, one has to endure insults and other abuses from people above oneself, from people equal to oneself and from people under oneself; because nobody shall in any way make waver the devout one of good endurance. And it is as if one threw flowers against an elephant, and these flowers cannot smash the elephant; and as if raindrops fell upon a stone, and these raindrops cannot melt the stone. Just so, insults and other abuses shall not in any way be able to make waver the devout one of good endurance.

691

VISIONS OF PARADISE IN MANICHAEAN MISSIONARY HISTORY

And when the Turan-Shah [i.e., the Prince of Turan in north eastern Baluchistan] saw that the Beneficent one, Mani, had got up, then he, indeed, from afar was on his knees. And he implored the Beneficent one and spoke to him respectfully: "Do not come hither before me!" Then the Beneficent one went there. The prince stood up and went to meet him. And he kissed him. Then he said to the Beneficent one: "You are the Buddha, and we are sinful men; it is not becoming that you come to us. Because of that. . . . As many steps as we come before you, so much merit and salvation will be to us. And as many steps as you come to us, so much non-merit and sin will be to us." Then the Beneficent one gave him his blessing. And he said to him: "Be blessed! Just as you now on earth amongst men are fully of glory and honored, in that very same way you on the last day of the soul, in the eyes of the gods, shall be full of glory and noble. And among the gods and the beneficent Righteous [viz., in Paradise] you shall be immortal forever and ever." Then . . . he seized the hand. . . .

. . . the Apostle led the Righteous one [i.e., here, in a vision, most probably one of the saved from Paradise] up into the atmosphere, and said: "What is still higher?" The Righteous one said: "My sphere!" The Apostle said: "Further, what is still greater?" He said: "The earth that bears everything." Further he said: "What is still greater than these things?" The Righteous one said: "The sky . . . ." "What is still greater?" He said: "The sun and the moon." "Further, what is still lighter?" He said: "The wisdom of the Buddha." Then the Turan-Shah said: "Of all these you are the greatest and lightest, for, in truth, you are the Buddha yourself." Then the Devout one said

to the Turan-Shah: "You shall act so. . . ." . . . apostles have come to various countries, pious and sinner, and the actions of the Electus and the Hearer. Then, when the Turan-Shah and the noblemen heard this word, they became happy, adopted the belief, and became well-disposed towards the Apostle and the religion. Further, when the Turan-Shah was with Mani in the garden, he found the daughter of the Turan-Shah and the brothers transported.

THE LIGHT OF PARADISE

The Meshun-Shah Mihrshah
Moreover Shahpuhr, the King of Kings, had a brother, Lord of Meshun [i.e., Mesene, a district of Basra in Mesopotamia], and his name was Mihrshah. And to the religion of the Apostle he was extraordinarily hostile. And he had arranged a garden, which was good, lovely, and extraordinarily large, so that there was none like it. Then the Apostle knew that the time of salvation had come near. He then rose and appeared before Mihrshah who with great merriment was seated at a feast in the garden. Then the Apostle . . . he commanded. Then he said to the Apostle: "Was there ever in the Paradise that you praise, such a garden as this garden of mine?" Then the Apostle understood this utterance of disbelief. Then by his miraculous power he showed him the Paradise of Light with all gods, divine beings, and the immortal breath of life and every kind of garden and also other splendid things there. Thereafter he fell to the ground unconscious for three hours, and what he saw he kept as a memory in his heart. Then the Apostle put his hand upon his head. He regained consciousness. When he had risen, he fell down at the Apostle's feet and seized his right hand.

"The gate of the eyes that is deceived

when seeing what is vain, is like the man who sees a mirage in the desert: a town, a tree, water, and many other things that demon makes him imagine and kills him. Further, it is like unto a castle on a rock to which the enemies found no access. Then the enemies arranged a feast, much singing and music. Those in the castle became greedy of seeing, and the enemies assaulted them from behind and took the castle. The gate of the ears is like unto that man who went along a secure road with many treasures. Then two robbers stood near his ear, deceived him through beautiful words, took him to a place far away, and killed him and stole his treasures. Further, it is like a beautiful girl who was kept locked up in a castle, and a deceitful man who sang a sweet melody at the base of the castle wall, until that girl died of grief. The gate of the smelling nose is like the elephant when it from a mountain above the garden of the king became greedy of the smell of the flowers, fell down from the mountains in the night and died.

If you wish, I will instruct you from the testimony of the fathers of old. The righteous Zarathustra, the savior, when talking with his soul (ie., self), said: "Deep is the drunkenness in which you sleep; awake and look at me! Grace upon you from the world of peace, whence I am sent for your sake." And it answered: "I, I am the tender innocent son of Sroshav [in Parthian texts, a name borrowed from Zoroastrianism, of the Father of Greatness], I am in the state of mixture [i.e., this material world] and see suffering; lead me out from the embrace of death." With "grace" Zarathustra asked of it: "Are you the Word of Old, my member? The power of the living and the peace of the highest worlds come upon you from your own home. Follow me, son of gentleness [i.e., son of the First Man], set the crown of Light upon your head [i.e., be redeemed]! You son of mighty ones that have become so poor that you even have to beg at every place."

PRAYER TO MANI AND OTHER POEMS*

Prayer to Mani

Father of our souls,
holy Mani
and Buddha,
our highest god.

*The Illuminator of our Hearts***

The illuminator of our hearts
is coming,
the lamp of Light
brightening even those in darkness.

---

*Revised by Willis Barnstone.
**From "Praise to the Apostle of Light."

693

The true upraiser of the dead
is coming
to heal us.

Mani, Son of Gods

Mani, son of gods,
Lord,
vivifier,
great center of region,
I pay homage to you,
Chosen One.
Be merciful, Father, Lord, Life-giver,
Mani.
You who vivify the dead
and light those in darkness,
raise me,
raise me,
Mani, Lord.

Salvation of the Soul (Old Turkish)

Like the gray wolf I will walk with you;
like the black raven I will stay on earth.
Like charcoal to the disease,
like the spittle to the whetstone I will be.
You are our powerful great ruler.
Like gold rounded,
like a ball rounded,
you are our glorious wise lord.
And your numerous people
at your wide breast,
at your long seam,
you keep and protect, you nurse, take care of.

Come to Me, My Kinsman, the Light, My Guide*

Come to me, my kinsman, the Light, my guide.
Since I went forth into the darkness I was given a water to drink. I bear up
  beneath a burden which is not my own.
I am in the midst of my enemies, the beasts surrounding me; the burden which I
  bear is of the powers and principalities.
They burned in their wrath, they rose up against me.
Matter and her sons divided me up amongst them, they burnt me in their fire,
  they gave me a bitter likeness.

---

*From Hans Jonas, *The Gnostic Religion*, 2d ed., rev. (1958; reprint, Boston:
Beacon Press, 3d printing, 1970), pp. 229–230.

694

The strangers with whom I mixed, me they know not; they tasted my sweetness, they desired to keep me with them.

I was life to them, but they were death to me; I bore up beneath them, they wore me as a garment upon them.

I am in everything, I bear the skies, I am the foundation, I support the earths, I am the Light that shines forth, that gives joy to the souls.

I am the life of the world: I am the milk that is in all trees: I am the sweet water that is beneath the sons of matter.

I bore these things until I had fulfilled the will of my Father; the First Man is my father whose will I have carried out.

Lo, the darkness I have subdued; lo, the fire of the fountains I have extinguished, as the sphere turns hurrying round, as the sun receives the refined part of life.

O soul, raise your eyes to the height and contemplate your bond, lo, your Fathers are calling you.

Now go aboard the Ship of Light and receive your garland of glory and return to your kingdom and rejoice with all the Aeons.

Paradise of Light (Middle Persian)

The shining sun
and the glittering full moon
shine and glitter
from the trunk of this tree.
Brilliant birds
are there sporting happily.
Sporting there are doves
and peacocks of all colors.

Mandaean Salvation and Ethics

Mandaean soteriology depicts the soul's salvation, its release from the body to return to the felicitous realm of light. Adam is a key figure, whose salvation gives hope to all of us. Kurt Rudolph describes the deliverance of the soul from the perishable body: "Death is the 'day of deliverance' when the soul leaves the body and begins a long and dangerous journey leading through seven or right supernatural 'places of detention' (the planetary spheres, including the sun and the moon and that of Rūhā). These places are considered altogether evil and hostile to the soul. They, therefore, seek to detain it, but can only succeed in the case of sinners and non-Mandeans, who then have to endure the punishments of hell."[1] For the "great day of the end" or day of judgment, the soul may fall into the Sea of Sūf and its blazing fire or be flown into the Pleroma.

The Ethics and Morality poems are concerned with ideal human virtue and its rewards. Mandaean morality was based on old Jewish practice: dietary laws, monogamy, alms-giving, ritual slaughtering and baptism and lustration. Women were held in poor regard. There was a certain paradox in their attitude toward sexuality—neither ascetic nor libertine—and while they rejected this world as a transitory prison, they lived rather comfortably and made beautiful objects as goldsmiths and silversmiths.

For further information, see part 1, "Creation of the World and the Alien Man" (Mandaean Gnosticism).

Note

1. Kurt Rudolph, *Gnosis: the Nature and History of an Ancient Religion*, trans. Robert McLachlan Wilson (San Francisco: Harper & Row, forthcoming), p. 359.

SOTERIOLOGY (SALVATION OF THE SOUL)*

The Messenger of Light Creates the Way of Salvation

I prepared a path for the good ones
and made a gateway for the world.
A gateway for the world I made
and erected a throne in it.
A throne for the good ones I erected
and set up a light beside it.
A light I set up beside it,
which is completely perfect.
And a watch-tower for the sons of perfection I erected,
in the place where they live and are without deficiency.
I set up thrones for them
and presented them with magnificent robes.
I established the Jordan of the Great Life
and appointed guardians over it.
I stationed two uthras beside it,
who were rich and without deficiency.
I set up a throne for the lord of the radiant beings
and erected a light before it.
A light, which I erected,
which was completely perfect.
With illumination and praise,
with what the Life had caused me to hear,
With illumination and praise
I arose and went to the House of the Mighty Life.
In the joy that I felt,
I reported to the Mighty Life.
The Mighty Life rejoiced and was glad,
he was overjoyed with me.
The Life thanked me
and gave me more glory than I had before.
He spoke to me:
"Kusta preserve you, good one,
and preserve the word you have spoken."
The Life spoke in his joy
to the uthras and said:
"Praise the strength of the man,
who healed the water through the fire.
Praise the strength of the man,
against whom the fire sinned not.

---

*From Werner Foerster, *Gnosis: A Selection of Gnostic Texts*, vol. 2, trans. R. McL. Wilson (Oxford: Clarendon Press, 1974), pp. 213–214, 224–225, 259, 261–262, 265, 270, 293, 295.

The fire did not sin against him;
the uthra shone in its brightness.
In its brightness the uthra shone
and prepared a path for the perfect ones.
For the perfect ones he prepared a path
and granted salvation to the perfect ones.
Salvation he granted to the perfect ones
and remembered their names in the house of the Mighty Life."

Adam's Deliverance

In the name of the Great Life
the sublime Light be glorified.
From the Place of Light I have come forth,
from you, everlasting (or, bright) dwelling-place,
From the Place of Light I have come forth,
and an uthra from the House of Life accompanied me.
The uthra who accompanied me from the House of the Great Life
held a staff of living water in his hand
The staff which he held in his hand
was completely full of leaves.
He gave me its branches,
of which the ritual books and prayers were full.
Then he gave me more of them,
and then my suffering heart was healed.
My suffering heart was healed
and my world-shy soul found peace.
A third time he gave me some of them,
and then he lifted up the eyes of my head.
The eyes of my head he lifted up,
so that I beheld my father and recognized him.
I beheld my father and recognized him.
and I put three questions to him:
I asked him about the calm in which there is no insubordination.
I asked him about a great, strong heart,
which can support both great and small.
I asked him about a smooth path,
in order to ascend and see the Place of Light.
The Life is worshiped and is victorious
and victorious is the man who has come hither.

Adam's Baptism

The planets stand there,
they are bound by fetters and say:
"When Adam fled from us
our watch-houses were destroyed.
When Adam rose from us,
our radiance was soon taken away."

He rose up and ascended to the House of Life;
they, the uthras, washed him in the Jordan and protected him.
They washed him and protected him in the Jordan;
they placed their right hand on him.
They baptized him with their baptism
and strengthened him with their pure words.

The Soul's Deliverance

Hail to you, hail to you, soul,
for you have departed from the world.
You have left corruption behind
and the stinking body in which you found yourself,
the abode, the abode of the wicked,
the place which is all sin,
the World of Darkness,
of hatred, envy, and strife,
the abode in which the planets live,
bringing sorrows and infirmities;
they bring sorrows and infirmities,
and every day they cause unrest.
Rise up, rise up, soul,
ascend to your first earth.
To your first earth, ascend,
to the place from which you were transplanted,
to the place from which you were transplanted,
to the fine abode of the uthras.
Bestir yourself, put on your garment of radiance
and put on your resplendent wreath.
Sit on your throne of radiance,
which the Life set up for you in the Place of Light.
Rise up, inhabit the skinas,
among the uthras, your brothers.
As you have learnt, pronounce the blessing
over your first father's house.
And curse this place
the house of your earthly guardian.
For the years that you spent in it,
the Seven were your enemies.
Your enemies were the Seven,
and the Twelve were your persecutors. . . .

Bliss and Peace

Bliss and peace there shall be
on the road which Adam built well.
Bliss and peace there shall be
on the road which the soul takes.
Go, soul, in victory
to the place from which you were transplanted,

the place of joy,
in which the face shines.
The face shines in it,
the form is illumined and does not grow dim.
The soul has loosened its chain
and broken its fetters.
It shed its bodily coat,
then it turned about, saw it, and shuddered.
The call of the soul is the call of life
which departs from the body of refuse.

The Soul in Its Coat of All Colors

The soul, the soul speaks:
"Who cast me into the Tibil, the earth,
Who cast me into the Tibil, the earth,
who chained me in the wall?
Who cast me into the stocks,
which matches the fullness of the world?
Who threw a chain round me,
that is without measure?
Who clothed me in a coat
of all colours and kinds?"

Wrapped in Sleep

I am wrapped and sleep
in a garment in which there is no defect.
In a garment in which there is no defect,
which has nothing missing or lacking.
The Life knew about me,
Adam, who slept awoke.
He the Helper took me by the palm of my right hand
and gave a palm-branch into my hand.
The light cast me into the darkness,
and the darkness was filled with light.
On the day when light arises,
darkness will return to its place.
He approached the clouds of light,
and his course was set to the Place of Light.

SONG OF ASCENT

I fly and proceed thither,
until I reach the watch-house of the sun.
I cry:
"Who will guide me past the watch-house of Šamiš?"

"Your reward, your works, your alms, and your goodness
will guide you past the watch-house of Šamiš."
How greatly I rejoice,
how greatly my heart rejoices.
How much I look forward
to the day when my struggle is over,
to the day when my struggle is over
and my course is set towards the Place of Life.
I hasten and proceed thither,
until I reach the watch-house of the moon.

When I arrived at the water-brooks,
a discharge of radiance met me.
It took me by the palm of my right hand
and brought me over the streams.
Radiance was brought and I was clothed in it,
light was brought and I was wrapped in it.
The Life supported the Life. . . .
Son of the good ones,
show me the way of the uthras
and the ascent upon which your father
rose up to the Place of Light.

ETHICS AND MORALITY
(MANDAEAN)

Instruction of Adam by an Uthra

Do not slumber and sleep,
and forget not what your lord commanded you.
Be no son of the House, the world,
and be not named as a guilty person in the Tibil.
Love not fragrant wreaths,
and have no liking for a seductive woman.
Love not pleasant odors,
and do not neglect the night prayer.
Love not treacherous spirits
and seductive courtesans.
Love not lust,
and lying phantoms.
Drink not and do not become intoxicated,
and do not forget your lord in your thoughts.
In your coming in and your going out
be careful not to forget your lord.
In your coming and going
be careful not to forget your lord.
In your sitting and in your standing
be careful not to forget your lord.

In your resting and your lying down
be careful not to forget your lord.
Do not say: I am a firstborn son,
in everything that I do I am proof against folly.
Adam, look upon the world,
which is a completely unreal thing.
It is an unreal thing,
in which you can put no trust.

Be Not Like a Pomegranate

My brothers! speak the truth
and lie not with lying lips.
Be not like a pomegranate,
whose outer face looks fine.
Its outer face looks fine,
but inside it is full of seed-corns or, rottenness.
Be like wine-jars
full of fragrant wine.
Their outside is clay and pitch,
but inside is fragrant wine.
The message of life cries,
ears of my chosen, hearken to me.

10
MYSTICAL DOCUMENTS

The Divine
Throne-Chariot

(Dead Sea Scrolls)*

The Divine Throne-Chariot draws its inspiration from Ezekiel (1:10) and is related to the Book of Revelation (4). It depicts the appearance and movement of the *Merkabah*, the divine Chariot supported and drawn by the cherubim, which is at the same time a throne and a vehicle. The "small voice" of blessing is drawn from 1 Kings 19:12: it was in a "still small voice" that God manifested himself to Elijah. In our Qumran text this voice is uttered by the cherubim and it is interesting to note that although the Bible does not define the source of the voice, the ancient Aramaic translation of 1 Kings (Targum of Jonathan) ascribes it to angelic beings called "they who bless silently."

The Throne-Chariot was a central subject of meditation in ancient as well as in medieval Jewish esotericism and mysticism, but the guardians of Rabbinic orthodoxy tended to discourage such speculation. The liturgical use of Ezekiel's chapter on the Chariot is expressly forbidden in the Mishnah; it even lays down that no wise man is to share his understanding of the *Merkabah* with a person less enlightened than himself. As a result, there is very little ancient literary material extant on the subject, and the Qumran text is therefore of great importance to the study of the origins of Jewish mysticism.

*Introduction by Geza Vermes.

THE DIVINE THRONE-CHARIOT*

... the ministers of the Glorious Face in the abode of the gods of knowledge fall down before him, and the cherubim utter blessings. And as they rise up, there is a divine small voice and loud praise; there is a divine small voice as they fold their wings.

The cherubim bless the image of the Throne-Chariot above the firmament, and they praise the majesty of the fiery firmament beneath the seat of his glory. And between the turning wheels, angels of holiness come and go, as it were a fiery vision of most holy spirits; and about them flow seeming rivulets of fire, like gleaming bronze, a radiance of many gorgeous colors, of marvelous pigments magnificently mingled.

The spirits of the Living God move perpetually with the glory of the wonderful Chariot. The small voice of blessing accompanies the tumult as they depart, and on the path of their return they worship the Holy One. Ascending, they rise marvelously; settling, they stay still. The sound of joyful praise is silenced and there is a small voice of blessing in all the camp of God. And a voice of praise resounds from the midst of all their divisions in worship. And each one in his place, all their numbered ones sing hymns of praise.

*From Geza Vermes, *The Dead Sea Scrolls*, 2d ed. (1962; reprint, New York: Penguin Books, 1962), pp. 212–213.

The Zohar, *the Book of Radiance*

*(Kabbalah)**

The method of Kabbalah is to comment on scriptures and so each part usually begins with a line from the Bible. The main part of the *Zohar* purports to be an ancient Midrash (commentary); another section is called *Midrash ha-Neelan* (The Secret Midrash). The practice of biblical exegesis also goes back to Alexandria and Philo (fl. 40 B.C.–A.D. 40), whose allegorical exegesis of the Bible were the model for later Christian allegorical and typological commentary.

The authors of Kabbalah were obsessed with letters, which had to be created before the Word. And in drawings they hung them like fruit from trees of life and placed them on vital parts of the human body. Numbers also had numerical meanings and, as in Pythagoras, represented mysteries of the universe. But the Kabbalists, in their poetic fantasy, go beyond mere numerology. In their descriptions they attribute physical forms and human qualities to signs and numbers, as we see in the depiction of *eyn sof*, the Infinite:

Within the most hidden recess a dark flame issued from the mystery of *eyn sof*, the Infinite, like a fog forming in the unformed— enclosed in the ring of that sphere, neither white nor black, neither red nor green, of no color whatsoever. Only after this flame began to assume size and dimension, did it produce radiant colors. From the innermost center of the flame sprang forth a well out of which colors issued and spread upon everything beneath, hidden in mysterious hiddenness of *eyn sof*.[1]

---

*For more information see Section 1, Kabbalah.

Note
1. Gershom Scholem, *Zohar: The Book of Splendor* (1949; reprint, New York: Schocken Books, 1963), p. 27.

HIGHEST GRADE OF FAITH

The "soul" *(nefesh)* stands in intimate relation to the body, nourishing and upholding it; it is below, the first stirring. Having acquired due worth, it becomes the throne for the "spirit" *(ruah)* to rest upon, as it is written, "until the spirit be poured upon us from on high" (Isa. 32: 15). And when these two, soul and spirit, have duly readied themselves, they are worthy to receive the "supersoul" *(neshamah)*, resting in turn upon the throne of the spirit *(ruah)*. The supersoul stands preëminent, and not to be perceived. There is throne upon throne, and for the highest a throne.

The study of these grades of the soul yields an understanding of the higher wisdom; and it is in such fashion that wisdom alone affords the linking together of a number of mysteries. It is *nefesh*, the lowest stirring, to which the body adheres; just as in a candle flame, the obscure light at the bottom adheres close to the wick, without which it cannot be. When fully kindled, it becomes a throne for the white light above it, and when these two come into their full glow, the white light becomes a throne for a light not wholly discernible, an unknowable essence reposing on the white light, and so in all there comes to be a perfect light.

It is the same with the man that arrives at perfection and is named "holy," as the verse says, "for the holy that are in the earth" (Ps. 16:3). It is likewise in the upper world. Thus, when Abram entered the land, God appeared before him, and Abram received *nefesh* and there erected an altar to the like grade (of divinity). Then he "journeyed toward the South" (Gen. 12:9), and received *ruah*. He attained at last to the summit of cleaving to God through *neshamah*, and thereupon he "built an altar to the Lord," whereby is meant the ineffable grade which is that of *neshamah*. Then seeing that he must put himself to the test, and pass through the grades, he journeyed into Egypt. There he resisted being seduced by the demonic essences, and when he had proved himself, he returned to his abode; and, actually, he "went up out of Egypt" (Gen. 13:1), his faith was strong and reassured, and he attained to the highest grade of faith. From that time, Abram knew the higher wisdom, and cleaved to God, and of the world he became the right hand.

MIDNIGHT*

The "soul" *[nefesh]*, stands in intimate relation to the body, nourishing and upholding it; it is below, the first stirring. Having acquired due worth, it becomes the throne for the "spirit" *[ruah]* to rest upon, as it is written, "until the spirit be poured upon us from on high" [Isa. 32:- 15]. And when these two, soul and spirit, have duly readied themselves, they are worthy to receive the "supersoul" *[neshamah]*, resting in turn upon the throne of the spirit *[ruah]*. The supersoul stands preeminent, and not to be perceived. There is throne upon throne, and for the highest a throne.

*All selections in the chapter are from Gershom Scholem, ed., *The Zohar, the Book of Radiance* (New York: Schocken Books, 1949), pp. 44–48, 70–74, 77–81, 91–94, 96–97, 113–115, 116–117, 118, 119–120.

The study of these grades of the soul yields an understanding of the higher wisdom; and it is in such fashion that wisdom alone affords the linking together of a number of mysteries. It is *nefesh*, the lowest stirring, to which the body adheres; just as in a candle flame, the obscure light at the bottom adheres close to the wick, without which it cannot be. When fully kindled, it becomes a throne for the white light above it, and when these two come into their full glow, the white light becomes a throne for a light not wholly discernible, an unknowable essence reposing on the white light, and so in all there comes to be a perfect light.

It is the same with the man that arrives at perfection and is named "holy," as the verse says, "for the holy that are in the earth" [Ps. 16:3]. It is likewise in the upper world. Thus, when Abram entered the land, God appeared before him, and Abram received *nefesh* and there erected an altar to the like grade of divinity. Then he "journeyed toward the South" [Gen. 12:9], and received *ruah*. He attained at last to the summit of cleaving to God through *neshamah*, and thereupon he "built an altar to the Lord," whereby is meant the ineffable grade which is that of *neshamah*. Then seeing that he must put himself to the test, and pass through the grades, he journeyed into Egypt. There he resisted being seduced by the demonic essences, and when he had proved himself, he returned to his abode; and, actually, he "went up out of Egypt" [Gen. 13:1], his faith was strong and reassured, and he attained to the highest grade of faith. From that time, Abram knew the higher wisdom, and cleaved to God, and of the world he became the right hand.

Rabbi Abba set out from Tiberias to go to the house of his father-in-law. With him was his son, Rabbi Jacob. When they arrived at Kfar Tarsha, they stopped to spend the night, Rabbi Abba inquired of his host: "Have you a cock here?" The host said: "Why?" Said Rabbi Abba: I wish to rise at exactly midnight." The host replied: "A cock is not needed. By my bed is a water-clock. The water drips out drop by drop, until just at midnight it is all out, and then the wheel whirls back with a clatter which rouses the entire household. This clock I made for a certain old man who was in the habit of getting up each night at midnight to study Torah." To this Rabbi Abba said: "Blessed be God for guiding me here."

The wheel of the clock whirled back at midnight, and Rabbi Abba and Rabbi Jacob arose. They listened to the voice of their host coming up from the lower part of the house where he was sitting with his two sons, and saying: It is written, "Midnight I will rise to give thanks to you for your righteous judgments" [Ps. 119:62]. The word "at" is not used, and so we ssume that "Midnight" is an appellation of the Holy one, be blessed, whom David speaks to thus because midnight is the hour when He appears with his retinue, and goes into the Garden of Eden to converse with the righteous. Rabbi Abba then said to Rabbi Jacob: "Now we indeed have the luck to be with the Presence."

And they went and seated themselves by their host, and said: "Tell us again that which you just said, which is very good. Where did you hear it?" He replied: "My grandfather told it me. He said that the accuser angels below are busy all about the world during the first three hours of the night, but exactly at midnight the accusations halt, for at this moment God enters the Garden of Eden."

He continued: "These ceremonies above occur nightly only at the exact midnight and this we know from what is written of Abraham, that 'the night was divided for them' [Gen. 14:15] and from the verse 'and it came to pass at the midnight,' in the story of the Exodus [Exod. 12:29], and from numerous other passages in the Scripture. David knew it,"

709

so the old man related, "because upon it depended his kingship. And so he was accustomed to get up at this hour and sing praises, and on this account he addressed God as Midnight. He said, too, 'I will rise to give thanks to you for your righteous judgments,' since he knew this sphere to be the source of justice, with judgments of earthly kings deriving therefrom, and for this reason David did not ever fail to rise and sing praises at this hour."

Rabbi Abba went up to him and kissed him, and said: "Surely, it is as you say. Blessed be God who has guided me here. In all places judgment is executed at night, and this we have certainly affirmed, discussing it before Rabbi Simeon."

At this, the young son of the innkeeper asked: "Why then does it say 'Midnight'?"

Rabbi Abba replied: "It is established that the heavenly King rises at midnight."

The boy said: "I have a different explanation."

Then Rabbi Abba said: "Speak, my child, because through your mouth will speak the voice of the Lamp.[1]"

He answered: "This is what I have heard. Truly, night is the time of strict judgment, a judgment which reaches out impartially everywhere. But midnight draws from two sides, from judgment and from mercy, the first half only of the night being the period of judgment, while the second half takes illumination from the side of mercy [hased]. Wherefore David said 'Midnight.' "

Upon this, Rabbi Abba stood up and put his hands on the boy's head and blessed him, and said: "I had thought that wisdom dwells only in a few privileged pious men. But I perceive that even children are gifted with heavenly wisdom in the generation of Rabbi Simeon. Happy are you, Rabbi Simeon! Woe to the generation when you will have left it!"

A SEAL UPON YOUR HEART

On a certain occasion, wishing to get away from the heat of the sun, Rabbi Eleazar and Rabbi Abba turned into a cave at Lydda. Rabbi Abba spoke: "Let us now compass this cave about with words of the Torah." Rabbi Eleazar then began, quoting the verse: " 'Set me as a seal upon your heart, as a seal upon your arm . . . the flashes thereof are flashes of fire, a very flame of the Lord' " [Cant. 8:6].

He said: "This verse has provoked great discussion. One night I was in attendance on my father, and I heard him say that it is the souls of the righteous, they alone, which effect the true devotion of the Community of Israel to God, and her longing for him, for these souls make possible the flow of the lower waters toward the upper, and this brings about perfect friendship and the yearning for mutual embrace in order to bring forth fruit. When they cleave one to the other, then says the Community of Israel in the largeness of her affection: 'Set me as a seal upon your heart.' For, as the imprint of the seal is to be discerned even after the seal is withdrawn, so I shall cling to you, even after I am taken from you and enter into captivity: thus says the Community of Israel.

"Thus, 'Set me as a seal upon your heart,' so that I may remain upon you in semblance, as the imprint of a seal.

" 'For love is strong as death' (Cant. 8:6), violent, as is the separation of the spirit from the body; for we have learned that when a man is come to leave this world and he sees wondrous things, his spirit, like an oarless boatmen tossing up and down and making no headway on the sea, also tosses up and down through his limbs, asking leave of each one; and only with great rending is its separation performed. Thus, violently, does the Community of Israel love God. 'Jealousy is cruel as the grave' (Cant. 8:

6). Without jealousy, it is not true love. Thus we learn that for a man's love of his wife to be perfect, he should be jealous, for then he will not look after any other woman."

As they sat, they heard Rabbi Simeon approaching on the road, with Rabbi Judah and Rabbi Isaac. When Rabbi Simeon came to the cave, Rabbi Eleazar and Rabbi Abba emerged from it. Said Rabbi Simeon: "From the walls of the cave I perceive that the Divine Presence hovers here." And they all sat down.

Rabbi Simeon asked: "What have you been discoursing of?"

Rabbi Abba replied: "Of the love that the Community of Israel bears to God." And Rabbi Eleazar cited in that connection the words: "Set me as a seal upon thy heart."

Rabbi Simeon said: "Eleazar, it was the celestial love and the ties of affection which you were in the act of perceiving." Then he remained silent for a time, and at last said: "Always silence is agreeable, save where the Torah is concerned. I possess a jewel which I would share with you. It is a profound idea which I came upon in the book of Rav Hamnuna the Elder. It is this:

"Always, it is the male who pursues the female seeking to stimulate her love, but in this case we see the female pursuing the male and paying court, a thing not ordinarily accounted fitting for the female. But in this there is a profound mystery, one of the most cherished treasures of the King. We know that three souls pertain to the divine grades. Nay, four, for there is one supernal soul which is unperceivable, certainly to the keeper of the lower treasury, and even to that of the upper. This is the soul of all souls, incognizable and inscrutable. All is contingent on it, which is veiled in a dazzling bright veil. From it are formed pearls which are tissued together like the joints of the body, and these it enters into, and through them manifests its energy. It and they are one, there being no division between them. Yet another, a female soul, is concealed amidst her hosts and has a body adhering to her through which she manifests her power, as the soul in the human body.

"These souls are as copies of the hidden joints above. Yet another soul is there, namely, the souls of the righteous below, which, coming from the higher souls, the soul of the female and the soul of the male, are hence preeminent above all the heavenly hosts and camps. It may be wondered, if they are thus preeminent on both sides, why do they descend to this world only to be taken thence at some future time?

"This may be explained by way of a simile: A king has a son whom he sends to a village to be educated until he shall have been initiated into the ways of the palace. When the king is informed that his son is now come to maturity, the king, out of his love, sends the matron his mother to bring him back into the palace, and there the king rejoices with him every day. In this wise, the Holy One, be blessed, possessed a son from the matron, that is, the supernal holy soul. He despatched it to a village, that is, to this world, to be raised in it, and initiated into the ways of the King's palace. Informed that his son was now come to maturity, and should be returned to the palace, the King, out of love, sent the matron for him to bring him into the palace. The soul does not leave this world until such time as the matron has arrived to get her and bring her into the King's palace, where she abides for ever. Withal, the village people weep for the departure of the king's son from among them. But one wise man said to them: 'Why do you weep? Was this not the king's son, whose true place is in his father's palace, and not with you? . . . '

"If the righteous were only aware of this, they would be filled with joy when their time comes to leave this world. For does it not honor them greatly that the matron comes down on their account, to take them into the King's palace, where the King may every day rejoice in them? For to God there is no joy save in the souls of the righteous. Only the souls of the righteous here on earth can stir the love of the Community of Israel for God, for they come from the King's side, the side of the male. This transport goes on to the female and excites her love, and thus does the male stir the love and fondness of the female, and the female is united with the male in love. In like manner the female's desire to pour forth lower waters to mingle with the upper waters[2] is incited only through the souls of the righteous. And so, happy are the righteous in this world and the world to come, for on them the upper and lower beings are based. Hence it stands written: 'The righteous is the foundation of the world' [Prov. 10:25]."

THE TEN SEFIROT

If one should ask: Is it not written, "For ye saw no manner of similitude" [Deut. 4:15], the answer would be: Truly, it was granted us to behold him in a given similitude, for concerning Moses it is written, "and the similitude of the Lord doth he behold" [Num. 12:8]. Yet the Lord was revealed only in that similitude which Moses saw, and in none other, of any creation formed by his signs. Therefore it stands written: "To whom then will ye liken God? Or what likeness will ye compare unto Him?" [Isa. 40:18]. Also, even that similitude was a semblance of the Holy One, be blessed, not as he is in his very place which we know to be impenetrable, but as the King manifesting his might of dominion over his entire creation, and thus appearing to each one of his creatures as each can grasp him, as it is written: "And by the ministry of the prophets have I used similitudes" [Hos. 12:11].[3] Hence says

he: "Albeit in your own likeness do I represent myself, to whom will you compare me and make me comparable?"

Because in the beginning, shape and form having not yet been created, he had neither form nor similitude. Hence is it forbidden to one apprehending him as he is before Creation to imagine him under any kind of form or shape, not even by his letters *hé* and *vav*,[4] not either by his complete holy Name, or by letter or sign of any kind. Thus, "For ye saw no manner of similitude" means, You beheld nothing which could be imagined in form or shape, nothing which you could embody into a finite conception.

But when he had created the shape of supernal man, it was to him for a chariot, and on it he descended, to be known by the appellation YHVH, so as to be apprehended by his attributes and in each particular one, to be perceived. Hence it was he caused himself to be named El, *Elohim*, *Shaddai*, *Zevaot* and YHVH, of which each was a symbol among men of his several divine attributes, making manifest that the world is upheld by mercy and justice, in accordance with man's deeds. If the radiance of the glory of the Holy One, be blessed, had not been shed over his entire creation, how could even the wise have apprehended him? He would have continued to be unknowable, and the words could not be verily said, "The whole earth is full of his glory" [Isa. 6:3].

However, woe to the man who should make bold to identify the Lord with any single attribute, even if it be his own, and the less so any human form existent, "whose foundation is in the dust" [Job 4:19], and whose creatures are frail, soon gone, soon lost to mind. Man dare project one sole conception of the Holy One, be blessed, that of his sovereignty over some one attribute or over the creation in its entirety. But if he be not seen under these manifestations, then there is neither attribute, nor likeness, nor form in him; as the very sea, whose waters lack form and solidity in themselves, having these only when they are spread over the vessel of the earth.

From this we may reckon it so: One, is the source of the sea. A current comes forth from it making a revolution which is *yod*.[5] This source is one, and the current makes two. Then is formed the vast basin known as the sea, which is like a channel dug into the earth, and it is filled by the waters issuing from the source; and this sea is the third thing. This vast basin is divided up into seven channels, resembling that number of long tubes, and the waters go from the sea into the seven channels. Together, the source, the current, the sea, and the seven channels make the number ten. If the Creator who made these tubes should choose to break them, then would the waters return to their source, and only broken vessels would remain, dry, without water.

In this same wise has the Cause of causes derived the ten aspects of his Being which are known as *sefirot*, and named the crown the Source, which is a never-to-be-exhausted fountain of light, wherefrom he designates himself *eyn sof*, the Infinite. Neither shape nor form has he, and no vessel exists to contain him, nor any means to apprehend him. This is referred to in the words: "Refrain from searching after the things that are too hard for you, and refrain from seeking for the thing which is hidden from you."[6]

Then he shaped a vessel diminutive as the letter *yod*, and filled it from him, and called it Wisdom-gushing Fountain, and called himself wise on its account. And after, he fashioned a large vessel named sea, and designated it Understanding *[binah]* and himself understanding, on its account. Both wise and understanding is he, in his own essence; whereas wisdom in itself cannot claim that title, but only through him who is wise and has made it full from his fountain; and so understanding in itself cannot claim that title, but only through him who filled it from his own essence, and it would be ren-

dered into an aridity if he were to go from it. In this regard, it is written, "As the waters fail from the sea, and the river is drained dry" [Job 14:11].

Finally, "He smites the sea into seven streams" [Isa. 11:15], that is, he directs it into seven precious vessels, the which he calls Greatness, Strength, Glory, Victory, Majesty, Foundation, Sovereignty;[7] in each he designates himself thus: great in Greatness, strong in Strength, glorious in Glory, victorious in Victory, "the beauty of our Maker" in Majesty, righteous in Foundation [cf. Prov. 10:25]. All things, all vessels, and all worlds does he uphold in Foundation.

In the last, in Sovereignty, he calls himself King, and his is "the greatness, and the strength, and the glory, and the victory, and the majesty; for all that is in Heaven and in the earth is yours; yours is the kingdom, O Lord, and you are exalted as head above all" [1 Chron. 29:11]. In his power lie all things, be it that he chooses to reduce the number of vessels, or to increase the light issuing therefrom, or be it the contrary. But over him, there exists no deity with power to increase or reduce.

Also, he made beings to serve these vessels: each a throne supported by four columns, with six steps to the throne; in all, ten. Altogether, the throne is like the cup of benediction about which ten statements are made in the Talmud, harmonious with the Torah which was given in Ten Words [the Decalogue], and with the Ten Words by which the world was created.

THE DESTINY OF THE SOUL

At the time that the Holy One, be blessed, was about to create the world, he decided to fashion all the souls which would in due course be dealt out to the children of men, and each soul was formed into the exact outline of the body she was destined to tenant. Scrutinizing each, he saw that among them some would fall into evil ways in the world. Each one in its due time the Holy One, be blessed, bade come to him, and then said: "Go now, descend into this and this place, into this and this body."

Yet often enough the soul would reply: "Lord of the world, I am content to remain in this realm, and have no wish to depart to some other, where I shall be in thralldom, and become stained."

Whereupon the Holy One, be blessed, would reply: "Your destiny is, and has been from the day of thy forming, to go into that world."

Then the soul, realizing it could not disobey, would unwillingly descend and come into this world.

The Torah, counsel of the entire world, saw this, and cried to mankind: "Behold, see how the Holy One, be blessed, takes pity on you! Without cost, he has sent to you his costly pearl, that you may use it in this world, and it is the holy soul. 'And if a man sell his daughter to be a maid-servant' [Exod. 21:7], that is, when the Holy One, be blessed, gives over to you his daughter the holy soul for your maid servant, to be held in bondage by you, I adjure you, in her due time, 'she shall not go out as the men-servants do' [Exod. 21:7], that is, stained with sin, but in freedom, in light, in purity, so that her Master may rejoice in her, and in rewarding her exceedingly with the glories of Paradise, as it stands written: 'And the Lord will . . . satisfy your soul with brightness" [Isa. 58:11], that is, when she shall have ascended back to that sphere, bright and pure.

"But 'if she please not her master' [Exod. 21:8], for that she is fouled with sin, then woe to the body that has eternally been deprived of its soul! The reason being, that those souls which ascend from this world in a condition of brightness and purity are put down in the King's archives, each by name; and he says: 'Here is the soul of this certain one; she appertains to the body which she left.'—As it stands written: 'Who hath espoused her to himself' [Exod. 21:8].

"But 'if she please not her master,' which means if she be fouled by sin and guilt, he refuses to designate the same body as before for her, and thus she is deprived of it forever, save if her Master grant her grace and lead her back again to the body by transmigration, for 'then he let her be redeemed' [Exod. 21:8], as it stands written: 'He redeems his soul from going into the pit' [Job 33:28]. This has the meaning that man is counseled to redeem his soul by his repentance. In truth, there is a twofold meaning in the words, 'then he let her be redeemed,' for they allude to a man's own redemption of his soul by repentance, and after it, the redemption from Gehinnom by the Holy One, be blessed.

" 'And if he espouse her unto his son, he shall deal with her after the manner of daughters' [Exod. 21:9]. How much heed should a man take lest he wander in a crooked path in this world! For if he shall have evidenced his worthiness in this world, having watched over his soul with every precaution, then the Holy One, be blessed, will be greatly content with him, and daily speak his praise before his supernal family, in this wise: 'See the holy son who is mine in that world below! Behold his deeds and the probity of his ways.'

"And when such a soul departs from this world, pure, bright, unblemished, the Holy One, be blessed, daily causes her to shine with a host of radiances and proclaims concerning her: 'Here is the soul of my son, such and such: let her be preserved for the body from which she has departed.'

"This is the significance of the words: 'And if he espouse her unto his son, he shall deal with her after the manner of daughters.' What mean the words, 'after the manner of daughters'? It is a secret held solely in the trust of the wise: A palace which is known as the Palace of Love sits amidst a vast rock, a most secret firmament. Here in this place the treasures of the King are kept, and all his kisses of love. Every soul loved by the Holy One, be blessed, enters into that palace. And when the King makes his appearance, 'Jacob kisses Rachel' [Gen. 29:11], which is to say, the Lord discerns each holy soul, and taking each in turn to himself, embraces and fondles her, 'dealing with her after the manner of daughters,' even as a father acts toward his beloved daughter, embracing and fondling her, and presenting her with gifts."

THE THREE ASPECTS OF THE SOUL

The names and grades of the soul of man are three: *nefesh* [vital soul], *ruah* [spirit], *neshamah* [innermost soul, super-soul]. The three are comprehended one within the other, but each has its separate abode.

While the body in the grave is decomposing and moldering to dust, *nefesh* tarries within it, and it hovers about in this world, going here and there among the living, wanting to know their sorrows, and interceding for them at their need.

Ruah betakes itself into the earthly Garden of Eden. There, this spirit, desiring to enjoy the pleasures of the magnificent Garden, vests itself in a garment, as it were, of a likeness, a semblance of the body in which it had its abode in this world. On Sabbaths, new moons, and festival days, it ascends up to the supernal sphere, regaling itself with the delights there, and then it goes back to the Garden. As it is written: "And the spirit [*ruah*] returneth unto God who gave it" [Eccles. 12:7], that is, at the special holidays and times we have mentioned.

But *neshamah* ascends forthwith to her place, in the domain from which she emanated, and it is on her account that the light is lit, to shine above. Never thereafter does she descend to the earth.

In *neshamah* is realized the One who embraces all sides, the upper and the lower. And until such time as *neshamah* has ascended to be joined with the Throne, *ruah* is unable to be crowned in the lower Garden and *nefesh* cannot rest easy in its place; but these find rest when she ascends.

Now when the children of men, being troubled and sorrowful, betake themselves to the graves of those who are gone, then *nefesh* is wakened, and it goes out to bestir *ruah*, which then rouses the patriarchs, and after, *neshamah*. Whereupon the Holy One, be blessed, has pity on the world. . . .

But if *neshamah* has for some reason been prevented from ascending to her proper place, then *ruah*, coming to the gate of the Garden of Eden, finds it closed against it, and, unable to enter, wanders about alone and dejected; while *nefesh*, too, flits from place to place in the world, and seeing the body in which it once was tenant eaten by worms and undergoing the judgment of the grave, it mourns for it, as the Scripture says: "But his flesh grieves for him, and his soul mourns over him" [Job 14:22].

So do they all undergo suffering, until the time when *neshamah* is enabled to reach to her proper place above. Then, however, each of the two others becomes attached to its rightful place; this is all because all three are one, comprising a unity, embraced in a mystical bond.

HYMNS IN HEAVEN

"And he shall go out unto the altar that is before the Lord" [Lev. 16:18]. In this connection Rabbi Judah quoted the verse: "God, God, the Lord, has spoken, and called the earth from the rising of the sun unto the going down thereof" [Ps. 50:1].

He said: "It has been taught us that at

the break of the day a chorus of a thousand and five hundred and fifty myriads sing out hymns to God, and at midday, a thousand and five hundred and forty-eight, and at the time which is known as 'between the evenings,' a thousand and five hundred and ninety myriads."

Rabbi Yose commented that at the dawning of the day all the heavenly hosts which are known as the "lords of shouting" greet it with utterances of praise, for then are all jubilant, and then judgment is lightened. At this moment the world rejoices and is blessed, and the Holy One, be blessed, rouses up Abraham, the representative of Mercy, and holds glad converse with him and allows him the sway over the world. But at the time known as "between the evenings" the angels called "masters of howling" raise their voices, and through the world, contentiousness prevails. Then the Holy One, be blessed, bidding Isaac, the representative of stern Judgment, rise up, moves to judge the transgressors of the precepts of the law. There come forth seven rivers of fire to descend on the heads of the wicked, and also the burning coals of fire. Now Abraham retreats back, the day departs, and in Gehinnom the evildoers, groaning, cry: "Woe unto us! for the day declines, for the shadows of the evening are stretched out" [Jer. 6:4].

Thus, at this hour, a man should take heed not to overlook the afternoon prayer. With the arrival of night, there are called forth from outside the curtain the other fifteen hundred and forty-eight myriads, and they intone hymns, whereupon the punishments from the netherworld are roused up and wander about the world, chanting praises until midnight, which is a watch-and-a-half. Then, the north wind having stirred up and gone out, all the remaining congregate to sing Psalms until the daylight breaks and the morning stirs up, and gladness and blessing come back to the world.

GOD'S LOVE

Rabbi Abba considered the verse: "O turn unto me, and be gracious unto me; give your strength unto your servant" [Ps. 86:16].

He said: "Does it mean David was the most beautiful that God could turn to? The meaning is that God, as we have learned, possesses another David, one who commands numbers of heavenly hosts and legions; and, desiring to bestow his grace upon the world, God directs a smiling countenance upon this 'David,' the Divine Presence, who then, by virtue of his beauty, illuminates the world and engraces it. His head is a golden skull embellished with seven gold ornaments. God loves him greatly, and so instructs him to turn and gaze at him with his surpassingly fair eyes, which, when he does, causes God's heart, so to speak, to be pierced with shafts of celestial affection. It was for the sake of that heavenly and comely David, the object of God's love and desire, that David said: 'O turn unto me, and be gracious unto me.'

"So it was when Isaac said to Jacob, 'See, the smell of my son is as the smell of a field which the Lord hath blessed' [Gen. 27:27]. We have been taught that this was so because accompanying Jacob when he went in was the Garden of Eden. We may ask, again: how could the Garden of Eden enter with him, stretching as it does an immense length and breadth, and with numerous sections and abodes? In reality, God possesses another holy garden. He has a special affection for it, and watches over it himself, and he charges it to accompany the righteous always. This garden it was that entered with Jacob.

"Likewise, when the story is told that the entire land of Israel came and put itself under Abram,[8] it signifies another land which God has, a holy and celestial land which is known also as "the land of

Israel." This land of Israel lies beneath the mystical abode of Jacob, and God, out of his love for them, has given it to Israel to be with them and lead them and stand guard over them; it is known as 'the land of the living.' "

THE ROSE OF SHARON

Discoursing on the verse: "I am a rose of Sharon, a lily of the valleys" [Cant. 2:1], Rabbi Simeon said: "The Holy One, be blessed, bears great love to the Community of Israel, wherefore he constantly praises her, and she, from the store of chants and hymns she keeps for the King, constantly sings his praises.

"Because she flowers splendidly in the Garden of Eden, the Community of Israel is called rose of Sharon; because her desire is to be watered from the deep stream which is the source of all spiritual rivers, she is called lily of the valleys.

"Also, because she is found at the deepest place is she designated lily of the valleys. At first, she is a rose with yellowish petals, and then a lily of two colors, white and red, a lily of six petals, changing from one hue to another. She is named 'rose' when she is about to join with the King, and after she has come together with him in her kisses, she is named 'lily.' "

THE TREE OF LIFE

Remark this: that God, when he made man and clothed him in great honor, made it incumbent that he cleave to him so as to be unique and of single heart, united to the One by the tie of the single-purposed faith which ties all together. But later, men abandoned the road of faith and left behind the singular tree which looms high over all trees, and ad-

hered to the place which is continually shifting from one hue to another, from good to evil and evil to good, and they descended from on high and adhered below to the uncertain, and deserted the supreme and changeless One. Thus it was that their hearts, shifting between good and evil, caused them at times to merit mercy, at others punishment, depending on what it was that they had cleaved to.

The Holy One, be blessed, spoke: "Man, life you have abandoned, and to death you cleave; truly, death awaits you." And so the decree was death, for him and for all the world.

But if Adam transgressed, in what did the rest of the world sin? We know that all creatures did not come and eat of the forbidden tree, no. But it was this way: when man stood upright, all creatures, beholding him, were seized with fear of him, and slavelike they followed after him. And hence when he addressed them: "Come, let us bow down to the Lord who did make us," they followed suit. But when they observed him making obeisance to the other place, adhering to it, again, they did the same, and in this wise did he bring about death for himself and all the world.

So did Adam move back and forth from one hue to another, from good to evil, from evil to good, from agitation to rest, from judgment to mercy, from life to death: never consistent in any one thing, because of the effect of that place, which is thus known as "the flaming sword which turned every way" [Gen. 3:24], from this direction to that, from good to evil, from mercy to judgment, from peace to war.

But the supreme King, out of compassion for his own handiworks, gave them warning, and said: "Of the tree of the knowledge of good and evil, you shall not eat" [Gen. 2:17]. Not heeding, man did as his wife, and was banished for ever, inasmuch as woman can come to this place, but not farther, and on her account death was decreed for all. But in time to come, "the days of my people shall be as the days of the tree" [Isa. 65: 22], like that singular tree we know of. Concerning that time it is written, "He will swallow up death for ever; and the Lord God will wipe away tears from all faces" [Isa. 25:8].

Notes

1. Throughout the *Zohar*, Rabbi Simeon ben Yohai is called "the holy lamp."

2. The upper and lower waters represent the "male" and the "female" forces, or active and passive principles in creation.

3. This verse is taken to mean that God manifests himself to each prophet according to his capacity of grasping God.

4. The four letters of the holy name YHVH are understood as symbols of the manifestations of God's creative power in every being.

5. The first letter in the name of God.

6. Ben Sira, as quoted in the Talmud, Hagigah 13a.

7. These designate the seven lower *sefirot*.

8. According to a midrash on Genesis 13: 15.

The Mystical Theology of Pseudo-Dionysius

(Christian)

Pseudo-Dionysius has been traditionally and incorrectly connected with Dionysius the Areopagite, whom Paul converted in Athens, and with St. Denis, patron saint of France. Pseudo-Dionysius, now most ungenerously called the "False Dionysius," was probably a Syrian clergyman from the sixth century. As a theologian and philosopher, as the inheritor of Christian Platonism and the Neoplatonism of Proclus, and as the model for virtually all later major Christian mystics, he is one of the most creative and seminal thinkers of the past. Dante and Milton used images and ideas from his *The Mystical Theology*. The basic ideas of Saint John of the Cross appear in full detail in the writings of Pseudo-Dionysius, which include *The Celestial Hierarchy*, *The Ecclesiastical Hierarchy*, *The Divine Names* (based in part on Kabbalah and a source for Luis de León's *The Names of Christ*), and *The Mystical Theology*.

The ways of the mystic were marked out in the Garden. When Eve and Adam ate from the Tree of Knowledge, they took the first step toward mystical salvation, toward a knowledge of spiritual light. They ate from the "Tree of Gnosis" and were for the Gnostics moving toward the possibility of mystical union. For traditional Christianity, Eve and Adam's step was a fall from innocence. Innocence, meaning "without knowledge," is a virtue and the mystic strives for agnosia— the opposite of *gnosis*—for darkness, ignorance, wordlessness in order to reach the silence and superessential gloom that is God. So Saint John of the Cross writes,

> Entréme donde no supe
> y quedéme no sabiendo,
> toda ciencia trascendiendo.
> ("I came into the unknown
> and stayed there unknowing,
> rising beyond all science" [i.e., systematized knowledge])

And in the same poem, he writes: "My mind had found a surer way: a knowledge by unknowing."[1] While the Gnostics sought internal light and knowledge, John of the Cross pursued his "negative way," another notion which comes directly from Pseudo-Dionysius. It may be argued that the Christian mystic also ultimately seeks light, the *via iluminativa*, before the final union, and that we are using different words to describe the same experience: the ineffable union with God. While the experience of mysticism may be the same whatever its description and interpretation (which may hold true for secular as well as religious mysticism), the methods of the Gnostic contrast with the traditional Christian, a contrast exemplified by its most important systematizer, Pseudo-Dionysius. For the Gnostic, ignorance is an error; darkness implies removal from God (who is Light). Conversely, the Christian moves toward the absolutely unknowable, in total ignorance, to a knowledge of unknowing; that is, to the cessation of thought and reason, to a wordless abstraction from earthly reality.

For Pseudo-Dionysius union with God comes as an ascent when the body and mind are annihilated, momentarily dead, as it were, and the spirit has escaped the laws of time. In absolute ecstasy, one rises to a contradiction, to a superluminous gloom where eyelessly one perceives glories of beauty. No longer distracted by the light of existing things, one reaches the ray of the divine darkness. To reach "Him who is beyond all," the way is "by knowing nothing." Inactivity of thought is the universal key, east and west, to meditation.

It is appropriate that *The Other Bible* end with the scriptures of the Pseudo-Dionysius. As with most of its texts, authorship is uncertain, despite the attribution, in this case false, to Dionysius the Areopagite. Pseudo-Dionysius is an amazingly syncretic figure, uniting basic notions of Greek Platonism and Alexandrian and Roman Neoplatonism, mystery religions such as Hermes Trismegistus, and primitive Christianity. His mystical ideas find an analogue in the Jewish mystics of Alexandria and earliest Kabbalah. His work continues in the mainstream of European mystical theology.

Pseudo-Dionysius was scarcely interested in organization, doctrine, proselytizing, or traditional eschatology. His was a personal experience, offered to the reader of his time, and which today is relevant and useful to anyone who wishes to understand the background and essential ideas of mystical speculation. Not concerned with the rewards of Heaven or the terrible punishments of Hell, he proposed salvation now through introspection. Despite his preoccupation with the darkness of the invisible and silent gloom, we may speak of him as enlightened. His lucid treatises have an appeal for religious and secular reader alike.

Note

1. Willis Barnstone, *The Poems of St. John of the Cross* (1968; reprint, New York: New Directions, 1972), pp. 58–59.

WHAT IS THE DIVINE GLOOM?*

Section I

Triad supernal, both super-God and super-good, guardian of the theosophy of Christian men, direct us aright to the super-unknown and super-brilliant and highest summit of the mystic oracles, where the simple and absolute and changeless mysteries of theology lie hidden within the super-luminous gloom of the silence, revealing hidden things, which in its deepest darkness shines above the most super-brilliant, and in the altogether impalpable and invisible, fills to overflowing the eyeless minds with glories of surpassing beauty. This then be my prayer; but you, O dear Timothy, by your persistent commerce with the mystic visions, leave behind both sensible perceptions and intellectual efforts, and all objects of sense and intelligence, and all things not being and being, and be raised aloft unknowingly to the union, as far as attainable, with him who is above every essence and knowledge. For by the resistless and absolute ecstasy in all purity, from yourself and all, you will be carried on high, to the superessential ray of the divine darkness, when you have cast away all, and become free from all.

Section II

But see that none of the uninitiated listen to these things—those I mean who are entangled in things being, and fancy there is nothing superessentially above things being, but imagine that they know, by their own knowledge, him, who has placed darkness as his hiding place. But, if the divine initiations are above such, what would any one say respecting those still more uninitiated, such as both portray the cause exalted

*All selections in this chapter are from a nineteenth century translation.

above all, from the lowest of things created, and say that it in no wise excels the no-gods fashioned by themselves and of manifold shapes, it being our duty both to attribute and affirm all the attributes of things existing to it, as cause of all, and more properly to deny them all to it, as being above all, and not to consider the negations to be in opposition to the affirmations, but far rather that it, which is above every abstraction and definition, is above the privations.

Section III

Thus, then, the divine Bartholomew says that theology is much and least, and the Gospel broad and great, and on the other hand concise. He seems to me to have comprehended this supernaturally, that the good cause of all is both of much utterance, and at the same time of briefest utterance and without utterance; as having neither utterance nor conception, because it is superessentially exalted above all, and manifested without veil and in truth, to those alone who pass through both all things consecrated and pure, and ascend above every ascent of all holy summits, and leave behind all divine lights and sounds, and heavenly words, and enter into the gloom, where really is, as the oracles say, he who is beyond all. For even the divine Moses is himself strictly bidden to be first purified, and then to be separated from those who are not so, and after entire cleansing hears the many-voiced trumpets, and sees many lights, shedding pure and streaming rays; then he is separated from the multitude, and with the chosen priests goes first to the summit of the divine ascents, although even then he does not meet with Almighty God himself, but views not him, for he is viewless, but the place where he is. Now this I think signifies that the most divine and highest of the things seen and contemplated are a sort of suggestive expression of the things subject to him who is above all, through which his wholly inconceivable presence is shown, reaching to the highest spiritual summits of his most holy places; and then Moses is freed from them who are both seen and seeing, and enters into the gloom of the *Agnosia;* a gloom veritably mystic, within which he closes all perceptions of knowledge and enters into the altogether impalpable and unseen, being wholly of him who is beyond all, and of none, neither himself nor other; and by inactivity of all knowledge, united in his better part to the altogether unknown, and by knowing nothing, knowing above mind.

HOW WE OUGHT BOTH TO BE UNITED AND RENDER PRAISE TO THE CAUSE OF ALL AND ABOVE ALL

Section I

We pray to enter within the super-bright gloom, and through not seeing and not knowing, to see and to know that the not to see nor to know is itself the above sight and knowledge. For this is veritably to see and to know and to celebrate superessentially the superessential, through the abstraction of all existing things, just as those who make a lifelike statue, by extracting all the encumbrances which have been placed upon the clear view of the concealed, and by bringing to light, by the mere cutting away [i.e., the abstraction], the genuine beauty concealed in it. And, it is necessary, as I think, to celebrate the abstractions in an opposite way to the definitions. For we used to place these latter by beginning from the foremost and descending through the middle to the lowest; but, in this case, by making the ascents from the lowest to the highest, we abstract everything, in order that, without veil, we may know that *Agnosia,* which is enshrouded under all the known, in all things that be, and may see that superessential gloom, which is hidden by all the light in existing things.

Appendix I
PLOTINUS

Plotinus, The Enneads

(Pagan)

With the exception of Hermes Trismegistus, who was a Pagan Gnostic, the figures whose scriptures appear in *The Other Bible* have all been Jewish, Christian, or Gnostic. The term Gnostic is itself problematic since some Gnostics were Jewish, others Christian—the true Christians, they said of themselves—while a major personage such as Mani introduced Zoroastrian and Buddhist elements into his Christian Gnosticism. But Plotinus (A.D. 205–270) was a Pagan who followed Plato and indeed wrote against the Gnostics. Why then should we include any work by Plotinus, even in the appendix? At least three reasons persuade me that a knowledge of Plotinus is indispensable.

As a Neoplatonist Plotinus developed Platonic notions that not only pervaded the texts of early Christian theologians such as Pseudo-Dionysius and Johannes Scotus Erigena, but his work continued to infiltrate and even dominate thought until the end of the Middle Ages. Renaissance humanism continued to favor Plotinus; and we feel his impact in the resurgence of Neoplatonism in Pletho, Ficino, and the Cambridge Platonists. A salient quality of the early competing religions and philosophies was their syncretic nature, that tendency to absorb and combine the thought of several systems. Syncretism is also the salient quality in Plotinus and suggests why early Christians favored his work as the conduit back to the Stoa, Aristotle, Pythagoras, and especially Plato.

A second reason for reading Plotinian texts is because of his ties with the Gnostics. Plotinus wrote against the Gnostics, as did Hippolytus, Irenaeus, and Clement; but while the early Christians were essential sources of our knowledge of the Gnostics, they totally rejected Gnostic doctrines as heretical. Plotinus rejected Gnosticism in principle, but in several important areas his own thought coincided with Gnostic speculation. First we should acknowledge that Plotinus vehemently rejected Gnostic pessimism, that acosmic view that considered human beings as alienated creatures in a hostile world created by an evil Creator God. For him the world was good and beautiful. He espoused optimism. Yet the material world was not our end; indeed, it was, as for the Gnostics, the source of ignorance, error, and even evil. The soul that redeems the physical world is immortal and in a doctrine similar to the Gnostics descends, in a downward journey, passing through planetary spheres, on its way to the body. Philip Merlan writes that Plotinus "sometimes comes dangerously close to the Gnostic theory that matter imprisons the soul and to a completely dualistic system."[1]

The third reason for examining Plotinus concerns ecstasy and mysticism. The notion of the soul returning to the One, to the realm of light, coincides with Gnostic thought and is essential to early Christian theology, particularly that of Pseudo-Dionysius, himself the model for much later western mysticism. The mystics read in Plotinus the notion of the One preceding all multiplicity, of the ineffability of the One, of rising to union with the One by stripping oneself of everything, and of going through light to light. Hans Jonas writes:

> [w]e are here again dealing with a phenomenon which Gnosticism shared with the broader religious tide of the age. In fact, the real *conceptual* elaboration of the whole idea of an inner ascent ending in mystical ecstasis, and its articulation into psychologically definable stages, was the work of no other than Plotinus and the Neoplatonic school after him—anticipated to some extent by Philo—i.e., of a "philosophy" turned mystical. . . .[2]

Plotinus was born in upper Egypt, probably in Lykopolis. He is thought to have been a Hellenized Egyptian rather than a Greek. He had an adventurous early life, joining an army that was to invade Persia where he wished to go in order to steep himself in Persian and Indian wisdom. Most of his life was spent in Rome, where he founded a school of philosophy. His writing, the *Enneads* (six books containing nine treatises each), was written in the last sixteen years of his life and arranged in their present form by his pupil Porphyry. Porphyry recounts that Plotinus was almost ashamed of existing in a human body since the whole material world was created by the soul and has no real existence in itself. When a painter asked permission to paint his portrait, Plotinus said, "Why paint an illusion of an illusion?" He died outside of Rome, probably of leprosy.

According to Plotinus the supreme source of the world is the One. It is the highest principle, a pure unity entirely undifferentiated, that is, without multiplicity. Plotinus states that the One is without cognition, ignorant even of itself, for self-cognition presupposes the duality of subject and object. The One can no more know itself than can the soul, upon ascending to the One, know the One, for at that point the soul *is* the One, subject and object are the same. One cannot see the sun when one is the sun; the seer cannot see the seen because the seer is the seen. And using other metaphors (the mystics always resort to metaphors), Plotinus states, explaining the monistic union and its ineffable nature:

> In this state the seer does not see or distinguish or imagine two things; he becomes another, he ceases to be himself and to belong to

himself. He belongs to him and is one with him, like two concentric circles; they are one when they coincide, and two only when they are separated. It is only in this sense that the Soul is other than God. Therefore this vision is hard to describe. For how can one describe, as other than oneself, that which, when one saw it, seemed to be one with oneself? *(Enneads, 6.9.11)*

In Plotinus the One causes the world. But it does not "create" the world as a separate entity, with an independent existence, as in Judaism, Christianity, and Islam. In the theistic religions of the west there is always a dualism of God and his creations. In Plotinus the world is an emanation or manifestation of the One, or rather a series of descending emanations. Since the cosmos descends from the One, it is not independent of it. God is pantheistically the world. The first emanation from the One is described as *nous*, Intelligence; and from Intelligence emanates the Soul. The final emanation which proceeds from the Soul is matter, the farthest from the sun and therefore the darkest. Utter darkness is pure nonbeing. If we use the same image of the sun to represent the One, the return to the One is the ascent of the soul to its mystical union.

Plotinus tells us the method of spiritual intuition: "Shut your eyes and change to and wake to another way of seeing." The soul apprehends the light and becomes the light. It accomplishes this by stripping itself of good and evil, and becoming alone as the One is alone. In one of his most memorable lines, the Alexandrian speaks of the communion with the One as "a liberation from all earthly bonds, a life that takes no pleasure in earthly things, a flight of the alone to the Alone." He describes deification:

> For he was then one with him, and retained no difference, either in relation to himself or to others. Nothing stirred within him, neither anger nor concupiscence nor even reason or spiritual perception or his own personality, if we may say so. Caught up in an ecstasy, tranquil and God-possessed, he enjoyed an imperturbable calm. (6.9.11)

Elaborating the communion, he says "it is rather another mode of seeing, an ecstasy and simplification, an abandonment of oneself." In the end the Soul "will not arrive at something else, but at itself, and so being in nothing else, it is only in itself alone; but that which is in itself alone and not in the world of Being is in the Absolute. It ceases to be Being; it is above Being, while in communion with the One." There will be some memory of the vision, at least enough to lead one to seek constant return:

> If then a man sees himself become one with the One, he has in himself a likeness of the One, and if he passes out of himself, as an image to its archetype, he has reached the end of his journey. And when he comes down from his vision, he can again awaken the virtue that is in him, and seeing himself fitly adorned in every part he can again mount upward through virtue to Spirit, and through wisdom to the One itself. (6.9.11)

Yet even such words as "vision" and "seeing" are misleading, for, as Walter Stace comments, that would "imply a duality of subject and object,"[3] and we know from his works that when one is the One, when "the flight of the alone to the Alone" is complete, there is a total commingling, an ineffable union *(enosis)*. This is the monistic mystical experience.

The ascent to God in Plotinus occurs in three stages of perfection. These levels were already anticipated in Philo (f. 20 B.C.–A.D. 40), who through his stages of purgation, illumination, and union, provided a chart of the mystical way. Both Philo and Plotinus speak of the knowledge of God as ineffable (a term not used in Greek philosophy prior to Philo); yet knowledge in itself, as in all Hellenic thought, is good, and the way to God is not to follow the mandate of ignorance of the Creator God but to follow reason as far as it will take us. Therein the Gnostics—who reversed the notion of the serpent by making the serpent provide us with virtuous knowledge in order for us to waken from the illusion of the world—are once more aligned with Plotinus, the author of polemical attacks on the Gnostics. In common is their mutual purpose of seeking self-knowledge in order to rise from the world of illusion to the God of total light.

Notes

1. Philip Merlan, "Plotinus," Edwards ed., *The Encyclopedia of Philosophy,* vol. 6 (New York: Macmillan, 1967), p. 358.
2. Hans Jonas, *The Gnostic Religion,* 2d. ed. rev. (1958; reprint, Boston: Beacon Press, 1970), p. 286.
3. Walter T. Stace, *The Teachings of the Mystics* (New York: New American Library, 1960), p. 122.

THE ASCENT TO UNION WITH THE ONE*

Here the greatest, the ultimate contest is set before our souls; all our toil and trouble is for this, not to be left without a share in the best of visions. The man who attains this is blessed in seeing that blessed sight, and he who fails to attain it has failed utterly. A man has not failed if he fails to win beauty of colors or bodies, or power or office or kingship even, but if he fails to win this and only this. For this he should give up the attainment of kingship and rule over all earth and

*From A. H. Armstrong, ed., *Plotinus* (London: George Allen & Unwin, 1953), pp. 136–137.

sea and sky, if only by leaving and overlooking them he can turn to that and see.

But how shall we find the way? What method can we devise? How can one see the inconceivable beauty which stays within the holy sanctuary and does not come out where the profane may see it? Let him who can follow and come within, and leave outside the sight of his eyes and not turn back to the bodily splendors which he saw before. When he sees the beauty in bodies he must not run after them; we must know that they are images, traces, shadows, and hurry away to that which they image. For if a man runs to the image and wants to seize it as if it was the reality (like a beautiful reflection playing on the water, which some story somewhere, I think, said riddlingly a man wanted to catch and sank down into the stream and disappeared) then this man who clings to beautiful bodies and will not let them go, will, like the man in the story, but in soul, not in body, sink down into the dark depths where *nous* has no delight, and stay blind in Hades, consorting with shadows there and here. This would be truer advice, "Let us fly to our dear country." Where then is our way of escape? How shall we put out to sea? (Odysseus, I think, speaks symbolically when he says he must fly from the witch Circe, or Calypso, and is not content to stay though he has delights of the eyes and lives among much beauty of sense.) Our country from which we came is there, our Father is there. How shall we travel to it, where is our way of escape? We cannot get there on foot: for our feet only carry us everywhere in this world, from one country to another. You must not get ready a carriage, either, or a boat. Let all these things go, and do not look. Shut your eyes and change to and wake another way of seeing, which everyone has but few use.

The discursive reason, if it wishes to say anything, must seize first one element of the truth and then another; such are the conditions of discursive thought. But how can discursive thought apprehend the absolutely simple? It is enough to apprehend it by a kind of spiritual intuition. But in this act of apprehension we have neither the power nor the time to say anything about it; afterwards we can reason about it. We may believe that we have really seen, when a sudden light illumines the Soul; for this light comes from the One and is the One. And we may think that the One is present, when, like another god, he illumines the house of him who calls upon him; for there would be no light without his presence. Even so the soul is dark that does not behold him: but when illumined by him, it has what it desired, and this is the true end and aim of the soul, to apprehend that light, and to behold it by that light itself, which is no other than the light by which it sees. For that which we seek to behold is that which gives us light, even as we can only see the sun by the light of the sun. How then can this come to us? Strip yourself of everything.

We must not be surprised that that which excites the keenest of longings is without any form, even spiritual form, since the Soul itself, when inflamed with love for it, puts off all the form which it had, even that which belongs to the spiritual world. For it is not possible to see it, or to be in harmony with it, while one is occupied with anything else. The soul must remove from itself good and evil and everything else, that it may receive the One alone, as the One is alone. When the soul is so blessed, and is come to it, or rather when it manifests its presence, when the soul turns away from visible things and makes itself as beautiful as possible and becomes like the One; (the manner of preparation and adornment is known to those who practice it;) and seeing the One suddenly appearing in itself, for there is nothing between, nor are they any longer two, but one; for you cannot distinguish between them, while the vision lasts; it is that union of which the union of earthly lovers, who wish to blend their being with each other, is a copy. The soul is no longer conscious of the body, and cannot tell whether it is a man or a living being or anything real at all; for the contemplation of such things would seem unworthy, and it has no leisure for them; but when, after having sought the One, it finds itself in its presence, it goes to meet it and contemplates it instead of itself. What itself is when it gazes, it has no leisure to see. When in this state the soul would exchange its present condition for nothing, no, not for the very Heaven of Heavens; for there is nothing better, nothing more blessed than this. For it can mount no higher; all other things are below it, however exalted they be. It is then that it judges rightly and knows that it has what it desired, and that there is nothing higher. For there is no deception there; where could one find anything truer than the true? What it says, that it is, and it speaks afterwards, and speaks in silence, and is happy, and is not deceived in its happiness. Its happiness is no titillation of the bodily senses; it is that the soul has become again what it was formerly, when it was blessed. All the things which once pleased it, power, wealth, beauty, science, it declares that it despises; it could not say this if it had not met with something better than these. It fears no evil, while it is with the One, or even while it sees him; though all else perish around it, it is content, if it can only be with him; so happy is it.

The soul is so exalted that it thinks lightly even of that spiritual intuition which it formerly treasured. For spiritual perception involves movement, and the soul now does not wish to move. It does not call the object of its vision spirit, although it has itself been transformed into spirit before the vision and lifted up into the abode of spirits. When the soul arrives at the intuition of the One, it leaves the mode of spiritual perception. Even so a traveler, entering into a palace, admires at first the various beauties which adorn it; but when the master appears, he alone is the object of attention. By continually contemplating the object before him, the spectator sees it no more. The vision is confounded with the object seen, and that which was before object becomes to him the state of seeing, and he forgets all else. The spirit has two powers. By one of them it has a spiritual perception of what is within itself, the other is the receptive intuition by which it perceives what is above itself. The former is the vision of the thinking spirit, the latter is the spirit in love. For when the spirit is inebriated with the nectar, it falls in love, in simple contentment and satisfaction; and it is better for it to be so intoxicated than to be too proud for such intoxication.

If you are perplexed because the One is none of those things which you know, apply yourself to them first, and look forth out of them; but so look, as not to direct your intellect to externals. For it does not lie in one place and not in another, but it is present everywhere to him who can touch it, and not to him who cannot. As in other matters one cannot think of two things at once, and must add nothing extraneous to the object of thought, if one wishes to identify oneself with it, so here we may be sure that it is impossible for one who has in his soul any extraneous image to conceive of the One while that image distracts his attention. Just as we said that matter must be without qualities of its own, if it is to receive the forms of all things, so *a fortiori* must the soul be formless if it is to receive the fullness and illumination of the first principle. If so, the soul must forsake all that is external, and turn itself wholly to that which is within; it will not allow itself to be distracted by anything external, but will ignore them all, as at first by not attending to them, so now last by not seeing them; it will not even know itself; and so it will come to the vision of the One and will be united with it; and then, after a sufficient converse with it, it will return and bring word, if it be possible, to others of its heavenly intercourse. Such probably was the converse which Minos was fabled to have had with Zeus, remembering which he made the laws which were the image of that converse, being inspired to be a lawgiver by the divine touch. Perhaps, however, a Soul which has seen much of the heavenly world may think politics unworthy of itself and may prefer to remain above. God, as Plato says, is not far from every one of us; he is present with all, though they know him not. Men flee away from him, or rather from themselves. They cannot grasp him from whom they have fled, nor when they have lost themselves can they find another, any more than a child who is mad and out of his mind can know his father. But he who has learnt to know himself will know also whence he is.

If a soul has known itself throughout

its course, it is aware that its natural motion has not been in a straight line (except during some deflection from the normal) but rather in a circle round a center; and that this center is itself in motion round that from which it proceeds. On this center the soul depends, and attaches itself thereto, as all Souls ought to do, but only the Souls of gods do so always. It is this that makes them gods. For a god is closely attached to this center; those further from it are average men, and animals. Is then this center of the soul the object of our search? Or must we think of something else, some point at which all centers as it were coincide? We must remember that our "circles" and "centers" are only metaphors. The Soul is no "circle" like the geometrical figure; we call it a circle because the archetypal nature is in it and around it, and because it is derived from this first principle, and all the more because the souls as wholes are separated from the body. But now, since part of us is held down by the body (as if a man were to have his feet under water), we touch the center of all things with our own center —that part which is not submerged—as the centers of the greatest circles coincide with the center of the enveloping sphere, and then rest. If these circles were corporeal and not psychic, the coincidence of their centers would be spatial, and they would lie around a center somewhere in space; but since the souls belong to the spiritual world, and the One is above even spirit, we must consider that their contact is through other powers—those which connect subject and object in the world of spirit, and further, that the perceiving spirit is present in virtue of its likeness and identity, and unites with its like without hindrance. For bodies cannot have this close association with each other, but incorporeal things are not kept apart by bodies; they are separated from each other not by distance, but by unlikeness and difference. Where there is no unlikeness, they are united with each other. The One, which

has no unlikeness, is always present; we are so only when we have no unlikeness. The One does not strive to encircle us, but we strive to encircle it. We always move round the One, but we do not always fix our gaze upon it: we are like a choir of singers who stand round the conductor, but do not always sing in time because their attention is diverted to some external object; when they look at the conductor they sing well and are really with him. So we always move round the One; if we did not, we should be dissolved and no longer exist; but we do not always look towards the One. When we do, we attain the end of our existence, and our repose, and we no longer sing out of tune, but form in very truth a divine chorus round the One.

In this choral dance the soul sees the fountain of life and the fountain of Spirit, the source of being, the cause of good, the root of soul. These do not flow out of the One in such a way as to diminish it; for we are not dealing with material quantities, else the products of the One would be perishable, whereas they are eternal, because their source remains not divided among them, but constant. Therefore the products too are permanent, as the light remains while the sun remains. For we are not cut off from our source nor separated from it, even though the bodily nature intervenes and draws us toward itself, but we breathe and maintain our being in our source, which does not first give itself and then withdraw, but is always supplying us, as long as it is what it is. But we are more truly alive when we turn towards it, and in this lies our well-being. To be far from it is isolation and diminution. In it our soul rests, out of reach of evil: it has ascended to a region which is pure from all evil; there it has spiritual vision, and is exempt from passion and suffering; there it truly lives. For our present life, without God, is a mere shadow and mimicry of the true life. But life yonder is an activity of the spirit, and by its peaceful activity it engenders gods also, through its contact with the One, and beauty, and righteousness, and virtue. For these are the offspring of a soul which is filled with God, and this is its beginning and end—its beginning because from this it had its origin, its end because the Good is there, and when it comes there it becomes what it was. For our life in this world is but a falling away, an exile, and a loss of the Soul's wings. The natural love which the Soul feels proves that the Good is there; this is why paintings and myths make Psyche the bride of Cupid. Because the Soul is different from God, and yet springs from him, she loves him of necessity; when she is yonder she has the heavenly love, when she is here below, the vulgar. For yonder dwells the heavenly Aphrodite, but here she is vulgarized and corrupted, and every soul is Aphrodite. This is figured in the allegory of the birthday of Aphrodite, and Love who was born with her. Hence it is natural for the soul to love God and to desire union with him, as the daughter of a noble father feels a noble love. But when, descending to generation, the soul, deceived by the false promises of a lover, exchanges its divine love for a mortal love, it is separated from its father and submits to indignities; but afterwards it is ashamed of these disorders and purifies itself and returns to its father and is happy. Let him who has not had this experience consider how blessed a thing it is in earthly love to obtain that which one most desires, although the objects of earthly loves are mortal and injurious and loves of shadows, which change and pass; since these are not the things which we truly love, nor are they our good, nor what we seek. But yonder is the true object of our love, which it is possible to grasp and to live with and truly to possess, since no envelope of flesh separates us from it. He who has seen it knows what I say, that the soul then has another life, when it comes to God and having come possesses him, and knows, when in that state, that it is in the presence of the dispenser of the true life, and that it needs nothing further. On the contrary, it must put off all else, and stand in God alone, which can only be when we have pruned away all else that surrounds us. We must then hasten to depart hence, to detach ourselves as much as we can from the body to which we are unhappily bound, to endeavor to embrace God with all our being, and to leave no part of ourselves which is not in contact with him. Then we can see him and ourselves, as far as is permitted: we see ourselves glorified, full of spiritual light, or rather we see ourselves as pure, subtle, ethereal, light: we become divine, or rather we know ourselves to be divine. Then indeed is the flame of life kindled, that flame which, when we sink back to earth, sinks with us.

Why then does not the soul abide yonder? Because it has not wholly left its earthly abode. But the time will come when it will enjoy the vision without interruption, no longer troubled with the hindrances of the body. The part of the soul which is troubled is not the part which sees, but the other part, when the part which sees is idle, though it ceases not from that knowledge which comes of demonstrations, conjectures, and the dialectic. But in the vision that which sees is not reason, but something greater than and prior to reason, something presupposed by reason, as is the object of vision. He who then sees himself, when he sees will see himself as a simple being, will be united to himself as such, will feel himself become such. We ought not even to say that he will *see*, but he will *be* that which he sees, if indeed it is possible any longer to distinguish seer and seen, and not boldly to affirm that the two are one. In this state the seer does not see or distinguish or imagine two things; he becomes another, he ceases to be himself and to belong to himself. He belongs to him and is one with him, like two concentric circles; they are one when they coincide, and two only when they are separated. It is only in this sense that the soul is other than God. Therefore this vision is hard to describe. For how can one describe, as other than oneself, that which, when one saw it, seemed to be one with oneself?

This is no doubt why in the mysteries we are forbidden to reveal them to the uninitiated. That which is divine is ineffable, and cannot be shown to those who have not had the happiness to see it. Since in the vision there were not two things, but seer and seen were one (for the seeing was no seeing but a merging), if a man could preserve the memory of what he was when he was mingled with the divine, he would have in himself an image of him. For he was then one with him, and retained no difference, either in relation to himself or to others. Nothing stirred within him, neither anger nor concupiscence nor even reason or spiritual perception or his own personality, if we may say so. Caught up in an ecstasy, tranquil and God-possessed, he enjoyed an imperturbable calm; shut up in his proper essence he inclined not to either side, he turned not even to himself; he was in a state of perfect stability; he had become stability itself. The soul then occupies itself no more even with beautiful things; it is exalted above the beautiful, it passes the choir of the virtues. Even as when a man who enters the sanctuary of a temple leaves behind him the statues in the temple, they are the objects which he will see first when he leaves the sanctuary after he has seen what is within, and entered there into communion, not with statues and images, but with the deity itself. Perhaps we ought not to speak of *vision*; it is rather another mode of seeing, an ecstasy and simplification, an abandonment of oneself, a desire for immediate contact, a stability, a deep intention to unite oneself with what is to be seen in the sanctuary. He who seeks to see God in any other manner, will find nothing. These are but figures, by which the wise prophets indicate how we may see this God. But the wise priest, understanding the symbol, may enter the sanctuary and make the vision real. If he has not yet got so far, he at least conceives that what is within the sanctuary is something invisible to mortal eyes, that it is the source and principle of all; he knows that it is by the first principle that we see the first principle, and unites himself with it and perceives like by like, leaving behind nothing that is divine, so far as the soul can reach. And before the vision, the soul desires that which remains for it to see. But for him who has ascended above all things, that which remains to see is that which is before all things. For the nature of the soul will never pass to absolute not-being: when it falls, it will come to evil, and so to not-being, but not to absolute not-being. But if it moves in the opposite direction, it will arrive not at something else, but at itself, and so, being in nothing else, it is only in itself alone; but that which is in itself alone and not in the world of being is in the absolute. It ceases to be being; it is above being, while in communion with the One. If then a man sees himself become one with the One, he has in himself a likeness of the One, and if he passes out of himself, as an image to its archetype, he has reached the end of his journey. And when he comes down from his vision, he can again awaken the virtue that is in him, and seeing himself fitly adorned in every part he can again mount upward through virtue to Spirit, and through wisdom to the One itself. Such is the life of gods and of godlike and blessed men; a liberation from all earthly bonds, a life that takes no pleasure in earthly things, a flight of the alone to the Alone.

Appendix II
GLOSSARY

Abathur. Keeper of the Scales. A fallen creature of light at the watch-house where the soul's journey ends.

Achamoth. Late Hebrew for "wisdom." A term used by some Valentinians for Mother Sophia. *See* Sophia.

Acta. Acts. Accounts of the lives and persecution of Christian martyrs and saints.

Adakas-Mana. Heavenly Adam.

Adakas-Ziwa. Radiant heavenly Adam.

Aeon. Originally, an age. One of the pretemporal beings ruling the Gnostic Pleroma; also, one of the sons or powers created by the Demiurge. *See* Pleroma.

Ahura Mazda. The Zoroastrian God of Light. *See* Ormuzd.

Albigensian. A Gnostic group in southern France, destroyed for religious and political reasons in the thirteenth century. *See* Cathari.

Angra Mainu. The Zoroastrian devil. God of Darkness, often associated among the Manichaean Gnostics with the Old and New Testament Creator God.

Anos. Enos. Messenger of light.

Apocalypse. A revelation of doctrinal significance often forecasting future events and frequently attributed to a great historical personage to increase the authority of the text.

Apocalyptist. Author of an apocalypse.

Apocrypha. Writings not admitted to the canon of sacred scriptures and of doubtful authority.

Apocryphon. A secret book or revelation to be read only by initiates of a particular sect.

Archon. One of the world rulers of planetary spirits, a governor of an Aeon, linked by some to the twelve signs of the zodiac, and by the Gnostics to Yahweh.

Avesta or Zend Avesta. Zoroastrian scriptures. Zend Avesta means "commentary on the law."

Bogomils. A Gnostic group in Bulgaria and the Balkans who flourished between the tenth and fifteenth centuries. *See* Cathari.

Cathari. The Cathari (Greek for "the pure") were a Gnostic group, deriving from Manichaeism, which was widespread in Europe from the Balkans to western Europe and England. They were known for their extreme asceticism and shared Gnostic belief in a rigidly dualistic universe. Its members were divided into believers and the Perfect. They were known by several names and appeared in diverse places in Europe, such as the Bogomils of Bulgaria and the Balkans and the Albigensians of southern France.

Cosmogony. Creation of the universe.

Demiurge. In Gnostic belief the Old Testament Creator God, subordinate to the Highest God. Also called Ialdabaoth, Samael, or Saclas. From the Greek for craftsman, the term appears in Plato's *Timaeus* as God the Creator.

Docetists. An early Christian sect that claimed Christ was a mere phantasm or simulacrum and who therefore did not live or suffer on the cross. Most of the Gnostics shared this view.

Eight (or *Ogdoad*). The sphere beyond the *Seven* or Hebdomad.

Encratites. A heretical sect that emphasized strict discipline or asceticism, some of whose members were influenced by Gnostic or docetic beliefs.

Ephebeion. A place where an *ephebos*, a young man, was disciplined for two years to bear arms and to learn the duties of citizenship.

Essenes. A devout apocalyptic sect identified by Josephus, Philo, Pliny, and Hippolytus, which flourished from the first century B.C. to the first century A.D. It is more or less established that the Qumran community, which gave us the Dead Sea Scrolls, was an Essene community.

Father of Light. The supreme Gnostic deity. Also called Father of Truth, Father of All, Father of Greatness, the Unknown Father.

Gemara. The Aramaic commentary in the Talmud.

Gnosis. The Greek word for knowledge, from which the term Gnostic derives.

Gymnasion. A center of activities where athletes exercised naked.

Haggadah. Legend. The oral tradition of stories, biblical commentary, biblical exegesis, which derives from oral law.

Hagiography. The biography of saints.

Halakha. The teachings and ordinance of written biblical law.

Hibil. Abel. Messenger of light.

Ialdabaoth. Probably from the Hebrew name for God—Yahweh Sabaoth—and used by the Gnostics in referring to the ignorant Demiurge. Also written Yaldabaoth.

Intertestamental. Sacred scriptures written between the Old and New Testaments.

Kusta. Truth. Also, personification of truth.

Mana. Great heavenly being of light.

Manda d'Haiye. Gnosis. Redeemer and chief messenger of light.

Mandaeans. Thought to have originated in Palestine and Syria, this baptizing sect, which still survives today in parts of Iran and Iraq, flourished from the second to the eighth centuries. The Mandaeans have affinities with the Gnostics, although they reject asceticism and emphasize fertility. Their chief holy book is the *Ginza Rba*.

Manichaeans. A Gnostic sect founded by Mani (c. A.D. 215–c.276), based on Persian and Judeo-Christian dualism, in which the forces of Light are pitted against darkness and matter. Followers believed Mani to be the last of a series of prophets, including Zoroaster, Buddha, Hermes, and Christ. The most organized of Gnostic sects, it survived into medieval times, extending from Chinese Turkestan to parts of Europe.

Merkabah. In Jewish scriptures the mystical Chariot of God.

Midrash. Jewish commentaries on the Bible written between Exile and ca. A.D. 1200. Midrashic commentary signifies Jewish exegesis.

Mishnah. The Hebrew text of the Talmud.

Montanist. The Montanists were followers of Montanus, a Phrygian bishop of the second century. He was at once an ecstatic and an ascetic, claiming that the Holy Spirit, the Paraclete, resided in him.

Nous. Mind or intelligence. *Nous* is used differently in different systems. For the Neoplatonist Plotinus, *nous* is the first emanation from God or the One. From *nous* in turn emanates the soul and from the soul emanates matter.

Ogdoad. The first eight Aeons in the Gnostic Pleroma.

Ormuzd. Manichaean god of Light. In other Gnostic systems he is called Primal Man. Ormuzd is a Manichaean version of the Zoroastrian god of Light, Ahura Mazda.

Pleroma. The thirty highest Aeons that constitute the attributes of the Supreme Being; or the beings who exist beyond the sensory world.

Pleromatogony. The creation of or origin of the Pleroma.

Prunicos. The Valentinian name for Sophia. In the *Apocryphon of John,* Prunicos is an element in Sophia.

Pseudepigrapha. In Greek the word means things falsely ascribed, and so pseudepigrapha (pl.) refer to those noncanonical texts by Jews from 200 B.C. to A.D. 200 and to Christians, A.D. 50 to 400, falsely ascribed to great figures in order to give them greater authority. The Song of Songs and Hymns of David are biblical examples of dubious authorship. Typical pseudepigrapha are the *Book of Enoch* (Jewish), the *Acts of Thomas* (Christian), and the *Gospel of Thomas* (Gnostic).

Ptahil. An uthra fallen from light. The Mandaean Demiurge.

Qumran or Khirbet Qumran. Site on the western shore of the Dead Sea where the Dead Sea Scrolls were found. The community at Qumran, thought to be Essenes, was called the Qumran Community. The Dead Sea Scrolls are frequently called the Qumran Scrolls.

Ruha. Evil female spirit. Mother of seven planets.

Saclas. The equivalent of Satan. Sometimes refers to the chief of angels opposed to the Highest God; also, Gnostic name for Yahweh, the biblical Creator God.

Samis. Sun. An evil being.

Sefirah. Sefiroi (pl.) In the Kabbalah each sefirot (sing.) has a virtue or ethical attribute.

Sheol. Hell in the Old Testament. For the ancient Jews Sheol was a dark and melancholy place for departed souls who wander unhappy, but untormented. Eventually, Sheol took on the characteristics of Gehenna, Hell in the New Testament, a place of punishment.

Sibyllines. Works attributed to sibyls, oracular women who proclaimed future events in a state of ecstasy. The sibylline tradition of prophecy came to Greece from Zoroastrian Persia and was much later adopted by both Jews and Christians.

Sitil. Seth. Pure soul and messenger of light.

Skina. Heavenly abode of beings of light and risen souls.

Sophia. Greek for "wisdom." The first female principle emanating either from the Highest God or a succession of Aeons. One of the Pleroma. As the Mother of Life she brings forth Primal man. A lower manifestation of Sophia brings forth God, the biblical Creator, the Demiurge. Sophia is then literally the mother of God, but not of Jesus—whom she later marries—but of his father, the Father of the Earth. In the Valentinian speculation she is ex-

...rom the Pleroma and wanders ...r pain; emphasis is on her suffering, rather than that of Jesus, who in his earthly form was considered a simulacrum and who therefore did not suffer. Sophia is also referred to by her Hebrew name, Mother Achamoth.

Talmud. A vast collection of Jewish writing completed from the post-biblical period of the fourth century A.D. for the Palestinian Talmud and the fifth and perhaps sixth century for the Babylonian Talmud.

Teacher of Righteousness. A messiah figure in the Dead Sea Scrolls. Probably a founder and leader of the sect. According to Theodor H. Gaster this "righteous teacher" is not one figure, but changes for each generation. For others he is a precursor of Jesus, but this notion has the same credentials as finding Jesus in Isaiah.

Theogony. Creation of the gods; usually giving their genealogy.

Thought. Sometimes identified with Sophia, this female principle is the first emanation from the Highest God.

Tibil. Earth.

Uthra. Good beings of light who inhabit the realm of light like angels.

Wicked Priest. In the Dead Sea Scrolls the Wicked Priest was probably the Hasmonean leader Jonathon or Simon, who represented the "wickedness" of worldly Jerusalem.

Zadokite. The sons of Zadok, the name by which members of the Qumran Community called themselves. The Zadokites are thought to be Essenes and to have composed the Dead Sea Scrolls.

Zohar. Sefer Ha-Zohar (The Book of Radiance). Attributed to the Spanish Kabbalist Moses de Leon who died in 1305. Its source is ancient Midrashic works of the first centuries A.D., written in Aramaic. Much of it is a mystical commentary on the Torah.

Bibliography

JEWISH PSEUDEPIGRAPHA

Ackroyd, Peter R. *Exile and Restoration.* Philadelphia: Westminster, 1968.

Bate, H. N. *The Sibylline Oracles*, books III–V. London: 1918.

Bensly, R. L. *The Fourth Book of Ezra*, with Introduction by M. R. James. *Texts and Studies*, vol. III, no. 2, Cambridge: 1892.

Bickerman, E. *From Ezra to the Last of the Maccabees.* New York: Schocken, 1962.

Black, Matthew. *Apocalypsis Henochi Graece.* PVTG 3 Leiden: Brill, 1970.

Bloch, J. *On the Apocalyptic in Judaism.* JQR Monographs, no. 2. Philadelphia, 1952.

Bonner, Campbell. *The Last Chapters of Enoch in Greek.* London: Chatto & Windus, 1937.

Box, G. H. *The Ezra-Apocalypse.* London: 1912.

Charles, R. H. *The Apocrypha and Pseudepigrapha of the Old Testament.* 2 vols. Oxford: Clarendon, 1912.

———. *The Ascension of Isaiah.* London: Black, 1900.

———. *The Book of Enoch.* Oxford: Clarendon, 1912.

———. *The Book of Enoch*, with an Introduction by W. O. E. Oesterley. London: 1917.

———. *The Ethiopic Version of the Book of Enoch.* Oxford: Clarendon, 1906.

———. *The Ethiopic Version of the Hebrew Book of the Jubilees*, Anecdota Oxoniensia. Oxford: Clarendon, 1895.

———. *Religious Development between the Old and New Testaments.* London: 1914.

Charlesworth, James H. *The Pseudepigrapha and Modern Research*, SBLSCS 7, rev. ed. Missoula: Scholars Press, no date.

———. *The Pseudepigrapha of the Old Testament.* Garden City, N.Y.: Doubleday, no date.

Collins, John H., and George W. E. Nicklesburg, eds. *Ideal Figures in Ancient Judaism: Profiles and Paradigms*, SBLSCS 12. Missoula: Scholars Press, 1980.

Collins, John J. *The Sibylline Oracles of Egyptian Judaism*, SBLDS 13. Missoula: Scholars Press, 1974.

Davenport, Gene L. *The Eschatology of the Book of Jubilees*, SPB 20. Leiden: Brill, 1971.

de Lange, Nicholas. *Jewish Literature of the Hellenistic Age.* New York: The Viking Press, 1978.

Deane, W. J. *Pseudepigrapha.* Edinburgh: 1891.

Fraser, Peter. *Ptolemaic Alexandria.* 3 vols. Oxford: Clarendon, 1972.

Frost, S. B. *Old Testament Apocalyptic.* London, 1952.

Geyer, J. *The Wisdom of Solomon.* London: S.C.M. Press, 1963.

Guignebert, C. *The Jewish World in the Time of Jesus.* Translated by S. H. Hooke. London, 1939.

Moses. *Aristeas to Philocrates*, New York: Harper, 1951.

...son, Paul D. *The Dawn of Apocalyptic*. Philadelphia: Fortress, 1975.

Harris, Rendel, and Mingana, A. *The Odes and Psalms of Solomon*. 2 vols. Manchester, 1916 and 1920.

Hengel, Martin. *Judaism and Hellenism*. 2 vols. Philadelphia: Fortress, 1974.

Herford, R. T. *Judaism in the New Testament Period*. London, 1928.

_____. *Talmud and Apocrypha*. London, 1953.

James, M. R. *The Biblical Antiquities of Philo*. London, 1917.

Klausner, J. *The Messianic Idea in Israel*. Translated by W. F. Stinespring. London: G. Allen and Unwin, 1956.

Knibb, Michael A. *The Ethiopic Book of Enoch: A New Edition in the Light of Aramaic Dead Sea Fragments*. Oxford: Clarendon, 1978.

Lieberman, S. *Greek in Jewish Palestine*. New York, 1942.

_____. *Hellenism in Jewish Palestine*. Jewish Theological Seminary in America. New York, 1950.

Moore, G. F. *Judaism in the First Centuries of the Christian Era*. 3 vols. Cambridge, Mass., 1927–30.

Morfill, W. R., and R. H. Charles. *The Book of the Secrets of Enoch*. Oxford: Clarendon, 1896.

Nickelsburg, George W. E., Jr. *Jewish Literature between the Bible and the Mishnah*. Philadelphia: Fortress, 1981.

Oesterley, W. O. E. *A History of Israel*, vol. II. Oxford: Clarendon, 1932.

_____. *The Jews and Judaism during the Greek Period*. London, 1941.

_____. *Judaism and Christianity*, vol. I: *The Age of Transition*. New York, 1937.

Pfeiffer, R. F. *Between the Testaments*. Grand Rapids, Mich.: Baker Book House, 1963.

Pfeiffer, Robert H. *History of New Testament Times*, with an Introduction to the Apocrypha. New York: Harper, 1949.

Russell, D. S. *The Method and Message of Jewish Apocalyptics*. London: S.C.M. Press, 1964.

Schurer, E. *History of the Jewish People in the Time of Jesus Christ*, div. II, vol. III. Translated by J. Macpherson, S. Taylor, and P. Christie. Edinburgh, 1890.

Torrey, C. C. *The Apocryphal Literature*. New Haven, 1945.

VanderKam, James C. *Textual and Historical Studies in the Book of Jubilees*, HSM 14. Missoula: Scholars Press, 1977.

Wicks, H. J. *The Doctrine of God in the Jewish Apocryphal and Apocalyptic Literature*. London, 1915.

Winston, David. *Wisdom of Solomon*, AB 43. Garden City, N.Y.: Doubleday, 1979.

THE DEAD SEA SCROLLS

Avigad, N., and Yigael Yadin. *A Genesis Apocryphon*. Jerusalem, 1956.

Barthelemy, D. *The Zadokite Fragments* (JQR Monograph Series, no. 1). Philadelphia: Dropsie College, 1952.

Barthelemy, D., and J. T. Milik. *Qumran Cave I* (Discoveries in the Judaean Desert I). Oxford: Clarendon Press, 1955.

Black, M. *The Scrolls and Christian Origins*. London, 1961.

Burrows, M. *The Dead Sea Scrolls*. London, 1956.

_____. *More Light on the Dead Sea Scrolls*. London, 1958.

Charlesworth, J. H., ed. *John and Qumran*. London, 1972.

Cross, F. M. *The Ancient Library of Qumran and Modern Biblical Study*. London, 1958.

DeVaux, R. *The Archaeology of the Dead Sea Scrolls*. London, 1973.

Driver, G. R. *The Judaean Scrolls*. Oxford, 1965.

Dupont-Sommer, A. *The Dead Sea Scrolls: A Preliminary Survey*. Translated by E. Margaret Rowley. Oxford, 1952.

_____. *The Jewish Sect of Qumran and the Essenes*. Translated by R. D. Barnett. London, 1954. Translated by G. Vermes. Oxford, 1961.

Fitzmeyer, Joseph A. *The Dead Sea Scrolls: Major Publications and Tools for Study,* SBLSBS 8. Missoula: Scholars Press, 1975.

———. *The Genesis Apocryphon of Qumran Cave I,* Bib Or 18a, 2d ed. Rome: Biblical Institute, 1971.

Gaster, T. H. *The Scriptures of the Dead Sea Sect.* London, 1957.

Gaster, T. H., and J. C. Greenfield, eds. *New Directions in Biblical Archaeology.* New York, 1971.

Leaney, A. R. C., ed. *A Guide to the Scrolls.* London, 1958.

Milik, J. T. *Ten Years of Discovery in the Wilderness of Judea.* Translated by J. Strugnell. London, 1959.

Rabin, C. *The Zadokite Documents.* Oxford: Clarendon Press, 1953.

Rowley, H. H. *Jewish Apocalyptic and the Dead Sea Scrolls.* London, 1957.

———. *The Zadokite Fragments and the Dead Sea Scrolls.* Oxford, 1955.

Schonfield, H. J. *Secrets of the Dead Sea Scrolls.* London, 1956.

Stendahl, K., ed. *The Scrolls and the New Testament.* London, 1958.

Vermes, G. *The Dead Sea Scrolls in English.* Harmondsworth, 1962.

Wallenstein, M. *Hymns from the Judean Scrolls.* Manchester, England: Manchester University Press, 1950.

Yadin, Yigael. *The Message of the Scrolls.* New York: Simon and Schuster, 1957.

KABBALAH

Ashlag, Yehudah. *An Entrance to the Tree of Life: A Key to the Portals of Jewish Mysticism.* Edited by Philip S. Berg. New York: Research Centre of Kabbalah, 1977.

Blau, Joseph Leon. *The Christian Interpretation of the Cabala in the Renaissance.* New York: Columbia University Press, 1944.

Bloom, Harold. *Kabbalah and Criticism.* New York: Seabury Press, 1975.

Bokser, Ben Zion. *From the World of the Cabbalah: the Philosophy of Rabbi Judah Loew of Prague.* New York: Philosophical Library, 1954.

———. *The Jewish Mystical Tradition.* New York: Pilgrim Press, 1981.

Franck, Adolphe. *The Religious Philosophy of the Hebrews.* Secaucus, N.J.: The Citadel Press, 1967.

Ginsburg, Christian David. *The Essenes: Their History and Doctrines; The Kabbalah: Its Doctrines, Development, and Literature.* New York: Macmillan, 1956.

Krakovsky, Levi Isaac. *Kabbalah, the Light of Redemption.* Brooklyn: Kabbalah Foundation, 1950.

Meltzer, David, ed. *The Secret Garden.* New York: Seabury Press, 1976.

Ponce, Charles. *Kabbalah, An Introduction and Illumination for the World Today.* San Francisco: Straight Arrow Books, 1973.

Rosenberg, Roy A. *The Anatomy of God: The Book of Concealment, the Zohar, the Assembly of the Tabernacle.* New York: Ktav, 1973.

Schaya, Leo. *The Universal Meaning of the Kabbalah.* Translated by Nancy Pearson. London: Allen & Unwin, 1971.

Scholem, Gershom. *Major Trends in Jewish Mysticism.* Jerusalem: Schocken, 1961.

———. *On the Kabbalah and Its Symbolism.* Translated by R. Manheim. London: Routledge and Kegan Paul, 1965.

Sperling, Harry, and Maurice Simon, trans. 5 vols. *The Zohar.* Introduction by Dr. John Abelson. London: The Soncino Press, 1931–34.

Unterman, Alan, trans. *The Wisdom of the Jewish Mystics.* New York: New Directions, 1976.

Waite, Arthur E. *The Doctrine and Literature of the Kabbalah.* London: Theosophical Pub. Society, 1902.

CHRISTIAN NEW TESTAMENT APOCRYPHA

Bickerman, E. J. *From Ezra to the Last of the Maccabees.* New York: Schocken Books, 1962.

R., *Primitive Christianity in Its rary Setting*. New York: ...an, 1956.

Burkitt, F. C. *Jewish and Christian Apocalypses*. London, 1914.

Charles, R. H. *The Apocrypha and Pseudepigrapha of the Old Testament*. 2 vols. London: Oxford University Press, 1913.

Charlesworth, J. H. *The Odes of Solomon*. New York: Oxford University Press, 1973.

Gaster, T. H. *Dead Sea Scriptures in English Translation*, third ed., rev. Garden City, N.Y.: Anchor Books, 1976.

Goodspeed, E. J. *The Story of the Apocrypha*. Chicago: University of Chicago Press, 1939.

Hadas, Moses. *The Third and Fourth Books of Maccabees*. New York: Ktav, 1953.

Hadas, Moses, ed. *Aristeas to Philocrates*. New York: Ktav, 1951.

Hengel, M. *Judaism and Hellenism*. 2 vols. Translated by J. Bowden. Philadelphia: Fortress Press, 1975.

Klausner, J. *The Messianic Idea in Israel from Its Beginning to the Completion of the Mishnah*. Translated by W. F. Stinespring. New York: Macmillan, 1955.

Metzger, B. M. *An Introduction to the Apocrypha*. New York: Oxford University Press, 1957.

Moore, G. F. *Judaism in the First Centuries of the Christian Era*. 2 vols. New York: Schocken Books, 1971.

Myers, J. M. I. *I and II Esdras*, a New Translation with Introduction and Commentary (Anchor Bible). New York: Doubleday, 1974.

Oesterley, W. O. E. *The Jews and Judaism during the Greek Period: The Background of Christianity*. Repr. of 1941 ed. Port Washington, N.Y.: Kennikat Press, 1970.

Oxford Annotated Apocrypha, expanded ed. *Greek Period: the Background of Christianity*. Repr. of 1941 ed. Port Washington, N.Y.: Kennikat Press, 1970.

Pfeiffer, R. H. *History of the New Testament Times*, with an Introduction to the Apocrypha. Repr. of 1949 ed. Westport, Conn.: Greenwood Press, 1972.

Porter, F. C. *The Messages of the Apocalyptical Writers*. London, 1905.

Rowley, H. H. *The Relevance of the Apocalyptic*. London: Lutterworth Press, 1947.

Sanders, J. A. *The Dead Sea Psalms Scroll*. Oxford: Clarendon Press, 1965.

Scholem, G. *Major Trends in Jewish Mysticism*. 3d ed. New York: Schocken Books, 1961.

Schurer, E. *A History of the Jewish People in the Time of Jesus Christ*. Various translators. New York: Schocken Books, 1961.

Surburg, R. F. *Introduction to the Intertestamental Period*. St. Louis: Concordia Publishing House, 1975.

Torrey, C. C. *The Apocryphal Literature: A Brief Introduction*. New Haven: Yale University Press, 1945. Second ed., Hamden, Conn.: Shoe String Press, 1963.

Vermes, G., trans. *The Dead Sea Scrolls in English*. 1962, New York: Bantam Books, 1968.

Weiss, J. *Earliest Christianity*. New York: Harper Torch Books, 1959.

GNOSTIC

Allberry, C. R. C., ed. and trans. *A Manichaean Psalm-book*. Stuttgart, 1938.

Angus, S. *The Mystery Religions and Christianity*. New York, 1925.

———. *The Religious Quests of the Graeco-Roman World*. New York, 1929.

Augustine, Saint. *De Natura Boni*. Translated by A. A. Moon. Washington, 1955.

Bevan, A. A., ed. and trans. *The Hymn of the Soul* (Texts and Studies 5, 3). Cambridge, England, 1897.

Boyce, M. *The Manichaen Hymn-cycles in Parthian*. Oxford, 1954.

Bullard, Roger A. *The Hypostasis of the Archons: The Coptic Text with Translation and Commentary*, with a Contribution by M. Krause. Berlin: Walter de Gruyter, 1970.

Burkitt, F. C. *Church and Gnosis*. Cambridge: University Press, 1932.

———. *The Religion of the Manichees*. Cambridge: University Press, 1925.

Butler, E. M. *The Fortunes of Faust*. Cambridge, England, 1952.

———. *The Myth of the Magus*. Cambridge, England, 1948.

Ceram, C. W. *Gods, Graves and Scholars*. New York: Alfred A. Knopf, 1951; rev. ed., 1967.

Charles, R. H. *The Apocrypha and Pseudepigrapha of the Old Testament*. Oxford, 1913.

Clark, G. H., ed. *Selections from Hellenistic Philosophy*. New York, 1940.

Cross, F. L., ed. *The Jung Codex, a Newly Recovered Gnostic Papyrus; Three Studies*. London: Mowbray, 1955.

Daniclou, J. *The Theology of Jewish Christianity*. Translated by J. H. Baker. London: Darton, Longman and Todd, 1964.

Doresse, J. *The Secret Books of the Egyptian Gnostics*. Translated by P. Mairet. London: Hollis & Carter, 1960.

Drower, E. S. *The Canonical Prayerbook of the Mandaeans*. Leiden, 1959.

———. *The Mandaeans of Iraq and Iran: Their Cults, Customs, Legends, and Folklore*. Oxford, 1937.

———. *The Secret Adam: A Study of Nasoraean Gnosis*. Oxford, 1960.

Drower, E. S., ed. and trans. *Diwan Abatur, or Progress through the Purgatories*. Bibl. apost. vaticana, 1950.

Foerster, Werner, ed. *Gnosis: a Selection of Gnostic Texts*. Translated and edited by R. McL. Wilson. Oxford: Clarendon Press, vol. I, 1972.

Goodenough, E. R. *An Introduction to Philo Judaeus*. New Haven, 1940.

———. *By Light, Light: the Mystic Gospel of Hellenistic Judaism*. Oxford, 1935.

Grant, F. C. *Hellenistic Religions: The Age of Syncretism*. New York, 1953.

Grant, R. M. *Gnosticism: An Anthology*. London: Collins, 1961.

———. *Gnosticism and Early Christianity*. London: Oxford University Press, 1955.

Grant, R. M., and David N. Freedman. *The Secret Sayings of Jesus*, with an English Translation of the Gospel of Thomas by W. R. Schoedel. Garden City, N.Y.: Doubleday, 1960.

Groebel, K. *The Gospel of Truth*. New York: Abingdon, 1960.

Guillaumont, A. *The Gospel According to Thomas*. Translated and edited by G. C. H. Puech, G. Quispel, W. Till, and Yasah 'Abal Al Masih. London: Collins, 1959.

Guitton, J. *Great Heresies and Church Councils*. London: Harvell Press, 1965.

Haardt, Robert. *Gnosis: Character and Testimony*. Translated by J. F. Hendry. Leiden: Brill, 1971.

Harnack, A. *The Mission and Expansion of Christianity in the First Three Centuries*. 2 vols. New York, 1908.

Harris, J. R., and A. Mingana. *The Odes and Psalms of Solomon*. 2 vols. Manchester, 1916–1920.

Helmbold, A. *The Nag Hammadi Gnostic Texts and the Bible*. Grand Rapids: Eerdmans, 1967.

Inge, W. R. *The Philosophy of Plotinus*, 3d ed. 2 vols. London, 1929.

Jackson, A. V. W. *Researches in Manichaeism, with Special Reference to the Turfan Fragments*. New York, 1932.

James, M. R., trans. *The Apocryphal New Testament*. Oxford, 1924.

Jonas, Hans. *The Gnostic Religion: The Message of the Alien God and the Beginnings of Christianity*. Boston: Beacon Press, 1963.

Kingsland, W. *The Gnosis or Ancient Wisdom in the Christian Scriptures*. London: Allen & Unwin, Ltd., 1937.

Lewy, H., trans. *Philo Selections* (Philosophia Judaica). Oxford, 1964.

Lietzmann, H. *The Beginnings of the Christian Church*. New York, 1937.

———. *History of the Early Church*. 4 vols. New York, 1938.

Mead, G. R. S., trans. *The Gnostic John the Baptizer: Selections from the Mandaean John-book*. London, 1924.

Moore, G. F. *Judaism in the First Centuries of the Christian Era*. 3 vols. Cambridge, 1927–1930.

Commentary on St. John's Gos- ed by E. Preuschen. Leipzig,

———. *Contra Celsum*. Edited by P. Koetschau. Leipzig, 1899.

———. *Id*. Edited and translated by H. Chadwick. Cambridge, England, 1953.

Pallis, S. A. *Mandaean Studies*. London, 1926.

Peel, Malcolm L. *The Epistle to Rheginos: A Valentinian Letter on the Resurrection*. Philadelphia: Westminster, 1969.

Robinson, James M., ed. *The Coptic Gnostic Library* (Edited with an English Translation, Introductions, and Notes). Leiden: Brill, 1975– .

———. *The Nag Hammadi Library*. San Francisco: Harper & Row, 1977.

Robinson, James M., and Helmut Koester. *Trajectories through Early Christianity*. Philadelphia: Fortress, 1971.

Runcimann, S. *The Medieval Manichee*. Cambridge, 1947.

Russell, David Syme. *The Method and Message of Jewish Apocalyptic 200 B.C.– A.D. 100*. Philadelphia: Fortress, 1964.

Schneemelcher, Wilhelm, ed. *New Testament Apocrypha*. Translated by R. McL. Wilson. Philadelphia: Westminster, 1963.

Scholem, Gershom. *Jewish Mysticism*, 2d ed. New York, 1965.

———. *Major Trends in Jewish Mysticism*. New York: Schocken, 1961.

Scholer, David M. *Nag Hammadi Bibliography 1948–1969*. Leiden: Brill, 1971.

Schurer, E. *History of the Jewish People in the Time of Jesus*. 5 vols. Edinburgh, 1885–91; New York, 1938.

Scott, W., and A. S. Ferguson, ed. and trans. *Hermetica*, vols. I–IV. Oxford, 1924–36.

Serapion of Thmuis. *Against the Manichees* (Harvard Theological Studies 15). Edited by R. B. Casey. Cambridge, 1931.

Summers, R. *The Secret Sayings of the Living Jesus: Studies in the Coptic Gospel According to Thomas*. Waco, Texas: Word Books, 1968.

Syrus, Ephraem. *S. Ephraim's Prose Refutations of Mani, Marcion and Bardaisan*. Edited and translated by C. W. Mitchell. Vols. I, II: London, 1912, 1921.

Turner, H. E. W., and H. Montefiore. *Thomas and the Evangelists*. London, 1962.

Van Unnik, W. C. *Newly Discovered Gnostic Writings*. London: S.C.M. Press, 1960.

Widengren, G. *The Great Vohu Manah and the Apostle of God; Studies in Iranian and Manichaean Religion*. Uppsala, 1945.

———. *Mani and Manichaeism*. London, 1965; New York, 1966.

———. *Mesopotamian Elements in Manichaeism: Studies in Manichaean, Mandaean, and Syrian-Gnostic Religion*. Uppsala-Leipzig, 1946.

Wilson, Robert McL. *Gnosis and the New Testament*. Philadelphia: Fortress, 1968.

———. *The Gnostic Problem*. London, 1958.

———. *The Gospel of Philip*. New York, 1962.

———. *Studies in the Gospel of Thomas*. London, 1960.

Yamauchi, E. *Mandaic Incantation Texts*. New Haven, 1967.

Zandee, J. *The Terminology of Plotinus and of Some Gnostic Writings, Mainly the Fourth Treatise of the Jung Codex*. Istanbul, 1961.